THE REGULATION OF PUBLIC UTILITIES

Theory and Practice

The Regulation of Public Utilities
Theory and Practice

CHARLES F. PHILLIPS, JR.

Robert G. Brown
Professor of Economics
Washington and Lee University

1988
PUBLIC UTILITIES REPORTS, INC.
Arlington, Virginia

© Public Utilities Reports, Inc., 1988

First Printing, May, 1984
Second Edition, June, 1988

Library of Congress Catalog Card No. 88-61684

ISBN 0-910325-27-8

Printed in the United States of America

To Three Very Special People:

Charles F. Phillips III
Susan H. Phillips
Anne D. Phillips

Preface

Modern regulation is increasingly in need of more headlights and [fewer] taillights.

—Francis X. Welch*

The late Francis X. Welch wrote the above statement over twenty years ago, but its relevance has never been greater than today. The public utility sector of the American economy has changed dramatically in the last two decades; a period that has severely tested both the regulated and the regulator, as well as the courts. Moreover, it has become all too obvious that while "taillights" provide important insights and experience, the changes require "headlights" that incorporate innovative analyses and procedures.

There is evidence that the need is being recognized. The literature on public utilities has grown significantly. Irwin Stelzer has been reminding us for years that there is "no free lunch," and this lesson has finally been learned. Electric, gas, telephone, and water services were promoted and supplied below their true costs for decades. Today, proper pricing principles are being recognized, so that consumers can (and will) act rationally. Further, technological change has eroded the traditional monopoly position of some public utilities, leading to substantial deregulation (thus, the transportation sector is not included in this volume) and to the dissolution of the Bell System. In other cases, competition is being introduced into segments of the public utility industries, resulting in a series of new issues that require resolution and a greater reliance upon antitrust policy. And the regulatory process has struggled to adapt to new pressures and problems, and literally dozens of proposals for reform have been put forth.

These changes are reflected in this revised text. The emphasis continues to be on the development of economic regulation (as opposed to social regulation, although there is often an overlap), and on recent and future issues confronting the public utility sector. The book includes extensive quotations from the growing volume of research on those issues and comprehensive footnotes for those who wish to pursue a particular topic further.

It would be impossible to acknowledge all of those who have contributed to this study, for over the years the author has discussed regulatory concepts and issues with hundreds of individuals. Many will find their ideas

*Francis X. Welch, "Changing Values in the Regulatory Mix," 80 *Public Utilities Fortnightly* 61, 69 (November 9, 1967).

included. My students at Washington and Lee University have constantly challenged concepts and regulation itself. Those who have attended the "Public Utility Executive Program" at The University of Michigan over the past eighteen years have contributed much to my understanding of the issues. Four people, however, must be mentioned: O. O. Ashworth, Jr., J. Rhoads Foster, the late Edward P. Larkin, and David W. R. Morgan, Jr. Friends over many years, they have been a source of both ideas and information.

In addition, several people provided detailed comments and suggestions on various chapters or sections of the book. With respect to the first edition, they include: Ernest Z. Adelman, Ward J. Campbell, Arthur A. Gladstone, David J. Muchow, Victor G. Rosenblum, and John F. Utley. With respect to both editions, Robert E. Evans (President, Economic Research Associates Ltd.) and Patrick C. Mann (Professor of Economics and Research Associate, Regional Research Institute, West Virginia University) were especially helpful; the former supplying information on regulation in Canada and the latter supplying information on the water industry. All of their assistance is acknowledged with deep gratitude. However, none of them is responsible either for the conclusions reached or for any errors.

Anna B. Claytor and Anne S. Zeigler typed the manuscript. Nina Seebeck and Wallace C. Stefany, on James M. McInnis' staff at Public Utilities Reports, edited and prepared the manuscript for publication. Their cheerful and dedicated assistance is appreciated. And, finally, the author thanks his wife for her continuous support and patience.

To those who use this book, it is hoped that the problems discussed will be as stimulating and challenging as they are to the author. Any comments and suggestions on the material included, or excluded, would be appreciated.

Charles F. Phillips, Jr.

Lexington, Virginia
June, 1988

Table of Contents

Introduction

Public Utilities: *Private Ownership. Public Regulation. An Obsolete Concept?* The Significance of Public Utilities: *Services to Consumers. Contribution to the Economy.* The Changing Environment Confronting Public Utilities: *The First Change: Late 1960s and 1970s. Some Implications. The Second Change: Mid-1970s and 1980s.* Plan of Study: *The Economic, Legal, and Administrative Concepts of Public Utility Regulation. The Theory of Public Utility Regulation. The Public Utility Industries. An Evaluation—And the Future.*

PART I. The Economic, Legal, and Administrative Concepts of Public Utility Regulation

Exceptions to Competitive Policy. Determinants of Market Structure: *Market Structure: Cost Considerations. Market Structure: Demand Considerations. Market Structure: Noneconomic Factors.* Competition, Pricing, and Discrimination: *A Review of Price Theory. Workable Competition. Competition and Price Discrimination. Interindustry Competition.* Economic Characteristics: A Matter of Degree.

The Legal Basis of Government Regulation: *Constitutional Provisions.* Origins of the Public Interest Concept: *Development in America.* Leading Judicial Opinions: *Munn v. Illinois. Budd v. New York. Brass v. Stoeser. German Alliance Insurance Co. v. Lewis. Wolff Packing Co. v. Court of Industrial Relations. Tyson & Brother v. Banton. Ribnik v. McBride. Williams v. Standard Oil Co. New State Ice Co. v. Liebmann. Nebbia v. New York. Some Implications of the Nebbia Case.* Obligations and Rights of Public Utilities: *Obligations. Rights.* Limitations on Government Regulation.

The *"Fair Value" Doctrine. Reproduction Cost versus Prudent Investment: 1898 to 1933. Judicial Shift to the "End Result": 1933 to the Present.* Property Valuation: Economic Concepts: *The Economics of Reproduction Cost. The Economics of Original Cost.* Property Valuation: Current Practices and Problems: *Current Measures of Value. Measures of Reproduction Cost. Used and Useful, Prudent Investment, and Excess Capacity. Mega Additions to Plant in Service: Phase-in Plans.* Accrued Depreciation: *Consistency with Depreciation Accounting. Accrued Depreciation and Original Cost Valuations. Accrued Depreciation and Fair Value.* Other Elements of Value: *Working Capital Allowance. Property Held for Future Use. Land. Intangibles. Customer Contributions.* Construction Work in Progress. The Rate Base: Confusion and Operationalism.

sions. Quality of Service: *Service Standards: Telephone Companies. Termination of Service: Electric and Gas Utilities.* Quantity of Service: *Restriction of Entry. Compulsory Extension of Service. Curtailment of Service: Interstate Gas Pipelines. Abandonment of Service.* Conservation: A Service-related Issue: *Residential Conservation Service Programs. Utility Insulation Programs. Some Unresolved Issues.* Safety Regulation: *Natural Gas Pipelines and LNG Facilities. Nuclear Power Plants.* Management Efficiency: *Management Audits, Incentive Systems.* Service, Safety, and Efficiency: The Future.

Appendix: Environmental Quality Control and the Quantity of Service: *Pipeline Projects: An Illustration. Many Unanswered Questions. Selected Bibliography on Environmental Quality Control.*

PART III. The Public Utility Industries

sions. The Carterfone *Decision: Foreign Attachments. First Computer Inquiry. The* Domsat *Decision: Domestic Communications Satellites.* Execunet *Decisions. A Concluding Note.* Deregulation and Divestiture: An Industry Is Restructured: *Second Computer Inquiry. Modification of Final Judgment. Third Computer Inquiry.* The Future of the Domestic Telecommunications Industry. Appendix: Antitrust Policy in a Transitional Era: *The Private Cases. Three Key Legal Issues. The Major Antitrust Issues. Some Concluding Observations.*

Historical Development and Structure: *Central Water Systems. Some Important Characteristics. Ownership and Regulation. Public Fire Protection.* Water Utility Rate Structures. *Existing Rate Structures. Future Rate Structures: Issues and Problems.* A Host of Unresolved Issues.

PART IV. An Appraisal—And a Challenge

The Regulatory Process: *Independence from Political Control. The Issue of Legitimacy. Lack of Meaningful (Consistent) Policy Standards. Regulatory Delay.* Regulation as a Substitute for Competition: *The Inherent Difficulties. The Role of Competition. Management: Divided Responsibility.* A Continuing Challenge: *The Need for Dynamic Standards. The Need for Performance Evaluation. The Need for Policy Review. The Future.*

Indexes

INTRODUCTION

| Chapter 1 | PUBLIC UTILITIES IN THE AMERICAN ECONOMY |

There is something quite special about government regulation of the public utility type: this is the way we behave when we are really keyed up about economizing, when we stop acquiescing and "going along," when we feel quite certain that, for reasons we can identify, the processes of the free market cannot be made satisfactorily to perform the economizing job we want done and, hence, that we must perform the economizing functions by specifically designed laws, agencies, and measures.

—*Ben W. Lewis**

The economy of the United States is often described as a competitive, private enterprise system. In such a system, the economy is organized on the decentralized lines of private property and private enterprise. Since competition is relied upon to promote the public welfare, the market is the central institution regulating economic activity. But it has long been recognized that some industries, in which competition is not fully effective, must be regulated by government to protect the public interest. "Here the visible hand of public regulation was to replace the invisible hand of Adam Smith in order to protect consumers against extortionate charges, restrictions of output, deterioration of service, and unfair discrimination."[1] By common usage, those businesses which have long been subjected to detailed public regulation are known collectively as "public utilities."

Public Utilities

As Bonbright has noted: "The term 'public utility' is one of popular usage rather than of precise definition. . . ."[2] As commonly used, the term refers to a diverse group of businesses which have been subjected over several decades to detailed local, state, and federal regulation as to rates and service. Public utilities can be divided into two major classes: "(1) those enterprises which supply, directly or indirectly, continuous or repeated services through more or less permanent physical connections between the plant of the supplier and the premises of the consumer; and (2) the public transportation agencies."[3] In the first class are enterprises supplying energy (electricity and natural gas), communications services (telephone and telegraph), and water and sewage. In the second class are firms providing local and interregional transportation (airlines, bus companies, motor freight carriers, gas and oil pipelines, railroads, and water carriers).[4]

A more comprehensive definition of the term has been offered by Glaeser:

> In its most extended sense the term public utilities is designed to cover certain industries which in the course of time have been classified apart from industry in general and have likewise been distinguished from governmental services with which, however, they often are intimately related. The basis of the classification is essentially economic and technological, although the meaning of the term is derived from the law.[5]

Public utilities, then, differ in several respects from other industries in the economy. These differences will be discussed at length in the following three chapters. To summarize: Public utilities (with some important exceptions, such as motor and domestic water carriers, natural gas producers, and some portions of the telecommunications industry) tend toward monopoly or, more accurately, the firms in these industries seem to operate more efficiently as monopolies. Yet, if economic power is not to be controlled by the market, it must be controlled by public authority, for a firm's contribution to the general welfare, rather than being the result of voluntary choice, must be compelled.[6] Some regulation, moreover, may be undertaken for social or political reasons, such as promoting regional development or for national defense purposes. There is a high degree of public interest attached to the services rendered by public utilities; a fact that is the primary legal basis of regulation. Finally, regulation is undertaken by administrative commissions that have been established with jurisdiction over the rates and services of these industries.[7]

There are two common characteristics of the industries under consideration that deserve further discussion. The first is the fact that private ownership is predominant. The second is the existence, in varying degrees, of public regulation.

Private Ownership

The provision of public utility services in the American economy is unique. In contrast to most other industrialized countries, which traditionally have provided these services by nationalized firms,[8] the United States has relied primarily on private ownership, controlled by state and federal agencies, to provide services which are more or less essential to the economy and which are public in their nature.[9] Argued Justice Harlan in the *Smyth* case: "A railroad is a public highway, and none the less so because constructed and maintained through the agency of a corporation deriving its existence and powers from the State. . . . It performs a function of the State."[10] And Justice Brandeis, in the *Southwestern Bell Telephone* case, remarked that "the company is the substitute for the State in the performance of the public service, thus becoming a public servant."[11]

The combination of private ownership and public control means that some conflicts are inevitable. In the first place, while regulation is essentially a legislative and legal concept, it is also an economic one. Accordingly, public utilities are economically motivated as are other private enterprises, but they render a public service and, hence, have been subjected historically to detailed governmental regulation, supervised by the judicial system.[12] Two important results are divided responsibility and ambiguous statutes. Explains Shapiro:

> . . . Regulatory statutes with one hand impose responsibility for a certain sector of the economy on a given agency, while with the other leaving ownership, initiative, and nearly all the actual decision-making power in private hands. The agency is apparently intended to get the private decision makers to act in the public interest not by telling them what to do but only by sporadically intervening to tell them what not to do. Furthermore, the statute maker typically invokes the public interest or public convenience and necessity without saying what he means. Just as typically he mixes a number of specific limitations on jurisdiction and a number of concrete policy standards with these rather open directives to the agency to use its discretion and take its own initiatives to meet new circumstances. In short, regulatory statutes represent an uneasy compromise between laissez faire and government-control visions of the economy. As such they are likely to embody the ambiguity and internal contradictions of contemporary economic philosophy. . . .[13]

In the second place, there often seems to be a conflict between private and public interests. The basic objective of private corporations is profit maximization, while the public interest demands adequate service at the lowest possible price. However, this conflict is more apparent than real for a public utility cannot maximize profit in the long run without providing adequate service at prices acceptable to the public, while the public in the long run cannot receive adequate service at reasonable prices except from a utility which is financially healthy.

In the third place, there is a difficult division of authority between the federal government and the fifty state governments. In theory, interstate activities are subject to federal regulation; intrastate activities to state control. In actual practice, however, the line is a hard one to draw as most public utilities provide both inter- and intrastate services. While many jurisdictional problems have been resolved by past commission and court decisions, new concerns (such as the attempt to establish a national energy policy and to deregulate certain activities) result in renewed conflicts. At a minimum, effective public policy under such circumstances requires continuous cooperation between federal and state agencies.

Finally, as private corporations, public utilities are entitled to due process of law in administrative proceedings and to judicial protection of private property. So, too, are their customers entitled to due process of law. At the commission level, due process of law frequently results in lengthy regulatory proceedings, thereby precluding rapid adjustment to changing economic conditions. In recent years, new procedures have been established in an attempt to overcome the problems created by lengthy, formal proceedings, but these newer procedures have not gained complete acceptance. Either public utilities or intervenors, moreover, may contest commission decisions and orders in the courts. Such appeals, while often necessary, further delay an already complex regulatory situation. At the same time, it is important to keep in mind that these legal requirements and protections are a vital part of the regulatory process.

Public Regulation

Given the facts that public policy historically has sought (*a*) to restrict competition and (*b*) to maintain private ownership, public regulation of the utility sector becomes necessary. As previously noted, uncontrolled economic power is economically, politically, and socially unacceptable in a democratic society. In the United States, regulation is carried on by local, state, and federal governments. Prior to 1934, regulation of the nontransportation utilities was an almost exclusive function of local and state governments. As these industries developed, however, they expanded beyond local and state boundaries, serving multiple states or the entire nation. In the telephone and telegraph industries, international operations became common. Federal regulation thus tended to become more important than state control. The more recent deregulation movement, which has basically affected interstate activities, has shifted much of the burden of *economic* regulation back to the states.[14]

It must be clearly stated and recognized at the outset that regulation has not developed in a smooth or always logical manner. On the contrary, regulation has experienced "a slow and fitful growth."[15] And every change in policy is certain to meet strong opposition. Compromise is frequently the ultimate outcome.

The fact that regulation is necessary does not imply how much or what kind of regulation is desirable. It is to be expected that public utilities tend to favor minimum regulation, while the public may demand the maximum. But economic conditions are changing constantly and, if regulation is to be up-to-date, public policy must change too. Further, since "antitrust and public regulation have, broadly speaking, been the characteristic response of American politics, government, and law to the problems posed by the modern corporation,"[16] a study of public regulation is vital to an evaluation of the desirability of its extension to nonregulated industries or of its curtailment (or withdrawal) from existing utilities.

An Obsolete Concept?

Gray, in a well-known article published in 1940,[17] argued that it is fallacious to suppose that the privilege of private monopoly can be harmonized with the public interest by the imposition of regulation. In fact, he contended, regulation has failed to limit the power of the very monopolies it has created. The public utility status has become "the haven of refuge for all aspiring monopolists who found it too difficult, too costly, or too precarious to secure and maintain monopoly by private action alone." He explained:

> Enough perhaps has been said to demonstrate the "institutional decadence" of the public utility concept. It originated as a system of social restraint designed primarily, or at least ostensibly, to protect consumers from the aggressions of monopolists; it has ended as a device to protect the property, i.e., the capitalized expectancy, of these monopolists from the just demands of society, and to obstruct the development of socially superior institutions. This perversion of the public utility concept from its original purpose was perhaps inevitable under capitalism. Here, as in other areas of our economic and social life, the compelling sanctions of private property and private profit, working within a framework of special privilege, determined the direction and outlook of public policy. Just as in the days of the Empire all roads led to Rome so in a capitalistic society all forms of social control lead ultimately to state protection of the dominant interest, i.e., property. The public utility concept has thus merely gone the way of all flesh.[18]

Gray also claimed that the public utility concept has become obsolete, since it is "incapable of securing the social objectives that are essential in the modern economy." To quote again from his article:

> . . . As previously noted, it was designed to attain limited objectives by negative means. One may read the early public utility statutes in vain to discover any express mandate for the positive promotion of public welfare; the whole tenor of these laws is negative and restrictive; they prohibit certain obvious forms of monopolistic misbehavior but fail to impose definite responsibility for socially desirable action. Thus, public utility companies are under no legal compulsion to conserve natural resources, to utilize capital efficiently, to employ the best known techniques and forms of organization, to treat labor fairly, to extend service to nonprofitable areas, to improve public health, to strengthen national defense, to promote technical research, to provide service to indigent persons, to institute rate and service policies that will foster cultural and social values, or to develop related benefits such as navigation, flood control, and irrigation. This being the case, private utility monopolists will have regard for these broad social objectives only when by so doing they can increase or maintain their own profit. Experience has shown that they will not voluntarily strive to attain these ends; moreover, it is clear that public utility regulation, as at present constituted, cannot compel them, against their own interest, to do so. . . .[19]

The attack on the public utility concept by Gray thus involves two elements.[20] In the first place, he argues that regulation has failed to serve as an efficient substitute for competition. Since publication of his article, however, many changes have taken place in the regulatory process. Procedures have been improved. The holding company abuses of the 1920s were corrected under the Public Utility Holding Company Act of 1935. The Supreme Court's restrictive "fair value" rule of ratemaking was modified by the *Hope* decision of 1944. Pricing theory and practice have been reexamined, particularly under the Public Utility Regulatory Policies Act of 1978. These and other developments have substantially improved the results of regulation.[21]

In the second place, Gray argues that the limited objectives of a fair profit or of a cost-price philosophy of ratemaking should be superseded by broad social and national goals. The phrase "social principles of ratemaking" has a variety of meanings, but generally "it refers to any policy of rate control designed to make the supply of utility services responsive to social needs and social costs, and rejecting as even tolerable measures of these needs and these costs the prices that consumers are able and willing to pay for the services and the money costs that the enterprise must incur in their production."[22] Ratemaking based upon social principles would be complex. How, for example, are social benefits and social costs to be measured?

Similarly, will not the use of the social principles philosophy lead to a distortion between utility rates and other prices, since the others do not reflect social benefits and costs (except for those required by legislation)? Business, as opposed to social, principles of ratemaking seem more desirable in the utility industry.[23]

The Significance of Public Utilities

In legal phraseology, public utilities are "affected with a public interest." The significance of these industries can be measured in at least two ways.

Services to Consumers

One measure of the importance of public utilities is in the services they provide to consumers. In 1986, residential customers spent $169.1 billion for public utility services, equal to 6 percent of personal consumption expenditures.[24] In the same year, the average residential electric bill was $674.95 (compared with $148.39 in 1970); the average residential gas bill was $531.25 (compared with $136.69 in 1970).[25]

Between 1920 and 1970, the use of electric energy doubled every ten years, reaching 1.391 trillion kilowatt-hours in 1970. Significantly higher prices in the 1970s dramatically slowed the growth in electricity demand (the growth rate fell about 50 percent), with the result that total sales were 2.361 trillion kilowatt-hours in 1986 (an increase of 1.9 percent over 1985). Electricity is now available to practically every American home, with more than 98 percent of all occupied homes, both urban and rural, connected for electric service. Residential customers used an average of 9,068 kilowatt-hours of electric power during 1986, at an average price of 7.44 cents per kilowatt-hour. The electric power industry currently supplies 104 million customers a year. The United States, with only 6 percent of the world's population, produces approximately 36 percent of all the electricity generated in the world.

The gas industry has experienced a similar growth pattern. In 1920, gas utilities supplied only 4 percent of domestic energy consumption; by 1970, the figure had risen to 25 percent (or about one-third of domestic energy production). Natural gas reserves, however, began to decline in the late 1960s and early 1970s, leading to severe service curtailments. The industry, presently serving 50 million customers annually, has just over a million-mile network of pipelines and mains that transport natural gas from wells to the consumer. Net production of natural gas, which continues to have the largest share of the total gas market, peaked at 22.6 trillion cubic feet in 1973 and totaled 16 trillion cubic feet in 1986. Proved recoverable reserves totaled 191.6 trillion cubic feet at the end of 1986 (versus 282.9 trillion cubic feet at the end of 1967).

The telephone industry also has experienced a rapid growth, as over 97 percent of American households have basic telephone service. The nearly 180 million telephones in use represent about 40 percent of the world's telephones. Telephone utilities, in 1981, carried approximately 321 billion domestic conversations, equal to an average daily volume of 786.3 million local calls and 93.7 million toll calls. These services required such equipment as 24.2 million poles, 1.2 billion miles of wire, and 21,987 central offices. In addition, the American Telephone and Telegraph Company, which handled an estimated 80 percent of the 1986 domestic long-distance telephone business, has one of the most efficient research laboratories in the world — Bell Laboratories — and is a major supplier of communications systems for national defense and outer space exploration. It is important to keep in mind, however, that the domestic telephone industry is only a part of the broader telecommunications industry; an industry that is undergoing a significant transition in market structure and, as a result of technological developments, in services offered.

Contribution to the Economy

A second measure of the importance of public utilities is their annual contribution to the economy. As Table 1-1 indicates, in 1986, 7.9 percent of national income originated in the public utility sector, while the sector's share of business investment was 25.8 percent. Other contributions, for the nontransportation utilities, included the following.[26] (*1*) Annual operating revenues were approximately $286.2 billion. Electric utilities accounted for 52.4 percent of this total; domestic communications for 25.5 percent; and gas utilities for 22.1 percent. (*2*) Net investment in utility plant and equipment was nearly $549 billion. Electric utilities accounted for 61.4 percent of this total; domestic communications for 29.9 percent; and gas utilities for 8.7 percent. (*3*) Investor-owned public utilities employed just over 2 million full-time workers. (*4*) New plant and equipment expenditures totaled $74.3 billion, with electric utilities accounting for nearly 49 percent of the total. (*5*) To carry out such construction programs, investor-owned public utilities raised $26.4 billion in the capital markets (*i.e.,* 88.7 percent by issuing bonds and 11.3 percent by issuing preferred and common stock); an amount equal to 13.1 percent of total corporate security issues. (*6*) Taxes collected for local, state, and federal governments totaled $43.6 billion.

By several economic measures, therefore, public utilities make a substantial annual contribution to the American economy. Yet, their full economic significance to the economy's productivity is even greater than these figures indicate, for the services of public utilities are just as essential to efficient production and distribution as money and credit are to exchange.

TABLE 1-1

Percentage of National Income and Business Investment
Originating in Public Utility Sector, 1986

Industry	Percentage of National Income	Percentage of Business New Plant and Equipment
Communications	2.1	8.7
Transportation	3.4	4.9
Utilities (electric, gas, and sanitary services)	2.4	12.2
Total	7.9	25.8

Source: U.S. Department of Commerce, 67 *Survey of Current Business* 10, 20 (June, 1987).

The Changing Environment Confronting Public Utilities[27]

The environment within which public utilities operate has changed dramatically over the last two decades. For some sixty years — up until about 1968 — the tremendous expansion of the entire public utility sector was accomplished in a favorable and supportive environment. Economic growth was unquestioned. Annual inflation rates, as well as interest rates, were low. Utilities could plan, construct, and finance new plant in a relatively short period of time, and without great difficulty. Six- to eight-year planning periods for new generating facilities, for instance, were common. Capacity and reserves were adequate. Rates, due to the achievement of economies of scale and sales growth, were relatively constant or declining (see Table 1-2). And there were many who indicated that these trends would continue. Thus, the 1964 *National Power Survey* projected that there would be "a reduction in the nationwide average price per kilowatt-hour from 1.7¢ today to about 1.2¢ in 1980."[28]

The regulatory process was geared to this environment. "[T]he task of state regulators," Perry notes, "was essentially one of distributing among ratepayers the benefits of the progressively higher efficiencies achieved by utility

TABLE 1-2

Average Charge per Kilowatt-hour, Residential Service

1935-1985

Date	250 kwh	500 kwh	750 kwh
Jan. 1, 1935	3.56¢	2.77¢	—
Jan. 1, 1940	2.95	2.11	—
Jan. 1, 1945	2.84	2.04	
Jan. 1, 1950	2.79	2.02	—
Jan. 1, 1955	2.87	2.06	—
Jan. 1, 1960	2.98	2.12	—
Jan. 1, 1965	2.95	2.08	1.91¢
Jan. 1, 1970	3.00	2.10	1.90
Jan. 1, 1975	4.60	3.59	3.30
Jan. 1, 1980	6.11	5.56	4.92
Jan. 1, 1985	9.04	8.37	7.71

Source: *Moody's Public Utility Manual*, various annual editions.

managers. Not bad work, if you can get it."[29] Consider: Many state commissioners were part-time, and often were seeking higher political offices. Rate cases — and generally rate decrease cases — occurred every five years or so. The emphasis in rate design was on promotion (via declining block rates and internal subsidies) and on fairness (via the development of detailed cost allocation methods).

For both the regulated and the regulator, however, the environment was to change — twice. The first change began in the late 1960s. It occurred because of the development of a hostile economic, social, and political environment, and resulted in a decade-long struggle for survival. The second change began in the mid-1970s. It occurred because of the shortcomings of the traditional regulatory process and/or because of technological changes, and resulted in the restructuring of significant portions of the public utility sector.

The First Change: Late 1960s and 1970s

Beginning in the late 1960s, a series of events impacted on the economy which altered the environment within which public utilities operated. The annual rate of inflation began to accelerate, affecting both operating and construction costs.[30] Productivity advances were no longer adequate to offset such cost increases. Interest rates started to rise, forcing the capital-intensive utilities to pay record-high costs for their new capital (see Table 1-3). The combination of rising costs and high interest rates caused almost immediate coverage problems, widespread bond downgradings, and even higher interest costs. Fuel prices, for electric and gas utilities, started to escalate; by the end of the 1970s, many had tripled. The adequacy of capacity and/or reserves became of concern, as construction cutbacks occurred[31] and proved natural gas reserves declined.

Inevitably, utility rates began to rise. Consumers started to organize and to intervene in rate cases[32] in opposition to such increases — increases which began to occur almost annually and which involved larger and larger requests — and to urge new rate design concepts (particularly lifeline rates for those having difficulty paying rising monthly utility bills). The consumer group quickly expanded from basically residential customers, to commercial and industrial customers, as well as the federal government.[33] Americans became seriously concerned about the environment, as reflected in policy measures which forced business enterprises to cover both private and social costs, and to invest millions of dollars in nonrevenue producing pollution control equipment.[34] Intervention by environmental groups became common. Summarizes Anderson:

> Coinciding with the awakened interest of consumers, a second new, more ideologically motivated group of intervenors began showing up at commission hearings in the early seventies: the environmentalists. Groups such as the Sierra Club and the Environmental Defense Fund (EDF) identified the electric power industry as a major source of environmental degradation. The industry's pro-growth ethos and pricing policies were especially suspect. Where the industry's engineers looked and saw modern, technically efficient generating units, environmentalists looked and saw foul air, scarred landscape, and polluted streams. They argued that utilities failed to "internalize" these social costs in their pricing structure and so encouraged their users to consume more electricity than was optimal. Moreover, because the price of electricity did not vary by time of use, they claimed that utilities built more power plants than were needed in order to meet their peak demands. Starting in 1973, the EDF and other groups began making appearances in rate cases in Wisconsin, Michigan, New York, and California to urge regulators to pay more attention to the environmental effects of the industry's building and pricing plans.[35]

The media, after years of neglect, began to cover utility hearings, often giving them top coverage,[36] and to discuss the major issues confronting the

TABLE 1-3

Consumer Price Index and Yields on Newly Issued
Public Utility Bonds

1960-1987

Year	Annual Increase in CPI	Moody's			
		Aaa	Aa	A	Baa
1960	1.6%	4.77%	4.78%	5.02%	5.33%
1961	1.0	4.51	4.59	4.73	5.10
1962	1.1	4.36	4.34	4.45	4.75
1963	1.2	4.31	4.35	4.41	4.64
1964	1.3	4.46	4.46	4.55	4.74
1965	1.7	4.57	4.62	4.70	4.95
1966	2.9	5.44	5.57	5.76	5.98
1967	2.9	5.85	5.98	6.18	6.28
1968	4.2	6.57	6.72	6.90	7.11
1969	5.4	7.75	7.88	8.07	8.54
1970	5.9	8.61	8.63	9.19	9.68
1971	4.3	7.50	7.68	7.93	8.32
1972	3.3	7.31	7.45	7.60	7.85
1973	6.2	7.81	7.80	8.05	8.25
1974	11.0	9.02	9.04	9.75	9.16
1975	9.1	9.11	9.46	10.25	11.39
1976	5.8	8.43	8.60	8.96	9.57
1977	6.5	8.18	8.30	8.48	8.92
1978	7.7	8.93	9.23	9.21	9.66
1979	11.3	9.86	10.48	10.74	11.12
1980	13.5	12.55	13.08	13.41	14.26
1981	10.4	15.90	15.92	16.35	17.20
1982	6.1	14.94	14.56	15.06	15.83
1983	3.2	12.30	11.92	12.70	13.26
1984	4.3	*	13.23	12.92	14.49
1985	3.6	11.51	11.72	11.92	11.66
1986	1.9	8.96	9.14	9.61	10.12
1987	3.7	8.43	9.61	9.85	10.43

*Suspended January 17- October 12, 1984.
  Source: *Economic Report of the President*, February 1988; *Moody's Public Utility Manual*, 1987; *Moody's Bond Survey*, various issues.

entire public utility sector.[37] The legislative branches, state and federal, became involved as hundreds of bills were introduced dealing with various aspects of regulation (*e.g.,* elected versus appointed commissioners, automatic fuel adjustment clauses, construction work in progress [CWIP] in the rate base).[38] Regulatory issues began to appear on state ballots, with nuclear-related measures predominate (*e.g.,* Idaho voters, in 1982, approved a measure requiring voter approval of nuclear power facilities; Maine voters, in 1980, 1982, and 1987, rejected measures to close the state's only nuclear power facility, Maine Yankee[39]). Utility-related issues became of significance in some statewide political campaigns.[40] The judicial branch also became more involved in the regulatory process.[41] First, rate cases were often appealed either by the affected utility or by an intervenor. Second, federal-state jurisdictional problems intensified throughout the 1970s, and these disputes had to be resolved. Third, new legislation had to be interpreted, especially the national energy legislation of 1978, but also environmental legislation.

The Northeast Power Failure[42] (in November 1965) indicated the electric power industry's potential vulnerability to widespread interconnections, while subsequent brownouts stressed the need for adequate capacity. The accident at Three Mile Island[43] (in March 1979) raised again the issue of nuclear safety and cast doubt over the future of nuclear power.[44] The rapid decline in natural gas reserves led to a widespread curtailment of service in the early 1970s and to an acute shortage during the winter of 1976-77.[45] Conservation began to be promoted as the major long-run solution to the "energy crisis."

For telecommunications utilities, continuous technological change in the post-World War II period (*e.g.,* microwave transmission, transistor, silicon chips, communication satellites, digital computers) made it possible for the industry to meet the demand for new types of communications services.[46] These same technological innovations, however, also made possible new options for supplying telecommunications services. Stated differently, new technology, new markets, and new potential suppliers rendered all but obsolete the traditional natural monopoly concept (except, perhaps only on a temporary basis, for local exchange service), thereby confronting policymakers with a series of issues affecting the very structure of the domestic telecommunications industry.[47]

Water utilities likewise felt the change. While there has been a continuous growth in the demand for this essential commodity (for which there is no substitute), there have been no major technological advances in recent years. Thus, rates have continued to escalate due to inflation, environmental requirements, the federal Safe Drinking Water Act, and the need to secure and protect new sources of supply. These factors are of considerable importance in view of the fact that the industry is the most capital-intensive of the utilities, with a ratio of capital required per dollar of annual revenue ranging from 6:1 to 10:1.[48]

Some Implications

As a consequence of these — and other — developments, the decade of the 1970s was one of strain, change, and experimentation for the public utility sector.[49] Many utilities and regulatory commissions were ill-equipped to deal with the new environment. From the point of view of the utilities, their marketing departments had effectively promoted the use of communications, energy, and water for decades.[50] Conservation; inverted, flat, and/or lifeline rates; and inflation all conflicted with this mission. It was almost impossible to obtain accurate load and financial projections from electric utilities. Further: (1) The electric power industry was not even in charge of its technological destiny; for decades, it had relied upon its equipment manufacturers for technological advances and, equally important, technological advances had slowed considerably.[51] (2) The Federal Power Commission's wellhead price regulation held natural gas prices well below the competitive level, thereby encouraging consumption but discouraging exploration and development, and contributing to the natural gas shortage.[52] (3) The telecommunications industry went through a decade of uncertainty and confusion, as the Federal Communications Commission and Congress, and then the court, debated the industry's future structure and the industry, in turn, tried to anticipate policy changes.

From the point of view of the regulatory commissions, annual appropriations were too small (particularly at the state level) to permit adequate staffs, both in terms of numbers and of composition.[53] The regulatory process was oriented toward the past (*e.g.,* past or historic test years, embedded or fully distributed cost pricing methodology) and for periodic rate reductions; some state commissioners, as already noted, were only part-time. Regulatory lag[54] became a serious problem just at a time when public utilities found it essential to request, and the commissions to grant, larger and larger annual rate increases.[55] Substantial rate relief occurred. Table 1-4 shows annual rate increases for electric and gas utilities for 1965 through 1981, *exclusive* of the fuel adjustment clauses.[56] Yet, despite this rate relief, the utility sector was in a precarious financial situation by 1974[57] and another group began to organize and to intervene in rate cases — utility shareholders (see Table 1-5).[58]

Several important consequences follow:

1. Utilities, as well as their customers and investors, learned some lessons from these events. Marketing departments (in many electric firms) were abolished; planning departments were created. The planning period, moreover, more than doubled, especially for new electric generating facilities — and construction costs skyrocketed.[59] Customers found that even though rates were increasing, service interruptions could, and did, occur.[60] Investors found that utility earnings could fluctuate both upward and downward, and that annual dividend increases were no longer "guaranteed." In

TABLE 1-4

Electric and Gas Utility Annual Rate Increases*

1965-1981

Year	Electric	Gas
1965	$ 0	$ 6,300,000
1966	33,432,000	8,615,000
1967	701,000	2,834,000
1968	20,657,000	43,349,000
1969	145,123,000	137,705,000
1970	430,578,000	229,573,000
1971	802,678,000	204,313,000
1972	827,090,000	130,309,000
1973	1,150,763,000	491,265,000
1974	2,337,746,000	401,191,000
1975	3,168,730,000	917,460,000
1976	2,385,900,000	503,090,000
1977	2,636,780,000	692,790,000
1978	2,362,670,000	993,620,000
1979	4,567,010,000	2,043,910,000
1980	5,667,393,621	1,500,266,000
1981	9,477,250,500	1,062,902,800

*All figures exclude automatic fuel adjustment clauses.
Source: Ebasco Business Consulting Company.

TABLE 1-5
Electric Utility Shareholders Associations

American Society of Utility Investors
Arizona Public Service Shareholders Association
Association of Detroit Edison Shareholders
Association of Investors in New York Utilities
Association of South Carolina Electric and Gas
    Company Investors
California Association of Utility Shareholders
Louisiana Utility Shareholders, Inc.
National Association of Shareholders
Utah Shareholders Association of Utah
Wisconsin Utility Investors, Inc.

Source: *Electric Perspectives,* Winter 1982, p. 46.

fact, dividends were no longer a certainty, as Con Ed's stockholders learned in April 1974.[61] Investors in electric utility stocks also found that an increasing percentage of their annual earnings per share was comprised of allowance for funds used during construction (AFUDC), a noncash item (see Table 1-6). The public's perception of utilities changed radically, and utilities tried several different approaches to regain confidence throughout the decade.[62] Natural gas companies began to invest time and money in alternative gas sources; electric and gas utilities began to study diversification moves into nonregulated activities[63]; telephone utilities began to reorganize to confront the new competitive challenges.[64]

2. Rate increase cases proliferated, and soon resulted in a growing burden on commission (and utility) staffs. Annual appropriations and staffs of the traditional regulatory commissions were enlarged.[65] Part-time commissioners became full-time. Increased consumer pressures resulted in a movement to elected, rather than appointed, commissioners. New duties were assigned to the commissions by state and federal legislatures or, in some cases, were simply assumed. Hearings became lengthy, drawn-out, and expensive battles, even though many attempts were made to shorten the regulatory process.[66] In an effort to enhance the economic and technical research capabilities available to state commissions, the National Regulatory Research Institute was established in 1977.[67]

Some important reorganizations occurred: the Atomic Energy Commission was abolished in 1974, and two new federal agencies were created — the Nuclear Regulatory Commission (to regulate the construction and licensing of nuclear power facilities) and the Energy Research and Development Administration (to supervise research and development).[68] The Federal Energy Regulatory Commission — an independent regulatory agency within the Department of Energy — replaced the Federal Power Commission in 1977. The Texas Public Utility Commission was created in 1975.[69]

3. New organizations outside of the traditional regulatory commissions were created at all levels of government to deal with many of the new public concerns or to represent consumers — air and water control or pollution boards, consumer protection agencies[70] or divisions (within the state attorney general's office),[71] and energy departments at the state level; the Environmental Protection Agency (1970), the Consumer Product Safety Commission (1972), the Occupational Safety and Health Administration (1973), the Mine Safety and Health Administration (1973), and the Department of Energy (1977), among others, at the federal level.[72]

Whatever their merits, the creation of these agencies added a new complexity to the regulatory process. Required licenses and permits, to illustrate, often involve appearances before several different agencies, each of which may be required to hold public hearings. For an electric utility contemplating a nuclear generating facility, it is not uncommon for the company to confront as many as twenty state and federal agencies for necessary licenses and permits, in addition to meeting all of the Nuclear Regulatory

TABLE 1-6

Selected Financial Data

1965-1986

| Year | Return on Average Equity | | Market Prices[1] | | Market/Book Ratios | | Pre-Tax Interest Coverage[2] | AFUDC as a Percentage of Earnings Per Share |
	Moody's 24 Utilities	S&P's 400 Industrials	Moody's 24 Utilities	S&P's 400 Industrials	Moody's 24 Utilities	S&P's 400 Industrials	Moody's 24 Utilities	Moody's 24 Utilities
1965	11.9%	13.1%	100.0	100.0	2.35	2.23	5.29	4.6%
1966	12.2	13.2	87.9	97.4	2.00	2.04	5.10	5.4
1967	12.5	12.0	87.0	106.1	1.90	2.13	4.66	7.8
1968	11.8	12.6	84.0	115.0	1.74	2.19	4.25	10.2
1969	11.7	12.0	80.8	114.6	1.60	2.10	3.73	13.9
1970	11.1	10.4	67.5	97.7	1.27	1.75	2.98	21.5
1971	11.0	11.1	71.9	115.9	1.29	2.01	2.86	26.3
1972	11.3	12.0	68.5	130.3	1.17	2.14	2.96	30.3
1973	10.6	14.7	60.8	128.8	1.00	1.99	2.79	31.9
1974	10.5	14.7	41.2	99.4	.67	1.42	2.51	35.9
1975	10.4	12.4	43.8	103.3	.69	1.39	2.53	34.2
1976	10.7	14.5	51.3	122.3	.79	1.55	2.75	31.5
1977	11.1	14.6	57.7	116.0	.87	1.37	2.89	29.4
1978	10.8	15.3	54.3	113.6	.80	1.24	2.94	37.4
1979	11.1	17.3	51.5	122.8	.75	1.22	2.57	46.8
1980	10.9	15.6	46.8	143.9	.68	1.30	2.39	56.0
1981	12.3	14.8	47.3	154.3	.67	1.28	2.44	52.9
1982	13.2	11.0	54.3	142.9	.77	1.11	2.49	56.1
1983	14.3	12.2	63.2	193.1	.89	1.50	3.17	51.3
1984	15.1	14.6	60.8	193.9	.85	1.48	3.25	46.8
1985	14.5	12.2	74.5	222.3	1.01	1.67	3.33	42.7
1986	14.7	11.5	94.9	280.5	1.25	2.09	—	—

[1]1965 = 100.
[2]Includes AFUDC.
Source: *Moody's Public Utility Manual, 1987; Standard & Poor's Current Statistics.*

Commission's requirements. And there is always the possibility of subsequent court action initiated by environmental (or other) groups. Furthermore, the multiplicity of agencies raises the important questions: Who is really in charge? Who has the "final" say?[73] Likewise, the growth of both public advocacy and of increased participation by previously underrepresented groups (such as environmentalists, antinuclear, and consumer groups), adds pressure for formal, rather than informal, regulatory proceedings (thereby contributing to regulatory delay).[74] Increased participation, in addition, has tended to transform "the traditional model of administrative law (the basic purpose of which was to limit the coercive power of government officials) into an interest representation model of administrative law (the basic purpose of which is to ensure the equitable exercise of discretionary policymaking power by administrators)."[75]

4. Federal-state jurisdictional problems have intensified. In 1978, Congress extended federal control to intrastate natural gas prices, despite strong opposition from gas producing states.[76] However, stiff state opposition defeated an attempt to establish mandatory federal standards for the regulation of electric and gas retail rates. Instead, state commissions were required to consider, and to adopt if appropriate (for electric utilities), the specified standards.[77] The Federal Communications Commission's procompetitive policy with respect to interstate markets and terminal equipment was opposed by a majority of the state commissions who feared that removal of separations support for basic exchange service would result in a significant increase in local exchange rates and in a demise of the "universal service" concept.[78] In Texas, two major electric utilities restricted their transmission of electric power to intrastate commerce so as to avoid federal jurisdiction,[79] but the state of New Hampshire was unsuccessful in its attempt to keep low-cost hydroelectric power for its consumers.[80]

5. The issues brought before the regulatory commissions have shifted in emphasis. The most significant shift has been from a utility's total revenue requirements to its rate design. Prior to the 1970s, utility rate structures were developed by the companies themselves and, especially, by their engineers. The theoretical basis for the resulting structures was often difficult to discern, other than an obvious emphasis on promoting usage. Today, perhaps as much as one-half or more of a typical rate case is devoted to rate design; an emphasis heightened by rising utility rates, by enactment of the Public Utility Regulatory Policies Act of 1978, and by the introduction of competition in the telecommunications industry. The relevant issues include embedded versus incremental costs, peak-load pricing, lifeline rates, and so forth. This shift in emphasis, moreover, highlights an underlying conflict in objectives; specifically, fairness versus economic efficiency.[81] Embedded or fully distributed cost pricing, for instance, may be defended on grounds of fairness and "regulated competition," but only incremental cost pricing can be defended on grounds of economic efficiency and competitive standards.

Nor was the shift to rate design the only important one. The proper regulatory treatment of construction work in progress (CWIP) and of deferred taxes ("phantom taxes") are two obvious examples. So, too, are advertising expenditures and the efficiency of management. (Management audits were the rage of the 1970s![82]) Faced with growing financial problems, the determination of a fair rate of return received major emphasis. Rapidly rising utility rates revived old issues (*e.g.*, deposit and service termination policies); shortages raised new issues (*e.g.*, curtailment priorities); both factors led to the widespread development of conservation programs. And, by the early 1980s, significant cost overruns (plus the development of excess capacity) resulted in a highly controversial dimension being added to regulation — prudency reviews, especially for nuclear power projects.[83]

The entire regulatory process thus became "highly adversarial, as well as analytically demanding."[84] Moreover: (*1*) The regulatory agencies found themselves involved in areas once considered management's prerogative — capacity expansion, financing, and management itself,[85] to cite but three illustrations — raising once again the vital, but often neglected, question: How far should the regulatory commissions go in substituting their judgment for that of management?[86] (*2*) Some saw the end of the long-standing (but unwritten) "regulatory compact"; a compact that had two aspects. "First, in return for a monopoly franchise, utilities accepted an obligation to serve all comers. Second, in return for agreeing to commit capital to the business, utilities were assured a fair opportunity to earn a reasonable return on that capital."[87]

The Second Change: Mid-1970s and 1980s

Given the strain on the regulatory process, it is little wonder that significant substantive reform occurred, if for no other reason (*and there were many other good reasons*) than the inability of understaffed and overworked regulatory agencies to handle the growing workloads and conflicting pressures. As Reagan has summarized:

By the late 1970s, and continuing even more strongly into the 1980s, strong doubts were being expressed about regulation:

about its effectiveness, by economists who doubted that it could be effective, and by environmental advocates who thought it could and should be stronger.

about its costs, mostly by business firms and their spokespersons, but also by a number of economists concerned about the possibly negative impact of regulatory costs on productivity.

about its necessity in many of the traditional areas of economic regulation, where the microeconomic theorists developed strong arguments that the competitive market could provide adequate social controls without governmental intervention.[88]

The substantive reform that occurred was deregulation.[89] To date, Congress has substantially deregulated the transportation utilities[90] and has removed federal controls from approximately one-half of all natural gas sold[91]; a bill to deregulate most of the oil pipeline industry has been introduced into Congress.[92] The 1982 Modification of Final Judgment required the divestiture of the Bell System and greatly enhanced the Federal Communications Commission's procompetitive policy of the past decade or so.[93] The Federal Energy Regulatory Commission's 1985 rule on natural gas transmission, when fully implemented, promises to result in even greater reliance on competitive forces in the natural gas industry.[94] And debate continues over the desirability of deregulating a portion of the electric power industry, *i.e.*, generation; a debate that the growth of cogeneration and the existence of excess capacity may make moot.[95]

Regulation, as a substitute for competition, has never enjoyed great popularity. "Among economists," concludes Dewey as one example, "the disdain and contempt for regulation is nearly universal: if effective, it is thought to be pernicious, and if ineffective, a waste of resources."[96] However, the introduction of competitive forces and pressures both simplify and complicate the regulatory process. They simplify the process in that public utility rates should increasingly be set by market forces, and not by regulatory action, whether those rates be the wellhead price of natural gas or prices at the burner tip, or interLATA (local access and transport area) telephone rates. Yet, at the same time, they complicate the process (especially where deregulation of an industry is only partial[97]) by presenting a series of new issues and challenges that will require imaginative solutions. The following issues are illustrative.

A Competitive Philosophy. Competition will force public utilities to reorganize and to adopt a competitive philosophy. The present structure of utilities (both organizational and financial) was predicated on the monopoly concept; *i.e.*, ". . . customers have no place else to go for service, prices are set by regulators, recovery of investment is assured, the utility retains economies of scale and is the low-cost producer, and competition is on the fringes (if anywhere)."[98] Continues Hyman:

That view has led to the following policies:

- Cross-subsidies so that certain customers do not carry their costs.
- Low rates of depreciation.
- High debt ratios on the theory that low business risk can be offset with high financial risk.
- Capitalization of costs on the theory that recovery of those costs can be assured through the regulatory process.
- Taking what have proved to be unexpectedly high risks for low returns because risk was ignored on the theory that regulators can and will bail out the utility.

- Use of mortgage debt because the assets were supposed to be valuable and solid.
- High dividend payout ratio because earnings were stable.
- Vertical integration to reach economies of scale to provide high-quality service.[99]

The fact of the matter is that these policies are no longer appropriate in the new competitive and economic environment. The examples are endless. Because of the competitive environment, the American Telephone and Telegraph Company, during its reorganization, wrote off some $5.2 billion of assets, in large part ($3.8 billion) reflecting a reduction in the book value of telephone equipment and network facilities, and shifted its accounting methods from the "uniform systems of accounts" to "generally accepted accounting principles." Deregulation, as telephone subscribers are learning, "means removing cross-subsidies, basing prices on costs, de-averaging prices, de-tariffing competitive services, introducing more realistic depreciation schedules, and permitting free and open entry into new lines of business."[100] It will require the separation of resource allocation objectives from social equity or income distribution considerations. Marketing will become a cornerstone of a competitive philosophy, as AT&T well recognizes; marketing programs that must conform to generally accepted competitive behavior.[101] Pricing will become more complex, as airline deregulation proved.[102]

Management, according to Bleeke, must "maintain a clear sense of corporate direction and avoid foreclosing options by reacting too hastily to an unfamiliar competitive environment."[103] Consider Braniff Airlines: "Prior to deregulation it differentiated itself from other competitors by serving very specialized markets and emphasized luxury. With deregulation it expanded its route system by 50 percent overnight. It immediately became an international carrier, got involved in price wars, found its profits disappearing, and went into bankruptcy."[104] In short: "Questions that once were thought routine must be considered within a broader context of competition and market forces."[105]

It is easy to predict, therefore, that the emphasis upon pricing and rate design, which occurred throughout the 1970s, will continue into the future, for it is essential in the new environment that consumers be given proper price signals. Take local telephone service. Competition will result in the elimination of the subsidies long enjoyed by local companies, thereby causing local rates to continue to increase. Proper price signals and, absent government subsidies, the old goal of universal service, can be achieved only by the introduction of measured local service. In the words of Stelzer:

> . . . Measured local service can cushion the effect of losing the subsidy, since the fixed monthly charge for access to local measured service can be set lower than the comparable rate for flat rate service, which would have to be high enough to cover the cost of free local calls as well as

access. With measured service, the customer has control over the size of his local service bill. He can keep his bill below what it would be under flat rate service by making fewer local calls. And a customer who highly values local calls will presumably continue to make many, but will now be guided by price to make only those calls whose value to him exceeds their cost. This, of course, is exactly as it should be.[106]

The introduction of measured local service, however, has not been easy, since it is abundantly clear that such service is unpopular with subscribers.[107]

Or, take gas pipeline rate design. The use of rolled-in pricing, argues former FERC Chairman O'Connor,

> . . . separates the commodity rate the consumer sees from the price the producer sees. If a pipeline has supplies of low-priced gas under contract, it may be more willing to pay a higher price to producers. Consumers never see the higher price paid to the producer. Instead, they see a much smaller price change as the high-priced gas is averaged in with low-priced gas. We need to examine the use of rolled-in pricing and explore better ways of communicating price and volume signals from producers to consumers.[108]

Knowing When Not to Regulate. One of the greatest challenges confronting regulation today is to know when *not* to regulate. As competitive forces strengthen, prices should be determined in the marketplace. But at just what point competitive forces are strong enough to permit the end of pervasive regulation is yet to be determined. The issue already is one confronting both federal and state commissions in the provision of telecommunications services. How long should the Federal Communications Commission maintain comprehensive control over AT&T Communications, Inc.'s interLATA, interexchange rates? How long should the state commissions maintain comprehensive control over intrastate, interLATA, interexchange rates?

In August of 1984, for example, the Virginia State Corporation Commission issued a landmark decision in this area, when it decided to permit unregulated competition in the provision of intrastate, interLATA, interexchange services. The order also applied to the dominant carrier, although AT&T was ordered not to de-average rates for particular services on a geographic basis "until such time as we are satisfied that competitive factors will control its rates."[109] To illustrate both its content and its tone, the following two paragraphs from the order are instructive:

> In our view, effective competition does not mean that all firms serve all markets or that more than one firm necessarily serves each market. We believe the threat of competition is, in itself, a potent check on a

firm's pricing policies. Nor do we believe effective competition requires that all companies provide exactly the same product under identical circumstances. Indeed, if this were the case, one would be hard pressed to find an example of effective competition anywhere in the economy. In any event, the consuming public benefits from the wider range of price-quality choices arising from these differences. New entrants to virtually any market face challenges, but that is the nature of competition. Profits or success are not guaranteed. However, as evidenced by numerous examples in other industries such as computers, through use of ingenuity new entrants can succeed against seemingly formidable odds. The competitors in this case include well-financed, sophisticated companies with considerable experience in the telecommunications market. Therefore, in our judgment, the potential for effective competition is very high.

If the present regulation of AT&T's rates were continued until all of these challenges no longer existed, a change to competitive rates would not occur in the foreseeable future. And that does not serve the public interest. To continue traditional regulation of AT&T while not regulating the other common carriers would maintain rates at artificially high levels. It may even contribute to higher rates for rural customers if AT&T, unable to freely compete, lost its high-volume, high-density market.[110]

The commission announced that its division of communications would "monitor" closely the interLATA, interexchange telecommunications market, including tariffs, consumer complaints, rate levels, financial condition, and rivalrous activity, and stated: "If we find competition inadequate to serve the public interest, we will not hesitate to reimpose traditional regulatory review."[111] Finally, the Virginia commission noted: "Our determination that the interexchange market is competitive is notice to all carriers that their conduct henceforth is in no manner exempted by this commission from the reach of antitrust laws. From the date of this order they must conduct their business accordingly."[112]

In making such decisions, detailed economic analysis will be required and regulatory agencies (and utilities) will confront an antitrust constraint. Above all, they will find that a proper monitoring function differs substantially from the traditional regulatory function and that it requires, among other things, great restraint.

The Need for Flexibility. The growing competitive environment will require much greater flexibility (the new buzzword of the 1980s?) in the coming years. Almost every critic of economic regulation has noted the rigidity of traditional regulation as compared with competition; a rigidity, in part, dictated by the necessity of satisfying the requirements of due process. Could one imagine competitive enterprises such as General Motors, International Business Machines, Kroger, or Safeway having to wait just over nine months to change their prices, once a decision had been made to do so? Competition has no respect for precedent and the traditional regulatory process.

There are numerous examples. "As burner-tip competition grows, gas will have to be marketed more vigorously with prices more responsive to the volatility of alternate fuel prices."[113] It is one thing to estimate a fair rate of return for a monopoly firm; it is quite another thing to estimate a fair rate of return for a competitive (or a partially competitive) enterprise. Moreover, even when a more traditional type of regulation must be maintained — and that is especially true at the state level — the new environment suggests a change in its focus, as well as greater flexibility. New procedures and long-term planning are required, despite the fact that existing economic, political, and social pressures make it difficult to avoid lengthy, formal proceedings and short-run expediency.[114] Efficient, long-term planning, in turn, might well be enhanced if it were undertaken on a regional basis.[115]

Plan of Study

The topics covered in this introductory chapter suggest the outline of the book. Admittedly, more questions are raised than are answered, but there are no definitive answers to many of the problems under consideration. It is only with more understanding and discussion that regulation (along with the introduction of competition) in the United States can be successful. Moreover, controversy is the essence of public policy. The book has been divided into four major sections.

The Economic, Legal, and Administrative Concepts of Public Utility Regulation

Public policy, with respect to the domestic economy, has been directed toward maintaining competition. The belief has been that a competitive, free enterprise economic system is the best means of achieving our basic goals, including an efficient allocation of resources, a higher standard of living, and the preservation of personal freedom. In many industries, however, competition is imperfect. Especially is this true of a group of industries which have been singled out and subjected to a vast amount of government regulation. From an economic point of view, such industries (again, with important exceptions) tend to be monopolistic; from a legal standpoint, they are "affected with a public interest." To carry out regulatory functions, various administrative agencies have been established by state and federal legislatures. All decisions of these agencies are subject to judicial review. The economic and legal concepts of public utility regulation, along with the development of administrative agencies, are discussed in Part I.

The Theory of Public Utility Regulation

Economic regulation is primarily concerned with rate and service control. Rate regulation occupies much of the time of the administrative agencies. Under this topic fall the questions of supervision of operating expenses, depreciation rates and practices, valuation of physical property, rate of return, and the rate structure. Closely connected are problems dealing with service and safety standards, and with management efficiency. Public utilities are expected to provide adequate and safe service at reasonable rates and with reasonable efficiency. And, in more recent years, greater emphasis has been placed upon environmental quality control. The theory of public utility regulation forms the subject matter of Part II.

The Public Utility Industries

In practice, the theory of public utility regulation often must be adapted to specific conditions. Each of the nontransportation utility industries has experienced a unique history and currently confronts a number of specific problems. Further, an attempt has been made to develop a national energy policy, for the first time in history; an effort which impacts on the electric and gas utilities. The telecommunications industry has been restructured, but the industry's future market structure has yet to be determined. Water utilities are perhaps the forgotten utility industry, probably in large part because private ownership is so limited. The development of each utility industry, and current public policy problems, are considered in Part III.

An Evaluation — And the Future

Regulation has resulted in many complex problems and policy issues, and countless proposals have been advanced as solutions. These issues can be divided into two broad categories. The first category includes the procedures of regulation, such as delay, quality of the administrative agencies, and the desirability of independent regulatory commissions. The second category includes the kind of regulation presently employed. As a means of improving economic performance, regulation has many limitations compared with competition. Some have argued in recent years that the real problem is too much regulation, as well as regulation of the wrong kind, and some significant structural changes have been made. But if the trend toward encouraging more competition in the public utility sector is to be successful, other policy issues must be resolved, such as the accommodation of antitrust and regulatory policies. The problems and future of regulation are discussed in Part IV.

Notes

*Ben W. Lewis, "Ambivalence in Public Policy toward Regulated Industries," 53 *American Economic Review* 38, 40 (1963).

[1]Walter Adams, "The Role of Competition in the Regulated Industries," 48 *American Economic Review* 527 (1958).

[2]James C. Bonbright, *Principles of Public Utility Rates* (New York: Columbia University Press, 1961), p. 3.

[3]*Ibid.*, p. 4. "Despite the distinction . . . between the transportation . . . and the nontransport utilities, even most of the latter utilities do a transportation business if we use 'transportation' in a broad sense to include what are more frequently called 'transmission' and (in gas and electricity parlance) 'distribution.' True, a local utility company may have a production or manufacturing department, as does an electric company which generates its own power or a gas company which manufacturers its own gas. But the transmission-distribution phase of the business is a vital part of most public utility systems and may constitute the major component of the total cost of service. Moreover, even though the entire utility system is usually subject to regulation, it is likely to have derived its recognized utility status from the department of the operations concerned with the transfer of the gas, or the electricity, or the telephone messages from one location to another." *Ibid.*, p. 5.

[4]The public utility concept usually encompasses several fields of economic activity not included in the above classification, such as ice plants, sanitation, elevators, stockyards, and warehouses. For an exhaustive classification of public utilities, see Martin G. Glaeser, *Public Utilities in American Capitalism* (New York: The Macmillan Co., 1957), pp. 9-10, n. 2.

[5]*Ibid.*, p. 8.

[6]"It is the fact that the competitive market *compels* the results of its processes which is the ultimate defense against the demand that economic decisions be made or supervised by politically responsible authorities. Without such market compulsion, that demand appears ultimately irresistible in a society committed to representative government." Carl Kaysen and Donald F. Turner, *Antitrust Policy: An Economic and Legal Analysis* (Cambridge: Harvard University Press, 1959), pp. 48-49.

[7]Several industries and activities, not discussed in this book, also are subject, in varying degrees, to commission regulation, including banking, broadcasting, and corporate securities at the federal level, and insurance and milk distribution at the state level.

[8]There are signs of change, particularly in telecommunications. See, *e.g.,* "Telecommunications: The Global Battle," *Business Week,* October 24, 1983, pp. 126-48; Marcellus S. Snow (ed.), *Marketplace for Telecommunications: Regulation and Deregulation in Industrialized Democracies* (New York: Longman, Inc., 1986). Thus, in Great Britain, British Telecommunications ($16.3 billion in assets) was separated from the Post Office under legislation passed in 1981, a new entity — Mercury Communications — was granted a license to provide competing telecommunications services, and the terminal equipment market was opened to competition. The industry is supervised by the Office of Telecommunications. (In 1984, 50.2 percent of British Telecom was sold to the public. See "For Sale: Pieces of the Public Sector," *Fortune,* October 31, 1983, pp. 78-84.) However, in a 1985 decision, the Canadian Radio-Television and Telecommunications Commission denied an application to offer long-distance service in com-

petition with Bell Canada and British Columbia Telephone. (*The Wall Street Journal*, August 30, 1985, p. 8.)

[9]There are certain exceptions to private ownership, such as the majority of water and sewage systems; some electric power generation, transmission, and distribution; and a limited number of transportation facilities, particularly at the local level.

[10]*Smyth v. Ames*, 169 U.S. 466, 544 (1898).

[11]*Missouri ex rel. Southwestern Bell Teleph. Co. v. Missouri Pub. Service Comm.*, 262 U.S. 276, 291 (1923).

[12]C. Woody Thompson and Wendell R. Smith, *Public Utility Economics* (New York: McGraw-Hill Book Co., Inc., 1941), p. 12.

[13]Martin Shapiro, *The Supreme Court and Administrative Agencies* (New York: The Free Press, 1968), pp. 260-61.

[14]"Economic (sometimes called 'business') regulation is generally used to cover most of the older, traditional regulatory areas in which the price of the product or service and the authority to enter or leave the industry are the main objects of regulation; the public purpose is to protect the economic interests of consumers from monopoly exactions, and in terms of quality and quantity of service. ... Social regulation, on the other hand, is a recent arrival on the scene, pursued through single-headed line agencies that are clearly under presidential authority as part of the executive branch, and focused essentially on matters of health, safety, environmental protection, and social practices (e.g., employment discrimination), rather than on prices and conditions for entry of new firms into an industry." Michael D. Reagan, *Regulation: The Politics of Policy* (Boston: Little, Brown and Co., 1987), pp. 17-18.

[15]Emery Troxel, *Economics of Public Utilities* (New York: Holt, Rinehart & Winston, Inc., 1947), p. 786.

[16]Abram Chayes, "The Modern Corporation and the Rule of Law," in Edward S. Mason (ed.), *The Corporation in Modern Society* (Cambridge: Harvard University Press, 1959), p. 37.

[17]Horace M. Gray, "The Passing of the Public Utility Concept," 16 *Journal of Land & Public Utility Economics* 8 (1940); reprinted in American Economic Association, *Readings in the Social Control of Industry* (Philadelphia: Blakiston Co., 1949), pp. 280-303.

[18]*Ibid.*, p. 15 (footnote omitted).

[19]*Ibid.*, p. 16.

[20]Bonbright, *op. cit.*, p. 25.

[21]"Regulation, like the Constitution under which it functions, is a living thing. It cannot be locked off into any permanent formula. It must change as the economic system in which it operates changes. The good, sound, practical regulation of one decade may not necessarily be the good, sound, practical regulation of another, and the United States Supreme Court has always wisely insisted upon preserving this elasticity." Francis X. Welch, "The Effectiveness of Commission Regulation of Public Utility Enterprise," 49 *The Georgetown Law Journal* 639, 672 (1961).

[22]Bonbright, *op. cit.*, p. 110.

[23]See, *e.g.*, David C. Sweet and Kathryn Wertheim Hexter, *Public Utilities and the Poor: Rights and Responsibilities* (New York: Praeger Publishers, 1987). The lifeline rate controversy is considered in Chapter 10.

[24]U.S. Department of Commerce, 67 *Survey of Current Business* 32 (July 1987).

[25]Moody's Investors Service, *Moody's Public Utility Manual*, 1987, p. a21; American Gas Association, *Gas Facts, 1986 Data* (Arlington, Va., 1986), p. 116. Average bills

vary considerably from one section of the country to another. Thus, in 1986, the average residential gas bill ranged from $329 in the Pacific division to $712 in the East North Central division; from $233 in Florida to $790 in Connecticut. *Ibid.*, p. 115. See, *e.g.*, Hans H. Landsberg and Joseph M. Dukert, *High Energy Costs: Uneven, Unfair, Unavoidable?* (Baltimore: The Johns Hopkins Press, 1981).

[26]The data in this section must be used with caution. In general, the data — all for 1985 — are for the investor-owned electric and gas utilities, and for communications firms. As a result, the data are not for the entire nontransport utility sector (*e.g.*, municipal, cooperative, and federal electric systems; some specialized communications firms; water and sewer utilities).

[27]Adapted by permission from two of the author's articles: "The Changing Environment of Public-Utility Regulation: An Overview," in Albert L. Danielsen and David R. Kamerschen (eds.), *Current Issues in Public-Utility Economics* (Lexington, Mass.: D.C. Heath & Co., 1983), pp. 25-39 and "The Changing Structure of the Public Utility Sector," 117 *Public Utilities Fortnightly* 13, 13-20 (January 9, 1986).

[28]Federal Power Commission, *National Power Survey* (Washington, D.C.: U.S. Government Printing Office, 1964), Vol. I, p. 277.

[29]Howard Perry, "The New Federalism, Free Market Economics, and Utility Regulation" (Speech before the 1981 Symposium on Regulation, Warrenton, Va., August 18, 1981) (mimeographed), p. 5.

[30]"From 1972 to 1975 the cost per kilowatt of new nuclear capacity rose 80 percent while the cost of new coal-fired plants doubled." Douglas D. Anderson, "State Regulation of Electric Utilities," in James Q. Wilson (ed.), *The Politics of Regulation* (New York: Basic Books, Inc., 1980), p. 22. See also W. R. Steur, "Increasing Power Plant Costs in the 1970's," 87 *Public Utilities Fortnightly* 29 (February 4, 1971).

[31]In the period 1975 through 1982, 103 generating units, totaling 100,917 megawatts, were canceled. Of these units, 73 were nuclear. *Electrical Week*, January 4, 1982, p. 3; *Electric Utility Week*, January 10, 1983, p. 3. "Much of the trimming back in construction programs to date has been efficient and cost effective. The stress on conservation is long overdue and it certainly saves money for both the consumer and the utility. But the pendulum is now swinging too far the other way. Cancellations are now beginning to occur simply because utilities can't raise the money, even for plants for which there will be an economical market. And utilities are not ordering the electric power plants the nation needs for the 1990s." S. David Freeman, quoted in 108 *Public Utilities Fortnightly* 12 (November 19, 1981).

[32]Consumer group received substantial assistance. See, *e.g.*, Richard E. Morgan and Sandra Jerabek, *How to Challenge Your Local Electric Utility: A Citizen's Guide to the Power Industry* (Washington, D.C.: Environmental Action Foundation, 1974); Richard E. Morgan, *The Rate Watcher's Guide: How to Shape Up Your Utility's Rate Structure* (Washington, D.C.: Environmental Action Foundation, 1980).

[33]For a discussion and list of "grassroots advocates," see William T. Gormley, Jr., *The Politics of Public Utility Regulation* (Pittsburgh: University of Pittsburgh Press, 1983), chap. 2. On government participation see Patrick C. Mann, *Government Agency Participation in the Regulatory Process* (Columbus, Ohio: National Regulatory Research Institute, 1987).

[34]At the end of 1984, investor-owned electric utilities had invested $20.5 billion in electric plant in service attributable to environmental protection facilities, with $9.9 billion in environmental construction work in progress. Energy Information Adminis-

tration, U.S. Department of Energy, *Financial Statistics of Selected Electric Utilities 1984* (Washington, D.C.: U.S. Government Printing Office, 1986), pp. 738-39.

[35]Anderson, *op. cit.*, p. 24.

[36]"In close pursuit of the consumers came television and newspaper reporters, ever eager to broadcast a confrontation. Regulators, who a few years before had enjoyed the relative obscurity of technical debates over such arcane matters as the proper valuation of a utility's rate base and the correct treatment of depreciation, now saw those same debates recast in emotional terms before a wide audience." *Ibid.*, pp. 23-24.

[37]The utilities also became the subject of movies and novels. Among the best: "The China Syndrome" and Arthur Hailey, *Overload* (New York: Doubleday & Co., 1979).

[38]"For example, a study of the Maryland State Legislature revealed that 215 utility-related bills were introduced between 1976 and 1979. Of these, only 33 were passed, and only two could be described as major pieces of legislation." Gormley, *op. cit.*, p. 25, citing Jackson Diehl, "Utility Lobbies Keep Power Turned on in Annapolis," *Washington Post*, March 30, 1980, p. 1.

[39]See "Anti-Nuke Forces Lose Bid to Close Facility in Maine," *The Wall Street Journal*, November 5, 1987, p. 6. [The five states with the highest percentage of their electric power supply generated by nuclear power: Vermont (77 percent), Maine (69 percent), South Carolina (61 percent), Virginia (54.9 percent), and Connecticut (49.8 percent). 117 *Public Utilities Fortnightly* 32 (February 6, 1986).]

[40]Perhaps the best known was the 1978 gubernatorial race in New Hampshire, where a major issue was the inclusion of construction work in progress (CWIP) in the rate base. See also Salomon Brothers, Inc., "The Elections, the Electrics — and Recent Rate Cases," November 5, 1982.

[41]Sometimes too involved, according to many. As Justice Rehnquist wrote in a 1978 decision: "Administrative decisions should be set aside in this context, as in every other, only for substantial procedural or substantive reasons as mandated by statute . . . not simply because the court is unhappy with the result reached. . . ." *Vermont Yankee Nuclear Power Corp. v. Natural Resources Defense Council*, 435 U.S. 519, 558 (1978).

[42]See, *e.g., Northeast Power Failure*, A Report to the President by the Federal Power Commission (Washington, D.C.: U.S. Government Printing Office, 1965); *Prevention of Power Failures*, Vol. I: *Report of the Commission* (Washington, D.C.: U.S. Government Printing Office, 1967).

[43]See, *e.g.*, Daniel Martin, *Three Mile Island: Prologue or Epilogue?* (Cambridge: Ballinger Publishing Co., 1980); David L. Sills, C. P. Wolfe, and Vivien B. Shelanski, *The Accident At Three Mile Island: The Human Dimension* (Boulder: Westview Press, 1981); Daniel F. Ford, *Three Mile Island: 30 Minutes to Melt Down* (New York: Viking Press, 1981). The later meltdown at Chernobyl (in April 1986) reinforced the safety concern. See, *e.g.*, Nuclear Regulatory Commission, *Report on the Accident at Chernobyl Nuclear Power Station* (Washington, D.C.: U.S. Government Printing Office, 1987); *Implications of the Accident at Chernobyl for Safety Regulation of Commercial Nuclear Power Plants in the United States* (Nuclear Regulatory Commission draft report, September 1987). See also "The Nuclear Bargain," *Newsweek*, May 12, 1986, pp. 40-49; *1986 Nuclear Power Safety Report* (Washington, D.C.: Critical Mass Energy Project, 1987).

[44]No nuclear reactors have been ordered in the United States since 1978, despite the fact that nuclear energy's growth is continuing in other industrial countries. One

major reason for the domestic situation "is the rising cost and uncertainty of building a nuclear plant and getting it licensed in light of increasing regulatory requirements, especially in the wake of the unfortunate incident at Three Mile Island." Robert W. Scherer, quoted in 108 *Public Utilities Fortnightly* 12 (November 19, 1981). See, *e.g.*, "Japan: The Unlikely Nuclear Giant," *Business Week*, September 19, 1983, pp. 66, 71; Energy Information Administration, U.S. Department of Energy, *Commercial Nuclear Power: Prospects for the United States and the World* (Washington, D.C.: U.S. Government Printing Office, 1986).

[45]In 1976, interstate pipelines were able to deliver only about three-quarters of the amount of gas they agreed to deliver under long-term contracts. See Federal Power Commission, *Gas Curtailment Report No. 22438: Requirements, Curtailments and Deliveries of Interstate Pipeline Companies* (1977).

[46]See, *e.g.*, Kurt Borchardt, *Structure and Performance of the U.S. Communications Industry* (Boston: Graduate School of Business Administration, Harvard University, 1970).

[47]See, *e.g.*, John R. Meyer et al., *The Economics of Competition in the Telecommunications Industry* (Cambridge: Oelgeschlager, Gunn & Hain, Publishers, Inc., 1980); Gerald W. Brock, *The Telecommunications Industry: The Dynamics of Market Structure* (Cambridge: Harvard University Press, 1981); David S. Evans (ed.), *Breaking Up Bell: Essays on Industrial Organization and Regulation* (New York: Elsevier Science Publishing Co., Inc., 1983); Manley R. Irwin, *Telecommunications America: Markets Without Boundaries* (Westport, Conn.: Quorum Books, 1984); Albert L. Danielsen and David R. Kamerschen (eds.), *Telecommunications in the Post-Divestiture Era* (Lexington, Mass.: D.C. Heath & Co., 1986); Gerald R. Faulhaber, *Telecommunications in Turmoil: Technology and Public Policy* (Cambridge: Ballinger Publishing Co., 1987).

[48]U.S. Environmental Protection Agency, *Survey of Operating and Financial Characteristics of Community Water Systems* (Washington, D.C., 1977).

[49]See Paul L. Joskow, "Inflation and Environmental Concern: Structural Change in the Process of Public Utility Price Regulation," 17 *Journal of Law & Economics* 291 (1974); Paul W. MacAvoy, "The Present Condition of Regulated Enterprise" (Working Paper No. 5, Series C, School of Organization and Management, Yale University, October 1978); L. H. Knapp, "Earthquakes and Aftershocks: The Regulatory Management Landscape of the 1980s," 107 *Public Utilities Fortnightly* 11 (January 1, 1981).

[50]The promotional practices of electric and gas utilities provided some regulatory nightmares in the late 1950s and early 1960s. See Irwin M. Stelzer and Bruce C. Netschert, "Hot War in the Energy Industry," 45 *Harvard Business Review* 14 (November-December 1967).

[51]See Edward Berlin, Charles J. Cicchetti, and William J. Gillen, *Perspectives on Power* (Cambridge: Ballinger Publishing Co., 1974), pp. 1-11.

[52]See Stephen G. Breyer and Paul W. MacAvoy, *Energy Regulation by the Federal Power Commission* (Washington, D.C.: The Brookings Institution, 1974), esp. chap. 3.

[53]See, *e.g.*, Charles F. Phillips, Jr., "The Effectiveness of State Commission Regulation," in Warren J. Samuels and Harry M. Trebing (eds.), *A Critique of Administrative Regulation of Public Utilities* (East Lansing: MSU Public Utilities Papers, 1972), pp. 71-89. Notes Perry: "What we are now witnessing in state regulation — and the rapid turnover among commissioners is the most visible symptom of this — is painful adaption to an environment that was once comfortable, and has now become hostile." Perry, *op. cit.*

[54]See, *e.g.*, Richard L. Norgaard and Michael J. Riley, "Regulatory Lag: Everyone Loses," 111 *Public Utilities Fortnightly* 29 (May 26, 1983).

[55]To illustrate: (*1*) In 1970, 46 investor-owned electric utilities received $430,578,000 in rate relief, an average of $9,360,391 per company. In 1981, 101 investor-owned electric utilities received $9,477,250,000 in rate relief, an average of $93,834,158 per company. [Data from Ebasco Business Consulting Company.] (*2*) In 1981, 988 rate cases — 223 electric, 200 gas, two combination electric and gas, 122 telephone, 373 water, 48 sewer, and 20 combination water and sewer — were filed with the state commissions. *1981 Annual Report on Utility and Carrier Regulation* (Washington, D.C.: National Association of Regulatory Utility Commissioners, 1982), pp. 281-347.

[56]Fuel clauses added $11 billion to consumers' electric and gas bills in 1977; approximately 80 percent of the total increase of $13.4 billion for that year. *Electric and Gas Utility Rate and Fuel Adjustment Clause Increases, 1977* (Committee Print, Subcommittee on Intergovernmental Relations and Subcommittee on Energy, Nuclear Proliferation and Federal Services, Senate, 95th Cong., 2d sess.) (Washington, D.C.: U.S. Government Printing Office, 1978), p. vii. The magnitude of rate increases is apparent when it is noted that electric and gas rates increased $6 billion in the twenty-five year period 1948 through 1973, compared with an increase of $48.3 billion in the four-year period 1974 through 1977. *Ibid.*

[57]See, *e.g.*, Paul G. Russell, "Developments in Utility Financing," in American Bar Association Annual Report, Section of *Public Utility Law, 1975*, pp. 33-47; Scott Fenn, *America's Electric Utilities: Under Siege and in Transition* (New York: Praeger Publishers, 1984); Leonard S. Hyman, *America's Electric Utilities: Past, Present, and Future* (2d ed.; Arlington: Public Utilities Reports, Inc., 1985).

[58]Most of the organized shareholder associations have three main goals: (*1*) "to improve the regulatory climate through interaction with legislative and administrative bodies"; (*2*) "to educate and inform utility shareholders about issues that may affect their investments"; and (*3*) "to promote good relations between association members and utilities." Their approach varies "from direct intervention in rate hearings and legal proceedings to subtle appeals to the general public." They "are managed by an Executive Board or Board of Directors, the members of which are volunteers. The day-to-day administrative duties are managed by an Executive Director or President, usually the chief spokesman for the association. A few of the financially stronger associations, such as the California Association of Utility Shareholders, have full-time directors. . . . Most shareholder associations are financed by membership dues. The dues usually range from $10 to $20 per member, and membership in dues-collecting associations range from 1,500 in the Association of South Carolina Electric and Gas Company Investors to 8,000 in the California Association of Utility Shareholders. The few associations financed through voluntary contributions tend to have larger memberships because marginally interested investors are more willing to join. The Wisconsin Utility Investors, Inc., for example, is financed entirely through voluntary contributions and claims 22,000 members." "Equity Shareholder Associations," *Electric Perspectives*, Winter 1982, p. 46.

[59]To cite just two examples. (*1*) When construction of the Zimmer nuclear power plant began in 1969 (Cincinnati Gas & Electric Company, responsible for the plant's construction, owns 46.5 percent; Dayton Power and Light Company owns 28.1 percent; and Columbus and Southern Ohio Electric Company owns 25.4 percent), the estimated cost was $240 million, with operations scheduled to commence in 1975. After spending $1.6 billion, the plant's owners faced a total cost of $3.5 billion, with

an uncertain operating date. The Nuclear Regulatory Commission halted all safety-related construction at the plant in November 1982, following allegations of misman-agement. In late-1984, the owners announced that the plant would be converted to a coal-fired unit (with American Electric Power Company in charge of the construction) at an additional cost of $1.7 billion, to be completed in 1991. [*The Wall Street Journal*, August 2, 1984, p. 2.] (2) The Midland nuclear power plant (owned by CMS Energy Corporation, formerly Consumers Power Company) was scheduled originally to be on line by 1975 at a cost of $276 million. When construction was halted in 1984, the company had spent $4.2 billion. (The plant was 85 percent complete.) In late 1986, the Michigan Public Service Commission approved a plan to convert the Midland plant into a gas-fired facility and, in early 1987, the Federal Energy Regulatory Commission certified the proposed plant as a qualifying cogeneration facility. The converted plant, estimated to cost $600 million, is expected to be in operation in early 1990. [See "The Midland Cogeneration Project: New Horizons for Electrics," 119 *Public Utilities Fortnightly* 42 (April 16, 1987.)] According to Smith: "The average book value of generating plant today is $210 per kilowatt, while new generating units are coming on stream at costs of $600 to over $2,000 per kilowatt." Darrell A. Smith, "Pricing Strategies for New Generating Plants," 111 *Public Utilities Fortnightly* 31, 32 (June 9, 1983) (footnote omitted).

[60]See, *e.g.*, Andrew S. Carron and Paul W. MacAvoy, *The Decline of Service in the Regulated Industries* (Washington, D.C.: American Enterprise Institute, 1981).

[61]Consolidated Edison Company of New York was hard hit by the 1973 oil embargo, since the utility was producing 75 percent of its electricity by burning foreign oil. "A black market for oil developed with Con Ed buying oil on the high seas at $23 to $24 per barrel — up from $4 to $5 per barrel earlier. . . Even though the New York Public Service Commission authorized a temporary increase of something like $75 million in February, 1974, in April the company was on the brink of bankruptcy because it couldn't raise working capital. . . . Banks were refusing to loan, and people weren't buying its bonds. When the commission refused to allow the company to use working capital to pay dividends, the company had to pass on its dividends in April. The stock stopped trading for a while." Anderson, *op. cit.*, p. 22. "It was to first time in eighty-nine years that the giant utility had failed to pay quarterly dividends on its common stock. . . . The shock of Con Ed's actions reverberated throughout the industry. The common stock of Boston Edison fell from over $25 on April 22 to about $15 on May 14. Duke Power's stock dropped over 12 percent." *Ibid.*, pp. 22-23.

[62]See, *e.g.*, Geraldine Alpert, "Consumer Advisory Boards and Investor-owned Utilities: Rhetoric and Reality," 108 *Public Utilities Fortnightly* 19 (August 27, 1981).

[63]During the 1960s, several electric utilities diversified into coal mining, in an attempt to secure assured and cheaper sources of supply. The more recent diversification move is into unrelated lines of business: FPL Group Inc. into cable TV and insurance; Gulf States Utilities Company into oil exploration; PacifiCorp into gold mining and telephone communications; Pacific Lighting Corporation into home building and drugstores; and Pinnacle West Capital Corporation (formerly AZP Group Inc.) into banking. See, *e.g.*, "A High-Risk Era for the Utilities," *Business Week*, February 23, 1981, pp. 76-86; "Utilities, Flush With Cash, Enter New Fields," *The Wall Street Journal*, July 1, 1986, p. 6. Warned one editorial: "Inevitably the attempts of the power companies to get their capital out of the utility industry brings to mind the sad history of the Penn Central and the collapse of what once called itself 'the

standard railroad of the World'." *Business Week, op. cit.*, p. 162. See *Utility Diversification Study* (Arlington: Public Utilities Reports, Inc., 1981); Stanley York and J. Robert Malko, "Utility Diversification: A Regulatory Perspective," 111 *Public Utilities Fortnightly* 15 (January 6, 1983); J. Robert Malko and George R. Edgar, "Energy Utility Diversification: Its Status in Wisconsin," 118 *Public Utilities Fortnightly* 20 (August 7, 1986).

[64]See, *e.g.*, "Behind AT&T's Change at the Top," *Business Week*, November 6, 1978, pp. 114-26; Alvin von Auw, *Heritage & Destiny: Reflections on the Bell System in Transition* (New York: Praeger Publishers, 1983); Leonard Schlesinger et al., *Chronicles of Corporate Change: Management Lessons from AT&T and Its Offspring* (Lexington, Mass.: D. C. Heath & Co., 1986).

[65]"Appropriations have increased in recent years, yet the increments have not been equal to rising work loads." David Welborn, *The Governance of Federal Regulatory Agencies* (Knoxville: University of Tennessee Press, 1977), p. 63.

[66]"A typical retail rate case for a medium to large utility costs about $300,000 to $500,000 in out-of-pocket costs and probably double that amount when company fixed expenses such as staff salaries are included." Michael Schmidt, *Automatic Adjustment Clauses: Theory and Application* (East Lansing: MSU Public Utilities Studies, 1980), p. 9. See also "Legal Expenses and Utility Rate Making," 102 *Public Utilities Fortnightly* 58 (October 26, 1978).

[67]See David C. Sweet, "Meeting the Research Needs of State Regulators," 102 *Public Utilities Fortnightly* 11 (August 17, 1978); Douglas N. Jones, "Three Years in the Life of the National Regulatory Research Institute," 107 *Public Utilities Fortnightly* 13 (January 15, 1981).

[68]The Energy Research and Development Administration was consolidated into the Department of Energy in 1977.

[69]See Jack Hopper, "A Legislative History of the Texas Public Utility Regulatory Act of 1975," 28 *Baylor Law Review* 777 (1976).

[70]See, *e.g.*, Note, "The Office of Public Counsel: Institutionalizing Public Interest Representation in State Government," 64 *Georgetown Law Journal* 895 (1976).

As Stelzer has noted: "Consumer advocacy is big business today." Between 1977 and 1979, for example, nearly $6 million was awarded by the Department of Energy "to state consumer offices to assist them in their role as consumer advocates. . . . There are approximately 170 nongovernmental Public Interest Research Groups nationwide. The Consumer Federation of America, a Washington-based lobby group, currently represents 200 so-called 'grass-roots' organizations." Irwin M. Stelzer, "A Policy Guide for Utility Executives: 'Know When to Hold'em; Know When to Fold'em'," 106 *Public Utilities Fortnightly* 62, 65 (October 9, 1980). See also "Reimbursing Intervenors for Attorney's Fees," 105 *Public Utilities Fortnightly* 42 (February 28, 1980). On the pros and cons of public advocacy, see Gormley, *op. cit.*, pp. 44-48.

[71]See, *e.g.*, *Attorney General's Intervention Before Regulatory Agencies* (Raleigh, N.C.: National Association of Attorneys General, 1975). These divisions may cause conflicts. "In Michigan, for example, the attorney general's Special Litigation Division represents the public in public service commission proceedings and the courts, while the attorney general's Public Service Division represents the public service commission staff." Gormley, *op. cit.*, p. 51.

[72]Both administrative and compliance costs grew dramatically. (*1*) "The first four years of the 1970s saw a doubling of the number of pages in the *Federal Register*, the primary document for notification of federal rules and regulations." (*2*) The adminis-

trative costs for economic regulation (in 1970 dollars) rose from $.4 billion in fiscal year 1971 to $.9 billion in fiscal year 1979; administrative costs for social regulation rose from $.8 billion to $4.6 billion in the same period. (For 57 federal agencies involved in both economic and social regulation, the overall employment in 1979 was approximately 87,500, "almost three times as large as in 1971.") (*3*) In 1976, the estimated compliance costs of business, for both economic and social regulation, were $62.3 billion. Kenneth W. Clarkson and Roger LeRoy Miller, *Industrial Organization: Theory, Evidence, and Public Policy* (New York: McGraw-Hill Book Co., 1982), pp. 452-53.

[73]*Re Southern California Edison Co.*, 86 PUR3d 482 (Cal. 1970), *rev'd sub nom. Orange County Air Pollution Control Dist. v. California Pub. Utilities Comm.*, 90 PUR3d 389 (1971). See, *e.g.*, Douglas N. Jones and Richard A. Tybout, "Environmental Regulation and Electric Utility Regulation: Compatibility and Conflict," 14 *Boston College Environmental Affairs Law Review* 31 (1986).

[74]See, *e.g.*, Richard B. Stewart, "The Reformation of American Administrative Law," 88 *Harvard Law Review* 1667 (1975). See also Ernest Gellhorn, "Public Participation in Administrative Proceedings," 81 *Yale Law Journal* 359 (1972); Roger C. Cramton, "The Why, Where, and How of Broadened Public Participation in the Administrative Process," 60 *Georgetown Law Journal* 529 (1972); Andrew McFarland, *Public Interest Lobbies: Decision Making on Energy* (Washington, D.C.: American Enterprise Institute, 1976).

[75]Stephen G. Breyer and Richard B. Stewart, *Administrative Law and Regulatory Policy* (Boston: Little, Brown & Co., 1979), p. 1014 (with a citation to Stewart, *op. cit.*).

[76]See *Oklahoma v. Federal Energy Regulatory Comm.*, 494 F. Supp. 636 (W.D. Okla. 1980), *aff'd*, 661 F. 2d 832 (10th Cir. 1981), *cert. denied sub nom. Texas v. Federal Energy Regulatory Comm.*, 102 S. Ct. 2902 (1982).

[77]See *State of Mississippi et al. v. Federal Energy Regulatory Comm.*, 38 PUR4th 284 (D. Miss. 1981), where a federal judge held unconstitutional certain provisions of the Public Utility Regulatory Policies Act of 1978 (PURPA). The act, declared Judge Cox, "usurps and dispells [sic] the intrastate jurisdiction and activity of the Mississippi Public Service Commission. ... The sovereign state of Mississippi is not a robot, or lackey which may be shuttled back and forth to suit the whim and caprice of the federal government, but was and is the prime benefactor of the power and authority designated by the Constitution and allocated as desired by this instrument as the supreme law of the land." *Ibid.*, pp. 284, 285 (footnote omitted). On appeal, the decision was reversed: *Federal Energy Regulatory Comm. v. State of Mississippi*, 456 U.S. 742, 47 PUR4th 1 (1982).

[78]See, *e.g.*, Edward P. Larkin, "Separations and Settlements in the Telephone Industry" (Washington, D.C.: National Association of Regulatory Utility Commissioners, 1979); "The Ruckus that Phone Rates will Raise," *Business Week*, June 13, 1983, pp. 39-43.

[79]*West Texas Utilities Co. v. Texas Elec. Service Co., 1979-2 Trade Cases*, Par. 62,851 (N.D. Tex. 1979). See A. Robert Thorup, "Electric Range War in Texas: A Case Study in Federal-State Energy Regulation," 48 *George Washington Law Review* 392 (1980).

[80]*Re New England Power Co.*, 120 NH 866 (1980), *rev'd*, 455 U.S. 331, 45 PUR4th 641 (1982).

[81]See, *e.g.*, Edward E. Zajac, *Fairness or Efficiency: An Introduction to Public Utility Pricing* (Cambridge: Ballinger Publishing Co., 1978).

[82]For a list of recent management audits, see *1985 Annual Report on Utility and*

Carrier Regulation (Washington, D.C.: National Association of Regulatory Utility Commissioners, 1987), pp. 501-09. See also Ralph C. Mitchell III and Richard J. Metzler, "The Second-generation Management Audits," 111 *Public Utilities Fortnightly* 21 (May 12, 1983).

[83]See, *e.g.*, Robert E. Burns et al., *The Prudent Investment Test in the 1980s* (Columbus, Ohio: National Regulatory Research Institute, 1985); "'Prudency Reviews' Are Changing the Way Utilities Set Rates," *The Wall Street Journal*, October 2, 1986, pp. 1, 21; Chapter 8.

[84]Perry, *op. cit.*

[85]Several senior utility executives have "retired" in part upon the urging of state regulatory officials. See, *e.g.*, "Departure of Consumers Power Head is Urged by State Official in Rate Case," *The Wall Street Journal*, August 6, 1984, p. 5; "Boston Edison Bid on Rate Rise Fails; Firm is Criticized," *The Wall Street Journal*, June 27, 1986, p. 12; "Philadelphia Electric Told to Cut Rates and Regulator Urges Chairman to Quit," *The Wall Street Journal*, February 16, 1988, p. 7.

[86]See "Managerial and Regulatory Functions Distinguished," 74 *Public Utilities Fortnightly* 67 (July 2, 1964); "Management — Utility and Commission Powers," 79 *Public Utilities Fortnightly* 57 (March 2, 1964); Charles F. Phillips, Jr., "The Thin Red Line," 57 *Bell Telephone Magazine* 10 (Summer 1978); Richard B. McGlynn, "The Regulator as Manager" (Paper presented at the Third Annual Utility Regulatory Conference, Washington, D.C., October 7, 1980) (mimeographed).

[87]Irwin M. Stelzer, "The Utilities of the 1990s," *The Wall Street Journal*, January 7, 1987, p. 20. With respect to the electric power industry: "Monopoly franchises are being eroded by the entry of new producers of power, ranging from entrepreneurs financing small hydroelectric developments to large chemical companies selling excess power. ... Regulators are now refusing utilities an opportunity to earn profits on their investments if subsequent developments provide them with the hindsight to see that a plant should not have been built — at least not just now or not just there or not just in that way. ... " *Ibid.*

[88]Reagan, *op. cit.*, p. 36.

[89]See, *e.g.*, Donald L. Martin and Warren F. Schwartz (eds.), *Deregulating American Industry: Legal and Economic Problems* (Lexington, Mass.: D.C. Heath & Co., 1977); Roger G. Noll and Bruce M. Owen, *The Political Economy of Deregulation: Interest Groups in the Regulatory Process* (Washington, D.C.: American Enterprise Institute, 1983); Martha Derthick and Paul J. Quirk, *The Politics of Deregulation* (Washington, D.C.: The Brookings Institution, 1985); Robert W. Poole, Jr., *Unnatural Monopolies: The Case for Deregulating Public Utilities* (Lexington, Mass.: D.C. Heath & Co., 1985); Leonard W. Weiss and Michael W. Klass (eds.), *Regulatory Reform: What Actually Happened* (Boston: Little Brown & Co., 1986); Marshall R. Goodman and Margaret T. Wrightson, *Managing Regulatory Reform: The Reagan Strategy and Its Impact* (New York: Praeger Publishers, 1987). But see, *e.g.*, Martin T. Farris, "The Case Against Deregulation in Transportation, Power, and Communications," 45 *I.C.C. Practitioners' Journal* 306 (1978); Susan J. Tolchin and Martin Tolchin, *Dismantling America: The Rush to Deregulate* (New York: Oxford University Press, 1983); Frederick C. Thayer, *Rebuilding America: The Case for Economic Regulation* (New York: Praeger Publishers, 1984).

[90]See Railroad Revitalization and Regulatory Reform Act of 1976 (Pub. Law 96-296, 94 Stat. 803); Airline Deregulation Act of 1978 (Pub. Law 95-504, 92 Stat. 1705); Motor Carrier Act of 1980 (Pub. Law 96-296, 94 Stat. 793); and Staggers Rail Act of 1980 (Pub. Law 96-448, 94 Stat. 1895). On airline deregulation, see, *e.g.*, John

R. Meyer and Clinton V. Oster, Jr. (eds.), *Airline Deregulation: The Early Experience* (Boston: Auburn House Publishing Co., 1981); J. Rhoads Foster et al. (eds.), *Airline Deregulation: Lessons for Public Policy Formation* (Washington, D.C.: Institute for Study of Regulation, 1983); John R. Meyer et al., *Deregulation and the New Airline Entrepreneurs* (Cambridge: The MIT Press, 1984); Steven Morrison and Clifford Winston, *The Economic Effects of Airline Deregulation* (Washington, D.C.: The Brookings Institution, 1986).

[91]See Natural Gas Policy Act of 1978 (Pub. Law 95-621, 92 Stat. 3351). On the act, see, *e.g.*, Richard J. Pierce, Jr., "The Natural Gas Policy Act of 1978," 47 *Journal of the Kansas Bar Association* 259 (1978); Paul W. MacAvoy, "The Natural Gas Policy Act of 1978," 19 *Natural Resources Journal* 811 (1979). On the issues, see Edward J. Mitchell (ed.), *The Deregulation of Natural Gas* (Washington, D.C.: American Enterprise Institute, 1983); Chapter 14.

[92]Jurisdiction over the oil pipeline industry was transferred from the Interstate Commerce Commission to the Federal Energy Regulatory Commission by the Department of Energy Organization Act of 1977 (Pub. Law 95-91, 91 Stat. 565, 584). On the FERC's regulation of the industry, see *Re Williams Pipe Line Co.*, Opinion No. 154 (FERC, 1982), *aff'd in part and rem'd in part sub nom. Farmers Union Central Exchange, Inc. v. Federal Energy Regulatory Comm.*, 734 F. 2d 1486, 59 PUR4th 1 (D.C. Cir. 1984), *cert. denied*, 105 S. Ct. 507 (1984), order on remand, 67 PUR4th 669 (FERC, 1985).

[93]See, *e.g.*, Herbert F. Forrest and Richard E. Wiley, *Regulation and Deregulation After the AT&T Divestiture* (New York: Practicing Law Institute, 1984) and *The New Telecommunications Era After the AT&T Divestiture: The Transition to Full Competition* (New York: Practicing Law Institute, 1985); Chapter 15. On international telecommunications, see Stuart Z. Chiron and Lise A. Rehberg, "Fostering Competition in International Telecommunications," 38 *Federal Communications Law Journal* 1 (1986).

[94]See Chapter 14.

[95]See, *e.g.*, Tom Alexander, "The Surge to Deregulate Electricity," *Fortune*, July 13, 1981, pp. 98-105; Paul L. Joskow and Richard Schmalensee, *Markets for Power: An Analysis of Electrical Utility Deregulation* (Cambridge: The MIT Press, 1983); John C. Moorhouse (ed.), *Electric Power: Deregulation and the Public Interest* (San Francisco: Pacific Research Institute for Public Policy, 1986); Chapter 13.

[96]Donald J. Dewey, "The New Learning: One Man's View," in Harvey J. Goldschmid, H. Michael Mann, and J. Fred Weston, *Industrial Concentration: The New Learning* (Boston: Little, Brown & Co., 1974), p. 10. "Unregulated, extra-legal monopolies are tolerable evils; but private monopolies with the blessing of regulation and the support of law are malignant cancers in the system." Henry C. Simons, "The Requisites of Free Competition," 26 *American Economic Review* 68, 74 (March, 1936). See also Peter Navarro, *The Dimming of America: The Real Cost of Electric Utility Regulatory Failure* (Cambridge: Ballinger Publishing Co., 1985) and "The Performance of Utility Commissions," in Moorhouse, *op. cit.*, chap. 10.

[97]See, *e.g.*, Sallyanne Payton, "The Duty of a Public Utility to Serve in the Presence of New Competition," in Werner Sichel and Thomas G. Gies (eds.), *Applications of Economic Principles in Public Utility Industries* (Ann Arbor: The University of Michigan, 1981), pp. 121-52; "Special Issue on Antitrust Implications of Deregulation," 28 *The Antitrust Bulletin* 1 (1983).

[98]Leonard S. Hyman, "Utility Finance: Looking Toward the Future or Parallel Lines Do Converge at the Horizon" (Paper presented at the Public Utilities Reports Financial Conference, New York City, February 25, 1985) (mimeographed), p. 2.

[99]*Ibid.*, p. 2, 3.

[100]William L. Weiss, quoted in 115 *Public Utilities Fortnightly* 12 (March 7, 1985).

[101]See, *e.g.*, *Maryland People's Counsel v. Federal Energy Regulatory Comm.*, 66 PUR4th 529 (D.C. Cir. 1985) and 66 PUR4th 542 (D.C. Cir. 1985).

[102]In the postderegulation period, discount plans offered by airlines proliferated. "In April, 1982, 77 percent of domestic coach traffic of the majors moved on discounted fares. This compares with about 67 percent in April, 1981, and 46 percent in April, 1978." George W. James, "The Deregulation Experience of the U.S. Airline Industry" (Presentation before the 1982 Symposium on Regulation, Warrenton, Va., August 19, 1982) (mimeographed), p. 6. See also Michael E. Levine, "Airline Competition in Deregulated Markets: Theory, Firm Strategy, and Public Policy," 4 *Yale Journal on Regulation* 393 (1987).

[103]Joel Bleeke, "Deregulation: Riding the Rapids," 26 *Business Horizons* 15, 25 (May-June, 1983).

[104]George A. Steiner and John F. Steiner, *Business, Government, and Society* (4th ed.; New York: Random House, Inc., 1985), p. 189.

[105]Raymond J. O'Connor, "Balancing Competition and Regulation in the Natural Gas Industry," 115 *Public Utilities Fortnightly* 15, 17 (January 24, 1985). See, *e.g.*, *Utility Restructuring: Strategies, Issues and Cases* (Arlington: Public Utilities Reports, Inc., 1987).

[106]Irwin M. Stelzer, "The Post-Decree Telecommunications Industry" (New York: National Economic Research Associates, Inc., 1982), p. 7.

[107]See "Phone Companies Draw Fire by Seeking to Base Local Phone Charges on Usage," *The Wall Street Journal*, January 6, 1987, p. 31.

[108]O'Connor, *op. cit.*, p. 16.

[109]*Re SouthernTel of Virginia, Inc.*, 62 PUR4th 245, 257 (Va., 1984).

[110]*Ibid.*, p. 256.

[111]*Ibid.*, p. 257.

[112]*Ibid.*, pp. 257, 258. See, *e.g.*, Franklin M. Fisher (ed.), *Antitrust and Regulation* (Cambridge: The MIT Press, 1985); David C. Hjelmfelt, *Antitrust and Regulated Industries* (New York: Wiley Law Publications, 1986). But see Jule R. Herbert, Jr., "An Antitrust Route to Re-regulation," *The Wall Street Journal*, July 26, 1985, p. 20.

[113]O'Connor, *op. cit.*

[114]It is of significance that the hostile economic environment which confronted regulation during the 1970s and early 1980s became somewhat friendlier by the mid-1980s. Annual inflation and interest rates declined dramatically, as did fuel prices. The natural gas shortage of the last decade became a surplus; in many sections of the country, excess capacity developed in the case of electricity as well. With the notable exception of those electric utilities with nuclear-related problems, the financial integrity of the public utility sector improved. Rate increase cases declined; in fact, substantial rate decreases occurred. *If* this economic environment continues in the next few years, those involved with utility regulation will have the opportunity to focus on the challenges resulting from structural reform.

[115]See, *e.g.*, Larry J. Wallace, "Reregulation of the Electric Utility Industry — A Neglected Alternative," 110 *Public Utilities Fortnightly* 13 (November 25, 1982); Sidney Saltzman and Richard E. Schuler, (eds.), *The Future of Electrical Energy: A Regional Perspective of an Industry in Transition* (New York: Praeger Publishers, 1986); Chapter 13.

PART I

The Economic, Legal, and Administrative Concepts of Public Utility Regulation

Chapter 2

THE ECONOMIC CONCEPTS OF REGULATION

At most, regulation is a supplement or partial alternative to competition, resorted to on a largely ad hoc basis to secure particular objectives which it is thought cannot be obtained by competition.

—*Lee Loevinger**

Regulation is an economic, legislative, and legal concept. The legislature usually decides what industries should be regulated. Such decisions may be based upon the economic characteristics of certain industries, prevailing social philosophies, or political considerations. The policies adopted, however, must conform to existing legal concepts and procedures. Compromise is thus a basic ingredient of economic policy.

In this chapter, emphasis is placed on the economic characteristics of public utilities. The legal concepts are discussed in the following chapter. It will become readily apparent that there is often a gap between the economic criteria justifying regulation on the one hand, and the legislative and legal concepts on the other. It is hoped that the subsequent discussion will help to bridge this gap. Likewise, it will become quickly apparent that while a differentiation can be made between regulated and unregulated industries[1] on the basis of their economic characteristics, the distinction is frequently "a matter of degree."

Exceptions to Competitive Policy

Kaysen and Turner have suggested that regulation or exemption from competitive policy may be either necessary or desirable when one or more of three situations are found within an industry:

1. Situations in which competition, as a practical matter, cannot exist or survive for long, and in which, therefore, an unregulated market will not produce competitive results.
2. Situations in which active competition exists, but where, because of imperfections in the market, competition does not produce one or more competitive results.
3. Situations in which competition exists, or could exist, and has produced or may be expected to produce competitive results, but where in light of other policy considerations competitive results are unsatisfactory in one or more respects.[2]

The first situation refers to the inherently noncompetitive market. From an economic point of view, such a market structure is due to the technology of an industry, so that one ("natural monopoly") or a small number ("natural oligopoly") of optimum-size firms have adequate productive capacity to supply the demand in a market. In the case of public utilities, there are also other bases for limiting competition, such as technical limitations and the unique position of the buyer. The second situation refers to interference with the market process to prevent ruinous competition or to promote conservation. The third situation refers to the alteration of market results to serve other public policy goals, including national defense, economic stabilization, regional development, and social equity. Political considerations, in other words, largely determine what activities fall within the third category. For this reason, primary attention is focused on the first two situations.

Each of these situations suggests different kinds of regulatory approaches to meet the various problems they pose. Moreover, more than one situation might well be found in the same industry, although such is not inevitable. At the same time, the justification for regulation implies neither the degree of regulatory activity that is desirable nor the goals that public policy should seek. Safety regulation does not necessarily require control of entry or rates; regulatory policy may seek maximum economic efficiency, equity or fairness, the promotion of an industry, or countless other goals.[3] Finally,

> ... regulation can easily expand beyond the scope appropriate to the conditions that first produced it, and often for reasons quite unrelated to those originally deemed pertinent. The new reasons may be sufficient to justify the extended reach, but intelligent policy-making requires that they be treated on their own merits. "Logical" extensions of

regulation are not always logical. Similarly, the conditions that first produced regulation may well change to the point that regulation should be reduced or drastically revised.[4]

Determinants of Market Structure

The market structure, market conduct, and market performance of public utility industries will be discussed at length in Part III.[5] What economic characteristics possessed by such industries distinguish them from other domestic industries? Specifically, why provide detailed regulation of electric, gas, and water firms (and, historically, telecommunications firms) and leave the large steel companies, drug manufacturers, and automobile producers free from comparable regulation? Clearly all of these industries are "affected with a public interest" and "render an essential service."

Market Structure: Cost Considerations

The classic *economic* case for extensive regulation of price, investment, service, and other managerial decisions of an industry is the inherently noncompetitive situation. Public utilities are frequently referred to as "natural monopolies."[6] The phrase is misleading.[7] Economies of scale may allow one firm to serve a market at a lower average cost than can several competing firms.[8] But in some cases, primarily transportation utilities, competition was limited for many years by legislative policy rather than by technological conditions. In such cases, there was nothing natural or inherent about the resulting market structure. Similarly, interindustry or intermodal competition may be present. While this type of competition may lead to different results than does intraindustry or intramodal competition, it can still serve to limit discretionary control over price. Many utility industries, therefore, exhibit both monopolistic and competitive elements.

It should be emphasized also that economic conditions are constantly changing. Market growth may make entry of new firms economically feasible; technological advances may lead to either larger or smaller optimum-size plants; substitute products or services may be developed. What is "natural" at one period of time, then, may become quite unnatural at another. One must distinguish, therefore, between a permanent and a temporary natural monopoly.[9] "Perhaps, as others have observed, the notion of a natural monopoly was invented to justify exclusive markets for utility companies after their ineffectual and sometimes wasteful rivalry proved unsatisfactory to both the investor and the consumer interests."[10]

Economies of Scale. In some fields, regulation is predicated on the idea that an enterprise can achieve lower costs if placed in the position of a monopolist in a market. As Stelzer has pointed out, there are three aspects of decreasing cost.

. . . The first is short-run decreasing cost. This reflects the fact that once an investment in facilities is made, output can be increased with unit costs declining until the physical capacity of the facilities is reached.

The second aspect of decreasing cost relates to the long run. This phenomenon arises from the fact that, at any point in time, the unit cost of adding capacity declines as the size of the additional facility increases. Note that whereas the short-run decreasing cost situation relates to fuller utilization of existing capacity, the long-run decreasing cost situation applies to the economies associated with larger rather than smaller additions to capacity.

The third aspect of decreasing cost reflects the fact of technological progress. Note that the second aspect is basically a static concept; at any point in time, with given technology, larger capacity increments tend to be associated with lower unit costs. But this third aspect of decreasing cost is dynamic: as technology changes, the real unit costs of adding capacity decline.[11]

As short-run decreasing cost is a characteristic of many industries, this phenomenon does not provide an economic rationale for detailed regulation. The long-run decreasing cost situation, however, does provide an economic justification for regulation, as illustrated in Figure 2-1. Assume a given state of technology. If four firms of equal size were competing in a market, the long-run price could not be less than P_3 (plant A). If two firms of equal size were serving the market, minimum average costs would fall to P_2 (plant B). But the situation would still be unstable, for if economies of scale permitted one of the firms to double its plant, it would be able to supply the entire market (plant C), charging P_1 and earning a monopoly profit equal to P_1CBA.[12]

FIGURE 2-1

The Natural Monopoly Situation

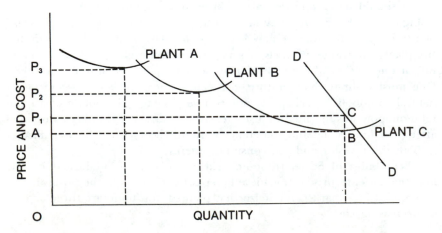

The inherently noncompetitive market structure, therefore, is determined by economies of scale, of the long-run variety.[13] Competition may exist for a time, but only until bankruptcy or merger leaves the field to one firm. Competition is self-destructive and results in a waste of scarce resources.[14] Conceivably, the two or three firms could make an agreement to share the market. Neither the firms nor the public would benefit should this occur. The firms would be high cost producers and the consumers would be denied the benefits derived from economies of scale. Moreover, nonprice rivalry between inefficient plants does not lead to an efficient allocation of resources. When economies of scale permit only one optimum-size producer in a market, it is highly desirable for public policy to allow a monopolistic supplier to operate. But the mere fact that a monopolist is allowed to exist does not assure the public of obtaining the benefits of whatever lower costs are achieved. In fact, the monopolist might absorb not only the benefits resulting from the lower cost, but also might raise prices. Consequently, the presence of a monopolist calls for some degree of public regulation.[15]

With respect to public utilities, significant (permanent) economies of scale indicating large-scale, monopolistic operations appear to be found in the transmission and distribution of electric power; the transportation by pipeline of natural gas and petroleum; the distribution of natural gas; and water and sewage services. The pipeline industry is illustrative. Unit costs of crude oil pipeline transport decline rapidly with increases in the designated capacity (throughput) per day and the diameter of the pipeline. Thus, a throughput of 25,000 barrels per day in a 10 3/4-inch line costs 0.237 cents per ton-mile as compared with a cost of .0513 cents per ton-mile for a daily throughput of 400,000 barrels in a 32-inch line.[16] The second cost is approximately 22 percent of the first.

In some markets, two or more competitors are found, all of which may be relatively efficient producers. Even when subjected to detailed regulation, this was true with respect to air, highway, and water transportation and to the production of natural gas. In these cases, regulation was based on considerations other than the existence of significant economies of scale and, consequently, it is not surprising that these activities have been subject to deregulation in recent years. Some economists, moreover, believe that the generation of electricity and the provision of telecommunications services may be only temporary natural monopolies, "since the tendency for average costs to decline with plant size may not continue indefinitely."[17] The telecommunications industry, in particular, is currently undergoing a significant change in market structure, as will be discussed in Chapter 15.

Fixed and Nonliquid Investment. Economies of scale often require large-scale plants. Such plants, in turn, require large fixed investments. Indeed, an important economic characteristic of public utilities (bus, highway freight, and water carriers are exceptions) is their heavy investment in durable equipment; and investment which is largely fixed (and, hence, unchanging irrespective of how many units are sold) and which represents a high percentage of total costs. One result is a low annual rate of capital turnover (the ratio of annual revenues to total investment). For electric utilities, the turnover is once every four to four and one-half years; for telephone utilities, it is once every two and one-half years. In contrast, the turnover for all manufacturing corporations is about twice every year.[18] Public utilities are highly capital intensive.

For most public utilities, their large investment has been irrevocably sunk in the original site; it is highly specialized and nonliquid. If the market for a utility's service began to disappear, its investment could not be moved to some other location where the prospects of success appear greater nor could its physical assets be sold to another firm to produce a different service. Should a company desire to retire from the utility field, a significant percentage of its total investment would be lost. To use an obvious example: A nuclear generating facility can be used only to produce electricity. In a similar manner, although perhaps to a somewhat lesser degree, little could be realized on such investments as hydroelectric plants, telephone cables and lines, and natural gas and petroleum pipelines. (In a few instances, natural gas pipelines have been converted into petroleum pipelines.)

The Problem of Unused Capacity. Closely connected with the limitation on intraindustry competition in the public utility sector arising from economies of scale is the problem of unused capacity.[19] This situation results from two factors: first, the diversity of consumer demand; second, engineering considerations, resulting from the general policy requirement that a public utility must have the necessary capacity to meet foreseeable increases in demand.

Consider the first factor — the peak demand problem. Most public utilities provide a service which is nonstorable (communications and electricity, but not natural gas or water). Yet, consumers expect, indeed demand, instantaneous service, despite the fact that they have different demands throughout a day, a season, or a year. Since storage is limited, at best, the companies must have adequate capacity to satisfy the peak demand, even though this maximum demand on a system may come only for a few minutes or a few hours at periodic intervals of time. There are many examples: The demand for electricity in the Northeast is greater in the summer than in the winter, while the demand for natural gas is just the opposite; telephone plant may be used more continuously during the day and early evening than during the night hours. Except for peak demand periods, therefore, utilities commonly have unused capacity.

Consider next the second factor — short-term overinvestment — due to engineering considerations. If there are significant economies of scale and if consumer demand is expected to increase in the foreseeable future, cost savings can be achieved by building an optimum-size plant, even though total capacity is greater than required to meet the existing demand. The same conclusion applies to the expansion of a plant. Frequently, such economies of scale result from the indivisibility of some factors of production. Pegrum has pointed this out with respect to the railroad industry, as follows:

> A railroad has to make large initial outlays to build a single-track line and acquire the necessary terminal facilities and rolling stock to operate it. When the plant is utilized to capacity, double-tracking will require a large additional investment which cannot profitably be made unless there is a prospect of a large proportionate increase in traffic. Expansion of this type entails difficult problems of market anticipation because the facilities have to be built well in advance of market opportunities. Meanwhile the traffic which is available will have to bear the burden of keeping the railroad in operation until the new traffic has been built up. If, instead of double-tracking, a new railroad were to be built, a complete duplication of the facilities of the existing road would be necessary, and the immediately available traffic would be inadequate to give either road a profit. The building of the second road would cost more than double-tracking the first, although doing this would give the two railroads only the same capacity as the double-tracked one, perhaps even less.[20]

For one or both of these reasons, therefore, unused capacity is another common characteristic of public utilities. But the utilization problem provides little support for economic regulation. Unused capacity due to the diversity of consumer demand is a persistent situation.[21] Firms, in order to attract off-peak users, will tend to cut their prices. Such price cuts (off-peak rates) are often economically defensible, but sometimes they result in discrimination among customers, products, or sections of the country, or in severe price wars, to the detriment of both the companies and their customers. Unused capacity due to engineering considerations is only temporary, until markets grow. Thus, while economies of scale provide a permanent reason for monopoly, the existence of unused capacity only provides a reason for controlling discrimination.[22]

The Limits to Size. It should not be assumed either that the present size of firms in the economy can be justified solely by economies of scale or that economies of scale are limitless. On the contrary, it appears that there are definite (if imprecise) limits to large-scale enterprises,[23] and public utilities are not exceptions. Thus, there are apparently few, if any, significant economies of scale in the air, highway, and water transportation industries[24] or in the production of natural gas. And local telephone (exchange) service is often considered to be subject to increasing costs.[25] In some cases, moreover, there may be other means of achieving cost savings. Two or more electric utilities may be interconnected, for example, thereby reducing the necessary reserve capacity. Finally, plant economies of scale, necessitating local monopoly operations, may be of far greater importance than multiplant economies, necessitating regional or national monopoly operations.[26]

Technical Limitations. Rivalry in the public utility sector is frequently confined to local or regional market areas. Such competition, in addition to economies of scale, may be limited by the fact that equipment must be located below, upon, or over public property. While the number of conduits or mains that can be buried below the street, the number of tracks that can be laid upon it, and the networks of wires that can be strung above it are limited, competing firms are usually possible. Yet, as the number of conduits or mains increases, the streets are torn up more frequently, thereby creating a public nuisance, and the available space is used up. The number of desirable sites also may be limited such as those for hydroelectric power plants and, increasingly, for nuclear generating facilities.

Local telephone service illustrates the technical limitations of competition. If such services were supplied by two competing companies — a situation which has existed in a number of cities in former years — subscribers might be forced to have two telephones in order to contact every other telephone subscriber in the city. Of course, the two companies might agree to interchange calls (either free or for a fee), but they might not.[27] Such a situation, however, also might require two sets of telephone poles and lines throughout the city. The tremendous cost for duplication of facilities is evident. Even if the firms agreed to an interchange of calls, it would be more difficult to achieve an efficient, integrated system (delay in completing calls might be either avoidable or unavoidable) than would be possible from a single telephone company serving the entire city.[28]

Market Structure: Demand Considerations

In legal terminology, there is a high degree of public interest attached to the services rendered by public utilities. While the major economic criteria justifying detailed regulation result from cost considerations, this statement implies that there are some demand characteristics of public utilities that distinguish their services from those of other industries, for many unregulated firms produce goods or render services that can be regarded as necessities (food, clothing and shelter, among many others).

The Diversity Problem. One important demand characteristic of public utilities is the diversity problem discussed above. Consumers demand instantaneous and uninterrupted service. In many cases, they can neither store the service nor defer its purchase. However, since consumers' demands for service differ considerably from one period of time to another, public utilities commonly have peak hours or peak seasons when their plant is used to capacity and other times when they have varying amounts of unused capacity. "For all these reasons, there has to be a heavy investment in capacity sufficient to meet the peak demands; and it is most efficiently provided by a single supplier, with a single fixed connection to the customer."[29]

The Elasticity of Demand. A second demand characteristic of the services provided by public utilities concerns the elasticity of demand. Two concepts are involved. Price elasticity of demand refers to the effect of a price increase or decrease on consumer expenditures for a good or service under given demand conditions. If the price for a service increases, demand is elastic if consumers decrease their expenditures for the service, inelastic if they increase their expenditures. Conversely, if the price falls, demand is elastic if consumers increase their expenditures for the service, inelastic if they decrease their expenditures. Income elasticity of demand refers to the effect of a change in consumer income on consumer expenditures for a good or service at a given price. If consumers change their expenditures for a service more than proportionately to a change in their incomes, demand is elastic; when they change their expenditures less than proportionately to a change in their incomes, demand is inelastic.

Historically, it has been common to argue (and studies supported the argument) that for many types of consumers and for many uses, demand (measured by both price elasticity and income elasticity) was inelastic for the services of public utilities. As a result, the revenues and earnings of these industries, with the significant exception of transport utilities, tended to show greater stability throughout the business cycle than did the revenues and earnings of unregulated industries. Such a situation reflected the fact that many consumers considered these services to be indispensable, preferring during a business recession to cut their expenditures for other goods and services before reducing their outlays for electric, gas, and telephone services.

Figures 2-2 and 2-3 reflect this characteristic by showing the sensitivity of dollar sales to income changes.[30] Figure 2-2 shows that sales of electric, gas, and telephone industries were less sensitive — in the 1929 to 1960 period — to changes in disposable personal income than were transportation services and all manufacturing sales. Figure 2-3, showing the major consumer groups for the nontransportation utilities, indicates that their sales to small consumers (residential) as well as local telephone service, were less sensitive to changes in disposable income than were sales to large consumers (commercial and industrial) and long-distance telephone service.

However, in recent years, utility prices have increased sharply, conservation has been urged as a partial solution to higher annual utility bills and to solving the "energy crisis," and more efficient appliances have been put on the market. According to studies by National Economic Research Associates, the conventional wisdom — that consumers of energy had highly inelastic demands — is no longer valid. With respect to electricity: ". . . .every 1 percent increase in (real) residential rates has been associated with between a 0.5 percent and 1.0 percent decrease in residential usage. The reactions of industrial users have varied, ranging from a 0.5 percent reduction in use in response to a 1 percent rate increase in the rubber industry, to a 1.2 percent cutback in use in the primary metal industry. . . ."[31] With respect to natural gas: ". . . every 1 percent increase in gas prices induced residential users to use 0.3 percent less gas. And industrial users proved even more

FIGURE 2-2
Income Sensitivity for Sales of Various Industries
(1929-60 average, growth trend removed)

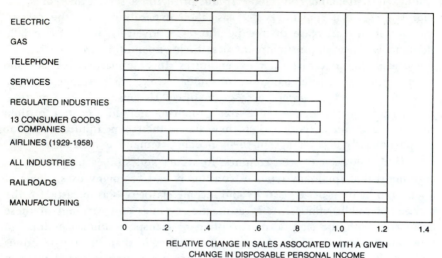

RELATIVE CHANGE IN SALES ASSOCIATED WITH A GIVEN
CHANGE IN DISPOSABLE PERSONAL INCOME

Source: Gerald W. Groepper, "Sensitivity of Corporate Sales to Income Changes,"
26 *Journal of Marketing* 47, 51 (1962). Reprinted with permission of the American
Marketing Association.

FIGURE 2-3
Income Sensitivity for Sales of the Nontransportation Utilities
(1929-60 average, growth trend removed)

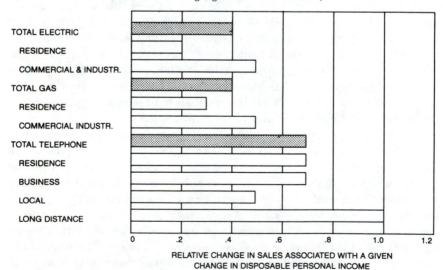

RELATIVE CHANGE IN SALES ASSOCIATED WITH A GIVEN
CHANGE IN DISPOSABLE PERSONAL INCOME

Source: Gerald W. Groepper, "Sensitivity of Corporate Sales to Income Changes,"
26 *Journal of Marketing* 47, 51 (1962). Reprinted with permission of the American
Marketing Association.

responsive: for example, every 1 percent increase in real price caused chemical and petroleum products firms to reduce their gas use by twice that amount. . . ."[32]

The Position of the Consumer. A final demand characteristic concerns the position of the buyer of services offered by public utilities. Most utilities' markets, as well as their customers' alternatives, are restricted by "the necessarily close connection between the utility plant on the one hand and the consumers' premises on the other."[33] With respect to the average consumer, and exempting some transportation services, intraindustry competition would offer few benefits. As explained by Lewis:

> Even though a utility service is furnished in any community by two or more companies, the position of any consumer is not significantly different from that which he would occupy if he were served by a monopolistic company. He is both free and able to buy his groceries daily from any of many competing stores, but it is not possible for him to buy gas, for example, elsewhere than from the concern with whose distribution system his gas-burning equipment is at the time physically connected. Nothing short of desperation borne of excessive and long-continued abuse would induce him to incur the cost and inconvenience of changing companies, and of course, once the new arrangement had been made he would find himself once more removed from the current of active competition. . . .[34]

Market Structure: Noneconomic Factors

These cost and demand characteristics partly explain the present market structures of the public utility industries and the need for detailed economic regulation. At the same time, noneconomic factors also have played a role in shaping public policy decisions. Entry into the public utility sector has been rigidly controlled. Evidence indicates that such control has been used for two basic purposes: to promote the maximum number of firms economically feasible in a given market and to protect existing firms in a market from new competition. The need to enforce safety requirements and the desire to promote the development of an industry (especially by offering subsidies), have likewise been advanced as justification for restricting competition. Particularly have these factors been of importance in the history of transportation regulation.[35] Regulation of natural monopolies has been justified (a) to avoid the transfer of income from consumers to investors, (b) to give consumers a recourse for grievances against the monopolists, and (c) to control the social and/or political power of monopolists controlling essential products or services.[36] The point being stressed is that public policy is determined on economic and on political and/or social grounds and, since not all public utilities possess the same economic and noneconomic characteristics, the basis for their regulation also differs.

Competition, Pricing, and Discrimination

The present market structures of the public utility industries vary considerably. Where a single firm serves a market, there is a presumption in favor of regulation to control prices, earnings, and service standards. Where a large number of firms serve a market, there is a presumption in favor of unregulated competition to protect the public interest. In between these two situations, the case for or against economic regulation is more complex and uncertain. A brief review of price theory will provide a background for further analysis.

A Review of Price Theory[37]

In economic theory, four models are usually recognized for purposes of analyzing pricing policies — pure or perfect competition, pure monopoly, oligopoly, and monopolistic competition. These are theoretical models, built upon certain limiting assumptions — assumptions which may not be valid in explaining the price behavior of a particular firm in real life. They are useful, nevertheless, as analytical aids.

Perfect Competition. Perfect competition refers to a market situation in which no seller has any influence over the market price of his product. Five assumptions concerning the structure of the market underlie this model. First, the products being offered are homogeneous, so that there is perfect substitutability among them. Buyers can thus shift quickly from one seller to another in response to a lower price. Second, there is a large number of buyers and sellers, each of them small, so that neither the quantity supplied nor the quantity demanded by any one of them will have an effect on the market price. Third, buyers and sellers possess complete knowledge of market conditions, so that no individual has an advantage over the others. Fourth, there are no restraints on the market or on the independence of any buyer or seller. Economic forces are free to operate in the market, and individuals are free to act in their own self-interests. Fifth, there are no obstacles preventing the complete mobility of resources, both into and out of an industry.[38]

Given this market structure, the final result is a situation in which no seller or buyer can become better off by altering his own behavior. Equilibrium, in the long run, requires that marginal revenue equals marginal cost (Figure 2-4),[39] for at that point, the firm is maximizing its profit. Producing more units would add more to total cost. Further, since price equals minimum average cost, the plant is being used efficiently. The model indicates that the market determines the price of a product and allocates resources. Each seller, by trying to maximize his own profit, works for the best interests of the economy as a whole.

FIGURE 2-4

Long-Run Equilibrium of a Firm in a Perfectly Competitive Industry

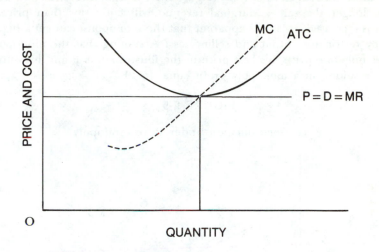

The final market equilibrium also defines in a precise way a socially efficient allocation of resources. In the first place, the firms are of optimum size, so that total production is maximized and all factors of production are fully utilized. Given existing consumer tastes and available technology and resources, no other arrangement of resources would result in an increase in the total value of production. In the second place, consumer satisfaction is maximized. Under conditions of perfect competition, the price represents what consumers are willing to pay for the last unit of a product. The price, in turn, is equal to the cost of producing the last unit — that is, marginal cost. It follows that the consumer's valuation of the last unit and the cost of producing that unit are equal. Producing more of one good involves giving the consumer additional units which are valued at less than the cost of production to society; producing less involves forgoing units that the consumer values more than the cost of production. Only when price is equal to marginal cost is consumer satisfaction maximized.

Pure Monopoly. Pure monopoly is at the opposite extreme to conditions of perfect competition. This situation means there is a single seller of a product. The extent of a monopolist's power, however, will depend on the closeness of available substitutes. As used here, pure monopoly implies a situation in which substitutes are lacking.

In the long run, a monopolist has the same objectives as a seller operating under conditions of perfect competition — the maximization of profit. Being the only supplier, the demand for the monopolist's product is the entire market demand for the product. In seeking to maximize profit, a seller operating under conditions of perfect competition will adjust his total output so that his marginal cost is equal to his marginal revenue. So, too, with the monopolist. But there is a vital difference, for what distinguishes the monopolist's position is the shape of the demand curve. As this curve slopes downward and to the right (Figure 2-5), marginal revenue and price are no longer the same. Marginal revenue will fall faster than price as output is increased. It is thus apparent that the monopolist can get a higher price by restricting output and selling less. Assuming that the monopolist charges only one price, his best price in the illustration is P and his output is OA, resulting in a monopoly profit equal to PECG.

FIGURE 2-5

Price Determination under Pure Monopoly

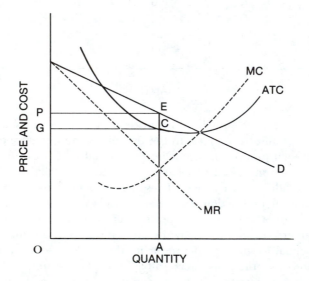

The results of pure monopoly differ in several important respects from those of perfect competition. The most profitable policy for the monopolist is to produce less, and charge more, than a firm operating under perfect competition. As noted above, the best allocation of resources for society as a whole is to carry production to the point where marginal cost equals price. Here, the value of the last unit of input just equals the value of the last unit of output. The most profitable adjustment for the monopolist, in contrast, is where price is greater than marginal cost. The difference is excess profit to the firm. Consequently, fewer resources are being employed than society would be willing to pay for at going rates. As long as price exceeds marginal cost, use of additional resources would add more to the value of output than in their present use. From the point of view of society, monopoly keeps output from being maximized. And, in addition, the monopolist's plant is not being used efficiently. Society does not get the full potential advantages of economies of scale. In short, price is higher, profits excessive, output smaller, and fewer resources are used under conditions of pure monopoly as compared with perfect competition.

Oligopoly. Both perfect competition and pure monopoly are uncommon market structures. An understanding of these markets does give a means of analyzing two more realistic types of markets found in the modern economy — oligopoly and monopolistic competition. Oligopoly is common in our basic industries, monopolistic competition in consumer goods industries and retailing.

Oligopoly exists when there is a small number of sellers in a market. Each seller, therefore, must take into account the effects of his own price and output decisions on those of his rivals. In other words, each seller recognizes that his actions have a definite effect on the final market outcome. The products produced by oligopolists may be virtually identical (cement, oil, steel), or differentiated but close substitutes (automobiles, cigarettes).

In theory, the condition for profit maximization under oligopoly is the output where marginal cost equals marginal revenue. But because of the existence of close substitutes, a seller must also consider what others are likely to do if he takes a certain course of action. Each seller, moreover, faces the same kind of problem. The result is uncertainty; the inherent characteristic of oligopoly.

To illustrate: A price reduction by one seller, assuming that rivals do not follow suit, might lead to a larger sales volume. Yet, can such an assumption be made? Given a small number of sellers, it could reasonably be expected that each will follow a known price reduction made by another. And if all firms reduce their prices, revenues may fall (depending on the elasticity of demand) with little or no change in market shares, but with smaller profits for each seller. The same considerations apply to price increases. No one seller, under normal conditions, will want his price to be far above that of his rivals. If one oligopolist wants to raise his price, he will consider whether or not the others will follow suit. Thus, the initiative taken by one seller to either raise or lower his price may be risky. It is not surprising, then, that price changes in oligopolistic markets may be few and far between. Price leadership is common. Rivalry tends to take the form of quality, advertising, research and development, and innovation. These forms of competition, more difficult for rivals to match, largely determine the market shares held by each producer.

Pricing behavior in oligopoly cannot be precisely formulated, but depends on the assumptions that one makes. Competitive prices, monopoly prices, or prices somewhere between these two extremes are likely outcomes of oligopoly. Some have argued that the most plausible outcome is monopoly pricing[40] or limited joint profit maximization.[41] Others have rejected the assumption of profit maximization altogether, substituting in its place the theory of games,[42] preventative pricing to forestall entry,[43] and organizational considerations (such as sales[44] or growth[45] maximization, and inter- and intrafirm objectives[46]). Clearly, there is little consensus on oligopoly price theory.

Monopolistic Competition. Monopolistic competition stands between perfect competition and oligopoly. Many industries have numerous suppliers, but each seller has a differentiated product. Products may differ because of quality, color, location, packaging, service, or a particular dealer's reputation. Since many sellers are supplying a similar product, joint action is not feasible. Moreover, there is reason for expecting active price competition. For example, while there is only one gasoline station on a given location, there may be many within a few blocks. Some may give lower prices, others trading stamps, and still others better service. Each automobile dealer normally enjoys an exclusive franchise in a given area, but competition among dealers is keen.

Firms operating under conditions of monopolistic competition will achieve maximum profits at the point where marginal cost equals marginal revenue, as depicted in Figure 2-6. Due to product differentiation, each seller faces a downward sloping demand curve. The seller will produce OA units and sell at price P, thus giving him the excess profit represented by GCEP. Such profits may attract new competition. A new producer, of course, cannot produce exactly the same product, but he can try for a close enough substitute to capture a share of the market. At the same time, existing competitors may pursue more aggressive policies through price reductions or advertising campaigns to attract some of the customers of the original firm. If either event occurs, the demand curve facing the original firm will shift to the left, as in Figure 2-7. In the long run, therefore, the equilibrium point may be where profits are normal (O'A' units, O'P' price). It should be noted, however, that such an equilibrium is at a point where price equals average total cost, indicating a smaller output and higher cost (due to advertising, research, promotional activities, and so forth) and price than under perfect competition.[47]

What effect does imperfect competition (oligopoly and monopolistic competition) have on economic efficiency? Clearly, imperfect competition does not result in a socially efficient allocation of resources in the same sense as perfect competition. Price is above marginal cost, so that what consumers are willing to pay for the last unit of a good is not equated to the cost to society of the last unit. Stated another way, price is higher and output is smaller under imperfect competition than under perfect competition, and plants are not being operated at their most efficient output levels. Taking a broader view of social efficiency, however, the perfectly competitive definition may not be applicable. If consumers want product differentiation, a situation ignored by the perfectly competitive model, imperfect competition is inevitable. In addition, research and development, technological and product innovation, and advertising are all part of imperfect competition, and again, the model of perfect competition ignores these factors. Perhaps, then, progress and efficiency, in line with consumer wants, will be greater

FIGURE 2-6

Price Determination under Monopolistic Competition

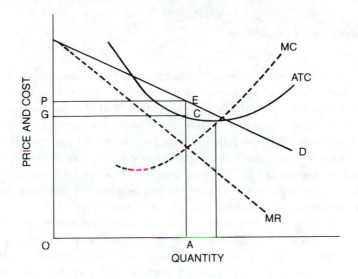

FIGURE 2-7

Long-Run Equilibrium under Monopolistic Competition

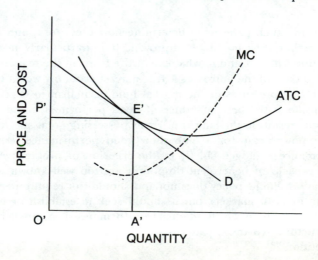

under conditions of oligopoly or monopolistic competition.[48] Whether or not this is true can only be determined from a case-by-case analysis of actual markets in the economy.

Workable Competition

In the economists' theoretical concept of perfect competition, and the added assumption of profit maximization, the market structure of an industry is a necessary and sufficient condition to define one unique market performance that will result. Under conditions of imperfect competition, the market structure of an industry may permit several patterns of market performance, so that there is no single one-to-one correlation between structure and performance. No modern industry conforms exactly to all the conditions necessary for perfect competition. Fortunately, evidences of competitive performance, adequate for public policy purposes, often can be found in markets in which structure is not ideal. In recent years, it has become common to study the workability of competition in various industries.

Workable or effective competition may result from conditions that are less exacting than those demanded for perfection.[49] The major elements of market structure are: (*1*) the number and size distribution of buyers and sellers; (*2*) the characteristics of demand; (*3*) the nature of the price structure; (*4*) the marketing or distribution channels utilized; (*5*) the geographical distribution of supply and demand; and (*6*) the conditions of entry into the industry. Similarly, the leading tests of market performance are: (*1*) price behavior; (*2*) capacity-output relationships; (*3*) progressiveness; (*4*) the level of profits; and (*5*) selling expenses.[50] The objective of studying these aspects of an industry's structure and performance has been well summarized by McKie:

> We study such patterns to determine how they work, and how well, and whether they might be improved. It is particularly necessary to determine whether and to what extent the firms in the market have the power to control the outcome. A free-market economy works best when the external pressures of the market hold each firm in check. Market compulsion is the best guarantee of good performance and optimum economic results in the long run. Firms possessing great and unchecked market power may for a time show good performance, especially if performance is judged chiefly by the criterion of progressiveness; but the drawbacks of benevolent despotism are too well known to require elaboration. Public policy does not and should not require perfect competition in most markets, but it should seek to establish or encourage market patterns in which adequate performance is compelled by market structure. To these patterns we give the generic name "workable competition."[51]

The concept of workable competition is admittedly less precise than that of perfect competition. By what standards, for example, should progressiveness, prices, or profits be measured? Further, complete flexibility or optimum resource allocation cannot be insured. The concept, however, does contribute toward these ends. And, since the utopia of perfect competition, with a total absence of market power, is not attainable (many would say undesirable), workable competition is a more useful goal of public policy. It assumes that a situation can be devised whereby the existing market power poses no economic or political threat to consumers.

Competition and Price Discrimination

Past experience suggests that unrestricted competition in some public utility industries (*1*) may become cutthroat, destructive, or ruinous and (*2*) may result in severe price discrimination. The latter is of far more importance than is the former, particularly with respect to current conditions and regulatory problems.

Inadequacy of Competition. Historically, it can be argued with a considerable measure of validity that competition within the public utility industries did not seem to afford a sufficient degree of protection for the public.[52] More specifically, whereas competition among automobile producers seemed to result in lower prices and/or a better product, unregulated competition among public utilities did not produce consistently lower rates for an equally good or improved product. Competition often became cutthroat or ruinous.[53]

Cutthroat competition may occur when investment in plant and equipment is large, fixed, and specialized and when competing firms have unused capacity. Except for motor and water carriers, these factors are all characteristics of public utility industries. If capital cannot be readily withdrawn from a business, a company will continue operations as long as it can make some return on the capital invested, for a significant portion of the money invested in the business is lost if operations cease. Therefore, companies will continue operations even at ruinously low rates. Rate wars are likely to occur as the firms try to increase their output or to utilize their plants more fully. Given a small number of competitors, rate reductions are usually met promptly by all rivals. Rates may even fall below marginal costs for a short time. Many examples can be found: a rate of 25 cents per person for carrying passengers from New York to Chicago, established by the railroads during a rate war; a rate of 2.5 cents a kilowatt-hour as a result of a rate war in Chicago. Whereas failure of a corner grocery store to show a profit may result (*a*) in sale of its stock — on which a large percentage of its cost will be realized — and retirement from business, (*b*) in conversion, for example, into a drugstore, or (*c*) in reorganization as a grocery store under different management, in the case of a public utility, reorganization is usually the only choice.

Any one or a combination of a number of results may follow from such severe competition. One possibility is continuance of the low rates so long that bankruptcy may occur. However, long before this will occur, the service offered by the firms will suffer. Adequate outlays cannot be made for improvements. Maintenance will be neglected. Finally, it is likely, and this is substantiated by past experience, that the competitors will take steps to reduce the severity of rate competition. And in making an agreement, the firms might extract a very high rate from the customer.

Thus, in the case of public utilities, competition may not succeed in a gradual elimination of the weaker firms, with business becoming concentrated in the hands of the more efficient.[54] However, it must be emphasized that both the actual existence of rate wars and the threat of rate wars have been overemphasized. There is substantial evidence that cutthroat competition was the exception and not the rule prior to the establishment of regulatory commissions. The spectacular nature of the rate wars which did occur may explain the attention which they have received.[55] But rate wars also exist among unregulated companies, as gasoline price wars so vividly demonstrate. There are many unregulated industries, such as steel, which have engaged in severe price wars during periods of general recession or when unused capacity existed.[56] Cutthroat competition, therefore, is not of particular significance in distinguishing between regulated and unregulated industries.

Price Discrimination. Price discrimination occurs when a seller establishes for the same product or service different rates which are not entirely justified by differences in cost, or the same rate where differences in cost would justify differences in price.[57] Such discrimination arises from the presence of high fixed costs, differences in the elasticity of demand, and the special nature of utilities' services. As noted above, fixed costs may result in competition driving rates below a point at which all costs are covered (assuming the existence of unused capacity). Moreover, consumers have different demands for these services, and since each consumer must usually deal directly with the company furnishing the service, it would be theoretically possible for a firm to charge each customer a different rate. That is, each customer represents a market for electric, gas, telephone, and water services. Whereas an individual can buy a car from a dealer and then resell it to a neighbor, a customer cannot do the same with the services rendered by utilities. While price discrimination is not a sole characteristic of public utilities, it is a more important one.

As a result of the possibility of adding to profits through price discrimination, this became a common practice in the early days of public utilities. Special rates were given to certain buyers, particular commodities, or favored places. Particularly was discrimination found in the railroad industry. With respect to personal discrimination, for example, Locklin has stated:

> . . . The railroad companies sometimes gave a practical monopoly to
> certain individuals or corporations in supplying wood or coal to partic-

ular towns and cities. The monopoly was enforced through preferential rates to the favored dealers and higher rates to the independent dealers. In the same way the buying of grain was monopolized by preferential rates to favored shippers. These monopolies could not have long endured if all shippers had been treated equally by the common carriers.[58]

The gradual realization that discrimination was substantially aiding certain firms to make tremendous profits (the classic example is Standard Oil of New Jersey) and to engage in selling at prices below those possible for companies not receiving special rates or rebates — and thus forcing these unfavored firms out of business — was one of the driving forces behind the movement for regulation. Since nineteenth century western agricultural regions were especially susceptible to discriminatory practices by the railroads, it is little wonder that the move to regulate the railroad industry was organized by midwestern farmers through the Grange.

It should be noted at this point that discrimination is accepted in the rate structures of public utilities, but that such discrimination must be "just and reasonable." Discrimination is both unintentional and purposive. It is unintentional in that some discrimination results from the efforts of utilities and commissions to simplify the rate structures by grouping customers into a limited number of classifications. It is purposive in that discrimination may be the only way in which service can be provided to some customers. Low-density routes may be subsidized by high-density routes (even under competition), small towns by large cities.[59] Rather than preventing discrimination, regulation merely seeks to control what discrimination takes place.

Interindustry Competition

For some of the public utility industries, interindustry competition is of far more significance than is intraindustry competition. Sometimes interindustry rivalry is between regulated firms: competition between electricity and gas; telephone and telegraph. Sometimes interindustry rivalry is between regulated and unregulated firms: electricity and gas compete with coal and oil; telephone and telegraph with private microwave. This type of competition raises two important regulatory problems.

In the first place, is interindustry competition an adequate substitute for intraindustry competition? In economic literature, the latter has been stressed, since

> . . . intraindustry competition has certain unique characteristics. It is only in competition between firms in the same industry that each competitor has similar cost structures and products, so that each can come near to duplicating a rival's prices and service. In contrast, interindustry competition must always be limited, for the differences in cost struc-

tures from one industry to another provide sheltered markets in which one industry has an inherent advantage over all rivals. For this reason, competition within an industry is considered necessary in both the literature of economics and the interpretations of antitrust laws in order to provide the competitive pressures necessary to fully promote efficiency, progress, and lower prices.[60]

Interindustry competition, then, may be imperfect.[61] A residential consumer, for example, will be even slower to switch from one type of fuel to another than from one gas company to another. The fuel change not only involves new equipment, but it also involves new appliances, thereby resulting in an even greater cost. Interindustry competition thus tends to be strongest for new customers, such as those deciding which fuel to use for heating when a new home is being constructed, and in the replacement market. It also tends to be stronger for larger customers than for smaller ones. Due to low volume, for instance, a residential user does not have the option of an industrial user of installing a private microwave system.

In the second place, interindustry competition presents difficult pricing problems, raising again the issue of "just and reasonable" discrimination. Assume that a regulated utility offers a basic service for which there are no close substitutes and another service for which there is a close substitute supplied by an unregulated firm. How can the commissions insure that the regulated enterprise does not use the power at its disposal in the "monopoly" area of its business to eliminate (via internal subsidies) competition in the "competitive" area? This complex issue will be considered in connection with the telecommunications industry.

Economic Characteristics: A Matter of Degree

The major economic characteristics of public utilities have been set forth. In part, they explain why certain enterprises are regulated. To summarize briefly[62]: For electric power generation, transmission, and distribution, for the transportation and distribution of natural gas, and for water and sewage services, the economic justification for regulation is based on the existence of significant economies of scale (long-run decreasing costs) in a given local or regional market. For telephone and telegraph services, the economic justification for regulation also is based on significant economies of scale, as well as on the expense and inconvenience to consumers of parallel competing systems.

For the production of natural gas and for the provision of transportation services, economies of scale are of less significance. Regulation of natural gas producers was based on the proposition that concentration was high enough to raise the probability of monopolistic pricing practices. Regulation of the railroads was initially based on their oligopolistic market structure over long-haul routes and their monopolistic market structure over short-haul routes. In both cases, discriminatory pricing proved profitable. The development of several competing modes of transport, however, reduced the economic justification for detailed regulation of the railroad industry. But instead of deregulating the railroads, regulation (in the 1930s) was extended to these competing modes. Bus, highway, and water transport regulation was largely predicated on the need to prevent cutthroat or destructive competition within each of these modes and to prevent undue price discrimination throughout the transportation industry. Airline regulation was primarily based on safety and promotional considerations. All of these industries have been, or are being, deregulated.

It should be apparent to the reader that the economic characteristics used to justify regulation do not belong solely to public utilities; rather, the distinction is one of degree. That is, most of the utility industries seem to possess these characteristics to a greater degree than do other industries. In many fields, economies of scale may explain the need for large-scale plants, such as typewriters and automobiles.[63] The necessity of enforcing competition in such industries caused Congress to enact the Sherman Antitrust Act in 1890 and to establish the Federal Trade Commission in 1914. Fixed costs and nonliquidity of capital are important in such industries as concrete and steel, so that some degree of cutthroat competition can and does exist. The monopoly element, inherent in public utilities, may be found in unregulated manufacturing and mining industries due to patents or control of raw materials. As mergers may reduce competition in unregulated industries, an antimerger policy was adopted in 1914 (Clayton Act) and amended in 1950 (Celler-Kefauver Act). Seasonal and cyclical unused capacity is common throughout American industry. And consumers have relatively inelastic demands for goods and services other than those of public utilities.

The tendency for many businesses to discriminate in price caused passage of a law limiting such discrimination as early as 1914 (Clayton Act) and strengthening of this law in 1936 (Robinson-Patman Act). Since imperfect competition is common in many industries, price competition is frequently avoided in favor of nonprice competition. As regards the lower cost of monopoly, it must be apparent that a lower immediate cost would be obtained in many fields by the creation of a monopoly. Many industries render essential services and yet escape public regulation. Even in the case of public utilities, services are not regarded as being so essential that they should be provided to everyone irrespective of the individual's ability to pay for them.[64] Safety requirements have been established and enforced, as in the automobile industry, without also imposing economic regulation. Finally, some manufacturing industries have avoided detailed regulation, not because they are more competitive, but rather because of the difficulties of extending regulation to the manufacturer of commodities. "Reliance on a certain degree of competition, fortified by antitrust laws, may therefore be deemed the lesser evil."[65]

What determines, then, which industries are to be regulated? It is the judgment of legislatures and, ultimately, of the Supreme Court. Regulation is applied when it is felt that competition cannot be relied on to provide adequate service at a reasonable price. This decision often has been based on proper economic criteria, but it has sometimes been predicated on political or social considerations.

Notes

*Lee Loevinger, "Regulation and Competition as Alternatives," 11 *The Antitrust Bulletin* 125, 139 (1966).

[1]"If anyone can find such a thing now as an 'unregulated industry' he can sell it at a profit to the Smithsonian." George Champion, quoted in 79 *Public Utilities Fortnightly* 10 (March 2, 1967).

[2]Carl Kaysen and Donald F. Turner, *Antitrust Policy: An Economic and Legal Analysis* (Cambridge: Harvard University Press, 1959), pp. 189-90. For a slightly different approach, see Francis M. Bator, "The Anatomy of Market Failure," 72 *Quarterly Journal of Economics* 351 (1958). See also Ronald H. Coase, "The Problem of Social Cost," 3 *Journal of Law and Economics* 1 (1960); E. J. Mishan, "The Postwar Literature on Externalities: An Interpretative Essay," 9 *Journal of Economic Literature* 1 (1971).

[3]See *e.g.*, Edward E. Zajac, *Fairness or Efficiency: An Introduction to Public Utility Pricing* (Cambridge: Ballinger Publishing Co., 1978); Richard Schmalensee, *The Control of Natural Monopolies* (Lexington, Mass.: D.C. Heath & Co., 1979). Trebing contends "that much of the current doubt about the adequacy of regulation stems from the failure of the commission system to demonstrate that it can resolve problems in a fashion that promotes the general welfare by effectively incorporating efficiency and equity criteria." Harry M. Trebing, "Equity, Efficiency, and the Viability of Public Utility Regulation," in Werner Sichel and Thomas G. Gies (eds.), *Applications of Economic Principles in Public Utility Industries* (Ann Arbor: The University of Michigan, 1981), p. 18.

[4]Kaysen and Turner, *op. cit.*, p. 190.

[5]"Theory tells us that market structure (the environment) determines market conduct (the behavior of economic agents within that environment) and thereby sets the level of market performance." Richard Caves, *American Industry: Structure, Conduct, Performance* (6th ed.; Englewood Cliffs: Prentice-Hall, Inc., 1987), p. 14. See also Joe S. Bain, *Industrial Organization* (2d ed.; New York: John Wiley & Sons, Inc., 1968); Douglas Needham, *The Economics of Industrial Structure, Conduct and Performance* (New York: St. Martin's Press, 1978); F. M. Scherer, *Industrial Organization and Public Policy* (2d ed.; New York: Macmillan Publishing Co., 1984); Michael Waterson, *Economic Theory of the Industry* (Cambridge: Cambridge University Press, 1984).

More recently, "the theory of contestable markets" has been advanced as a "new theory of industry structure. . . . The notion of contestable markets offers a generalization of the notion of purely competitive markets, a generalization in which fewer assumptions need to be made to obtain the usual efficiency results. Using contestability theory, economists no longer need to assume that efficient outcomes occur only when there are large numbers of actively producing firms, each of whom bases its decisions on the belief that it is so small as not to affect price. What drives contestability theory is the possibility of costlessly reversible entry. Where such entry is possible, efficient outcomes are shown to be consistent with the relatively large scales of operation that characterize many industrial technologies." William J. Baumol, John C. Panzar, and Robert D. Willig, *Contestable Markets and the Theory of Industrial Structure* (New York: Harcourt Brace Jovanovich, Inc., 1982), p. xix. See also Michael Spence, "Contestable Markets and the Theory of Industry Structure: A Review Article," 21 *Journal of Economic Literature* 981 (1983); Elizabeth E. Bailey and William J. Baumol, "Deregulation and the Theory of Contestable Markets," 1 *Yale Journal on Regulation* 111 (1984). With respect to the airline industry, see, *e.g.*, Elizabeth E. Bailey and John C. Panzar, "The Contestability of Airline Markets During the Transition to Deregulation," 44 *Law and Contemporary Problems* 125 (1981); Elizabeth E. Bailey et al., *Deregulating the Airlines* (Cambridge: The MIT Press, 1985). But see Michael E. Levine, "Airline Competition in Deregulated Markets: Theory, Firm Strategy, and Public Policy," 4 *Yale Journal on Regulation* 393, esp. pp. 403-08 (1987).

[6]On the natural monopoly concept, see Edward D. Lowry, "Justification for Regulation: The Case for Natural Monopoly," 92 *Public Utilities Fortnightly* 17 (November 8, 1973); William W. Sharkey, *The Theory of Natural Monopoly* (Cambridge: Cambridge University Press, 1982), chap. 2.

[7]"One of the most unfortunate phrases ever introduced into law or economics was the phrase 'natural monopoly.' Every monopoly is a product of public policy. No present monopoly, public or private, can be traced back through history in a pure form. . . . '[N]atural monopolies' in fact originated in response to a belief that some goal, or goals, of public policy would be advanced by encouraging or permitting a monopoly to be formed, and discouraging or forbidding future competition with this monopoly." James R. Nelson, "The Role of Competition in Regulated Industries," 11 *The Antitrust Bulletin* 1, 3 (1966). For a critical analysis of the natural monopoly concept as a justification for regulation, see Harold Demsetz, "Why Regulate Utilities?," 11 *Journal of Law and Economics* 55 (April, 1968) and "On the Regulation of Industry: Reply," 79 *Journal of Political Economy* 356 (1971); Richard Posner, "Natural Monopoly and Its Regulation," 21 *Stanford Law Review* 548 (1969); Walter J. Primeaux, *Direct Electric Utility Competition: The Natural Monopoly Myth* (New York: Praeger Publishers, 1986).

[8]The traditional theory assumes that a firm sells a homogeneous product or service. In fact, many public utilities supply multiple services to several distinct markets (*i.e.*, intercity motor carriers and telecommunications firms). In such cases, one can no longer talk about a decline in average total costs over the entire extent of the market, since there is no relevant industry output aggregate. Baumol, among others, has attempted to develop a natural monopoly concept based on a multiproduct firm. See William J. Baumol, "On the Proper Cost Tests for Natural Monopoly in a Multiproduct Industry," 67 *American Economic Review* 809 (1977). See also Robert D. Willig, "Multiproduct Technology and Market Structure," 69 *American Economic Review* 346 (Papers and Proceedings, 1979); Sharkey, *op. cit.*, chap. 4. But see Kenneth D. Boyer, "Testing the Applicability of the Natural Monopoly Concept," in Sichel and Gies, *op. cit.*, pp. 1-15.

[9]See William G. Shepherd, *The Treatment of Market Power* (New York: Columbia University Press, 1975), chap. 9, for an argument that no permanent natural monopolies exist.

[10]Emery Troxel, *Economics of Public Utilities* (New York: Holt, Rinehart & Winston, Inc., 1947), p. 27. Or, in Kahn's view: "It was out of this experience that the concept

of 'natural monopoly' gradually emerged, as an attempt on the one hand to explain the persistent tendency of competition to produce inferior results and to disappear and, on the other, to justify its abandonment." Alfred E. Kahn, *The Economics of Regulation: Principles and Institutions* (New York: John Wiley & Sons, Inc., 1971), Vol. II, p. 118.

[11]Irwin M. Stelzer, "Incremental Costs and Utility Rate-Making in the Competitive Era," in American Bar Association Annual Report, Section of *Public Utility Law, 1967*, pp. 30-31.

[12]The theoretical treatment of long-run decreasing cost resulting from technological advances is the same as depicted in Figure 2-1: Over time, only one firm of optimum size will survive in a market. Historically, technological advances have been of major importance in explaining decreasing costs in American industries.

[13]These economies of scale, moreover, must be *internal* to the individual firm. As Kahn has noted: "Economies of scale might instead be *external* to the individual firm. It could be, for example, that as an entire industry grows it can acquire some of its inputs at decreasing average costs, because its growth enables the suppliers of those inputs to take advantage of potential economies of scale internal to *their* industry. Increasing returns of this kind are compatible with a competitive organization of the first industry: all firms in it could benefit equally from these emergent external economies, no matter what the scale of their individual outputs." Kahn, *op. cit.*, p. 119, n. 15.

[14]Once a natural monopoly has been established, should entry be permitted into some or all of the firm's markets? This question has resulted in growing literature on the "sustainability" of natural monopoly. The possibility has been pointed out "that a set of commodities can involve natural monopoly (by globally subadditive costs), and yet a monopoly producer may not be immune to profit-seeking entry. That is, even if a single firm produces all the relevant commodities and even if prices are regulated so that costs are just covered, outside firms may be able to offer a subset of the commodities at prices below those charged by the regulated firm. The conclusion is that there can exist situations in which entry restrictions are necessary in order to sustain efficient production." Schmalensee, *op. cit.*, p. 35. See, *e.g.*, Gerald R. Faulhaber, "Cross-subsidization: Pricing in Public Enterprises," 65 *American Economic Review* 966 (1975); John C. Panzar and Robert D. Willig, "Free Entry and the Sustainability of Natural Monopoly," 8 *Bell Journal of Economics* 1 (1977); William J. Baumol et al., "Weak Invisible Hand Theorems on the Sustainability of Prices in a Multiproduct Natural Monopoly," 67 *American Economic Review* 350 (1977); Sharkey, *op. cit.*, esp. chap. 5. Panzar, for example, has argued that the airlines may have had nonsustainable natural monopolies when the industry's markets were smaller and that deregulation could have been harmful earlier in the industry's history. John C. Panzar, "Regulation, Deregulation, and Economic Efficiency: The Case of the CAB," 70 *American Economic Review* 311 (Papers and Proceedings, 1980). But see, *e.g.*, G. Knieps and I. Vogelsang, "The Sustainability Concept Under Alternative Behavioral Assumptions," 13 *Bell Journal of Economics* 234 (1982); William G. Shepherd, "Competition and Sustainability," in Thomas G. Gies and Werner Sichel (eds.), *Deregulation: Appraisal Before the Fact* (Ann Arbor: The University of Michigan, 1982), pp. 13-34.

[15]Nationalization, of course, is an alternative to regulation, but it "is less popular in the United States than elsewhere in the world." Stephen Breyer, *Regulation and Its Reform* (Cambridge: Harvard University Press, 1982), p. 181. On the pros and cons of nationalization, see *ibid.*, pp. 181-83. But see William G. Shepherd et al., *Public*

Enterprise: Economic Analysis of Theory and Practice (Lexington, Mass,: D.C. Heath & Co., 1976).

Even regulation, however, may not be able to achieve minimum costs. See, *e.g.*, Harvey Leibenstein, "Allocative Efficiency vs. 'X-Efficiency'," 56 *American Economic Review* 392 (1966); William S. Comanor and Harvey Leibenstein, "Allocative Efficiency, X-Efficiency, and the Measurement of Welfare Losses," 36 *Economica* 304 (1969). But see George J. Stigler, "The Existence of X-Efficiency," 66 *American Economic Review* 213 (1976).

[16]Leslie Cookenboo, Jr., "Costs of Operating Crude Oil Pipe Lines," *Rice Institute Bulletin* (April, 1954).

[17]Schmalensee, *op. cit.*, p. 5. See, especially, studies by Leonard W. Weiss ("Antitrust in the Electric Power Industry") and Leonard Waverman ("The Regulation of Intercity Telecommunications") in Almarin Phillips (ed.), *Promoting Competition in Regulated Markets* (Washington, D.C.: The Brookings Institution, 1975). On economies of scale in electric power generation, see, *e.g.*, P. J. Dhrymes and M. Kurz, "Technology and Scale in Electric Generation," 32 *Econometrica* 287 (1964); M. Galatin, *Economies of Scale and Technological Change in Thermal Power Generation* (Amsterdam: North-Holland Publishing Co., 1968); L. R. Christensen and W. H. Greene, "Economies of Scale in U.S. Electric Power Generation," 84 *Journal of Political Economy* 655 (1976); D. A. Huettner and J. H. Landon, "Electric Utilities: Scale Economies and Diseconomies," 44 *Southern Economic Journal* 883 (1978); T. G. Cowing and V. K. Smith, "The Estimation of a Production Technology: A Survey of Econometric Analyses of Steam-Electric Generation," 54 *Land Economics* 56 (1978). On economies of scale in telecommunications, see, *e.g.*, John R. Meyer et al., *The Economics of Competition in the Telecommunications Industry* (Cambridge: Oelgeschlager, Gunn & Hain, Publishers, 1980), chap. 4; David S. Evans (ed.), *Breaking Up Bell* (New York: Elsevier Science Publishing Co., 1983), chaps. 6 and 10.

[18]Stated another way, electric utilities require an investment in plant and equipment of between $4 and $4.50 to produce one dollar in revenue; telephone utilities require $2.50 per dollar of revenue. In comparison, all manufacturing corporations require an investment in plant and equipment of $0.52 per dollar of sales. Thus, electric utilities require at least eight times the capital investment of typical manufacturing firms doing equivalent volumes of business.

[19]Unused capacity is not synonymous with excess capacity. Both are usually thought of in the investment sense — that is, a commitment to an industry of factors of production in excess of current demand. As used in this book, however, unused capacity refers to short-term overinvestment due to seasonal or cyclical fluctuations in demand, or to engineering considerations, while excess capacity refers to large and persistent maladjustments between capacity and long-run demand.

[20]Dudley F. Pegrum, *Transportation: Economics and Public Policy* (rev. ed.; Homewood, Ill.: Richard D. Irwin, Inc., 1968), p. 139.

[21]"The wide divergence between peak and off-peak demand does not in itself contribute to economies of scale or natural monopoly. As far as this factor alone is concerned, the requisite capacity could be provided just as efficiently by a large number of suppliers, with an average load factor corresponding to that of the single one. . . ." Kahn, *op. cit.*, p. 120, n. 17.

[22]Nor does excess capacity provide a strong case for economic regulation. "The kind of intervention usually demanded is that which is likely not to cure the situation but rather to insure that it will persist much longer than it otherwise would. What is

usually sought is price support, by public authority or by authorized private agreement, and production quotas are often necessary to make the price support effective. It may be that not even these steps will improve the affected industry's lot — if demand for the product concerned is highly elastic, a raising of price may well make the industry's losses more acute than before. This is likely to be the case where the decline in demand has been caused by the rise of competitive substitutes, as has happened to railroads, coal, and a host of less significant industries. But to the extent that price-fixing restores the profits or cuts the losses of the industry's producers, cure of the basic problem — excess capacity — is simply postponed, and meanwhile resources are being uneconomically used from an overall standpoint. . . ." Kaysen and Turner, *op. cit.,* p. 196.

[23]See, *e.g.,* Joe S. Bain, *Barriers to New Competition: Their Character and Consequences in Manufacturing Industries* (Cambridge: Harvard University Press, 1956), esp. chap. iii; F. M. Scherer et al., *The Economics of Multi-Plant Operation: An International Comparisons Study* (Cambridge: Harvard University Press, 1975).

[24]H. D. Koontz, "Domestic Air Line Self-Sufficiency," 42 *American Economic Review* 103 (1952); Merrill J. Roberts, "Some Aspects of Motor Carrier Costs: Firm Size, Efficiency and Financial Health," 32 *Land Economics* 228 (1956); Edward W. Smykay, "An Appraisal of the Economies of Scale in the Motor Carrier Industry," 34 *Land Economics* 143 (1958); John R. Meyer et al., *The Economics of Competition in the Transportation Industries* (Cambridge: Harvard University Press, 1959), pp. 86-101, 135-36; Ann F. Friedlaender and Richard H. Spady, *Freight Transport Regulation: Equity, Efficiency, and Competition in the Rail and Trucking Industries* (Cambridge: The MIT Press, 1981).

[25]Local exchange service may be subject to increasing costs because as the number of subscribers increases, the amount of central office equipment required per telephone increases even more rapidly. But there are economies of scale in circuits and switching equipment to provide any given number of connections. Consequently, the judgment as to whether costs are increasing or decreasing depends primarily upon the unit of measurement of output. If calls are taken as the unit, local exchange service clearly shows economies of scale. If the number of subscribers is the measure, it appears that there may be diseconomies. See Charles W. Meyer, "The Cost Function for Local Telephone Service: Increasing or Decreasing?" (Ph.D. dissertation, The Johns Hopkins University, 1961); David A. Bowers and Wallace F. Lovejoy, "Disequilibrium and Increasing Costs: A Study of Local Telephone Service," 41 *Land Economics* 31 (1965).

"Despite the apparent presence of increasing costs, . . . monopoly is still natural because one company can serve any *given* number of subscribers (for example, all in a community) at lower cost than two." Kahn, *op. cit.,* p. 123 (footnote omitted). More generally, as Bonbright has noted, "even if the unit cost of supplying a given area with a given type of public utility service must increase with an enhanced rate of output, any specified required rate of output can be supplied most economically by a single firm or single system." James C. Bonbright, *Principles of Public Utility Rates* (New York: Columbia University Press, 1961), pp. 14-15.

[26]Bain, *Barriers to New Competition, op. cit.;* Scherer et al., *op. cit.*

[27]See James M. Herring and Gerald C. Gross, *Telecommunications* (New York: McGraw-Hill Book Co., Inc., 1936), pp. 62-66.

[28]A word of caution: Kahn has correctly argued that "as with the phenomenon of heavy fixed costs, it is not the fact of duplication alone that makes for a natural

monopoly, but the presence of economies of scale or decreasing costs in the provision and utilization of these facilities. . . . It is only when the entire demand can most efficiently be supplied via a single set of telephone poles and gas mains that it becomes inefficient to duplicate them, to have two companies digging up the streets at various times rather than one. So, duplication is inefficient — indeed, one might prefer to say that only in this event does it in fact constitute duplication — only in the presence of the economies of scale that make for natural monopoly." Kahn, *op. cit.*, pp. 121-22 (footnotes omitted).

[29]*Ibid.*, p. 120.

[30]The sensitivity of *dollar sales* to income changes must be distinguished from the concept of income elasticity of demand. The second refers to the correlation of *unit sales* with income. Thus, income sensitivity is a broader concept and includes more factors which influence sales than does income elasticity.

[31]Irwin M. Stelzer, "Alternative Responses to the Energy Crisis: The 70s As Guide to the 80s" (New York: National Economic Research Associates, Inc., 1981), p. 7. See also Lester D. Taylor, "The Demand for Electricity: A Survey," 6 *Bell Journal of Economics* 74 (1975); Michael P. Murray et al., "The Demand for Electricity in Virginia," 60 *Review of Economics and Statistics* 585 (1978).

[32]Stelzer, "Alternative Responses to the Energy Crisis . . .," *op. cit.*, p. 8. As Stelzer is careful to note, these elasticity estimates "have inherent limitations. The most obvious is that they all are bound by the historic data base, and of necessity are using experience with price changes much smaller and to much lower levels than those of the post-OPEC era." *Ibid.* On natural gas wholesale sales, see Paul W. MacAvoy, "Relative Prices on Regulated Transactions of the Natural Gas Pipelines," 4 *Bell Journal of Economics and Management Science* 212 (1973).

On demand studies for telephone services, see, *e.g.*, S. C. Littlechild, "Peak-load Pricing of Telephone Calls," 1 *Bell Journal of Economics and Management Science* 191 (1970); A. R. Dobell et al., "Telephone Communications in Canada: Demand, Production, and Investment Decisions," 3 *Bell Journal of Economics and Management Science* 175 (1972); B. E. Davis et al., "An Econometric Planning Model for American Telephone and Telegraph Company," 4 *Bell Journal of Economics and Management Science* 29 (1973); Lester D. Taylor, *Telecommunications Demand: A Survey and Critique* (Cambridge: Ballinger Publishing Co., 1980). On water service, see H. S. Houthakker and L. D. Taylor, *Consumer Demand in the United States: Analyses and Projections* (2d ed.; Cambridge: Harvard University Press, 1970), p. 89.

[33]Bonbright, *op. cit.*, pp. 12-13.

[34]Ben W. Lewis, "Public Utilities," in L. S. Lyon and V. Abramson, *Government and Economic Life* (Washington, D.C.: The Brookings Institution, 1940), Vol. II, p. 621.

[35]Airline regulation, for example, began in the 1930s when the federal government was subsidizing the industry (through airmail contracts) to promote its development. Argues Breyer: "But, at least in theory, a subsidy offer provides one perfectly sensible rationale for 'excessive competition:' the airlines' belief that the ICC would increase the subsidy award to a firm under contract provided an incentive to bid for the initial contract at a price well below cost. By doing so, an airline could expand the size of its route system, with the government making up the difference. Indeed, each airline would charge low prices to all customers, for the objective of each would be to expand system size and not to earn profits or to minimize losses. Thus, a government seeking to minimize the amount of subsidy required would have to

prevent prices that were 'unreasonably low,' and regulation would be justified in order to minimize government outlay." Breyer, *op. cit.,* pp. 29-30 (footnote omitted).

[36]*Ibid.,* pp. 19-20.

[37]For exhaustive studies on pricing, see Edwin Mansfield, *Microeconomics: Theory and Applications* (3d ed.; New York: W. W. Norton & Co., 1979); Donald S. Watson and Malcolm Getz, *Price Theory and Its Uses* (5th ed.; Boston: Houghton Mifflin Co., 1981). The welfare concepts of competition are discussed by J. de V. Graaff, *Theoretical Welfare Economics* (Cambridge: Oxford University Press, 1957).

[38]Pure, as opposed to perfect, competition is a less restrictive concept. It assumes imperfect knowledge, so that instantaneous market adjustments do not result.

[39]It is assumed throughout the book that all cost curves include a "normal" profit, defined as the net return required to maintain the equity capital in the business.

[40]See G. W. Stocking and M. W. Watkins, *Monopoly and Free Enterprise* (New York: Twentieth Century Fund, Inc., 1951), chap. iv.

[41]William Fellner, *Competition Among the Few* (New York: Alfred A. Knopf, 1949).

[42]John von Neumann and Oskar Morgenstern, *Theory of Games and Economic Behavior* (3d ed.; Princeton: Princeton University Press, 1953); Martin Shubik, *Strategy and Market Structure: Competition, Oligopoly, and the Theory of Games* (New York: John Wiley & Sons, Inc., 1959); James W. Friedman, *Oligopoly and the Theory of Games* (Amsterdam: North-Holland Publishing Co., 1977).

[43]Bain, *Barriers to New Competition, op. cit.;* Paolo Sylos-Labini, *Oligopoly and Technical Progress,* trans. Elizabeth Henderson (Cambridge: Harvard University Press, 1962). See also Avinash Dixit, "Recent Developments in Oligopoly Theory," 72 *American Economic Review* 12 (Papers and Proceedings, 1982).

[44]William J. Baumol, *Business Behavior, Value and Growth* (rev. ed.; New York: Harcourt, Brace & World, 1967).

[45]Robin Marris, *The Economic Theory of "Managerial" Capitalism* (New York: Macmillan Co., 1964).

[46]See, *e.g.,* Almarin Phillips, *Market Structure, Organization and Performance* (Cambridge: Harvard University Press, 1962); R. M. Cyert and J. G. March, *A Behavioral Theory of the Firm* (Englewood Cliffs: Prentice-Hall, Inc., 1963); O. E. Williamson, *The Economics of Discretionary Behavior: Managerial Objectives in the Theory of the Firm* (Englewood Cliffs: Prentice-Hall, Inc., 1964). For a summary and critique of these nonprofit maximizing theories of the firm, see Kenneth W. Clarkson and Roger LeRoy Miller, *Industrial Organization: Theory, Evidence, and Public Policy* (New York: McGraw-Hill Book Co., 1982), chap. 2. See also Michael Jensen and William Meckling, "Theory of the Firm: Managerial Behavior, Agency Costs, and Ownership Structure," 3 *Journal of Financial Economics* 305 (1976).

[47]Above-normal profits may still persist in the long run. The original firm might increase its own advertising campaign, thus checking the inroads of its competitors so that price will not fall to $O'P'$. See Edward H. Chamberlin, *The Theory of Monopolistic Competition* (8th ed.; Cambridge: Harvard University Press, 1962).

[48]The outstanding exponent of this view was Joseph Schumpeter. See his *Capitalism, Socialism, and Democracy* (3d ed.; New York: Harper & Bros., 1950), esp. chap. vii.

[49]See, *e.g.,* Stephen H. Sosnick, "A Critique of Concepts of Workable Competition," 72 *Quarterly Journal of Economics* 380 (1958); Charles E. Ferguson, *A Macroeco-*

nomic Theory of Workable Competition (Durham: Duke University Press, 1964); Scherer, *op. cit.;* Needham, *op. cit.*

[50]Edward S. Mason, "The Current Status of the Monopoly Problem in the United States," 62 *Harvard Law Review* 1265 (1949).

[51]James W. McKie, *Tin Cans and Tin Plate* (Cambridge: Harvard University Press, 1959), p. 7.

[52]See W. Z. Ripley, "Economic Wastes in Transportation," 21 *Political Science Quarterly* 381 (1906).

[53]On cutthroat or ruinous competition, see A. T. Hadley, *Railroad Transportation* (New York: Putnam, 1885), pp. 63-74; E. Jones, "Is Competition in Industry Ruinous?," 34 *Quarterly Journal of Economics* 473 (1920); J. M. Clark, *Studies in the Economics of Overhead Costs* (Chicago: University of Chicago Press, 1923), esp. chap. xxi; Kaysen and Turner, *op. cit.,* pp. 195-98.

[54]In fact, a reorganized company may well find itself in a position from which it may even force into bankruptcy a competitor who, up to that time, had been the low-cost producer. Such a possibility follows from the opportunity for a significant write-down of plant and equipment during a reorganization, with an accompanying decrease in capitalization. Accordingly, the company can show profits with a smaller return than was possible preceding the reorganization.

[55]Troxel, *op. cit.,* p. 40.

[56]See Arthur R. Burns, *The Decline of Competition* (New York: McGraw-Hill Book Co., Inc., 1936).

[57]A satisfactory definition of price discrimination is elusive. Thus, what costs — marginal or average, short-run or long-run, out-of-pocket or fully allocated, including or excluding either some or a uniform rate of return — are relevant to a determination of discrimination? Further, what are the same or like services? Is business exchange service, for instance, the same as residential exchange service, or are they different? These problems are considered at greater length in Chapter 10.

[58]D. Philip Locklin, *Economics of Transportation* (7th ed.: Homewood, Ill.: Richard D. Irwin, Inc., 1972), p. 213.

[59]Price discrimination, that is, may offset — at least in part — the tendency of an unregulated monopolist to restrict output. "The seriousness of the classical 'output curtailment' problem depends upon the practicality of determining appropriate price classifications, which in turn depends upon the firm's knowledge of how demand responds to price changes." Breyer, *op. cit.,* p. 18.

[60]Meyer et al., *The Economics of Competition in the Transportation Industries, op. cit.,* pp. 240-41 (footnote omitted).

[61]For some statistical documentation, see J. B. Vermitten and J. Plantinga, "The Elasticity of Substitution of Gas with Respect to Other Fuels in the United States," 35 *Review of Economics and Statistics* 140 (1953); John F. Felton, "Competition in the Energy Market Between Gas and Electricity," 4 *Nebraska Journal of Economics and Business* 1 (Autumn 1965).

[62]This summary is partly based on Bain, *Industrial Organization, op. cit.,* pp. 635-37.

[63]See Bain, *Barriers to New Competition, op. cit.,* pp. 53-113.

[64]Lewis, *op. cit.,* p. 622.

[65]Bonbright, *op. cit.,* p. 11.

Chapter 3

THE LEGAL CONCEPTS OF PUBLIC UTILITY REGULATION

All business is subject to some kinds of public regulation, but when the public becomes so peculiarly dependent upon a particular business that one engaging therein subjects himself to a more intimate public regulation is only to be determined by the process of exclusion and inclusion, and to gradual establishment of a line of distinction.

—Chief Justice Taft*

For many years, the courts attempted to establish a separate category of businesses that were "affected with a public interest" and that required detailed government regulation. A business so designated, known as a public utility, was privately owned and rendered an indispensable service to the community under economic conditions of imperfect competition. In the Supreme Court's words:

Property does become clothed with a public interest when used in a manner to make it of public consequence, and affect the community at large. When, therefore, one devotes his property to a use in which the public has an interest, he, in effect grants to the public an interest in that use, and must submit to be controlled by the public for the common good. . . .[1]

In 1934, the Court upheld price regulation of the milk industry without classifying that industry as a public utility.[2] As a result, while there is still a distinct public utility concept, some regulation may be applied to any industry when deemed essential to protect the public interest.

By what right does government regulate these activities? How does an activity become classified as a public utility? What are the obligations and rights of public utility enterprises? Is government free to go as far as it likes in regulating these activities, or are there certain limitations? These legal concepts are discussed in this chapter.

The Legal Basis of Government Regulation

In the United States, federal regulation of business proceeds under the interstate commerce clause, state regulation under the police power of the state. In both federal and state constitutions, there are constitutional safeguards for individual rights. All acts of administrators and legislatures are subject to judicial review.

Constitutional Provisions

Article I, Section 8 of the Constitution enumerates the economic powers delegated to the federal government by the states. From the viewpoint of public regulation of business, the most important clause is the one usually referred to as the interstate commerce clause that gives Congress power "to regulate commerce . . . among the several states. . . ." In addition, there are the implied powers that have been inferred from the final clause of the same article which authorizes Congress "To make all laws which shall be necessary and proper for carrying into Execution the foregoing Powers, and all other Powers vested by this Constitution in the Government of the United States. . . ." The Supreme Court has interpreted this clause broadly, with the result that the federal government is permitted to do both things expressly stated in the Constitution and things the Court is willing to infer. Said Chief Justice Marshall, in one of his most frequently quoted passages:

Let the end be legitimate, let it be within the scope of the Constitution, and all means which are appropriate, which are plainly adapted to that end, which are not prohibited, but consistent with the letter and spirit of the Constitution, are constitutional.[3]

All governmental powers, except those denied them by the Constitution, are reserved for the several states. State regulation of business proceeds under the police power of the state — that is, the power of the state to regulate business to safeguard the health, safety, morals, and general welfare of its citizens. While not mentioned in the Constitution, this power has long been recognized by the courts.[4]

In many areas, this distribution of powers between the federal and state governments causes conflicts. In such cases, the former must prevail. According to Article VI: "This Constitution and the Laws of the United States which shall be made in Pursuance thereof . . . shall be the supreme Law of the Land."

The Interstate Commerce Clause. After decades of court decisions, the interstate commerce clause has been broadly interpreted by the courts, and it seems that the clause is unlikely to impose significant limits on federal regulatory powers in the future.[5] The first Supreme Court definition of the word "commerce" was in 1824. Commerce, said Chief Justice Marshall, "is traffic, but it is something more: it is intercourse. It describes the commercial intercourse between nations, and parts of nations, in all its branches, and is regulated by prescribing rules for carrying on that intercourse."[6] Thus, Chief Justice Marshall, in refusing to limit the definition of commerce to "buying and selling, or the interchange of commodities,"[7] extended the concept to embrace all processes through which trade is carried on. Further, the phrase "among the several States" also was interpreted broadly.

> The word "among" means intermingled with . . . . Commerce among the States cannot stop at the external boundary line of each State, but may be introduced into the interior.
>
> Comprehensive as the word "among" is, it may very properly be restricted to that commerce which concerns more States than one. . . . The genius and character of the whole government seem to be, that its action is to be applied to all the external concerns of the nation, and to those internal concerns which affect the States generally; but not to those which are completely within a particular State, which do not affect other States, and with which it is not necessary to interfere, for the purpose of executing some of the general powers of the government. The completely internal commerce of a State, then, may be considered as reserved for the State itself.[8]

Subsequently, this interpretation was applied to railways and communication services.[9]

In 1871, the Court upheld federal regulation of a steamer carrying goods between two ports in Michigan, ruling that the out-of-state origin and destination of these goods made the vessel "an instrument" of interstate commerce.[10] The Court, in 1914, permitted the federal government to fix railway rates between points within the borders of a state because "in all matters having such a close and substantial relation to interstate traffic . . . the control is essential or appropriate. . . ."[11] In 1922, the Court approved the regulation of grain elevators, saying that such enterprises, though tied to one location, were situated in the "stream" or "flow" of interstate commerce.[12] Similarly, in the same year, federal regulation of stockyards was approved. While stockyards "are not a place of rest or final destination," stated the Court, they are "a throat through which the current flows, and the transactions which occur therein are only incident to this current from the West to the East, and from one State to another."[13]

Later cases have served to reinforce and extend these early decisions.[14] In 1937, the Court upheld the constitutionality of the National Labor Relations Act, saying that Congress cannot be held powerless to regulate "when industries organize themselves on a national scale, making their relation to interstate commerce the dominant factor in their activities. . . ." The relevant test, the Court added, was whether an interstate activity had a "close and intimate effect" on interstate commerce.[15] In 1938, it ruled that the law applied to a cannery that shipped only a third of its output to other states,[16] and to a power company that sold an insignificant percentage of its current across state lines.[17] In 1941, the Court upheld a law forbidding interstate shipment of goods made by persons paid less than legally determined wages or required to work for more than legally determined hours (Fair Labor Standards Act), holding that "Congress . . . may choose the means reasonably adopted to the attainment of the permitted end, even though they involve control of intrastate activities."[18] The following year, when the Court upheld the power of Congress to regulate the quantity of wheat a farmer could sell (under the Agricultural Adjustment Act of 1938), Justice Jackson stated:

> Even if the appellee's activity be local and though it may not be regarded as commerce, it may still, whatever its nature, be reached by Congress if it exerts a substantial economic effect on interstate commerce, and this irrespective of whether such effect is what might at some earlier time have been defined as "direct" or "indirect."[19]

In the same year, the Court held that Congress could regulate both building employees who serviced interstate operations[20] and oil drillers.[21] In 1944, it upheld the application of a federal statute to the insurance business[22]; in 1945, to retail trade[23]; and in 1946, to a newspaper which sold only 45 copies out of the state.[24]

It would seem that federal authority is almost unlimited. As the Court put it in 1946, federal power to regulate commerce among the several states "is as broad as the economic needs of the nation."[25] Further, federal authority may even be extended to intrastate commerce when necessary to prevent intrastate commerce from imposing a burden on interstate commerce. Thus, in 1914, when it upheld an Interstate Commerce Commission order that required a group of railroads to raise intrastate rates so that they would not be discriminatory against interstate commerce, the Court said that "Congress in the exercise of its paramount power may prevent the common instrumentalities of interstate and intrastate commercial intercourse from being used in their intrastate operations to the injury of interstate commerce."[26] Eight years later, in upholding a similar ICC order with respect to an intrastate passenger rate, Chief Justice Taft argued:

> Commerce is a unit and does not regard state lines, and while, under the Constitution, interstate and intrastate commerce are ordinarily subject to regulation by different sovereignties, yet when they are so mingled together that the supreme authority, the nation, cannot exercise complete effective control over interstate commerce without incidental regulation of intrastate commerce, such incidental regulation is not an invasion of state authority. . . .[27]

Federal regulation of intrastate commerce is subject to one limit: it may be used only to remove "undue or unreasonable advantages, preferences, or prejudices" or "unjustly discriminatory" inequalities.[28] But since the mere existence of inequality is not necessarily proof of an undue burden, federal-state jurisdictional conflicts remain.[29]

The Police Powers of the States. The Tenth Amendment provides that those powers not delegated to the federal government and not specifically prohibited to them may be exercised by the states. States have the broad authority to legislate for protection of the health, safety, morals, and general welfare of their citizens. These are collectively known as the "police powers" of the states.

The courts have given the states wide latitude under these police powers to regulate business enterprises. In an early case, Chief Justice Waite recognized that ". . . this is a power which may be abused; but that is no argument against its existence. For protection against abuses by legislatures the people must resort to the polls, not the courts."[30] And in 1934, the Court said:

> . . . a state is free to adopt whatever economic policy may reasonably be deemed to promote the public welfare, and to enforce that policy by legislation adapted to its purpose. The courts are without authority either to declare such policy, or, when it is declared by the legislatures, to override it. . . . With the wisdom of the policy adopted, with the adequacy or practicability of the law enacted to forward it, the courts are both incompetent and unauthorized to deal. . . . Price control, like any other form of regulation, is unconstitutional only if arbitrary, discriminatory, or demonstrably irrelevant to the policy the legislature is free to adopt. . . .[31]

There has been a partial retreat from, or perhaps a refinement of, this position in more recent years. In 1956, for instance, the Oregon Supreme Court ruled that the right of an owner to sell his property at a price agreeable to him was a valuable property right which the legislature could not take away except in a lawful exercise of its police power to protect the public interest. The Court said: ". . . to be a valid exercise of the police power, the statute and the regulations thereunder must have a well-recognized and direct bearing upon the health, happiness, and well-being of the public as a whole."[32]

Constitutional Safeguards for Corporate Rights. The rights of citizens are protected against invasion by the acts of government in both federal and state constitutions. The limitations on control of business by the federal government are found in the Fifth Amendment: "No person shall . . . be deprived of life, liberty, or property without due process of law; nor shall private property be taken for public use, without just compensation." The limitations on state power over business are contained in the contracts clause in Article I, Section 10 of the Constitution: "No state shall . . . pass any . . . Law impairing the Obligation of Contracts"; and in the Fourteenth Amendment: "No State shall make or enforce any law which shall abridge the privileges or immunities of citizens of the United States; nor shall any State deprive any person of life, liberty, or property, without due process of law; nor deny to any person within its jurisdiction the equal protection of the laws."

In both amendments, reference is made to *persons* and *citizens*. Since business enterprises have never been held to qualify as citizens, the clause relating to privileges and immunities has never been applied to limit governmental regulation. The other clauses, however, have been held applicable ever since the Supreme Court declared in 1886 that a corporation is a person.[33]

The significance of these amendments was well summarized by Justice Roberts in a 1934 decision:

> The Fifth Amendment, in the field of federal activity, and the Fourteenth, as respects state action, do not prohibit government regulation for the public welfare. They merely condition the exertion of the admitted power, by securing that the end shall be accomplished by methods consistent with due process. And the guaranty of due process, as has often been held, demands only that the law shall not be unreasonable, arbitrary, or capricious, and that the means selected shall have a real and substantial relation to the object sought to be attained. It results that a regulation valid for one sort of business, or in given circumstances, may be invalid for another sort, or for the same business under other circumstances, because the reasonableness of each regulation depends upon the relevant facts.[34]

Judicial Review. Under our constitutional system, all acts of legislatures and decisions of administrators are subject to judicial review. The term "judicial review," as Shapiro has noted, has both a particular and a general meaning. "The particular meaning, and the one most often invoked in the United States, is the power to declare statutes and the regulations and acts of government officials and agencies unconstitutional."[35] The courts interpret the Constitution as acts and laws are brought before them. State courts can find a local ordinance or a state law to be in violation of either state or federal constitutions. Federal courts can find state or federal laws to be in violation of the federal Constitution. The final authority is the Supreme Court of the United States.

In the more general sense, judicial review "is the power of a court to review the interpretations made by government agencies and officers (including other courts and judges) in order to determine what interpretation of the statute, regulation or previous ruling, and/or findings of fact supporting them shall be taken as binding upon the parties."[36] It has been well established that orders of a commission

> ... are final unless (1) beyond the power which it could constitutionally exercise; or (2) beyond its statutory power; or (3) based upon a mistake of law. But questions of fact may be involved in the determination of questions of law, so that an order, regular on its face, may be set aside if it appears that (4) the rate is so low as to be confiscatory and in violation of the constitutional prohibition against taking property without due process of law; or (5) if the Commission acted so arbitrarily and unjustly as to fix rates contrary to evidence, or without evidence to support it; or (6) if the authority therein involved has been exercised in such an unreasonable manner as to cause it to be within the elementary rule that the substance, and not the shadow, determines the validity of the exercise of the power. . . . In determining these mixed questions of law and fact, the court confines itself to the ultimate question as to whether the Commission acted within its power. It will not consider the expediency or wisdom of the order, or whether, on like testimony, it would have made a similar ruling.[37]

Origins of the Public Interest Concept

There are four recognizable antecedents of our "public interest" concept. First, there was the "just price" doctrine of medieval times. As Glaeser has explained:

> Regulation of private industry has been attempted by government from the earliest times. All attempts at such regulation owed much to a very ancient ideal of social justice, which, as applied to economic life

by the early Church Fathers, became their very famous doctrine of *justum pretium;* i.e., "just price." They opposed this idea to the contemporaneous doctrine of *verum pretium;* i.e., "natural price," which the Roman law had derived from Stoic philosophy. As contrasted with the doctrine of natural price, which justified any price reached by agreement in effecting exchanges between willing buyers and willing sellers, the "just price" doctrine drew attention to the coercion which may reside in economic circumstances, such as a food famine where a buyer is made willing by his economic necessities. Hence, in order to draw the sting of coercion, the early Church Fathers, following St. Augustine, considered only that trading to be legitimate in which the trader paid a "just price" to the producer, and in selling, added only so much to the price as was customarily sufficient for his economic support. There was to be no unjust enrichment. . . .[38]

The Emperor, during the decline of the Roman Empire, issued price edicts setting maximum prices for some 800 articles, based upon their estimated cost of production. His edicts were supported by the Church Fathers under the "just price" doctrine; a doctrine firmly established by the Middle Ages.

Second, during the Middle Ages, guilds operated. These guilds were similar to modern craft unions — members of the same craft belonged to the same guild. The obligation of the crafts was to provide service to anyone who wanted it at reasonable prices. The various crafts were known, therefore, as "common carriers," "common innkeepers," "common tailors," and so forth. As each craft had a monopoly of its trade, they were closely regulated. Third, the idea of an exclusive privilege to monopolize a line of commerce was further developed in France during the sixteenth century. Royal charters were given by the government to plantations and trading companies, granting them monopolies. A charter was the equivalent of the franchise granted to public utilities today. Here, regulation was strictly applied to these companies to carry out governmental objectives. To quote Glaeser again:

> Thus, the grant of monopoly was regarded as a method of accomplishing social results. Since franchises were royal grants, they conferred the special privilege of performing functions which the state itself, for various reasons, did not care to undertake, but which the mercantilist authorities conceived to be governmental in character. These grants of monopoly provided an incentive for the investment of capital and the assumptions of risks. That they turned out, in many cases, to be extremely profitable to their grantees, and would in turn need curbing, should not conceal the fact that they were originated by the state as a means of attaining public objects. No distinct line can be drawn between the guilds, the regulated commercial companies of the fourteenth and fifteenth centuries, and the new, joint-stock companies that

sprang into being in the sixteenth century with the discoveries and colonizations. In this development, however, is to be found the origin of our modern notion of a public service corporation. . . .[39]

Finally, there was the common law of England from which the legal antecedent of our public interest concept was developed. The common law courts displaced the authorities of the guilds, manors, and towns. Under the common law, certain occupations or callings were singled out and subjected to special rights and duties. These occupations became known as "common callings," and were explained primarily by the conduct of the business. That is, a person who practiced such a calling, as distinguished from a private calling, sought public patronage. Lord Chief Justice Hale (1609-76) of England, in his treatise, *De Portibus Maris,* stated:

> A man, for his own private advantage, may, in a port or town, set up a wharf or crane, and may take what rates he and his customers can agree for cranage, wharfage, housellage, pesage; for he doth no more than is lawful for any man to do, vis., makes the most of his own. . . . If the king or subject have a public wharf, unto which all persons that come to that port must come and unlade or lade their goods as for the purpose, because they are the wharfs only licensed by the king, . . . or because there is no other wharf in that port, as it may fall out where a port is newly erected; in that case there cannot be taken arbitrary and excessive duties for cranage, wharfage, pesage, etc., neither can they be enhanced to an immoderate rate; but the duties must be reasonable and moderate, though settled by the king's license or charter. For now the wharf and crane and other conveniences are affected with a public interest and they cease to be *juris privati* only; as if a man set out a street in new building on his own land, it is now no longer bare private interest, but is affected by a public interest.[40]

The list of common or public occupations regulated by the English Parliament included those of bakers, brewers, cab drivers, ferrymen, innkeepers, millers, smiths, surgeons, tailors, and wharfingers. A person engaged in a common employment had special obligations that were not attached to private employment, particularly the duty to provide, at reasonable prices, adequate service and facilities to all who wanted them. Closely connected was the "just price" of medieval times. These occupations, then, were to charge a reasonable price that was ethically controlled and not market determined.

Development in America[41]

The same regulations of business which existed in England were tried in the English colonies in North America. In the years prior to the American Revolution, a few colonies attempted to regulate prices for such products as beer, bread, corn, and tobacco, although the most detailed control was exercised over common carriers by land and water. "During the Revolution, generally at the instigation of the Continental Congress, at least eight of the thirteen states passed laws fixing the price of almost every commodity in the market."[42] Some of these laws even provided for the establishment of rates for various kinds of skilled and unskilled labor.

In the course of time, especially after the War of 1812, many, if not all, of these restrictions were either repealed or allowed to become inoperative. America had developed an economic and political liberalism which was adverse to government regulation. Competition was regarded as the best form of control for the general welfare. "Growing up in this environment, public utility regulation was a small cross current in the general economic life of the nation."[43] Only two public interest industries — carriers and waterworks — were subjected to special obligations, and both required franchises to use or cross public streets, highways, and waterways.

Following the war between the states, the doctrine of public interest was revived. Competition did not prove to be so perfect as economic theory had indicated. As agriculture became less important in the total economic activity of the country, and as technological changes resulted in the growth of corporate concentration, competition in business enterprise began to disappear. Financiers, too, used various devices to bring rival companies under common control, culminating in the great merger movement of 1898 to 1902. And management frequently seized the opportunities at hand to increase profits. Gradually, the liberal tradition was modified. Railroad companies were the first to feel this change in economic philosophy. As summarized by Troxel:

> When the railroad industry was new, the companies were encouraged to expand freely throughout the country. They received land grants from the federal and state governments, the voters gave them tax exemptions and public funds, and their securities were sold to the towns and persons to which they brought transportation service. Yet, even though the legislatures and voters helped the struggling railroad companies, they did not always get low rates. And they did not experience much competition between railroad companies. Railroading never was destined to be a competitive business in the same degree, for instance, that farming was. There never were so many companies serving every hamlet and city that competition controlled the freight rates. Often only one and never more than a few railroads served each town or area. Consequently most of the railroads operated under monopolistic or imperfectly competitive conditions. And the companies took advantage of their pricing situations, exploiting some of the people and towns from which financial aid was obtained. Being built ahead of the demand for railroad service and needing earnings, the railroad

systems resorted to discriminatory and noncompetitive pricing, and forgot the promises of their promoters to the populace.[44]

The Grangers (the Patrons of Husbandry) led a nationwide movement for the regulation of railroad companies during the long depression of the 1870s.[45] Regulation began in the Middle West, but soon spread throughout the country. Regulatory commissions, often ineffective, were established.[46] But in subsequent years, commissions were to be strengthened and the list of public utilities expanded. Today, the legal concept of common callings, with its many duties and obligations, is not static. Stated simply, the public interest with which some businesses are affected is one created by the public policy of the people.

Leading Judicial Opinions

Unless something is unusual about the industry involved, government regulation of private business would violate rights guaranteed by the Fifth and Fourteenth Amendments to the Constitution. When, therefore, is an industry so affected with a public interest that the usual privileges of private property give way to the duties attached to public service? Certainly, meat packing has a direct bearing on the health of the inhabitants of a state, but meat packing has been held by the courts as not sufficiently affected with a public interest to be a public utility.[47] Certainly, the sanitary conditions of drugstores as well as the care with which prescriptions are compounded affect public welfare, yet drugstores are not public utilities. In contrast, such an activity as the operation of a grain elevator has been held by the Supreme Court as sufficiently affected with a public interest to allow a considerable degree of regulation.[48] How have the courts distinguished among these and other activities?

At the outset, it must be recognized that there is no definite way of foretelling the necessary characteristics for distinguishing an industry affected with a public interest from one that is not sufficiently affected to require detailed public regulation. In practice, a business becomes so classified when the courts declare it to be, and they make such declarations only when a business is

> . . . so pervasive and varied as to require constant detailed supervision and a very high degree of regulation. Where this is true, it is common to speak of the business as being a "public" one, although it is privately owned. It is to such businesses that the designation "public utility" is commonly applied; or they are spoken of as "affected with a public interest."[49]

This statement is not very helpful. There are, however, three important steps in getting into this classification. First, the public at large or a smaller group must demand regulation. Second, the legislature must deem it necessary to regulate the particular industry in the interest of people. Third, the courts must recognize the need of regulation. The Supreme Court has long held:

> ... the mere declaration by a legislature that a business is affected with a public interest is not conclusive. ... The circumstances of its alleged change from the status of a private business and its freedom from regulation into one in which the public have come to have an interest are always a subject of judicial inquiry.[50]

In the course of passing on regulations imposed on various industries, the courts have laid down certain characteristics of these industries as justifying the regulations allowed. The following illustrative Supreme Court cases will indicate what reasons have been accepted by the courts as grounds for declaring an industry to be affected with a public interest and thus subject to broad regulation.

Munn v. Illinois

Beginning in 1877, in the well-known case of *Munn v. Illinois*,[51] and continuing until 1934, the courts attempted to establish a separate category of businesses affected with a public interest, and confined regulation to those that they so defined. In general, businesses placed in this category were known as public utilities. The *Munn* case was the first important statement of the Supreme Court on the public interest concept.

The Illinois constitution of 1870 contained a provision granting to the legislature power to prescribe rates and service for several businesses. In 1871, the state legislature passed a law establishing regulation for grain elevators and warehouses in the city of Chicago. The statute required elevator owners to obtain a license, file a schedule of rates for the storage of grain, and charge no more than the maximum rate specified in the law. The following year, Munn and his partner Scott, who had operated a grain elevator business in Chicago for about eight years, were sued for failure to comply with all the provisions of the statute.[52] Believing that they had a private business, Munn and Scott contested the law on the grounds that it constituted state regulation of interstate commerce and that they were being deprived of property without due process of law.

The important facts of the case are essentially as follows: In 1874, fourteen grain storage plants operated in Chicago. These plants were owned by about thirty people and were controlled by nine companies. It was shown that the possible number of sites on which to build such elevators was strictly limited. Moreover, the leaders of these nine firms met periodically to agree on grain storage rates. The situation was described by Chief Justice Waite:

> Thus it is apparent that all the elevating facilities through which these vast [wheat] productions "of seven or eight great States of the West" must pass on the way "to four or five of the States on the sea-shore" may be a "virtual monopoly." . . . They stand, to use again the language of their counsel, in the very "gateway of commerce," and take toll from all who pass. Their business most certainly "tends to a common charge, and is become a thing of public interest and use." Every bushel of grain for its passage "pays a toll, which is a common charge," and, therefore, according to Lord Hale, every such warehouseman "ought to be under public regulation, viz.: that he . . . take but a reasonable toll." Certainly, if any business can be clothed "with a public interest, and cease to be *juris privati* only," this has been. It may not be made so by the operation of the Constitution of Illinois or this statute, but it is by the facts.[53]

The Court also recognized the growing importance of the Chicago warehouses to midwestern farmers. The Court said the fact that the people of Illinois revised their constitution in 1870 to permit legislative statutes protecting shippers, producers, and consumers,

> . . . indicates very clearly that during the twenty years in which this peculiar business had been assuming its present "immense proportions," something had occurred which led the whole body of the people to suppose that remedies such as are usually employed to prevent abuses by virtual monopolies might not be inappropriate here. For our purposes we must assume that, if a state of facts could exist that would justify such legislation, it actually did exist when the statute now under consideration was passed. For us the question is one of power, not of expediency. If no state of circumstances could exist to justify such a statute, then we may declare this one void, because in excess of the legislative power of the State. But if it could, we must presume it did. Of the propriety of legislative interference within the scope of legislative power, the legislature is the exclusive judge.[54]

The majority opinion was not decided by the precedent rule, as no earlier parallel case involving a utility enterprise existed. The Chief Justice said it was not

> . . . a matter of any moment that no precedent can be found for a statute precisely like this. It is conceded that the business is one of recent origin, that its growth has been rapid, and that it is already of great importance. And it must also be conceded that it is a business in which the whole public has a direct and positive interest. It represents,

therefore, a case for the application of a long-known and well-established principle in social science, and this statute simply extends the law so as to meet this new development of commercial progress. There is no attempt to compel these owners to grant the public an interest in their property, but to declare their obligations, if they use it in this particular manner.[55]

The court recognized, however, that unless the restrictions in question involved special and peculiar circumstances, the statute would violate the Fourteenth Amendment. Chief Justice Waite, quoting extensively from an essay written by Lord Chief Justice Hale two centuries before, said:

> This brings us to inquire as to the principles upon which this power of regulation rests, in order that we may determine what is within and what without its operative effect. Looking, then, to the common law, from whence came the right which the Constitution protects, we find that when private property is "affected with a public interest, it ceases to be *juris privati* only." This was said by Lord Chief Justice Hale more than two hundred years ago ... and has been accepted without objection as an essential element in the law of property ever since. Property does become clothed with a public interest when used in a manner to make it of public consequence, and affect the community at large. When, therefore, one devotes his property to a use in which the public has an interest, he, in effect, grants to the public an interest in that use, and must submit to be controlled by the public for the common good, to the extent of the interest he has thus created. He may withdraw his grant by discontinuing the use; but, so long as he maintains the use, he must submit to the control.[56]

Finally, the Court argued:

> It matters not in this case that these plaintiffs in error had built their warehouses and established their business before the regulations complained of were adopted. What they did was from the beginning subject to the power of the body politic to require them to conform to such regulations as might be established by the proper authorities for the common good. They entered upon their business and provided themselves with the means to carry it on subject to this condition. If they did not wish to submit themselves to such interference, they should not have clothed the public with an interest in their concerns.[57]

Justice Bradley, who concurred with the majority opinion, said later of the *Munn* case:

> The inquiry ... was as to the extent of the police power in cases

where the public interest is affected; and we held that when an employment or business becomes a matter of such public interest and importance as to create a common charge or burden upon the citizens; in
other words, when it becomes a practical monopoly, to which the citizen is compelled to resort, and by means of which a tribute can be
exacted from the community, it is subject to regulation by the legislative
power.[58]

The Court thus held that the state, under the police power, could
regulate grain elevator rates in Chicago, since such a large part of all grain
passed through the city that a "virtual monopoly" existed. Hence, the principle of monopoly — an economic condition — as a basis for broad regulation was established.[59]

An important dissent in the *Munn* case was written by Justice Field and
concurred in by Justice Stone. Two positions were taken. First, Justice Field
thought that the state's right to regulate a privately owned business must be
based upon some privilege (franchise) conferred on the owner. In his words:

It is only where some right or privilege is conferred by the government or municipality upon the owner, which he can use in connection
with his property, or by means of which the use of his property is
rendered more valuable to him, or he thereby enjoys an advantage over
others, that the compensation to be received by him becomes a legitimate matter of regulation. . . . When the privilege ends, the power to
regulate ceases.[60]

Second, Justice Field believed the grain elevator business was of no
greater public interest than many other businesses. To quote him again:

If this be sound law, if there be no protection, either in the principles
upon which our republican government is founded, or in the prohibitions of the Constitution against such invasion of private rights, all
property and all business in the State are held at the mercy of a
majority of its legislature. The public has no greater interest in the use
of buildings for the storage of grain than it has in the use of buildings
for the residences of families, nor, indeed, anything like so great an
interest; and according to the doctrine announced, the legislature may
fix the rent of all tenements used for residences, without reference to
the cost of their erection. If the owner does not like the rates prescribed, he may cease renting his houses. He has granted to the public,
says the court, an interest in the use of the buildings, and "he may
withdraw his grant by discontinuing the use; but, so long as he maintains the use, he must submit to the control." The public is interested in
the manufacture of cotton, woolen, and silken fabrics, in the construction of machinery, in the printing and publication of books and period-

icals, and in the making of utensils of every variety, useful and orna-
mental; indeed, there is hardly an enterprise or business engaging the
attention and labor of any considerable portion of the community, in
which the public has not an interest in the sense in which that term is
used by the court in its opinion; and the doctrine which allows the
legislature to interfere with and regulate the charges which the owners
of property thus employed shall make for its use, that is, the rates at
which all these different kinds of business shall be carried on, has
never before been asserted, so far as I am aware, by any judicial tribu-
nal in the United States.[61]

Budd v. New York

In 1892, the Supreme Court, following the precedent of the *Munn*
decision, declared that the business of elevating, weighing, and discharging
grain from ships was rendered under monopoly conditions and thus was
"affected with a public interest."[62] The significance of this case, however, lies
in the dissenting opinion.

Three justices (Brewer, Brown, and Field) dissented. Their philosophy
was one of opposition to the expansion of governmental control over business. Justice Brewer first distinguished between property devoted to a public
use and property in whose use the public has an interest:

> The vice of the doctrine is, that it places a public interest in the use
> of property upon the same basis as a public use of property. Property
> is devoted to a public use when, and only when, the use is one which
> the public in its organized capacity, to wit, the State, has a right to
> create and maintain, and, therefore, one which all the public have a
> right to demand and share in. The use is public, because the public
> may create it, and the individual creating it is doing thereby and *pro
> tanto* the work of the State. The creation of all highways is a public duty.
> Railroads are highways. The State may build them. If an individual does
> the work, he is *pro tanto* doing the work of the State. He devotes his
> property to a public use. The State doing the work fixes the price for
> the use. It does not lose the right to fix the price, because an individual
> voluntarily undertakes to do the work. But this public use is very differ-
> ent from a public interest in the use. There is scarcely any property in
> whose use the public has no interest. No man liveth unto himself alone,
> and no man's property is beyond the touch of another's welfare. Every-
> thing, the manner and extent of whose use affects the well-being of
> others, is property in whose use the public has an interest. . . . I cannot
> bring myself to believe that when an owner of property has by his
> industry, skill, and money made a certain piece of his property of large
> value to many, he has thereby deprived himself of the full dominion

over it which he had when it was of comparatively little value; nor can I believe that the control of the public over one's property or business is at all dependent upon the extent to which the public is benefited by it.[63]

Justice Brewer recognized three limitations to the proposition that property "honestly acquired" should be controlled by the owner.

> . . . First, that he shall not use it to his neighbor's injury, and that does not mean that he must use it for his neighbor's benefit; second, that if he devotes it to a public use, he gives to the public a right to control that use; and, third, that whenever the public needs require, the public may take it upon payment of due compensation.[64]

None of these limitations, he argued, were applicable in the present case. Nor was the majority's concern with monopoly conditions persuasive:

> It is suggested that there is a monopoly, and that that justifies legislative interference. There are two kinds of monopoly; one of law, the other of fact. The one exists when exclusive privileges are granted. Such a monopoly, the law which creates alone can break; and being the creation of law justifies legislative control. A monopoly of fact anyone can break, and there is no necessity for legislative interference. It exists where any one by his money and labor furnishes facilities for business which no one else has. A man puts up in a city the only building suitable for offices. He has therefore a monopoly of that business; but it is a monopoly of fact, which any one can break who, with like business courage, put his means into a similar building. Because of the monopoly feature, subject thus easily to be broken, may the legislature regulate the price at which he will lease his offices? So here, there are no exclusive privileges given to these elevators. They are not upon public ground. If the business is profitable, any one can build another; the field is open for all the elevators, and all the competition that may be desired. If there be a monopoly, it is one of fact and not of law, and one which any individual can break.[65]

Justice Brewer's dissent contained a prediction, but one which has not come true. He argued:

> I believe the time is not distant when the evils resulting from this assumption of a power on the part of government to determine the compensation a man may receive for the use of his property, or the performance of his personal services, will become so apparent that the courts will hasten to declare that government can prescribe compensation only when it grants a special privilege . . . or when the service

which is rendered is a public service, or the property is in fact devoted to a public use.[66]

The majority of the Court, as will be shown below, in fact continued to expand the list of businesses subject to detailed regulation.

Brass v. Stoeser

In 1894, the Court gave a further definition of the public interest concept.[67] The North Dakota legislature, in 1891, passed a law fixing the maximum rates for grain storage. Within the state, there were in operation 600 elevators controlled by 125 different owners. While the economic power of these elevator owners was not so great as that enjoyed by the owners of the Chicago elevators, the statute was upheld by the Court.

Unlike the *Munn* case, in which the noncompetitive practices of the storage companies were an important consideration, the Court did not discuss pricing practices in the *Brass* case. Rather, the Court recognized the size of the elevators and the volume of business, as well as the judgment of the North Dakota legislature. Stated Justice Shiras: ". . . as we have no right to revise the wisdom of expediency of the law in question, so we would not be justified in imputing an improper exercise of discretion to the legislature of North Dakota."[68] In short, since the legislature obviously sought to protect the state's farmers, the Supreme Court approved the regulatory statute. The *Munn* case was reaffirmed, and the state legislatures were free to exercise their prerogatives in assigning a public utility status to industries.[69]

German Alliance Insurance Co. v. Lewis

The next important step in defining the public interest concept was taken in 1914 when the Court upheld regulation of the fire insurance business.[70] The state of Kansas, through its superintendent of insurance, had ordered a 12 percent reduction in fire insurance premiums in 1909. The German Alliance Insurance Company contended that the fire insurance business was private and not dependent on special privileges conferred by the state and, therefore, that there was no constitutional power for state regulation of rates and charges for services rendered by it. Justice McKenna, speaking for a divided Court, stated:

> We may put aside, therefore, all merely adventitious considerations and come to the bare and essential one, whether a contract of fire insurance is private and as such has constitutional immunity from regulation. Or, to state it differently and to express an antithetical proposition, is the business of insurance so far affected with a public interest as to justify legislative regulation of its rates? And we mean a broad and

definite public interest. In some degree the public interest is concerned in every transaction between men, the sum of the transaction constituting the activities of life. But there is something more special than this, something of more definite consequence, which makes the public interest that justifies regulatory legislation. We can best explain by examples. The transportation of property — business of common carriers — is obviously of public concern and its regulation is an accepted governmental power. The transmission of intelligence is of cognate character. There are other utilities which are denominated public, such as the furnishing of water and light, including in the latter gas and electricity. We do not hesitate at their regulation or at the fixing of the prices which may be charged for their service. The basis of the ready concession of the power of regulation is the public interest. . . .

Against that conservatism of the mind, which puts to question every new act of regulating legislation and regards the legislation invalid or dangerous until it has become familiar, government — state and national — has pressed on in the general welfare; and our reports are full of cases where in instance after instance the exercise of regulation was resisted and yet sustained against attacks asserted to be justified by the Constitution of the United States. The dread of the moment having passed, no one is now heard to say that rights were restrained or their constitutional guaranties impaired.[71]

After reviewing preceding cases in which state regulation of business was upheld, Justice McKenna continued:

The cases need no explanatory or fortifying comment. They demonstrate that a business, by circumstances and its nature, may rise from private to be of public concern and be subject, in consequence, to governmental regulation. And they demonstrate . . . that the attempts made to place the right of public regulation in the cases in which it has been exerted, and of which we have given examples, upon the ground of special privilege conferred by the public on those affected cannot be supported. "The underlying principle is that business of certain kinds holds such a peculiar relation to the public interest that there is superinduced upon it the right of public regulation."[72]

Did the insurance business come within the principle? Answered the Court:

We have shown that the business of insurance has very definite characteristics, with a reach of influence and consequence beyond and different from that of the ordinary business of the commercial world, to pursue which a greater liberty may be asserted. The transactions of the latter are independent and individual, terminating in their effect with the instances. The contracts of insurance may be said to be interdependent. They cannot be regarded singly, or isolatedly, and the effect of their relation is to create a fund of assurance and credit, the companies becoming the depositories of the money insured, possessing great power thereby and charged with great responsibility. How necessary their solvency is, is manifest. On the other hand to the insured, insurance is an asset, a basis of credit. It is practically a necessity to business activity and enterprise. It is, therefore, essentially different from ordinary commercial transactions, and, as we have seen, according to the sense of the world from the earliest times — certainly the sense of the modern world — is of the greatest public concern. It is therefore within the principle we have announced. . . .[73]

The Court thus expanded the public interest doctrine to include more than the mere rendering of service by means of tangible, physical property. The customary legal characteristics of a public utility — monopoly conditions and an indispensable commodity — were not found. Rather, fire insurance was referred to as "practically a necessity," thereby justifying public regulation. As Justice Lamar argued in his dissent (an opinion concurred in by Chief Justice White and Justice Van Devanter): if the state can regulate the premiums of fire insurance contracts, "then the price of everything within the circle of business transactions can be regulated."[74]

Wolff Packing Co. v. Court of Industrial Relations

In the *Wolff Packing Company* case of 1923,[75] the Supreme Court unanimously held that a state of Kansas statute undertaking extensive controls of commodity prices and wage rates was unconstitutional. The Kansas legislature, in 1920, enacted a statute declaring that the manufacture and preparation of food for human consumption, the production of clothing and all fuels, the transportation of these commodities, and the ordinary public utility businesses were affected with a public interest. The Court of Industrial Relations, created to fix wages and other terms for the conduct of such industries, ordered the Wolff Packing Company to increase the wages being paid to its workers by over $400 weekly, despite the fact that the company had lost $100,000 the previous year. The statute was held unconstitutional on the grounds that it was in conflict with the Fourteenth Amendment. The order of the Court of Industrial Relations, accordingly, was canceled.

In reaching this decision, Chief Justice Taft said the concept of public interest involved a "peculiarly close relation" between the public and those businesses so classified. He then proceeded to divide those industries affected with a public interest into three classes:

(1) Those which are carried on under the authority of a public grant

of privilege which either expressly or impliedly imposes the affirmative duty of rendering a public service demanded by any member of the public. Such are the railroads, other common carriers and public utilities.

(2) Certain occupations, regarded as exceptional, the public interest attaching to which, recognized from earliest times, has survived the period of arbitrary laws by Parliament or Colonial legislatures for regulating all trades and callings. Such are those of the keepers of inns, cabs, and gristmills. . . .

(3) Businesses which, though not public at their inception, may be fairly said to have risen to be such and have become subject in consequence to some governmental regulation. They have come to hold such a peculiar relation to the public that this is superimposed upon them. In the language of the cases, the owner, by devoting his business to the public use, in effect grants the public an interest in that use, and subjects himself to public regulation to the extent of that interest, although the property continues to belong to its private owner, and to be entitled to protection accordingly. . . .

It is manifest from an examination of the cases cited under the third head that the mere declaration by a legislature that a business is affected with a public interest is not conclusive of the question whether its attempted regulation on that ground is justified. The circumstances of its alleged change from the status of private business and its freedom from regulation into one in which the public has come to have an interest are always a subject of judicial inquiry. . . .

In nearly all the businesses included under the third head above, the thing which gave the public interest was the indispensable nature of the service and the exorbitant charges and arbitrary control to which the public might be subjected without regulation.[76]

Justice Taft's classification of businesses affected with a public interest is as good a general statement as will be found in court decisions, but he did not discuss the characteristics of such enterprises. The first category was based upon the belief that a special privilege, the right of eminent domain or the issuance of a franchise, was the legal basis for detailed regulation. As previously discussed, this was the position taken by those dissenting in the earlier grain elevator cases. It was not until 1934, in the *Nebbia* case, that this problem was finally clarified.[77] The franchise is not the evidence of public interest; rather, it can be possessed only as a result of that status. The second category was no more than a statement of historical facts. And the third category, one for which Justice Taft gave no illustrations, simply implied the industries that already were subject to regulation. "The whole classification, in fact, was scarcely more than a tautology."[78]

Moreover, as Justice Taft pointed out:

In a sense, the public is concerned about all lawful business because it contributes to the prosperity and well-being of the people. The public may suffer from high prices or strikes in many trades, but the expression "clothed with a public interest," as applied to a business, means more than that the public welfare is affected by continuity or by the price at which a commodity is sold or a service rendered. The circumstances which clothe a particular kind of business with a public interest, in the sense of *Munn v. Illinois* and the other cases, must be such as to create a peculiarly close relation between the public and those engaged in it, and raise implications of an affirmative obligation on their part to be reasonable in dealing with the public.[79]

The Court thus gave a classification of the businesses considered to be affected with a public interest, but did not attempt to define a public utility. Justice Taft clearly implies that the two concepts are not synonymous, foreshadowing a development made in the later *Nebbia* case.

Tyson & Brother v. Banton

The state of New York, trying to control the pricing practices of ticket scalpers, enacted a law which declared that the business of reselling tickets of admission to theaters and other places of amusement or entertainment was affected with a public interest and which limited the advance in the printed price of theater tickets sold through brokers to 50 cents per ticket. In 1927, the Supreme Court, in a five-to-four decision, decided the law was unconstitutional.[80] In the words of the majority:

The significant requirement is that the property shall be devoted to a use in which the public has an interest, which simply means . . . that it shall be devoted to a "public use." Stated in another form, a business or property, in order to be affected with a public interest, must be such or be so employed as to justify the conclusion that it has been devoted to a public use and its use thereby, in effect, granted to the public. . . .

A theatre is a private enterprise, which, in its relation to the public, differs obviously and widely, both in character and degree, from a grain elevator, standing at the gateway of commerce and exacting toll, amounting to a common charge, for every bushel of grain which passes on its way among the states; or stock yards, standing in like relation to the commerce in live stock; or an insurance company, engaged, as a sort of common agency, in collecting and holding a guaranty fund in which definite and substantial rights are enjoyed by a considerable portion of the public sustaining interdependent relations in respect of their interests in the fund. Sales of theatre tickets bear no relation to the commerce of the country; and they are not interdependent transactions, but stand, both in form and effect, separate and apart from each other, "terminating in their effect with the instances." And, certainly, a place of entertainment is in no legal sense a public utility; and, quite as certainly, its activities are not such that their enjoyment can be regarded under any conditions from the point of view of an emergency.

The interest of the public in theatres and other places of entertainment may be more nearly, and with better reason, assimilated to the like interest in provision stores and markets and in the rental of houses and apartments for residence purposes; although in importance it falls below such an interest in the proportion that food and shelter are of more moment than amusement or instruction. As we have shown, there is no legislative power to fix the prices of provisions or clothing or the rental charges for houses or apartments, in the absence of some controlling emergency; and we are unable to perceive any dissimilarities of such quality or degree as to justify a different rule in respect of amusements and entertainments.[81]

Justice Sutherland, who wrote the majority opinion, even noted the danger of carrying governmental price-fixing too far. He argued:

If it be within the legitimate authority of government to fix maximum charges for admission to theatres, lectures (where perhaps the lecturer alone is concerned), baseball, football, and other games of all degrees of interest, circuses, shows (big and little), and every possible form of amusement, including the lowly merry-go-round with its adjunct, the hurdy-gurdy, . . . it is hard to see where the limit of power in respect of price-fixing is to be drawn.[82]

There were three dissenting opinions in the case. Justice Holmes, in a dissent concurred in by Justice Brandeis, said:

. . . I think the proper course is to recognize that a state legislature can do whatever it sees fit to do unless it is restrained by some express prohibition in the Constitution of the United States or of the State, and that courts should be careful not to extend such prohibitions beyond their obvious meaning by reading into them conceptions of public policy that the particular court may happen to entertain. Coming down to the case before us I think . . . that the notion that a business is clothed with a public interest and has been devoted to the public use is little more than a fiction intended to beautify what is disagreeable to the sufferers. The truth seems to me to be that, subject to compensation when compensation is due, the legislature may forbid or restrict any business when it has a sufficient force of public opinion behind it. . . .

But if we are to yield to fashionable conventions, it seems to me that theatres are as much devoted to public use as anything well can be. We have not that respect for art that is one of the glories of France. But to many people the superfluous is the necessary, and it seems to me that Government does not go beyond its sphere in attempting to make life livable for them. I am far from saying that I think this particular law a wise and rational provision. That is not my affair. But if the people of the State of New York speaking by their authorized voice say that they want it, I see nothing in the Constitution of the United States to prevent their having their will.[83]

Justice Stone wrote a second dissent, concurred in by Justice Brandeis and Holmes. He, too, was unable to find anything in the Constitution that would prohibit the state of New York from regulating the price of brokerage charges. Of more significance, however, was his questioning of the usefulness of the phrase "business affected with a public interest." Justice Stone argued that it

> . . . seems to me to be too vague and illusory to carry us very far on the way to a solution. It tends in use to become only a convenient expression for describing those businesses, regulation of which has been permitted in the past. To say that only those businesses affected with a public interest may be regulated is but another way of stating that all those businesses which may be regulated are affected with a public interest. It is difficult to use the phrase free of its connotation of legal consequences, and hence when used as a basis of judicial decision, to avoid begging the question to be decided. The very fact that it has been applied to businesses unknown to Lord Hale, who gave sanction to its use, should caution us against the assumption that the category has now become complete or fixed and that there may not be brought into it new classes of business or transactions not hitherto included, in consequence of newly devised methods of extortionate price exaction.[84]

Thus, price control was appropriate, contended Justice Stone, whenever there existed "a situation or a combination of circumstances materially restricting the regulative force of competition, so that buyers or sellers are placed at such a disadvantage in the bargaining struggle that serious economic consequences result to a very large number of members of the community."[85]

Justice Sanford, in the third dissent, argued that the relevant question was "whether the business of ticket brokers who intervene between the theatre owners and the general public in the sale of theatre tickets is affected with a public interest, and may, under the circumstances disclosed in this case, be regulated by the legislature to the extent of preventing them from selling tickets at more than a reasonable advance upon the theatre prices."[86] He concluded that such regulation was proper:

> . . . ticket brokers, by virtue of arrangements which they make with the theatre owners, ordinarily acquire an absolute control of the most

desirable seats in the theatres, by which they deprive the public of access to the theatres themselves for the purpose of buying such tickets at the regular prices, and are enabled to exact an extortionate advance in prices for the sale of such tickets to the public.

In *Munn v. Illinois* . . . — although there was no holding that the sale of grain was in itself a business affected with a public interest which could be regulated by the legislature — it was held that the separate business of grain elevators, which "stood in the very gateway of commerce" in grain, "taking toll" from all who passed and tending to a common charge, had become by the facts, clothed "with a public interest" and was subject to public regulation limiting the charges to a reasonable toll. So, I think, that here — without reference to the character of the business of the theatres themselves — the business of the ticket brokers, who stand in "the very gateway" between the theatres and the public, depriving the public of access to the theatres for the purchase of desirable seats at the regular prices, and exacting toll from patrons of the theatres desiring to purchase such seats, has become clothed with a public interest and is subject to regulation by the legislature limiting their charges to reasonable exactions and protecting the public from extortion and exorbitant rates.[87]

Ribnik v. McBride

The *Ribnik* decision closely parallels that of the *Tyson* case. The state of New Jersey became concerned over the abuses of private employment agencies, and passed a law requiring such agencies to secure a license to operate. One of the terms for securing the license was the filing of the agency's proposed charges. Ribnik's application for a license was rejected by the Commissioner of Labor on the ground that his proposed fees were excessive and unreasonable.

In a six-to-three decision, the Supreme Court ruled that the law was unconstitutional.[88] Again, the Court held that the interest of the public in the matter of employment is not "that *public interest* which the law contemplates as the basis for legislative price control." Argued Justice Sutherland:

The business of securing employment for those seeking work and employees for those seeking workers is essentially that of a broker, that is, of an intermediary. While we do not undertake to say that there may not be a deeper concern on the part of the public in the business of an employment agency, that business does not differ in substantial character from the business of a real estate broker, ship broker, merchandise broker or ticket broker. In the *Tyson* case . . . we declared unconstitutional an act of the New York legislature which sought to fix the price at which theatre tickets should be sold by a ticket broker, and it is not

easy to see how, without disregarding that decision, price-fixing legislation in respect of other brokers of like character can be upheld.[89]

In his dissent, Justice Stone, supported by Justices Brandeis and Holmes,
strongly criticized the antisocial practices of employment agencies.[90] But of
greater importance, he could not understand the majority's distinction between price control and other forms of regulation. He thought it obvious
that,

> ... even in the case of businesses affected with a public interest,
> other control than price regulation may be so inappropriate as to be
> arbitrary or unreasonable, and hence unconstitutional. To me it seems
> equally obvious that the Constitution does not require us to hold that a
> business, subject to every other form of reasonable regulation, is im-
> mune from the requirement of reasonable prices, where that require-
> ment is the only remedy appropriate to the evils encountered. In this
> respect I can see no difference between a reasonable regulation of price
> and a reasonable regulation of the use of property, which affects its
> price or economic return. The privilege of contract and the free use of
> property are as seriously cut down in the one case as in the other.
> To say that there is constitutional power to regulate a business or a
> particular use of property because of the public interest in the welfare
> of a class peculiarly affected, and to deny such power to regulate price
> for the accomplishment of the same end, when that alone appears to
> be an appropriate and effective remedy, is to make a distinction based
> on no real economic difference, and for which I can find no warrant in
> the Constitution itself nor any justification in the opinions of this Court.[91]

Williams v. Standard Oil Co.

In 1927, the state of Tennessee adopted a statute enabling the Commissioner of Finance and Taxation to fix the prices at which gasoline could be
sold within the state.[92] A "proper" differential between the wholesale and
retail price was to be maintained; rebates, price concessions, and price discrimination between persons or localities were forbidden. Suit was brought
to declare the statute unconstitutional. Justice Sutherland, speaking for the
majority,[93] argued:

> It is settled by recent decisions of this Court that a state legislature is
> without constitutional power to fix prices at which commodities may be
> sold, services rendered, or property used, unless the business or prop-
> erty involved is "affected with a public interest." ... Nothing is gained
> by reiterating the statement that the phrase is indefinite. By repeated
> decisions of this Court, beginning with *Munn v. Illinois*, ... that phrase,

however it may be characterized, has become the established test by which the legislative power to fix prices of commodities, use of property, or services, must be measured. As applied in particular instances, its meaning may be considered both from an affirmative and a negative point of view. Affirmatively, it means that a business or property, in order to be affected with a public interest, must be such or be so employed as to justify the conclusion that it has been *devoted* to a public use and its use thereby in effect *granted* to the public. . . . Negatively, it does not mean that a business is affected with a public interest merely because it is large or because the public are warranted in having a feeling of concern in respect of its maintenance. . . .

In support of the act under review it is urged that gasoline is of widespread use; that enormous quantities of it are sold in the State of Tennessee; and that it has become necessary and indispensable in carrying on commercial and other activities within the state. But we are here concerned with the character of business, not with its size or the extent to which the commodity is used. Gasoline is one of the ordinary commodities of trade, differing, so far as the question here is affected, in no essential respect from a great variety of other articles commonly bought and sold by merchants and private dealers in the country. The decisions referred to above make it perfectly clear that the business of dealing in such articles, irrespective of its extent, does not come within the phrase "affected with a public interest." Those decisions control the present case.

There is nothing in the point that the act in question may be justified on the ground that the sale of gasoline in Tennessee is monopolized by appellees, or by either of them, because, objections to the materiality of the contention aside, an inspection of the pleadings and of the affidavits submitted to the lower court discloses an utter failure to show the existence of such monopoly.[94]

The Court ruled, therefore, that the statute was unconstitutional. There was no monopoly in the sale of gasoline. More importantly, since earlier decisions were controlling, the selling of gasoline was not a business "affected with a public interest."

New State Ice Co. v. Liebmann

In 1925, the state of Oklahoma enacted a statute declaring that the manufacture, sale, and distribution of ice was a "public business" and conferring on the Corporation Commission the power of regulation. Among the regulations was the power to license new enterprises on a showing that they were necessary to meet the public need. Liebmann began to construct an ice plant in competition with the New State Ice Company without first obtaining the required license, contending that he was not engaged in a public business but in a common calling and, therefore, no license from the state was necessary.[95]

The majority of the Court found no monopoly conditions or emergency conditions that justified regulation, believing, instead, that a restriction of the number of ice manufacturing companies might result in monopoly, thereby jeopardizing the interests of consumers. In the words of Justice Sutherland:

> It has been said that the manufacture of ice requires an expensive plant beyond the means of the average citizen, and that since the use of ice is indispensable, patronage of the producer by the consumer is unavoidable. The same might, however, be said in respect of other articles clearly beyond the reach of restriction like that here under review. . . . We know, since it is common knowledge, that today, to say nothing of other means, wherever electricity or gas is available (and one or the other is available in practically every part of the country), anyone for a comparatively moderate outlay may have set up in his kitchen an appliance by means of which he may manufacture ice for himself. Under such circumstances it hardly will do to say that people generally are at the mercy of the manufacturer, seller, and distributor of ice for ordinary needs. Moreover, the practical tendency of the restriction . . . is to shut out new enterprises, and thus create and foster monopoly in the hands of existing establishments, against, rather than in aid of, the interest of the consuming public.[96]

Justice Brandeis, in one of his most famous dissents, concurred in by Justice Stone, showed his willingness to expand public regulation greatly. First, he argued that the Court should not substitute its judgment for that of the legislature with respect to the desirability of regulation. To quote from his dissent:

> Oklahoma declared the business of manufacturing ice for sale and distribution a "public business"; that is, a public utility. So far as appears, it was the first State to do so. Of course, a legislature cannot by mere legislative fiat convert a business into a public utility. . . . But the conception of a public utility is not static. The welfare of the community may require that the business of supplying ice be made a public utility, as well as the business of supplying water or any other necessary commodity or service. If the business is, or can be made, a public utility, it must be possible to make the issue of a certificate a prerequisite to engaging in it. . . .
> The business of supplying ice is not only a necessity, like that of supplying food or clothing or shelter, but the legislature could also consider that it is one which lends itself peculiarly to monopoly. Char-

acteristically the business is conducted in local plants with a market narrowly limited in area, and this for the reason that ice manufactured at a distance cannot effectively compete with a plant on the ground. In small towns and rural communities the duplication of plants, and in large communities the duplication of delivery service, is wasteful and ultimately burdensome to consumers. At the same time the relative ease and cheapness with which an ice plant may be constructed exposes the industry to destructive and frequently ruinous competition. Competition in the industry tends to be destructive because ice plants have a determinate capacity, and inflexible fixed charges and operating costs, and because in a market of limited area the volume of sales is not readily expanded. Thus, the erection of a new plant in a locality already adequately served often causes managers to go to extremes in cutting prices in order to secure business. Trade journals and reports of association meetings of ice manufacturers bear ample witness to the hostility of the industry to such competition, and to its unremitting efforts, through trade associations, informal agreements, combination of delivery systems, and in particular through the consolidation of plants, to protect markets and prices against competition of any character. . . .

The advisability of treating the ice business as a public utility and of applying to it the certificate of convenience and necessity has been under consideration for many years. Similar legislation has been enacted in Oklahoma under similar circumstances with respect to other public services. The measure bore a substantial relation to the evils found to exist. Under these circumstances, to hold the Act void as being unreasonable, would, in my opinion involve the exercise not of the function of judicial review, but the function of a super-legislature. If the Act is to be stricken down, it must be on the ground that the Federal Constitution guarantees to the individual the absolute right to enter the ice business, however detrimental the exercise of that right may be to the public welfare. Such, indeed, appears to be the contention made. . . .

The claim is that manufacturing ice for sale and distribution is a business inherently private, and, in effect, that no state of facts can justify denial of the right to engage in it. To supply one's self with water, electricity, gas, ice, or any other article, is inherently a matter of private concern. So also may be the business of supplying the same articles to others for compensation. But the business of supplying to others, for compensation, any article or service whatsoever may become a matter of public concern. Whether it is, or is not, depends upon the conditions existing in the community affected. If it is a matter of public concern, it may be regulated, whatever the business. The public's concern may be limited to a single feature of the business, so that the needed protection can be secured by a relatively slight degree of regulation. Such is the concern over possible incompetence, which dictates the licensing of dentists . . . or the concern over possible dishonesty, which led to the licensing of auctioneers. . . . On the other hand, the public's concern about a particular business may be so pervasive and varied as to require constant detailed supervision and a very high degree of regulation. Where this is true, it is common to speak of the business as being a "public" one, although it is privately owned. It is to such businesses that the designation "public utility" is commonly applied; or they are spoken of as "affected with a public interest." . . .

A regulation valid for one kind of business may, of course, be invalid for another; since the reasonableness of every regulation is dependent upon the relevant facts. But so far as concerns the power to regulate, there is no difference in essence, between a business called private and one called a public utility or said to be "affected with a public interest." Whatever the nature of the business, whatever the scope or character of the regulation applied, the source of the power invoked is the same. And likewise the constitutional limitation upon that power. The source is the police power. The limitation is that set by the due process clause, which, as construed, requires that the regulation shall not be unreasonable, arbitrary or capricious; and that the means of regulation selected shall have a real or substantial relation to the subject sought to be obtained. The notion of a distinct category of business "affected with a public interest," employing property "devoted to a public use," rests upon historical error. The consequences which it is sought to draw from those phrases are belied by the meaning in which they were used centuries ago, and by the decision of this court, in *Munn v. Illinois*, . . . which first introduced them into the law of the Constitution. In my opinion, the true principle is that the State's power extends to every regulation of any business reasonably required and appropriate for the public protection. I find in the due process clause no other limitation upon the character or the scope of regulation permissible.[97]

Second, Justice Brandeis rejected the majority's contention that regulation would result in monopoly. Instead he argued:

It is settled that the police power commonly invoked in aid of health, safety and morals, extends equally to the promotion of the public welfare. The cases just cited show that, while, ordinarily, free competition in the common callings has been encouraged, the public welfare may at other times demand that monopolies be created. Upon this principle is based our whole modern practice of public utility regulation. It is no objection to the validity of the statute here assailed that it fosters monopoly. That, indeed, is its design. The certificate of public convenience and necessity is a device — a recent social-economic invention — through which the monopoly is kept under effective control by vesting in a commission the power to terminate it whenever that course is required in the public interest. To grant any monopoly to any person as a favor is forbidden even if terminable. But where, as here, there is reasonable ground for the legislative conclusion that in order to secure a necessary service at reasonable rates, it may be necessary to curtail the right to enter the calling, it is, in my opinion, consistent with the due process clause to do so, whatever the nature of the business. The existence of such power in the legislature seems indispensable in our ever-changing society.[98]

Finally, it was suggested that an emergency of sufficient importance to warrant experimental legislative regulation had been created by the depression. Said Justice Brandeis:

To stay experimentation in things social and economic is a grave responsibility. Denial of the right to experiment may be fraught with serious consequences to the Nation. It is one of the happy incidents of the federal system that a single courageous State may, if its citizens choose, serve as a laboratory; and try novel social and economic experiments without risk to the rest of the country. This Court has the power to prevent an experiment. We may strike down the statute which embodies it on the ground that, in our opinion, the measure is arbitrary, capricious, or unreasonable. We have power to do this, because the due process clause has been held by the Court applicable to matters of substantive law as well as to matters of procedure. But in the exercise of this high power, we must be ever on our guard, lest we erect our prejudices into legal principles. If we would guide by the light of reason, we must let our minds be bold.[99]

Nebbia v. New York

The last attempt of the Supreme Court to define the public interest concept is found in the *Nebbia* case of 1934.[100] In addition, this case marks the Court's abandonment of its attempt to distinguish a peculiar category of industries "affected with a public interest."

In 1933, the New York legislature passed a statute which declared that the milk industry was affected with a public interest. The statute set up a Milk Control Board and provided for control of prices and trade practices of milk producers and distributors. The board proceeded to fix nine cents as the price below which a store could not resell a quart of milk. A grocer in Rochester, named Nebbia, had sold two quarts of milk, plus a five-cent loaf of bread, for eighteen cents. Promptly sued for violating the law, Nebbia argued that the milk business was competitive rather than monopolistic, that it had none of the characteristics of a public utility, and that the federal

Constitution prohibited a state from regulating the price charged for milk. The Supreme Court, in a five-to-four decision, rejected this defense. Said Justice Roberts:

> We may as well say at once that the dairy industry is not, in the accepted sense of the phrase, a public utility. We think the appellant is also right in asserting that there is in this case no suggestion of any monopoly or monopolistic practice. It goes without saying that those engaged in the business are in no way dependent upon public grants or franchises for the privilege of conducting their activities. But if, as must be conceded, the industry is subject to regulation in the public interest, what constitutional principle bars the state from correcting existing maladjustments by legislation touching prices? We think there is no such principle. . . .
>
> It is clear that there is no closed class or category of businesses affected with a public interest, and the function of courts in the application of the Fifth and Fourteenth Amendments is to determine in each case whether circumstances vindicate the challenged regulation as a reasonable exertion of governmental authority or condemn it as arbitrary or discriminatory. . . . The phrase "affected with a public interest" can, in the nature of things, mean no more than that an industry, for adequate reason, is subject to control for the public good. In several of the decisions of this court wherein the expressions "affected with a public interest," and "clothed with a public use," have been brought forward as the criteria of the validity of price control, it has been admitted that they are not susceptible of definition and form an unsatisfactory test of the constitutionality of legislation directed at business practices or prices. These decisions must rest, finally, upon the basis that the requirements of due process were not met because the laws were found arbitrary in their operation and effect. But there can be no doubt that upon proper occasion and by appropriate measures the state may regulate a business in any of its aspects, including the prices to be charged for the products or commodities it sells.
>
> So far as the requirement of due process is concerned, and in the absence of other constitutional restriction, a state is free to adopt whatever economic policy may reasonably be deemed to promote public welfare, and to enforce that policy by legislation adapted to its purpose. The courts are without authority either to declare such policy, or, when it is declared by the legislature, to override it. If the laws passed are seen to have a reasonable relation to a proper legislative purpose, and are neither arbitrary or discriminatory, the requirements of due process are satisfied, and judicial determination to that effect renders a court *functtus officio*.[101]

Justice Roberts clearly discards monopoly as a prerequisite of the public interest concept, substituting the principle of imperfect competition — a concept covering both monopoly and excessive competition. The Court thus observed:

> ... If the law-making body within its sphere of government con-cludes that the conditions or practices in an industry make unrestricted competition an inadequate safeguard of the consumer's interests, produce waste harmful to the public, threaten ultimately to cut off the supply of a commodity needed by the public, or portend the destruction of the industry itself, appropriate statutes passed in an honest effort to correct the threatened consequences may not be set aside because the regula-tion adopted fixes prices reasonably deemed by the legislature to be fair to those engaged in the industry and to the consuming public. And this is especially so where, as here, the economic maladjustment is one of price, which threatens harm to the producer at one end of the series and the consumer at the other. The Constitution does not secure to any one liberty to conduct his business in such fashion as to inflict injury upon the public at large, or upon any substantial group of the people. Price control, like any other form of regulation, is unconstitutional only if arbitrary, discriminatory, or demonstrably irrelevant to the policy the legislature is free to adopt, and hence an unnecessary and unwarranted interference with individual liberty.[102]

Justice McReynolds, in his dissent concurred in by Justices Butler, Suth-erland, and Van Devanter, stated:

> Is the milk business so affected with public interest that the Legisla-ture may prescribe prices for sales by stores? This Court has approved the contrary view; has emphatically declared that a State lacks power to fix prices in similar private businesses. . . . Regulation to prevent recog-nized evils in business has long been upheld as permissable legislative action. But fixation of the price at which "A," engaged in an ordinary business, may sell, in order to enable "B," a producer, to improve his condition, has not been regarded as within legislative power. This is not regulation, but management, control, dictation — it amounts to the deprivation of the fundamental right which one has to conduct his own affairs honestly and along customary lines. The argument advanced here would support general prescription of prices for farm products, groceries, shoes, clothing, all the necessities of modern civilization, as well as labor, when some legislature finds and declares such action advisable and for the public good. This Court has declared that a State may not by legislative fiat convert a private business into a public util-ity. . . . And if it be now ruled that one dedicates his property to public use whenever he embarks on an enterprise which the Legislature may think is desirable to bring under control, this is but to declare that

rights guaranteed by the Constitution exist only so long as supposed public interest does not require their extinction. To adopt such a view, of course, would put an end to liberty under the Constitution.[103]

Some Implications of the Nebbia Case

The *Nebbia* decision established a new basic doctrine which has become a vital part of our constitutional law. While the exact meaning of the doctrine cannot be precisely determined,[104] two major implications emerge. First, as argued by the dissent in the case, the Court's broadened definition of "affected with a public interest" virtually brings within the regulatory power all modern business enterprises.[105] Second, the "affected with a public interest" concept is no longer synonymous with the traditional "public utility" concept; the latter concept is broader than, and includes, the former.

Extension of Regulation. Since the *Nebbia* case, the Supreme Court has allowed state and federal governments to extend regulation over many businesses. The Court has upheld state laws fixing maximum warehouse charges for handling and selling leaf tobacco,[106] and curtailing the output of petroleum[107]; and federal laws requiring inspection of tobacco,[108] restricting quantities of tobacco that can be marketed,[109] and providing for establishment of minimum prices for milk.[110] In a 1941 case in which the Supreme Court upheld a state statute fixing maximum compensation that could be collected by a private employment agency, it was argued that "The drift away from *Ribnik v. McBride* has been so great that it can no longer be deemed a controlling authority."[111] The Court even referred to the concept of "affected with a public interest" as "discarded" in the *Nebbia* case.[112] And in 1950, the Court upheld a state law fixing minimum prices for natural gas at the wellhead without invoking the concept at all. The Court simply stated: "Like any other regulation, a price-fixing order is lawful if substantially related to a legitimate end sought to be attained."[113]

Public Utility Status. The most extensive public regulation has been reserved for those activities which have been designated as public utilities (or regulated industries). The public utility status generally has been conferred on an industry that possesses those distinct economic characteristics which indicate that administrative, as opposed to market, regulation can improve the industry's economic performance. Such activities are those closely associated with the processes of transportation and distribution. As summarized by Judge Vinson in a 1943 dissenting opinion:

> The participation by a business in activities *intimately connected with the processes of transportation and distribution* . . . was the characteristic which caused it to be subjected to the impositions implicit in public utility regulation. A somewhat exhaustive enumeration of the businesses which frequently have been designated, operated, and regulated as public util-

ities illustrates that the gradual growth of the family has involved no departure from the initial concept, but merely reflected scientific progress in the facilities, auxiliaries, and varieties of transportation and distribution.[114]

Judge Vinson then proceeded to state the essential elements of the public utility concept.

> ... If a business is (1) affected with a public interest, *and* (2) bears an intimate connection with the processes of transportation and distribution, *and* (3) is under an obligation to afford its facilities to the public generally, upon demand, at fair and nondiscriminatory rates, *and* (4) enjoys, in a large measure an independence and freedom from business competition brought about either (a) by its acquisition of a monopolistic status, or (b) by the grant of a franchise or certificate from the State placing it in this position, it is ... a public utility.[115]

The Supreme Court's decisions, however, do not provide consistent criteria from which a more precise definition of the public utility concept may be formulated. Thus, "while monopoly and lack of competition are present in the case of some undoubted public utilities, there are others, carriers by motor vehicle for example, whose business is highly competitive."[116] The Court, in other words, has permitted detailed regulation of some industries with economic characteristics which differ from those possessed by traditional public utilities. At the same time, a legislature cannot confer public utility status on *any* business merely by passing a statute.[117]

Obligations and Rights of Public Utilities

The English courts evolved a group of obligations and rights which they attached on common callings or public interest occupations. The obligations were not voluntary but compulsory, and could be avoided only by withdrawal from service. They were later adopted by the American courts. Today, such obligations and rights have been incorporated into, and amplified by, state and federal statutes. As with other matters, however, the courts still retain their prerogative of reviewing the reasonableness of all statutory provisions and their administrative applications. Because these obligations and rights are discussed at length in succeeding chapters, the following paragraphs merely summarize the major requirements.

Obligations

Public utilities have four major obligations or responsibilities imposed on them because of their special status. First, they are obligated to serve all who apply for service.[118] Within a market (service) area, and within the limit of its capacity (ability to serve), a public utility must be prepared to serve any customer who is willing and able to pay for the service. At times, this requirement means that a business must provide capital investment in rural areas where it is not profitable to do so or must maintain an unprofitable type of service. The price of services in such cases may not be based on cost, but often are subsidized by other services offered by the company. More commonly, this requirement means that a public utility must build capacity ahead of demand growth (reserve capacity or margin).

Second, public utilities are obligated to render safe and adequate service. Consequently, there exist regulations of voltage requirements for electricity, and heat value and pressure requirements for gas. Each service must be supplied by means of the safest equipment available to the industry involved. Moreover, the service rendered must be adequate. For the utility industries, this requirement means service must be provided twenty-four hours a day. All utilities must be prepared for foreseeable increases in demand. In short, utility firms must be ready to give instantaneous service on demand.

Third, public utilities have the obligation to serve all customers on equal terms. Unjust or undue discrimination among customers is forbidden. Under conditions of near monopoly, discrimination in price and perhaps service may become profitable to a business. As there are few substitute services available, customers would be helpless in such a situation. If reasonable, regulation does permit the classification of customers for the purpose of ratemaking. But within each class, the same rate structure must apply. Regulation also permits the use of graduated rate structures; again, they must be reasonable.

Finally, public utilities are obligated to charge only a "just and reasonable" price for the services rendered. It is up to the various commissions and the courts to interpret this duty. Nonregulated businesses are under no such restraint, as competition is assumed to regulate prices in the public interest. As will be demonstrated throughout the book, this provision has resulted in considerable controversy between the industries, commissions, and courts.

Rights

All businesses, regulated and nonregulated, have certain rights. The most important general right is the legal protection of private property. In addition, however, public utilities have four rights that are largely the result of their special status.

First, public utilities have the right to collect a reasonable price for their services. Regulatory authorities may not force such a business to operate at a loss.[119] At the same time, a reasonable return is not guaranteed, and under adverse economic conditions it may happen that no rate will cover the cost of service. Barring such a possibility, the courts have insisted on the right to a reasonable price.

Second, public utilities have the right to render service subject to reasonable rates and regulations. The public has certain rights and can demand that public utilities live up to their obligations. For their part, these industries have the right to reasonable office hours, prompt customer payments, service deposits, and contracts, among others. Moreover, these businesses have the right to withdraw service under prescribed conditions and after giving due notice to their customers.

Third, when they furnish adequate service at reasonable rates, public utilities have the right of *protection* from competition from an enterprise offering the same service in the same service area. A public utility must receive a certificate of public convenience and necessity from the appropriate regulatory agency, and a franchise (generally dealing with the use of city streets and with city utility service) from the relevant local governmental unit, prior to commencing operations. In turn, such certificates and franchises, while not exclusive, offer a public utility some freedom from competition in its service area.

Finally, the specific right of eminent domain has been given to most public utilities. This right enables them to condemn private property and take it for "public use," when necessary to the proper conduct of their business. Public utilities are required to pay a just compensation for any property so condemned. Land may be taken, for instance, for electric or telephone pole lines or for water mains, to enable a public utility to provide adequate service for the public.[120]

Limitations on Government Regulation

Once the right to regulate an industry has been established under the police powers of the state or the interstate commerce clause of the federal Constitution, are there any limits on the actions of the regulatory commissions? The answer is very definitely in the affirmative. The Fifth and Fourteenth Amendments to the Constitution guarantee due process of law. As the courts have long held the right to profits as a fundamental characteristic of property, these two Amendments mean that no regulation by a unit of government can reduce profits below a confiscatory level and be upheld as constitutional.

It is to this limitation on the actions of regulatory commissions that many of the difficulties in the effort to achieve effective regulation can be traced. In fact, this limitation is directly responsible for the frequent overruling of a so-called expert body (the regulatory commission) by a legal body that is often untrained in the problems of regulation (the court). As a result, to test the reasonableness of the commissions' orders, the regulated companies have taken to the courts many important decisions made by the commissions. And the companies cannot necessarily be blamed in their actions. The companies are privately owned and privately operated. Regulation, therefore, involves the question of private rights versus public needs, and the line between them often requires judicial interpretation. But from the point of view of effective regulation, this often results in very slow enforcement of the commissions' decisions.[121]

Thus, there is a good deal of uncertainty both as to the fields over which the units of government may practice regulation and as to how far such regulation may be carried. In both instances, the courts have the final word. In both instances, while the courts have laid down some general rules, they continue to take each specific case under review, and the general rules are so vague and flexible that no commission can accurately forecast just what the final court decision will be. Under such conditions, regulation has proceeded by trial and error. Before taking up these matters in greater detail, the following chapter discusses the independent regulatory commissions.

Notes

*Chief Justice Taft, *Wolff Packing Co. v. Court of Industrial Relations*, 262 U.S. 522, 538-39 (1923).

[1]*Munn v. Illinois*, 94 U.S. 113, 126 (1877).

[2]*Nebbia v. New York*, 291 U.S. 502 (1934).

[3]*McCulloch v. Maryland*, 4 Wheaton 316 (1819).

[4]*Brown v. Maryland*, 12 Wheaton 419 (1827); *Charles River Bridge v. Warren Bridge*, 11 Peters 420 (1837).

[5]While the trend of court decisions favors the federal government, it should not be inferred that it has been a smooth and continuous trend. In 1887 and in 1895, the Supreme Court ruled that manufacturing was not commerce, thus excluding the entire sector from federal power (*Kidd v. Pearson*, 128 U.S. 1 [1887]; *United States v. E. C. Knight Co.*, 156 U.S. 1 [1895]. In 1918, it invalidated a law prohibiting interstate shipment of the products of child labor, ruling that their production was not interstate (*Hammer v. Dagenhart*, 247 U.S. 251). And in 1936, the Court invalidated a law providing for wage- and price-fixing in the coal industry, asserting that the effect on interstate commerce was "close and substantial," but not "direct" (*Carter v. Carter Coal Co.*, 298 U.S. 238). In later decisions, these rulings have been explicitly reversed. For a review of the cases in this area, see Charles P. Light, Jr., "The Federal Commerce Power," 49 *Virginia Law Review* 717 (1963).

[6]*Gibbons v. Ogden*, 9 Wheaton (22 U.S.) 1, 189-90 (1824).

[7]*Ibid.*

[8]*Ibid.*, pp. 194-95.

[9]*Railway v. Van Husen*, 95 U.S. 465 (1872); *Pensacola Telegraph Co. v. Western Union*, 96 U.S. 1 (1877).

[10]*Steamer Daniel Bell v. United States*, 10 Wallace 557 (1871).

[11]*Houston, East & West Texas Ry. Co. v. United States*, 234 U.S. 342 (1914). See also

Swift & Co. v. United States, 196 U.S. 375 (1905); *Southern Ry. v. United States*, 222 U.S. 20 (1911).

[12]*Lemke v. Farmers Grain Co.*, 258 U.S. 50 (1922).

[13]*Stafford v. Wallace*, 258 U.S. 495, 515-16 (1922).

[14]See Robert L. Stern, "The Commerce Clause and the National Economy, 1933-1946," 59 *Harvard Law Review* 645, 883 (1946).

[15]*National Labor Relations Board v. Jones & Laughlin Steel Corp.*, 301 U.S. 1, 38, 41 (1937). See also *National Labor Relations Board v. Fruehauf Trailer Co.*, 301 U.S. 49 (1937); *National Labor Relations Board v. Friedman-Harry Marks Clothing Co.*, 301 U.S. 58 (1937).

[16]*Santa Cruz Fruit Packing Co. v. National Labor Relations Board*, 303 U.S. 453 (1938).

[17]*Consolidated Edison Co. v. National Labor Relations Board*, 305 U.S. 197 (1938).

[18]*United States v. Darby Lumber Co.*, 312 U.S. 100, 121 (1941).

[19]*Wickard v. Filburn*, 317 U.S. 111, 125 (1942).

[20]*Kirschbaum Co. v. Walling*, 316 U.S. 517 (1942).

[21]*Warren-Bradshaw Drilling Co. v. Hall*, 317 U.S. 88 (1942).

[22]*United States v. South-Eastern Underwriters Ass'n*, 322 U.S. 533 (1944).

[23]*United States v. Frankfort Distilleries*, 324 U.S. 293 (1945).

[24]*Mabee v. White Plains Publishing Co.*, 327 U.S. 178 (1946).

[25]*American Power & Light Co. v. Securities & Exchange Comm.*, 329 U.S. 90, 104 (1946).

[26]*Houston, East & West Texas Ry. Co. v. United States*, op. cit., p. 353.

[27]*Wisconsin Railroad Comm. v. Chicago, B. & Q. R. Co.*, 257 U.S. 563, 588 (1922). In 1942, the Court said: "The commerce power is not confined in its exercise to the regulation of commerce among the states. It extends to those activities intrastate which so effect interstate commerce, or the exertion of the power of Congress over it, as to make regulation of them appropriate means to the attainment of a legitimate end, the effective execution of the granted power to regulate interstate commerce," *United States v. Wrightwood Dairy Co.*, 315 U.S. 110, 119 (1942). See also *Stafford v. Wallace*, op. cit.; *Chicago Board of Trade v. Olsen*, 262 U.S. 1 (1923).

[28]*North Carolina v. United States*, 325 U.S. 1 (1923).

[29]See Chapter 4, pp. 145-48.

[30]*Munn v. Illinois*, op. cit., p. 134.

[31]*Nebbia v. New York*, op. cit., pp. 537, 539.

[32]*General Elec. Co. v. Wahle*, 207 Ore. 302 (1956).

[33]*Santa Clara County v. Southern Pacific R.R. Co.*, 118 U.S. 394 (1886).

[34]*Nebbia v. New York*, op. cit., p. 525.

[35]Martin Shapiro, *The Supreme Court and Administrative Agencies* (New York: The Free Press, 1968), p. 2.

[36]*Ibid.*, p. 3. "In this sense judicial review is the power to declare an act or decision of a government official not unconstitutional but simply illegal — not beyond the totality of powers that government may legitimately exercise, but simply beyond the authorization of the statute or other legal rule by which he is supposed to conduct himself." *Ibid.*

[37]*Interstate Commerce Comm. v. Union Pacific R.R. Co.*, 222 U.S. 541, 547 (1912). See, *e.g.*, *Arkansas Power & Light Co. v. Arkansas Pub. Service Comm.*, 546 S.W. 2d 720 (1977); *United Inter-Mountain Teleph. Co. v. Tennessee Pub. Service Comm.*, 19 PUR4th

589 (1977); *Southern California Gas Co. v. California Pub. Utilities Comm.*, 591 P. 2d 34 (1979).

[38]Martin G. Glaeser, *Public Utilities in American Capitalism* (New York: The Macmillan Co., 1957), p. 196.

[39]*Ibid.*, p. 201.

[40]Quoted in *Munn v. Illinois, op. cit.*, p. 127.

[41]Ronald E. Seavoy, "The Public Service Origins of the American Business Corporation," 52 *Business History Review* 30 (1978).

[42]Note, "State Regulation of Prices Under the Fourteenth Amendment," 33 *Harvard Law Review* 838, 838-39 (1920) (citations omitted).

[43]Emery Troxel, *Economics of Public Utilities* (New York: Holt, Rinehart & Winston, Inc., 1947), p. 5.

[44]*Ibid.*, p. 7. It has been estimated, for example, that the land grants made by the federal government alone (not all railroads received land grants) were equal to about 10 percent of the total land area of the continental United States. Charles L. Dearing and Wilfred Owen, *National Transportation Policy* (Washington, D.C.: The Brookings Institution, 1949), p. 11.

[45]See S. J. Buck, *The Granger Movement* (Cambridge: Harvard University Press, 1913); Charles R. Dietrick, "The Effects of the Granger Acts," 11 *Journal of Political Economy* 237 (1903); A.E. Paine, "The Granger Movement in Illinois," 1 *University of Illinois Studies* 335 (1905); Charles Fairman, "The So-Called Granger Cases, Lord Hale, and Justice Bradley," 5 *Stanford Law Review* 587 (1953).

[46]See Chapter 4, pp. 121-23.

[47]*Wolff Packing Co. v. Court of Industrial Relations, op. cit.*

[48]*Munn v. Illinois, op. cit.*

[49]Dissenting opinion of Justice Brandeis in *New State Ice Co. v. Liebmann*, 285 U.S. 262, 301 (1932).

[50]*Wolff Packing Co. v. Court of Industrial Relations, op. cit.*, p. 536. See also *Tyson & Brother v. Banton*, 273 U.S. 418 (1927).

[51]94 U.S. 113.

[52]The Criminal Court of Cook County, Illinois, found Munn and Scott guilty and fined them $100.

[53]*Munn v. Illinois, op. cit.*, pp. 131-32.

[54]*Ibid.*, pp. 132-33.

[55]*Ibid.*, p. 133.

[56]*Ibid.*, pp. 125-26. See Walton H. Hamilton, "Affectation with Public Interest," 39 *Yale Law Journal* 1089 (1930); Breck P. McAllister, "Lord Hale and the Business Affected with a Public Interest," 43 *Harvard Law Review* 759 (1930).

[57]*Munn v. Illinois, op. cit.*, p. 133.

[58]*Sinking Fund Cases*, 99 U.S. 700, 747 (1878).

[59]McAllister (*op. cit.*, p. 769) argues that "Chief Justice Waite's references to monopoly seem to be for the purpose of emphasizing the size and importance of the business and not of delimiting a necessary condition to regulate." This argument is difficult to support, however, in view of the Court's subsequent references to the *Munn* case and to monopoly conditions. See, *e.g.*, *Nebbia v. New York, op. cit.*, pp. 531-32.

[60]Dissenting opinion, *Munn v. Illinois, op. cit.*, pp. 146-47.

[61]*Ibid.*, pp. 140-41.

[62]*Budd v. New York*, 143 U.S. 517 (1892).

[63]Dissenting opinion, *ibid.*, p. 549-50.

[64]*Ibid.*, p. 550.

[65]*Ibid.*, pp. 550-51. As Troxel (*op. cit.*, p. 15) has pointed out, "a monopoly of law was a consequence of private privilege, and was subject to regulation. But the idea of a monopoly of fact involved some strange legal reasoning."

[66]Dissenting opinion, *Budd v. New York, op. cit.*, p. 552.

[67]*Brass v. North Dakota ex rel. Stoeser*, 153 U.S. 391 (1894).

[68]*Ibid.*, p. 403.

[69]Troxel, *op. cit.*, p. 16. Justices Brewer, Field, Jackson and White dissented.

[70]*German Alliance Insurance Co. v. Lewis*, 233 U.S. 389 (1914).

[71]*Ibid.*, pp. 406-7, 409.

[72]*Ibid.*, p. 411 (citation omitted).

[73]*Ibid.*, pp. 414-15.

[74]Dissenting opinion, *ibid.*, p. 420. The dissent also argued that the statute was discriminatory and represented a denial of equal protection of the law, since insurance rates were to be fixed for stock companies but not for either mutual companies or individual persons selling insurance. *Ibid.*, pp. 433-34.

[75]*Wolff Packing Co. v. Court of Industrial Relations, op. cit.*

[76]*Ibid.*, pp. 535-36, 538.

[77]*Nebbia v. New York, op. cit.*

[78]Troxel, *op. cit.*, p. 17.

[79]*Wolff Packing Co. v. Court of Industrial Relations, op. cit.*, p. 536.

[80]*Tyson & Brother v. Banton, op. cit.*

[81]*Ibid.*, pp. 433-34, 439-40.

[82]*Ibid.*, p. 442.

[83]Dissenting opinion, *ibid.*, pp. 446-47.

[84]Dissenting opinion, *ibid.*, p. 451.

[85]*Ibid.*, pp. 451-52.

[86]Dissenting opinion, *ibid.*, p. 454.

[87]*Ibid.*, p. 455.

[88]*Ribnik v. McBride*, 277 U.S. 350 (1928).

[89]*Ibid.*, pp. 356-57.

[90]"For thirty years or more the evils found to be connected with the business of employment agencies in the United States have been the subject of repeated investigations, official and unofficial, and of extensive public comment. They have been the primary reason for the establishment of public employment offices in the various states." Dissenting opinion, *ibid.*, pp. 363-64.

[91]*Ibid.*, pp. 373-74.

[92]*Williams v. Standard Oil Co.*, 278 U.S. 235 (1929).

[93]Justice Holmes dissented, but did not write an opinion. Justices Brandeis and Stone dissented from the majority's reasoning, but concurred in the result.

[94]*Williams v. Standard Oil Co., op. cit.*, pp. 239-40.

[95]*New State Ice Co. v. Liebmann, op. cit.*

[96]*Ibid.*, pp. 277-78.

[97]Dissenting opinion, *ibid.*, pp. 283-84, 291-93, 300-03.

[98]*Ibid.*, p. 304.

[99]*Ibid.*, p. 311. The majority had argued that there were "certain essentials of liberty with which the state is not entitled to dispense in the interest of experiments." *Ibid.*, p. 280.

[100]*Nebbia v. New York, op. cit.*

[101]*Ibid.*, pp. 531-32, 536-37.

[102]*Ibid.*, p. 538-39.

[103]Dissenting opinion, *ibid.*, pp. 552, 554-55.

[104]The implications of the *Nebbia* case are discussed by Irving B. Goldsmith and Gordon W. Winks, "Price Fixing: From Nebbia to Guffey," 31 *Illinois Law Review* 179 (1936); R. L. Hale, "The Constitution and the Price System: Some Reflections on Nebbia v. New York," 34 *Columbia Law Review* 401 (1934); Irwin S. Rosenbaum, "Ruling on Milk Price Control," 14 *Public Utilities Fortnightly* 795 (1934); R. W. Harbeson, "The Public Interest Concept in Law and in Economics," 37 *Michigan Law Review* 181 (1938).

[105]"In truth, it would appear that the *Nebbia* case, in attempting to define 'affected with a public interest' in a manner sufficiently broad to sustain price regulation, destroyed that concept." Ronald A. Anderson, *Government and Business* (4th ed.; Cincinnati: South-Western Publishing Co., 1981), p. 225.

[106]*Townsend v. Yeomans*, 301 U.S. 441 (1937).

[107]*Railroad Comm. v. Rowan & Nichols Oil Co.*, 310 U.S. 573 (1940).

[108]*Currin v. Wallace*, 306 U.S. 1 (1939).

[109]*Mulford v. Smith*, 307 U.S. 38 (1939).

[110]*United States v. Rock Royal Co-operative*, 307 U.S. 533 (1939).

[111]*Olsen v. Nebraska*, 313 U.S. 236, 244 (1941).

[112]*Ibid.*, p. 245.

[113]*Cities Service Gas Co. v. Peerless Oil & Gas Co.*, 340 U.S. 179, 186 (1950).

[114]*Davies Warehouse Co. v. Brown*, 137 F. 2d 201, 212-13 (1943).

[115]*Ibid.*, p. 217. Judge Vinson recognized that the "formula is a limited one," amounting to an affirmative test only. "My formula has no negative or exclusive implications. What I do say is that, at least, *any* business which *does* possess and practice and operate under each and all of these features, is by a preponderance of considered judicial opinion a business in the public utility class." *Ibid.*

[116]*Ibid.*, majority opinion by Judge Maris, p. 207.

[117]Francis X. Welch, *Cases and Text on Public Utility Regulation* (rev. ed.; Arlington, Va.: Public Utilities Reports, Inc., 1968), p. 3.

[118]For a recent analysis of this obligation, see Sallyanne Payton, "The Duty of a Public Utility to Serve in the Presence of New Competition," in Werner Sichel and Thomas G. Gies (eds.), *Applications of Economic Principles in Public Utility Industries* (Ann Arbor: The University of Michigan, 1981), pp. 121-52.

[119]Certain services offered by a particular company may be operated at a loss, but a company cannot be forced to operate at an overall loss.

[120]See, *e.g.,* "Eminent Domain Laws and Electric Utilities," 106 *Public Utilities Fortnightly* 49 (July 31, 1980). Conversely, the lack of eminent domain has been a major factor hindering the development of coal slurry pipelines. See Comment, "Coal Slurry Pipelines and Railroad Crossings: Court Decisions Favor the Pipeline Sponsors," 18 *Houston Law Review* 1075 (1981). On the coal slurry pipeline issue, see also Note, "Do State Restrictions on Water Use by Slurry Pipelines Violate the Commerce Clause?," 53 *University of Colorado Law Review* 655 (1982).

[121]This paragraph should not be interpreted to mean that judicial review is a bad thing. Quite the contrary. "Court review has been a public benefit. . . . The courts are the constitutional guardians of the powers of the legislatures and of the rights of those affected by legislation." E. R. Johnson, *Government Regulation of Transportation* (New York: D. Appleton-Century Co., (1938), p. 102. In other words, while judicial review has resulted in slow regulation, it is a lesser evil to have judicial review than it would be to abolish it.

Chapter	THE INDEPENDENT
4	REGULATORY
	COMMISSIONS

The need for a commission arises ... when the legislative body finds that particular conditions call for continual and very frequent acts of legislation, based on a uniform and consistent policy, which in themselves require intimate and expert knowledge of numerous and complex facts, a knowledge which can only be obtained by processes of patient, impartial, and continued investigation.

—*Joseph B. Eastman**

Regulatory functions may be exercised by administrative agencies or by executive departments. The agency has become the most important form of economic regulation at both the federal and state levels in the United States. Such was not always the case. Competition was relied on to protect the consumer during the early developmental stages of all now-regulated utilities. As a result, charters and franchises to operate in certain specified areas were granted almost indiscriminately by cities and states. Denver, in 1880, granted a general electric utility franchise "to all comers."[1] New York City, in 1887, gave franchises to six electric utility companies at the same time.[2] In fact, the general policy throughout the country was to grant a franchise to any company that applied.[3]

The impossibility of relying on competition as a regulatory force gradually became evident. As outlined in Chapter 2, the economic characteristics of certain industries indicate that they operate more efficiently as monopolies. Detailed government regulation was needed, however, to insure that these potential economic advantages were realized by consumers. Attention in this chapter is focused on early methods of public control and on the development of commission regulation, as well as on relations between federal and state commissions, and between commissions and the three branches of government.

Pre-Commission Methods of Regulation

Three early methods of government regulation were: (*1*) by the terms of decisions handed down by courts at common law; (*2*) by the terms of charters granted by state legislatures; and (*3*) by the terms of franchises issued by local governments. These methods frequently overlapped, but they are treated separately for discussion purposes.

Judicial Regulation

Present-day regulation is based upon statutes and ordinances enacted by local, state, or federal governments' legislative bodies. As previously noted, however, statutory law was preceded by the common law — the nonlegislative body of principles built up by court decisions. The common law was developed in England during and following the last part of the Middle Ages, and resulted from decisions handed down by the courts in cases brought by private litigants.

There were no preventative features in the common law. Any person who thought himself injured could sue. As conditions changed and new problems arose, many different issues were brought before the courts. Each decision, therefore, either built upon an old precedent or created a new precedent. The common law thus developed from case to case, from one individual lawsuit to another.

Two major principles of the common law unfolded. First, monopoly and restraints of trade were held to be contrary to the public interest. Damages might even be awarded in case of proven injury. The modern parallel is our antitrust laws. Second, certain occupations were recognized as "common callings." In these occupations, the general right of refusal to sell was denied. Instead, the common law imposed on such callings the duty of serving all customers, at reasonable prices and without discrimination. The modern parallel is the public utility sector.

As a method of regulation, the common law had many limitations. Litigation was (and still is) expensive. An individual might not have known that he had been injured and, even when he did, he might have lacked the funds necessary to sue. Not being provided with staffs of trained accountants, economists, engineers, and rate experts, the courts lacked special competence to deal with the issues brought before them, especially those involving intricate industry problems. Expertise was required for effective regulation. Further, even when the courts found a business practice unreasonable, only negative action could be taken. The problem of deciding on new rates and regulation for a future period is a legislative, not a judicial, function. The courts, moreover, could only decide the cases brought before them; they could not take the initiative. And the court system was not able to handle the required volume of cases which arose from regulatory adjudication. Under such limitations, regulation was discontinuous, expensive, and often slow.

Direct Legislative Regulation

Prior to the enactment of general incorporation laws, public utilities were incorporated through the passage of special legislative acts. These charters contained both the usual corporate rights and a number of special privileges, such as the power of eminent domain. Their regulatory provisions varied considerably, but frequently prescribed only maximum rates and/or limited the yield on common stock to stated percentages. In 1886, to illustrate, the New York legislature passed a law to incorporate the New York Mutual Gas Light Company which provided that:

> Whenever the profits which shall be earned by said company, after deducting all expenses and necessary outlays for labor and materials used in carrying on and extending the business of said company shall exceed in any one year the sum of 10 percent upon the whole capital stock of said company, then, and in that event, the excess over the said sum of 10 per cent shall be divided, one half of such excess between the consumers of the gas furnished by said company pro rata according to the amount consumed by them respectively, and the other half shall be paid as dividend to such owners and holders of the stock of said company as may be consumers of the gas furnished by said company; provided that no individual owner or holder of said stock shall be entitled to, or shall receive, nor shall there be paid to him, such dividend upon more than fifty shares of said stock.[4]

Toward the end of the nineteenth century, the states started to enact general incorporation laws. The regulatory provisions in these laws were equally ineffective, since they continued to be written in broad, general terms.

Direct legislative regulation of this sort was, above all else, inflexible. Economic conditions were constantly changing as modern technology was developed. Adjustments were required if regulation was to be up-to-date.

Each adjustment, however, necessitated an amendment of the law. But legislatures were in session only a small percentage of the time and found their attention being claimed by many other matters. Under such circumstances, continuous regulation was impossible.[5] Little effort was expended to enforce regulatory provisions contained in charters, and in the absence of effective accounting and financial control, rate regulation was inadequate. And just as the courts lacked specialized knowledge of regulatory problems, so did the members of state legislatures. In practice, therefore, noneconomic considerations would often dictate the type of regulation followed. It should be stressed also that the proper function of a legislative body is to enact and formulate policy and not to engage in administrative work. For all of these reasons, direct statutory regulation proved to be a poor method of controlling an industry.

Local Franchise Regulation

Some local (municipal) control was exercised by the enactment of city ordinances, but particularly did local regulation rely on the franchise.[6] In order to enter a field, certain businesses had to acquire a franchise from the relevant city council before they could commence operations. When well-drawn, the franchise set exact standards for service to be rendered, rates to be charged or methods of arriving at the rates, accounting methods to be employed, and in the case of term franchises, the method of renewing the franchise or provision for the locality's taking over the company at expiration of the franchise. Such agreements usually were to run for a definite period, although many franchises were granted in perpetuity.

While use of the well-drawn franchise had some merit, in the main the franchise as actually used proved a defective instrument for detailed regulation. When franchises were issued indiscriminately, little regard was paid to the interest of the public. When they were issued in perpetuity, franchises were often exclusive. In either case, they tended to be poorly drafted due to the inexperience of city councilmen.[7] And even when they were well-drawn, the company often benefited, since it was common for the utility's lawyers to draft the franchise and then present it to the city council for approval.

Changes in the prescribed rates or in the service standards were made with great difficulty. This difficulty was due to a Supreme Court decision which held that a franchise had the status of a contract which a state could not impair[8]; thus both parties had to approve a change. As expected, the companies resisted downward rate changes and the city councils upward adjustments. Nor was it easy to change the prescribed service standards, especially when the companies were asked to raise the standards at the same level of rates. In the case of a franchise issued for a definite period of time, another problem arose. Service often became poor as the termination date on the franchise drew near. The company would try to keep its investment as small as possible to avoid loss if the contract were not renewed. The agreements also failed to provide for administrative machinery to keep check on the company to see that it met the terms of its franchise. It was often possible, therefore, for the actual service rendered to fall for long periods of time below the level specified in the franchise.

It was often impossible, consequently, for franchise or charter provisions to be changed, "however ill-considered or antiquated with respect to current needs for regulation they might be."[9] Especially where exclusive franchises were issued, authorities "found themselves in the disagreeable situation of having bargained away their right to allow competition without having retained effective control over rates and service."[10] Thus, as with direct legislative regulation, franchise regulation proved to inflexible. Detailed requirements were unsatisfactory under changing conditions. New York City granted to a subway corporation a franchise that provided for a five-cent fare, and in Georgia a franchise given a street railway company required it to run cars over its lines as often as every thirty minutes, day and night. Such detailed requirements obstructed adjustments to changing consumer demands. Moreover, franchises were frequently sought by speculators to be sold to the highest bidder. Some cities, feeling that a franchise carried with it valuable rights, issued one only for a monetary consideration. Chicago, for instance, issued to its utilities franchises that required annual payments of 3 percent of their gross incomes.[11]

In addition, a more serious drawback to franchise regulation soon became apparent — the significant change in scope of operations. Whereas at first each company usually serviced but one market area (community), technological developments gradually made it both feasible and advisable to have one company serve two or more towns. As this change took place, it became obvious that state regulation would have to succeed the earlier regulation obtained through the local franchise.

Many cities continue to issue franchises to public utilities serving their areas. In a few instances, these franchises are a method of regulation. In Texas, incorporated cities may control the rates and services of electric, gas, and private water utilities within their boundaries, with the public utility commission exercising appellate jurisdiction over electric and water rates within municipalities (and primary jurisdiction over telephone rates) and the railroad commission exercising appellate jurisdiction over gas rates within municipalities (and primary jurisdiction over gas rates in unincorporated areas). In Nebraska, municipalities grant permits and set rates for gas utilities (there are no private electric utilities in that state). But in most cases, city franchises are limited in function, usually dealing with the use of city streets. Economic regulation is carried out by state and federal commissions.

Commission Regulation

Each of the early methods of regulation proved ineffective. Court control was expensive, slow, and negative in character. Direct legislative control was inflexible, as well as slow. Local franchise control had the same defects. Each of these methods was incapable of adapting to the development of an industrialized and highly complex society — a development requiring expertise, flexible regulation, and continuity of policy.[12] Further, there were no clear lines of authority between state and local governments. "Owing often to the lack of clearness in the general laws, serious questions arose whether a city, in granting the special franchise, was authorized to impose conditions upon applicant companies in addition to those imposed by general statute."[13] Under these conditions, regulation failed to safeguard the interests of consumers, investors, and the companies involved. Gradually the demand for more stringent and continuous control arose, and the states responded by turning to regulatory commissions. These commissions, operating under general legislative statutes, are referred to as "independent" regulatory commissions (agencies).

The initial state commissions, generally those created prior to 1870, were largely fact-finding and advisory bodies, with jurisdiction limited to the railroads. Six states set up such commissions before the Civil War: Rhode Island in 1839, New Hampshire in 1844, Connecticut in 1853, New York and Vermont in 1855, and Maine in 1858. Ohio, in 1867, and Massachusetts, in 1869, followed right after the war. These commissions made recommendations to their state legislatures[14] and to railroad managements, appraised property taken by railroads under the right of eminent domain, and enforced railroad safety standards, but they had no control over rates. Thus, they had to rely heavily on publicity and public opinion to obtain enforcement of their orders.[15]

Shortly after the beginning of the Granger movement in the Midwest, the first commissions with mandatory powers were established. Between 1871 and 1874, Illinois, Iowa, Minnesota, and Wisconsin established commissions with power to set maximum rates, prevent discrimination, and forbid mergers of competing railroad lines. While the Granger laws, except in Illinois, were repealed by the end of the seventies, they established a pattern followed by other states. By 1887, when Congress created the Interstate Commerce Commission (partly patterned after the British Railway Commission of 1873) to regulate the nation's railroads, "twenty-five states had established commissions to assist the legislature in this work."[16]

Commission regulation of other industries was slower to develop, reflecting in part their later development. In 1859, an Office of Inspector of Gas Meters was established by the New York legislature; two years later, electric light companies were added to its jurisdiction. But most nontransportation industries were not subjected to commission regulation until the beginning of the twentieth century. Many abuses long went unrecognized. Despite evidence of ineffective control long before this time, local authorities were reluctant to give up their regulatory power. In the absence of public agitation, state legislatures were slow to act.

The public clamor for reform, however, became widespread early in the twentieth century as notorious abuses began to appear. In New York, Charles Evans Hughes was elected governor primarily because of his 1905 expose of insurance scandals. Under his leadership, the legislature enacted the Public Service Commissions Law in May, 1907, creating two district commissions: the First District Commission with jurisdiction over rapid transit, railroad, gas and electric companies in New York City, and the Second District Commission with jurisdiction over the same industries in the remainder of the state.[17] Little more than a month later the Wisconsin legislature, largely on the urging of Governor Robert M. LaFollette, expanded the powers and duties of its existing railroad commission to cover such utilities as gas, light, power, and telephone companies. These powerful state commissions became the models, and gradually other states followed suit, either by establishing new commissions or by extending the powers and duties of existing ones.

By 1920, more than two-thirds of the states had regulatory commissions.[18] Their jurisdictions and powers were often limited, as was clearly shown after the stock market crash of 1929 and the resulting financial scandals. Thereafter, state commissions were strengthened, their jurisdictions extended, and their powers increased. Today, all fifty states, plus the District of Columbia, have commissions (listed in Table 4-1), known as public utilities or public service commissions, corporation commissions, or commerce commissions. Four federal commissions also have been established with jurisdiction over the interstate activities of the industries under consideration.

The State Regulatory Commissions[19]

The jurisdiction (sometimes limited) of the state commissions, including the District of Columbia, is shown in Table 4-1 and can be summarized as follows:

Telephone and telegraph 51
Electric utilities 50
Gas utilities 50
Water utilities 43
Municipal: electric and/or gas 27
Electric cooperatives 23
Steam heating 15

Fifty of the regulatory commissions have jurisdiction over one or more additional businesses and/or activities, including transportation utilities, toll bridges, sewage systems, warehouses, CATV systems, security laws, and blue-sky laws. Moreover, in states where one or more of the public utilities are not subject to commission control, the statutes frequently provide other methods of insuring service at a reasonable rate. The most common of these methods, as noted earlier, is local regulation.

TABLE 4-1

Jurisdiction of State Regulatory Commissions, 1985

Commission	E	G	SH	W	M	ECO	TT	O[b]
				Utilities Regulated[a]				
Alabama Public Service Commission	E	G	SH	W			TT	O
Alaska Public Utilities Commission	E	G	SH	W			TT	O
Arizona Corporation Commission	E	G		W		ECO	TT	O
Arkansas Public Service Commission	E	G		W	M[e]	ECO	TT	O
California Public Utilities Commission	E	G	SH	W			TT	O
Colorado Public Utilities Commission	E	G	SH	W	M	ECO	TT	O
Connecticut Department of Public Utility Control	E	G		W			TT	O
Delaware Public Service Commission	E	G		W		ECO	TT	O
District of Columbia Public Service Commission	E	G					TT	O
Florida Public Service Commission	E	G		W	M	ECO[f]	TT	O
Georgia Public Service Commission	E	G					TT	O
Hawaii Public Utilities Commission	E	G		W			TT	O
Idaho Public Utilities Commission	E	G					TT	O
Illinois Commerce Commission	E	G		W	M[g]		TT	O
Indiana Public Service Commission[c]	E	G		W	M	ECO	TT	O
Iowa Public Utilities Board	E	G		W	M[h]	ECO	TT	O
Kansas State Corporation Commission	E	G		W	M	ECO	TT	O
Kentucky Public Service Commission	E	G		W		ECO	TT	O
Louisiana Public Service Commission	E	G		W			TT	O
Maine Public Utilities Commission	E	G		W	M	ECO	TT	O
Maryland Public Service Commission	E	G	SH	W	M	ECO	TT	O
Massachusetts Department of Public Utilities	E	G		W	M		TT	O
Michigan Public Service Commission	E	G	SH	W		ECO	TT	O
Minnesota Public Utilities Commission	E	G			M	ECO	TT	O
Mississippi Public Service Commission	E	G		W	M[i]		TT	O
Missouri Public Service Commission	E	G	SH	W	M[i]		TT	O
Montana Public Service Commission	E	G		W	M		TT	O
Nebraska Public Service Commission							TT	O
Nevada Public Service Commission	E	G		W		ECO	TT	O
New Hampshire Public Utilities Commission	E	G	SH	W	M	ECO	TT	O
New Jersey Board of Public Utilities	E	G	SH	W	M		TT	O
New Mexico Public Service Commission	E	G		W	M[j]			
New Mexico State Corporation Commission							TT	O
New York Public Service Commission	E	G	SH	W	M		TT	O
North Carolina Utilities Commission	E	G		W			TT	O
North Dakota Public Service Commission	E	G					TT	O
Ohio Public Utilities Commission	E	G	SH	W			TT	O
Oklahoma Corporation Commission	E	G				ECO	TT	O
Oregon Public Utility Commissioner[d]	E	G	SH[k]	W			TT	O
Pennsylvania Public Utility Commission	E	G	SH	W	M[l]		TT	O

TABLE 4-1 *(Continued)*

Commission	Utilities Regulated[a]							
	E	G	SH	W	M	ECO	TT	O[b]
Rhode Island Public Utilities Commission	E	G		W	M	ECO	TT	O
South Carolina Public Service Commission	E	G		W			TT	O
South Dakota Public Utilities Commission	E	G					TT	O
Tennessee Public Service Commission	E	G		W			TT	O
Texas Public Utility Commission	E			W^m	M^n	ECO	TT	O
Texas Railroad Commission		G			M^g			O
Utah Public Service Commission	E	G		W		ECO	TT	O
Vermont Public Service Board	E	G		W	M	ECO	TT	O
Virginia State Corporation Commission	E	G		W		ECO	TT	O
Washington Utilities and Transportation Commission	E	G		W	M^g		TT	O
West Virginia Public Service Commission	E	G		W	M^o	ECO	TT	O
Wisconsin Public Service Commission	E	G	SH	W	M		TT	O
Wyoming Public Service Commission	E	G	SH	W	M^l	ECO	TT	O

[a]E = Electric. G = Gas. SH = Steam Heating. W = Water. M = Municipal Electric and Gas Plants. ECO = Electric Cooperatives. TT = Telephone and Telegraph. O = Other.

[b]Other includes a variety of activities, such as transportation utilities, radio-common carriers, toll bridges, sewage systems, warehouses, security laws, CATV systems, and blue-sky laws.

[c]Name changed to Indiana Utility Regulatory Commission, effective July 1, 1987.

[d]New commission, Oregon Public Utility Commission, effective April 1, 1987.

[e]Municipal gas utilities only for service outside city limits.

[f]Rate structure regulation only.

[g]Municipal gas utilities only.

[h]Service rules, plant siting, and safety matters only.

[i]Municipal gas utilities for safety only.

[j]Only when municipality petitions for such regulation.

[k]Regulation phased out on June 30, 1986.

[l]Municipal electric and gas rates only to service rendered beyond a municipality's corporate limits.

[m]Jurisdiction over water and sewer companies transferred to Texas Water Commission, effective March 1, 1986.

[n]Appellate jurisdiction over municipal electric rates outside city limits.

[o]Municipal electric utilities only.

Source: *1985 Annual Report on Utility and Carrier Regulation* (Washington, D.C.: National Association of Regulatory Utility Commissioners, 1987), pp. 799-806.

State commissions vary somewhat in regulatory powers. A majority have authority to issue licenses, franchises, or permits for the initiation of service, for construction or abandonment of facilities, and related matters. With respect to rates, commissions generally have power to require prior authorization of rate changes, to suspend proposed rate changes, to prescribe interim rates, and to initiate rate investigations. Most commissions have authority to control the quantity and quality of service, to prescribe uniform systems of accounts, and to require annual reports. Over three-fourths of the commissions are authorized to regulate the issuance of securities.

TABLE 4-2

State Regulatory Commissions and Selected Statistics, 1985, 1986

State	Number of Commissioners	Term, Years	Method of Selection[a]	Yearly Salary[b] Chairman	Yearly Salary[b] Commissioners	No. of Full-Time Employees	Expenditures[c] ($000 omitted)
Alabama	3	4	E	$44,550	$44,000	139	$ 4,832
Alaska	5	6	G-S	66,816	66,816	49	3,877
Arizona	3	6	E	45,000	45,000	215	4,399[d]
Arkansas	3	6	G-S	52,204	50,311	114	4,701
California	5	6	G-S	78,495	76,079	987	53,962
Colorado	3	6	G-S	48,400	48,400	96	3,826[e]
Connecticut	5	4	G-L	f	f	83	3,171[e]
Delaware	5	5	G-S	15,585[g]	12,540[g]	20	1,692
District of Columbia	3	4	M-C	63,700	63,700	45	1,931
Florida	5	4	G-S	64,217	64,217	346	13,419[h]
Georgia	5	6	E	60,321	60,321	137	7,239[i]
Hawaii	3	6	G-S	61,560	55,404	24	655[d]
Idaho	3	6	G-S	36,500	36,500	55	2,400
Illinois	7	5	G-S	65,000	55,000	380	13,182
Indiana	5	4	G-S	j	j	108	4,045
Iowa	3	6	G-S	k	k	117	4,961
Kansas	3	4	G-S	63,664	61,974	276	9,479
Kentucky	3	4	G-S	54,744	l	106	2,665[e]
Louisiana	5	6	E	37,800[g]	37,800[g]	110	2,883
Maine	3	6	G-L	53,185	50,149	54	2,498

TABLE 4-2 (Continued)

State	Number of Commissioners	Term, Years	Method of Selection[a]	Yearly Salary[b] Chairman	Yearly Salary[b] Commissioners	No. of Full-Time Employees	Expenditures[c] ($000 omitted)
Maryland	5	5	G-S	62,100	60,000	125	5,713
Massachusetts	3	4	G	61,093	56,037	134	7,504
Michigan	3	6	G-S	60,000	55,100	200	10,029
Minnesota	5	6	G-S	44,850	44,850	28	1,123
Mississippi	3	4	E	40,000	40,000	111	3,777
Missouri	5	6	G-S	62,100	62,100	191	9,431
Montana	5	4	E	37,363	36,141	44	—
Nebraska	5	6	E	35,000	35,000	54	1,574
Nevada	5	4	G	51,740	48,671	91	—
New Hampshire	3	6	G-GC	58,940	58,940	55	1,987
New Jersey	3	6	G-S	90,000	85,000	375	11,155
New Mexico PSC	3	6	G-S	51,420	50,040	51	2,703[h]
New Mexico SCC	3	6	E	40,425	40,425	119	2,382
New York	6	6	G-S	83,407	72,051	620	36,666
North Carolina	7	8	G-L	62,044	61,044	136[m]	5,202
North Dakota	3	6	E	46,000	46,000	54	4,075
Ohio	5	5	G-S	61,000	53,000[n]	455	16,274
Oklahoma	3	6	E	52,000	50,000	438	20,876[d]
Oregon	1[o]	4	G-S	62,988		388	15,735
Pennsylvania	5	10	G-S	57,500	55,000	583	22,536

TABLE 4-2 (Continued)

State	Number of Commissioners	Term, Years	Method of Selection[a]	Yearly Salary[b] Chairman	Yearly Salary[b] Commissioners	No. of Full-Time Employees	Expenditures[c] ($000 omitted)
Rhode Island	3	6	G-S	57,130	39,991	38	908
South Carolina	7	4	L	50,510	46,688	145	4,462[h]
South Dakota	3	6	E	36,000	36,000	24	1,196[h]
Tennessee	3	6	E	57,480	57,480	159	5,352
Texas PUC	3	6	G-S	60,976	60,976	204	10,667
Texas RC	3	6	E	73,233	73,233	954	2,741[p]
Utah	3	6	G-S	59,675	57,650	21	4,273
Vermont	3	6	G-S	49,500	15,000[g]	12	794
Virginia	3	6	L	75,843	74,399	474	21,579
Washington	3	6	G-S	60,400	54,400	220	8,797
West Virginia	3	6	G-S	44,675	41,000	177	6,423
Wisconsin	3	6	G-S	q	q	180	6,457
Wyoming	3	6	G-S	r	r	41	2,135[h]

ᵃE = Elected. G = Governor. G-GC = Governor, confirmed by Governor's Council. G-L = Governor, confirmed by Legislature. G-S = Governor, confirmed by Senate. L = Legislature (General Assembly). M-C = Mayor, confirmed by Council.

ᵇAs of June, 1986.

ᶜExpenditures, unless otherwise noted, are for the fiscal year ending in 1985 and exclude amounts transferred to the state treasury and/or put into the revolving fund.

ᵈAuthorized for fiscal year ending in 1986.

ᵉFiscal year ending in 1983.

ᶠChairman: $64,209-$78,821; commissioners: $59,681-$72,875.

ᵍPart-time.

ʰFiscal year ending in 1984.

ⁱFiscal year ending in 1986.

ʲChairman: $45,000-$69,576; commissioners: $40,586-$63,154.

ᵏ$42,400-$45,600.

ˡVice-Chairman: $51,696; commissioner: $52,512.

ᵐCommission staff: 58; Public Staff: 78.

ⁿOne commissioner receives $55,660.

ᵒThree-member commission, effective April 1, 1987.

ᵖGas utilities division only.

ۋChairman: $54,319-$62,698; commissioners: $52,500-$59,535.

ʳChairman: $44,300-$70,800; commissioners: $40,150-$64,200.

SOURCE: *1985 Annual Report on Utility and Carrier Regulation* (Washington, D.C.: National Association of Regulatory Utility Commissioners, 1987), pp. 821-51, 855-57.

Personnel. The vast majority of the states have either three- or five-member commissions, but three states (Illinois, North and South Carolina) have seven-member commissions (Table 4-2).[20] Commissioners are appointed by the governor or mayor (thirty-eight agencies), selected by the legislature (two agencies), or elected by popular vote (thirteen agencies[21]). The most common legal qualifications are that commissioners must be qualified electors, citizens, and residents without financial interests in the industries regulated. Other more specific requirements vary widely. For example, fifteen states have a minimum age requirement (ranging from eighteen in Arizona and New York to thirty in Georgia, Nebraska, Oklahoma, Pennsylvania, Texas PUC and Utah); one state (Nebraska) specifies a maximum age of sixty-eight; one state (South Carolina) requires the appointment of "the best qualified people"; and one state (Arizona) requires that a candidate for commissioner be "able to speak, write, and read the English language." Only eight states have specific statutory professional requirements. The Alaska statute, for instance, specifies that "one member shall be a graduate of an accredited school of law; one member shall be a graduate of an accredited university with a major in engineering; one member shall be a graduate of an accredited university with a major in finance, accounting, or business administration; and two members shall be consumers."[22]

Most commissioners have had professional training and practice (the legal profession predominates over either a business or engineering background),[23] although one in four does not have a college degree.[24] However, only a few had previous experience with a regulatory commission prior to their appointment or election. Their understanding of the complex legal, economic, accounting, and engineering problems confronting them as commissioners increases with their tenure of service. The terms fixed by law run from four to ten years, with either four- or six-year terms being the most frequent. While some commissioners are reappointed or reelected, most of them serve a single term or less. (The average tenure for state commissioners is just under four years.) Moreover, commissioners are sometimes appointed because of political considerations rather than because of their qualifications for the job. Removal from office, while rare (only six known removals since 1933), is provided for in many of the legislative statutes. Generally, removal may be made by executive order or by impeachment for "just cause." The most common reasons for such action are neglect of duty, misconduct in office, incompetence, and malfeasance. With respect to their motives and goals, finally, Aman has summarized:

> For commissioners with political ambitions in mind, protecting the consumer and cutting every last ounce of fat out of a utility rate filing may be his or her publicly proclaimed goal. For others, a more rule-oriented approach may be taken: What does the evidence in the record justify in the way of an increase? For others, efficiency concerns and

dedicated efforts to approximate a market result may be a primary goal. Still other commissioners may see the ratemaking process as a political bargaining process: How much will the utility be willing to live with and how much will the public tolerate?....[25]

State commission staffs, varying in size from twelve (Vermont) to 987 (California), totaled 10,262 full-time employees in mid-1986.[26] A 1967 study suggested that, with the exception of the larger state commissions, both the size and the composition of the professional staffs were inadequate to undertake an extensive regulatory program.[27] Since then, full-time staff employees have been increased by over 71 percent,[28] salaries have been raised, and there is a better composition of the professional staffs.[29] In addition, in an effort to maintain highly skilled staffs, the National Association of Regulatory Utility Commissioners (NARUC; an association of state and federal regulatory personnel[30]) has established for its members an annual regulatory development course which covers regulatory principles and their applications.

Financial Matters. In 1986, the median salary for full-time commissioners was just over $50,000, compared with a 1967 median salary of just under $16,000. Staff salaries vary widely, but a majority pay top professional personnel above $40,000 a year. Other staff salaries, however, are often considerably lower, making it difficult to attract and retain trained people. As a result, the annual turnover in commission staffs is relatively high, as better paying jobs open up.

All public utilities, and hence their customers, pay their own expenses of regulation. Since 1930, commission funds also have come increasingly from assessments and/or fees imposed on the utilities under their jurisdiction. Thirty-eight state agencies receive a portion or all of their annual expenditures in this manner; the remaining seventeen receive all of their annual expenditures from general tax funds. The assessments to cover the annual costs of regulation usually take the form of a percentage tax on each utility's gross revenues. Special assessments are usually made for specific types of investigations or cases. In fiscal year 1985, the expenditures for fifty-one agencies (shown in Table 4-2) totaled just over $399.5 million, with the largest seven agencies accounting for nearly one-half of this amount.[31] Many continue to maintain that limited financial resources inhibit more effective state regulation.

Organization. State commissions are organized along functional lines, with separate departments for rates, engineering, accounting, financial, and legal work; along industry lines, with separate departments for each type of industry regulated; or some combination of the two. Typical of a larger agency is the New York Public Service Commission, whose organization chart is shown in Figure 4-1.

FIGURE 4-1

Organization Chart
New York Public Service Commission

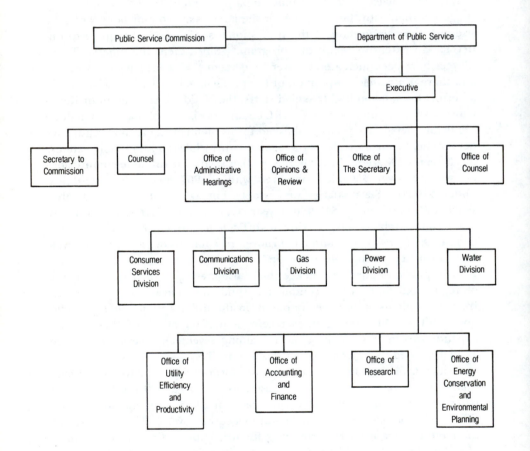

Source: *1985 Annual Report on Utility and Carrier Regulation* (Washington, D.C.: National Association of Regulatory Utility Commissioners, 1987), p. 118.

Duties and Responsibilities. The range and complexity of issues that come before the regulatory commissions are vast. The duties and responsibilities of a commissioner were outlined several years ago by a former member of the Massachusetts commission as follows:

> ... to be familiar with the history of regulation; to understand the meaning of objectivity in the light of the dual capacity of a public utility commissioner as a party and as judge, and to cultivate in his own judgments this quality; to become familiar with the fundamental characteristics of the industries over which he exercises control; to exercise a wide discretion over the procedures followed before the commission, having in mind the basic guides of fairness to the parties and uniformity of application; and, FINALLY, to cultivate a public awareness of the limitations of regulatory control over the basic economic conditions which give rise to increasing rates in some industries and diminishing services in others.[32]

These duties, which have become even more complex in recent years, impose a time-consuming task on regulatory commissions. Further, all of the commissions have found their work loads increasing rapidly since the late 1960s. The Michigan Public Service Commission reported that in 1985, 150 new electric, gas, and telephone proceedings were instituted and that 178 public hearings involving the same three industries were held (involving 414 days of hearings and thousands of pages of testimony and exhibits). In addition, 2,002 complaints were received from electric, gas, and telephone customers involving service, billing, and miscellaneous matters.[33] Michigan's work load is typical of that confronting most other state commissions.

The Federal Regulatory Commissions

There are four federal commissions with jurisdiction over interstate activities of public utilities. These commissions are organized to handle particular functional groups (Table 4-3).

The *Federal Communications Commission* (FCC), established in 1934, succeeded the Federal Radio Commission of 1927, which regulated radio and television broadcasting. From the Interstate Commerce Commission (ICC), the FCC took over regulation of interstate and foreign telephone and telegraph services in 1934.

The *Federal Energy Regulatory Commission* (FERC), an independent regulatory agency within the Department of Energy (DOE), was established in 1977. The FERC inherited many of the functions of the former Federal Power Commission (FPC). The latter was first set up in 1920 with three Cabinet officers to regulate power projects on navigable rivers and was reorganized in 1930 with five full-time commission-

TABLE 4-3

Selected Statistics for Federal Regulatory Agencies, 1986

Agency	Date Established	Number of Commissioners	Term, Years	Number of Full-Time Employees	Budget, Fiscal 1986 ($000 omitted)	Jurisdiction
Federal Communications Commission	1934	5	7	1,793	$ 90,341	Radio, television, telephone, telegraph, cables, satellite communication
Federal Energy Regulatory Commission	1977	5	4	1,688	91,459	Electric power, natural gas, natural gas and oil pipelines, water-power sites
Nuclear Regulatory Commission	1974	5	5	3,369	400,026	Civilian nuclear energy, nuclear research, certain import and export responsibilities
Securities and Exchange Commission	1934	5	5	1,900	106,323	Securities and financial markets, electric and gas utility registered holding companies

Source: *1985 Annual Report on Utility and Carrier Regulation* (Washington, D.C.: National Association of Regulatory Utility Commissioners, 1987), pp. 845-48; *Budget of the United States, 1988 - Appendix* (Washington, D.C.: U.S. Government Printing Office, 1987).

ers. Besides the FPC's original duties, Congress gave it authority in 1935 to regulate the transmission and sale at wholesale of electric energy in interstate commerce and in 1938 (under the Natural Gas Act) to regulate the transmission and sale for resale of natural gas in interstate commerce. When the FERC was established, Congress transferred to the agency (from the ICC) jurisdiction over oil pipeline rates.

The *Nuclear Regulatory Commission* (NRC) was established in 1974, when the Atomic Energy Commission (AEC, established in 1946) was abolished. The duties transferred to the NRC include the licensing and regulation of civilian nuclear energy to ensure the protection of public health and safety, the maintenance of national security, and compliance with the antitrust laws. The NRC also administers a program of research in such areas as reactor safety, fuel cycle, and environmental protection, and licenses the export of nuclear reactors, as well as the export and import of special nuclear materials.

The *Securities and Exchange Commission* (SEC) was organized in 1934 to administer the Securities Act of 1933 and the Securities Exchange Act of 1934. The commission regulates the conditions of sale of new securities, and some of the practices of the stock exchanges. In 1935, the SEC was given power, under the Public Utility Holding Company Act of that year, to regulate the finances and corporate structures of electric and gas utility holding companies.[34]

Personnel and Financial Matters. Each of the federal regulatory agencies has five commissioners, appointed by the President, with Senate approval, for terms ranging from four to seven years. The agencies are bipartisan by law, and members must be citizens with no financial interest in the industries they regulate. No other qualifications for commissioners have been established. A majority of federal commissioners have had a legal background (with the notable exception of the Nuclear Regulatory Commission). The 1986 salary of a federal commissioner was $72,300 ($73,600 in the case of the NRC); for a chairman, $73,600 ($75,100 for the chairman of the NRC). These salaries, while somewhat below those of private industry, appear adequate to attract and retain the caliber of people required. However, Mitnick concludes that "the pattern seems to be one of mediocre politically-colored appointments of people with diverse backgrounds who are not in general well-prepared in the specifics of the regulated area."[35] One problem: The tenure of commissioners, which varies considerably among the commissions, has been relatively short. In the period 1933-1965, commissioners averaged just over one term for the former FPC, 69 percent of a term for the FCC, and 67 percent of a term for the SEC.[36] As a result, commissioners "have not remained in office long enough to develop the necessary expertness or to give the government the full advantage of what competence they possess."[37] Another problem: Commissioners have frequently departed for jobs that were in, or related to, public utilities.[38]

Congressional appropriations for the four federal commissions totaled $688.1 million in fiscal 1986.[39] The NRC had the largest staff — 3,369; the FCC and FERC had staffs of nearly 1,800 and 1,700, respectively. In 1949, the Hoover Commission found these staff members to be well-qualified and conscientious[40] — a finding that appears equally true today. But the annual turnover rate, with the possible exception of top-level staff positions,[41] remains relatively high.

Organization and Duties. The organization of the federal commissions is similar to that of the state agencies. The organization chart of the Federal Communications Commission is shown in Figure 4-2. The statutory duties of the federal commissions also are comparable to those of the state commissions. And, finally, the federal commissions have found their work loads increasing. In fiscal year 1985, for example, as shown in Table 4-4, the Federal Energy Regulatory Commission instituted 72,065 proceedings and concluded 73,863 proceedings, and held 194 hearings (involving 700 hearing days). The table also reflects another regulatory issue of major significance: The commissions have found it increasingly difficult to keep up with their greater work loads. Thus, at the end of the 1985 fiscal year, the FERC had 20,910 proceedings pending. This issue, considered in later chapters, is referred to as "regulatory lag."

TABLE 4-4

Total Volume of Proceedings Before the Federal
Energy Regulatory Commission - Fiscal Year 1985

	Hydro	*Electric*	*Gas*[a]	*Total*
Number of Proceedings:				
Pending as of 9/30/84	1,355	512	20,841	22,708
Instituted in FY 1985	2,158	1,881	68,026	72,065
Concluded in FY 1985	2,212	1,919	69,732	73,863
Pending as of 9/30/85	1,301	474	19,135	20,910
Number of Hearings[b]	——	——	——	194
Number of Hearing Days	——	——	——	700
Number of Orders Appealed to Courts	——	——	——	186

[a]Excludes oil pipeline proceedings, but includes wellhead pricing items.
[b]Total of all new cases set for hearing.

Source: *1985 Annual Report on Utility and Carrier Regulation* (Washington, D.C.: National Association of Regulatory Utility Commissioners, 1987), p. 6.

FIGURE 4-2

Organization Chart
Federal Communications Commission

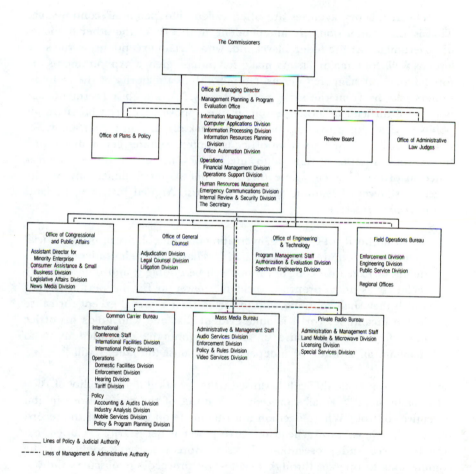

Source: *1985 Annual Report on Utility and Carrier Regulation* (Washington, D.C.: National Association of Regulatory Utility Commissioners, 1987), p. 3.

Status and Functions of the Commissions

At both the state and federal levels, the regulatory agencies occupy a unique position in the structure of American government. Their independent status and combined functions deserve brief discussion.

Independence of the Commissions

The regulatory agencies are often called "independent" commissions. That is, the commissions are independent, in theory, of the other branches of government. At the federal level and, with certain exceptions, at the state level as well, four major factors make for independence. Appointments are for definite, but staggered, terms. No more than a majority of the commissioners may be from the same political party. "Although a President may not find it difficult to locate persons in the opposition party who share his points of view, this provision does insure a lack of partisan responsibility."[42] Removal of commissioners from office is limited. Statutes generally confine the executive's power of removal to "inefficiency, neglect of duty, or malfeasance in office."[43] Even where there are not statutory limitations on the executive's power of removal, legal barriers exist. Argued Justice Sutherland in the *Humphrey's* case:

> The authority of Congress, in creating quasi-legislative or quasi-judicial agencies, to require them to act in discharge of their duties independently of executive control cannot well be doubted; and that authority includes, as an appropriate incident, power to fix the period during which they shall continue, and to forbid their removal except for cause in the meantime. For it is quite evident that one who holds his office only during the pleasure of another cannot be depended upon to maintain an attitude of independence against the latter's will.[44]

Removal also may be difficult because of the "political inadvisability of such a traumatic step."[45] Finally, procedural features of the commissions inhibit executive control. "Where decision must be made on the basis of the record made in hearings, an overhead directive power is necessarily excluded, except to choice and prosecution of cases. Moreover, the tendency of the commissions to operate through case-to-case proceedings obscures the opportunity to develop policy by overhead directives."[46]

Independent status was aimed at keeping political influence over commission work and decisions at a minimum and, hence, making the agencies more efficient. They were to have the advantages of expertise, continuity, flexibility, and impartiality. But this independent status was quickly challenged in the courts. Under our constitutional law, a legislature cannot divest itself of its powers. Consequently, since regulatory agencies operate under general legislative powers, their creation was challenged as an unconstitutional delegation of legislative power. To this contention the Supreme Court declared in 1894:

> ... there can be no doubt of the general power of a state to regulate the fares and freights which may be charged and received by railroad or other carriers, and that this regulation can be carried on by means of a commission. Such a commission is merely an administrative board created by the state for carrying into effect the will of the state as expressed by its legislation.[47]

It is thus firmly established that an administrative body may be delegated legislative power as long as the legislature lays down general provisions or standards to guide the agency. "... Congress cannot delegate any part of its legislative power except under the limitation of a prescribed standard...."[48] In practice, however, the legislative standards are frequently broad — such as the general requirement that rates must be "just and reasonable" — and commissions, therefore, have wide discretion. Many regulatory problems arise from these broad, delegated powers because of their interpretation by the commissions or by the courts.

How Independent Are the Commissions?

While in theory the regulatory agencies are independent, they nevertheless have a direct relationship to the executive, legislative, and judicial branches of their respective governments. Sometimes referred to as the "headless fourth branch of government," the regulatory agency is created by, and dependent on, the other three. As a result, the administrative process is inherently a political activity, closely connected with other governmental policies.

Relation to the Executive Branch.[49] The executive branch of government comes into contact with regulatory commissions in several ways. The President and the governor (in many states) have the power to appoint commissioners as terms expire or members resign and, with some exceptions, to name the chairmen.[50] Appointments to high positions in the commissions also may be cleared with the executive branch before being made by the various chairmen. And, while the statutory and legal power of removal is limited, a governor or the President can use, and has used, a variety of means to force the resignation of a commissioner whose conduct or policies the Chief Executive disapproves.

The commissions' budgets and legislative matters generally are handled by the executive branch. At the federal level, for example, the Office of Management and Budget (formerly the Bureau of the Budget), which is part of the executive office of the President, "is the Cerberus at the gate of any program."[51] Proposed testimony before congressional committees must be cleared through the office. All budget requests and legislative recommendations must pass through it for ultimate approval by the White House. Moreover, while Congress does not always adopt appropriations or enact legislation recommended by the President, the fact remains that presidential backing is usually required to obtain budget requests and legislative proposals. "Thus a hostile or unsympathetic President or budget officer can severely cripple the activities of a commission."[52]

The executive branch frequently consults with the commissioners. It can initiate legislation affecting regulatory policy or appoint special study commissions. It can express preferences about general policy. At times, the executive branch has tried to influence the initiation of specific investigations or the outcome of specific decisions. The commissions also are dependent on the executive branch (through the offices of the state attorneys general or the Department of Justice) to enforce and defend their orders.[53]

Finally, various executive offices have an interest in particular cases before the commissions, or are directly involved with the industries controlled by the commissions. Governments are large buyers of public utilities' services. It is not uncommon, therefore, to find an executive office (such as the General Services Administration) intervening in a rate case. Many states have established consumer protection divisions or sections within their attorney generals' offices[54] to intervene in cases before the commissions. Further, a regulatory commission may not have complete jurisdiction over an industry. In establishing the Department of Energy, for instance, Congress transferred energy functions from some nine federal agencies or parts of federal agencies.[55] But there remain energy functions with more than a dozen other federal agencies (such as those of the Nuclear Regulatory Commission).[56] In addition, the Department of Justice is concerned with the antitrust aspects of regulation, and the Rural Electrification Administration with the promotion of rural electric and telephone services.

The involvement of more than one agency[57] raises two problems. First, coordination of policy is more difficult. Second, the executive branch can turn to any one of these agencies for advice and counsel. Assuming that the policy-making role of a regulatory agency is of minimal importance, the Chief Executive "is likely to give only passing attention to appointments to that body," while the executive agencies, "not being judicial in nature, can take a much freer policy line."[58]

Relation to the Legislative Branch. Being an administrative body, a regulatory commission is created by legislative authority and depends on legislation for its powers. Moreover, a commission may exercise only such powers as the legislature confers on it. Early attempts to prescribe detailed standards by franchise or statute were unsuccessful. It was gradually realized, therefore, that regulatory laws must be written in very general terms, and that the exact meaning and application of these statutes must be left to the commissions subject, of course, to judicial review. A majority of the commissions are thus authorized to prescribe "just and reasonable" rates and to prevent "undue" discrimination, but no criteria are found in the laws as to what constitutes a reasonable rate or when a rate is unduly discriminatory. The legislative branch cannot be expected to specify rules to govern every possible situation. Thus, a commission is vested with broad authority to apply general legislative principles to many specific instances that arise.

A commission is dependent also on the legislature for its annual appropriations[59] and for both the number and salaries of its staff. Budget control, in particular, gives legislative committees the opportunity to direct commissions, as the following quote from the 1964 report of the House Appropriations Committee indicates:

> The Federal Power Commission is an important agency, but it has grown almost 40 percent in jobs since 1960. Along with growth in jobs there is much complaint that the agency is footdragging in its disposal of cases. The committee urges the commission to cut down its delay in disposing of cases as it is hurting the industries it has to regulate. . . . The commission is spending too much time in empire building and trying to expand its jurisdiction.[60]

Because they are created by the legislative branch, regulatory commissions must report directly to this body. The legislature has the right to conduct investigations or to hold hearings on all aspects of a commission's policy or performance.[61] Two-thirds of the state legislatures have statutory authority to review proposed rules and regulations of their agencies before their adoption.[62] Where sunset laws have been adopted (such as Florida), the state legislature must make a periodic review of its regulatory commission. Finally, in many states and at the federal level, commissioners must be confirmed by the whole legislature or by the Senate.

The legislative branch thus has a large responsibility for the strength or weakness of commission regulation. If a commission receives a statute that clearly defines its objectives, a grant of sufficient jurisdiction and powers, and adequate appropriations and staff to carry out its responsibilities, the legislative branch has done its part. If, however, goals and objectives are poorly defined, jurisdiction and powers inadequate, and control over the budget used to exert legislative influence, the effectiveness of a regulatory commission will be sharply diminished.

Relation to the Judicial Branch.[63] As the power given to a regulatory commission is of necessity broad, there is always danger that the constitutional rights of parties involved will be endangered by the arbitrary and unreasonable exercise of this power. To avoid this danger, the courts must act to check on the actions of administrative agencies. The courts also must interpret the rulings of regulatory commissions from the point of view of the Constitution and of existing legislation. Judicial review is well established and the courts have the power to review and set aside, if necessary, commission orders. Yet,

> . . . it is difficult to determine just how far the courts should go in interfering with the acts of administrative bodies; for if the courts insist upon reopening matters supposedly determined by a commission and substitute their judgment for that of the commission, the latter becomes a worthless body which impedes rather than aids in the regulating process.[64]

In the early days of railroad regulation, difficulties were experienced because the courts exercised an unlimited right of review over ICC decisions. The courts insisted on reviewing all evidence, both old and new. As a result, the railroads refused to take seriously the commission's hearings, and the commission's orders, in turn, frequently were reversed by the courts. The situation is well illustrated by the *Alabama Midland* case, decided by the Supreme Court in 1897.[65] In making a decision as to the reasonableness of rates to Troy, Alabama, a knowledge as to the existence or nonexistence of water competition was essential. In the evidence presented before the commission at its hearing, the presence of water competition was shown. Later, when evidence was presented to the Court, it was shown that the river — the water competition shown in evidence before the ICC — was dry half of the year, that it was but three feet deep, and that the presence of overhanging trees made the use of boats impossible.[66]

In 1910, the Supreme Court clarified the proper scope of judicial review. Recognizing the advantages of commission regulation, the Court held that review must be confined to questions of power and right, and not to matters which could be left to the administrative discretion of a commission. In the words of the Court:

> Beyond controversy, in determining whether an order of the commission shall be suspended or set aside, we must consider (*a*) all relevant questions of constitutional power or right; (*b*) all pertinent questions as to whether the administrative order is within the scope of the delegated authority under which it purports to have been made; and (*c*) . . . whether, even although the order be in form within the delegated power, nevertheless it must be treated as not embraced therein, because the exertion of authority which is questioned has been manifested in such an unreasonable manner as to cause it, in truth, to be within the elementary rule that the substance, and not the shadow, determines the validity of the exercise of the power.[67]

As a result of this, and of subsequent decisions, the findings of fact of a regulatory commission are ordinarily conclusive. Except in reparation cases, the courts will not substitute their judgment for that of a commission in determining the facts of a particular case. Yet, until 1942, the Supreme

Court did not hesitate to specify the factors that should guide commission decisions. It enumerated specific measures of value to be considered in determining a fair value in 1898[68] and listed a number of factors to be considered in determining a fair rate of return in 1923.[69] The Court narrowed the boundaries of judicial review in 1942 stating:

> The Constitution does not bind rate-making bodies to the service of any single formula or combination of formulas. Agencies to whom this legislative power has been delegated are free, within the ambit of their statutory authority, to make the pragmatic adjustments which may be called for by particular circumstances. Once a fair hearing has been given, proper findings made, and other statutory requirements satisfied, the courts cannot intervene in the absence of a clear showing that the limits of due process have been overstepped. If the commission's order, as applied to the facts before it and viewed in its entirety, produces no arbitrary result, our inquiry is at an end.[70]

The courts have other functions in the regulatory process. As a commission is not a court, it has only limited power to compel observance of its orders. The courts, therefore, must enforce orders and laws by injunctions or mandamus. The courts also may compel a commission to perform its duties under the law. Often, when a statute is broad and lacking in precise objectives, a commission may simply refuse to act. In such situations, the courts may compel action.[71]

Independence: An Outdated Concept? In creating regulatory commissions, legislatures sought to establish agencies that were free from control of the executive and of the legislature, in order to insure continuity of policy and to keep political pressures to a minimum. But both branches of government have potential influence over the commissions. As former SEC Chairman Cary has put it: ". . . government regulatory agencies are stepchildren whose custody is contested by both Congress and the Executive, but without very much affection from either one."[72]

For many years, the *concept of independence* has been challenged, and the argument advanced that administrative and policy-making functions should be transferred to executive departments or agencies. The essence of the argument supporting this view is that commissions performing these functions — functions which are closely related to the broadest objectives of government — should be politically responsible. Further, the commissions would be left to perform their quasi-judicial functions for which they should be independent.[73] Such a transfer of functions, however, has long been opposed by the legislative branch. As stated by former Congressman Harris: "These agencies should not in any way be subservient to the White House or anyone else."[74] This important issue is examined in Chapter 17.

A Combination of Functions

Regulatory commissions have been characterized as quasi-judicial and quasi-legislative. Contrary to the basic pattern of American government, which is based upon the doctrine of separation of powers, a commission assumes the tasks of administrator, judge, and legislator. When investigating rates or service and safety standards, a commission is performing an administrative function. When holding hearings, examining evidence, and making decisions, a commission is acting as judge of a utility's conduct. Moreover, a commission can even determine the rules it wants to administer, and it can decide to prosecute a utility and to gather evidence against the firm. It then considers its own evidence, as well as the evidence presented by the company and intervenors, and makes a decision. When prescribing certain rules of conduct for a utility, such as fixing rates, a commission is acting in a legislative capacity. As explained by the Supreme Court:

> The function of rate-making is purely legislative in its character, and this is true, whether it is exercised directly by the legislature itself or by some subordinate or administrative body, to whom the power of fixing rates in detail has been delegated. The completed act derives its authority from the legislature and must be regarded as an exercise of the legislative power.[75]

That regulatory commissions combine various functions has been the subject of considerable controversy. Argues a former chairman of the FCC: "I do not believe it is possible to be a good judge on Monday and Tuesday, a good legislator on Wednesday and Thursday, and a good administrator on Friday."[76] The American Bar Association (ABA), in particular, has long been critical of the adjudicating function of administrative bodies. The ABA believes that administrative exercise of judicial powers "violates the fundamental 'rule of law.'"[77] Thus, the association has recommended the abolition of all independent commissions and the establishment of an administrative court system.[78] In the absence of abolition, the ABA has sought "to judicialize administrative procedure."[79] The aim has been "to establish a meaningful concept of due process of law with reference to administrative proceedings, thereby protecting the citizen under the jurisdiction of administrative agencies."[80] While the commissions have been concerned with due process, they also have been conscious of regulatory lag. Consequently, they have developed various procedures to speed the regulatory process, consistent with due process of law.[81]

There is a related issue that has caused considerable debate, particularly with respect to the Federal Communications Commission. The procedure long followed by the FCC in rate proceedings, "permits the same staff members to investigate, initiate, participate as parties, advocate, inform, and advise the commission ex parte, and then participate in the decision process both as advisers and draftsmen to the commission."[82] Former FCC Commissioner Loevinger has argued that the procedure

... is unfair to the telephone company, it is unfair to the public (which is denied effective representation), it is an inefficient and impractical way to conduct an inquiry of this nature, it is contrary to the intent of Congress and to the recommendations of the Administrative Conference of the United States, and it is an unreasonable method of seeking to arrive at an informed, wise, and impartial decision.[83]

Regardless of the legality of the dual role of the FCC's staff,[84] the procedure raises the question of fairness to the parties of record. In more recent years, the FCC has separated the trial staff from making *ex parte* presentations to the presiding administrative law judge and the commissioners.[85] Such a separation of functions also has been undertaken by many states.[86]

The Federal-State Jurisdictional Problem[87]

For many years, state commissions and even some public utilities were opposed to federal regulation. Opposition was especially strong prior to 1935. Opponents generally argued that federal regulation was unnecessary, that it would raise the cost of regulation, and that it was bureaucratic. "Federal regulation was even likened to Communism and Socialism."[88] One state commissioner put it this way: "There can be no such thing as concurrent jurisdiction or even co-operation between the states and the federal government on the subject of rate-making."[89] And two leaders of the electric industry argued:

> The interests of the public are already fully safeguarded. . . . Federal regulation would only lead to confusion and besides it would greatly increase the cost of service.
> [Federal regulation will] raise from the several states the last vestige of utility control and deprive them of rights which distinctly belong to the states. . . . It would substitute for a regulation sensitive to local public opinion the absentee treatment of a federal bureau in Washington.[90]

After 1935, opposition to federal regulation sharply declined. In part, this was due to a change in the political climate brought about by the depression and the New Deal. And, in part, it was due to the uncovering of notorious abuses, particularly through the use of the holding company device, and the growing realization that the states were unable to regulate interstate activities effectively. The conclusion should not be drawn, however, that harmony between federal and state commissions has been achieved. The state commissions, in particular, fear the continual encroachment of the federal agencies into areas once exclusively the province of the states. Argues former Chairman Karber of the Illinois Commerce Commission:

It is not clear that the best interests of all the users of utility services can best be served by federal control over all the utility operations. Yet there are indications that this is the path which most of the federal agencies seem to be taking. . . . In their desire to expand their powers, however, the federal agencies ignore the constitutional rights of the state legislatures to decide how much regulation is necessary for the public interest. The federal agencies do not have the constitutional power to impose their own ideas of appropriate regulatory standards and procedures upon all the state commissions.[91]

Federal-State Conflicts

In the preceding chapter, it was pointed out that the courts have long recognized three fields of jurisdiction in the United States: (*1*) the field in which the federal power is exclusive; (*2*) the field in which the state power is exclusive; and (*3*) the field in which state and federal governments have concurrent power. Concurrent power means that either may act, but if both legislate on the same subject matter, the federal law supersedes the state law. Only in the absence of federal legislation can the state act in this field.[92] In general, all interstate activities are under the jurisdiction of federal agencies, and intrastate activities are under the control of state commissions. The courts have restricted the jurisdiction of the states, however, if intrastate activities interfere with federal regulation of interstate commerce.[93]

Efforts to Alleviate Jurisdictional Disputes. Congress, in order to alleviate jurisdictional disputes, has tried to outline federal authority in its legislation. For example, the Public Utility Act of 1935, which extended the authority of the former Federal Power Commission, reads in part:

> The provisions of this Part shall apply to the transmission of electric energy at wholesale in interstate commerce, but shall not apply to any other sale of electrical energy or deprive a state or state commission of its lawful authority now exercised over the exportation of hydroelectric energy which is transmitted across a state line. The commission shall have jurisdiction over all facilities for such transmission or sale of electric energy, but shall not have jurisdiction, except as specifically provided in this Part . . . over facilities used for the generation of electric energy or over facilities used in local distribution or only for the transmission of electric energy in intrastate commerce, or over facilities for the transmission of electric energy consumed wholly by the transmitter.[94]

Attempts also have been made to ease jurisdictional conflicts through closer federal-state cooperation. By statute, the federal commissions are authorized to confer with state authorities and to hold joint hearings with them on matters within federal jurisdiction which affect the ratemaking authority of the states. The former Federal Power Commission had statutory authority to assist the state commissions by making cost studies, supplying information and reports, and loaning its rate or other experts. The Federal Communications Commission, by statute, must refer certain matters (*e.g.,* the jurisdictional separation of common property and expenses between interstate and intrastate operations) to a Federal-State Joint Board for a recommended decision.[95] And both state and federal commissioners are brought together in the National Association of Regulatory Utility Commissioners and in regional associations.

Some Illustrations: The FPC. Despite years of experience, jurisdictional boundaries have not been firmly established, as illustrated by the following Supreme Court decisions concerning the jurisdiction of the former Federal Power Commission. In 1942, the Court held that an order requiring an intrastate subsidiary of an interstate natural gas pipeline to make an extension was properly to be issued by the FPC and not by the state commission.[96] In 1947, the Court ruled that a company which produced and bought gas in Louisiana and, in turn, sold the gas in the same state to three interstate pipeline companies was subject to federal regulation.[97] In 1950, the Court upheld the right of the FPC, at the request of the city of Cleveland, to determine the cost of transporting gas from the southern border of Ohio through the pipelines of the East Ohio Gas Company, a large distributor, and to determine the value of the company's facilities, even though all were confined within the state.[98] In 1954, despite language to the contrary in the Natural Gas Act, the Court decided that the FPC had jurisdiction over all natural gas producers.[99]

In 1964, the Court ruled that the FPC and not state agencies had jurisdiction over all wholesale rates of electricity for resale within a single state, even if only a small part of a company's power is brought in from another state.[100] Early in 1965, the Court upheld the FPC's claim of jurisdiction over natural gas sales to an interstate pipeline which were subject to "restricted use" agreements providing that the gas either would be used within a state or that it would be transported to another state for use in the pipeline company's own facilities.[101] Later in the same year the Court held that construction of pumped storage hydroelectric projects which utilize headwaters of navigable rivers to generate energy for interstate power systems required licenses from the FPC, regardless of whether such projects affected commerce on navigable waters.[102] In 1972, the Court upheld the FPC's jurisdiction over an intrastate electric company on the grounds that it connects with another utility which in turn connects with an out-of-state utility.[103]

Some Current Areas of Conflict. There are five more recent examples that deserve brief mention, since they will be considered in later chapters. In 1978, Congress extended federal control to intrastate natural gas prices,[104] legislation unsuccessfully challenged by several producing states.[105] However, strong state opposition defeated an attempt to establish mandatory federal standards for the regulation of electric and gas retail rates. Instead, state commissions were required to consider, and to adopt if appropriate, twelve specific standards.[106] The Federal Communications Commission's procompetitive policy with respect to intercity markets and markets for terminal equipment has been opposed by a majority of the state commissions who fear that the removal of separations support for basic exchange service will result in a significant increase in local exchange rates.[107]

In a 1983 decision, the Supreme Court upheld California's so-called "nuclear laws," which prohibit the issuance of a certificate for construction of a new nuclear power plant until the California Energy Commission finds that the Nuclear Regulatory Commission "has approved and there exists a demonstrated technology or means for the disposal of high-level nuclear waste."[108] Finally, in 1987, the Supreme Court agreed to hear an appeal in a case involving Middle South Utilities' Grand Gulf nuclear plant. The Federal Energy Regulatory Commission allocated the plant's costs among the integrated electric utility system's four operating companies,[109] but the Mississippi Supreme Court held that a subsequent Mississippi commission rate increase of $326 million for Mississippi Power & Light (one of the operating subsidiaries) was improperly approved because the commission failed to consider whether the company's investment in the plant was "prudent."[110]

A Resume

It has been suggested that regulatory commissions were established to meet existing problems and as a result were not based on a carefully developed philosophy of government.[111] Summarize Corley and Black:

> As our industrial society has grown and become more and more complex, the social and economic problems which confront government have multiplied fantastically. Not only have these problems increased in number, but interrelationships and conflicting social goals have complicated their solution. Also, advances in technology have required special training and experience to make an intelligent attempt at the solution of problems in many areas. Having decided that regulation of one sort or another is desirable, governments of necessity have employed the device of the administrative agency to lighten the burdens imposed on the executive branch, legislative bodies, and courts by this growth and development. The multitude of administrative agencies performing governmental functions today has resulted from limitations due to the lack of time to devote to making, enforcing, and interpreting laws and the lack of expert familiarity with all aspects of all these problems to make informed and effectual decisions concerning them.[112]

Irrespective of their origin, Woll has noted that the rise of the administrative branch poses many serious questions "both for constitutional government and for the more newly created democratic norms of our society." He explains:

> Constitutional government requires limitation through counterbalancing the departments and through the requirement that governmental agencies act in accordance with traditional legal rights protected by the Constitution. Democratic government requires participation by the people in the formulation of public policy. There is no provision in the Constitution designed to control administrative agencies, and the very ambiguities of the Constitution permit Congress to create a "headless fourth branch," the independent regulatory commissions. The constitutional limitations, then, which are operative with respect to the three traditional branches of government do not control the activities of administrative agencies.[113]

Should, therefore, administrative commissions be abolished and administrative courts established in their place? Should the present commissions remain, but with their administrative and policy-making functions transferred to the executive branch? To date, negative answers have been given to these and other questions concerning the status of independent regulatory commissions. As Senator Cummings argued many years ago:

> ... the whole policy of our regulation of commerce is based upon our faith and confidence in administrative tribunals. If we are not willing to entrust the commercial fortunes of the United States to the honor, the learning, and the integrity of administrative tribunals, we had better suspend and cease any attempted regulation of commerce.[114]

And yet, regulatory commissions have been severely criticized in recent years. The caliber of commissioners and adequacy of staffs have been questioned. Regulatory lag has resulted in continuing debate over commission procedures and practices.[115] It has been argued that the commissions have tended to become protectors of the regulated rather than guardians of the public interest — that their performance has been deficient.[116] Such criticisms are partly responsible for the deregulation movement over the past decade.

Moreover, the broad problem concerning the proper jurisdiction of state and federal agencies remains unresolved. While accepting federal regulation, many believe that federal agencies have gone too far in regulating essentially "fringe interstate matters" and, unless this trend is reversed, that "the entire fabric of state regulation of local matters may well disintegrate."[117] But there is no easy or obvious solution to the jurisdictional problem, and it is likely to remain unresolved as long as an attempt is made to distinguish between intrastate and interstate commerce for regulatory purposes.

Notes

*Joseph B. Eastman, "The Place of the Independent Commission," 12 *Constitutional Review* 95, 97 (1928).

[1]Martin G. Glaeser, *Outlines of Public Utility Economics* (New York: The Macmillan Co., 1931), p. 204. The resolution contained one provision: "that said companies do not obstruct the public thoroughfares." *Ibid.*

[2]Burton N. Behling, *Competition and Monopoly in Public Utility Industries* (Urbana: The University of Illinois Press, 1938), p. 19.

[3]*Ibid.*, p. 23.

[4]New York State Public Service Commission, "Utility Regulatory Bodies in New York State, 1855-1953" (Albany, N.Y., 1953), p. 13.

The law also warned the promoters of the new company that: "In case the directors of the said corporation hereby created shall consolidate with or transfer the franchise hereby granted to any of the organized gas companies of the City of New York, the director or directors voting for such consolidation or transfer shall be deemed guilty of a misdemeanor, and, upon conviction, shall be punished by imprisonment in the penitentiary of said county for a period of not less than six, nor more than twelve months." *Ibid.*

[5]As Welch has noted: "It has been stated that the U.S. Supreme Court, when it decided Smyth v. Ames (1898) . . ., sounded the death knell of the earlier efforts of the legislature to regulate utilities directly by statute. It did this by setting up such an exacting set of standards . . . for determining the reasonableness of utility rates, that it became apparent that regulation was a full-time job. . . . [A]s a result of Smyth v. Ames state regulatory commissions, meaning specifically organized boards, with powers over specified utility operations, became a virtual necessity." Francis X. Welch, *Cases and Text on Public Utility Regulation* (rev. ed.; Arlington, Va.: Public Utilities Reports, Inc., 1968), p. 577.

[6]For a more complete analysis of franchise regulation, see Delos F. Wilcox, *Municipal Franchises* (Rochester, N.Y.: The Gervaise Press, 1910), Vol. I; Leonora Arent, *Electric Franchises in New York City* (New York: Columbia University Press, 1919); Herman H. Trachsel, *Public Utility Regulation* (Homewood, Ill.: Richard D. Irwin, Inc., 1950), chaps. iv and v.

[7]"The city of Dayton, Ohio, once contracted with a corporation for the 'disposal of *all* garbage.' In carrying out the provisions of the contract it developed that the city could not require all the people to give their garbage to the collectors, and the company collected many thousands of dollars in damage. Nevertheless, a few years later a new group of officials, unfamiliar with conditions, were willing to incorporate the same provisions in a new contract." Trachsel, *op. cit.*, p. 78.

[8]*Trustees of Dartmouth College v. Woodward*, 4 Wheaton 518, 643 (1819).

[9]Behling, *op. cit.*, p. 24. Following the *Dartmouth College* decision, clauses reserving the right to amend franchise or charter provisions were often inserted, but with limited results.

[10]*Ibid.*, p. 25.

[11]Many cities continue to charge annual fees for their franchises.

[12]Peter Woll, *Administrative Law: The Informal Process* (Berkeley and Los Angeles: University of California Press, 1963), pp. 7-8.

[13]Glaeser, *op. cit.*, p. 204.

[14]As a result of a recommendation of the three commissioners, the New York Railroad Commission was abolished by the legislature in 1857.

[15]See L. D. White, "The Origin of Utility Commissions in Massachusetts," 29 *Journal of Political Economy* 177 (1921).

[16]Glaeser, *op. cit.*, p. 234.

[17]The two district commissions were abolished in 1921 when the New York State Public Service Commission was established.

[18]The development of state regulatory commissions is discussed by Glaeser, *op. cit.*, pp. 233-63; William E. Mosher and Finla G. Crawford, *Public Utility Regulation* (New York: Harper & Bros., 1933), pp. 14-26; Robert E. Cushman, *The Independent Regulatory Commissions* (New York: Oxford University Press, 1941), pp. 19-41; Irston R. Barnes, *The Economics of Public Utility Regulation* (New York: F. S. Crofts & Co., Inc., 1942), pp. 173-75; *1985 Annual Report on Utility and Carrier Regulation* (Washington, D. C.: National Association of Regulatory Utility Commissioners, 1987), pp. 184-236.

[19]Unless otherwise noted, the data in this section are from *1985 Annual Report on Utility and Carrier Regulation, op. cit.*

[20]For many years, Oregon had a single commissioner. Effective April 1, 1987, a three-member commission was established.

[21]Elections are either statewide (eight agencies — Alabama, Arizona, Georgia, New Mexico SCC, North Dakota, Oklahoma, Tennessee, and Texas RC) or by districts (five agencies — Louisiana, Mississippi, Montana, Nebraska, and South Dakota). The pros and cons of appointed versus elected commissioners have been debated for many years. See, *e.g.,* Merton K. Cameron, "The Experience of Oregon with Popular Election and Recall of Public Service Commissioners," 5 *Journal of Land & Public Utility Economics* 48 (1929); Charles O. Ruggles, "Public Utilities," 20 *Business History Review* 57 (1946); William T. Gormley, Jr., "Nonelectoral Participation as a Response to Issue-Specific Conditions: The Case of Public Utility Regulation," 62 *Social Science Quarterly* 527 (1981); Peter Navarro, "Public Utility Commission Regulation: Performance, Determinants, and Energy Policy Impacts," 3 *Energy Journal* 119 (1982); Patrick C. Mann and Walter J. Primeaux, Jr., "The Controversial Question of Commissioner Selection," 111 *Public Utilities Fortnightly* 21 (March 17, 1983) and "Elected Versus Appointed Commissioners: Does It Make a Difference in Utility Prices?," in *Adjusting to Regulatory, Pricing, and Marketing Realities* (East Lansing: MSU Public Utilities Papers, 1983), pp. 56-72; Walter J. Primeaux, Jr. and Patrick C. Mann, "Regulator Selection Methods and Electricity Prices," 62 *Land Economics* 1 (1986).

[22]Former Chairman Lundy of the New York commission once remarked: "The task of the utility regulator is one which requires the wisdom of Solomon, the patience of Job, the determination of a bulldog, and the hide of a rhinoceros." *Annual Proceedings, 1966* (Washington, D.C.: National Association of Regulatory Utility Commissioners, 1967), p. 14.

[23]See Francis X. Welch, "The Trend from Lawyers to Laymen as Commissioners," 4 *Public Utilities Fortnightly* 801 (1929); and three subsequent articles by Lincoln Smith, "Trend from Lawyers to Laymen on State Commissions," 54 *Public Utilities Fortnightly* 630 (1954), "Professional Backgrounds of Regulatory Commissioners," 76 *Public Utilities Fortnightly* 20 (August 5, 1965), and "State Utility Commissioners — 1978," 101 *Public Utilities Fortnightly* 9 (February 16, 1978).

Of the 198 commissioners from fifty-two of the state commissions listed in Table 4-1 (Texas RC was excluded; there were seven vacancies), seventy (or 35 percent) had a legal background; forty-five (or 23 percent) were women. *NARUC Bulletin* Nos. 20-1987 (May 18, 1987), 22-1987 (June 1, 1987), and 24-1987 (June 15, 1987).

[24]William T. Gormley, Jr., *The Politics of Public Utility Regulation* (Pittsburgh: University of Pittsburgh Press, 1983), p. 189.

[25]Alfred C. Aman, Jr., *Energy and Natural Resources Law: The Regulatory Dialogue* (New York: Matthew Bender & Co., 1983), p. 3-23.

[26]In many states the commissions can obtain assistance from the state attorney general and his or her staff, as well as employ experts in utility regulatory matters when needed or request assistance from federal commissions. But such part-time assistance hinders the development of a comprehensive program.

[27]*State Utility Commissions* (Committee Print, Subcommittee on Intergovernmental Relations, Committee on Government Operations, Senate, 90th. Cong., 1st sess.) (Washington, D.C.: U.S. Government Printing Office, 1967). To illustrate: About half of the state commissions had two or fewer attorneys; three or fewer engineers; three or fewer accountants; and two or fewer rate analysts. Four state commissions had no engineers; six had no rate analysts; seven had no accountants; eight had no full-time attorneys; and 26 had no security analysts. Only five state commissions had economists on their staffs." *Ibid.*

[28]All data for the late 1960s are from Charles F. Phillips, Jr., *The Economics of Regulation: Theory and Practice in the Transportation and Public Utility Industries* (rev. ed.; Homewood, Ill.: Richard D. Irwin, Inc., 1969), pp. 96-100.

[29]See Anthony F. Campagna et al., *Commission Personnel Policy Assessment — 1981* (Columbus, Ohio: National Regulatory Research Institute, 1981). Still larger staffs are probably required. See Gormley, *The Politics of Public Utility Regulation, op. cit.,* pp. 191-92.

[30]See *The NARUC Was There: A History of the NARUC* (Washington, D.C.: National Association of Regulatory Utility Commissioners, 1978). Note: the NARUC's original name was National Association of Railroad and Utilities Commissioners.

[31]Table 4-2 overstates the annual expenditures related to public utility regulation, since the figures represent total agency expenditures. Some agencies (see Table 4-1) have jurisdiction over other industries. For purposes of making a general comparison, total expenditures of the state agencies in fiscal year 1967 were nearly $65 million.

[32]David M. Brackman, quoted in 66 *Public Utilities Fortnightly* 981 (1960).

[33]*1985 Annual Report on Utility and Carrier Regulation, op. cit.,* pp. 88-89. Summarized Commissioner Stalon, then of the Illinois commission: ". . . The Commission must regulate more than two utilities per person on the public utility side. Each hearing examiner must carry 40 to 60 cases at a time and the Commission's weekly agenda contains 100-150 items for decision. Hundreds more items are currently decided by division managers. Contested cases, depending on the breadth assigned to the definition, could easily run to 30 per week and, if the procedures of contested cases are accepted for rate cases, it could go three or four per week higher." Charles G. Stalon, "Some Observations on the Problem of Excessive Regulation of Regulators in the Current Climate of Anti-Regulation" (Paper presented at the 1982 Symposium on Regulation, Warrenton, Va., August 20, 1982 (mimeographed), p. 19.

[34]Two federal regulatory commissions exercise jurisdiction over the transportation utilities: (*1*) the *Interstate Commerce Commission,* established in 1887 to regulate the railroads, had its jurisdiction extended to oil pipelines (1906; transferred to the Federal Energy Regulatory Commission in 1977), telephone and telegraph services

(1910; transferred to the Federal Communications Commission in 1934), motor carriers (1935), and water carriers (1940); and (2) the *Federal Maritime Commission,* created in 1961 (succeeding the Federal Maritime Board) to control shipping in domestic and foreign offshore commerce. [The *Civil Aeronautics Board,* created in 1938 with economic control of commercial air transportation, was abolished at the end of 1984. Some of its functions were transferred to the Department of Transportation.] There are other independent federal regulatory agencies, including the *Board of Governors of the Federal Reserve System* (1913), the *Federal Trade Commission* (1914), the *Federal Home Loan Bank Board* (1932), the *Federal Deposit Insurance Corporation* (1933), and the *Postal Rate Commission* (1970). In addition, there are a number of federal agencies, primarily concerned with social regulation, that have an important impact on public utilities, such as the *Equal Employment Opportunity Commission* (1964), the *Environmental Protection Agency* (1970), and the *Occupational Safety and Health Administration* (1973).

[35]Barry M. Mitnick, *The Political Economy of Regulation: Creating, Designing, and Removing Regulatory Forms* (New York: Columbia University Press, 1980), p. 231. The observed lack of quality "is not a matter of venality or corruption or even stupidity; rather, it is a problem of mediocrity." *Study on Federal Regulation,* Vol. I: *The Regulatory Appointments Process* (Committee Print, Committee on Governmental Affairs, Senate, 95th Cong., 1st sess.)(Washington, D.C.: U.S. Government Printing Office, 1977), p. 10. See, *e.g.,* E. Pendleton Herring, *Federal Commissioners: A Study of Their Careers and Qualifications* (Cambridge: Harvard University Press, 1936); David T. Stanley, Dean E. Mann, and Jameson W. Doig, *Men Who Govern: A Biographical Profile of Federal Political Executives* (Washington, D. C.: The Brookings Institution, 1967); *Federal Regulation and Regulatory Reform* (Committee Print, Subcommittee on Oversight and Investigations, Committee on Interstate and Foreign Commerce, House, 94th Cong., 2d sess.)(Washington, D.C.: U.S. Government Printing Office, 1976). But see Thomas K. McCraw, *Prophets of Regulation* (Cambridge: Belknap Press of Harvard University Press, 1984).

[36]Stanley, Mann, and Doig, *op. cit.,* chap. iv. See also James M. Graham and Victor H. Kramer, *Appointments to the Regulatory Agencies: The Federal Communications Commission and the Federal Trade Commission (1949-1974)* (Committee Print, Committee on Commerce, Senate, 94th Cong., 2d sess.)(Washington, D.C.: U.S. Government Printing Office, 1976), esp. pp. 406-7; *Federal Regulation and Regulatory Reform, op. cit.,* esp. p. 452.

[37]Herring, *op. cit.,* p. 98.

[38]Graham and Kramer, *op. cit.,* pp. 413-18. The so-called "revolving door" issue is discussed in Chapter 17.

[39]Welborn argues that appropriations have not kept pace with rising work loads. David Welborn, *The Governance of Federal Regulatory Agencies* (Knoxville: University of Tennessee Press, 1977).

[40]Commission on Organization of the Executive Branch of the Government, *Task Force Report on Regulatory Commissions* (Washington, D.C.: U.S. Government Printing Office, 1949), p. 23.

[41]Herring observed the appearance of "a career corps of permanent officials" in the older agencies. Herring, *op. cit.,* p. 91. See also Robert C. Fellmeth et al., *The Interstate Commerce Omission: The Public Interest and the ICC* (New York: Grossman Publishers, 1970), p. 14.

[42]Emmette S. Redford, *American Government and the Economy* (New York: The Macmillan Co., 1956), p. 550.

[43]At the federal level, there is no statutory authority to remove an FCC commissioner. Most of the states have statutory provisions regarding removal. See *State Utility Commissions, op. cit.*, Table I and pp. 65-67; *1985 Annual Report on Utility and Carrier Regulation, op. cit.*, pp. 245-50.

[44]*Humphrey's Executor v. United States*, 295 U.S. 602, 629 (1935). The principle of security was reaffirmed in *Wiener v. United States*, 357 U.S. 349 (1958). See Reginald Parker, "The Removal Power of the President and Independent Administrative Agencies," 36 *Indiana Law Journal* 63 (1960).

[45]William L. Cary, *Politics and the Regulatory Agencies* (New York: McGraw-Hill Book Co., Inc., 1967), p. 10.

[46]Redford, *op. cit.* More recently, "both the necessity and constitutional legitimacy of commissions that are independent of presidential direction have been subjected to renewed discussion. Congress's attempt to check abuses of executive power by creating 'executive' agencies outside of presidential control has been challenged by some commentators as a violation of the separation of powers." Charles N. Steele and Jeffrey H. Bowman, "The Constitutionality of Independent Regulatory Agencies Under the Necessary and Proper Clause: The Case of the Federal Election Commission," 4 *Yale Journal on Regulation* 363 (1987) (footnotes omitted). See, *e.g.*, Peter L. Strauss, "The Place of Agencies in Government: Separation of Powers and the Fourth Branch," 84 *Columbia Law Review* 573 (1984); *Synar v. United States*, 626 F. Supp. 1374 (D.D.C. 1986), *aff'd sub nom. Bowsher v. Synar*, 106 S. Ct. 3181 (1986) (Court held that ruling should not be seen as "casting doubt on the status of 'independent' agencies").

[47]*Reagan v. Farmers' Loan & Trust Co.*, 154 U.S. 362, 393-94 (1894).

[48]*United States v. Chicago, Milwaukee, St. Paul & Pacific R.R. Co.*, 282 U.S. 311, 324 (1931).

"Some courts have taken the view that the legislature cannot delegate its lawmaking function at all, but have concluded that authorizing an administrative agency to 'fill in the details' of legislation is valid as not being an exercise of the legislative power. Other courts have stated that the legislation *can* delegate part of its function to an agency as long as sufficient general standards to be used by the agency are included in the grant of authority. The difference in the two foregoing approaches to delegation is largely a matter of semantics...." Robert N. Corley and Robert L. Black, *The Legal Environment of Business* (2d ed.; New York: McGraw-Hill Book Co., Inc., 1968), p. 99. Compare *Yakus v. United States*, 321 U.S. 414 (1944) with *Panama Refining Co. v. Ryan*, 293 U.S. 388 (1935).

[49]For a more complete discussion, upon which this summary is largely based, see Marver H. Bernstein, *Regulating Business by Independent Commission* (Princeton: Princeton University Press, 1955), pp. 109-13, 126-54; Bernard Schwartz, *The Professor and the Commissions* (New York: Alfred A. Knopf, Inc., 1959), pp. 205-34; Emmette S. Redford, "The President and the Regulatory Commissions," 44 *Texas Law Review* 288 (1965); David M. Welborn, "Presidents, Regulatory Commissioners and Regulatory Policy," 15 *Journal of Public Law* 1 (1966).

[50]The President has the power to name all federal regulatory chairmen. Governors have the power to appoint the chairmen of thirty state agencies.

Presidential and gubernatorial control of the bureaucracy is subject to dispute. Compare, *e.g.*, Thad Beyle and J. Oliver Williams (eds.), *The American Governor in Behavioral Perspective* (New York: Harper & Row Publishers, 1972) with Martha Wagner Weinberg, *Managing the State* (Cambridge: The MIT Press, 1977).

[51]Cary, *op. cit.*, p. 12. See also testimony of Elmer M. Staats, *Federal Administrative*

Procedure (Hearings before the Subcommittee on Administrative Practice and Procedure of the Committee on the Judiciary, Senate, 86th Cong., 2d sess.)(Washington, D.C.: U.S. Government Printing Office, 1960), pp. 22-46; *Budget Bureau Censorship and Control of Independent Agency Fiscal and Other Matters* (Study by the staff of the Special Subcommittee on Legislative Oversight for the Committee on Interstate and Foreign Commerce, House, 86th Cong., 2d sess.)(Washington, D.C.: U.S. Government Printing Office, 1960).

[52]D. Philip Locklin, *Economics of Transportation* (7th ed.; Homewood, Ill.: Richard D. Irwin, Inc., 1972), p. 303.

[53]See Robert L. Stern, "The Solicitor General's Office and Administrative Agency Litigation," 46 *American Bar Association Journal* 154 (1960).

[54]A few states have established "independent" consumer protection agencies; *e.g.*, Office of People's Counsel in the District of Columbia and Maryland, Office of the Public Counsel in Florida. See *1985 Annual Report on Utility and Carrier Regulation, op. cit.*, pp. 892-94.

[55]The Energy Research and Development Administration; the Federal Energy Administration; the Federal Power Commission; the Alaska, Bonneville, Southeastern and Southwestern Power Administrations (from the Department of the Interior); power marketing functions of the Bureau of Reclamation (also from the Department of the Interior); and certain functions of the Interstate Commerce Commission (oil pipeline regulation), and the Departments of Commerce, Housing and Urban Development, the Navy and the Interior.

[56]See Kenneth W. Clarkson and Roger LeRoy Miller, *Industrial Organization: Theory, Evidence, and Public Policy* (New York: McGraw-Hill Book Co., 1982), Table 20-2, p. 457.

[57]Most states have established state energy offices to coordinate energy policy at the state level. These offices, too, frequently intervene in cases before the state regulatory commissions. See *1985 Annual Report on Utility and Carrier Regulation, op. cit.*, pp. 895-97.

[58]Hugh S. Norton, *Modern Transportation Economics* (Columbus: Charles E. Merrill Books, Inc., 1963), pp. 229-30.

[59]Even in the case of state commissions that receive part or all of their annual appropriations from assessments levied on the industries under their jurisdiction, the legislatures establish their annual budgets.

[60]*Report on Independent Offices Appropriation Bill, 1964* (House Report No. 824, Appropriations Committee, 88th Cong., 1st sess.)(Washington, D.C.: U.S. Government Printing Office, 1963), p. 9.

[61]See, *e.g.*, *Study on Federal Regulation*, Vol. II: *Congressional Oversight of Regulatory Agencies* (Committee on Governmental Affairs, Senate, 95th Cong., 1st sess.)(Washington, D.C.: U.S. Government Printing Office, 1977). See also Arthur L. Litke and Thomas F. O'Connor, "The Changing Role and Influence of The General Accounting Office on Regulation," 106 *Public Utilities Fortnightly* 25 (September 25, 1980).

[62]See Alan Rosenthal, *Legislative Life: People, Process, and Performance in the States* (New York: Harper & Row Publishers, 1981), pp. 321-22.

[63]See Frank E. Cooper, *Administrative Agencies and the Courts* (Ann Arbor: University of Michigan Law School, 1951); Louis L. Jaffe, *Judicial Control of Administrative Action* (Boston: Little, Brown & Co., Inc., 1965); Martin Shapiro, *The Supreme Court and Administrative Agencies* (New York: The Free Press, 1968).

[64]Locklin, *op. cit.*, p. 293.

[65]*Interstate Commerce Comm. v. Alabama Midland Ry. Co.*, 168 U.S. 144 (1897).

[66]"The same case is not tried before the court which is tried before the Commission. The trial before the Commission, therefore, with all its attendant expense and consumption of time, goes practically for nothing ... A procedure like the present one tends to bring the body into disrepute and is grossly unfair to it and to the complainants who appear before it." Interstate Commerce Commission, *Annual Report, 1897,* pp. 31-32.

[67]*Interstate Commerce Comm. v. Illinois Central R.R. Co.*, 215 U.S. 452, 470 (1910).

[68]*Smyth v. Ames*, 169 U.S. 466, 546-47 (1898).

[69]*Bluefield Water Works & Imp. Co. v. Pub. Service Comm. of West Virginia*, 262 U.S. 679, 692-93 (1923).

[70]*Federal Power Comm. v. Natural Gas Pipeline Co.*, 315 U.S. 575, 586 (1942)

[71]See, *e.g.*, *Phillips Petroleum Co. v. Wisconsin*, 347 U.S.672 (1954).

[72]Cary, *op. cit.*, p. 4. In recent years, concludes Gormley, "commissions remain independent not because politicians respect their integrity but because they recognize a political liability when they see one. Public utility commissions today have little to fear from the governor or the state legislature. Both are bogeymen whose power to scare vanishes with the light of day." Gormley, *The Politics of Public Utility Regulation, op. cit.*, p. 88.

[73]See President's Committee on Administrative Management, *Report with Special Studies* (Washington, D.C.: U.S. Government Printing Office, 1937), pp. 39-42; Frederick F. Blachly and Miriam E. Oatman, *Federal Regulatory Action and Control* (Washington, D.C.: The Brookings Institution, 1940), chap. ix; James M. Landis, *Report on Regulatory Agencies to the President-Elect* (Washington, D.C.: U.S. Government Printing Office, 1960); Redford, "The President and the Regulatory Commissions," *op. cit.*, pp. 297-98.

[74]Oren Harris, quoted in 67 *Public Utilities Fortnightly* 222 (1961).

[75]*Knoxville v. Knoxville Water Co.*, 212 U.S. 1 (1909).

[76]Newton N. Minow, quoted in 72 *Public Utilities Fortnightly* 11 (December 5, 1963).

[77]Roy L. Cole, "Administrative Agencies and Judicial Powers," 44 *American Bar Association Journal* 953, 954 (1958).

[78]See Woll, *op. cit.*, pp. 15-18.

[79]*Ibid.*, p. 19.

[80]*Ibid.*, p. 21.

[81]See Chapter 5, pp. 190-93.

[82]Concurring opinion of Commissioner Loevinger, *Re American Teleph. & Teleg. Co.*, 70 PUR3d 129, 227 (FCC, 1967).

[83]*Ibid.* See also preliminary concurring statement of Commissioner Johnson, *ibid.*, p. 234; Carl A. Auerbach, "The Controversy over the Role of the FCC's Common Carrier Bureau in Rate Cases," American Bar Association Annual Report, Section of *Public Utility Law, 1966*, pp. 6-24; Kenneth Culp Davis, "Advocating and Deciding in Rate Cases," *Ibid.*, pp. 25-38.

[84]The FCC's position has been upheld on three occasions: *Wilson & Co. v. United States*, 335 F. 2d 788 (7th Cir. 1964), *cert. denied*, 380 U.S. 951 (1965); *American Trucking Ass'ns, Inc. v. Federal Communications Comm.*, 377 F. 2d 121 (D.C. Cir. 1966), *cert. denied*, 386 U.S. 943 (1967); *American Teleph. & Teleg. Co. v. Federal Communications Comm.*, 449 F. 2d 439 (2d Cir. 1971).

[85]See, *e.g.*, *Re American Teleph. & Teleg. Co.*, 46 FCC 2d 169 (1974).

[86]See, *e.g.*, Thomas L. Peterson, "The Hawaii Public Utilities Commission: Separating the Advocative and Advisory Roles of Counsel," 80 *Public Utilities Fortnightly* 73 (September 28, 1967).

[87]While major jurisdictional problems have concerned state and federal regulatory spheres, there have been a number of cases involving local and state authority. See, *e.g.*, *Re East Ohio Gas Co.*, 41 PUR3d 75 (Ohio, 1961); *Florida v. Dade County*, 178 So. 2d 703 (1965); *Re Northwest Natural Gas, Inc.*, 67 PUR3d 523 (N.J., 1967).

[88]C. Woody Thompson and Wendell R. Smith, *Public Utility Economics* (New York: McGraw-Hill Book Co., Inc., 1941), p. 229.

[89]*Annual Proceedings, 1931* (Washington, D.C.: National Association of Regulatory Utility Commissioners, 1932), p. 150.

[90]From addresses by H. Erickson and H. Sands, respectively, delivered at a conference, August 29, 1928, and published by the National Electric Light Association, as cited in Thompson and Smith, *op. cit.*, p. 229.

[91]James W. Karber, "Challenge: A Way of Life for the Future," 80 *Public Utilities Fortnightly* 19, 24 (November 9, 1967). See also "Proper Spheres of State and Federal Regulation," in *Annual Proceedings, 1963* (Washington, D.C.: National Association of Regulatory Utility Commissioners, 1964), pp. 320-38; "Report of the Committee on Regulatory Procedure," in *Annual Proceedings, 1965* (Washington, D.C.: National Association of Regulatory Utility Commissioners, 1966), pp. 62-70; James W. Karber, "The Regulatory Jurisdictional Problem: State or Federal?," 82 *Public Utilities Fortnightly* 17 (October 24, 1968).

[92]An 1851 Supreme Court decision suggested that federal inaction should be interpreted as implying that no regulation should be exercised, thus prohibiting state action. *Cooley v. The Board of Wardens of the Port of Philadelphia*, 53 U.S. 298 (1851). Later decisions indicate otherwise. See, *e.g.*, *Munn v. Illinois*, 94 U.S. 113 (1877); *Peik v. Chicago & Northwestern Ry. Co.*, 94 U.S. 164 (1877).

[93]See Chapter 3, pp. 78-79.

[94]Public Utility Act of 1935, Title II, Part II, Sec. 201(b).

[95]A Federal-State Joint Board is composed of three FCC commissioners and four state commissioners. Its recommended decision is for review and action by the FCC. See, *e.g.*, "State Commissioners Testify in House on Federal-State Joint Board Proposal on Subscriber Line Charges, Federal Lifeline Assistance, High Cost Assistance, and Pooling of Common Line Costs," *NARUC Bulletin* No. 14-1987 (April 6, 1987), pp. 22-26. Experience under all these provisions has shown limitations. See David M. Welborn, "National-State Cooperation in Regulatory Administration," 33 *State Government* 199 (1960); Karber, "Challenge: A Way of Life for the Future," *op. cit.*, pp. 24-25.

[96]*Illinois Natural Gas Co. v. Central Illinois Pub. Service Co.*, 314 U.S. 498 (1942). Said the Court: ". . . the proposed extension . . . is so intimately associated with the commerce [of gas transportation], and would so affect its volume moving into the state and distribution among the states, as to be within the Congressional power to regulate those matters which materially affect interstate commerce, as well as the commerce itself." *Ibid.*, p. 509.

[97]*Interstate Natural Gas Co. v. Federal Power Comm.*, 331 U.S. 682 (1947). Argued the Court: ". . . it is clear that the sales in question were quite as much in interstate commerce as they would have been had the pipes of the petitioner crossed the state line before reaching the points of sale." *Ibid.*, pp. 687-88.

[98]*Federal Power Comm. v. East Ohio Gas Co.*, 338 U.S. 464 (1950). In response,

Congress in 1954 enacted the Hinshaw amendment to the Natural Gas Act which exempts any company from the Act if it buys and consumes all gas within one state and its rates, services, and facilities are regulated by a state commission.

[99]*Phillips Petroleum Co. v. Wisconsin, op. cit.* See Chapter 11, pp. 456-58.

[100]*Federal Power Comm. v. Southern California Edison Co.,* 376 U.S. 205 (1964).

[101]*California v. Lo-Vaca Gathering Co.,* 379 U.S. 366 (1965). Argued Justice Douglas: "Were suppliers of gas and pipeline companies free to allocate by contract gas from a particular source to a particular use, havoc would be raised with the federal regulatory scheme. . . ." *Ibid.,* p. 369. See also *Re United Gas Pipe Line Co.,* 50 PUR3d 186 (1963).

[102]*Federal Power Comm. v. Union Electric Co.,* 381 U.S. 90 (1965).

[103]*Federal Power Comm. v. Florida Power & Light Co.,* 404 U.S. 453 (1972).

[104]Natural Policy Gas Act of 1978 (Pub. Law 95-621).

[105]*Oklahoma v. Federal Energy Regulatory Comm.,* 494 F. Supp. 636 (W.D. Okla. 1980), *aff'd,* 661 F. 2d 832 (10th Cir. 1981), *cert. denied sub nom. Texas v. Federal Energy Regulatory Comm.,* 102 S. Ct. 2902 (1982).

[106]Public Utility Regulatory Policies Act of 1978 (Pub. Law 95-617). Argued Joseph C. Swidler, a former chairman of both the Federal Power Commission and the New York Public Service Commission, in testimony opposing mandatory standards before the Senate Subcommittee on Energy Conservation and Regulation: "There is full authority in the bill to make the state commissions virtual branch offices of the Department of Energy. . . . The justification for this vast extension of Federal authority is slender indeed. . . . It is one of the great strengths of state regulation that it can give attention to the specifics of individual company conditions and consumer needs and practices in adopting rate policies to particular cases." Testimony on S. 1469 (mimeographed, July 28, 1977). The state of Mississippi and the Mississippi Public Service Commission unsuccessfully challenged portions of the act. *State of Mississippi et al. v. Federal Energy Regulatory Comm. et al.,* 38 PUR4th 284 (D. Miss. 1981), *rev'd,* 456 U.S. 742, 47 PUR4th 1 (1982). But compare Maurice Van Nostrand, "Federal-State Relationships in Energy Regulation: A State Commissioner's Perspective," in Harry M. Trebing (ed.), *Issues in Public Utility Regulation* (East Lansing: MSU Public Utilities Papers, 1979), pp. 22-30 with Jay B. Kennedy, "DOE Mandates: Taking Power Away from the States," 106 *Public Utilities Fortnightly* 11 (November 6, 1980).

[107]See (a) on the entry of specialized common carriers: *Re Specialized Common Carrier Services,* 24 F.C.C. 2d 318 (1970), 29 F.C.C. 2d 870 (1971), 31 F.C.C. 2d 1106 (1971), *aff'd sub nom. Washington Utils. & Transp. Comm. v. Federal Communications Comm.,* 513 F. 2d 1142 (9th Cir. 1974), *cert. denied,* 423 U.S. 836 (1975); (b) on interconnection policy: *Re Telerent Leasing Corp.,* 45 F.C.C. 2d 204 (1974), *aff'd sub nom. North Carolina Utils. Comm. v. Federal Communications Comm.,* 537 F. 2d 787 (4th Cir. 1975), *cert. denied,* 429 U.S. 1027 (1976); (c) on federal registration of terminal equipment: *Re Interstate & Foreign MTS and WATS,* 56 F.C.C. 2d 593 (1975), *aff'd sub nom. North Carolina Utils. Comm. v. Federal Communications Comm.,* 552 F. 2d 1036 (4th Cir. 1977), *cert. denied,* 434 U.S. 874 (1977); (d) on interstate access charges: *Re MTS & WATS Market Structure,* Third Report & Order, 93 F.C.C. 2d 241 (1983), *aff'd in principal part and rem'd in part sub nom. National Ass'n of Reg. Util. Comm'rs v. Federal Communications Comm.,* 737 F. 2d 1095 (D.C. Cir. 1984); and (e) on federal preemption of certain depreciation practices: *Re Amendment of Uniform System of Accounts for Class A and Class B Telephone Companies,* 83 F.C.C. 2d 267, 40 PUR4th 251 (1980), 92 F.C.C. 2d 864, 50 PUR4th 298 (1982), *aff'd sub nom. Virginia State Corp. Comm. v.*

Federal Communications Comm., 737 F. 2d 388, 60 PUR4th 171 (4th Cir. 1984), *rev'd sub nom. Louisiana Pub. Service Comm. v. Federal Communications Comm.*, 106 S. Ct. 1890, 74 PUR4th 1 (1986).

[108]*Pacific Gas & Elec. Co. v. State Energy Resources Conservation and Development Comm.*, 489 F. Supp. 699 (E.D. Cal. 1980), *rev'd*, 659 F. 2d 903 (9th Cir. 1981), *aff'd*, 103 S. Ct. 1713, 52 PUR4th 169 (1983). See, *e.g.*, Omer F. Brown and Edward M. Davis, "The Implications of the Supreme Court's California Nuclear Moratorium Decision," 111 *Public Utilities Fortnightly* 35 (May 26, 1983). See also J. F. Seiberling, "Radioactive Waste Disposal: The Emerging Issue of States' Rights," 13 *Akron Law Review* 261 (1979); L. M. Trosten and M. R. Anncarrow, "Federal-State-Local Relationships in Transporting Radioactive Materials: Rules of the Nuclear Road," 68 *Kentucky Law Journal* 251 (1979-1980); C. B. Wiggins, "Federal Balancing and the Burger Court: California's Nuclear Law as a Preemptive Case Study," 13 *U.C. Davis Law Review* 1 (1979-1980); S. Bernstein, "Nuclear Law: A Battle Over Atomic Power in the Courts," 16 *Trial* 42 (1980).

[109]*Re Middle South Energy, Inc.*, 67 PUR4th 341 (FERC, 1985), order on rehearing, 32 FERC Par. 61,425 (1985), *aff'd sub nom. Mississippi Industries v. Federal Energy Regulatory Comm.*, Nos. 85-1611 et al. (D.C. Cir. 1987).

[110]*The Wall Street Journal*, October 6, 1987, p. 6. See Sheldon L. Bierman, "A Lesson from Grand Gulf: A Gap in Jurisdiction," 118 *Public Utilities Fortnightly* 15 (September 4, 1986); "Jurisdictional Conflicts in the Regulation of Integrated Interstate Electric Utility Systems," 119 *Public Utilities Fortnightly* 47 (March 5, 1987).

[111]Cushman, *op. cit.*, pp. 28-29. For a further discussion of this topic, see Mitnick, *op. cit.*

[112]Corley and Black, *op. cit.*, p. 97.

[113]Woll, *op. cit.*, pp. 1-2.

[114]LI *Congressional Record*, Part II (June 25, 1914), p. 11104.

[115]"Delay is inherent in any decision-making procedure that is formalized. But the peculiar nature of the administrative process is to accentuate that delay and to make the period of delay responsive to the actions of the parties. In particular, any party disadvantaged by the prospective decision is granted the right to delay that decision for many years. The extensive delay is not automatic. The easing of standing criteria and the promotion, by the courts, of interest group representation have increased the importance of this right." Bruce M. Owen and Ronald Braeutigam, *The Regulation Game: Strategic Use of the Administrative Process* (Cambridge: Ballinger Publishing Co., 1978), p. 20 (citation omitted).

[116]For a more complete discussion, see *ibid.*, esp. chap. 1.

[117]Albert L. Sklar, former chairman of the Maryland Public Service Commission, quoted in 72 *Public Utilities Fortnightly* 68 (November 21, 1963). "In light of these congressional purposes I would not superimpose federal regulation on top of state regulation in case of *de minimis* transmissions not made by prearrangement or in case of wholesale transactions. . . . If we allow federal preemption on this case, then we have come full cycle, leaving local authorities control of electric energy only insofar as municipal plants are concerned. The federal camel has a tendency to occupy permanently any state tent." Dissenting opinion of Justice Douglas, *Federal Power Comm. v. Florida Power & Light Co.*, *op. cit.*, pp. 475-76.

PART II

The Theory of
Public Utility
Regulation

Chapter	THE GOALS,
5	PROCEDURES, AND
	THEORIES OF
	PUBLIC UTILITY
	REGULATION

We are asking much of regulation when we ask that it follow the guide of competition. As Americans, we have set up a system that indicates we have little faith in economic planning by the government. Yet, we are asking our regulators to exercise the judgment of thousands of consumers in the evaluation of our efficiency, service, and technical progress so that a fair profit can be determined. Fair regulation is now, and always will be, a difficult process. But it is not impossible.

—Ralph M. Besse*

Regulation, as it has developed in the United States, is concerned with rates, service, safety, and, to a growing extent, the efficiency of management. In most of the industries under consideration, rate regulation has occupied much of the commissions' time and has been the subject of continuous controversy. Rate regulation has two aspects: control of the rate level (earnings) and control of the rate structure (prices). As to the rate level, public utilities are entitled to cover all allowable operating costs and to have the opportunity to earn a "fair" rate of return. Collectively, these items comprise a company's total revenue requirements. As to the rate structure, public utilities are permitted to establish rates that, at a minimum, will cover their revenue requirements. Such rates must be "just and reasonable," with no "undue" discrimination.

While rate regulation has been the major concern of the commissions and the courts, attention also has been paid to the problems of quality and quantity of service, safety of operations, and efficiency of management. Consumers expect high standards of service from public utilities, for "it does the buyer no good to pay a lower price if the quality or quantity he gets for his money is lowered in the same proportion, giving him gas, for instance, of four-fifths the former heating power for four-fifths the former price."[1] They also expect safe service, because the best service available is useless if gas leaks cause explosions or accidents cause blackouts, brownouts, or plant shutdowns. And, "it does the buyer no good to compel the producer to accept half the former net earnings if he gets in exchange a management half as efficient, for the poor management will add more to the costs of operation than the regulating commission can take away in reduced earnings."[2]

The goals of regulation, the task and phases of rate regulation, various theories of regulation, and commission procedures are discussed in this chapter. In the following six chapters, accounting and financial control, the rate level, the rate of return, and the rate structures of public utilities are examined in detail. Finally, service and safety standards, as well as management efficiency, are considered in Chapter 12.

The Goals of Public Utility Regulation

The job of a public utility is "to provide the public with as much and as good service as the public wants and is willing to pay for. The goal of regulation, within the limits set by its authority and its capacity, is to translate this task into operating terms, and see to it that it is carried out."[3] Five basic objectives have been employed by the regulatory commissions in translating this task into operating terms:

1. Commissions have sought to prevent excessive (monopoly) profits and unreasonable (inequitable) price discrimination among customers and places. This objective is essentially a negative or restrictive one.

2. Commissions have tried to assure adequate earnings so that the public utility sector could continue to develop and expand in accordance with consumer demand. Profits, however, are not guaranteed, and incentives to efficiency have received little attention.

3. Commissions have sought to provide service to the maximum number of customers. In some instances, competition has been limited to permit internal subsidy (low-density routes may be subsidized by earnings on high-density routes). More recently, conservation and new entry have resulted in a growing emphasis upon cost-based rates, thereby forcing commissions to reevaluate the use of internal subsidies to achieve this objective.

4. Commissions have often promoted the development of an industry. Rate structures have been designed to promote growth (declining block rates) or subsidies (from Congress) have been given to achieve this objective (rural electric cooperatives and rural telephone service). Federal public power projects were undertaken to promote the industrial development of specific regions.

5. Commissions, in some instances, have been — or are rapidly becoming — concerned with insuring maximum public safety and management efficiency. Safety has been an important objective in the provision of natural gas and in the country's nuclear power program. Concern about the efficiency of management has resulted in countless "management audits" since the early 1970s.

These are not the only possible alternative goals or objectives for regulation. A few have argued that regulation should seek "social," as opposed to "business" or "economic," objectives. The term is difficult to define, but generally "refers to any policy of rate control designed to make the supply of utility services responsive to social needs and social costs, and rejecting as even tolerable measures of these needs and these costs the prices that consumers are able and willing to pay for the services and the money costs that the enterprise must incur in their production."[4] A larger number have argued that regulation is too often conceived of as a restrictive or negative force; that it must become more dynamic with greater emphasis on achieving (a) maximum economic performance, by providing explicit incentives to reward efficiency and penalize inefficiency, and (b) proper resource allocation.[5]

Public utilities are no longer, if they ever were, isolated from the rest of the economy. It is possible that the expanding utility sector has been taking too large a share of the nation's resources, especially of investment.[6] At a minimum, regulation must be viewed in the context of the entire economy — and evaluated in a similar context. Public utilities have always operated within the framework of a competitive system. They must obtain capital, labor, and materials in competition with unregulated industries. Adequate profits are not guaranteed to them. Regulation, then, should provide incentives to adopt new methods, improve quality, increase efficiency, cut costs, develop new markets, and expand output in line with consumer demand. In short, regulation is a substitute for competition and should attempt to put the utility sector under the same restraints competition places on the industrial sector.

When it is stated that regulation should follow the guide of competition, much is being asked. In the first place, such a goal has an inherent limitation, as pointed out by former FCC Commissioner Loevinger:

> The basic strength of the competitive system is that it avoids such problems [*i.e.*, the necessity of securing, organizing, and weighting data adequate to make a complex economic decision] by distributing market power among numerous diverse enterprises, so that operation of the market rests upon the action of many independent decision makers. The vice of monopoly is that it concentrates market power and thus eliminates the diverse independent decision makers. . . . Regulation preserves a number of independent decision makers, but it reduces the number from that which might otherwise exist, and it concentrates decision-making power with respect to the areas of regulatory control. The difficulty is that no regulatory agency can acquire or utilize effectively the range of data which influence a competitive market. Consequently, the ability of regulation to substitute for competition has an inherent limitation which cannot be wholly overcome by any improvement in the regulatory structure or process.[7]

In the second place, policies are shaped by various economic, social, and political pressures, so that regulation may seek other than competitive objectives (*i.e.*, internal subsidies, lifeline rates).[8] But even when economic objectives are sought, it is not easy to specify with any precision that competitive standard which regulation should seek, for competition throughout the economy is imperfect (*i.e.*, it is not the perfect form of competition envisioned by Adam Smith). Consequently, as Lewis has pointed out:

> It is probably true that regulation can never achieve more than a rough approximation of the results which perfect competition probably would have worked out in these industries — that is, it must be regarded as a "make-shift" for a condition of competition which never has existed and never can exist — and society must be prepared to accept some degree of maladjustment as inevitable.[9]

Consider, for example, the marginal cost pricing principle and the "problem of the second best."[10] Summarizes Schmalensee:

> . . . Suppose an economy has twenty-six markets, labeled A to Z, with only the price charged in A subject to direct government control. Suppose further that because of uncontrolled monopoly, excise taxation, or other distortions, buyers in markets B to Z do not face prices equal to marginal costs. The best government policy would be to eliminate all

the distortions in the economy and to induce marginal cost pricing in all markets. But if this is not feasible, Lipsey and Lancaster show that the *second-best* price policy for industry A alone is not always marginal cost pricing. In an economy with distortions elsewhere, second-best analysis establishes that efficiency-seeking monopoly control should not necessarily require marginal cost pricing.[11]

In short, unless marginal cost pricing is being followed uniformly throughout the economy, it will not necessarily provide a correct guide for pricing in the public utility sector.

In the third place, the regulatory process is inherently slower than the competitive process and, equally important, creates vested interests itself. Regulation "must satisfy the requirements of due process: investigate, give notice, hold hearings, study the record, make findings, issue orders, permit appeals. All this takes time and delays action."[12] Further, as Bernstein has concluded:

> It is impossible to avoid the conclusion that regulation of particular industries by independent commissions tends to destroy rather than promote competition. The historical tradition of commissions is anti-competitive. Their basic methods, especially their reliance upon the case-by-case approach, place small business firms at a disadvantage. The growing passivity of the commissions' approach and the inconvenience of dealing with large numbers of firms strengthen the commissions' tendency to identify their view of the public interest with the position of the dominant regulated firms. In short, regulation of particular businesses stacks the cards against the small competitive firms and weakens the force of competition.[13]

Finally, it is difficult to adopt regulatory laws and concepts to meet changing economic conditions. Rostow, for example, has argued that the statutes which our regulatory agencies seek to enforce are

> ... usually out of date, often confused, ill-drawn, and needlessly complex. Many of their rules echo forgotten battles, and guard against dangers which no longer exist. They comprise vast codes, understood only by a jealous priesthood which protects these swamps and thickets from all prying eyes. In the main, the agencies follow routines established for the control of local gas companies and street railways. The relevance of the model is not immediately apparent, in dealing with progressive and expanding industries like air transport or trucking.[14]

All four of these factors suggest that the development of consistent regulatory goals, and the adoption of policies to achieve these goals, is exceedingly difficult. Adding to the problem have been technological developments which have greatly increased the competitive relationships between the public utility industries, and between the regulated and unregulated sectors of the economy. As will be demonstrated in the following chapters, regulation is now, and always will be, a difficult process. It is only with better understanding and increased knowledge of economic, political, and social factors that regulation can be an efficient substitute for competition.

The Task of Rate Regulation

Before discussing the theory of public utility regulation in detail, it is desirable to outline the overall task of rate regulation. The method of establishing rates constitutes one of the most fundamental differences between public utilities and the remainder of our private enterprise system. In the nonregulated sector, rates are largely determined by the action of competitive forces — market supply and demand. In the regulated sector, because of the absence or the control of these competitive forces, rates are generally determined by a regulatory commission acting under broad powers conferred on it by the legislature, subject, of course, to judicial review.

Each aspect of rate regulation is treated separately in the next few chapters, but in reality they overlap in many instances. Thus, annual depreciation must be included in operating costs and accrued depreciation subtracted from the value of a utility's tangible and reproducible property; service and safety standards have an important relation to the rates which a utility must charge its customers. For these and other similar reasons, the various problems of regulation are closely interwoven.

The Revenue-Requirement Standard

The basic standard of rate regulation is the revenue-requirement standard, often referred to as the rate base-rate of return standard. Simply stated, a regulated firm must be permitted to set rates which will (a) cover operating costs and (b) provide an opportunity to earn a reasonable rate of return on the property devoted to the business. This return must enable the utility to maintain its financial credit as well as to attract whatever capital may be required in the future for replacements, expansion, and technological innovation, and it must be comparable to that earned by other businesses with corresponding risks.

There are two aspects of rate regulation: the rate level or determination of a utility's general level of rates and the rate structure or determination of specific rates and the relationships between rates. In the words of the Supreme Court:

> The establishment of a rate for a regulated industry often involves two steps of different character, one of which may appropriately precede the other. The first is the adjustment of a general revenue level to

the demands of a fair return. The second is the adjustment of a rate schedule conforming to that level, so as to eliminate discriminations and unfairness from its details.[15]

The Rate Level. The first aspect of rate regulation, the determination of a utility's total revenue requirement, can be expressed as a formula:

$$R = O + (V - D)r$$

where R is the total revenue required,
O is the operating costs,
V is the gross value of the tangible
and intangible property,
D is the accrued depreciation of
the tangible and reproducible
property, and
r is the allowed rate of return.

The formula indicates that determining the total revenue required (generally for a twelve-month period) involves three major steps. First, allowable operating costs must be ascertained. These include all types of operating expenses (wages, salaries, fuel, maintenance, advertising, research, and charitable contributions) plus annual charges for depreciation and operating taxes. Operating costs represent the largest percentage of a utility's total revenue requirement. Many of these costs are determined by normal competitive factors (wages, salaries, fuel, and maintenance) or by various levels of government (taxes). Others are determined by the individual firms (expenditures on advertising, research and development, and charitable contributions; purchases from affiliated subsidiaries) or by the regulatory commissions (annual depreciation rates). A public utility legally may spend any amount it chooses for such purposes, but a commission may not allow all expenditures made for ratemaking purposes. When an expenditure is disallowed it, in effect, is charged to a utility's stockholders rather than to its customers.[16]

Second, the net or depreciated value of the tangible and intangible property, or net investment in the property, of the enterprise must be determined. This net value or investment (V − D) is referred to as the *rate base*; the process of determining its value as "valuation." Referring again to legal phraseology, a public utility is entitled to the opportunity to earn a "fair rate of return" on this net value or investment; *i.e.,* on the rate base. The determination of the rate base has been the source of major controversies between public utilities and the commissions ever since the early days of regulation.

Tangible property represents the value of, or investment in, plant and equipment "used and useful" in providing a particular utility's services. Methods of arriving at the value of a company's property differ. In recent years, with an increasing price level, the utilities have argued in favor of reproduction cost valuations or the value of plant and equipment expressed in current dollars, while the commissions generally have favored original cost valuations or the cost of plant and equipment when purchased or built. Regardless of the measure used, accrued depreciation must be subtracted so as to reflect the depreciated cost or value of the property. Land is usually separated from other tangible property. It is commonly valued either at its original cost or at the value of adjacent property, although qualified appraisals are sometimes accepted by the commissions. No depreciation is subtracted since land tends to appreciate in value over time.

In addition to "used and useful" tangible property, the rate base includes an allowance for working capital and, depending on the circumstances, amounts for water rights and leaseholds. In former years, the utilities also argued that several intangibles — especially franchise value, going concern value, and good will — should be considered in ratemaking, but current commission practices exclude these items. Considerable controversy, however, surrounds the proper inclusion or exclusion of plant under construction; an item that is of major significance to expanding utilities. The issue: Should construction work in progress (CWIP) be included in the rate base and a current return earned or should it be excluded from the rate base and the allowance for funds used during construction (AFUDC) capitalized?

The foregoing discussion assumes that the rate base is determined from the left-hand or asset side of the balance sheet, which represents the depreciated original cost of assets "used and useful" in the enterprise as well as an allowance for working capital. The rate base also may be determined from the right-hand side of the balance sheet, which constitutes the capital employed in the business. This second method is known as the invested-capital or prudent-investment rate base, and was long advocated by Justice Brandeis. "The thing devoted by the investor to the public use," he argued in the *Southwestern Bell* case, "is not specific property, tangible and intangible, but capital embarked in the enterprise."[17] Regulatory statutes permit some commissions to use either method, while limiting other commissions to only one.

Third, a "fair rate of return" must be determined. This rate is usually expressed as a percentage of the depreciated value of a utility's property. Thus, a rate base of $250 million combined with a 12.00 percent fair rate of return will result in an annual allowance of $30 million as the fair return component of the firm's revenue requirement. (To this figure must be added the allowable operating expenses, depreciation, and taxes to determine the firm's rate level.)

Whatever rate of return is allowed, it should perform two functions. It should be fair to investors so as to avoid the confiscation of their property. It should also preserve the credit standing of the utility to enable it to attract new capital to maintain, improve, and expand its services in response to consumer demand. Public utilities must compete for investment funds in the capital market with nonregulated businesses. Moreover, they are not guaranteed a fair rate of return; they are entitled to a fair return only if it can be earned. As expressed by the Supreme Court:

> ... it may be safely generalized that the due process clause never has been held by this Court to require a commission to fix rates on the present reproduction value ... or on the historical valuation of property whose history and current financial statements showed the value no longer to exist. ... The due process clause has been applied to prevent governmental destruction of existing economic values. It has not and cannot be applied to insure values that have been lost by the operation of economic forces.[18]

The Rate Structure. The second aspect of rate regulation, the determination of a utility's rate structure, involves the establishment of rates (prices) to be charged consumers. The problem is complex. For many public utilities, nonallocable (common or joint) costs represent a significant percentage of total costs. All public utilities have various degrees of monopoly power in the market areas they serve and all have unused capacity some of the time. For these reasons, rate structures are differentiated: both supply (cost of service) and demand (value of service) considerations enter into their development. Utilities, for example, sell the same service to different classes of buyers with the classes largely determined by differences in demand elasticities. They do not charge each class the same rate. Often, differences in rates can be justified by differences in costs. Sometimes they cannot, and discrimination occurs.

In the absence of regulation, price discrimination may be favorable to the supplying companies and to some buyers but unfavorable to the vast majority of consumers. As has already been pointed out, there is a potential for a firm with monopoly power to charge more where demand is relatively inelastic and alternatives are lacking, and less where demand is relatively elastic and alternatives are available. Moreover, special prices or rebates may be given to those in the strongest bargaining position. Yet, under conditions of decreasing costs, price discrimination may be socially desirable. The seller who discriminates might well enjoy higher sales, lower costs, and larger profits, while the seller who is forbidden to discriminate might have smaller sales, higher costs, and smaller profits or even losses. Consumers, too, may benefit from discrimination: lower prices usually result in a greater demand for — and, hence, consumption of — the utility's services. For many years the commissions and the courts supervised the utilities' rate structures to prevent undue and unjust discrimination and to insure that the benefits of discrimination were realized.

In more recent years, increasing utility rates and competition have added a new dimension to the rate structure problem. Indeed, rate design has become the most important single issue in ratemaking (at least in terms of time devoted by all the parties in the typical commission proceeding). Economists, in particular, have contended that the traditional approach, based on average total or embedded cost, must be replaced with a marginal cost approach to insure economic efficiency and promote conservation; competition has forced such a reexamination, since rates are forced toward the cost of service as internal cross-subsidies among services are no longer tenable. But the adoption of marginal cost pricing involves numerous theoretical and practical problems, and the concept is even "feared" by some competitors and customers. And then there are those who contend that they are unable to afford utility services, regardless of how the prices for such services are determined.

The Phases of Rate Regulation

A former electric utility executive has pointed out that the history of public utility regulation consists of three major phases — legislative, judicial, and administrative.[19] The legislative phase began with the *Munn v. Illinois* decision in 1877,[20] when the Supreme Court upheld the right of the state of Illinois to regulate grain elevators under its police power. By implication, the constitutionality of other state laws regulating private firms also was established. The Court ruled, however, that the regulation of rates was a legislative function and that recourse against the abuse of that function must be at the polls and not from the courts. In 1890, the Court reversed its position, saying that the reasonableness of rates was subject to judicial review.[21] This decision marked the beginning of the judicial phase that was to last over four decades.

Throughout this period, the judiciary was to dominate regulatory policy. The *Smyth v. Ames* decision in 1898[22] listed a number of factors that the commissions should consider in determining the value of a company's property, but it did not assign a weight to each one. So started the valuation controversy concerning original cost versus reproduction cost, which was to occupy much of the commissions' and utilities' time for many years. The Court, especially after the first World War, emphasized reproduction cost, as did the utilities, while many commissions favored original cost. Then, in the *Bluefield* case of 1923,[23] the Supreme Court enumerated a number of factors the commissions should consider in determining the rate of return. Again, however, no weights were assigned to the various factors. In general, the Court found that a utility was entitled to a return "equal to that generally being made at the same time and in the same general part of the country on investments and in other business undertakings which are attended by corresponding risks and uncertainties."[24] The comparable earnings standard, which had been developed in earlier cases, was reaffirmed.

These two judicial decisions, in particular,

... put the regulatory commissions on the spot. The rule of *Smyth v. Ames* required that full consideration be given to the many economic factors pertinent to valuation. It limited regulation to those factors arising as a result of the elimination of competition, since valuation of property would be changed only as a result of changing economic conditions. The Bluefield case said that the fair rate of return for a utility should be gauged by that received in competitive industry of similar risk. Regulators were faced with the choice of either searching out the facts and reaching a decision in line with those facts, or having their decisions overruled by the courts.[25]

The *Hope Natural Gas* case of 1944[26] marks the beginning of the administrative phase, although the reasoning of this decision was foreshadowed in a number of earlier cases.[27] The Supreme Court held that the procedure and method of determining both the rate base and the rate of return should be left to the commissions.[28] Thus began the doctrine of the "end result." Only in cases of obvious injustice would the Court interfere with the rulings of the regulatory agencies.

According to Kahn: "The most important thing the Hope Natural Gas decision did was to invite regulatory commissions to break out of the mold into which they had been confined for forty-five years by *Smyth v. Ames* and start thinking about the economic requirements of effective public utility regulation."[29] In accepting this invitation, the commissions have been faced with the task of determining the criteria to be used in rate regulation. In establishing a reasonable or fair return, for instance, they have found "reasonableness" and "fairness" difficult terms to define. "The Supreme Court's concept of a reasonable return is really a notion of a zone of reasonableness. Confiscation of the property of a private company is the lower limit of the zone; exploitation of buyers, which is revealed by pricing practices and monopoly profits, is the upper limit. If the return is reasonable, it must fall between these limits."[30] Clearly, then, the required earnings of a utility cannot be represented by a specific sum, nor determined by a precise formula. Rather, they will vary with the economic conditions of both the company and the economy. And what appears to be reasonable to one person or at one time may seem unreasonable to another person or at another time.

Historically, far fewer cases involving questions of rate structure have been appealed to the courts. Most of these questions have been settled at the commission level. In many cases, commissions have been satisfied with the rate structures suggested by the utilities and have adopted them without significant change. Moreover, until the late 1960s, rates were declining, with the result that there was little consumer participation in the ratemaking process. In other cases, particularly at the federal level, rate structures different from those proposed by the utilities have been prescribed by the commissions. But as rates have moved upward sharply and as competition has increased in intensity, the commissions have become more involved in rate structure problems and in the development of proper pricing criteria and objectives.

The administrative phase of regulation, therefore, is relatively new. Freed from court domination, the federal and state commissions, acting within broad legislative provisions, have the responsibility for establishing their own criteria to determine both the rate level and the rate structure. And as long as the "end result" is just and reasonable, the courts (at least the Supreme Court) will not interfere. As will become readily apparent in the following chapters, there are few established or consistent criteria, so that regulatory practices vary considerably from commission to commission. Some, for example, use original cost valuations; others, reproduction cost valuations; still others, a combination of the two (known as "fair value"). For each problem raised, there are as many potential solutions as there are commissions and utilities. Whether any uniform criteria can or should be established and accepted by all interested parties is doubtful, for the present diversity, despite its complexity, permits experimentation. Such experimentation, in turn, helps to prevent rigidity in the entire regulatory process.

Theories of Regulation

Over the years, four major (and often overlapping) theories of regulation have been put forth to explain either the rationale for regulation or the behavior of regulatory agencies.[31] These theories are summarized below.

Public Interest Theory

The public interest theory of regulation — the oldest and one that is more often implied than articulated — holds that regulation is undertaken to protect the consumer from the abuses of market imperfections (or, more broadly, is established for "public interest-related objectives"[32]). Regulation thus is viewed as the law's substitute for competition, with its basic goal being to seek "economic" objectives. The theory, argues Posner, is based on two underlying assumptions: (1) "that economic markets are extremely fragile and apt to operate very inefficiently (or inequitably) if left alone" and (2) "that government regulation is virtually costless."[33] Given these assumptions,

> . . . it was very easy to argue that the principal government interventions in the economy — trade union protection, public utility and common carrier regulation, public power and reclamation programs, farm subsidies, occupational licensure, the minimum wage, even tariffs — were simply responses of government to public demands for the rectification of palpable and remedial inefficiencies and inequities in the operation of the free market. Behind each scheme of regulation could be discerned a market imperfection, the existence of which supplied a complete justification for some regulation assumed to operate effectively and without cost.[34]

But regulation is not costless (either in terms of money[35] or in terms of resource misallocation[36]); "social" objectives may be sought over "economic" objectives[37]; and commissions may find it difficult, if not impossible, to adopt policies that promote the public interest.[38] With respect to the latter, for example, inadequate appropriations and staffs, the lack of meaningful (consistent) policy standards, and the excessive judicialization of procedures are among the reasons often cited for the difficulty of promoting the public interest.[39] Nor, finally, is it obvious that any concept of market failure could justify regulation of such industries as natural gas production,[40] airlines,[41] or motor and water carriers.[42]

Capture Theories

The capture theories of regulation held either (*a*) that regulatory agencies were created to protect consumers, but that subsequently they became captives of the industries they regulate[43] or (*b*) that regulatory agencies were created to serve the interests of the industries they regulate, in response to the demands of the industries for cartel management placed upon the legislature.[44] Some interest groups (including the regulated firms) have sought regulation, but the capture theory fails to explain subsequent regulatory policies that may be against their interests.[45] The "life cycle" theory of regulation requires further analysis.

The Life Cycle Theory.[46] Some have described the evolution of a regulatory commission in terms of a biological metaphor.[47] The life of a commission, they say, can be divided into four periods: gestation, youth, maturity, and old age.[48]

The gestation phase includes the period during which legislation is enacted, providing for a regulatory commission. Since most legislative statutes calling for the regulation of an activity or industry have resulted from a publicly recognized problem, two decades or more may be required to produce such a statute, as illustrated by the political agitation preceding the creation of the ICC in 1887. During this gestation period, so the theory runs, the various contestants seek and oppose government regulation to eliminate the designated evil. As those favoring regulation are concerned more with receiving immediate relief than in developing a long-term philosophy, the net result is a legislative statute that often is lacking in clarity and provides few clear directives to the new commission. Indeed, the proponents of the theory contend that the long period of struggle may well produce a statute that is out-of-date at the time of its enactment.[49]

Once established, the new commission is apt to be aggressive and to act with vigor. Davis summarizes:

Characteristically, the great federal regulatory agencies in the early years of their existence have been fired with an inspiration to achieve the goals laid down for them by Congress. During those years the political pressures which have given birth to the agency are still felt, and the agency is acutely aware of its responsibility. Alertness is natural and necessary, for the agency is pioneering; new paths must constantly be broken. The newness of the tasks and the absence of familiar patterns force the agency and its staff to draw constantly upon their own resourcefulness. Young agencies are dominated by the qualities of youth — energy, ambition, imagination.[50]

The youth phase, according to this view, therefore involves a crusading commission. Since the legislative statute resulted from public agitation, the new agency has popular support and attracts a highly qualified staff. The issues are challenging and present ample opportunities for initiative and imagination. The FCC's telephone investigation in the late thirties, to illustrate, provided for many years the groundwork for the commission's regulation of that particular industry.

Gradually, in the cycle theory, a commission matures. Redford describes this phase as follows:

Later, there comes a period of maturity, when the agency has lost the original political support, when it has found its position among the contending forces in society, and when it has crystallized its own evolved program. It then becomes part of the status quo and thinks in terms of the protection of its own system and its own existence and power against substantial change. Its primary function in government is to operate the mechanisms which have been developed in its creative stage and adjust these as circumstances change. This is not to say that it may not still initiate constructive changes, for changes, and even leaps, in administrative program are sometimes made as conditions change, and agencies also may go to the Congress for new directive; but it is too much to expect that, after maturity is reached, government will find all the organization and perspective which it needs in its administrative institutions alone.[51]

During the maturity phase, say the cyclists, both public support and political leadership diminish. The agency tends to become identified with the industry it regulates. Its basic function shifts from one of protecting the public interest to one of protecting the economic health of the industry. "Precedent, rather than prospect, guides the commission. Its goals become routine and accepted."[52]

According to the cycle theory, inertia and a loss of vitality are symptoms of the final phase in a commission's life cycle, old age. The agency no longer enjoys public support or confidence and, cut off from political leadership, it tends to become even more closely allied with the interests of those it regulates. The agency becomes passive and seeks to maintain the status quo in the industry regulated. It tends to become outdated, failing to keep pace with changing technology and economic conditions. To quote Bernstein:

> In the phase of old age the regulatory objectives of a commission are no longer meaningful and appropriate. Not only are there growing doubts about the original objectives laid down vaguely in the enabling statute, but there is even greater doubt about what the objectives ought to be. In their declining days commissions can be described as retrogressive, lethargic, sluggish, and insensitive to their wider political and social setting. They are incapable of securing progressive revision of regulatory policies and fall further and further behind in their work.[53]

Those who support the cycle theory thus hold that a commission is systematically transformed from a vigorous protector of the public interest into an organization captured by the interests being regulated. They contend, further, that in its old age regulation becomes obsolete in that it fails to keep pace with the dynamic changes occurring throughout the economy. The ICC has been the traditional target of the cyclists.[54] Yet, the cycle theory leaves some unanswered questions. If industry-mindedness is a function of a commission's life cycle, why is it that many believed the CAB, a relatively young agency, to be as industry-oriented, if not more so, than the older ICC?[55] Is not industry-mindedness as closely related to a commission's personnel as to the agency's life cycle?[56] And Noll and Owen note that there are several factors which, in the long run, "militate against the full 'capture' of an agency," including (a) "the protection against it afforded by the constitutional design of the federal government," (b) "the continuing scrutiny of regulatory policy by scholars in economics, law, and political science," and (c) "the nature of government service." With respect to the third factor, they point out: "Regulators have no direct financial incentive to operate as efficient cartel managers."[57]

Interest Group Theories

Interest group theories of regulation focus on the formation of political coalitions to explain both the creation of regulation and the behavior of regulatory agencies.[58] With respect to the former, regulation is viewed as a good "sold" by the legislature in return for the votes of those who are benefited. "Much regulation," suggests Posner, "may be the product of coalitions between the regulated industry and customer groups, the former obtaining some monopoly profits from regulation, the latter obtaining lower prices (or better service) than they would in an unregulated market — all at the expense of unorganized, mostly consumer groups."[59] With respect to the latter, regulators are viewed as "arbitrators" between various "special interest groups in an effort to maximize support gained or lost at the margin."[60]

Interest group theories explain some aspects of traditional public utility regulation. Price discrimination, for example, has been permitted as a means of enhancing capacity utilization and expanding service. The latter occurs when excess earnings in some markets are used to provide uneconomic services, thus broadening "the base of participation in the coalition."[61] The theories also have some important implications for regulatory reform. Concludes Trebing:

> ... efforts to strengthen consumer representation will probably be counterproductive in improving the position of residential users. A growth in consumerism will simply mean more cross-subsidization, and this could ultimately translate into higher average prices for the monopolistic residential markets. The theory suggests that any efforts toward reform must involve major changes in regulatory objectives if they are to correct the propensity toward cross-subsidization and income redistribution.[62]

At the same time, the applicability of the interest group theories appears limited due to a number of shortcomings. As an explanation of regulation, the theories fail to enable a prediction as to what specific industries will be regulated. "That is because the theory does not tell us what (under various conditions) is the number of members of a coalition that maximizes the likelihood of regulation."[63] Moreover, where interest groups have the ability to impact the political process in their favor, society "might establish institutions that enable genuine public interest considerations to influence the formation of policy."[64] More broadly, "the theory provides little basis for judging the circumstances under which regulation enhances the general welfare of society. . . . In practice, the theory can say very little about the conditions which will promote the public interest because it describes a system which is inherently indeterminate."[65] As an explanation of regulatory behavior, the interest group theories fail to recognize the facts that commission actions may be limited by judicial review, that regulators may have little to gain by broadening their base of support or power,[66] and that "it may be virtually impossible to anticipate the priorities and values of a broad based constituency."[67]

Equity-Stability Theory

The equity-stability theory of regulation

> ... purports to explain the growth of regulation in terms of the desire of legislators to replace markets with administrative-judicial types of institutional arrangements which are better qualified to promote fairness, social values, and stability. According to this theory, public intervention occurs not because markets are inefficient, but rather be-

cause legislators seek to protect society from the unimpeded operation of market forces. In recognition of this legislative intent, commissions and other regulatory agencies place great emphasis on equity and fairness — to the point of rejecting efficiency-oriented solutions if these solutions impinge upon equity considerations. As a consequence, regulation tends to control the rate at which income is redistributed, while at the same time bringing about a degree of stability that would not prevail in the absence of market intervention. Of course, such stability is also conducive to maintaining the status quo and reducing the risk and uncertainty associated with change. . . .[68]

The equity-stability theory thus emphasizes social as opposed to economic goals (equity and fairness in place of economic efficiency) and stability as opposed to rapid change. It also explains some regulatory behavior: average, rolled-in, or embedded cost pricing, for one example; the development of cost allocation methods for overhead or fixed costs, for another. But the theory does not explain either the reorganization of particular agencies or the deregulation movement of the last few years, where the legislature concluded that efficiency would be improved. Nor does the theory offer any concrete guidance to regulators. Which group or groups, for instance, should be given preferential treatment? Equity and fairness are highly judgmental, and regulatory decisions based upon such concepts tend to result in distorted economic signals (prices) to consumers.[69]

The Four Theories: Their Significance

One can find several examples to support all four of the major theories of regulation. None, however, provides a general theory of commission regulation, for they lack predictive value. But their development, "spanning more than two decades, serves to indicate the growing importance of equity-related issues as an explanation of the motivation and objectives of regulatory agencies."[70] At the same time, as will become readily apparent in the following chapters, the debate continues over the relative weight to be given by regulatory agencies to equity and fairness considerations vis-a-vis efficiency solutions.

Commission Procedures[71]

Commissions, as previously discussed, have considerable authority to regulate the earnings and rates of many important industries in the economy. Much of their work originates in requests filed by public utilities and in complaints made by customers or competitors. A formal proceeding may be initiated by either a commission or a public utility. In the background of such a proceeding "is a network of state and federal constitutional provisions and principles, general and specific statutes governing procedures at the state and federal levels, the rules and regulations of the commission, prior opinions of the commission, and precedents and usages in other states."[72]

There are two types of proceedings: "rule-making" and "adjudicatory." Rule-making proceedings are usually legislative in effect and are initiated for the purpose of establishing procedures, policies, and practices (*e.g.*, rules of practice and procedure for persons and entities doing business with the commission, uniform systems of accounts, allowed depreciation rates, and safety standards) or to investigate a specific issue (*e.g.*, proper pricing principles, advertising practices, and conservation programs[73]). Rule making generally is applicable to a large group of affected parties and is always looking to the future. Adjudication is initiated for the purpose of settling a contested issue and generally relates to an action which took place in the past. In contrast to rule making, adjudication always involves specifically named persons or entities.

Rule-making and adjudicatory proceedings may be either formal ("on the record") or informal ("off the record").[74] Contested issues are dealt with by formal methods; customer complaints generally are handled by informal methods. A rule-making proceeding may or may not require a formal hearing, depending upon the applicable statutory requirement. In recent years, with workloads increasing rapidly, there have been several attempts made to shorten formal proceedings.

Rule-making Procedures[75]

If the relevant statute requires a formal hearing in a rule-making proceeding, such a proceeding, while legislative in nature, becomes a hybrid and approximates the adjudicatory hearing. In general, rule-making proceedings follow the provisions of the Federal Administrative Procedure Act, which provides:

Sec. 553. *Rule Making*

(a) This section applies, according to the provisions thereof, except to the extent that there is involved —

(1) a military or foreign affairs function of the United States; or

(2) a matter relating to agency management or personnel or to public property, loans, grants, benefits, or contracts.

(b) General notice of proposed rule making shall be published in the *Federal Register,* unless persons subject thereto are named and either personally served or otherwise have actual notice thereof in accordance with law. The notice shall include —

(1) a statement of the time, place, and nature of public rule-making proceedings;

(2) reference to the legal authority under which the rule is proposed; and

(3) either the terms or substance of the proposed rule or a description of the subjects and issues involved.

Except when notice or hearing is required by statute, this subsection does not apply —

(A) to interpretative rules, general statements of policy, or rules of agency organization, procedure, or practice; or

(B) when the agency for good cause finds (and incorporates the finding and a brief statement of reasons thereof in the rules issued) that notice and public procedure thereon are impracticable, unnecessary, or contrary to the public interest.

(c) After notice required by this section, the agency shall give interested persons an opportunity to participate in the rule making through submission of written data, views, or arguments with or without opportunity for oral presentation. After consideration of the relevant matter presented, the agency shall incorporate in the rules adopted a concise general statement of their basis and purpose. When rules are required by statute to be made on the record after opportunity for an agency hearing, Sections 556 and 557 of this title apply instead of this subsection.

(d) The required publication or service of a substantive rule shall be made not less than 30 days before its effective date, except —

(1) a substantive rule which grants or recognizes an exemption or relieves a restriction;

(2) interpretative rules and statements of policy; or

(3) as other wise provided by the agency for good cause found and published with the rule.

(e) Each agency shall give an interested person the right to petition for the issuance, amendment, or repeal of a rule.

Rule-making proceedings, particularly where a formal hearing is not required, may be relatively brief. Further, many commissions "have a 'constituency' — the groups for whose particular benefit they operate and the groups whose conduct they regulate. These more often than not are organized. Their organizations are consulted and informed during all stages of the rule making."[76] As already noted, rule-making proceedings have been widely used for such purposes as establishing uniform systems of accounts and safety regulations. But there has been a trend toward using such proceedings for other purposes. Two examples are illustrative.

Natural Gas Prices. In 1974, the Federal Power Commission established a single uniform national base rate for the wellhead price of "new" natural gas in a rule-making proceeding.[77] In its April 11, 1973, notice of proposed rule-making, the commission "made all large producers respondents to the rule-making proceeding, provided for the submission of written comments (submitted under oath) from all interested parties and the named respondents, and was accompanied by a staff study on the estimated nationwide cost of finding and producing new nonassociated natural gas supplies."[78] The rate order was subsequently affirmed,[79] as was another national rate order, issued in 1976.[80]

Rate of Return Determination. Since 1978, the Interstate Commerce Commission has set a single overall rate of return for the railroad industry, using a rule-making approach.[81] The industrywide rate of return is updated each year. The procedure is as follows:

> ... All class 1 railroads are automatically made parties to the proceeding and other interested parties may participate if they wish. Notice of the proceeding is given by April 30 of each year, and the railroads, individually or collectively, are required to file cost of capital evidence by June 30. Reply comments are permitted, including cost of capital evidence, and the railroads are given an opportunity to file rebuttal statements. The ICC regulations indicate the type of data required to be filed as evidence (*e.g.*, debt costs, percent of capital financed with debt), but the regulations do not prescribe any particular technique for estimating the cost of capital. The parties are permitted to demonstrate the cost of capital in ways deemed most suitable under conditions prevailing at the time of a particular proceeding.
>
> By October 30, the ICC issues its decision setting the industywide cost of capital. The single cost of capital figure ... may be used by railroads in their rate filings, or the ICC can authorize departure from use of this rate of return for individual railroads if warranted by special circumstances. Railroads are not allowed to use some portion of the rate of return, like the equity rate of return, and apply that to their individual capital structure. If departure from the generically derived rate of return is permitted, the railroads must use individual company data for all of the components of the overall rate of return. To date, no requests for waiver of the regulation have been made.[82]

Adjudicatory Hearings

Formal adjudicatory hearings are generally held to settle contested issues of fact based on the evidence produced at the hearing (*i.e.*, based "on the record"). The adjudicatory provisions of the Federal Administrative Procedure Act provide:

Sec. 554. *Adjudications*

(a) This section applies, according to the provisions thereof, in every case of adjudication required by statute to be determined on the record after opportunity for an agency hearing, except to the extent that there is involved —

(1) a matter subject to a subsequent trial of the law and the facts de novo in a court;

(2) the selection or tenure of an employee, except an administrative law judge appointed under Section 3105 of this title;

(3) proceedings in which decisions rest solely on inspections, tests, or elections;

(4) the conduct of military or foreign affairs functions;

(5) cases in which an agency is acting as an agent for a court; or

(6) the certification of worker representatives.

(b) Persons entitled to notice of any agency hearing shall be timely informed of —

(1) the time, place, and nature of the hearing.

(2) the legal authority and jurisdiction under which the hearing is to be held; and

(3) the matters of fact and law asserted.

When private persons are the moving parties, other parties to the proceeding shall give prompt notice of issues controverted in fact or law; and in other instances agencies may by rule require responsive pleading. In fixing the time and place for hearings, due regard shall be had for the convenience and necessity of the parties or their representatives.

(c) The agency shall give all interested parties opportunity for —

(1) the submission and consideration of facts, arguments, offers of settlement, or proposals of adjustment when time, the nature of the proceeding, and the public interest permit; and

(2) to the extent that the parties are unable so to determine a controversy by consent, hearing and decision on notice and in accordance with Sections 556 and 557 of this title.

(d) The employee who presides at the reception of evidence pursuant to Section 556 of this title shall make the recommended decision or initial decision required by Section 557 of this title, unless he becomes unavailable to the agency. Except to the extent required for the disposition of ex parte matters as authorized by law, such an employee may not —

(1) consult a person or party on a fact in issue, unless on notice and opportunity for all parties to participate; or

(2) be responsible to or subject to the supervision or direction of an employee or agent engaged in the performance of investigative or prosecuting functions for an agency.

An employee or agent engaged in the performance of investigative or prosecuting functions for an agency in a case may not, in that or a factually related case, participate or advise in the decision, recommended decision, or agency review pursuant to Section 557 of this title, except as witness or counsel in public proceedings. This subsection does not apply —

(A) in determining applications for initial licenses;

(B) to proceedings involving the validity or application of rates, facilities, or practices of public utilities or carriers; or

(C) to the agency or a member or members of the body comprising the agency.

(e) The agency, with like effect as in the case of other orders, and in its sound discretion, may issue a declaratory order to terminate a controversy or remove uncertainty.

***

Sec. 556. *Hearings; Presiding Employees; Powers and Duties; Burden of Proof; Evidence; Record as Basis of Decision*

(a) This section applies, according to the provisions thereof, to hearings required by Section 553 or 554 of this title to be conducted in accordance with this section.

(b) There shall preside at the taking of evidence —

(1) the agency;

(2) one or more members of the body which comprise the agency; or

(3) one or more administrative law judges appointed under Section 3105 of this title.

This subchapter does not supersede the conduct of specified classes of proceedings, in whole or in part, by or before boards or other employees specially provided for by or designated under statute. The functions of presiding employees and of employees participating in decisions in accordance with Section 557 of this title shall be conducted in an impartial manner. A presiding or participating employee may at any time disqualify himself. On the filing in good faith of a timely and sufficient affidavit of personal bias or other disqualification of a presiding or participating employee, the agency shall determine the matter as a part of the record and decision in the case.

(c) Subject to published rules of the agency and within its powers, employees presiding at hearings may —

(1) administer oaths and affirmations;

(2) issue subpoenas authorized by law;

(3) rule on offers of proof and receive relevant evidence;

(4) take depositions or have depositions taken when the ends of justice would be served;

(5) regulate the course of the hearing;

(6) hold conferences for the settlement or simplification of the issues by consent of the parties;

(7) dispose of procedural requests or similar matters;

(8) make or recommend decisions in accordance with Section 557 of this title; and

(9) take other action authorized by agency rule consistent with this subchapter.

(d) Except as otherwise provided by statute, the proponent of a rule or order has the burden of proof. Any oral or documentary evidence may be received, but the agency as a matter of policy shall provide for the exclusion of irrelevant, immaterial, or unduly repetitious evidence. A sanction may not be imposed or rule or order issued except on consideration of the whole record or those parts thereof cited by a party and supported by and in accordance with the reliable, probative, and substantial evidence. The agency may, to the extent consistent with the interests of justice and the policy of the underlying statutes administered by the agency, consider a violation of Section 557 (d) of this title sufficient grounds for a decision adverse to a party who has knowingly committed such violation or knowingly caused such violation to occur. A party is entitled to present his case or defense by oral or documentary evidence, to submit rebuttal evidence, and to conduct such cross-examination as may be required for a full and true disclosure of the facts. In rule making or determining claims for money or benefits or applications for initial licenses an agency may, when a party will not be prejudiced thereby, adopt procedures for the submission of all or part of the evidence in written form.

(e) The transcript of testimony and exhibits, together with all papers and requests filed in the proceeding, constitutes the exclusive record for decision in accordance with Section 557 of this title and, on payment of lawfully prescribed costs, shall be made available to the parties. When an agency decision rests on official notice of a material fact not appearing in the evidence in the record, a party is entitled, on timely request, to an opportunity to show the contrary.

Sec. 557. *Initial Decisions; Conclusiveness; Review by Agency; Submissions by Parties; Contents of Decisions; Record*

(a) This section applies, according to the provisions thereof, when a hearing is required to be conducted in accordance with Section 556 of this title.

(b) When the agency did not preside at the reception of the evidence, the presiding employee or, in cases not subject to Section 554 (d) of this title, an employee qualified to preside at hearings pursuant to Section 556 of this title, shall initially decide the case unless the agency requires, either in specific cases or by general rule, the entire record to be certified to it for decision. When the presiding employee makes an initial decision, that decision then becomes the decision of the agency without further proceedings unless there is an appeal to, or review on motion of, the agency within time provided by rule. On appeal from or review of the initial decision, the agency has all the powers which it would have in making the initial decision except as it may limit the issues on notice or by rule. When the agency makes the decision without having presided at the reception of the evidence, the presiding employee or an employee qualified to preside at hearings pursuant to Section 556 of this title shall first recommend a decision, except that in rule making or determining applications for initial licenses —

(1) instead thereof the agency may issue a tentative decision or one of its responsible employees may recommend a decision; or

(2) this procedure may be omitted in a case in which the agency finds on the record that due and timely execution of its functions imperatively and unavoidably so requires.

(c) Before a recommended, initial, or tentative decision, or a decision on agency review of the decision of subordinate employees, the parties are entitled to a reasonable opportunity to submit for the consideration of the employees participating in the decisions —

(1) proposed findings and conclusions; or

(2) exceptions to the decisions or recommended decisions of subordinate employees or to tentative agency decisions; and

(3) supporting reasons for the exceptions or proposed findings or conclusions.

The record shall show the ruling on each finding, conclusion, or exception presented. All decisions, including initial, recommended, and tentative decisions, are a part of the record and shall include a statement of —

(A) findings and conclusions, and the reasons or basis thereof, on all the material issues in fact, law, or discretion presented on the record; and

(B) the appropriate rule, order, sanction, relief, or denial thereof.

(d)(1) In any agency proceeding which is subject to subsection (a) of this Section, except to the extent required for the disposition of ex parte matters as authorized by law —

(A) no interested person outside the agency shall make or knowingly cause to be made to any member of the body comprising the agency, administrative law judge, or other employee who is or may reasonably be expected to be involved in the decisional process of the proceeding, an ex parte communication relevant to the merits of the proceeding;

(B) no member of the body comprising the agency, administrative law judge, or other employee who is or may reasonably be expected to be involved in the decisional process of the proceeding, shall make or knowingly cause to be made to any interested person outside the agency an ex parte communication relevant to the merits of the proceeding;

(C) a member of the body comprising the agency, administrative law judge, or other employee who is or may reasonably be expected to be involved in the decisional process of such proceeding who receives, or who makes or knowingly causes to be made, a communication prohibited by this subsection shall place on the public record of the proceeding:

(i) all such written communications;

(ii) memoranda stating the substance of all such oral communications; and

(iii) all written responses, and memoranda stating the substance of all oral responses, to the materials described in clauses (i) and (ii) of this subparagraph;

(D) upon receipt of a communication knowingly made or knowingly caused to be made by a party in violation of this subsection, the agency, administrative law judge, or other employee presiding at the hearing may, to the extent consistent with the interests of justice and the policy of the underlying statutes, require the party to show cause why his claim or interest in the proceeding should not be dismissed, denied, disregarded, or otherwise diversely affected on account of such violation; and

(E) the prohibitions of this subsection shall apply beginning at such time as the agency may designate, but in no case shall they begin to apply later than that time at which a proceeding is noticed for hearing unless the person responsible for the communication has knowledge that it will be noticed, in which case the prohibitions shall apply beginning at the time of his acquisition of such knowledge.

(2) This subsection does not constitute authority to withhold information from Congress.

Formal hearings — whether rule making on the record or adjudication — normally follow these procedures and take time, work, and money. Assume, for example, that Utility X files for a rate increase. The commission will generally suspend the proposed rate increase for a period of time.[83] The company, with the concurrence of the commission or its staff, will generally select a "test year," frequently the latest 12-month period for which complete data are available. The purposes of such a test year are as follows. In the first place, the commission's staff must audit the utility's books. For ratemaking purposes, only just and reasonable expenses are allowed; only used and useful property (with certain exceptions) is permitted in the rate base. In the second place, the commission must have a basis for estimating future revenue requirements. This estimate is one of the most difficult problems in a rate case. A commission is setting rates for the future, but it has only past experience (expenses, revenues, demand conditions) to use as a guide. *"Philosophically, the strict test year assumes the past relationship among revenues, costs, and net investment during the test year will continue into the future."*[84] To the extent that these relationships are not constant, the actual rate of return earned by a utility may be quite different from the rate allowed by the commission.[85] For many years, commissions have adjusted test-year data for "known changes"; *i.e.,* a change that actually took place during or after the test period (such as a new wage agreement that occurred toward the end of the year). More recently, due largely to inflation, a few commissions have modified the traditional historic test-year approach by using a forward-looking test year (either a partial or a full forecast)[86] or by permitting pro forma expense and revenue adjustments.

The case will be set down on the commission's docket for future public hearings, and due notice will be given to the utility's customers.[87] Before the case is called, the utility, the commission's staff, and intervenors (interested parties)[88] will file their testimony (prefiled "canned" testimony). Such testimony usually is presented by outside experts, as well as by both company and staff personnel. Any of the parties in the case may make data requests to the others.[89] When the case is called, the hearing is conducted by an administrative law judge,[90] a panel (one or more) of the commissioners, or the full commission. All witnesses are sworn, the evidence is recorded (transcribed), and witnesses may be questioned by the administrative law judge or commissioners and cross-examined by counsel for the staff and other parties. In some instances, hearings will be held in the community or communities affected. Individual consumers, even though not represented by counsel, are permitted to testify and, in a few states, to cross-examine witnesses.[91]

After all evidence has been received, the record is closed. Briefs may be filed by the various parties. When an administrative law judge presides, an "initial" or "recommended" decision is subsequently issued by the judge.[92] The decision must be written and accompanied by formal findings of fact and conclusions of law. It is then subject to review by the full commission[93] (usually through the filing of briefs that take exception to part or all of the initial decision,[94] but sometimes in an oral presentation). Once the commission has issued its decision and order, petitions may be filed for reconsideration and rehearing.[95] The final commission order, in turn, may be appealed to the courts.

It is not uncommon for important cases to require many days or weeks of hearings and to take a year or more (from date of filing to date of a commission order).[96] When an order is appealed to the courts, another two to four years may be added, particularly when the reviewing court remands the case to the commission.[97] As a result, formal proceedings often involve delay to the disadvantage of many of the parties involved.[98]

Shortened Procedures.[99] In an attempt to save both time and expense, shortened procedures have been developed. One of the most important and widely used is the prehearing conference, generally called by and held before the presiding administrative law judge. The Rules of Practice of the former Civil Aeronautics Board are typical:

> The purpose of such a conference is to define and simplify the issues and the scope of the proceeding, to secure statements of the positions of the parties, . . . to schedule the exchange of exhibits before the date set for hearing, and to arrive at such agreements as will aid in the conduct and disposition of the proceeding. For example, consideration will be given to: (*1*) matters which the Board can consider without the necessity of proof; (*2*) admissions of fact and the genuineness of documents; (*3*) admissibility of evidence; (*4*) limitation of the number of witnesses; (*5*) reducing of oral testimony to exhibit form; (*6*) procedure at the hearings, etc. . . .[100]

Following the prehearing conference, the administrative law judge "shall issue a report of the prehearing conference, defining the issues, giving an account of the results of the conference, specifying a schedule for the exchange of exhibits and rebuttal exhibits, the date of hearings, and specifying a time for the filing of objections to such report."[101] The report is sent to all parties in the proceeding and, based upon their objections, may be revised by the administrative law judge. The final report "shall constitute the official account of the conference and shall control the subsequent course of the proceeding, but it may be reconsidered and modified at any time to protect the public interest or to prevent injustice."[102] Finally, the presiding administrative law judge has the right to "hold conferences, before or during the hearings, for the settlement or simplification of issues."[103]

The regulatory agencies have adopted other informal methods as well to shorten formal proceedings. The Interstate Commerce Commission, for instance, used a "modified procedure." As explained by Woll:

> The Rules of Practice of the ICC provide that if modified procedure is to be used, either by order of the Commission or by desire of the parties, statements of fact with regard to a particular case, together with exhibits, are to be filed in writing by the defendant, followed by the rebuttal of the complaint. Further, "if cross-examination of any witness is desired the name of the witness and the subject matter of

the desired cross-examination shall, together with any other request for oral hearings, including the basis thereof, be stated. . ." And, "the order setting the proceeding for oral hearing, if hearing is deemed necessary, will specify the matters upon which the parties are not in agreement and respecting which oral evidence is to be introduced." In this manner, under modified procedure, the ICC has adopted a selective formal procedure with regard to witnesses and evidence.[104]

The purposes of prehearing conferences and other informal methods are to simplify and clarify the issues in the case at hand and to dispose of minor issues prior to the initiation of formal proceedings. "The facts with respect to a particular case can be developed either independently by the agency or through the introduction of various forms of exhibits and stipulations of fact."[105] In both theory and practice, shortened procedures result in speedier regulatory decisions.

Informal Procedures

Informal procedures are frequently used to deal with customer complaints.[106] Any customer may present a complaint directly to a regulatory commission. After an investigation, if the complaint has merit, a solution satisfactory to all concerned is usually arrived at without undue delay. But, absent a settlement, formal adjudication is required. Customer complaints commonly concern such matters as service interruptions, inaccurate metering, disputes over bills, poor voltage, and other similar grievances. Moreover, some commissions adopt informal procedures even when such issues as rates and rate of return are under consideration, as the following two examples illustrate.

The FCC and Constant Surveillance.[107] In 1938, the Federal Communications Commission explained the need for constant or continuing surveillance of the telephone industry:

> Many of the problems of interstate telephone rate regulation are continuing in nature, calling at all times for frank, informal discussion between company and commission representatives. The atmosphere of the council table seems ordinarily much more conducive to the development of positive results in such matters than does the adversary air which tends to surround most formal proceedings. The aspect of a game or contest which inevitably envelopes the respective advocates (be they lawyers, accountants, engineers, or what not) in formal cases makes for bickering and bitterness, as well as for delay and expense.
>
> If the essential factors can be soundly defined and weighted, and if their factual background can be fully and frankly developed, the positive and direct methods of informal negotiation should prove effective,

and desired ends should be attainable with a minimum expenditure of time, money and effort. Only through some such concept of regulatory functions can an end apparently be brought to the sorry spectacle of "ten year rate cases." *In rate making, time is always of the essence,* and certain of the state commissions are today making notable progress in the development of informal regulatory machinery.[108]

To implement this policy,[109] the FCC and the Bell System developed routines for submitting regular reports (about 300 yearly) on a monthly, quarterly, and semiannual basis. Special reports were submitted when needed. At all times, therefore, the commission had at its disposal "a veritable fluoroscope of Bell telephone system operating performance."[110] Informal proceedings were usually initiated by the FCC's Common Carrier Bureau. "The agenda for those conferences is decided and prepared, and in the final stages the full commission may sit to hear the informal and uninhibited discussion by company spokesmen and experts called in to explain the company's position under various topics on the agenda."[111] The commission also inspected and audited Bell System operations throughout the country through its field offices.

Between the investigation ordered by Congress in 1935 and the full-scale investigation initiated late in 1965, the FCC did not hold a formal hearing on the entire interstate telephone rate structure. (The commission did hold many formal hearings on specific issues and rates.) But the FCC was not lax in regulating such rates. Some fifty negotiated interstate telephone rate changes during this period resulted in a net savings to the public of over $1.5 billion annually, based on 1967 volumes of business. Interstate rates decreased by 24 percent between 1940 and 1967. There were similar reductions in interstate revenue requirements, totaling more than $350 million annually, based on 1967 volumes of business, due to changes in separations procedures.[112]

The FERC and Settlement Proceedings. The Federal Energy Regulatory Commission (and the former Federal Power Commission) generally resolve electric and gas wholesale rate applications by settlement. (In fiscal year 1980, forty-seven of the fifty-four electric cases concluded were resolved by settlement.[113]) A case is initiated when the commission issues notice of the filing and invites public comment. Then, after a review of both the filing and any public comments,

> . . . the FERC's advisory staff recommends to the Commission, for action by it within 60 days of the filing date, one of three options: that the filing be accepted without suspension; that it be rejected in whole or in part; or that it be suspended and set for hearing. . . .
>
> If a filing is suspended, the suspension order sets a date, usually 90 to 120 days after the order is issued, for trial staff to complete and file its analysis of the rate request.

The project of trial staff's analysis is referred to in the jargon of the trade as "top sheets." Both the cost-of-service analyst and the rate of return analyst provide input. The cost-of-service analyst checks the company's figures for each account and makes recommendations about allocation of demand, energy and other classes, and assignments to specific categories. The rate of return analyst, after a further review of the company's financial position, makes an overall rate of return recommendation. . . .

The cost of service analysis and rate of return analysis yield staff recommended revenue requirements; *i.e.,* those revenues a company would have to collect to cover costs, including return on equity. The calculation of the revenue requirement is completed by a computer model, based on each analyst's input, and is compared with the company's requested revenues on the top sheets.

Within 10 days of circulation of the top sheets to all parties, a settlement conference among the staff and al parties is convened. The focus of settlement negotiations is generally upon the total dollar amount of revenue requested by the company in comparison to the revenue that the staff analysis indicates is justified. Sometimes intervenors in a proceeding will have estimated a lesser dollar amount of increased revenues and may bargain for this amount. . . .

. . . it is during the settlement proceedings that the three major paths for suspended filings diverge. The settlement negotiations may produce a total package to which all participants agree. Or it may result in what is referred to as a contested settlement. Finally, negotiations may fail and the proceeding will go to a formal on-the-record hearing before an administrative law judge. . . .

A case frequently is resolved by settling some issues and reserving others for adjudication, thus following two of the paths.[114]

Some Observations. The advantages of informal procedures are three-fold. First, time and money are saved. Decisions which might take several months to reach in formal hearings can often be made in several days of concentrated conferences or negotiations.[115] Thus, the average (median) processing time for electric rate filings completed by the FERC in fiscal year 1980 was fifty months for litigated cases, thirty-seven months for contested settlements, and fourteen months for uncontested settlements.[116] Second, an informal atmosphere is usually more conducive to mutual understanding and respect than is a formal, courtroom-type proceeding.[117] Third, the data considered are generally more current than found in a formal proceeding. Decisions, therefore, are likely to be more up-to-date and more responsive to the current situation.

At the same time, there are two potential disadvantages of informal procedures. Such procedures are sometimes cited by potential intervenors as a denial of due process. While interested parties may participate in the FERC's settlement proceedings, they could not in the FCC's constant surveillance proceedings.[118] Further, since any data used are not subject to detailed cross-examination, reliability may be a problem.[119] It seems clear that safeguards can be developed to overcome these potential problems, while preserving the advantages of informal procedures.

Summary

As the American economy has developed, the regulatory process has become extremely complex. "Technological and economic change have revolutionized traditional relationships, and eroded conventional conceptions of market structure, conduct, and performance. And the future promises more of the same."[120] Modern technology has tended to blur the common distinction between public utilities and nonregulated industries. One result is a growing tendency to treat public utilities "as only one part of the economy, rather than as isolated entities."[121] Significant competition, particularly in the telecommunications industry, has developed. "Behavior which might be reasonable given a market structure approximating a natural monopoly may be fraught with disaster once that structure is exposed to potential erosion by competitive product or process innovations."[122]

To cope with these complexities (a) new procedures have been, and are being, developed and (b) deregulation of some industries or services has been, and is being, undertaken. Increasingly is emphasis being placed on informal procedures as opposed to formal procedures, where strictures of law permit. Despite criticism, informal procedures have been adopted in an attempt to reduce regulatory lag and to cope with rapid technological change. Deregulation is taking place in natural gas production and in the supplying of some telecommunications services; it has already taken place in the transportation industry. At the same time, much research has been devoted to analyzing the economic effects of regulation and to considering regulatory goals.

Consider, for example, criticisms of current regulation. There are three distinct conceptions of the central problem confronting modern regulation.[123] The first conception of regulatory failure is economic. Regulation has failed to pursue economic efficiency as the appropriate objective. Instead, regulators appear to be primarily concerned with questions of fairness and justice, and with the welfare of the industries they regulate. The second conception of regulatory failure is political. Regulation has failed to be responsive to the "whole spectrum of legitimate interest group pressures."[124] The third conception of regulatory failure is administrative. Regulation has failed because of "the delays and costs inherent in case-by-case decision making."[125] Each conception calls for different prescriptions. But of greater importance is the multiplicity of goals and their inherent conflicts. Schmalensee contends that "economic efficiency should be the only objective of government control of natural monopoly industries. . . ."[126] Flax argues that "economic theory cannot and must not control despite its promises of multiple benefits such as conservation, equity, economic efficiency, and optimal resource allocation."[127]

One final point: In considering the problems of regulation, it should be emphasized that they are policy problems. As explained by Lewis:

> . . . They are not problems of right and wrong, for which there is only one right solution as distinct from all other solutions — which are, perforce, wrong. The "principles" of public-utility regulation are not "scientific principles" or "natural laws." Essentially, regulation has an identifiable job to do, and its organization and operation should be established and determined functionally in the light of that job; it is a matter of defining a goal and proceeding economically to achieve it. Regulation involves the human adjustment of resources to accomplish humanly established ends. Regulation is limited and guided both by what we want and by what we are willing to give in order to get what we want. To say that there are no immutable laws of regulation is not to say that regulation is, by nature, amorphous, loose, aimless, adrift. It can be just as purposeful and tight and firm as we care to make it. The point is that regulation and regulatory policies must be *made;* they are not revealed to us, nor do we discover them.[128]

Notes

*Ralph M. Besse, "Seventy-five Years of Public Utility Regulation in a Competitive Society" (Speech before the American Bar Association's Annual Meeting, Boston, August 25, 1953) (mimeographed), p. 4.

[1]J.M. Clark, *Social Control of Business* (2d ed.; New York: McGraw-Hill Book Co., Inc., 1939), p. 337.

[2]*Ibid.*

[3]Ben W. Lewis, "Emphasis and Misemphasis in Regulatory Policy," in William G. Shepherd and Thomas G. Gies (eds.), *Utility Regulation: New Directions in Theory and Policy* (New York: Random House, 1966), p. 219.

[4]James C. Bonbright, *Principles of Public Utility Rates* (New York: Columbia University Press, 1961) p. 110. On social objectives see *ibid.,* chap. vii; Horace Gray, "The Passing of the Public Utility Concept," 16 *Journal of Land & Public Utility Economics* 8 (1940).

[5]See Shepherd and Gies, *op. cit.;* Harry M. Trebing (ed.), *Performance Under Regulation* (East Lansing: MSU Public Utilities Studies, 1968).

[6]Harvey Averch and Leland L. Johnson, "Behavior of the Firm under Regulatory Constraint," 52 *American Economic Review* 1052 (1962); Stanislaw H. Wellisz, "Regulation of Natural Gas Pipeline Companies: An Economic Analysis," 71 *Journal of Political Economy* 30 (1963). This thesis is discussed in Chapter 17.

[7]Lee Loevinger, "Regulation and Competition as Alternatives," 11 *The Antitrust Bulletin* 101, 125 (1966).

[8]"Society may, of course, quite appropriately seek other than 'competitive' ends.

But it should not depart from a program of harmonizing the processes and policies of public utility regulation with a larger competitive economy, without conscious purpose, and without seeking to ascertain the extent and implications of its departure." Ben W. Lewis, "Public Utilities," in L.S. Lyon and V. Abramson, *Government and Economic Life* (Washington, D.C.: The Brookings Institution, 1940), Vol. II, pp. 625-26.

[9]*Ibid.*, p. 625.

[10]R.G. Lipsey and Kelvin Lancaster, "The General Theory of Second Best," 24 *Review of Economic Studies* 11 (1956).

[11]Richard Schmalensee, *The Control of Natural Monopolies* (Lexington, Mass.: D.C. Heath & Co., 1979), p. 30.

[12]Clair Wilcox, *Public Policies Toward Business* (3d ed.; Homewood, Ill.: Richard D. Irwin, Inc., 1966), p. 477.

[13]Marver H. Bernstein, in *Airlines* (Report of the Antitrust Subcommittee of the Committee on the Judiciary, House, 85th Cong., 1st sess.)(Washington, D.C.: U.S. Government Printing Office, 1957), p. 4.

[14]E.V. Rostow, *Planning for Freedom* (New Haven: Yale University Press, 1959), pp. 311-12.

[15]*Federal Power Comm. v. Natural Gas Pipeline Co.*, 315 U.S. 575, 584 (1942).

[16]In regulatory terminology, expenditures allowed for ratemaking purposes are charged "above-the-line"; expenditures disallowed in determining net operating income are charged "below-the-line."

[17]Concurring opinion in *Missouri ex rel. Southwestern Bell Teleph. Co. v. Missouri Pub. Service Comm.*, 262 U.S. 276, 290 (1923).

[18]*Market Street Ry. Co. v. California Railroad Comm.*, 324 U.S. 548, 567 (1945).

[19]Besse, *op. cit.* See also William H. Anderson, "The Supreme Court and Recent Public Utility Valuation Theory," 21 *Journal of Land & Public Utility Economics* 12 (1945).

[20]94 U.S. 113 (1877).

[21]*Chicago, Milwaukee & St. Paul Ry. Co. v. Minnesota*, 134 U.S. 418 (1890).

[22]169 U.S. 466 (1898).

[23]*Bluefield Water Works & Imp. Co. v. Pub. Service Comm. of West Virginia*, 262 U.S. 679 (1923).

[24]*Ibid.*, p. 692.

[25]Besse, *op. cit.*, p. 8.

[26]*Federal Power Comm. v. Hope Natural Gas Co.*, 320 U.S. 591 (1944).

[27]*McCardle v. Indianapolis Water Co.*, 272 U.S. 400 (1926); *Los Angeles Gas & Elec. Corp. v. Railroad Comm. of California*, 289 U.S. 287 (1933); *Federal Power Comm. v. Natural Gas Pipeline Co.*, *op. cit.*

[28]The *Hope Natural Gas* decision applies only to the federal commissions and to appeals from state courts. State regulatory commissions are still bound by their own constitutional or statutory requirements.

[29]Alfred E. Kahn, "Inducements to Superior Performance: Price," in Trebing, *op. cit.*, p. 88 (citations omitted).

[30]Emery Troxel, *Economics of Public Utilities* (New York: Holt, Rinehart & Winston, Inc., 1947), p. 224.

[31]For a more complete discussion, upon which this section draws heavily, see Barry M. Mitnick, *The Political Economy of Regulation: Creating, Designing, and Removing Regulatory Forms* (New York: Columbia University Press, 1980), chap. III.

[32]*Ibid.*, p. 91. See *Munn v. Illinois, op. cit.;* Frederick F. Blachly and Miriam E. Oatman, *Federal Regulatory Action and Control* (Washington, D.C.: The Brookings Institution, 1940); Robert E. Cushman, *The Independent Regulatory Commissions* (New York: Oxford University Press, 1941; reprinted, Octagon Books, 1972); Bonbright, *op. cit.;* Kenneth C. Davis, *Administrative Law Treatise* (2d ed.; San Diego: K.C. Davis, 1978 and 1980 Supplements).

[33]Richard A. Posner, "Theories of Economic Regulation," 5 *Bell Journal of Economics & Management Science* 335, 336 (1974).

[34]*Ibid.*

[35]See Paul W. MacAvoy, *The Regulated Industries and the Economy* (New York: W.W. Norton & Co., 1979), chap. 1; Kenneth W. Clarkson and Roger LeRoy Miller, *Industrial Organization: Theory, Evidence, and Public Policy* (New York: McGraw-Hill Book Co., 1982), pp. 452-54.

[36]Averch and Johnson, *op. cit.* See also William M. Capron (ed.), *Technological Change in Regulated Industries* (Washington, D.C.: The Brookings Institution, 1971); Stephen G. Breyer and Paul W. MacAvoy, *Energy Regulation by the Federal Power Commission* (Washington, D.C.: The Brookings Institution, 1974).

[37]See, *e.g.*, Gray, *op. cit.*

[38]See Marver H. Bernstein, *Regulating Business by Independent Commission* (Princeton: Princeton University Press, 1955) and "Independent Regulatory Agencies: A Perspective on Their Reform," in W.J. Samuels and H.M. Trebing (eds.), *A Critique of Administrative Regulation of Public Utilities* (East Lansing: MSU Public Utilities Papers, 1972), pp. 3-23.

[39]See, e.g., Henry J. Friendly, *The Federal Administrative Agencies: The Need for Better Definition of Standards* (Cambridge: Harvard University Press, 1962). Conversely, the implication is that if these matters were corrected, regulation would serve its original purpose.

[40]Breyer and MacAvoy, *op. cit.;* Paul W. MacAvoy, "The Regulation-Induced Shortage of Natural Gas," 14 *Journal of Law & Economics* 167 (1971).

[41]William A. Jordan, *Airline Regulation in America: Effects and Imperfections* (Baltimore: The Johns Hopkins Press, 1970).

[42]John R. Meyer et al., *The Economics of Competition in the Transportation Industries* (Cambridge: Harvard University Press, 1959).

[43]Bernstein, *Regulating Business by Independent Commission, op. cit.*

[44]Gabriel Kolko, *Railroads and Regulation, 1877-1916* (Princeton: Princeton University Press, 1965); Mark J. Green and Ralph Nader, "Economic Regulation versus Competition: Uncle Sam and the Monopoly Man," 82 *Yale Law Journal* 871 (1973). But see Robert W. Harbeson, "Railroads and Regulation, 1877-1916: Conspiracy or Public Interest?," 27 *Journal of Economic History* 230 (1967). See also Paul W. MacAvoy, *The Economic Effects of Regulation: The Trunk-Line Railroad Cartels and the Interstate Commerce Commission before 1900* (Cambridge: The MIT Press, 1965); George W. Hilton, "The Consistency of the Interstate Commerce Act," 9 *Journal of Law & Economics* 87 (1966).

[45]"For example, the ICC's policy of preserving excess rail capacity can hardly be cited as evidence of good cartel management — especially when the effect of this policy is equivalent to levying a high surcharge on rail revenues for the benefit of a relatively small number of shippers. Similarly, neither AT&T nor the natural gas producers would agree that the FCC and FPC were sympathetic to their objectives." Harry M. Trebing, "Equity, Efficiency, and the Viability of Public Utility Regulation,"

in Werner Sichel and Thomas G. Gies (eds.), *Applications of Economic Principles in Public Utility Industries* (Ann Arbor: The University of Michigan, 1981), p. 23.

[46]The life cycle model discussed here is attributed to Bernstein, *Regulating Business by Independent Commission, op. cit.,* chap. II. For a critique of this and other life cycle models, see Mitnick, *op. cit.,* chap. II.

[47]". . . regulatory bodies, like the people who comprise them, have a marked life cycle. In youth they are vigorous, aggressive, evangelistic, and even intolerant. Later they mellow, and in old age — after a matter of ten or fifteen years — they become, with some exceptions, either an arm of the industry they are regulating or senile." John K. Galbraith, *The Great Crash* (Boston: Houghton Mifflin Co., 1955), p. 171.

[48]"The length of each phase varies from one commission to another, and sometimes a whole period seems to be skipped. Some commissions maintain their youthfulness for a fairly long time, while others seem to age rapidly and apparently never pass through a period of optimistic adolescence. Some are adventurous, while others are bound more closely to the pattern established by the oldest commission, the ICC. Such differences add an element of interest and reality to the evolution of commission regulation, but they do not invalidate generalizations about the administrative history of regulation." Bernstein, *Regulating Business by Independent Commission, op. cit.,* p. 74.

[49]"Because of the rapidity of technological and industrial change and continuing modifications in the economic structure of industry, the regulatory treaty finally hammered out by the House and Senate conferees will be focused on remedying problems that have been acute for many years. The battle to adapt regulatory policy and practices to problems currently emerging in the industrial scene will be fought bitterly during subsequent decades." *Ibid.,* pp. 76-77.

[50]Kenneth C. Davis, *Administrative Law* (St. Paul: West Publishing Co., 1951), p. 164.

[51]Emmette S. Redford, *Administration of National Economic Control* (New York: The Macmillan Co., 1952), p. 386.

[52]Bernstein, *Regulating Business by Independent Commission, op. cit.,* p. 88.

[53]*Ibid.,* pp. 94-95.

[54]The pros and cons of the "railroad-mindedness" of the ICC were discussed in a series of articles in the *Yale Law Journal* in 1952 and 1953. See Samuel P. Huntington, "The Marasmus of the ICC," 61 *Yale Law Journal* 467 (1952); Charles S. Morgan, "A Critique of 'The Marasmus of the ICC,'" 62 *Yale Law Journal* 171 (1953); C. Dickerman Williams, "Transportation Regulation and the Department of Commerce," 62 *Yale Law Journal* 563 (1953); "The ICC Reexamined: A Colloquy," 63 *Yale Law Journal* 44 (1953).

[55]Jaffe, among others, has argued that agency reliance on the affected interests generally exists from its inception and is administratively rather than industry determined. He explains: "There are those who say that the ICC is 'railroad-minded,' as if actions of the ICC favorable to the railroads were a deviation from the expected and relevant norm. The criticisms of the ICC are tendentiously documented and ultimately evasive. There can surely be no question that it was an essential element of the philosophy of the Motor Carrier Act to protect (as the drafters saw the problem) the *regulated* railroad from the *unregulated* motor carrier by subjecting both types of carrier to the same regime of regulation. In the words of a Senate Committee at a somewhat later date (1939), this was not a 'railroad philosophy' but a 'transportation philosophy.' Obviously the implementation of this philosophy as against the pre-

viously unregulated motor carrier would favor the railroads. It may be that the ICC is more 'railroad-minded' than 'motor carrier-minded,' but recent criticism has failed to distinguish to what extent it goes beyond the likely consequences of the kind of regulation which presently obtains in this field. The criticism pinning the blame on the ICC, and proposing perhaps this or that reshuffling of administrative power, refuses to face the problems created by regulation as such." Louis L. Jaffe, "The Effective Limits of the Administrative Process: A Reevaluation," 67 *Harvard Law Review* 1105, 1108-9 (1954). See also James Q. Wilson, "The Dead Hand of Regulation," 25 *The Public Interest* 48 (1971); Kenneth J. Meier and John P. Plumlee, "Regulatory Administration and Organizational Rigidity," 31 *Western Political Quarterly* 80 (1978).

[56]Trebing, for example, has argued that the capture theory (*a*) "gives inadequate recognition to recent changes on the regulatory scene" (*e.g.*, growing consumer intervention; a "new generation of state commissioners, who have been independent, highly active, and quite willing to experiment — much to the chagrin of the established utilities.") and (*b*) "takes too simplistic a view of who are the captors and who are the captives." Trebing, "Equity, Efficiency, and the Viability of Public Utility Regulation," *op. cit.*, p. 24.

[57]Roger G. Noll and Bruce M. Owen, "What Makes Reform Happen?," 7 *Regulation* 19, 22-23 (March/April 1983).

[58]See, *e.g.*, David B. Truman, *The Governmental Process: Political Interests and Public Opinion* (2d ed.; New York: Alfred A. Knopf, Inc., 1971); George J. Stigler, "The Theory of Economic Regulation," 2 *Bell Journal of Economics & Management Science* 3 (1971); Posner, *op. cit.*; Milton Russell and Robert B. Shelton, "A Model of Regulatory Agency Behavior," 20 *Public Choice* 47 (1974); Sam Peltzman, "Toward a More General Theory of Regulation," 19 *Journal of Law & Economics* 211 (1976). For an excellent overview, see Mancur Olson, Jr., *The Logic of Collective Action: Public Goods and the Theory of Groups* (rev. ed.; Cambridge: Harvard University Press, 1971).

[59]Posner, *op. cit.*, p. 351, with a reference to the author's "Taxation by Regulation," 2 *Bell Journal of Economics & Management Science* 22 (1971).

[60]Trebing, "Equity, Efficiency, and the Viability of Public Utility Regulation," *op. cit.*, p. 25. As Trebing correctly notes, interest group theories differ substantially from the public interest and capture theories. "Regulation is not perceived as a means for curbing monopoly abuses, nor is it a pawn, vulnerable to capture or manipulation. Instead, it emerges as an institutional form that seeks political support by redistributing wealth in favor of its constituency." *Ibid.*, p. 26.

A slightly different approach has been suggested by Goldberg. A regulatory agency, he contends, may be regarded as an "agent" for consumer groups, negotiating and administering a "relational contract" between suppliers and consumers; a contract which gives suppliers the right to serve and consumers the right to be served under an agreement which limits their future options in order to minimize costs and/or uncertainties. Victor P. Goldberg, "Regulation and Administered Contracts," 7 *Bell Journal of Economics* 426 (1976). This concept, however, "seems inconsistent with the theory of administrative law, wherein the regulator is supposed to be an impartial arbiter of the public interest (where 'public interest' includes the interest of the firm being regulated)." Bruce M. Owen and Ronald Braeutigam, The *Regulation Game: Strategic Use of the Administrative Process* (Cambridge: Ballinger Publishing Co., 1978), p. 17.

[61]Trebing, "Equity, Efficiency, and the Viability of Public Utility Regulation," *op. cit.*, p. 26.

[62]*Ibid.*, pp. 26-27.

[63]Posner, "Theories of Economic Regulation," *op. cit.*, p. 347.

[64]*Ibid.*, p. 350. Posner gives as examples the constitutional establishment of an independent judiciary and the constitutional requirement of just compensation in eminent domain cases.

[65]Trebing, "Equity, Efficiency, and the Viability of Public Utility Regulation," *op. cit.*, p. 27. As Judge Breyer notes: Interest group theories "cannot fully explain environmental, health, safety regulation, or even traditional utility and transportation regulation. While such a theory may help explain the origins of railroad regulation, it does not explain airline regulation, which arose not as a method of cartelizing the industry but, rather, as an effort to stop corruption in the awarding of airline subsidies." Stephen Breyer, *Regulation and Its Reform* (Cambridge: Harvard University Press, 1982), p. 388, n. 38.

[66]The "bureaucratic" theories of regulatory behavior have failed, at least to date, to specify the goals or objectives regulators seek to maximize (*e.g.*, their jurisdiction, their budgets, a legislative mandate, personal goals, and so forth). See, *e.g.*, Anthony Downs, *Inside Bureaucracy* (Boston: Little, Brown & Co., 1967); Lee Loevinger, "The Sociology of Bureaucracy," 24 *The Business Lawyer* 7 (November 1968); Roger G. Noll, "The Behavior of Regulatory Agencies," 29 *Review of Social Economy* 15 (1971); Paul L. Joskow, "Pricing Decisions of Regulated Firms: A Behavioral Approach," 4 *Bell Journal of Economics & Management Science* 118 (1973); Herbert Kaufman, *Red Tape: Its Origins, Uses, and Abuses* (Washington, D.C.: The Brookings Institution, 1977).

[67]Trebing, "Equity, Efficiency, and the Viability of Public Utility Regulation, *op. cit.*, p. 27. "As an illustration, the inclusion of construction work in progress (CWIP) in the rate base appears to have been instrumental in the defeat of a conservative governor and the removal of a conservative commission chairman in New Hampshire in 1978. On the basis of the conservative history of that state, the inclusion of CWIP should have earned the governor and the chairman the wholehearted support of the voters." *Ibid.*, pp. 27-28.

As Judge Breyer has argued: ". . . All regulatory rules and programs benefit some group or other. One could 'explain' any deviation from 'optimal' regulation as a response to the political power of the affected group. This criticism can be avoided only if the theory is strong enough to predict in advance precisely how and when regulators would respond to political pressures, but so far it is not." Breyer, *op. cit.*, p. 388, n. 38.

[68]Trebing, "Equity, Efficiency, and the Viability of Public Utility Regulation," *op. cit.*, pp. 28-29. The theory is developed and illustrated by Owen and Braeutigam, *op. cit.*

[69]See, *e.g.*, Edward E. Zajac, *Fairness or Efficiency: An Introduction to Public Utility Pricing* (Cambridge: Ballinger Publishing Co., 1978). "When it comes to issues of economic or social justice, regulation's ability to effect social goals makes it potentially more effective than the competitive market place. Unfortunately, the available economic justice theory falls short of what is desired. A positive theory which describes how the public in fact views economic justice is almost nonexistent." *Ibid.*, pp. 104-5.

[70]Trebing, "Equity, Efficiency, and the Viability of Public Utility Regulation," *op. cit.*, p. 30.

[71]For a more complete analysis of this topic, see Frank E. Cooper, *State Adminis-*

trative Law (Indianapolis: The Bobbs-Merrill Co., Inc., 1965), Vols. I and II; Francis X. Welch, *Cases and Text on Public Utility Regulation* (rev. ed.; Arlington, Va.: Public Utilities Reports, Inc., 1968), chap. xiii; Louis L. Jaffe and Nathaniel L. Nathanson, *Administrative Law: Cases and Materials* (4th ed.; Boston: Little, Brown & Co., 1976), esp. chap. vii; Stephen G. Breyer and Richard B. Stewart, *Administrative Law and Regulatory Policy* (Boston: Little, Brown & Co., 1979); Lief H. Carter, *Administrative Law and Politics: Cases and Comments* (Boston: Little, Brown & Co., 1983); Florence Heffron, *The Administrative Regulatory Process* (New York: Longman, 1983).

[72]Richard J. Pierce, Jr., Gary D. Allison, and Patrick H. Martin, *Economic Regulation: Energy, Transportation and Utilities* (Indianapolis: The Bobbs-Merrill Co., Inc., 1980), p. 129.

[73]Such investigations are known as "generic" proceedings. See, *e.g., Re Generic Hearings Concerning Electric Rate Structure*, 36 PUR4th 6 (Colo., 1979); *Re Advertising Practices of Telephone, Electric, and Gas Distribution Companies*, 35 PUR4th 361 (N.J., 1980); *Re Residential Conservation Service Program*, 35 PUR4th 515 (Conn., 1980).

[74]"Procedural change in the past ten to fifteen years has consisted, for the most part, of judicial imposition of increasingly strict formal procedural requirements. The courts, expanding the application of the 'due process' clause of the Constitution, have required adjudications to be conducted with increasing legal formality. They have required agencies, when they 'legislate' through 'informal rulemaking,' to conduct their proceedings with greater formality, giving all parties greater opportunity to examine the evidence upon which the agency bases its decision." Breyer, *op. cit.,* p. 346 (footnotes omitted).

[75]See, *e.g.,* William F. West, *Administrative Rulemaking: Politics and Processes* (Westport, Conn.: Greenwood Press, 1985).

[76]Jaffe and Nathanson, *op. cit.,* p. 26.

[77]*Re National Rates for Natural Gas* (Opinion No. 699), 4 PUR4th 401 (FPC, 1974). A nationwide base rate for "old" natural gas at the wellhead was established a year later. *Re National Rates for Natural Gas* (Opinion No. 749), 12 PUR4th 493 (FPC, 1975).

[78]*Ibid.* (4 PUR4th 401), p. 405.

[79]*Shell Oil Co. v. Federal Power Comm.,* 520 F. 2d 1061 (5th Cir. 1975), *cert. denied sub nom. California Co. v. Federal Power Comm.,* 426 U.S. 941 (1976).

[80]*Re National Rates for Natural Gas* (Opinion No. 770), 15 PUR4th 21 (FPC, 1976), *aff'd sub nom. American Pub. Gas Ass'n v. Federal Power Comm.,* 567 F. 2d 1016 (D.C. Cir. 1976), *cert. denied,* 435 U.S. 907 (1977). See also *Phillips Petroleum Co. v. Federal Power Comm.,* 475 F. 2d 842 (10th Cir. 1973), *cert. denied,* 414 U.S. 1146 (1974).

[81]*Establishment of Adequate Railroad Revenue Levels,* 358 ICC 855 (1978), *modified,* 359 ICC 270 (1978).

[82]"Establishing the Rate of Return on Equity for Wholesale Electric Sales: Potential Regulatory Reforms," A Discussion Paper on Electric Rate of Return by a Staff Study Group, Federal Energy Regulatory Commission (mimeographed, December 15, 1980), pp. 83-84 (citation omitted).

In 1984, the Federal Energy Regulatory Commission established a rule for determining benchmark rates of return on common equity and applying them in individual electric utility rate cases. [Order No. 389, 28 FERC par. 61,068.] The rule provides for annual commission proceedings to determine the industry's average cost of common equity and a procedure for updating the cost on a quarterly basis. [See *Re Generic Determination of Rate of Return on Common Equity for Public Utilities,* Docket No.

RM84-15, Order No. 420, 50 *Fed. Reg.* 21,802 (FERC, 1985; first annual proceeding); Docket No. RM85-19, Order No. 442, 51 *Fed. Reg.* 343 (FERC, 1986; second annual proceeding) and Docket No. RM85-19-001 et al., Order No. 442-A, 75 PUR4th 219 (FERC, 1986; order on rehearing).] The benchmark rates of return established in the first two annual proceedings were "advisory" only. The third annual proceeding will determine a rate of return on common equity that will constitute a "rebuttable presumption" in individual rate cases.

[83]Most regulatory commissions have statutory authority (a) to suspend proposed rate changes for a period of time and (b) to prescribe temporary ("interim") rates pending a full investigation. With respect to the first, statutory provisions range from four months to indefinite periods, with six to nine months being the most common. [See *1985 Annual Report on Utility and Carrier Regulation* (Washington, D.C.: National Association of Regulatory Utility Commissioners, 1987), p. 419.] At the end of this statutory period, the applicant may put the change into effect, generally under bond, unless the commission has ruled otherwise. Proposed rate changes must usually be filed thirty days before they can become effective. With respect to the second, if temporary rates are authorized, any subsequent refunds ordered after an investigation generally must be made to consumers with interest. [See *ibid.*, p. 426.]

[84]Pierce, Allison, and Martin, *op. cit.*, p. 238.

[85]"To the extent that expenses and the rate base increase faster (slower) than revenues, the realized rate of return will fall short of (exceed) the fair rate of return." *Ibid.*

[86]See "Alternative Test Year Methods in Public Utility Rate Proceedings" (Washington, D.C.: National Association of Regulatory Utility Commissioners, 1980); *1985 Annual Report on Utility and Carrier Regulation, op. cit.*, pp. 429-30.

[87]Due notice involves either an advertisement in newspapers serving the utility's service area or notification of each customer by mail.

[88]The FCC's requirements for intervention are typical. Petitions for leave to intervene in a formal proceeding must be filed within thirty days from the date of publication of the hearing issues in the *Federal Register*. Each petition "must set forth the interest of petitioner in the proceedings, must show how such petitioners' participation will assist the commission in the determination of the issues in question, and must be accompanied by the affidavit of a person with knowledge as to the facts set forth in the petition. The presiding officer, in his discretion, may grant or deny such petition or may permit intervention by such person limited to particular issues or to a particular stage of the proceeding." For a more complete discussion, see Charles F. Phillips, Jr., "Interveners in the Telephone Investigation," 78 *Public Utilities Fortnightly* 26 (December 22, 1966). Many commissions offer assistance to intervenors. See *1985 Annual Report on Utility and Carrier Regulation, op. cit.*, pp. 864-65; "California Rule Forces Utilities to Pay Critics," *The Wall Street Journal*, December 8, 1986, p. 29.

[89]Typical is the data request used by the Kansas commission: "Answers to this data request shall rely upon and divulge and provide all information in the possession of or available to the answering party, its agents, employees, contractors, attorneys, and other representatives of the answering party which is responsive in whole or in part to the request. This data request is intended to be continuing in nature and requires supplemental answers if additional data is generated or obtained which is responsive in whole or in part to the request. As used in this Data Request the term 'document' includes publication in any format, workpapers, letters, memoranda, notes, reports, analyses, computer printouts, test results or data, audio recordings,

photographs, drawings, maps, charts, video recordings, transcriptions, and printed, typed or handwritten materials of any kind." An individual or company receiving such a data request must "answer fully within seven days after service thereof."

[90]An administrative law judge (formerly a hearing examiner) is an official in the federal and in some of the state administrative agencies who performs the function of a judge — hearing evidence, listening to lawyers' arguments, and rendering an opinion. All such opinions may be appealed to the full commission. On the role of the administrative law judge, see Victor G. Rosenblum, "The Administrative Law Judge in the Administrative Process: Interrelations of Case Law With Statutory and Pragmatic Factors in Determining ALJ Roles," in *Recent Studies Relevant to the Disability Hearings and Appeals Crisis* (Subcommittee on Social Security, Committee on Ways and Means, House, 94th Cong., 1st sess.)(Washington, D.C.: U.S. Government Printing Office, 1975), pp. 171-245; Arthur A. Gladstone, "The Administrative Process — Yesterday, Today, Tomorrow," in Charles F. Phillips, Jr. (ed.), *Regulation, Competition and Deregulation — An Economic Grab Bag* (Lexington, Va.: Washington and Lee University, 1979), pp. 145-70. See *1985 Annual Report on Utility and Carrier Regulation, op. cit.,* pp. 868-73.

[91]In some states, individual consumers are represented by public counsel or by the attorney assigned to the case from the state attorney general's office. Consumers may be permitted to testify during the regular hearing or a particular time may be set aside for such testimony (such as an evening or a Saturday.)

[92]In some instances, the record is certified to the full commission for decision, without an initial decision by the presiding administrative law judge or panel of commissioners. See, *e.g., Re Ohio Edison Co.,* 61 PUR4th 241, 242-43 (Ohio, 1984).

[93]A majority of the regulatory commissions are subject to freedom of information ("sunshine") statutes which, among other things, require deliberations in rate cases to be held in open meetings. See *1985 Annual Report on Utility and Carrier Regulation, op. cit.,* pp. 883-89.

[94]"Typically, and I say this without humor, exceptions are filed to everything but the caption of the case and the judge's name at the end of the decision." Gladstone, *op. cit.,* p. 159.

[95]In general, petitions for reconsideration and rehearing must present "newly discovered evidence, . . . not in existence, or . . . not discoverable through the exercise of due diligence, prior to the expiration of the time within which to file a petition for rehearing . . ." and must raise "new and novel arguments not previously heard, or considerations which appear to have been overlooked or not addressed by the commission." *Duick v. Pennsylvania Gas & Water Co.,* 51 PUR4th 284, 288-89 (Pa., 1983).

[96]The typical rate case takes just under one year. To illustrate a more complex proceeding: The record in the Phase 1A "Interim Decision and Order" in the FCC's telephone investigation (Docket No. 16258, FCC 67-776, July 5, 1967) consisted of 101 exhibits (3,471 pages) submitted by the Bell System, the commission's staff, and the 103 intervenors; five exhibits (forty-two pages) submitted by "nonparties"; 76 volumes of transcript (10,499 pages); and briefs and prepared findings of fact filed by twelve parties (1,011 pages). There were three days of prehearing conferences, seventy-one days of hearings (sixty-six witnesses), and two days of oral arguments before the full commission. (The record was certified to the full commission for decision without an initial decision, in this case, by the Telephone Committee.) Phase 1A was completed in approximately twenty months (not including the subsequent

time for a rehearing on certain issues). Data from Charles F. Phillips, Jr., "Phase 1A of the Telephone Investigation," 80 *Public Utilities Fortnightly* 15, 16 (August 31, 1967).

[97]See, *e.g., Re Williams Pipe Line Co.,* Opinion No. 154 (FERC, 1982), *aff'd in part and rem'd in part sub nom. Farmers Union Central Exchange, Inc. v. Federal Energy Regulatory Comm.,* 734 F. 2d 1486, 59 PUR4th 1 (D.C. Cir. 1984), *cert. denied,* 105 S. Ct. 507 (1984), Order on remand, 67 PUR4th 669 (FERC, 1985).

[98]See *e.g.,* Richard L. Norgaard and Michael J. Riley, "Regulatory Lag: Everyone Loses," 111 *Public Utilities Fortnightly* 29 (May 26, 1983).

[99]For a more complete discussion of this topic, see Peter Woll, *Administrative Law: The Informal Process* (Berkeley and Los Angeles: University of California Press, 1963).

[100]Civil Aeronautics Board, Procedural Regulations, Part 302 — "Rules of Practice in Economic Proceedings" (Washington, D.C.: U.S. Government Printing Office, 1961), p. 7.

[101]*Ibid.*

[102]*Ibid.*

[103]*Ibid.*

[104]Woll, *op. cit.,* pp. 39-40 (footnotes omitted).

[105]*Ibid.,* p. 57.

[106]See *ibid.,* chap. iv.

[107]See Francis X. Welch, "Constant Surveillance: A Modern Regulatory Tool," 8 *Villanova Law Review* 340 (1963).

[108]Federal Communications Commission, "Final Report of the Telephone Rate and Research Department" (Washington, D.C., 1938), p. 68 (footnote omitted; emphasis in original). Some regulatory statutes require formal hearings, while others leave the type of proceeding to the commission. For a discussion on the use of informal procedures by the state commissions, see *Annual Proceedings, 1965* (Washington, D.C.: National Association of Regulatory Utility Commissioners, 1966), pp. 65-67.

[109]The FCC's use of constant surveillance has been tested and upheld in the courts. See *Pub. Utilities Comm. of State of California v. United States,* 356 F. 2d 236 (9th Cir. 1966), *cert. denied,* 385 U.S. 816 (1966).

[110]Welch, "Constant Surveillance. . .," *op. cit.,* p. 352.

[111]*Ibid.*

[112]"We have not repudiated continuing surveillance. We agree with Bell that it is often an effective and highly efficient method of regulation and we appreciate the cooperation which has contributed to its past success. Under appropriate circumstances, we intend to use the method again. Indeed, we believe that the standards and criteria developed on the record here will enable us to employ continuing surveillance even more effectively in the future." Federal Communications Commission, "Memorandum Opinion and Order," Docket No. 16258 (FCC 65-1144, December 22, 1965), p. 6.

[113]"Establishing the Rate of Return on Equity for Wholesale Electric Sales. . .," *op. cit.,* p. B-6. "However, not all those settlements completely resolve the case since differences regarding return on equity and other issues may have been reserved for a separate hearing." *Ibid.*

[114]*Ibid.,* pp. B-1 - B-5 (footnotes omitted). All settlement agreements, whether contested or uncontested, are reviewed by the Commission. "The Commission has generally been inclined to accept the results of the bargaining among the parties that produced the settlement." *Ibid.,* p. B-5.

[115]"Informal settlement of rate level cases is especially desirable since it eliminates the need for expensive litigation and very often makes it possible for customers to begin paying lower rates much sooner than would be possible if full litigation were necessary." Former Chairman White, Federal Power Commission, quoted in *Annual Proceedings, 1966* (Washington, D.C.: National Association of Regulatory Utility Commissioners, 1967), p. 403.

[116]"Establishing the Rate of Return on Equity for Wholesale Electric Sales. . . ," *op. cit.*, p. 34.

[117]"Many tasks call for round tables and unbuttoned vests, not for witness chairs and courtroom trappings." Kenneth C. Davis, *Administrative Law Treatise* (St. Paul: West Publishing Co., 1958), Vol. 1, p. 284.

[118]See, *e.g.*, *Pub. Utilities Comm. of State of California v. United States, op. cit.* A related concern: A settlement ("stipulation") "can be seen as a 'secret deal.' It is sometimes felt that if each and every decision is not made at an open hearing somehow it looks to the public as if 'deals' have been made." Marilyn C. O'Leary, "Negotiated Settlements in Utility Regulation," 118 *Public Utilities Fortnightly* 11, 14 (August 21, 1986).

[119]In upholding the FPC's national rate order, Judge Leventhal commented: "Looking at objective data, we are constrained to find that there is a bare minimum to support the FPC's ruling. We can and do caution that on any future rate order there will be need for a more solid undergirding of result. . . . At this juncture we announce our approval, but with more of a sigh than a whoop." *American Pub. Gas Ass'n v. Federal Power Comm., op. cit.*, p. 1044.

[120]Walter Adams and Joel B. Dirlam, "Market Structure, Regulation, and Dynamic Change," in Trebing, *op. cit.*, p. 131.

[121]William G. Shepherd, "Conclusion," in Shepherd and Gies, *op. cit.*, p. 270.

[122]Adams and Dirlam, *op. cit.*, p. 138.

[123]Schmalensee, *op. cit.*, pp. 11-13.

[124]*Ibid.*, p. 12.

[125]*Ibid.*

[126]*Ibid.*, p. 20. "If those charged with the control function are instructed or encouraged to consider other goals as well, effective administrative or judicial review of their actions becomes all but impossible because there can be no clear standard for appropriate trade-offs among the many conflicting and imprecise goals that governments nominally pursue. This ambiguity makes it more likely that decisions will reflect the values and objectives of the administrators involved or those of other special interests than any defensible conception of the public interest." *Ibid.*, p. 143.

[127]Louis Flax, "Will the Utility Service Obligation Become a Victim of Economic Theory?," in *Proceedings of the 1980 Rate Symposium on Problems of Regulated Industries* (Columbia: University of Missouri-Columbia, 1981), p. 39.

[128]Lewis, "Emphasis and Misemphasis in Regulatory Policy," *op. cit.*, pp. 214-15.

Chapter	ACCOUNTING
6	AND
	FINANCING

The overriding purposes of the uniform systems of accounts are twofold: uniformity and consistency. In the exercise of their responsibilities, regulatory commissions must investigate and review the operations of utilities within their jurisdiction. For the most part, this requires accounting-oriented information. In order to ensure that the actions of regulators are reasonable and consistent and that utilities are regulated on a comparable basis, uniformity of accounting treatment, as well as consistency of treatment from period to period, is necessary.

—Robert L. Hahne and Gregory E. Aliff*

Two aspects of regulation, while of vital significance in over-all regulatory activity, are largely historical. At the turn of the century and continuing into the early 1930s, methods of both accounting and financing were abused by American industry. This situation was partly due to the infancy of the accounting profession and of business. However, it was also a result of the opportunities for enormous profits which often accrued to the unscrupulous.

From the point of view of the public utility sector, the development of uniform systems of accounts and of control over financing by the commissions has decreased the *opportunity* for abuses in this area. Of equal importance, the *desire* has decreased as the business system has matured. Despite

these changes, it is essential that the need for, and development of, accounting and financing regulation be examined. Moreover, several issues, such as
cost allocation methods and supervision of capital structures, deserve attention. These are the topics of the present chapter.

Regulation of Accounting

In the early days of regulation, little attention was paid to the methods
of accounting used by public utilities. Notorious abuses appeared. Operating
expenses were overstated, the investment in plant and equipment was impossible to ascertain, utility and nonutility businesses were not separated,
and overcapitalization — often at the expense of the investor — was common due to the lack of reliable figures.[1] Under these conditions, the goals
of regulation were frustrated; effective regulation requires commission control of accounting procedures.

The Objectives of Accounting Regulation

Several basic objectives of accounting regulation can be realized under
uniform systems of accounts. In the first place, rate regulation requires
accurate records of revenues, operating costs, depreciation expenses, and
investment in plant and equipment, among others. Here, uniformity is essential to effective commission staff audits, and where applicable, when rate
regulation is undertaken on an industrywide basis. Uniformity also is desirable so that public utilities are not subject to different accounting regulations in each of the states in which they operate — a situation that would
require keeping several different sets of records.[2]

In the second place, accounting regulation is needed so as to distinguish between expenditures that should be charged to capital and those that
should be charged to income. (This control is exercised for all business by
the Securities and Exchange Commission and independent auditors.) Expenditures that represent investment in capital assets (plant and equipment)
should be charged to fixed asset accounts rather than to operating expense
accounts. Similarly, expenditures that represent costs of doing business should
be charged to operating expense accounts rather than to capital. If these
distinctions are not made, earnings can be inflated by charging operating
expenses to capital, or concealed by charging capital to operating expenses.
Again, uniformity is essential, for without it the accounting practices of the
various companies would differ. One firm might charge all replacements to
operating expenses, even if the expenditures were for improved equipment.
Another firm might distinguish between an expenditure that represented a
replacement in kind and one that represented an improvement, charging
the first to operating expenses and the second to capital. Such varied practices would make industrywide comparisons impossible.

In the third place, as public utilities are entitled to a fair rate of return on the fair value of their property, an accurate statement of a utility's property account is one of the most important objectives of accounting regulation and uniform systems of accounts. Prior to the mid-1930s, some of the worst abuses occurred with respect to property valuations: values were often increased arbitrarily, and property was exchanged between affiliated companies at inflated prices. As explained by Troxel:

> These write-ups and "inside" property exchanges were parts of holding company finance, parts of the reckless expansion and questionable business conduct of public utility promoters. Sometimes a plant was exchanged several times, or was included in several successive consolidations. And as each exchange or consolidation was effected, the plant was recorded at higher and higher book values. Some affiliated companies exchanged properties, indeed, because they wanted to write up their property values. When holding companies or their management companies added fees to the acquisition prices of properties, further write-ups occurred. Some write-ups were imaginary "overhead" expenses of construction work. And another kind of book value revision was common too: managers made an "inside" revaluation of property and credited the increment to the capital surplus account. Other companies wrote up book values to the reproduction costs of their properties; or they wrote up property accounts to whatever figures suited their financial purposes.[3]

Regulatory commissions, therefore, must have control over a utility's property account. But at this point, an important distinction must be made. All commissions require that property accounts show the original cost of property items. The rate of return, moreover, is based on the value of, or investment in, property used and useful in providing a particular service. However, the value of a utility's property in an accounting sense is not necessarily the same as the value of a utility's property for ratemaking purposes. In rate cases, valuation may be based upon original cost, reproduction cost, or some figure between these two measures.[4]

In the fourth place, utility business must be separated from nonutility business. Public utilities are permitted to earn a fair rate of return on the property devoted to utility purposes. A great majority of such companies, however, have other investments, expenses, and sources of revenue. They may have investments or make loans to other companies; they may own other businesses; they may sell electric or gas appliances. With a few exceptions, these outside expenses and revenues, *in theory,* are not subject to regulation. The commissions can permit a utility to earn neither more than a fair return to make up for other unprofitable undertakings nor less when a utility has additional sources of income that are profitable.

In the fifth place, accounting regulation is of aid to the commissions and utilities in evaluating the reasonableness of rates. Public utilities provide many different types of services. Unit cost information is essential in controlling price discrimination and in determining the profitability of competitive rates. It must be emphasized, however, that the cost of providing a particular service cannot be determined from accounting data alone.[5] Directly allocated costs can be charged to different service accounts; common or joint costs cannot. This problem will be discussed below.

Finally, accounting regulation is beneficial to investors. Before effective accounting regulation was undertaken, accounts were frequently misrepresented and earnings raised or lowered to suit a utility's immediate purpose. Investors lacked reliable information on which to make intelligent investment decisions. Commissions, too, lacked reliable data and found it impossible to regulate the issuance of new securities. Overcapitalization, stock watering, and excessive indebtedness became common. During the depression of the thirties, millions were lost by investors when reorganizations (railroads) were necessary and holding company (electric and gas) abuses were uncovered.[6]

The Development of Uniform Systems

The courts have long upheld the commissions' right to prescribe accounting practices. In 1912, the Supreme Court said:

> If the Commission is to successfully perform its duties in respect to reasonable rates, undue discriminations, and favoritism, it must be informed as to the business of the carriers by a system of accounting which will not permit the possible concealment of forbidden practices. . . . Further, the requiring of information concerning a business is not regulation of that business.[7]

A year later, the Court rejected a challenge to the ICC's accounting regulations:

> Congress, in authorizing the Commission to prescribe a uniform system of accounts, recognized that accounting systems were not then uniform; and in reiterating this authorization in 1906, and adding a prohibition against the keeping of other accounts than those prescribed, manifested a purpose to standardize and render uniform the accounts of the different carriers with respect to matters that entered into property and the improvements thereof, on the one hand, and the current operations of the company, on the other. . . . Plainly, the law-making body recognized the essential distinctions between property accounts and operating accounts, between capital and earnings; it recognized that the practice of different carriers varied in respect to those matters; and that no system of supervision and regulation would be complete without requiring the accounts of all the carriers to speak a common language.[8]

In a later case, the Court went even further, implying its approval of almost any method of accounting regulation adopted by the commissions. The Court argued:

> Whether the Commission should make specific classifications to fit exceptional cases lies within the discretion conferred, and courts ought not to be called upon to interfere with or correct alleged errors with respect to accounting practice. If we were in disagreement with the Commission as to the wisdom and propriety of the order, we are without power to usurp its discretion and substitute our own.[9]

Uniform systems of accounts, however, developed slowly.[10] Early legislative statutes either made no provision for commission control of accounting methods, or, when provision was made, the commissions often did not act. Massachusetts was the first state to direct its commission to prescribe uniform accounting systems: for railroads in 1876, gas companies in 1885, and electric utilities in 1887. The regulatory agencies of New York and Wisconsin were given jurisdiction over the accounting practices of public utilities in 1905 and 1907, respectively, and they prescribed uniform systems for electric and gas utilities in 1909.

In other instances, public utilities develop their own uniform accounting systems. The National Electric Light Association, an organization of private electric utilities, devised the first important standard classification of electric accounts. In 1907, the Association of American Railway Accountants in cooperation with the Interstate Commerce Commission developed a similar system of accounting for the nations's railroads. In 1913, the ICC established a uniform system for telephone companies (over which it then had jurisdiction), and in 1922, the National Association of Railroad and Utilities Commissioners (NARUC) prescribed uniform systems of accounts for electric and gas companies. These systems served as models, and by 1925, forty states had adopted or approved such uniform classifications.[11] These early systems, though better than no systems at all:

> ... had significant defects. They gave too much accounting authority to the utility companies. When the first draft of the uniform electric system was drawn up in 1920, representatives of private electric companies did much of the work. And the accounting ideas of private electric systems were evident in the final draft of the uniform system. Managers of utility companies could fix, in part, the book valuation standard for property, and could choose the method of depreciation accounting.[12]

Major revisions in accounting control of electric, gas, and telephone companies were made during the depression of the thirties. The Federal Communications Commission adopted in 1935, with only minor modifications, the uniform system for the telephone companies which had been promulgated by the ICC in 1913, and in 1937, the NARUC approved a similar system for intrastate telephone companies. In 1936, systems of accounts were developed for electric companies by the Federal Power Commission and the NARUC, for gas companies by the NARUC, and for holding companies by the Securities and Exchange Commission. Shortly after Congress passed the Natural Gas Act in 1938, the FPC prescribed a uniform system of accounts for all interstate natural gas companies. Since this time, the uniform systems have been modified on numerous occasions — "due to the introduction of new technology of accounting interpretations by professional accounting organizations or regulatory bodies"[13] — but they remain substantially as developed during the thirties.

The uniform systems prescribed by the federal commissions went into effect immediately, but the state commissions had to adopt the systems before they became effective. Today, most of the state commissions have adopted either the federal or the NARUC accounting systems, although they are often modified in detail to fit local situations or problems. Thus, forty-six of the state commissions regulating private electric utilities prescribe the FERC or the NARUC systems of accounts and three prescribe their own systems, while forty-eight of the state commissions regulating telephone companies prescribe the FCC uniform systems of accounts and three prescribe their own systems.[14]

Comparability and Rate Regulation

The ultimate objective of uniform systems of accounts "must be comparability in financial reporting both among companies within a single industry and among companies in different industries, so that substantial factual matters are not hidden from the public view by accounting flexibility."[15] Yet, as is true with almost all regulatory procedures, uniform systems of accounts represent a tool. There are many important differences of opinion with respect to scope, content, and application of the various provisions of any uniform system. Because of alternative accounting principles, uniform accounting standards have not been adopted by the regulatory commissions.[16] Consequently, while there is widespread comparability of financial reports filed by companies within each jurisdiction, interjurisdictional comparisons must be made with some care.[17]

In this connection, it must be kept in mind that a commission

> . . . is not bound in its rate proceedings by any system of accounts it may have prescribed or by what is revealed in a review of the systems of accounts. Utility regulation, the making of business decisions, and the determination of values cannot be reduced to an automatic process by which the correct decision can be made by reference to books of accounts.[18]

In rate proceedings, therefore, a commission may (and often does) disallow certain expenditures for ratemaking purposes or may (on occasion) place a value on a utility's property in determining the rate base that exceeds the original cost of that property as shown in the uniform system of accounts. These problems are considered in succeeding chapters.

Finally, it is important to note that while "generally accepted accounting principles" apply to all industries, there are cases where their application results in differences for public utilities because of economic regulation. As noted by Suelflow:

> ... One of the main differences that occurs is in the timing of when certain items enter into net income — matching of expenses and revenues. For example, extraordinary losses are recognized by nonregulated firms in the accounting period in which they occur; regulated utilities often defer these items, amortizing them over a future time period. While at variance with generally accepted principles, the practice is acceptable, but only if cost recovery is sure. The other possible difference which exists between regulated and nonregulated firms concerns certain charges that may be written off to retained earnings when generally accepted accounting principles would consider the item as a charge against current income of the nonregulated firm.[19]

Uniform Systems of Accounts[20]

The uniform systems of accounts used by regulatory commissions can be illustrated with reference to the uniform system prescribed by the Federal Energy Regulatory Commission (as of 1986) for Major Electric Utilities.[21]

Balance Sheet Accounts. A condensed balance sheet form is shown in Figure 6-1. On the asset side, the most important account for ratemaking purposes is "Utility Plant."[22] The FERC, along with the other federal and state commissions, requires that property accounts show the original cost of all items entered. It is important to realize, however, that the term "original cost" has a special meaning — that is, it represents "the cost of such property to the person first devoting it to public service." This definition is not the conventional accounting meaning, for accountants generally value property at its cost to the existing company (the investment cost). Thus, when a utility builds its own plant, the total cost of construction is entered under the appropriate utility plant account. When property is acquired as a gift, it is entered on the basis of the estimated value at the time of donation. But when property is purchased from another company, it is recorded in the plant account on the basis of its original cost, even though the acquiring firm may have paid more or less than this figure for the property.[23]

The costs of additions and improvements are added when incurred, whether paid for from accrued depreciation, retained earnings, or the proceeds of security issues; any excess cost of replacing property in kind over

FIGURE 6-1

Condensed Balance Sheet Accounts

Assets and Other Debits	*Liabilities and Other Credits*
Utility Plant[a]	Proprietary Capital[e]
Other Property and Investments[b]	Long-term Debt[f]
Current and Accrued Assets[c]	Other Noncurrent Liabilities[g]
Deferred Debits[d]	Current and Accrued Liabilities[h]
	Deferred Credits[i]

[a]Electric plant in service less accumulated provision for depreciation and amortization, construction work in progress — electric, plant acquisition adjustments less accumulated provision for amortization, nuclear fuel (*e.g.*, nuclear fuel assemblies in reactor less accumulated provision for amortization, nuclear fuel under capital leases).

[b]Nonutility property less accumulated provision for depreciation and amortization, investment in associated companies, other investments, special funds (*e.g.*, sinking funds, depreciation funds, amortization funds — Federal).

[c]Cash, special deposits (*e.g.*, interest and dividend special deposits), working funds, temporary cash investments, notes and accounts receivable, accumulated provision for uncollectible accounts — credit, notes receivable from associated companies, materials and supplies.

[d]Unamortized debt expense, extraordinary property losses, other deferred debits (*e.g.*, preliminary survey and investigative charges, clearing accounts), research, development, and demonstration expenditures, unamortized loss on reacquired debt, accumulated deferred income taxes.

[e]Common and preferred stock (issued, subscribed, and liability for conversion), premium on capital stock, donations received from stockholders, appropriated and unappropriated retained earnings.

[f]Bonds, reacquired bonds, advances from associated companies, other long-term debt.

[g]Obligations under capital leases — noncurrent, accumulated provision for: property insurance, injuries and damages, pensions and benefits, rate refunds.

[h]Notes payable, accounts payable, notes and accounts payable to associated companies, customer deposits, accrued liabilities (*e.g.*, taxes, interest, dividends declared), obligations under capital leases — current.

[i]Customer advances for construction, accumulated deferred investment tax credits, deferred gains from disposition of utility plant, unamortized gain on reacquired debt, accumulated deferred income taxes — accelerated amortization (property, other property, and other).

the original cost of the property retired is added to the account. Abandoned property is written off (although it is sometimes amortized over a period of years). The cost of construction work in progress is added.

As previously discussed, the regulatory commissions must make a distinction between charges made to capital and charges made to income. The commissions have prescribed lists of retirement units to handle this problem. A retirement unit list contains those property items whose costs are recorded in the plant account when they are acquired, whose costs are charged to depreciation expense during their useful lives, and which are withdrawn from the plant account when they are retired. While the commissions prescribe these lists, specifying the grouping of similar items of plant, a utility may subdivide each of the commission-prescribed categories for its own analysis.

All federal commissions and most of the state commissions also require the maintenance of continuing property records of inventories.[24] Property items found in the list of retirement units are arranged according to their technical characteristics, location (usually by plants, taxing districts, or the operating systems of each company), date of installation, and original cost. When a property item is retired, it is withdrawn from the continuing property record. In addition to showing the original cost of property, such records provide useful information for measuring the service life of property and for aiding in the computation of depreciation rates. And when reproduction cost valuations are desired, they can be obtained by multiplying each property item by its current price, including the current cost of installation. Such a procedure is quicker and cheaper than taking a complete inventory every time a new valuation is required.

Finally, the uniform balance sheet requires the separation of utility and nonutility businesses, and provides special accounts to record transactions among affiliated companies. The first is necessary for rate regulation; the second to prevent abuses or excessive charges among affiliated enterprises.

Income Accounts. Whereas the balance sheet shows the financial position of a company at a specific moment of time, the income statement reflects the results of operations over a specified period of time. If commissions are to supervise operating expenses, they must have accurate and reliable uniform data. This information is contained in the prescribed income accounts.

The income accounts illustrated in Figure 6-2 are largely self-explanatory. As with balance sheet accounts, detailed instructions for each type of expense are given to indicate in which account they should be entered. It should be noted that nonutility income is reported separately from utility income. For regulatory purposes, the most important account is "Utility Operating Income," which represents the company's income from utility operations. It should also be noted that donations to, and expenditures for, charitable, social, and civic purposes are charged to "Other Income Deductions," as are penalties and fines levied by the commissions for violating regulatory statutes. The ratemaking treatment of these items differs among the commissions.

All uniform systems of accounts require depreciation accounting. Over the past half century, the depreciation practices of the regulated industries have changed significantly. Prior to the thirties, most of the companies, with

FIGURE 6-2

Condensed Income Accounts

Utility Operating Income
    Operating Revenues
    Operating Expenses[a]
Other Income and Deductions[b]
Interest Charges[c]
Extraordinary Items[d]

[a]Includes operating expenses; maintenance expense; depreciation expense; amortization of limited-term electric plant; amortization of electric plant acquisition adjustments; amortization of property losses and unrecovered plant and regulatory study costs; taxes other than income taxes, utility operating income; income taxes, utility operating income; provisions for deferred income taxes; investment tax credit adjustments; revenues from, and expenses of, electric plant leased to others.

[b]Includes Other Income (*e.g.*, net revenue from merchandising, jobbing, and contract work; revenues from, and expenses of, nonutility operations; nonoperating rental income; interest and dividend income; gain on disposition of property), Other Income Deductions (*e.g.*, loss on disposition of property; donations; life insurance; penalties; expenditures for certain civic, political and related activities), and Taxes Applicable to Other Income and Deductions.

[c]Includes interest on long-term debt, amortization of debt discount and expense, interest on debt to associated companies, allowance for borrowed funds used during construction-credit.

[d]Extraordinary income, deductions, and associated income taxes.

the notable exception of the Bell System, practiced retirement accounting, whereby either the whole investment cost of property is charged to depreciation expense only when retired from service, or part of the investment cost is charged to a partial reserve and accumulated during the useful life of the property. As a result, the utilities were able to control their annual reported earnings: when actual earnings were high, they could make large charges to depreciation expense, thereby lowering reported earnings and avoiding regulatory rate and earnings reductions; when actual earnings were low, they could make few, if any, charges to depreciation expenses, thereby making it possible to pay some common stock dividends by overstating reported earnings. Nor were the rates of depreciation uniform. In its 1926 investigation of depreciation accounting, for instance, the Interstate Commerce Commission found that wooden freight cars had been given service lives ranging from three to sixty years by different carriers; steam locomotives from four to fifty-five years; steel passenger cars from five to fifty years; and wooden passenger cars from five to sixty-six years.[25]

During the thirties and early forties, the commissions gradually required the regulated utilities to accrue depreciation, making annual charges to depreciation expense so as to distribute the original cost over the service life of the property. This practice is known as depreciation accounting,[26] as distinguished from retirement accounting. In addition, the commissions have prescribed the various plant accounts for which depreciation charges are to be set up, and have established rates of depreciation for the most important types of property. Depreciation charges generally are computed on the basis of the original cost of the property.

Cost Allocation Methods: Telephone Services

The property of many public utilities is used in common to (a) furnish service to different customer classes, (b) provide different services, or (c) supply both intrastate and interstate services. In these circumstances, cost allocation methods are required. The methods used to allocate common or joint costs[27] for ratemaking purposes are discussed in later chapters. One case, however, deserves separate treatment: the separation of costs between interstate and intrastate telephone services. Detailed cost allocation methods — known as "separations procedures" — were adopted.[28] But with the growth of competition, they are obsolete.

Accounting regulation offers little guidance in developing cost allocation methods, since common or joint costs cannot generally be identified with any customer class, specific service, or jurisdiction. As Justice Douglas has put it:

A separation of properties is merely a step in the determination of costs properly allocable to the various classes of service rendered by a utility. But where as here several classes of services have a common use of the same property difficulties of separation are obvious. Allocation of costs is not a matter for the slide-rule. It involves judgment on a myriad of facts. It has no claim to an exact science.[29]

Stated another way, any cost allocation method contains elements of arbitrariness. The results obtained by the application of a particular method are affected by the method employed.

Jurisdictional Separations — The Past. The Bell System furnished both interstate and intrastate communications services.[30] Interstate services, which included message toll telephone and wide area telephone services (MTS/ WATS), private-line telephone, telegraph, data, and program transmission (video and audio), were subject to the jurisdiction of the Federal Communications Commission. Intrastate services, which represented local exchange and intrastate toll services (similar to the interstate services listed above), were subject to the jurisdiction of the state commissions. The Long Lines Department of AT&T was engaged solely in interstate and overseas activities. Much of the property of the Bell System operating companies (as well as the nearly 1,500 independent telephone companies) was used in common for both interstate and intrastate services. Further, it was basically nontraffic-sensitive plant (*e.g.*, the local distribution plant and terminal equipment on the customer's premises). The costs incurred in rendering such services cannot be directly assigned to those services. The state and federal regulatory agencies thus cooperated in developing uniform methods of allocating common costs between the various jurisdictions.[31]

Separations procedures evolved from many years of study by all interested parties. Moreover, they were changed and modified on numerous occasions.[32] Separations methods were built around the "actual use" principle; namely, that (*1*) all costs of plant used solely for one service were assigned directly to that service, and (2) all costs of plant used jointly for two or more services were allocated among the services on an actual use basis which considered both relative occupancy and relative time in use measurements.[33] Measurements of time in use were determined on a unit basis (*e.g.*, traffic units per call) in studies of traffic handled or work performed during a representative test period, and applied to a full 24-hour period rather than busy hour volumes.[34] Thus, telephone circuit plant was separated on the basis of minutes of use (*i.e.*, minutes of holding time or conversation time), manual switching plant on the basis of operator work time, and dial switching plant on the basis of minutes of use; while reserves, expenses, and taxes generally were separated on the same basis as the current costs or the book costs of the related plant.[35]

For settlements within the Bell System, all revenues collected from interstate operations were pooled each month, and expenses and taxes allocated to interstate operations by each company were repaid to them out of those revenues.[36] The remaining net revenues, which represented the amount for return, were distributed to the Long Lines Department and the operating companies on the basis of the net investment each contributed to the total net investment of interstate services. If the Long Lines Department, for example, provided 35 percent of the total net investment, it would receive 35 percent of the remaining net revenues.

The methods used to allocate common costs have been subject to criticism and review.[37] Between 1945 and 1961, interstate toll rates, particularly for very long distances, decreased significantly, while intrastate toll rates increased moderately. This rate behavior resulted in the so-called "disparity problem"; *i.e.*, rates for interstate toll calls generally below those for intrastate toll calls of approximately equal distances.[38] Although the relationship between interstate and intrastate rates changed over time, on July 1, 1967, when the last study was made, intrastate long-distance rates averaged 15 to 30 percent higher than interstate rates for comparable distances for station-to-station calls; 30 to 80 percent higher for person-to-person calls.[39] Some critics maintained that the separations procedures placed too great a burden on intrastate service. But application of the actual use principle under conditions of decreasing unit costs for long-haul plant and relatively constant unit costs for both short-haul and local exchange plant accounted for the diverse movement of interstate and intrastate rates.[40] Moreover, as a result of (a) a larger percentage increase in interstate toll calls relative to intrastate calls and (b) cooperative changes in separations procedures,[41] the disparity began to narrow in the late 1960s.

Despite basic differences of opinion over methodology, therefore, the toll rate disparity was not the result of separations procedures alone. Fundamentally, the disparity problem was created by the jurisdictional division of authority between the federal and state governments. Costs differed substantially among the jurisdictions that regulated toll telephone rates, reflecting primarily differences in length of haul and, to some degree, differences in terrain, density of population, volume of calls, plant investment, and other miscellaneous factors.[42] The disparity problem would have disappeared completely if responsibility for interstate and intrastate toll calls had been transferred to one jurisdiction. Some, including Hatfield, supported such a transfer:

> ... the present jurisdictional split which puts local exchange and intrastate toll under state jurisdiction and interstate toll under federal jurisdiction is in need of revision. Since long distance or interexchange service is virtually the same whether or not it crosses state lines, the existing jurisdictional arrangement is not a natural point of division on technical, economic, or regulatory grounds. For one thing, the long haul services — both interstate and intrastate — are generally open to competition while local service in many areas will likely remain a virtual monopoly for some time to come. Moreover, it complicates the separations process by requiring an added allocation of toll facility costs between the two jurisdictions. Because of these and other factors, we have consistently advocated that jurisdiction over intrastate toll be shifted to the FCC.[43]

Competition and Access Charges — The Future. Separations procedures were developed under monopoly conditions. In more recent years, the FCC has permitted interstate competition, first in private-line services and then in MTS-like services. The new competitors, however, did not carry the MTS/WATS separations burden (*i.e.,* since they only purchased local exchange service, they were not party to the division of revenues/settlements process) which, in 1983, amounted to an estimated $11.6 billion (for interstate alone); an amount equal to over 40 percent of MTS/WATS revenues or over $1 per MTS message. At the same time, if competition is to be fostered in the industry, all competing carriers must have access to local exchange facilities and, therefore, must make contributions to the nontraffic-sensitive costs.[44]

Late in 1982, the FCC voted to approve (the order was issued early in 1983[45]) a new system of tariffed access charges (also known as "subscriber line charges") to be administered by the National Exchange Carrier Association (NECA),[46] effective January 1, 1984. Under the system, most of the nontraffic-sensitive costs would be recovered through end-user access charges, rather than through usage-sensitive interstate toll rates (for those nontraffic-sensitive costs assigned to the interstate jurisdiction). The decision, as modified in 1983,[47] proved to be highly controversial.[48] Critics argued that flat, monthly access charges (*a*) would impose a severe financial burden on many residential users, thereby contributing to a decline of universal service[49] and (*b*) would encourage businesses to bypass the public network.[50] Yet, as Kahn has argued:

> . . . a large portion of the costs of providing access to the telephone network are recovered in charges for *using* the system, even though those costs are largely independent of usage: customers impose access costs on the system when they are connected to it, regardless of whether they then proceed to place or to receive calls. This practice has two adverse consequences, each the counterpart of the other. On the one hand, the basic monthly service charge is far too low: people are encouraged to become customers — and, even more flagrantly undesirable, to order additional lines — when the value to them of that access is less than the cost to society of providing it. And, on the other side, the charges for using the long distance network are artificially inflated (on the order of 60 percent), because customers are required by the jurisdictional separations and settlements process to contribute to costs that would not be avoided if that usage were curtailed. The result is very inefficient: the artificial, 60 percent tax discourages people from making calls by grossly exaggerating the cost burden that they place on society when they do so.[51]

Regulation of Financing

Prior to the 1930s the financing of utilities, except for the railroads, was almost completely unregulated. The general attitude of the times toward overcapitalization was expressed by Senator LaFollette: "The public need not concern itself with all the villainies of overcapitalization."[52] And the chairman of the Wisconsin commission stated the general feeling toward the control of corporate securities: "Regulation of corporate securities is . . . for the benefit of investors and . . . it has no bearing . . . upon the question of rates."[53] After the stock market crash of 1929, however, the public attitudes changed completely as a result of the many abuses uncovered — overcapitalization, stock watering, excessive dividends, and the like.[54] These abuses, it should be noted again, were not limited to public utilities, but were widespread throughout American industry. Many of the regulatory commissions were granted jurisdiction over the financing of the utility companies.

The abuses which brought about this type of regulation have long since been removed through the surveillance of the commissions, the reorganization of electric and gas holding companies under the Public Utility Holding Company Act of 1935, and refinements in the art of accounting and auditing. It is important, nevertheless, to understand why the commissions were granted these powers and the methods by which they corrected the abuses.

Control of Capitalization

For many years, it was widely believed by the commissions that the financial policies of public utilities had no effect upon either rates or service. Among the commissions, only those of California, Massachusetts, New York, Texas, and Wisconsin, in addition to the Interstate Commerce Commission, exercised active supervision of financial matters prior to 1930.[55] Most of the commissions apparently accepted the proposition that financial decisions should be the responsibility of management.

Relation of Capitalization to Rates and Service. The capitalization of a company refers to the amount of outstanding securities — long-term debt, preferred and common stock. A company is considered to be undercapitalized when the amount of outstanding securities is below the value of its property (assets); overcapitalized when the amount of outstanding securities exceeds the value of its property. For public utilities, a distinction must be made between capitalizable and noncapitalizable assets. Simply stated, the first refers to property devoted to utility business, the second to property devoted to nonutility purposes. This distinction, and the reasons for making it, are the same as those discussed under accounting regulation. It is sufficient to state again, therefore, that rates should be set on the basis of a fair rate of return on the value of the property devoted to utility business.[56]

It is now generally recognized that abuses of capitalization can prevent effective regulation. In extreme cases, overcapitalization has resulted in higher rates charged by a company or in deteriorating quality and quantity of service offered. This situation arose because utility rates are set by regulation. Under competitive conditions, capitalization cannot affect rates. Even if a company were overcapitalized, it would be unable to raise its rates above those of its competitors. Likewise, under monopoly conditions, capitalization is unrelated to rates. While an overcapitalized company might find it possible to raise its rates to earn a profit on its inflated capitalization, a monopolist has the power to charge excessive rates whether overcapitalized or not.[57] Under regulation, however, capitalization may affect rates.

In theory, a public utility is entitled to earn a fair rate of return on the fair value of its property. If the theory were strictly adhered to, capitalization would have no affect on rates. But such does not occur in practice. Assume that the value of a utility's property, on an original cost basis, is $5 million. If the commission allows a 10 percent rate of return, the utility will earn $500,000. Further, assume that the utility's capitalization is $10 million; that is, the company is overcapitalized. On $4 million of bonds at 8 percent, it must pay $320,000, leaving $180,000. On $3 million of preferred stock at 7 percent, it must pay $210,000. Obviously, this is impossible. In other words, the utility is unable to meet its fixed obligations. To do so, the utility would need a rate of return of 10.6 percent, and even then, it would be unable to pay any dividends on its common stock.

In practice, therefore, commissions would be faced with a difficult decision when confronted with such a situation. Unless the utility were allowed, through increased rates, a rate of return sufficient to meet its fixed obligations, it would be forced into bankruptcy and reorganization — an alternative which may be less desirable over the long run than higher rates. Bankruptcy not only inflicts losses upon investors, making it difficult or impossible for the utility to attract capital in the future, but service improvements and growth may be deferred. In extreme cases, the provision of any service at all may be imperiled. "As between the two alternatives — high rates or poor service — the public will usually choose the former."[58]

For these reasons, overcapitalization does affect the rates and services of public utilities. The solution, of course, is for the commissions to exercise supervision over the financing of these companies so as to prevent the problem of overcapitalization from arising.

Commission Control of Capitalization. There are three important problems concerning commission supervision of capitalization. What is the proper measure of a utility's capitalization? How can overcapitalization be corrected? How can overcapitalization be prevented?

Measures of Capitalization. It was earlier noted that a public utility's capitalization should not exceed the value of its capitalizable assets. But what is the proper basis of valuation to use? The value of a company's assets can be measured by original or actual cost, reproduction cost, and market values. While the terms are the same, the considerations which govern the choice of the proper valuation method as a basis of capitalization are not the same as those governing the choice of a standard for determining the rate base.[59] The commissions, for sound reasons, commonly use the original or actual cost as a basis for capitalization.[60]

Reproduction cost fluctuates with the price level. If capitalization were based on this value, a utility might be properly capitalized at one time but overcapitalized at another simply because of a change in the price level. Such a situation would be undesirable, for a utility cannot easily change its capitalization, especially if the price level and, hence, reproduction cost is falling. A utility's capitalization should not fluctuate with the price level.[61] Nor can a utility's capitalization be based upon the market value of its assets or its capitalized earnings, because circular reasoning would be involved. The earnings of a utility depend on the rates established by a commission. Thus, whereas an unregulated company may have a proper capitalization when its outstanding securities equal its capitalized earnings, even though the resulting capitalization is higher than the original or actual cost of its assets, this is improper for a regulated company whose earnings are not determined by market forces.[62]

The commissions have long held, therefore, that the proper measure of a utility's capitalization is the original or actual cost of the company's capitalizable assets.[63] Except in unusual circumstances, such as reorganizations, capitalization will be permitted to increase only as the investment in property rises, and a commission may try to reduce a utility's capitalization as investment falls. This statement does not imply that a utility should be considered as overcapitalized when its earnings are insufficient to meet its fixed obligations. While in such a situation it might be desirable for a utility to reduce its capitalization, so long as its "securities outstanding represent funds actually invested in the property," the company is not overcapitalized.[64]

Methods of Correcting Overcapitalization. Particularly in the electric, gas, and railroad industries was overcapitalization a serious problem following the stock market crash of 1929. Use of the holding company device was primarily responsible for the financial difficulties of the electric and gas utilities. In the case of the railroads, construction costs were inflated because of the widespread use of the construction company,[65] property purchased at excessive prices, securities sold at a discount when investors were unwilling to pay par for them, and excessive amounts of securities issued in reorganization cases when companies offered to replace defaulted bonds with securities whose par values were even higher.

The commissions used several methods to correct the excessive capitalizations which occurred before they were given jurisdiction over the financial affairs of public utilities. The most common method was reorganization and will be discussed below. Capitalization readjustments were made in at least four other ways. First, the current book value of common stock was scaled down by writing off excessive values of property. Second, earned surplus was accumulated by restricting or entirely withholding dividend payments. Third, stockholders contributed cash or securities to a utility. Fourth, authority to issue new securities was denied when the proceeds were to be used to reimburse the company's treasury for construction expenditures already made. While all of these methods were used,[66] they had obvious disadvantages. Reorganization remained as the most effective and most frequently used way of eliminating excessive overcapitalization.

Methods of Preventing Overcapitalization. It is far easier to prevent than to correct overcapitalization. A majority of the state commissions have the power to regulate or control purchases, mergers, and consolidations (forty-nine states and the District of Columbia); issuance of securities (forty-four states and the District of Columbia)[67]; property and security transactions with affiliated companies (forty-three states and the District of Columbia); and purchase of securities of other utilities (thirty-five states and the District of Columbia). In addition, a few state commissions (fifteen) have the authority to regulate dividends.[68] The federal commissions, except for natural gas and telephone companies, have similar powers. The commissions have frequently exercised these powers to prevent overcapitalization.[69] Most of the commissions have made certain exceptions so that the companies have some necessary flexibility.[70] Short-term debt (notes under one year), for instance, are frequently exempt unless they exceed a specified percentage (5 percent is common) of a utility's total capitalization.

In regulating security issues, a few commissions control the selling prices of the securities. The most active commission in this respect is the Massachusetts commission, which fixes the issuing prices of the common stocks of electric and gas utilities.[71] More common is regulation of the selling costs of new security issues by requiring competitive bidding. These costs, known as "flotation costs," represent the difference between the amount paid by investors and the amount received by the issuing company.

It was the long-standing practice of public utilities to float issues of new securities through one or more of the large investment banking houses. Which investment bank a company would use often depended on tradition or which bank was represented on the company's board of directors. Prior to 1940, however, investment banking houses frequently made excessive charges for their services by agreeing not to compete against each other.[72] The commissions, in an effort to reduce flotation charges, began to require competitive bidding as opposed to direct placement. A 1919 Massachusetts statute required competitive bidding on electric and gas bonds; the Interstate Commerce Commission started competitive bidding on railroad equipment-trust obligations in 1926; and other commissions followed suit during the thirties and early forties.[73] Exceptions will be made for small issues (the Securities and Exchange Commission exempts all issues under one million dollars), when a utility can show that direct placement of securities will result in a better price, or when market conditions are unfavorable for competitive bidding. Otherwise, competitive bidding for mortgage bonds and debentures is required by eight states and for the underwriting of new common stock by six states.[74]

Control of the Capital Structure

Regulatory commissions are not only concerned with a utility's total capitalization, but also with the capital structure. The term capital structure refers to the composition of a company's capitalization; that is, to the proportion between debt and equity that makes up the capitalization. Historically, public utilities have issued about 50 percent of their securities in the form of bonds,[75] 15 percent in preferred stock, and 35 percent in common stock. These proportions, however, vary widely among individual companies. Manufactured gas companies and railroads, which have often used even larger amounts of debt financing, have undergone many bankruptcy proceedings. Other utilities, which have maintained lower debt to equity ratios, have been criticized as being too conservative. Since the early 1970s, the concern has been that utilities' debt ratios have become too high.

Importance of Capital Structure. A utility's capital structure is important for three major reasons. First, if the proportion of debt to equity is high, fixed charges also will be high, thereby creating difficulties for a utility in times of low earnings. A utility must meet its fixed charges or go through the process of reorganization. During the depression of the thirties, the dangers of large debt ratios were evident. To illustrate: In 1932, 122 out of 162 Class I railroads, operating nearly 74 percent of the total mileage of Class I roads, failed to earn their fixed charges.[76]

Second, it is widely held that the cost of capital is related to a utility's capital structure.[77] As the proportion of debt increases, "the added *financial risks* for both the debt and equity holders result in higher and higher costs for both debt and equity capital."[78] The commissions, in determining a fair rate of return, commonly consider the cost of capital as the minimum necessary return needed to maintain a utility's credit standing.[79] Therefore, the higher the cost of capital, the higher a utility's total earnings (and, hence, rates) must be to preserve its credit rating.[80]

Third, the capital structure determines control of a utility. Before the commissions exercised supervision over their capital structures, public utilities often issued large amounts of bonds and preferred stock, incurring heavy interest and fixed dividend obligations, in addition to nonvoting common stock, to avoid losing control by issuing voting common stock. Particularly was this true of the electric and gas holding companies. While this situation may have benefited those in control, it was detrimental to the debt holders, stockholders, and the economy, for bankruptcy often resulted from these burdensome capital structures. For all these reasons, effective regulation requires commission supervision of capital structures.

What Is a Proper Capital Structure? At the outset, it must be recognized that there is no one proper or ideal capital structure. Rather, a utility's capital structure is a function of its business risks (which include all of the economic, physical, political, and technological risks to which a particular investment is exposed) and, thus, is largely a matter of business judgment. For manufacturing firms, whose earnings are subject to sharp fluctuations, a debt ratio of 30 percent or under is common, compared with a 58.6 percent ratio (bonds and preferred stock) for investor owned electric utilities (year-end 1984). Further, it should be noted that

> . . . a capital structure evolves. It is rooted in the history of the firm, and is the present reflection of financial decisions made at various times in the past and in the light of considerations then obtaining. Ordinarily, a firm's capital structure cannot be changed radically overnight — short of Draconian measures which would probably entail a cost greater than the benefits sought to be obtained by such a radical change.[81]

Too Little Debt? In the 1950s and 1960s, some commissions expressed concern that particular utilities had too little debt. The American Telephone and Telegraph Company, for example, maintained a debt to total capital ratio of about one-third. Critics of AT&T's postwar financing argued that the company had been too conservative. A higher debt ratio, they argued, would have reduced the overall cost of capital and increased the market price of the company's common stock. Financing by debt costs less than by equity — 5 to 6 percent interest on debt compared to 10 to 11 percent earnings on equity (at that time). Moreover, interest charges on debt are deductible from income subject to taxes. As a result (assuming a 48 percent corporate income tax rate), a utility must earn $1.92 to pay a dollar in dividends, compared with only $1.00 to pay a dollar in interest. It was estimated that if the debt ratio had increased from 35 to 40 percent in 1959, AT&T could have saved nearly $100 million in taxes and lower capital costs, and could have saved nearly double that amount if the debt ratio had risen to 45 percent.[82]

Such calculations assume that equity and debt holders would have taken the same return on their investment, even though the debt ratio had risen. The critics maintained that they would have done so, first, because other utilities had maintained a higher debt ratio and their securities were rated as high as those of AT&T; second, since with a higher debt ratio there is greater leverage for any given level of return on total capital, the earnings on each share are higher. Higher earnings, in turn, would have made it possible to increase dividends, which would have tended to result in a rise of the stock's market price. Finally, the critics concluded, even if the company were forced to pay somewhat higher interest rates as its debt ratio increased, this would have been offset by the tax savings.

AT&T took issue with all of those contentions. In the immediate postwar years, the company's debt ratio reached 54 percent, but its bond rating dropped and it had trouble placing its bonds. Summarized a former company official:

> ... once the System's debt ratio rises appreciably, there is an immediate reaction in the market and it becomes more expensive to finance by debt. In other words, higher debt adds to investment risks — both debt and equity, and even the bond buyers, whose investments in effect are underwritten by the share owners, demand a greater return for the greater risk taken. The share owners, in turn, also demand (and are entitled to) a greater return for their greater risks. When all of these factors are added up, the claimed cost of capital advantages realized from financing by debt are actually nonexistent. Over the long-run, it is the over-all risks of the business that determine the over-all capital costs, regardless of how these risks are divided among the classes of investors. No one has been able to prove successfully to the contrary.[83]

The company also maintained that it must keep "a reserve of borrowing capacity." Explained former treasurer Scanlon:

A business like ours, faced with the necessity for frequent and heavy new borrowings, must maintain a high grade credit rating on its debt. Such a credit rating cannot be achieved with a debt burden which the financial markets consider to be high for that business. In our case this need is underscored by the fact that shortly we shall have to commence the refunding of our large volume of existing debt. This refunding will be over-laid on the heavy requirements for additional new debt financing to finance current growth.[84]

For these reasons, AT&T's management contended "that its policy of maintaining its debt ratio in the 30-40 percent range is proper, considering the kind of business it is, its riskiness and its future prospects and problems."[85]

Too Much Debt? By the early 1970s, many commissions began to express concern that some utilities had too much debt. AT&T's debt ratio, to illustrate, increased to nearly 50 percent at the end of 1974. Utilities' stock market prices declined (below book value) and, to avoid dilution, new capital requirements were met to a large extent by debt issues. But when further "increases in debt and preferred stock ratios became unacceptable in the market and, in many instances, were prohibited by the terms of bond indentures and other investment contracts," common stock financing by utilities

... became necessary to prevent a further rise of the debt ratio, to maintain borrowing capacity, to protect bond ratings, and to arrest the rapid decline in the coverage of fixed charges. Most common stock offerings were at prices below book equity, thus further diluting the market value of already outstanding shares. A large majority of electric utility bonds were derated. The cost of both debt and equity capital increased because of the loss of investor confidence.[86]

The issue confronting the commissions, then, was no longer excessive conservatism; rather, the issue was too much debt, combined with the need to raise huge amounts of capital at high costs. The utilities were forced to adopt imaginative financing — convertible securities, issues with warrants, preference stock, short-term notes (five years) and intermediate-term bonds (seven to ten years), pollution control facilities financed with industrial development bonds or pollution abatement revenue bonds, and employee stock option and dividend reinvestment plans.[87] Leasing and project financing became viable options.[88] With high interest rates, refunding and debt-equity swaps were carried out.[89] A few utilities have offered common stock to their customers through a monthly installment plan[90]; a few electric utilities have established an energy trust to finance nuclear power plants or the purchase of nuclear fuel. Utility financing, in short, has changed substantially over the years.[91]

Commission Control of Capital Structures. The most important problem faced by the commissions historically has been excessive indebtedness.

Two questions are raised. How do commissions control indebtedness? How can indebtedness be reduced?

Control of Indebtedness. Past experience showed the commissions that large amounts of debt securities often are undesirable, but no satisfactory method of limiting indebtedness has been developed. A few state commissions have fixed the ratio of bonds to stock that a public utility may not exceed. Others have refused to approve increases in indebtedness when companies already have large amounts of debt securities, have restricted bond issues, or have ruled that stock instead of bonds should be issued.[92] These methods, however, have limitations. For example, since the financial conditions of individual utilities vary, no one ratio of debt to equity is correct. The refusal to approve a bond issue may lead to no issue at all, for if a utility's earnings are insufficient to maintain its stock at par, it is in no position to issue more stock; bonds are the only way new capital can be raised. As a result of these problems, few commissions are willing to substitute their judgments for those of management, except in reorganization cases.[93]

Rather than adopt an arbitrary debt limit, some commissions have established requirements for additional bond issues, particularly for mortgage bonds. "Today the SEC and several state commissions regularly examine the values of mortgaged properties, control the issuance of additional bonds under each mortgage, require sinking funds for most bond issues, specify provisions for depreciation and maintenance costs, and limit the payments of common stock dividends."[94] Restriction on dividend payments also is used when a utility is in financial difficulty. Some commissions will prescribe minimum amounts of earned surplus that must be available before dividends can be paid, or will prohibit dividend payments altogether.[95]

Methods of Reducing Indebtedness. Short of reorganization, indebtedness can be reduced in four principal ways. First, the debt to equity ratio can be lowered by confining new security issues to common stock.[96] Second, bonds can be retired by issuing common stock or out of earnings.[97] Unless bonds have a "call provision," only maturing issues can be retired in this manner. Some commissions now require such a provision so that bonds can be repaid and retired before their maturity at the utility's option.[98] When earnings and stock market conditions are favorable, redemption may be a desirable way to reduce indebtedness. Retirement also may be accomplished out of earnings. In a few cases, as noted above, commissions have prohibited or restricted dividend payments until indebtedness has been reduced. Oftentimes, however, retirement from earnings is impossible; unless a utility has adequate earnings, it will have to use all available resources for improvements and additions.

Third, the refunding of bond and note issues offers another method of reducing indebtedness. When these issues mature, they must be paid. Commonly, new issues are sold in order to obtain the money for the maturing bonds and notes. Commissions sometimes will require that stock issues be used to refund debt, thereby reducing a utility's debt.[99] Callable bonds can be refunded before maturity. Here, new bonds are sold at lower interest rates and the proceeds used to retire higher interest bonds. While the capital structure remains unchanged, the burden of debt is reduced, as the utility's annual interest charges are lower.

Indebtedness can be reduced, finally, through voluntary agreements with bondholders. Income bonds and common stock have been substituted for fixed interest securities, the maturity date of bonds extended, and the rate of interest reduced.[100] While not a popular method, bondholders are often willing to accept such adjustments when a company faces bankruptcy.

Reorganization

Financial reorganization offers the most effective, but also the most drastic, way of revising a utility's capitalization and capital structure. Reorganization may come about in one of two ways: (*a*) bankruptcy or (*b*) legislative mandate. The railroad industry illustrates the first; electric and gas utilities the second.

Railroad Reorganization.[101] Since 1872, the nation's railroads have been undergoing continuous financial reorganizations. As of April 30, 1948, the Interstate Commerce Commission had approved reorganization plans resulting in the elimination of over $2.5 billion of debt, and a reduction of over $111 million in fixed charges.[102] The procedure for railroad reorganization cases, under Section 77 of the Bankruptcy Act of 1933, has been summarized by Locklin:

> Section 77 provides that a railroad corporation, or creditors having claims which aggregate 5 percent or more of the corporation's indebtedness, may file a petition in the appropriate court, stating that the company is insolvent and unable to meet its debt and that a financial reorganization is desirable. Upon approval of the petition the court must appoint one or more trustees to take charge of the carrier's property. Within six months after approval of the petition the debtor corporation is required to file a plan of reorganization with the court and with the Interstate Commerce Commission. Reorganization plans may also be filed by the trustees, creditors, stockholders, or other interested parties. After public hearings on the reorganization plans the Commission is to render a report approving a plan of reorganization. This plan may be different from that presented by any party. Before approving a plan, however, the Commission must find that it conforms to certain requirements. Among these are the following: (*1*) The plan must be "compatible with the public interest"; (*2*) the fixed charges must be within the earning capacity of the carrier; and (*3*) the plan must be fair and equitable, affording due recognition to the rights of

each class of creditors and stockholders, and conforming to the requirements of the law of the land regarding the participation of the various classes of creditors and stockholders. The plan of reorganization approved by the Commission is then submitted to the court for its approval. The court is not empowered to approve a plan that has not been approved by the Commission. If the court will not accept the plan approved by the Commission, the matter is referred back to the Commission for reconsideration. After a plan has been approved by the court, it is submitted for approval to such classes of creditors and stockholders as under the circumstances may be necessary. After approval by creditors or stockholders representing two-thirds of the amount of such claims or stock, the judge must confirm the plan. Upon confirmation of the plan it is binding upon all parties.[103]

With respect to security issues, the statute states that a reorganization plan

> ... shall provide for fixed charges (including fixed interest on funded debt, interest on unfunded debt, amortization of discount on funded debt, and rent for leased railroads) in such an amount that, after due consideration of the probable prospective earnings of the property in light of its earnings experience and all other relevant facts, there shall be adequate coverage of such fixed charges by the probable earnings available for the payment thereof.[104]

In general, the commission's policy has been to limit a company's total capitalization to an amount based upon a conservative estimate of future earnings, rather than upon property valuations. As explained by the commission in an early case: "If this reorganization is to be successful, the capital structure of the reorganized company must be realistically related to its actual earning power, and consideration given to the investment in its property only to the extent that such investment is justified by the probable earnings reasonably foreseeable in the future."[105] And, in 1943, this position was upheld by the Supreme Court:

> A basic requirement of any reorganization is the determination of a capitalization which makes it possible ... to give the new company a reasonable prospect for survival. ... Only "meticulous regard for earning capacity" ... can give the new company some safeguards against the scourge of overcapitalization. Disregard of that method of valuation can only bring ... "a harvest of barren regrets."[106]

Similar views have been expressed by the Securities and Exchange Commission and some state commissions in other public utility reorganization cases.[107]

Electric and Gas Utility Reorganizations. The consolidation movement in the electric and gas industries in the late 1910s and throughout the 1920s took place by means of the holding company. While there were many advantages, holding company abuses came to light after the stock market crash in 1929, when millions were lost by investors.[108] Some went bankrupt: Between September 1, 1929, and April 15, 1936, fifty-three holding companies with combined securities of a par value of $1.7 billion went into bankruptcy or receivership. Twenty-three others were forced to default on interest payments or to offer extension plans.[109] When the Insull system fell ($238 million investment), holders of debentures received $8.34 per $100 in the final distribution, while other security holders received nothing.[110] But particularly did reorganization of electric and gas utilities take place under the Public Utility Holding Company Act (Title I of the Public Utility Act of 1935) — "the most stringent corrective measure ever applied to American business."[111]

Among other things, the act required holding companies to register with the SEC and gave the commission power (Section 11) to simplify the holding company structures in two ways: technical integration and financial reorganization. With respect to the latter,[112] the SEC was instructed to take steps to "ensure that the corporate structure or continued existence of any company ... does not unduly or unnecessarily complicate the structure, or unfairly or inequitably distribute voting power among security holders. ..." Companies were given a year (with extensions permitted) to comply voluntarily or the commission could order an investigation and reorganization. During the period June 15, 1938 to June 30, 1962, 2,419 electric and gas utilities and natural gas pipeline companies came under the jurisdiction of the commission, either as registered holding companies or as subsidiaries thereof. Of these companies, 928, with assets aggregating approximately $13 billion, were subject to divestiture.[113]

"Like a reorganization of an insolvent company, a financial revision under Section 11 has three main dimensions: the total capitalization, the composition of the capital structure, and proration of the new securities to the old security holders."[114] Specifically, guided by prospective earnings, excessive capitalizations were scaled down by eliminating write-ups. Debt-heavy capital structures were revised by replacing debt and preferred stock with common stock. It has been estimated that long-term debt for ten large holding company systems decreased from $526 million to $268 million in the period 1934 to 1944.[115] The commission required, and continues to require, competitive bidding for new security issues. And, especially when a company was in arrears of preferred stock dividends, voting rights were redistributed to reduce the control of common stockholders who had small investments in a holding company.[116] These financial reorganizations

> ... simplified the corporate organizations. As a consequence of the changes, some systems were perhaps able to borrow investable funds and to make investments that were deferred for a long time. If straitened financial conditions, such as large amounts of unpaid preferred

dividends, limited the borrowing capacity of a company, a recapitalization obviously facilitated new investments and service expansion. Alteration of top-heavy capital structures also improved borrowing conditions. . . .[117]

Bankruptcy: A Current Option for Electric Utilities?[118] Two types of bankruptcy are possible under present laws: debt reorganization, under Chapter 11, and liquidation, under Chapter 7. In view of the financial problems of electric utilities with nuclear power projects since the late 1970s, several state commissions have faced the possibility that an electric utility might declare bankruptcy and file for Chapter 11 reorganization.[119] These include the New Hampshire and Maine commissions with respect to Seabrook,[120] and the Michigan commission with respect to Midland.[121] In each of these instances, the commissions have rejected bankruptcy as a solution to financial problems, citing (*a*) possible loss of regulatory control over rates and operations, and (*b*) possible interruptions of utility services. While these concerns "may be largely unfounded," the

> . . . financial ramifications for the utility are not optimistic . . . The utility's reduced borrowing capacity, market restrictions on additional credit, and the domino effect on the company's economic future demonstrate the financial difficulties a utility would face. Yet without sufficient refinancing, the utility cannot expand its customer base or encourage industrial development and may be strangled by its new debt. While bankruptcy may be a source of immediate, short-term freedom, and a utility may be able to emerge from reorganization virtually intact, the length and expense of bankruptcy and refinancing proceedings makes bankruptcy appear to be more of a revolving door than a solution.[122]

All of these issues will soon be tested, since Public Service Co. of New Hampshire was forced to file for protection from creditors under Chapter 11 early in 1988.[123]

A Concluding Comment of Caution

At the outset of this chapter, it was stated that the material covered in the chapter was largely of historical importance. This point needs reemphasis. With respect to accounting procedures, the establishment of uniform systems of accounts has solved the earlier abuses which resulted from irregular accounting practices. Moreover, there is no disagreement concerning the need for such systems. They are used as a starting point in evaluating a public utility's rates and in developing cost allocation methods. But since uniform systems only specify an accounting form, there remain differences of opinion over the scope, content, and application of the various provisions.[124] Public utility industries take the general position that accounting principles should be the same for both regulated and nonregulated business. There-fore, they argue, the principal objective of the regulatory commissions in this area should be the uniform application of these principles.[125] Current accounting and depreciation problems center on the proper statement of income, inflation, and competition, and will be considered at length in subsequent chapters.

Similarly, with respect to financial matters, the excesses brought to light in the early 1930s have been corrected. There is no evidence, for example, that public utilities (in general) are overcapitalized at the present time, or that their capital structures are unjustified. Disagreements as to the proper capital structure for a particular company are to be expected, but overcapi-talization, stock watering, excessive dividends, and so forth are primarily problems of the past.

Notes

*Robert L. Hahne and Gregory E. Aliff, *Accounting for Public Utilities* (New York: Matthew Bender & Co., Inc., 1983; 1987 Revision), p. 11-3.

[1]Earl H. Barbee, "As Represented: Adventures in Public Utility Accounting," 11 *Journal of Land & Public Utility Economics* 25 (1935).

[2]Complete uniformity in state and federal commission accounting requirements has not been achieved. Where conflicts occur, federal commission requirements take precedence. *Re Appalachian Power Co.*, 46 PUR3d 440 (FPC, 1962).

[3]Emery Troxel, *Economics of Public Utilities* (New York: Holt, Rinehart & Winston, Inc., 1947), pp. 123-24.

[4]The problem is discussed at length in Chapter 8.

[5]"Without belaboring the problems relating to the accounting system or enumer-ating all its deficiencies, we need simply say that we recognize the inadequacies of the Uniform System of Accounts for our regulatory purposes. In recent decisions involv-ing AT&T interstate services, . . . we were hampered in our ability to determine the lawfulness of Bell's rates and rate structure by the lack of information as to invest-ment, expenses and revenues associated with specific services and sub-services." *Re American Teleph. & Teleg. Co.*, Docket No. 19129, par. 213 (FCC, 1977). In 1978, the FCC initiated a proceeding to consider revisions of the Uniform System of Accounts (Docket No. 78-196, 70 FCC 2d 719). See *Re Amendment of Part 31*, 85 FCC 2d 818 (1981).

[6]Accounting information has many other potential uses for decision making in the utility sector. See, *e.g.*, Roland F. Salmonson (ed.), *Public Utility Accounting: Mod-els, Mergers, and Information Systems* (East Lansing: MSU Public Utilities Papers, 1971); James E. Suelflow, *Public Utility Accounting: Theory and Application* (East Lansing: MSU Public Utilities Studies, 1973), chaps. 13 and 14; Hahne and Aliff, *op. cit.*, esp. Part IV.

[7]*Interstate Commerce Comm. v. Goodrich Transit Co.*, 224 U.S. 194, 211 (1912).

[8]*Kansas City So. Ry. Co. v. United States*, 231 U.S. 423, 442-43 (1913).

[9]*Norfolk & Western Ry. Co. v. United States*, 287 U.S. 134, 141 (1932). Four years

later, the Court stated: "Error or unwisdom is not equivalent to abuse. What has been ordered must appear to be 'so entirely at odds with fundamental principles of correct accounting' . . . as to be the expression of a whim rather than an exercise of judgment." *American Teleph. & Teleg. Co. v. United States*, 299 U.S. 232, 236-37 (1936).

[10]See Jay H. Price, Jr., Richard Walker, and Leonard Spacek, "Accounting Uniformity in the Regulated Industries," 30 *Law and Contemporary Problems* 824, 830-35 (1965).

[11]*Re Montana Power Co.*, 42 PUR3d 241, 252 (Mont., 1962).

[12]Troxel, *op. cit.*, p. 121.

[13]Suelflow, *op. cit.*, p. 35.

[14]*1985 Annual Report on Utility and Carrier Regulation* (Washington, D.C.: National Association of Regulatory Utility Commissioners, 1987), pp. 484-85. Only a few state commissions have authority to prescribe uniform systems of accounts for cooperatively-owned and publicly-owned utilities. *Ibid.*

[15]Price, Walker, and Spacek, *op. cit.*, p. 849. This objective can be accomplished, the authors believe, "without incurring a costly burden of detailed or straitjacket uniformity." *Ibid.*

[16]See *ibid.*, pp. 839-47; Gordon R. Corey, "Some Controversial Aspects of Accounting," 79 *Public Utilities Fortnightly* 46 (January 5, 1967) and "Problems in Uniform Accounting," 79 *Public Utilities Fortnightly* 23 (January 19, 1967); Dhia D. Alhashim, "Uniform Accounting in the Regulated Industries," 23 *Federal Accountant* 43 (June 1974).

[17]See Alfred L. Burke, "The Investor Looks at Accounting Problems in the Utility Industry," 21 *Financial Analysts Journal* 27 (September-October 1965); Homer E. Sayad, "Consistency in Utility Financial Statements," 80 *Public Utilities Fortnightly* 17 (September 14, 1967).

A related issue: The Federal Power Commission assumed jurisdiction over financial reporting to the public, by requiring that reports to stockholders conform to the accounting requirements set forth in its uniform systems of accounts. Its authority was upheld in 1964. [*Appalachian Power Co. v. Federal Power Comm.*, 328 F. 2d 237, 52 PUR3d 449 (4th Cir. 1964), *cert. denied*, 379 U. S. 829 (1964).] The FPC subsequently revised its regulations to require electric utilities and natural gas pipeline companies to add to their annual reports a statement from independent certified, or licensed, public accountants attesting to the conformity of certain schedules in the reports with the commission's accounting requirements. [FPC, News Release No. 15288 (December 29, 1967).] "This has not been a significant problem in recent years because utility companies, with minor differences, generally present their published financial statements in the format required by the FERC." Hahne and Aliff, *op. cit.*, p. 11-6. No other commission has claimed jurisdiction over published financial statements.

[18]*Re Montana Power Co.*, *op. cit.*, p. 253. See also *Federal Power Comm. v. Hope Natural Gas Co.*, 320 U.S. 591, 643-44 (1944).

[19]Suelflow, *op. cit.*, pp. 40-41 (citation omitted). In 1962, the Accounting Principles Board (APB) issued Opinion No. 2, Addendum, "Accounting Principles for Regulated Industries." In 1982, the Financial Accounting Standards Board (FASB) issued Statement No. 71, "Accounting for the Effects of Certain Types of Regulation." In early 1984, the FASB began a reconsideration of Statement No. 71, with specific reference to accounting for phase-in plans, plant abandonments, and disallowances of newly completed plants. On these issues, see Hahne and Aliff, *op. cit.*, chap. 12.

[20]See J. Rhoads Foster and B. S. Rodey, *Public Utility Accounting* (New York: Prentice Hall, Inc., 1951); Leon E. Hay and D. J. Grinnell, *Water Utility Accounting* (New York: Municipal Finance Officers Association and American Water Works Association, 1970); Suelflow, *op. cit.;* Hahne and Aliff, *op. cit.,* esp. chap. 11.

[21]The current uniform systems of accounts prescribed by (*a*) the FERC for electric and gas utilities can be found in Title 18 of the *Code of Federal Regulations* (CFR) and (*b*) the FCC for telephone companies can be found in Title 47. The systems are updated annually. The accounts shown in Figures 6-1 and 6-2 are from this publication.

[22]Each specific account is broken down into one or more subdivisions; that is, Utility Plant into Electric Plant in Service; Electric Plant in Service into Intangible Plant, Production Plant, Transmission Plant, Distribution Plant, and General Plant; and so forth. Many accounts specify what items should *not* be included or the specific accounts into which items must be placed.

[23]The difference between the original cost and a higher purchase price (known as an "acquisition adjustment") is either added to operating expenses or amortized (sometimes "below-the-line") over a period of years. [See Chapter 7.] Many state commissions, it should be noted, use the accountants' concept of original cost, thereby charging the entire purchase price to the plant account.

[24]See Suelflow, *op. cit.,* chap. 7.

[25]*Depreciation Charges of Steam Railroad Companies,* 118 ICC 295, 336-37 (1926).

[26]Depreciation accounting is considered in greater detail in Chapter 7.

[27]Common and joint costs are similar in that they arise when the production of one product results in the output of another. But there is a theoretical distinction between the two: joint costs require that the joint products be produced in fixed proportions (i.e., beef and hides), while the proportions can vary when common costs are involved. Moreover, common and joint costs can be both variable and fixed with respect to changes in output. That is, while fixed costs generally belong to the business as a whole, they may be partially traceable to particular services and, conversely, while variable costs generally are traceable to particular services, they may be partially common or joint to two or more services.

[28]Telephone separations were discussed in *Smith v. Illinois Bell Teleph. Co.,* 282 U.S. 133 (1930).

[29]*Colorado Interstate Gas Co. v. Federal Power Comm.,* 324 U.S. 581, 589 (1945).

[30]There were three related procedures. (*1*) *Separations* was a procedure for allocating costs and revenues between federal and state jurisdictions. (*2*) *Settlements* was a procedure for allocating long-distance revenues between the Bell System and the independent telephone companies. (*3*) *Division of revenues* was an internal procedure for allocating Bell System long-distance revenues between AT&T's Long Lines Department and the Bell System operating companies.

[31]See *Separations Manual — Standard Procedures for Separating Telephone Property Costs, Revenues, Expenses, Taxes, and Reserves* (Washington, D.C.: National Association of Regulatory Utility Commissioners, 1971). The *Separations Manual* also applied to independent telephone companies. It was used in rate case presentations by some independent companies before state commissions and for developing independent company costs underlying intercompany settlements between independents and the Bell System and between two independent companies.

[32]See Richard Gabel, *Development of Separations Principles in the Telephone Industry* (East Lansing: MSU Public Utilities Studies, 1967); testimony of H. L. Baker, "Background Information and History of Separations for the Telephone Communications

Industry," FCC Docket No. 16258 (FCC Staff Exhibit No. 25, dated November 14, 1966). Major revisions were made on five occasions, the last one being in 1971.

[33]Telephone plant was divided into two broad classifications: interexchange plant, which was plant used primarily to furnish long-distance services; and exchange plant, which was plant used primarily to furnish local service.

[34]While the *Separations Manual* was designed for interstate-intrastate separations only, some of its procedures were used without modifications or were adapted for use in intrastate toll-exchange services separations. One state commission — California — required such separations in intrastate rate cases and approved separations procedures for that purpose. The remaining state commissions generally determined a fair rate of return on the combined investment devoted to local exchange and intrastate toll services.

[35]*Separations Manual, op. cit.,* pp. 16-17.

[36]In addition to expenses and taxes, from total interstate revenues were deducted the amount of settlements between Bell System companies and independent companies for the independents' share of the revenues for interstate services furnished jointly by the independent companies and the Bell System. The amount of these settlements was based upon separation studies of independent company costs incurred in providing the joint services. The settlement received by each independent company was made in accordance with an agreement between the independent and a Bell System associated company. Most independent companies were covered by a settlement agreement employing uniform settlement schedules based on nationwide cost studies negotiated for the independents by the United States Independent Telephone Association (now the U. S. Telephone Association). The remaining independent companies had agreements calling for settlements based on individual company cost studies. While the latter type of agreement involved only a small proportion of the total independent companies, such agreements covered about one-half of the total settlements.

[37]See Curtis M. Bushnell, "Regulatory Responsibilities in Telephone Cost Allocations," Part I: 72 *Public Utilities Fortnightly* 52 (November 7, 1963); Part II: 72 *Public Utilities Fortnightly* 32 (November 21, 1963); Gabel, *op. cit.,* chap. vi.

[38]Delaware and Pennsylvania based their entire intrastate toll rate structure on the interstate structure, so that the rates for both services were the same for comparable distances. See also "Telephone Toll Settlements in Alaska and Hawaii: 'Transitional Supplements'," 119 *Public Utilities Fortnightly* 49 (April 30, 1987).

[39]*A Study of Message Toll Telephone Rate Disparities* (Washington, D.C.: National Association of Regulatory Utility Commissioners, 1967); Sanford F. Smith, "Disparities in Message Toll Telephone Rates," 79 *Public Utilities Fortnightly* 25 (March 30, 1967).

[40]Major technological advances were occurring in the longer haul interstate toll service field. In addition, a number of service extensions and improvements were introduced into the exchange field (*e.g.,* the establishment of extended and metropolitan area exchange services, the elimination of most multiparty subscriber lines) which necessitated increases in monthly and nonrecurring exchange service charges.

[41]From 1959 to 1970, separations changes totaled nearly $500 million; that is, the "contribution" from interstate services toward the costs of intrastate services increased by that amount.

[42]"States having a predominance of short-haul traffic are necessarily burdened with higher unit costs than states with an average longer haul traffic. In the interstate

area there is a very high volume of long-haul traffic over high density routes. This, in turn, reduces the cost per mile of the long lines plant. The effect of such high volume of long-haul traffic over high-density routes is reflected in the cost per message minute mile. To put it another way, the average length of haul for intrastate calls is 47 miles, while for interstate calls it is 400 miles." E. William Henry, "Communications Problems — 1965," in *Annual Proceedings, 1965* (Washington, D.C.: National Association of Regulatory Commissioners, 1966), p. 506.

[43]Dale N. Hatfield, "Contributions from Interstate Services for Use of Intrastate Facilities," in *Proceedings of the 1980 Rate Symposium on Problems of Regulated Industries* (Columbia: University of Missouri-Columbia, 1981), pp. 354-55. Certainly, "such a course would destroy the authority and discretion vested in the regulatory body of each separate state. It would also be contrary to the basic principle of our federal system, in which the individual states maintain and play a fundamental regulatory role in intrastate matters." Henry, *op. cit.,* p. 506. The development of LATAs, discussed in Chapter 15, represents a step in the direction of Hatfield's recommendation.

[44]Until access charges were imposed, the specialized common carriers paid for local access under a negotiated formula (the "ENFIA" tariff), which represented about 35 percent of the burden borne by MTS. [Data from Richard A. Genthner, "Contributions from Interstate Services," in *Proceedings of the 1980 Rate Symposium on Problems of Regulated Industries, op. cit.,* pp. 369, 371.] However, these carriers did not have equal access at that time. On the ENFIA tariff and equal access, see Chapter 15.

[45]*Re MTS and WATS Market Structure,* Third Report and Order, 93 F.C.C. 2d 241 (1983), modified on recon., 97 F.C.C. 2d 682 (1983), further modified on recon., 97 F.C.C. 2d 834 (1983), *aff'd in principal part and rem'd in part sub nom. National Ass'n of Reg. Util. Comm'rs v. Federal Communications Comm.,* 737 F. 2d 1095 (D.C. Cir. 1984), *cert. denied,* 105 S. Ct. 1224, 1225 (1985). See, *e.g.,* Clark A. Mount-Campbell et al., *A Study of Telephone Access Charges: An Empirical Analysis of Bell Companies in Five Regions* (Columbus, Ohio: National Regulatory Research Institute, 1983); Richard A. Romano, "Nontraffic-sensitive Telephone Costs: Examining the Components," 118 *Public Utilities Fortnightly* 18 (November 27, 1986).

[46]See Jane L. Racster, *The National Exchange Carrier Association, Inc.: Structure and Operation* (Columbus, Ohio: National Regulatory Research Institute, 1985). The NECA has three purposes: the filing of common access charge tariffs, administering access charge revenue pools, and distributing the pool revenues.

[47]Under the 1983 modified plan, residential users would have paid flat monthly charges of $2 (1984), $3 (1985), and $4 (1986); business customers would have paid $6 per month per line (1984 through 1986); and both customers would have borne an increasing percentage of the "residue amount of non-traffic sensitive costs" in the final three years of the six-year transition period (1984 through 1989).

[48]*NARUC Bulletin* No. 43-1983 (October 24, 1983), pp. 5-6. Of particular concern were access charges on residential customers and single-line business users, as well as higher access charges on specialized common carriers. After the House, in November, 1983, voted *to repeal* the FCC's access charges on these customers, the Commission voted to postpone their imposition until mid-1985. (Access charges on multi-line business customers were imposed in May, 1984.) A $1 monthly residential and single-line business access charge was implemented on June 1, 1985; a charge increased to $2 on June 1, 1986. In April, 1987, the FCC adopted a $1.50 per

month increase, in three phases: sixty cents on July 1, 1987, sixty cents on December 1, 1988, and thirty cents on April 1, 1989.

In addition to interstate access charges, the state commissions have authority to determine intrastate access charges. See, *e.g., Re Intrastate Access Charges (Primary Toll Carrier Designation),* 68 PUR4th 90 (Ill., 1985); *Re Revenue Transfer from Long-distance Carriers to Local Exchange Customers,* 82 PUR4th 271 (Or., 1987). But see *Re Idaho Public Utilities Commission Order No. 19663* (FCC, 1985).

[49]To help in maintaining universal service, the FCC established (*a*) a "universal service fund" — paid for by interexchange carriers — to assist high cost areas (*i.e.,* where local costs exceed 115 percent of the national average) and (*b*) a mechanism for providing lifeline assistance to low-income households. But see V. Louise McCarren and Paul F. Levy, "The Mandatory Carrier Common Line Pool Should Go," 119 *Public Utilities Fortnightly* 23 (March 19, 1987).

[50]Bypass has several definitions, but generally refers to a situation where a customer secures telecommunications services without using the telephone company's local exchange and toll networks. [See Chapter 15.] "The usage rate charged by the local exchange carrier to the interexchange carrier includes a 'contribution' toward the payment of the fixed costs of providing a network of subscriber loops. In order to pay this 'contribution,' the interexchange carrier must charge its customers rates that are higher than the costs of providing long-distance service. These higher-than-cost rates are only charged when an end user's call passes through the local 'switch' to the interexchange carrier." Mark S. Fowler, Albert Halprin, and James D. Schlichting, " 'Back to the Future': A Model for Telecommunications," 38 *Federal Communications Law Journal* 145, 180, n. 98 (1986). See, *e.g.,* Jane L. Racster, *The Bypass Issue: An Emerging Form of Competition in the Telephone Industry* (Columbus, Ohio: National Regulatory Research Institute, 1984); *Re Telephone Services that Bypass Local Exchange or Toll Networks,* 70 PUR4th 1 (N.Y., 1985); "The Bypass of Local Telephone Facilities: How Serious a Threat?," 117 *Public Utilities Fortnightly* 49 (May 1, 1986). See also Michael A. Einhorn and Bruce L. Egan, "How to Set Long-Distance Access Charges: A Multi-Tariff Approach," 119 *Public Utilities Fortnightly* 19 (May 14, 1987).

[51]Alfred E. Kahn, "Some Thoughts on Telephone Access Pricing" (New York: National Economic Research Associates, 1983), pp. 3-4 (footnote omitted).

[52]Cited in Troxel, *op. cit.,* p. 141.

[53]*Ibid.*

[54]See, *e.g.,* Harold H. Young, *Forty Years of Public Utility Finance* (Charlottesville: The University Press of Virginia, 1965).

[55]See D. Philip Locklin, *Regulation of Security Issues by the Interstate Commerce Commission, 13 University of Illinois Studies in the Social Sciences* (No. 4, 1927); D. F. Pegrum, *Regulation of Public Utility Security Issues in California* (Berkeley: University of California Press, 1937).

[56]*Securities of Louisville & Nashville R.R.,* 76 ICC 718 (1923).

[57]D. Philip Locklin, *Economics of Transportation* (7th ed.; Homewood, Ill.: Richard D. Irwin, Inc., 1972), p. 552.

[58]*Ibid.,* p. 553.

[59]See Chapter 8.

[60]Original cost has two common meanings: the cost of assets when first devoted to public service and the cost of assets to the existing company. While a majority of the commissions use the first meaning when valuing assets for capitalization pur-

poses, some of the state commissions, as well as the Federal Energy Regulatory Commission and the Securities and Exchange Commission, use the second.

[61]"An estimate of what it would cost to reproduce the properties now, ... or even what a purchaser may have agreed to pay ..., are too fanciful to warrant serious consideration." *Re California Water Supply Co.*, PUR1928C 516, 525 (Cal., 1928). See also *Chicago Junction Case*, 71 ICC 631 (1922); *Grand Trunk Western R.R. Co., Unification & Securities*, 158 ICC 117 (1929); *Re Mondovi Teleph. Co.*, PUR1931C 439 (Wis., 1931); *Re Stoughton Light & Fuel Co.*, 26 PUR (NS) 160 (Wis., 1936); *Re Central Illinois Elec. & Gas Co.*, 5 SEC 115 (1939); *Re Waynesboro Gas Co.*, 53 PUR (NS) 247 (Pa., 1944); *Re Winnebago Nat. Gas Corp.*, 31 PUR3d 79 (Wis., 1959).

[62]"... we do not consider the capitalized value of earning capacity as an appropriate basis for the issue of securities under the provisions of Section 20a." *Grand Trunk Western R.R. Co., op. cit.*, pp. 134-35.

[63]For many years, the Massachusetts commission restricted utility's capitalization to the amount of cash contributed by investors, not to the company's actual investment. The effect was to exclude investment from retained earnings, on the ground that such funds were contributed by consumers rather than investors. This practice was overturned by the Massachusetts Supreme Court in 1951. *New England Teleph. & Teleg. Co. v. Dept. of Pub. Utilities*, 327 Mass. 81, 97 N.E. 2d 509 (1951).

[64]Locklin, *Economics of Transportation, op. cit.*, p. 559.

[65]In the 1860s and 1870s, a railroad's directors would frequently organize a construction company for the purpose of voting profitable contracts to themselves — as the construction company — for construction of the railroad. As payment for construction, the company would receive the land grants and state and local bonds offered to the railroad as a subsidy, or bonds and stock of the railroad. To illustrate: "The Logan, Crawfordsville & South Western Railroad voted all its municipal bonds, capital stock, and bonds to the director-contractors. The road actually cost about a million dollars, while $4 million in securities were issued." *Ibid.*, p. 139.

[66]See, *e.g.*, *Re Michigan Gas & Elec. Co.* (SEC), Holding Co. Act Release No. 4780 (December, 1943); *Re Niagara Falls Power Co.* (SEC), Holding Co. Act Release No. 4911 (February 1944); *Re Commonwealth Teleph. Co.*, PUR1932D 299 (Wis.); *Re Laclede Gas Light Co.*, 11 SEC 40 (1942); *Securities of St. Louis-San Francisco Ry.*, 79 ICC 92 (1923).

[67]There is some controversy, however, over the scope of a commission's authority. Specifically, can a commission — in a proceeding to authorize the issuance of securities — inquire into the reasonableness of the project for which the securities are to be issued or must the inquiry be limited to the lawfulness of the proposed project? See *Kelley v. Michigan Pub. Service Comm.*, 316 N.W. 2d 187 (1982); *Re Pub. Service Co. of N.H.*, 454 A. 2d 435, 51 PUR4th 298 (1982), *reversing* 47 PUR4th 167 (1982); Shippen Howe, "Utility Security Issues: The Scope of Commission Inquiry," 110 *Public Utilities Fortnightly* 61 (October 14, 1982). See also Russell J. Profozich et al., *Commission Preapproval of Utility Investments* (Columbus, Ohio: National Regulatory Research Institute, 1981).

[68]*1985 Annual Report on Utility and Carrier Regulation, op. cit.*, pp. 516-24. See "Regulatory Restrictions on Dividends," 79 *Public Utilities Fortnightly* 71 (March 30, 1967); Robert H. Plattner, "State Regulatory Control of Dividend Policy," 81 *Public Utilities Fortnightly* 29 (February 15, 1968); *New York Pub. Service Comm. v. Jamaica Water Supply Co.*, 386 N.Y.S. 2d 230 (1976).

[69]See, *e.g.*, *Securities Application of Detroit & Toledo Shore Line R. R.*, 70 ICC 322

(1921); *Re White Mt. Power Co.*, 18 PUR (NS) 321 (N.H., 1937); *Re Federal Water & Gas Corp.* (SEC), Holding Co. Act Release No. 6052 (September, 1945); *Rochester Gas & Elec. Corp. v. Maltbie*, 76 N.Y.S. 2d 671 (1948); *Re Old Dominion Elec. Cooperative*, 86 PUR (NS) 129 (Va., 1950).

[70]Further flexibility was provided when the Securities and Exchange Commission adopted a temporary rule (Rule 415) in March, 1982, "which allows a firm to preregister all or any of the securities that it reasonably expects to sell in the next two years. This allows the issuing firm to keep securities 'on the shelf' (register) and then take securities 'off the shelf' (issue) any time it chooses; therefore, the name shelf registration has been associated with the rule." M. W. Marr and G. R. Thompson, "SEC Rule 415: Do Utilities Save Issue Costs?," 111 *Public Utilities Fortnightly* 62 (June 9, 1983). As the authors note, the rule "alters the traditional underwriter-client relationship. The issuing firm now has the ability to call several investment bankers on the day the firm decides to sell its securities and bargain for the best possible price." *Ibid.* See also David S. Kidwell, M. W. Marr, and G. R. Thompson, "Shelf Registration of Utility Securities," 115 *Public Utilities Fortnightly* 41 (February 21, 1985).

[71]Troxel, *op. cit.*, p. 151. See also *Re Long Island Light Co.*, 5 PUR (NS) 456 (N.Y., 1934); *Re Pennsylvania Elec. Co.*, 6 PUR (NS) 22 (Pa., 1934); *Re California-Oregon Teleph. Co.*, 32 PUR (NS) 317 (Cal., 1940).

[72]See Irston R. Barnes, *The Economics of Public Utility Regulation* (New York: F. S. Crofts & Co., 1942), pp. 729-39.

[73]See, *e.g.*, *Western Maryland Equipment Trust*, 111 ICC 434 (1926); *Re New Hampshire Gas & Elec. Co.*, 40 PUR (NS) 285 (N.H., 1941); Securities and Exchange Commission, *Seventh Annual Report* (1941), pp. 98-102; *In re Competitive Bidding in Sale of Securities*, 257 ICC 129 (1944); *Re Competitive Bidding Rule for Public Utility Securities*, 63 PUR (NS) 140 (Cal., 1946); *Re Rochester Teleph. Corp.*, 64 PUR (NS) 30 (N.Y., 1946).

[74]*1985 Annual Report on Utility and Carrier Regulation, op. cit.*, p. 527. Thirty-six state commissions have authority to require competitive bidding on mortgage bonds and debentures; thirty-three on underwriting of new common stock. *Ibid.*, p. 526. The FERC requires competitive bidding for electric utilities. See also "Exemptions from Competitive Bidding Requirements," 61 *Public Utilities Fortnightly* 417 (March 13, 1958) and 75 *Public Utilities Fortnightly* 71 (January 21, 1965); L. H. Ederington, "Negotiated versus Competitive Underwriting of Corporate Bonds," 31 *Journal of Finance* 17 (March, 1976); Edward A. Dyl and Michael D. Joehnk, "Competitive versus Negotiated Underwriting of Public Utility Debt," 7 *Bell Journal of Economics* 680 (1976).

[75]Three types of bonds are commonly issued by public utilities: (*1*) first mortgage bonds, which are secured by the entire property of the issuing utility; (*2*) debenture bonds, which are secured by the general credit of the issuing utility, but which are subject to the prior claim of the first mortgage bonds; and (*3*) revenue or income bonds, which are secured by the earnings of the issuing utility after interest on any outstanding first mortgage or debenture bonds has been paid. For a complete discussion, see John F. Childs, *Encyclopedia of Long-Term Financing and Capital Management* (Englewood Cliffs: Prentice-Hall, Inc., 1976), esp. chap. 4.

[76]Locklin, *Economics of Transportation, op. cit.*, p. 567.

[77]The assumption that the average cost of capital is a function of a utility's capital structure is questioned by Franco Modigliani and Merton H. Miller, "The Cost of

Capital, Corporation Finance and the Theory of Investment," 48 *American Economic Review* 261 (1958). See Chapter 9, pp. 396-97, n. 63.

[78]J. J. Scanlon, *Financial Expansion and the Problems of Corporate Capital Structure* (Urbana: University of Illinois Bulletin, 1968) (Weinstein Lecture series, Department of Finance), p. 5.

[79]See Chapter 9.

[80]Utility bonds are rated by the three principal rating agencies (*i.e.*, Duff and Phelps, Moody's Investors Service, and Standard & Poor's Corporation). Bond ratings are important for at least four reasons: (*a*) they are used by investors in determining the quality of debt investment; (*b*) they are used in determining the breadth of the market, since some large institutional investors are prohibited from investing in the lower grades; (*c*) they determine, in part, the cost of new debt, since both the interest charges on new debt and the degree of difficulty in marketing new issues tend to rise as the rating decreases; and (*d*) they have an indirect bearing on the status of a utility's common stock and on its acceptance in the market. See Fergus J. McDiarmid, "Interest Coverage and Bond Ratings," 89 *Public Utilities Fortnightly* 19 (May 11, 1972).

[81]Scanlon, *op. cit.*, p. 8.

[82]Gilbert Burck, "Is AT&T Playing It Too Safe?," *Fortune* (September, 1960), p. 276. One authority estimated that for electric utilities, "a change of 10 percent of capitalization from equity to debt saves 1.10 percentage points in the cost of capital, or a saving of about 11 percent." Donald C. Cook, "Special Problems of Electric Regulation," Part II, 74 *Public Utilities Fortnightly* 30, 31 (November 19, 1964).

[83]L. Chester May, "Bell System Financing," *Bell Telephone Magazine* (Autumn, 1960), p. 28.

[84]Scanlon, *op. cit.*, p. 15. During the 1950s and 1960s, the Bell System's annual financing increased from $321 million (1950) to $2.5 billion (1969).

[85]May, *op. cit.*, p. 29.

[86]J. Rhoads Foster, "Fair Return Criteria and Estimation," 28 *Baylor Law Review* 883, 890-91 (1976). See, *e.g.*, David M. Brooks, III and Malcolm C. Harris, "The Case for Higher Equity Ratios in Electric Utilities," 110 *Public Utilities Fortnightly* 35 (September 2, 1982).

[87]See, *e.g.*, Barnard Seligman, "Analysis of Utility Convertible Bonds," 86 *Public Utilities Fortnightly* 31 (December 3, 1970); Richard A. Stevenson, "Utilities Issuing Warrants: Rationale and Evaluation," 93 *Public Utilities Fortnightly* 26 (April 11, 1974); Albert C. Barkwill, "The Single Payment Bond: An Innovative Financing Technique," 93 *Public Utilities Fortnightly* 31 (May 9, 1974); Barry W. Huff, "Financing with Industrial Development Bonds," 96 *Public Utilities Fortnightly* 32 (July 3, 1975); Joseph F. Bradley and Petros Christofi, "Pollution Abatement Revenue Bonds As a Source of Finance," 105 *Public Utilities Fortnightly* 25 (January 31, 1980); Morris A. Nunes and Haig Kevitch, "The Employee Stock Ownership Plan — An Opportunity for Electric Utilities," 99 *Public Utilities Fortnightly* 22 (January 20, 1977); Herbert B. Mayo, "Savings from Dividend Reinvestment Plans," 94 *Public Utilities Fortnightly* 36 (September 12, 1974). See also Michael von Clemm, "Eurodollar Financing for U. S. Utilities," 107 *Public Utilities Fortnightly* 21 (May 7, 1981).

[88]See, *e.g.*, Arthur L. Litke, "Leasing — Phantom Financing?," 87 *Public Utilities Fortnightly* 27 (April 15, 1971); David G. Crane, "Behind the Increasing Use of Lease

Financing by Utilities," 119 *Public Utilities Fortnightly* 24 (February 19, 1987); Charles H. Lee, Jr. and Thomas J. Healey, "Project Financing of Large-scale Energy Programs," 99 *Public Utilities Fortnightly* 17 (April 14, 1977); Jacob J. Worenklein, "Project Financing of Joint Ventures," 108 *Public Utilities Fortnightly* 39 (December 3, 1981).

[89]See, *e.g.*, Susan G. Pollack, "Tender Offers and Other Debt Refunding," 100 *Public Utilities Fortnightly* 28 (December 8, 1977); Anthony H. Meyer and Jon M. Jetmore, "Swapping Stock for Bonds: A Perspective for Utilities," 109 *Public Utilities Fortnightly* 29 (February 18, 1982).

[90]See Timothy C. Jochim, "Consumer Stock Ownership Plans in Public Utility Financing," 109 *Public Utilities Fortnightly* 32 (January 21, 1982). In the case of Dominion Resources (formerly Virginia Electric and Power Company), to illustrate, its first two subscriptions attracted 20,500 of its 1.15 million customers, who supplied $15.1 million in new capital. *Ibid.*, p. 34.

[91]See, *e.g.*, H. Guttman (ed.), *Alternatives for Electric Utility Financing* (Albany: New York State Department of Public Service, 1975); Jerome S. Katzin, "Electric Utility Financing Today," 55 *Oregon Law Review* 479 (1976).

[92]See, *e.g.*, *Bonds of Chesapeake & Ohio Ry.*, 105 ICC 748 (1926); *Securities of Yankton, Norfolk & Southern R.R. Co.*, 154 ICC 669 (1929); *Re Nelson Teleph. Co.*, 28 PUR (NS) 116 (Wis., 1939); *Re El Paso Elec. Co.*, 8 SEC 366 (1941).

[93]For ratemaking purposes, however, a few commissions have used a hypothetical capital structure for a utility's actual capital structure. See Chapter 9.

[94]Troxel, *op. cit.*, p. 160.

[95]See, *e.g.*, *Re Interstate Light & Power Co.*, PUR1933A 319 (Wis.,); *Re Luzerne County Gas & Elec. Corp.*, 9 SEC 359 (1941); *Re Missouri Edison Co.*, 11 SEC 1125 (1942); *Laclede Gas Light Co.*, 11 SEC 40 (1942); *Re Stockbridge & Sherwood Teleph. Co.*, 37 PUR3d 313 (Wis., 1960).

[96]*Re Consolidated Edison Co. of N.Y., Inc.*, Case No. 22092 (N.Y., 1962).

[97]Frequently, the redemption of sinking fund and serial bonds is scheduled so as to match depreciation accruals. In this way, the cash generated through depreciation is used to retire outstanding bonds; when the asset is fully depreciated, the bonds used to finance it originally also are retired.

[98]A "call premium" or "call penalty" is often added before a callable bond issue will be accepted by investors. See "Limitations on the Redemption of Senior Securities," 60 *Public Utilities Fortnightly* 417 (1957).

[99]*Re Mid-Georgia Nat. Gas Co.*, 35 PUR3d 477 (Ga., 1960).

[100]These procedures have been used on numerous occasions in the railroad industry.

[101]See William H. Moore, "Railroad Fixed Charges in Bankruptcy Proceedings," 47 *Journal of Political Economy* 100 (1939); Robert T. Swaine, "A Decade of Railroad Reorganization under Section 77 of the Federal Bankruptcy Act," 56 *Harvard Law Review* 1037, 1193 (1943); De F. Billyou, "Railroad Reorganization since Enactment of Section 77," 96 *University of Pennsylvania Law Review* 793 (1948).

[102]Locklin, *Economics of Transportation, op. cit.*, pp. 569, 572. In more recent years, the number of railroads in receivership or trusteeship has declined, "but two important railroads were added to the list in 1970; namely, the Penn Central and the Boston & Maine." *Ibid.*, p. 569.

[103]*Ibid.*, pp. 570-71. Two further provisions should be noted. First, "the acceptance

of the reorganization plan by stockholders is not necessary if the Commission and the court find that the equity of the stockholders has no value." Second, the court may confirm a reorganization plan rejected by a particular class of creditors or stockholders provided it "is satisfied that the plan makes adequate provision for fair and equitable treatment of their interests, and that rejection of the plan was not reasonably justified." *Ibid.* See also Max Lowenthal, "The Railroad Reorganization Act," 47 *Harvard Law Review* 18 (1933); Leslie Craven and Warner Fuller, "The 1935 Amendments of the Railroad Bankruptcy Law," 49 *Harvard Law Review* 1254 (1936).

[104]49 Stat. 911 (1935), 11 U.S.C. Sec. 205 (b) (4) (1958).

[105]*Western Pacific R.R. Co. Reorganization*, 230 ICC 61, 87 (1939). The policy has been criticized, largely on the ground that by underestimating the future earnings of a company, stock has been declared worthless needlessly; that is, future earnings have been higher than estimated at the time of reorganization. See William Polatsek, "The Wreck of the Old 77," 34 *Cornell Law Quarterly* 532 (1949); *Railroad Reorganizations* (Committee Print, Committee on Interstate and Foreign Commerce, Senate, 82d Cong., 2d sess.) (Washington, D.C.: U. S. Government Printing Office, 1952).

[106]*Group of Investors v. Chicago, Milwaukee, St. Paul & Pacific R. R. Co.*, 318 U. S. 523, 540-41 (1943).

[107]See, *e.g.*, *Re United Teleph. & Elec. Co.*, 3 SEC 679 (1938); *Re Louer*, 35 PUR (NS) 351 (N.Y., 1940); *Re George*, 41 PUR (NS) 193 (Pa., 1941).

[108]See Merwin H. Waterman, *Financial Policies of Public Utility Holding Companies* (Ann Arbor: University of Michigan Press, 1932); Young, *op. cit.*

[109]Securities and Exchange Commission, *Ninth Annual Report* (1943), p. 25.

[110]Robert H. O'Brien, "Some Current Problems under the Public Utility Holding Company Act," 28 *Public Utilities Fortnightly* 639-47 (1941).

[111]William G. Shepherd and Clair Wilcox, *Public Policies Toward Business* (6th ed.; Homewood, Ill.: Richard D. Irwin, Inc., 1979), p. 325.

[112]Other aspects of the act are discussed in Chapter 13.

[113]Securities and Exchange Commission, *Twenty-Eighth Annual Report* (1962), pp. 82-84. Of the remaining companies, 793 were released from the commission's jurisdiction as the result of dissolutions, mergers, and consolidations, and 514 by exemption. Today, some two dozen holding companies are registered under the act.

[114]Troxel, *op. cit.*, p. 186.

[115]R. A. Finlayson, "The Public Utility Holding Company," 19 *Journal of Business*, Part 2, p. 27 (1946). See also Melvin G. Dakin, "Public Utility Debt Ratios and the Public Interest — Reasonable Fixed Charges and Just and Reasonable Rates," 15 *Vanderbilt Law Review* 195 (1961).

[116]As of December 31, 1938, $1.4 billion of a total of $2.5 billion of the preferred stock of holding companies registered with the SEC was in arrears in dividends, representing $363 million or 26 percent of the par value of the stock. [Securities and Exchange Commission, *Ninth Annual Report (1943)*, p. 25.] See E. M. Dodd, "Fair and Equitable Recapitalization," 55 *Harvard Law Review* 780 (1942) and "Relative Rights of Preferred and Common Stockholders in Recapitalization Plans under the Holding Company Act," 57 *Harvard Law Review* 295 (1944); S. H. Galfand, "Determination of Common Stock Participation in Plans under Section 11(e) of the Public Utility Holding Company Act," 93 *University of Pennsylvania Law Review* 308 (1945).

[117]Troxel, *op. cit.*, p. 188.

[118]See Alvin Kaufman and Donald Dulchinos, *Utility Bankruptcy: Thinking the Unthinkable* (Washington, D.C.: Congresional Research Service, Library of Congress, 1984).

[119]See, *e.g.*, "Kansas G&E Sees Bankruptcy If Rate Increase Isn't Approved," *The Wall Street Journal*, August 29, 1985, p. 6; "Gulf States Treads Fine Line in Request for Rate Rise, Firm's Threat to Seek Chapter 11 Protection Is Making Matters Worse," *ibid.*, January 28, 1987, p. 6; "How Seabrook Plant Sends Utility to Brink of Bankruptcy Courts," *ibid.*, September 22, 1987, pp. 1, 22.

[120]*Re Pub. Service Co. of New Hampshire*, 66 PUR4th 349 (N.H., 1985); *Re Maine Pub. Service Co.*, 67 PUR4th 101 (Me., 1985).

[121]*Re Consumers Power Co.*, 66 PUR4th 1 (Mich., 1985).

[122]Diane Sponseller, "Utility Bankruptcy: A Negative Option?," 117 *Public Utilities Fortnightly* 53, 55-56 (February 6, 1986).

[123]"PS New Hampshire Asks Chapter 11 Status," *The Wall Street Journal*, January 28, 1988, p. 2.

[124]"A prescribed system of accounts is a prerequisite to effective control of utilities by a regulatory body. However, by no stretch of the imagination can the system of accounts be viewed as furnishing an interpretation of the accounting results." *Re Montana Power Co.*, *op. cit.*, p. 253.

[125]For a discussion of one relevant question — who will develop accounting principles? — see Robert N. Anthony, "Showdown on Accounting Principles," 41 *Harvard Business Review* 99 (May-June, 1963). See also William J. Powell, "The Case for the Regulatory Accountant," 75 *Public Utilities Fortnightly* 36 (January 7, 1965); Hahne and Aliff, *op. cit.*, chap. 12.

Chapter 7

OPERATING EXPENSES, DEPRECIATION, AND TAXES

Expenses (using that term in its broad sense to include not only operating expenses but depreciation and taxes) are facts. They are to be ascertained, not created, by the regulatory authorities. If properly incurred, they must be allowed as part of the composition of the rates. Otherwise, the so-called allowance of a return upon investment, being an amount over and above expenses, would be a farce.

—*Judge Prettyman**

Previously, it was seen that the problem of rate regulation can be expressed by the formula $R = O + (V - D)r$, where R is the total revenue to be obtained, O is the operating costs, V is the value of the tangible and intangible property, D is the accrued depreciation of the tangible and reproducible property, and r is the rate of return. Establishment of the total revenue thus involves three steps: (*1*) determination of the costs of operation, (*2*) determination of the value of the property minus accrued depreciation, known as the rate base, and (*3*) determination of the rate of return.

Operating costs make up the largest sum that must be covered in fixing

rates. Commonly, they range from three-fourths to four-fifths of total revenues for most public utilities. These costs include all types of operating
expenses (fuel, wages and salaries, maintenance, among others), as well as
annual depreciation charges and taxes. For a typical private electric utility,
operating expenses average about 60 percent of revenues, depreciation about
7 percent, and taxes about 14 percent; for a typical gas utility, the comparable figures are 85 percent for operating expenses, 3 percent for depreciation, and 6 percent for taxes.

Some operating costs are determined by normal competitive forces and
by tax authorities; others basically are determined by individual companies.
Yet, commission supervision as to their reasonableness is essential for effective regulation.

The Necessity for Supervision

The need for commission supervision of operating expenses might seem
questionable given the development of uniform systems of accounts and the
self-interest of public utilities. As earlier noted, however, uniform systems
only specify the form and content of the statement of expenses; they do not
solve controversies over permissible expenditures or their computation. Nor
is self-interest always sufficient. Commissions seldom challenge expenditures
controlled by competitive forces, such as those for plant maintenance, raw
materials, and labor. Conflicts do arise over whether certain expenditures
should be charged to operating expenses or be paid for by owners out of
earnings.

Management might vote itself high salaries and pensions. Payments to
affiliated companies for fuel and services might be excessive. Expenses for
advertising, rate investigations, litigation, and public relations should be closely
scrutinized by the commissions to determine if they are extravagant or if
they represent an abuse of discretion. In all cases, moreover, the commissions should require proof as to the reasonableness of a utility's charges to
operating expenses.

Depreciation and taxes, too, receive special attention by the regulatory
commissions. The accounting for depreciation affects rate regulation in two
ways: (*1*) as a current operating cost and (*2*) as a deduction from the value
of the tangible and reproducible property in determining a utility's rate
base. For many years, some regulated companies made large depreciation
charges to operating costs in years of good earnings and low charges in
years of poor earnings, while deducting little for accrued depreciation in
determining the rate base. Such practices benefited investors, but not consumers. Taxes present important regulatory problems. Public utilities often
are referred to as "tax collectors *par excellence*." As taxes are included in
operating costs (with a few exceptions), they can usually be passed on to the
consumer in the form of higher rates. There is a conflict, therefore, between

the commissions and consumers who seek minimum rates and tax authorities who seek maximum revenues.

The Legal View and Managerial Judgment

The right of the commissions to exercise supervision over all three component parts of operating costs — operating expenses, depreciation, and taxes — has been approved by the courts.

Operating Expenses

As early as 1892, the Supreme Court recognized that the power to determine reasonable rates required supervision of operating expenses. As expressed by Justice Brewer:

> ... It is agreed that the defendant's operating expenses for 1888 were $2,404,516.54. Of what do these operating expenses consist? Are they made up partially of extravagant salaries; fifty to one hundred thousand dollars to the president, and in like proportion to subordinate officers? Surely, before the courts are called upon to adjudge an act of the legislature fixing the maximum passenger rates for railroad companies to be unconstitutional . . . , they should be fully advised as to what is done with the receipts and earnings of the company; for if so advised, it might clearly appear that a prudent and honest management would, within the rates prescribed, secure to the bondholders their interest, and to the stockholders reasonable dividends. While the protection of vested rights in property is a supreme duty of the courts, it has not come to this, that the legislative power rests subservient to the discretion of any railroad corporation which may, by exorbitant and unreasonable salaries, or in some other improper way, transfer its earnings into what it is pleased to call "operating expenses."[1]

In upholding the commissions' right of supervision over operating expenses, however, the courts have distinguished between expenditures resulting from "arm's-length bargaining" and have recognized the functions of management. With respect to the first, when expenditures are controlled by competitive forces, they are seldom challenged. For example, public utilities engage in collective bargaining with their employees as do nonregulated enterprises. Except in rare circumstances, the resulting contracts are not questioned by the commissions. But in the absence of arm's-length bargaining, particularly when transactions occur between affiliated companies, commission supervision is required.

With respect to the second, how far can and should a commission be allowed to go in exercising supervision over a utility's operating expenses?

Two cases provide a partial answer to this question. In 1923, the Missouri commission refused to include in Southwestern Bell's operating expenses the 4.5 percent of its gross revenue that the company was paying to the American Telephone and Telegraph Company as rent for telephone instruments and for managerial services. The Supreme Court overruled the commission, saying:

> The commission is not the financial manager of the corporation and it is not empowered to substitute its judgment for that of the directors of the corporation; nor can it ignore items charged by the utility as operating expenses unless there is an abuse of discretion in that regard by the corporate officers.[2]

Thirteen years later, in a case involving regulation of stockyard charges by the Secretary of Agriculture, the Supreme Court approved rejection of certain marketing costs on the grounds that they were unwise. Said Justice Roberts:

> The contention is that the amount to be expended for these purposes is purely a question of managerial judgment. But this overlooks the consideration that the charge is for a public service, and regulation cannot be frustrated by a requirement that the rate be made to compensate extravagant or unnecessary costs for these or any other purposes.[3]

To disallow an expenditure, then, a commission must prove "an abuse of discretion" on the part of management. Such an abuse, in turn, results from "a showing of inefficiency or improvidence"[4] or from "extravagant or unnecessary costs."[5] Public utilities, in other words, cannot spend freely and expect all expenditures to be included as allowable operating expenses. In effect, this means the commissions are permitted to question both the judgment and integrity of management. And if rates must be high enough to yield sufficient revenue to cover all operating expenses, the consumer has the right to expect that such expenditures will be necessary and reasonable.

At the same time, managerial good faith is presumed.[6] Public utilities must be given the opportunity to prove the necessity and reasonableness of any expenditure challenged by a commission (or intervenor). To justify an expenditure, a company must show that the expense was actually incurred (or will be incurred in the near future), that the expense was necessary in the proper conduct of its business, and that the amount of the expenditure was reasonable.[7] Moreover, it must be emphasized again that a public utility may still spend its money in any way it chooses. Management's function is to set the level of expenses; the commission's duty is to determine what expense burden the ratepayer must bear.[8]

Depreciation and Depletion

The right of a public utility to a depreciation cost allowance was stated by the Supreme Court in 1909. In the *Knoxville Water Company* decision, the Court recognized that a plant "begins to depreciate in value from the moment of its use," and added:

> Before coming to the question of profit at all the company is entitled to earn a sufficient sum annually to provide not only for current repairs but for making good the depreciation and replacing the parts of the property when they come to the end of their life. The company is not bound to see its property gradually waste, without making provision out of earnings for its replacement.[9]

In later cases, the Court also approved depreciation provisions for the effects of obsolescence and inadequacy.[10]

Public utilities are expected to account fully for the depreciation of their plants. In the Court's words:

> It is not only the right of the company to make such a provision, but it is its duty to its bond and stockholders, and, in the case of a public service corporation at least, its plain duty to the public. . . . If, however, a company fails to perform this plain duty and to exact sufficient returns to keep the investment unimpaired . . . the fault is its own.[11]

If, therefore, public utilities fail to make adequate charges to cover depreciation costs and do not accumulate the necessary depreciation reserves, they cannot increase their charges at a later time in order to recover the deficiencies from consumers. The key phrase is "adequate charges" and has been the subject of considerable dispute between the companies and the commissions.

In 1934, the Supreme Court held that an allowance for the depletion of irreplaceable natural resources was required.

> To withhold from a public utility the privilege of including a depletion allowance among its operating expenses, while confining it to a return of 6-1/2 percent upon the value of its wasting assets, is to take its property away from it without due process of law, at least where the waste is inevitable and rapid. . . . Plainly the state must either surrender the power to limit the return or else concede to the business a compensating privilege to preserve its capital intact.[12]

Taxes

The Supreme Court decided in the *Galveston* case of 1922 that taxes, including the federal income tax, were operating costs rather than reductions of investors' returns. Said Justice Brandeis:

> In calculating whether the five-cent fare will yield a proper return, it is necessary to deduct from gross revenue the expenses and charges; and all taxes which would be payable if a fair return were earned are appropriate deductions. There is no difference in this respect between state and federal taxes or between income taxes and others.[13]

In practice, all kinds of taxes — property, income, sales, franchise, social security, and miscellaneous taxes — are classified as reasonable costs of service. The significant exceptions to this rule are state taxes on capital stock and excess profits taxes levied during World War II and the Korean conflict.

Commission Supervision of Expenses

Commissions have the legal right to supervise a utility's operating expenses. Thus, for ratemaking purposes, they can control the cost of service. Moreover, since commissions have authority over accounting procedures, they can prescribe general rules for expenditures. In practice, however, commissions have not been vigorous in prescribing such rules. Operating expenses are normally subject to careful scrutiny in rate proceedings, and a commission's decisions provide guides during interim periods.

Methods of Supervision

Operating expenses may be controlled in two broad ways: (*1*) by disallowing improper charges already incurred in rate proceedings and (*2*) by prohibiting extravagant or unnecessary charges before they are incurred.

In a rate proceeding, a commission has the opportunity to separate the reasonable and unreasonable costs of service. This method of supervision consists of refusing to permit a utility to charge a particular expense to operating expenses. In so doing, the expense is charged to investors. As a method of control, however, the disallowance technique has one important limitation. If a commission disallows a significant percentage of a utility's operating expenses (expenses which have already been incurred), the revenue of the company will be inadequate to attract sufficient capital.

For this reason, authority to question expenditures before they are incurred is more satisfactory. At least nineteen state commissions have authority to require that annual budgets be submitted in advance of their effective dates.[14] A majority of the state statutes also require that all intracompany contracts be filed with the commissions. In both cases, the commissions have the opportunity to consider a company's expenditures before they are incurred. And, finally, in their orders, commissions may offer guidance as to the probable future ratemaking treatment of certain expenditures.

Supervision of Specific Expenses

An examination of several important costs usually scrutinized by the commissions will illustrate the problems and principles involved in this area.

Fuel Costs. For electric and gas utilities, fuel costs represent between 50 and 60 percent of operating expenses. Twenty-three commissions have automatic fuel adjustment clauses for electric utilities; thirty have automatic purchased gas adjustment clauses for gas utilities.[15] Generally, these clauses provide for automatic adjustments (sometimes after a hearing), thereby tracking fluctuations in the cost of fuel to the fuel costs embedded in the base rates. Such clauses, which "relieve utilities of the burden of constantly filing for rate increases or decreases as fuel costs change,"[16] were of particular significance during the 1970s when fuel costs rose substantially.

Criticism of automatic fuel clauses has centered on four issues. First, they permit rates to increase (decrease) automatically without a full hearing or a determination of the cost of service. While formal hearings are frequently not held, notice of their filing must be given and the utility has the burden of showing their justness and reasonableness. Further,

> . . . although they involve only one element of cost, it is unrealistic to believe that a major element, such as fuel, will move against the trend in a period of rising costs. When fuel costs rise and fluctuate beyond the control of management, the use of fuel adjustment clauses tends to avoid multiple rate proceedings and, consequently, serves a useful regulatory purpose.[17]

Second, they permit other than fuel costs to be passed on to ratepayers. While in theory only fuel costs are to be passed through, there are instances where other costs may have been involved.[18] Third, they reduce a utility's incentive to minimize fuel costs.[19] Even with an automatic fuel clause, there may be time lags in recovering the increased cost of fuel through billing. Further, many commissions hold that a utility must use reasonable care in negotiating a fuel supply contract and, should the contract not be fulfilled, must seek either its enforcement or compensation for damages.[20] Fourth, where fuel is purchased from subsidiaries, automatic fuel adjustment clauses may permit a subsidiary exorbitant profits. As will be discussed below, the commissions control such intracompany transactions.

Regulation or Rate Case Expenses. In a majority of states, regulatory expenses of the commissions are assessed to public utilities in the form of special taxes. Such assessments are allowable expenses. Allowed, too, is the amount spent in preparing the various reports required by the commissions.

But in the case of a company's being fined for failing to comply with (*a*) a statutory requirement, commission order, or rate tariff or (*b*) a safety regulation, the expense is not allowable.[21]

A more complex problem arises with respect to a utility's rate case expenses, for consumers should not be forced to pay for "elaborate defenses of private interest."[22] Companies must spend money preparing testimony and exhibits, and hiring lawyers and experts. These expenditures, if reasonable and necessary, are allowed and generally amortized over a period of two to five years.[23] However, expenses for a rate increase that has no merit[24] or advertising expenses incurred by a company to present its case in the newspapers for a rate increase[25] are generally not included in operating expenses. When a utility exercises its right to appeal a commission decision to the courts, the motives of the company are crucial. The expenses of appeal will be allowed if the rates established by the commission, for instance, are found to be confiscatory. The expenses of appeal will not be allowed when a utility merely wants to delay enforcement of a commission decision or, under certain circumstances, when the appeal is unsuccessful.[26]

Salaries, Wages, and Fringe Benefits. Commissions do not attempt to control wage rates, as they are subject to usual labor-management collective bargaining agreements.[27] Salary and fringe benefit costs, however, have been occasionally challenged. If excessive, they would constitute a source of concealed profit; excessive earnings could be turned into high salaries or fringe benefits rather than into rate reductions.

In questioning a utility's salaries, a commission normally considers gross revenues, total operating costs, and the quality and duties of management. The New Mexico commission, holding that a salary of $25,000 for a nonresident proprietor of a gas utility was excessive in relation to the company's total operating revenues of less than $700,000, reduced the allowable figure to $12,000.[28] The Connecticut commission held a general officer salary expense of nearly $13,000 excessive for a bus company having total operating expenses of $66,000.[29] The California commission disallowed $2,150,000 of supervisory salaries actually paid by a telephone company when the record disclosed no reason for a substantial increase in the number of management personnel at division level and higher.[30] The North Carolina commission disallowed 50 percent of executive officers' salaries on the theory that the company's management perform functions designed to benefit common shareholders.[31] But the Louisiana Supreme Court held that the commission's disallowance of part of the utility executive officers' salaries of a small, family-owned telephone company was arbitrary, since most if not all of such salaries appeared to have been earned.[32]

One reason for the sparsity of cases in this area is the fact that such salaries of public utilities as a whole are not excessive.[33] Even though they are regulated, they must still compete with the nonregulated sector of the economy for top executives. The general commission practice, therefore, is to leave the determination of officers' salaries to each company. As the

Michigan commission held many years ago, the directors are the "best judges of the value of executive officers . . . both to the utility and to the public."[34] It is only in holding company structures, in cases where company officers are also important stockholders, or where smaller utilities are involved, that serious problems arise regarding executive salaries.

Public utilities, like nonregulated industries, offer a number of fringe benefits, including pension and stock option plans. They are regarded as legitimate costs, since they are considered as part of an employee's total compensation and necessary to attract and retain good personnel. The cost of such plans must be reasonable, and the plans must be in existence at the time of the rate case.[35] A problem sometimes arises over unfunded pension liability when a plan covers both existing and retired employees, as well as new employees. "The unfunded liability problems exist because the retirement fund is deficient, at the time it is established, in the amount of the accruals due on past services performed by all but new employees."[36] A majority of the commissions have held that the unfunded liability should be amortized over a twenty to thirty year period and included in operating expenses, but a few commissions have disallowed such expenses on the ground that they involved costs related to past services.[37]

Advertising, Promotion, and Public Relations. While there is general agreement that the cost of public relations activities — including lobbying and political expenses, as well as dues paid to organizations that support legislative activities — should be disallowed for ratemaking purposes,[38] commission supervision of utility advertising and promotional expenses has undergone a significant change over the years. Prior to the 1970s, public utilities were constantly seeking new customers and larger sales in order to attain the full utilization of their facilities and to realize economies of scale. Advertising costs, expended to increase the demand for service or to retain existing customers, were classified as operating expenses. As the Supreme Court put it: "A business never stands still. It either grows or decays. Within the limits of reason, advertising or development expenses to foster normal growth are legitimate charges upon income for rate purposes. . . ."[39]

During this period, as interfuel competition intensified, promotional activities of electric and gas utilities expanded rapidly, and were scrutinized by the commissions, the courts, and Congress. Promotional activities fell into seven categories:

    I. Advertising cost sharing programs.
   II. Construction cost allowances.
  III. Sales bonuses.
  IV. Maximum cost guarantees.
   V. Financing assistance.
  VI. Equipment and appliance rental programs.
 VII. Varied sales promotion activities such as Open House Parties, Prize

Contests, and the lending of company personnel for showing houses and apartments.[40]

Several of these allowances and practices were challenged by competing suppliers, but their use was generally upheld as long as they were granted on a uniform basis, and were reasonable and nondiscriminatory.[41] Thus, allowances for conversion to gas or electric heat had to be uniform regardless of from what type of fuel the conversion was made; utilities were prohibited from guaranteeing maximum annual costs, and electric utilities could not provide free underground line extensions to all-electric customers.[42]

In the early 1970s, utility rates started to rise. The commissions began to scrutinize advertising and promotional activities.[43] Illustrative is a 1977 policy statement issued by the New York commission.[44] Advertising expenses were subdivided into two categories: "promotional — advertising intended to stimulate the purchase of utility services — and institutional and informational, a broad category inclusive of all advertising not clearly intended to promote sales." With respect to promotional advertising, the commission generally prohibited any such advertising for electric and gas utilities, including all promotional activities designed to acquire new customers or increase sales to existing customers. Telephone companies were permitted to advertise, as long as adequate capacity exists to provide the advertised service "without adversely affecting existing subscribers" and as long as "the advertising expenditures themselves together with the expansion of the service which they seek to promote will tend to reduce rates for telephone service." With respect to institutional advertising, the commission held that (a) civic and political advertising (including matters of public controversy, such as nuclear power) "will not be considered a legitimate cost of doing business" and, further, that bill inserts on such matters (even when paid for by stockholders) will not be permitted, and (b) informational advertising (conservation, notification of emergency conditions and procedures) "are a legitimate expense of doing business," for which an allowance of between 1/10 and 1/25 of one percent of operating revenues ("in inverse relationship to the size of the companies") will "probably" be permitted.[45]

Among the commissions, there are few areas of agreement over what advertising expenses will be allowed.[46] Moreover, supervision of utility advertising raises a related issue: freedom of speech under the First Amendment. In 1971, the Supreme Judicial Court of Massachusetts held invalid the commission's disallowance of $300,000 for institutional advertising, holding that the company was "no less entitled to advertise by reason of the fact that it is a regulated public utility than is the ordinary business corporation. The type and quality of such advertising, and the means, media, or vehicle used therefor are matters to be decided originally by the duly authorized managers of the company's business."[47] But the California Supreme Court, in 1972, upheld the commission's disallowance of $1,400,000 for institutional advertising.[48] Then, in 1980, the Supreme Court invalidated two of the New

York commission's rules: the rule banning electric utilities from advertising to promote use[49] and the rule prohibiting the use of bill inserts to express the utility's views on nuclear power.[50] In neither decision, however, did the Court deal directly with the ratemaking treatment of such advertising expenditures.[51]

Contributions, Donations, and Dues. American industry spends significant amounts annually in the form of contributions, donations, and dues. Contributions to charity and educational institutions are often included in operating expenses, if they are reasonable, since they benefit a utility by building good will and strengthening the economic well-being of the community.[52] Refusal to include contributions is based on the belief that they might be a means of influencing public opinion and on the fact that their inclusion would place consumers in the position of becoming involuntary contributors to charity.[53]

When donations to industrial and economic development funds or dues to professional associations (including local and state chambers of commerce) are at issue, they have usually been included in operating expenses.[54] Such donations and dues make a direct contribution to the well-being of the utility involved. But dues in civic and service clubs are generally excluded on the grounds that they do not directly benefit a utility in providing service to its customers,[55] as are any portion of dues to trade associations used for lobbying purposes.[56]

Merchandising and Jobbing Expenses. Some electric and gas utilities sell appliances as a promotional activity. These appliances are sold to customers either directly or indirectly by means of sales to architects and builders. In many cases, appliance sales do not show a profit; the utility gains through an increased use of its service or through a more efficient use.

The merchandising of appliances by utilities has been the subject of constant controversy. Local merchants often claim that such sales represent a form of "unfair" competition, because utilities can write off their appliance sales losses to general business expenses, have larger financial resources, and can obtain quantity discounts from manufacturers.[57] Others argue that appliance merchandising, like general sales promotion, is simply another method of obtaining new business. This position has been summarized by Troxel:

> Before domestic consumers can buy more electricity or gas, they often must buy more stoves, refrigerators, and other equipment.... Perhaps they do not buy more water heaters or other appliances because the appliance prices are too high. If this is true, a reduction of appliance prices can increase the sales of electricity or gas. The losses are new business expenses. And the losses, like general advertising expenditures, can be covered by the additional earnings that the company obtains from the demand increases. Appliance sales can be sensibly classed as a part of public utility operations.[58]

The commissions require, for accounting purposes, that expense and revenue accounts for the appliance business of an electric or gas utility be separated from other accounts. Salaries and commissions of salesmen, the cost of appliance advertising, and any losses on appliance sales, generally are excluded from operating expenses for purposes of ratemaking — even when a utility's efforts are directed toward the use of efficient, conservation-rated appliances.[59] Similarly, any profits on appliance sales are not included in a company's annual utility earnings. The merchandising of appliances, therefore, is treated as a nonutility business.

Replacement Power Costs; Repair and/or Cleanup Costs. Generating plant outages, particularly in the case of nuclear plants (whether due to an accident or to an NRC mandate), raise two issues: Who should pay the replacement power costs and the repair and/or cleanup costs? The cause of the outage is crucial. If due to mismanagement or imprudence, replacement power costs, as well as any related repair and/or cleanup costs, generally are disallowed.[60] In the words of the New York commission:

> ... the company's conduct should be judged by asking whether the conduct was reasonable at the time, under all the circumstances, considering that the company had to solve its problems prospectively rather than in reliance on hindsight. In effect, our responsibility is to determine how reasonable people would have performed the tasks that confronted the company.[61]

Under this standard, Consolidated Edison Company was required to refund $33.7 million (plus interest) in replacement power costs "because of lack of reasonable care in its management and operation of the Indian Point No. 2 nuclear facility. . . ."[62] Under similar standards, Philadelphia Electric Company had to absorb $53.2 million in replacement power costs as a result of two outages (in 1983 and 1984) at Salem Unit No. 1,[63] and Utah Power & Light Company's cleanup costs from a toxic waste spill were disallowed.[64] But the Pennsylvania commission permitted Metropolitan Edison Company and Pennsylvania Electric Company to fully recover their replacement power costs as a result of events at Three Mile Island, since "the current purchases of power by respondents were direct and immediate costs of providing service."[65]

Transactions among Affiliated Companies.[66] The widespread existence of holding companies results in two important problems in the control of expenditures. Operating companies normally pay either the holding company or a subsidiary service company an annual fee for accounting, financial, and legal services. Operating companies also commonly purchase all or some of their equipment, materials, and supplies from affiliated manufacturing firms. In addition, other electric and gas utilities own fuel subsidiaries, from which they purchase all or part of their annual fuel requirements. All of these transactions, because of the absence of arm's-length bargaining, require careful scrutiny by the commissions, but they "should not be given any consideration in the absence of evidence of unfair dealing."[67]

With respect to annual service fees, a majority of the state commissions have authority over the management contracts that are signed by operating companies, and copies of such contracts must be filed with the commissions. In some cases, the contracts must be submitted for approval before they become effective. In other cases, the contracts are subject to approval or disapproval after they have become effective. But in either situation, a commission always has the opportunity in a rate case to question a payment made to an affiliated company.

In general, service fees will not be approved unless the company can show some specific services rendered by the management firm. This requirement follows the principle expressed by the SEC in a 1943 case:

> Each service company should confine itself to functions which the operating subsidiaries cannot perform as efficiently and economically themselves. These services should be limited to services of an "operating nature" as distinguished from managerial, executive, or policy-forming functions.[68]

At the federal level, the service contracts of electric and gas holding companies are closely controlled by the SEC. In the Public Utility Holding Company Act of 1935, the commission was authorized to approve service companies if it finds that services will be performed efficiently and economically "at a cost fairly and equitably allocated among" operating subsidiaries and "at a reasonable saving over the cost of comparable services or construction performed or goods sold by independent persons."[69] The commission prescribes a standard system of accounts for service companies. Charges are limited to the costs of the services performed; all proposed modifications in service contracts must be approved by the commission.[70]

At the state level, service fees are regularly reviewed in rate proceedings and, on occasion, adjustments are made. Prior to divestiture, for example, the American Telephone and Telegraph Company had a general service and license contract with each Bell System operating company. The license contract was for a variety of services, including accounting, legal, and financial services; research and development; and advice and assistance in engineering, plant, traffic, commercial, and other operating fields. Prior to 1974, the operating subsidiaries paid to AT&T one percent of exchange and toll revenues annually. No state commission found it necessary to revise the service charges under the license contract.[71] Between 1974 and 1983, AT&T charged the actual costs of its services to the Bell operating companies on an allocation formula (not to exceed 2 1/2 percent of collectible gross operating revenues).[72] As a result, substantial scrutiny occurred in some cases. The Illinois commission, for instance, deducted those allocated costs attributable to AT&T's Washington office, press relations, and special projects, and all allocated costs attributed to charitable contributions and dues,[73] while the Louisiana Supreme Court upheld the commission's requirement that the portion of the license contract attributable to research and development be capitalized and amortized over a twenty-year period.[74] A few adjustments have been made by state commissions in non-Bell System rate cases as well.[75]

With respect to prices for equipment charged operating companies by affiliated manufacturing firms, the commissions generally consider two criteria of reasonableness, both based on Supreme Court decisions: (1) whether the prices charged operating companies are lower than those charged by other manufacturers for comparable equipment and supplies and (2), of greater importance, whether the profits earned on sales to operating companies are lower than those of comparable large manufacturing companies.[76] Using these criteria, there are a few cases in which commissions have made disallowances, either in operating expenses or in the rate base. Further, in those instances where significant disallowances have been made, it has generally been because of a belief that an affiliated manufacturer should earn no more than a commission permits a regulated utility, rather than a finding that the affiliated manufacturer's prices were too high.[77]

Similar criteria have been applied to utility fuel purchases from affiliated subsidiaries. Coal purchases are illustrative. First, the "transfer price" is monitored to make sure that it is similar to, or below, market generated prices of coal.[78] Second, the profits earned on a subsidiary's coal sales to a parent are scrutinized. In several cases, significant disallowances have been made, often on the theory that an affiliated supplier should earn no more than allowed a regulated utility.[79] Such a position, it should be noted, assumes that the risks are similar; a position that is subject to dispute.

Amortization of Expenses. Potentially, there are several items that might be amortized for ratemaking purposes. Under such a procedure, the amount involved — for accounting purposes — is placed in an appropriate reserve account and — for ratemaking purposes — is amortized as an expense over an appropriate number of years, but the unamortized reserve is generally excluded from a utility's rate base.[80]

Rate case expenses and unfunded pension liabilities, as noted earlier, may be treated in this manner. So, too, are unusual casualty-related losses, due to ice storms,[81] flood damage,[82] or high winds and rain.[83] One commission amortized a utility's expenses for a computerized financial model[84]; another for the expenses of a special study[85]; and a third for a utility's expenses associated with the early termination of a coal supply contract.[86] Acquisition adjustments are another example. Such an adjustment represents the price paid to another utility[87] for an asset that exceeds the seller's depreciated original cost. As explained by the Iowa commission: ". . . the sale of utility property for more than its cost does not result in establishing an increased cost for ratemaking purposes since there is actually no increased investment in plant to be used in rendering service."[88]

In dealing with obsolete or abandoned plant that was in service (such as the abandonment of gas manufacturing plants with the advent of natural gas pipelines), and assuming the original investment decision was prudent, commissions have often permitted the unrecovered portion of the investment to be recovered through amortization charges.[89] Even in the case of plant abandonment (cancellation) prior to completion, due in large part to revised demand projections made in the 1970s and early 1980s, utilities have been permitted to recover their investment, again assuming the abandonment decision was prudent.[90] But the most complex issue in this regard has yet to be determined: the ratemaking treatment of a nuclear accident.[91]

Evaluation of Commission Control

The above items do not represent a complete list of the costs of service incurred by public utilities, nor are they the only expenses scrutinized in rate cases. Rather, they are representative, and illustrate the problems and nature of commission control of operating expenses. One conclusion stands out: few of the commissions have formulated rules or established standards to govern expenditures, but supervision of expenses has been vigorous in ratemaking proceedings.

Clemens has argued that more effective commission control of operating expenses would require use of expense ratios.[92] By comparing the expense ratios of different companies — expenses as a percentage of revenues, expenses per unit of consumption, and expenses per customer — the commissions would have a basis for analyzing company expenditures. More elaborate measures of efficiency (productivity) have been or are being developed, particularly with respect to the electric utility industry. These studies include the econometric efforts of Iulo and Pace[93] (using levels of unit output costs as the measure); the total productivity factor method of Dodge, Trebing, and Stevenson[94] (to measure the output of a firm to its total physical volume); and the "Red Flag" approach of Smith[95] (ranking a utility against other like utilities in terms of various operating ratios). Shepherd has noted that attempts to measure, explain, and predict the performance of electric utility firms are difficult because of "the multiplicity of elements in performance and the problem of weighting them, data scarcities, difficulty in disentangling cause and effect, and so on" and that they "will not be easy to extend to other utilities, whose products are even more heterogeneous than in electric supply."[96] It remains true, as Trebing stated several years ago, that their applicability "to the general process of regulation or to a given commission problem can only be judged after greater research and investigation."[97]

Depreciation as a Cost

The concern in this section is with depreciation as an annual charge to operating costs, thereby shown in the income statement. Accrued depreciation, recorded in the depreciation reserve (a balance sheet account) as a deduction from the value of a utility's tangible and reproducible property for rate base purposes, will be discussed in the following chapter.

The Meaning of Depreciation

The National Association of Regulatory Utility Commissioners has defined depreciation as follows:

(a) Depreciation is the expiration or consumption, in whole or in part, of the service life, capacity, or utility of property resulting from the action of one or more of the forces operating to bring about the retirement of such property from service;

(b) The forces so operating include wear and tear, decay, action of the elements, inadequacy, obsolescence, and public requirements;

(c) Depreciation results in a cost of service.[98]

Depreciation thus involves the gradual deterioration and eventual destruction in the value of physical facilities used in the process of providing service. The several causes of depreciation are commonly divided into two broad categories. (*1*) Physical depreciation is caused by usage, rust, rot, and decay — all through the passage of time. Trucks and tires wear out; telephone and electric poles slowly rot; gas and water mains gradually corrode. Physical depreciation also results from unforeseeable and uninsurable contingencies such as accidents and disasters. (*2*) Functional depreciation occurs when facilities are rendered obsolete by new technology, are made inadequate by growth in demand, or are made useless by changes in public requirements. As will be discussed below, functional depreciation represents a special regulatory problem.

The basic purpose of depreciation accounting is to recover through revenues the costs invested in the physical plant contributing to the production of those revenues. By matching capital recovery with capital consumption, a more accurate measure of current costs of operation is possible. Stated another way, depreciation accounting is necessary to reimburse those supplying the capital used to purchase the related assets and should properly be charged to consumers as a cost of the service they receive. "It is the exhaustion of service life, not the particular cause of retirement, that is important."[99]

It should be noted that the basic purpose of depreciation accounting is *not* to finance replacements. Even if facilities are not to be replaced, depreciation must be charged to operating expenses in order to record the cost of property consumed in providing service, thereby maintaining the integrity of the investment. Nor does depreciation result in a fund. "The depreciation reserve is an account *contra* to the plant account."[100] Further, a distinction must be made between provisions for depreciation and for maintenance. While both are costs, maintenance keeps facilities in good condition while they are in use, but does not reimburse those supplying capital. Only depreciation charges perform the reimbursement function. This important distinction was stated by Chief Justice Hughes as follows:

> Broadly speaking, depreciation is the loss, not restored by current maintenance, which is due to all the factors causing the ultimate retirement of the property. These factors embrace wear and tear, decay, inadequacy, and obsolescence. Annual depreciation is the loss which takes place in a year. In determining reasonable rates for supplying public service, it is proper to include in the operating expenses, that is, in the cost of producing the service, an allowance for consumption of capital in order to maintain the integrity of the investment in the service rendered.[101]

Depreciation Accounting[102]

The regulatory commissions require depreciation accounting.[103] Under this accounting system, and assuming the age-life or whole-life method,[104] balances are established in the depreciation reserve account. Credits to this account result from annual charges during the service life of the property.[105] With certain exceptions, the annual charge depends on three factors: (*1*) the value of the property, plus cost of removal less estimated salvage value, (*2*) the estimated service life of the property over which this sum is written off, and (*3*) the method used in distributing the sum over this life.

As will be discussed in the following section, property may be valued at its original cost, at its replacement cost, or at some intermediate point between these two. In 1930, the Supreme Court held that the annual depreciation accrual of public utilities should be based on the "present value" of the depreciable property[106] — a ruling consistent with its earlier decisions emphasizing fair value in determining the rate base. If followed, the annual depreciation charge would fluctuate with price changes, rising as the price level increased and falling as prices declined. The Court subsequently overruled the *United Railways* case on this point (as well as on fair value), thus recognizing that the recovery of past investments is the main purpose of depreciation accounting.[107] As a result, original cost accounting is now the general rule for valuating depreciable property. The estimated cost of removal[108] is then added to, and the estimated salvage value[109] is deducted from, the original cost in order to determine the amount to be recovered through depreciation charges.

The service life of the various property items, which determines the length of the depreciation period, is established in three basic ways. First, and the most frequently used method, is a combination of a review of past retirement experience and engineering estimates of future service lives. Second, when estimates made by the company and/or by the commission differ or when it is desirable to adopt a uniform depreciation rate, the length of the depreciation period may be set by negotiation.[110] Third, as commissions are reluctant to allow depreciation rates in excess of those permitted for tax purposes, tax policy may determine the depreciation period.[111] Particularly is the third method important when accelerated depreciation (discussed below) is permitted for tax purposes. Welch has stated that the process of estimating the useful life of property items

> ... is something very similar to the actuarial experience used by insurance companies for fires, accidents, and other hazards covered by insurance, even human life. Given a broad enough experience, such actuarial tables can be surprisingly accurate. Thus, a single pole for a pole line might be assigned a life expectancy of twenty years and be knocked down by an automobile the day after it is put into service. Or it may be destroyed by lightning ten years after that. And it may be standing and giving good service thirty years later. But given enough experience with enough poles, and making due adjustments for local hazards (such as sleet in the North, and termites in the South), the average life table assignment will generally be found to work out very close to actual experience.[112]

In practice, a separate rate is not computed for each item of property. Rather, property items are grouped (either by like property items or by functional groups of plant accounts) and an average rate is applied to all items within each group.[113]

Finally, the depreciation charge can be distributed over the expected service life of the property[114] in three ways. The *straight line method,* by which rates (annual depreciation charges) remain the same each year, is the simplest and most commonly used. Thus, a piece of property costing $10,000, with no removal cost or salvage value and an estimated service life of ten years, would be depreciated at the rate of $1,000 per year. In a growing utility, the accruals (*i.e.,* the annual depreciation charges, which are allowable operating costs and thus are recovered through annual revenue requirements) are reinvested in the business, but they are not credited with interest.[115] The annual depreciation charges are intended to add up to the original cost of the property when retired, after considering removal cost and salvage value. The *sinking fund* method is more complicated. A reserve is set up on the utility's books and equal charges assigned to it each year. It is assumed, moreover, that the annual depreciation charges are invested and interest earned. Therefore, the fixed portion of the annual depreciation charge need not be so large as under the straight line method, but only large enough so that the yearly charges plus the accumulated compound interest will be equal to the cost of the property at the time of retirement.

Using the same illustration as above, an annual charge of $758.68 and the addition of compound interest at 6 percent would bring the reserve up to $10,000 at the end of ten years. The *accelerated method*, which is permitted for tax purposes but which is not generally used for book purposes, originally was of two types: sum-of-the-years' digits method and double-declining balance method. Under an accelerated method, the annual depreciation expense is greater in the early years of the asset's life. "The assumptions are that an asset makes a greater contribution to revenues during the earlier part of its life and that service value expires more rapidly in the early years."[116] The three methods (using the double-declining balance method for accelerated[117]) are compared in Table 7-1.

A new accelerated method — the Accelerated Cost Recovery System (ACRS) — was initiated by the Economic Recovery Tax Act of 1981,[118] and was modified by the Tax Reform Act of 1986.[119] The ACRS is based upon the concept of a "recovery period" (three- , five- , ten- , or fifteen-year periods, originally), rather than on the useful life of the depreciable asset, for depreciable property placed in service after 1980. The system also disregards salvage value. The original purpose of the ACRS was to stimulate capital formation by increasing depreciation expenses and, thereby, reducing taxable income[120]; the new purpose of the ACRS "is to more evenly match class lives with the economic or useful lives of particular assets."[121] The ACRS is available only if a utility uses a normalization method of accounting for ratemaking purposes.

Current Depreciation Problems

While the use of depreciation accounting is firmly established, two problems frequently arise in rate cases. First, how should the commissions deal with functional depreciation? Second, what is the proper depreciation rate when competition has been introduced? In addition, in view of a constant inflationary trend in prices, should depreciation allowances be based upon reproduction cost? Each of these issues will be discussed in turn. Accelerated depreciation is considered in the following section.

The Problem of Obsolescence. Functional depreciation may be of more importance than physical depreciation. Functional depreciation is due to changes in technology, demand, or public requirements.[122] Dial telephone systems have been substituted for manual switchboards and electronic offices have replaced electromechanical equipment, leading to the retirement of much equipment. Electric companies have installed more economical boilers, stokers, turbines, and generators, resulting in the retirement of many small plants and their equipment. And governmental bodies have required that underground cables be used in place of overhead lines in the interest of beautification. In these and many other cases, plant and equipment have been outdated and retired. Functional depreciation, however, raises a seri-

TABLE 7-1

Age-Life Methods of Calculating Depreciation*

Year	Straight Line		Sinking Fund			Accelerated	
	Annual Depreciation Expense	Depreciation Reserve Accumulation	Annual Depreciation Expense	Annual Interest Accumulation	Depreciation Reserve Accumulation	Annual Depreciation Expense	Depreciation Reserve Accumulation
1	$ 1,000	$ 1,000	$ 758.68	$ ...	$ 758.68	$ 2,000	$ 2,000
2	$ 1,000	$ 2,000	758.68	45.52	1,562.88	1,600	3,600
3	$ 1,000	$ 3,000	758.68	93.77	2,415.33	1,280	4,880
4	$ 1,000	$ 4,000	758.68	144.92	3,318.93	1,024	5,904
5	$ 1,000	$ 5,000	758.68	199.14	4,276.75	819	6,723
6	$ 1,000	$ 6,000	758.68	256.61	5,292.04	655	7,378
7	$ 1,000	$ 7,000	758.68	317.52	6,368.24	524	7,902
8	$ 1,000	$ 8,000	758.68	382.08	7,509.01	419	8,321
9	$ 1,000	$ 9,000	758.68	450.54	8,718.23	336	8,657
10	$ 1,000	$10,000	758.68	523.09	10,000.00	268	8,925
Total	$10,000		$7,586.80	$2,413.20		$8,925	

*The following assumptions underlie the computations: original investment, $10,000; no removal cost or salvage value; estimated service life, ten years; annual interest, 6 percent; accelerated method, double-declining balance.

ous regulatory problem: engineers can estimate with some accuracy physical depreciation, but the rate of obsolescence is determined by changing technology or public requirements. As a result, no separate allowance is made for obsolescence in depreciation accounting, but it is a major consideration in setting overall depreciation rates.[123]

The Investment Decision. A business firm, in deciding whether it should replace existing equipment with more efficient equipment, should

> ... compare the average *variable* cost of producing with it (AVC_o) with the average *total* cost of production with new equipment (ATC_n). Only the variable costs of the old can be saved by turning to the new; the choice therefore is between continuing to incur those AVC, on the one hand, or incurring the ATC — including the capital costs as well — involved in purchasing a new machine. If the AVC_o are smaller than the ATC_n it is economical to continue to use the old capital goods. But if, *regardless* of the fixed costs on the old, the AVC_o are the greater, it is foolish not to scrap; every moment of continued production with the old means a greater drain on the company's resources, a greater avoidable cost of production, than would be involved in replacement.[124]

In making such a decision, fixed costs — including any unrecovered depreciation on the current equipment — are irrelevant. But a public utility cannot ignore such fixed costs. Assume that a replacement is economically justified, but that the current asset is not fully depreciated. If a commission refuses to permit the utility to write off (amortize) the unrecovered investment, management may decide to withhold the replacement.

> ... Suppose, for example, that the average variable costs under the old process are a constant $7 per unit, the average fixed costs (depreciation and return on the unamortized part of the investment) $3, and the regulated price is $10. Suppose then a new process becomes available with the same capacity as the old, with average variable costs of $4.50 and average fixed costs of $2. Such an investment would be economically efficient; every unit that continued to be produced under the old process (at an avoidable cost of $7) would be involving society as well as the firm in the unnecessary expenditure of 50 cents worth of resources (since the *total* unit costs under the new are only $6.50).[125]

If a commission cut the utility's price to $6.50, once replacement had been made, and removed the old assets from the rate base, "the company would find itself in a position of having incurred *additional* capital costs of $2 a unit, and yet had its gross return on capital (depreciation and profit) reduced from $3 a unit to $2 a unit. It obviously would have been better for the company to postpone the new investment and continue to take in the $3 per unit of depreciation and return on the old assets until the latter had been completely written off."[126]

Regulatory Policy. The regulatory commissions have dealt with the depreciation problem due to obsolescence in four basic ways. First, they may permit utilities to take future obsolescence into account in establishing annual depreciation rates. Second, when required to meet emergencies or maximum peak service demands, the obsolete equipment may be defined as standby capacity and left in the rate base, with the equipment being depreciated at the normal rate. Third, the unrecovered depreciation on the obsolete equipment may be amortized. By amortizing the costs over a five-year period, for example, the costs would be recovered gradually and some of the benefits of the new technology could be passed on to consumers immediately. Fourth, the obsolete equipment may be written-off immediately, without or with only partial recovery. Regulatory policy, therefore, is far from consistent. Typical is a 1957 Minnesota Supreme Court decision:

> The principle of law which should guide the discretion of the commission in determining whether the customer or investor should be charged with the amount of alleged loss due to obsolescence is twofold: (*1*) the future customer may not be charged for obsolescence through any method of accounting unless the investor has suffered an actual loss by not having fully recovered prudently invested funds, and (*2*) even if such loss has occurred, it is unreasonable to charge the customer if the investor has been compensated for assuming the risk of obsolescence. . . .
>
> Where an actual loss has occurred due to obsolescence, the commission may, in the exercise of its judgment, apportion one-half of all such actual loss to the investor and charge the remaining one-half to future customers by amortization as an operating expense over a period of years.[127]

Depreciation and Competition. As portions of the telecommunications industry were opened to competition, some critical issues were raised with respect to depreciation policy. The industry's depreciation practices were developed under monopoly conditions; long capital recovery periods (up to thirty-five years) were the rule. Such practices are not proper under competitive conditions. Some assets are being, or will be, used to provide competitive services ("enhanced" services), while others will be subjected to competition. Take terminal equipment: The FCC ordered that all terminal equipment must be removed from rate base. Much of this equipment has a net book value considerably greater than its economic value. How should telephone utilities recover their investment?[128] Or, take station connections (primarily labor and wiring costs associated with the installation and removal of customer equipment): The FCC decided that this investment will be recovered by amortization over a four- to five-year period.[129] An even broader issue is whether the commission should continue to establish depreciation rates for competitive services.[130]

The Reproduction Cost Controversy.[131] The basic purpose of depreciation accounting is the recovery of past investment in plant and equipment, and is properly a cost of providing service. In recent years, moreover, because of inflationary price trends, many have argued that annual depreciation charges should be based upon current cost rather than upon original cost.[132] Only in this way, it is argued, will a company be able to maintain unimpaired the capital invested in the enterprise.

Consider an inflationary situation (Table 7-2). If a company purchases a machine for $2,000, with an estimated life of five years and no removal cost or salvage value, straight line depreciation would result in an annual charge of $400 based upon original cost. Now assume that the price level rises throughout the five-year period. In terms of the purchasing power of the dollar, the company has recovered only $1,691 of its original investment. As a result, the current-cost advocates argue, depreciation based upon original cost has failed to measure the real consumption of capital. Further, when taxes are levied on taxable income which reflects original cost depreciation allowances, a portion of the tax represents a tax on capital as well as on real income. The capital invested in the enterprise, therefore, is eroded. This situation can be corrected by expressing depreciation allowances in current dollars, as illustrated. The result is to return to the company its original $2,000 investment in terms of constant purchasing power.[133] In times of deflation, the opposite adjustments would be made, and depreciation allowances would be decreased.

Representatives of public utilities are not the only ones advocating reproduction cost depreciation. Any industry with a large investment in plant and equipment in relation to annual revenues will be severely hit by changes in the price level. Assume two industries: one with an investment in plant and equipment equal to four times annual revenues, the other with investment equal to one-half annual revenues. If the price level rises 50 percent, it takes either an 8 percent increase in revenues or a 22 percent decrease in operating expenses to offset the tax burden for the first, as compared to a one percent increase in revenues or a one percent decrease in operating expenses for the second.[134]

The economics of original and reproduction costs will be considered at length in the next chapter. At this point, however, three comments are pertinent. First, if the reproduction cost concept is accepted, it should apply to all American industry, not just to public utilities. Second, acceptance of the reproduction cost concept should involve a change in tax policy. There is no logical reason why depreciation methods for accounting purposes should not be the same as for tax purposes. And, from a practical standpoint, commissions are reluctant to allow depreciation rates in excess of those permitted for tax purposes. Assuming a 46 percent income tax rate, a utility

TABLE 7-2

Original Cost versus Reproduction Cost Depreciation Allowance*

Year	Depreciation Accruals Based on Original Cost	Consumer Price Index	Depreciation Accruals Based on Price Index	Capital Recovered in Terms Of Year One Dollars	
				With Original Cost Depreciation	With Reproduction Cost Depreciation
1	$ 400	100	$ 400	$ 400	$ 400
2	400	110	440	364	400
3	400	120	480	333	400
4	400	130	520	308	400
5	400	140	560	286	400
Totals	$2,000		$2,400	$1,691	$2,000

*The following assumptions underlie the computations: original investment, $2,000; no removal cost or salvage value; estimated service life, five years; straight line depreciation.

must collect $1.85 from its customers for each $1.00 it retains for the extra depreciation allowance. Only a few commissions, therefore, have permitted depreciation allowances in excess of those allowed by current tax laws.[135] Third, consistency requires that if the reproduction cost concept is accepted, it should apply in periods of rising prices and in periods of falling prices. As a result, the annual depreciation charges will fluctuate with the price level.

Depletion Accounting

The object of depreciation accounting is to charge consumers the cost of maintaining intact the capital funds of a company. For the minerals industries, however, other problems arise, of which two are major. First, the fair market value of a mine, quarry, or well cannot be determined accurately for tax purposes; they usually have an unknown content. Second, these industries are subject to increasing costs in the exploration and discovery of new domestic reserves. Increasing costs result because as more easily accessible deposits are depleted, their replacement comes from less accessible deposits. The processes of exploration and discovery, moreover, are expensive, and the risk of loss is large. Finally, there is often a lag of five years or more between exploration and production. The President's Materials Policy Commission explained:

> It is customary under U.S. tax laws to permit a business to recover tax free its investment in physical assets as they wear out or become obsolete. Ordinarily the recovered investment can be applied toward replacing physical assets. But for many minerals there is considerable uncertainty as to whether reserves can be replaced, and considerable risk entailed in attempting to replace them. Moreover, for some major minerals the real cost of replacement keeps rising because of the progressive depletion of natural resources.[136]

The natural gas industry, therefore, must account for the depletion of the natural gas fields. "This usually is done on a unit-of-production basis for each leasehold or field. A cost for the period is arrived at by applying a predetermined unit rate to the total number of units produced during the period. Several different methods may be used to determine the unit rate. One is to divide the net book cost of depletable plant by the estimated number of units to be recovered; a second is to divide the gross book cost by the total past plus estimated future units to be extracted."[137] The depletable base generally includes the leasehold costs, plus the intangible drilling and development costs.[138]

Taxes as a Cost

Since 1922, taxes, with but minor exceptions, have been included in operating costs.[139] The local, state, and federal tax payments of public utilities have increased rapidly and now represent a substantial percentage of their gross revenues. For private electric utilities, for example, the ratio of taxes paid or tax expenses to operating revenues was 17.4 percent in 1984, compared with 6.5 percent in 1917.[140] As tax payments are costs of service, conflicts between the regulation and taxation of public utilities are inevitable.[141] Moreover, public utilities are taxed even more heavily than nonregulated businesses.[142]

Public Utilities as Tax Collectors

Why are public utilities often called "tax collectors *par excellence*"?[143] In the first place, they are generally large corporate enterprises, which simplifies the administration and collection of taxes. In the second place, their investment in plant and equipment in relation to annual revenue is greater than that of most industries. Public utilities, consequently, are peculiarly subject to the property tax.[144] In the third place, given relatively inelastic demand curves for some of their services, higher prices are unlikely to lead to significant decreases in consumer demand. When rates are below the value of service, higher prices can be charged (with regulatory approval), resulting in more revenues and more taxes.

In the fourth place, many communities derive a significant portion of their annual revenues from taxes levied on the property of public utilities. Finally, with public utilities lacking strong political support and, prior to the 1970s, often showing good earnings, legislatures appeared to consider that further taxation of them was a safe way to increase tax revenues. Some punitive taxes also have been levied on these industries. In short, public utilities are often used as tax collectors, and are a politically acceptable source of local, state, and federal governmental revenues.[145] As explained by one lawmaker:

> . . . a continuation of the excise tax on telephone and telegraph service will not, after all, jeopardize a continued profit in the business of the public utilities affected, because each one of them operates under rates set by public regulatory bodies which allow rates sufficiently high to enable the companies to meet their tax situations and at the same time operate at a profit, *even if their business should be slightly reduced.*[146]

Categories of Taxes

The types of taxes imposed on public utilities can be grouped into three categories. First, some of the taxes applied to public utilities are also applied uniformly to nonregulated industries. These include corporate and state income taxes, social security taxes, state unemployment compensation taxes, and the federal excess profits tax (levied during World War II and the Korean conflict).[147] Second, other taxes are applied to all businesses, but unequally. Public utilities, for instance, frequently pay more property (ad valorem) tax per dollar of investment than are paid by other business property owners. Third, some taxes are levied only on public utilities, such as franchise taxes, federal excise taxes on telephone and telegraph services, and local consumer utility taxes.

The Incidence of Taxes

Treatment of taxes as an operating cost means there is a tendency, in the long run, to shift them to consumers, but it does not follow that such a shift is always successful. Two exceptions should be noted.[148] (*1*) If there is a lag in the regulatory process, tax increases are borne, in the short run, by the regulated companies. Regulatory procedure is often slow, and a utility seldom finds it possible to obtain an immediate offsetting rate increase when a new tax is placed on it or an old tax is increased. The situation may be serious for a utility that was just earning a fair return, or less than a fair return, before the tax was added or increased. (*2*) When a utility is already charging rates close to the value of service, so that an increase in rates will result in either a decline in profits or an increase in deficits, taxes are borne by the utility.[149]

There is an important tax problem concerning the incidence of local taxes. In most cases, a public utility serves a large area and is subject to several local tax jurisdictions. Where should local taxes rest: on the consumers of the utility throughout its market area, or on the consumers of the jurisdiction which levied the tax? In practice, the commissions tend to follow the first alternative when the tax in question is a franchise tax and the second for gross receipts and consumer utility taxes. Franchise taxes are "going concern" taxes, it is argued, and should be included in general operating expenses. But if all taxes were so handled, one city would be permitted, in effect, to tax service users in other cities.[150] Moreover, many commissions require public utilities to pass local taxes on to consumers in each of the cities levying such taxes by making a surcharge on each bill. The Idaho commission, in making such a requirement, indicated that unless handled in this manner, consumers would not realize that these "hidden taxes" were being passed on to them, thereby tending to lull the public into a frame of mind which allows government expenditures to be increased without strong opposition.[151]

Interperiod Income Tax Allocation[152]

Although public utilities are subject to many types of taxes, federal income taxation presents the most complex and controversial issues. At the outset, it must be recognized that there is commonly a difference between income and expenses for accounting (book) purposes and for income tax purposes. As explained by the Accounting Principles Board of the American Institute of Certified Public Accountants:

> The principal problems in accounting for income taxes arise from the fact that some transactions affect the determination of net income for financial accounting purposes in one reporting period and the computation of taxable income and income taxes payable in a different reporting period. The amount of income taxes determined to be payable for a period does not, therefore, necessarily represent the appropriate income tax expense applicable to transactions recognized for financial accounting purposes in that period. A major problem is, therefore, the measurement of the tax effects of such transactions and the extent to which the tax effects should be included in income tax expense in the same periods in which the transactions affect pretax accounting income.[153]

Where there are book/tax timing differences,[154] income taxes must be apportioned among accounting periods. That process is known as *interperiod income tax allocation*. Three major areas that require allocation follow: accelerated depreciation, investment (job development) tax credit, and consolidated tax returns.

Accelerated Depreciation: The "Phantom Tax" Issue. Under the Revenue Act of 1954, business firms are permitted to adopt accelerated depreciation in calculating taxable income, thereby charging higher depreciation expenses in the early years of the service life of assets than would be allowed under straight line depreciation and lower rates in later years. The effect is to produce lower tax payments with respect to the early years which are offset by increased tax payments in the remaining years. The act posed a problem for the regulatory commissions: should they include, for ratemaking purposes, as operating costs the higher income taxes to which utilities would be subject were they to report taxable income on a straight line basis ("normalization" method) or should they include only the taxes actually paid ("flow through" method) by the utilities? If the normalization method is adopted, the utilities, in effect, are granted during the early years of the property's life an interest-free loan of the difference between taxes paid and taxes due under the straight line method.[155] The implication is that the act results in a tax deferral rather than a permanent tax saving. The difference could be used for modernization and expansion or for other financial needs. If the flow through principle is adopted, the tax deferrals are denied to the utilities and the reduced tax expense can be used to raise reported earnings or to reduce consumer rates.

The normalization and flow through methods are compared in Table 7-3. Assume that a utility invests $10,000 in new equipment, that its esti-

TABLE 7-3

Illustration of Effect of Accelerated Depreciation, for Tax Purposes, on Net Income*

A. NORMALIZATION ACCOUNTING

Year	Straight Line Depreciation (a)	Accelerated Depreciation (b)	Effect On Taxable Income (c=b−a)	Effect On Taxes Payable (d=c×.46)	Credit (or Charge) to Deferred Taxes (e=−d)	Effect On Net Income (f=d+e)
1	$ 892.50	$ 2,000.00	$−1,107.50	$−509.45	$+509.45	0
2	892.50	1,600.00	− 707.50	− 325.45	+ 325.45	0
3	892.50	1,280.00	− 387.50	− 178.25	+ 178.25	0
4	892.50	1,024.00	− 131.50	− 60.49	+ 60.49	0
5	892.50	819.00	+ 73.50	+ 33.81	− 33.81	0
6	892.50	655.00	+ 237.50	+ 109.25	− 109.25	0
7	892.50	524.00	+ 368.50	+ 169.51	− 169.51	0
8	892.50	419.00	+ 473.50	+ 217.81	− 217.81	0
9	892.50	336.00	+ 556.50	+ 255.99	− 255.99	0
10	892.50	268.00	+ 624.50	+ 287.27	− 287.27	0
	$ 8,925.00	$ 8,925.00	0	0	0	0
Salvage value	$ 1,075.00	$ 1,075.00				
Total	$10,000.00	$10,000.00				

TABLE 7-3 (Continued)

B. FLOW THROUGH ACCOUNTING

Year	Straight Line Depreciation (a)	Accelerated Depreciation (b)	Effect on Taxable Income (c=b−a)	Effect on Taxes Payable (d=c×.46)	Effect on Net Income (e=−d)
1	$ 892.50	$ 2,000.00	$ −1,107.50	$ −509.45	$ +509.45
2	892.50	1,600.00	− 707.50	− 325.45	+ 325.45
3	892.50	1,280.00	− 387.50	− 178.25	+ 178.25
4	892.50	1,024.00	− 131.50	− 60.49	+ 60.49
5	892.50	819.00	+ 73.50	+ 33.81	− 33.81
6	892.50	655.00	+ 237.50	+ 109.25	− 109.25
7	892.50	524.00	+ 368.50	+ 169.51	− 169.51
8	892.50	419.00	+ 473.50	+ 217.81	− 217.81
9	892.50	336.00	+ 556.50	+ 255.99	− 255.99
10	892.50	268.00	+ 624.50	+ 287.27	− 287.27
	$ 8,925.00	$ 8,925.00			
Salvage value	$ 1,075.00	$ 1,075.00	0	0	0
Total	$10,000.00	$10,000.00			

*The following assumptions underlie the computations: original investment, $10,000; no removal cost; salvage value, $1,075.000; estimated service life, ten years; accelerated depreciation, 20 percent declining balance method; 46 percent federal income tax rate.

mated useful service life is ten years, that it has no removal cost, and that the estimated salvage value is $1,075. Using the straight line method, $892.50 would be charged to depreciation expense annually. Using accelerated depreciation (assuming the double-declining balance method), the annual depreciation charge would start at $2,000 and decline to $268 over the ten-year period. In either case, the utility would receive a tax saving during the first four years. However, the effect on net income would not be identical: normalization accounting would result in no effect on net income, while under flow through accounting net income would be increased in the first four years and decreased in the last six years of the equipment's service life.

The Controversy. Income tax normalization has been the subject of considerable controversy. It is charged by many consumer groups that normalization results in ratepayers paying "phantom taxes."

> ... The argument relies on the assumption that because the utility's business will probably continue to grow, the deferred tax account will also continue to grow indefinitely. The phantom tax advocates contend that, as the deferred taxes grow at a rapid pace, there will always be more revenues collected to cover the deferred tax expense than deferred taxes paid out. They further allege that such a method gives rise to a "permanent tax savings" rather than a "tax deferral" that would eventually be paid out when the timing differences reach a reversal point (*i.e.,* the book expense is higher than the tax expense).[156]

The phantom tax argument is fallacious. As explained by Hahne and Aliff:

> The error of the phantom tax argument may be seen by analogy with the growth of a long-term debt account. As any issue of long-term debt reaches maturity, it must be repaid. At the same time, new plant additions may require that capital be raised through additional long-term borrowing to finance the additions. That new issues may exceed repayment of maturing debt over any period so as to result in net growth of long-term debt in no way means that the debt is not being repaid nor that, in the future, when the new issue matures, it will not have to be repaid.[157]

For many years, the utilities themselves debated the wisdom of adopting accelerated depreciation, even when permitted by the commissions. The Bell System, to illustrate, did not take advantage of accelerated depreciation until 1970. Its decision to use straight line depreciation for both accounting and tax purposes was based on three considerations:

1. Congress might suspend, modify, or repeal the accelerated tax depreciation provisions at some future date, thereby resulting in a

sudden decline in per share earnings and a possible drop in the market price of a utility's stock.

2. A multistate utility, subject to several jurisdictions, might find some commissions permitting normalization and others flow through; a situation which would result in confusion on the part of investors and expensive record keeping on the part of a utility.

3. Flow through, which was required by many of the commissions, impairs the financial integrity of a utility by: (*a*) failing to recognize current costs, since a tax cost is understated during the early life of the property; (*b*) increasing investor risk, since future depreciation deductions might not be available to offset the past costs which were not recognized under this method, while economic conditions or regulatory commissions might not allow future rate increases; and (*c*) endangering the ability of a utility to raise funds because of large amounts of unprovided-for costs overhanging the business.[158]

Commission Treatment. Prior to 1969, the regulatory commissions were split over the proper method to employ. The Federal Power Commission, which at first permitted normalization,[159] adopted the flow through method early in 1964.[160] The Federal Communications Commission, until 1971, required the flow through method. As of July 1, 1967, twenty state commissions permitted various forms of the normalization method for ratemaking purposes, twenty-three (including the District of Columbia commission) had either ordered or favored the flow through method, and two permitted either method.[161]

Then, in the Tax Reform Act of 1969, public utilities were required to use either straight line depreciation or accelerated depreciation with normalization for tax purposes. Most commissions, therefore, beginning in 1970, permitted normalization of deferred taxes for both book and ratemaking purposes (although some continued to use flow through on pre-1970 property).[162] In such instances, a utility is not permitted to earn a return on the deferred taxes; that is, they are either deducted from a utility's rate base or included in a utility's capitalization at a zero cost rate.[163] Further, it should be noted again that normalization is required for a utility to elect the accelerated cost recovery system under current tax laws.

"Excess" Deferred Income Taxes. The Revenue Act of 1978[164] lowered the maximum federal corporate income tax rate from 48 to 46 percent. How should the commissions recognize the fact that deferred income taxes had been accumulated at the higher rate for many years? Some commissions held that the deferred tax reserves should be reversed at the original rate of 48 percent.[165] Others took the position that the deferred tax reserves were excessive, and that the "excess" deferred taxes should be amortized over one to ten years.[166] The latter method, which resulted in a reversal of the tax

deferred over a period shorter than the remaining life of the underlying assets, did not appear to meet the statutory normalization requirements, thereby resulting in the disallowance of accelerated tax depreciation.[167]

Similarly, the Tax Reform Act of 1986 reduced the maximum federal corporate income tax rate from 46 to 34 percent, effective July 1, 1987. The new tax law specified that if the excess deferred tax reserve is reduced, it must be normalized using a method that reduces the tax reserve over the remaining life of the assets which generated the deferral. "Flow through of the excess tax reserves over a period shorter than the remaining life of the underlying asset will result in the loss of a utility's eligibility to use accelerated depreciation."[168]

The Investment (Job Development) Tax Credit. The Revenue Act of 1962,[169] as an incentive to investment, provided for the investment tax credit; a credit that was repealed retroactively (as of December 31, 1985) by the Tax Reform Act of 1986.

The version of the investment tax credit in effect just prior to its repeal[170] provided that all businesses were eligible for a credit graduated up to 10 percent on property placed in service during a taxable year and on qualified progress expenditures.[171] The tax credit was linked to the recovery period of the property, rather than to its useful life. To qualify for the full credit (by then also known as the job development investment tax credit), property had to have a recovery period of five years or more; qualified progress expenditures (for qualified property requiring two or more years to construct) had to be for property expected to be classified as five- , ten- , or fifteen-year recovery property when placed in service. Further, the law provided that no credit would be allowed unless (for ratemaking purposes) it was spread over the useful life of the property giving rise to the credit (normalization).[172]

Prior to 1964 for federal commissions, and 1971 for state commissions, there was considerable debate as to how the investment tax credit should be treated for ratemaking purposes.[173] Unlike accelerated depreciation, which only affects the time when such depreciation may be used for tax purposes, the investment tax credit resulted in a permanent savings to the utility. The flow through method resulted in the entire tax credit being reflected as an increase in net income (or reduction of taxes) in the year the credit was received, thereby giving all benefits of the tax credit to a utility's customers, while the normalization method resulted in spreading the tax credit over the productive life of the property, thereby sharing the benefits of the tax credit with a utility's shareholders and customers. Normalization was the general practice.[174]

Consolidated Tax Returns. Under the Internal Revenue Code, an affiliated group of companies is permitted to file a consolidated tax return. Certain benefits accrue to companies that file such returns. The losses of any affiliate can be set off against the taxable income of other affiliates in the group[175]; the parent company is freed from paying federal income taxes on dividends from its subsidiaries. In determining a regulated affiliate's cost of service, for ratemaking purposes, the common practice is to allocate to that company a share of the consolidated taxes.[176]

When a parent company has both utility and nonutility or jurisdictional and nonjurisdictional affiliates, a question arises as to the proper allocation procedure. A 1964 FPC decision, involving United Gas Pipe Line Company, a subsidiary of United Gas Corporation, is illustrative.[177] United Gas elected to file consolidated federal income tax returns for the years 1957-1961. Because its two oil and gas production and exploration affiliates (Union and Overseas) had net losses over the five-year period, the group's tax liability was thereby reduced. In the rate case, United Gas Pipe Line claimed that its allowance for federal income taxes should be the full 52 percent rate (the rate then applicable) or about $12 million for the test year. The FPC rejected this claimed allowance and allocated the actual consolidated taxes paid among the companies in the group or approximately $9.9 million for United Gas Pipe Line for the test period.[178]

On appeal, the company claimed that the FPC improperly applied nonjurisdictional losses to jurisdictional income. But the Supreme Court upheld the commission, saying in part:

> There is no frustration of the tax laws inherent in the commission's action. The affiliated group may continue to file consolidated returns and through this mechanism set off system losses against system income, including United's fair return income. The tax law permits this, but it does not seek to control the amount of income which any affiliate will have. Nor does it attempt to set United's rates. This is the function of the commission, a function performed here by rejecting that part of the claimed tax expense which was no expense at all, by reducing cost of service and therefore rates, and by allowing United only a fair return on its investment.[179]

In short, when a group of affiliated companies elects to file a consolidated tax return, a commission *may* pass on to customers — in the form of lower rates — any resulting benefits. But the Court was careful to note that the decision to file such a return belongs to the companies.

However, during the 1970s, the FPC (and later the FERC) adopted a "stand-alone" policy; that is, the computation of the income tax expense component of the cost of service as if the subsidiaries had filed separate federal income tax returns. In a 1972 decision, the commission held that a pipeline company should be permitted to retain the consolidated tax savings generated by losses incurred by an affiliate engaged in gas exploration and development.[180] Five years later, the commission adopted a similar treatment in wholesale electric rate cases, holding that the stand-alone policy was appropriate in those situations where jurisdictional customers had not paid the expenses that generated the consolidated tax savings.[181] But in a 1981 decision, a court of appeals remanded a case to the FERC, holding that while the commission had legal authority to use a stand-alone policy, its order contained insufficient evidence to support the concept.[182] That support was put forth in a subsequent decision, when the commission held:

> [2] Because deductions are given for expenses incurred in producing income, the necessary causal link between the ratepayers and the deductions is the expense the company incurs in providing service. Accordingly, the proper way to allocate deductions is to match the deductions with the expenses included in the cost of service. Thus, when an expense is included in the cost of service, the corresponding tax deduction is also allocated to the ratepayers. In this way any tax-reducing benefits, or savings, the company realizes in providing the service are recognized in calculating the tax allowance for the benefit of the ratepayers.
>
> The corollary to this is that when an expense is not included in the cost of service (because the company did not incur that expense in providing service), the deduction created by that expense is not allocated to the ratepayers. To do otherwise would result in the tax savings the company realizes from expenses incurred in providing services to other groups and periods or for its own benefit being used to reduce rates for a particular group of ratepayers. The tax allowance would then be lower or higher than is warranted by the profit each group provides the company. Since the amount of profit to be provided is the measure of the tax cost the company will incur in providing service, none of the rates for the groups would be cost justified. Subsidization would inevitably result. One group would bear the burden, but another group would gain the benefit.[183]

Severance and "First Use" Taxes: A Digression

There are two tax issues that are of particular importance to electric and gas utilities and that require brief discussion. Both affect the prices paid by these utilities for their fuel supplies.

Severance Taxes. Thirty-two states impose severance taxes on depletable resources. In fiscal 1983, these taxes generated $7.4 billion in tax revenues, with 78 percent going to just five states (Texas, Alaska, Louisiana, Oklahoma, and Wyoming).[184] Of particular concern in more recent years has been the severance taxes on coal which, with one possible exception (North Dakota's severance tax on lignite), are the highest such taxes in the country. Montana levies a maximum rate of 30 percent of the "contract sales price," Wyoming a 17 percent rate (including local charges). These two states account for 40 percent of domestic coal reserves and 68 percent of reserves of low-sulfur coal. Further, in the case of Montana, some 90 percent of the coal mined in the state is shipped to other states and a significant percentage of the state's coal-bearing land — 70 to 75 percent — is owned by the federal government.[185]

The issues are numerous. To what extent are severance taxes shifted to out-of-state consumers?[186] What is the likelihood that "price leadership" in the western states will result in an informal cartel, pursuing a policy of "OPEC-like revenue maximization"?[187] To what extent will severance taxes result in a massive transfer of wealth from energy-poor states to energy-producing states in the coming years?[188] Equally important, should Congress place a ceiling on state severance taxes, in recognition of the fact that "the natural resources being taxed by energy-rich states actually are 'national' resources that should benefit all states"?[189]

"First Use" Tax. Louisiana, in 1978, enacted a tax of seven cents per thousand cubic feet of natural gas on the "first use" of any gas imported into the state (primarily from offshore wells in the outer continental shelf) which was not previously subjected to taxation by either another state or the federal government. The tax, precisely equal to the severance tax the state imposes on Louisiana gas producers, was intended (*a*) "to reimburse the people of Louisiana for damages to the state's water bottoms, barrier islands and coastal areas resulting from the introduction of natural gas into Louisiana from areas not subject to state taxes," (*b*) "to compensate for the costs incurred by the state in protecting those resources," and (c) "to equalize competition" between gas produced in the state and subject to the state severance tax and gas produced elsewhere that was not subject to a similar tax.[190] The tax, imposed upon pipeline companies and producers, was passed on to ultimate customers.[191] Varying estimates were made of the annual revenues that Louisiana would receive from the tax (ranging from $150 to $275 million).

In 1981, the Supreme Court held that the first use tax of Louisiana violated the Supremacy Clause (because it interfered with federal regulation of the transportation and sale of natural gas in interstate commerce) and was unconstitutional under the Commerce Clause (because it discriminated against purchasers of gas moving through Louisiana in interstate commerce, due to various exemptions and tax credits).[192]

Conclusions: "The Thin Red Line"

Commission supervision of operating costs raises one broad question and countless specific problems. The latter have been outlined in some detail in this chapter. They are part of the broader question: How far should the regulatory commissions go in substituting their judgment for that of management.[193] The answer to this question, in turn, will largely depend on one's personal philosophy.

Some feel that since public utilities operate within a free enterprise system, they should be subjected to the same general rules that are applicable to nonregulated firms. If nonregulated firms can make annual contributions to charitable and educational institutions, or if they are permitted to benefit from filing consolidated income tax returns, so, too, should public utilities be afforded the same opportunities. Others believe that the very existence of regulation indicates that public utilities can and should be treated differently from nonregulated firms. As they are public service enterprises, their basic obligation is to render adequate service at the lowest possible rates. Thus, charitable and educational contributions, they feel, should not be allowed as operating expenses, since they contribute little toward the achievement of this basic obligation, while the benefits from consolidated income tax returns should be passed on to consumers.

When a commission does substitute its judgment for that of management, two issues arise. First, the process may be costly. "Regulators have frequently disallowed some expenditures, and curtailed others as being excessive or unwarranted. But the policing job is endless, aimless, and dubious, mainly because of the sheer impossibility of small staffs tracking myriads of payments."[194] The end result is a major contribution to regulatory lag, as rate cases are extended. Second, an underlying assumption in the process may be incorrect. Wilcox has put it this way:

> . . . the regulated industry comes, in the end, to have two masters: its own management and the regulatory agency. Essential functions of management are duplicated. Managerial decisions are reviewed. Where the regulatory agency finds them to be wise, it allows them to stand. Where it finds them to be unwise, it exercises a veto power. It thus acts to protect management against the consequences of its own mistakes.
>
> If there were assurance that the business judgment of commissioners would be superior to that of managers in more than half of the cases (weighted by their importance), we might conclude that duality of management would produce a net gain. But commissioners, in fact, are unlikely to be the better businessmen. And even if they were, there would be offsetting costs.[195]

The broad issue becomes of even greater importance as commissions have extended their challenges into areas other than the reasonableness of operating expenses; into such areas as innovation, capacity additions, and so forth. "Commissioners," a former one has warned, "have neither the training, nor the skills, nor the incentives to manage."[196]

The dilemma is clear. A commission has the authority to overrule management if the latter abuses its discretion. But an abuse of discretion is a matter of judgment. Moreover, failing to draw a line between regulatory and managerial discretion results in serious consequences, including a heavier administrative burden, delay, a diversion of effort, and the loss of managerial incentives. The dilemma has led some to propose that commissions must develop an incentive system of regulation; one that would demand high performance, but which would let management decide the ways in which service is to be provided. The issue is considered in later chapters.

Notes

Mississippi River Fuel Corp. v. Federal Power Comm., 163 F. 2d 433, 437 (1947).

[1]*Chicago & Grand Trunk Ry. Co. v. Wellman*, 143 U.S. 339, 345-46 (1892).

[2]*Missouri ex rel. Southwestern Bell Teleph. Co. v. Missouri Pub. Service Comm.*, 262 U.S. 276, 289 (1923), quoting from *Illinois Pub. Service Comm. ex rel. Springfield v. Springfield Gas & Elec. Co.*, 291 Ill. 209, 234 (1920).

[3]*Acker v. United States*, 298 U.S. 426, 430-31 (1936). See also *Smith v. Illinois Bell Teleph. Co.*, 282 U.S. 133 (1930); *Western Distributing Co. v. Pub. Service Comm. of Kansas*, 285 U.S. 119 (1932).

[4]*West Ohio Gas Co. v. Pub. Utilities Comm. of Ohio*, 294 U.S. 63, 72 (1935).

[5]*Acker v. United States, op. cit.*, p. 31.

[6]*West Ohio Gas Co. v. Pub. Utilities Comm. of Ohio, op. cit.; Re New England Teleph. & Teleg. Co.*, 79 PUR (NS) 508 (Vt., 1949).

[7]*Re Ripon United Teleph. Co.*, PUR1924A, 171 (Wis., 1923); *Commerce Comm. v. Pub. Service Co. of No. Illinois*, 4 PUR (NS) 1 (Ill., 1934).

[8]*Re Honolulu Gas Co.*, 36 PUR3d 309 (Hawaii, 1960). As one expert has put it: "Utility managements may not be arbitrary and capricious. And neither may regulators." A.J.G. Priest, "Utility Advertising and Other Operating Expenses," 75 *Public Utilities Fortnightly* 23, 27 (April 29, 1965).

[9]*Knoxville v. Knoxville Water Co.*, 212 U.S. 1, 13 (1909).

[10]*Denver v. Denver Union Water Co.*, 246 U.S. 178 (1918); *Kansas City Southern Ry. Co. v. United States*, 231 U.S. 423 (1913); *Lindheimer v. Illinois Bell Teleph. Co.*, 292 U.S. 151 (1934).

[11]*Knoxville v. Knoxville Water Co., op. cit.*, p. 14.

[12]*Columbus Gas & Fuel Co. v. Pub. Utilities Comm. of Ohio*, 292 U.S. 398, 404-5 (1934).

[13]*Galveston Elec. Co. v. Galveston*, 258 U.S. 388, 399 (1922). See also *Georgia Ry. & Power Co. v. Railroad Comm. of Georgia*, 262 U.S. 625, 632-33 (1923).

[14]*State Utility Commissions* (Committee Print, Subcommittee on Intergovernmental Relations, Committee on Government Operations, Senate, 90th Cong., 1st sess.) (Washington, D.C.: U.S. Government Printing Office, 1967), Table V facing p. 34. Thirty-five state commissions have authority to require advance submission of budgets on capital expenditures. *1985 Annual Report on Utility and Carrier Regulation* (Washington, D.C.: National Association of Regulatory Utility Commissioners, 1987), p. 521.

[15]*Ibid.*, pp. 427-28. On automatic fuel clauses, see *State Commission Regulation and Monitoring of the Fuel Adjustment Clause, Purchased Gas Adjustment Clause, and Electric and Gas Utility Fuel Procurement Practices* (Washington, D.C.: National Association of Regulatory Utility Commissioners, 1978); Michael Schmidt, *Automatic Adjustment Clauses: Theory and Application* (East Lansing: MSU Public Utilities Studies, 1980); Roger D. Blair and David L. Kaserman, "Automatic Fuel Cost Adjustment Clauses: Issues and Evidence," 110 *Public Utilities Fortnightly* 27 (November 25, 1982).

[16]"Recent Cases on Automatic Fuel Adjustment Clauses," 105 *Public Utilities*

Fortnightly 45 (March 13, 1980). See Elizabeth Warren, "Regulated Industries' Automatic Cost of Service Adjustment Clauses: Do They Increase or Decrease Cost to the Consumer?," 55 *The Notre Dame Lawyer* 333 (1980); Roger G. Clarke, "The Effect of Fuel Adjustment Clauses in the Systematic Risk and Market Values of Electric Utilities," 35 *Journal of Finance* 347 (Papers and Proceedings, 1980).

[17]*Re New England Power Co.*, 97 PUR3d 41, 45 (FPC, 1972). There has been a trend towards closer regulatory scrutiny, including more formal hearings. See, *e.g.*, *Re Detroit Edison Co.*, 72 PUR4th 585 (Mich., 1986); *Re Arizona Pub. Service Co.*, 76 PUR4th 399 (Ariz., 1986).

[18]See, *e.g.*, *Re Louisville Gas & Elec. Co.*, 6 PUR4th 520 (Ky., 1974); *Western Massachusetts Elec. Co. v. Massachusetts Dept. of Pub. Utilities*, 366 N.E. 2d 1232 (1977); *Wisconsin's Environmental Decade, Inc. v. Wisconsin Pub. Service Comm.*, 260 N.W. 2d 712 (1978); *Re San Diego Gas & Elec. Co.*, 29 PUR4th 613 (Cal., 1979); *Re Pennsylvania Power & Light Co.*, 27 PUR4th 609 (FERC, 1979).

[19]"Since aggregate fuel cost is a weighted average of expenditures on the individual fuels that comprise this aggregate, this distortion may manifest itself in two distinct ways. First, to the extent that fuel markets are less than perfectly competitive in the sense that a single uniform price does not exist for a given quality, utility companies that are subject to an automatic fuel adjustment clause may invest fewer resources in searching out the relatively lower-priced supply sources than firms that have no adjustment clause. Thus, this regulatory mechanism may increase aggregate fuel price by encouraging firms to pay higher prices for the individual fuels that they purchase. Second, given some variation in the rates at which specific fuel prices are increasing, those firms with adjustment clauses may have a reduced incentive to switch their existing plants to the fuel that exhibits a slower rate of escalation, especially when such fuel switching is costly. Thus, the adjustment clause may lead to a further increase in aggregate fuel price by encouraging an overutilization of the relatively expensive fuels; e.g., oil." Blair and Kaserman, *op. cit.*, p. 30. For an attempt to measure this effect, see David L. Kaserman and Richard C. Tepel, "The Impact of the Automatic Adjustment Clause on Fuel Purchase and Utilization Practices in the U.S. Electric Utility Industry," 48 *Southern Economic Journal* 687 (1982).

It has been argued that, in the long run, automatic fuel adjustment clauses will result in the overutilization of fuel inputs (relative to labor and capital). [This possible distortion is similar to the Averch-Johnson thesis with respect to the overutilization of capital. (See Chapter 17, pp. 809-10.)] See, *e.g.*, F. M. Gollop and S. H. Karlson, "The Impact of the Fuel Adjustment Mechanism on Economic Efficiency," 60 *Review of Economics and Statistics* 574 (1978); S. E. Atkinson and R. Halvorsen, "A Test of Relative and Absolute Price Efficiency in Regulated Industries," 62 *Review of Economics and Statistics* 81 (1980).

[20]See, *e.g.*, *Re Pub. Service Co. of New Hampshire*, 29 PUR4th 242 (FERC, 1979). Attempts have been made to incorporate incentives into automatic fuel adjustment clauses. See Daniel M. Violette and Michael D. Yokell, "Fuel Cost Adjustment Clause Incentives: An Analysis with Reference to California," 109 *Public Utilities Fortnightly* 33 (June 10, 1982); "Partial Passthrough [Incentive] Fuel Clauses," 116 *Public Utilities Fortnightly* 52 (August 8, 1985); *Re Salem Nuclear Generating Station*, 70 PUR4th 568 (Pa., 1985). See also D. P. Baron and R. D. DeBondt, "On the Design of Regulatory Price Adjustment Mechanisms," 24 *Journal of Economic Theory* 70 (1981).

[21]See "Fines and Penalties against Utilities," 79 *Public Utilities Fortnightly* 62 (April 13, 1967).

[22]Emery Troxel, *Economics of Public Utilities* (New York: Holt, Rinehart & Winston, Inc., 1947), p. 240.

[23]See *e.g., Re Pacific Power & Light Co.*, 34 PUR3d 36 (Or., 1960); *Re Continental Oil Co.*, 42 PUR3d 1 (FPC, 1962); *Re Allied Utilities Corp.*, 10 PUR4th 237 (Ark., 1975); *Re Hudson Water Co.*, 28 PUR4th 617 (N.H., 1979); *Re Ohio Power Co.*, 76 PUR4th 121 (Ohio, 1986). See also "Proper Period for Amortization of Rate Case Expense," 67 *Public Utilities Fortnightly* 59 (January 5, 1961); "Rate Case Expense must be Reasonable and Necessary," 77 *Public Utilities Fortnightly* 65 (March 3, 1966).

[24]See *Re Union Light, Heat & Power Co.*, 97 PUR (NS) 33 (Ky., 1953); *Re Carolina Water Co.*, 32 PUR3d 462 (N.C., 1960); *Re New England Teleph. & Teleg. Co.*, 13 PUR4th 65 (Me., 1976); *Re Millinocket Water Co.*, 70 PUR4th 387 (Me., 1985).

[25]See *Re New England Teleph. & Teleg. Co.*, 83 PUR (NS) 414 (Vt., 1950); *City of Fort Smith v. Southwestern Bell Teleph. Co.*, 247 S.W. 2d 474 (1952); *Southern Bell Teleph. & Teleg. Co. v. Louisiana Pub. Service Comm.*, 118 So. 2d 372 (1960).

[26]See, *e.g., Ohio Edison Co. v. Pub. Utility Comm.*, 45 PUR3d 1 (Ohio, 1962); *Pennsylvania Pub. Utility Comm. v. York Teleph. & Teleg. Co.*, 53 PUR3d 146 (Pa., 1963). Nonservice related legal expenses are generally not includable. See, *e.g., Washington Utils. & Transp. Comm. v. Pacific Northwest Bell Teleph. Co.*, 26 PUR4th 495 (Wash., 1978).

[27]See "Rate Making as Affected by Negotiations for Wage Increases," 71 *Public Utilities Fortnightly* 60 (March 14, 1963). Wage increases that occur during a test year generally are regarded as a "known change" and annualized. See, *e.g., Re Lockhart Power Co.*, 26 PUR4th 540 (FERC, 1978); *Re Arizona Pub. Service Co.*, 77 PUR4th 542 (Ariz., 1986). Anticipated or expected wage increases (after the test year) generally are excluded. See, *e.g., Re Brooklyn Union Gas Co.*, 17 PUR4th 451 (N.Y., 1976); *Re Southwest Bell Teleph. Co.*, 74 PUR4th 624 (Okla., 1986).

[28]*Re Vernah S. Moyston, d/b/a Hobbs Gas Co.*, 48 PUR3d 459, 462 (N.M., 1963). See also *Re Cascade Town Co.*, 41 PUR3d 256 (Colo., 1961).

[29]*Re Airfield Service Co.*, 46 PUR3d 246 (Conn., 1962). See also *Re Pleasant Green Water Co.*, 55 PUR (NS) 99 (Utah, 1944); *Re Wilkinson County Teleph. Co.*, 31 PUR3d 318 (Ga., 1959); *Re Bozrah Light & Power Co.*, 34 PUR3d 398 (Conn., 1960); *Re Henderson Teleph. Co., Inc.*, 36 PUR3d 458 (Nev., 1960); *Re Cherokee Teleph. Co.*, 45 PUR3d 91 (Ga., 1962).

[30]*Re Pacific Teleph. & Teleg. Co.*, 53 PUR3d 513, 568-70 (Cal., 1964), *aff'd*, 401 P. 2d 353 (1965).

[31]*Re Carolina Power & Light Co.*, Docket No. E-26, Sub 481 (N.C., 1984). See also *Re Duke Power Co.*, 49 PUR4th 483 (N.C., 1982).

[32]*Lafourche Teleph. Co., Inc. v. Louisiana Pub. Service Comm.*, 367 So. 2d 1174 (1979).

[33]See a summary of a 1967 study by National Economic Research Associates concerning electric and gas utilities compensation in 80 *Public Utilities Fortnightly* 45 (July 20, 1967); David H. Ciscel, "Executive Compensation in Regulated Industries," 100 *Public Utilities Fortnightly* 20 (July 7, 1977); Charles M. Cumming, "Electric Utilities are Ready for Better Executive Pay Plans," 115 *Public Utilities Fortnightly* 44 (June 13, 1985).

[34]*Re Detroit Edison Co.*, 16 PUR (NS) 9, 25 (Mich., 1936). See also *Latourneau v. Citizens Utilities Co.*, 209 A. 2d 307 (1965). A. J. G. Priest recalls "... when the president of a large electric utility in the Pacific Northwest was asked on the witness stand (some years ago and with sour sarcasm) whether he *really* thought he was

worth $40,000 a year, he replied smilingly, 'No, I don't. But my directors do. And who am I to question their judgment?' The executive in question was unduly modest, but his answer was sound, because his directors were entitled to manage that utility." A. J. G. Priest, *Principles of Public Utility Regulation* (Charlottesville: The Michie Co., 1969), Vol I, p. 48.

[35]See "Pension Expense," 78 *Public Utilities Fortnightly* 66 (September 15, 1966); *Central Maine Power Co. v. Maine Pub. Utilities Comm.*, 109 A. 2d 512 (1954); *United Gas Corp. v. Mississippi Pub. Service Comm.*, 127 So. 2d 404 (1961); *East Ohio Gas Co. v. Pub. Utilities Comm.*, 12 N.E. 2d 765 (1978); *Re So. California Gas Co.*, 27 PUR4th 63 (Cal., 1978).

[36]Paul J. Garfield and Wallace F. Lovejoy, *Public Utility Economics* (Englewood Cliffs: Prentice-Hall, Inc., 1964), p. 51.

[37]Amortization was allowed in *Re Utilities & Industries Corp.*, 52 PUR3d 37 (N.Y., 1963) and *Re Alaska Elec. Light & Power Co.*, 70 PUR3d 481 (Alaska, 1967); disallowed in *Re Chesapeake & Potomac Teleph. Co.*, 57 PUR3d 1 (D.C., 1964) and *Re Peoples Gas System, Inc.*, 1 PUR4th 464 (Fla., 1973).

[38]". . . we conclude that Bell's customers, who are not given an opportunity either to advocate or decide which legislative proposals should be supported, should not bear the cost of lobbying, and that such expenditures should be excluded from the operating expenses which are to be taken into consideration in fixing rates." *Illinois Bell Teleph. Co. v. Illinois Commerce Comm.*, 3 PUR4th 36, 48 (1973). See "Accounting and Rate Case Treatment of Political Advertising Expenses," 66 *Public Utilities Fortnightly* 417 (1960); "Public Relations Expenses," 77 *Public Utilities Fortnightly* 67 (January 20, 1966); "Recent Cases on Political and Lobbying Expense," 99 *Public Utilities Fortnightly* 44 (March 17, 1977). See also *Re Pub. Service Co. of Colorado*, 13 PUR4th 40 (Colo., 1975); *Re Boston Edison Co.*, 16 PUR4th 1 (Mass., 1976); *Re Southwestern Bell Teleph. Co.*, 28 PUR4th 519 (Kan., 1979); *Re Sierra Pacific Power Co.*, 73 PUR4th 306 (Nev., 1985).

[39]*West Ohio Gas Co. v. Pub. Utilities Comm. of Ohio, op. cit.*, p. 72. See also *Southern Bell Teleph. & Teleg. Co. v. Georgia Pub. Service Comm.*, 49 S.E. 2d 38 (1948); *Central Maine Power Co. v. Maine Pub. Utilities Comm.*, 136 A. 2d 726 (1957); *City of El Dorado v. Arkansas Pub. Service Comm.*, 362 S.W. 2d 680 (1962).

[40]Wallace R. Burke, "Promotional Activities," in National Association of Regulatory Utility Commissioners, *Annual Proceedings*, 1966 (Washington, D.C., 1967), p. 39.

[41]See *Re Savannah Elec. & Power Co.*, 45 PUR3d 88 (Ga., 1962); *Re Delaware Power & Light Co.*, 56 PUR3d 1 (Del., 1964); *Watkins v. Atlantic City Elec. Co.*, 60 PUR3d 213 (N.J., 1965); *Gifford v. Central Maine Power Co.*, 63 PUR3d 205 (Me., 1965), aff'd, 217 A. 2d 200 (1966); *Rossi v. Garton*, 211 A. 2d 806 (1965); *Virginia State Corp. Comm. v. Appalachian Power Co.*, 65 PUR3d 283 (Va., 1966); *Re Promotional Practices of Electric and Gas Utilities*, 65 PUR3d 405 (Conn., 1966); *Re Promotional Activities by Gas and Electric Corporations*, 68 PUR3d 162 (N.Y., 1967); *Re Promotional Practices of Electric and Gas Utilities*, 69 PUR3d 317 (Ill., 1967). See also Peter B. Spivak, "The Regulator's Views of Utility Competition," 79 *Public Utilities Fortnightly* 28 (February 2, 1967); Grant S. Lewis, "Promotional Activities of Public Utilities," 80 *Public Utilities Fortnightly* 44 (October 26, 1967); "Regulatory Policy and Promotional Practices," 80 *Public Utilities Fortnightly* 72; T. Justin Moore, Jr., "Competitive Activities of Regulated Utilities," American Bar Association Annual Report, Section of *Public Utility Law, 1967*, pp. 15-25; Burke, *op. cit.*, pp. 38-51; "Promotional Rates and Allowances for Electric Service," 81 *Public Utilities Fortnightly* 99 (June 6, 1968); *Promotional Practices by Public*

Utilities and Their Impact upon Small Business (Hearings before the Subcommittee on Activities of Regulatory Agencies, House, 90th Cong., 2d sess.) (Washington, D.C.: U.S. Government Printing Office, 1968) and, under the same title, House Report No. 1984, 90th Cong., 2d sess. (1968).

[42]See cases cited in preceding footnote and "Underground Wiring Conjoined with Promotional Allowances," 80 *Public Utilities Fortnightly* 58 (July 20, 1967).

[43]State Commission scrutiny of advertising expenses by electric and gas utilities also was required by the Public Utility Regulatory Policies Act of 1978. That act established a *federal* standard: No electric or gas utility "may recover from any person other than the shareholders (or other owners) of such utility any direct or indirect expenditure . . . for promotional or political advertising. . . ." Almost every state commission subsequently placed some kind of restriction on the recovery of advertising costs. But see Lee M. Cassidy, "Why Regulators Should Take a Longer View of Utility Advertising," 117 *Public Utilities Fortnightly* 27 (May 29, 1986).

[44]New York Public Service Commission, "Statement of Policy on Advertising and Promotional Practices of Public Utilities" (17 NY PSC 1-R, dated February 25, 1977). The 1977 policy statement amended a 1972 statement.

[45]See also "Curbs on Promotional Practices of Electric and Gas Utilities," 87 *Public Utilities Fortnightly* 53 (February 18, 1971); *Re Promotional Practices of Electric Utilities*, 8 PUR4th 268 (Fla., 1975); *Re Utility Advertising Expenditures*, Order No. 76-467 (Or., 1976); *Re Rules and Regulations Covering Rate Case Treatment of Certain Expenses*, 30 PUR4th 338 (N.M., 1979); *Re Advertising Practices of Telephone, Electric, and Gas Distribution Companies*, 35 PUR4th 361 (N.J., 1980).

[46]See "Advertising Expenses Examined," 104 *Public Utilities Fortnightly* 51 (November 8, 1979). To illustrate: (*a*) institutional and goodwill advertising disallowed: *Re General Teleph. Co. of Florida*, 19 PUR4th 227 (Fla., 1977); *Re Georgia Power Co.*, 30 PUR4th 409 (Ga., 1979); (*b*) conservation, safety, and proper use of appliances advertising allowed: *Re Pub. Service Co. of North Carolina*, 19 PUR4th 109 (N.C., 1977); *Re Idaho Power Co.*, 29 PUR4th 183 (Idaho, 1979); *Re Iowa Gas Co.*, 76 PUR4th 425 (Iowa, 1985); (*c*) informational, institutional, and goodwill advertising limited to 1/10th of one percent of operating revenues: *Re Laclede Gas Co.*, 27 PUR4th 241 (Mo., 1978); (*d*) promotional advertising disallowed: *Re Southwestern Pub. Service Co.*, 27 PUR4th 302 (N.M., 1978); *Re Northern States Power Co.*, 73 PUR4th 395 (Minn., 1985); and (*e*) economic development advertising allowed: *Re Nat. Fuel Gas Distribution Corp.*, 74 PUR4th 346 (N.Y., 1986); *Re Ohio Power Co.*, *op. cit.*

[47]*New England Teleph. & Teleg. Co., v. Dept. of Pub. Utilities*, 275 N.E. 2d 493, 517 (1971). See also *Alabama Power Co. v. Alabama Pub. Service Comm.*, 359 So. 2d 776 (1978).

[48]*City of Los Angeles v. Pub. Utilities Comm.*, 497 P. 2d 785 (1972).

[49]*Central Hudson Gas & Elec. Corp. v. New York Pub. Service Comm.*, 100 S. Ct. 2343, 34 PUR4th 178 (1980). In a concurring opinion by Justices Blackmun and Brennan, they expressed serious "doubt whether suppression of information concerning the availability and price of a legally offered product is ever a permissible way for the state to 'dampen' demand for or use of the product. Even though 'commercial' speech is involved, such a regulatory measure strikes at the heart of the First Amendment. . . . If the First Amendment guarantee means anything, it means that, absent clear and present danger, government has no power to restrict expression because of the effect the message is likely to have on the public." *Ibid.*, p. 189.

[50]*Consolidated Edison Co. of New York, Inc. v. New York Pub. Service Comm.*, 100 S.

Ct. 2326, 34 PUR4th 208 (1980). "The customer ... may escape exposure to objectionable material simply by transferring the bill insert from envelope to wastebasket." *Ibid.*, p. 215. See also Note, "Utility Companies and the First Amendment: Regulating the Use of Political Inserts in Utility Bills," 64 *Virginia Law Review* 921 (1978).

In 1986, the Supreme Court vacated an order of the California commission that required utilities to include messages from outside groups in the "extra space" (defined as the additional weight that might be added to the envelopes after inclusion of the bill and other required notices without increasing the postal charge) of their monthly billing envelopes. The billing envelopes, held the Court, are the property of the utility. *Pacific Gas & Elec. Co. v. California Pub. Utilities Comm.*, 106 S. Ct. 903, 72 PUR4th 634 (1986).

[51]See "Utility Free Speech," 106 *Public Utilities Fortnightly* 48 (August 14, 1980).

[52]"Reasonable charitable contributions are very much an obligation of a business enterprise to the community it serves and upon which it is dependent for its revenues. To ignore a commitment to the general welfare would be unthinkable and very much in contradiction to the spirit of the times. This is particularly applicable to a regulated enterprise whose identification with the public interest is instinctive in the legislation which gives rise to its regulation." *Re El Paso Nat. Gas Co.*, 90 PUR3d 462, 473 (FPC, 1971). See also *Re General Teleph. Co. of Florida*, 44 PUR3d 247 (Fla., 1962); *Re Northwestern Bell Teleph. Co.*, 8 PUR4th 75 (Minn., 1974); *Re Southwestern Bell Teleph. Co.*, 28 PUR4th 519 (Kan., 1979). Some limits have been placed on charitable contributions; *e.g.*, .04 percent of operating expenses: *Re Consolidated Edison Co. of New York, Inc.*, 29 PUR4th 327 (N.Y. , 1979); .1 percent of gross revenues: *Re Ohio Power Co.*, 29 PUR4th 298 (Ohio, 1979).

[53]"Dues, donations, and contributions, if included as an expense for ratemaking purposes, become an involuntary levy on ratepayers, who, because of the monopolistic nature of utility service, are unable to obtain service from another source and thereby avoid such a levy. Ratepayers should be encouraged to contribute directly to worthy causes and not involuntarily through an allowance in utility rates." *Re Pacific Teleph. & Teleg. Co.*, 53 PUR3d 513, 586 (Cal., 1964), *aff'd*, 401 P. 2d 353 (1965). See also *Re Michigan Bell Teleph. Co.*, 32 PUR3d 395 (Mich., 1960); *Re Chesapeake & Potomac Teleph. Co.*, 57 PUR3d 1 (D.C., 1964); *Re Mountain States Teleph. & Teleg. Co.*, 8 PUR4th 514 (Colo., 1974); *Re Laclede Gas Co.*, 27 PUR4th 241 (Mo., 1978); *New England Teleph. & Teleg. Co. v. Maine Pub. Utilities Comm.*, 390 A. 2d 8 (1978); *Alabama Power Co. v. Alabama Pub. Service Comm.*, 359 So. 2d 776 (1978).

[54]See *Re Southwestern Bell Teleph. Co.*, 34 PUR3d 257 (Kan., 1960); *Re Consumers Power Co.*, 38 PUR3d 355 (Mich., 1961); *Re Gas Service Co.*, 6 PUR4th 99 (Mo., 1974); *In re Communications Satellite Corp.*, 56 F.C.C. 1101 (1975); *Re Chesapeake & Potomac Teleph. Co.*, Case No. 9358 (W.Va., 1979); *Re Virginia Elec. & Power Co.*, 75 PUR4th 315 (Va., 1986).

[55]See *Re Accounting Treatment for Donations, Dues, and Lobbying Expenditures*, 71 PUR3d 440 (N.Y., 1967); *Re Florida Power & Light Co.*, 9 PUR4th 146 (Fla., 1975); *Re Intermountain Gas Co.*, 26 PUR4th 442 (Idaho, 1978).

[56]See "EEI and AGA Dues Reviewed in State Rate Cases," 117 *Public Utilities Fortnightly* 48 (January 23, 1986); *Re Southeastern Michigan Gas Co.*, 72 PUR4th 410 (Mich., 1986); *Washington Utils. & Transp. Comm v. Puget Sound Power & Light Co.*, 74 PUR4th 536 (Wash., 1986). See also *Report of the Committee on EEI Oversight* (Washington, D.C.: National Association of Regulatory Utility Commissioners, 1985).

[57]Richard A. Harvill, "The Opposition to Public Utility Appliance Merchandising," 8 *Journal of Land & Public Utility Economics* 290 (1932).

[58]Troxel, *op. cit.*, p. 244.

[59]See *Re Nevada Power Co.*, 43 PUR3d 511 (Nev., 1962); *Re Northern Gas Co.*, 70 PUR3d 260 (Wyo., 1967); *Re Elizabethtown Gas Co.*, 3 PUR4th 182 (N.J., 1973); *Re Promotional Practices of Electric and Gas Utilities*, 8 PUR4th 268 (Fla., 1975); *Re Nat. Fuel Gas Distribution Corp.*, 28 PUR4th 42 (N.Y., 1978).

[60]See "Replacement Power Costs Due to Nuclear Outages: A Higher Standard of Care?," 109 *Public Utilities Fortnightly* 56 (April 1, 1982); "Nuclear Plant Outages: Refueling, Management Prudence, and Replacement Power," 120 *Public Utilities Fortnightly* 39 (October 29, 1987).

Another related issue: Should a state commission rely upon its own assessment of an accident or upon the Nuclear Regulatory Commission's assessment? See, *e.g.*, *Florida Power Corp. v. Florida Pub. Service Comm.*, 424 So. 2d 745 (1982) and 456 So. 2d 451 (1984); *Re Salem Nuclear Generating Station*, 70 PUR4th 568 (Pa., 1985); David V. Stivison, "State Commissions and the NRC: A Nuclear Utility's Two Masters," 115 *Public Utilities Fortnightly* 37 (June 13, 1985).

[61]*Re Consolidated Edison Co. of New York, Inc.*, Opinion 79-1 (N.Y., 1979), as quoted in *Re Consolidated Edison Co. of New York, Inc.*, 45 PUR4th 325, 331 (N.Y., 1982).

[62]*Ibid.* (45 PUR4th 325, 364).

[63]*Re Salem Nuclear Generating Station, op. cit.*

[64]*Re Utah Power & Light Co.*, 63 PUR4th 13 (Idaho, 1984). See David V. Stivison, "When the Big Plants Shut Down: State Commissions Respond to Nuclear Outrages," 117 *Public Utilities Fortnightly* 29 (February 6, 1986).

[65]*Pennsylvania Pub. Utility Comm. v. Metropolitan Edison Co.*, 37 PUR4th 77, 91 (Pa., 1980). See also *Pennsylvania Pub. Utility Comm. v. Metropolitan Edison Co.*, 29 PUR4th 502 (Pa., 1979), *aff'd*, 467 A. 2d 1367 (1983); *Re Baltimore Gas & Elec. Co.*, Order No. 66951 (Md., 1985); *Re Carolina Power & Light Co.*, 69 PUR4th 278 (N.C., 1985); *Pennsylvania Pub. Utility Comm. v. Philadelphia Elec. Co.*, 58 Pa PUC 743 (Pa., 1985).

[66]See Robert E. Burns et al., *Regulating Electric Utilities with Subsidiaries* (Columbus, Ohio: National Research Regulatory Institute, 1986); *Re Affiliated Relationships of Telecommunications Exchange Carriers*, 83 PUR4th 205 (Utah, 1987).

[67]*Southwestern Bell Teleph. Co. v. Kansas State Corp. Comm.*, 386 P. 2d 515, 552 (1963). See "Transactions with Affiliates," 99 *Public Utilities Fortnightly* 48 (March 31, 1977); "Payments to Affiliates," 99 *Public Utilities Fortnightly* 52 (April 14, 1977); "Recent Cases on Payments to Affiliates," 101 *Public Utilities Fortnightly* 45 (March 30, 1978).

[68]*Re Columbia Engineering Corp.* (SEC), Holding Co. Act Release No. 4166 (March, 1943).

[69]Securities and Exchange Commission, "General Rules and Regulations under the Public Utility Holding Company Act of 1935" (Washington, D.C.: U.S. Government Printing Office, 1958), Rule 88, pp. 26-27.

[70]See, *e.g.*, *Re Columbia Gas System Service Corp.* (SEC), Holding Co. Act Release No. 14699 (September, 1962).

[71]One state commission, California, has long required that service charges be determined by the cost of service. See *Re Pacific Teleph. & Teleg. Co.*, 53 PUR3d 513, 582-86 (Cal., 1964), *aff'd*, 401 P. 2d 353 (1965). The annual fee (which at that time was 1 1/2 percent) was found reasonable by a committee of state commission and FCC representatives in 1945. See *Report on Service Charges by the American Telephone &*

Telegraph Company to the Associated Bell Telephone Companies and Long Lines Department (New York: National Association of Regulatory Utility Commissioners, 1945). See also Joseph R. Rose, "The Bell Telephone System Rate Cases," 37 *Virginia Law Review* 699, 722-23 (1951); A.J.G. Priest, "Operating Expenses in the Spotlight," 77 *Public Utilities Fortnightly* 15, 19-24 (February 3, 1966).

[72]In 1973, the Illinois Supreme Court held it improper to include in operating expenses for ratemaking purposes a license fee based on a percentage of revenues. *Illinois Bell Teleph. Co. v. Illinois Commerce Comm., op. cit.*

[73]*Re Illinois Bell Teleph. Co.*, 13 PUR4th 482 (Ill., 1976).

[74]*South Central Bell Teleph. Co. v. Louisiana Pub. Service Comm.*, 352 So. 2d 964 (1977).

Since divestiture, the regional holding companies equally own Bell Communications Research, Inc. (Bellcore); a company established to provide technical and other services to the regional holding companies, and "to serve as a single point of contact for coordination of communication services associated with national security and emergency preparedness." [*Re New England Teleph. & Teleg. Co.*, 71 PUR4th 652, 667 (Vt., 1985).] The cost of Bellcore projects are shared equally ("core" projects) or only by those regional companies which elect to participate ("noncore" projects). See, *e.g.*, *Multi-State Audit Team's Investigation of Bell Communications Research, Inc.* (Washington, D.C.: National Association of Regulatory Utility Commissioners, 1985); *Re Mountain States Teleph. & Teleg. Co.*, 71 PUR4th 598 (Utah, 1985).

[75]See, *e.g.*, *Re General Teleph. of the Southeast*, 2 PUR4th 228 (N.C., 1973); *Re General Teleph. of the Midwest*, 3 PUR4th 113 (Iowa, 1974); *Re Boston Gas Co.*, 12 PUR4th 405 (Mass., 1975); *Re Boise Water Corp.*, 18 PUR4th 251 (Idaho, 1976); *Re Mountain Home Teleph. Co., Inc.*, Docket No. U-2732 (Ark., 1977).

[76]*Houston v. Southwestern Bell Teleph. Co.*, 259 U.S. 318, 323 (1922); *Smith v. Illinois Bell Teleph. Co., op. cit.*, pp. 152-53. See also *Illinois Bell Teleph. Co. v. Gilbert*, 3 F. Supp. 595 (N.D. Ill. 1933).

[77]See *e.g. Re Pacific Teleph. & Teleg. Co.*, 53 PUR3d 513 (Cal., 1964), *aff'd*, 401 P. 2d 353 (1965); *Re General Teleph. Co. of Upstate New York*, Case No. 22522 (N.Y., 1963), *aff'd sub nom. General Teleph. Co. of Upstate New York v. Lundy*, 17 N.Y. 2d 373 (1966); *Re New York Teleph. Co.*, 7 PUR4th 496 (Conn., 1974); *Re New England Teleph. & Teleg. Co.*, 10 PUR4th 132 (R.I., 1975); *Re General Teleph. Co. of the Northwest, Inc.*, 10 PUR4th 382 (Or., 1975); *Re Jamestown Teleph. Co.*, 11 PUR4th 55 (N.Y., 1975). The North Carolina commission limited the General Telephone Directory Company to a return on equity equal to that permitted on the telephone company's operations in the state. *Re General Teleph. Co. of the Southeast*, 18 PUR4th 440 (N.C., 1976).

[78]See, *e.g.*, Burns et al., *op. cit.*, esp. pp. 159-72.

[79]". . . the chief concern is not the level of price, but instead the level of earnings by the unregulated arm of the utility at a rate higher than the utility is authorized and would be allowed to achieve if no corporate device were utilized. The wholly owned affiliate should be in the same position as an integrated producing arm of a utility." *Re Washington Water Power Co.*, 24 PUR4th 39, 54 (Idaho, 1978). See also *Re Montana-Dakota Utilities Co.*, 21 PUR4th 1 (S.D., 1977), *aff'd*, 278 N.W. 2d 189 (1979); *Re Montana Power Co.*, Order No. 4714a (Mont., 1980).

[80]By not including an unamortized reserve in a utility's rate base, the expenses are shared between ratepayers and stockholders, since no return is paid on the exclusion. But see *Re Jersey Central Power & Light Co.*, 19 FERC Par. 61,208 (1982), 20 FERC Par. 61,083 (1982), *aff'd sub nom. Jersey Central Power & Light Co. v. Federal*

Energy Regulatory Comm., 730 F. 2d 816 (D.C. Cir. 1984), *vacated and rem'd on rehearing*, 768 F. 2d 1500 (D.C. Cir. 1985), *rehearing order vacated and rem'd*, Docket No. 82-2004 (D.C. Cir. 1986); "The Hope Case and the 'End-result' Test — A Re-appraisal," 117 *Public Utilities Fortnightly* 50 (March 6, 1986).

[81]See *Re United Illum. Co.*, 7 PUR4th 417 (Conn., 1974); *Re Long Island Lighting Co.*, 9 PUR4th 21 (N.Y., 1975); *Re So. New England Teleph. Co.*, 9 PUR4th 301 (Conn., 1975).

[82]See *Pennsylvania Pub. Utility Comm. v. Bell Teleph Co. of Pennsylvania*, 2 PUR4th 417 (Pa., 1973); *Pennsylvania Pub. Utility Comm. v. Pennsylvania Gas & Water Co.*, 12 PUR4th 165 (Pa., 1975).

[83]See *Re Detroit Edison Co.*, 43 PUR4th 478 (Mich., 1981).

[84]*Re Savannah Elec. & Power Co.*, 30 PUR4th 219 (Ga., 1979).

[85]*Re New Haven Water Co.*, Docket No. 770323 (Conn., 1977).

[86]*Re Kansas City Power & Light Co.*, 75 PUR4th 1 (Mo., 1986).

[87]Thus, in a 1967 decision, the FPC required no acquisition adjustment when a utility had purchased a transmission line from the federal government, since the line had not previously been devoted to public service. [*Re Virginia Elec. & Power Co.*, 38 FPC 487 (1967).] But, in a 1979 decision, a circuit court upheld an FERC decision that such an adjustment was proper when a utility purchased a transmission line from a regulated railroad. [*Montana Power Co. v. Federal Energy Regulatory Comm.*, 599 F. 2d 295 (9th Cir. 1979).]

[88]*Re Davenport Water Co.*, 76 PUR3d 209, 227 (Iowa, 1968). See "Acquisition Adjustments Considered in Recent Cases," 105 *Public Utilities Fortnightly* 65 (February 14, 1980); "Cost-of-Service [Acquisition] Adjustments for Purchased Utility Assets," 116 *Public Utilities Fortnightly* 58 (October 31, 1985). In a few cases, when a utility has purchased assets at a price below the seller's depreciated original cost, the unamortized "credit" or "negative" acquisition adjustment has been included in the rate base. See, *e.g.*, *Re Southwestern Bell Teleph. Co.*, 19 PUR4th 1 (Kan., 1977); *Providence Gas Co. v. Burman*, 22 PUR4th 103 (R.I., 1977). But see *Re Davenport Water Co.*, *op. cit.*; *Re Broward Water Supply Co.*, 76 PUR3d 161 (Fla., 1968); *Re Vermont Gas Systems, Inc.*, 100 PUR3d 202 (Vt., 1973).

[89]See "Abandoned or Lost Property," 99 *Public Utilities Fortnightly* 59 (March 3, 1977); *Re Jacksonville Gas Corp.*, 40 PUR3d 372 (Fla., 1961); *Re Consolidated Edison Co. of New York, Inc.*, 56 PUR3d 337 (N.Y., 1964); *Re Newport Gas Light Co.*, 85 PUR3d 257 (R.I., 1970).

[90]See "Recouping Abandoned Construction Losses," 107 *Public Utilities Fortnightly* 60 (February 26, 1981); "Regulatory Treatment of Plant Cancellation Costs," 111 *Public Utilities Fortnightly* 52 (March 31, 1983); *Re San Diego Gas & Elec. Co.*, 31 PUR4th 435 (Cal., 1979); *Re Central Vermont Pub. Service Corp.*, 49 PUR4th 372 (Vt., 1982); *Re Potomac Elec. Power Co.*, 50 PUR4th 500 (D.C., 1982); *Re Fitchburg Gas & Elec. Light Co.*, 52 PUR4th 197 (Mass., 1983); *Re Maine Pub. Service Co.*, 74 PUR4th 209 (Me., 1986). But see *Office of Consumers' Counsel v. Ohio Pub. Utilities Comm.*, 423 N.E. 2d 820 (1981) (holding that Ohio statute does not permit recovery); *Washington Utils. & Transp. Comm. v. Pacific Power & Light Co.*, 51 PUR4th 158 (Wash., 1983) (rejecting amortization, but permitting higher return on equity capital — 2.5 percentage points — as alternative); *Citizens Action Coalition of Indiana, Inc. v. Northern Indiana Pub. Service Co.*, 485 N.E. 2d 610 (1985) (holding that Indiana statute does not permit recovery). On the issues, see Energy Information Administration, U.S. Department of Energy, *Nuclear Plant Cancellations: Causes, Costs and Consequences* (Wash-

ington, D.C.: U.S. Government Printing Office, 1983); Richard J. Pierce, Jr., "The Regulatory Treatment of Mistakes in Retrospect: Cancelled Plants and Excess Capacity," 132 *University of Pennsylvania Law Review* 497 (1984); Richard D. Gary and Edgar M. Roach, Jr., "The Proper Regulatory Treatment of Investment in Cancelled Utility Plants," 13 *Hofstra Law Review* 469 (1985); Warren J. Samuels, "A Consumer View on Financing Nuclear Plant Abandonment," 115 *Public Utilities Fortnightly* 24 (January 10, 1985).

[91]See George A. Avery, "The Costs of Nuclear Accidents and Abandonments in Rate Making," 104 *Public Utilities Fortnightly* 17 (November 8, 1979).

[92]Eli W. Clemens, *Economics and Public Utilities* (New York: Appleton-Century-Crofts, Inc., 1950), pp. 131-38.

[93]William Iulo, *Electric Utilities — Costs and Performance* (Pullman: Bureau of Economic and Business Research, Washington State University, 1961); Joe Pace, "Relative Efficiency in the Electric Utility Industry" (unpublished Ph.D. dissertation, The University of Michigan, 1970).

[94]William H. Dodge, "Productivity Measures and Performance Evaluation," in Harry M. Trebing (ed.), *Performance under Regulation* (East Lansing: MSU Public Utilities Studies, 1968), pp. 3-19; Rodney E. Stevenson, "Productivity in the Private Electric Utility Industry," in Walter L. Balk and Jay M. Shafritz (eds.), *Public Utility Productivity: Management and Measurement* (Albany: New York State Department of Public Service, 1976), pp. 11-33; Thomas G. Cowing and Rodney E. Stevenson (eds.), *Productivity Measurement in Regulated Industries* (New York: Academic Press, 1981).

[95]J. Edward Smith, Jr., *The Measurement of Electric Utility Efficiency* (Washington, D.C.: National Association of Regulatory Utility Commissioners, 1975). This study utilized an earlier FPC study: Federal Power Commission, Office of Economics, Division of Reports and Statistical Analysis, *Performance Profiles: Private Electric Utilities in the United States 1963-1970* (Washington, D.C., 1973). See also J. Edward Smith, Jr., *The Measurement of Electric Utility Cost Performance: A Proposed Methodology* (Washington, D.C.: National Association of Regulatory Utility Commissioners, 1976).

[96]William G. Shepherd, "Comment," in Trebing, *Performance under Regulation, op. cit.*, pp. 33, 34. See William Iulo, "Problems in the Definition and Measurement of Superior Performance," in *ibid.*, pp. 3-19; Balk and Shafritz, *op. cit.*

[97]Harry M. Trebing, "Toward an Incentive System of Regulation," 72 *Public Utilities Fortnightly* 22, 33 (July 18, 1963). See also Luc Anselin et al., *The Measurement of Electric Utility Performance: Preliminary Analysis* (Columbus, Ohio: National Regulatory Research Institute, 1981) and *A Decision Support System for Utility Performance Evaluation* (Columbus, Ohio: National Regulatory Research Institute, 1985).

[98]*Report of the Committee on Depreciation, 1943* (Washington, D.C.: National Association of Regulatory Utility Commissioners, 1943), p. xiv. On utility depreciation practices, see *Public Utility Depreciation Practices* (Washington, D.C.: National Association of Regulatory Utility Commissioners, 1968); James E. Suelflow, *Public Utility Accounting: Theory and Application* (East Lansing: MSU Public Utilities Studies, 1973), chaps. 5-7; Robert L. Hahne and Gregory E. Aliff, *Accounting for Public Utilities* (New York: Matthew Bender & Co., Inc., 1983; 1987 Revision), chap. 6. See also *Glossary of Depreciation Terms* (Washington, D.C.: National Association of Regulatory Utility Commissioners, 1980).

[99]*Report of the Committee on Depreciation, 1943, op. cit.*, p. xv.

[100]*Ibid.*

[101]*Lindheimer v. Illinois Bell Teleph. Co., op. cit.*, p. 167.

[102]"Depreciation accounting is a system of accounting which aims to distribute cost or other basic value of tangible capital assets, less salvage (if any), over the estimated useful life of the unit (which may be a group of assets) in a systematic and rational manner. It is a process of allocation, not of valuation." American Institute of Certified Public Accountants, as quoted in Hahne and Aliff, *op. cit.,* p. 6-6.

[103]For many years, some public utilities favored retirement accounting whereby replacements are not charged to operating costs until they are actually made. See H. E. Riggs, "The Two Radically Different Concepts of Depreciation," 9 *Public Utilities Fortnightly* 559 (1932). See also, by the same author, *Depreciation of Public Utility Properties* (New York: McGraw-Hill Book Co., 1922); Perry Mason, *Principles of Public Utility Depreciation* (Chicago: American Accounting Association, 1937); L. R. Nash, *Anatomy of Depreciation* (Arlington, Va.: Public Utilities Reports, Inc., 1947).

[104]Some have advocated use of the remaining life method. Compare, *e.g.,* John S. Ferguson, "The Remaining Life Concept in Modern Depreciation Analysis," 99 *Public Utilities Fortnightly* 19 (June 23, 1977) with William F. Fox, "The Remaining Life Depreciation Concept: A Regulator's View," 102 *Public Utilities Fortnightly* 19 (July 6, 1978).

[105]"The annual depreciation estimate for a company within a particular industry is a tailor-made proposition. No two companies are ever alike. There is a whole host of reasons why this is so. The more obvious are natural causes. Companies that operate in tropical areas are much more familiar with the ravages caused by hurricanes, high humidity, tropical rot, fungus, and other familiar phenomena in such areas. Companies that operate in northern climates are familiar with the ravages of wind and snow and ice, of alternate freezing and thawing. Companies that operate near the seashore where there are prevailing winds from the sea know the damage done by salt air." Edward C. Edgar and G. R. Faust, "System Growth and Obsolescence — Their Effect on Depreciation," 81 *Public Utilities Fortnightly* 15, 17 (February 15, 1968).

[106]*United Railways & Elec. Co. v. West,* 280 U.S. 234 (1930).

[107]*Federal Power Comm. v. Hope Natural Gas Co.,* 320 U.S. 591 (1944).

[108]Cost of removal "means the cost of demolishing, dismantling, tearing down or otherwise removing utility plant, including the cost of transportation and handling incidental thereto." *Uniform System of Accounts for Class A and B Electric Utilities* (Washington, D.C.: National Association of Regulatory Utility Commissioners, 1976), p. 2. See Stuart G. McDaniel, "Accounting for Cost of Removal," 103 *Public Utilities Fortnightly* 25 (February 15, 1979).

Decommissioning costs associated with nuclear power plants present special problems. See, *e.g., Re Connecticut Yankee Atomic Power Co.,* Opinion No. 102 (FERC, 1980); *Re Decommissioning Cost of Nuclear Powered Generators,* 47 PUR4th 357 (Fla., 1982); *Re Nuclear Facility Decommissioning Costs,* 52 PUR4th 632 (Cal., 1983); *Re Wolf Creek Nuclear Generating Facility,* 70 PUR4th 475 (Kan., 1985); *Re Connecticut Light & Power Co.,* 73 PUR4th 725 (Conn., 1986). See also "Financing of Nuclear Decommissioning Costs," 117 *Public Utilities Fortnightly* 57 (March 20, 1986); "Estimating the Cost of Nuclear Decommissioning," 117 *Public Utilities Fortnightly* 47 (May 15, 1986); Kenneth W. Sieving, "Estimating the Funding Levels for Nuclear Plant Decommissioning," 120 *Public Utilities Fortnightly* 17 (August 20, 1987).

[109]Salvage value "means the amount received for property retired, less any expenses incurred in connection with the sale or in preparing the property for sale, or, if retained, the amount at which the material recoverable is chargeable to materials

and supplies, or other appropriate account." *Uniform System of Accounts for Class A and B Electric Utilities, op. cit.,* p. 3. See also G. Robert Faust, "A Positive Rationale for Negative Net Salvage," 98 *Public Utilities Fortnightly* 25 (July 29, 1976).

[110]The Federal Communications Commission, for example, has frequently used this method, with negotiations conducted by the commission's staff, state commission staffs, and representatives of the companies. See, *e.g., Re General Teleph. of the Northwest,* FCC 79-801 (December 17, 1979).

[111]Prior to 1971, the Internal Revenue Service (IRS) provided the taxpayer either with an item-by-item listing of useful lives for calculating depreciation (Bulletin F, issued in 1942) or with guidelines for depreciation arranged in broad industry classes of assets (1962). In 1971, the IRS commenced the Asset Depreciation Range System (ADR); a system based on broad industry classes of assets, but one permitting the taxpayer to select a depreciation period within the asset depreciation range pre-scribed for a class (a range between 80 and 120 percent of the guidelines). As a result, the depreciation period for tax purposes may be shorter than the asset's physical or book life. "If a public utility elects to use the ADR System, it must normalize the deferral for rate-making purposes." Suelflow, *op. cit.,* p. 92.

[112]Francis X. Welch, *Cases and Text on Public Utility Regulation* (rev. ed.; Arlington, Va.: Public Utilities Reports, Inc., 1968), p. 415.

[113]"The group concept has been an integral part of utility depreciation accounting practice for many years. Though the concept is as applicable to nonregulated entities, it is not often applied. Under the group concept, no attempt is made to keep track of the depreciation reserve applicable to individual items of property. This does not imply any loss of control, but rather is a practical approach for utilities because they possess millions of items of property.

"Under the group concept each depreciable property group has some 'average' life. For accounting purposes, every item in the group is assumed to have the life of the group and to be fully depreciated at the time of retirement. The average is the result of a calculation, and there is no assurance that any of the property items in the group is average." Hahne and Aliff, *op. cit.,* p. 6-10.

[114]Under certain circumstances, the depreciation charges may be distributed over production rather than over service life. "The units-of-production procedure is used when facilities produce a distinctive pattern, such as an electric generating unit or a natural gas field." *Ibid.,* p. 6-28.

[115]In a few states (such as Indiana), utilities are required by statute to maintain a depreciation fund. See Suelflow, *op. cit.,* pp. 106-9.

[116]*Ibid.,* p. 97.

[117]Under this method, salvage value is ignored in the calculation of the deprecia-tion expense. Moreover, the method leaves an unexpired cost at the end of the depreciation period which, under current law, is recovered by permitting the firm to switch to a straight line method. "Since the initial calculation ignores salvage value when the double-declining rate is applied, salvage value must be deducted before dividing the undepreciated balance among the remaining years of the asset's life." *Ibid.,* pp. 96-97 (citation omitted).

[118]Pub. Law 97-34 (1981). See Lindsay Johnson and John W. Weber, Jr., "The Economic Recovery Tax Act of 1981 and Public Utilities," 109 *Public Utilities Fortnightly* 31 (March 4, 1982).

[119]Pub. Law 99-514 (1986).

[120]On this objective, see Carl G. K. Weaver and Mark S. Gerber, "The Accelerated

Cost Recovery System — A Catch 22?," 109 *Public Utilities Fortnightly* 38 (May 13, 1982).

The scheduled increases in rates of accelerated depreciation for 1985 and 1986, for property placed in service after 1984, were repealed by the Tax Equity and Fiscal Responsibility Act of 1982 [Pub. Law 97-248 (1982)]. The repeal was mandated by growing concern over the anticipated size of the federal deficits. See, *e.g.*, *Tax Equity and Fiscal Responsibility Act of 1982* (Chicago: Arthur Andersen & Co., 1982).

[121] *Tax Reform 1986: Analysis and Planning* (Chicago: Arthur Andersen & Co., 1987), p. 111. Thus, the lives of utility property are longer (up to twenty years) under the new law.

[122] For a more complete discussion, see Edgar and Faust, *op. cit.*, pp. 15-28.

[123] For example, a basic purpose in the revised depreciation guidelines announced in 1962 was to give greater weight to obsolescence. See U.S. Treasury Department, Internal Revenue Service, "Depreciation Guidelines and Rules" (Washington, D.C.: U.S. Government Printing Office, 1962).

[124] Alfred E. Kahn, *The Economics of Regulation: Principles and Institutions* (New York: John Wiley & Sons, Inc., 1970), Vol. I, p. 118 (footnote omitted).

[125] *Ibid.*, pp. 118-19.

[126] *Ibid.*, p. 119.

[127] *Minneapolis Street Ry. Co. v. City of Minneapolis*, 86 N.W. 2d 657, 659, 660 (1957) (quotations from court's syllabus).

[128] In 1983, AT&T announced a $5.2 billion charge against 1983 net income, or $5.50 per share. About $3.8 billion ($7.3 billion pre-tax) reflected a reduction in the book value of telephone equipment and network facilities, in the form of an increase in depreciation reserves, to bring book value more in line with market value. About $1.4 billion reflected bookkeeping changes due to a shift in accounting methods, from the "uniform system of accounts" to "generally accepted accounting principles." The charge was taken on December 31, 1983, coincident with the divestiture of the Bell System. *The Wall Street Journal*, October 20, 1983, p. 3.

[129] See *Re Amendment of Uniform System of Accounts for Class A and Class B Telephone Companies*, 50 PUR4th 298 (FCC, 1982). It has been estimated that local telephone companies have $26 billion worth of "reserve deficiencies" on their books, but the FCC was unsuccessful in attempting to preempt state commissions regarding depreciation rates and practices. *Louisiana Pub. Service Comm. v. Federal Communications Comm.*, 106 S. Ct. 1890, 74 PUR4th 1 (1986).

[130] See Walter G. Bolter and David A. Irwin, *Depreciation Reform — A Critical Step in Transforming Telecommunications to a Free Market* (Washington, D.C., 1980); Mark C. Griffith and Terence D. Robinson, "Economic Value and Capital Recovery: A Regulatory Model," 116 *Public Utilities Fortnightly* 30 (July 11, 1985); Joseph R. Fogarty, "Telephone Company Capital Recovery: Crisis and Dilemma Persist," 117 *Public Utilities Fortnightly* 23 (February 6, 1986).

[131] The discussion in this section is limited to the controversy over the use of reproduction cost in determining annual depreciation allowances. The property valuation — rate base — controversy is considered in the following chapter.

It should be noted that there are other concepts of "economic" depreciation. See, *e.g.*, William J. Baumol, "Optimal Depreciation Policy: Pricing the Products of Durable Assets," 2 *Bell Journal of Economics and Management Science* 638 (1971); Alan Kraus and Ronald J. Huefner, "Cash-Flow Patterns and the Choice of a Depreciation Method," 3 *Bell Journal of Economics and Management Science* 316 (1972); Bruce L.

Jaffee, "Depreciation in a Simple Regulatory Model," 4 *Bell Journal of Economics and Management Science* 338 (1973); U. Sankar, "Depreciation, Tax Policy and Firm Behavior under Regulatory Constraint," 44 *Southern Economic Journal* 1 (July, 1977).

[132]The terms current cost, reproduction cost, and price level depreciation are used synonymously. On the controversy, see Francis J. Walsh, Jr., *Inflation and Corporate Accounting* (New York: The National Industrial Conference Board, 1962). Commonwealth Edison Company has estimated that its "1976 depreciation provision of $197 million (per books) would be more than doubled, to $465 million, if restated to reflect replacement costs." Gordon R. Corey, "Some Observations on the Taxation of Regulated Utilities," 100 *Public Utilities Fortnightly* 13, 15 (October 13, 1977) (citation omitted).

[133]Current cost depreciation allowances differ from replacement depreciation. To use the same example depicted in Table 7-2, the $2,400 resulting from current cost depreciation may be greater than or less than the amount needed to replace the machine.

[134]F. Warren Brooks, "Needed Reform for Utility Tax Depreciation," 52 *Public Utilities Fortnightly* 407, 412 (1953). Brooks states that "for the average large electric utility in 1952, 83 percent of the income taxes paid were levied on real income and 17 percent were levied on capital." *Ibid.*, p. 411.

[135]In a 1957 Indiana decision, a utility was permitted to accrue depreciation upon the cost of property repriced in current dollars. *Re Indiana Teleph. Corp.*, 16 PUR3d 490, 497 (Ind., 1957). A few commissions have granted additional depreciation allowances over those allowed for tax purposes and have granted higher rates to cover partly the additional income taxes of the companies. See *Re The Peoples Gas Light & Coke Co.*, 97 PUR (NS) 33 (Ill., 1953). See also Louis E. Mullen, "Tax Depreciation Adjusted for Price Level Changes," 82 *Public Utilities Fortnightly* 29 (August 29, 1968); Joel L. Lebowitz, Chong Ouk Lee, and Peter B. Linhart, "Some Effects of Inflation on a Firm with Original Cost Depreciation," 7 *Bell Journal of Economics* 463 (1976).

[136]The President's Material Policy Commission, *Resources for Freedom* (Washington, D.C.: U.S. Government Printing Office, 1952), Vol. I, pp. 34-35.

[137]Suelflow, *op. cit.*, p. 109.

[138]For tax purposes, Congress has long granted special allowances to the mineral industries. The last depletion allowance for the gas and oil industries was as follows: (*1*) With minor exceptions, drilling, exploration, and development costs could be fully depreciated in the year in which they were incurred. (*2*) In place of the fair market value of property, 22 percent of the gross income from a gas or oil well could be deducted from taxable income, provided that such allowance did not exceed 50 percent of the net income from a well. Depletion allowances have been debated for years. See, *e.g.*, *Compendium of Papers on Broadening the Tax Base* (Committee on Ways and Means, House) (Washington, D.C.: U.S. Government Printing Office, 1959), Vol. 2, pp. 933-1060. Except for small companies, the depletion allowance was terminated in 1975.

[139]One writer concludes that the history of utility taxation can be divided into three periods: those of (*a*) subsidy, terminating at about the end of the nineteenth century, (*b*) neutral treatment, terminating with the depression of the 1930s, and (*c*) "special burdens," from the 1930s to date. Harold M. Groves, *Financing Government* (5th ed.; New York: Holt, Rinehart & Winston, Inc., 1958), p. 336.

[140]In 1984, private electric utilities paid $20.9 billion in local, state, and federal

taxes; private telephone utilities paid $13 billion; and private gas utilities paid $7.1 billion.

[141]Legislatures and tax authorities, seeking revenue for governmental purposes, sometimes disregard the relation between utility taxes on the one hand, and rates, investment, and service improvements on the other. The commissions commonly wish to use any excess earnings either to reduce rates or for service improvements. If utilities have excess earnings and taxes are increased, the earnings are diverted to tax revenues rather than to consumers.

[142]For an excellent overview, see Donald J. Reeb, Howard Shapiro, and Louis R. Tomson, "State and Local Taxes and Electric Utilities," 110 *Public Utilities Fortnightly* 29 (August 19, 1982).

[143]Clemens, *op. cit.*, pp. 526-27. See also Patrick C. Mann and John L. Mikesell, "The Public Utility: A Taxpayer or a Tax Collector?," 7 *Business and Economic Decisions* 14 (January 1971).

[144]". . . states may classify property for taxation; may set up different modes of assessment, valuation, and collection; may tax some kinds of property at higher rates than others; and in making these differentiations may treat railroads and other utilities with that separateness which their distinctive characteristics and function in society make appropriate." *Nashville, Chattanooga & St. Louis Ry. Co. v. Browning,* 310 U.S. 362, 368 (1940). In a 1968 decision, the Supreme Court cautioned states against attempting to levy on interstate corporations property taxes that represent more than a fair share of a company's facilities within the state. *Norfolk & Western Ry. Co. v. Missouri State Tax Comm.,* 88 S. Ct. 995 (1968).

[145]For a discussion of the problems and inequities of assessments in Nebraska, see F. O. Woodward, "The Assessment Value of Telephone Properties," *Nebraska Journal of Economics and Business,* Spring 1962, pp. 49-59.

[146]Senator S. L. Holland, quoted in 66 *Public Utilities Fortnightly* 101 (1960) (emphasis added).

Troxel has argued that a case can be made for the lighter taxation of public utilities. Many nonutility companies "often have a better opportunity to get excessive returns than that of even a poorly regulated utility company. Considering these facts, tax authorities can justify higher tax rates on some nonutility earnings than on utility company earnings." Troxel, *op. cit.*, p. 257. See also Peter S. Spiro, "The Corporate Income Tax and Electric Utilities," 117 *Public Utilities Fortnightly* 17 (June 26, 1986).

[147]The federal excess profits tax is discussed by Troxel, *op. cit.*, pp. 253-54.

[148]See, *e.g.*, Jesse V. Burkhead, "The Changing Incidence of Public Utility Taxation," *Journal of Land & Public Utility Economics* 383 (1939); Thomas W. Calmus, "Regressivity of Excise Taxes on Public Utilities," 84 *Public Utilities Fortnightly* 19 (November 20, 1969); Martin T. Farris, "The Incidence of Public Utility Taxes," 85 *Public Utilities Fortnightly* 28 (April 9, 1970).

[149]Even when taxes are shifted to consumers, the burden is unequally distributed. Public utilities are allowed to practice price discrimination by classifying customers into various groups and charging different rates for each group. Price discrimination is discussed in Chapter 10.

[150]*State ex rel. Pacific Teleph. & Teleg. Co. v. Dept. of Pub. Service,* 52 PUR (NS) 6, 54 (Wash., 1943).

[151]*Re Intermountain Gas Co.,* 35 PUR3d 342 (Idaho, 1960). See also *Re Bell Teleph. Co. of Nevada,* 31 PUR3d 392 (Nev., 1959); *Re Florida Water Service,* 32 PUR3d 320 (Fla., 1960); *Re Missouri Utilities Co.,* 43 PUR3d 423 (Mo., 1962). In Illinois, and in a

few other jurisdictions, even franchise taxes are treated in this manner. See, *e.g.*, *Village of Maywood v. Illinois Commerce Comm.*, 178 N.E. 2d 345 (1962). For an overview, see "Gross Receipts Taxes: Regulatory Fees or Revenue Raising Techniques?," 117 *Public Utilities Fortnightly* 52 (April 3, 1986).

[152]For a more comprehensive discussion, see Hahne and Aliff, *op. cit.*, chap. 17.

[153]Accounting Principles Board, Opinion No. 11, "Accounting for Income Taxes" (1967).

[154]Differences may be either timing (differences between book income and tax income that will reverse in subsequent periods, *i.e.*, deferred income taxes) or permanent (differences between book income and tax income that will not reverse in some future period, *i.e.*, interest on governmental obligations, which is exempt for tax purposes but is recognized for book purposes). Timing differences, in turn, may refer to items that relate to revenues (gains or losses from sale of utility property), expenses (fuel expenses), or property (due to depreciation methods). For examples of major timing differences, see Hahne and Aliff, *op. cit.*, Chap. 17, Appendix C.

[155]For accounting purposes, the tax effect of the depreciation difference is placed in a reserve for deferred income taxes.

[156]Hahne and Aliff, *op. cit.*, pp. 17-22 — 17-23. Compare, *e.g.*, *Re Alabama-Tennessee Nat. Gas Co.*, 52 PUR3d 118 (FPC, 1964), *aff'd*, 359 F. 2d 318 (1966), *cert. denied*, 385 U.S. 847 (1966), with *Colorado Municipal League v. Pub. Utilities Comm.*, 597 P. 2d 586 (Colo., 1979). See also D. Kiefer, *Accelerated Depreciation and the Investment Tax Credit in the Public Utility Industry: A Background Analysis* (Columbus, Ohio: National Regulatory Research Institute, 1979).

[157]Hahne and Aliff, *op. cit.*, pp. 17-23.

[158]See Gerald J. Glassman, "Objections to Taking Liberalized Depreciation," 77 *Public Utilities Fortnightly* 29 (March 31, 1966); Herman Green, "Proper Regulatory Treatment of Liberalized Depreciation," 78 *Public Utilities Fortnightly* 31 (July 7, 1966); C. N. Ostergreen, "Accelerated Depreciation and Rate Making Once More," 81 *Public Utilities Fortnightly* 48 (January 18, 1968). But see Donald C. Cook, "The Flow Through of Tax Benefits," 77 *Public Utilities Fortnightly* 170 (June 9, 1966), for an argument that accelerated depreciation should be adopted even if flow through is required.

It has been estimated that if the Bell System had elected to use accelerated depreciation in 1954, its income tax liabilities would have been reduced by a total of $1.6 billion by the end of 1965, resulting in cumulative reductions in charges to consumers of about $3 billion. Testimony of A. L. Stott, FCC Docket No. 16258 (Bell Exhibit 38, October 17, 1966) Attachment C; Testimony of William J. Powell, FCC Docket No. 16258 (FCC Staff Exhibit No. 29), p. 10.

[159]*Re Panhandle Eastern Pipe Line Co.*, 3 PUR3d 396 (FPC, 1954), *aff'd sub nom. City of Detroit v. Federal Power Comm.*, 230 F. 2d 810 (D.C. Cir. 1955); *Re El Paso Nat. Gas Co.*, 29 PUR3d 469 (FPC, 1959). See Note, "Liberalized Depreciation: About-Face by the FPC," 50 *Virginia Law Review* 298 (1964).

[160]*Re Alabama-Tennessee Nat. Gas Co., op. cit.* Further, in 1966, the FPC held that the increased federal income tax payments resulting from the decision of a natural gas pipeline company to discontinue the use of accelerated depreciation were not a reasonable and prudent business expense. *Re Midwestern Gas Transmission Co.*, 64 PUR3d 433, 444 (FPC, 1966).

[161]Federal Power Commission, *Federal and State Commission Jurisdiction and Regulation, Electric, Gas, and Telephone Utilities, 1967* (Washington, D.C.: U.S. Government Printing Office, 1968), p. 38. See Eugene F. Brigham, "Public Utility Depreciation

Practices and Policies," 19 *National Tax Journal* 144 (1966); H. Bierman, Jr., "Accelerated Depreciation and Rate Regulation," 44 *Accounting Review* 65 (1969). For typical decisions, compare *Re Gulf Power Co.*, 10 PUR3d 273 (Fla., 1956) (normalization permitted) with *City of Pittsburgh v. Pennsylvania Pub. Utility Comm.*, 17 PUR3d 249 (1957) (flow through required).

[162]The most publicized exception was in California, where the commission's decision to permit normalization in 1970 (Decision No. 77984, November 24, 1970) was overturned by the California Supreme Court [*San Francisco v. California Pub. Utility Comm.*, 91 PUR3d 209 (1972)]. If the 1969 act did prohibit utilities from using accelerated depreciation and the investment tax credit with flow through, the court's position would have resulted in Pacific Telephone and General Telephone of California having tax liabilities in excess of $2.2 billion for delinquent taxes, penalties, and interest. In fact, in 1978, the Internal Revenue Service sent Pacific Telephone a deficiency notice. Congress resolved the dispute by adding an amendment to federal gasoline tax legislation which made more specific "the rules under which public utilities lose the investment credit and accelerated depreciation when these tax benefits are flowed through too rapidly to consumers" and which resulted in compromise payments of $321 million by Pacific Telephone and $97.7 million by General Telephone. 49 *Telecommunications Reports* 1, 26 (January 10, 1983). On the dispute, see Albin J. Dahl, "The California Remand Case: Controversy over Normalization," 104 *Public Utilities Fortnightly* 13 (December 30, 1979).

A few other state commissions continue to use the flow through method [see, *e.g., Gulf States Utilities Co. v. Louisiana Pub. Service Comm.*, 364 So. 2d 1266 (1978)] or the flow through method for computing a utility's state income tax expense [see, *e.g., Continental Teleph. Co. of Maine v. Maine Pub. Utilities Comm.*, 397 A. 2d 1001 (1979)]. See also "Recent Decisions on Accelerated Depreciation and Normalization," 105 *Public Utilities Fortnightly* 49 (May 8, 1980).

[163]See, *e.g.,* Eugene F. Brigham and James L. Pappas, *Liberalized Depreciation and the Cost of Capital* (East Lansing: MSU Public Utilities Studies, 1970).

[164]Pub. Law 95-600 (1978).

[165]See, *e.g., Re Southwestern Bell Teleph. Co.*, 36 PUR4th 283 (Mo., 1980).

[166]See, *e.g., Re Chesapeake & Potomac Teleph. Co. of West Virginia*, 40 PUR4th 279 (W.Va., 1980).

[167]See, *e.g., Kansas Power & Light Co. v. Kansas State Corp. Comm.*, 620 P. 2d 329 (1980).

[168]"The Effect of the Tax Reform Act of 1986 on Regulatory Treatment of Excess Deferred Tax Reserves," 118 *Public Utilities Fortnightly* 48, 50 (December 11, 1986). It must be noted that the act also provides for a new corporate alternative minimum tax. Thus, public utilities, who have enjoyed relatively low effective income tax rates (due to the benefits of accelerated depreciation and the availability of the investment tax credit) may experience an overall tax increase under the act.

[169]Pub. Law. 87-834 (1962).

[170]Under the Tax Reduction Act of 1975 (Pub. Law 94-12), as modified by the Economic Recovery Tax Act of 1981. Under the original (1962) act, nonregulated firms, as well as natural gas producers and pipeline companies and transportation firms received a percentage that was graduated up to 7 percent, depending on the estimated life of the new property; other public utilities received a percentage graduated up to 3 percent. To qualify for the full credit, the property had to have a life of eight years or more. The act further provided that the tax base of the eligible

property was to be lowered by an amount equal to the tax credit. The Revenue Act of 1964 (Pub. Law 88-272), among other things, prohibited the *federal* commissions from adopting the flow through method without the consent of the taxpayer and provided that the tax credit was not to be used to reduce the tax base. The investment tax credit was suspended by Congress on October 10, 1966; reinstated effective March 10, 1967; terminated in the Tax Reform Act of 1969; and reinstated again in the Revenue Act of 1971. The latter act increased the 3 percent rate for most public utilities to 4 percent.

[171]The Revenue Act of 1971 also provided for an additional one percent if the firm had an Employee Stock Ownership Plan (ESOP) for the benefit of employees. The ESOP credit expired on December 31, 1982. Under the Economic Recovery Act of 1981, this credit has been replaced by a payroll-based credit for taxable years 1983 through 1987.

Under the latter act, the carryover period for the investment tax credit was extended from seven to fifteen years.

[172]The Revenue Act of 1971 provided three specific options (rules) for ratemaking treatment of the tax credits. Option 3, which permitted flow through, was available to those utilities which were flow through companies under the accelerated depreciation rules enacted as part of the Tax Reform Act of 1969. A utility had to elect the option within ninety days after enactment of the act; it could not be imposed by a regulatory commission. The Tax Reduction Act of 1975 continued the three ratemaking opinions. Very few utilities, in fact, elected Option 3 and it was eliminated by the Economic Recovery Tax Act of 1981 for all property placed in service after 1980.

[173]See Francis X. Welch, "Utility Accounting and Investment Tax Credit," in American Bar Association Annual Report, Section of *Public Utility Law, 1963* (Chicago, 1963), pp. 52-65; *Federal and State Commission Jurisdiction and Regulation, Electric, Gas, and Telephone Utilities, 1967, op. cit.,* p. 38.

[174]The accumulated tax credit is frequently included in a utility's capitalization and receives either the overall rate of return or the cost of common equity. Some state commissions permit a utility a return only on the post-1971 investment tax credits. See *1985 Annual Report on Utility and Carrier Regulation, op. cit.,* pp. 562-66.

[175]A net loss in any year can be carried back to the three preceding years or carried forward to the succeeding five years.

[176]See, *e.g., Re South Central Bell Teleph. Co.,* Docket No. U-6402 (Tenn., 1977); *Re General Teleph. Co. of the Southwest,* 29 PUR4th 379 (Ark., 1979); *Re Mid-Carolina Teleph. Co.,* 46 PUR4th 575 (N.C., 1982); *General Teleph. Co. of Florida v. Florida Pub. Service Comm.,* 446 So. 2d 1063 (1984); *Pennsylvania Pub. Utility Comm. v. Western Pennsylvania Water Co.,* 72 PUR4th 103 (Pa., 1986).

[177]*Re United Gas Pipe Line Co.,* 54 PUR3d 285 (FPC, 1964). See also *Re Missouri Cities Water Co.,* 29 PUR4th 1 (Mo., 1979).

[178]The FPC's allocation was based on a formula developed in an earlier decision, whereby (1) the companies are separated into regulated (jurisdictional) and non-regulated (nonjurisdictional) groups, (2) the net aggregate taxable income is determined for each group, and (3) the net total consolidated tax liability is apportioned over a representative period of time between the two groups, and among the companies in the regulated group, on the basis of their respective taxable incomes; "provided that the allowance so computed for the regulated company shall not exceed

what its tax liability would be for rate-making purposes, if computed on a separate return basis." *Re Cities Service Gas Co.*, 49 PUR3d 229, 236 (FPC, 1963).

[179]*Federal Power Comm. v. United Gas Pipe Line Co.*, 386 U.S. 237, 246-47 (1967). In a dissenting opinion, Justice Harlan (joined by Justices Douglas and Stewart), argued: ". . . no allocation whatever could be required by the commission in this case because nonjurisdictional income was more than sufficient to absorb all nonjurisdictional losses and there was no showing that jurisdictional activities would actually benefit from nonjurisdictional losses. To permit the FPC in such circumstances to allocate would in effect extend the commission's jurisdiction to areas not encompassed within the authority given the commission by the Natural Gas Act." Dissenting opinion, *ibid.*, pp. 256-57.

[180]*Re Florida Gas Trans. Co.*, 47 FPC 341, 93 PUR3d 477 (FPC, 1972). The stand-alone method "is one that takes into account the revenues and costs entering into the regulated cost of service without increase or decrease for tax gains or losses related to other activities." *Ibid.*, Exhibit 11, p. 4.

[181]*Re So. California Edison Co.*, 23 PUR4th 44 (FPC, 1977). See also "Consolidated Tax Savings and Affiliated Utilities: New Life for an Old Issue," 108 *Public Utilities Fortnightly* 62 (November 5, 1981).

[182]*City of Charlottesville v. Federal Energy Regulatory Comm. and Columbia Gas Trans. Corp.*, 661 F. 2d 945 (D.C. Cir. 1981), 48 PUR4th 682 (1982).

[183]*Re Columbia Gulf Trans. Co.*, 54 PUR4th 31, 37 (FERC, 1983). "The mechanics of calculating a stand-alone allowance are as follows: From the total return allowed on rate base are deducted interest expenses (computed by multiplying the rate base by the weighted cost of long-term debt used in determining the rate of return), permanent tax differences, and the effect of the surtax exemption to arrive at the tax base. The tax base is then multiplied by the factor of 48 percent over 52 percent (now 46 percent over 54 percent) to produce the tax allowance, which includes recognition of the fact that the tax allowance itself is subject to tax when received by the utility and is not deductible. The amount so calculated is the tax allowance." *Ibid.*, p. 38.

[184]William A. Testa, "State Taxation of Energy Production: Regional and National Issues," 8 *Economic Perspectives* 3, 8 (September/October, 1984). See also Andy Plattner, "Severance Taxes on Energy Seen Widening Gap Between Rich, Poor Areas of Nation," 40 *Congressional Quarterly* 319 (February 20, 1982).

[185]All data from *Commonwealth Edison Co. et al. v. Montana*, 453 U.S. 609, 40 PUR4th 159 (1981).

[186]Compare Charles E. McLure, Jr., "Economic Constraints on State and Local Taxation of Energy Resources," 31 *National Tax Journal* 257 (1978), with Albert M. Church, "Conflicting Federal, State and Local Interest Trends in State and Local Energy Taxation: Coal and Copper — A Case in Point," 31 *National Tax Journal* 269 (1978). See also Kenyon N. Griffin and Robert B. Shelton, "Coal Severance Tax Policies in the Rocky Mountain States," 7 *Policy Studies Journal* 29 (1978).

[187]Church, *op. cit.*, p. 272.

[188]Some feel that the transfer could go over $200 billion during the 1980s. Plattner, *op. cit.*, p. 317.

[189]*Ibid.* Several bills have been introduced in Congress to this effect, with a 12.50 percent ceiling commonly suggested. See, *e.g.*, *Coal Severance Tax* (Hearings on S. 2695 Before the Committee on Energy and Natural Resources, Senate, 96th Cong., 2d sess.) (Washington, D.C.: U.S. Government Printing Office, 1980). In upholding

Montana's coal severance tax in 1981 (*Commonwealth Edison Co. et al. v. Montana, op. cit.*), the Supreme Court suggested that such a ceiling was constitutional. See, *e.g.,* Stephan F. Williams, "Severance Taxes and Federalism: The Role of the Supreme Court in Preserving a National Common Market for Energy Supplies," 53 *University of Colorado Law Review* 281 (1982). See also W. Hellerstein, "Constitutional Constraints on State and Local Taxation of Energy Resources," 31 *National Tax Journal* 245 (1978).

[190]*Maryland et al. v. Louisiana,* 451 U.S. 725, 40 PUR4th 1, 5 (1981).

[191]See, *e.g., Re State of Louisiana First Use Tax in Pipeline Rate Cases,* Docket No. RM78-23, Order No. 10 (FERC, 1978).

[192]*Maryland et al. v. Louisiana, op. cit.* Outer continental shelf gas moving out of the state, to illustrate, was subject to the first use tax while, because of tax credits, outer continental shelf gas used within the state was exempt. *Ibid.,* p. 20. See, *e.g.,* Note, "The Louisiana First Use Tax: Does It Violate the Commerce Clause?," 53 *Tulane Law Review* 1474 (1979); W. Hellerstein, "State Taxation in the Federal System: Perspectives on Louisiana's First Use Tax on Natural Gas," 55 *Tulane Law Review* 601 (1981).

[193]See "Managerial and Regulatory Functions Distinguished," 74 *Public Utilities Fortnightly* 67 (July 2, 1964); "Management — Utility and Commission Powers," 79 *Public Utilities Fortnightly* 57 (March 2, 1967); Charles F. Phillips, Jr., "The Thin Red Line," 57 *Bell Telephone Magazine* 10 (Summer, 1978).

[194]Sidney Weintraub, "Rate Making and an Incentive Rate of Return," 81 *Public Utilities Fortnightly* 23, 25 (April 25, 1968).

[195]Clair Wilcox, *Public Policies Toward Business* (4th ed.; Homewood, Ill.: Richard D. Irwin, Inc., 1971), pp. 477-78.

[196]Richard B. McGlynn, "The Regulator as Manager" (Paper presented at the Third Annual Utility Regulatory Conference, Washington, D.C., October 7, 1980) (mimeographed), p. 8. States former CAB Chairman Kahn: "Hell, I don't know how to run an airline." *The Wall Street Journal,* October 4, 1983, p. 35.

Chapter	THE RATE BASE
8	

Original cost and the practice of using it as the base for rate of return measurements are not mere regulatory artifacts. Putting the distinction between original cost and historical cost . . . to one side for the moment, books of account are kept, financial statements prepared, and rates of return calculated on original cost throughout the economy. Hence the traditional regulatory emphasis on original cost is in large measure a mere reflection of long-standing business and financial practice. Of course, that practice has been much criticized of late. In an age of inflation it looks unreal.

—*Federal Energy Regulatory Commission**

Determination of the rate base — the value of a utility's property used and useful in the public service minus accrued depreciation — is one of the most important and most difficult problems confronting both the commissions and the utilities. No other conflict in the history of regulation has received so much attention or been the subject of so much litigation. There has always been agreement that the price for the service of a public utility should be high enough to cover operating expenses, depreciation, and taxes, and also allow a fair return on the fair value of the capital invested in the business. Consumers expect to pay "just and reasonable" prices for the services they demand; investors expect to receive a "fair" return on the capital they invest. How should the commissions establish the value of a utility's property?

The major controversy has been over the determination of the depreciated value of tangible and reproducible property and is discussed in the first four sections of this chapter. The fifth section concerns other elements of value, while construction work in progress is considered in the final section.

Elements versus Measures of Value

At the outset, it will be useful to distinguish between the elements of value or the things to be valued and the measures of value or the ways in which they are valued.[1]

The Elements of Value. The elements of value refer to the tangible and intangible assets of a utility which together comprise the rate base. The elements may be listed under four headings. Of these the first element is tangibles, which includes "used and useful" land, buildings, and equipment (plant). The decision as to what property is "used and useful" is normally left to management, although certain items claimed by utilities may be questioned and excluded from the rate base by the commissions. As listed by Welch, these items are:

> (*1*) Duplicate and unnecessary property; (*2*) obsolete and inadequate property; (*3*) property to be abandoned; (*4*) abandoned and superseded property; (*5*) overdeveloped property and facilities for future needs; (*6*) real estate: buildings, leaseholds, and water rights; (*7*) incomplete and contemplated construction; (*8*) property used for nonutility purposes; (*9*) property of other utility departments (as in the case of a combination gas and electric utility company); (*10*) property not owned; (*11*) property donations — voluntary or involuntary; (*12*) deposits and moneys advanced by customers.[2]

The second, other elements of value, includes working capital, property held for future use, and intangibles. The third, customer contributions and tax deferrals, is frequently deducted from the rate base, since those components do not represent investor-supplied capital. The fourth, construction work in progress, has become one of the most controversial issues in rate making. A typical electric utility rate base is illustrated in Table 8-1.

The Measures of Value. Once the items of property to be included in the rate base have been determined, their value must be established. The measures of value refer to the various methods of computation used in determining the total value of a utility's investment.

A word of caution: In discussing the rate base valuation problem, it must be recognized that "fair value" is not value in the economic sense. Regulatory commissions are not finding the value of property; they are

TABLE 8-1

Electric Utility Rate Base[a]

Total Utility Plant in Service	$569,544,820
Total Accumulated Depreciation	$103,464,587
TOTAL NET PLANT	$466,080,233
Eliminate Amounts Recorded on Books in Excess of Original Cost — Mystic Lake	$ (1,883,582)
LESS: Customer Contributed Capital	
Accumulated Deferred Income Taxes	
Amortization of Plant Acquisition	
Adjustment	$ 105,194
Accelerated Depreciation	1,816,954
Liberalized Depreciation	29,775,539
Accumulated Deferred Investment Tax	
Credits (Pre-1971)	1,340,566
Customer Advances for Construction	1,120,638
TOTAL CUSTOMER CONTRIBUTED CAPITAL	$ 34,158,891
PLUS: Working Capital	
Gross Cash Requirements	$ 6,979,821
Credit for Accrued Taxes	(5,457,809)
Fuel	1,544,915
Materials & Supplies	5,862,088
Net Kerr Rentals	3,393,786
TOTAL WORKING CAPITAL	$ 12,322,801
COMPANY ADJUSTED TOTAL ELECTRIC UTILITY RATE BASE	$442,360,561
PLUS: Commission Adjustment for Excess Accumulated Deferred Taxes[b]	$ 345,750
COMMISSION ADOPTED TOTAL ELECTRIC UTILITY RATE BASE	$442,706,311

[a]The rate base was calculated on a thirteen-month average test period, ended September 30, 1979, adjusted for known changes.

[b]To adjust the accumulated deferred tax account for the reduction in the corporate income tax rate from 48 to 46 percent.

Source: *Re Montana Power Co.*, Order No. 4714a (Mont., 1980), p. 20.

making it. In the case of nonregulated companies, value is the result of market processes. The value of a company's property is determined by the profitability of the business, and represents the capitalized sum of the earnings above all operating costs at the current rate of interest or rate of return. In the case of public utilities, this cannot be done, for the earnings depend on the rates established by the regulatory commissions. If rates are set high, value will be high; if low rates are set, value will be low. Circular reasoning is thus involved if fair value for ratemaking purposes is thought of in the economic sense — rates cannot be based on a value which is dependent on the rates. This distinction, long overlooked, was finally recognized by the Supreme Court in 1944:

> The fixing of prices, like other applications of the police power, may reduce the value of the property which is being regulated. But the fact that the value is reduced does not mean that the regulation is invalid. . . . It does, however, indicate that "fair value" is the end product of the process of rate making, not the starting point as the Circuit Court of Appeals held. The heart of the matter is that rates cannot be made to depend upon "fair value" when the value of the going enterprise depends on earnings under whatever rates may be anticipated.[3]

For purposes of ratemaking, therefore, value depends on the measures of value used by the companies and commissions.

Throughout commission and court decisions, several measures of tangible and reproducible property value, some subsequently rejected, have been discussed and employed. While these measures will be discussed at length in the following sections, they can be summarized as follows.[4]

I. Measures of Construction Cost Value
   1. *Actual, "First" Original, or Original Cost.* The amount actually paid for installing the original plant and equipment, plus additions, when first devoted to public service.
   2. *Book or Investment Cost.* The amount actually paid for installing the present plant and equipment, plus additions, as shown in the investment accounts on the utility's books.
   3. *Historical Cost or Prudent Investment.* The original cost minus any fraudulent, unwise, or extravagant expenditures.
   4. **Capitalization Cost.* The capital invested in the business as measured by the outstanding bonds, stock, and other securities.

II. Measures of Reproduction Cost Value
   5. *Current or Reproduction Cost; Price Level Accounting.* The cost of plant and equipment, plus additions, estimated at price levels prevailing at the date of valuation.
   6. **Split Inventory Value.* The original cost (reproduction cost) of plant and equipment installed before a specific date, and the reproduction cost (original cost) of property installed thereafter.
   7. **Taxation Value.* The value of property as assessed for taxation purposes.
   8. **Market Value.* The capitalized value of a utility (*i.e.*, its probable earnings capacity).
   9. **Exchange or Purchase Value.* The value of a utility as determined by the price another party is willing to pay for the property.

There is a third measure of value, which depends upon these two: fair value. *Fair value* is a figure somewhere between original cost and reproduction cost, arrived at by the exercise of "enlightened judgment" or by a specific formula.

Property Valuation: Legal Concepts

Prior to the famous case of *Smyth v. Ames* in 1898,[5] determining the rate base was a commission and legislative problem. Deciding an 1877 case, the Supreme Court took the position that ratemaking was a legislative rather than a judicial function. As explained by the Court:

> Rights of property which have been created by the common law cannot be taken away without due process; but the law itself . . . may be changed at the will, or even at the whim, of the legislature, unless prevented by constitutional limitations. . . . To limit the rate of charge for services rendered in a public employment . . . is only changing a regulation which existed before. . . .
>
> We know that this is a power which may be abused; but that is no argument against its existence. For protection against abuses by legislatures the people must resort to the polls, not to the courts.[6]

In 1886, the Court reversed its position, recognizing that "this power to regulate is not a power to destroy, and limitation is not the equivalent of confiscation."[7] Rates fixed under legislative authority, therefore, were subject to judicial review and might be set aside if they were found to deprive investors of their property without due process of law. And a few years later, for the first time, the Court held that a rate-fixing statute of Texas confiscated the property of a railroad company.[8] But the Court established no standards by which to judge the reasonableness of commission valuations until the *Smyth* decision.

The "Fair Value" Doctrine

The state of Nebraska in 1893 passed a law which established a Board of Transportation. Among other things, the board was given the authority to determine the rates charged for hauling freight. One of its first orders, setting maximum rates, was challenged by the railroads on the basis that the rates were confiscatory. The railroads contended that much of their property had been constructed during and after the Civil War when prices were high and that they were entitled to a return on their original cost. The state, represented by William Jennings Bryan, based its measure of reasonable earnings on the lower reproduction cost. The property valuation problem thus came to the front.

The Supreme Court held that the rates were confiscatory by any measure. This finding was not, however, the importance of the decision, for the Court went on, in a dictum not essential to its decision, to state the measures of value by which confiscation could be judged. This dictum later became the legal basis of the "fair value" doctrine. Said Justice Harlan:

> The corporation may not be required to use its property for the benefit of the public without receiving just compensation for the services rendered by it. How such compensation may be ascertained, and what are the necessary elements in such an inquiry, will always be an embarrassing question. . . .
>
> We hold, however, that the basis of all calculations as to the reasonableness of rates to be charged by a corporation . . . must be the fair value of the property being used by it for the convenience of the public. And in order to ascertain that value, the original cost of construction, the amount expended in permanent improvements, the amount and market value of its bonds and stock, the present as compared with the original cost of construction, the probable earning capacity of the property under particular rates prescribed by statute, and the sum required to meet operating expenses, are all matters for consideration, and are to be given such weight as may be just and right in each case. We do not say that there may not be other matters to be regarded in estimating the value of the property. What the company is entitled to ask is a fair return upon the value of that which it employs for the public convenience. On the other hand, what the public is entitled to demand is that no more be extracted from it . . . than the services rendered by it are reasonably worth.[9]

The Court thus enumerated six specific measures of value to be considered in determining fair value: (*1*) the original cost of construction and the amount spent on permanent improvements, (*2*) the amount of bonds and stock, (*3*) the market value of bonds and stock, (*4*) the present as compared with the original cost of construction, (*5*) the probable earning capacity of the property, and (*6*) operating expenses. Perhaps fearing that something might have been forgotten, the Court added: "We do not say that there may not be other matters to be regarded. . . ." However, the Court did not say which measure is controlling. Each must be considered and be given "such weight as may be just and right. . . ."

Of the measures specifically mentioned, four were subsequently rejected as proper measures of value.[10] Earning capacity and the market value of bonds and stock involve circular reasoning, because they depend on the utility's earnings which, in turn, depend on the rates charged.[11] The amount of bonds and stock also has been rejected, for to base a valuation for ratemaking purposes on this amount would encourage stock watering and overcapitalization.[12] And operating expenses have nothing to do with the determination of the rate base.[13] As a result, two measures remain: (*1*) original cost, including expenditures on permanent improvements; and (*2*) present, current, or reproduction cost.

The Court's measures of value have been criticized and defended at length ever since 1898. Some have argued that the decision presented so many broad and vague measures as to make it useless as a guide to the commissions for ratemaking purposes. Justice Frankfurter, for example, later referred to the "hodgepodge of the rule in *Smyth v. Ames*,"[14] calling it a "mischievous formula for fixing utility rates" and "useless as a guide to adjudication."[15] Others have argued that the Court was simply trying to place emphasis on the concept of reasonableness without being too doctrinaire about the use of any particular formula to achieve it. Consequently, the commissions were given considerable latitude in determining a proper valuation measure.[16] "But it is important to remember that it did lay down the 'fair return on fair value formula' for determining the reasonableness of utility rates, and it is still followed by the regulatory commissions in a number of states. . . ."[17]

Reproduction Cost versus Prudent Investment: 1898 to 1933

Before World War I, public utilities generally based their valuation estimates on original cost, while commissions based theirs on reproduction cost. But during the war, construction costs soared, and reproduction cost became higher than original cost. Consequently, the two parties changed sides. The utilities now began to demand consideration of reproduction cost; the commissions started to urge original cost. This switch led one observer to comment: "On the issue of original cost versus reproduction cost the position of the various contestants has been largely opportunistic."[18]

Until the early thirties, the Supreme Court was divided. The majority's leading spokesman was Justice Butler, a railroad lawyer appointed to the Court by President Harding, while the minority's leading spokesman was Justice Brandeis, a liberal appointed by President Wilson. Justice Butler emphasized reproduction cost; Justice Brandeis, prudent investment. A brief discussion of the leading decisions will illustrate the valuation controversy, as far as the Court was concerned, during this period.

Emphasis on Reproduction Cost. Around the turn of the century, the majority emphasized reproduction cost largely because the original cost of property was difficult, if not impossible, to determine. As discussed earlier, accounting practices varied widely among public utilities, and costs were often inflated by extravagant and fraudulent expenditures. Referring to original cost in one case, the Court said: "The property may have cost more than it ought to have cost. . . ."[19] A few years later, the same view was expressed when the Court argued that "the only evidence in favor of a higher value in the present case, is the original cost of the work seemingly inflated by improper charges to that account and by injudicious expenditures.... No doubt cost may be considered, and will have more or less importance according to circumstances."[20]

As the price level began to rise, however, the principle that reproduction cost was a better measure of value than original cost became firmly established. In 1909, and again in 1913, the Court argued that utilities were entitled to any increase in property values. Said the Court:

> There must be a fair return upon the reasonable value of the property at the time it is being used for the public.... And we concur with the court below in holding that the value of the property is to be determined as of the time when the inquiry is made regarding the rates. If the property, which legally enters into the consideration of the question of rates, has increased in value since it was acquired, the company is entitled to the benefit of such increase.[21]

* * *

> It is clear that in ascertaining the present value we are not limited to the consideration of the amount of the actual investment. If that has been reckless or improvident, losses may be sustained which the community does not underwrite. As the company may not be protected in its actual investment, if the value of its property be plainly less, so the making of a just return for the use of the property involves the recognition of its fair value if it be more than its cost. The property is held in private ownership and it is that property, and not the original cost of it, of which the owner may not be deprived without due process of law.[22]

In several postwar cases, the Supreme Court continued to emphasize reproduction cost. The Court overruled the Missouri commission in 1923 on the grounds that the property of the utility had been valued at prewar prices. In the Court's words: "It is impossible to ascertain what will amount to a fair return upon properties devoted to public service without giving consideration to the cost of labor, supplies, etc., at the time the investigation is made."[23] In the same year, a decision of the West Virginia commission was overruled. The Court argued:

> The record clearly shows that the commission in arriving at its final figure did not accord proper, if any, weight to the greatly enhanced costs of construction in 1920 over those prevailing about 1915 and before the war, as established by uncontradicted evidence; and the company's detailed estimated cost of reproduction new, less depreciation, at 1920 prices, appears to have been wholly disregarded. This was erroneous.[24]

The greatest judicial emphasis on reproduction cost came in the *Indianapolis Water Company* case of 1926. The original cost of the utility's property was $10 million. Its estimated reproduction cost was $22 million. The Indiana commission valued the property at $15.3 million, while the utility insisted on $19 million. The Supreme Court, accepting the utility's claim, held that rates based on any valuation below $19 million would be confiscatory. Said Justice Butler:

> ... in determining present value, consideration must be given to prices and wages prevailing at the time of the investigation; and, in the light of all the circumstances, there must be an honest and intelligent forecast as to probable price and wage levels during a reasonable period in the immediate future. In every confiscation case, the future as well as the present must be regarded. It must be determined whether the rates complained of are yielding and will yield, over and above the amounts required to pay taxes and proper operating charges, a sum sufficient to constitute just compensation for the use of the property employed to furnish the service; that is, a reasonable rate of return on the value of the property at the time of the investigation and for a reasonable time in the immediate future.... It is well established that values of utility properties fluctuate, and that owners must bear the decline and are entitled to the increase.[25]

Three years later, the Court set aside the valuation of railroad properties that had been made over many years by the Interstate Commerce Commission. Although holding that the weight to be accorded to the various measures of value was not at issue and recognizing that "there are some, perhaps many, railroads the ultimate value of which should be placed far below the sum necessary for reproduction," the Court ruled that the commission had failed to give sufficient consideration to reproduction cost.[26]

Measurement of "Fair Value." There are two pertinent comments concerning the Court's emphasis on reproduction cost. First, the Court consistently refused to adopt this measure of value as the only controlling one. Instead, it merely stated that "consideration" must be given to reproduction cost in rate cases. In upholding the Georgia commission's refusal to base a valuation entirely on reproduction cost, the Court said:

> Here the commission gave careful consideration to the cost of reproduction; but it refused to adopt reproduction cost as the measure of value. It declared that the exercise of a reasonable judgment as to the present "fair value" required some consideration of reproduction costs as well as of original costs, but that "present fair value" is not synonymous with "present replacement cost," particularly under abnormal conditions....

The refusal of the commission and of the lower court to hold that, for ratemaking purposes, the physical properties of a utility must be valued at the replacement cost less depreciation was clearly correct.[27]

The same position was taken in the *Los Angeles Gas* case: "This Court has . . . declared that, in order to determine present value, the cost of reproducing the property is a relevant fact which should have appropriate consideration. . . . But again, the Court has not decided that cost of reproduction furnishes an exclusive test." [28]

Second, the Court refused, just as consistently, to adopt a precise formula for measuring fair value. In the *Minnesota Rate Cases,* the Court said: "The ascertainment of . . . value is not controlled by artificial rules. It is not a matter of formulas, but there must be a reasonable judgment having its basis in a proper consideration of all relevant facts."[29] In several cases, the Court suggested that the commissions should determine a relatively "normal" level of prices based on "an honest and intelligent forecast" of future price trends. But in a 1922 case, it accepted a reproduction cost valuation that was 33 percent above original cost, even though it was argued that prices had risen 110 percent; while in a 1923 case, it rejected a 25 percent increase in valuation, even though it was shown that prices had risen 100 percent.[30]

In 1923, the so-called "split inventory" method was introduced, in which value was based upon prewar reproduction cost for prewar investment and original cost for investment made during and after the war.[31] And, in a 1935 case, the Court rejected the Maryland commission's method of measuring fair value. As Troxel has explained, the commission

. . . used sixteen indexes of general prices and construction costs. These indexes ranged from the wholesale price index of the Bureau of Labor Statistics to an index of Western Electric prices. Arbitrary weights were assigned to each index. Then the composite index was used to translate a fair property valuation of 1923 and the cost of subsequent property additions (less property abandonments and accrued depreciation) into a fair value in 1932. The Supreme Court rightly objected to this strange method of reproduction-cost valuation.[32]

In general, the commissions based their estimates of reproduction cost on averages of past prices, frequently using the preceding five-year period. And the Court, despite its suggestion that consideration should be given to "probable future values," usually accepted these estimates.

Prudent Investment and Dissent. During this period, the minority of the Supreme Court repeatedly rejected the emphasis being given to reproduction cost. Justice Brandeis characterized the *Smyth* rule of determining fair value as "legally and economically unsound," and argued that its application, in practice, has shown it to be "delusive."[33] In a series of separate opinions, he argued that the proper measure of value should be prudent investment — that is, the original cost minus any fraudulent, unwise, or extravagant expenditures that should not be a burden on the public. Perhaps the best statement of his position was in the *Southwestern Bell* case:

> The thing devoted by the investor to the public use is not specific property, tangible and intangible, but capital embarked in the enterprise. Upon the capital so invested the Federal Constitution guarantees to the utility the opportunity to earn a fair return. Thus, it sets the limit to the power of the state to regulate rates. . . .
>
> The investor agrees, by embarking capital in a utility, that its charges to the public shall be reasonable. His company is the substitute for the state in the performance of the public service; thus becoming a public servant. The compensation which the Constitution guarantees an opportunity to earn is the reasonable cost of conducting the business. . . . The reasonable rate to be prescribed by a commission may allow an efficiently managed utility much more. But a rate is constitutionally compensatory, if it allows to the utility the opportunity to earn the cost of service as thus defined.
>
> The adoption of the amount prudently invested as the rate base and the amount of the capital charge as the measure of the rate of return would give definiteness to these two factors involved in rate controversies which are now shifting and treacherous, and which render the proceedings particularly burdensome and largely futile. Such measures offer a basis for decision which is certain and stable. The rate base would be ascertained as a fact, not determined as a matter of opinion. It would not fluctuate with the market price of labor, or materials, or money. It would not change with hard times or shifting populations. It would not be distorted by the fickle and varying judgments of appraisers, commissions, or courts.[34]

The prudent investment standard would shift attention from the left-hand or asset side to the right-hand side of the balance sheet which constitutes the capital embarked in the enterprise. The aim of Justice Brandeis was to achieve a measure of value that would be "certain and stable" and that would "not be determined as a matter of opinion." Instead of fluctuating rate base valuations, he was perfectly willing to vary the allowable rate of return as conditions warranted. In part, Justice Brandeis' prudent investment measure has been adopted. The uniform system of accounts requires original cost entries. With the steady inflationary trend in the economy, however, his hope that this measure would represent a readily ascertainable value for ratemaking purposes proved too optimistic; original cost is not synonymous with fair value.

Justice Brandeis was not alone in attacking the Court's fair value doctrine. Justice Stone argued:

In assuming the task of determining judicially the present fair replacement value of the vast properties of public utilities, courts have been projected into the most speculative undertaking imposed upon them in the entire history of English jurisprudence. . . . When we arrive at a theoretical value based upon such uncertain and fugitive data we gain at best only an illusory certainty.[35]

Three years later, Justice Black wrote:

Whenever the question of utility valuation arises today, it is exceedingly difficult to discern the truth through the maze of formulas and the jungle of metaphysical concepts sometimes conceived, and often fostered, by the ingenuity of those who seek inflated valuations to support excessive rates. . . . Completely lost in the confusion of language — too frequently invented for the purpose of confusing — commissions and courts passing upon rates for public utilities are driven to listen to conjectures, speculations, estimates and guesses, all under the name of "reproduction costs."[36]

As far as the Court was concerned, therefore, the valuation controversy was between the merits of prudent investment and reproduction cost. Consistently it refused to resolve the controversy. Even the majority, while placing considerable emphasis on reproduction cost, refused to say how much weight should be given to this measure of value, and declined to determine a uniform procedure for the utilities and commissions to follow. The Court simply held that "fair value" demanded consideration of reproduction cost as well as original cost and directed the commissions to exercise their enlightened judgment.

Outside the Court itself, dissent was equally strong. The Interstate Commerce Commission criticized the fair value doctrine as early as 1927 and defended the use of either original cost or prudent investment in making rate base valuations.[37] The position of most economists was well stated by Lewis when he referred to the "hybrid 'fair value' ('trance') method"[38] as "the unpredictable product of incalculable considerations"[39] which

. . . consists of an examination by the commission of evidence relating to reproduction cost and prudent investment, together with evidence of intangible values and observed condition of the property, the application of judgment whose processes defy analysis or description, and the selection of a final value figure which bears no derivative relation to any figures in evidence and no ascertainable relation to any functional purpose of rate making. The determination is typically accompanied by explicit denials that a formula was employed or that the result is a compromise, together with a statement that the commission is quite incapable of retracing and setting forth the processes by which the value figure was reached. . . . The peculiar contribution of the "fair value" method to rate regulation is indecision and confusion.[40]

Judicial Shift to the "End Result": 1933 to the Present

With dissatisfaction being expressed both inside and outside of the Supreme Court, it was perhaps inevitable that a shift in emphasis would be forthcoming. That shift began with the *Los Angeles Gas* case in 1933 and culminated with the *Hope Natural Gas* case in 1944.

In the *Los Angeles Gas* case, the California commission made two valuations — one based on "historical cost" and the other on "fair value." It then reduced the company's gas rates. The new rates were estimated to produce a 7.7 percent rate of return on historical cost and 7 percent on fair value. The Court, upholding the order, held that the choice of valuation measures was within the discretion of the commission. Said Chief Justice Hughes:

> The legislative discretion implied in the rate-making power necessarily extends to the entire legislative process, embracing the method used in reaching the legislative determination as well as that determination itself. We are not concerned with either, so long as constitutional limitations are not transgressed. When the legislative method is disclosed, it may have a definite bearing upon the validity of the result reached, but the judicial function does not go beyond the decision of the constitutional question. That question is whether the rates as fixed are confiscatory. And upon that question the complainant has the burden of proof and the Court may not interfere with the exercise of the State's authority unless confiscation is clearly established.[41]

In four valuation cases decided in 1934 and 1938, the Court approved measures of value based upon original cost.[42] In a 1935 decision, it rejected a reproduction cost valuation based upon several price indices.[43] And in a 1942 case, the Court upheld an order of the Federal Power Commission reducing pipeline rates. While the issue of original versus reproduction cost did not arise, the Court said: "The Constitution does not bind rate-making bodies to the service of any single formula or combination of formulas. Agencies to whom this legislative power has been delegated are free . . . to make the pragmatic adjustments which may be called for by particular circumstances."[44] It was the minority's concurring opinion (Justices Black, Douglas, and Murphy), however, that attracted the attention:

> . . . we think this is an appropriate occasion to lay the ghost of *Smyth v. Ames*, . . . which has haunted utility regulation since 1898. . . .
> As we read the opinion of the Court, the Commission is now freed from the compulsion of admitting evidence on reproduction cost or of

giving any weight to that element of "fair value." The Commission may now adopt, if it chooses, prudent investment as a rate base — the base long advocated by Mr. Justice Brandeis.[45]

The Hope Natural Gas Case. Two years later, the Court abandoned the *Smyth* rule that prescribed the use of a fair value rate base. The Federal Power Commission ordered a company to reduce its wholesale gas rates by more than 60 percent ($3.6 million annually). In making this decision, the commission used the "actual legitimate cost" of $33.7 million as the rate base and allowed a return of 6.5 percent. The company, which estimated that the reproduction cost of its property was $97 million and the trended original cost was $105 million, claimed it should be allowed to earn 8 percent on a $66 million fair value rate base. In a five-to-three decision, the Court upheld the commission. Speaking for the majority, Justice Douglas said:

> We held in *Federal Power Commission v. Natural Gas Pipeline Co.* . . . that the Commission was not bound to the use of any single formula or combination of formulae in determining rates. Its rate-making function, moreover, involves the making of "pragmatic adjustments." And when the Commission's order is challenged in the courts, the question is whether that order "viewed in its entirety" meets the requirements of the Act. Under the statutory standard of "just and reasonable" it is the result reached not the method employed which is controlling. . . . It is not theory but the impact of the rate order that counts. If the total effect of the rate order cannot be said to be unjust and unreasonable, judicial inquiry under the Act is at an end. The fact that the method employed to reach that result may contain infirmities is not then important. Moreover, the Commission's order does not become suspect by reason of the fact that it is challenged. It is the product of expert judgment which carries a presumption of validity. And he who would upset the rate order under the Act carries the heavy burden of making a convincing showing that it is invalid because it is unjust and unreasonable in its consequences. . . .
> . . . Rates which enable the company to operate successfully, to maintain its financial integrity, to attract capital, and to compensate its investors for the risks assumed certainly cannot be condemned as invalid, even though they might produce only a meager return on the so-called "fair value" rate base. . . .[46]

All three of the dissenting opinions argued that there is a connection between the method of determining the "end result" and the end result itself. "My disagreement with the Court," stated Justice Reed, "arises primarily from its view that it makes no difference how the Commission reached the rate fixed so long as the result is fair and reasonable. For me the statutory command to the Commission is more explicit."[47] Justice Frank-furter expressed a similar view when he argued:

> It will not do to say that it must all be left to the skill of experts. Expertise is a rational process and a rational process implies expressed reasons for judgment. It will little advance the public interest to substitute for the hodge-podge of the rule in *Smyth v. Ames* . . . , an encouragement of conscious obscurity or confusion in reaching a result, on the assumption that so long as the result appears harmless its basis is irrelevant.[48]

And Justice Jackson, approving the prudent investment theory in utility rate cases, thought natural gas belonged in a separate category from other public utility industries. In his opinion:

> The heart of this problem is the elusive, exhaustible, and irreplaceable nature of natural gas itself. Given sufficient money, we can produce any desired amount of railroad, bus, or steamship transportation, or communications facilities, or capacity for generation of electric energy, or for the manufacture of gas of a kind. In the service of such utilities one customer has little concern with the amount taken by another, one's waste will not deprive another, a volume of service can be created equal to demand, and today's demands will not exhaust or lessen capacity to serve tomorrow. But the wealth of Midas and the wit of man cannot produce or reproduce a natural gas field. We cannot even reproduce the gas, for our manufactured product has only about half the heating value per unit of nature's own.[49]

Implications of the Hope Decision. There are two important, but conflicting, implications of the *Hope* decision. On the one hand, it removed an obstacle to effective regulation that had been created by the courts. Comments Welch:

> . . . the departure from the old fair return-fair value doctrine, in effect, frees the regulatory commissions from the federal court domination and close supervision which prevailed in former years. This does not mean that the regulatory problem of fixing reasonable rates is all settled. To the contrary, reasonable rates will probably be a troublesome question as long as there is regulation. This does, however, place a greater responsibility on commissions, since reasonable rates now become more a matter of expert commission judgment and less a matter of rules or formulas.[50]

Moreover, attention was shifted from the rate base to the rate of return — a shift that many believed was long overdue. As long as the "end result" is reasonable, "judicial inquiry . . . is at an end."[51]

On the other hand, the Court still has the right of review. But it presented no criteria by which the end result was to be judged. Troxel argues:

> If many commission decisions are reviewed in a thorough and factual manner, the Court cannot escape measurements of fair returns; it cannot fail to recognize that the choice of methods affects the ends. If the decisions are not reviewed for their reasonableness, the Court really turns back to the Munn decision without admitting the reversion.[52]

Consequently, the Court at some future date may be forced to reconsider its position in the property valuation controversy.

Most of the regulatory commissions continue to use the rate base/rate of return concept in rate regulation. But there have been attempts to experiment with alternative approaches. In a 1947 decision, the Wisconsin commission attempted to fix telephone rates without determining either a rate base or a rate of return.[53] The decision was reversed by the Wisconsin circuit court. Argued Judge Reis:

> The Commission . . . disavowed its own accepted precept of rate making. *It outlawed rate base.* It denied the *need* of finding fair value — or making any finding whatever, other than the elicitation of the end result that old rates were unreasonable and new rates are reasonable. . .
>
> Our conclusion is that by failing to find, and by decrying its duty to find, *a base upon which to fix the fair profit* — the commission has gone beyond the four quarters of the statute which vitalize it; and perchance has impinged upon the due process clause of the Constitution itself.[54]

In a 1956 decision, the Florida commission used the "cost of capital" as a substitute for the rate base. While it based rates on the utility's revenue requirements, it also determined the value of the firm's physical rate base and then translated the amount of revenue required into a percentage of such rate base.[55] And, finally, for a period of time in regulating natural gas producers, the FPC set rates on an area basis, rather than upon an individual utility cost of service basis.[56]

Property Valuation: Economic Concepts

Over the past several decades, many arguments, sometimes conflicting, have been presented in favor of, as well as against, each of the various measures of value. More recently, the various measures of value have been discussed extensively in two oil pipeline cases.[57] In this section, the major economic arguments will be analyzed. Although a distinction is frequently made between "reproduction cost" (or "current cost") and "replacement cost" on the one hand, and among "original cost," "book cost," and "prudent investment" on the other, these terms will be used synonymously and referred to as reproduction cost and original cost, respectively.

The Economics of Reproduction Cost

The economic case for reproduction cost is based upon its effectiveness in obtaining a proper allocation of the nation's resources.[58] During inflation — and assuming a constant rate of return — if the rates of public utilities are based upon original cost valuations, according to the argument, they will be lower than the rates of nonregulated industries, which would tend to reflect reproduction costs.[59] The rates of public utilities, in other words, will not be covering current costs of production. Such a situation will result in an excessive increase in the demand for the services of public utilities relative to the demand for other commodities and, in turn, will require an expansion in the capacity of public utilities' plants in order to satisfy the new demand.

On two grounds, economic resources will be improperly allocated. First, because consumers will not be paying current production costs, public utilities will be supplying services for wasteful consumption. Second, the new investment required will result in a disproportionate amount of resources being allocated to these industries. Likewise, when prices fall and the rates of public utilities are maintained above those of nonregulated industries, consumption and investment in public utilities are unduly restricted, again resulting in a poor allocation of resources.[60]

The argument of public utilities in favor of reproduction cost valuations is similar, although often expressed in a different manner. Their position can be summarized as follows. The earnings of nonregulated industries rise during inflation. For public utilities to (*1*) obtain necessary replacement funds, (*2*) maintain the real income of investors and prevent confiscation of their property, and (*3*) preserve their credit standing, their earnings also should rise. Increased earnings can be obtained by making adjustments in property valuations (and annual depreciation charges) in line with changes in the price level.[61]

While there is merit to these arguments, four basic problems arise from the concept and use of reproduction cost that make questionable its use as a proper measure of value.

The Resource Allocation Argument. The proposition that reproduction cost valuations will lead to a better allocation of resources is subject to three limitations. First, rates based on reproduction cost valuations will not result in "optimum" prices. The reproduction cost measure

. . . identifies reasonable rates with rates sufficient, in the aggregate, to cover total costs of service replacement including a capital-attracting rate of return on the hypothetical investment in a new plant. With a public utility or railroad system still operating at a scale at which further enhancements in rates of output can take place with less than a proportionate increase in operating and capital costs (conditions of decreasing unit costs), such rates will exceed the incremental or marginal costs of service. Yet, under the economists' theory of optimum pricing, the important relationship between prices and costs is an equality, under equilibrium conditions, between prices and *marginal* costs. Hence, if optimum resource allocation were to be accepted as the primary objective of rate-making policy, as the replacement-cost advocates insist, what would be required is not a mere transfer from an actual-cost standard to a replacement-cost standard, but rather a transfer from *any* standard of total cost to a standard of incremental cost.[62]

Second, the resource allocation argument fails to take into account the tax factor. In the preceding chapter, it was pointed out that public utilities are subject to heavy local, state, and federal taxes, and that these taxes represent a significant percentage of the utilities' annual revenues. Bonbright argues:

> Viewed from the standpoint of the consumers and of the companies that render utility service, the payment of these taxes is a part of the necessary costs of service. Viewed, however, from the standpoint of the nation or of the community, this payment cannot be relied upon to reflect, even in a rough and ready way, the *social* costs of service rendition — the burdens that the community as a whole could save by refraining from supplying the service. Yet the resource-allocation defense of replacement-cost rate control involves the assumption that the expenses incurred by the private producer of the service reflect social costs.[63]

Third, the resource allocation argument is valid only if an original cost valuation is further removed from a reproduction cost valuation for the property of public utilities than it is for the property of nonregulated industries. Both types of industries have plant and equipment that are the result of separate investments made over many years. At any given time, therefore, the depreciated original cost of each property item will differ. However, if replacement takes place at a more or less uniform rate, in addition to new construction, the total depreciated original cost is kept close to replacement cost. For example, on the assumption that a utility's property is retired at a uniform rate, that straight-line depreciation is used, and that net investment is 5 percent annually, Bernstein estimates that,

> . . . if the average length of useful life of the property were ten years,

20.9 percent of the property in a prudent investment valuation would be valued at the prices of the current year, and 77 percent of the property would be valued at the prices of the five most recent years. If the average length of useful life of the property were twenty years, 12.6 percent of the property would be valued at the prices of the current year, and 52 percent of the property would be valued at the prices of the five most recent years.[64]

Whether these assumptions are fully valid is not at issue.[65] The important point is that unless the ratio of reproduction cost to original cost for public utilities differs significantly from the comparable ratio for nonregulated industries, the resource allocation argument is invalid.[66]

An Imaginary Measure. Reproduction cost is an imaginary cost. The inherent uncertainties of the concept have been summarized by Wilcox:

(1) What is it that is being reproduced: a modern replacement for an old plant, the old plant in its original condition, or the old plant as it stands today? The assumption made in the McCardle case was that the company, starting fresh, would build its old plant in its depreciated condition, a purely imaginary procedure in which sane managements are unlikely to engage.

(2) Under what conditions is reproduction cost to occur: those originally existing or those existing at the present time? If the former, are allowances to be made to cover the possible cost, today, of cutting paths through forest long since razed, and hauling supplies by horse and wagon rather than train or truck? If the latter, are sums to be allowed for tearing down the buildings that might conceivably be standing where a railroad has lines, or for ripping up and then relaying pavements that did not exist when a water company first laid its mains? Company lawyers have lively imaginations. And though the more absurd of their inventions have been rejected by the courts, a certain residue remains.

(3) What methods of reproduction are to be assumed: simultaneous rebuilding of the whole plant involving large-scale operations and employing modern techniques, or piecemeal reconstruction on a small scale with techniques no longer in use? The latter assumption is the usual rule. And here, again, a procedure is imagined that no sane management would countenance.

(4) What prices are to be taken as representing reproduction cost: the spot prices of a particular day, the average prices of a recent period, or figures based on forecasts of the future? If spot prices, they change from day to day; the chosen day may not be represen-

tative. If average prices, they may be raised or lowered by changing the selected period. If either, the costs computed are those of the past and not the future. But if future prices are to be employed, valuation becomes a matter of guesswork, with the companies, presumably, guessing high and the commissions guessing low. Yet is was said by Justice Butler, speaking for the Court in the McCardle case, that forecasts of future prices should be made.[67]

As a result of these inherent uncertainties, three conclusions follow. First, even expert and enlightened judgment will lead to vastly different fair value estimates of the same property. In the *New York Telephone* case, six estimates were made: the majority of the commission, $367 million; a federal court, $397 million; the minority of the commission, $405.5 million; the court-appointed "master," $518 million; and two independent appraisals — one of $529 million, the other of $615 million.[68] Under these conditions, the determination of property valuations becomes a matter of bargaining between the utilities and the commissions. The final valuation chosen cannot be explained or defended on any economic grounds.

Second, the use of reproduction cost adds to regulatory delay. A typical rate case takes many months before the commission issues its final decision. The utility then may appeal the decision to the courts, hoping for a more favorable valuation. And litigation is not only expensive but also results in delay.

Finally, reproduction cost valuations are expensive. There are two frequently used methods of taking a utility's inventory for valuation purposes. (*1*) Prior to the establishment of continuing property records, utility and commission engineers had to spend months obtaining an inventory of the entire plant and equipment, and estimating its current value. "In theory, it means counting and valuing every nut and bolt and other items of property. . . . Even for a small utility company, this could be a burdensome, costly, and time-consuming job."[69] (*2*) When continuing property records are required, the inventory procedure is simplified. There still remains the problem, however, of valuing the property items, in addition to the problem of estimating accrued depreciation. The most widely used and inexpensive method of valuing property items is by "trending" original cost, which will be considered later in the chapter.

Maintenance of Investors' Real Income. The argument that the real income of investors should be maintained also has shortcomings. The argument assumes that the cost of reproducing a utility's property is a good measure of changes in the cost-of-living index. However, the index of construction costs, which should be used in reproduction cost valuations, and the index of living costs, which measures investors' purchasing power, are not the same. While they generally move in the same direction, the construction cost index has been considerably above the cost-of-living index for many years. In order to maintain investors' real income, reproduction cost valuations must be based upon the cost-of-living index. Yet, if this index is below the index of construction costs, the utilities would receive less than the necessary "reproduction cost"; if it is above, they would receive more.

More importantly, the use of either index overcompensates a utility's common stockholders when prices rise, and undercompensates them when prices fall. As interest on bonds and dividends on preferred stock are fixed or subject to a limited return, they do not change with the price level. Earnings on common stock, therefore, will change by more than the price level.[70] Thus, to maintain the real income of all investors, the returns on each type of security would necessarily have to be flexible. To maintain the real income of common stockholders, only their investment needs to be revalued as the price level rises.[71] Conversely, if the cost-of-living index declines, the earnings on common stock will fall even more sharply. "Just as regulation is not likely to permit the latter exigency to develop as a mere incident of a falling price level, so public policy need not support the magnifying of profits produced by a fortuitous rise in prices." [72]

The reproduction cost argument implies a second assumption — namely, that the allowable fair rate of return is firmly fixed. In fact, the rate of return is flexible and, if an inflationary adjustment is necessary (a subject considered in the next chapter), the commissions can increase it as the cost of capital changes. Public utilities contend that this solution is socially and politically unacceptable, as the rate of return would be much higher than that customarily looked on as the reasonable earning power of money. Furthermore, they argue, the adjustment would be in the wrong place, since it is the value of the property which is affected by inflation. But, as Wilcox has observed, the public "does not complain when the same effect is achieved through revaluation. For here, it does not realize what is going on. The companies center their attention on the rate base rather than the rate of return because valuation is a mystery and earnings can thus be boosted with greater ease." [73] In theory, by stabilizing property valuations, regulatory attention can be shifted to the rate of return — that is, to the earnings a utility needs to maintain its credit standing. Earnings regulation is thereby tied in with a utility's investment and service requirements. In practice, however, there is some truth to the utilities' contention, especially when one considers actual versus authorized rates of return over the past two decades.

Preservation of Utilities' Credit Standing. Closely connected with maintenance of investors' real income is the argument that public utilities must preserve their credit standing in order to attract additional capital for improvement and expansion. There is no one who would deny the validity of this argument. The question arises, therefore, as to whether the use of reproduction cost valuations will accomplish this goal better than will the use of original cost valuations.

Reproduction cost valuations result in a constantly fluctuating rate base. The Interstate Commerce Commission, for example, pointed out in the *St. Louis & O'Fallon* case that if the nation's railroads were valued on the basis of 1914 prices, their value would have been nearly $18 billion; in 1920, their value would have become $41 billion; and in 1923, their value would have dropped to $31 billion.[74] And, as pointed out above, only the common stockholders receive the gains and losses from reproduction cost valuations. "Obviously any method of valuation which concentrates upon the stockholders the gains and losses arising from charges in rates, tends to increase risks and introduces a speculative element in the provision for capital that is not conducive to obtaining capital at the lowest cost."[75]

The Economics of Original Cost

On *economic* grounds, reproduction cost valuations are exceedingly difficult to defend. Original cost valuations have two major advantages, but the measure is not devoid of controversy.

Administrative Advantages. Original cost is easily understood, results in inexpensive valuations, and can be efficiently administered. The accounting practices of public utilities are controlled and are based upon original cost. Therefore, because the commissions can easily obtain original cost valuations that are not subject to estimates and speculation, they are able to dispose of rate cases in the shortest possible period of time and with a minimum expense to all concerned. It must not be implied that ratemaking should become a mechanical or routine process based solely on accounting data and formulas. On the contrary, while this danger is always present, by simplifying the process of establishing the rate base, attention is shifted to the rate of return; a determination that will always be the subject of controversy.[76] Rather, the advantages of original cost valuations lie in that they (*1*) reduce the number of controversial issues per rate case and (*2*) force the utilities and commissions to consider the relation of rate regulation to investment needs.[77] This consideration represents the basic purpose of rate regulation and is of much more significance than property valuations. As Troxel has put it:

> Trying to achieve these ends [successful operation, financial integrity, and attraction of capital], commissions must look to the future; even if they rely on past experiences and allow enough earnings to cover the present interest and dividend obligations, they still must keep their eyes on the future demands for service, future operating expenses, and other future investment conditions. The future is more significant than the past; earnings and costs in years to come are more important than historical facts about property costs, past earnings, and recorded expenses.[78]

It should be emphasized again that there may be some controversy, under an original cost basis, among the three frequently used measures —

original cost, book or investment cost, and prudent investment. However, compared with the controversy and uncertainty which inevitably arise over the proper determination of reproduction cost, these differences are relatively minor.

Credit Standing and Capital Attraction. The use of an original cost rate base enables public utilities to maintain their credit standing and to attract new capital. Investors receive a rate of return on the money which they have invested in the utility. At the time an investment decision is made, investors consider the expected future rate of return. The expected or anticipated rate, of course, will vary with the financial position of the utility and the general economic situation of the country. For this reason, the allowable rate of return cannot be inflexible. The important point, however, is that an original cost rate base serves this purpose better than one based upon reproduction cost. As Bonbright has explained: "Whatever scheme of rate regulation will put investors in a position to draw this balance between present outlay and anticipated future return with the most confidence is the scheme most likely to permit a well-managed company to maintain sound financial health at a minimum 'cost of capital' to the consumers."[79]

Many executives of public utilities will agree with the validity of these advantages of original cost valuations, at least in theory. Yet, somewhat ironically, they frequently use the same arguments when advocating reproduction cost valuations. Their argument for reproduction cost is predicated on two beliefs: the inevitability of continuing inflation in the economy, so that reproduction cost valuations will remain above, or at least equal to, those based on original cost; and the previously mentioned factor that commissions are unlikely to make the necessary adjustments for inflation in the allowable rate of return. The truth of the first belief can be proven quickly: if the price level should fall sharply, many present supporters of reproduction cost valuations and price level depreciation would become advocates of original cost measures. The second belief will be discussed in the following chapter.

Property Valuation: Current Practices and Problems

The Supreme Court has indicated its willingness to leave the choice of proper measures of value to the commissions. What measures do the commissions employ? When reproduction cost or fair value measures are used, how are values determined? What are the current problems with respect to property valuations? The issues raised by these questions are considered in this section.

Current Measures of Value

The two federal commissions concerned with the valuation problem —

the FCC and the FERC — base property valuations on original cost.[80] Among the state commissions, practices vary. In a study of the impact of the *Hope* decision on utility valuations, Rose found that twenty-seven state commissions changed from fair value to original cost.[81] That trend has continued. As of 1985, in regulating electric, gas, or telephone utilities, forty-three commissions (including the District of Columbia commission) use original cost or prudent investment, eight use fair value or current value, and two consider all evidence presented.[82]

Measures of Reproduction Cost

Where reproduction cost or fair value measures are employed, two important issues arise.[83] First, how should reproduction cost be determined? Second, what weight should the commissions attach to this measure in arriving at a fair value rate base? Only generalized answers can be given to these questions, for each rate case is unique in that the evidence presented and accepted varies according to the case, industry, state, and year.

With respect to the first question, reproduction cost estimates usually are obtained in three ways. (*1*) General price indices are used. These indices include the Bureau of Labor Statistics' "Consumer Price Index" or the Gross National Product deflator. The resulting estimate, frequently referred to as "reproduction cost new," represents the original cost of the property expressed in dollars of current purchasing power.[84] (*2*) Construction cost indices are used. The most widely employed construction cost index is the "Handy-Whitman Index of Public Utility Construction Costs." The resulting valuation is known as "trended" original cost.[85] As with general price indices, the purpose of the index is to translate original costs into values expressed in current dollars. (*3*) Unit cost pricing is employed. This method involves pricing like units of property directly by means of price indices representing the price movement of the specific property under consideration.[86]

The advantages and disadvantages of each of these methods have been enumerated in journal articles, as well as in commission and court decisions, for many years.[87] If reproduction cost valuations are to be made, unit cost pricing would seem to be the most desirable. General price indices measure purchasing power changes and are entirely unrelated to the cost of reproducing the property of any particular utility. Such a valuation represents an imaginary figure. Construction cost indices, while more closely related to the actual cost of constructing buildings and equipment, have the same general drawbacks. However, when like units of property cannot be easily identified or separated, either general price indices or construction cost indices must be used in obtaining a reproduction cost valuation.

With respect to the second question concerning the weighting problem, the commissions generally do not allow the full valuation estimate based upon reproduction cost or trended original cost. As a result, the final valuation figure chosen represents a compromise. In his 1962 study, for example, Rose concluded:

> The Illinois Commission has assigned one-quarter weight to reproduction cost and three-quarters to original cost; Alabama has assigned one-third to reproduction cost and two-thirds to original cost; Minnesota, Delaware, Pennsylvania, and Arizona have given approximately equal weight to each element. North Carolina and Indiana have also attributed equal weight to each in some proceedings, but in others have given greater weight to original cost. New Mexico, Maryland, and New Jersey have used original cost as the principal factor and added an increment to compensate for reproduction cost, while Missouri has given "greater weight" to original cost than to reproduction cost. And in Kentucky, Nebraska, and Montana, where the statutes also require fair value, no generalization at all can be made concerning the findings of the regulatory authorities.[88]

Used and Useful, Prudent Investment, and Excess Capacity

There are several valuation issues that are of particular significance to the electric utility industry. Under traditional ratemaking principles, public utilities are entitled to recover "prudent" investments when they become "used and useful." Certain items may be excluded from the rate base, including "excess capacity." But since the late 1970s, it has become clear that all three terms lack precise definitions.

Used and Useful. For decades, used and useful referred to needed capacity; that is, a determination as to whether a plant was actually used in service and was useful in providing service. If not, or if any expenditures were imprudent, all or part of the investment in a plant would be excluded from rate base. Today, however, used and useful has been held by some commissions to be a broader concept. The Massachusetts commission, to cite one example, holds that under the used and useful standard it must "determine whether a utility investment is needed *and economically desirable.*"[89] Explains the commission:

> ... Need for a new electric utility production plant is established if it can be shown that the investment in question can provide either capacity which is required by the utility or energy, at a net cost which is lower than the cost of the capacity which it displaces. Once need for capacity or reliability, as the case may be, and/or energy savings has been established, the [Commission] then must determine the extent to which an investment is useful and thus the extent to which a return should be allowed on the investment. . . .[90]

Thus, a threshold issue arises: Are the used and useful test and the prudent investment test two distinct tests and, if so, must both tests be satisfied before an investment will be included in the rate base?

Prudent Investment.[91] Prudence, according to *The Random House Dictionary*, "is care, caution, and good judgment, as well as wisdom in looking ahead. . . ."[92] Prudence thus involves foresight, not hindsight. Decisions must be judged as to their reasonableness at the time they were made and not after the fact. To quote two commissions:

> A prudence review must determine whether the company's actions, based on all that it knew or should have known at the time were reasonable and prudent in light of the circumstances which then existed. It is clear that such a determination may not properly be made on the basis of hindsight judgments, nor is it appropriate for the [commission] merely to substitute its best judgment for the judgments made by the company's managers.[93]

* * *

> . . . the company's conduct should be judged by asking whether the conduct was reasonable at the time, under all the circumstances, considering that the company had to solve its problems prospectively rather than in reliance on hindsight. In effect, our responsibility is to determine how reasonable people would have performed the task that confronted the company.[94]

In their prudence investigations, commissions have disallowed billions of dollars due to imprudence, generally running between 8 and 15 percent of a plant's final cost,[95] but sometimes much higher. The New York commission, for instance, found that $1.395 billion of Long Island Lighting's Shoreham plant (about 30 percent of the estimated total cost of $4.62 billion) was incurred because of construction imprudence.[96] Construction-related issues, however, are only one aspect of prudence reviews. Disallowances have been made because (*a*) of excess capacity (discussed below), (*b*) a plant should have been canceled sooner,[97] (*c*) the capacity cost more than it should have cost in terms of alternative energy sources[98] or the optimal supply alternative,[99] and/or (*d*) cost overruns related to Nuclear Regulatory Commission (or other regulatory bodies) policy changes were not supported.[100] In some of these cases, it should be noted, disallowances were based upon the used and useful test; they were not found to be imprudent.[101]

Excess Capacity. Excess capacity has been defined as "capacity over and above that necessary to meet peak demand plus that capacity to insure that there is a margin to allow for day-to-day variations in the operating condition of installed generation."[102] For electric utilities, a 15 to 20 percent reserve margin has been viewed historically as necessary. But ever since the

Arab oil embargo in 1973, the industry's reserve margin has climbed, remaining above 30 percent over the last decade (and nearer to 50 percent for some firms). Notes Studness: "The recent frightful cost escalations of nuclear plant construction, of course, proved to be the catalyst that finally precipitated the realization that the industry's excess capacity is no longer an unavoidable product of unforeseeable events. Similarly, disallowance has emerged as the vehicle with which ratepayers are attempting to shift the costs of excess capacity onto shareholders."[103]

The possibility of excess capacity raises several regulatory problems. How, for example, should excess capacity be identified? The most common method is physical excess capacity: capacity determined to be over-and-above a required reserve margin.[104] Is excess capacity plant specific or system specific? It is generally considered to be plant specific. To illustrate: The Pennsylvania commission determined that 945 megawatts of Pennsylvania Power & Light's interest in Susquehanna Unit 2 were excess and disallowed $443.2 million,[105] while the Kansas commission determined that 327 megawatts of Kansas Gas & Electric's interest in Wolf Creek were excessive and disallowed $716.3 million.[106] In contrast, in an earlier case, the Pennsylvania commission determined that Philadelphia Electric's investment in Salem Unit 1 resulted in 775 megawatts of excess capacity and disallowed $25 million based on *"the least economical units."*[107]

Ratemaking Treatment. Whenever disallowances are made, the issue of their proper ratemaking treatment arises. Construction-related imprudent investment is generally excluded from the rate base and written off.[108] All other disallowances, including these for excess capacity, are generally shared between the ratepayers and the stockholders by (*a*) excluding the excess investment from the rate base, allowing no return[109] or a return to be deferred until the investment is deemed used and useful[110] or (*b*) including the excess investment in the rate base, but deducting from revenue requirements a complete[111] or partial[112] equity return, while permitting annual operating and maintenance expenses and annual depreciation.[113] In the Kansas commission's original decision regarding Kansas Gas & Electric's investment in Wolf Creek, for example, 10 percent was disallowed as construction imprudence (without recovery), 68 percent was excluded from the rate base (but with recovery through annual depreciation charges), and 22 percent was included in the rate base (with recovery of and full return on).[114]

Critics of such significant disallowances have argued that risk-sharing methodologies have both financial consequences (including higher capital costs and, possibly, bankruptcy) and future investment disincentives.[115] And while the actual treatment adopted by a commission has been constrained by its impact on the financial strength of the particular utility, far too little attention has been paid to the investment disincentive issue.[116]

Mega Additions to Plant in Service: Phase-in Plans

For electric utilities adding new generating capacity, the cost of a new power plant — even after disallowances — may represent a large proportion of the net book cost of the firm's existing assets.[117] Long Island Lighting's Shoreham nuclear power station, to illustrate, was estimated (in 1983) to increase the company's rate base by approximately 150 percent (from $1.8 billion to more than $4.4 billion) and to increase the average cost per kilowatt-hour supplied to its customers by 40 to 50 percent. What ratemaking procedures should be adopted to cushion or avoid such rate shocks (also known as front-end charges) to consumers?

The inclusion of construction work in progress (CWIP) in the rate base (without an AFUDC offset) would spread the rate impact over the entire construction period and would smooth out the rate increases associated with such plant additions. In most cases, as discussed in a later section, the full inclusion of CWIP in the rate base has not been permitted. As a result, several commissions have adopted phase-in plans, whereby the investment in a plant (found used and useful and/or prudent) is placed in the rate base over a number of years, along with the associated carrying charges. Thus, the Missouri commission authorized an eight-year phase-in plan for Union Electric's Callaway nuclear plant, involving six years of rate increases (14 percent the first year, 10 percent the second, and 7.29 percent in each of the third through sixth years) and two years of recovery of deferred charges (in this instance, deferred equity return).[118] At least four critical questions underlie all such phase-in proposals. Does the plan contribute adequately to the cash flow position of the utility?[119] What is the added risk to the firm from deferring the recovery of invested capital?[120] Are lower rates to current ratepayers favored over higher rates to future ratepayers?[121] Is the plan in conformity with FASB Statement No. 71?[122]

A similar situation applies to natural gas and oil pipelines. Consider the proposed Alaska Natural Gas Transportation System. Argues Streiter:

> ... A project such as the Alaska gas pipeline may never be built, despite the fact that on a present worth basis it more than pays off. The *value* of the gas will rise with inflation, but under current regulatory practices the *price* will fall over time, starting at a level of up to $20 per Mcf (or three times market prices) and ending up at $6 per Mcf. (By this time the real value of Alaskan gas will exceed the tariff rate many times over.) The Alaska pipeline may be the extreme example, but such absurdities are repeated continually. ... [123]

Various trended original cost methodologies have been proposed to level tariffs in such situations.[124] Yet, their application raises a number of both practical and policy issues, including "avoiding cash-flow problems during the transition, obtaining agreement on what the new rules are to be, and assuring investors that future regulators cannot change the rules to eliminate past write-ups."[125] Cash flows, for instance, would be relatively low during the early years under the proposed trending methods, which might require the indexing of bonds.[126] Trending might be applied to the entire rate base, to equity only, or only to new plant.[127] Investors would have to accept rate base write-ups instead of current income.[128]

Accrued Depreciation

Whatever measure of value is used to determine the rate base, depreciation must be deducted. In accounting terms, this deduction from a utility's property valuation is known as "accrued depreciation." And, as with other regulatory problems, both the role and measurement of accrued depreciation have been the subject of controversy. A former president of the National Association of Regulatory Utility Commissioners has stated:

> More confusion has arisen with respect to, or has been injected into, regulatory thinking with regard to depreciation in rate making than seems possible.
>
> In rate making, the deduction has run the gamut from
> (1) no deduction at all, to
> (2) deduction of an engineering determination,
> (3) deduction of the accumulated accounting reserve for depreciation, and
> (4) to the deduction of a computed amount which it is alleged the accountants *should* have accumulated if they had known what they were doing.
>
> The pendulum has indeed swung far, and the process hasn't been free from political influence.[129]

The meaning of, and need for, depreciation accounting have already been discussed.[130] The need for accrued depreciation was succinctly stated by the Interstate Commerce Commission in a 1931 case:

> An article when new contains a certain number of units of service and as those units are exhausted the article depreciates. In order to make any figure, whether of original cost or cost of reproduction, representative of the condition of the property at the time of the inquiry it would seem on principle to be necessary to make due allowance for the expired units of service life.[131]

Consequently, if the straight-line method of depreciation is used, a unit of property that has a life of thirty years and that has been employed for fifteen years in providing service would be depreciated 50 percent.[132]

Consistency with Depreciation Accounting

Closely connected with the above is the need for consistency; depreciation in the accounting sense and in the valuation sense are the same. Property that is used up in service is a charge to operating costs. As it is consumed, the investment in the property is decreased by an equal deduction from its value. In the words of the Federal Power Commission:

> The determination of the annual allowance (annual expenses) for depletion, depreciation, and amortization (sometimes referred to jointly as depreciation) and the accrued depreciation in the properties must be consistent. This is a simple statement of what should be regarded as a universal truth in the regulation of rates. It is so regarded by the overwhelming majority of the regulatory authorities of the country, and by students and writers on the subject. It is so regarded by sound business management outside of the utility rate case field.[133]

The need for consistency, however, has not always been recognized. Following the *Knoxville Water Company* case of 1909, "observed depreciation" was usually accepted as a measure of accrued depreciation.[134] According to this concept, depreciation is "a subnormal or rundown condition of a physical plant — one which is below the proper maximum condition in which the plant can be and should be permanently maintained in order to render adequate service."[135] The physical deterioration of a plant, as estimated by expert engineers, was commonly measured as the "percent condition" of old equipment relative to new. Thus, a percent condition of 90 would mean that small amounts of deferred maintenance and accrued depreciation should be deducted from the property valuation. In approving observed depreciation in one 1926 case, the Court held: "The testimony of competent valuation engineers who examined the property and made estimates in respect of its condition is to be preferred to mere calculations based on averages and assumed probabilities."[136] Yet, the inconsistency of the Court can be seen from another 1926 decision in which it rejected a commission's effort to deduct accrued depreciation, saying: "Consumers pay for service, not for the property used to render it. Their payments are not contributions to depreciation . . . or to capital of the company."[137]

When depreciation accounting is used in computing operating costs and either observed depreciation or no depreciation in determining the rate base, the utility gains at the expense of consumers, and the whole concept of accrued depreciation becomes void of meaning. The first would increase revenues by increasing allowable operating costs. The second would also increase revenues by decreasing the deduction from the property value and, in addition, would force consumers to pay a rate of return on an investment already charged to operating costs. The two positions are inconsistent.[138] The Supreme Court has never explicitly accepted the depreciation reserve as the proper measure of accrued depreciation. In the *Hope* case, however, the

Federal Power Commission rejected a percent condition deduction for accrued depreciation.[139] The Court did not comment on this position.

Accrued Depreciation and Original Cost Valuations

The vast majority of the commissions deduct the depreciation reserve as shown on the utility's books when an original cost rate base valuation is used. As noted at length above, this position is economically sound.[140] But under certain conditions, commissions deduct what is called the "reserve requirement." The reserve requirement is simply a commission's estimate of what a utility's depreciation reserve should be. Compared with this hypothetical reserve, a utility may have either an excessive or, more commonly, a deficient depreciation reserve. Excessive reserves occur when a utility makes conservative estimates of service life and obsolescence by fixing high annual rates of depreciation or when a commission prescribes conservative rates.[141] Deficient reserves result from low annual depreciation rates, the use of retirement accounting prior to effective commission control, the inability to recover from earnings the depreciation which has already occurred, and unexpected technological obsolescence.

When a commission uses the reserve requirement for ratemaking purposes, care must be exercised. If, for example, a utility has a deficient depreciation reserve and a higher reserve requirement is deducted from the property valuation, the financial condition of the company can be seriously affected. Especially is this true when original cost valuations are used in determining property values. For this reason, many commissions refuse to adjust the depreciation reserve unless a utility ignores depreciation expenses so that dividends can be higher. But commission procedure is not uniform.[142]

Accrued Depreciation and Fair Value

In fair value jurisdictions, the proper measure of accrued depreciation is subject to wide differences of opinion. Frequently, the deduction for depreciation is based on the "field method" and/or "office method." The field method involves a physical inspection of representative samples of the various types of the utility's property "in order to ascertain outward manifestation of depreciation."[143] The office method involves "an age-life study of the property existing in the various plant accounts; *i.e.*, a study of the relationship of the age of the property as determined from book records to the expected life of such property."[144] The two methods may be used together, with each given a specific weight so as to determine a composite percentage of depreciation. As explained by the Ohio commission:

The commission's engineering staff, on the basis of their own studies, estimated that the depreciation to be deducted from the reproduction cost new as of the date certain was 8.4 percent. Their estimate was based upon both a field study and an actuarial or office study. The field study consisted of an actual inspection of all of the company's larger installations, as well as an actual inspection of samples of those types of property that are commonly designated as the "mass accounts." The latter include poles, pole lines, aerial wire, etc. The results of the field inspections were converted into percentages by accounts and an average percentage of depreciation was determined for each property account.

The staff's office study consisted of age-life analyses by property accounts. The average service life and the average expired life was estimated for the property in each account. The ratios of expired life to average service life were then applied to depreciation curves. Each of these curves is derived from property mortality data and represents the loci of points each of which shows the percentage of depreciation associated with a given percentage of expired life. Thus, once the type of curve appropriate to the particular account is selected and the ratio of expired life to average service life is determined for the property in the account, the percentage of depreciation is simply the point on the vertical axis corresponding to the point on the curve given by the ratio of expired life to average service life. In this way a percentage of depreciation was estimated for each property account. The results of the office study and the field study were then averaged by accounts to arrive at the staff's final estimate of depreciation.[145]

Bonbright has argued that it is difficult to reconcile commission treatment of depreciation "with any basic 'theory' of reasonable public utility rates."[146] When fair value is used, he suggests:

If this [fair] value were to be derived from a record of actual construction cost, the allowance for "depreciation" should reflect any fall in value, not otherwise recognized, that may have taken place since the date of the construction. If, as is more plausible for older properties, the value were to be deducted from an estimate of current replacement cost — and the relevant replacement cost, despite some judicial opinions to the contrary, is the cost of a modern substitute plant — the deduction for "depreciation" should summarize the value inferiority of the existing property, including the inferiority due to liability to earlier retirement. This deduction, moreover, should be subject to a partial offset for any superior quality of the present plant over the hypothetical modern substitute — a superiority often claimed in the early railroad valuations, in the form of allowances for roadbed solidification.[147]

At the same time, it is difficult to explain the logic of deducting observed depreciation, however measured, from a reproduction cost or fair value rate base determined by general price indices. Such a property valuation, as noted earlier, represents a purely imaginary figure.

Other Elements of Value

While the determination of the depreciated value of the tangible and reproducible property has occupied most of the courts', commissions', and utilities' time, several other elements of value also have received attention — working capital allowances, property held for future use, land, intangibles, and customer contributions. Each will be briefly discussed below. The issues surrounding construction work in progress will be considered in the next section.

Working Capital Allowance

The question of working capital must be considered in every rate case and several important problems are raised in determining a suitable allowance. Working capital — the funds representing necessary investment in materials and supplies, and the cash required to meet current obligations and to maintain minimum bank balances — is included in the rate base so that investors are compensated for capital they have supplied to a utility. The amount required largely depends on a utility's purchasing and billing methods, as well as its construction program. When purchases are made on credit, when deposits or payments are required in advance, when accruals are made for the payment of taxes in advance of payment dates, or when customers pay for the service at the time it is used, working capital requirements may be small. When materials and supplies must be purchased long before use, when customers are billed monthly, quarterly, semiannually, or even annually, or when the business is seasonal, such requirements may be large.

The calculation of an electric utility's working capital allowance is illustrated in Table 8-2. The cash component may be determined in three basic ways. (1) A detailed lead/lag study, which measures the amount of time before expenses must be paid (expense lead) and compares it with the amount of time before revenues are received (revenue lag). (2) A formula approach (developed to avoid a costly lead/lag study in every case), which commonly uses one-eighth of a utility's annual operating and maintenance expenses, excluding fuel and purchased power. The factor of one-eighth equates to a forty-five-day time lag between the rendering of the service by a utility and payment by the customer.[148] (3) The balance sheet method, representing the difference between a utility's current assets and current liabilities.[149] The allowance for materials and supplies is based upon a utility's

TABLE 8-2

Working Capital Allowance

Cash Component	
One-eighth of Adjusted Operation and Maintenance Expense, Excluding Fuel and Purchased Power	$ 43,106,000
Fuel Lag	5,145,000
TOTAL CASH COMPONENT	$ 48,251,000
PLUS: Materials and Supplies	$ 35,369,000
Fossil Fuel Inventory	59,679,000
Deferred Nuclear Fuel (Net of Tax)	6,544,000
Deferred Quarto Coal (Net of Tax)	23,289,000
TOTAL	$124,881,000
LESS: Customer Deposits	$ 3,734,000
Tax Offset	
One-fourth of Adjusted Taxes, Excluding FICA, Deferred Taxes, and ODOE	31,638,000
TOTAL	$ 35,372,000
WORKING CAPITAL ALLOWANCE	$137,760,000

Source: *Re Ohio Edison Co.,* 61 PUR4th 241, 258 (Ohio, 1984).

inventories that are held for future operation and use.[150] In addition to these two items, a credit is frequently made for accrued taxes[151] and/or customer deposits,[152] while an allowance may be made for fuel (such as coal or oil inventories, gas storage underground, unrecovered fuel costs)[153] and for compensating balances.[154]

Property Held for Future Use

Property held for future use is the amount of investment in property and plant which is not being used currently by a utility to provide service. Generally, such property is land, purchased when available, for potential future use (such as an office building or a generating site). The rule that most commissions follow in deciding whether to include or exclude such property is one based upon a time limitation; that is, if the property has an expected in-service data within a reasonable time period (commonly two to ten years),[155] it is included in the rate base. As the District of Columbia commission noted in a 1979 case, suitable generating sites in the Washington metropolitan area were scarce and rapidly increasing in value. Inclusion in the rate base would provide an incentive to the utility to acquire suitable sites as soon as possible.[156]

Land

Except for natural gas utilities, the valuation of land is of little importance in ratemaking cases. Unlike most other items in the rate base, land represents a small portion of total property, has no cost of production, and tends to appreciate in value. Generally, commissions value land on an original cost basis, although an estimate of its current value is used when fair value property valuations are made.[157]

The Supreme Court approved the Federal Power Commission's procedure of valuing natural gas land on an original cost basis in 1934.[158] Troxel has argued that this is the proper measure:

> The market price of gas land is not altogether independent of utility service prices: utility consumers buy most of the gas of Appalachian fields, and they buy much of the natural gas output in other areas. If circular reasoning is avoided, a property value cannot be based on the prices that are subject to public control. Another consideration goes against a return on the market price of natural gas land. Gas companies obtain revenue from consumers that is used to cover the gas exploration costs. Since buyers pay some or all of the costs of gas discoveries, they should not pay a return, too, on increases in land prices.[159]

Intangibles

It will be recalled that the Supreme Court, in the *Smyth* case, listed six specific measures of value and then added: "We do not say that there may not be other matters to be regarded in estimating the value of the property."[160] Almost immediately, public utilities claimed allowances for several intangibles, the most important being good will, franchise value, water rights, leaseholds, and going concern value. These items should properly be included in the rate base, they argued, because the value of a utility is more than just the value of its physical property. While the commissions and courts have often supported this contention and have made allowances for these items in the past, few are currently included in rate bases.

Good Will. Good will has been defined by the Superior Court as "that element of value which inheres in the fixed and favorable consideration of customers, arising from an established and well-known and well-conducted business."[161] It is, in short, the value of customer loyalty and is recognized as an element in the market value of competitive firms.

When consumers have no alternative sources of supply, however, as is the case with most public utilities, no special value can be attached to the company-customer relationship. As early as 1909, in the *Consolidated Gas* case, the Court recognized this point: "The complainant has a monopoly in fact, and a consumer must take gas from it or go without. He will resort to the 'old stand' because he cannot get gas anywhere else."[162] To include good will in the rate base would involve circular reasoning: its value depends on a utility's earnings which, in turn, depend on the rates established by the commission. Its inclusion, therefore, would permit the capitalization of expected future earnings. Good will has not been accepted for purposes of ratemaking.[163]

Franchise Value. A public utility must receive a franchise (or a certificate of public convenience and necessity) before it may serve a market area. As only one utility usually is authorized to serve a given market, it represents a monopoly grant. If the utility is then permitted to earn an excessive return, the franchise will become valuable. "To measure a separate franchise value, the company estimates the future earnings above a reasonable return on the tangible property value, and discounts these excess earnings at the probable fair rate of return. A franchise valuation is a capitalization of the earnings that regulators should take away from a utility firm."[164]

Inclusion of a franchise value in the rate base, therefore, would require consumers to pay a permanent return on a monopoly privilege which they granted. Moreover, it would prevent justifiable rate reductions to consumers. Only in a few cases when a city has made a charge for a franchise does the sum so invested belong in the rate base. The Court has supported this position since 1912.[165]

Water Rights. Electric, irrigation, and water utilities possess water rights to use and dispose of flowing water. Some of these rights are acquired when a utility purchases a piece of land — streams and rivers flowing through the land and subsurface water recovered by sinking wells. Other rights are given by local, state, and federal governments. Especially important are the rights granted by the Federal Energy Regulatory Commission which controls the power sites on navigable streams and federal government land. Like franchises, however, these rights have no special value for regulatory purposes; the value of the rights is determined by the expected future earnings of a utility.

Only a few cases involving water rights have come before the Supreme Court. In 1914 and again in 1923, water rights valuations were granted.[166] Three years later, the Court said, "the evidence sustains an amount in excess of 10 percent to cover water rights and going value...."[167] But in the *Indianapolis Water Company* case, when the utility claimed water rights had a value of at least $1 million, Justice Black, in his dissenting opinion, could not believe

> ... that, even if the people of Indianapolis and the surrounding community have permitted the Water Company to use this stream for a public service, there has been a grant of a prescriptive right which can be capitalized by the Company, in order to exact higher water rates from the very people who granted the privilege.[168]

No Supreme Court decision since that time has dealt with the issue of water rights. However, the cost of acquiring water rights, as well as waterpower sites, is usually included in the rate base.[169]

Leaseholds. A common practice of gas utilities is to lease, rather than purchase, the land from which they hope to obtain natural gas. The leases are usually bought and paid for, and their cost included in the rate base. If gas is discovered, the market value of a leasehold will tend to rise. Should the increased value also be included in the rate base?

For many years, a few commissions thought so, allowing some or all of the increases in the market value of leases. While affording an incentive to exploration, this practice also granted the utilities an unearned increment on which to base an annual return. Moreover, as pointed out above, consumers pay for the costs of developing natural gas land. The present practice, and one followed by the Federal Energy Regulatory Commission in determining pipeline rates, is to value leaseholds at their original cost. While the Supreme Court has not always agreed, it approved this measure of value in 1945.[170]

Going Concern Value. Going concern value can be defined as "the difference in value existing between a plant in successful operation and a similar plant assembled but not yet functioning."[171] No cost measure of this value has ever been devised, making it "purely hypothetical" and the "most intangible of all the intangibles."[172]

Going concern value has sometimes been thought of in terms of development costs: establishing an organization, recruiting and training personnel, developing administrative procedures, acquiring a market, and soliciting business. It has also been thought of as compensating a firm for the accumulated deficits it may have sustained in the earlier years of its development. Both concepts have been rejected by the Supreme Court.[173] Development costs have already been charged to operating costs; the losses of previous years cannot be compensated unless excess profits can also be recovered and, in any event, past deficits should not be capitalized. There seems to be no cost basis for going concern value.[174]

Until 1933, however, going concern value was recognized by the commissions and courts, and a separate allowance was usually included in the rate base. In the *Knoxville Water Company* case in 1909, the Supreme Court said there was an "added value of the plant as a whole over the sum of the values of its component parts, which is attached to it because it is in active and successful operation and earning a return."[175] And in the *McCardle* decision of 1926, Justice Butler said the "evidence is more than sufficient to sustain 9.5 percent for going value."[176] As the Court neither required a separate going concern allowance nor said how such values were to be measured, most commissions simply added a flat 10 percent to the value of tangible property in determining the rate base. But the Court reversed its position in 1933, when it upheld the California commission's rejection of a claimed allowance of $9 million. The Court observed that "an examination of the evidence offered by the company ... shows it to be of a highly speculative and uncertain character."[177] Similarly, in the *Natural Gas Pipeline* case, the Court could not find a basis for a separate going concern value.[178]

Although they may still be influenced by the concept when they determine the value of tangible property, few commissions now add a separate allowance for value as a going concern in ratemaking cases.[179] As Troxel has observed, this is as it should be: "The going-concern value depends on a franchise or certificate; it is, in fact, another name for a franchise or certificate value. It is a social value, and belongs to the public instead of the public utility company."[180]

Customer Contributions

Since the purpose of establishing a rate base is to determine the dollar amount of the investment in used and useful utility plant that has been supplied by investors, there are various deductions that must be considered when capital contributions are made by customers. Three items are frequently considered.[181] First, customer deposits. Where customers are required to make deposits, they are deducted from the rate base so that ratepayers are not providing a return on money which they have supplied to the utility. However, since interest is paid on such deposits, the interest must be charged to operating expenses. Second, customer advances for construction and/or contributions in aid of construction. When a new customer is not near existing facilities or requires unusual facilities, utilities may require advances.[182] When advances are made by customers for construction work, they are frequently refunded at some future date and, for accounting purposes, are recorded in the account "Customer Advances for Construction." But when advances represent donations or contributions in cash, services, and/or property, and when they are not subject to future refund, they are recorded in the account "Contributions in Aid of Construction." For ratemaking purposes, the commissions generally deduct such customer advances from a utility's rate base, although "utilities always have been allowed to include depreciation on contributed property as a legitimate operating expense."[183] Third, deferred taxes, resulting from accelerated depreciation, and the investment tax credit (pre-1971). These items are generally deducted from the rate base, unless they are included in a utility's capital structure (at a zero cost rate).

Construction Work in Progress[184]

For many years, it was a common practice to include in the rate base an allowance for "overhead" construction costs. Such an allowance included the costs of incorporation; legal, engineering, and administrative services; and interest, insurance, and taxes during construction. Prior to the development of uniform systems of accounts, 15 percent of the total value of the property was the frequent allowance, although several commissions never accepted any percentages without supporting figures showing actual cost.[185]

With the development of uniform systems of accounts, utilities were required to enter all costs incurred during construction. The FPC's Uniform System of Accounts (effective January 1, 1937), to illustrate, provided that the "cost of construction properly includable in the electric plant accounts shall include," among other overhead costs, "interest during construction," defined as "the net cost of borrowed funds used for construction purposes and a reasonable rate upon the utility's own funds when so used." Interest during construction was capitalized and, when the plant went into service, the accumulated interest was added to the book cost of such plant and the total amount included in the rate base. For ratemaking purposes, the utility then depreciated the total amount over the useful life of the plant.[186]

In 1971, the FPC abandoned the term "interest during construction" and substituted "allowance for funds used during construction" (AFUDC) in its systems of accounts. The commission developed a formula for computing the maximum AFUDC rate annually; a formula which includes the net cost of borrowed funds used for construction purposes and a reasonable rate on other funds when so used.[187] Under the formula, the embedded book-cost rates for the prior year are used for debt and preferred stock, while the cost rate for common equity "shall be the rate granted common equity in the last rate proceeding before the rate-making body having primary rate jurisdiction. If such cost rate is not available, the average rate actually earned during the preceding three years shall be used." Further, since 1977, AFUDC has been segregated into two component parts — borrowed funds and other funds. The former have been assigned to the "interest charges" section of the income statement; the latter remain in the "other income and deductions" section.

While many support this procedure from an accounting point of view and while consumer groups universally contend that the procedure results in a correct match of costs and benefits between present and future customers,[188] economic events over the past decade have caused a reevaluation for ratemaking purposes. Starting in the late 1960s, costs of both construction and capital began to increase dramatically, and construction periods (particularly for electric utilities) were greatly extended.[189] The AFUDC accounts became very large. Such accounts, it must be noted, even though properly included in a utility's income statement, are "paper" rather than cash earnings.[190] By 1980, AFUDC had increased to over 50 percent of the electric industry's return on common equity, equal to $1.38 per share of common stock.[191] Since the typical electric utility has a pay-out ratio in excess of 50 percent, companies were in effect being forced to borrow funds to pay common stock dividends. Further, the investment community gradually began to question the quality of a utility's earnings when AFUDC was a significant amount.[192] As the Oklahoma commission summarized:

> In theory, AFUDC as a component of construction cost, to recognize that capital is tied up, was acceptable, but in practice (today) it is not proving satisfactory or viable. An unacceptably high percent of net income is reflected by AFUDC, which does not help cash flow or generation (it is "funny money," however, it is an actual capitalized dollar figure); nor does it improve the company's earnings coverage of interest charges or its ability to finance at the lowest and reasonable rates.[193]

Confronted with severe cash flow problems and inadequate coverage ratios, many commissions began to permit all or part of CWIP in the rate base.[194] However, actual practices vary considerably as to the amount of, and the conditions under which, CWIP will be included. Thus, several commissions permit its inclusion on projects expected to be completed within a reasonable time (six months to a year is a common requirement[195]); the FERC, which for years permitted inclusion only where a utility was in "severe financial stress," now permits electric utilities to file for wholesale rates based on the inclusion of up to 50 percent of CWIP in the jurisdictional rate base (subject to a rate impact limit of 6 percent in each of the first two years)[196]; Ohio, by statute, includes CWIP — at the discretion of the commission — if 75 percent complete on date certain and the allowance for CWIP does not exceed 20 percent of total valuation[197]; while New Hampshire and Oregon prohibit all CWIP from the rate base by statute. There are other commissions that include CWIP in the rate base, but with a full or partial AFUDC offset, thereby permitting a utility cash earnings at a rate equal to the difference between the allowed overall cost of capital and the AFUDC rate.[198]

The Rate Base: Confusion and Operationalism

In 1898, the Supreme Court declared that rates must be calculated to yield a fair return on the "fair value" of utility property,[199] and thereby started a continuing debate over the meaning and measurement of value. Even the Supreme Court's 1944 *Hope* decision, which "removed fair value, and indeed valuation, as a constitutional requirement,"[200] failed to terminate the long-standing controversy. And, during the 1970s and early 1980s, the issue was revived as the annual rate of inflation accelerated.

Part of the confusion can be traced to statutory provisions — provisions which "do not include the essentials of an operational concept."[201] In a careful analysis of state statutory enactments, Rose found wide diversity in the definition of "value" and in the association of value with rates. He concluded:

> It is obvious that the instruction that is the essence of "fair value" — to give the matters for consideration (principally original cost and reproduction cost) such weight as may be just and right — is not operational. It offers no criterion or rule to determine what is "just and right" and, therefore, does not provide a method to ascertain a uniquely determinate value of the weight to be assigned to each of the "matters for consideration" in a finding of fair value. In practice, the weights attributed to original cost and reproduction cost in the application of the fair value concept are the results of a purely subjective and arbitrary process, which is characterized euphemistically as the "judgment" of the regulatory authorities. The weights vary from jurisdiction to jurisdiction and from case to case within the same jurisdiction. The fact is that fair value is an indeterminate magnitude lying anywhere between original cost and reproduction cost.[202]

Part of the confusion also can be traced to the conflicting nature of the objections to an original cost rate base. As Bonbright has explained:

> A close reading of the literature written in recent years in support of the fair value rule revealed two greatly different asserted objections to an actual cost rate base. According to one objection, which is in line with the older legal tradition of property rights, investors are entitled to a reasonable return on the value of their property and not on its cost, not even on its replacement cost except to the extent to which this latter cost may happen to serve as a measure or clue to the real value of the property. But according to the other objection, which now is receiving much greater emphasis in this postwar period of price inflation, what makes the original cost standard of rate making so deficient in the opinion of those who object to it is not any failure to reflect value rather than cost, but rather its failure to reflect original cost itself when restated in terms of current dollars.
>
> Now, both of these objections to an orthodox original cost or actual cost standard of rate making have some plausibility on the grounds of fairness or of economic analysis; and it would therefore be very nice if both of them could be avoided at one and the same time by the adoption of a fair value rule of rate making. But, unhappily, they cannot both be avoided in this manner — for that matter, in any other man-

ner. By this I mean that a rate base if designed to protect stockholders against the impairment of their capital investment or their real income in terms of purchasing power could be very different from a rate base designed to reflect the actual current values of the current assets as determined by a skillful, hard-boiled appraiser who takes full account of the ravages of obsolescence.[203]

In more recent years, original cost methodology, combined with huge cost overruns — due to high annual inflation rates and environmental concerns — and conservation, have raised new problems (especially for the electric utility industry). Contends Studness:

> . . . the institutional arrangements under which utilities have planned and built power plants for over half a century have been irreparably changed by the expanded use of disallowances during the last two years. Unfortunately, there is not a very broad understanding of how risks have changed for utilities or the limited extent to which risks can be shifted onto shareholders without compensation. Yet it is imperative that new institutional arrangements be established promptly. A failure to do so will needlessly lead to the industry's current excess capacity giving way to inadequate capacity with the attendant inconvenience for ratepayers and misallocation of resources in the economy. . . .[204]

The long-standing "regulatory compact," in short, has been broken, resulting in an adverse impact on utility investment decisions.[205]

The determination of the rate base thus remains a source of uncertainty and leads to confusion. The gap between theory and practice is often wide.

Notes

Re Williams Pipe Line Co., Opinion No. 154 (FERC, 1982), pp. 226-27 (footnotes omitted).

[1]This distinction is drawn by Francis X. Welch, *Cases and Text on Public Utility Regulation* (rev. ed.; Arlington, Va.: Public Utilities Reports, Inc., 1968), pp. 292-93.

[2]*Ibid.*, p. 360, "Not all of the foregoing classes have invariably been excluded from rate bases in rate cases. Some have been partially allowed under particular circumstances. Some have been included on a 'de minimis' basis in case of very small items. Property held for future use, for example, has been included at full value where it was scheduled to go into public service at a very early date and where no claim was made for interest during construction." *Ibid.*

[3]*Federal Power Comm. v. Hope Natural Gas Co.*, 320 U.S. 591, 601 (1944).

[4]The measures marked with an asterisk have been generally rejected as proper measures of value.

[5]169 U.S. 466 (1898).

[6]*Munn v. Illinois,* 94 U.S. 113, 134 (1877).

[7]*Stone v. Farmers' Loan & Trust Co.,* 116 U.S. 307, 331 (1886).

[8]*Reagan v. Farmers' Loan & Trust Co.,* 154 U.S. 362 (1894).

[9]*Smyth v. Ames, op. cit.* pp. 546-47.

[10]In later cases, two other measures also were rejected: taxation value as being unreliable for ratemaking purposes [*Brooklyn Union Gas Co. v. Prendergast,* 7 F. 2d 628 (1925)] and exchange value because public utilities are not commonly bought and sold in the market [dissenting opinion of Justice Brandeis in *Missouri ex. rel. Southwestern Bell Teleph. Co. v. Missouri Pub. Service Comm.,* 262 U.S. 276 (1923)].

[11]*Knoxville v. Knoxville Water Co.,* 212 U.S. 1 (1909); *Minnesota Rate Cases,* 230 U.S. 352 (1913).

[12]*Knoxville v. Knoxville Water Co., op. cit.* In the absence of either stock watering or overcapitalization, a utility's total capitalization (*i.e.,* the amount of capital contributed to the enterprise) may be used in rate cases. See discussion below on the prudent investment measure.

[13]See Chapter 7.

[14]Dissenting opinion in *Federal Power Comm. v. Hope Natural Gas Co., op. cit.,* p. 627.

[15]Concurring opinion in *Driscoll v. Edison,* 307 U.S. 104, 122 (1939). See also Robert L. Hale, "Conflicting Judicial Criteria of Utility Rates — the Need for Judicial Restatement," 38 *Columbia Law Review* 959 (1938).

[16]A. J. G. Priest, "Major Public Utility Decisions in Perspective," 46 *Virginia Law Review* 1327 (1960).

[17]*Welch, op. cit.,* p. 280. See also G. Stanley Joslin and Arthur S. Miller, "Public Utility Rate Regulation: A Re-examination," 43 *Virginia Law Review* 1027 (1957).

[18]D. Philip Locklin, *Economics of Transportation* (7th ed.; Homewood, Ill.: Richard D. Irwin, Inc., 1972), p. 380.

[19]*San Diego Land & Town Co. v. National City,* 174 U.S. 739, 757 (1899).

[20]*San Diego Land & Town Co. v. Jasper,* 189 U.S. 439, 443 (1903).

[21]*Willcox v. Consolidated Gas Co.,* 212 U.S. 19, 41, 52 (1909).

[22]*Minnesota Rate Cases, op. cit.,* p. 454.

[23]*Missouri ex rel. Southwestern Bell Teleph. Co. v. Missouri Pub. Service Comm., op. cit.,* pp. 287-88.

[24]*Bluefield Water Works & Imp. Co. v. West Virginia Pub. Service Comm.,* 262 U.S. 679, 689 (1923).

[25]*McCardle v. Indianapolis Water Co.,* 272 U.S. 400, 408-9, 410 (1926).

[26]*St. Louis & O'Fallon Ry. Co. v. United States,* 279 U.S. 461, 487 (1929).

[27]*Georgia Ry. & Power Co. v. Railroad Comm.,* 262 U.S. 625, 629-30 (1923). As will be discussed in the next section, reproduction cost and replacement cost are not synonymous.

[28]*Los Angeles Gas & Elec. Co. v. Railroad Comm. of Calif.,* 289 U.S. 287, 307 (1933).

[29]*Minnesota Rate Cases, op. cit.,* p. 434. See similar opinions expressed in *McCardle v. Indianapolis Water Co., op. cit.,* p. 410; *Los Angeles Gas & Elec. Co. v. Railroad Comm. of Calif., op. cit.,* p. 308.

[30]*Galveston Elec. Co. v. Galveston,* 258 U.S. 388 (1922); *Missouri ex. rel. Southwestern Bell Teleph. Co. v. Missouri Pub. Service Comm., op. cit.*

[31]*Georgia Ry. & Power Co. v. Railroad Comm., op. cit.*

[32]Emery Troxel, *Economics of Public Utilities* (New York: Holt, Rinehart & Winston,

Inc., 1947), p. 296n. See *West v. Chesapeake & Potomac Teleph. Co.,* 295 U.S. 662 (1935).

[33]Dissenting opinion (supported by Justice Holmes) in *Missouri ex. rel. Southwestern Bell Teleph. Co. v. Missouri Pub. Service Comm., op. cit.,* pp. 290, 291.

[34]*Ibid.,* pp. 290-91, 306-7.

[35]Dissenting opinion (supported by Justices Brandeis and Cardozo) in *West v. Chesapeake & Potomac Teleph. Co., op. cit.,* p. 689.

[36]Dissenting opinion in *McCart v. Indianapolis Water Co.,* 302 U.S. 419, 428-29 (1938).

[37]*Excess Income of St. Louis & O'Fallon Ry. Co.,* 124 ICC 3, 26-39 (1927).

[38]Ben W. Lewis, "Public Utilities," in L. S. Lyon and V. Abramson (eds.), *Government and Economic Life* (Washington, D.C.: The Brookings Institution, 1940), Vol. II, p. 692.

[39]*Ibid.,* p. 696.

[40]*Ibid.,* pp. 692-93.

[41]*Los Angeles Gas & Elec. Co. v. Railroad Comm. of Calif., op. cit.,* pp. 304-5.

[42]*Lindheimer v. Illinois Bell Teleph. Co.,* 292 U.S. 151 (1934); *Dayton Power & Light Co. v. Pub. Utilities Comm. of Ohio,* 292 U.S. 290 (1934); *Railroad Comm. of Calif. v. Pacific Gas & Elec. Co.,* 320 U.S. 388 (1938); *Denver Union Stock Yard Co. v. United States,* 304 U.S. 470 (1938).

[43]*West v. Chesapeake & Potomac Teleph. Co., op. cit.*

[44]*Federal Power Comm. v. Natural Gas Pipeline Co.,* 315 U.S. 575, 586 (1942).

[45]Concurring opinion, *ibid.,* pp. 602, 606. See Robert L. Hale, "Does the Ghost of Smyth v. Ames Still Walk?," 55 *Harvard Law Review* 1116 (1942).

[46]*Federal Power Comm. v. Hope Natural Gas Co., op. cit.,* pp. 602, 605 (citations omitted).

[47]Dissenting opinion, *ibid.,* p. 623.

[48]Dissenting opinion, *ibid.,* p. 627.

[49]Dissenting opinion, *ibid.,* p. 629. This problem is discussed in Chapter 14.

[50]Welch, *op. cit.* (1961 ed.), p. 311. It should be emphasized again that the Court did not forbid use of the fair value doctrine; instead, it merely removed the *Smyth v. Ames* requirement that prescribed the use of a fair value rate base.

[51]In determining the "end result," however, the courts require the use of fair and proper procedures. Thus, a year after the *Hope* decision, the Supreme Court set aside an FPC order on the ground that the commission had failed to furnish sufficient evidence to support its findings. "We have repeatedly emphasized," said Justice Douglas, "the need for clarity and completeness in the basic or essential findings on which administrative orders rest . . . Their absence can only clog the administrative function and add to the delays in rate-making." *Colorado-Wyoming Gas Co. v. Federal Power Comm.,* 324 U.S. 626, 634 (1945).

[52]Troxel, *op. cit.,* p. 278. See "The *Hope* Case and the 'End-result' Test — A Re-appraisal," 117 *Public Utilities Fortnightly* 50 (March 6, 1986).

[53]*City of Two Rivers v. Commonwealth Teleph. Co.,* 70 PUR (NS) 5 (Wis., 1947).

[54]*Commonwealth Teleph. Co. v. Wisconsin Pub. Service Comm.,* 71 PUR (NS) 65, 69, 71 (1947), *aff'd,* 32 N.W. 2d 247 (1948). See also *New England Teleph. & Teleg. Co. v. State,* 64 A. 2d 9 (1949); *Milwaukee & Suburban Transp. Corp. v. Wisconsin Pub. Service Comm.,* 108 N.W. 2d 729 (1961).

[55]*Re Peninsula Teleph. Co.,* 17 PUR3d 109 (Fla., 1956). This approach is defended in two articles by Harold M. Somers: "'Cost of Money' as the Determinant of Public

Utility Rates," 4 *Buffalo Law Review* 289 (1955) and "The 'End Result' Approach to Public Utility Regulation," 16 *Buffalo Law Review* 689 (1967).

[56]The approach is discussed in Chapter 11.

[57]The Hepburn Act of 1906 brought oil pipelines within the jurisdiction of the ICC. The commission subsequently adopted a "valuation" methodology (a weighting of original cost and reproduction cost). [See Testimony of Jessee C. Oak in *Valuation of Common Carrier Pipelines,* FERC Docket No. RM78-2 (formerly ICC Ex Parte 308).] In 1977, the FERC was given regulatory responsibilities for interstate oil pipelines. See testimony in *Re Trans Alaska Pipeline System,* FERC Docket No. OR78-1; *Re Williams Pipe Line Co.,* FERC Docket No. OR79-1, *et. al.* See also P. Navarro, B. C. Petersen, and T. R. Stauffer, "A Critical Comparison of Utility-Type Ratemaking Methodologies in Oil Pipeline Regulation," 12 *Bell Journal of Economics* 392 (1981).

[58]James C. Bonbright, *Principles of Public Utility Rates* (New York: Columbia University Press, 1961), p. 225. This discussion draws heavily from Bonbright's study.

[59]"In the absence of rapid technological change, the value of capital assets in a competitive industry grows at approximately the rate of growth of the cost of reproducing them. The reason for this is simple: they can be resold to other investors at this cost, less a discount for cumulative 'wear and tear.' Prices charged consumers are based on current, not historical assets values. As asset prices appreciate, prices charged consumers appreciate also." Testimony of Stewart C. Myers in *Re Williams Pipe Line Co., op. cit.* (mimeographed, 1979), p. 41.

[60]The classic economic defense of reproduction cost is made by Harry G. Brown in two articles: "Railroad Valuation and Rate Regulation," 23 *Journal of Political Economy* 505 (1925) and "Economic Basis and Limits of Public Utility Regulation," 53 *American Bar Association Reports* 717 (1928).

[61]William A. Paton and Howard C. Greer, "Utility Rates Must Recognize Dollar Depreciation," 51 *Public Utilities Fortnightly* 333 (1953); H. A. Coxe, "The Modern Case for Fair Value," 76 *Public Utilities Fortnightly* 15 (December 3, 1965).

[62]Bonbright, *op. cit.,* pp. 229-30. It is important to emphasize that this same argument applies to any rates which are based upon costs, no matter how the costs are measured. "Reliance upon costs does serve, however, to keep utility prices somewhere within the range of . . . standards relied upon almost universally in our private enterprise economy, and, as well, within an acceptable area of 'fairness' to utility owners and users." Lewis, *op. cit.,* p. 686. The marginal cost pricing proposal is discussed in Chapter 10.

[63]Bonbright, *op. cit.,* p. 231. The tax factor creates an interesting paradox. During inflationary periods, it is argued, the rates of public utilities will be too low if based upon original cost valuations, thereby encouraging wasteful consumption. "But if this danger were really believed to exist despite the heavy prevailing levels of utility taxation, the remedy would not need to be sought for by the adoption of a replacement-cost principle of rate making. Instead, it could be secured far more easily and expeditiously by an increase in utility taxes!" *Ibid.,* p. 232.

[64]E. M. Bernstein, *Public Utility Rate Making and the Price Level* (Chapel Hill: University of North Carolina Press, 1937), p. 124. See also *Chesapeake & Potomac Teleph. Co. v. Pub. Service Comm.,* 187 A. 2d 475 (1963).

[65]The assumption as to replacement and/or new construction may not be valid in the case of natural gas and oil pipelines, and is discussed in a later section.

[66]A long period of hyperinflation or deflation would undoubtedly result in distortions in the allocation of resources between public utilities and nonregulated in-

dustries. However, as Lewis has argued: "It should be borne in mind that any really cataclysmic changes in the general price level could not be handled effectively, in the case of public utility rates, by employing either reproduction cost valuations or variable rates of return on prudent investment. If general price increases, for instance, should occur suddenly and on a tremendous scale the situation probably would call for the bold application of an emergency percentage increase directly to the rates themselves, without resort to any time-consuming intermediate procedure." Lewis, *op. cit.*, p. 690.

[67]Clair Wilcox, *Public Policies Toward Business* (4th ed.; Homewood, Ill.: Richard D. Irwin, Inc., 1971), pp. 305-6 (citations omitted).

[68]Cited in Felix Frankfurter, *The Public and Its Government* (New Haven: Yale University Press, 1930), p. 105.

[69]Welch, *op. cit.*, p. 317. The New York Telephone Company paid $6 million for property inventories and reproduction cost valuations during the twenties, and the New York Edison Company nearly $5 million for a single valuation, while the Interstate Commerce Commission paid $45 million and the railroads nearly $138 million to determine property valuations on the basis of 1914 prices. Leland Olds, "The Public Utility Issues," 24 *Yale Review* 704 (1935); John Bauer and Nathaniel Gold, *Public Utility Valuation for Purposes of Rate Control* (New York: The Macmillan Co., 1934), p. 120.

[70]Assume that a utility has an $8 million capitalization, an original cost property valuation of $8 million, and an allowable rate of return of 10 percent. Its annual earnings will be $800,000. On $3 million of bonds at 8 percent, it pays $240,000. On $2 million of preferred stock at 7 percent, it pays $140,000. The amount remaining is $420,000. On $3 million of common stock, it earns 14 percent. Now assume that the cost-of-living index doubles, and the utility is revalued at $16 million. With its return still at 10 percent, its annual earnings are $1,600,000. It still pays $380,000 on its bonds and preferred stock. But it now has $1,220,000 left, resulting in a yield of 40.7 percent on its common stock.

[71]See, *e.g.*, Murray L. Swanson and Richard Swanson, "The Critical Problem of Inflation in Utility Rate Making," 109 *Public Utilities Fortnightly* 29 (January 7, 1982), for such a proposal.

[21]Lewis, *op. cit.*, pp. 687-88.

[73]Wilcox, *op. cit.*, p. 305.

[74]*Excess Income of St. Louis & O'Fallon Ry. Co.*, *op. cit.*, pp. 31-32.

[75]Locklin, *op. cit.*, p. 382.

[76]In fact, there is always the possibility that rate regulation will become routine under any valuation procedure. As will be discussed in the following chapter, during the long period that reproduction cost was emphasized by the judiciary, the rate of return was usually based upon a conventional, traditional, or customary return. Only in the past few years has any attempt been made to establish a rationale for, or basic principles of, setting the allowable rate of return.

[77]"While the question of what constitutes a 'fair' rate of return, as an ethical or political matter, would seem to be just as potentially productive of controversy as the question of what constitutes 'fair value,' the economic question, though in a sense unchanged and no easier to solve than before, is at least subject to the pragmatic test suggested by the Supreme Court itself — are the regulated companies succeeding in attracting the capital they require?" Alfred E. Kahn, *The Economics of Regulation* (New York: John Wiley & Sons, Inc., 1970), Vol. I, p. 41.

[78]Troxel, *op. cit.*, pp. 305-6.

[79]Bonbright, *op. cit.*, p. 187.

[80]One exception: The FERC decided to use a trended original cost rate base, rather than the ICC's "valuation" methodology, for oil pipelines (except possibly for the Trans Alaska Pipeline System) in *Re Williams Pipe Line Co.*, 21 FERC Par. 61,260 (1982), *aff'd in part and rem'd in part sub nom. Farmers Union Central Exchange, Inc. v. Federal Energy Regulatory Comm.*, 734 F. 2d 1486, 59 PUR4th 1 (D.C. Cir. 1984), *cert. denied sub nom. Williams Pipe Line Co. v. Farmers Union Central Exchange, Inc.*, 469 U. S. 1034 (1984), Order on remand, 67 PUR4th 669 (FERC, 1985).

[81]Joseph R. Rose, "The Hope Case and Public Utility Valuation in the States," 54 *Columbia Law Review* 188 (1954).

[82]*1985 Annual Report on Utility and Carrier Regulation* (Washington, D.C.: National Association of Regulatory Utility Commissioners, 1987), pp. 443-44. Some commissions use a particular measure of value by statute or because of a state supreme court decision; others, where the statutory language is in general terms, have adopted a particular measure of value in rate cases. The fair value commissions are: Arizona, Indiana, Kentucky, Maryland, Missouri, Nebraska, New Mexico PSC, and Texas RC. The commissions which consider all evidence submitted are: New Jersey and Washington. See "States Consider Rate Base Methodology," 105 *Public Utilities Fortnightly* 46 (March 27, 1980).

[83]A third issue, concerning accrued depreciation, is considered in the next section.

[84]See Myron J. Gordon, "Comparison of Historical Cost and General Price Level Adjusted Cost Rate Base Regulation," 31 *Journal of Finance* 1501 (1977).

[85]The process of trending original cost is explained by Ezra B. Whitman and Ernest C. North, "Trending Public Utility Construction Cost Indices," 52 *Public Utilities Fortnightly* 285 (1953); Ernest C. North, "Trending Utility Plant Costs," 66 *Public Utilities Fortnightly* 88 (1960). See also "Trended Original Cost as Substitute for Reproduction Cost," 50 *Public Utilities Fortnightly* 273 (1957); "Use of Trended Original Cost in Fixing a Rate Base," 66 *Public Utilities Fortnightly* 665 (1960).

[86]The process of unit cost pricing is explained by Henry E. Crampton, "A Practical Approach to the Development of the Current Cost of Utility Plant" (Speech at the Public Utility Valuation and Rate Making Conference, Iowa State University, 1983) (mimeographed).

[87]See, *e.g.*, *Re El Paso Elec. Co.*, 29 PUR4th 427 (N.M., 1979); *Pennsylvania Pub. Utility Comm. v. Philadelphia Elec. Co.*, 37 PUR4th 381 (Pa., 1980).

[88]Joseph R. Rose, "Confusion in Valuation for Public Utility Rate-Making," 47 *Minnesota Law Review* 1, 23-24 (1962) (citations omitted). To illustrate: In a 1976 case, the North Carolina commission determined the utility's net original cost to be $87.3 million and its net replacement cost to be $143.9 million and, using a 70/30 weighting factor, found a fair value rate base of $104.2 million; a rate base that was about 20 percent above the net original cost. See S. Kumar, "How Fair Is Fair Valuation of Rate Base?," 104 *Public Utilities Fortnightly* 27, 28 (July 19, 1979).

[89]*Re Western Massachusetts Elec. Co.*, 80 PUR4th 479, 520 (Mass., 1986) (emphasis added).

[90]*Ibid.* In Kansas, the statutory phrase is "used and required to be used." See *Re Wolf Creek Nuclear Generating Facility*, 70 PUR4th 475 (Kan., 1985).

[91]See Robert E. Burns et al., *The Prudent Investment Test in the 1980s* (Columbus, Ohio: National Regulatory Research Institute, 1985); Howard E. Lubow and Richard

Ganulin, "Regulatory Considerations in Assessments of Blame," 120 *Public Utilities Fortnightly* 11 (July 23, 1987).

"Between 1945 and 1975, fewer than a dozen prudence cases were brought. Since 1975, however, over fifty cases have been undertaken by state PUCs." "Regulating Independent Power Producers: A Policy Analysis," A Staff paper prepared by the Office of Economic Policy, Federal Energy Regulatory Commission (mimeographed, October 13, 1987), p. 18 (footnotes omitted).

[92]*The Random House Dictionary of the English Language* (College Ed.; New York: Random House, Inc., 1968), p. 1066. Argued Justice Brandeis: "The term 'prudent investment' is not used in a critical sense. There should not be excluded from the finding of the base, investments which, under ordinary circumstances, would be deemed reasonable. The term is applied for the purpose of excluding what might be found to be dishonest or obviously wasteful or imprudent expenditures. Every investment may be assumed to have been made in the exercise of reasonable judgment, unless the contrary is shown." Dissenting opinion in *Missouri ex rel. Southwestern Bell Teleph. Co. v. Missouri Pub. Service Comm.*, *op. cit.*, p. 289, n. 1.

[93]*Re Western Massachusetts Elec. Co.*, *op. cit.*, p. 501 (citation omitted).

[94]*Re Consolidated Edison Co. of New York, Inc.*, Opinion No. 79-1 (N.Y., 1979), pp. 5-6.

[95]For the twelve nuclear plants completed in the period 1984 to 1987, disallowances for management imprudence totaled $6.6 billion, or about 16 percent of the $41.7 billion of investment. [Michael A. Laros and Samuel A. Haubold, "The Shifting Standard of Prudence: Implications for Utilities," 120 *Public Utilities Fortnightly* 21, 22 (October 29, 1987).] These figures do not include other disallowances, such as for excess capacity. On construction-related disallowances, see Morris H. Jacobs, "Cost Impact Quantification in Construction Prudence Studies," 120 *Public Utilities Fortnightly* 19 (July 23, 1987).

[96]*Re Long Island Lighting Co.*, 71 PUR4th 262 (N.Y., 1985). Three commissioners would have disallowed $1.875 billion. *Ibid.*, pp. 333-38.

[97]See, *e.g.*, *Re Boston Edison Co.*, 46 PUR4th 431 (Mass., 1982); *Re Houston Lighting & Power Co.*, 50 PUR4th 157 (Tex., 1982).

[98]See, *e.g.*, *Re Wolf Creek Nuclear Generating Facility, op. cit.*; *Re Kansas City Power & Light Co.*, 75 PUR4th 1 (Mo., 1986). But see *Montana Power Co. v. Montana Dept. of Pub. Service Regulation*, 68 PUR4th 521 (Mont. Dist. Ct. 1985).

[99]See, *e.g.*, *Re Western Massachusetts Elec. Co.*, *op. cit.* But see *Re Duke Power Co.*, 79 PUR4th 145 (S.C., 1986).

[100]See "Nuclear Plant Cost Overruns: The Effect of the NRC Policy Changes on State Commission Review," 118 *Public Utilities Fortnightly* 46 (October 30, 1986).

[101]As a result of significant disallowances, countless lawsuits have been filed by project owners against participants, vendors and architect-engineers, or contractors; by shareholders against utility management; and by financial institutions against utility companies. See Joseph E. Manzi, "When a Utility Faces Disallowances on New Plant Investment," 117 *Public Utilities Fortnightly* 39 (March 20, 1986); "Consumers Power, Dow Chemical Agree on Midland Conversion Plan, End Suits," *The Wall Street Journal*, January 28, 1987, p. 10; "CMS to Enter Nuclear Venture with Bechtel," *ibid.*, October 8, 1987, p. 4.

[102]*Pennsylvania Pub. Utility Comm. v. Philadelphia Elec. Co.*, *op. cit.* More recently, several states have passed laws redefining excess capacity. To illustrate: (*1*) A 1984 Kansas Act defines excess capacity as "any capacity in excess of the amount used and

required to be used to provide adequate and reliable service to the public within the state of Kansas as determined by the commission." [See, *e.g., Re Wolf Creek Nuclear Generating Facility, op. cit.;* Robert Vancrum, "The Wolf Creek Excess Cost-Excess Capacity Bill," 33 *Kansas Law Review* 475 (1985).] (2) A 1986 Pennsylvania act states, in part: ". . . a rebuttable presumption is created that a unit or units or portion thereof shall be determined to be excess unless found to be needed to meet the utility's customer demand plus a reasonable reserve margin in the test year or the year following the test year, or if it is a base load unit, it is also found to produce annual economic benefits which will exceed the total annual cost of the plant during the test year or within a reasonable period following the test year." [See, *e.g., Pennsylvania Pub. Utility Comm. v. West Penn Power Co.*, 84 PUR4th 198 (Pa., 1987).]

[103]Charles M. Studness, "Excess Capacity and the Threat of Rate Base Disallowances," 115 *Public Utilities Fortnightly* 42, 43 (March 7, 1985).

[104]For an argument that excess capacity should be "capacity not needed to provide reliable service at minimum cost," see Michael D. Yokell and Bruce A. Larson, "Excess Capacity: What It Is and What To Do About It," 118 *Public Utilities Fortnightly* 13, 15 (December 11, 1986). For examples in other utility industries, see *Re Continental Teleph. Co. of North Carolina*, 67 PUR4th 280 (N.C., 1985); *Re Quapaw Water Co.*, 82 PUR4th 31 (Ark., 1987).

[105]*Pennsylvania Pub. Utility Comm. v. Pennsylvania Power & Light Co.*, 67 PUR4th 30, 39 (Pa., 1985).

[106]*Re Wolf Creek Nuclear Generating Facility, op. cit.*, p. 515. The decision was later modified: *Re Kansas Gas & Elec. Co.*, 82 PUR4th 539 (Kan., 1987).

[107]*Pennsylvania Pub. Utility Comm. v. Philadelphia Elec. Co., op. cit.*, p. 388 (emphasis in original). See also *Pennsylvania Pub. Utility Comm. v. Pennsylvania Power & Light Co.*, 55 PUR4th 185 (Pa., 1983).

[108]After the New York commission placed a cap of $4.16 billion on the amount of the Nine Mile Point 2 nuclear plant's costs that could be passed on to ratepayers [*Re Nine Mile Point 2 Nuclear Generating Facility*, 78 PUR4th 23 (N.Y., 1986)], the plant's five owners had to write off some $2.2 billion (about 35 percent) of the $6.3 billion generating facility. *The Wall Street Journal*, July 24, 1987, p. 11.

[109]See, *e.g., Pennsylvania Pub. Utility Comm. v. Pennsylvania Power & Light Co., op. cit.* (55 PUR4th 185). (Note: The Company subsequently signed a long-term sale of the 945 megawatts determined to be excess capacity to Jersey Central Power & Light. *Ibid.*, p. 35.)

[110]See, *e.g., Re South Carolina Elec. & Gas Co.*, 59 PUR4th 244 (S.C., 1984) and 84 PUR4th 460 (S.C., 1987) (carrying charges on 400 megawatts previously excluded from rate base amortized over a ten-year period); *Re Pacific Corp.*, 68 PUR4th 473 (Wyo., 1985) (excluding one-half of company's investment in Colstrip Unit 3 from rate base, but allowing carrying charges equal to overall rate of return).

[111]See, *e.g., Pennsylvania Pub Utility Comm. v. Pennsylvania Power & Light Co., op. cit.* (67 PUR4th 30); *Re Iowa Power & Light Co.*, 55 PUR4th 530 (Iowa, 1983).

[112]See, *e.g., Re Kansas City Power & Light Co.*, 75 PUR4th 1 (Mo., 1986) (allowing one-half equity return on 75 percent of Company's jurisdictional investment in Wolf Creek deemed excess capacity).

[113]There are two options. Thus, for a period of time, the Massachusetts commission treated "unuseful" capacity as abandoned plant (an extraordinary loss), thereby permitting the investment to be amortized, after reducing the amount by the equity return portion of AFUDC and denying carrying charges for the unamortized bal-

ance during the amortization period. See, *e.g.*, *Re Fitchburg Gas & Elec. Co.*, 52 PUR4th 197 (Mass., 1983); *Re Western Massachusetts Elec. Co., op. cit.*

[114]*Re Wolf Creek Nuclear Generating Facility, op. cit.*

[115]On the risk-sharing concept, see Roger D. Colton, "Excess Capacity: Who Gets the Charge From the Power Plant?," 34 *Hastings Law Journal* 1133 (1983); John Stutz, "Risk Sharing in a Regulated Industry," 117 *Public Utilities Fortnightly* 29 (April 3, 1986). But see "New Approaches to Prudence Issue Receiving Attention, Undergoing Testing," *Electric Utility Week*, May 18, 1987, pp. 9-10.

For an analysis of the consequences of significant disallowances, see Burns et al., *op. cit.*, esp. chap. 5.

[116]Several utilities have cited a need for new generating capacity, but have stated a reluctance to build new capacity under current prudence review procedures. Other utilities have sought to purchase power under long-term contracts or to build smaller generating plants. See, *e.g.*, Gerald Charnoff, "Nuclear Prudence Audits: A Performance Review," 119 *Public Utilities Fortnightly* 18 (June 11, 1987); "Retreating from Used-and-Useful Rule, Mass. DPU Mulls Pre-Approval Method," *Electric Utility Week*, April 27, 1987, pp. 1-3.

[117]There is another potential problem: The fuel savings in the early years of the plant's life may be less than the capital-related revenue requirements, resulting in a "money-saving rate increase." See Sally Hunt Streiter, "Avoiding the 'Money Saving' Rate Increase," 109 *Public Utilities Fortnightly* 18 (June 24, 1982).

[118]*Re Union Elec. Co.*, 66 PUR4th 202 (Mo., 1985). See also *Re Utah Power & Light Co.*, 66 PUR4th 32 (Wyo., 1985); *Re Wolf Creek Nuclear Generating Facility, op. cit.; Re Niagara Mohawk Power Corp.*, 74 PUR4th 97 (N.Y., 1986); *Re Western Massachusetts Elec. Co., op. cit.*

[119]See, *e.g.*, *Re Kansas Gas & Elec. Co., op. cit.*

[120]This risk basically arises from the fact that a commission may change an approved plan at a later date. See, *e.g.*, *Ex parte Louisiana Power & Light Co.*, 80 PUR4th 353 (La., 1987).

[121]See, *e.g.*, *Washington Utils. & Transp. Comm. v. Puget Sound Power & Light Co.*, 62 PUR4th 557 (Wash., 1984); *Re Utah Power & Light Co.*, 63 PUR4th 13 (Utah, 1984).

[122]Under current rules, a utility can capitalize for accounting purposes only costs deferred pursuant to a formal plan which specifies the timing of and schedules recovery of all deferred costs within ten years. Any other costs must be written off as a loss in the current period. "Rate increases scheduled under a plan must not be backloaded; that is, rate increases called for under a plan may not exceed the initial rate increase that is authorized pursuant to the phase-in plan." Deloitte Haskins & Sells, "Public Utility Briefs," March 27, 1987, p. 2. See also Michael Foley, "Proposed Reforms of Accounting Standards — A Cure Worse Than the Disease?," 117 *Public Utilities Fortnightly* 19 (May 29, 1986). But see *Re Western Massachusetts Elec. Co., op. cit.*, p. 547 (holding that "arbitrary accounting standards" must not determine the commission's "treatment of a jurisdictional company").

[123]Sally Hunt Streiter, "Trending the Rate Base," 109 *Public Utilities Fortnightly* 32 (May 13, 1982).

[124]See *ibid.*; T. R. Stauffer and P. Navarro, "A Critique of Public Utility Rate-making Methodologies," 107 *Public Utilities Fortnightly* 25 (February 26, 1981); Navarro, Petersen, and Stauffer, *op. cit.*; Swanson and Swanson, *op cit.*; S. Myers, L. Kolbe, and W. Tyre, "Inflation and Rate of Return Regulation" (Boston: Charles River Associates, Inc., 1982) (mimeographed); A. Lawrence Kolbe, "Inflation-driven Rate Shocks:

The Problem and Possible Solutions," 111 *Public Utilities Fortnightly* 26 (February 17, 1983). The use of a trended rate base was discussed and rejected in *Re So. California Edison Co.*, 64 PUR4th 452 (Cal., 1984).

There are other potential solutions. See, *e.g.*, Darrell A. Smith, "Pricing Strategies for New Generating Plants," 111 *Public Utilities Fortnightly* 31 (June 9, 1983); Edward M. Barrett, "Proposed Regulatory Treatment of Costs of Extraordinary Large Additions to Plant in Service," in J. Rhoads Foster et al. (eds.), *Regulatory Reform: The State of the Regulatory Art; Emerging Concepts and Procedures* (Washington, D.C.: Institute for Study of Regulation, 1984), pp. 117-36; "Rate Base Phase-in Plans for Electric Utilities — A Case Update," 116 *Public Utilities Fortnightly* 51 (July 25, 1985).

[125]Kolbe, *op. cit.*, p. 29 (footnote omitted). See also R. N. Morrison and R. J. Schultz (eds.), *Pipeline Regulation and Inflation: An Evaluation of Tariff Levelling* (Montreal: Center for the Study of Regulated Industries, McGill University, 1983).

[126]See Sally Hunt Streiter, "Indexing Bonds and Other Issues," 109 *Public Utilities Fortnightly* 40 (June 10, 1981).

[127]See Swanson and Swanson, *op. cit.*

[128]"The fundamental difference between prices under OC and unregulated prices is the way in which investors are compensated for inflation. Under OC, the allowed rate of return applied to the equity share of rate base to calculate net income is supposed to equal the nominal cost of equity capital, which includes an 'inflation premium.' *The problems with OC regulation are caused by compensating equity holders for inflation in current cash earnings, instead of through appreciation in the value of the company's assets.*" Kolbe, *op. cit.*, p. 27 (emphasis in original). See also Myers, Kolbe, and Tyre, *op. cit.*, for a discussion of other practical details, such as the choice of index for trending the rate base and the effect of income tax laws.

[129]Cited by Ralph M. Besse, "Deductibility of Depreciation Reserves for Rate Base Purposes" (Speech before the National Conference of Electric and Gas Utility Accountants, 1950) (mimeographed), p. 1.

[130]See Chapter 7, pp. 259-62.

[131]*Excess Income of Richmond, Fredericksburg & Potomac R.R. Co.*, 170 ICC 451, 568 (1931).

[132]When the sinking-fund method is used, the depreciation reserve is not deducted from the rate base, since the utility is required to pay interest on the amount in the reserve. The annual charges to depreciation would be insufficient unless interest is earned on the entire fund already accumulated.

[133]*Re Canadian River Gas Co.*, 43 PUR (NS) 205, 218 (1942).

[134]*Knoxville v. Knoxville Water Co.*, *op. cit.*

[135]H. E. Riggs, "The Two Radically Different Concepts of Utility Depreciation," 9 *Public Utilities Fortnightly* 559, 560 (1932). Observed depreciation, also known as deferred maintenance, is closely related to retirement accounting.

[136]*McCardle v. Indianapolis Water Co.*, *op. cit.*, p. 416.

[137]*Board of Pub. Utility Commrs. v. New York Teleph. Co.*, 271 U.S. 23, 31-32 (1926).

[138]See *Re Yankers R.R. Co.*, PUR1933D 61 (N.Y., 1932). Moreover, "engineers took some very substantial liberties with what we would now consider to be the realities. Many were the instances of 50 to 75-year old office buildings considered in 98 percent condition. Overall condition of total utility property was seldom conceded to be less than 90 percent." Besse, *op. cit.*, p. 2. In one case, for example, a utility's depreciation reserve totaled approximately $48 million, but it claimed only $15.8 million as observed depreciation. *Lindheimer v. Illinois Bell Teleph. Co.*, *op. cit.*

[139]"The fallacy of the 'percent condition' theory of accrued depreciation is plain here. To illustrate, under the hypothesis of the company's witness . . . the property would be found to have depreciated only 25 percent throughout its life . . . , and then suffer a precipitous loss in the brief final stage of service. Such a theory is opposed by reason and facts." *Cities of Cleveland & Akron v. Hope Natural Gas Co.*, 44 PUR (NS) 1, 17 (1942).

[140]For a summary of commission depreciation policies and practices, see *1985 Annual Report on Utility and Carrier Regulation, op. cit.*, pp. 450-51.

[141]In the *Hope* case, to illustrate, the commission found that the utility had an excessive reserve and deducted a reserve requirement of approximately $22 million, nearly $18 million less than the actual reserve of $50 million. *Cities of Cleveland & Akron v. Hope Natural Gas Co., op. cit.*

[142]See Troxel, *op. cit.*, pp. 348-51; "Accrued Depreciation Not Measured by Accounting Computations," 66 *Public Utilities Fortnightly* 60 (1960).

Some have argued that the depreciation reserve should not be deducted from the property value when a utility has failed to earn a fair rate of return, since its customers have not provided all the depreciation accruals. But see Bonbright (*op. cit.*, pp. 211-12) for an argument that the full reserve should be deducted even if it is not earned.

[143]*Ohio Edison Co. v. City of Mansfield*, 41 PUR3d 452, 456 (Ohio, 1961).

[144]*Ibid.*, p. 457. See "Accrued Depreciation Not Measured by Accounting Computations," *op. cit.*

[145]*Re Citizens Teleph. Co.*, 43 PUR3d 471, 474 (Ohio, 1962).

[146]Bonbright, *op. cit.*, p. 193, n.2.

[147]*Ibid.*, p. 195.

[148]The formula approach was used in *Re Oklahoma Gas & Elec. Co.*, 26 PUR4th 123 (Ark., 1978), but rejected in *Re Hudson Water Co.*, 28 PUR4th 617 (N.H., 1979).

[149]The balance sheet approach was utilized in *Re Granite State Elec. Co.*, 28 PUR4th 240 (N.H., 1978), but rejected in *Re The Peoples Gas Light & Coke Co.*, 27 PUR3d 209 (Ill., 1959). See also *Re Working Capital Allowances of Gas, Electric, and Telephone Utilities*, 68 PUR4th 177 (Mich., 1985).

[150]See, *e.g.*, *Re National Fuel Gas Distribution Corp.*, 28 PUR4th 42 (N.Y., 1978); *Re Southwestern Bell Teleph. Co.*, 28 PUR4th 519 (Kan., 1979); *Re Intermountain Gas Co.*, 30 PUR4th 231 (Idaho, 1979).

[151]See "Tax Offsets against Working Capital," 79 *Public Utilities Fortnightly* 59 (March 16, 1967); *Re Iowa Pub. Service Co.*, 74 PUR4th 405 (Iowa, 1986).

[152]Because of the procedure of using accrued taxes and customers' deposits to offset cash requirements, it is possible to have a *negative* working capital allowance. In such cases, some commissions have deducted this amount from the rate base. See, *e.g.*, *Re Pacific Teleph. & Teleg. Co.*, 53 PUR3d 513 (Cal., 1964); *Re Southern Bell Teleph. & Teleg. Co.*, 66 PUR3d 1 (Fla., 1966). See also *Re American Teleph. & Teleg. Co.*, 70 PUR3d 129 (FCC, 1967).

[153]See, *e.g.*, *Re Pacific Teleph. & Teleg. Co.*, (63 PUR4th 13); *Re Piedmont Nat. Gas Co., Inc.*, 71 PUR4th 531 (N.C., 1985).

[154]Compensating balances were included in *Re Citizens Utilities Co.*, 26 PUR4th 553 (Idaho, 1978), but excluded in *Pennsylvania Pub. Utility Comm. v. Pennsylvania Power Co.*, 27 PUR4th 426 (Pa., 1978). See "Compensating Bank Balances Discussed," 99 *Public Utilities Fortnightly* 48 (January 20, 1977).

[155]*Re Northwestern Bell Teleph. Co.*, 29 PUR4th 7 (Minn., 1978); *Re Interstate Power*

Co., Docket No. 78-0161 (Ill., 1979). See also *Re Southwestern Pub. Service Co.*, 27 PUR4th 302 (N.M., 1978).

[156]*Re Potomac Elec. Power Co.*, 29 PUR4th 517 (D. C., 1979). The commission added, however, that should such property subsequently be sold, any gain would be reflected as an above-the-line item, thereby benefiting ratepayers.

[157]Welch has argued that all land should be valued at its present value regardless of the measure used for other property items. "Assume that a utility enterprise whether by foresight or good luck, is located on land which is rapidly increasing in real estate market value. Keeping that increased value out of the rate base penalizes or handicaps the utility in comparison with other enterprises. It tends to undermine incentive for advance progressive planning. The utility's earnings are to that extent kept below the earnings of the others." Welch, *op. cit.*, p. 359.

[158]*Dayton Power & Light Co. v. Pub. Utilities Comm. of Ohio, op. cit.*

[159]Troxel, *op. cit.*, p. 281. Yet, beginning in 1954, when the FPC adopted an area rate approach, a present value standard, in effect, was permitted. See Chapter 11, pp. 460-65.

[160]*Smyth v. Ames, op. cit.*, p. 547.

[161]*Des Moines Gas Co. v. Des Moines*, 238 U. S. 153, 165 (1915).

[162]*Willcox v. Consolidated Gas Co., op. cit.*, p. 52.

[163]*Omaha v. Omaha Water Co.*, 218 U. S. 180 (1910); *Des Moines Gas Co. v. Des Moines, op. cit.; Los Angeles Gas & Elec. Co. v. Railroad Comm. of Calif., op. cit.; General Teleph. Co. of the Midwest v. Iowa State Commerce Comm.*, 275 N.W. 2d 364 (1979).

[164]Troxel, *op. cit.*, p. 310.

[165]*Cedar Rapids Gas Light Co. v. Cedar Rapids*, 223 U.S. 655 (1912); *Galveston Elec. Co. v. Galveston, op. cit.* A franchise value was permitted in an earlier case because the state of New York had approved a franchise valuation in 1884 and had permitted the utility to issue securities on the basis of this valuation. *Willcox v. Consolidated Gas Co., op. cit.*

[166]*San Joaquin & Kings River Co. v. County of Stanislaus*, 233 U.S. 454 (1914); *Bluefield Water Works & Imp. Co. v. Pub. Service Comm. of West Virginia, op. cit.*

[167]*McCardle v. Indianapolis Water Co., op. cit.*, p. 421.

[168]Dissenting opinion in *McCart v. Indianapolis Water Co., op. cit.*, p. 433.

[169]See *Central Maine Power Co. v. Maine Pub. Utilities Comm.*, 36 PUR3d 19 (1960).

[170]*Colorado-Interstate Gas Co. v. Federal Power Comm.*, 324 U.S. 581 (1945); *Panhandle Eastern Pipe Line Co. v. Federal Power Comm.*, 324 U.S. 635 (1945).

[171]M. C. Waltersdorf, "Going Value in Utility Valuation," 17 *American Economic Review* 26 (1927).

[172]Wilcox, *op. cit.*, p. 312.

[173]*Galveston Elec. Co. v. Galveston, op. cit.*

[174]Several other cost measures of going value have been presented in rate cases, including a dollar value for each customer or meter, a percentage of the utility's gross revenue for a year or more, and the estimated reproduction cost of developing the business. See two articles by Ben W. Lewis, "Going Value and Rate Regulation," 26 *Michigan Law Review* 720 (1928) and "Going Value," 6 *Public Utilities Fortnightly* 77 (1930).

[175]*Knoxville v. Knoxville Water Co., op. cit.*, p. 9. No separate allowance was permitted in *Cedar Rapids Gas Light Co. v. Cedar Rapids, op. cit.*, but an allowance was included in *Des Moines Gas Co. v. Des Moines, op. cit.*

[176]*McCardle v. Indianapolis Water Co., op. cit.,* p. 415.

[177]*Los Angeles Gas & Elec. Co. v. Railroad Comm. of Calif., op. cit.,* p. 317. See also *Dayton Power & Light Co. v. Pub. Utilities Comm. of Ohio, op. cit.,* p. 309.

[178]*Federal Power Comm. v. Natural Gas Pipeline Co., op. cit.*

[179]But see *Re Kansas City Power & Light Co.,* 43 PUR3d 433 (Mo., 1962). When valuation is being undertaken for the purpose of a sale, going concern value generally is included.

[180]Troxel, *op. cit.,* p. 327.

[181]See "Customer Contributions as Rate Base Items," 99 *Public Utilities Fortnightly* 48 (May 12, 1977); "Recent Cases on Customer Contributions," 103 *Public Utilities Fortnightly* 45 (February 15, 1979).

[182]"An electric company properly required a customer to pay for the installation of electric service where the company had no power line in the immediate vicinity of the customer's premises, where the company had to acquire rights-of-way across other properties, and where there was no contention that the charge demanded was unreasonable." *Douthit v. Arkansas Power & Light Co.,* 398 S.W. 2d 521 (1966).

[183]James E. Suelflow, *Public Utility Accounting: Theory and Application* (East Lansing: MSU Public Utilities Studies, 1973), p. 187. For a more complete discussion, see *ibid.,* pp. 181-87. Under the Tax Reform Act of 1986, contributions in aid of construction must be recorded as taxable income. See "CIAC Issues: Depreciation, Negative Rate Base, and Tax Reform," 119 *Public Utilities Fortnightly* 38 (February 5, 1987).

[184]See Lawrence S. Pomerantz and James E. Suelflow, *Allowance for Funds Used During Construction: Theory and Application* (East Lansing: MSU Public Utilities Studies, 1976).

[185]Typical is the following 15 percent claimed allowance (*Re Alton Water Co.,* 35 PUR3d 284 [Ill., 1960]):

1. Organization expense	1.00%
2. Engineering and supervision during design and construction	5.00%
3. Administrative and legal costs	2.00%
4. Omissions and contingencies	2.00%
5. Interest lost on nonproductive investment during construction	4.95%
Total claimed	14.95%

[186]Several commissions continued to permit utilities to include construction work in progress in the rate base, particularly where plant under construction was expected to be in service within a reasonable period of time. See *Re American Teleph. & Teleg. Co.,* 71 PUR3d 273, 288 (FCC, 1967).

[187]AFUDC is not generally compounded, although many feel that it should be. See Paul B. Coughlan, "Allowance for Funds in Construction: Accounting Stepchild and Regulatory Football," 98 *Public Utilities Fortnightly* 26 (November 4, 1976); Johnny R. Johnson, "The Income Quality of Allowances for Funds Used during Construction," 99 *Public Utilities Fortnightly* 32 (June 9, 1977).

[188]But see Robert R. Trout, "A Rationale for Preferring Construction Work in Progress in the Rate Base," 103 *Public Utilities Fortnightly* 22 (May 10, 1979); Wilfred H. Comtois, "Construction Work in Progress in the Rate Base: A Benefit to the Consumer," 105 *Public Utilities Fortnightly* 19 (May 8, 1980); Roger A. Morin, "An Empirical Study of the Effects of CWIP on Cost of Capital and Revenue Require-

ments," Part I: 118 *Public Utilities Fortnightly* 21 (July 10, 1986), Part II: 118 *Public Utilities Fortnightly* 24 (July 24, 1986). See also U. S. General Accounting Office, *Construction Work in Progress Issue Needs Improved Regulatory Response for Utilities and Consumers* (Washington, D.C., 1980), esp. chaps. 4 ("Effect of CWIP on Consumer Utility Bills Is Not Clear") and 5 ("Does Allowing CWIP in Rate Base Shift the Burden of Paying for New Construction from Investors to Consumers?").

[189]In 1967, private electric utilities had CWIP balances of $4.4 billion, compared with 1980 CWIP balances of $60.4 billion. In the latter year, twenty-one companies had CWIP balances of $1 billion or more. *Statistics of Privately Owned Electric Utilities in the United States* (Washington, D.C.: U.S. Government Printing Office, 1981), p. 4.

[190]See Robert E. Frazer and Richard C. Ranson, "Is Interest during Construction 'Funny Money'?," 90 *Public Utilities Fortnightly* 20 (December 21, 1972). The alternative minimum tax provision in the Tax Reform Act of 1986 includes a financial statement ("book") adjustment. AFUDC is one such book-income item, even though it is not a cash-flow item. See *Tax Reform Act of 1986: Analysis and Planning* (Chicago: Arthur Andersen & Co., 1986), pp. 248-49; Benjamin J. Ewers, Jr., "Capitalized Interest During Construction in Utility Rate Making," 119 *Public Utilities Fortnightly* 27 (January 8, 1987).

[191]*Statistics of Privately Owned Electric Utilities in the United States, op. cit.*, p. 8. AFUDC "dollars alone often account for 25 to 30 per cent of final plant costs, and can add $20 to $30 million for each month near the completion of a project." Charnoff, *op. cit.*, p. 24.

[192]See Dennis B. Fitzpatrick and Thomas E. Stitzel, "Capitalizing an Allowance for Funds Used during Construction: The Impact on Earnings Quality," 101 *Public Utilities Fortnightly* 18 (January 19, 1978); P. R. Chandy and Wallace N. Davidson, III, "AFUDC and Its Impact on the Profitability of Electric Utilities," 112 *Public Utilities Fortnightly* 34 (August 4, 1983). See also Ganas K. Rakes and William C. Boynton, "AFUDC: An Overlooked Impact on Balance Sheets and Some Broader Implications for Financial Reporting," 105 *Public Utilities Fortnightly* 19 (June 5, 1980).

[193]*Re Pub. Service Co. of Oklahoma*, 22 PUR4th 118, 123 (Okla., 1978). In 1974, a federal court ruled in favor of allowing CWIP in the rate base under the "used and useful" test. The court noted that "funds are not necessarily 'used and useful' only when they are currently invested in completed plants." *Goodman v. Pub. Service Comm. of D.C.*, 497 F. 2d 661 (D.C. Cir. 1974).

[194]"As of 1978, 34 state regulatory commissions had allowed CWIP. Since 1975, a total of 12 states have allowed CWIP for the first time." William W. Muhs and David A. Schauer, "State Regulatory Practices with Construction Work in Progress: A Summary," 105 *Public Utilities Fortnightly* 29, 31 (March 27, 1980). See also "Recent Cases on Construction Work in Progress," 103 *Public Utilities Fortnightly* 39 (February 1, 1979); "CWIP and the Financial Needs Standard — An Update," 116 *Public Utilities Fortnightly* 62 (November 28, 1985). Pollution control equipment and other nonrevenue producing items (including fuel conversion) are almost universally included in the rate base. See, *e.g.*, *Pennsylvania Pub. Utility Comm. v. Peoples Nat. Gas Co.*, 28 PUR4th 180 (Pa., 1978).

[195]See, *e.g.*, *Re Oklahoma Gas & Elec. Co., op. cit.*; Docket No. 19129 (FCC, 1979); *Re Georgia Power Co.*, 30 PUR4th 409 (Ga., 1979).

[196]*Re Construction Work in Progress for Public Utilities*, Order No. 298, 48 *Fed. Reg.* 24323 (FERC, 1983), Order No. 298-A, 48 *Fed. Reg.* 46012 (FERC, 1983), *aff'd in part and rem'd in part sub nom. Mid-Tex Elec. Cooperative, Inc. v. Federal Energy Regulatory*

Comm., 773 F. 2d 327, 70 PUR4th 62 (D.C. Cir. 1985) (remanded regarding potential anticompetitive effects), Order No. 448 (FERC, 1986).

[197]See *Office of Consumers' Counsel v. Ohio Pub. Utilities Comm.,* 388 N.E. 2d 1370 (1979).

[198]*1985 Annual Report on Utility and Carrier Regulation, op. cit.,* p. 447; *Ex parte Louisiana Power & Light Co.,* Order No. U-14690-A (La., 1981).

[199]*Smyth v. Ames, op. cit.*

[200]Rose, "Confusion in Valuation . . .," *op. cit.,* p. 2. To repeat the Court's words: "Rates which enable the company to operate successfully, to maintain its financial integrity, to attract capital, and to compensate its investors for the risks assumed certainly cannot be condemned as invalid, even though they might produce only a meager return on the so-called 'fair value' rate base." *Federal Power Comm. v. Hope Natural Gas Co., op. cit.,* p. 605.

[201]Rose, "Confusion in Valuation . . . ," *op. cit.,* p. 23.

[202]*Ibid.*

[203]James C. Bonbright, "The Ill-Defined Meaning of a Fair Value Rate Base" (Paper before the Iowa State Conference on Public Utility Valuation and the Rate Making Process, May 7-8, 1962) (mimeographed), pp. 49-50.

To these two factors must be added a third, to be discussed in the following chapter: uncertainty over the meaning and measurement of a "fair rate of return."

[204]Charles M. Studness, "Rate Base Disallowances and Future Utility Generating Capacity," 118 *Public Utilities Fortnightly* 33, 35 (September 4, 1986). Argue Gary and Roach: "The logic of penalizing a utility when it has acted in a prudent manner so that a utility will act in a prudent manner in the future is elusive." Richard D. Gary and Edgar M. Roach, Jr., "The Proper Regulatory Treatment of Investment in Cancelled Utility Plants," 13 *Hofstra Law Review* 469, 502-3 (1985).

[205]See, *e.g.,* Vincent Butler, "A Social Compact to Be Restored," 116 *Public Utilities Fortnightly* 17 (December 26, 1985); Irwin M. Stelzer, "The Utilities of the 1990s," *The Wall Street Journal,* January 7, 1987, p. 20.

THE RATE

OF RETURN

From the investor or company point of view it is important that there be enough revenue not only for operating expenses but also for the capital costs of the business. These include service on the debt and dividends on the stock. . . . By that standard the return to the equity owner should be commensurate with returns on investments in other enterprises having corresponding risks. That return, moreover, should be sufficient to assure confidence in the financial integrity of the enterprise, so as to maintain its credit and attract capital.

—*Justice Douglas**

While the property valuation problem, from an historical perspective, has received too much emphasis, determination of the rate of return has received too little. In recent years, however, the combined effects of the *Hope* decision and of inflation have been to shift regulatory attention from the rate base to the rate of return.[1] At a minimum, a public utility must be afforded the opportunity not only of assuring its financial integrity so that it can maintain its credit standing and attract additional capital as needed, but also of achieving earnings comparable to those of other companies having corresponding risks. Further, regulation may use the rate of return as an incentive by awarding returns that are higher than the minimum to those utilities with relatively greater efficiency. But in determining a rate, a commission may not set it so high as to exploit consumers. The concept of a fair rate of return, therefore, represents a range or a zone of reasonableness. And its quantitative importance is evident: given the rate base, earnings are 25 percent higher under a 10 percent return than under an 8 percent rate.

For regulatory purposes, the rate of return is the amount of money earned by a public utility, over and above operating costs, expressed as a percentage of the rate base. In other words, the rate of return includes interest on long-term debt, dividends on preferred stock, and earnings on common stock (including surplus or retained earnings). As Garfield and Lovejoy have put it, "the return is that money earned from operations which is available for distribution among the various classes of contributors of money capital. In the case of common stockholders, part of their share may be retained as surplus."[2] The important point to note is that the rate of return includes profit (in the traditional sense), as well as interest on debt capital and dividends on preferred stock.

The problems associated with determination of the rate of return are considered in this chapter. The leading judicial concepts and commission decisions are discussed in the first two sections.[3] The remainder of the chapter is devoted to an examination of the cost of capital standard as an estimate of a fair rate of return.

Judicial Concepts

The judicial concepts of a fair rate of return are few and far between. In some cases, the Supreme Court has enumerated a number of factors that should be considered. In general, however, the Court has limited its discussions on this matter to the question of confiscation. At the same time, the Court has made it clear that a fair rate of return may be higher than a rate which avoids confiscation, that no single rate of return is always fair, and that public utilities are not guaranteed a fair return.

The Court's Standards of "Fair"

The valuation problem was considered at length in the case of *Smyth v. Ames* in 1898, but no attempt was made to define a fair rate of return until 1909. Then, in the *Consolidated Gas* case of that year, the Supreme Court said:

> There is no particular rate of compensation which must in all cases and in all parts of the country be regarded as sufficient for capital invested in business enterprise. Such compensation must depend greatly upon circumstances and locality; among other things, the amount of risk in the business is a most important factor, as well as the locality where the business is conducted and the rate expected and usually realized there upon investments of a somewhat similar nature with

regard to the risk attending them. There may be other matters which in some cases might also be properly taken into account in determining the rate which an investor might properly expect or hope to receive and which he would be entitled to without legislative interference. The less risk, the less right to any unusual returns upon the investments. One who invests his money in a business of somewhat hazardous character is very properly held to have the right to a larger return without legislative interference, than can be obtained from an investment in Government bonds or other perfectly safe security. . . .[4]

According to the Court, therefore, a fair rate of return involved two elements — a return on invested capital and a return for risk. In this case, a 6 percent rate of return was held to be nonconfiscatory.

In the *Bluefield* case of 1923, the Court extended and elaborated on these principles and, in so doing, presented a lengthy list of factors for determining a fair rate of return. The Court argued:

What annual rate will constitute just compensation depends upon many circumstances and must be determined by the exercise of a fair and enlightened judgment, having regard to all relevant facts. A public utility is entitled to such rates as will permit it to earn a return on the value of the property which it employs for the convenience of the public equal to that generally being made at the same time and in the same general part of the country on investments in other business undertakings which are attended by corresponding risks and uncertainties; but it has no constitutional right to profits such as are realized or anticipated in highly profitable enterprises or speculative ventures. The return should be reasonably sufficient to assure confidence in the financial soundness of the utility and should be adequate, under efficient and economical management, to maintain and support its credit and enable it to raise the money necessary for the proper discharge of its public duties. A rate of return may be reasonable at one time, and become too high or too low by changes affecting opportunities for investment, the money market, and business conditions generally.[5]

As in *Smyth v. Ames,* the Court listed a number of factors for consideration, including (*1*) comparisons with other companies having corresponding risks, (*2*) the attraction of capital, (*3*) current financial and economic conditions, (*4*) the cost of capital, (*5*) the risks of the enterprise, (*6*) the financial policy and capital structure of the utility, (*7*) the competence of management, and (*8*) the company's financial history. The Court did not define these factors, nor did it indicate the relative weight that should be assigned to each. Rather, the commissions were to consider "all relevant facts" and to exercise an "enlightened judgment."

Since the *Bluefield* case, little has been added by Court decisions. In the

McCardle case of 1926, the Court found: "The evidence is more than sufficient to sustain the rate of 7 per cent found by the Commission. And recent decisions support a higher rate of return."[6] In the *United Railways* case of 1930, the Court decided that a 7.5 percent to 8 percent return was necessary under the attraction of capital standard. Said the Court:

> What is a fair return ... cannot be settled by invoking decisions of this Court made years ago based upon conditions radically different from those which prevail today. The problem is one to be tested primarily by present day conditions. Annual returns upon capital and enterprises, like wages of employees, cost of maintenance and related expenses, have materially increased the country over.... What will constitute a fair return in a given case is not capable of exact mathematical demonstration.... There is much evidence in the record to the effect that in order to induce the investment of capital in the enterprise or to enable the company to compete successfully in the market for money to finance its operations, a net return upon the valuation fixed by the commission should not be far from 8 percent.[7]

During the depression years of the thirties, the Court recognized the decline in interest rates and in business earnings throughout the country, and was willing to accept lower rates of return. In the *Dayton Power and Light* case of 1934, it approved a 6.5 percent return rather than the 8 percent sought by the utility.[8] A year later, the Court made no mention of a 6 percent rate of return allowed by the commission in the *Chesapeake and Potomac Telephone* case.[9] A 6 percent return also was upheld in the *Driscoll* case of 1939, in which the Court said:

> When bonds and preferred stocks of well seasoned companies can be floated at low rates, the allowance of an overall rate of return of a modest percentage will bring handsome yields to the common stock. Certainly the yields of the equity issues must be larger than that for the underlying securities. In this instance, the utility operates in a stable community, accustomed to the use of electricity and close to the capital markets, with funds readily available for secure investment. Long operation and adequate records make forecasts of net operating revenues fairly certain. Under such circumstances a 6 percent return after all allowable charges cannot be confiscatory.[10]

In two natural gas cases decided in the early forties, the Court approved 6.5 percent rates of return (on original cost rate bases), pointing out that the rate of return to the equity owner should be commensurate with returns on investments in other companies having corresponding risks, as well as sufficient to maintain the credit of the company and to attract capital. In the 1942 case, Chief Justice Stone argued:

The evidence shows that profits earned by individual industrial corporations declined from 11.3 percent on invested capital in 1929 to 5.1 percent in 1938. The profits of utility corporations declined during the same period from 7.2 percent to 5.1 percent. For railroad corporations the decline was from 6.4 percent to 2.3 percent. Interest rates were at a low level on all forms of investment, and among the lowest that have ever existed. The securities of natural gas companies were sold at rates of return of from 3 percent to 6 percent, with yields on most of their bond issues between 3 percent and 4 percent. The interest on large loans ranged from 2 percent to 3.25 percent.... The regulated business here seems exceptionally free from hazards which might otherwise call for special consideration in determining the fair rate of return.[11]

And in the 1944 case, Justice Douglas stated:

The rate-making process under the [Natural Gas] Act; *i.e.,* the fixing of "just and reasonable" rates, involves a balancing of the investor and the consumer interests.... From the investor or company point of view it is important that there be enough revenue not only for operating expenses but also for the capital costs of the business. These include service on the debt and dividends on the stock.... By that standard the return to equity owner should be commensurate with returns on investments in other enterprises having corresponding risks. That return, moreover, should be sufficient to assure confidence in the financial integrity of the enterprise, so as to maintain its credit and to attract capital.... The conditions under which more or less might be allowed are not important here. Nor is it important to this case to determine the various permissible ways in which any rate base on which the return is computed might be arrived at. For we are of the view that the end result in this case cannot be condemned under the Act as unjust and unreasonable from the investor or company viewpoint.[12]

The *Hope* decision thus represented a restatement of the rate of return principles listed by the Court in its earlier *Bluefield* decision.[13] These principles, moreover, remain as the judicial "guidelines" for determining a fair rate of return.[14] "Just as jurists try to make reasonable decisions, so the members of the Supreme Court expect reasonable-return judgments from commissions."[15]

Reasonable versus Nonconfiscatory Rates

The earnings of a public utility cannot be unduly restricted, or such earnings would be confiscatory and would violate the constitutional guarantees of "due process" and "equal protection of the law." Held the Court in an early railroad case:

The question of the reasonableness of a rate of charge for transportation by a railroad company, involving as it does the element of reasonableness both as regards the company and as regards the public, is eminently a question for judicial investigation, requiring due process of law for its determination. If the company is deprived of power of charging reasonable rates for the use of its property, and such deprivation takes place in the absence of an investigation by judicial machinery, it is deprived of the lawful use of its property, and thus, in substance and effect, of the property itself, without due process of law and in violation of the Constitution of the United States; and in so far as it is thus deprived, while other persons are permitted to receive reasonable profits upon their invested capital, the company is deprived of the equal protection of the laws.[16]

Is a reasonable or fair rate of return, then, the same as a nonconfiscatory rate? Or, conversely, is an unreasonable or unfair rate one that is confiscatory? The Supreme Court has held that a fair rate of return may be higher than one necessary to avoid confiscation. To quote from a 1925 decision:

A commission or other legislative body, in its discretion, may determine to be reasonable and just a rate that is substantially higher than one merely sufficient to justify a judicial finding in a confiscation case that it is high enough to yield a just and reasonable return on the value of the property used to perform the service covered by the rate. The mere fact that a rate is nonconfiscatory does not indicate that it must be deemed to be just and reasonable.[17]

Several state commissions and state supreme courts also have made this distinction, holding that a "just and reasonable" rate may be higher than a confiscatory rate.[18]

No Single Rate Always Fair

The Supreme Court has clearly indicated that no single rate of return is always fair. Rather, a fair return varies with investment opportunities, the location of a utility, the nature of the business, and general economic conditions. In the *Consolidated Gas* case, the Court said a fair rate of return depends on "circumstances and locality."[19] Following World War I, the Court recognized that prices were rising and "that annual returns upon capital and enterprise the world over have materially increased, so that what would have been a proper rate of return for capital invested in gas plants and similar public utilities a few years ago furnishes no safe criterion for the present or for the future."[20]

A few years later in the *Bluefield* case, the Court argued: "A rate of return may be reasonable at one time, and become too high or too low by changes affecting opportunities for investment, the money market, and business conditions generally."[21] Furthermore, because of differences in risk, a fair rate of return also will vary by industry or company. For example, a higher rate may be necessary for a street railway than for an electric or gas company.[22]

No Guarantee of a Fair Return

The Supreme Court also has stated that public utilities are not guaranteed a fair rate of return. In a 1933 case, the Court argued:

> The due process clause of the Fourteenth Amendment safeguards against the taking of private property, or the compelling of its use, for the service of the public without just compensation. . . . But it does not assure to public utilities the right under all circumstances to have a return upon the value of the property so used. The use of, or the failure to obtain, patronage, due to competition, does not justify the imposition of charges that are exorbitant and unjust to the public. The clause of the Constitution here invoked does not protect public utilities against such business hazards.[23]

In the *Market Street Railway* case, the Court stated: "The due process clause has been applied to prevent governmental destruction of existing economic values. It has not and cannot be applied to insure values or to restore values that have been lost by the operation of economic forces."[24] Public utilities, in other words, are protected against arbitrary action of commissions, but not from normal "business hazards" or from the operation of "economic forces."

Summary of Judicial Decisions

Throughout all of its decisions, the Supreme Court has formulated no specific rules for determining a fair rate of return, but it has enumerated a number of guidelines. The Court has made it clear that confiscation of property must be avoided, that no one rate can be considered fair at all times, and that regulation does not guarantee a fair return. The Court also has consistently stated that a necessary prerequisite for profitable operations is efficient and economical management.[25] Beyond this is a list of several factors the commissions are supposed to consider in making their decisions, but no weights have been assigned.

The relevant economic criteria enunciated by the Court are three: financial integrity, capital attraction, and comparable earnings. Stated another way, the rate of return allowed a public utility should be high enough: (*1*) to maintain the financial integrity of the enterprise; (*2*) to enable the utility to attract the new capital it needs to serve the public; and (*3*) to provide a return on common equity that is commensurate with returns on investments in other enterprises of corresponding risk. These three economic criteria are interrelated and have been used widely for many years by regulatory commissions throughout the country in determining the rate of return allowed public utilities.[26]

In reality, the concept of a fair rate of return represents a "zone of reasonableness."[27] As explained by the Pennsylvania commission:

> There is a range of reasonableness within which earnings may properly fluctuate and still be deemed just and reasonable and not excessive or extortionate. It is bounded at one level by investor interest against confiscation and the need for averting any threat to the security for the capital embarked upon the enterprise. At the other level it is bounded by consumer interest against excessive and unreasonable charges for service.[28]

As long as the allowed return falls within this zone, therefore, it is just and reasonable. "As the fair value of the property is a judgment figure so is the denominated fair rate of return a judgment determination."[29] It is the task of the commissions to translate these generalizations into quantitative terms.

Commission Decisions

Bonbright has warned that those "familiar with the actual practice of American rate regulation need no reminder about the uncertain relationship between the supposed 'principles' of rate-of-return determination . . . and the considerations that actually lead commissions to allow whatever rates of return they do allow in specific cases."[30] He continues:

> In the opinions that accompany their rate orders, commissions seldom attempt to disclose the reasons why they find, say, 5.85 percent fair in one case and 6.2 percent fair in another. Especially in fair-value jurisdictions, some of the decisions lead one to suspect that the commissions have first reached a conclusion as to reasonable revenue requirements in terms of dollars per annum and then have proceeded to translate these requirements into whatever combination of a rate base and a percentage rate of return will be likely to pass muster with the appellate courts or with public sentiment.[31]

To illustrate: The New York commission, in a 1915 decision, reduced the rates of the Edison Company to yield "6 percent on nearly $100,000,000, which it seems . . . must certainly cover the value of the 'capital actually expended in the enterprise.'"[32] In a 1933 Texas decision, all mention of the rate of return was confined to a single sentence: "We find that an annual rate of return equal to 7 percent of the present fair value of the properties as herein found is adequate."[33] The North Carolina commission, in a 1949 decision, explained that the allowed rate of return was determined after consideration of several factors:

> In arriving at a rate of return . . . the Commission has given consideration to the financial history of the company; to its earnings in the past as compared with the present; to the cost of rendering service under existing high prices; to the ratio of its debt capital to its equity capital; to the general market trends in the cost of labor, materials, and capital; to the opportunity of investors to invest in other business undertakings of comparable stability and soundness; to the opportunity for growth and expansion and to public demand thereof; to the protection afforded against destructive competition; to the value of the service to telephone users and to the probability of diminishing returns from rates and charges that approach burdensome proportions.[34]

In a 1963 decision, the Arkansas commission concluded: "In order to be conservative, the commission has decided that a rate of return from 6.25 percent to 6.50 percent would be reasonable in this case."[35] The New Jersey commission, in a 1971 decision, found a fair rate of return of 7.9 percent, based upon "a review of the entire record and consideration of petitioner's proposed capital structure, costs of capital, attrition, and erosion. . . ."[36] And, in finding a return of 8.372 percent on a fair value rate base in a 1980 decision, the Illinois commission said that

> . . . the commission's decision regarding a fair rate of return must be one based on reasoned judgment. The commission, in reaching its decision on a fair rate of return, has considered the continuing inflation in our economy, the volatile nature of current interest rates, the generally depressed condition of electric utility common stocks, the deratings of the company's debt, the limitations of current regulatory tools, and the decision to include certain construction work in progress in rate base.[37]

Allowed Rates of Return

Before turning to the standards underlying commission decisions, it is desirable to summarize the rates of return which have been allowed in the past. In discussing allowed rates of return, however, it must be emphasized that any rate by itself is meaningless unless considered in connection with a commission's entire order; that is, with the type of rate base and test year employed, with the inclusion or exclusion of CWIP, and so forth. To illustrate: It is obvious that a 10 percent rate of return, say, on an original cost rate base of $100 million that excludes CWIP is far different from an 8.50 percent rate of return on a reproduction cost or fair value rate base of $150 million (or an original cost rate base of $150 million that includes CWIP).

The relationship between the allowed rate of return and the type of rate base employed by the commissions has been analyzed in five studies.[38] In each case, it was concluded that when commissions adopt either reproduction cost or fair value rate bases, they partially offset the effect of the larger bases by granting lower percentage rates of return, but that the combined effect of the larger rate base and the lower rate of return is to permit higher levels of earnings in reproduction cost and fair value jurisdictions. Eiteman, for example, found that the average rate of return for telephone companies in original cost cases was 5.93 percent, compared with *an equivalent return* of 7.98 percent on original cost in reproduction cost jurisdictions, and 6.62 percent on original cost in fair value cases. The average returns, therefore, were approximately 35 percent higher for reproduction cost companies and 12 percent higher for fair value companies than they were for original cost companies.

The conclusion of these studies supports the argument often advanced by representatives of public utilities to the effect that since commissions are reluctant to allow high rates of return, adequate earnings are more easily achieved when a reproduction cost or fair value rate base is employed. Further, the conclusion also is consistent with Bonbright's contention that some commissions appear to determine a firm's total revenue requirement before either the rate base or the rate of return is established.

One further factor should be kept in mind. Because of attrition (see Table 9-6), there is commonly a difference between the rate of return prescribed by a commission and the rate of return earned by a utility.

Electric, Gas, Telephone, Water Utilities. The prescribed or allowed rate of return for electric, gas, telephone, and water utilities has varied considerably, depending on the industry and the company, as well as the period of time. During the height of the rate base measurement controversy, many commissions maintained a "standard" rate of return for long periods of time — 8 percent in New York and 7 percent in Pennsylvania, for instance, during the twenties.[39] A utility's total earnings, therefore, were closely related to the type of rate base used by a commission. Then, as interest rates declined, the standard rate also fell. During the thirties, the standard rate of return became 6 percent in New York; a rate defended by the commission in the following words:

> It exceeds the actual cost of raising funds for a public utility in this state which is soundly financed and properly conducted. Any utility corporation which cannot earn for its stockholders an adequate return

upon the basis of a 6 percent return has neglected to conduct its affairs upon the basis of sound finance and engineering.[40]

In the 1950s, allowed rates of return centered around 6 percent, with somewhat higher rates for utilities in fast-growing areas and for utilities under the jurisdiction of more liberal commissions.[41] In the 1960s, allowed rates of return started upward, often exceeding 7 percent.[42] This upward trend continued throughout the 1970s and early 1980s, as rates of return in excess of 10 percent became common, due to inflation and high interest rates. Table 9-1 gives recent (1985) rates of return established by representative state commissions. In 1976, the FCC prescribed a rate of return for the American Telephone and Telegraph Company in the range of 9.5 to 10 percent; in April of 1981, a return of 12.75 percent was authorized.[43] The FPC, in 1965, approved a return of 12 percent on average production investment for natural gas producers, noting the greater financial risks of exploration and production[44]; a return that went to 15 percent in the 1970s.[45] In its 1980 settlement orders, the FERC permitted rates of return ranging from 8.67 to 10.75 percent in electric rate cases.[46] In recent years, due to falling interest rates and an improved stock market, allowed rates of return have declined. Thus, in August of 1986, the FCC authorized a return of 12.2 percent for AT&T Communications.[47]

Pipelines. While under the jurisdiction of the Interstate Commerce Commission, pipeline companies transporting crude oil were permitted an 8 percent rate of return on a valuation rate base.[48] In defending this rate, the commission argued: "The hazards and uncertain future of the common-carrier business of the pipelines suggest the fairness of a somewhat larger rate of return than it would be reasonable to expect would be applied in industries of a more stable character, where the volume of traffic is more accurately predicted."[49] In the case of pipelines used for the transportation of gasoline and other liquid products of petroleum — the "products lines" — a 10 percent return on valuation was established by the ICC.[50] Jurisdiction over oil pipelines was transferred to the FERC in 1977 and, until 1985, the commission struggled to develop the methodology that it would use.[51]

For natural gas pipeline companies, the FPC found rates of 6.125 to 6.50 percent on original cost rate bases in the early 1960s,[52] and somewhat higher rates in the late 1960s (6.625 and 6.875 percent, for example[53]) and in the 1970s (9.25, 9.66, and 10.157 percent, in three cases[54]) and early 1980s (a range of 11.73 to 14.05 percent in 1985 cases[55]). The great majority of all natural gas pipeline cases, it should be noted, are terminated by settlement.

The Cost of Capital Standard[56]

Since the end of World War II, there has been a significant shift in

TABLE 9-1

Rate of Return Allowed by Representative State Commissions[a]

Commission	Electric Utilities Rate of Return on:		Gas Utilities Rate of Return on:		Telephone Utilities Rate of Return on:		Water Utilities Rate of Return on:	
	Rate Base	Equity	Rate Base	Equity	Rate Base	Equity	Rate Base	Equity
Alaska PUC	12.96%	16.50%	—	—	12.96%	15.68%	13.98%	16.00%
California PUC	12.37	15.00	13.05%	15.25%	12.72	15.50	11.75	14.00
District of Columbia PSC	—	—	—	—	12.29	15.10	—	—
Florida PSC	9.81	14.50	10.58	15.75	11.15	15.00	13.46	14.62
Illinois CC	12.63	15.40	12.22	15.28	12.00	14.76	13.17	14.28
Kansas SCC	—	—	12.28	15.35	9.86	15.71	—	—
Michigan PSC	10.30	14.50	9.26	14.82	11.17	13.50	—	—
Mississippi PSC	11.85	15.50	11.68	12.02	—	—	—	—
Missouri PSC	12.17[b]	15.62	13.06	15.08	11.36	14.74	—	—
Montana PSC	11.24	14.00	—	—	11.64	14.00	—	—
New Mexico PSC	11.72	14.50	—	—	—	—	12.98	12.13
New York PSC	12.09	15.00	12.08	14.00	11.85	14.00	12.40	13.70
Ohio PUC	13.43	16.65	12.04	14.56	12.22	14.58	—	—
Pennsylvania PUC	11.18	15.82	12.42	14.50	12.38	15.15	12.50	15.00
Tennessee PSC	—	—	12.92	15.20	—	—	10.57	14.50
Texas PUC	12.56	16.30	—	—	—	—	9.48	14.93
Virginia SCC	—	—	11.17	14.50	10.35	15.00	11.53	14.50
Washington UTC	11.53	14.80	—	—	12.04	14.52	11.93	14.35
Wisconsin PSC	11.82	14.50	11.46	14.50	—	—	—	—

[a]The decisions are generally those made in 1985.
[b]Fair value rate base.
Source: *1985 Annual Report on Utility and Carrier Regulation* (Washington, D.C.: National Association of Regulatory Utility Commissioners, 1987), pp. 332-79.

regulatory emphasis, with the fair rate of return becoming a more important part of rate cases. This shift in emphasis, moreover, has become even more pronounced since 1968, when rapidly spiraling costs (due to inflation, environmental protection, rising fuel prices, etc.) forced utilities across the country to seek almost continuous rate increases.

During this period, the cost of capital standard — sometimes referred to as the "differentiated rate of return" — has been developed. Since many commissions consider that the determination of the cost of capital is at least a first step in arriving at a fair rate of return, this section is devoted to an analysis of its meaning, application, and interpretation by the agencies and by financial experts.[57]

Definition of Cost of Capital

Justice Brandeis expounded the cost of capital concept in his 1923 dissenting opinion in the *Southwestern Bell* case:

> In essence, there is no difference between the capital charge and operating expenses, depreciation, and taxes. Each is a part of the current cost of supplying the service; and each should be met from current income. When the capital charges are for interest on the floating debt paid at the current rate, this is readily seen. But it is no less true of a legal obligation to pay interest on long-term bonds, entered into years before the rate hearing and to continue for years thereafter; and it is true also of the economic obligation to pay dividends on stock, preferred or common.[58]

As used by Justice Brandeis and by most commissions in recent years, the term "cost of capital" may be defined as the annual percent which a utility must receive to maintain its credit, to pay a return to the owners of the enterprise, and to insure the attraction of capital in amounts adequate to meet future needs. Mathematically, the cost of capital is the composite of the cost of the several classes of capital used by a utility — debt, preferred (and preference) stock, and common stock (par value plus earned and capital surplus) — weighted on the basis of an appropriate capital structure. If short-term debt has become a permanent part of a utility's financing, it is included.[59] Tax deferrals, resulting from the pre-1971 investment tax credit and/or accelerated depreciation, are included at a zero cost rate (unless they have been deducted from the rate base); the job development tax credit is either included in common equity or as a separate item (at the overall cost of capital).[60] A typical capital structure is shown in Table 9-2, illustrating the determination of an overall cost of capital of 10.12 percent. It should be noted that unless a utility has significant investments in nonutility assets, its invested capital should approximate its original cost rate base, except for investment in construction work in progress.[61]

TABLE 9-2

Estimated Cost of Capital

	Percentage of Capital Structure	Annual Cost	Weighted Cost
Long-term Debt	41.25%	9.87%	4.07%
Short-term Debt	2.13	9.00	.19
Preferred Stock	7.22	8.92	.64
Common Stock	34.71	14.00	4.86
Unamortized Investment Tax Credits:			
Pre-1971	1.14	0	—
Post-1971	3.51	10.12	.36
Deferred Federal Income Taxes	10.04	0	—
Overall Cost of Capital	100.00%		10.12%

In applying the cost of capital standard, commissions face numerous and difficult problems "which almost defy solution."[62] Two major and three related problems will be analyzed below: (1) the appropriate capital structure, (2) the allowable cost of senior capital and common equity, (3) the incentive to efficiency, (4) "earnings erosion" during periods of inflation, and (5) "gradualism" during volatile markets.

The Capital Structure

The first step in estimating the overall cost of capital involves the appropriate capital structure. There are two important issues. First, the traditional theory of business finance holds that the average cost of capital to a firm varies with the capital structure upon which it is based.[63] The interest rate on debt is normally lower than the cost of equity capital.[64] Consequently, within limits determined by such factors as the risk of a business, the overall cost may be somewhat lower when the debt-equity ratio is high than when the debt-equity ratio is low. Given this theory, some argue that the regulatory commissions should base their cost of capital estimates on what they consider an "ideal" or "typical" capital structure without regard to the actual capitalization of a particular utility being considered. Others argue that cost estimates should be based upon either the actual capital structure or the structure that is expected in the near future.

Second, when the utility under consideration is a subsidiary of another company, whose capital structure should be used — that of the subsidiary or that of the consolidated system? The widespread existence of holding companies in the public utility sector, plus the trend toward diversification, makes this an important consideration in many cases.

Actual versus Hypothetical Capital Structure. Locklin has argued that most commissions "disregard actual capital structures and set up an ideal or normal structure for the purpose. To do otherwise would burden the public with the higher costs of obtaining capital that result from a capital structure that is something less than ideal, and may, in fact, be quite unsound."[65] And Rose argues: "When a commission in determining cost of capital disregards the actual capital structure or a capital structure proposed by management it is no more invading the domain of management than when it disregards unreasonable expenses for labor, fuel, or other productive factors in prescribing rates."[66]

Others maintain that in normal circumstances the actual or planned capital structure should be used in computing the cost of capital. As was discussed in Chapter 6,[67] a utility's existing capitalization may well have resulted from sound and economical decisions when made, although a different structure might attract capital at a lower cost at the time of a rate case. While hindsight is often superior to foresight, financial decisions must be made on the basis of judgment of present and future conditions.[68] Moreover, as Bonbright has argued, "the use of a hypothetical or 'typical' capitalization substitutes an estimate of what the capital cost *would be* under nonexisting conditions for what it *actually* is or *will soon be* under prevailing conditions."[69] Unless the rate of return to equity capital is adjusted upward, and it seldom is, the utility is forced to adopt the hypothetical debt ratio to earn its allowed rate. But if the hypothetical debt ratio is significantly higher than the actual debt ratio, it may take several years of financing exclusively by means of debt to attain the higher ratio. During this period, the utility is unable to realize the rate on equity found to be required. Further, issuance of securities is under the control of the vast majority of the regulatory commissions, so that there is a check on unsound financing. "It seems, then, that it is economically sound to leave with management the decision as to proper debt ratio, at least within that area where the directors are not usurping or defaulting on their duties as directors."[70]

During the 1950s and 1960s, many commissions sought an approximation of an ideal capital structure through the use of a hypothetical capitalization, particularly in telephone cases. As explained by the Alabama Supreme Court:

> The ideal capital structure would allow a debt-equity ratio in amounts that the company would get its full benefit in the amount of debt capital, and yet not have the debt component so high as to discourage prudent investors. This ideal capital structure is not static. However, many commissions and courts for rate-making purposes have concluded that a debt-equity ratio of 45 percent debt 55 percent equity most nearly approximates a proper debt-equity ratio.[71]

The Massachusetts commission thus rejected both the actual capitalization (62 percent debt) and one proposed by the company (35 percent debt), adopting a hypothetical capital structure of 45 to 50 percent debt. The commission pointed out that the company's actual capital structure had a debt ratio that was too high, while the proposed ratio represented an inefficient capital structure because it did not include an amount of debt which could be reasonably assumed by the company.[72] The Mississippi commission, in a 1956 decision, held:

> (4) Southern Bell's capital structure during the test period, with an average debt ratio of 21.7 percent, is imprudent and uneconomical, and imposes an unjust and unwarranted financial burden on the telephone subscribers. For the purpose of assessing the priority of the company's intrastate rates which prevail during the test period, we have reformed the capital structure on the basis of a debt ratio in the range of 45 percent to 50 percent, which we find is prudent, fair, and equitable.[73]

And the District of Columbia commission rejected a telephone company's actual capital structure of 15 percent debt and 85 percent equity as being unrealistic, adopting for ratemaking purposes a hypothetical capital structure of 40 percent debt and 60 percent equity. "In our judgment," said the commission, "this capital structure, when applied to the cost of debt and equity, will amply afford sufficient earnings to pay a reasonable dividend and allow an increment for surplus."[74]

Other commissions, during this same period, adopted the actual capitalization. The New York commission declared that to disregard the "actual historic structure" created with the commission's approval "would unsettle investors" and remove from management control over the capital structure. It added that "having approved a company's capital structure . . . the company and the public have the right to rely upon our using the capital structure which we have approved as the basis for determining its rate of return."[75] The commission later indicated, however, that it would disregard the actual capital structure when it was "wasteful."[76] The Colorado commission said that it "could adopt a hypothetical structure for rate making in the event that applicants' actual financial structure is not in the long run public interest . . . keeping in mind that responsibility for financial decisions rests with management."[77] The Arizona commission rejected the use of hypothetical capital structures on the grounds that they involve "pure speculation," while actual capitalizations are "more realistic."[78] The Florida commission held that capital structures "fall within the prerogatives of management" and that "invasion of the field of management in such a sensitive area is justified only when the public interest requires the exercise of extreme measures for its protection and benefit."[79] Finally, the FCC rejected the adoption of a hypothetical capital structure for the American Telephone and

Telegraph Company in a 1967 decision, but noted that in fixing the allowable rate of return it would take into account the "extraordinary amount of risk insurance respondents have given its stockholders by its low debt ratio policy."[80]

Debt ratios began to rise during the late 1960s and early 1970s, and the financial condition of the public utility sector began to deteriorate. It became the common practice to use actual or expected capitalizations; actual where an historic test year is used, expected when a projected or future test year is used.[81] The objective, in short, shifted from minimization of the short-term cost of capital to protection of a utility's ability "to raise capital at all times. This objective requires that a public utility make every effort to keep indebtedness at a prudent and conservative level."[82] A hypothetical capital structure is used only where a utility's actual capitalization is clearly out of line with those of other utilities in its industry or where a utility is diversified.[83]

Consolidated Capital Structure and Double Leverage. Where a utility is a wholly owned subsidiary which obtains its equity capital through its parent corporation, commissions commonly use the capital structure of the consolidated system.[84] When (*a*) no substantial minority interest exists and (*b*) risks are similar between parent and subsidiary, a consolidated capital structure is appropriate, for "market evaluations of the parent's stock afford the primary evidence of the current cost of equity to the subsidiary. . . . Moreover, it would be inappropriate to use either the subsidiary's own cost of debt or its capital structure because the capital structure ratios would be inconsistent with the respective cost rates and the composite cost of total capital would be distorted."[85]

Use of a consolidated capital structure, however, must be distinguished from the "double leverage" concept. The latter concept "prescribes the use of the cost of total capital (the composite cost of debt and equity) to the parent company as the measure of the cost of common equity to the operating subsidiary."[86] Double leverage, it is argued by advocates, has the advantage of using the actual data for the subsidiary for which a fair rate of return is being estimated.[87] But the concept is a controversial one, since its use may result in a "cost" of common equity that is lower than the opportunity cost.[88]

When a substantial minority interest exists or when there are substantial differences in risks between a subsidiary and its parent, neither a consolidated capital structure nor the double leverage approach is appropriate.[89] The following case is illustrative. The Maine commission (see Table 9-3) attempted to use the double leverage approach in a case involving the New England Telephone and Telegraph Company. First, the commission noted that the subsidiary was 86 percent owned by AT&T and 14 percent owned by outside (minority) investors. Second, it determined AT&T's capital structure and associated cost rates. Third, it determined the subsidiary's capital structure and associated embedded cost of debt. It then used the overall

TABLE 9-3

Example of Double Leverage

A) AT&T's Capital Structure and Cost of Capital

	Capital Structure	Cost	Weighted Cost
Debt	25%	6.50%	1.63%
Preferred Stock	9	7.80	.70
Common Equity	66	11.50	7.59
Overall Cost of Capital			9.92%

B) Subsidiary's Capital Structure and Cost of Capital

	Capital Structure	Cost	Weighted Cost
Debt	45.0%	6.99%	3.15%
Common Equity:			
AT&T Supplied	47.3	9.92	4.69
Minority Supplied	7.7	11.50	.89
Overall Cost of Capital			8.73%

Source: *New England Teleph. & Teleg. Co. v. Maine Pub. Utilities Comm.*, 27 PUR4th 1, 38, 39 (1978).

cost of capital for AT&T's capital structure and associated embedded cost of debt. It then used the overall cost of capital for AT&T as the cost of equity capital on 86 percent of the subsidiary's common stock and a cost of 11.5 percent on the remaining 14 percent of common equity held by outside investors. In overturning the commission's decision on this approach, the Maine Supreme Judicial Court noted, among other things, that "the commission is unable to cite to us any authority in which a double leveraging adjustment or a consolidated capital structure has been applied where a substantial minority interest exists."[90]

The Annual Cost of Capital

The second step in estimating the overall cost of capital involves the determination of the cost of senior capital and of equity capital. These costs are then applied to the capitalization of a utility to find the weighted cost of capital.

The Cost of Senior Capital. Few problems arise in computing the cost of senior capital. By common practice, the cost of senior capital is the embedded cost: the actual fixed charges on long-term debt and the annual dividend requirements of preferred (and preference) stock.[91] When a future test year is used, the embedded cost is used for existing debt and the current cost for additional indebtedness contemplated in the projected test year.[92] When a hypothetical capital structure is used which contains "imputed debt" (*i.e.,* the hypothetical debt is higher than the utility's actual debt outstanding), the embedded cost is used for outstanding debt and the current cost for the imputed debt.[93] Except for these circumstances, the embedded cost of senior capital is appropriate. Basing the cost of existing senior capital upon the hypothetical cost of doing senior financing under current conditions of the bond and stock market would represent (just as in the case of reproduction cost property valuations) an alternative not available to a utility.[94]

In addition, allowances are usually made for the costs of financing, such as discounts and premiums on sale, call premiums paid when bonds are retired before maturity, underwriting fees, and other flotation costs. Such allowances, however, are not uniform. For example, with respect to call premiums, some commissions have charged such costs of refunding bonds to stockholders,[95] while others have charged them to ratepayers by amortizing the premiums over a reasonable period[96]; with respect to flotation costs, some commissions deny them unless a new stock issue is planned.[97]

The Cost of Equity Capital. The most difficult problem in determining the overall cost of capital arises in estimating the cost of equity capital. The relevant question is: How much must a utility earn to induce investors to hold and to continue to buy common stock? In answering this question, it is important to realize that circular reasoning is involved. In the absence of a fixed, expressed, or implied commitment as to the dividend rate, the actual cost of floating a stock issue is indeterminate. Investors' decisions are largely based on a utility's expected earnings and upon their stability, as well as upon alternative uses of investment funds. Yet, since the allowable amount of earnings is the object of a rate case, a commission's decision, in turn, will affect investors' decisions.

There are several approaches for estimating the cost of equity capital, but two principal ones have evolved in recent years: the "market-determined" standard and the "comparable earnings" standard.[98] The former is a market-oriented approach that focuses on investor expectations in terms of a utility's earnings, dividends, and market prices. The latter is an alternative investment approach that focuses on what capital can earn in various alternatives with comparable risk.

The Market-Determined Standard. The market-determined standard relies upon stock market transactions and estimates of investor expectations. Three major approaches have been, or are being, employed: e/p ratios (earnings/price ratios), the DCF or Discounted Cash Flow Model, and the CAPM or Capital Asset Pricing Model.

The earnings/price ratio approach holds that the cost of equity capital to a utility is equal to the ratio of current earnings per share to the market price per share. Thus, if a utility's annual earnings are $5 per share and the average market price of its common stock for that same period is $38, the earnings/price ratio is 13.16 percent. (The ratio must be increased to allow for flotation costs. An allowance of 5 percent would result in an adjusted ratio of 13.85 percent — 13.16 percent divided by .95.) The method was widely used in the 1950s and early 1960s, although there was growing recognition of an underlying theoretical problem: The earnings/price ratio approach ignores the fact that investors purchase common stock for future growth and not for past or current earnings alone.[99] As a result, a growth factor must be added in computing the cost of equity capital.

Finance theory holds that the cost of common equity capital

> . . . is the equity investors' capitalization rate, or required market rate of return, competitively determined in the capital markets, adjusted by an appropriate allowance for underpricing in connection with sales of additional shares, including allowance for market pressure and for costs of flotation and underwriting. The capitalization rate before the allowance for underpricing is the discount rate that equates all expected dividends in the future plus the market price that investors eventually expect to realize to the present market price. While this is a simple enough concept, it is difficult to measure since measurement requires the estimation of the expectations of the investors who determine the present market price. Such estimates, of course, involve the exercise of informed judgment.[100]

The discounted cash flow model (DCF) represents an attempt to estimate the equity investors' capitalization rate. Mathematically,

$$k = \frac{d}{p} + g$$

where: k is the investor's capitalization or discount rate (*i.e.*, the cost of capital);
   d is the current dividend per share;
   p is the current market price per share; and
   g is the expected rate of growth in dividends per share.[101]

Thus, if the stock of a particular utility pays a $3 dividend, which is expected to grow at a rate of 6 percent per year, and if investors are willing to pay $38 for the stock, the required return on common equity (assuming a 5 percent allowance for flotation costs) is 14.31 percent.[102] However, use of the

DCF model for regulatory purposes involves both theoretical and practical difficulties.

The theoretical issues include the assumption of a constant retention ratio (*i.e.*, a fixed payout ratio) and the assumption that dividends will continue to grow at rate "g" in perpetuity. Neither of these assumptions has any validity, particularly in recent years. Further, the investors' capitalization rate and the cost of equity capital to a utility for application to book value (*i.e.*, an original cost rate base) are identical only when market price is equal to book value.[103] Indeed, DCF advocates assume that if the market price of a utility's common stock exceeds its book value, the allowable rate of return on common equity is too high and should be lowered; and vice versa.[104] Many question the assumption that market price should equal book value, believing that "the earnings of utilities should be sufficiently high to achieve market-to-book ratios which are consistent with those prevailing for stocks of unregulated companies."[105]

Most frequently, the major practical issue involves the determination of the growth rate; a determination that is highly complex and that requires considerable judgment.[106] The crux of the measurement problem is this: How can investors' expectation of *future* growth be measured? When past growth rates are used as a proxy for future growth rates, which is a common practice, it is far from obvious as to (*a*) which time periods have the most relevance to investors and (*b*) whether the prospective growth rate should be determined by using trends in dividends per share, earnings per share, and/or book value per share and exactly how the information contained in these various measures is used by investors.[107] Indeed, one study showed that the expectations of security analysts outperformed the extrapolation of historical trends in explaining share prices.[108] But when future growth rates are used, it is not clear whether the prospective growth rate should be determined by using analysts' estimates, surveys of institutional investors, or the expected return on common equity times the retention ratio.[109] And, even when all of these issues have been settled, there remains the circularity problem: Since regulation establishes a level of authorized earnings which, in turn, implicitly influences dividends per share, estimation of the growth rate from such data is an inherently circular process. For these reasons, the DCF model "suggests a degree of precision which is in fact not present"[110] and leaves "wide room for controversy and argument about the level of k."[111]

The newest entrant[112] is the capital asset pricing model (CAPM), which holds that the cost of equity capital or expected return on a utility's common equity is equivalent to that on a riskless security plus a risk premium related to the risk inherent in a particular utility's stock; that is, the model combines risk and return in a single measure.[113] The formula is as follows:

$$R = R_f + (R_m - R_f)\,\beta$$

> *where:* R   is the total return;
> R_f is the risk free return;
> R_m is the stock market return (or the expected return on a stock market portfolio); and
> β   is the beta coefficient (or the utility's relevant market risk).

Thus, assuming a stock market return of 13.9 percent, a risk free return (Treasury bills) of 7.8 percent, and a beta of 1.057, the total return or cost of equity capital would be 14.25 percent.[114]

Despite its appeal, the CAP model also has both theoretical and practical problems. The theoretical issues include the reliability of the model's basic assumptions[115] and the static nature of the model.[116] The practical problems surround the beta coefficient; "the only variable in the CAPM equation that is unique to the particular firm for which the cost of equity capital is being determined."[117] They include: How should beta be measured — stock market price alone or total return on investment (*i.e.*, dividends plus capital gains)? What period of time should be used for such measurement? What is the proper measure of stock market performance (*i.e.*, Dow Jones index, Standard & Poor's index, etc.)? Finally, the evidence suggests that betas are unstable over time and that they move in the opposite direction from investors' perceptions of risk.[118] For these reasons, many would agree that the CAP model, at least at this stage in its development, "is inaccurate, incomplete, and unreliable as a measure of a firm's equity cost of capital."[119]

The Comparable Earnings Standard. The comparable earnings standard[120] recognizes a fundamental economic concept; namely, opportunity cost. This concept states that the cost of using any resource — land, labor and/or capital — for a specific purpose is the return that could have been earned in the next best alternative use. The opportunity cost to a farmer using his land for beef grazing is what the land would yield after expenses if used for raising tobacco or for growing wheat; the opportunity cost to a worker in accepting one job is what he forgoes by not accepting the next best alternative. Likewise, the opportunity cost to an investor in a utility's common stock is what that capital would yield in an alternative investment — in another utility's or industrial's common stock; in utility, corporate, or government bonds; in real estate; etc. Stated another way, the opportunity cost of capital concept holds "that capital should not be committed to any venture unless it can earn a return commensurate with that prospectively available in alternative employments of similar risk."[121]

The relevance of the opportunity cost concept was recognized by Judge Hand in a 1920 case:

> The recurrent appeal to a just rate and a fair value assumes that the effort is to insure such a profit as would induce the venture originally and that the public will keep its faith so impliedly given. That, I think, involves a tacit comparison of the profit possible under the rate with

profits available elsewhere; *i.e.*, under those competitive enterprises which offer an alternative investment. The implication is that the original adventurer would compare future rates, varying as they would with the going profit, and would find them enough, but no more than enough, to induce him to choose this investment. By insuring such a return it is assumed that the supply of capital will be secured necessary to the public service. As the profits in the supposed alternative investment will themselves vary, so it is assumed to be a condition of the investors' bargain that their profit shall measurably follow the general rates. It is, of course, not relevant here to discuss these presuppositions, since they have now the support of authoritative law.[122]

The comparable earnings approach is implemented by examining earnings on book common equity for enterprises that have comparable risks *or* by examining earnings on book common equity for enterprises that have different risks and then making an allowance for those risk differences. Earnings on book common equity are used since the resulting cost of common equity is to be applied to an original cost rate base (in most jurisdictions).[123] The comparable earnings approach, further, requires that comparisons be made with both regulated and nonregulated alternatives, if the results are to have any validity, for two basic reasons. First, the alternatives confronting investors include both regulated and nonregulated enterprises. There is active competition for investor capital; no company enjoys a monopoly of the capital markets. Investors will seek the opportunity which provides the greatest profit, commensurate with the risks involved. Second, returns of regulated firms always must be used with extreme caution. At best, they reflect what the informed judgments of regulatory commissions have permitted such utilities to earn and may not be indicative of what could have been earned in the competitive market.[124]

The most difficult problem in applying the comparable earnings standard is the determination of relative risk. Prior to the 1970s, it was frequently argued that regulation tended to eliminate some of the risks to which nonregulated enterprises are subject, so that utilities' overall or business risk tended to be less than the corresponding business risk of industrial firms. As a result, utilities financed with larger amounts of senior capital (*i.e.*, they had significantly higher debt ratios). But there is clear evidence that the risk of public utilities has increased in more recent years, particularly with the introduction of competition and significant disallowances,[125] and there is also support for the proposition that regulation itself is a risk.[126] Yet, the fact remains that there is no accepted method of measuring relative risk. Some have argued that risk can be measured by instability of earnings; statistically, by use of the standard deviation or coefficient of variation. Some advocate the use of market price-book value ratios and/or market price-earnings ratios to reflect how investors appraise relative risk.[127] Beta has received attention in some cases although, as noted earlier, betas tend to be unstable over time. Still others maintain that the higher debt ratios of utilities serve to offset their overall lower business risk, with the result that the financial or equity risks of utilities and industrials are similar under current economic conditions. And, finally, some rely upon the various indices published by Merrill Lynch (the Merrill Lynch Suitability Rating), Standard & Poor's (the S&P's Quality Rating), and/or Value Line (the Value Line Safety and Timeliness Ratings).

Despite the difficulty of measuring relative risk, the comparable earnings standard is no harder to apply than is the market-determined standard. The DCF method, to illustrate, requires a subjective determination of the growth rate the market is contemplating. Moreover, as Leventhal has argued: "Unless the utility is permitted to earn a return comparable to that available elsewhere on similar risk, it will not be able in the long run to attract capital."[128]

Other Methods. Several other approaches have been used to estimate the cost of common equity. Two of these should be noted. First, there is the risk premium method which is based upon the premise that common equity carries a higher risk than debt.[129] This approach is relatively straightforward: (1) determine the historic spread between the return on debt and the return on common equity and (2) add this risk premium to the current debt yield to derive an approximation of current equity return requirements. Thus, the Federal Communications Commission, in its 1981 decision regarding the American Telephone and Telegraph Company, determined that the appropriate risk premium (for an Aaa-rated utility) was 2.5 percentage points which, when added to the then-current cost of debt of 14.9 percent, resulted in a cost of equity capital of 17.4 percent.[130]

Like other methods, however, there are a number of specific problems. Over what historic period of time should the spread be established? Does the spread between the return on debt and the return on equity remain constant over time and at all interest levels?[131] Should the spread be expressed on a before- or after-tax basis to the investor? What debt instruments should be used (*e.g.*, government securities versus corporate or utility bonds)? What equity securities should be used? How should the resulting return requirement be adjusted for the risk that corresponds to a given utility? At this stage, the risk premium approach is only a subsidiary method.

Second, and at least as another possible subsidiary method, one can test the likely results of the recommended cost of equity or overall cost of capital. In the 1970s, due to low interest coverages, many electric utilities had difficulty financing. Several commissions sought an allowed return that would result in sufficient interest coverage.[132] Other factors which have been considered are cash flow, internal funds for construction expenditures, and cash earnings for dividends. Many utilities have detailed financial models which permit such results to be readily estimated.[133]

Conclusions on Cost of Capital. It is clear that determining the cost of capital is not an exact science. It is based on as objective and comparable data as possible, but experience and judgment must be used in drawing conclusions from that data. In the words of the National Energy Board:

> One of the few things upon which the regulated industries, the regulatory agencies, and the courts which review their decisions have all been agreed is that the consideration of the two objectives, just and reasonable rates or prices to the consumer, and just and reasonable return to the regulated enterprise, is a function requiring informed and scrupulous judgment. Many tests and techniques for assisting the process of reaching a just decision have been used, but no single test is conclusive, nor is any group of them definitive: whatever tests may be used, in the last analysis the adjudicating body cannot escape the responsibility of exercising judgment as to what, in a stated set of circumstances, is a just and reasonable return or rate of return, or what is a range of justness and reasonableness of return or rate of return.
>
> ... While such tests as the earnings of comparable enterprises and the interest coverages of the Applicant and of other enterprises can be applied, it is difficult to assign precise weights to these respective considerations. The final conclusion as to what is enough but not too much in the way of return, and rate of return, is not precisely supportable on a mathematical basis. If it were, one computer and a few programmers could replace all the regulatory boards in North America, and dispense undeniable justice instantaneously.... [134]

It is especially difficult to estimate the cost of equity capital.[135] Given the variety of approaches, it is little wonder that estimates of the cost of equity capital differ significantly. To cite AT&T's 1981 rate case before the FCC once again, seven witnesses presented the estimates, shown in Table 9-4, ranging from 12.50 to 17.60 percent. The FCC's trial staff recommended a cost of equity of 14.25 percent, the administrative law judge found 14.60 percent, and the full commission allowed 17.40 percent. Here, as is true with many other aspects of regulation, the quality of the commissions is crucial.

The Incentive to Efficiency

The cost of capital standard, as discussed above, has one serious limitation: it makes no specific allowance for efficiency. Justice Brandeis argued that an efficient utility might properly be allowed more than a rate of return barely above the level of confiscation.[136] And the Florida commission has stated:

TABLE 9-4

Estimates of the Cost of Equity Capital

Witness	Cost
Dwyer	16.40-17.60%
Curley	15.50-16.00%
Friend	15.33-16.00%
Gordon and Gould	14.50%
Kosh	13.00%
Langsam	12.50-13.50%
FCC Trial Staff	14.25%
ALJ Luton	14.60%
Full Commission	17.40%

Source: *Re American Teleph. & Teleg. Co.*, 86 FCC 2d 221 (1981).

... Inefficient operations sometimes penalize the guilty utility and this matter of efficiency compared with inefficiency in the operations of a public utility has given rise to considerable controversy in regulatory circles as to the impact efficiency, or the lack of it, should have in fixing the allowable return. It does not appear to be reasonable to penalize a public utility's customers or subscribers for the inefficiencies of the utility. It would seem to be more reasonable that a utility should be allowed something more in the rate of return if it has demonstrated its ability to operate efficiently. While it is difficult to accurately evaluate this factor because of its imponderable nature, it would appear reasonable to conclude that a public utility is operating efficiently if it has a minimum of service complaints, is continually improving its service, but is still able to produce higher earnings on lower rates than comparable or similar utilities in the general area.[137]

Competition is supposed to compel management efficiency as firms seek ways of reducing costs in order to maximize profits and increase sales. Under regulation, however, if rates are fixed so as to enable all companies — those that are well managed and those that are not — to cover their costs plus receive a fair rate of return, there is no stimulus for efficiency comparable to the stimulus of competition. Based upon the experience of the 1950s, Bonbright concluded:

American experience with regulated private ownership hardly justifies the unqualified indictment that some writers have made against it on this score. But a plausible case, at least, could be made for the thesis that what has saved regulation from being a critical influence in the direction of mediocrity and tardy technological progress has been its very "deficiencies" in the form of regulatory lags and in the form of acquiescence by commissions in fairly prolonged periods of theoretically "excessive" earnings on the part of companies whose public repute and whose comparative rates of charge for service have not made them vulnerable to popular attack.[138]

Perhaps the most significant incentive to efficiency is regulatory lag. Prior to the advent of rapid inflation, most commissions considered a fair return to represent a range, and utilities had an incentive to bring their earnings into the upper portion of the allowable range. More recently, the incentive has been to earn the allowable rate of return, although it is doubtful that efficiency can overcome a high rate of inflation. There is also an incentive for small utilities to be efficient, since their earnings as a group are often lower than the rate authorized by the regulatory commissions.[139] And a few commissions have made a specific allowance for efficiency in setting a fair rate of return.[140]

Various proposals have been made to deal with this problem. The most frequently stated suggestion is for commissions to make adjustments in the rate of return according to some measure(s) of performance, and some commissions have adopted versions of this proposal.[141] Particularly difficult, however, is the problem of inefficiency. Should a commission find it necessary to impose a penalty for inefficiency, a serious obstacle might be placed on the ability of a utility to attract and to hold capital. A reduction in earnings would almost certainly make it more difficult for a utility to confront investors, thereby causing efficiency to decline even further.[142] But penalties have been imposed for service deficiencies: rate increase applications have been denied[143]; the North Carolina commission imposed an 0.45 percent penalty on rate base in one case[144] and a 5.5 percent penalty reduction in return on common equity in another[145]; the California commission imposed an 0.50 percent penalty (equivalent to $7.4 million in revenue requirements) on common equity[146]; and the Iowa commission imposed a 1 percent penalty on common equity under its recently adopted management efficiency standards.[147]

Finally, the absence of specific incentives does not mean that commissions can ignore the problem. At a minimum, regulatory agencies must make sure they avoid policies that penalize efficiency. For example, if a commission requires the deduction from the rate base of the unamortized cost of assets unexpectedly retired because of obsolescence, but permits their retention in the rate base as long as the assets are not replaced by superior, but available, substitutes, efficiency is discouraged.[148] The same is true "if every act that raises profit is offset by a regulatory act that reduces it. . . ."[149]

Earnings Erosion during Periods of Inflation

Since the *Hope* decision in 1944, the majority of federal and state commissions have adopted the original cost less accrued depreciation method of determining the rate base and have applied a rate of return estimated by the cost of capital standard. The resulting earnings, it is argued, should be sufficient to meet the contractual obligations of the utility, to reward common stockholders, and to attract new capital. But owing to price inflation in the economy since World War II, and at a greatly accelerated annual rate in the 1968 to 1982 period, this procedure has become a source of controversy before the regulatory commissions. Specifically, should investors be compensated for inflation? Such compensation could be made in two ways: by converting either the original cost rate base or the equity portion of the investment into dollars of the current year, or by making an appropriate adjustment in the rate of return. It was argued in the preceding chapter[150] that the second method is preferable to the first if an adjustment is necessary.

Two arguments are commonly advanced in support of a policy of raising earnings during inflation. The first is ethical: unless commissions allow an adjustment in relation to the current purchasing power of the dollar, there is an unfair expropriation of the real value of the utility's property and, hence, of the common stockholders' investment. The second is economic: unless earnings are kept in line with those in other industries, public utilities will not be able to attract needed capital on reasonable and equitable terms.

> To be sure, these claims are not independent of each other, since the question whether existing investors have a fair claim to indemnity for *past* inflation may be held to depend on the question whether uncommitted prospective investors are willing to supply new capital without receiving any protection against *future* inflation. Nevertheless, the answer to the one issue does not necessarily carry with it the answer to the other.[151]

The two arguments will be considered in turn.

Fairness to Stockholders. The first argument in support of an inflation adjustment has been advanced by Morton. In an article published in 1952, he argued that in computing the cost of capital, the equity portion should be adjusted upward by the use of a general price index, with 1946 as the base year. To deny such an inflation adjustment to the common stockholders of utilities, he continued, is unfair and constitutionally confiscatory. Interestingly enough, his argument is based on the grounds of fairness and not financial necessity. To quote from the article:

... Instead of giving a utility a reasonable return because it is just, we now ask what rate is necessary to maintain it as a going concern and to attract new capital. Justice is a moral concept, necessity is a power concept. The demands of fairness are not always those of power. We have already shown that a utility will continue to function as a going concern and attract new capital even if no compensation is made for inflation to capital already irrevocably committed. An inflation adjustment is not necessary to maintain the financial soundness and integrity of the concern. As long as necessity is the sole guide to action, the property of a utility can be taken without compensation by means of inflation, provided the will to do so is accompanied by legal and political power. Under these circumstances, holders of utility property can hardly be expected to submit to expropriation without trying to use political power to protect themselves. Within the constitutional framework, political power is after all the ultimate arbiter of all rights to liberty and property.

The erroneous notion that the market somehow automatically compensates for inflation rests on the belief that economic power is capable of protecting itself. In unregulated industry this is true. Any interest having economic power to compel a fair return can exert that power; it does not need to resort to the courts. Appeal to the courts under the 14th Amendment is made when the individual is incapable of defending himself against arbitrary action. A utility cannot protect itself against inflation by its power to control the supply of services because that power is limited and circumscribed by regulation. Potential investors can exert some economic power by withholding capital, but past investors are wholly dependent upon constitutional interpretation.[152]

Morton's argument rests upon two basic assumptions: first, that inflation results in the impairment of stockholders' "real" capital and, second, that nonregulated industries can protect their stockholders from such capital impairment by exercising their "economic power." The first assumption is valid, but the second is questionable (although it is true that industrial earnings tend to rise during inflationary periods).[153] These comments aside, the most significant drawbacks to an inflationary adjustment made on the basis of fairness are that such an adjustment would be selective and not remedial[154] and that in being fair to the common stockholders of public utilities, unfairness to others would result.[155]

In the first place, the holders of bonds and preferred stocks receive no safeguards against inflation. While they receive other safeguards (such as less risk), justice or fairness would seem to indicate that they, too, should share in any inflation allowance, for inflation also results in the impairment of their "real" capital. In the second place, the buyers of common stocks, whether of utilities or nonregulated companies, were never promised a return that would protect their capital against price inflation. (In fact, they were never promised any return at all.) Provided that investors are fully informed about the facts of their investments, as required by the Federal Securities Act, and that commissions are consistent in their policies,[156] common stockholders have no claim to preferential treatment.[157] In the third place, inflation adjustments would tend to "unsettle regulation." As Thatcher puts it:

> It would strengthen the very inflationary forces against which representatives of the companies warn us. Principles such as those proposed by witnesses urging an inflation adjustment, like those urged by proponents of "fair value" or "reproduction cost," if consistently carried onward into the future, as they should be if they are recognized in rate cases, would in fact endanger the future stability of companies in times of falling prices and hopelessly confuse the regulatory process.[158]

Finally, an inflation adjustment might not achieve its intended goal. In the short run, as Clemens has argued, it is likely that such an adjustment

> . . . would stabilize the *expected* purchasing power of the market value of the equity investment — something entirely different and of limited desirability. This arises from the fact that the formula consists of two variables, the cost of money and the price or inflation adjustment. The inflation adjustment standing alone would give the investor an income of constant purchasing power, but it would not do so if it were coupled with the cost of money computed from market yields. Investors would simply discount expected inflation or deflation and bid up, or bid down, the value of the stock accordingly. Under conditions of expected inflation, yields would be lower than otherwise; under conditions of expected deflation, yields would be higher. . .
> It is likely that in the long-run the return would move upward with prices but, assuming inflation, the inflationary adjustment might be offset to a degree by the lower yield at which inflation-protected securities would probably sell. However, a cyclical pattern would be imposed upon the income flow: income would be higher in times of expected deflation; lower in times of expected inflation.[159]

The Attraction of Capital. Until 1968, all of the evidence available suggests that utilities were able to attract capital on terms comparable with nonregulated industries.[160] However, during this period, most commissions permitted utilities under their jurisdictions to earn incomes in excess of the minimum cost of capital. This fact, combined with an average payout ratio of 70 percent and the flotation of new common stock issues at prices in excess of the book values of old stocks, provided an upward trend in earnings per share. Investors found that the market values of their stocks more than kept pace with changes in the cost of living index.[161]

However, beginning in the late 1960s, the situation changed dramatically, as the annual rate of inflation accelerated and interest rates soared. As a result, the financial integrity of the entire public utility sector deteriorated. Embedded debt costs rose; interest coverage declined; bonds were downgraded. Market prices of utilities' common stock fell below book values; new stock issues resulted in dilution. Consider, for example, the financial position of a large combination utility — Consumers Power Company (now the principal subsidiary of CMS Energy Corporation) — summarized in Table 9-5. Between 1965 and 1982, the utility's (a) embedded cost of debt increased 172 percent; (b) indenture coverage declined from 8.43 to 2.67 times (and twice fell below the 2.00 times required to issue new long-term debt); (c) market price declined 74.9 percent and has been below book value since 1973; and (d) return on common equity, which fluctuated significantly (-18.7 to 13.2 percent), was comprised of a growing percentage of AFUDC (70.81 percent in 1982). During the 1970s, the utility generated only about 34 percent of its construction expenditures internally.

Many factors account for the deterioration of the utilities' financial integrity, but a major cause is "attrition." As explained by the Florida commission:

> "Attrition" is the term frequently used to describe the eroding effects which increased costs caused by inflation have upon the rate of return of a utility, which must apply fixed rates for its services. A regulated utility may encounter such increasing costs in securing additional capital (capital cost attrition), in adding new plant to service at incrementally higher per unit costs (rate base attrition), or in the operating expenses normally incurred to provide service (NOI attrition).[162]

Rate base attrition can be illustrated by the following example. Suppose a commission sets a utility's rate base at $10 million and allows a 10 percent rate of return, resulting in annual earnings of $1 million. If, however, the utility completes construction of a $2 million new plant and puts it into operation during the next year, and if total earnings increase to $1,105,000, the rate of return will be 9.20 percent. And because rate regulation is not continuous, this situation may exist for a year or more before the commission can complete a new rate case. This problem is especially important for utilities that are expanding. The results of attrition are shown in Table 9-6 for the electric utility industry. Notice that in 1980, the difference between the allowed rate of return on common equity and the earned rate of return was 2.8 percentage points (or 280 basis points).

The commissions use several methods to deal with the problem of attrition (inflation). First, they may modify or replace the historic or past test-year method by (a) adjusting historic test-year data for "known changes"[163]; (b) using a "year-end" rate base, rather than an "average" rate base, for the

TABLE 9-5

Consumers Power Company
1965-1986

Year	Construction Expenditures (millions)	Source of Funds		Embedded Cost of Debt	Indenture Coverage	Market Price[a]	Market/Book Ratio	Return on Average Equity	AFUDC as a Percentage of Net Income
		Internal	External						
1965	$109.9	80.5%	19.5%	3.70%	8.43	100.0	2.48	12.8 %	1.03 %
1966	147.0	50.8	49.2	3.97	7.26	88.5	2.08	13.2	3.47
1967	140.8	58.7	41.3	4.21	6.11	87.6	1.96	12.9	3.72
1968	208.3	44.6	55.4	4.60	4.92	81.8	1.76	11.2	7.82
1969	205.1	49.2	50.8	5.06	3.93	75.8	1.56	11.5	12.58
1970	241.9	34.0	66.0	5.54	3.31	64.9	1.28	11.6	19.38
1971	253.8	41.2	58.8	5.80	2.46	63.6	1.21	10.2	30.46
1972	379.4	33.7	66.3	5.99	2.34	58.1	1.06	9.9	32.57
1973	368.7	31.6	68.4	6.16	2.39	53.1	.97	8.7	28.71
1974	342.8	12.5	87.5	6.80	1.99	31.4	.56	4.8	25.53
1975	220.4	78.4	21.6	7.36	2.58	32.2	.59	9.3	24.66
1976	353.2	22.6	77.4	7.60	2.90	41.9	.76	13.1	23.42
1977	544.8	13.4	86.6	7.89	2.42	46.9	.86	11.4	34.97
1978	665.1	36.6	63.4	8.35	2.36	45.9	.88	11.3	41.75
1979	824.0	30.9	69.1	8.82	2.17	43.4	.78	11.2	56.67
1980	640.9	30.0	70.0	10.50	1.81	36.7	.67	11.0	61.68
1981	706.2	39.8	60.2	10.27	2.26	34.5	.62	11.1	58.86
1982	855.0	29.3	70.7	10.38	2.06	35.6	.66	11.4	70.81
1983	909.0	29.8	70.2	10.72	2.14	38.6	.74	11.9	69.40
1984	605.0	45.5	54.5	11.11	2.25	15.6	.30	4.4	68.69
1985	139.5	56.4	43.6	10.83	2.30	14.1	.33	(18.7)	b
1986	149.0	44.3	55.7	10.08	2.67	25.1	.57	3.4	.34

[a]1965 = 100.
[b]Net loss of $269.8 million before preferred and preference dividends; AFUDC was $2.6 million.

Source: Company records.

TABLE 9-6

Electric Utility Industry Returns on Equity Allowed
In Rate Cases versus Returns Earned

1976-1986

Year	Allowed[a]	Earned[b]	Spread
1976	13.1%	12.0%	110bp
1977	13.3	11.9	140
1978	13.2	11.8	140
1979	13.5	11.7	180
1980	14.3	11.5	280
1981	15.3	12.8	250
1982	15.8	13.6	220
1983	15.3	14.6	70
1984	15.3	15.1	20
1985	15.2	14.1	110
1986	13.9	13.6	30

[a]Unweighted average of rate cases each year for 100-company universe, *excluding* FERC decisions.

[b]Earned return on average equity.

Source: Salomon Brothers Inc., "Electric Utility Regulation — Semiannual Review," September 1, 1987, p. 3.

test period[164]; or (c) using a fully "projected" or "forecast" test-year approach.[165] While a year-end or projected rate base is more representative of the future period for which rates are being set, a year-end rate base creates a mismatch unless revenues and expenses for the test year are adjusted to reflect year-end conditions.

Second, a separate allowance for attrition may be added (a) to the revenue requirement ($15 million in one case by the Louisiana commission[166]); (b) to the rate base valuation (the New Jersey commission added $25.5 million in one case, while the Maryland commission added an attrition allowance of $146,000 — about 3 percent — to the net investment rate base of a gas utility[167]); or (c) to the rate of return (the Virginia Supreme Court added 20 basis points in one case, the New York commission added 50 basis points for a utility, and the Florida commission added 76 basis points to offset attrition[168]). And, even where no separate attrition adjustment is made, the commissions have frequently stated that they take this factor — along with others — into account in determining a fair rate of return.[169]

Third, some commissions have adopted interim rate procedures, whereby rates are put into effect, subject to refund provisions, while the case is in progress,[170] while others have adopted annual review or "make-whole" proceedings, where the issues are usually confined to changes in expenses and capital costs, revenues, and investment since the last review or proceeding.[171] Fourth, a variety of indexing arrangements have been utilized. Under the original (1975) New Mexico Cost of Service Plan, for instance, there were automatic quarterly adjustments of Public Service Company of New Mexico's base rates to allow the utility an opportunity to earn between 13.50 and 14.50 percent on common equity.[172]

Finally, several other procedures have been adopted to reduce regulatory lag (and, hence, to minimize attrition). Greater use of prehearing conferences (to narrow the disputed issues) and settlement procedures; at the state level, the hiring of administrative law judges (called hearing examiners, agents, or referees in some jurisdictions) or the use of panels of commissioners; and the adoption of methods to speed the formal hearing process (control over cross-examination, for instance), provide but a few examples.

Conclusions on Inflation Adjustment. With high annual rates of inflation, an inflation adjustment is necessary if public utilities are to be given an opportunity to earn their cost of capital and to attract new capital on reasonable terms. There is substantial evidence that utilities failed to earn their capital costs throughout most of the 1970s.[173] While many commissions permitted attrition allowances, they were often inadequate and other commissions refused to deal with the inflation problem.[174] As a result, utilities (and their customers) paid high capital costs, in addition to the fact that construction expenditures were cut back.[175] On the basis of capital attraction, therefore, an inflation adjustment is necessary.[176] And, if due to political pressures, the commissions are unable to grant adequate rates of return, an "overt" or systematic adjustment for inflation may well be required.

Gradualism during Volatile Markets

As the economic environment became more favorable in the early- to mid-1980s, a new issue arose: With money costs falling dramatically, but with significant volatility, should authorized returns on common equity be reduced rapidly or gradually? In arguing for the latter, the Virginia commission said in a 1986 decision:

> The commission has no control over a rapidly changing economy or volatile interest rates. We do, however, have the power to regulate authorized returns on equity. The commission feels that stability in the cost of equity is in the interest of utilities, ratepayers and the economic environment of the commonwealth. When interest rates soared and the prime rate exceeded 20%, we did not allow exorbitant authorized re-

turns which would have exacerbated the situation. We allowed returns to gradually increase, recognizing the trends of the day but avoiding extreme reaction. Recently interest rates have plummeted. Our appropriate reaction should not be to cut authorized equity returns drastically, but to once again gradually move in the direction of the trend. Our goal is a fair and stable environment which will allow Virginia's utilities to better plan for the future and continue to provide economical, reliable service.[177]

Given volatile markets, combined with a trend toward greater reliance upon market forces, the issue of gradualism cannot be ignored.

The Rate of Return: "Between Scylla and Charybdis"

Justice Holmes once commented that rate regulation involved a middle course, determined by judgment and fairness, "between Scylla and Charybdis." As he explained:

> On the one side, if the franchise is taken to mean that the most profitable return that could be got, free from competition, is protected by the Fourteenth Amendment, then the power to regulate is null. On the other hand if the power to regulate withdraws the protection of the Amendment altogether, then the property is nought. This is not a matter of economic theory, but of fair interpretation of a bargain. Neither extreme can have been meant. A midway between them must be hit.[178]

The search for this midway position involves consideration of many complex factors. Despite significant advances in finance theory, the method of determining a fair rate of return is far from settled. The frequently used cost of capital standard is a beginning and represents a significant improvement over the earlier commission practices of basing the allowable return on a customary or traditional figure. But such a return is a minimum. It "determines a floor, below which rate of return is so low as to become confiscatory. . . . If a utility cannot recover its capital cost, it cannot continue indefinitely to serve the public and, per se, present investors in the enterprise will suffer the loss of all or a part of their investment."[179]

Yet, while there have been substantial advances in techniques for estimating the cost of capital, the fact remains that regulation

> . . . has been unable to respond promptly or adequately in recent years to changing economic conditions, particularly the impact of inflation and higher energy costs. Regulation of public utility earnings has not been efficient because the commissions, as well as utilities, are identified as responsible for rapid price increases. Regulatory agencies are

understandably sensitive to the loss of public esteem which follows from even cost-justified rate increases. Perhaps only a broader public understanding and acceptance of relevant economic criteria will alleviate this problem.[180]

Finally, failure to maintain the financial integrity of utilities is against the interests of consumers, as well as investors:

> An immediate effect of low earnings and earnings of low quality is to increase the financial risks of investors, and thus lead to the downgrading of securities by the rating agencies. Downrating, in turn, means that the bonds must carry higher interest rates, a charge which is passed along to customers. Such downgrading has become a familiar phenomenon in the utility scene. . . . The bonds of many utilities are now rated at levels so low that many institutional investors are barred by law from purchasing them, and interest rates must be raised in order to sell the securities within a much smaller market. These additional capital costs force rate increases which otherwise would not be necessary, without improving the financial condition of the utilities or their ability to raise money on a low cost basis. An equally serious result of limited capability to raise money is the inability of the utilities to make the investments required in order to achieve the optimum economies of service.[181]

Notes

*Justice Douglas, *Federal Power Comm. v. Hope Natural Gas Co.*, 320 U.S. 591, 603 (1944).

[1]It must be emphasized that the fair rate of return is not independent of the rate base to which it will be applied. A utility's earnings are a product of the rate of return and the rate base, and a fair rate of return on a fair value rate base may not constitute a fair rate of return on an original cost rate base.

[2]Paul J. Garfield and Wallace F. Lovejoy, *Public Utility Economics* (Englewood Cliffs: Prentice-Hall, Inc., 1964), p. 116.

[3]For an exhaustive analysis of these problems, see Ellsworth Nichols, *Ruling Principles of Utility Regulation: Rate of Return* (Arlington, Va.: Public Utilities Reports, Inc., 1955); Ellsworth Nichols and Francis X. Welch, *Ruling Principles of Utility Regulation: Rate of Return-Supplement A* (Arlington, Va.: Public Utilities Reports, Inc., 1964).

[4]*Willcox v. Consolidated Gas Co.*, 212 U.S. 19, 48-49 (1909).

[5]*Bluefield Water Works & Imp. Co. v. Pub. Service Comm. of West Virginia*, 262 U.S. 679, 692-93 (1923). See also *Missouri ex rel. Southwestern Bell Teleph. Co. v. Missouri Pub. Service Comm.*, 262 U.S. 276 (1923); *Lincoln Gas & Elec. Light v. City of Lincoln*, 250 U.S. 256 (1919).

[6]*McCardle v. Indianapolis Water Co.*, 272 U.S. 400, 419 (1926).

[7]*United Railways & Elec. Co. v. West,* 280 U.S. 234, 249, 251 (1930). Justice Sutherland also argued: "Sound business management requires that after paying all expenses of operation, setting aside the necessary sums for depreciation, payment of interest and reasonable dividends, there should still remain something to be passed to the surplus account. . . ." *Ibid.,* pp. 251-52. Justice Brandeis dissented: "A net return of 6.26 percent upon the present value of the property of a street railway enjoying a monopoly in one of the oldest, largest and richest cities on the Atlantic Seaboard would seem to be compensatory." *Ibid.,* p. 255.

[8]*Dayton Power & Light Co. v. Pub. Utilities Comm. of Ohio,* 292 U.S. 290, 311 (1934).

[9]*West v. Chesapeake & Potomac Teleph. Co.,* 295 U.S. 662 (1935). Justice Stone, dissenting from the decision, even suggested that a 4.5 percent rate of return would not be confiscatory, noting (among other things) that both railroads and other corporations listed on the stock exchange were averaging less than 4 percent on their invested capital. *Ibid.,* pp. 682-83.

[10]*Driscoll v. Edison Light & Power Co.,* 307 U.S. 104, 120(1939).

[11]*Federal Power Comm. v. Natural Gas Pipeline Co.,* 315 U.S. 575, 596-97 (1942).

[12]*Federal Power Comm. v. Hope Natural Gas Co., op. cit.,* p. 603. A year later, the Court stated: "We are unable to say . . . that the return [of 6.5 percent] is not commensurate with the risks, that confidence in petitioner's financial integrity has been impaired, or that petitioner's ability to attract capital, to maintain its credit, and to operate successfully and efficiently has been impeded." *Panhandle Eastern Pipe Line Co. v. Federal Power Comm.,* 324 U.S. 635, 650 (1945).

[13]However, the *Bluefield* statements that the allowable rate of return must be (*a*) applied to the "value" of the company's property and (*b*) based upon regional comparisons were omitted by the Court.

[14]The criteria were reiterated in two subsequent Supreme Court decisions: *Permian Basin* in 1968 and *Memphis Light* in 1973. Said the Court in the former, for example: "Third, the court must determine whether the order may reasonably be expected to maintain financial integrity, attract necessary capital, and fairly compensate investors for risks they have assumed, and yet provide appropriate protection to the relevant public interests, both existing and foreseeable." *Permian Basin Area Rate Cases,* 390 U.S. 747, 792 (1968). See also *Federal Power Comm. v. Memphis Light Gas & Water Division,* 411 U.S. 458 (1973).

[15]Emery Troxel, *Economics of Public Utilities* (New York: Holt, Rinehart & Winston, Inc., 1947), p. 378.

[16]*Chicago, M. St. P. Ry. Co. v. Minnesota ex rel. Railroad & Warehouse Comm.,* 134 U.S. 418, 458 (1890).

[17]*Banton v. Belt Line Ry. Corp.,* 268 U.S. 413, 422-23 (1925). See Nathaniel T. Guernsey, "The Test of Reasonable Rates," 14 *Virginia Law Review* 1 (1927).

[18]*Peoples Gas Light & Coke Co. v. Slattery,* 373 Ill. 31 (1939); *Re Pacific Teleph. & Teleg. Co.,* 89 PUR (NS) 414 (Cal., 1950); *Re Southwestern Bell Teleph. Co.,* 87 PUR (NS) 97 (Ark., 1951); *Iowa-Illinois Gas & Elec. Co. v. Perrine,* 351 Ill. App. 195 (1953). In a 1976 decision, the Kentucky Supreme Court held that the *lowest* reasonable rate is one which is constitutionally not confiscatory. *Kentucky ex rel. Stephens v. South Central Bell Teleph. Co.,* 545 S.W. 2d 927 (1976). The Montana commission has held that if a public utility is earning a fair rate of return from its consolidated operations, the fact that it may be required to operate one segment of its business at a loss is not

confiscation of its property. *Re Montana-Dakota Utilities Co.*, 14 PUR4th 115 (Mont., 1976).

[19]*Willcox v. Consolidated Gas Co.*, *op. cit.*, p. 48. See also *Driscoll v. Edison Light & Power Co.*, *op. cit.*

[20]*Lincoln Gas & Elec. Light v. City of Lincoln*, *op. cit.*, p. 268.

[21]*Bluefield Water Works & Imp. Co. v. Pub. Service Comm. of West Virginia*, *op. cit.*, p. 693.

[22]*Wabash Elec. Co. v. Young*, 287 U.S. 234, 252 (1930).

[23]*Pub. Service Comm. of Montana v. Great Northern Utilities Co.*, 289 U.S. 130, 135 (1933).

[24]*Market Street Ry. Co. v. Railroad Comm. of Calif.*, 324 U.S. 548, 567 (1945).

[25]See, *e.g.*, "Objective Standards on Management Efficiency Have Arrived for Regulated Utilities," 118 *Public Utilities Fortnightly* 48 (November 27, 1986).

[26]"The Constitutional standard setting forth the economic test for a fair rate of return was enunciated by the United States Supreme Court in the *Bluefield* and *Hope* cases. These two cases provide the foundation for state regulatory commissions in deciding the cost of capital." *Re Appalachian Power Co.*, Case No. 19723, p. 11 (Va., 1977). See also *Re Southwestern Pub. Service Co.*, 27 PUR4th 302 (N.M., 1978).

[27]*Federal Power Comm. v. Natural Gas Pipeline Co.*, *op. cit.*

[28]*Pennsylvania Pub. Utility Comm. v. Bell Teleph. Co. of Pennsylvania*, 43 PUR3d 241, 246 (Pa., 1962).

[29]*Re Eastern Rowan Teleph. Co.*, 44 PUR3d 379, 382 (N.C., 1962).

[30]James C. Bonbright, *Principles of Public Utility Rates* (New York: Columbia University Press, 1961), p. 281.

[31]*Ibid.*

[32]*Stadtlander v. The New York Edison Co.*, PUR1915B 685 (N.Y. 1915).

[33]*Texas Border Gas Co. v. Laredo*, 2 PUR (NS) 503, 516 (1933).

[34]*Re Southern Bell Teleph. & Teleg. Co.*, 79 PUR (NS) 109, 112 (N.C., 1949).

[35]*Re Fort Smith Gas Corp.*, 50 PUR3d 105, 111 (Ark., 1963).

[36]*Re New Jersey Water Co.*, 90 PUR3d 215, 222 (N.J., 1971).

[37]*Re Commonwealth Edison Co.*, 35 PUR4th 49, 79-80 (Ill.,1980).

[38]David K. Eiteman, "Independence of Utility Rate-Base Type, Permitted Rate of Return, and Utility Earnings," 17 *Journal of Finance* 38 (1962); Fredric Stuart, "Rate Base *versus* Rate of Return," 70 *Public Utilities Fortnightly* 395 (1962); John Pike, "Residential Electric Rates and Regulation," 7 *Quarterly Review of Economics & Business* 45 (1967); H. Craig Petersen, "The Effect of Fair Value Rate Base Valuation in Electric Utility Regulation," 31 *Journal of Finance* 1487 (1976); Richard B. Edelman, "Rate Base Valuation and Its Effect on Rate of Return for Utilities," 110 *Public Utilities Fortnightly* 40 (September 2, 1982).

[39]See Joseph R. Rose, "The Rate of Utility Returns," 23 *Public Utilities Fortnightly* 113 (1939); W. R. Buckwalter, "The Rate of Return on Pennsylvania Utilities," 91 *University of Pennsylvania Law Review* 626 (1943).

Such standard returns die slowly; see Lee Metcalf and Vic Reinemer, *Overcharge* (New York: David McKay Co., 1967).

[40]Temporary National Economic Committee, *Economic Standards of Government Price Control*, Monograph No. 32 (Washington, D.C.: U.S. Government Printing Office, 1941), p. 38.

[41]Bonbright, *op. cit.*, p. 282. See also *Electric World*, May 5, 1958, pp. 97-100; Fred

P. Morrissey, "Relation of Growth and Rate of Return for Utilities," 60 *Public Utilities Fortnightly* 361 (1957); *Re Peoples Water & Gas Co.*, 99 PUR (NS) 516 (Fla., 1953).

[42]See *Federal Power Commission, Federal and State Commission Jurisdiction and Regulation of Electric, Gas, and Telephone Utilities, 1973* (Washington, D.C.: U.S. Government Printing Office, 1974), pp. 50-51.

[43]*Re American Teleph. & Teleg. Co.*, 57 FCC 2d 960 (1976); *Re American Teleph. & Teleg. Co.*, 86 FCC 2d 221 (1981), 87 FCC 2d 34 (1981), *aff'd sub nom. United States v. Federal Communications Comm.*, 707 F. 2d 610 (D.C. Cir. 1983).

[44]*Re Area Rate Proceedings for Permian Basin*, 59 PUR3d 417, 473 (FPC, 1965).

[45]*Re National Rates for Natural Gas*, 17 PUR4th 317 (FPC, 1976). A return of 20 percent was found necessary for small producers of natural gas. *Re Small Producers Regulation*, 11 PUR4th 179 (FPC, 1975).

[46]"Establishing the Rate of Return on Equity for Wholesale Electric Sales: Potential Regulatory Reforms," A Discussion Paper on Electric Rate of Return by a Staff Study Group, Federal Energy Regulatory Commission (mimeographed, December 15, 1980), Appendix D.

[47]*Re Authorized Rates of Return for the Interstate Services of AT&T Communications and Exchange Telephone Carriers*, CC Docket No. 84-800 (Phase III) (FCC, 1986).

Annual surveys of rate cases (including rates of return granted) for electric, gas, and telephone utilities are published in *Public Utilities Fortnightly*.

[48]*Re Reduced Pipe Line Rates & Gathering Charges*, 243 ICC 115 (1940); *Petroleum Rail Shippers Ass'n v. Alton and S.R.*, 243 ICC 589 (1941); *Minnelusa Oil Corp. v. Continental Pipe Line Co.*, 258 ICC 41 (1944); *Re Petroleum Products, Williams Pipe Line Co.*, 351 ICC 102 (1975), aff'd full commission, 355 ICC 479 (1976).

[49]*Reduced Pipe Line Rates & Gathering Charges*, op. cit., p. 142.

[50]*Minnelusa Oil Corp. v. Continental Pipe Line Co.*, op. cit., p. 53.

[51]See *Re Williams Pipe Line Co.*, 67 PUR4th 669 (FERC, 1985). "The commission is providing a guide to its action in future and pending oil pipeline cases. The commission is establishing a methodology pursuant to which it will test the reasonableness of oil pipeline rates on a case-by-case basis. At that time, the commission will determine whether the 'end result' of this methodology produces just and reasonable rates." *Ibid.*, p. 678 (footnote omitted). With respect to TAPS, Administrative Law Judge Kane, in his initial decision, recommended use of an original cost rate base and an 11.50 percent rate of return. [*Re Trans-Alaska Pipeline System*, Docket No. OR78-1 (1980).] The commission remanded the decision for further proceedings in light of the *Williams* decision.

[52]See *Re Southern Nat. Gas Co.*, 35 PUR3d 179 (FPC, 1960); *Re Kansas-Nebraska Nat. Gas Co., Inc.*, 38 PUR3d 136 (FPC, 1961); *Re Panhandle Eastern Pipe Line Co.*, 38 PUR3d 307 (FPC, 1961); *Re Alabama-Tennessee Nat. Gas Co.*, 44 PUR3d 19 (FPC, 1962).

[53]*Panhandle Eastern Pipe Line Co.*, Docket No. RP68-15 (Phase I) (FPC, 1968); *Nat. Gas Pipeline Co. of America*, Docket Nos. RP67-21 and RP68-17 (Phase I) (FPC, 1968).

[54]*Re Tennessee Gas Pipeline Co.*, 20 PUR4th 355 (FPC, 1977); *Re Nat. Gas Pipeline Co. of America*, Opinion No. 762 (FPC, 1976); *Re United Gas Pipe Line Co.*, 23 PUR4th 234 (FERC, 1977).

[55]*1985 Annual Report on Utility and Carrier Regulation* (Washington, D.C.: National Association of Regulatory Utility Commissioners, 1987), p. 405.

[56]For exhaustive studies, see A. Lawrence Kolbe and James A. Read, Jr., with George R. Hall, *The Cost of Capital: Estimating the Rate of Return for Public Utilities*

(Cambridge: The MIT Press, 1984); Roger A. Morin, *Utilities' Cost of Capital* (Arlington, Va.: Public Utilities Reports, Inc., 1984).

[57]While the two terms "cost of capital" and "fair rate of return" are frequently used interchangeably, there is a significant distinction found in the literature on public utility regulation. The cost of capital is a *minimum* return, often referred to as the "bare-bones" return; a return that any firm must earn if it is to maintain its financial integrity. The allowed rate of return (usually referred to as the "fair rate of return") may well be higher than the cost of capital (*a*) to provide an incentive to management for efficiency [*New England Teleph. & Teleg. Co. v. New Hampshire*, 44 PUR3d 498 (1962)], (*b*) to reward management for good performance under incentive systems [*Re Consumers Power Co.*, 25 PUR4th 167 (Mich., 1978)], (*c*) to provide an attrition allowance to permit the utility an opportunity to earn its cost of capital [*Re Tampa Elec. Co.*, Order No. 9599 (Fla., 1980)], (*d*) to produce a necessary cash flow level [*Pennsylvania Pub. Utility Comm. v. Philadelphia Elec. Co.*, 33 PUR4th 319 (Pa., 1980)], and/or (*e*) to compensate for extraordinary risk [*Pennsylvania Pub. Utility Comm. v. Metropolitan Edison Co.*, 56 PUR4th 230 (Pa., 1983)].

[58]Dissenting opinion in *Missouri ex rel. Southwestern Bell Teleph. Co. v. Missouri Pub. Service Comm., op. cit.*, p. 306.

[59]*Re New England Teleph. & Teleg. Co.*, 13 PUR4th 65 (Me., 1976); *Re Arkansas Power & Light Co.*, 66 PUR4th 167 (Ark., 1985). Short-term debt also may be included where it is soon to be converted into permanent long-term capital [*Re Huntington Water Corp.*, Case No. 84-173-W-42T (W. Va., 1985)] or where its inclusion provides a closer matching of rate base and capitalization [*Re Sierra Pacific Power Co.*, 73 PUR4th 306 (Nev., 1985)]. But especially where short-term debt is relatively small, it may be excluded because it is "volatile and difficult to measure" [*Re Arizona Pub. Service Co.*, Decision No. 53761 (Ariz., 1983)].

[60]Two additional items are often considered. First, where customers are required to make deposits, they are sometimes included in the capital structure at the annual interest rate which a commission requires the utility to pay its customers on such deposits. [*Re Northern Indiana Pub. Service Co.*, Cause No. 36689 (Ind., 1982).] Second, customer advances, where appropriate, may be included in the capital structure.

[61]See, *e.g.*, Mark Cicchetti, "Reconciling Rate Base and Capital Structure: The Balance Sheet Method," 115 *Public Utilities Fortnightly* 41 (June 27, 1985).

[62]Joseph R. Rose, "'Cost of Capital' in Public Utility Rate Regulation," 43 *Virginia Law Review* 1079, 1082 (1957). See also A. B. Jackson, "The Determination of the Fair Return for Public Utilities," 7 *Canadian Public Administration* 343 (1964); Harry M. Trebing and R. Hayden Howard (eds.), *Rate of Return Under Regulation: New Directions and Perspectives* (East Lansing: MSU Public Utilities Studies, 1969); W. Truslow Hyde, Jr., "Rate of Return — An Art or a Science?," 96 *Public Utilities Fortnightly* 27 (December 18, 1975); J. Rhoads Foster, "Fair Return Criteria and Estimation," 28 *Baylor Law Review* 883 (1976); Basil L. Copeland, Jr., "Alternative Cost-of-Capital Concepts in Regulation," 54 *Land Economics* 348 (1978).

[63]As previously noted, Franco Modigliani and Merton H. Miller have questioned this assumption. "The Cost of Capital, Corporate Finance, and the Theory of Investment," 48 *American Economic Review* 261 (1958). These two authors concluded that the cost of capital is primarily a function of basic business risk and not of how that risk may be apportioned between debt and equity holders. They subsequently modified their position to acknowledge the effect of savings in federal income tax charges resulting from the deductibility of bond interest payments. "Corporate Income Taxes

and the Cost of Capital: A Correction," 53 *American Economic Review* 433 (1963). But see two comments by Joseph R. Rose and by David Durand, 49 *American Economic Review* 638, 639 (1959); Alexander Barges, *The Effect of Capital Structure on the Cost of Capital* (Englewood Cliffs: Prentice-Hall, Inc., 1963); J. Fred Weston, "A Test of Cost of Capital Propositions," 30 *Southern Economic Journal* 105 (1963); Robert H. Dodge, "How Leverage Affects the Cost of Capital to a Public Utility," 51 *Management Accounting* 39 (August 1969); A. James Heins and Case M. Sprenkle, "A Comment on the Modigliani-Miller Cost of Capital Thesis," 59 *American Economic Review* 590 (1969) and the authors' "Reply to Heins and Sprenkle," 59 *American Economic Review* 592 (1969); Joseph Stiglitz, "A Re-Examination of the Modigliani-Miller Theorem," 59 *American Economic Review* 784 (1969); Robert W. Resek, "Multidimensional Risk and the Modigliani-Miller Hypothesis," 25 *Journal of Finance* 47 (1970); Thomas J. Velk and William L. Baldwin, "The Modigliani-Miller Cost of Capital Thesis: A Further Comment," 10 *Quarterly Review of Economics and Business* 75 (1970); Merton H. Miller, "Debt and Taxes," 32 *Journal of Finance* 261 (1977); Alan J. Auerbach, "Taxation, Corporate Financial Policy, and the Cost of Capital," 21 *Journal of Economic Literature* (1983); Stewart C. Myers, "The Capital Structure Puzzle," 39 *Journal of Finance* 575 (1984); Cleveland S. Patterson, "The Effects of Leverage on k," in J. Rhoads Foster et al., (eds.), *Regulatory Reform: The State of the Regulatory Art; Emerging Concepts and Procedures* (Washington, D.C.: Institute for Study of Regulation, 1984), pp. 237-60; Eugene F. Brigham, Louis C. Gapenski, and Dana A. Aberwald, "Capital Structure, Cost of Capital, and Revenue Requirements," 119 *Public Utilities Fortnightly* 15 (January 8, 1987). For empirical studies of the electric utility industry, see Merton H. Miller and Franco Modigliani, "Some Estimates of the Cost of Capital to the Electric Utility Industry, 1954-57," 56 *American Economic Review* 333 (1966); three comments by J. Crockett and I. Friend, by Myron J. Gordon, and by A. A. Robichek, R. C. Higgins, and J. G. McDonald, 57 *American Economic Review* 1258, 1267, 1278 (1967) and a reply by the authors, 57 *American Economic Review* 1288 (1967); Eugene F. Brigham and Myron J. Gordon, "Leverage, Dividend Policy, and the Cost of Capital," 23 *Journal of Finance* 85 (1968); A. A. Robichek, R. C. Higgins, and M. Kinsman, "The Effect of Leverage on the Cost of Equity Capital of Electric Utility Firms," 28 *Journal of Finance* 353 (1973).

[64]As interest rates rose to record levels in the late 1970s, some contended that the cost of new debt was greater than the current cost of equity capital. "Bonds are denoted in nominal terms. A substantial risk to holding bonds is that the inflation rate may increase in the future, raising the cost of debt and lowering the market price of existing bonds. This risk was fairly slight when inflation rates were low and stable. In the current environment of high and uncertain rates of inflation, this risk has increased and risen to a level where inflation risk is large in relation to any risk premium for holding equities." Robert M. Spann, "Inflation Risk and the Cost of Debt and Equity Capital" (Washington, D.C.: ICF Incorporated, mimeographed, 1982), p. 2. There is little empirical evidence to support the premise. See, *e.g.*, Joseph F. Brennan, "Does Utility Long-Term Debt Really Cost More than Common Equity?," 109 *Public Utilities Fortnightly* 34 (February 18, 1982); Gordon T. C. Taylor and Charles F. Peake, "A Utility's Cost of Common Equity May Be Less Than Its Cost Rate for New Debt," 109 *Public Utilities Fortnightly* 23 (June 24, 1982); Dennis B. Fitzpatrick, "Does the Negative Risk Premium Really Exist?," 110 *Public Utilities Fortnightly* 27 (July 8, 1982); and three articles — Basil L. Copeland, Jr., "Inflation, Monetary Policy, and the Equity Risk Premium," Dennis B. Fitzpatrick, "A Review of the

Theoretical and Empirical Evidence Regarding Equity-Debt Risk Premia for Electric Utilities," and Charles M. Linke, "Equity-Debt Risk Premia Issues in Utility Rate Regulation" — in Foster et al., *op. cit.,* pp. 183-236.

[65]D. Philip Locklin, *Economics of Transportation* (6th ed.; Homewood, Ill.: Richard D. Irwin, Inc., 1966), p. 382 (footnotes omitted).

[66]Rose, "'Cost of Capital' in Public Utility Rate Regulation," *op. cit.,* pp. 1088-89.

[67]See Chapter 6, pp. 223-25.

[68]A utility's financing decision at any point of time depends upon such factors as the condition of the market, the availability of funds, and the financial condition of the company. These factors are constantly changing.

[69]Bonbright, *op. cit.,* pp. 243-44.

[70]G. Stanley Joslin and Arthur S. Miller, "Public Utility Rate Regulation: A Reexamination," 43 *Virginia Law Review* 1027, 1060 (1957). See also *Peoples Nat. Gas Division of Northern Nat. Gas Co. v. Colorado Pub. Utilities Comm.,* 567 P. 2d 377 (1977).

[71]*Alabama v. Southern Bell Teleph. & Teleg. Co.,* 47 PUR3d 65, 67 (1962).

[72]*New England Teleph. & Teleg. Co. v. Dept. of Pub. Utilities,* 327 Mass. 81, 97 N.E. 2d 509 (1951).

[73]*Mississippi Pub. Service Comm. v. Southern Bell Teleph. & Teleg. Co.,* 16 PUR3d 415, 461 (Miss., 1956).

[74]*Re The Chesapeake & Potomac Teleph. Co.,* 57 PUR3d 1, 39 (D.C., 1964). See also *Re Mountain States Teleph. & Teleg. Co.,* 2 PUR3d 75 (Utah, 1953); *Re Southern Bell Teleph. & Teleg. Co.,* 4 PUR3d 195 (Ala., 1954); *Re Illinois Bell Teleph Co.,* 7 PUR3d 493 (Ill., 1955); *Re Northwestern Bell Teleph. Co.,* 20 PUR3d 385 (S.D., 1957); *Re New England Teleph. & Teleg. Co.,* 42 PUR3d 57 (N.H., 1961); *Re Southern New England Teleph. Co.,* 42 PUR3d 310 (Conn., 1962).

[75]*Re New York Teleph. Co.,* 84 PUR (NS) 267, 290 (N.Y., 1950).

[76]*Re New York Teleph. Co.,* 11 PUR3d 320, 332 (N.Y., 1955).

[77]*Re Mountain States Teleph. & Teleg. Co.,* 1 PUR3d 129, 140 (Colo., 1954).

[78]*Re Mountain States Teleph. & Teleg. Co.,* 7 PUR3d 115, 122 (Ariz., 1954).

[79]*Re Florida Power & Light Co.,* 67 PUR3d 113, 162 (Fla., 1966).

[80]*Re American Teleph. & Teleg. Co.,* 70 PUR3d 129, 193 (FCC, 1967).

[81]See, *e.g., Re Southern New England Teleph. Co.,* 23 PUR4th 251 (Conn., 1977); *Re Consumers Power Co., op. cit.*

[82]Foster, *op. cit.,* p. 891. "A slightly lower return now might well result in sharply higher financial costs in the future and would be self-defeating in the long-run." *Re Orange & Rockland Utilities,* 92 PUR3d 479, 490 (N.Y., 1971).

[83]See, *e.g., Re Carrabassett Light & Power Co.,* 17 PUR4th 246 (Me., 1976); *Re Gas Co. of New Mexico,* 28 PUR4th 20 (N.M., 1978); *Mars Hill & Blaine Water Co. v. Maine Pub. Utilities Comm.,* 397 A. 2d 570 (1979); *Re Walnut Hill Teleph. Co.,* 56 PUR4th 501 (Ark., 1983); *Re Cook Inlet Pipe Line Co.,* 66 PUR4th 77 (Alaska, 1985); *Re Citizens Utilities Co.,* 72 PUR4th 340 (Idaho, 1986).

In 1977, a lower court rejected the FCC's use of an imputed capital structure for the Communications Satellite Corporation (COMSAT): "The fault of the Commission's action in this opinion is to deny COMSAT even the opportunity to make that choice and begin to phase in debt. As of the moment the opinion was issued, COMSAT shareholders were subjected to a less than adequate rate of return." *Communications Satellite Corp. v. Federal Communications Comm.,* 611 F. 2d 883, 908 (D.C. Cir. 1977). Indiana [*Re Indianapolis Water Co.,* 65 PUR4th 368 (Ind., 1985)] and Ohio [*Re Cincinnati Gas & Elec. Co.,* 63 PUR4th 585 (Ohio, 1984)] have rejected use of hypothetical capital structures. The FERC has "a general policy" favoring actual capital structures [*Re Williams Pipe Line Co., op. cit.*].

[84]See, *e.g., Re Bell Teleph. Co. of Nevada*, 75 PUR3d 92 (Nev., 1968); *Re New York Teleph. Co.*, 92 PUR3d 321 (N.Y., 1971); *Re The Chesapeake & Potomac Teleph. Co. of Virginia*, 19 PUR4th 349 (Va., 1977); *Re Kentucky-West Virginia Gas Co.*, 24 PUR4th 349 (FERC, 1978); *Re Southern Bell Teleph. & Teleg. Co.*, 35 PUR4th 1 (S.C. 1980); *Re Ohio Power Co.*, 76 PUR4th 121 (Ohio, 1986).

[85]Foster, *op. cit.*, p. 889.

[86]*Ibid.*

[87]See Basil L. Copeland, Jr., "Double Leverage One More Time," 100 *Public Utilities Fortnightly* 19 (August 18, 1977); *Re Hawkeye State Teleph. Co.*, 2 PUR4th 166 (Iowa, 1973); *Re United Teleph. Co. of New Jersey*, 2 PUR4th 299 (N.J., 1974); *Re Continental Teleph. Co. of Minnesota, Inc.*, 14 PUR4th 310 (Minn., 1976); *Re Mountain States Teleph. & Teleg. Co.*, 29 PUR4th 97 (Mont., 1978); *Re General Teleph. Co. of the Southwest*, 63 PUR4th 663 (Ark., 1984); *Re Tennessee-American Water Co.*, 67 PUR4th 630 (Tenn., 1985).

[88]See Eugene M. Lerner, "What Are the Real Double Leverage Problems?," 91 *Public Utilities Fortnightly* 18 (June 17, 1973); James E. Brown, "Double Leverage: Indisputable Fact or Precarious Theory?," 93 *Public Utilities Fortnightly* 26 (May 9, 1974); Dennis B. Fitzpatrick, "Subsidiaries' Capital Costs — A Compromise Approach," 99 *Public Utilities Fortnightly* 23 (June 23, 1977); John Robert Jones and John L. O'Donnell, "Double Leverage — Lawful and Based on Sound Economics?," 101 *Public Utilities Fortnightly* 26 (June 8, 1978); Robert S. Stich, "The Four Fables of Double Leverage," 116 *Public Utilities Fortnightly* 6 (August 8, 1985).

[89]"If the risks are not comparable, the relevant cost rates are those which relate to the capital structure of the operating company." Foster, *op. cit.*, pp. 889-90. But see *Central Teleph. Co. of Virginia v. Virginia State Corporation Comm.*, 252 S.E. 2d 575 (1979), in which the Virginia Supreme Court upheld the commission's use of a consolidated capital structure in a case involving a telephone subsidiary, despite the fact that the parent company owns electric and water utilities, as well as telephone companies, on other states.

In a 1976 decision, the North Carolina commission rejected the double leverage approach because the underlying assumption "that the equity of a subsidiary is provided by its parent from the parent's permanent capital in the same proportion that the parent has historically developed its own capital structure" was "contrary to the known facts." *Re General Teleph. Co. of the Southeast*, 18 PUR4th 440, 470 (N.C., 1976).

[90]*New England Teleph. & Teleg. Co. v. Maine Pub. Utilities Comm.*, 27 PUR4th 1, 42 (1978) (citation omitted).

[91]See "Determination of Debt Cost in the Rate of Return," 81 *Public Utilities Fortnightly* 53 (May 23, 1968).

[92]See, *e.g., Re Georgia Power Co.*, 22 PUR4th 321 (Ga., 1977).

[93]See, *e.g., Re Alberta Nat. Gas Co. Ltd.* (NEB, 1980).

[94]But see Eugene M. Lerner, "The FCC's 7.5 Per Cent Ruling," 80 *Public Utilities Fortnightly* 40, 41-43 (October 12, 1967).

[95]See, *e.g., Chicopee Mfg. Co. v. Pub. Service Co. of New Hampshire*, 93 A. 2d 820 (1953).

[96]See, *e.g., Re New England Teleph. & Teleg. Co.*, F.C. No. 2213 (Me., 1977) (amor-

tization permitted over a thirty-three-year period; a period equal to the full life of the repurchased bonds).

[97]See, *e.g., Re Washington Gas Light Co.,* Order No. 6051 (D.C., 1979). But see Eugene F. Brigham, Dana A. Aberwald, and Louis C. Gapenski, "Common Equity Flotation Costs and Rate Making," 115 *Public Utilities Fortnightly* 28 (May 2, 1985).

[98]See Trebing and Howard, *op. cit.;* Walter A. Morton, "Guides to a Fair Rate of Return," 86 *Public Utilities Fortnightly* 17 (July 2, 1970); Ezra Solomon, "Alternative Rate of Return Concepts and Their Implications for Utility Regulation," 1 *Bell Journal of Economics and Management Science* 65 (Spring, 1970); Stewart C. Myers, "The Application of Finance Theory to Public Utility Rate Cases," 3 *Bell Journal of Economics and Management Science* 58 (Spring, 1972); Myron J. Gordon, *The Cost of Capital to a Public Utility* (East Lansing: MSU Public Utilities Studies, 1974); Foster, *op. cit.;* Robert L. Hagerman, "Finance Theory in Rate Hearings," 5 *Financial Management* 18 (Spring, 1976); Robert E. Levy, "Fair Return on Equity for Public Utilities," *Business Economics* 46 (September, 1978); J. Rhoads Foster and Stevan R. Holmberg (eds.), *Earnings Regulation Under Inflation* (Washington, D.C.: Institute for Study of Regulation, 1982); Harold Bierman, Jr., "We Cannot Measure the Cost of Equity Capital Exactly," 114 *Public Utilities Fortnightly* 31 (August 16, 1984).

[99]See Eli W. Clemens, "Some Aspect of the Rate-of-Return Problem," 30 *Land Economics* 32 (1954); Lionel W. Thatcher, "Cost-of-Capital Techniques Employed in Determining the Rate of Return for Public Utilities," 30 *Land Economics* 85 (1954); Fred P. Morrissey, "Current Aspects of the Cost of Capital to Utilities," 62 *Public Utilities Fortnightly* 217 (1958); Ralph E. Badger, "Important Concepts as to Fair Return and Cost of Money," 66 *Public Utilities Fortnightly* 93 (1960); Arnold H. Hirsch, "Earnings-Price Ratios and the Current Cost of Common Equity," 67 *Public Utilities Fortnightly* 225 (1961); John H. Bickley, "What Is Wrong with Earnings-Price Ratios? Part II," 70 *Public Utilities Fortnightly* 18 (July 5, 1962); Stephen H. Fletcher, "Current Problems in the Determination of the Cost of Equity Capital for Rate of Return Purposes," American Bar Association Annual Report, Section of *Public Utility Law, 1963,* pp. 46-50; "Earnings-Price Ratios Test Equity Capital Costs," 81 *Public Utilities Fortnightly* 59 (January 18, 1968); Robert J. Gelhaus and Gary D. Wilson, "An Earnings-Price Approach to Fair Rate of Return in Regulated Industries," 20 *Stanford Law Review* 287 (1968) and comment by L. M. Ross, 21 *Stanford Law Review* 644 (1969). See also *Re Pacific Teleph. & Teleg. Co.,* 5 PUR3d 306 (Cal., 1954); *Re Southern Bell Teleph. & Teleg Co.,* 66 PUR3d 1 (Fla., 1966).

[100]*Re American Teleph. & Teleg. Co.,* CC Docket No. 79-63, Bell Statement No. 2, Testimony of Irwin Friend (mimeographed, December, 1979), p. 2. (Hereinafter "Testimony of Irwin Friend.")

[101]There are many versions of the basic DCF model. Some use d_1: the expected dividend per share in the next twelve months. There are constant and varying growth models. [See, *e.g.,* Louis E. Buck, Jr. and John C. Groth, "Yes, Dear Friends, We Can Improve Our Discounted Cash Flow Estimate of a Utility's Cost of Equity," 113 *Public Utilities Fortnightly* 38 (March 1, 1984); Robert Rosenberg, "Dealing With Varying Expected Growth In a Discounted Cash Flow Analysis," 118 *Public Utilities Fortnightly* 28 (December 11, 1986).] The FERC establishes both a "cost of equity" and a "rate-making rate of return on common equity." The latter, which is lower than the former, attempts to recognize (among other things) that "any return investors expect to receive from dividend reinvestment is not part of the return required from invest-

ment in the firm." *Re Generic Determination of Rate of Return*, 75 PUR4th 219, 227 (FERC, 1986).

[102]k = $3/$38 = 7.89%/.95 = 8.31% + 6% = 14.31%.

[103]To illustrate, assume market price is above book value. The sum of d/p plus g (which is a measure of what an investor anticipates on *market value*), when applied to a lesser *book value* figure, will produce insufficient earnings to provide the indicated dividend and the indicated growth. In fact, over time, the earnings will be insufficient to pay the dividends, and both earnings and book value will necessarily decline.

[104]See, *e.g.*, David A. Kosh, "Recent Trends in Cost of Capital," 72 *Public Utilities Fortnightly* 19, 21-26 (September 26, 1963). But see Win Whittaker and Robert Sefton, "The Discounted Cash Flow Methodology: A Fair Return in Today's Market?," 120 *Public Utilities Fortnightly* 16 (July 9, 1987).

[105]Foster, *op. cit.*, p. 919. Bonbright has argued that "market prices are beyond the control, though not beyond the influence, of rate regulation. Moreover, even if a commission did possess the power of control, any attempt to exercise it [so as to prevent the market prices of utility equities from rising to substantial premiums above book values] . . . would result in harmful, uneconomic shifts in public utility rate levels. . . . Regulation is simply powerless to assure the purchasers of public utility equities that future corporate earnings will suffice to maintain market prices on par with book values or with any other dollar figure." Bonbright, *op. cit.*, pp. 255, 256. And Solomon contends that if regulation were to maintain the market price to book value equality, utility common stocks would be "transformed into a peculiar hybrid form of security which is neither contractual debt nor equity; it can best be described as a perpetual low-grade subordinated debenture which offers neither upside price potential nor any guarantee of dividend or capital recoupment, but which does offer a differential rate of return above the rate on bonds if rates allowed by regulation are actually earned." Ezra Solomon, "Comments on Commission's Proposed Statement of Policy," FPC Docket No. RM77-1 (mimeographed, February, 1977), p. 17.

Throughout the 1970s, for most utilities, market prices fell below book values. See Thomas G. Marx, "Market-to-Book Return on Equity Correlation," 96 *Public Utilities Fortnightly* 28 (December 4, 1975).

[106]See, *e.g.*, *Re Narragansett Elec. Co.*, 52 PUR4th 271 (R.I., 1983).

[107]Only under the assumption of a constant payout ratio will the growth rates of dividends per share, earnings per share, and book value per share be the same.

[108]B. G. Malkiel and J. G. Cragg, "Expectations and the Structure of Share Prices," 60 *American Economic Review* 601 (1970).

[109]See, *e.g.*, "Testimony of Irwin Friend," *op. cit.*, pp. 4-9.

[110]Foster, *op. cit.*, p. 915.

[111]Solomon, "Comments on Commission's Proposed Statement of Policy," *op. cit.*, p. 13. See also Robert S. Stich, "'K' Is Not the Cost of Capital," 85 *Public Utilities Fortnightly* 30 (March 12, 1970); Joseph F. Brennan and Paul R. Moul, "Does the Constant Growth Discounted Cash Flow Model Portray Reality?," 121 *Public Utilities Fortnightly* 24 (January 21, 1988).

Argued the National Energy Board in a 1979 decision: "The Board considers that, as a measurement of the cost of common equity capital, the adjusted DCF rate has some merits and should be given some consideration, notwithstanding the difficulty in estimating future growth rates, the susceptibility of stock prices to erratic movements based on factors that may be unrelated to a particular stock's anticipated performance, and the difficulty of segregating the regulated business from that of the corporate entity as a whole." *Re Westcoast Transmission Co. Ltd.* (NEB, September, 1979), pp. 4-7.

[112]Diana R. Harrington, "The Changing Use of the Capital Asset Pricing Model in Utility Regulation," 105 *Public Utilities Fortnightly* 28 (February 14, 1980) and "Trends in Capital Asset Pricing Model Use," 108 *Public Utilities Fortnightly* 27 (August 13, 1981). See also *Re Portland General Elec. Co.*, 23 PUR4th 209 (Or., 1977), *aff'd*, 30 PUR4th 468 (1979).

[113]See Eugene F. Brigham and Roy L. Crum, "On the Use of the CAPM in Public Utility Cases," 6 *Financial Management* 7 (Summer, 1977) and "Discussion," 7 *Financial Management* 52 (Autumn, 1978); Ronald W. Melicher, "Risk Measurement and Rate of Return under Regulation," in Harry M. Trebing (ed.), *Issues in Public Utility Regulation* (East Lansing: MSU Public Utilities Papers, 1979), pp. 325-41; Robert Litzenberger, Krishna Ramaswamy, and Howard Sosin, "On the CAPM Approach to the Estimation of A Public Utility's Cost of Equity Capital," 35 *Journal of Finance* 369 (Papers and Proceedings, 1980); Joseph I. Rosenberg, "Risk, Return, and Regulation Among Energy Industries," 118 *Public Utilities Fortnightly* 31 (August 7, 1986).

[114]7.8% + (13.9% − 7.8%) 1.057 = 14.25%. See "Recent Cases Discuss the Capital Asset Pricing Model," 101 *Public Utilities Fortnightly* 41 (December 21, 1978).

[115]"These assumptions are: (*1*) Investors are risk averse. . . . (*2*) All investors compose their portfolios (with regard to anticipated risk and return) using a common single investment period. . . . (*3*) Investors make decisions to maximize their expected utility of wealth. . . . (*4*) Capital markets are perfect. . . . (*5*) All investors form, on the basis of this common information, identical subjective expectations of future returns, the variance of these returns for specific securities and the covariance among securities. . . . (*6*) There is a riskless rate of return investment opportunity with no variance or covariance commonly available to all with the same rate of return prospect for each investor. . . ." Robert F. Vandell and James K. Malernee, "The Capital Asset Pricing Model and Utility Equity Returns," 102 *Public Utilities Fortnightly* 22, 24 (July 6, 1978).

[116]*Ibid.* See also Richard W. Roll, "A Critique of the Asset Pricing Theory's Tests," Part I: "On Past and Potential Testability of the Theory," 4 *Journal of Financial Economics* 129 (1977).

[117]Vandell and Malernee, *op. cit.*, p. 27. "The beta coefficient compares the volatility and direction of movement of the return on an investment with those of the market as a whole. Specifically, the beta coefficient of a particular stock measures the degree to which the return on the stock follows the trend of the market. It indicates that change in the rate of return on a stock associated with a one percentage point change in the rate of return on the market. The beta coefficient thus measures the degree to which that stock shares the same risk as the market as a whole. . . . A stock with a beta coefficient of one can be expected, on the average, to follow closely the market trend in return so that investment in such a stock would be subject to the same market risk as that characterizing stocks as a whole. . . ." "Testimony of Irwin Friend," *op. cit.*, p. 11.

[118]For example: "Investments in electric utilities involved more risk in the mid-1960s than they do today. Considering that industry conditions deteriorated substantially between the 1960s and the present time, we reject that interpretation and consider it absurd." Leonard S. Hyman and Joseph M. Egan, "The Utility Stock Market: Regulation, Risk, and Beta," 105 *Public Utilities Fortnightly* 21, 24 (February

14, 1980). See also Gerald J. Glassman, "Discounted Cash Flow versus the Capital Asset Pricing Model (Is 'g' Better than 'β'?)," 102 *Public Utilities Fortnightly* 30 (September 14, 1978); William J. Breen and Eugene M. Lerner, "On the Use of β in Regulatory Proceedings," 3 *Bell Journal of Economics and Management Science* 612 (1972) and comment by Stewart C. Myers, 3 *Bell Journal of Economics and Management Science* 622 (1972); Richard H. Pettway, "On the Use of β in Regulatory Proceedings: An Empirical Examination," 9 *Bell Journal of Economics and Management Science* 239 (1978).

[119]Vandell and Malernee, *op. cit.*, p. 23. See also J. Chartoff, G. Mayo, Jr., and W. Smith, Jr., "The Case Against the Use of the Capital Asset Pricing Model in Public Utility Ratemaking," 3 *Energy Law Journal* 67 (1982).

Stated the Nova Scotia Board of Commissioners of Public Utilities in a 1981 decision: "The Board considers that the 'state of the art' seems to have advanced to a point where the earnings/price ratio test has been largely supplanted by the discounted cash-flow method, except perhaps in limited circumstances, and the capital asset pricing model has not yet been developed to a point where it can yield a reliable indicator of a utility's required return on common equity." *Re Maritime Teleg. & Teleph. Co., Ltd.* (MT-1373, 1981), p. 12.

The Arbitrage Pricing Theory (APT) has been proposed as an alternative to the CAPM. See, *e.g.*, Stephen A. Ross, "The Arbitrage Theory of Capital Asset Pricing," 13 *Journal of Economic Theory* 341 (1976); Richard W. Roll and Stephen A. Ross, "An Empirical Investigation of the Arbitrage Pricing Theory," 35 *Journal of Finance* 1073 (1980) and "Regulation, the Capital Asset Pricing Model, and the Arbitrage Pricing Theory," 111 *Public Utilities Fortnightly* 22 (May 26, 1983); Jay Shanken, "The Arbitrage Pricing Theory: Is It Testable?," 37 *Journal of Finance* 1129 (1982).

[120]See Harold Levanthal, "Vitality of the Comparable Earnings Standard for Regulation of Utilities in a Growth Economy," 74 *Yale Law Review* 989 (1965); Herman G. Roseman, "Comparable Earnings and the Fair Rate of Return," American Bar Association Annual Report, Section of *Public Utility Law, 1970*, pp. 26-40; Richard H. Adelaar and Leonard S. Hyman, "The Comparable Earnings Approach as a Useful Tool in Utility Regulation," 87 *Public Utilities Fortnightly* 30 (March 4, 1971); David R. Kamerschen and Richard L. Wallace, "Opportunity Cost and the Capital Attraction for Utility Rate Regulation," 91 *Public Utilities Fortnightly* 43 (February 15, 1973).

[121]*Re Tampa Elec. Co.*, Docket No. 800011-EU, Testimony of Stephen F. Sherwin (mimeographed, February 1980), p. 16. (Hereinafter "Testimony of Stephen F. Sherwin.")

[122]*Consolidated Gas Co. of New York v. Newton*, 267 Fed. 231, 237 (S.D. N.Y. 1920).

[123]The comparable earnings standard logically implies an original cost rate base. Nonregulated enterprises report earnings on an original cost basis. Therefore, to argue that a 15 percent return on equity capital, for instance, indicated by the comparable earnings standard, should be applied to a fair value rate base would be inconsistent.

[124]"These standards of comparison may include both regulated and unregulated companies. Indeed, this commission has never advocated basing allowed rates of return solely on what other regulated companies have been allowed to earn in the past. Such a process, rather like observing an endless series of duplicate images in multiple mirrors, would be hopelessly circular. . . ." *Re Union Elec. Co.*, 94 PUR3d 87, 100 (FPC, 1972).

Another consideration: During periods of rapid inflation, regulated firms find it nearly impossible to earn what regulatory commissions determine to be fair (due to "attrition"). At a minimum, therefore, comparisons must be made with commission decisions, and not with actual returns.

[125]See, *e.g.,* Richard S. Bower and H. Dorthy, "Risk and the Valuation of Common Stock," 77 *Journal of Political Economy* 349 (1969); R. Hayden Howard (ed.), *Risk and Regulated Firms* (East Lansing: MSU Public Utilities Studies, 1973); Ronald W. Melicher, "Risk and Return in the Electric Utility and Natural Gas Industries," 23 *MSU Business Topics* 48 (Spring, 1975); G. K. Rakes, "Risk Factors Affecting Power Company Securities," 96 *Public Utilities Fortnightly* 22 (July 31, 1975); H. G. Mulle, "Some Testimony on Risk: The Case for the Utilities and Regulation," 97 *Public Utilities Fortnightly* 22 (January 15, 1976); Stevan R. Holmberg, "Investor Risk and Required Rate of Return in Regulated Industries," 16 *Nebraska Journal of Economics and Business* 61 (Autumn 1977); J. Gordon Christy and George A. Christy, "Who Says Utilities Are Less Risky?," 105 *Public Utilities Fortnightly* 11 (May 8, 1980); P. R. Chandrasekaran and William P. Dukes, "Risk Variables Affecting Rate of Return of Public Utilities," 107 *Public Utilities Fortnightly* 32 (February 26, 1981); William P. Dukes and P. R. Chandy, "Rate of Return and Risk for Public Utilities," 112 *Public Utilities Fortnightly* 35 (September 1, 1983); Jay A. Copan, "The Case for Higher Common Equity Ratios for Natural Gas Companies," 116 *Public Utilities Fortnightly* 24 (July 11, 1985).

[126]Jeffery A. Dubin and Peter Navarro, "The Effect of Rate Suppression on Utilities' Cost of Capital," 111 *Public Utilities Fortnightly* 18 (March 31, 1983); Louis E. Buck, Jr., and John C. Groth, "Regulatory Uncertainty and the Cost of Capital for Utilities," 117 *Public Utilities Fortnightly* 23 (February 20, 1986); Philip Fanara, Jr., and Raymond Gorman, "The Effects of Regulatory Risk On the Cost of Capital," 117 *Public Utilities Fortnightly* 32 (March 6, 1986).

[127]See, *e.g.,* Robert S. Stich, "An Additional Standard for Measuring Common Equity Costs," 97 *Public Utilities Fortnightly* 34 (February 26, 1976).

[128]Harold Leventhal, Testimony filed before the Federal Communications Commission (mimeographed, September, 1962). "As typically applied under the 'just and reasonable' standard, original cost rate-making attempts to set the rate of return for a regulated enterprise at the same level as the rate of return of an unregulated enterprise with similar associated risks." *Farmers Union Central Exchange, Inc. v. Federal Energy Regulatory Comm.,* 734 F. 2d 1486, 1515, 59 PUR4th 1, 31 (D.C. Cir. 1984), *cert. denied,* 469 U.S. 1034 (1984).

[129]See, *e.g.,* Eugene F. Brigham, Dilip K. Shome, and Steve R. Vinson, "The Risk Premium Approach to Measuring a Utility's Cost of Equity," 14 *Financial Management* 33 (Spring, 1985).

[130]*Re American Teleph. & Teleg. Co., op. cit.* (86 FCC 2d 221).

[131]See, *e.g., Stocks, Bonds, Bills and Inflation: 1987 Yearbook* (Chicago: Ibbotson Associates, 1987).

[132]See, *e.g., Re Alabama Power Co.,* Docket No. 17094 (Ala., 1976).

[133]See, *e.g.,* Carl W. Treleaven, "The Use of Financial Planning Models in Utility Rate Making," 108 *Public Utilities Fortnightly* 33 (July 16, 1981).

[134]*Re Trans-Canada Pipe Lines Ltd.* (NEB, December, 1971), pp. 6-2 — 6-3, 6-6. As Judge Breyer has concluded: "This discussion is meant to suggest that setting a rate of return cannot — even in principle — be reduced to an exact science. To spend hours of hearing time considering elaborate rate-of-return models is of doubtful value, and suggestions of a proper rate, carried out to several decimal places, give an

air of precision that must be false." Stephen Breyer, *Regulation and Its Reform* (Cambridge: Harvard University Press, 1982), p. 47.

[135]In an effort to overcome the problems inherent in determining the cost of equity capital, it has been proposed that common stock be placed on a contractual basis. See Arthur P. Becker, "Fixed Dividends for All Public Utility Stock," 21 *Journal of Land & Public Utility Economics* 243 (1945); John Bauer, *Transforming Public Utility Regulation* (New York: Harper & Bros., 1950); Chaps. x and xi. There is little support, however, for such a proposal.

[136]Dissenting opinion in *Missouri ex rel. Southwestern Bell Teleph. Co. v. Pub. Service Comm.*, op. cit., p. 290.

[137]*Re General Teleph. Co. of Florida*, 44 PUR3d 247, 255 (Fla., 1962).

[138]Bonbright, *op. cit.*, p. 262.

[139]Richard B. Blatz, "Efficiency Incentives for Telephone Companies," 72 *Public Utilities Fortnightly* 19 (September 12, 1963).

[140]Thus, the New Hampshire commission allowed 0.20 percent in excess of the cost of capital as an efficiency allowance [*New England Teleph. & Teleg. Co. v. New Hampshire*, op. cit., p. 506], while the New Mexico commission allowed an extra 0.50 percent on common equity, partly because of efficiency [*Re Southwestern Pub. Service Co.*, op. cit., p. 313]. More commonly, commissions state that efficiency is taken into account in determining the overall rate of return.

[141]See Chapter 12, pp. 536-37.

[142]*Re Rochester Teleph. Corp.*, 24 PUR3d 262 (N.Y., 1958); dissent of Commissioner Smith in *Hogan v. Hampden Teleph. Co.*, 36 PUR4th 480, 497-98 (Me., 1980). See also *Texas Pub. Utility Comm. v. Houston Lighting & Power Co. et al.*, 715 S.W. 2d 98 (Tex. App. 1986).

[143]See, *e.g.*, *Re Western Light & Teleph. Co., Inc.*, 17 PUR3d 422 (Okla., 1957); *Ex parte Southern Bell Teleph. & Teleg. Co.*, 26 PUR3d 55 (La., 1959); *Re North Missouri Teleph. Co., Inc.*, 49 PUR3d 313 (Mo., 1963). Such a penalty was upheld in *North Carolina ex rel. Utilities Comm. v. General Teleph. Co. of the Southeast*, 208 S.E. 2d 681 (1974).

[144]*Re Norfolk & Carolina Teleph. & Teleg. Co.*, 18 PUR4th 592 (N.C., 1977).

[145]*Re Virginia Elec. & Power Co.*, Docket No. E-22, Sub 257 (N.C., 1981). The penalty was removed a year later. See *Re Virginia Elec. & Power Co.*, 48 PUR4th 327, 359-60 (N.C., 1982).

[146]*Re General Teleph. Co. of California*, 37 PUR4th 127 (Cal., 1980).

[147]*Re Iowa Gas Co.*, 76 PUR4th 425 (Iowa, 1986). See *Re Standards for Public Utility Management Efficiency*, 65 PUR4th 189 (Iowa, 1985).

[148]Bonbright, *op. cit.*, p. 265.

[149]Walter A. Morton, "Creative Regulation," 39 *Land Economics* 367, 371 (1963).

[150]See Chapter 8, pp. 320-21.

[151]Bonbright, *op. cit.*, p. 267. It should be emphasized again that the arguments supporting an inflation adjustment pertain to original cost jurisdictions; a reproduction cost or fair value rate base makes a full or partial allowance for inflation.

[152]Walter A. Morton, "Rate of Return and the Value of Money in Public Utilities," 28 *Land Economics* 91, 119 (1952).

[153]"Regulation of public utilities is generally viewed as a substitute for competition. Under competition, the level of profits will vary with the business cycle, but will in the long run be equal to the cost of attracting or retaining physical resources whose earning power is related to dollars of current purchasing power as distin-

guished from nominal dollar values. Under competitive conditions, however, investors are not always able to achieve the preservation of real capital values and protect their assets against the ravages of inflation. The competitive principle requires that utility investors should be given an opportunity — not a guarantee — to preserve the real value of their capital to no greater, but also to no lesser, a degree than that to which investors in industrial companies (of similar risk to utilities) can achieve a preservation of real capital values." "Testimony of Stephen F. Sherwin," *op. cit.,* pp. iv-v. Proper use of the comparable earnings standard achieves this objective.

[154]Martin G. Glaeser, *Public Utilities in American Capitalism* (New York: The Macmillan Co., 1957), p. 399.

[155]See, *e.g., Re New York Teleph. Co.,* 91 PUR (NS) 231 (N.Y., 1951); *Re Michigan Bell Teleph. Co.,* 91 PUR (NS) 129 (Mich., 1951); *Re Wisconsin Elec. Power Co.,* 93 PUR (NS) 97 (Wis., 1952).

[156]Consistency in regulatory ratemaking policy is closely connected to the fairness issue. Stockholders who purchase the common stocks of utilities which are in fair value jurisdictions, for example, have the right to expect that commissions will continue to adhere to a fair value theory. See Bonbright, *op. cit.,* pp. 272-73.

[157]In the words of the California commission: ". . . the law contemplates that people who buy securities are charged with the knowledge that certain risks will be attached to their ownership and that one of the risks is the possibility of the decline in purchasing power of the dollar." Quoted in Glaeser, *op. cit.,* p. 398.

[158]Thatcher, *op. cit.,* p. 111. See also *Re Mountain States Teleph. & Teleg. Co.,* 2 PUR3d 75 (Utah, 1953); *Re New York Teleph. Co.,* 5 PUR3d 33 (N.Y., 1954); *Re Pacific Teleph. & Teleg. Co.,* 5 PUR3d 396 (Cal., 1954).

[159]Clemens, *op. cit.,* pp. 38-39.

[160]See, *e.g.,* Fergus J. McDiarmid, "Are Public Utility Stocks an Inflation Hedge?," 80 *Public Utilities Fortnightly* 33 (October 12, 1967); Morrissey, "Current Aspects of the Cost of Capital to Utilities," *op. cit.*

[161]See Fred P. Morrissey, "Inflation and Public Utility Regulation," 1 *California Management Review* 74 (1959); Ralph E. Badger, "Important Concepts as to Fair Return and Cost of Money," 66 *Public Utilities Fortnightly* 93 (1960).

[162]*Re Tampa Elec. Co.,* Order No. 9599 (Fla., 1980), p. 14. See also Peter C. Manus and Charles F. Phillips, Jr., "Earnings Erosion during Inflation," 95 *Public Utilities Fortnightly* 17 (May 8, 1975); David R. Kamerschen and Chris W. Paul, II, "Erosion and Attrition: A Public Utility's Dilemma," 102 *Public Utilities Fortnightly* 21 (December 21, 1978); Walter G. French, "On the Attrition of Utility Earnings," 107 *Public Utilities Fortnightly* 19 (February 26, 1981).

[163]There is an obvious limitation to this method: Inflation is not generally considered to be a "known change."

[164]See, *e.g.,* "Use of a Year-end Rate Base to Offset Effects of Inflation," 64 *Public Utilities Fortnightly* 241 (July 30, 1959); "The Year-end Rate Base," 78 *Public Utilities Fortnightly* 53 (August 16, 1979); *Re Commonwealth Edison Co.,* 71 PUR4th 81 (Ill., 1985).

[165]See J. Michael Harrison, "Forecasting Revenue Requirements," 103 *Public Utilities Fortnightly* 11 (March 15, 1979); "Alternative Test Year Methods in Public Utility Rate Proceedings" (Washington, D.C.: National Association of Regulatory Utility Commissioners, 1980), pp. 37-43. A few commissions have experimented with a split-year approach; *e.g.,* six months actual, six months projected.

[166]*Ex parte Louisiana Power & Light Co.,* Order No. U-14690-A (La., 1981).

[167]*Re New Jersey Bell Teleph. Co.*, 31 PUR3d 453 (N.J., 1959); *Re Columbia Gas of Maryland*, 57 PUR3d 460 (Md., 1965). See also "Rate Base Allowance for Attrition," 80 *Public Utilities Fortnightly* 59 (December 7, 1967).

[168]"Offsets to Attrition and Regulatory Lag," 66 *Public Utilities Fortnightly* 585, 587 (1960); *Re Consolidated Edison Co. of New York*, 41 PUR3d 305 (N.Y., 1961); *Re Tampa Elec. Co., op. cit.*, p. 14. See also "Attrition Factor Affecting Return Allowance," 98 *Public Utilities Fortnightly* 44 (November 18, 1976) and 99 *Public Utilities Fortnightly* 51 (June 9, 1977).

[169]"Offsets to Attrition and Regulatory Lag," *op. cit.*, pp. 585-86; *Re Montana Power Co.*, 42 PUR3d 241 (Mont., 1962).

[170]"Interim Rate Relief Discussed," 104 *Public Utilities Fortnightly* 53 (September 13, 1979).

[171]See Edward L. Flippen and Daniel M. Walker, "Financial Review of Utilities: The Virginia Plan," 108 *Public Utilities Fortnightly* 30 (July 30, 1981).

[172]*Re Pub. Service Co. of New Mexico*, 9 PUR4th 113 (N.M., 1975). In 1978, the commission eliminated the quarterly adjustment and the return on common equity range, and provided for an annual adjustment and a 13.50 percent return on common equity. *Re Pub. Service Co. of New Mexico*, Case No. 1419 (N.M., 1978). See David S. Cohen and Charles F. Noble, "Cost of Service Indexing: An Analysis of New Mexico's Experiment in Public Utility Regulation," 9 *New Mexico Law Review* 287 (1979); *The New Mexico Cost of Service Index, an Effort in Regulatory Innovation* (Columbus, Ohio: National Regulatory Research Institute, 1979); Michael Schmidt, *Automatic Adjustment Clauses: Theory and Application* (East Lansing: MSU Public Utilities Studies, 1980), pp. 49-53.

In 1980, the Michigan commission adopted an experimental indexing approach for Michigan Bell Telephone Company, under which the allowable annual rate increase (decrease), from October, 1980, through October, 1982, was computed as follows: the annual rate of inflation (December-to-December), less a 4 percent productivity offset, times 90 percent (10 percent was treated as an offset to regulatory lag, since a case was filed in July of each year and the rates were in effect in October). Thus, if the annual inflation rate were 12 percent, the allowed increase would be 7.20 percent (12 percent − 4 percent = 8 percent × .90 = 7.20 percent). See Schmidt, *op. cit.*, pp. 57-58.

The New Jersey commission has experimented with indexing plans [see, *e.g.*, *Re New Jersey Power & Light Co.*, 53 PUR (NS) 1 (N.J., 1944); *Re Adjustment Clauses in Telephone Rate Schedules*, 3 PUR4th 298 (N.J., 1974)] and cost-of-service adjustments are common in Canada for gas transmission companies [see, *e.g.*, *Re Westcoast Transmission Co. Ltd., op. cit.*]. But the Illinois commission rejected a comprehensive "cost and efficiency" proposal filed by the Illinois Bell Telephone Company. See *Re Illinois Bell Teleph. Co.*, Cause No. 58916 (Ill., 1975).

[173]See, *e.g.*, Paul L. Joskow and Paul W. MacAvoy, "Regulation and the Financial Condition of the Electric Power Companies in the 1970's," 65 *American Economic Review* 295 (1975); M. W. Keran, "Inflation, Regulation, and Utility Stock Prices," 7 *Bell Journal of Economics* 268 (1976); Paul W. MacAvoy, "The Present Condition of Regulated Enterprise" (Working Paper No. 5, Series C, School of Organization and Management, Yale University, April, 1978); Eugene M. Lerner, "Competition for the Funds of Investors and the Cost of Capital for Utilities," 105 *Public Utilities Fortnightly* 15 (February 28, 1980).

[174]Said the Massachusetts Supreme Court, in reversing a commission decision:

"The department has been proceeding for years on the assumption that the company's rate base will remain constant during the period following a decision of the department. In substance this is an assumption that there will be no inflation. That assumption is not only speculative and uncertain; it is clearly erroneous. It has proved wrong, year after year, and the department errs when it stubbornly persists in an erroneous assumption." *New England Teleph. & Teleg. Co. v. Mass. Department of Pub. Utilities,* 16 PUR4th 346, 350 (1976). Yet, in 1979, the U.S. Supreme Court dismissed an appeal by the California Association of Utility Shareholders which urged, among other things, that the California commission be compelled to account for inflation in rate decisions. The association claimed that its members lost more than $270 million through stock dilution since 1973. *California Ass'n of Utility Shareholders v. Pub. Utilities Comm.,* 444 U.S. 986 (1979).

[175]See "For the Utilities, It's a Fight for Survival," *Fortune,* March, 1975, pp. 97-101, 184-89.

[176]During the 1970s, as the utility sector's financial position deteriorated, security analysts began to rate the regulatory commissions. [See, *e.g.,* Salomon Brothers Inc., "Electric Utility Regulation — Semiannual Review," September 1, 1987, p. 7.] There is evidence that such ratings or evaluations have an impact on the cost of capital. See Robert R. Trout, "The Regulatory Factor and Electric Utility Common Stock Investment Values," 104 *Public Utilities Fortnightly* 28 (November 22, 1979); Stephen H. Archer, "The Regulatory Effects on Cost of Capital in Electric Utilities," 107 *Public Utilities Fortnightly* 36 (February 26, 1981). See also Thomas M. Tole and Sammy O. McCord, "A Bond Rating Agency's Influence on Utilities' Cost of Capital," 117 *Public Utilities Fortnightly* 34 (January 9, 1986).

[177]*Re Potomac Edison Co.,* 74 PUR4th 428, 432 (Va., 1986).

[178]*Cedar Rapids Gas Light Co. v. Cedar Rapids,* 223 U.S. 655, 669 (1912).

[179]Badger, *op. cit.,* p. 101.

[180]Foster, *op cit.,* p. 884.

[181]Report of an Informal Task Force to the Energy Transition Team, "Recommendations for Restoration of Financial Health to the U.S. Electric Power Industry" (mimeographed, December 17, 1980), pp. 11-12.

Chapter 10

THE RATE STRUCTURE

> *There are two basic functions of price; to discourage the buyer of a commodity (or service) from using up too much of it, and to induce the supplier to produce enough. But what is the right amount? What is enough and not too much?*
>
> —*Abba P. Lerner**

The preceding three chapters concerned determination of the rate level. The end result is the total revenue requirement of a public utility. The next step is the rate structure — determination of the specific rates that will yield the required revenues.

Historically, public utility rate structures were developed by the companies themselves and, more particularly, by their engineers. The theoretical basis for the resulting structures was too often difficult to discern, other than an obvious emphasis on promoting usage. Like most private firms, utilities considered market (demand) factors as well as cost (supply) factors in determining their rate structures. Discrimination often resulted; discrimination, some contended, that was not "just and reasonable."

The situation has changed completely, as the emphasis in regulatory proceedings has shifted to rate design. The theoretical principles are being developed. This shift in emphasis has resulted from three developments. First, as Kahn has noted, management generally has adopted "increasingly sophisticated economic criteria and techniques in formulating investment and price policies."[1] Second, the development of competition has forced utilities to abandon their traditional pricing policies, as rates have been forced toward cost of service. Finally, the acceleration in the rate of inflation, the environmental movement, rising fuel prices, and conservation have affected public utility costs and, hence, rates. These pressures too have compelled both the regulated and the regulator to rethink proper pricing principles.

Nor can the role of the federal government in this reexamination process be overlooked. On the one hand, competition has been promoted by federal agencies, often over objections from the state commissions. On the other hand, the federal government assumed an important input into rate design through enactment of the national energy plan in 1978. Specifically, the Public Utility Regulatory Policies Act (*a*) required the state commissions to consider, and to implement or adopt if appropriate, any or all of twelve specified standards in the case of electric utilities, (*b*) initiated a gas utility rate design study, and (*c*) gave to the Department of Energy the right to intervene in state electric and gas utility rate proceedings to advocate reforms.

The legal standards guiding the regulatory commissions are broad. Each specific rate must be "just and reasonable." Further, "undue" or "unjust" discrimination among customers is prohibited. The rate structure thus involves determination of specific rates and determination of rate relationships.

The theory of rate design is discussed in the first sections of this chapter: the criteria of a sound rate structure, the bases for price differentiation, the economics of price discrimination, and the theory of marginal cost pricing. A special case — lifeline rates — is discussed in the fifth section. The concluding section considers rate design with respect to the electric utility industry.[2]

Criteria of a Sound Rate Structure

Bonbright, in his study on public utility rates, lists eight criteria of a sound or desirable rate structure. They are as follows:

1. The related, "practical" attributes of simplicity, understandability, public acceptability, and feasibility of application.
2. Freedom from controversies as to proper interpretation.
3. Effectiveness in yielding total revenue requirements under the fair-return standard.
4. Revenue stability from year to year.
5. Stability of the rates themselves, with a minimum of unexpected changes seriously adverse to existing customers. (Compare "The best tax is an old tax.")
6. Fairness of the specific rates in the apportionment of total costs of service among the different consumers.
7. Avoidance of "undue discrimination" in rate relationships.
8. Efficiency of the rate classes and rate blocks in discouraging wasteful

use of service while promoting all justified types and amounts of use:

(a) in the control of the total amounts of service supplied by the company;

(b) in the control of the relative uses of alternative types of service (on-peak versus off-peak electricity, Pullman travel versus coach travel, single-party telephone service versus service from a multi-party line, etc.).[3]

Admittedly, these criteria are broad and ambiguous (what, for example, is "undue" discrimination?). They also overlap without offering any rules of priority in case of conflicts. How is the "cost of service" to be measured — marginal cost, average cost, or fully distributed cost? Clearly, the measure largely depends on the purpose that a rate is to fulfill. Further, is the dominant objective one of "fairness" or one of "efficiency"?[4] But the criteria are of value "in reminding the rate maker of considerations that might otherwise escape his attention, and also useful in suggesting one important reason why problems of practical rate design do not readily yield to 'scientific' principles of optimum pricing."[5]

Bonbright further suggests that the three primary criteria are numbers 3, 6, and 8; namely,

... (a) the revenue-requirement or financial-need objective, which takes the form of a fair-return standard with respect to private utility companies; (b) the fair-cost-apportionment objective, which invokes the principle that the burden of meeting total revenue requirements must be distributed *fairly* among the beneficiaries of the service; and (c) the optimum-use or consumer-rationing objective, under which the rates are designed to discourage the wasteful use of public utility services while promoting all use that is economically justified in view of the relationships between costs incurred and benefits received.[6]

Cost and Demand: Price Differentiation[7]

There are two bases for price differentiation. The first is differences in costs or the "cost of service." The second is differences in demand or the "value of service." A seller does not discriminate when rates are based upon costs, even though some customers pay more than others. But when rates are based upon demand, discrimination occurs.

Cost of Service

Differences in rates may be due to differences in costs. It is more expensive to serve some customers than others. Those who use the service only occasionally are more expensive to serve than those who use it continuously. The costs of billing each type of customer, for example, may be approximately the same, so that average costs are higher for the first group than for the second. For the telephone industry, terminal costs are as high for short distances as for long distances, so that costs per mile decline with distance. In the case of electric utilities, little of the distribution plant is applicable to large industrial sales, resulting in a significant cost difference between industrial and residential or small commercial users.

Costs also vary according to the time of use. Customers who use the service during the peak demand period are more expensive to serve than off-peak users. A basic factor in determining the size of a utility plant is the peak demand. Therefore, it costs less to serve those customers who use the service without burdening the business as a whole by adding to the peak demand period. Further, if off-peak usage is increased, the utility may obtain a better utilization of its plant throughout the day, thereby resulting in a larger total output over which fixed costs may be spread.

Value of Service

Differences in rates may be due to differences in demand. A customer's demand is based upon the need or desire for the service, the ability to pay for it, and the availability of substitutes. Customers have relatively elastic demands when they have little need for the service, when they have insufficient incomes to pay for the service, or when they can provide it for themselves or purchase it from a competing seller. Customers have relatively inelastic demands when their need and ability to pay for the service are great and when no alternative sources of supply or substitutes are available.

From the seller's point of view, discrimination may offer marked advantages. When a supplier can fully utilize his plant and earn a fair rate of return by charging a single price, he is unlikely to practice price discrimination. But a price low enough to maintain full production may yield insufficient revenues to cover costs, while one set high enough to cover costs may result in unused capacity. In such a situation, the supplier will be able to increase his revenues by charging a higher price where demand is inelastic and a lower price where demand is elastic.

This situation is illustrated in Table 10-1. Assume that an enterprise has a plant with a capacity of 3,800 units. Assume further that total cost includes a fair return on the investment in the plant, so that the final column represents either excess profit or loss. If the firm's output is sold at a single price, the rate will be $8.00 and sales will be 400 units. Profits are maximized. At this price, the plant is not fully utilized. A glance at the table will show that it is impossible for the firm to both cover costs and maintain full production as long as a single price is charged.

If discrimination is practiced, however, the situation is quite different, as shown in Table 10-2. Now, by dividing customers into separate classes and

TABLE 10-1

Enterprise Selling at a Single Price

Price	Sales	Total Revenue	Total Cost	Profit Or Loss
$11.00	100	$1,100	$ 1,600	− $ 500
10.00	200	2,000	2,150	− 150
9.00	300	2,700	2,650	+ 50
8.00	400	3,200	3,100	− 100
7.00	500	3,500	3,500	0
6.00	700	4,200	4,250	− 50
5.00	1,000	5,000	5,400	− 400
4.00	1,400	5,600	6,700	− 1,100
3.00	2,000	6,000	8,200	− 2,200
2.00	2,800	5,600	10,000	− 4,400
1.00	3,800	3,800	13,000	− 9,200

TABLE 10-2

Enterprise Practicing Price Discrimination

Price	Sales	Sales in Each Class	Revenue from Each Class	Total Revenue	Total Cost	Profit Or Loss
$11.00	100	100	$1,100	$ 1,100	$ 1,600	− $ 500
10.00	200	100	1,000	2,100	2,150	− 50
9.00	300	100	900	3,000	2,650	+ 350
8.00	400	100	800	3,800	3,100	+ 700
7.00	500	100	700	4,500	3,500	+ 1,000
6.00	700	200	1,200	5,700	4,250	+ 1,450
5.00	1,000	300	1,500	7,200	5,400	+ 1,800
4.00	1,400	400	1,600	8,800	6,700	+ 2,100
3.00	2,000	600	1,800	10,600	8,200	+ 2,400
2.00	2,800	800	1,600	12,200	10,000	+ 2,200
1.00	3,800	1,000	1,000	13,200	13,000	+ 200

charging each one a different price, total revenue will increase. Prices will range from a high of $11.00 to a low of $3.00, output will expand to 2,000 units, and excess profits will rise to $2,400. Yet, as will be demonstrated below, such a schedule would be considered as "unduly" discriminatory.

The Economics of Price Discrimination

When a firm sells the same service at rates which are not proportional to costs, discrimination results. Stated another way, discrimination occurs when rates are based upon differences in demand, rather than differences in costs. Consequently, some buyers will pay more than the cost of the particular service; others will pay less. It must be noted, however, that discrimination is not unlimited. As sellers cannot force customers to pay more than they believe the service is worth, the upper ceiling is the value of service. A price set above this limit would result in reduced sales. The lower limit is the seller's marginal (sometimes referred to as out-of-pocket) costs. Any sales made at a price below this limit would result in losses, since these costs can be avoided by not producing the output. When fixed costs are high, as in most of the utility industries, these limits are wide, thereby leaving considerable latitude for discrimination.

Unavoidable versus Intentional Discrimination

Discrimination is partially unavoidable. The cost of providing a particular service is difficult, if not impossible, to determine accurately. Some variable costs, such as labor and fuel, are easily identified with a unit of output. Other costs, however, are commonly or jointly incurred in rendering different types of service. Rather than varying directly with output, they decline in importance as output increases. These costs include interest, depreciation, investment in plant and equipment, and administrative overhead. When investment is large, such costs represent a significant percentage of total costs. When the same plant or equipment is used to provide several types of service, there is no one correct way to allocate these costs among the different units of service. Any method of apportionment is subject to dispute, as was demonstrated in Chapter 6 when separations procedures were discussed.[8] Even if firms tried to base their rates upon costs, therefore, a substantial element of judgment is involved.

Discrimination is also intentional. As previously shown, when one rate is charged for a service, a company may not be able to utilize its capacity fully. Only by discrimination may idle capacity be eliminated. Furthermore, discrimination is often socially desirable. If it allows a company to expand its sales and utilize its facilities more fully, average costs are reduced as fixed costs are spread over more units of output and the firm's profits are increased. Fuller utilization, in turn, may result in lower prices for *all* customers and in a wider use of the utility's services. Some services might be offered that would not be available under uniform rates or only available at substantially higher rates: interstate toll calls over low density routes often are subsidized by revenues from high density routes. Regional development also may be encouraged: low electric rates encouraged its use and attracted industry to the TVA area. These advantages, however, are unlikely to be realized unless rates are controlled. As Sharfman has pointed out, there is an inherent danger in discrimination:

> The "value of service" principle, as a basis for rate-making, provides at best a vague and indeterminate formula, rather easily construed as justifying any system of rates found expedient by the carrier. Taking the words in their most obvious sense, no rate can exceed the value of service and still continue to be paid by the shipper.[9]

The Conditions for Discrimination

Rate discrimination is not possible unless the market can be separated into distinct sectors so that (*1*) customers who are charged the higher rate cannot buy in the low-rate sector and (2) those buying at the lower rate cannot resell in the high-rate sector. For industries selling transferable products, this is usually not possible.[10] However, for public utilities which sell services, such a division of the market is possible. Moreover, they are able to control the use of their services, since they generally deliver them to the customer as they are consumed. If a telephone company charges a business customer more than it charges a residential user, the business subscriber cannot obtain the lower rate by connecting his telephone with the residential subscriber's lines. Customers of utilities cannot shift between the established sectors. This condition further implies that the discriminating firm is either free from competition or that competition is controlled. If two firms supplied the same market, their rivalry for business would force rates down.

Two other conditions for discrimination also must exist.[11] The elasticities of demand in the established sectors of the market must be considerably different. That is, if the elasticities are equal or similar, so, too, will be the marginal revenue curves, and discrimination would serve no purpose. Finally, the cost of separating the market into sectors must not be too large. Rate discrimination involves some extra expense. Different bills, for example, usually must be printed for each type of customer, and bookkeeping becomes more complex. For discrimination to be profitable, the increase in revenues must be greater than the additional expenses incurred.

The Case for Discrimination

Discrimination may be advantageous for two reasons. First, it may result in a fuller utilization of a firm's plant and equipment, and a wider consumption of its service. Second, it may lead to lower prices for all customers. The first was illustrated above, where adoption of price discrimination raised output from 400 units to 2,000 units. The second can be seen in Table 10-3. Here, the prices, sales, and costs are the same as those in the previous tables. But now it is assumed that a regulatory commission controls the firm's rate structure. It was suggested earlier that the rate structure shown in Table 10-2 involves "undue" discrimination because of the presence of excess profits. If discrimination were not allowed, therefore, the commission would force the seller to produce 500 units, which would sell for $7.00 each, as shown in Table 10-1. At this price, there would be no excess profits.

TABLE 10-3

Enterprise Practicing Price Discrimination under Regulation*

Price	Sales	Sales in Each Class	Revenue from Each Class	Total Revenue	Total Cost	Profit Or Loss
$5.00	1,000	1,000	$5,000	$ 5,000	$ 5,400	− $ 400
4.00	1,400	400	1,600	6,600	6,700	− 100
3.00	2,000	600	1,800	8,400	8,200	+ 200
2.00	2,800	800	1,600	10,000	3,100	0
1.00	3,800	1,000	1,000	11,000	13,000	− 2,000

*This rate structure is only one of several possible structures that might be established by a company and accepted by a commission.

By allowing discrimination, the commission could establish the rate schedule shown in Table 10-3. A fair return is earned from a scale of prices that begins at $2.00 and rises to $5.00, while the volume of output is raised to 2,800 units. It should be noted that every price is well below the $7.00 that would have to be charged if discrimination were not allowed. This schedule is made possible because by serving the low-rate customers who cannot afford the service at a higher rate, the firm's fixed costs are spread over more units. As a result of the adoption of such a schedule, no customers are harmed. On the contrary, all of them have been helped: the $5.00 customers have saved $2.00 per unit, while the $4.00, $3.00, and $2.00 rates are required to obtain customers that otherwise could not afford the service.

Such discrimination cannot be justified, however, unless (a) there are high fixed costs and chronic unused capacity, so that costs per unit are reduced as the fixed costs are spread over a larger volume of output; (*b*) the lower rates are needed to attract new business; (*c*) all rates cover at least variable costs and make some contribution to fixed (overhead) costs; and (*d*) regulation is undertaken to keep total earnings reasonable and to keep discrimination within bounds. If these conditions exist, discrimination is desirable, since it leads to either an increased use of the facilities or to a lower rate for the customers discriminated against. At the same time, it is important to remember that each rate must be set with the thought that all rates together should return to the utility sufficient revenue to cover its total cost of service, including the rate of return allowed by the commission. This statement does not imply that such revenue is guaranteed; rather it simply means that this end should be kept in view.

The Case against Discrimination and Embedded Costs

Under conditions of decreasing costs, and assuming a goal of expanding service to a maximum number of consumers, few would challenge the desirability of discrimination.[12] But such discrimination does not promote economic efficiency, particularly under conditions of increasing costs, for consumers are given improper price signals. Correct price signals — and the achievement of economic efficiency — require marginal cost pricing, and herein lies the controversy concerning rate design.

Utility rate structures, as they were developed over the years, represented a complex and confusing mixture of cost of service and value of service considerations, with the promotion of use as the dominant objective. To the extent that rate structures were cost-justified, they were based upon historical embedded (average or fully distributed) costs. In the words of the Colorado commission:

> For example, a utility will establish an actual test year for determining revenue requirements and utilize the historical costs for purposes of functionalizing and allocating the costs to various classes of customers for purposes of establishing rates. In that fashion, both the revenue requirements and the rates ultimately determined are based upon the average costs for the historical test year. . . .[13]

In many instances, however, discrimination was not justified. Further, rate structures contained countless internal subsidies: off-peak users subsidized on-peak users, industrial and commercial customers subsidized residential customers (electric and gas), and long-distance (toll) calls subsidized local exchange service (telephone), to cite only a few examples. Many customers, in short, paid a rate that did not reflect "the marginal social opportunity cost of supply."[14] Those who paid less were encouraged to demand more service; those who paid more were encouraged to demand less service.

By the early 1970s, recognition was growing that such rate structures were incompatible with the new economic environment. Promotion was no longer rational, since new capacity resulted in higher average costs. And competition was forcing some rates toward marginal costs, since internal subsidies require monopoly conditions.[15] Not only were customers being given improper price signals, but utilities found that rates based upon past costs and sales, during inflation, resulted in constant revenue deficiencies. For these and other reasons, the emphasis began to shift to marginal cost pricing.

Marginal Cost Pricing: Theory and Practice

The economic literature has long provided the theoretical framework of marginal cost pricing; that is, the pricing of all goods and services at marginal cost.[16] Until recently, however, little attention has been devoted to the problem of translating abstract theory to practical application, particularly with respect to public utilities,[17] although the marginal cost pricing principle has been widely employed in France and England.[18] But with the exposure of public utilities to competitive market forces, rising costs, and more elastic demand conditions, marginal cost pricing principles have received increased attention in the literature and in regulatory proceedings.

The Theory and Qualifications

Under the equilibrium conditions of pure competition, as explained in Chapter 2, price, which represents what consumers are willing to pay for the last unit of a good or service, is equal to the cost of producing that last unit; that is, marginal cost. As a result, the consumers' valuation of the last unit and the cost of producing the last unit are equal. This equilibrium results in a socially optimum volume of output and a minimum cost of producing the volume. The theory, however, is subject to two qualifications:

> . . . The first qualifying consideration is the cost of administering such a pricing system: obviously, economic efficiency requires that we move toward marginal cost pricing only so long as the additional cost of developing and administering a closer approximation to it is exceeded by the incremental benefit. Notice that even in this decision marginal costs remain the controlling criterion. The second qualification is the principle of second-best: in deciding to what extent and whether to price at marginal cost in a particular market, it is essential to take into account the presence of imperfections elsewhere in the system, in particular the extent and direction in which prices in other markets may diverge from that standard. Both of these qualifications counsel taking into account such other considerations as the possible desirability of avoiding excessive fluctuation of rates over time.[19]

The first qualification is self-evident; the second requires brief consideration. It has been shown that unless prices are equal to marginal costs in *all* industries, an optimum allocation of resources (in the Paretian sense) cannot be achieved.[20] The "problem of the second best" is both a disturbing and a serious one "in an economy shot through with imperfections of competition, monopoly power, and government taxes and subsidies, causing all prices to diverge in varying directions and degrees from marginal costs."[21] At a minimum, the problem suggests that second-best considerations must be taken into account in designing rates. Contends Baumol:

> Over the whole of the discussions . . . there looms most menacingly the injunction of the theorem of the second best: Thou shalt not optimize piecemeal. But I would argue that in practice this admonition must be softened lest otherwise all effective policy be stultified. I would propose, instead, that one should shun piecemeal ameliorative measures that have not been sanctioned by careful analysis and the liberal use of common sense. Many policies may plausibly be expected to yield improvements even though things elsewhere are not organized optimally.[22]

Marginal Cost Pricing: From Theory to Practice

Despite these qualifications, economic efficiency requires marginal cost pricing. Implementation of marginal cost pricing, however, raises a number of issues, considered below as threshold issues, time-of-day considerations, and minimum rates.

Threshold Issues. Marginal cost pricing raises three basic threshold issues. The first issue concerns the proper time frame; that is, short-run versus long-run marginal costs. The term short-run refers to a period of time in which some productive services are fixed in amount; most typically, the plant capacity (capital) is fixed.[23] Here, a distinction must be made between fixed or constant costs and variable costs. Only variable costs affect the calculation of short-run marginal costs, for they are the only costs which vary with changes in the rate of plant utilization. Thus, if a plant is operating at less than full capacity and fixed costs are high, short-run marginal costs will represent a small fraction of average total costs. In a long-run period of time, the capacity of a plant can be varied. All costs are variable. The long-run marginal costs, therefore, represent the increments in total costs as plants of different sizes (capacities) are put into operation.

Strict application of marginal cost pricing requires that price equal short-run marginal costs. As Kahn has noted: "no airplane should take off unfilled so long as there exists some potential passenger who would place a greater value on making that single flight than the almost negligible short-run variable cost of adding him to the flight roster; and no sale should be made, whatever the possibly lower costs of making it on a continuing basis, whose incremental variable costs exceed the value of that single unit of service to a customer."[24] Put another way, price-output decisions should be governed by short-run marginal costs. Such costs, however, are extremely volatile. As the volume of output expands, for example, short-run marginal costs change more rapidly than do average costs. Rates, in turn, would have to be changed frequently in accordance with variations in the volume of output. Further, it is long-run marginal costs which should govern investment decisions.

There is a variant of the theoretical marginal cost principle which has greater practical application; that is, the long-run incremental cost (LRIC) concept. This concept, unlike the concept of short-run marginal cost, recognizes that utilities add capacity in discrete units and on a continuous basis. The long-run incremental cost concept thus includes the future costs of supplying utility services, as opposed to the average cost of serving existing customers. Stated the Wisconsin commission in its 1974 *Madison Gas and Electric Company* decision:

> We believe that the appropriate bench mark for the design of electric rates in the case is marginal cost as represented by the practical variant, long-run incremental cost. If electric rates are designed to promote an efficient allocation of resources, this is a logical starting point.
>
> It must be understood that the "long-run" concept is pursued as the most appropriate and most practicable cost measurement. The fact that "long-run" incremental cost is being used does not imply that the resulting rates will be valid for a long time into the future, nor that they will compensate for inflationary cost increases. The primary objective that the LRIC-based rates are intended to accomplish is to guarantee an efficient allocation of resources directed toward the production of electricity. . . .[25]

The relevant future time frame is largely a matter of judgment. Argues Kahn:

> . . . What we are trying to measure is how costs will differ, after a span of time sufficiently long for the system planners to adapt the supplying system to the change, by virtue of taking on some specified incremental block of sales on a continuing basis, as compared with not taking it on. Measurement is, to be sure, another matter. What I suspect we are likely to have, mainly, is a measure of the average, full additional costs, for all additional sales undertaken on a continuing basis, over whatever is the reasonable planning period for additions to capacity — possibly on the order of ten to twelve years for electricity, perhaps three to five years in communications. . . .[26]

It is the very indefiniteness of the relevant time frame that leads Melody, among others, to question the long-run incremental cost concept:

> ... The framework for marginal cost analysis assumes a planning horizon sufficiently distant that all the effects of all alternative decision possibilities can be taken into account. But all of this information is hypothetical and subject to the forecasting ability of the decision maker. Once the optimum alternative is selected and pursued, the firm must await the judgment of reality to see if its decision was good or bad. If the firm correctly perceived and made perfect forecasts for all alternative decision possibilities, its decision indeed will have been optimum. If it did not, its marginal cost calculations will have been inaccurate. As a practical matter we know in advance that our hypothesis of optimization will be disproved by reality.[27]

Closely connected is a second threshold issue; namely, the calculation of marginal or incremental costs. With respect to electric utilities, for example, several different methodologies have been developed for the calculation of incremental costs.[28] Consider the issue of estimating the annualized capacity cost per kilowatt of new capacity. There are two major methods used for making such an estimate, as summarized by Crespi:

> ... One method developed by the National Economic Research Associates (hereafter referred to as the NERA method) uses as an estimate the annualized average cost per kilowatt of a gas-fired peaking generation unit plus the annualized average cost per kilowatt of the associated incremental transmission and distribution investment. The other major method considers what changes will take place in a utility's actual system expansion plan as a result of an upward shift in the trend path of system peak demand, calculates the present value of the resulting change in overall system costs over time, and converts this figure to a per kilowatt basis. This method was developed by Charles J. Cicchetti and others (herein referred to as the CGS method).
>
> The strength of the NERA method is that the cost of a new gas-fired peaking unit is relatively easy to determine. The major weakness is that, by law, no more such peaking units may be installed so that it is not clear what relation, if any, such hypothetical figure would bear to actual system marginal capacity costs.
>
> The main strength of the CGS method is that it is based on the actual expansion plan of the system. The major weakness is that to apply it one must have reasonable estimates of various system costs many years in advance; figures that are notably unreliable.
>
> Once one has estimated by some method the annualized marginal costs of one kilowatt of new system capacity one must determine how these costs will be allocated to the kilowatt-hours provided in each of

the costing periods. One method is to apportion the marginal capacity costs equally over all hours of the "peak" costing period (the CGS method). This method implicitly assumes that any hour in this period has an equal probability of being the actual capacity-determining system peak hour, and that no hour outside this period has any positive probability of becoming the system peak. Another method is to assign these marginal capacity costs to costing periods in proportion to the average "loss-of-load" probabilities for hours in each costing period. Again, subjective, challengeable judgments are required of the analyst.[29]

The third threshold issue concerns the required adjustments to incremental costs. The required adjustments fall into three categories. First, adjustments may be required because of the theory of the second best, as previously discussed. Second, adjustments may be required to meet a utility's total revenue requirement; a revenue requirement that is determined on the basis of embedded (average) costs. Whenever incremental costs exceed embedded costs for a utility, overcollection of revenues will occur; whenever embedded costs exceed incremental costs, undercollection of revenues will occur. Several methods of making rate adjustments exist. Assume an overcollection situation. One adjustment method, widely supported by economists, is the inverse elasticity rule; departures from marginal cost pricing should be inversely proportional to the elasticity of demand.[30] Those customers with elastic demands would be charged marginal cost-based rates; those customers with inelastic demands, would be charged rates below marginal costs. In this way, prices below marginal cost "would distort consumption decisions as little as possible."[31] Another method is to lower or eliminate the customer charge.[32] A third method is to adopt an inverted rate structure, in which the tailblock rate reflects marginal costs and "the initial block or blocks are set at a low enough level to meet the revenue requirement."[33]

Third, adjustments may be necessary to account for social costs. As summarized by the Department of Energy:

> Although there are external or social costs associated with the production of electric power, to a large extent these social costs have already been internalized and accounted for in the determination of electric utility rates. As a result of both Federal and State environmental and safety regulations, electric utilities have been required to incur considerable expense to reduce these social costs; and these expenses for pollution abatement and the maintenance of public health and safety are now included by the utilities and their regulators in the prices that consumers must pay for electricity.
>
> Other important social costs associated with the production of electricity at the margin may be found to exist, which have not been imposed on the producers of electricity. In such cases if the magnitude of

these social costs can be quantified, these costs should be included in the calculation of marginal costs.[34]

Time-of-day Considerations. Marginal cost pricing requires time-of-day (peak-load) rates, since marginal costs vary at different times of the day (and, perhaps, by different seasons). It must be emphasized, however, that time-of-day considerations also are relevant when embedded costs are utilized.[35]

Public utilities historically have paid some attention to peak and off-peak pricing. Commercial and industrial electric rates, for example, have included a separate demand charge although, until recently, the charge was generally based on the maximum kilowatts of electricity used by the customer, regardless of when that demand occurred. Today, the demand charge is frequently based on the maximum kilowatts of demand of the user during the utility's expected peak period. Many electric utilities, moreover, have offered residential customers special rates for off-peak water heating. In more recent years, many electric utilities have adopted a seasonal rate structure (*i.e.*, a summer/winter differential), where there is a high or significant seasonal peak. Long-distance telephone rates, since the mid-1960s, have reflected time-of-day considerations (although such rates were not based on marginal costs).

Time-of-day rates require a significant investment in metering equipment, thereby raising a cost-benefit question. Are the metering costs (as well as other administrative costs associated with a more complex rate structure) outweighed by the potential for minimizing peak usage and the required, associated plant capacity? Or, conversely, will time-of-day rates simply result in a shift in a utility's peak period, rather than in a real peak period reduction? (In the mid-1960s, when the Bell System reduced long-distance rates after 9 P.M., the System's peak was shifted from business hours to evening hours.)

Nissel has argued that peak-load rates, for electric utilities, "are . . . not a suitable device for producing capacity or energy savings," for two basic reasons: first, because "price signals do not work," and second, because peak periods may be too long; *i.e.*, twelve to fourteen hours.[36] Acton and Mitchell contend, however, that the evidence clearly shows that time-of-day rates have changed industrial load curves, both in the United States and abroad.[37] But there is little concrete evidence to date about residential time-of-day effects, although seasonal rates (which require little or no additional metering and administrative costs) have been beneficial.

So, too, may interruptible rates be beneficial, when they involve relatively large loads. Under such rates, an electric or gas utility can turn off service for specified periods of time during system peaks. There are appliances which permit interruption for limited times, while still providing the customer with a satisfactory level of service — air conditioners, water heaters, swimming pool heaters, space heaters, and certain types of pumps and compressors, to name a few of the more obvious examples. Under interruptible rates, customers receive lower rates, since they do not have any demand or capacity costs. Interruptible service can be an important load management technique.

Minimum Rates. There is another use of the marginal cost concept that is more familiar in ratemaking. Frequently, commissions have stated their refusal to allow rates to fall below out-of-pocket costs. If out-of-pocket costs are the same as marginal costs, commissions may be employing marginal costs as measures of minimum rates.

Bonbright has pointed out that the terms out-of-pocket cost and marginal cost may be only approximate synonyms as used by the commissions. In his words:

> "Out-of-pocket cost," itself an ambiguous term, is the popular partial equivalent of "marginal cost," especially in railroad parlance. But it is sometimes used to refer merely to the additional *cash* outlay imposed directly by the production of additional output, where "marginal cost" also includes any enhancements in noncash costs (such as depreciation due to wear and tear of equipment) attributable to an increase in rate of output.[38]

Moreover, whether minimum rates should be based upon short-run or long-run marginal costs represents an important dilemma. The argument in favor of short-run marginal costs as a basis of minimum rates is that rates should be determined by the current costs of providing the service. The aim is to increase consumption in order to make full use of the existing capacity or, when present plant capacity is inadequate to satisfy demand, to raise rates in order to limit consumption. This position,

> ... that utility rates should approximate short-run marginal costs, at least to the maximum extent permitted by the requirement that rates in the aggregate must cover total costs, is in accord with the view that public utility rate making should accept competitive price standards of reasonable rates and rate differentials. For, under the theories of pure or perfect competition, prices are supposed to tend to come much more quickly into accord with short-run marginal costs than in accord with long-run marginal costs.[39]

The argument in favor of long-run marginal costs as the correct measure of minimum rates is based on a conviction that a firm's rate level and rate structure should be as stable as possible. If short-run marginal costs were employed, rates would change rapidly as the volume of production increased or decreased. This change, in turn, would pose an increased burden on the regulatory commissions. Further, many argue that consumers often consider long-run, anticipated rates when deciding between substitute services (oil versus gas heating, gas versus electric ranges). Bonbright argues:

> Once these commitments have been made, the demand for utility services consequent thereon will be largely predetermined by the consumers' investment in equipment and will depend only to a minor extent on any temporary changes in rates of charge. In other words, the demand for public utility services is likely to be much less elastic in the short-run than in the long-run.[40]

On balance, should minimum rates be determined by short-run or long-run marginal costs? Despite the greater difficulty of measurement, most economists would probably favor the long-run.[41] In using the concept of long-run marginal costs, the added costs of providing a service (*e.g.*, the additional operating expenses and the cost of any additional construction, including a full rate of return thereon) would be taken into account. Only when a firm has significant and continuing excess capacity (such as off-peak periods) may short-run marginal costs be a better guide to pricing decisions.

It is important to emphasize, however, that marginal costs set the lower boundary — the floor below which rates should not fall.[42] But they should not determine rates, for the upper boundary is set by demand conditions and regulation.[43]

The issue of minimum rates has occupied much of the time of the Interstate Commerce Commission, due to the existence of intermodal competition.[44] But the issue, particularly during the 1970s, also became of importance for the telecommunications industry.

Lifeline Rates: A Special Case

The basic principles of rate design have been considered in the previous sections. There is an additional issue, however, that has been of growing concern over the last decade; namely, lifeline rates. While the lifeline concept has been subject to various interpretations, the major premise of those advocating lifeline rates is that low-income and elderly customers can no longer pay for "basic" utility services and, since such basic services are both "essential" and inelastic, they should be provided at "an 'affordable' rate, even if that rate is below the cost of service."[45] Some, moreover, contend that lifeline rates also will promote conservation; *i.e.*, an initial low-priced block of electricity, for instance, will result in a higher price for usage above the lifeline threshold level.

The Issues

The issues surrounding the lifeline concept are as complex as they are numerous.[46] The following discussion is intended to be illustrative and not all-inclusive.

Perhaps the initial question is whether the lifeline concept should be considered by the legislative branches or by the regulatory commissions. Some maintain that the legislative branches should properly be concerned with social welfare programs and that only the legislative branches can consider all of the options to lifeline rates; *i.e.*, tax credits, energy or telephone stamps, and direct subsidy programs.[47] Lifeline rates, in other words, have limitations: they are of no aid to those who pay for utility services indirectly through their rent.

When regulatory commissions have considered the lifeline concept — and most of them have, since such an inquiry is required under the Public Utility Regulatory Policies Act of 1978[48] — concern has been expressed, first, about unfair preference and, second, about the proper mechanism for establishing lifeline rates. Unfair preference may arise when a special, low-priced block is offered to a limited segment of a class without regard to the character of the service provided.[49] Even where statutes permit a distinction based on age or income, the issues of administrative costs and increased costs to other customers must be considered. Such unfair preference could be avoided by providing a low-priced block for *all* customers in a class and thereby avoiding a distinction based on age or income. But in that case, several other questions arise.

Are the poor or elderly minimum users, or does energy use (to illustrate) depend upon such other variables as type of dwelling, family size, and life-style?[50] If lifeline rates are available to all customers in a class, the initial low-priced block might have to be sufficiently high that many users in that class would actually experience lower bills, thereby encouraging consumption and discouraging conservation. The problem, of course, is that while most lifeline proposals are based upon end uses, it is not easy to identify individual customer's "essential" needs; they "would vary monthly depending on temperatures, amount of time spent at home, number of loads of wash, and other factors."[51] And, when the initial low-priced block is kept below the cost of service, who would pay the subsidy (*i.e.*, the revenue deficiency): all residential users above the lifeline threshold level or commercial and industrial users? If the revenue deficiency were placed on the residential class (above the initial block), high-usage but low-income consumers would face significant rate increases. If the revenue deficiency were shifted to the commercial or industrial class, they "might be able to pass their higher electric costs back to the poor in the form of higher prices for food, rent, and transportation" while, at the same time, making businesses in a state "less competitive, reducing the level of economic activity in the state and injuring the poor by decreasing employment opportunities and reducing the tax base that provides the source of existing income supplements."[52]

Lifeline in Practice

In the case of telephone service, the separations process (discussed in Chapter 6) long provided a subsidy to local exchange service. However, partly in response to pressure for lifeline rates, the industry began to introduce a new option to flat rate service throughout the country — measured service. Under measured service, a subscriber can elect the so-called "economy" service; for a flat rate per month the subscriber is tied into the network and then pays for each outgoing local call.[53] A few states have implemented lifeline rates.[54] And there are three FCC lifeline plans available to states that are certified by the commission, that waive the federal subscriber (access) line charges and provide assistance toward phone-service connection charges for qualifying low-income households.[55]

In the case of electric and gas service, several different types of lifeline rates have been approved. Four examples are illustrative:

1. California was one of the first regulatory commissions to institute lifeline rates. Rate schedules for residential users of electricity and gas were inverted. Under the Miller-Warren Energy Lifeline Act, "the lifeline rate shall not exceed rates in effect as of January 1, 1976," and "no increase in the lifeline rate [shall be authorized] until the average system rate in kilowatt-hours or cents per therm has increased 25 per cent or more over the [level prevailing on January 1, 1976]." Further, in determining basic domestic needs, the act directed the commission to consider only five residential end uses: (*1*) lighting, (*2*) cooking, (*3*) refrigeration, (*4*) water heating, and (*5*) space heating.[56]

2. North Carolina approved a special rate schedule (a discount for basic monthly energy usage not exceeding 350 kilowatt-hours) for blind, disabled, or aged customers receiving supplemental security income from the Social Security Administration (SSA).[57]

3. Rhode Island approved an experimental residential rate schedule (a 30 percent discount) for all "heads of households" and "principal wage earners" sixty-five years of age or older receiving supplemental security income from the SSA.[58]

4. Montana instituted a four-month "winter" seasonal discount for the first 15 Mcf per month for *all* firm customers. The revenue loss from the discount is made up on Mcf sold in excess of 15 in the winter months and on all Mcf sold in other months, all within the firm class, as follows:

		Winter (*January-April*)	*Remainder of Year* (*May-December*)
First	15 Mcf per Month	$2.287 per Mcf	$3.049 per Mcf
Excess of	15 Mcf per Month	$3.049 per Mcf	$3.049 per Mcf[59]

One final consideration: In addition to lifeline rates, many other programs have been tried or instituted to aid those unable to pay rising energy bills.[60] Two pilot projects utilizing energy stamps were undertaken in the mid-1970s, in Lehigh Valley, Pennsylvania, and Denver, Colorado, both funded by the Federal Community Services Administration (formerly the Office of Economic Opportunity). Investment tax credits have been available for homeowners and renters for insulation and other energy conservation devices. Utilities across the country have undertaken various optional conservation programs, including free or low-cost energy audits and low or interest-free loans to customers insulating their homes. Since 1980, Congress has provided a winter heating assistance program to provide aid to individuals receiving supplemental security income and block grants to the fifty states.[61] And many electric and gas utilities have instituted company-customer programs (*i.e.*, HeatShare, EnergyShare, and so forth) to provide funds for those needing assistance, with the funds generally being disbursed by local organizations.

Rate Structures in Practice: Electric Utility Rates[62]

In its early history, most electricity was sold for lighting uses. Electric utilities charged either flat or uniform rates. Under a flat rate, the customer was charged a fixed amount per month or season, irrespective of the quantities of electricity used. (A variant was the fixture rate, which was a fixed amount per month on the basis of the number of lamps or outlets on the customer's premises.[63]) Under a uniform rate, the customer was charged a fixed amount for each kilowatt-hour of electricity used. The former rate encouraged waste because it ignored differences in consumption, while the latter rate ignored demand costs. As the industry developed, recognition of decreasing costs was made by means of progressive discounts for additional use. A customer's bill, to illustrate, might have been discounted 10 percent if fifty kilowatt-hours were used, whereas the discount might have been 20 percent if 100 kilowatt-hours were consumed.[64] Such discounts, of course, were inequitable and were replaced by the step rate. An example of this rate:

50 Kwh or less per month	10¢ per Kwh
50 to 100 Kwh per month	9¢ per Kwh
100 to 150 Kwh per month	8¢ per Kwh
etc.[65]	

An examination of the step rate quickly reveals that it encouraged waste as a user approached a turning point. Thus, forty-eight kilowatt-hours would cost $4.80, but fifty-one kilowatt-hours would cost only $4.59.

Embedded Costs and Traditional Types of Electric Rates

As electric utilities began to acquire other classes of customers (the most important being residential, commercial, and industrial, as shown in Table 10-4), they established different rates for each class, partly based upon cost differences.

TABLE 10-4

Percentage of Electric Customers, Sales, and
Revenues by Customer Classes, 1986

Classification	Percentage of Customers	Percentage of Sales	Percentage of Revenues
Residential & Rural	88.4	34.8	40.0
Commercial	10.8	26.8	29.9
Industrial	.5	34.6	26.7
Other	.3	3.8	3.4
Total	100.0	100.0	100.0

Source: Edison Electric Institute.

Embedded Cost Considerations. The variations in the cost of serving different customers can be illustrated by noting three important technical concepts — the load factor, the utilization factor, and the diversity factor.

The *load factor* is the average load expressed as a percentage of the peak load. Electric utilities are primarily concerned with two types of load curves — annual and customer. Thus, if the average load for a year is 12,000 kilowatts and the peak at any moment of time is 18,000, the annual load factor is 66 2/3 percent. Since electricity cannot be stored, and since a utility must provide instantaneous and uninterrupted service, the size of a utility plant is determined by the amount of service taken by its customers at any particular time (peak period). The peak, it should be noted, may occur only for a short period of time once a year. Utilities attempt to keep their load factor as high as possible, for the higher the average output relative to the peak load, the more units over which to spread the fixed costs. Customers, too, have load factors: the average consumption expressed as a percentage of the maximum consumption. A customer whose average load is high relative to his maximum demand is a more desirable customer than one whose load factor is low.

The *utilization factor* is the peak load expressed as a percentage of the system capacity. Electric utilities must have some reserve capacity to meet emergencies. The necessary reserve will depend on a number of factors, including the size of the area served and the size of the generators and transformers in use. As desirable as a high utilization factor may be, it also serves as a warning to the utility that its excess reserve capacity is declining.[66]

The *diversity factor* is the ratio of the sum of noncoincident maximum demands of a system's customers to maximum demand on the whole system. If all customers registered their maximum demands at exactly the same time, the diversity factor would equal one. But because of differences in time of use, the sum of the noncoincident maximum demands is greater than the system's load at any moment of time — that is, the diversity factor is greater than one. A high diversity factor is desirable, since an electric utility seeks to achieve full utilization on its plant and equipment.

These factors indicate that the cost of supplying electricity to different customers is a function of many variables. Moreover, these factors are interrelated. As Clemens has pointed out,

> . . . a high diversity factor will compensate for low customer load factors. A customer who used only one kilowatt for one hour a day would be an expensive customer. But twenty-four such customers, each using electricity at a different hour, would give the utility a load factor of 100 percent. Conversely, a good load factor customer contributes little to the diversity factor. He uses his equipment continuously and increases the peak load as much as he increases the average load. In short a utility can achieve a desirable load factor for itself by having customers with good load factors, or by a high diversity factor, but either is achieved at the expense of the other.[67]

For ratemaking purposes, electric utilities have historically performed embedded cost-of-service studies. In such studies, it is assumed that an electric utility's total costs are variable. The allocation of these costs among the different classes of customers, however, represents a difficult task since a major portion of total costs are common or joint. The most frequently used division of total costs is a threefold one: (*1*) demand, capacity, or load costs; (*2*) energy, output, or volumetric costs; and (*3*) customer costs.

Demand costs vary with a customer's maximum demand. These costs include investment charges and expenses in connection with generating plants, transmission lines, substations and part of the distribution system. Suppose two customers have equal monthly consumptions but different demands. Customer A has a load of ten kilowatts which he operates 200 hours per month, thus consuming 2,000 kilowatt-hours monthly. Customer B has a load of twenty kilowatts which he operates 100 hours per month, resulting in a monthly use of 2,000 kilowatt-hours or the same as for customer A. The cost of serving B, however, is greater than A's cost, because more equipment is needed to supply the larger load.

Output costs vary with the number of kilowatt-hours consumed and are largely composed of fuel and labor expenses. If customer A uses fifty kilowatt-hours per month and customer B uses 500 kilowatt-hours per month, more fuel and labor will be required to produce the electricity demanded by B than by A.

Customer costs vary with the number of customers. These costs include a portion of the distribution system, local connection facilities, metering equipment, meter reading, billing, and accounting. Customer costs, moreover, are independent of consumption. Assume the monthly consumption of three customers to be ten, fifty, and 500 kilowatt-hours. Despite the differences in consumption, each customer requires a meter, each meter must be read, and a bill must be sent to each customer.

Traditional Types of Electric Rates. The block meter rate or, more precisely, a variation of this type known as the initial charge rate, became the traditional rate schedule for residential and other small users. An example of this rate:

First	12 Kwh per month	$1.75
Next	36 Kwh per month	3.82¢ per Kwh
Next	42 Kwh per month	3.59¢ per Kwh
Next	420 Kwh per month	2.56¢ per Kwh
Next	990 Kwh per month	2.15¢ per Kwh
Excess of	1,500 Kwh per month	1.94¢ per Kwh

Minimum charge: $1.75 per meter per month, exclusive of fuel adjustment.

Under this rate schedule, customer costs are partially recovered by making a flat charge for the first kilowatt-hour block or by making a minimum charge even though nothing is consumed. The demand cost element is recognized only indirectly, however, since it is assumed that demand costs are recovered in the higher earlier blocks. Moreover, the use of the block rate permits the rates in each succeeding block to be lower since only output costs need to be covered. And, from the utility's point of view, the major advantage of this rate schedule is its simplicity, making it easily understood by customers.

The Wright demand rate became common for commercial customers, and at times, for industrial loads. This schedule emphasizes the customer's load factor (demand cost). An example of this rate:

First 100 Kwh per kilowatt of demand per month ..	6¢ per Kwh
Over 100 Kwh per month	3¢ per Kwh

Under this rate schedule, all customers with the same load factor would pay the same price per kilowatt-hour, regardless of their monthly consumption. As there is no inducement to install additional equipment, the Wright rate is not promotional. Moreover, an examination of the schedule indicates that it contains a hidden demand charge of $3.00 per kilowatt and a uniform energy charge of three cents per kilowatt-hour. Yet, there is no assurance that the full demand cost will be collected by the utility: when a buyer's monthly consumption is less than 100 kilowatt-hours, for example, this would be true.

A two-part Hopkinson demand rate came into use for medium- and large-sized commercial and some industrial customers. This schedule has block demand and block energy charges. An example of the Hopkinson rate schedule:

Demand Charge
First	50 Kw of demand per month	$2.50 per Kw
Next	100 Kw of demand per month	$2.00 per Kw
Over	150 Kw of demand per month	$1.75 per Kw

Energy Charge
First	100 Kwh per month	5.5¢ per Kwh
Next	900 Kwh per month	3.0¢ per Kwh
Next	4,000 Kwh per month	2.3¢ per Kwh
Over	5,000 Kwh per month	2.0¢ per Kwh

There are two frequently used ways of measuring a customer's demand. One is to measure with a meter the average consumption during the maximum fifteen- or thirty-minute interval during any three- or six-month period. The second is to compute the total horsepower rating of a customer's connected equipment.

In actual practice, industrial rate schedules are more complex, as indicated in Table 10-5. There may be a service charge, making a three-part rate. Off-peak service may be offered at a lower rate than is charged for peak service. Utilities may have a uniform rate for each kilowatt of demand instead of block demand rates. Monthly minimums are common. Discounts may be given for payment of bills within a specified number of days, with an additional charge if bills are not paid within the time limit. Other discounts may be given to industrial buyers who own transformers (voltage discount) or who purchase electricity at the supply-line voltage. When a customer requires additional voltage regulation (power factor), a special charge may be made.[68] A fuel cost adjustment has long been used to permit a utility to follow the variations in fuel costs either upward or downward. "The special provisions of industrial price schedules (*e.g.,* power factor adjust-

TABLE 10-5

Illustrative Industrial Power Schedule

Availability

Available in the entire territory of the company for any purpose for single-phase and three-phase loads of 50 kilowatts or more.

Monthly Rate

Demand charge:

First 50 Kw @ $2.50 gross per Kw of billing demand

Next 100 Kw @ $2.00 gross per Kw of billing demand

Additional @ $1.75 gross per Kw of billing demand

Voltage discount:

20 cents per kilowatt when the service voltage is 22 kilovolts.

Power factor charge:

25 cents gross per reactive kilovolt-ampere in excess of 50 per cent of the kilowatt demand. The reactive kilovolt-ampere demand shall be determined in the same way as the kilowatt demand.

Energy charge:

First 25,000 Kwh @ 10.0¢ gross per Kwh

Additional @ 0.8¢ gross per Kwh

Fuel cost adjustment:

Increase or decrease of 0.01 cent gross per kilowatt-hour for each change of 0.50 cents per million Btu above or below 15 cents per million Btu for the average cost of fuel on hand and delivered at company's generating stations during the second calendar month preceding the billing date.

Prompt payment discount:

2 per cent for payment within ten days.

Determination of Billing Demand

The billing demand for any month shall be the highest of the following:

1. The kilowatt demand, which shall be the maximum 15-minute kilowatt demand of the on-peak period plus 50 per cent of the excess of the maximum 15-minute kilowatt demand of the off-peak period over the on-peak demand.

2. 50 per cent of the maximum kilowatt demand of the preceding 11 months.

3. 50 kilowatts.

The off-peak period shall be from 10 P.M. until 6 A.M. daily, and from 12 noon Saturday until 6 A.M. Monday.

Term

Minimum of one year.

Source: Russell E. Caywood, *Electric Utility Rate Economics* (New York: McGraw-Hill Book Co., Inc., 1956), p. 66. Used by permission of McGraw-Hill Book Company.

ments) show distinctly the influence of the engineer in the formulation of pricing practices. Because engineers influence the shape of these schedules, only an engineer, indeed, can interpret and apply their technical provisions."[69]

Discrimination in Practice. The above typical electric utility rate schedules are highly differentiated and discriminatory. Such discrimination occurred in at least three ways. First, there are many different block sizes and block rates which could have been chosen. In determining these sizes and rates, both cost and demand considerations were taken into account. If a utility tried to recover its total demand and customer costs in the first block, the initial block rate might be so high that it would discourage more consumption. These costs were thus spread throughout succeeding blocks, largely according to differences in elasticities of demand. Explains Wilcox:

> Big industrial users have the alternative of generating their own power; their demand, therefore, is highly elastic; their rates are low. Other users lack this alternative; their demand is less elastic; their rates are higher. Householders can use gas rather than electricity for cooking; for this purpose their demand is elastic; the additional kilowatt-hours used in cooking fall in the quantity blocks where rates are low. Householders, on the other hand, are unlikely to substitute gas, kerosene, or candles for electricity in lighting; their demand for this purpose is inelastic; the hours used in lighting fall in the first block where rates are high.[70]

Consequently, both block sizes and block rates were established by the utility companies on the basis of differences in the value of service for each class of customer.

The second way in which discrimination is evident in the above electric utility rate structures is that allocation of demand, output, and customer costs among the different classes of customers is largely arbitrary. Particularly is this true of demand costs, "the treatment of which has made a nightmare of utility cost analysis. For the problem which it presents is that of imputing joint costs to joint products or byproducts and not merely that of distributing those common but nonjoint costs which vary more or less continuously with number of customers or with rates of output."[71]

In his book on electric rates, Caywood discusses three formulas for allocating demand costs among different classes of customers.[72] (*1*) The "peak responsibility method." Under this formula, the entire demand costs are allocated to those services rendered at the time of the system's peak demand, in proportion to the kilowatt demand at this peak load. Service rendered off-peak would not be apportioned demand costs. (*2*) The "noncoincident demand method." Here, demand costs are allocated among services in proportion to the maximum demands of the various classes regardless of when each class's maximum demand occurs. (*3*) The "average and excess demand method." Under this method,

. . . the assumed cost of that portion of the company's plant capacity which would be needed even if all consumers were taking their power at 100 per cent load factor is apportioned among customers in proportion to their average loads. . . . But the assumed cost of the excess in actual plant capacity over this lower, hypothetical capacity is apportioned "by applying the noncoincident peak method to the difference between maximum loads and average loads."[73]

The three methods lead to quite different results. Assuming three class loads comprising a system load having a peak of 1,000 kilowatts (Figure 10-1), the results are shown in Table 10-6.

For many years, the most frequently used means of allocating demand costs was the second method — the noncoincident demand method. Three steps are involved. An aggregate maximum demand is obtained by adding together the separate maximum demands of all classes of customers. Then, the percentage of this aggregate that is attributable to each class is determined. Finally, demand costs are allocated to each class in accordance with these percentages. The noncoincident demand method, despite its widespread use, is based upon two fallacies and, in fact, is not really a cost analysis at all. As Wilcox succinctly states:

> First, it involves circular reasoning. The differences in demand that are used as a guide in allocating costs are not independent of differences in rates, but are themselves determined by these differences. The companies first fix the rates they want to charge. These rates, in turn, affect the quantities demanded. These quantities are then used to govern the distribution of costs. And the costs are presented, finally, to justify the rates. Q.E.D. Second, the method does not make proper allowance for the factor of diversity. The concept of maximum coincident demand for a utility system as a whole is meaningful. The concept of aggregate noncoincident maximum demands of customer classes is not. A company does have to build a plant big enough to meet the peak of coincident demand. It does not have to build one big enough to meet the aggregate of noncoincident demands. For such demands, by definition, occur at different times. If a customer's maximum comes at the same time as the system's maximum, he may properly be charged with more responsibility for the size of the investment that is required. If it comes at any other time, he should be charged with less. But how much more and how much less is open to debate.[74]

Perhaps no formula of apportionment is perfect. Bonbright has argued, however, that from the standpoint of cost analysis, the "peak responsibility method" would undoubtedly come the closest to receiving support from economists. He points out two major difficulties in using the formula. In the first place, as the periods of peak demand are subject to constant

FIGURE 10-1

Hypothetical Loads

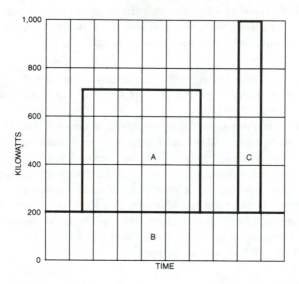

Source: Russell E. Caywood, *Electric Utility Rate Econom-ics* (New York: McGraw-Hill Book Co., Inc., 1956), p. 162. Used by permission of McGraw-Hill Book Company.

TABLE 10-6

Results of Demand Allocation Formulas*

Load	Maximum Demand	Load Factor	Allocation		
			PR Method	NCD Method	AED Method
A	500 Kw	50%	0 Kw	333 Kw	371 Kw
B	200	100	200	133	200
C	800	10	800	534	429
	1,500 Kw		1,000 Kw	1,000 Kw	1,000 Kw

*Assumption: Three classes of loads comprising a system load having a peak demand of 1,000 kilowatts.

Source: Russell E. Caywood, *Electric Utility Rate Economics* (New York: McGraw-Hill Book Co., Inc., 1956), p. 163. Used by permission of McGraw-Hill Book Company.

change, apportionment on this basis would necessitate frequent changes in the structure of rates. Such changes may have disruptive effects on consumption. But if the system's annual peak were used and if changes were announced in advance and at stated intervals, gradual adjustments in rates could overcome this difficulty. More important is a second often-voiced objection that the utility plant is required for the service of both on-peak and off-peak users and that both, therefore, should make some contribution toward its capital cost.[75] Once again, the question of how much must be raised.[76]

Closely connected is a third way in which discrimination enters into the rate structures: rates within each class do not vary according to time of use. (There are certain exceptions. Rates did vary by time of use for some large industrial customers; in a few instances, they varied for residential water heating; and, in even fewer instances, for residential space heating.) It was previously pointed out that the size of a utility plant and, hence, the total investment in the business, is determined by the quantity of service it must render during periods of peak demand. Just as in the case of apportioning total demand costs among classes, customers within each class who use the service during peak demand periods should contribute a larger percentage toward the class's share of the capital costs than should off-peak users. As there is no attempt to separate those two groups of customers, the rate schedule discriminates against those who use the service in off-peak hours.

Marginal (Incremental) Costs and Recent Trends

A fundamental shift in rate design philosophy began to occur in the late 1960s. Inflation, rising fuel prices, and environmental concerns were the major factors accounting for the shift, with enactment of the Public Utility Regulatory Policies Act (in 1978) and the emergence of surplus capacity (in the 1980s) added factors. Two changes occurred almost immediately. First, automatic fuel adjustment clauses were included in electric tariffs; by 1977, all but six states had adopted such clauses.[77] Second, summerwinter differentials gained widespread acceptance. The following residential (general service) rate schedule is illustrative:

		June to September	October to May
First	12 Kwh per month..	$1.75	$1.75
Next	36 Kwh per month..	3.82¢ per Kwh	3.82¢ per Kwh
Next	42 Kwh per month..	3.59¢ per Kwh	3.59¢ per Kwh
Next	420 Kwh per month..	2.56¢ per Kwh	3.56¢ per Kwh
Next	990 Kwh per month..	2.36¢ per Kwh	2.15¢ per Kwh
Excess of	1,500 Kwh per month..	2.36¢ per Kwh	1.94¢ per Kwh

Minimum charge: $1.75 per meter per month, exclusive of fuel adjustment.

For summer peaking utilities, the use of a summer-winter differential reflects the higher costs of adding capacity to serve the summer load (peak). Further, as rates continued to rise, blocks were gradually eliminated and inverted summer rates were introduced. Consider the following rate structure, which represents a later refinement of the above structure.

	June to September	*October to May*
Customer Charge	$5.60 per month	$5.60 per month
First 800 Kwh per month	6.622¢ per Kwh	6.622¢ per Kwh
Excess of 800 Kwh per month	7.439¢ per Kwh	5.124¢ per Kwh[78]

It is important to emphasize, however, that these rate structures were still based upon an embedded cost-of-service philosophy.

Incremental Cost Pricing. The long-run incremental cost (LRIC) concept has gained increased recognition in rate proceedings. This concept, unlike the concept of marginal cost, recognizes that electric utilities add capacity in discrete units and on a continuous basis. The long-run incremental cost concept thus includes the future costs of supplying electricity, as opposed to the traditional philosophy of basing rates on past or embedded costs of serving customers.

With respect to residential rates and based upon its analysis of long-run incremental cost, the Wisconsin commission in 1974 abandoned the traditional declining block rate structure, substituting an essentially flat rate for energy (and a fixed customer charge, which did not recover all customer-related costs) and instituted a summer-winter differential. The commission established the following rate structure, as compared to the structure authorized in a 1970 decision:[79]

	1970 Rates	*New Rates*	
Residential (rg-1)		*Winter*	*Summer*
Fixed Charge	$ .75	$1.50	$1.50
First 100 Kwh per month ..	2.85¢	2.50¢	2.50¢
Next 400 Kwh per month ..	2.03¢	2.20¢	2.20¢
Next 500 Kwh per month ..	2.03¢	2.20¢	2.20¢
Next 500 Kwh per month ..	1.56¢	2.20¢	2.20¢
Over 1,500 Kwh per month ..	1.56¢	1.50¢	2.20¢

In commenting on the new rate structure, Commissioner Cudahy noted:

... the economic evidence (insofar as it points to a definite movement away from "decreasing" costs) offers substantial support to the concept of flat rates as a starting point, bearing some presumption of reasonableness. But I am persuaded that each class and subclass of customers must also be analyzed on its own merits (with particular emphasis on contribution to annual — or, if applicable, seasonal —

peaks). For purposes of efficient blocking the essential question is whether additional usage results in lower or higher per kilowatt-hour costs. As a simplistic matter (and this is one of the arguments advanced for declining-block rates), it would appear that spreading additional usage over the same fixed costs would produce lower average costs. An important facet of this concept is illustrated by current utility distress over loss of revenues due to conservation. This line of reasoning seems to be correct in the case of "customer" costs, but beyond that it reflects only *short-run* considerations and is valid *in the long run* only if contribution to annual or seasonal (cost-causing) peaks is less than directly proportional to the corresponding increase in usage.

In the case of the summer residential rate we have assumed that increased usage (containing air conditioning) contributes at least proportionately to the annual (temperature-sensitive) peak. We have thus, after recovery of customer costs (in the fixed charge and in the first block), constructed a flat rate. No doubt this approach incorporates only a rough tracking of costs through the rate blocks. But with current metering techniques, these seem to be the best cost approximations which can be achieved. . . .[80]

Finally, the Wisconsin commission recognized that full peak-load pricing

. . . applied to electric rates must take the form of time-of-day metering. Under such a plan, rates would vary with the time of day in order to reflect the true cost of peak demand. Customers are compelled to pay for the actual cost they are imposing on society and are rewarded for shifting consumption to an off-peak time, thereby improving the utility's load factor. The winter/summer differential does not offer such an alternative. Summer air-conditioning use cannot be postponed until winter.[81]

Since the *Madison Gas and Electric* decision, incremental cost studies have been submitted in countless rate cases, experimental (or demonstration) time-of-day projects have been undertaken by a number of electric utilities, and time-of-day rates have been put into effect for industrial and commercial customers, as well as for some large residential customers (see Table 10-7). Based upon an analysis of 34 state commissions, Weiss concludes:

By early 1980 at least eight states were explicitly using some sort of marginal-cost or incremental-cost concepts in setting rates. These are Arizona, California, Michigan, New York, Ohio, Oregon, Vermont, and Wisconsin. In estimating incremental costs, all of these states use present or future costs to estimate the investments in plant and equipment. Most state commissions have seasonal rates for both industrial and residential customers, but some of these go back many years. A majority of

TABLE 10-7

Experimental Time-of-day Residential Rate Structure

	June to September	*October to May*
Customer Charge	$11.00 per month	$11.00 per month
Demand Charge		
Onpeak Kw of demand ...	$ 3.28 per Kw	$ 2.68 per Kw
Energy Charge		
Onpeak per Kwh	4.429¢ per Kwh	3.691¢ per Kwh
Offpeak per Kwh	2.760¢ per Kwh	2.760¢ per Kwh

Demand Charge: The highest average kilowatt load measured in any 30-minute interval during the onpeak hours of the current month.

Onpeak Hours: 10 A.M. to 10 P.M., EDT (9 A.M. to 9 P.M., EST), Mondays through Fridays.

Source: Virginia Electric and Power Company (1980).

states have time-of-day rates for industrial customers, and Arkansas, Michigan, Ohio, Oregon, Pennsylvania, Texas, and Wisconsin base industrial-demand charges on demand at system peak rather than at customer peak. Seventeen states have some residential time-of-day rates, but most of these were experimental or optional. Some of the experiments have used sophisticated statistical techniques. The findings to date are that consumers do respond to seasonal and time-of-day rate differences, but it still is not clear that the gains are worth the cost of the more elaborate metering required.[82]

PURPA and Further Rate Reform. In 1978, Congress enacted the Public Utility Regulatory Policies Act (PURPA), as part of the national energy plan.[83] That act required the state commissions to consider, and to implement or adopt if appropriate, six ratemaking standards[84] and five regulatory standards for electric utilities to further three statutory purposes: end-use conservation, utility efficiency, and equitable rates. The ratemaking standards, contained in Section III, in summary form, are:

1. Cost of service — the rates for each class of customer shall be designed, to the maximum extent practicable, to reflect the cost of providing service to that class. Section 115 (a) provides that costs shall be "determined on the basis of methods prescribed by the state and regulatory authority."

2. Declining block rates — the *energy* component of a rate for any class of service may not decrease as consumption increases unless the utility demonstrates that those energy costs in fact decrease as consumption increases.
3. Time-of-day rates — the rates for each class of service shall be on a time-of-day basis which reflects the cost of providing service at different times of day unless such rates are not cost effective for that class.
4. Seasonal rates — rates charged for the provision of service to each class of customer shall be on a seasonal basis which reflects the costs of providing such service to each class of consumer at different seasons to the extent that costs vary seasonally for the utility.
5. Interruptible rates — each utility shall offer industrial and commercial customers interruptible rates which reflect the cost of providing such service.
6. Load management techniques — each utility shall offer to its customers load management techniques where (a) practicable and cost effective, (b) reliable, and (c) useful to the utility for energy or capacity management.[85]

The act provided that the state commissions should consider and implement these ratemaking standards, if appropriate, within three years (*i.e.*, by November, 1981). The Department of Energy was given authority to intervene in any state proceeding related to rate design and to appeal the resulting decision in the courts. Various technical (*e.g.*, load management techniques, methods for determining cost of service) and financial assistance was provided to state commissions. Finally, funding was authorized for two programs established by the Energy Conservation and Production Act of 1976: grants to state offices of consumer services to assist consumers in making presentations before state commissions and grants to fund development of innovative rate structures.

A full assessment of these aspects of PURPA will take some time, although most of the state commissions have already adopted and/or implemented one or more of the standards.[86]

Competition and Surplus Capacity: Some Unresolved Issues. There are three additional pricing issues that remain unresolved, yet are of significance as competition and surplus capacity evolve in the industry. First, there are "wheeling" rates; rates for transporting electric energy from a seller of power to a buyer over the transmission lines of one or more utilities and/or government entities.[87] The demand for transmission services has grown in recent years, due in part to expanded sales of economy energy,[88] but also due to the development of surplus capacity (*e.g.*, large wholesale and retail customers desire to "shop around" for low-priced power) and to the growth of nonutility-owned cogeneration and small power production (discussed below). Greater transmission access, some argue, would remove a major impediment to increased competition in bulk power markets and, possibly, enhance generation deregulation.[89] But too often, they contend, wheeling is not economically feasible because of high wheeling rates.[90] While there are a variety of wheeling rate schedules,

> ... the most common is a "postage stamp rate" under which a customer is charged a fixed rate per unit of service; *e.g.*, miles per kilowatt-hour for nonfirm wheeling or dollars per kilowatt for firm wheeling. In approving rates for firm power wheeling, the FERC has employed an (embedded) "rolled-in" costing methodology; *i.e.*, all transmission-related costs are aggregated and uniformally allocated to firm transmission customers based on their respective demand. The commission has also approved numerous transmission rate schedules utilizing the costs of specific transmission facilities where it can be argued that those facilities are the principal ones employed in providing the service. . . .[91]

Second, there is the problem of the "full avoided cost rule." Title II of the Public Utility Regulatory Policies Act encouraged both cogeneration and small power production. The former "is the combined production of electrical power and useful thermal energy, such as heat or steam."[92] The latter are those producers which use biomass, waste, geothermal resources, or renewable resources (such as wind, solar energy, and water) to produce electric power and whose power production capacity is no greater than eighty megawatts.[93] Plants meeting PURPA requirements are termed "qualifying facilities" (QFs). Their encouragement has come from a requirement in the act (Section 210) that electric utilities purchase power produced from such facilities at their full avoided costs, defined by the FERC as "the incremental costs to an electric utility of electric energy, or capacity, or both which, but for the purchase from the qualifying facility or qualifying facilities, such a utility would generate itself or purchase from another source."[94]

To date, the states have not adopted a uniform calculation of avoided costs.[95] Moreover, the issue has become even more complex with the emergence of surplus capacity. A district court, for example, has ruled that PURPA does not require electric utilities to purchase power from QFs at a higher than market price.[96] And one state commission has approved "anticogeneration" rate contracts.[97]

Third, there are special discount rates; rates that have been proposed and adopted (often on an experimental basis) that are commonly known as "incentive" or "economic development" rates. Such rates "are designed both to promote increased sales to existing industrial customers and to attract new firms to a utility's service territory" and "are advanced as a means for lowering the short-run average total cost of an electric utility (and thereby the rates for all customer classes) as well as being more in line with efficient pricing in view of today's market conditions."[98] Such rates, however, raise issues of undue discrimination, from a statutory standpoint (*e.g.*, they are offered to only one class of customers), although they are based upon short-run marginal or long-run incremental costs. Three state commission decisions are typical:

1. In approving a discounted industrial rate (on a two-year experimental basis), the Rhode Island commission noted that the company's marginal costs were below its average embedded costs. While the proposed rate was discriminatory, it was in the "interest of the public," since its purpose was "to stimulate the local economy and provide new jobs" for the state, by being "attractive to growing New England companies who currently consider Rhode Island to be 'invisible.'"[99]

2. In approving a proposal for an "economic redevelopment" tariff, the Michigan commission agreed that the proposal resulted "in a form of discrimination." However, the rate was "designed to accomplish a rational purpose which includes encouraging minimum consumption, increasing manufacturing activity, increasing employment, and securing revenues to cover the utility's fixed costs. Furthermore, by increasing such business activity, the economic redevelopment rate will contribute to the eradication of the dismal economic climate in certain portions of the applicant's service territory within the state of Michigan."[100]

3. In approving a "special industrial contract policy," the New Hampshire commission concluded that as long as "an incremental customer pays a price that is above marginal cost, he is sharing the fixed costs with the company's nonincremental customers, thus reducing the responsibility of the nonincremental customer to pay those fixed costs."[101]

Notes

*Abba P. Lerner, "Conflicting Principles of Public Utility Price Regulation," 7 *Journal of Law and Economics* 61 (1964).

[1] Alfred E. Kahn, *The Economics of Regulation* (New York: John Wiley & Sons, Inc., 1970), Vol. I, p. 64.

[2] The water industry is considered in Chapter 16.

[3] James C. Bonbright, *Principles of Public Utility Rates* (New York: Columbia University Press, 1961), p. 291. See also Russell E. Caywood, "Electric Utility Rate Making Today," 81 *Public Utilities Fortnightly* 51, 53-54 (June 6, 1968).

[4] For an excellent analysis of this issue, see Edward E. Zajac, *Fairness or Efficiency: An Introduction to Public Utility Pricing* (Cambridge: Ballinger Publishing Co., 1978).

[5] Bonbright, *op. cit.*

[6]*Ibid.*, p. 292. See also John M. Clark, *Studies in the Economics of Overhead Costs* (Chicago: University of Chicago Press, 1932), p. 322.

[7]The content and outline of the first two sections closely follow Clair Wilcox, *Public Policies Toward Business* (4th ed.; Homewood, Ill.: Richard D. Irwin, Inc., 1971), pp. 321-27, and are used with the late author's permission.

[8]See Chapter 6, pp. 215-18. In discussing the problem of cost allocation for railroad service, Hadley once remarked that "God Almighty did not know the cost of carrying a hundred pounds of freight from Boston to New York." Quoted by Winthrop M. Daniels, *The Price of Transportation* (New York: Harper & Bros., 1932), p. 48.

[9]I. Leo Sharfman, *The Interstate Commerce Commission* (New York: Commonwealth Fund, 1936), Vol. IIIB, pp. 321-22.

[10]This statement does not imply that price discrimination is unimportant in the nonregulated sector of the economy. When competition is imperfect and when sellers lack complete information about each product, discrimination may occur.

[11]George J. Stigler, *The Theory of Price* (3d ed.; New York: The Macmillan Co., 1966), p. 210.

[12]Assuming decreasing costs, there is an additional justification for discrimination. Marginal cost pricing would result in losses, since marginal cost is below average cost. The most obvious solution — a subsidy to make up the difference between marginal and average cost — is not an option available to regulatory commissions, and no legislative body has ever indicated a willingness to pay such a subsidy.

[13]*Re Generic Hearings Concerning Electric Rate Structure*, 36 PUR4th 6, 50 (Colo., 1979) (footnote omitted).

[14]Alfred E. Kahn, "Efficient Rate Design: The Transition from Theory to Practice," in *Proceedings of the Symposium on Rate Design Problems of Regulated Industries* (Columbia: University of Missouri-Columbia, 1975), p. 35.

[15]If entry were permitted, competitors would enter into those markets where rates are above marginal costs; a situation frequently referred to as "cream-skimming." For an analysis of the issue, see Kahn, *The Economics of Regulation, op. cit.*, Vol. II (1971), pp. 220-50. See also Alan Reynolds, "A Kind Word for 'Cream Skimming,'" 52 *Harvard Business Review* 113 (November-December, 1974).

[16]See Nancy Ruggles, "The Welfare Basis of the Marginal Cost Pricing Principle," 17 *Review of Economic Studies* 29 (1949-50) and "Recent Developments in the Theory of Marginal Cost Pricing," 17 *Review of Economic Studies* 107 (1949-50).

[17]The classic article is by Harold Hotelling, "The General Welfare in Relation to Problems of Taxation and of Railway and Utility Rates," 6 *Econometrica* 242 (1938). See also William S. Vickrey, "Some Implications of Marginal Cost Pricing for Public Utilities," 45 *American Economic Review* 605 (Papers and Proceedings, 1955).

[18]Since the mid-1950s, the Electricite de France, a public electric power system, has used the principle as a basis of setting rates and for investment policy. See Thomas Marschak, "Capital Budgeting and Pricing in the French Nationalized Industries," 33 *Journal of Business of the University of Chicago* 133 (1960); James R. Nelson, "Practical Applications of Marginal Cost Pricing in the Public Utility Field," 53 *American Economic Review* 474 (1963); Ronald L. Meek, "An Application of Marginal Cost Pricing: The 'Green Tariff' in Theory and Practice," Part I, "The Theory," 11 *Journal of Industrial Economics* 217 (1963), Part II, "The Practice," 12 *Journal of Industrial Economics* 45 (1963); Marcel Boiteux, "The Green Tariff of the Electricite de France," as translated by Eli W. Clemens and Lucienne C. Clemens, 40 *Land Economics* 185

(1964); Eli W. Clemens, "Marginal Cost Pricing: A Comparison of French and American Industrial Power Rates," 40 *Land Economics* 389 (1964); James R. Nelson (ed.), *Marginal Cost Pricing in Practice* (Englewood Cliffs: Prentice-Hall, Inc., 1964). Recent developments are discussed by Hans E. Nissel, "Electricite de France Revises Its Green Tariff," 108 *Public Utilities Fortnightly* 22 (July 30, 1981). In England, a Bulk Supply Tariff, based on the marginal cost pricing concept, was put into use in 1967. See Haskell P. Wald, "The Theory of Marginal Cost Pricing and Utility Rates," 79 *Public Utilities Fortnightly* 15, 23-24 (June 22, 1967).

[19]Kahn, "Efficient Rate Design . . .," *op. cit.*, p. 35.

[20]R. G. Lipsey and K. J. Lancaster, "The General Theory of the Second Best," 24 *Review of Economic Studies* 11 (1956-57). But see E. J. Mishan, "Second Thoughts on Second Best," 14 *Oxford Economic Papers* 205 (1962).

[21]Kahn, *The Economics of Regulation, op. cit.*, Vol. I, p. 69.

[22]William J. Baumol, *Welfare Economics and the Theory of the State* (2d ed.; Cambridge: Harvard University Press, 1965), p. 30. See also M. J. Ferrell, "In Defense of Public-Utility Price Theory," 10 *Oxford Economic Papers* 112 (1958); J. Wiseman, "The Theory of Public Utility Price: A Further Note," 11 *Oxford Economic Papers* 92 (1959); Otto A. Davis and Andrew B. Whinston, "Welfare Economics and the Theory of Second Best," 32 *Review of Economic Studies* 1 (1965); R. Dusansky and J. Walsh, "Separability, Welfare Economics and the Theory of Second Best," 43 *Review of Economic Studies* 49 (1976); T. Hatta, "A Theory of Piecemeal Policy Recommendations," 44 *Review of Economic Studies* 1 (1977); K. Kawamata, "Price Distortion and the Second Best Optimum," 44 *Review of Economic Studies* 23 (1977).

[23]Stigler, *op. cit.*, chaps. v-x.

[24]Kahn, "Efficient Rate Design . . .," *op. cit.*, p. 38.

[25]*Re Madison Gas & Elec. Co.*, 5 PUR4th 28, 35-36 (Wis., 1974).

[26]Kahn, "Efficient Rate Design . . ., *op. cit.*, p. 39.

[27]William H. Melody, "The Marginal Utility of Marginal Analysis in Public Policy Formulation," 8 *Journal of Economic Issues* 287, 295 (1974). See also Joseph M. Cleary, "Marginland: A Magic Place Where Costs Disappear," 112 *Public Utilities Fortnightly* 23 (July 21, 1983).

[28]For a summary, see Ernst & Whinney, "An Evaluation of Ten Marginal Costing Methodologies" (A Report Prepared for the Electricity Consumers Resource Council, August 1979). For an analysis of the Cicchetti, Gillen, Smolensky (CGS) approach, see Charles J. Cicchetti and William J. Gillen, *The Marginal Cost and Pricing of Electricity* (Cambridge: Ballinger Publishing Co., 1977). Similarly, for an analysis of the National Economic Research Associates (NERA) approach, see three reports prepared for the Electric Utility Rate Design Study: "A Framework for Marginal Cost-Based Time-Differentiated Pricing in the United States: Topic 1.3" (February 1977), "How to Quantify Marginal Costs: Topic 4" (March 1977), and "Ratemaking: Topic 5" (June 1977).

[29]Gregory Crespi, "Marginal Cost-of-Service Studies: Some Practical Difficulties," 106 *Public Utilities Fortnightly* 19, 21 (December 4, 1980).

[30]See William J. Baumol and David F. Bradford, "Optimal Departures from Marginal Cost Pricing," 60 *American Economic Review* 265 (1970).

[31]Leonard W. Weiss, "State Regulation of Public Utilities and Marginal-cost Pricing," in Leonard W. Weiss and Michael W. Klass (eds.), *Case Studies in Regulation: Revolution and Reform* (Boston: Little, Brown and Co., 1981), p. 273.

[32]Both the California and New York commissions have held that customer costs

should be excluded from marginal cost calculations. See *Re Pacific Gas & Elec. Co.*, 34 PUR4th 1, 64-65 (Cal., 1979); *Re Consolidated Edison Co. of New York, Inc.*, 29 PUR4th 284, 291 (N.Y., 1979).

[33]Department of Energy, "Voluntary Guideline for the Cost of Service Standard under the Public Utility Regulatory Policies Act of 1978; Proposed Guideline and Public Hearing," 45 *Fed. Reg.* 58760, 58767 (September 4, 1980).

[34]*Ibid.*

[35]As the New York commission has put it: "The application of marginal cost pricing principles to electric rates would require peak-load pricing, since the cost of supplying additional consumption ordinarily varies (whether little or much need not concern us at this point) by the time of day and season of the year. If we adopt the former, we must be prepared to adopt the latter. The converse, however, is not true: the case for rates varying with time of consumption is not dependent on the case for marginal cost pricing; it is possible to justify and base time-related rates on average costs, embedded costs, fully allocated costs, as well as marginal." *Re Determining Relevance of Marginal Costs to Electric Rate Structures*, Case No. 26806 (N.Y., 1976).

[36]Hans E. Nissel, "Federal Rate Design Standards and Energy Conservation," 103 *Public Utilities Fortnightly* 16, 24 (May 24, 1979). See also, by the same author, "Peakload Pricing, Facts and Fancy," 106 *Public Utilities Fortnightly* 17 (September 11, 1960).

The relatively long peak periods arise from the fact that it would be impossible to establish a rate structure that tracked costs hour-by-hour and day-by-day. Thus, for ratemaking purposes, costs are grouped into "rating periods," and an average of these costs used within those periods.

[37]Jan Paul Acton and Bridger M. Mitchell, "The Effect of Time-of-use Rates: Facts versus Opinions," 107 *Public Utilities Fortnightly* 19 (April 23, 1981).

[38]Bonbright, *op. cit.*, p. 317, n. 2.

[39]*Ibid.*, p. 332.

[40]*Ibid.*, p. 333.

[41]See William J. Baumol and Associates, "The Role of Cost in the Minimum Pricing of Railroad Services," 35 *Journal of Business of the University of Chicago* 357, 361-62 (1962).

[42]"For maximum economic efficiency, rates should be related to costs, but not to an arbitrary allocation of costs. . . . 'Cost-oriented rates' in the true economic sense are related to the economist's concept of marginal cost — the increase in total expenses as a result of carrying additional ton-miles of traffic. In order to ensure efficiency, marginal, rather than average, cost should be the principal regulatory criterion in applications for rate reductions. . . . [W]here competition and new technology dictate rate reductions, competitive rates could be lowered to the level of marginal cost." "Annual Report of the Council of Economic Advisers" in *Economic Report of the President* (Washington, D.C.: U.S. Government Printing Office, 1966), p. 127.

[43]Baumol and Associates, *op. cit.*, p. 362. See also John J. Coyle, "Dissimilar Pricing: A Logical Approach to Regulated Rates," 78 *Public Utilities Fortnightly* 32 (September 15, 1966); James C. Nelson, "Economic Standards for Competitive Freight Rates," 48 *Journal of Farm Economics* 1408 (1966); Irwin M. Stelzer, "Incremental Costs and Utility Rate-Making in the Competitive Era," American Bar Association Annual Report, Section of *Public Utility Law, 1967*, pp. 26-42; Haskell P. Wald, "The Theory of Marginal Cost Pricing and Utility Rates," 79 *Public Utilities Fortnightly* 15

(June 22, 1967); Ronald H. Coase, "The Theory of Public Utility Pricing and its Application," 1 *Bell Journal of Economics & Management Science* 113 (1970).

[44]See, *e.g.*, the famous "Big John" case: *Grain in Multiple-Car Shipments — River Crossings to the South*, I&S Docket No. 7656 (January 21, 1963) and 321 ICC 582 (July 1, 1963), *rev'd sub nom. Cincinnati, New Orleans, & Texas Pacific Ry. Co. v. United States*, 229 F. Supp. 572 (1964), *vacated and remanded sub nom. Arrow Transportation Co. v. Cincinnati, New Orleans & Texas Pacific Ry. Co.*, 379 U.S. 642 (1965), final commission decision, 325 ICC 752 (1965).

[45]*Re Rate Design for Electric Corporations*, 26 PUR4th 280, 285 (N.Y., 1978).

[46]See, *e.g.*, "Moving toward Lifeline Rates," 101 *Public Utilities Fortnightly* 54 (June 22, 1978); "The Lifeline Rate Issue," 104 *Public Utilities Fortnightly* 42 (October 11, 1979); "Telephone Lifeline Rates After the AT&T Divestiture," 117 *Public Utilities Fortnightly* 57 (June 12, 1986).

[47]This was the position taken by the New Hampshire commission and by the Oregon commissioner: *Re Public Service Co. of N.H.*, 95 PUR3d 401 (N.H., 1972); *Re Rate Concessions to Poor Persons and Senior Citizens*, 14 PUR4th 87 (Or., 1976) and *Re Investigation into Rate Structures of Electric Utilities*, 38 PUR4th 409 (Or., 1980). But see *Re Montana-Dakota Utilities Co.*, 21 PUR4th 1 (S.D., 1977); *Re Telephone Lifeline Rates*, 72 PUR4th 407 (Utah, 1986). In California, the legislature mandated lifeline rates for residential electric and gas customers under the Miller-Warren Energy Lifeline Act of 1975 and for telephone subscribers under the Moore Universal Telephone Service Act of 1984; and in Michigan, residential lifeline rates for electricity were mandated by a 1980 amendment to the Public Service Commission Act [see *Re Lifeline Rates*, 42 PUR4th 432 (Mich., 1981). The act was repealed in 1984. See *Re Detroit Edison Co.*, 81 PUR4th 144 (Mich., 1987)]. In Maine, the legislature rejected the lifeline concept in 1977. For an argument that energy conservation and appropriate programs for public assistance to those truly eligible are preferable to lifeline rates, see J. B. Roll and Ellen Beth Lande, "Lifeline Rates: Impact and Significance," 106 *Public Utilities Fortnightly* 13 (July 31, 1980); H. Craig Petersen, "Gainers and Losers with Lifeline Electricity Rates," 110 *Public Utilities Fortnightly* 33 (November 25, 1982).

[48]Section 114 of the act.

[49]See, *e.g.*, *Re New England Teleph. & Teleg. Co.*, 84 PUR3d 130 (Mass., 1970); *Re New England Teleph. & Teleg. Co.*, 89 PUR3d 417 (R.I., 1971); *Pennsylvania Pub. Utility Comm. v. Philadelphia Elec. Co.*, 91 PUR3d 321 (Pa., 1971); *Mountain States Legal Foundation v. Colorado Pub. Utilities Comm.*, 28 PUR4th 609 (1979). It also has been held that undue discrimination occurs when rates are based upon ability to pay [*Re Washington Gas Light Co.*, Order No. 5542 (D.C., 1972)], unless a commission is directed to do so by the legislature [*Re Interstate Residential Subscriber Line Charge Waiver Mechanism*, Docket No. P-100, Sub 80 (N.C., 1986)].

[50]One study concluded that "the minimum use customer is likely to be the relatively affluent, middle-aged apartment or condominium dweller who uses his residence only part of the year, who eats out frequently, and who finds much of his entertainment away from home." Thus, a lifeline rate in New York might well result in the poor and elderly "subsidizing the affluent." Statement of Jules Joskow, speech before the Southeastern Association of Regulatory Utility Commissioners, as summarized in 96 *Public Utilities Fortnightly* 34 (May 8, 1975). Concluded the New York commission, after an extensive generic investigation: ". . . the relationship between

electricity consumption and income is far more complex than the lifeline proponents assumed." *Re Rate Design for Electric Corporations, op. cit.,* p. 293.

[51]*Re Investigation into Rate Structures of Electric Utilities, op. cit.,* p. 412. In that case, a Pacific Power and Light witness testified that "on average, individual electric consumption varies by 275 kilowatt-hours from month to month." *Ibid.* In the mid-1970s, to further illustrate the problem, a lifeline bill introduced in the Massachusetts legislature provided for an initial block of 300 kilowatt-hours per month (for residential customers), while a similar bill introduced in the Florida legislature provided for an initial block of 700 kilowatt-hours per month. In 1980, the Washington commission found that "the level of electric service meeting 'essential needs' falls in a range of approximately 400 to 600 kwh per month." *Re Pacific Power & Light Co.,* 40 PUR4th 405, 424 (Wash., 1980).

[52]*Re Rate Design for Electric Corporations, op. cit.,* p. 286.

[53]See, *e.g., Re Indiana Bell Teleph. Co., Inc.,* 82 PUR4th 402 (Ind., 1987). Such service, however, is not popular. See "Phone Companies Draw Fire by Seeking To Base Local Phone Charges on Usage," *The Wall Street Journal,* January 6, 1987, p. 31.

[54]See, *e.g., Re Moore Universal Telephone Service Act,* Decision No. 84-04-053 (Cal., 1984), as amended, Decision No. 86-02-021 (Cal., 1986); *Re Telephone Lifeline Rates, op. cit.; Re Nevada Bell,* 81 PUR4th 110 (Nev., 1987). See also *Re Specialized Telephone Equipment Provided to Disabled Subscribers,* 83 PUR4th 427 (Cal., 1987).

[55]See "Half of the States Now Offer Lifeline Aid Under One of FCC's Three Plans," 5 *State Telephone Regulation Report* 1 (October 8, 1987). See also U.S. General Accounting Office, *Telephone Communications: Cost and Funding Information on Lifeline Telephone Service* (Gaithersburg, Md., 1987).

[56]For electricity, the commission established (for single-family dwellings), 250 kilowatt-hours per month for lighting, cooking, and refrigeration; 250 kilowatt-hours per month for water heating; and from 550 to 1,420 kilowatt-hours per month, depending upon four climatic zones, for space heating. For natural gas, the commission established six therms per month for cooking; twenty therms per month for water heating; and from fifty-five to 140 therms per month, depending upon the four climatic zones, for space heating. California Pub. Utilities Comm., Decision No. 86087 (1976). On the California experience, see Albin J. Dahl, "California's Lifeline Policy," 102 *Public Utilities Fortnightly* 13 (August 13, 1978); William Symons, Jr., "California Rate Experiments: Lifeline or Lead-weight?," 102 *Public Utilities Fortnightly* 11 (October 26, 1978).

[57]*Re Duke Power Co.,* 26 PUR4th 241 (N.C., 1978).

[58]*Re Narragansett Elec. Co.,* 23 PUR4th 576 (R.I., 1978). Yet, the Maine commission rejected a similar proposal for an elderly, low-income residential rate schedule (a 20 percent credit against base monthly electric rates for the first 500 kilowatt-hours of consumption), on the grounds that the commission should not make "social judgments of the nature suggested by this rate" and that there was no evidence on the record "to support any contention that customers who would qualify for the elderly low-income rate are in need of rate relief any more than other low-income customers." *Re Central Maine Power Co.,* 26 PUR4th 388 (Me., 1978).

[59]*Re Montana Power Co.,* Order No. 4521b (Phase II) (Mont., 1979).

[60]See Jean H. Standish et al., *Trends Report of Energy Assistance Programs in the Fifty States, 1979-1984* (Columbus, Ohio: National Regulatory Research Institute, 1985).

[61]Pub. Law 96-126 (1979). Under the original program, $400 million was distributed directly to individuals receiving supplemental security income; $800 million

was given to the states in block grants, with each state's plan for distributing its block grant subject to the approval of the Department of Health, Education, and Welfare. See "Energy Assistance Checks Sent to Low-income Individuals," 105 *Public Utilities Fortnightly* 42 (January 17, 1980).

[62]In addition to the references cited in the following pages, the studies and reports of the Electric Power Research Institute (Palo Alto, California) provide a wealth of information on electric utility rate design.

[63]There were many other interesting variations in existence, including a New England utility with an ingenious block rate structure which used the number of cows on a farm as a substitute for a demand meter; a western utility with a schedule for "bachelor residential service"; and another which furnished "free service to widows, a majority of whom are not metered." See Louis Zanoff, "How New Are the 'New' Rate-making Principles?," 105 *Public Utilities Fortnightly* 6, 8 (January 17, 1980).

[64]C. Woody Thompson and Wendell R. Smith, *Public Utility Economics* (New York: McGraw-Hill Book Co., Inc., 1941), p. 394.

[65]*Ibid.*

[66]The widespread use of interconnections with other electric utilities reduces the necessary reserve capacity. Under these arrangements, utility A can buy power from utility B during peak or emergency situations. See Chapter 13.

[67]Eli W. Clemens, *Economics and Public Utilities* (New York: Appleton-Century-Crofts, Inc., 1950), p. 284.

[68]"The power factor is the ratio of the power to the volt-amperes. For direct current, volts multiplied by amperes equals watts. For alternating current, which is most widely used, volt-amperes are the equivalent of watts for lighting uses but not where the energy is transformed into mechanical power. Here at a given wattage a power user may require alternating generators, conductors and transformers of nearly a third greater capacity than the kilowatts he employs and for which he is supposed to pay. The power factor is the coefficient which expresses the significance of this element in the situation. The relation between the kilowatt-hours consumed and the necessary generating capacity and other equipment is in inverse ratio to the power factor of the consumer's apparatus." Emerson P. Schmidt, *Public Utility Economics* (St. Louis: John S. Swift Co., Inc., 1940), p. 134.

[69]Emery Troxel, *Economics of Public Utilities* (New York: Holt, Rinehart & Winston, Inc., 1947), p. 609.

[70]Wilcox, *op. cit.*, p. 331. See also Ralph K. Davidson, *Price Discrimination in Selling Gas and Electricity* (Baltimore: The Johns Hopkins Press, 1955).

[71]Bonbright, *op. cit.*, p. 350.

[72]Russell E. Caywood, *Electric Utility Rate Economics* (New York: McGraw-Hill Book Co., Inc., 1956), pp. 156-69. Bonbright notes that there are at least twenty-nine such formulas in existence. "Most of them have no claim whatever to validity from the standpoint of cost determination, and only a dubious claim to acceptance as compromise measures of reasonable rates." Bonbright, *op. cit.*, p. 351.

[73]Bonbright, *op. cit.*, p. 353.

[74]Wilcox, *op. cit.*, p. 333.

[75]"It is obvious that this method is not entirely satisfactory because a class load at the time of the system peak might be zero, while at some other time it might be of considerable size; yet no expense would be allocated to it." Caywood, *Electric Utility Rate Economics, op. cit.*, p. 156.

[76]Bonbright, *op. cit.*, p. 350-68.

[77]Irwin M. Stelzer, "Rate Structure Reform — A Federal or State Problem?" (New York: National Economic Research Associates, Inc., 1977).

[78]These two illustrative rate schedules are for the Virginia Electric and Power Company, as adopted by the Virginia commission in rate cases decided in 1970 and 1985, respectively.

[79]*Re Madison Gas & Elec. Co., op. cit.,* p. 46.

[80]*Ibid.,* concurring statement by Commissioner Richard D. Cudahy, pp. 52-53.

[81]*Ibid.,* commission decision, p. 36.

[82]Weiss, *op. cit.,* p. 287. See also William G. Shepherd, "Price Structures in Electricity," in Albert L. Danielsen and David R. Kamerschen (eds.), *Current issues in Public-Utility Economics: Essays in Honor of James C. Bonbright* (Lexington, Mass.: D. C. Heath & Co., 1983), chap. 9.

[83]See, *e.g.,* Paul L. Joskow, "Public Utility Regulatory Policies Act of 1978: Electric Utility Rate Reform," 19 *Natural Resources Journal* 787 (1979).

[84]The state commissions also were required to consider and adopt, if appropriate, lifeline rates.

[85]The regulatory standards, contained in Section 113, are (*1*) Master metering — master metering of new buildings shall be prohibited or restricted to the extent necessary to meet the objectives of the rate reform provisions. (*2*) Automatic adjustment clauses — no utility may increase any rate under an automatic adjustment clause unless the clause is reviewed (a) at least once every four years to ensure that it provides incentives for efficient use of resources and (b) at least once every two years to ensure maximum economies in operations and purchases that impact utility rates. (*3*) Information to consumers — a utility shall provide the following types of rate information to consumers: (a) an explanation of the existing rate schedule, (b) an explanation of any new rate schedule applied for or proposed, (c) at least once a year, a summary of existing rate schedules for each class of customer having a separate rate, and (d) on request, a statement of consumption for each billing period for the prior year. (*4*) Advertising — a utility may not recover from ratepayers the costs of promotional or political advertising. (*5*) Termination of service — service shall not be terminated except pursuant to certain enumerated procedures; specifically, reasonable prior notice, including notice of rights and remedies, and reasonable provisions for (a) elderly and handicapped consumers and (b) consumers who have established inability to pay, where termination would be especially dangerous to health. Standards (*4*) and (*5*) apply to both electric and gas utilities. The state commissions were to consider and to adopt these standards, if appropriate, by November 1980. See Economic Regulatory Administration, U.S. Department of Energy, *Annual Report to Congress, May 1980* (Washington, D.C.: U.S. Government Printing Office, 1980), Vols. 1 and 2. For representative state commissions decisions regarding the five standards, see (*1*) *Re Investigation of Master Metering,* 37 PUR4th 110 (S.D., 1980); *Re Master Metering Standards,* 37 PUR4th 119 (Idaho, 1980); (*2*) *Re Energy Cost Adjustment Clauses,* 41 PUR4th 81 (Cal., 1980); *Re Uniform Fuel Adjustment Clauses,* 45 PUR4th 1 (Ill., 1981); (*3*) *Re Public Utility Regulatory Policies Act Standards,* 46 PUR4th 39 (Alaska, 1982); *Re Public Utility Regulatory Policies Act,* Case Nos. U-6490, U-8455 (Mich., 1986); (*4*) *Re Potomac Elec. Power Co.,* 36 PUR4th 139 (D.C., 1980); *Re Rule Making Relating to Advertising Expenditures,* 39 PUR4th 295 (N.C., 1980); (*5*) *Re Termination of Services Standard,* 83 PUR4th 444 (Mich., 1987).

[86]See *Annual Report to Congress, May 1980, op. cit.;* two reports by the National Association of Regulatory Utility Commissioners, "State Commission Progress Under

the Public Utility Regulatory Policies Act of 1978" (Washington, D.C., 1980) and "Second Report on State Commission Progress Under the Public Utility Regulatory Policies Act of 1978" (Washington, D.C., 1982). For an overview, see *1985 Annual Report on Utility and Carrier Regulation* (Washington, D.C.: National Association of Regulatory Utility Commissioners, 1987), pp. 681-93. For representative state commission decisions regarding the six ratemaking standards, see *(1) Re Potomac Elec. Power Co.*, 36 PUR4th 139 (D.C., 1980); *Re Cost-of-Service Ratemaking Standards*, 44 PUR4th 33 (Tex., 1981); *(2) Re Carolina Power & Light Co.*, 49 PUR4th 188 (N.C., 1982); *Re Potomac Elec. Power Co.*, 62 PUR4th 1 (D.C., 1984); *(3) Re Commonwealth Edison Co.*, 35 PUR4th 49 (Ill., 1980); *Re Virginia Elec. & Power Co.*, 64 PUR4th 636 (W.Va., 1984); *(4) Re Commonwealth Edison Co., op. cit., Re Time-of-day and Seasonal Electric Rates*, 42 PUR4th 494 (Iowa, 1981); *(5) Re Dept. of Pub. Service*, 37 PUR4th 497 (Minn., 1980); *Re Virginia Elec. & Power Co., op. cit.; (6) Re Interruptible Rate and Load Management Standards*, 43 PUR4th 163 (Iowa, 1981); *Re Electric Utility Conservation and Load Management*, 55 PUR4th 351 (Pa., 1983).

[87]See John A. Casazza, "Understanding the Transmission Access and Wheeling Problem," 116 *Public Utilities Fortnightly* 35 (October 31, 1985). The FERC has limited authority to mandate wheeling [see *e.g., Southeastern Power Administration v. Kentucky Utilities Co.*, 25 FERC Par. 61,204 (1983)], but it has preempted jurisdiction over all interstate wheeling rates [*Re Florida Power & Light Co.*, 29 FERC Par. 61,140 (1984), and 40 FERC Par. 61,045, 85 PUR4th 1 (1987)]. On state activity, see *Re Electric Transmission Service*, 82 PUR4th 473 (Conn., 1987). The NRC may impose limited wheeling obligations as part of nuclear plant license conditions under the antitrust provisions of the Atomic Energy Act of 1954. [See Federal Energy Regulatory Commission, *Power Pooling in the United States* (Washington, D.C.: U.S. Government Printing Office, 1981), p. 58.] On antitrust issues, see *Otter Tail Power Co. v. United States*, 410 U.S. 366, 97 PUR3d 209 (1973) (holding that transmission lines are "essential facilities" under the antitrust laws when they cannot be economically duplicated); *City of Chanute et al. v. Kansas Gas & Elec. Co.*, 564 F. Supp. 1416, 54 PUR4th 162 (D. Kan. 1983).

[88]Economy energy refers to large-scale power transfers, where it is less expensive to purchase than to produce electricity. In 1982 and 1983, for example, both the Power Authority of the State of New York and the New England Power Pool signed long-term contracts with Hydro-Quebec to import up to 111 billion kilowatt-hours and 33 billion kilowatt-hours of electricity, respectively. The New England Power Pool estimated that the contract would save its members $1 billion over its life when compared with the cost of power from oil-fired generating stations. *The Wall Street Journal*, March 18, 1983, p. 10.

[89]See, *e.g.*, David W. Penn, "A Municipal Perspective on Electric Transmission Access Questions," 117 *Public Utilities Fortnightly* 15 (February 6, 1986). But see, *e.g.*, Jerry L. Pfeffer, "Policies Governing Transmission Access and Pricing: The Wheeling Debate Revisited," 116 *Public Utilities Fortnightly* 26 (October 31, 1985); Michael B. Rosenzweig and Joshua Bar-Lev, "Transmission Access and Pricing: Some Other Approaches," 118 *Public Utilities Fortnightly* 20 (August 21, 1986).

[90]"This may be either to cover the full costs imposed by wheeling or to gather a large share of the profits available because of the cost differential between buyer and seller." Kevin Kelly et al., *Some Economic Principles for Pricing Wheeling Power* (Columbus, Ohio: National Regulatory Research Institute, (1987), p. 2. See also Kevin Kelly

(ed.), *Non-Technical Impediments to Power Transfers* (Columbus, Ohio: National Regulatory Research Institute, 1987).

[91]Pfeffer, *op. cit.,* p. 29. See Oak Ridge National Laboratory, "Analysis of Power Wheeling Services" (A report prepared for the Federal Energy Regulatory Commission, 1984); Pfeffer, Lindsay and Associates, Inc., "A Review of Current Practice and Emerging Issues in the Design of Rates for Transmission Service" (A report prepared for the Edison Electric Institute, 1985); Kelly et al., *op. cit.,* esp. Appendix F.

[92]*American Elec. Power Service Corp., et al. v. Federal Energy Regulatory Comm.,* 675 F. 2d 1226, 45 PUR4th 364, 366 (D.C. Cir. 1982). "Cogeneration usually refers to the use of heat that would otherwise be wasted after electricity is generated ('topping cycle'); the term also applies to systems that generate electricity from heat left over from an industrial process ('bottoming cycle'). Because both heat and electricity are created in a single process, about half as much fuel is used to produce electricity and heat as would be needed to produce the two separately. While cogeneration is not a new concept, its popularity had declined steadily since the turn of the century as energy from central station power plants became relatively inexpensive. With the rise in utility rates in recent years, however, it became apparent that cogeneration might again become economical on a broad scale." *Ibid.* See also U.S. General Accounting Office, *Industrial Cogeneration — What It Is, How It Works, Its Potential* (Gaithersburg, Md., 1980).

[93]"Combined estimates of installed capacity and firm project commitments by independent producers are in the 20,000-megawatt range, while less certain undertakings could substantially increase that total. The amount of independently generated electricity has more than doubled since 1978, and should repeat that performance in the next ten or fifteen years." "PURPA: Still Hazy After All These Years," 118 *Public Utilities Fortnightly* 33 (July 10, 1986). See, *e.g.,* Howard J. Brown (ed.), *Decentralizing Electricity Production* (New Haven: Yale University Press, 1983).

[94]Order No. 69, 45 *Fed. Reg.* 12214 (FERC, 1980). The FERC's Rules were upheld in *American Elec. Power Service Corp., et al. v. Federal Energy Regulatory Comm., op. cit., rev'd sub nom. American Paper Institute, Inc. v. American Elec. Power Service Corp.,* 461 U.S. 402, 52 PUR4th 329 (1983).

The act also provides for the provision of backup service from utilities at just and reasonable rates [see, *e.g., Re Standby Rates for Electric Utilities,* 81 PUR4th 1 (Fla., 1987)] and for interconnections with utilities under terms and conditions consistent with reliable system operation [see, *e.g., Re Transmission System Operations for Cogeneration and Small Power Production Development,* 64 PUR4th 537 (Cal., 1985)]. The FERC may exempt qualifying facilities from certain state and federal regulations [see, *e.g., Federal Energy Regulatory Comm. v. State of Mississippi,* 456 U.S. 742, 47 PUR4th 1 (1982)]. See also Robert D. Stewart, Jr., "The Law of Cogeneration in Oklahoma," 118 *Public Utilities Fortnightly* 22 (November 27, 1986).

[95]See, *e.g.,* "Calculating Capacity Costs in Cogeneration Rates," 108 *Public Utilities Fortnightly* 57 (September 24, 1981); *The Appropriateness and Feasibility of Various Methods of Calculating Avoided Costs* (Columbus, Ohio: National Regulatory Research Institute, 1982); *Re Electric Avoided Cost Rates,* 73 PUR4th 138 (Mont., 1986) (discussing nine methods for calculating avoided costs); "Recent Decisions on Avoided Cost Methodologies and Standard Offer Cogeneration Contracts," 118 *Public Utilities Fortnightly* 46 (September 18, 1986); "Cogeneration and Small Power Production: Recent Regulatory Developments," 119 *Public Utilities Fortnightly* 46 (June 25, 1987); Hethie S. Parmesano, "Avoided Cost Payments to Qualifying Facilities: Debate Goes On," 120 *Public Utilities Fortnightly* 34 (September 17, 1987). See also Steven R. Miles,

"Full-Avoided Cost Pricing Under the Public Utility Regulatory Policies Act: 'Just and Reasonable' to Electric Consumers?," 69 *Cornell Law Review* 1267 (1984). On related issues, see "PURPA Still Hazy After All These Years," *op. cit.*

For representative state decisions, see *Re Cogenerators and Small Power Producers*, 51 PUR4th 369 (Ark., 1983); *Re Cogeneration and Small Power Production*, 51 PUR4th 399 (Wyo., 1983); *Re Rates for Sale and Purchase of Electricity Between Electric Utilities and Qualifying Facilities*, 64 PUR4th 369 (N.C., 1985); *Re Cogeneration and Small Power Production*, 83 PUR4th 19 (Utah, 1987).

[96]*Greensboro Lumber Co. v. Georgia Power Co.*, 643 F. Supp. 1245 (N.D. Ga. 1986).

[97]*Resolution*, E-3017 (Cal., 1987).

[98]Kenneth W. Costello, O. Douglas Fulp, and Calvin S. Monson, "Incentive and Economic Development Rates as a Marketing Strategy for Electric Utilities," 117 *Public Utilities Fortnightly* 27, 28 (May 15, 1986). See also Louis R. Jahn and Mark S. Berndt, "A Cost-of-Service Basis for Utility Marketing Programs," 116 *Public Utilities Fortnightly* 42 (September 19, 1985).

[99]*Re Narragansett Elec. Co.*, 57 PUR4th 120, 131 (R.I., 1983).

[100]*Re Detroit Edison Co.*, 57 PUR4th 540, 541 (Mich., 1984).

[101]*Re Pub. Service Co. of N.H.*, 57 PUR4th 563, 587 (N.H., 1984). See also *Re Hoosier Energy Rural Elec. Cooperative, Inc.*, 78 PUR4th 120 (Ind., 1986).

<table>
<tr><td>

Chapter

11

</td><td>

THE RATE
STRUCTURE
(Continued)

</td></tr>
</table>

The central policy prescription of microeconomics is the equation of price and marginal cost. If economic theory is to have any relevance to public utility pricing, that is the point at which the inquiry must begin.

—Alfred E. Kahn*

In this chapter, the rate structures of natural gas and telephone utilities are analyzed. In both industries, however, public policy is changing rapidly, as competition has been or is being introduced. Rate structures, in turn, are developing just as rapidly.

Rate Structures in Practice: Gas Utility Rates

Supplying natural gas to consumers involves three functions: (*1*) the production and gathering of natural gas in the field,[1] (*2*) the intra- and interstate transmission of the gas by pipeline from the producing fields to consumer markets, and (*3*) local distribution of the gas to consumers. There are three corresponding marketing transactions. The "field price" refers to rates on sales by the producer at the wellhead, or by producers and gatherers at the ends of their gathering lines, or by processors at the tail gates of their processing plants to gatherers, processors, and pipeline companies. The "city gate rate" refers to wholesale rates on sales by pipeline companies to local distribution companies. The "resale rate" refers to the rate charged on retail sales to ultimate customers by local distribution companies.

The Field (Wellhead) Price

The Natural Gas Act of 1938 appeared to exempt "the production or gathering of natural gas" from federal regulation. As a result, prior to the Supreme Court's 1954 *Phillips* decision,[2] the price paid to independent producers for gas at the wellhead or gathering points was determined by contract between producer and pipeline, and was taken by the Federal Power Commission as a datum not subject to its control.[3] When regulating city gate rates charged by integrated pipeline companies, the commission did have to consider the costs incurred or the price paid to obtain gas in the field in determining the reasonableness of the price charged local distributors. The commission did this by using the utility rate base, cost-of-service method — a company's operating costs (including dry-hole costs on nonproductive lands) plus a return of 6 percent on the original cost of its producing properties less reserves for depreciation.[4]

The 1954 Phillips Case. On October 28, 1948, the commission initiated an investigation of the Phillips Petroleum Company[5] to determine (*a*) whether the firm was a natural gas company within the meaning of the Natural Gas Act and, if so, (*b*) whether any of its rates were unjust or unreasonable.[6] Hearings were held before an administrative law judge from April 3, 1951 to May 23, 1951.[7] In general, gas-consuming states supported federal regulation, while producers and gas-producing states supported state regulation. The record was certified to the commission, which held arguments on July 9 and 10, 1951. Its opinion, issued on August 22, 1951, held that the commission lacked jurisdiction over Phillips on the grounds that all its activities were a part of its producing and gathering business exempt under the act, and that federal regulation of the company's sales made during the course of production and gathering would interfere with effective state conservation efforts.[8] The commission ordered the proceedings terminated.

The commission's decision was appealed by the state of Wisconsin, the cities of Kansas City, Milwaukee, and Detroit, and the county of Wayne, Michigan.[9] On June 7, 1954, the Supreme Court, in a 5-to-3 decision, held that Phillips was subject to the jurisdiction of the FPC and directed the commission to determine whether the firm's prices were just and reasonable. The majority argued, in part:

> . . . we believe that the legislative history indicates a congressional intent to give the Commission jurisdiction over the rates of all wholesales of natural gas in interstate commerce, whether by pipeline company or not and whether occurring before, during, or after transmis-

sion by an interstate pipeline company. There can be no dispute that the overriding congressional purpose was to plug the "gap" in regulation of natural gas companies resulting from judicial decisions prohibiting, on federal constitutional grounds, state regulation of many of the interstate commerce aspects of the natural gas business. A significant part of this gap was created by cases holding that "the regulation of wholesale rates of gas and electric energy moving in interstate commerce is beyond the constitutional powers of the States." . . . The committee reports on the bill that became the Natural Gas Act specifically referred to two of these cases and to the necessity of federal regulations to occupy the hiatus created by them. Thus, we are satisfied that Congress sought to regulate wholesales of natural gas occurring at both ends of the interstate transmission systems.

Regulation of the sales in interstate commerce for resale made by a so-called independent natural gas producer is not essentially different from regulation of such sales when made by an affiliate of an interstate pipeline company. In both cases, the rates charged may have a direct and substantial effect on the price paid by the ultimate consumer. Protection of consumers against exploitation at the hands of natural gas companies was the primary aim of the Natural Gas Act. . . . Attempts to weaken this protection by amendatory legislation exempting independent natural gas producers from federal regulation have repeatedly failed, and we refuse to achieve the same result by a strained interpretation of the existing statutory language.[10]

Justice Clark, in his dissent, stated:

By today's decision, the Court restricts the phrase "production and gathering" to "the physical activities, facilities, and properties" used in production and gathering. Such a gloss strips the words of their substance. If the Congress so intended, then it left for state regulation only a mass of empty pipe, vacant processing plants, and thousands of hollow wells with scarecrow derricks, monuments to this new extension of federal power. It was not so understood. . . . There can be no doubt, as the Commission has found, that federal regulation of production and gathering will collide and substantially interfere with and hinder the enforcement of . . . regulatory measures.[11]

The Court thus handed the Federal Power Commission the complex task of certificating thousands of independent natural gas producers and determining the wellhead price of natural gas. Instead of the 157 natural gas companies subject to its jurisdiction at the end of 1953, the *Phillips* decision extended the commission's power to 4,365 independent producers who sold to interstate pipelines. In July, 1954, the commission issued an order freezing the wellhead price of natural gas. It directed all producers to apply for certificates, both for present operations and for new service, and to file their rates. By June 30, 1963, 17,809 certificate applications had been filed; of these applications, 5,483 were for services rendered prior to the 1954 decision.[12]

Individual Company Cost-of-Service. In regulating the field price of gas of interstate pipeline companies, the commission, until the late 1960s, used the traditional rate base, individual company cost-of-service approach to ratemaking and, until 1960, the commission processed rate filings by independent natural gas producers on the same basis. Costs were segregated among three principal functions: exploration and development, production, and gas processing. Thereafter, it was necessary to assign the identifiable costs and to allocate the joint costs to particular products. The cost of all gas produced and sold, finally, had to be allocated between jurisdictional and nonjurisdictional sales. The commission soon found, however, that this method had serious drawbacks in regulating independent gas producers.[13]

The first problem faced by the commission was one of administrative feasibility. Since the largest 266 producers accounted for roughly 91 percent of interstate sales, most were small and their records, in turn, were often incomplete. Despite attempts to lessen the impact of regulation (for example, by releasing independent producers from maintaining accounts in accordance with the uniform systems and from submitting certain reports), the cost-of-service method, requiring a separate rate determination for each producer, would have resulted in an intolerable administrative burden. The commission itself concluded in a 1960 case when it rejected the method: ". . . if our present staff were immediately tripled, and if all new employees would be as competent as those we now have, we would not reach a current status in our independent producer rate work until 2043 A.D. — eighty-two and one-half years from now."[14]

In the second place, determining the cost of producing natural gas involves an allocation problem. Natural gas is produced to a considerable degree jointly with liquids: with crude oil from oil casinghead reservoirs and with lease liquids (called condensates) from gas condensate reservoirs.[15] The joint production and joint nature of many of the exploration (or finding) and production costs of oil and gas are the source of many of the difficulties in regulating the price of gas sold in interstate commerce, for the "cost" of gas largely depends on the allocation method chosen.

Three allocation methods have been widely employed. (*1*) *Sales Realization.* Annual costs, including operating expenses, depreciation, depletion, exploration, and development, are allocated in proportion to the revenues received from the products during the test period. Fixed costs, including net plant and working capital, are allocated in proportion to the value of the reserves remaining in the ground in the test period. (*2*) *Btu Method.* Joint costs are allocated in proportion to the British thermal unit content (*i.e.*, the energy content) of the products. (*3*) *Relative Cost Method.* The joint costs of gas and oil are divided in proportion to the costs of the two products in pure gas and pure oil wells. Each of these methods has serious weaknesses.[16] Moreover, since all allocation methods are partly arbitrary, so are the resulting "cost" figures.

Finally, the relationship between investment and service is nebulous in the case of natural gas production. As Justice Jackson observed in the *Hope Natural Gas* case: "The service one renders to society in the gas business is measured by what he gets out of the ground, not by what he puts into it, and there is little more relation between the investment and the results than in a game of poker."[17] Stated another way: "A huge investment might yield only a trickle of gas, while a small investment might lead to a bonanza."[18] The rate base, cost-of-service method would erase any bonanza or windfall profits to successful speculators. Yet, in an industry such as this one, where in the search for gas the elements of risk and chance are so important, the method also tends to penalize the "more astute, fortunate, and efficient" producer.[19] Indeed, as Howard has observed, "the rate base itself can, conceivably, vanish."[20]

Two consequences of the rate base, individual company cost-of-service approach also must be considered. First, the rate base method resulted in a structure of field prices described by Justice Jackson as "delirious." In his words:

> To let rate base figures, compiled on any of the conventional theories of rate-making, govern a rate for natural gas seems to me little better than to draw figures out of a hat. These cases confirm and strengthen me in the view I stated in the *Hope* case that the entire rate-base method should be rejected in pricing natural gas, though it might be used to determine transportation costs. . . . These orders in some instances result in three different prices for gas from the same well. The regulated company buys all of the gas for its interstate business. It is allowed to pay as operating expenses an unregulated contract price for its co-owner's share and a different unregulated contract price for the royalty owner's share, but for its own share it is allowed substantially less than either. Any method of rate-making by which an identical product from a single well, going to the same consumers, has three prices, depending on who owns it, does not make sense to me.[21]

Second, the cost-of-service approach discouraged vertical integration since it discriminated against pipeline-produced gas. Discrimination occurred because with the market price of natural gas rising, independent producers were receiving a higher rate of return than were integrated producers on their gas producing properties. Noted Lindahl:

> The role of the pipelines in providing gas for interstate use has fallen off greatly since the inception of rate control. Eight major interstate pipeline companies produced about 47 percent of the gas which they

transported and sold in 1940, whereas these systems produced less than 30 percent of their requirements in 1951. None of the seven large systems which have been created to serve large consuming markets since the Natural Gas Act became effective produces any substantial amount of gas. Taken together these fifteen large major transmission systems produced only 18 1/2 percent of their requirements in 1952.[22]

Area Rates. In April, 1954, just two months before the Supreme Court's *Phillips* decision, the commission rejected the rate base, individual company cost-of-service approach in a case involving Panhandle Eastern Pipe Line Company.[23] In valuing the gas produced by the company, the commission determined a "fair field price" by taking a weighted average of the prices paid by the pipeline company to independent producers in the same area. Prices so determined, argued the commission, resulted from arm's length bargaining and would encourage the exploration for, and development of, gas reserves. A year later, the procedure was held improper by a Court of Appeals.[24] The commission might use the average field method, ruled the Court, but the rate base, cost-of-service method must be used as a "point of departure." Then, if the resulting rates under the field price method were higher than those based on the cost-of-service method, the rates would have to be justified by specific evidence showing that they were just and reasonable. The Supreme Court refused to review the case.

The decision forced the commission to return to the rate base, cost-of-service approach in fixing wellhead prices for integrated producers, and it complicated the FPC's attempt to devise new regulatory methods. In 1956, the commission dismissed a number of rate increase applications of producers on the grounds that the evidence presented was insufficient to indicate whether the rates requested were needed to encourage exploration and development.[25]

In the meantime, the commission had before it the remand in the *Phillips* case, and was investigating the lawfulness of the company's interstate rates. The administrative law judge, in April, 1959, fixed the maximum wellhead price that Phillips could charge by computing the cost of production and adding a fair rate of return on the investment.[26] Over a year later, the commission issued its opinion in which it concluded that (*a*) the cost-of-service approach was "not a sensible, or even a workable, method of filing the rates of independent producers" since it would "produce fallacious results" and (*b*) the "ultimate solution" to producer regulation lay in the area rate approach — that is, "the determination of fair prices for gas, based on reasonable financial requirements of the industry and not on the particular rate base and expenses of each natural gas company."[27] Concurrently, the commission issued a "Statement of General Policy" to implement its new procedure.[28] The gas fields of the country producing for interstate shipments were divided into twenty-three geographical areas. Two price levels or ceilings were established for each area — initial service rates for new contracts

and increased rates ("escalated rates") for existing contracts, in recognition
of the fact that "initial prices in new contracts are, and in many cases by
virtue of economic factors, must be higher than the prices contained in old
contracts." These rates were "for the purpose of guidance and initial action
by the commission," and it was announced that in the absence of compel-
ling evidence the commission would not certificate initial rates, and would
suspend increased rates, that exceeded the set levels. The commission also
announced that it would begin a series of hearings, one on each of seven
major producing areas,[29] to determine final area prices.

The following year, the Court of Appeals affirmed the commission's
decision.[30] And in 1963, in a 5-to-4 decision, the Supreme Court did likewise.[31]
Justice Harlan argued:

> . . . to declare that a particular method of rate regulation is so sancti-
> fied as to make it highly unlikely that any other method could be
> sustained would be wholly out of keeping with this Court's consistent
> and clearly articulated approach to the question of the Commission's
> power to regulate rates. It has repeatedly been stated that no single
> method must be followed by the Commission in considering the just-
> ness and reasonableness of rates . . . and we reaffirm that principle
> today.
>
> More specifically, the Court has never held that the individual com-
> pany cost-of-service method is a *sine qua non* of natural gas regulation.
> Indeed the prudent investment, original cost, rate base method which
> we are now told is lawful, established, and effective is the very one the
> Court was asked to declare impermissible in the *Hope* case, less than
> twenty years ago.
>
> To whatever extent the matter of costs may be a requisite element in
> rate regulation, we have no indication that the area method will fall
> short of statutory or constitutional standards. The Commission has stated
> in its opinion in this proceeding that the goal is to have rates based on
> "the reasonable financial requirements of the industry" in each produc-
> tion area . . . and we were advised at oral argument that composite
> cost-of-service data will be considered in the area rate proceedings.
> Surely, we cannot say that the rates to be developed in these proceed-
> ings will in all likelihood be so high as to deprive consumers, or so low
> as to deprive producers, of their right to a just and reasonable rate.
>
> We recognize the unusual difficulties inherent in regulating the price
> of a commodity such as natural gas. We respect the Commission's con-
> sidered judgment, backed by sound and persuasive reasoning, that the
> individual company cost-of-service method is not a feasible or suitable
> one for regulating the rates of independent producers. We share the
> Commission's hopes that the area approach may prove to be the ulti-
> mate solution.[32]

For present purposes, it is only necessary to review the first area rate proceeding, initiated by the commission on December 23, 1960 — Permian Basin (west Texas and southeastern New Mexico). The commission's decision was issued on August 5, 1965, and was modified in an opinion issued on October 4, 1965.[33] The commission declined to calculate area rates from prevailing field prices. In arriving at costs, it used the cost-of-service technique (a composite of all producer costs in the area as reported by them for the test year 1960) for casinghead and residue gas, and a cost computed from industry-wide statistics (using such components as volumes of reserves added versus exploration and development costs, production operating expenses, regulatory expenses, depletion, and royalties) for new nonassociated gas.[34] Each of the cost calculations included a rate base on which a return on investment was allowed. For new gas-well gas, an average rate base approach, based on a twenty-year production life, was adopted. For all other gas, the traditional cost-of-service approach of total net investment in the test year (1960) was followed. The rate of return allowed, determined by a comparable earnings standard, was 12 percent on each producer's investment.

A two-price system was adopted (Figure 11-1) — a higher price for new gas-well gas (contracts since January 1, 1961) and a lower price for all other gas.[35] Refunds were ordered for rates that exceeded the ceilings back to the start of the case in 1961 (estimated at more than $68 million), a two and one-half year moratorium (until January 1, 1968) was imposed on filings for prices in excess of the applicable area maximum rate, and restrictions were placed on escalation clauses in existing contracts.[36] A minimum rate of nine cents per thousand cubic feet was fixed for Permian Basin gas of standard pipeline quality, with provisions for adjustment to reflect deviations from that standard.[37] Finally, the commission initiated a rulemaking proceeding for the purpose of relaxing the certificate and rate filing requirements for small producers (sales of 10 billion cubic feet per year or under).[38]

The economic rationale of the commission's two-price system[39] requires brief consideration.[40] The separate and higher price for new nonassociated (gas-well) gas was established to encourage the search for new gas reserves, and the lower price for all other gas was aimed at preventing producers from receiving excessive profits (rents). The commission attempted to recognize, in other words, that the costs of exploration and development were rising sharply. A one-price system based on costs already incurred would not provide the necessary incentive for exploration, while a one-price system based on the costs required to replace current production would overcompensate producers on gas already discovered, for which no incentive was needed and for which lower costs were incurred. The two-price system also reflected the fact that the industry can direct its exploration activity to some extent (known as "directionality") toward the search for gas, whereas most gas in the past was discovered as a by-product of the search for oil. Here,

FIGURE 11-1

Area Price Levels for Independent Producer Natural Gas Sales in Permian Basin Area Per Docket No. AR61-1 Proceedings (Opinion No. 468)

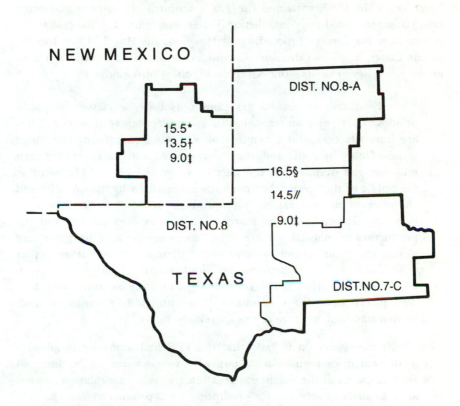

*Base area rate plus production taxes in effect September 1, 1965, for gas well gas and residue gas derived therefrom for gas sales contracts dated on and after January 1, 1961.

†Base area rate plus production taxes in effect September 1, 1965, for gas well gas and residue gas derived therefrom for gas sales contracts dated prior to January 1, 1961, and for all casinghead gas and residue gas derived therefrom.

‡Minimum rate for all gas sales of pipeline quality in Permian Basin.

§Base area rate for gas well and residue gas derived therefrom for gas sales contracts dated on and after January 1, 1961.

//Base area rate for gas well gas and residue gas derived therefrom for gas sales contracts dated prior to January 1, 1961, and for all casinghead gas and residue gas derived therefrom.

Note: All rates are subject to adjustment for deviations in gas quality.

Source: Federal Power Commission, *Annual Report, 1966,* p. 132.

again, the higher price for new nonassociated gas was to provide an incentive by rewarding the successful directional search for gas, while no incentive was needed for casinghead gas that would be forthcoming anyway as a result of the successful search for oil.

Predictably, the Permian Basin decision was appealed to the courts. A lower court, in 1967, sustained the FPC's authority to impose maximum area rates upon producers' jurisdictional sales, but remanded the case to the commission for further proceedings.[41] However, on May 1, 1968, the Supreme Court, in a 7-to-1 decision, sustained the commission's orders in their entirety.[42] After reviewing the background, the Court said:

> ... Producers of natural gas cannot usefully be classed as public utilities. They enjoy no franchises or guaranteed areas of service. They are intensely competitive vendors of a wasting commodity they have acquired only by costly and often unrewarded search. Their unit costs may rise and decline with the vagaries of good fortune. The value to the public of the service they perform is measured by the quantity and character of the natural gas they produce, and not by the resources they have expended in its search. ... The exploration for and the production of natural gas are thus "more erratic and irregular and unpredictable in relation to investment than any phase of any other utility business." ... Moreover, the number both of independent producers and of jurisdictional sales is large, and the administrative burdens placed upon the Commission by an individual company cost-of-service standard were therefore extremely heavy.[43]

The Court then went on to hold that the FPC had authority to adopt a system of area price regulation, to impose a moratorium on the filing of new rates in excess of the maximum area rates, to restrict escalation clauses, and to make special provisions for exempting small producers. The commission's methods also were approved, although with some reservations. For example, with respect to the prescribed rate structure, the Court noted:

> ... We do not suggest that the Commission need not continuously evaluate the revenue and other consequences of its area rate structures. A principal advantage of area regulation is that it centers attention upon the industry's aggregate problems, and we may expect that, as the Commission's experience with area regulation lengthens, it will treat these important questions more precisely and efficaciously. We hold only that, in the circumstances here presented, the Commission's rate structure has not been shown to deny producers revenues consonant with just and reasonable rates.[44]

And the Court concluded: "Although the Commission's position might at several places usefully be clarified, the producers have not satisfied the 'heavy burden' placed upon those who would set aside its decision."[45]

Nationwide Rates. In subsequent decisions, the FPC proceeded to establish rates for the other six geographical areas[46] and to prescribe new rates (where it found appropriate).[47] But the commission continued to confront difficulties, the most important of which was the fact that while producers' interstate sales were regulated, it had no jurisdiction over intrastate sales; and intrastate rates, in the late 1960s, were beginning to rise well above the FPC's ceilings. "Thus, in times of shortage, producers were able to sell gas intrastate, where prices were allowed to rise, particularly to industrial purchasers on the margin of choice between petroleum, natural gas, and other sources of hydrocarbons. The gas that these industries purchased was likely to be diverted from retail distributors willing to pay a much higher price but unable under regulation to do so."[48]

Consequently, the commission, in a December, 1974, opinion (an opinion which modified a June, 1974, order[49]), established a uniform national base rate[50] of fifty cents per thousand cubic feet for sales of gas by natural gas producers (a) from wells commenced on or after January 1, 1973, and (b) for new dedications of natural gas to interstate commerce on or after January 1, 1973.[51] The commission provided for annual escalations of one cent per thousand cubic feet and for biennial review procedures. The stated aim of the FPC was to establish a uniform base rate that would provide incentives to stimulate and encourage the exploration and development efforts necessary to produce the required level of new natural gas supplies. In establishing the new base rate, the commission found that the industry's costs would fall in the range of 47.82 cents to 51.46 cents per thousand cubic feet.[52] In its initial opinion, however, the commission admitted that the "cost" of new gas supplies "is an imprecise and elusive quantity."[53]

In December, 1975, the commission established a nationwide base rate of 23.5 cents per thousand cubic feet for old gas (*i.e.,* gas produced from wells commenced before January 1, 1973, or gas dedicated to the interstate market prior to January 1, 1973); a base rate increased to 29.5 cents per thousand cubic feet effective on or after July 1, 1976.[54] And, finally, in July, 1976, the commission adopted a new natural gas base rate structure: for natural gas newly discovered or newly dedicated to the interstate market (a) after January 1, 1975, $1.42 per thousand cubic feet, escalating one cent per quarter; (b) after January 1, 1973, but before January 1, 1975, $1.01 per thousand cubic feet; and (c) before January 1, 1973, $0.52 per thousand cubic feet.[55]

With respect to integrated pipelines and affiliated producers, the commission adopted an area rate approach in 1969, whereby gas produced from leases acquired after October 7, 1969, would be priced at the applicable area rate.[56] Five years later, the commission decided to apply the uniform national base rate to all qualifying production from leases owned by pipelines or their affiliates, regardless of the date the lease was acquired. "The existing natural gas shortage," said the commission, "requires the best efforts of all persons whether producer, pipeline, or pipeline affiliate to explore for and develop new supplies of gas to satisfy existing unfulfilled demands."[57]

Deregulation Efforts.[58] While the Federal Power Commission was struggling with producer regulation, the issue also was considered by Congress on several occasions. In 1949, Congressman Harris introduced a bill in the House exempting sales by independent producers to interstate pipelines, which was passed later in the year, 183 to 131. A companion bill was introduced by Senator Kerr in the Senate where, after strong opposition, it was approved the following year by a vote of 44 to 38.[59] However, President Truman, on April 18, 1950, vetoed the bill, stating that the

> . . . authority to regulate such sales is necessary in the public interest. . . . [T]o withdraw entirely from this field of regulation, however, impelled only by imaginary fears, and in the face of a record of accomplishment under present law which is successful from the standpoint of consumer, distributor, carrier and producer alike, would not be in the public interest.[60]

A report in March, 1955, by the President's special Advisory Committee on Energy Supplies and Resources, concluded that state, rather than federal, regulation of gas production was preferable.[61] Identical bills to exempt independent producers from FPC jurisdiction were introduced: one by Representative Harris in the House and the other by Senator Fulbright in the Senate. The House passed the measure in 1955, 209 to 203, and the Senate passed the bill the following year, 53 to 38. During the course of the Senate debate on the bill, a senator revealed that an oil company lawyer had offered to contribute $2,500 to his campaign fund in an apparent effort to influence his vote. President Eisenhower, while stating that he was "in accord with its basic objectives," nevertheless vetoed the bill, arguing that he could not sign the legislation before the "arrogant" tactics of its supporters had been fully investigated.[62]

In his budget message of January, 1957, President Eisenhower again endorsed exemption of natural gas producers from federal regulation, and some fourteen bills were subsequently introduced in Congress during the year. But in February, 1958, while the matter was pending in the House, it was disclosed that a Texas politician had issued invitations to a $100-a-plate dinner for the House minority leader, noting that his support and influence were needed to insure passage of the measure.[63] Congress took no further action on the proposed legislation and, for the next sixteen years, other proposals also failed. Then, in 1975, the Senate passed a bill (S. 2310), supported by President Ford, that would have eliminated federal price regulation over sales by producers, but the House balked and, instead, passed a bill (H.R. 9464) that would have extended federal regulation to intrastate sales. The impass could not be reconciled and no legislation resulted.

Finally, after some eighteen months of deliberation and negotiations, Congress enacted the Natural Gas Policy Act of 1978 (NGPA).[64] With respect to wellhead pricing, the act did two things. First, intrastate natural gas was put under federal price controls.[65] Second, Congress sought to bring natural gas prices into parity with oil prices by 1985. Specifically, "new" natural gas (generally, new gas-well gas) was subject to a mandated phased deregulation from 1977 through January 1, 1985. An initial ceiling price of $1.75 per thousand cubic feet was set for April 20, 1977, to escalate monthly at an annual rate of 3.5 percent until April 20, 1981, and thereafter at 4 percent, in addition to an annual inflation adjustment (based on the GNP Deflator). Other categories of gas were accorded escalating maximum ceilings and other price provisions which varied with each category. "High-cost" natural gas (*i.e.,* new gas below 15,000 feet, geopressured gas, occluded gas from coal seams, and gas from Devonian shale) was deregulated in 1979, while "gas produced under such other conditions as the Commission determines to present extraordinary risks or costs" was allowed special incentive prices to be determined by the FERC.[66] As a result of these provisions, federal controls have been removed from approximately one-half of all natural gas sold.

The City Gate Rate

Natural gas is transported from the producing fields to local distributors or industrial users by pipeline companies. However, pipeline companies are not common carriers; they generally own the gas which they transport. Natural gas pipeline companies make two types of sales. Interstate sales for resale (*i.e.,* sales to local gas distributors) are referred to as "jurisdictional" (city gate) sales. All others, including interstate sales to industrial customers ("direct" sales) and intrastate sales, are referred to as "nonjurisdictional" sales.[67] This classification recognizes that the Federal Energy Regulatory Commission's control over pipeline companies is limited to jurisdictional sales.[68] It also indicates that in determining pipeline rates, the commission must allocate joint costs.

Cost Allocation: The Seaboard Formula. In setting rates on interstate sales for resale, the FERC must first determine a pipeline company's overall system cost of service, and then must allocate this total cost between jurisdictional and nonjurisdictional sales. The allocation process, based upon the *Seaboard* formula of 1952,[69] involves five steps:

1. Total costs are grouped by operating functions: production costs, transmission costs, distribution costs and, where applicable, underground storage costs.

2. The items of cost in each of these categories are classified as variable or fixed (constant) costs.
3. Such costs are then classified as commodity or demand costs. Commodity costs include all variable costs (except that portion of purchased gas costs billed as demand costs and manufactured gas costs) and 50 percent of the fixed costs. Demand costs include the remaining 50 percent of fixed costs.
4. Commodity and demand costs are allocated to jurisdictional and nonjurisdictional sales. Demand costs are allocated in proportion to peak period volumes; commodity costs in proportion to annual volumes. In both cases, volumes alone are used to allocate production costs and volumes weighted by mileage to allocate transmission costs.
5. The final step involves the allocation of jurisdictional demand and commodity costs between rate zones or market areas served by the pipeline company on the basis of peak demand volumes and annual volumes respectively. This step thus involves the design of a company's rate structure.

The *Seaboard* formula has been the subject of sharp criticism, particularly the requirement that capacity (fixed) costs be distributed 50-50 between the commodity and demand charges instead of being assigned exclusively to the latter.[70] As Kahn has observed:

> . . . Since the demand costs are distributed among customers in proportion to their shares in the volume of sales at the system's (three-day) peak, while the commodity costs are borne in proportion to their annual volume of purchases, the consequence of the 50-50 formula is to shift a large proportion of capacity costs to off-peak users. This produces an uneconomic encouragement to sales at the peak (whose price falls short of the true marginal costs of peak service) and an uneconomic discouragement of off-peak. . . . Among other alleged harmful consequences of *Atlantic Seaboard* has been a tendency to discourage distribution companies from installing storage capacity: demand and commodity charges more fully reflecting the true respective marginal costs of peak and off-peak purchases would have increased their incentive to "shave" their purchases of the former by installing storage, which they could fill by low-cost purchases off-peak and draw on at the peak.[71]

In practice, the commission has not "slavishly followed Atlantic Seaboard but has made adjustments in individual cases in the area of rate design in order to achieve a reasonable and just result. While this procedure may not satisfy the rate purists, it does serve to treat the pertinent economic factors involved."[72] Such adjustments, known as "tilts," were made at first because competition required them — commodity rates were kept below their theoretical, *Seaboard* level so that interruptible gas sales were competitive with other fuels (particularly coal), thereby improving a system's load factor and lowering costs to firm users.[73] In the 1970s, due to the critical natural gas supply situation, the commission established the *United* formula, under which 75 percent of the fixed costs are assigned to the commodity charge and only 25 percent to the demand charge, thereby making natural gas more expensive to those customers (*i.e.,* interruptible customers) who usually have alternative fuel burning equipment.[74] In the mid-1980s, due to changes in market and gas supply conditions, the commission adopted a modified fixed-variable (MFV) approach, under which the allocation of fixed costs to the commodity charge is decreased, thereby making it "more responsive to competitive markets."[75]

Rate Structures. The goal of the cost allocation formula is to determine the relative levels of commodity and demand charges to be fixed in each zone. In turn: "The objective of rate design is to determine rates that enable the pipeline to sell its gas at charges which recover from the various types of loads their reasonably associated costs of service, keeping in mind the factors pertinent in this regard."[76] What are the factors to be considered? They include:

> ... the magnitude of the different classes of sales; load factors and load patterns of the pipeline and its customers; the kind of service rendered, i.e., firm or interruptible, peak or off-peak, seasonal or annual, etc.; the comparative prices of competing fuels in the market, and the ability of the company and its customers to make necessary competing sales of gas; and any minimum bill, penalty for unauthorized overruns, or other conditions of service contained in the tariff.[77]

The issues involved in rate design can best be illustrated by an example. Table 11-1 summarizes three sets of rates proposed for the Michigan Wisconsin Pipe Line Company in a 1963 case: the rates filed by the company, the administrative law judge's rates, and rates reflecting costs classified in accordance with the *Seaboard* formula. The terms of the company's rate schedule are also summarized in a note to the table.[78] At the outset, it should be noted that the rates proposed by both Michigan Wisconsin and the law judge depart from the *Seaboard* formula: the company's rates would result in the demand charge producing demand revenues some 29 percent, and the law judge's rates some 13 percent, in excess of the costs resulting from the *Seaboard* formula's classification to demand.[79] Two customers of Michigan Wisconsin supported the company's rate schedule since it would produce a relatively low commodity charge which would facilitate their industrial sales. In contrast, Michigan Gas and Electric Company, a distributing company customer of Michigan Wisconsin, and several "coal interve-

TABLE 11-1

Proposed Rates: Michigan Wisconsin Pipe Line Company, 1963*

	Filed Rates *Of Mich. Wis.*	*Rates Approved* *By Examiner*	*Rates Reflecting* *Seaboard Classification*
ACQ-1 rate			
Demand	$3.50	$3.05	$2.65
Commodity	26 cents	27.85 cents	29.67 cents
Developmental rate	46 cents	45 cents	33 cents
OS-1	26 cents	30 cents	
SGS-1	46 cents		

*Terms: Michigan Wisconsin's contract year is the twelve months beginning each September 1. For service under the ACQ-1 schedule, the company and each customer agree on a maximum daily quantity (MDQ) for each year, which fixes the maximum volume of gas Michigan Wisconsin is obligated to deliver to the customer on any single day. These deliveries are subject to a schedule of monthly contract demands. During the four cold months, November through February, the buyer is entitled to demand 100 percent of his maximum daily quantity, but only 85 percent from March 1-March 15, and 75 percent for the other months of the year. The total volume of gas the customer is entitled to purchase during the contract year, called the annual contract quantity (ACQ), may be stated in terms of the permitted number of days' use of the maximum daily quantity. For example, during the contract year 1961-62, each customer was entitled to a total of 190 days' use of his maximum daily quantity. In 1960-61, each customer's ACQ was 185 days' use of the MDQ. A customer's purchases in excess of his MDQ on a particular day (daily overrun), or in excess of his ACQ in a particular year (annual overrun), if authorized by Michigan Wisconsin, are billed as overrun gas under the OS-1 schedule. If not authorized, a penalty is charged. The SGS-1 rate is a small general service rate.

Source: *Re American Louisiana Pipe Line Co.,* 48 PUR3d 321, 327, n. 13, n. 14 (FPC, 1963).

nors" (Fuels Research Council, Inc.; National Coal Association; United Mine Workers of America; Mid-West Coal Producers Institute, Inc.; Upper Lake Docks Coal Bureau, Inc.; and The Chesapeake and Ohio Railway Company) contended that the *Seaboard* formula rates should be adopted with no deviation, thereby favoring a relatively high commodity charge. Thus, the company's rates would be advantageous to industrial gas users; the rates determined by the *Seaboard* formula would be competitively advantageous to coal.

The commission upheld the law judge's decision, as illustrated in Table 11-2. The commission argued, in part:

TABLE 11-2

Approved Rates: Michigan Wisconsin Pipe Line Company, 1963

Rate Schedule ACQ-1:
$3.05 per month per Mcf of billing demand
27.85 cents per Mcf of gas delivered
13.75 cents per Mcf of released gas purchased
10 cents per Mcf demand charge adjustment for impaired delivery
Alternative rate during development period: 45 cents per Mcf of gas
delivered
Rate Schedule SGS-1:
For customers whose maximum daily quantity is 6,000 Mcf or less:
45 cents per Mcf of all gas delivered
10 cents per Mcf demand charge adjustment for impaired delivery
Rate Schedule OS-1:
30 cents per Mcf for all gas delivered

Source: *Re American Louisiana Pipe Line Co.,* 48 PUR3d 321, 342 (FPC, 1963).

... the evidence of Michigan Wisconsin and some of the distributing companies supports some deviation to demand, for the resulting lower commodity rate will facilitate industrial sales by the customer companies that would benefit Michigan Wisconsin, the customer companies, and the public. ... However, in our view, a deviation to demand as large as the 29 percent deviation proposed under the filed rate, and the resulting shift of a greater share of costs onto the firm gas users (principally domestic consumers), is not supported by evidence of offsetting benefits to the final status of the distributing companies, the firm gas users, or the pipeline sufficient to justify such a request. Moreover, the Iowa utilities did not convincingly show that the examiner's rate would in fact harm their operations by causing a loss of present industrial sales. On balance, therefore, we conclude that the examiner's ACQ-1 rate with its some 13 percent deviation to demand represents a reasonable accommodation of the conflicting interests presented by this record.[80]

The foregoing discussion emphasizes once more that the allocation of costs "is not a matter for the slide rule" and "has no claim to an exact science," but "involves judgement on a myriad of facts."[81]

"Incremental Pricing." The Natural Gas Policy Act (NGPA) of 1978 mandated "incremental pricing." The FERC was required to establish by rulemaking a procedure under which certain large industrial interstate users (primarily boiler fuel users[82]) would bear the initial burden of increases in natural gas prices. Once the price paid for natural gas by large industrial users reached the price of alternative fuels (subsequently determined to be high-sulfur No. 6 fuel oil), higher natural gas prices would then be passed on to all users. The FERC implemented Phase I incremental pricing in 1979,[83] but its Phase II rule (extending incremental pricing to "other" industrial facilities[84]), was rejected by the House in 1980.[85]

Project Incremental Pricing. In an attempt to offset the shortages from traditional supply sources that occurred in the 1970s, some pipeline companies embarked on such projects as imported liquefied natural gas (LNG) and coal gasification. Gas from these supplemental projects generally is more expensive than the price paid for gas from conventional sources. Should pipelines sell the more expensive gas under a separate tariff (project incremental pricing) instead of averaging the cost of the new gas with the cost of existing supplies (rolled-in pricing)?

In a 1972 decision, the FPC mandated incremental pricing for the Columbia LNG project[86] and, in 1977, for the Trunkline LNG project.[87] In both instances, however, the incremental pricing conditions were later removed — in the first, because the LNG was required to maintain high-priority markets[88]; in the second, because the project was not financially feasible with the condition.[89] In subsequent decisions, the commission has not required incremental pricing for any supplemental fuel project.[90]

Special Marketing Programs. As the natural gas shortage of the 1970s turned into a surplus in the early 1980s, the statutory maximum price for new gas under the NGPA reached or exceeded the market clearing price in many geographic markets. Several pipelines sought regulatory approval for special marketing programs. In exchange for being released from "take-or-pay" and minimum daily purchase levels, pipelines would transport "released" gas sold directly by a producer or producers to end users (generally industrial users with alternative sources of fuel).[91] The programs were challenged, largely on the ground that they excluded core or captive customers (such as firm residential customers). Even though the original FERC orders were no longer in effect, a circuit court (in 1985) held that the orders were "invalid," since the commission failed to articulate its rationale for special marketing programs that helped "those who do not need the commission's protection while hurting those who do."[92]

The Resale Rate

Gas resale or distribution rates are similar to, but less complicated than, electric rates.[93] In the late nineteenth and early twentieth centuries, when natural gas was plentiful, cheap, and transported short distances, flat or uniform rates were the rule. Block rates became predominant in the 1920s, as the industry began to feel the competitive pressure from electric service.[94]

TABLE 11-3

Percentage of Gas Customers, Sales,
and Revenues by Customer Classes, 1986

Classification	Percentage of Customers	Percentage of Sales	Percentage of Revenues
Residential	91.9	39.4	48.3
Commercial	7.7	20.1	22.0
Industrial	.3	39.0	28.3
Other	.1	1.5	1.4
Total	100.0	100.0	100.0

Source: *Gas Facts, 1986 Data* (Arlington, Va.: American Gas Association, 1987), p. 2.

Customers were divided into three major classes (residential, commercial, and industrial, as shown in Table 11-3), and different rates were established for each class, partly based upon cost considerations,[95] but also based on differences in the elasticities of demand. Other gas distributors established a "general service rate" schedule that was applicable to all or many classes of firm service. Such schedules usually provided for monthly minimum charges and contained fuel adjustment clauses. Space heating fell into the last blocks, thereby making the service more competitive with other fuels. The following general service rate schedule is illustrative:[96]

First	2 Mcf or less per month	$2.06
Next	6 Mcf per month	40.0¢ per Mcf
Next	6 Mcf per month	26.5¢ per Mcf
Next	40 Mcf per month	23.4¢ per Mcf
Next	246 Mcf per month	19.4¢ per Mcf
Excess of 300 Mcf per month		16.3¢ per Mcf

Minimum charge: $2.06 per meter per month, exclusive of gas adjustment.

Still other gas distributors offered special, promotional space heating rates. Finally, gas distributors commonly had more complex rate structures for industrial customers (structures which sometimes took into account a customer's demand and load factor, as well as gas energy used), and one or more seasonal, off-peak, and interruptible rate schedules. The latter rate structures were designed to help even out the industry's annual load curve, which generally exhibits a winter (heating) peak.

Marginal Cost Pricing and Recent Trends. In the early 1970s, the nation's natural gas supplies began to decline and curtailments were common. Many urged the adoption of marginal cost pricing for gas distribution utilities. Typical is a 1980 report to Congress on gas rate design by the Department of Energy.[97] DOE contended that marginal cost pricing (referred to in the report as "economic cost rates") would promote three purposes: (*1*) end-use conservation (promoted because "the commodity charge for gas usage 'on the margin' reflects the cost of supplying additional gas"); (*2*) efficient use of utility resources (promoted because "the utility will be encouraged to make sensible decisions of its own regarding the need for supplemental gas supplies and expensive imports"); and (*3*) equitable rates (promoted because utilities will "charge all customer classes on the basis of the national consequences of customer usage decisions").[98] To achieve economic cost rates, state regulatory commissions could order that

> . . . distribution company rates reflect the price of alternative fuels or, if lower, the cost of new incremental supplies of gas which are not price regulated. Use of such rates for all customers may lead to revenue collection problems for a distribution company, however. In general, rates based on alternative fuel prices will exceed the city gate price a distribution company pays for gas. . . .
>
> Where excess revenues would result, one way to meet the revenue requirement would be to reduce or eliminate any customer charges. If customer charge reductions did not eliminate the excess revenues, the rate for initial blocks of usage could be reduced for some or all customer classes. In such an inverted rate structure, two different rates are charged for gas, a low rate for a base (and relatively inelastic) level of consumption and a high rate for all consumption above the base level. The low rate, called the initial block rate, is set at a level which will provide revenues consistent with the revenue requirement when the high tailblock rate reflects economic costs.
>
> In the event that inadequate revenues would be obtained from economic cost rates, fixed charges can be employed. Such fixed charges might be in the form of a customer charge which would allow a distribution company to just meet its revenue requirement. Alternatively a demand charge reflecting the costs of expanding storage, or peaking supplies, or the capacity to deliver gas could be used for this purpose.[99]

The most significant trend in gas resale rate design has been a consistent movement away from declining block rates, and the development of flat commodity (energy) rates within each customer class.[100] The flat commodity rate, however, has not been determined on a uniform basis: sometimes it has been based upon a customer classes' alternative fuel and sometimes upon the distribution company's current or future cost of gas supply. Gas rate schedules have been consolidated[101]; and some special promotional rates have been eliminated. A few commissions have gone further. Wisconsin, to illustrate, has adopted inverted, benchmark, and seasonal rates, as well as flat rates. Thus, the following inverted rate structure for residential customers served by Madison Gas and Electric Company was in effect in 1981:

Fixed Charge, per month $3.00
    First 150 Therms per month .... .44128¢ per Therm
    Over 150 Therms per month .... .48128¢ per Therm

A benchmark rate for large (over 75,000 therms in 1977) firm commercial and industrial customers of Wisconsin Power and Light Company was authorized in 1978. Under this rate:

Fixed Charge, per month $2.00
Commodity Charge, per month: *the greater of*
    (1) all consumption at 22.2¢ per Therm
       or
    (2) benchmark[a] use at 26.25¢ per Therm, with
       (a) consumption over benchmark at +30.00¢ per Therm
       (b) consumption under benchmark at −30.00¢ per Therm

[a]Each customer's current monthly use is compared to the customer's benchmark, computed as the average use during the same month in the three-year period 1976 through 1978.

In the case of the inverted rate structure, the tailblock rate was based upon "the customer's lowest cost alternative; *i.e.,* the sum of his marginal opportunity cost plus the distribution utility's cost of providing service to him."[102] In the case of the benchmark rate structure, the higher block rate was based upon "the average delivered cost on an equivalent per therm basis for No. 2 fuel oil as available to large commercial and industrial customers."[103]

Finally, the Wisconsin commission also adopted seasonal rate structures, consisting of flat winter and summer rates, with a differential of approximately four cents per therm. The higher winter rate, in effect for five or six months, was designed to reflect the greater costs incurred by a distribution utility in supplying the winter peak and to provide an incentive for conservation.[104]

As with electric rates, marginal cost pricing for natural gas is not without its practical problems or critics.[105] Two issues are of particular importance with respect to resale rates. First, if tailblock rates are linked to the price of alternative fuel, and that fuel is oil, natural gas prices may be influenced by OPEC decisions and not by the free market. Further, if tailblock rates are raised to such a level, as under "incremental pricing," customers (especially large users) may switch to oil, thereby forcing other customers to pay higher rates to cover a larger percentage of a utility's fixed costs. The issue is further complicated by the fact that the natural gas shortage turned around in the early 1980s, as gas utilities (both pipelines and distribution utilities) had more than sufficient gas to serve both present and prospective customers. Second, city gate rates tend to reflect rolled-in pricing and the relevant "avoidable cost" to a distribution utility is the price that it must pay to its pipeline supplier(s). In the words of the New York commission:

> . . . the companies subject to our regulation are mainly distributors who simply receive gas in New York from one or more interstate pipeline companies who, in turn, may be purchasing gas from various producers. In these circumstances, the relevant commodity costs for this Commission to consider are those which the companies under our jurisdiction pay their suppliers, for it is those costs that might be saved by gas consumption changes by New York's consumers.[106]

Flexible Rates and Transportation Service. Since the early 1980s, due to basic changes in the industry's environment (*i.e.,* the development of a natural gas surplus, volatile prices of alternate fuels, the growth of a "spot" market,[107] and the efforts of the FERC to promote an open access transportation policy in the interstate market[108]), local distribution utilities have been confronted with a number of policy issues, often involving pricing. Competition from industrial customers (mainly interruptible sales) with dual fuel capability has resulted in "flexible" rates in several states. To prevent the loss of large industrial sales, distributors have been permitted to negotiate contracts with such customers, subject only to an established price floor (generally based on the distributor's cost of gas or weighted cost of gas, but sometimes also including related taxes and a contribution to nongas service costs). Further, any revenues received above the floor, known as the "margin," are shared between the utility and its other customers on a predetermined basis. A typical justification for flexible rates is provided by the Virginia commission:

> . . . We are confident that a flexible rate is required in order for the company to remain in the competitive market of interruptible customers. . . . If the company were to lose its entire interruptible load, there would be an automatic shifting of significant non-gas costs to all firm customers. Hence, the economic viability of the company hinges upon its ability to generate revenues from interruptible customers, and to do so it must have a flexible pricing structure to compete in that market.[109]

Competition for gas supply has raised the issue of intrastate transportation services and rates. Specifically, should intrastate pipelines and local distribution utilities be required to transport gas for large end users (gas acquired directly from producers) and, if so, how should transportation rates be determined? The trend is to require mandatory transportation "to the extent there is available capacity."[110] There is little agreement, however, on transportation rates. Some commissions have adopted "margin-based" rates, with the margin "typically calculated as the customer's general service rate less the cost of the distributor's system supply."[111] Others have adopted (or stated a preference for) cost-of-service rates, frequently based on an embedded cost approach.[112] A few commissions have even permitted flexible transportation rates[113] and a "standby service" rate (for customers who elect to purchase their own supplies).[114]

Rate Structures in Practice: Telephone Rates[115]

In discussing domestic telephone rates,[116] a distinction must be made between local exchange service, toll service (MTS), and bulk communications services (WATS). Special services and equipment are charged for independently of the basic telephone service.

Local Exchange Service

The basic unit for the application of local rates is an exchange — a unit which usually embraces a city, town, or village, and its environs. Telephone rates vary widely among states and localities.[117] One of the most important reasons for rate variations among localities is the number of telephones in the exchange that can be called without a toll charge. The Bell System, for example, established a number of rate groups (commonly eight, although there has been a trend toward a smaller number) in each state, ranging in size from the smallest village and surrounding rural area to the largest city. The rates in the smallest exchanges may vary up to 45 percent of those in the largest. The types of service offered also vary to some extent according to the size of an exchange.

Flat Rate Service. Historically, with the exception of a few of the largest cities where message rate service is common, most local exchange service is offered at a flat rate. Subscribers are divided into two broad categories — business and residential. An example of a flat rate schedule for a city of 100,001 to 300,000 telephones is the following:

Business:
    One-party service .... $26.50 per main telephone per month
    Two-party service .... 20.55 per main telephone per month

Residential:
    One-party service .... $ 9.30 per main telephone per month
    Two-party service .... 7.60 per main telephone per month

Such rates are differentiated on the basis of elasticities of demand. Business subscribers are charged higher rates than are residential users. Since they have higher calling rates, and since a greater portion of their calls are concentrated during peak periods, on average, than residential subscribers, commercial subscribers tend to be more expensive customers. The value of service, moreover, is greater for business users. Differentiation is based also upon the number of subscribers on each line. One-party subscribers are charged more because the cost of serving them is greater and because they are willing to pay for added convenience. Conversely, multiple-party subscribers are charged less because the value of their service (privacy) and its costs are lower. Low rates are needed to encourage the widest possible use of the service,[118] since the more widely the service is used, the more valuable it is to all subscribers.

It has long been argued that flat rates do not economize the use of telephone plant:

1. Flat rates encourage economic waste. Patrons make unnecessary calls for which equipment and facilities must be provided. This increases the cost of service.
2. The high uniform rate prevents the expansion of service to marginal patrons who would be willing to take limited service on a cost basis.
3. The flat rate is inequitable between customers.
4. The flat rate produces a high peak load that might be avoided in part by measured, off-peak rates.
5. By encouraging calls that are both unduly numerous and unduly long, cheap multiple-party line service is made undesirable.[119]

These criticisms of flat rates have validity and there is a trend toward measured rate service. The historic use of flat rates is due to several important advantages. Flat rates encourage customers to use the service more freely, thus enhancing the value of telephone service to all. They help to build up habits of telephone use which further the steady growth of the business and the continuous widening of its field of usefulness. Subscribers generally prefer flat rates because of this freedom of use and the ability to know in advance the amount of their monthly local bills. Flat rates also are simpler for the subscriber to understand and for the telephone companies to operate and administer, thereby avoiding possible disputes as to local charges.

Further, some question that a more efficient use of plant could be gained by eliminating residential flat rates and substituting message rates or that such a change would result in large cost savings. While the costs of handling calls would be reduced, the costs of metering would be added and subscribers might well curtail their usage. Since a large portion of the costs of furnishing telephone service is independent of message use, the total savings would be less than proportionate to the reduction of usage.

Message Rate Service. In addition to flat rate service, message or measured rates[120] commonly are offered to business subscribers and, in many states, to residential subscribers.[121] A wider spread of telephone charges is sought, since a high proportion of business users have very large and specialized communications requirements, while the larger residential markets cover a wider range of income groups than that found in most small communities. The use of message rate service permits the telephone companies to offer a lower rate service to those who do not wish to pay for unlimited service. (In a limited number of cities, local calls are timed.) The following, for the same exchange as in the preceding example, is an illustrative message rate schedule:

Business:
   One-party service . . . $10.05 per main telephone per month (a)
   Two-party service . . . not offered
Residential:
   Option #1
       One-party service . . . $5.60 per main telephone per month (a)
       Two-party service . . . not offered
   Option #2
       One-party service . . . $3.85 per main telephone per month (b)
       Two-party service . . . not offered

(a) Monthly message charge — first 50 messages, no message charge; balance, each at 9¢.
(b) Monthly message charge — all messages, each at 9¢.

The boundary of an exchange's local calling area is a matter of judgment based on local conditions. If the local calling area is too large, local rates may be too high to promote maximum development. Conversely, if the area is too small, normal use of the service may be curtailed, and local service will have less value. Moreover, a desirable local calling area once established is not regarded as static. Especially is this true around the larger cities where conditions tend to change rapidly. Local calling area boundaries, therefore, are changed from time to time, thereby changing traffic over certain routes from toll to local. (An option is to zone a primary calling area. In New York City, for example, a subscriber's call within a zone is not timed, but a call outside a zone uses multi-message units which are timed.) Frequently, to meet varying customer requirements, optional services with different initial calling areas are offered. In many metropolitan service areas, finally, extended area service is offered, whereby a subscriber's service extends beyond an exchange or zone at higher exchange rates rather than at toll rates.

The regulatory commissions have been subjected to pressure to provide special telephone rates for low-income customers. In response, particularly in the early 1970s, a number of telephone companies established "economy" "low-usage," "Basic Budget," or "Lifeline" services, all of the message rate variety. In California, to illustrate, "Lifeline" service was initiated at $2.50 per month with a thirty message unit allowance and with additional message units billed at five cents each. In New York metropolitan areas, "Basic Budget" service was initiated at $4.03 per month, plus a charge of 8.2 cents for each outgoing call.[122]

Public Telephone Service.[123] Telephone companies furnish public telephone service for the use of the transient public. Facilities are provided at the telephone company's option at locations selected as most suitable and convenient for public use. For facilities equipped with coin boxes, a uniform price — ranging from ten to twenty-five cents per local call — is charged. At busy locations (large airports, military installations) an attendant may be provided to assist in making connections and to collect the charges for calls and/or coinless telephones may be provided for long-distance credit card calls.

Semipublic service is provided and used mainly at locations where there is some transient use (restaurants, gas stations), but not enough to justify public telephone service. Users of the semipublic service pay the same price per call as public users. In some states, the subscriber to the service guarantees a monthly minimum income to the telephone company. The amounts deposited by the public apply toward the guarantee and may substantially reduce the amounts which the subscribers must pay.

PBX Service. When private-branch exchanges (PBX service) are provided for hotels and motels, large companies, office buildings, and other institutions, telephone companies normally charge for each trunk from the switchboard to the central office. In addition, unless equipment is owned by the customer, there are monthly rental charges for the PBX switchboard and the telephones on the customers' premises connected to the switchboard.[124]

Special Charges. Telephone companies have long furnished many extras or auxiliary services at separate installations and monthly rental rates for those willing to pay for them. These include extension bells, buzzer circuits, longer desk cords, extension telephones, night-lights, and special telephone sets (the "Princess" or the "Ericofon"). Now that customers may own their own terminal equipment, separate monthly rates have been established for those leasing telephone stations (commonly $1.00 to $1.25 per month).[125] Formerly flat charges for service connections (installations) are now broken down into several elements, with charges varying with the amount of work required.[126] In recent years, it has become common to impose charges for directory assistance (ranging from ten to twenty-five cents per call), although most companies provide some free calls (ranging from three to ten, with unlimited calls for disabled or handicapped subscribers) per month.[127] Finally, separate — and unregulated — rates are charged for advertising in the Yellow Pages.[128]

Toll Rates

Message toll service (MTS) or long-distance message toll rates vary according to (*1*) distance, (*2*) whether the call is dialed directly or is operator assisted, (*3*) time-of-day, and (*4*) length of conversation (holding time).[129] In general, these rates are differentiated due to the costs involved, the value of service, and simplicity and ease of understanding.

Generally, as the distance of the toll call increases, costs per unit rise because of the greater length of circuits and the additional facilities required to secure satisfactory transmission. The costs per mile, however, do not vary directly with increasing distance, since terminal costs become relatively less important in the total cost of any particular call. Consequently, toll charges increase with distance, but at a decreasing rate.[130] Further, long-haul calls tend, on average, to have greater value to customers, since alternative means of communication involve greater expenditures of time or money, or both.

Toll charges are lower on calls dialed directly than on operator assisted calls. Operator assisted service charges, in turn, vary according to the amount of time involved by the operator: rates rise in three categories — credit card, station-to-station, and person-to-person. Overtime charges on operator assisted calls are not generally the same as the overtime charges on direct distance dialed messages.

Toll rates depend on the time of day. Three rate periods are common for such calls: day, evening, and night and weekend (Table 11-4). The aim is to offer users an incentive to increase or shift their calls without burdening the business as a whole by building up traffic in off-peak hours, thus gaining a better twenty-four-hour utilization of telephone plant.

Finally, toll rates vary with the length of the conversation. Lower initial period rates are thereby made possible and the service is further developed. Moreover, it is the customer who decides how long a conversation is worth the charge. Conversations are not needlessly prolonged, tying up expensive toll circuits and unnecessarily increasing toll costs. Yet, the customer is able to use the service as long as the additional conversation time has real value. Lower initial period rates thus are made practicable by both the overtime revenues derived from the longer conversations and the economical use of the circuit.

The interstate message toll rate schedule (as of mid-1982) is shown in Table 11-4.

Local versus Statewide Exchange and Toll Rates. While each exchange is a distinct unit for rate-quoting purposes, the Bell System companies have generally established rates on a statewide basis. Essentially, the statewide basis provides that the total costs of furnishing telephone service and the resulting revenue requirements are considered for the state as a unit. This

TABLE 11-4

Interstate Message Toll Rates
United States Mainland, 1982

DIRECT DIAL (DAY RATES)

Mileage Band	One Minute Initial Period	One Minute Additional Period
1-10	$.32	$.16
11-22	.40	.22
23-55	.48	.28
56-124	.57	.37
125-292	.58	.39
293-430	.59	.42
431-925	.62	.43
926-1910	.64	.44
1911-3000	.74	.49

RATE APPLICATION PERIODS

	MON.	*TUES.*	*WED.*	*THURS.*	*FRI.*	*SAT.*	*SUN.*
8 A.M. TO 5 P.M.	DAY RATE PERIODS FULL RATE						
5 P.M. TO 11 P.M.	EVENING RATE PERIOD 40% DISCOUNT						EVE. 40%
11 P.M. TO 8 A.M.	NIGHT & WEEKEND RATE PERIOD 60% DISCOUNT						

OPERATOR-ASSISTED SERVICE CHARGES

Mileage Band	Credit Card	Station To Station	Person To Person
1-10	$ .60	$ .75	$3.00
11-22	.80	1.10	3.00
23-3000	1.05	1.55	3.00

Notes:

—Operator-assisted service charges are in addition to the direct dial initial period.

—Operator-assisted service charges do not receive discounts for time-of-day.

Source: American Telephone and Telegraph Company (May, 1982).

practice recognizes that telephone service, both exchange and toll, furnished by a given company throughout a state is, in reality, an integrated whole, all portions of which are interdependent. The objective is to apply throughout the state a well-balanced and coordinated pattern of rate treatment, providing rates which are uniform under substantially like conditions and producing, in the aggregate, reasonable earnings on the company's total telephone operations within the state.

The statewide basis has five important advantages over consideration of individual exchanges. First, the statewide basis permits more people to have better service at a reasonable price. Some small areas, if forced to pay their own way, might have no service at all. Needed plant replacements or additions might be postponed if local customers had to cover their full costs, resulting in deterioration of local service within the exchange and of toll service to and from it. Second, on the statewide basis, customers pay like charges for like amounts of service. If each exchange had to stand on its own feet, customers' charges would vary with physical characteristics of the exchange area, age of plant, type of equipment, and other factors affecting costs, but not necessarily affecting the service rendered. The statewide basis averages out such factors.

Third, customers seem better satisfied with statewide rates, because the application of uniform schedules avoids any question of discrimination or unfair advantage to pressure groups in individual exchanges. Fourth, the statewide basis tends to stabilize rate levels by providing a broad rate base. Risks are spread so that a community suffering from flood, storm, or other natural disaster or from some local economic difficulty (*e.g.*, the removal of a major industry) need not pay higher telephone rates such as would be required if telephone operations in that exchange had to meet these conditions single-handedly. Finally, the statewide basis is more workable and makes the regulatory process less cumbersome and expensive to both the public and the company involved. It avoids multiplicity of rate cases for each individual exchange. It simplifies handling of questions and complaints by the regulatory commissions and administration by the companies.

At the same time, it should be pointed out that the statewide basis results in some subscribers subsidizing other subscribers. Because exchange telephone service is more valuable to customers in the larger local service areas, they are willing to pay more for their service. Since their average cash incomes are greater, they are able to pay more. Lower rates in the small towns and rural areas, where average money incomes are relatively low, encourage telephone use and development in these places. Once again, this is an example of how rate discrimination is used to achieve a socially desirable objective, in this case the widespread development of telephone usage throughout the country.

Nationwide Averaging — Interstate Toll Rates. For many years, nationwide averaging has been used in establishing interstate toll rates, under which toll rates are the same for equal distances throughout the continental

United States, despite differences in the costs involved. Such a rate structure has all of the advantages discussed above with respect to statewide rates, but results in internal subsidization. High-density routes, for example, subsidize low-density routes. Such a rate structure also invites selective entry (usually referred to as "cream-skimming") into high-density, low-cost markets.[131] Thus, MCI, Southern Pacific, and others who have been permitted to enter into the telecommunications industry, generally wish to serve such markets. In turn, if AT&T is to compete with such entrants, it may be forced to sacrifice geographical rate uniformity, as the FCC has recognized,[132] which would tend to raise rates in low-density, high-cost markets.

There is a related issue — the relevant measure of cost for use in pricing telephone services. As competitive entry began to occur in selective markets, the commission was forced to struggle with the development of ratemaking principles for individual services. Many economists, in particular, took the position that if cross-subsidization of one service by another is to be prevented, and if competition is to be encouraged, the relevant measure of cost must be marginal (incremental), not fully allocated (or fully distributed). Johnson has contended, for example, that the fully allocated cost criterion is incompatible with liberalized freedom of entry:

> The mere fact that a new entrant's rates for a particular route or for a particular service are lower than those of the established carrier does not indicate that the new entrant's costs are necessarily lower than the existing carrier's long-run incremental costs for comparable service. In order to discourage uneconomic entry, it is essential to permit the carriers to respond by adjusting their rates toward their own incremental costs. Existing rates must not be frozen to provide an umbrella protecting uneconomic competitive activity.[133]

Nevertheless, throughout the 1970s, the commission adopted a fully distributed cost approach[134] and, in 1981, it adopted an "interim" fully distributed cost manual.[135]

Bulk Communications Services

In addition to local exchange and toll services, telephone companies offer several services to customers with heavy (bulk) communications needs. Many of these service offerings have been highly controversial, since they have been viewed by actual or potential competitors as discriminatory and predatory pricing schemes. Further, these service offerings show the difficulties of a regulated industry moving into a competitive environment and of a commission struggling to develop proper ratemaking principles. Three AT&T offerings are illustrative: TELPAK, MPL (Multi-Schedule Private Line), and WATS (Wide Area Telephone Service).

TELPAK. AT&T filed its TELPAK tariff in 1961. TELPAK made available packages of channels in various band widths which could be used between specific locations to carry both voice and nonvoice communications. Facilities were furnished on a seven-day per week, twenty-four hour per day basis only, with a minimum subscription period of one month. The TELPAK rate structure, as originally filed, was composed of two elements: a monthly charge per airline mile for designated maximum capacities and a monthly rate per terminal for individual activated channels up to the maximum capacity.[136]

The TELPAK tariff was challenged by Western Union (a supplier of private-line services) and Motorola (a microwave equipment manufacturer). In December 1964, the commission held that: (*a*) the tariff was discriminatory, since TELPAK lines were indistinguishable from ordinary private lines purchased one at a time, (*b*) TELPAK A and B were not justified by competitive necessity, and (*c*) while TELPAK C and D were justified by competitive necessity, additional cost information was required.[137] (The interim TELPAK rate structure is shown in Table 11-5.) Twelve years later, the commission held that TELPAK C and D were noncost justified and ordered the tariffs withdrawn by June, 1977.[138] But several users petitioned for reconsideration and the commission subsequently rescinded its order to withdraw

TABLE 11-5

Interim TELPAK Rate Structure

A. TELPAK CHANNELS AND CHARGES

Classification	Carrier Spectrum Assignment (Kilocycles per Second)	Maximum Equivalent Telephone Grade Channels	Monthly Charge per Airline Mile
TELPAK C	240	60	$28
TELPAK D	1000 (approximate)	240	60

B. TERMINAL EQUIPMENT CHARGES

	First Station Exchange		Each Additional Station in Exchange	
	A Installation Charge	B Monthly Charge	C Installation Charge	D Monthly Charge
Telephone	$20	$ 25	$20	$10
Teletypewriter	20	25	20	10
Telephotograph	20	100	20	15
Data	20-200	25-625	20-200	20-375

Source: American Telephone and Telegraph Company (August, 1968).

TELPAK and ordered new hearings.[139] The tariffs were voluntarily canceled in June, 1977, by AT&T, after the commission ruled (in a separate proceeding) that the restrictions imposed by AT&T on the resale of shared use of its services were illegal.[140] But TELPAK users (including the federal government) obtained an appeals court order maintaining TELPAK in effect for existing customers while litigation continued.[141]

MPL. In November, 1973, AT&T filed a new tariff for private-line voice service. Under the so-called "High/Low Tariff," the country was divided into regions of high-density lines and low-density lines. For lines between high-density centers, the rate was eighty-five cents per mile; for lines between low-density centers or between a high-density center and a low-density center, the rate was $2.50 per mile. After receiving complaints from competitors, the commission found the tariff noncost justified in 1976, but permitted it to remain in effect pending AT&T's filing of replacement rates.[142]

The replacement rates were known as the MPL tariff. Like the previous tariff, it divided the country into centers served by low-capacity facilities and by high-capacity facilities, with lower rates for the high-capacity areas. But in place of the previous flat rate per mile (for the two density centers), the MPL tariff contained a decreasing charge per mile with increases in the line distance.

This tariff, also opposed by specialized carriers, went into effect in August, 1976 (after a three-month suspension). The commission's investigation into its lawfulness continued and, in September, 1979, the FCC concluded that "the MPL rates are unjust and unreasonable and that the support material is unreliable and the Phase I record does not support a prescription of rates."[143] However, the MPL tariff was permitted to remain in effect, pending the outcome of a new inquiry into the general structure of AT&T's private-line tariffs.

WATS. Under the original WATS offering, filed by AT&T in 1961, subscribers could purchase flat rate service (a customer could call six progressively larger interstate zones in the continental United States and Alaska for a flat monthly rate, and could call as often and talk as long as desired within the zone) or measured service (fifteen hours of conversation per month, with additional use charged by the hour). (See Table 11-6.) Subscribers also could transmit record messages by utilizing data-phone subsets and teletypewriter machines for which a rental fee was charged.[144]

The WATS tariff, like those for TELPAK and MPL, has been subject to continuous scrutiny before the FCC. However, unlike TELPAK, the basic issue did not concern predatory pricing, since both MTS and WATS earned over 10 percent on capital utilized (compared with a return of 0.3 percent for TELPAK).[145] The real issues have been discrimination[146] and cost methodology, with the result that AT&T was unable to develop a legal WATS tariff in the 1970s.[147] Said FCC Commissioner Washburn in 1976:

TABLE 11-6

WATS Rate Schedule: Illinois-North

		Measured Time	
	Full Time	*First 15 Hours*	*Each Additional Hour*
Intrastate	$ 575	$140	$10.50
Interstate			
Zone 1	700	180	14.00
Zone 2	900	180	16.50
Zone 3	1,200	250	19.50
Zone 4	1,400	270	21.50
Zone 5	1,500	280	22.00
Zone 6	1,950	335	25.50

Source: American Telephone and Telegraph Company (August, 1968).

In today's action, we have found the last four WATS tariffs filed by AT&T to be unlawful. Some of these tariffs have been in effect for over three years. . . . The result is a series of Bell tariffs, all of which the Commission finds unlawful but which customers must pay. Refunds cannot be made, despite the accounting order, because we have no legal tariff with which to compare and compute any overcharges. The Commission, therefore, has essentially lost control over the rates Bell charges customers.[148]

And a court of appeals expressed a similar view, concluding that the FCC's inability to determine the lawfulness of rates within a reasonable time suggests that the commission "verges on losing its ability to effectively regulate at all."[149]

Since its original WATS tariff, AT&T has made substantial modifications. An illustrative interstate WATS schedule is shown in Table 11-7. A subscriber pays a monthly access line charge and a monthly usage rate based on hours of use, with set prices within three time periods.[150] Thus, the WATS tariff is a multi-element one.

The Future: Some Current Trends

The 1982 Modification of Final Judgment provided for the designation of "LATAs" (Local Access and Transport Areas).[151] Intra-LATA service is provided by regulated telephone companies and (in many states) by resellers.[152]

TABLE 11-7

Interstate WATS Rate Schedule: Maryland—Service Area 5*

(A) Access Line Charge
$30.40 per access line per month
(B) Monthly Usage Rate (per hour of use per access line)

	Business Day	Evening	Night/Weekend
First 15 Hours	$22.00	$14.30	$7.65
Next 25 Hours	19.57	12.72	7.65
Next 40 Hours	17.16	11.15	7.65
Over 80 Hours	14.51	9.43	7.65

---

*Continental United States.
Source: American Telephone and Telephone Company (July, 1981).

Federal and state (where applicable) access or subscriber line charges have been established,[153] so that inter-LATA service (the service commonly known as long distance or message toll service) can be provided by competitive interexchange carriers. Since competition is inconsistent with the maintenance of internal subsidies (particularly through the separations process), the latter are gradually disappearing. Both intra- and interexchange services are certain to be more cost-based, and services (*e.g.*, installation, inside wiring[154]) are being "unbundled." The FCC's *Computer II* and *III* decisions, along with the Modification of Final Judgment, contemplate active competition in the terminal equipment market, with customers owning their own terminal equipment and being responsible for its maintenance.

While policy is still being developed, several comments and trends are noteworthy. First, at the federal level: (*1*) The FCC has ordered six reductions in AT&T's basic long-distance rates, totaling approximately 36 percent, since divestiture.[155] (*2*) The FCC has established a policy or guidelines with respect to long-distance discount plans (*e.g.*, AT&T's "Reach Out" America plan).[156] (*3*) In August of 1987, the FCC issued a Notice of Proposed Rule Making to obtain comments on a new regulatory system for AT&T; namely, to replace the traditional rate base/rate of return procedure with regulation by price caps.[157] Second, at the state level: (*1*) Local exchange rates have increased (by 20 percent according to one source[158]) and lifeline rates have been introduced across the country.[159] (*2*) Most states with more than one LATA (there are twelve single-LATA states) have authorized intra-state, inter-LATA competition. Where intra-LATA competition is permitted, various degrees of pricing flexibility have been granted to both carriers and resellers.[160] (*3*) Where permitted by statute, some services have been deregulated.[161]

Notes

*Alfred E. Kahn, *The Economics of Regulation* (New York: John Wiley & Sons, Inc., 1970), Vol. I, p. 65.

[1]Natural gas usually is gathered from various wellheads in a network of field pipes, processed to extract valuable byproducts (liquid hydrocarbons) and to remove impurities (sulfur compounds, nitrogen, and water, among others), and delivered to pipelines. Many of the field and gathering lines that transport gas from individual wells to compressor stations, processing points, or main-line transmission systems are owned and operated by the producer whose gas is transported. A few are owned by long-distance pipeline companies or by independent organizations, and some gathering systems have been developed jointly by pipelines and individual producers.

[2]*Phillips Petroleum Co. v. Wisconsin*, 347 U.S. 672 (1954).

[3]See, *e.g.*, *Re Columbian Fuel Corp.*, 2 FPC 200 (1940). But the commission did note: "Further experience with the administration of the Natural Gas Act may reveal that the initial sales of large quantities of natural gas which eventually flow in interstate commerce are by producing or gathering companies which, through affiliation, field agreement, or dominant position in a field, are able to maintain an unreasonable price despite the appearance of competition. Under such circumstances the Commission will decide whether it can assume jurisdiction over arbitrary field prices under the present act or should report the facts to Congress with recommendations for such broadening of the Act and provision of additional machinery as may appear necessary to close this gap in effective regulation of the natural gas industry." *Ibid.*, p. 208.

[4]See *Re Canadian River Gas Co.*, 43 PUR (NS) 205 (1942); *Cities of Cleveland and Akron v. Hope Natural Gas Co.*, 44 PUR (NS) 1 (1942); *Re Interstate Natural Gas Co.*, 48 PUR (NS) 267 (1943); *Re Cities Service Gas Co.*, 50 PUR (NS) 65 (1943); *Re Colorado Interstate Gas Co.*, 3 FPC 32 (1942), *aff'd*, 142 F. 2d 943 (10th Cir., 1944), 324 U.S. 581 (1945).

[5]*Re Phillips Petroleum Co.*, 7 FPC 983 (1948). At the time of the investigation, Phillips was the nation's largest seller of natural gas to interstate pipelines. It owned 4,380 miles of gathering lines in five states (some lines crossed the state border between Oklahoma and Texas) and thirty-five processing plants. It also purchased and gathered gas from other producers. Its sales were made to five interstate transmission companies.

[6]In August, 1947, the commission issued Order 139, declaring that the 1938 Natural Gas Act denied it jurisdiction over sales by independent producers to pipeline companies. A year later, it completed its natural gas investigation (initiated in September, 1944) and split (one vacancy existed): Commissioners Smith and Wimberly favored Congressional exemption of the field sales of independents, and Commissioners Draper and Olds opposed any amendment. (See Federal Power Commission, *Natural Gas Investigation: Smith-Wimberly Report* and *Natural Gas Investigation: Draper-Olds Reports* [Docket G-580, 1948].) The vacancy was filled in 1949 by Thomas Buchanan, who sided with Commissioners Draper and Olds; thus, a 3-2 majority of the commission was opposed to amending the 1938 Act.

[7]The record made included nearly 5,800 pages of testimony and approximately 4,000 pages of exhibits. Eight states, three cities, a county, and numerous private groups were permitted to intervene in the proceeding.

[8]*Re Phillips Petroleum Co.*, 90 PUR (NS) 325 (1951).

[9]The FPC's decision was reversed by the D.C. Circuit Court of Appeals [*Wisconsin v. Federal Power Comm.*, 205 F. 2d 706 (D.C. Cir. 1953)]. The Supreme Court denied Phillips' petition for writ of certiorari [346 U.S. at 896 (1953)], then changed its mind [346 U.S. at 934 (1953)]. In addition to the above named petitioners, the FPC and the state of Texas also filed petitions for rehearing for writ of certiorari.

[10]*Phillips Petroleum Co. v. Wisconsin, op. cit.*, pp. 682-84, 685.

[11]Dissenting opinion, *ibid.*, pp. 695-96.

[12]Federal Power Commission, *Annual Report*, 1963, p. 140.

It is important to emphasize that both producers and the commission faced three immediate tasks under the Natural Gas Act. First, producers had to meet certain reporting requirements. Second, producers had to file applications for certificates of public convenience and necessity under Section 7(c). Third, producers had to file "initial" rate schedules and changes of rates under Sections 4 and 5.

For sales being made under contracts in effect on June 7, 1954, contract prices generally were accepted as the "initial prices," but any subsequent increases required a filing under Section 4, even if the existing contract contained price escalation clauses. [See, *e.g., United Gas Pipe Line Co. v. Mobil Gas Service Corp.*, 350 U.S. 332 (1956).] "Thousands of such rate increases were filed, and thousands were suspended and later placed in effect subject to refund, pending Commission decision under Section 4. As a result, millions of dollars were collected subject to refund commencing in 1954, awaiting Commission decisions, to be made years later, as to the 'just and reasonable' rate under Section 4." Carroll L. Gilliam, "Wellhead Regulation Under the Natural Gas Act and the Natural Gas Policy Act," in American Gas Association (ed.), *Regulation of the Gas Industry* (New York: Matthew Bender & Co., Inc., 1983), Vol. I, pp. 20-30.

For sales initiated on or after June 7, 1954, "initial prices" became more controversial, were subject to hearings, and to several significant changes in policy. To illustrate: Following a 1959 Supreme Court decision [*Atlantic Refining Co. v. New York Pub. Service Comm.*, 360 U.S. 378 (1959)], the FPC evolved a system for determining the maximum initial price (known as the "in-line" price) at which natural gas could move, under sales contracts, during the interval preceding the establishment of "just and reasonable" rates. After determining the "in-line" prices (based largely on current prices for gas in the area of the proposed sale), the commission conditioned permanent certificates so as to limit the level to which prices might be raised (pursuant to escalation clauses) during a given period or until the relevant area rates had been determined. In granting permanent certificates, the commission also ordered refunds of amounts collected by producers in the past under temporary certificates which contained no refund conditions. The commission's procedures were upheld in *Federal Power Comm. v. Sunray DX Oil Co.*, 391 U.S. 9 (1968).

[13]See *Re Phillips Petroleum Co.*, 35 PUR3d 199, 208-15 (FPC, 1960).

[14]*Ibid.*, p. 210. The commission had 3,276 producer rate increase filings under suspension awaiting hearings.

[15]In recent years, over 70 percent of domestic gas production has come from gas-only and gas-condensate wells.

[16]See Otto Eckstein, "Natural Gas and Patterns of Regulation," 36 *Harvard Business Review* 126, 129-33 (1958).

The Btu Method was most often used to allocate exploration costs; the Relative Cost Method to allocate production costs. The two separate allocation methods were used because production costs can be more readily identified with a particular type of production (or lease type), whereas exploration costs (such as geological expenditures) are more general and are therefore said to be incurred "in the indiscriminate search for hydrocarbons." However, in the Area Rate Proceedings (discussed below), the FPC accepted the "directionality" thesis; namely, that producers can direct their exploration efforts towards oil or gas and can assign certain costs respectively.

[17]*Federal Power Comm. v. Hope Natural Gas Co.*, 320 U.S. 591, 649 (1944).

[18]*Wisconsin v. Federal Power Comm.*, 373 U.S. 294, 299 (1963).

[19]Martin L. Lindahl, "Federal Regulation of Natural Gas Producers and Gatherers," 46 *American Economic Review* 532, 538 (1956).

[20]Marshall C. Howard, "Regulation and the Price of Natural Gas," 23 *Southern Economic Journal* 142, 145 (1956).

[21]*Colorado Interstate Gas Co. v. Federal Power Comm., op. cit.*, p. 610.

[22]Lindahl, *op. cit.*, p. 536. The advantages of vertical integration are summarized by Edward Falck, "Area Gas Pricing for Pipelines?," 73 *Public Utilities Fortnightly* 34 (January 30, 1964).

[23]*Re Panhandle Eastern Pipe Line Co.*, 3 PUR3d 396 (1954).

[24]*City of Detroit v. Federal Power Comm.*, 230 F. 2d 810 (D.C. Cir. 1955), *cert. denied*, 352 U.S. 829 (1955).

[25]*Re Union Oil Co. of California, et al.*, Opinion No. 300 (FPC, 1956).

[26]*Re Phillips Petroleum Co.*, 24 FPC 590 (1959). The law judge and the company were far apart. The law judge allowed a cost of $57 million, compared to Phillips' claim of $92 million. The law judge allocated 30.50 percent of the cost of exploration to gas; the company allocated 62 percent. The law judge allowed a return of 9.25 percent on investment; the company asked for 18 percent.

[27]*Re Phillips Petroleum Co.*, 35 PUR3d 199 (1960). The commission decided, however, in the case at hand, to use cost-of-service evidence, since the whole case had been tried on that basis. See Note, "FPC Regulation of Independent Producers of Natural Gas," 75 *Harvard Law Review* 549 (1962); Edmund W. Kitch, "Regulation of the Field Market for Natural Gas by the Federal Power Commission," 11 *Journal of Law and Economics* 243 (1968).

[28]*Re Statement of General Policy No. 61-1*, 35 PUR3d 195 (1960). The policy statement was subsequently revised on several occasions.

[29]The seven areas: (*1*) Permain Basin Area; (*2*) Southern Louisiana Area; (*3*) Texas Gulf Coast Area; (*4*) Hugoton-Anadarko Area; (*5*) Other Southwest Area; (*6*) Appalachian and Illinois Basins; and (*7*) Rocky Mountain Area.

[30]*Wisconsin v. Federal Power Comm.*, 303 F. 2d 380 (D.C. Cir. 1961).

[31]373 U.S. 294 (1963).

[32]*Ibid.*, pp. 309-10. Justice Clark, in his dissenting opinion, argued: "The Sisyphean labors of the Commission continue as it marches up the hill of producer regulation only to tumble down again with little undertaken and less done. . . . In this summary fashion [the issuance of the Statement of General Policy] the Commission junked its cost-of-service regulation program, wasted a half dozen years of work thereon, and is now experimenting with a new, untried, untested, inchoate program which, in addition, is of doubtful legality. As a consequence the consumers of gas all over the United States . . . will pay for the Commission's area pricing wild-goose chase. I predict that in the end the consumer will find himself to be the biggest goose of the hunt and the small producer the dead duck." *Ibid.*, pp. 315, 317. See also Sterling W.

Steves, "FPC Gas Tariff — Solution to the Rate Change Dilemma of the Independent Producer?," 15 *Southwestern Law Journal* 46 (1961).

[33]*Re Permian Basin Area Rates*, 34 FPC 159 (1965), 34 FPC 1068 (1965). The commission's decision generally followed the recommendations of its administrative law judge. (Before the law judge, the proceeding involved 250 days of hearings, 30,365 pages of testimony, 337 exhibits, and ninety witnesses). The initial decision is summarized in 74 *Public Utilities Fortnightly* 86, 86-90 (October 8, 1964). See also Harold Leventhal, "Reviewing the Permian Basin Area Gas Price Hearings," 73 *Public Utilities Fortnightly* 19 (March 12, 1964); A. J. G. Priest, "Factors Leading up to the Permian Basin Decision," 79 *Public Utilities Fortnightly* 13 (March 2, 1967).

[34]The cost-of-service technique used by the commission differed from the usual individual company cost-of-service approach in that (*1*) the costs of all producer respondents were averaged together and (*2*) costs were only determined for gas-well gas leases; *i.e.*, costs were not computed for gas produced on casinghead-oil or combination leases. The commission felt that the allocation of costs to gas on these leases was more difficult to compute. It held, however, that the cost of such gas could not be greater than, and is probably less than, the cost of flowing gas-well gas.

[35]The ceiling prices for gas from the Permian Basin produced in New Mexico were lower, reflecting the lower production tax level in that state. In the proceedings before the commission, the producers had sought a one-price ceiling for all Permian Basin gas of about twenty cents per thousand cubic feet; the FPC staff sought a 13.7-cent ceiling for all gas except casinghead, which would be nine cents.

[36]Escalation clauses are discussed in Chapter 14, pp. 648-49.

[37]On the Permian Basin decision, see Comment, "Regulating Independent Gas Producers: The First Area Approach," 115 *University of Pennsylvania Law Review* 84 (1966); James C. Loughlin, "Controversies in the Area Rate Proceedings," 79 *Public Utilities Fortnightly* 36 (February 2, 1967); Stanley Learned, "The Biggest Goose of the Hunt," 20 *New Mexico Business* 4 (April, 1967); Edmund W. Kitch, "The Permian Basin Area Rate Cases and the Regulatory Determination of Price," 116 *University of Pennsylvania Law Review* 191 (1967).

[38]See *Re Exemption of Small Producers from Regulation*, 45 FPC 454 (1971), as amended, 45 FPC 548 (1971), *rev'd sub nom. Texaco Inc. v. Federal Power Comm.*, 474 F. 2d 416 (D.C. Cir. 1972), *vacated and remanded*, 417 U.S. 380 (1974); *Re Small Producers Regulation*, 11 PUR4th 179 (FPC, 1975).

[39]In subsequent area rate proceedings, three- and four-tier pricing systems were adopted.

[40]See Irwin M. Stelzer, "Economic Rationale of the Permian Two-price System," 76 *Public Utilities Fortnightly* 51 (December 9, 1965).

[41]*Skelly Oil Co. v. Federal Power Comm.*, 375 F. 2d 6 (10th Cir. 1967), 375 F. 2d 35 (10th Cir. 1967).

[42]*In re Permian Basin Area Rate Cases*, 390 U.S. 747 (1968). Justice Douglas dissented; Justice Marshall took no part in the decision.

[43]*Ibid.*, pp. 756-57, quoting from *Federal Power Comm. v. Hope Natural Gas Co.*, *op. cit.*, p. 649 (footnotes omitted).

[44]*Ibid.*, p. 822.

[45]*Ibid.*, pp. 812-13. Justice Douglas, in his dissent, said: "The area rate orders challenged here are based on averages. No single producer's actual costs, actual risks, actual returns are known. The 'result reached' as to any producer is not known. The 'impact of the rate order' on any producer is not known. The 'total effect' of the rate

order on a single producer is not known. . . . In absence of knowledge, we cannot possibly perform our function of judicial review, limited though it be. . . . If the task of regulating producer sales within the framework of the Natural Gas Act is as difficult as the present case illustrates, perhaps the problem should be returned to Congress. But certainly we do little today to advance the cause of responsible administrative action. With all respect, we promote administrative irresponsibility by making an agency's *fiat* an adequate substitute for supported findings." *Ibid.*, pp. 829-30, 831, 841.

[46](*1*) *Re Area Rate Proceeding for Southern Louisiana,* 40 FPC 530 (1968), on rehearing, 41 FPC 301 (1969), *aff'd sub nom. Austral Oil Co. v. Federal Power Comm.,* 428 F. 2d 407 (5th Cir. 1970), *on rehearing,* 444 F. 2d 125, *cert. denied sub nom. Municipal Distribs. Group. v. Federal Power Comm.,* 400 U.S. 950 (1970). (*2*) *Re Area Rate Proceeding for Texas Gulf Coast Area,* 45 FPC 674 (1971), on rehearing, 46 FPC 827 (1971), *rev'd and remanded sub nom. New York Pub. Service Comm. v. Federal Power Comm.,* 487 F. 2d 1043 (D.C. Cir. 1973), *vacated and remanded sub nom. Shell Oil Co. v. New York Pub. Service Comm.,* 417 U.S. 964 (1974). (*3*) *Re Area Rate Proceeding for Hugoton-Andarko Area,* 44 FPC 761 (1970), *aff'd,* 466 F. 2d 974 (9th Cir. 1972). (*4*) *Re Area Rate Proceeding for Other Southwest Area,* 46 FPC 900 (1971), on rehearing, 47 FPC 99 (1972), *aff'd sub nom. Shell Oil Co. v. Federal Power Comm.,* 484 F. 2d 469 (5th Cir. 1973), *cert. denied,* 417 U.S. 973 (1974). (*5*) *Re Area Rate Proceeding for Appalachian and Illinois Basins,* 44 FPC 1112 (1970), on rehearing, 44 FPC 1334 (1970) and 44 FPC 1487 (1970). (*6*) *Re Area Rate Proceeding for Rocky Mountain Area,* 49 FPC 924 (1973), on rehearing, 49 FPC 1279 (1973).

[47]See, *e.g., Re Area Rate Proceeding for Permian Basin,* 50 FPC 390 (1973), on rehearing, 50 FPC 932 (1973); *Re Area Proceeding for Southern Louisiana,* 46 FPC 86 (1971), on rehearing, 46 FPC 633 (1971), *aff'd sub nom. Placid Oil Co. v. Federal Power Comm.,* 483 F. 2d 880 (5th Cir. 1973), *aff'd sub nom. Mobil Oil Corp. v. Federal Power Comm.,* 417 U.S. 283 (1974).

[48]Stephen G. Breyer and Paul W. MacAvoy, *Energy Regulation by the Federal Power Commission* (Washington, D.C.: The Brookings Institution, 1974), p. 69. The two authors note two other flaws in the two-price system: "For one, it provided no way to ration the low-price gas. For another, there was no assurance that the two prices (for old and new gas) were equal to the long-term marginal costs of production." *Ibid.*

[49]*Re National Rates for Natural Gas* (Opinion No. 699), 4 PUR4th 401 (FPC, 1974).

[50]In all of the national rate proceedings, adjustments to the base rates were made for Btu content, state or federal taxes (such as production and/or severance taxes), and gathering allowances. Moreover, all of the national rate proceedings were rule-making proceedings, as noted in Chapter 5.

[51]In August, 1972, the commission adopted its so-called "optional procedure," which permitted producers to file applications for gas sales at prices which exceeded commission-established rates if found to be in the public interest. See *Re Optional Procedure for Certificating New Producer Sales of Natural Gas,* 48 FPC 218 (1972), amended, 48 FPC 477 (1972), *aff'd sub nom. Moss v. Federal Power Comm.,* 502 F. 2d 461 (D.C. Cir. 1974), as amended, FPC Order No. 455-B (1974).

[52]*Re National Rates for Natural Gas* (Opinion No. 699-H), 8 PUR4th 209 (FPC, 1974), *aff'd sub nom. Shell Oil Co. v. Federal Power Comm.,* 520 F. 2d 1061 (5th Cir. 1975), *cert. denied sub nom. California Co. v. Federal Power Comm.,* 426 U.S. 941 (1976). The lower court, however, emphasized that it was applying "a standard of review

requiring heightened deference to the Commission's expertise in such experimental regulations," expressed regret that the commission "continues to issue orders which would be inadequate but for our 'kid glove' treatment," and warned that "as experiment lapses into experience, the courts may well expect the Commission to justify its policies with reasoned projections of that once-prototypic policy's probable net effect. The principle of *stare decisis* may only lightly touch the standard of subsequent review." *Ibid.*, p. 1072.

[53]4 PUR4th 401, 424 (FPC, 1974).

[54]*Re National Rates for Natural Gas* (Opinion No. 749), 12 PUR4th 493 (FPC, 1975), on rehearing (Opinion No. 749-C), 15 PUR4th 1 (FPC, 1976), *aff'd sub nom. Tenneco Oil Co. v. Federal Power Comm.*, 571 F. 2d 834 (5th Cir. 1978), *dismissed*, 439 U.S. 801 (1978).

[55]*Re National Rates for Natural Gas* (Opinion No. 770), 15 PUR4th 21 (FPC, 1976), *aff'd sub nom. Am. Pub. Gas Ass'n v. Federal Power Comm.*, 567 F. 2d 1016 (D.C. Cir. 1976), *cert. denied*, 435 U.S. 907 (1977). Here, again, the lower court was concerned with the commission's underlying data: "Looking at objective data, we are constrained to find that there is a bare minimum to support the FPC's rulings. We can and do caution that on any future rate order there will be need for a more solid undergirding of result. . . . At this juncture we announce our approval, but with more of a sigh than a whoop." *Ibid.*, p. 1044.

[56]*Re Pipeline Production Area Rate Proceeding* (Phase I, Opinion No. 568), 42 FPC 738 (1969), as amended, 42 FPC 1089 (Opinion No. 568-A, 1969), *aff'd sub nom. City of Chicago v. Federal Power Comm.*, 458 F. 2d 731 (D.C. Cir. 1971), *cert. denied*, 405 U.S. 1074 (1972). The appropriate rate treatment for gas produced from leases acquired prior to October 7, 1969, would be decided in each pipeline rate proceeding, although the commission generally allowed cost-of-service treatment. See, *e.g.*, *Re El Paso Nat. Gas Co.*, 51 FPC 764, 52 FPC 406 (1974). Phase II was terminated by the commission in 1972: 47 FPC 1523 (1972).

[57]*Re National Rates for Natural Gas* (Opinion No. 699-H), 8 PUR4th 209, 235 (FPC, 1974).

[58]See M. Elizabeth Sanders, *The Regulation of Natural Gas: Policy and Politics, 1938-1978* (Philadelphia: Temple University Press, 1981).

[59]During the Senate debates, the confirmation of Commissioner Olds' reappointment to the FPC came before the Senate Committee. "In an endeavor to break the majority opposition of the Commission to such amendatory legislation and deliver a personal rebuff to Olds, gas and oil interests joined forces with the proponents of the legislation in the Senate to defeat Olds' confirmation." Richard W. Gable, "The Jurisdiction of the Federal Power Commission over the Field Prices of Natural Gas," 32 *Land Economics* 39, 49-50 (1956). See also Joseph P. Harris, "The Senatorial Rejection of Leland Olds: A Case Study," 45 *American Political Science Review* 674 (1951).

[60]96 *Cong. Rec.* 5304 (1950).

[61]Advisory Committee on Energy Supplies and Resources, *Report to the President* (Washington, D.C.: U.S. Government Printing Office, 1955).

Following the *Phillips* decision, an intensive public relations program was undertaken by producers and trade associations to persuade the public that federal regulation of independent producers was unnecessary. The legislatures of Oklahoma and Kansas enacted laws empowering their state regulatory commissions to establish minimum wellhead prices for natural gas even if they were above the maximum prices set by the FPC. Both statutes were later held unconstitutional on the ground that they were in conflict with the *Phillips* decision. See *Natural Gas Pipeline Co. v. Panama Corp.*, 349 U.S. 44 (1955); *Cities Service Gas Co. v. Corp. Comm. of Kansas*, 355 U.S. 391 (1958).

[62]102 *Cong. Rec.* 2793 (1956).

[63]*The Washington Post,* February 11, 1958, p. 1.

[64]Pub. Law 95-621 (1978). See, *e.g.,* Paul W. MacAvoy, "The Natural Gas Policy Act of 1978," 19 *Natural Resources Journal* 811 (1979).

[65]Federal control was upheld in *Oklahoma v. Federal Energy Regulatory Comm.*, 494 F. Supp. 636 (W.D. Okla. 1980), *aff'd,* 661 F. 2d 832 (10th Cir. 1981), *cert. denied sub nom. Texas v. Federal Energy Regulatory Comm.*, 102 S. Ct. 2902 (1982).

[66]See Chapter 14, Tables 14-4 and 14-5.

[67]Jurisdictional sales are "firm" sales; *i.e.,* they are sales which the pipeline is committed to supply continuously. Most nonjurisdictional sales are "interruptible" sales; *i.e.,* such sales may be interrupted in favor of firm sales at times of insufficiency of gas supply or pipeline capacity to meet its requirements.

[68]The FERC, however, does have control over the facilities added to a pipeline to serve industrial customers, as well as control over construction of a pipeline by an industrial customer. Further, the FERC has control over a pipeline company's "off-system" sales; *i.e.,* generally sales to other pipeline companies, which are for a specified period of time and on an interruptible basis. See, *e.g., Re Northern Nat. Gas Co.,* Docket No. CP81-236-000 (FERC, 1981).

[69]See *Re Atlantic Seaboard Corp., et al.,* 43 PUR (NS) 235 (FPC, 1952); *Re Northern Nat. Gas Co.,* 95 PUR (NS) 289 (FPC, 1952), *aff'd mem.* 346 U.S. 922 (1954). For the commission's earlier allocation decisions, see *Re Colorado Interstate Gas Co., op. cit.; Re Mississippi River Fuel Co.,* 4 FPC 340 (1945).

[70]See Stanislaw H. Wellisz, "The Public Interest in Gas Industry Rate Structures," Part II, 70 *Public Utilities Fortnightly* 145 (August 2, 1962); Homer R. Ross, "How Practical Is the Seaboard Formula?," 21 *Public Utilities Fortnightly* 26 (January 3, 1963).

[71]Kahn, *op. cit.,* pp. 98-100.

[72]*Re Southern Nat. Gas Co.,* 47 PUR3d 113, 137 (FPC, 1963).

[73]"We recognize fully the infirmities in the formula and, as indicated by us on a number of recent occasions, we do not consider ourselves bound thereto, as evidenced by our readiness to make substantial adjustments from straight Seaboard rates where warranted. This is particularly so where such adjustments have been necessary to meet competitive circumstances." *Re Midwestern Gas Trans. Co.,* 61 PUR3d 241, 251-52 (FPC, 1965). See also *Re Nat. Gas Pipeline Co. of America,* 45 PUR3d 415 (FPC, 1962); *Re United Fuel Gas Co.,* 31 FPC 1342 (1964).

[74]*Re United Gas Pipe Line Co.,* 3 PUR4th 491 (FPC, 1973), rehearing denied, 51 FPC 1014 (1974), *aff'd sub nom. Consolidated Gas Supply Corp. v. Federal Power Comm.,* 520 F. 2d 1176 (D.C. Cir. 1975).

[75]*Re Tennessee Gas Pipeline Co.,* 76 PUR4th 220, 234 (FERC, 1986). Under a straight fixed-variable (SFV) approach, 100 percent of fixed costs are allocated to the demand charge. Under MFV procedures, transmission and storage fixed costs are assigned to both the commodity charge and the demand charge, while 50 to 100 percent of the return on equity and associated taxes are assigned to the commodity charge. MFV procedures use either a single demand rate or a two-part demand rate (one based on traditional peak period volumes and one on annual volumes). The commission's use of the approach has been upheld: *Re Nat. Gas Pipeline Co. of*

America, 56 PUR4th 488 (FERC, 1983), *rem'd on other grounds sub nom. Northern Indiana Pub. Service Co. v. Federal Energy Regulatory Comm.,* 782 F. 2d 730 (7th Cir. 1986). See also *Re Texas Eastern Trans. Corp.,* 65 PUR4th 1 (FERC, 1985).

[76]*Re American Louisiana Pipe Line Co.,* 48 PUR3d 321, 334 (FPC, 1963).

[77]*Ibid.,* p. 334, n. 25.

[78]In this case, only one rate zone was involved. When rates for two or more zones are at issue, the level of revenues to be recovered in each zone must be considered in determining the demand and commodity components.

[79]Put another way, the company's rate deviates to demand by some 29 percent and the law judge's rate by some 13 percent. "The percentage of the deviation to demand is computed by determining what is the amount of commodity costs that cannot be recovered by the commodity charge because of competition from other fuels or otherwise (this amount of commodity costs must be recovered by the demand charge and so is transferred to demand costs); and then dividing the amount of such commodity costs by the total of the strictly Seaboard demand costs. *Re American Louisiana Pipe Line Co., op. cit.,* p. 324, n. 6.

[80]*Ibid.,* pp. 334-35.

[81]*Colorado Interstate Gas Co. v. Federal Power Comm.,* 324 U.S. 581, 589, 591 (1945).

[82]Electric utilities using natural gas as a boiler fuel in generating electricity, and certain agricultural users, were excluded from incremental pricing.

Under the NGPA, local distribution companies were required to pass through directly any surcharge paid to the incrementally priced industrial facilities they serve and states were prohibited from modifying any method of allocating costs.

[83]FERC Order No. 49, Docket No. RM79-14 (1979).

[84]45 *Fed. Reg.* 31622 (1980).

[85]126 *Cong. Rec.* H3855 (May 20, 1980). The House was presented evidence that Phase I incremental pricing caused large industrial users to switch from gas to oil and resulted in a subsidy to other gas users. See, *e.g.,* W. A. Mogel and W. R. Mapes, Jr., "Assessment of Incremental Pricing Under the Natural Gas Policy Act," 29 *Catholic University Law Review* 763 (1980). On August 1, 1980, the FERC revoked the Phase II rule. However, a circuit court, in January, 1982, held that the one-house veto provision was unconstitutional and that the commission's revocation of the Phase II rule was invalid. *Consumer Energy Council of America v. Federal Energy Regulatory Comm.,* 673 F. 2d 425 (D.C. Cir. 1982), *summarily aff'd,* 103 S. Ct. 3556 (1983).

[86]*Re Columbia LNG Corp.,* 47 FPC 1624 (1972), 48 FPC 723 (1972), *rem'd,* 491 F. 2d 651 (5th Cir. 1974).

[87]*Re Trunkline LNG Co.,* Opinion No. 796 (FPC, 1977).

[88]*Re Columbia LNG Corp.,* Opinion No. 789, 18 PUR4th 359 (FPC, 1977).

[89]*Re Trunkline LNG Co.,* Opinion No. 796-A, 20 PUR4th 310 (FPC, 1977).

[90]For an analysis of the associated problems, see Randall K. Anderson, "The Problems of Marginal Cost Pricing and Its Progeny," 102 *Public Utilities Fortnightly* 17, 19-20 (October 12, 1978).

[91]25 FERC Par. 61,220 (1983), 26 FERC Par. 61,031 (1984). See, *e.g., Re Transcontinental Gas Pipe Line Corp.,* 25 FERC Par. 61,219 (1983); *Re Tenneco Oil Co.,* 25 FERC Par. 61,234 (1983).

[92]*Maryland People's Counsel v. Federal Energy Regulatory Comm.,* 761 F. 2d 768, 66 PUR4th 529, 541 (D.C. Cir. 1985) (*MPC I*). On the same day, the circuit court also vacated the commission's "blanket" certification orders for special marketing programs [Order No 234-B, 48 *Fed. Reg.* 34,872 (FERC, 1983), Order No. 319, 48 *Fed.*

Reg. 34,875 (FERC, 1983), Order No. 319-A, 48 *Fed. Reg.* 51,436 (FERC, 1983)]; orders which allowed fuel-switchable end users, but not local distribution companies or other captive customers, to obtain blanket certificates. *Maryland People's Counsel v. Federal Energy Regulatory Comm.*, 761 F. 2d 780, 66 PUR 4th 542 (D.C. Cir. 1985) (*MPC II*). In subsequent *per curiam* opinions, however, the court allowed the orders regarding both special marketing programs and blanket certification to expire by their own terms or to remain in effect until October 31, 1985: 768 F. 2d 250 (D.C. Cir. 1985) (*MPC I*) and 768 F. 2d 1354 (D. C. Cir. 1985) (*MPC II*). "Second-generation" special marketing programs also were overturned: *Maryland People's Counsel v. Federal Energy Regulatory Comm.*, 768 F. 2d 450 (D.C. Cir. 1985) (*MPC III*).

[93]For a more complete analysis of gas rates, see American Gas Association, *Gas Rate Fundamentals* (3rd ed.; Arlington, Va., 1978).

[94]In the 1930s, the industry even experimented with demand rate schedules, such as the Wright and Hopkinson types, containing separate demand and commodity charges. The experiment had a short life, however, since demand costs for a gas distributor are far lower in relation to total costs than those of an electric utility.

[95]Like the electric industry, embedded cost-of-service studies involve the allocation of common or joint costs. See *Gas Rate Fundamentals, op. cit.,* chap. 12.

[96]Some gas distribution utilities bill on a therm basis (one therm = 100,000 Btu's) instead of on a volume of gas metered basis (Mcf or M = 1,000 cubic feet). The therm rate was established in the 1930s to avoid a loss of revenue as distributors switched from manufactured gas (approximately 500 Btu's per cubic foot) to natural gas (about 1,000 Btu's per cubic foot) service.

[97]Section 306 of the Public Utility Regulatory Policies Act required the Secretary of Energy to study and report to Congress on gas rate design by May 9, 1980. See Economic Regulatory Administration, U.S. Department of Energy, *Natural Gas Rate Design Study* (Washington, D.C.: U.S. Government Printing Office, 1980). On the study, see Stephen S. Skjei, "The Gas Rate Design Study," in *Proceedings of the 1980 Rate Symposium on Problems of Regulated Industries* (Columbia: University of Missouri-Columbia, 1981), pp. 235-43.

[98]*Natural Gas Rate Design Study, op. cit.,* p. 1.

[99]*Ibid.,* pp. 21-22 (footnote omitted). As an alternative, the FERC could set pipeline company rates "to reflect the costs of the most expensive source of gas purchased that is not subject to price controls." *Ibid.,* p. 22. See also Jean-Michel Guldmann, *Marginal Cost Pricing for Gas Distribution Utilities: Preliminary Analyses and Models* (Columbus, Ohio: National Regulatory Research Institute, 1980); *Re North Attleboro Gas Co.,* 78 PUR4th 437 (Mass., 1986).

[100]See, *e.g., Re Northwest Nat. Gas Co.,* Order No. 77-292 (Or., 1977); *Re Wisconsin Power & Light Co.,* Docket No. 6680-GR-3 (Wis., 1978); *Re Hawaiian Elec. Co., Inc.,* Order No. 6034 (Hawaii, 1980); *Pennsylvania Pub. Utility Comm. v. Philadelphia Elec. Co.,* 33 PUR4th 319 (Pa., 1980).

[101]In Montana, for example, three classes were established: Firm, Interruptible, and Utility, with one uniform commodity rate prescribed for each class. *Re Montana Power Co.* (Phase II), Order No. 4521b (Mont., 1979). For an analysis, see John D. Haffey, "Trends and Issues in Retail Rate Design — The Montana Experience," in *Proceedings of the 1980 Rate Symposium on Problems of Regulated Industries, op. cit.,* pp. 261-327.

[102]*Re Wisconsin Power & Light Co.* (initial order), Docket No. 6680-GR-3, *op. cit.,* p. 13.

[103]Teri L. Vierima and J. Robert Malko, "Natural Gas Rate Design: Innovative Activities in Wisconsin," 108 *Public Utilities Fortnightly* 28, 29 (October 22, 1981). See also Harold A. Meyer and J. Robert Malko, "Natural Gas Rate Design: A State Regulatory Perspective," in *Proceedings of the 1982 Rate Symposium on Problems of Regulated Industries* (Columbia: University of Missouri-Columbia, 1983), pp. 200-12.

[104]*Re Wisconsin Power & Light Co.*, Docket No. 6680-GR-11 (Wis., 1981). For a critical analysis of the Wisconsin experience, see James G. Miller, "Natural Gas Rate Design in Wisconsin," in *Proceedings of the 1980 Rate Symposium on Problems of Regulated Industries, op. cit.*, pp. 244-60. The Wisconsin commission also adopted an auction rate for interruptible customers, but subsequently changed to a flat rate (with an auction option). Vierima and Malko, *op. cit.*, p. 31. See also *Re Pacific Gas & Elec. Co.*, 62 PUR4th 466 (Cal., 1984).

[105]See, *e.g.*, Anderson, *op. cit.*, for a more complete discussion of the issues.

[106]*Re Long-Range Plans of New York State's Gas Distribution Companies*, Opinion No. 79-19 (N.Y., 1979), p. 6. The FERC has considered, but has not adopted, marginal cost pricing for pipeline companies. See, *e.g.*, *Re Texas Gas Trans. Corp.*, Docket No. RP75-19 (remand) (FERC, 1983); *Re Texas Eastern Trans. Corp.*, 51 PUR4th 359 (remand) (FERC, 1983) and 65 PUR4th 1 (FERC, 1985).

[107]See, *e.g.*, Michael A. Toman, "The Outlook for 'Spot' Trade in Natural Gas," 118 *Public Utilities Fortnightly* 28 (July 10, 1986).

[108]Order No. 436, 33 FERC Par. 61,007 (1985), *vacated and rem'd sub nom. Associated Gas Distributors v. Federal Energy Regulatory Comm.*, 824 F. 2d 981, 83 PUR4th 459 (D.C. Cir. 1987). See, *e.g.*, Jeremiah D. Lambert and Jay D. Pedelty, "Mandatory Contract Carriage: The Changing Role of Pipelines in Competitive Natural Gas Markets," 115 *Public Utilities Fortnightly* 26 (February 7, 1985). The issue is discussed in Chapter 14.

[109]*Re Washington Gas Light Co.*, 57 PUR4th 705, 707 (Va., 1984). See also *Re So. Connecticut Gas Co.*, 64 PUR4th 393 (Conn., 1985); *Re Incentive Rates for Natural Gas Customers and Electric Utility Customers*, 77 PUR4th 381 (Iowa, 1986); *Re Michigan Consol. Gas Co.*, 80 PUR4th 412 (Mich., 1987). But see *Pennsylvania Pub. Utility Comm. v. Equitable Gas Co.*, 59 PUR4th 470 (Pa., 1984). The margin is shared 90/10 in the District of Columbia and New Jersey: *Re District of Columbia Nat. Gas*, 77 PUR4th 589 (D.C., 1986); *Re Elizabethtown Gas Co.*, 85 PUR4th 231 (N.J., 1987).

[110]*Re Natural Gas Transportation Policies*, 81 PUR4th 453, 457 (W.Va., 1987). See "The Carriage Obligations of Gas Pipelines and Distributors," 115 *Public Utilities Fortnightly* 54 (February 21, 1985). See also *Re Transportation of Customer-owned Gas*, 54 PUR4th 627 (N.Y., 1984); *Re Transportation of Natural Gas Owned by End Users*, 59 PUR4th 636 (N.C., 1984); *Re Interstate Sales and Transportation of Gas*, 80 PUR4th 1 (Md., 1986); *Re Dome Pipeline Corp.*, 78 PUR4th 1 (Mich., 1986); *Re Transportation of Natural Gas*, 82 PUR4th 121 (Mo., 1987).

[111]J. Stephen Henderson et al., *Natural Gas Rate Design and Transportation Policy Under Deregulation and Market Uncertainty* (Columbus, Ohio: National Regulatory Research Institute, 1986), p. 21. The margin may be either "simple" or "gross." See "Rate Design for Intrastate Natural Gas Transportation Service — A Move Toward Cost-based Rates?," 118 *Public Utilities Fortnightly* 47 (December 25, 1986). [Compare *North Penn Industrial Coalition v. North Penn Gas Co.*, Docket No. C-850117 (Pa., 1986) with *Re Intermountain Gas Co.*, 74 PUR4th 696 (Idaho, 1986).] The "cost of the distributor's system supply" may be either the average cost or the marginal cost.

[112]See, *e.g., Re Natural Gas Industrial Rates and Transportation Policies,* 78 PUR4th 57 (Va., 1986).

[113]See, *e.g., Re Northern States Power Co.,* 73 PUR4th 395 (Minn., 1985); *Re Natural Gas Transportation Policies, op. cit.*

[114]See, *e.g., Re Michigan Consol. Gas Co., op. cit.* "Clearly, if a customer elects transportation and should not also elect a standby service, the utility company does not have a continuing public service obligation to sell gas to that customer." *Re Natural Gas Industrial Rates and Transportation Policies, op. cit.,* p. 70.

[115]This section basically describes the evolution of telephone rate structures prior to the divestiture of the Bell System, but concludes with some comments on more recent developments. Telephone rate structures were developed under monopoly and regulation. Future rate structures will be shaped by competition and regulation, upon the restructuring of the telecommunications industry.

[116]Overseas rates are established on the basis of direct negotiations between the carriers and representatives of the foreign countries involved and are filed with the FCC. See *Re International Competitive Carrier Policies,* CC Docket No. 85-107, 102 FCC 2d 812 (1985).

[117]See "Bell Operating Companies Exchange Service Telephone Rates," (Washington, D.C.: National Association of Regulatory Utility Commissioners, 1985).

[118]When subscribers share a line, investment and expenses for outside plant and those items of central office equipment which vary with the number of lines are reduced. At the same time, the usefulness of party line service is limited by its possible effect on the quality of service. The greater the number of parties per line, the more unsatisfactory the service is likely to be both for the party line customers and for other users who might encounter serious delays in calling party lines. It is for this reason that lines with four or more parties have virtually disappeared.

[119]Eli W. Clemens, *Economics and Public Utilities* (New York: Appleton-Century-Crofts, Inc., 1950), p. 333.

[120]"Message rate service" refers to a service differentiated by frequency and, on occasion, by duration. "Local measured service" refers to a multi-element method of charging by frequency, duration, distance, and time-of-day.

[121]See *1985 Annual Report on Utility and Carrier Regulation* (Washington, D.C.: National Association of Regulatory Utility Commissioners, 1987), pp. 638-43.

[122]See Carl Stern, "Usage-Sensitive Pricing for Telephone Service," 92 *Public Utilities Fortnightly* 53 (October 11, 1973).

[123]In 1984, the FCC permitted the interconnection of commission-approved customer-owned, coin-operated telephones to the telephone network and used for interstate calling. *Re Registration of Coin-operated Telephones Under Part 68 of the Commission's Rules and Regulations,* FCC 84-270, 49 *Fed. Reg.* 27,766 (1984). Many states have followed with respect to local and intrastate long-distance calling. See, *e.g., Re Customer-owned, Coin-operated Telephones,* 66 PUR4th 632 (Pa., 1985); *Re Customer-owned Pay Telephones,* 73 PUR4th 485 (N.C., 1986); *Re Customer-owned Telephone Coin Equipment,* 81 PUR4th 61 (Md., 1986). In Iowa, coin telephones have been deregulated. On customer-owned, coinless pay telephones, see *Re Network Connection of Customer-owned Instrument-implemented Coin Telephones,* 84 PUR4th 281 (Cal., 1987). See also "Pay-Phone Vendors Reshaping Industry," *The Wall Street Journal,* June 16, 1986, p. 8.

[124]In a December, 1943, order, the FCC barred hotels and motels from imposing a surcharge on their guests' telephone bills. To help defray the administrative costs of providing service to guests and to encourage the placement of telephones in guests'

rooms, AT&T began to pay commissions: 15 percent on long-distance interstate calls billed to a guest's room; five cents per call on collect calls and calls billed to a third party from a guest's room; and 15 cents on credit card calls from hotel guests. In 1980, the domestic hotel and motel industry received approximately $65 million in commissions. The FCC removed its ban on surcharges by hotels and motels as of June 1, 1980, and AT&T is in the process of eliminating all annual commission payments. (The payment of commissions on intrastate long-distance calls varies across the country.)

[125]In the two previous examples of rate structures, the rate "per main telephone per month" has been replaced with a rate "per access line per month."

[126]One local telephone company, for instance, has identified six steps in the installation process. A residential installation requiring all six steps costs $54.25 (versus $66.75 for a one-party business installation), but if inside wiring and jacks are in place, and the customer has the telephone(s), the installation charge is $22.00.

[127]See, *e.g.*, *Re Pacific Teleph. & Teleg. Co.*, 38 PUR4th 385 (Cal., 1980).

[128]While rates are unregulated, directory advertising revenues are commonly considered in state ratemaking. See *1985 Annual Report on Utility and Carrier Regulation, op. cit.*, pp. 654-55. See also "The Rush to Mine Gold From Yellow Pages," *Fortune*, September 29, 1986, pp. 133-34.

[129]For ratemaking purposes, a distinction is made between intrastate and interstate toll service. The theory of toll rates, however, is basically the same for both types of service. See "Long Distance Message Toll Telephone Rates" (Washington, D.C.: National Association of Regulatory Utility Commissioners, 1983).

[130]Distances within most states are measured point-to-point between toll rate centers for short hauls, and between the centers of specified blocks for the longer hauls and still larger sections for the longest hauls. The distance between rate centers is determined in accordance with the "V-H System" of mileage measurement. Under this system, the distance is computed from the originating rate center to the center of an area which encloses the terminating rate center. This area becomes progressively larger as the distance increases. Rate distance does not depend upon the actual routing of the call.

[131]For an analysis of the cream-skimming issue, see Kahn, *op. cit.*, Vol. II, pp. 220-50.

[132]In announcing its policy of free entry by specialized carriers, for example, the commission stated that the common carriers may depart from nationwide average rate levels. 37 *Telecommunications Reports* 1 (June 1, 1971).

[133]Leland L. Johnson, "Technological Advance and Market Structure in Domestic Telecommunications," 60 *American Economic Review* 204, 205-06 (Papers and Proceedings, 1970). For the opposite view, see William H. Melody, "Interservice Subsidy: Regulatory Standards and Applied Economics," in Harry M. Trebing (ed.), *Essays on Public Utility Pricing and Regulation* (East Lansing: MSU Public Utilities Studies, 1971), pp. 167-210. See also David Chessler and Li-King Ferng, "On the Limited Use of Marginal Cost Pricing in Telephone Regulation," in Jane L. Racster (ed.), *Issues in Regulating Imperfectly Competitive Telecommunications Markets* (Columbus, Ohio: National Regulatory Research Institute, 1986), pp. 43-94.

[134]See, *e.g.*, *Re American Teleph. & Teleg. Co., Private Line Service (TELPAK)*, Docket No. 18128, 61 FCC 2D 587 (1976).

[135]*Re American Teleph. & Teleg. Co., Manual and Procedures for the Allocation of Costs*, 84 FCC 2d 384 (1981), *aff'd sub nom. MCI Telecommunications Corp. v. Federal Communi-*

cations Comm., 675 F. 2d 408 (D.C. Cir. 1982). The manual, it should be noted, adopted a different fully distributed cost methodology than the methodology adopted in the 1976 TELPAK decision. The interim manual provides for allocating costs to three categories — MTS, WATS, and private line — using separations-based procedures.

[136]At the time of the filing, private-line rates were flat, and varied with distance. To illustrate: AT&T's rate for a 100-mile private line was $315 per line per month. The customer had unlimited use of the private line. Multiple lines were charged for at multiples of the single-rate line. The original TELPAK tariff offered a discount of 51 percent for twelve lines (TELPAK A), 64 percent for twenty-four lines (TELPAK B), 77 percent for sixty lines (TELPAK C), and 85 percent for 240 lines (TELPAK D). "Thus, for a set of 240 lines over a distance of 100 miles, a customer would have paid $75,600 per month under the old rates and $11,700 per month under the new rates." Gerald W. Brock, *The Telecommunications Industry: The Dynamics of Market Structure* (Cambridge: Harvard University Press, 1981), p. 207.

[137]37 FCC 1111 (1964). The tariffs for TELPAK A and B were canceled. "The post-1964 proceedings examined the relationship of Telpak C and D prices and costs. That question could not be answered without specifying accounting conventions in considerably more detail than the commission had previously. Telpak used the same facilities and personnel as other services and many possible methods of apportioning the costs existed. Some methods showed Telpak prices above costs and some did not. The Telpak hearings were combined with other issues related to cost allocation. Many years of hearings were held. . . ." Brock, *op. cit.*, p. 208.

[138]61 FCC 2d 587 (1976), 64 FCC 2d 971 (1977).

[139]60 *Radio Regulation 2d* 1289 (1977). See 65 FCC 2d 295 (1977).

[140]*Re Regulatory Policies Concerning Resale and Shared Use of Common Carrier Services and Facilities*, Docket No. 20097, 60 FCC 2d 261 (1976), modified in part, 62 FCC 2d 588 (1977), *aff'd sub nom. American Teleph. & Teleg. Co. v. Federal Communications Comm.*, 572 F. 2d 17 (2d Cir. 1978), *cert. denied*, 439 U.S. 875 (1978).

[141]See *Aeronautical Radio, Inc. v. Federal Communications Comm.*, 642 F. 2d 1222 (D.C. Cir. 1980), *cert. denied*, 451 U.S. 920 (1981). Interstate TELPAK service was terminated on May 7, 1981.

[142]*Re American Teleph. & Teleg. Co., Private Line Service (High Density-Low Density Rate Structure)*, Docket No. 19919, Interim Decision, 55 FCC 2d 224 (1975), Final Decision, 58 FCC 2d 362 (1976).

[143]45 *Telecommunications Reports* 11 (September 24, 1979). See Docket No. 20814, 74 FCC 2d 1 (1979).

[144]In addition to Outward WATS, AT&T introduced Inward WATS (800 Service), which permits individuals to call the given WATS subscriber toll free. AT&T also proposed to offer WADS (Wide Area Data Service), but the FCC rejected the initial tariff and ordered the company to cancel its offering. *Re Regulations and Charges for Development Line Switching Service*, Docket No. 14154 (August 5, 1963).

[145]9 FCC 2d 30, 37 (1967). The study, made by AT&T on a fully distributed cost basis (and known as the "Seven-Way Cost Study"), was for the year ending August, 1964.

[146]Under Section 202(a) of the Communications Act of 1934, the commission must consider whether services are dissimilar or "like," and must require consistent charges for "like" services, unless found to be both compensatory *and* justified by competitive necessity. The FCC found, in 1978, that MTS and WATS are "like" ser-

vices, and ordered AT&T either to offer similar terms and conditions or to cost justify any tariff differences that remain between these services.

[147]AT&T's revisions of the WATS tariff, filed between 1972 and 1974, were allowed to become effective under an accounting order which would permit refunds. *Re American Teleph. & Teleg. Co. (WATS Revisions)*, 46 FCC 2d 81 (1974). AT&T's revisions, filed in 1975, were rejected. *Re American Teleph. & Teleg. Co. (Interstate Service Tariff Revisions)*, 51 FCC 2d 619 (1975). In 1976, the FCC held that AT&T's 1974 to 1976 filings were unacceptable. *Re American Teleph. & Teleg. Co. (Revisions to WATS)*, 59 FCC 2d 671 (1976). AT&T's revisions, filed in 1977, also were rejected. *Re American Teleph. & Teleg. Co., Long Lines Department*, 66 FCC 2d 9 (1977), reconsideration denied, 69 FCC 2d 1672 (1978).

[148]59 FCC 2d 671, 703 (1976).

[149]*Nader v. Federal Communications Comm.*, 520 F. 2d 182, 207 (D.C. Cir. 1980). The same court, in another decision, said: ". . . there must be some reasonably prompt decision-making point at which the FCC says: 'To the best of our knowledge and expertise at this time, the rates are just and reasonable. Perfect, perhaps not, but just and reasonable, yes.' That is all the statute requires." *MCI Telecommunications Corp. v. Federal Communications Comm.*, 627 F. 2d 322, 340 (D.C. Cir. 1980).

[150]There are other rates and regulations, such as installation charges, timing and minimum lines.

[151]See Table 15-5.

[152]There are two basic types of carriers: facilities-based carriers and resellers. The former own all or part of their transmission facilities. The latter subscribe to communications services and facilities from facilities-based carriers "for reoffer of services to the public for profit." *1985 Annual Report on Utility and Carrier Regulation, op. cit.*, p. 667, n. 1. On resellers, see Comment, "Resale, Shared Use and Deregulation: Can the 'Invisible Hand' hold on to Ma Bell?," 35 *Federal Communications Law Journal* 209 (1983).

[153]See Chapter 6, pp. 217-18.

[154]See, *e.g.*, *Re Deregulation of Inside Wiring*, 81 PUR4th 134 (N.C., 1986).

[155]*The Wall Street Journal*, January 4, 1988, p. 4. "At the present time, only the interstate and foreign basic services of the local exchange carriers, AT&T, Alascom and Comsat remain subject to 'cost-of-service' or 'rate-of-return' regulation." *Re Policy and Rules Concerning Rates for Dominant Carriers*, CC Docket No. 87-313 (FCC, 1987), p. 2. All other carriers have been found to be "non-dominant" and have been granted "forebearance" from federal tariff regulation. See *Re Competitive Carriers*, CC Docket No. 79-252, First Report, 85 FCC 2d 1 (1980), Second Report, 91 FCC 2d 59 (1982), Third Report, 48 *Fed. Reg.* 46,791 (1983), Fourth Report, 95 FCC 2d 554 (1983), Fifth Report, 98 FCC 2d 1191 (1984), Sixth Report, 99 FCC 2d 1020 (1985), *rev'd and rem'd sub nom. MCI Telecommunications Corp. v. Federal Communications Comm.*, 765 F. 2d 1186 (D.C. Cir. 1985).

[156]*Re Guidelines for Dominant Carriers' MTS Rates and Rate Structure Plans*, CC Docket No. 84-1235, 50 *Fed. Reg.* 42,945 (FCC, 1985).

[157]"Under a price cap approach, there is a presumption that as long as a carrier's adjusting rate levels for a capped service does not result in rates exceeding the preset cap, the new rates are not unlawful." *Re Policy and Rules Concerning Rates for Dominant Carriers, op. cit.*, p. 8. However, there are various interpretations as to what is meant by a price cap. "At one extreme, the cap requirement could be interpreted to impose a ceiling on the average rates of capped services overall. . . . At the other extreme,

the cap requirement could mean a ceiling on the rate associated with each rate element of a service." *Ibid.* See, *e.g.*, *Re New York Teleph. Co.*, Opinion No. 85-17 (N.Y., 1985), Opinion No. 85-17(A), 74 PUR4th 590 (N.Y., 1986), Opinion No. 85-17(B), 77 PUR4th 119 (N.Y., 1986), Opinion No. 85-17(C) (N.Y., 1987), Opinion No. 85-17(D), 85 PUR4th 178 (N.Y., 1987).

This alternative to traditional regulation is often referred to as the social contract regulatory scheme. See *A Perspective on Social Contract and Telecommunications Regulation* (Columbus, Ohio: National Regulatory Research Institute, 1987); Sushil K. Bhattacharyya and Dan J. Laughhunn, "Price Cap Regulation: Can We Learn from the British Telecom Experience?," 120 *Public Utilities Fortnightly* 22 (October 15, 1987). But see Jack L. Landau, "Social Contract Regulation Is a Bad Bargain for Ratepayers," 120 *Public Utilities Fortnightly* 21 (July 9, 1987); "AT&T Profits on Price-Cap Alternative, Ending Margin Limit Aids Firm in Some States," *The Wall Street Journal,* September 2, 1987), p. 6; "FCC Proposal for Phone Deregulation Is in Trouble," *ibid.*, February 12, 1988, p. 4.

[158]*Ibid.*, December 30, 1986, p. 46. The estimate was made by the Consumer Federation of America.

[159]See Chapter 10, pp. 425-28.

[160]For a fifty-state summary, see 5 *State Telephone Regulation Report* 3 (September 24, 1987). For typical state decisions on intra-LATA competition, see *Re Inter- and Intra-LATA Intrastate Competition*, 60 PUR4th 24 (Ky., 1984); *Re Intrastate Telecommunications Competition*, 60 PUR4th 301 (N.J., 1984); *Re Intrastate Access Charges*, 69 PUR4th 69 (Pa., 1985); *Re Competition in the IntraLATA Telecommunications Market*, 77 PUR4th 1 (Mo., 1986); *Re Ideal-Z-Tel, Inc.*, 82 PUR4th 632 (Neb., 1987). Where intra-LATA competition is not permitted, several state commissions have considered the unauthorized use of intra-LATA facilities. See, *e.g.*, *Re Competitive Intrastate Offerings of Long-distance Telephone Service*, 69 PUR4th 629 (N.C., 1985); *Re Investigation to Consider Impact of Modified Final Judgment*, 83 PUR4th 672 (Va., 1987).

[161]As of September 1, 1987, twenty-two states had enacted telecommunications deregulation statutes. See 5 *State Telephone Regulation Report* 1, 6-9 (September 24, 1987). See, *e.g.*, *Re SouthernTel of Virginia, Inc.*, 62 PUR4th 245 (Va., 1984); *Re Intrastate Telephone Access Charges*, 80 PUR4th 112 (N.C., 1986); *Re Chicago SMSA Limited Partnership*, 81 PUR4th 287 (Ill., 1987); *Washington Utils. & Transp. Comm. v. Pacific Northwest Bell Teleph. Co.*, 83 PUR4th 380 (Wash., 1987).

Chapter 12

SERVICE, SAFETY, AND MANAGEMENT EFFICIENCY

Whenever the commission, after a hearing after reasonable notice had upon its own motion or upon complaint, finds that the service of any public utility is unreasonable, unsafe, inadequate, insufficient or unreasonably discriminatory, the commission shall determine the reasonable, safe, adequate, sufficient service to be observed, furnished, enforced or employed and shall fix the same by its order, rule or regulation.

—*Uniform Public Utilities Act**

The second primary duty of the regulatory commissions involves service and safety regulation, and the overseeing of management efficiency. These aspects of regulation are extremely important, because there is no such thing as a reasonable rate for service that is deficient. It will be remembered that common callings were required by the common law to render adequate and safe service without undue or unjust discrimination. Most of the common-law obligations have been incorporated within state and federal legislation dealing with public utilities.

The legislative standards and commission decisions relating to the quality and quantity of service, safety, and management efficiency will be discussed in this chapter. Some aspects of environmental quality are considered in the Appendix. One word of caution: The importance of this phase of regulation should not be minimized simply because it is covered in a single chapter. Service and safety regulation can be discussed in such a manner because far fewer problems have been raised by this aspect of regulation than by rate regulation. With but few exceptions, public utilities have maintained high service and safety standards, although some believe that there has been a deterioration in the quality of service in the last decade[1] and the volume of complaints has increased dramatically. (In 1985, for instance, the New York Public Service Commission received over 47,000 customer complaints, as detailed in Table 12-1.) Further, there are a number of specific issues, particularly those surrounding the termination of service, nuclear power safety, and management efficiency, that require analysis.

TABLE 12-1

Customer Complaints Received by
The New York Public Service Commission, 1985

	Telephone	Electric	Gas	Combination Elec. & Gas	Water
Service	7,738	21	271	1,330	144
Tariff	—	97	34	159	22
Billing	4,407	130	5,379	20,689	1,555
Safety	—	4	20	61	0
Miscellaneous	752	63	646	3,490	22
Totals	12,897	315	6,350	25,729	1,743

Source: *1985 Annual Report on Utility and Carrier Regulation* (Washington, D.C.: National Association of Regulatory Utility Commissioners, 1987), p. 117.

Relation of Service, Safety, and Efficiency to Rates

There is a relation — perhaps an obvious one — between the quality and quantity of service, safety, and efficiency and the rates charged consumers. In many cases, an increase in service or safety results in a rise of a utility's costs, and higher rates must be charged. Such is the case with the frequency of electric and gas meter tests or with one-party versus four-party telephone service.[2]

A utility also may be required to extend service to a small rural area that cannot afford to pay the full cost, thereby resulting in subsidization from service users in larger areas. The type of equipment which a utility uses is directly related to the cost of providing the service. And higher safety and/or environmental standards will usually result in higher costs, such as with nuclear power generating equipment, while higher costs than necessary will result from management inefficiencies.

The regulatory commissions cannot ignore this relation between service, safety, efficiency, and rates.[3] Equally important, their policies regarding rate regulation will directly affect the quality and quantity of service a utility will offer. Take, for instance, the depreciation problem. If a utility is permitted to accrue adequate depreciation or to amortize the unrecovered depreciation on its equipment when more modern or higher quality equipment is installed, technological improvements will be encouraged. If, however, a utility is not allowed adequate depreciation rates on equipment actually in use, it may not install new equipment until the old is fully depreciated. In short, commission policies have important effects on the quantity and quality of service a public utility will offer.

There are some types of service, as Thompson and Smith have pointed out, that bear little relation to rates:

> . . . It should cost but little to train employees to be courteous or to require the meter reader to clean his shoes before crossing the customer's threshold. In general, however, there is some connection between the quality of service and rates. And it goes without dispute that no higher quality or quantity can be demanded of a utility than the users are willing to pay for, assuming the usual economy of management.[4]

Not only is there a relationship between service, safety, efficiency, and rates, but there exists the possibility that service competition might become discriminatory. According to Welch:

> . . . Clearly, no utility can refuse service to any customer, otherwise qualified, because of race, color, creed, or political consideration. It can, however, refuse demands for free service or service to persons outside of the service area, or to those who refuse to comply with regulations governing special charges that cover the extra expense of furnishing special or unusual service demands. It can also refuse to serve persons who abuse or forfeit their right to service. . . .[5]

There are several examples involving the airline industry, prior to deregulation. Thus, in 1966, the Civil Aeronautics Board's Bureau of Enforcement filed formal complaints against nine domestic airlines, alleging that their special airport lounges ("clubs") constituted "unjust discrimination" because they provided "special and superior services" to selected passengers, while denying such services to other passengers who had paid the same fares.[6]

Legislative Provisions

The legislative provisions dealing with service and safety requirements are broad. The Colorado public utility law, for example, contains the following provisions:

(1) Whenever the commission, after a hearing upon its own motion or upon complaint, finds that the rules, regulations, practices, equipment, facilities, or service of any public utility or the methods of manufacture, distribution, transmission, storage, or supply employed by it are unjust, unreasonable, unsafe, improper, inadequate, or insufficient, the commission shall determine the just, reasonable, safe, proper, adequate, or sufficient rules, regulations, practices, equipment, facilities, service, or methods to be observed, furnished, constructed, enforced, or employed and shall fix the same by its order, rule, or regulation.

(2) The commission shall prescribe rules and regulations for the performance of any service or the furnishing of any commodity of the character furnished or supplied by any public utility, and upon proper tender of rates, such public utility shall furnish such commodity or render such service within the time and upon the conditions provided in such rules.[7]

Likewise, the legislative provisions concerning management efficiency are broad. The Maine public utility law, to illustrate, states:

The commission shall have authority to inquire into the management of the business of all public utilities and shall keep itself informed as to the manner and method in which each is conducted; and shall have the right to obtain from any public utility all necessary information to enable the commission to perform its duties.[8]

Further, in determining just and reasonable rates, the commission "may consider whether the utility is operating as efficiently as possible and is utilizing sound management practices."[9]

The application of these provisions has been left to the regulatory commissions, subject to judicial review. Traditionally, the commissions either acted only in response to consumer complaints or established broad service standards. Perhaps, argued Wilcox, that was fortunate:

The danger of prescribing service standards is that technology will be frozen, progress impeded, and managerial initiative impaired. This is a danger that the utility commissions have been able to avoid. In practice, little has been done in the way of developing and enforcing standards of quality. The utilities take the initiative; the commissions intervening only on complaint. On the whole the results appear to be good. With most utilities the quality of service is high.[10]

Despite this danger, a combination of rising utility rates and increasing consumer intervention (and complaints) has resulted in many commissions prescribing detailed service quality and performance standards, with staff members making periodic inspections and tests to insure adherence to the required standards. Efforts to promote conservation have placed a relatively new issue before the regulatory agencies and the utilities. Many commissions also have ordered so-called "management audits," in large part to provide an analysis of management efficiency, and both performance and productivity measures are being developed.

Quality of Service

The quality aspects of service include the following: accuracy of meters, methods of billing, continuity of service, voltage and frequency requirements, deposits and repayments, quality of equipment, treatment of complaints, courtesy to customers, and health standards. With respect to electric and gas meters, for instance, the New York commission:

1. ". . . allows use of only those types of meters which have been found to be operating satisfactorily,"
2. requires the companies "to remove meters from customer premises for inspection and tests at specified intervals,"
3. requires "gas and electric utilities to provide approved meter testing stations and then makes periodic tests of the meter-proving equipment to make certain that its high standards of accuracy are maintained at all times,"
4. maintains laboratories "where tests and inspections are made to insure adherence to proper standards," and
5. maintains a field staff to check on such matters as voltage levels, the heating value of gas, gas pressure, service interruptions, and load growth.[11]

The commissions have long prescribed a system for receiving and promptly resolving quality complaints from customers. They also specify when cash deposits are required for the purpose of establishing credit, their amount (usually a percentage of the customer's or applicant's estimated monthly bill), the conditions under which deposits are to be refunded, and the annual interest that must be paid on such deposits. Courtesy to customers is stressed by both the commissions and the utilities.

Service Standards: Telephone Companies

Typical of the more detailed, specific service standards are those of the Illinois Commerce Commission for telephone companies. Table 12-2 contains the "Table of Contents" from General Order 197. The following quality of service standards are from Section 600:

TABLE 12-2

General Order 197

Standards of Service for Telephone Companies
In the State of Illinois

TABLE 12-2 *(Continued)*

Table of Contents

Source: Illinois Commerce Commission, General Order 197 (adopted November 6, 1970, as amended in subsequent orders), pp. III-V.

1. Traffic studies shall be made and records maintained to the extent and frequency necessary to determine that sufficient equipment and an adequate operating force are provided. (Section 601-2)

2. Each telephone company shall maintain records of its operations in sufficient detail as is necessary to permit review and such records shall be made available for inspection by the Commission upon request at any time within the period prescribed for retention of such records. (Section 602-8)

3. When an operator is notified by a customer that he has reached a wrong number, been cut off, or experienced poor transmission, the customer shall be given credit when the claim has been substantiated. (Section 603-3).

4. The average speed of answer for toll and assistance calls will be in the range of 90 percent to 92 percent within ten seconds. Whenever the answering time falls below 88 percent on a monthly basis, the company shall take corrective action and provide a report of the matter to the Commission. (Section 604b)

5. Central office capacity and equipment shall be engineered to provide dial tone within three seconds on 98 percent of calls during the busy hour and this shall be maintained at 95 percent or above. (Section 605-2)

6. Local inter- and intra-office trunks shall be engineered so that at least 98 percent of telephone calls placed should not encounter an All Trunks Busy condition. When the completion rate falls below 96 percent for three consecutive months, corrective action shall be initiated and such action reported to the Commission. (Section 606-1)

7. In each exchange at least one coin telephone will be available to the public on a 24-hour basis. This coin telephone shall be located in a prominent location, provided with a directory, and lighted at night. (Section 609-1)

8. Each telephone company shall make all reasonable efforts to prevent interruptions of service. When interruptions occur, the telephone company shall reestablish service with the shortest possible delay. The minimum monthly objective should be to clear 95 percent of all out-of-service troubles within 24 hours of the time such troubles are reported, except when such service interruptions are caused by emergency situations or acts of God affecting large numbers of customers. Whenever a telephone company fails to meet the monthly objective hereinabove set forth, it shall report that fact, together with a verified statement of the reasons thereof, to the Commission within 15 days after the end of each such month. (Section 610-1)

9. The telephone company shall normally complete 90 percent of its regular service (business and residence 1, 2 and 4-party service) installations within five working days. The interval commences with the receipt of application unless a later date is requested by the

applicant, and when all tariff requirements related thereto have been complied with. Whenever, due to company reasons, the completion rate by report entity falls below 82 percent within five working days for three consecutive months, the company shall report to the Commission. (Section 611-1)[12]

Termination of Service: Electric and Gas Utilities

Public utilities have long had the right (a) to render service subject to reasonable rules and regulations and (b) to withdraw service under prescribed conditions (*e.g.,* violation of a rule, nonpayment of a bill), after giving due notice to their customers. The termination of service because of nonpayment, however, became of significance by the mid-1970s — particularly for electric and gas utilities — due to rapidly escalating customer bills.[13] Many new rules and regulations have been adopted in recent years.

Typical of these rules are those established by the Colorado commission for electric utilities.[14] Discontinuance of service requires due notice, meaning

... written notice mailed by first class mail, or delivered at least ten days in advance of the proposed termination date, advising the customer in what particular such rule has been violated for which service will be discontinued, and/or the amount due and the date by which the same shall be paid. In the event the customer previously has executed a third-party notification form indicating a third party to whom notice of discontinuance or termination is to be sent, written notice also shall be mailed by first class mail or delivered at least ten days in advance of the proposed termination date to said third party. The notice of discontinuance shall be conspicuous in nature and in easily understood language. The heading of the notice of discontinuance shall be in block capital letters and shall be bilingual, in English and in Spanish, as a minimum containing the notification that,

"THIS IS A FINAL NOTICE OF DISCONTINUANCE OF ELECTRIC UTILITY SERVICE. THIS NOTICE CONTAINS IMPORTANT INFORMATION INVOLVING YOUR LEGAL RIGHTS AND REMEDIES. IF YOU DO NOT READ ENGLISH YOU SHOULD REQUEST SOMEONE WHO UNDERSTANDS SPANISH AND ENGLISH TO TRANSLATE THIS NOTICE FOR YOU."

This rule shall not apply where a bypass is discovered on a customer's service meter, or any hazardous condition on a customer's premises, or in the case of a customer utilizing service in such a manner as to make it dangerous for occupants of the premises, thus making an immediate discontinuance of service to the premises imperative.[15]

The written notice, at a minimum, must advise the customer of certain information (*e.g.*, "how to contact the utility, without expense to the customer of a toll call, to resolve any dispute. . . .") and rights (*e.g.*, "a hearing in person, before termination of service, at a reasonable time and place within fourteen days of the date of the notice of discontinuance before the manager of the utility, or his designee"; an informal complaint to the commission or a request, in writing, of a hearing before the commission).

Service may not be discontinued under certain specific circumstances:

(1) if all current bills are paid when due and all past due amounts are being amortized by reasonable installment payments. The due date shall be no earlier than ten days subsequent to the mailing or delivery of the bill. Current bill means that portion of the bill which is not thirty days past due. The minimum reasonable installment payment is that which pays a current bill in full and is at least one-sixth of any past due balance. A reasonable installment payment plan may require that a past due balance be paid off in no more than six equal monthly installments. A utility has the right, in the event there is a breach in the installment agreement, to discontinue service. . . .

(2) between 12 noon on Friday and 8 A.M. the following Monday, or between 12 noon on the day prior to and 8 A.M. on the day following any federal holiday or utility observed holiday.

(3) during any period when termination of service would be especially dangerous to the health or safety of the customer or a permanent resident of the customer's household and such customer establishes that he is unable to pay for the service regularly billed by the utility, or he is able to pay for such service but only in reasonable installments.

   Termination of service that would be especially dangerous to the health or safety of the customer or a permanent resident of a customer's household means that termination of service would aggravate an existing medical condition or create a medical emergency for the customer or a permanent resident of the customer's household. Such shall be deemed to be the case when a physician licensed by the state of Colorado makes a certification thereof in writing and said certification is received by the utility.

   In the event a medical certification as aforesaid is delivered to or received by the utility, the nondiscontinuance of service as herein prescribed shall be effective for sixty days from the date of said medical certification. . . .

(4) until the utility has made a reasonable effort to give notice of the proposed discontinuance in person or by telephone to the customer or to a resident of the customer's household eighteen years of age

or over and to any third party who is listed by the customer on a third party notification form.

(5) in the event a customer at any time proffers full payment of any utility bill by cash or bona fide check to a utility service representative or field employee. The provision herein shall not preclude the utility, by tariff rule and rate, from making a reasonable charge for a service call.[16]

Finally, the rules require a utility to provide residential customers, both new and on an annual basis, "a list of major federal, state, or local government agencies, known to the utility, which provide customer assistance or benefits relating to utility service" and to all customers, upon request, "a list of all organizations and agencies, public and private, known to the utility," which provide such assistance or benefits.[17]

A few commissions have gone even further, adopting rules which make it extremely difficult to terminate service during the winter heating season.[18] In 1981, for example, the Missouri commission adopted a "cold weather" utility service termination rule (in effect from November 15 through March 15), under which customers are protected against discontinuance if they make a good faith attempt to pay their bill. "Under the provisions of the rule, a utility customer will not be terminated if he agrees to pay a minimum of 25 percent of the bill, or $75, whichever is greater. The customer, however, must make arrangements with the company to pay off his outstanding balance before the next winter season."[19] Other commissions and utilities have taken entirely different approaches. Many have adopted programs which allow customers to pay their electric and gas bills in levelized monthly amounts.[20] Others have placed emphasis upon making houses more energy-efficient and, thereby, more affordable.[21] And some utilities have experimented with "service limiters"; *i.e.*, devices that mechanically cut electric or gas supplies to the minimum level required for certain end uses (primarily heating, refrigeration, and lighting).[22]

Quantity of Service

The second aspect of service regulation involves the quantitative element. Four problems are predominant — entry restrictions, compulsory extension of existing services, curtailment of service, and service abandonment. Each will be examined in turn.

Restriction of Entry

Entry, including both the certification of a new company and the certification of an existing company to serve a new area, is rigidly controlled by the regulatory commissions.[23] Certificates of public convenience and necessity are required to provide public utility services. Each applicant must show that the proposed service is required by public convenience and necessity, and that it is "fit, willing, and able" to perform properly the proposed service and to conform to all relevant regulations. The exceptions to entry control are the construction of oil pipelines and municipal power production. The intended purpose of such control is to regulate competition *within* each industry, thereby preventing overinvestment in high fixed-cost industries and encouraging the achievement of economies of scale.[24]

Restriction of entry raises few problems in the electric, gas distribution, and water industries. The existing companies are usually willing to expand their operations in line with customer demands, and few new suppliers apply for certificates. Such is not the case, however, in the telephone and natural gas transmission industries.

Natural Gas Transmission.[25] Under the Natural Gas Act of 1938, as amended in 1942,

> No natural-gas company or person which will be a natural-gas company upon completion of any proposed construction or extension shall engage in the transportation or sale of natural-gas, subject to the jurisdiction of the Commission, or undertake the construction or extension of any facilities thereof, or acquire or operate any such facilities or extensions thereof, unless there is in force with respect to such natural-gas company a certificate of public convenience and necessity issued by the Commission authorizing such acts or operations. . . .[26]

The amended act gives the commission power to determine "reasonable terms and conditions as the public convenience and necessity may require"[27] and to determine the service areas to which each authorization is limited. But the commission may issue a certificate to another pipeline company within a service area if it finds that additional service is necessary.[28]

The criteria developed by the Federal Power Commission for certification included adequacy of natural gas reserves, physical facilities, financial resources, and market demand.[29] The commission soon found, however, that its exercise of the certificate power raised broad policy questions. In particular, should the certificate provision be employed to promote social goals?

Since the commission allowed interested parties to intervene extensively, certification cases, argues Huitt,

> . . . became the battleground upon which coal, labor, and railroad interests sought to stay the invasion by natural gas of coal-burning market areas. Their case for restricting the growth of the natural-gas industry rested on the basic fact that, while both coal and gas are exhaustible resources, gas reserves are estimated in decades and coal reserves in centuries. From this premise, three arguments were made:
> 1) The coal and railroad industries are large-scale employers of skilled

labor; natural-gas pipe-lines are not. Miners and railroad workers displaced by the substitution of gas for coal cannot be replaced when the gas is gone. Therefore, natural gas should be kept out of markets adequately supplied by coal.

2) Industrialization of major producing states in the South and Southwest, based on natural gas as a fuel, would help decentralize industry, foster regional development, and balance the economies of those sections. Therefore, the industrial needs of producing states should be considered in certificate cases.

3) Natural gas is a "luxury" commodity, having great value as a fuel for domestic consumption and as a raw material for the chemical industries, and perhaps for conversion into a liquid fuel. It is economic waste to burn vast quantities at low prices as boiler fuel. Therefore, the certificate power should be used for the selective control of end uses of gas.

These contentions clearly go beyond anything the Congress had in mind when it passed the Natural Gas Act. . . .[30]

As a general proposition, the FPC rejected the arguments advanced by various interested competitors. In a 1953 decision, for example, the commission held that allegations of possible economic loss to competing interests (railroads and labor) were insufficient to foreclose the issuance of a certificate. "If such a standard had been applied since enactment of the Natural Gas Act, the natural-gas industry, as an interstate supplier of one of the nation's most important fuels, would have been completely stultified."[31] Likewise, the FPC tended to reject the arguments advanced by existing pipelines when new entry was proposed. In 1967, in authorizing Transco's entry into the Washington, D.C., and Richmond, Virginia, market areas (previously served exclusively by affiliates of the Columbia System), the commission cited several cases involving competition and concluded that "the cases favor the introduction of an element of competition where its operative effect will tend to promote the public interest. This reflects sound regulatory policy which is based squarely upon the policies underlying the Natural Gas Act."[32]

Finally, with respect to conservation, the FPC tended to view end use as but one factor to be considered in granting a certificate. In an early decision, the commission said: "We have repeatedly held that the end use of natural gas as boiler fuel is an inferior usage and that, while it is not to be denied in all situations, it should be permitted only on a positive showing that it is required by public convenience and necessity."[33] Thus, in a 1961 decision, the commission rejected a certificate under which Con Ed proposed to contract with Transco to transport gas from producing fields in the Southwest for use as boiler fuel to generate electricity in New York. It held that the price to be paid for the gas was too high and would unbalance the area price level, and that the consumption of natural gas for boiler fuel was an "inferior" use which should be discouraged. The Supreme Court agreed.[34]

Compulsory Extension of Service

There are two aspects to the problem of service extension. First, service may be extended within the same general market area that a utility presently serves. Second, service may be extended into a new market area. The state and federal legislative provisions are similar to those found in the Natural Gas Act, as amended, which provide that the commission, after a hearing,

> ... may by order direct a natural-gas company to extend or improve its transportation facilities, to establish physical connection of its transportation facilities with the facilities of, and sell natural gas to, any person or municipality engaged or legally authorized to engage in the local distribution of natural or artificial gas to the public, and for such purpose to extend its transportation facilities to communities immediately adjacent to such facilities or to territory served by such natural-gas company, if the Commission finds that no undue burden will be placed upon such natural-gas company thereby: *Provided,* That the Commission shall have no authority to compel the enlargement of transportation facilities for such purposes, or to compel such natural-gas company to establish physical connection or sell natural gas when to do so would impair its ability to render adequate service to its customers.[35]

Extension within Market Area. A public utility is required to serve all who ask for, and are willing to pay for, service within the area where it holds itself out to serve.[36] This area is usually specified in the commission's certificate or the city's franchise. As stated by the Supreme Court:

> Corporations which devote their property to a public use may not pick and choose, serving only the portions of the territory covered by their franchises which is presently profitable for them to serve, and restricting the development of the remaining portions by leaving their inhabitants in discomfort without the service which they alone can render.[37]

As a rule, therefore, a public utility can be required to extend its service as its specified market area grows. Most companies are willing to do so voluntarily in order to expand or grow with their markets. At times, however, an extension within a market area is not profitable. Here, the commissions will consider the prospective costs and revenues, as well as the social benefits, of such an extension. Some service extensions may be ordered even though costs are greater than revenues. The key issues are the effect of the extension on (a) the total return of the company involved[38] and (b) the ability to render "adequate" service to "existing customers."[39]

The commissions have an alternative to requiring service extension by the existing company: they have the authority to issue a certificate to a new company when the existing company is providing deficient service in its market area.[40] Neither a certificate nor a franchise, in other words, protects a utility from the entry of a competitor if a commission finds such entry to be in the public interest.[41]

Extension into New Market. A different problem arises when considering the extension of service beyond a company's present market area, for substantial investment in new plant and equipment is usually required. While many of the commissions have authority to require expansion into a new area, that authority is limited and has been used sparingly. Thus, the Federal Energy Regulatory Commission is authorized to order natural gas pipeline extensions to communities that are "immediately adjacent" to a transmission line or "to territory served" by a transmission company, but no farther. And a few commissions lack authority to require extensions into new markets.[42]

As with extensions within a market area, a utility is usually willing to expand voluntarily into a new market area. Few cases have resulted and only two have reached the Supreme Court. In the first case, the New York commission ordered a gas company to extend its service to several communities adjacent to the city where the firm operated. After giving considerable attention to the prospective costs and revenues, the Court upheld the commission's order for the extension as a reasonable one. The Court warned, however, that:

> Under the guise of regulation, the state may not require the company to make large expenditures for the extension of its mains and service into new territory when the necessary result will be to compel the company to use its property for the public convenience without just compensation.[43]

The second case involved the only extension of a railroad line ever ordered by the Interstate Commerce Commission. The commission ordered a subsidiary of the Union Pacific to make a 187-mile extension in Oregon that would cost nearly $9 million. The Court refused to uphold the order, believing that the commission's authority did not "embrace the building of what is essentially a new line to reach new territory."[44] The Court concluded:

> We should expect, if Congress were intending to grant to the Commission a new and drastic power to compel the investment of enormous sums for the . . . service of a region which the carrier had never theretofore entered or intended to serve, the intention would be expressed in more than a clause in a sentence dealing with car service.[45]

When companies, because of the prospective costs and revenues, are unwilling to extend service to new market areas voluntarily, commissions can often make such extensions attractive. A company may be permitted to charge higher rates in the new market than are charged in the old market. In this way, the new customers will pay the costs of extending the service. A company may be permitted to raise its rates in the old market, thus charging more for the same service than in the new market.[46] The old customers will thereby subsidize part of the new service. Finally, a company may be permitted to raise rates in both markets, so that the new and old customers will pay the same rates. Both groups will pay the costs of extending the service. Commissions generally prefer either the first or second alternative, and there are many instances where each has been employed. Suburban bus rates commonly are higher than downtown city rates; city telephone service is usually more expensive, relative to cost, than rural service.

Curtailment of Service: Interstate Gas Pipelines[47]

Beginning in the early 1970s (and continuing until 1979), the demand for natural gas exceeded the supply in the interstate market, resulting in pipelines curtailing deliveries of gas to some of their customers. In April, 1971, the Federal Power Commission issued Order No. 431, requiring every jurisdictional pipeline (*a*) to report to the commission whether curtailment of its deliveries to customers would be necessary because of inadequate supplies and, if curtailment were deemed necessary, (*b*) to file a revised tariff to control deliveries to *all* customers.[48] Thereby began a debate over issues of the basis for curtailment (*e.g.*, curtailment based on end use versus curtailment based on pro rata reduction of contract entitlements), the method of implementation (*e.g.*, fixed base period versus moving base period), and curtailment-related compensation.

In Order No. 467 (issued January 8, 1973), the FPC set forth eight curtailment priorities based on end-use criteria, but stated that "in specific cases, opportunity will be afforded interested parties to challenge or support this policy through factual or legal presentation as may be appropriate in the circumstances presented."[49] Substantial controversy surrounded both the order itself[50] and proposed curtailment plans, with the result that it took years of hearings (and numerous court appeals) before final commission decisions were made.[51] A typical FPC curtailment plan, however, is the one approved in 1976 for Panhandle Eastern Pipe Line Company. Five priorities were established:

(1) residential and small commercial (less than 50 Mcf per peak day) requirements;

(2) large commercial (50 Mcf or more per peak day) requirements without alternate fuel capabilities, industrial requirements for feedstock, plant protection and process use, and pipeline customer storage injection requirements;

   (3) all industrial and commercial requirements not specified in (1), (2), (4), or (5);
   (4) industrial and commercial requirements of more than 300 Mcf per day, where alternate fuel capabilities can meet such requirements, other than requirements for boiler fuel use;
   (5) industrial and commercial requirements for boiler use of more than 300 Mcf per day where alternate fuel capabilities can meet such requirements.[52]

In establishing these priorities, the commission rejected its "firm-interruptible dichotomy," contained in Order No. 467-B, primarily on the grounds that curtailing interruptible service first incorrectly assumes that such sales service inferior end-uses.[53] The commission adopted a fixed, pre-curtailment base period to implement the plan — a fixed thirty-month base period (April 1, 1969 to October 31, 1971) — with entitlements calculated according to the twelve months of maximum takes during the period and with curtailments on a monthly basis.[54]

The issue of curtailment-related compensation arose in most curtailment plan proceedings. Any curtailment of supply (and the subsequent curtailment of sales) has an adverse impact on the curtailed customers. Both the FPC and the FERC took the position that they lacked the power to approve compensation proposals.[55] That position was reversed in several cases,[56] but the FERC has never approved a compensation proposal.[57] A second curtailment-related compensation issue involves liability for contractual damages (*i.e.*, breach of contract). Thus, in 1978, a customer was awarded $23.8 million in damages[58] and, in 1984, two customers were awarded $84.7 million.[59] Many similar cases are pending in state and federal courts against pipeline and distribution companies.

As a consequence of the various energy-related acts passed in the late 1970s, jurisdiction over interstate pipeline curtailment policy has been bifurcated. Under the Department of Energy Organization Act, the Secretary of Energy has the authority to establish curtailment priorities.[60] That authority, however, is subject to the specific priorities contained in the Natural Gas Policy Act. First, "high-priority user," meaning:

   ... any person who—
   (A) uses natural gas in residence;
   (B) uses natural gas in a commercial establishment in amounts of less than 50 Mcf on a peak day;
   (C) uses natural gas in any school, hospital, or similar institution; or
   (D) uses natural gas in any other use the curtailment of which the Secretary of Energy determines would endanger life, health, or maintenance of physical property.[61]

Second, "essential agricultural use," meaning:

... any use of natural gas—
  (A) for agricultural production, natural fiber production, natural fi-
      ber processing, food processing, food quality maintenance, irri-
      gation pumping, crop drying, or
  (B) as a process fuel or feedstock in the production of fertilizer,
      agricultural chemicals, animal feed, or food,
which the Secretary of Agriculture determines is necessary for full food
and fiber production.[62]

Third, "essential industrial process or feedstock use" meaning:

> ... any use of natural gas in an industrial process or as a feedstock
> which the Secretary determines is essential.[63]

Under the same act, the FERC retains authority to implement curtailment priorities (*i.e.,* approve curtailment plans). However, its authority is
subject to a provision in the Public Utility Regulatory Policies Act which
specifies that if the commission permits revision of any base period in a
curtailment plan, it must do so in a manner that preserves for local gas
distribution companies any gas that would otherwise be available to them
under the prior base period "by reason of the implementation of ... conservation measures."[64]

While litigation continues, the further development of curtailment plans
has been slowed because of the more recent surplus of natural gas throughout the country.

Abandonment of Service

Abandonment of service may be voluntary or involuntary. Voluntary
abandonment, either partial or complete, must be approved by the regulatory commissions. Involuntary abandonment involves the commission's revocation or suspension of a utility's certificate, permit, or license. It is important to note that abandonment refers to a partial or complete withdrawal of
service as opposed to a reduction in a plant's output. To date, discontinuance of service has been a relatively minor regulatory problem, since the
commissions have been dealing with expanding industries. Troxel has pointed
out, however: "Before the twentieth century ends, many flourishing utility
companies probably will stop expanding; some may be decadent. Given
time, commissions will face far more petitions for partial or complete abandonment of utility operations than they have encountered in past years."[65]

Complete Abandonment. In practice, the regulatory commissions have
little power to prevent complete abandonment of service. When a natural
gas field is exhausted (*i.e.,* depleted), for instance, abandonment is inevitable.[66]
Moreover, a public utility is not obligated to provide service at a loss. Thus,

in a 1924 railroad case, the Supreme Court argued that a utility devotes its property to public service

> ... on the condition that the public shall supply sufficient traffic on a reasonable basis to yield a fair return. And if at any time it develops with reasonable certainty that future operations must be at a loss, the company may discontinue operation and get what it can out of the property by dismantling the road. To compel it to go on at a loss, or to give up the salvage value, would be to take its property without just compensation which is a part of due process of law.[67]

Partial Abandonment. When partial abandonment of service is proposed by a public utility, the commissions have the authority to either approve or disapprove the request. As long as a company earns an adequate total return, it can be required to continue the operation of unprofitable services. If, however, a company's earnings are not reasonable, partial abandonment may be necessary to prevent the impairment of service throughout the whole system. To illustrate: The Missouri commission ruled that a company must be allowed to abandon a rural electric line "unless the customers are willing to pay the proper rates. ..."[68]; the Montana and Wisconsin commissions permitted electric companies to abandon unprofitable steam heating service[69]; the New Hampshire commission allowed a telephone company to discontinue service for summer customers "in view of a continuing financial loss"[70]; and the ICC permitted the New York Central to abandon a branch line because losses on the service were affecting the profitability of the whole system.[71]

The Supreme Court's position regarding partial abandonment has not always been clear. In a 1925 case involving a request by a street railway company to abandon less than a mile of its twenty-two-mile route, the Court decided:

> A public utility cannot, because of loss, escape obligations voluntarily assumed. ... A railway may be compelled to continue the service of a branch or part of a line, although the operation involves a loss. ... This is true even where the system as a whole fails to earn a fair return upon the value of the property. So far as appears, this company is at liberty to surrender its franchise and discontinue operations throughout the city. It cannot, in the absence of contract, be compelled to continue to operate its system at a loss. ... But the Constitution does not confer upon the company the right to enjoy the franchise of indeterminate permit and escape from the burdens incident to its use.[72]

A year later, the Court apparently reversed its position. The Court, in placing considerable emphasis on the total earnings of the company, ruled:

Expenditures in the local interest may be so large as to compel the carrier to raise reasonable interstate rates, or to abstain from making an appropriate reduction of such rates, or to curtail interstate service, or to forego facilities needed in interstate commerce. Likewise, excessive local expenditures may so weaken the financial condition of the carrier as to raise the cost of securing capital . . ., and thus compel an increase in rates.[73]

In the first case, the Court placed emphasis on the public's interest; in the second case, on the utility's earnings. While both must receive attention in any case involving partial abandonment, the relative weight assigned to the two factors varies from commission to commission.[74]

Revocation, Suspension, and Modification of Certificates. A majority of the commissions have the power to revoke, suspend, or modify a certificate, permit, or license they have issued.[75] Generally, revocation is limited to situations where the holder has never or is no longer providing service, or where the holder fails to serve every customer and/or to render continuous and adequate service.[76] Thus, in a 1978 decision, the Arkansas commission revoked a telephone company's certificate when it found that the company (*a*) was in violation of the commission's special rules regarding service, (*b*) repeatedly thwarted efforts by the commission to upgrade its service by ignoring commission orders and refusing to respond to commission inquiries, and (*c*) was unwilling to cooperate, in good faith, with the commission's enforcement efforts.[77]

With respect to the public utility sector, the most important instances of revocation, suspension, or modification occur with respect to nuclear plant operating licenses. These powers of the Nuclear Regulatory Commission are considered in a later section.

Conservation: A Service-related Issue

Programs explicitly designed by electric and gas utilities to promote conservation were rare prior to the 1970s; the emphasis was upon promoting usage. Rising energy rates and new environmental concerns, however, have changed that situation dramatically. As the California commission stated in a 1975 decision: "Today, the overriding task for this commission, the utilities, and the public is conservation."[78]

At first, conservation was viewed in the context of rate design (*e.g.*, elimination of declining block rates, initiation of marginal cost-based rates).[79] But it quickly spread to other programs, including increased consumer information (*e.g.*, residential energy audits, advertising to promote conservation), the development of alternate energy sources (*e.g.*, solar and wind power, cogeneration), activities designed for implementation by consumers and builders (*e.g.*, insulation, energy saving appliances and devices,[80] the construction of energy conservation-oriented buildings), and programs designed to improve operating efficiency (*e.g.*, load management, voltage regulation).[81] Then, in 1978, Congress enacted the National Energy Conservation Policy Act,[82] as amended by the Energy Security Act of 1980.[83] Conservation has been made a cornerstone of the nation's energy policy.

Residential Conservation Service Programs

The National Energy Conservation Policy Act (NECPA), as amended, provides for the establishment of utility-sponsored Residential Conservation Service (RCS) programs.[84] Such programs, subject to state commission hearings and approval, and to approval by the Secretary of Energy,[85] must involve procedures for disseminating conservation information to "residential customers."[86] The conservation information required includes suggested "conservation measures"; potential energy cost savings; the availability of (*a*) energy inspections, (*b*) arrangements for installation and financing, and (*c*) lists of approved contractors and lenders; and suggested conservation techniques not involving installation of conservation measures. "Conservation measures," in turn, are defined as caulking and weather stripping; certain furnace efficiency modifications; ceiling, attic, wall, and floor insulation; water heater insulation; storm windows and doors; load management technique devices; and solar and wind-powered heating or cooling devices. These conservation measures must be warranted by the manufacturers for no less than three years. An onsite "energy inspection" or "audit," performed at the request of the customer, is for the purpose of determining the customer's conservation needs, and to advise the customer of the cost of installing conservation measures and of the potential savings.[87] The actual installation may be performed either by the utility or by an approved contractor, with the necessary financing either by the utility or by an approved lender.[88]

Finally, the act, as amended, contains a number of related provisions. All amounts expended or received by a utility attributable to its RCS program must be accounted for separately. All amounts expended to provide the required information to customers are to be treated as current operating expenses for ratemaking purposes. The utility is permitted to recover the general administrative costs of carrying out a program, but the permitted fee for conducting an energy inspection is limited to the lesser of $15 or the actual cost. Any costs charged directly to the customer must be included as a separate item on the customer's regular bill, but termination of service for default is prohibited. Where a utility has arranged for a loan for purchase and/or installation of energy conservation measures, the lender may request repayment through the customer's regular billing and, in that case, the utility may recover from the lender the costs incurred in carrying out repayment.[89]

Utility Insulation Programs[90]

Electric and gas utilities have developed a variety of conservation programs. The following two residential insulation programs are among the most comprehensive established to date.

PacifiCorp. In the late 1970s, Pacific Power & Light Company (PP&L, now PacifiCorp) submitted a plan for improving the thermal efficiency of its customers' homes to the proper authorities in the six states in which the utility operates. The major aspects of the program are:

1. PP&L conducts free home energy audits.
2. PP&L determines a set of "economic" insulation and weatherization options (generally weather-stripping and caulking, attic insulation, and storm windows and doors).
3. PP&L estimates its marginal cost per kilowatt-hour and its average revenue per kilowatt-hour. Conservation investments found to cost less than marginal cost are recommended to the customer as "economic," and PP&L offers to provide financing. (Note; PP&L estimates that its marginal cost exceeds its average price.)
4. To ensure that nonparticipants benefit, the overall program is based upon the constraint that the difference between marginal cost per kilowatt-hour and average price per kilowatt-hour must exceed the average cost of the conservation per kilowatt-hour saved.
5. Customers are advised of the set of "economic" measures and asked for permission to proceed with installation. If the customer approves, PP&L contracts for the work through open bidding. PP&L provides the contractor with specifications of work to be performed, conducts post-installation inspections, and pays the contractor directly.
6. Customers are charged no interest, but must repay the principal amount at such time as the home is sold or title is transferred.
7. Amounts paid contractors for conservation measures are added to the rate base. These amounts are not amortized to operating expenses, but as loans are repaid, the rate base is reduced by the amount of loans.
8. Administrative expenses incurred by PP&L in the operation of the program are charged to rate base and are amortized to operating expenses over a ten-year period.[91]

Pacific Gas and Electric Company. Early in 1981, Pacific Gas and Electric Company (PG&E) was authorized by the California commission to embark on a weatherization zero interest program (known as ZIP).[92] Under the program, PG&E will make interest-free loans to finance the installation of up to twelve energy conservation measures in residences. These measures were separated into two groups (see Table 12-3).

TABLE 12-3

Conservation Measures Eligible for ZIP Financing

Class 1 (with or without prior energy audit):

1. Ceiling insulation.
2. When performed as a package job including all of the following measures unless either already installed or unnecessary in the residence.*
   a. Weather stripping.
   b. Water heater blankets.
   c. Low-flow shower heads.
   d. Caulking.
   e. Duct wrap.

Class 2 (after audit shows cost effective):

1. Wall insulation.
2. Floor insulation.
3. Clock thermostats.
4. Lighting conversion.
5. Storm or thermal windows or doors.
6. Intermittent ignition devices.
7. Any of the Class 1 measures.

*The administrative cost of financing these relatively minor improvements individually would be excessive.

Source: John E. Bryson and Jon F. Elliott, "California's Best Energy Supply Investment: Interest-free Loans for Conservation," 108 *Public Utilities Fortnightly* 19, 20 (November 5, 1981).

The first group contains measures that are so cost effective that ZIP financing will be provided even without an individualized prior energy audit. PG&E will provide a ZIP loan for measures in the second group only after they have been shown to be cost effective in the particular residence by an energy audit conforming to the requirements of the federal residential conservation service (RCS) program. All work performed under ZIP financing will be subject to postinstallation inspection by PG&E. . . .

Upon request PG&E will furnish each participant in the ZIP program with a list of eligible contractors and average price information for the local area within which the residential property is located. PG&E is authorized to provide ZIP financing up to a ceiling which is PG&E's marginal cost for the energy estimated to be saved as a result of installation of the ZIP program measures, but in no case more than $3,500 per residence.

Participants ultimately must repay the full principal of their ZIP loans, so PG&E will absorb less than half the total cost of ZIP-financed conservation. Participants may choose between two repayment schedules with roughly the same present value but very different monthly payments. Each participant will choose by deciding how to use the proceeds of a California state income tax credit of 40 percent of the installed costs of selected energy conservation measures. If the participant keeps the proceeds, he or she will repay 2 percent of the ZIP principal per month over fifty months. To reduce the size of the monthly payment, the participant instead can pay PG&E the tax credit proceeds and repay the remaining 60 percent of principal over one hundred months. Under either option, repayment does not begin until June of the year following installation, a grace period of up to eighteen months. No new ZIP loans will be made for installations after December 31, 1986.[93]

Some Unresolved Issues

Conservation offers significant potential savings. PG&E's ZIP program, for instance, is estimated to cost the utility $1.3 billion in financing and administrative costs over a fifteen-year period (present value $800 million), compared to estimated energy savings over a thirty-year period with a present value of $4.2 billion.[94] The implementation of conservation programs, however, is not without controversy, as a further examination of the above two illustrative programs suggests.[95]

First, are such programs cost-effective?[96] "If it costs more to conserve than to consume, then PG&E and its customers will save money if people continue to consume, assuming each alternative is priced correctly."[97] The key phrase, of course, is "assuming each alternative is priced correctly." Most utility rate structures do not reflect marginal costs[98]; many conservation impacts are ignored.[99] Further, several commissions have questioned gas conservation programs. Concluded the Idaho commission with respect to Intermountain Gas Company's (IGC) proposed zero-interest loan weatherization program:

> . . . the marginal cost economics that justify our zero-interest weatherization loan program for Idaho electric utilities simply does not exist for IGC. The need to produce added electricity has caused the average cost of electric energy to increase at a phenomenal rate, and for this reason electric utilities have much to gain by investing in conservation. Intermountain Gas Company is a distributor of energy, and is not faced with similar incremental costs. In fact, the more gas IGC sells, the less is its per unit cost. While laudable, IGC's efforts to minimize the impact of this reality by offering subsidized financing for weatherization in conjunction with financing for gas heating devices

provides a benefit only to those customers who can afford to commit themselves to the interest expense of the cost of the subsidized weatherization. . . .[100]

Second, are nonparticipants, particularly those who have already implemented conservation measures, and both commercial and industrial customers, being discriminated against? To protect nonparticipants, several commissions have adopted the following rule: investment in conservation measures will be undertaken whenever the cost is less than the utility's marginal minus average price. "In such instances, nonparticipants pay less than they would have if new supply rather than increased efficiency met the demand."[101] Third, is utility financing necessary for a successful RCS program and, if so, can a commission mandate such a financing program? The answer to the former question generally has been in the affirmative. Low-income homeowners, for example, often are unable to participate in such programs because of insufficient funds and the inability to obtain the required funds at credit institutions and/or because they live in substandard housing.[102] The answer to the latter question largely depends on a state's enabling legislation.[103]

Safety Regulation

In addition to the quality and quantity of service, regulation is concerned with safety standards. Few safety standards have been established for public utilities.[104] These industries, almost from their inception, have maintained stringent safety standards. Commissions have safety codes, however, to prevent explosions from breaks or leaks in gas transmission and distribution mains, and fires from faulty wiring. Many states require that gas have an odor to aid in early detection of leaks; in the case of natural gas, an artificial odorant is added. All accidents must be reported promptly. In most instances, customers are responsible for installing facilities within their premises in conformity with local building and/or safety codes.[105] The Federal Communications Commission is concerned with a different type of safety: the commission must allocate the spectrum space for public safety radio services, such as police, fire, disaster communications, and governmental operations.

The most comprehensive safety regulations govern natural gas pipelines and LNG facilities, and nuclear power plants.[106]

Natural Gas Pipelines and LNG Facilities

The Natural Gas Pipeline Safety Act of 1968, as amended,[107] gave to the Secretary of Transportation authority to establish minimum federal safety standards for "the transportation of gas and pipeline facilities."

... Such standards may apply to the design, installation, inspection, emergency plans and procedures, testing, construction, extension, operation, replacement, and maintenance of pipeline facilities. Standards affecting the design, installation, construction, initial inspection, and initial testing shall not be applicable to pipeline facilities in existence on the date such standards are adopted. Such Federal safety standards shall be practicable and designed to meet the need for pipeline safety. . . .[108]

State commissions or legislatures may require additional or more stringent standards, provided that they are compatible with the federal standards. Monitoring and enforcement powers are vested in the Secretary of Transportation (technically, in the Office of Pipeline Safety). Every pipeline is required to file a plan for inspection and maintenance of each facility, and to inform the Office of Pipeline Safety of any pipeline leaks.[109] Since passage of the act, the Federal Energy Regulatory Commission, in certificate cases, has required the applicant to attest to compliance with the minimum safety standards.

The Pipeline Safety Act of 1979 further expanded and defined the authority of the Department of Transportation with respect to pipeline safety. In addition, the act authorized the Secretary of Transportation to establish:

(A) minimum safety standards for determining the location of any new LNG facility, and

(B) minimum safety standards for the design, installation, construction, initial inspection, and initial testing of any new LNG facility.[110]

Further, no LNG facility may be operated without prior submittal of a contingency plan

... which sets forth those steps which are to be taken in the event of an LNG accident and which is determined to be adequate by the Department of Energy or the appropriate State agency, in the case of any facility not subject to the jurisdiction of the Department under the Natural Gas Act.[111]

Nuclear Power Plants

The March 28, 1979, accident at Three Mile Island[112] raised once again serious questions about the safety of nuclear energy and the ability of the Nuclear Regulatory Commission (NRC) to deal with safety issues. As of mid-January 1987, there were 107 domestic nuclear power generating plants with operating licenses and eighteen with construction permits (of which thirteen were actually under construction).[113] However, the NRC has not granted a new construction permit since the Three Mile Island accident and no domestic utility has ordered a new plant from a reactor manufacturer since 1978.[114] Moreover, over 100 nuclear generating units have been canceled since the mid-1970s, while several others have been postponed indefinitely.[115]

The Development of Public Policy.[116] Prior to 1954, the government exercised complete control over the industrial development and promotion of nuclear power. Under the Atomic Energy Act of 1946 (the McMahon Act),[117] private ownership, production, exploration, and importation of fissionable materials were forbidden, as was private ownership of nuclear productive facilities and patents covering productive processes. The Atomic Energy Commission (AEC), set up by the law, was authorized to construct its own nuclear facilities and to enter into contracts for research and production.[118] The AEC undertook a comprehensive program of basic research and experimental development that demonstrated the technical feasibility of nuclear power. But it was not until 1951 and 1952 that private industry was invited by the AEC to investigate the possibility of producing nuclear power.[119]

The field was opened up to private enterprise by the Atomic Energy Act of 1954.[120] The AEC, which retained control, was authorized to license the private construction, ownership, and operation of nuclear facilities, and the possession, but not ownership, of fissionable materials. The commission was forbidden from entering into the commercial production of nuclear power, but it could sell power generated in experimental plants. Public agencies were granted an equal right with private utilities to apply for licenses. There were two preference provisions: one gave preference in granting licenses and the other in disposing of energy produced at AEC experimental installations.[121] Private industry was permitted to use government patents and to patent new technology.[122] The patent privilege was not absolute in that compulsory licensing might be required on inventions found by the AEC to be "of primary importance."

Under the 1954 act, the AEC promoted the development of a civilian nuclear power program. First, the agency carried on an extensive research and development program "on a laboratory scale to investigate and understand the basic science and to develop and prove out the general technology."[123] Second, the agency carried on a "power demonstration" program of utility installations "to verify technology in actual practice, to yield economic information and to provide experience on which to base improvements."[124] In some cases, the commission built and operated reactors.[125] In cases where private utilities built their own reactors, public assistance was provided in other ways. Nuclear fuel, controlled by the government until 1964, apparently was provided at less than its full cost.[126] Research and development assistance was provided free of charge, but the commission paid private reactor operators for all economic and technical data they provided. The government also was liable for millions in the event of a nuclear accident.[127] In 1966 and 1967, nuclear power accounted for nearly half of all new generating capacity ordered by domestic utilities. By the end of 1973, forty domestic nuclear power generating units were in operation, and 177 additional units were being built or planned.

The Nuclear Regulatory Commission. Under the Energy Reorganization Act of 1974,[128] the Atomic Energy Commission was abolished and two new agencies were created: the Nuclear Regulatory Commission and the Energy Research and Development Administration (ERDA, presently consolidated in the Department of Energy). The act transferred to the NRC all responsibilities for carrying out the regulatory provisions of the Atomic Energy Act of 1954, as amended; specifically, regulating civilian nuclear energy activities to ensure that they are conducted in a manner which will protect public health and safety, maintain national security, and comply with the antitrust laws. In addition, under the National Environmental Policy Act of 1969,[129] the NRC is responsible for evaluating the environmental impact of major nuclear facilities proposed for licensing. The NRC's primary functions are carried out by five operating offices:

1. *Office of Nuclear Reactor Regulation.* This office evaluates all applications for permits to build, and licenses to operate, nuclear reactors. The office licenses the receipt, possession, ownership and use of special nuclear materials (*e.g.,* plutonium, uranium 233) and byproduct materials (*i.e.,* any radioactive material) used at reactor facilities; evaluates the health, safety and environmental aspects of nuclear sites and facilities; licenses reactor operators; analyzes reactor design concepts; evaluates methods of transporting nuclear materials and radioactive wastes on reactor sites; monitors and tests operating reactors; recommends upgrading of facilities or modifications of regulations; and provides assistance in matters involving reactors or critical facilities exempt from licensing. Four major divisions oversee these responsibilities: Operating Reactor, Project Management, Site Safety and Environmental Analysis, and Systems Safety.

2. *Office of Nuclear Material Safety and Safeguards.* This office licenses and regulates all facilities and materials associated with the processing, transportation, and handling of nuclear materials. The office reviews and assesses the licensee's safeguards against potential threats, thefts, and sabotage of those materials.

3. *Office of Nuclear Regulatory Research.* This office plans, recommends, and implements those nuclear research programs related to the NRC's licensing and regulatory functions. The office has two divisions: Reactor Safety Research and Safeguards, and Fuel Cycle and Environmental Research.

4. *Office of Standards Development.* This office focuses on NRC rules, regulations, standards, and guides governing the licensing of nuclear facilities and the commercial use of nuclear materials. The office has

two divisions: Engineering Standards and Siting, Health and Safeguards.

5. *Office of Inspection and Enforcement.* This office (consisting of a headquarters group and five regional offices) ascertains compliance with the NRC's licensing regulations, orders, and conditions through the development of policies and programs for the inspection of licensees, applicants, and their contractors and suppliers. It ensures safety by identifying potential adverse conditions (adverse to public health and safety or to the environment); makes recommendations on the issuance of authorizations, permits, or licenses; determines the adequacy of the licensee's quality assurance systems; and develops enforcement policies and recommends or takes appropriate action regarding incidents or accidents.[130]

The Responses to Three Mile Island. Numerous investigations were made into the causes of the Three Mile Island accident and countless proposals were made to improve safety and its regulation. Concluded the President's Commission:

... while the major factor that turned this incident into a serious accident was inappropriate operator action, many factors contributed to the action of the operators, such as deficiencies in their training, lack of clarity in their operating procedures, failure of organizations to learn the proper lessons from previous incidents, and deficiencies in the design of the control room. These shortcomings are attributable to the utility, to suppliers of equipment, and to the federal commission that regulates nuclear power. Therefore — whether or not operator error "explains" this particular case — given all the above deficiencies, we are convinced that an accident like Three Mile Island was eventually inevitable.[131]

The NRC, after studying these reports and proposals, issued the TMI Action Plan in May, 1980, which set forth all new requirements for granting future operating licenses.[132] In August, 1980, the NRC approved new emergency planning requirements.[133] President Carter submitted Reorganization Plan No. 1 to Congress in March, 1980, which delineated the respective roles of the NRC commissioners and designated the chairman as principal executive officer of the commission.[134] The industry established two new organizations — The Nuclear Safety Analysis Center and The Institute of Nuclear Power Operations — to enhance the safety of nuclear power plants through improved safety analysis, plant design, personnel training, and operating procedures.[135]

Regardless of their desirability and/or necessity, these developments have had two major impacts on the nuclear industry. First, the licensing process has been lengthened. It now takes up to fifteen years to get a nuclear plant on line.[136] Second, the cost of nuclear plants has increased significantly. In announcing cancellation of a nuclear plant in November, 1982, for instance, the Virginia Electric and Power Company estimated that new requirements imposed since Three Mile Island would have added about $1 billion to the projected completion cost.[137] At the same time, many important safety issues remain to be resolved, ranging from "embrittlement" (*i.e.*, brittle pressure vessels)[138] to the disposal of radioactive waste.[139] And the NRC is still assessing the potential safety issues from the meltdown at Chernobyl.[140]

Management Efficiency

Rising utility costs and rates, combined with lower productivity, have put new pressures on regulatory commissions (and on management) to make sure that utilities operate as efficiently as possible. Efficiency, however, has received little historic attention, despite the Supreme Court's statement in *Bluefield* that a fair rate of return must be consistent with "efficient and economical management."[141] The commissions generally assumed efficient operations, acting only in rate cases by disallowing "unreasonable" costs and/or by considering efficiency in establishing a fair rate of return. Indeed, some contended that regulatory lag — the inevitable delay imposed by regulation on an upward or downward adjustment in a utility's rates — induced public utilities to perform at high levels of efficiency.[142] Beginning in the early 1970s, management efficiency and performance became significant issues. Contends a former state commissioner:

> ... regulation must be fashioned to penetrate traditional management prerogatives, and in the place of management autonomy, pressures of regulation must be structured so as to reward economic efficiency and penalize inefficiency. Because there does not exist a "competitive standard" intrinsic to the market system itself, and because regulators do have a strong impact upon the shape of our future economic and social development, there is no alternative but to construct such explicit efficiency standards — based on a pragmatic, means-ends calculus — and to use them as the basis for establishing regulated economic price. This is the new wave which will shape the future of regulation in the United States.[143]

There are several reasons which explain the commissions' neglect of efficiency. These include "the difficulties of distinguishing the characteristics of good and bad performance, and relatedly, constructing benchmarks against which performances can be evaluated."[144] But attempts have been, and are being, made to develop efficiency and performance measures.

Management Audits

One approach to management efficiency and performance, widely used by regulatory commissions throughout the 1970s, is the management audit. Such an audit, generally mandated by a commission and conducted by an outside consulting firm (selected by the commission), can identify poor management practices and suggest organizational and procedural changes for more efficient operation. Yet, after nearly 100 audits, they remain controversial. Summarize Hertz and Braun:

> So far, however, these audits, in our opinion (however competently carried out by the consultants involved), have been disappointing. The constraints under which such studies have had to be done are such that they have not provided the anticipated benefits to the consumer, the commission, or the utility. And under the circumstances, we see little hope that they will be able to do so in the future. Therefore, we suggest that all concerned with these studies (both those statutorily required and those ordered independently by commissions) would be well advised to reconsider the manner in which they should be authorized and undertaken. Commissions should be wary of being placed in the position of supporting their chosen auditors' positions, or verifying them, or having them verified, or even rejecting them — hardly an effective stance for quasi-judicial proceedings. The public may have to accept the influence of an "official" report on a company that has not been a part of the regular processes of its duly appointed representatives and guardians. The utility company may find itself in an informal adversary relationship in which any attempt to be either helpful or to make corrections of fact can be construed as uncooperative defensiveness. And, finally, the consultant undertaking the audit may be completely frustrated in carrying out his presumed objectives — to help all three of the concerned parties analyze and improve the costs, service, and reliability of the company under scrutiny.[145]

When these potential pitfalls are fully recognized and when an audit is carefully planned, there is evidence that the approach can be beneficial to all parties.[146]

Incentive Systems[147]

A second approach to management efficiency and performance is the incentive system. Regulatory lag is one such system, and some have proposed the institutionalization of this device.[148] So, too, are executive incentive compensation programs, directly linking compensation to performance, although few utilities have implemented such programs.[149] Most of the specific incentive systems, either employed or proposed, involve varying the allowed rate of return according to some indicator(s) of performance. The FERC, to illustrate, has tied the return on common equity for the proposed Alaska gas pipeline to the minimization of cost overruns[150] and has implemented the "Performance Incentive Provision" for the Virginia Electric and Power Company, providing for a sliding rate of return tied to generating unit performance.[151]

Sliding Scale Plans. A few commissions have adopted various sliding scale plans, which "have varied all the way from a very simple agreement with respect to the sharing of the company's surplus profits to very elaborate schemes for establishing the company's dividend and depreciation policies."[152] The famous "Washington Plan," in effect from 1925 to 1955, is typical. The basic or normal rate of return originally was 7 1/2 percent on rate base. Whenever the actual return exceeded that figure, rates were to be reduced in the next year so as to eliminate one-half of the excess; whenever the return fell below that figure (*i.e.,* an average return of less than 7 1/2 percent for five consecutive years, or less than 7 percent for three consecutive years, or less than 6 1/2 percent for one year), rates were to be raised to restore the entire deficiency. "Since demand grew rapidly in this period and may also have been elastic, returns kept rising during the first two decades; what broke down the plan was the inflation after World War II. It also had the defect of providing no penalty for inefficiency."[153]

The Michigan Plans. Beginning in 1976, the Michigan commission began to implement incentive regulation for private electric utilities under its jurisdiction. Step one involved a new comprehensive fuel and purchased power adjustment clause, under which utilities were permitted — on a monthly basis — to recover 90 percent of the increase in fuel and purchased power costs and to retain 90 percent of the decrease in fuel and purchased power costs above or below a base level set in the last rate case. "After a rate case, these incurred costs do show up in rate levels. This use of regulatory lag as an incentive mechanism, although far from ideal, appears to be the best means available."[154]

Step two involved adoption of a power plant "availability incentive program." As summarized by Schmidt:

> This incentive provision offers a bonus of 25 basis points to the common equity rate of return for system power plant availability ranging from 80.1 percent to 85.0 percent and a bonus of 50 basis points for power plant availability over 85 percent. There is a neutral zone standard for routine expected availability from 70 percent to 80 percent. The plan provides for a disincentive of 25 basis points for availability below 70 percent.
>
> The commission estimates that an improvement of 5 percentage points in availability, for instance, can save Detroit Edison approximately $12 million. Yet, 25 basis points for Detroit Edison amounts to approximately $5.5 million. Thus, there can be substantial gain both to utility stockholders and consumers.[155]

Step three involved adoption of the "Other O & M Indexing System." As explained by Schneidewind and Campbell:

The system begins with a base level of allowed other expenses determined by a projected test year in a traditional rate case. Starting in 1979, each year Edison is allowed to increase its rates on account of expenses by a percentage equal to the change in the Consumer Price Index. The dollar amount is calculated by multiplying the Other O & M indexing base times the change in the CPI. The original 1978 base plus all previously allowed annual Other O & M increases is the base in each future year.

In this fashion, the utility gets a timely annual adjustment of its rates on account of these expenses. However, the utility has adequate incentive to operate efficiently because the annual increases produced by the indexing mechanism are the only increases allowed by the commission on these expenses. If the utility's Other O & M expenses increase more rapidly than the CPI, then the excess must be absorbed by the firm. Conversely, if these expenses increase at a lower rate than the CPI, the utility will retain the amount of the increase over expenses. The cost-plus aspect of the traditional regulatory system is abolished for this category of expenses.[156]

Performance Measures. Incentives tied to efficiency and performance require the development of comparative performance ratios.[157] In 1973, the Federal Power Commission's Office of Economics published its *Performance Profiles,* identifying an array of "performance indicators" which could be used to compare performance among utilities.[158] "While *Performance Profiles* seeks to distinguish between those cost determinants which can be controlled by company management and those which cannot, it does not come to grips with the problem of determining the relative impact of the various exogenous factors."[159]

The total factor productivity (TFP) approach, developed by Kendrick,[160] has received much academic attention,[161] but only limited commission interest.[162] This approach measures the relationship between input (*e.g.*, fuel, purchased power, capital) and output (*e.g.*, kilowatt-hours of electricity generated or sold, cubic feet of gas delivered). If the ratios increase over time, then more input is needed to produce the same output and, hence, productivity is declining.[163] There are several approaches to measuring total factor productivity. Iulo, in 1961[164] and Pace, in 1970,[165] attempted to determine quantitatively, by the use of multiple regression analysis, the major factors determining the individual costs of electric utilities. Both authors

... used what they termed "cost functions" to predict either the average or total cost per kilowatt-hour for each of the companies in their samples. They argued that each company's actual, incurred cost would come close to the cost predicted by the model if the company were conducting its operations with the "average efficiency" of the other companies in the sample. If a company's actual cost was considerably above the predicted value, this would be viewed as an indication of relative inefficiency. Conversely, a company whose cost was below the predicted value would be considered efficient.[166]

These studies also have been subject to theoretical controversies. For example, the independent cost-determining variables in the Iulo study (*e.g.,* consumption per residential customer, the distribution of sales among different classes of customers) may not be truly independent of management actions. They might be influenced by rate structures and/or promotional efforts. Thus, one cannot be sure that the difference between predicted cost and actual cost measures overall operating efficiency (or inefficiency).[167] Further, in the words of one administrative law judge, it is

... practically impossible to achieve comparability between past and future periods, and even if this could be overcome, it would remain highly arbitrary to project past productivity trends forward into a particular future year. Moreover, there is no point in seeking great precision as to one small aspect of highly imprecise rate determinations; and an attempt to do so would only divert effort from other vital tasks.[168]

Service, Safety, and Efficiency: The Future

Service, safety, and utility efficiency have assumed greater attention by the regulatory commissions and by management in recent years. Some believe that the quality of service has declined. To quote Carron and MacAvoy:

Regulation under economic conditions like those of the 1970s reduces the growth and quality of service in the controlled sector of the economy. Service has been reduced in almost all cases, as the companies have reacted to narrowed rate-cost margins by cutting back growth. The special considerations for home and rural consumers in electricity, natural gas, and telephone have all but disappeared, because these industries have not made the capital investments necessary to maintain and expand production. Reduced investment and consequent service quality reductions were noted first in the late 1960s in the natural gas and telephone industries. The same service deterioration would have appeared in electric power by the late 1970s, except for unexpected reduced demand growth resulting from the 1973-74 energy crisis and economy-wide fuel inflation.[169]

Safety regulation is of particular importance with respect to nuclear power plants. Renewed national concern about safety issues, an aftermath of the accident at Three Mile Island, has virtually halted the further development of the domestic nuclear power industry.

Much more research remains to be undertaken on utility efficiency, performance, and productivity. Conclude Cowing and Stevenson:

> ... Although many of the current measures of performance can be criticized as incomplete and potentially misleading, the task of performance measurement is no more heroic than that of identifying the minimum return expectations of investors of equity capital or the calculation of the marginal cost of utility services. Progress is being made by researchers in designing accurate and meaningful efficiency measurement techniques, and it is quite likely that both the utilization of productivity measures and the accuracy of such instruments will continue to grow.[170]

Efficiency and productivity, however, involve much more than the development of statistical measures. Marginal cost pricing, to illustrate, promotes economic efficiency. So, too, does intercompany coordination, such as the interconnection of transmission networks, and power pooling and interchange agreements in the electric utility industry. And, where feasible, competition can be promoted to stimulate efficiency and technological innovation.

Appendix: Environmental Quality Control and the Quantity of Service

With passage of the National Environmental Policy Act (NEPA) of 1969,[171] the federal government established a national policy for environmental protection. The act requires that federal decisionmakers undertaking "major federal actions significantly affecting the quality of the human environment" take into account the following factors:

1. the environmental impact of the proposed action,
2. any adverse environmental effects which cannot be avoided should the proposal be implemented,
3. alternatives to the proposed action,
4. the relationship between local short-term uses of man's environment and the maintenance and enhancement of long-term productivity, and
5. any irreversible and irretrievable commitments of resources which would be involved in the proposed action should it be implemented.[172]

Following passage of the NEPA, a substantial number of new federal statutes and amendments to preexisting statutes were enacted. The major federal legislation that affects utility facilities is listed in Table 12-4. Further, both state and local governments have become heavily involved in environmental issues.

> . . . For example, all states are obligated to enact standards for water, air, and solid waste under the provisions of the federal Water Pollution Control Act, the Clean Air Act, and the Solid Waste Act. In addition, many states have enacted state Environmental Protection Acts, state Wild and Scenic Rivers Acts, statewide land-use programs, state Coastal Zone Acts, and state Power Plant Siting Laws. . . .
>
> To complicate further the regulatory situation, local and regional building and zoning ordinances, quasi-legal codes — e.g., National Fire Protection Association standards, Building Officials and Code Administrators codes — and various industry standards — e.g., American National Standards Institute, American Society of Mechanical Engineers, etc. — are often imposed as permit requirements and become part and parcel of the terms and conditions which must be met before facility operation (in some cases, construction) can commence. In addition, certain technical specifications or operating conditions are also made part of the license or permit which controls or sets limits on facility operation for the life of the facility — e.g., the Environmental Protection Agency national pollution discharge elimination system (NPDES) permit or the Nuclear Regulatory Commission operating license.[173]

All of these statutes and requirements affect utility facilities, including planning, site selection, design, construction, and operation, with the result that the licensing process has become both costly and lengthy.[174]

Pipeline Projects: An Illustration

It would be impossible to discuss each statute in detail, but the extent and nature of environmental quality control can be illustrated by considering two natural gas pipeline projects. First, for a typical interstate or outer continental shelf pipeline project, the following are the necessary permits that may be required.[175]

1. *Environmental Protection Agency (EPA).* The EPA has responsibility for setting and enforcing the limits on the pollution a firm may discharge into the air, water, or earth. The basic requirement is the Environmental Impact Statement which analyzes the potential environmental impacts of, and alternatives to, proposed projects.[176] Five permits are required under present procedures:

TABLE 12-4

Major Federal Legislation Affecting Utility Facilities

I. *General*
1. National Environmental Policy Act of 1969
2. Atomic Energy Act of 1954
3. Endangered Species Act of 1973
4. National Historic Preservation Act of 1966
5. National Trails Systems Act
6. Fish and Wildlife Coordination Act
7. Wilderness Act
8. Federal Coal Mine Health and Safety Act of 1969
9. Surface Mining Control and Reclamation Act
10. Mining and Minerals Policy Act of 1970
11. Outer Continental Shelf Lands Act
12. Powerplant and Industrial Fuel Use Act of 1978, as modified by the Omnibus Budget Reconciliation Act of 1981
13. Outer Continental Shelf Lands Act Amendments of 1978
14. Toxic Substances Control Act of 1980

II. *Air Quality*
1. Clean Air Act of 1970
2. Clean Air Act Amendments of 1977

III. *Water Quality*
1. Rivers and Harbors Act of 1899
2. Water Quality Improvement Act of 1970
3. Federal Water Pollution Control Act
4. Coastal Zone Management Act
5. Federal Water Pollution Control Act Amendments of 1972
6. Wild and Scenic Rivers Act
7. Water Resources Planning Act
8. Marine Protection, Research, and Sanctuaries Act of 1972
9. Oil Pollution Act Amendments of 1973

IV. *Solid Waste*
1. Resource Conservation and Recovery Act of 1976
2. Solid Waste Act

Source: Adapted from Daniel C. Kasperski, "Licensing and Regulatory Affairs as an Engineering Discipline," 106 *Public Utilities Fortnightly* 28, 29 (July 3, 1980).

(*a*) Under the Clean Air Act, the EPA has established National Ambient Air Quality Standards for seven critical pollutants (*e.g.,* nitrogen dioxide, lead). Two permits are required under the 1977 amendments — Prevention of Significant Deterioration permit and Offset permit. The former applies to clean air areas; the latter to nonattainment areas.

(*b*) Under the Federal Water Pollution Control Act (commonly known as the Clean Water Act), the EPA was given administration of the National Pollutant Discharge Elimination System, which requires a permit to discharge pollutants into navigable waters. In addition, the EPA was given administration of the Spill Prevention Control and Countermeasure program, which requires the owner or operator of any onshore facility that has oil discharges into navigable waters or adjoining shorelines to prepare a Spill Prevention Control and Countermeasure Plan.

(*c*) Under the Resource Conservation and Recovery Act, the EPA was given authority to establish guidelines to promote the demonstration, construction, and application of solid waste management, resource recovery, and resource conservation systems and to establish a regulatory program for the generation, transportation, and ultimate disposal of hazardous waste. The latter, hazardous waste disposal, requires a permit.

(*d*) Under the Safe Drinking Water Act, the EPA was required to develop minimum requirements for state underground injection control programs, in order to protect the quality of domestic drinking water. A permit is required for underground injection.[177]

2. *U.S. Army Corps of Engineers (COE).* If the proposed pipeline project involves dredging activity or will cross wetlands or streams, a permit must be obtained from the COE, under the Federal Water Pollution Control Act.[178]

3. *Department of Interior.* There are two potential requirements that must be met:

(*a*) If the proposed pipeline project passes through a National Wildlife Refuge, the U.S. Fish and Wildlife Service and one of its regional directors must determine that the right-of-way is "compatible" with the purposes of the Wildlife Refuge.

(*b*) Under the Outer Continental Shelf Lands Act, the Secretary of the Interior has authority to grant rights-of-way for pipeline projects. Such authorization is given either by the Bureau of Land Management (BLM) or by the U.S. Geological Survey (USGS).[179]

4. *Department of Transportation.* Three potential applications may be required:

(*a*) The U.S. Coast Guard has several responsibilities for both pollution and safety under the Outer Continental Shelf Lands Act Amendments of 1978, the Oil Pollution Act, and the Federal

Water Pollution Control Act. These responsibilities include the control of pollution by discharge of oil or hazardous substances, and discharge removal from the waters of the United States.[180]

(b) The Federal Highway Administration has been charged with implementing the "Policy on the Accommodation of Utilities on Freeway Rights-of-Way." The policy requires that "maximum use of the highways be made for other purposes where such use does not adversely affect the design, construction, integrity, and operational characteristics of the freeway." An application must be filed with the Federal Highway Administration whenever a proposed pipeline project crosses an existing federal highway or federal-aid highway.[181]

(c) The Research and Special Programs Administration, Materials Transportation Bureau, requires the development of a Damage Prevention Program (or participation in an existing program) to reduce the risk of excavation damage to buried pipelines in populated areas.

In addition to these federal environmental-related applications, permits, and licenses, there are two other important filing requirements: safety-related standards (under the Office of Pipeline Safety, Department of Transportation) and the "certificate of public convenience and necessity" from the FERC. The latter two requirements were discussed earlier in the chapter. Finally, there are several liability requirements. Thus, an owner or operator of offshore facilities must apply for a Certificate of Financial Responsibility from the U.S. Coast Guard in case of an oil spill and its subsequent damages. And, under the Comprehensive Environmental Response, Compensation, and Liability Act of 1980, two trust funds will be set up to finance cleanups and grant compensation should hazardous substances be released into the environment and to finance the cleanup of inactive hazardous waste disposal sites.

Second, typical state requirements can be illustrated by considering a proposed pipeline project that began at a point offshore of the state of Texas and crossed both Texas state parklands and a National Wildlife Refuge. As shown in Table 12-5, the transmission company was required to file permit applications with nine state agencies.

Many Unanswered Questions

Since the early 1970s, state and federal legislatures have enacted numerous environmental quality statutes. Countless state and federal agencies have struggled with setting standards, preparing state implementation plans, and applying the established standards in specific cases — all under sub-

TABLE 12-5

Texas State Agencies Requiring Permit
Application for Pipeline Project

Agency	Information Required
Department of Water Resources	(1) Map and description of facilities
General Land Office	(1) Map and description of facilities
	(2) Fee of $5 per lineal rod
State Highway Department	(1) Map and description of facilities
State Historical & Preservation Office	(1) Map and description of facilities
Texas Air Control Board	(1) Map and description of facilities
Texas Antiquities Committee	(1) Map and description of facilities
	(2) Survey of offshore path to insure no shipwrecks would be disturbed
Texas Historical Commission	(1) Map and description of facilities
	(2) Archaeological survey and study of onshore path, including literature search and aerial survey, to insure no archaeological mounds would be disturbed
Texas Parks & Wildlife Department	(1) Map and description of facilities

TABLE 12-5 *(Continued)*

Agency	Information Required
	(2) Assessment of the environmental effect of proposed facilities
Texas Railroad Commission	(1) Map and description of facilities
	(2) Statement as to the effect the proposed facilities will have upon water quality

Source: Adapted from American Gas Association, *Regulation of the Gas Industry* (New York: Matthew Bender & Co., 1987 Supplement and Revision), Vol. 1, pp. 10-44 — 10-45.

stantial judicial challenge and interpretation. Today, environmental quality issues affect nearly every phase of utility construction and operations, with the result that environmental quality control has become almost as important as economic regulation in determining the quality (and cost) of utility service.[182]

The illustrations are familiar. An endangered species — the snail darter — halted construction of the TVA's 95 percent completed ($116 million) Tellico Dam.[183] Relations between the United States and Canada have become strained over "acid rain," a little-known form of air pollution just a few years ago.[184] Environmentalists were successful in halting the proposed construction of an 1,800-megawatt combination hydroelectric and pumped-storage project (the Blue Ridge project), after Appalachian Power Company had received both an FPC license (in 1974) and court approval (in 1976).[185] Texas Eastern Gas Pipeline Corporation, in the largest settlement of an EPA case in history, agreed to undertake a $400 million cleanup of toxic PCBs (polychlorinated biphenyls) contamination along its 10,600-mile pipeline network.[186]

But behind these and all other environmental issues remain a series of unanswered questions relating to scientific data, the reliability of new technology, and the costs and benefits of each particular standard. For example, is sulfur dioxide, by itself, as important a health hazard as the "ambient air-quality standards" developed by the EPA, under the Clean Air Act, suggest? If it is, are scrubbers cost effective? To what extent are tall stacks, low-sulfur fuel, and intermittent controls (*e.g.*, switching to low-sulfur fuel during periods of high-sulfur dioxide concentration, operating at a reduced level) adequate substitutes?[187] Given these, and many other, unanswered questions, it is not surprising that a major project can involve a utility with dozens of state and federal agencies in an effort to obtain approvals, licenses, and permits and with an almost certain court challenge.

Selected Bibliography on Environmental Quality Control

There is a growing volume of literature on environmental quality control, primarily dating from the early 1970s. The following represents a selected bibliography, which will provide hundreds of additional citations.

Ackerman, B.A., and Hassler, W.T., *Clean Coal/Dirty Air.* New Haven: Yale University Press, 1981.

Alexander, M.O., and Livingstone, J.L., "What Are the Real Costs and Benefits of Producing 'Clean' Electric Power?." 92 *Public Utilities Fortnightly* 15 (August 30, 1973).

Axelrod, R.S. (ed.), *Energy and the Environment.* Lexington, Mass.: Lexington Books, 1980.

Ball, R.H., et al., *California's Electricity Quandary: Planning for Power Plant Siting.* Santa Monica, Calif.: The Rand Corp., 1972.

Bingham, G., *Resolving Environmental Disputes: A Decade of Experience.* Washington, D.C.: The Conservation Foundation, 1986.

Biondo, S.J., "Flue Gas Desulfurization: The Magnitude of the Financial Pressure." 100 *Public Utilities Fortnightly* 18 (September 1, 1977).

Bronstein, D.A., "State Regulation of Powerplant Siting." 3 *Environmental Law* 273 (Summer 1973).

Carter, A.P., "Energy, Environment, and Economic Growth." 5 *Bell Journal of Economics and Management Science* 578 (Autumn 1974).

Cohn, H.B., "Environmentalism — Costs and Benefits." 96 *Public Utilities Fortnightly* 17 (July 31, 1975).

Comment, "The 'Best Location' Standards and PUC Review of Proposed Transmission Line Routes: *In Re Bangor Hydro-Electric Co.*" 27 *Maine Law Review* 331 (1975).

Crandall, R.W., *Controlling Industrial Pollution: The Economics and Politics of Clean Air.* Washington, D.C.: The Brookings Institution, 1983.

Downing, P.B., *Environmental Economics and Policy.* Boston: Little, Brown & Co., 1984.

Erbes, R.E., "Acid Rain in the West: Separating Politics and Environmental Fact." 115 *Public Utilities Fortnightly* 17 (May 16, 1985).

French, H.E., III, "Pricing of Pollution: The Coase Theorem in the Long Run." 4 *Bell Journal of Economics and Management Science* 316 (1973).

Friedlaender, A.F. (ed.), *Approaches to Controlling Air Pollution.* Cambridge: The MIT Press, 1978.

Greenwood, R., "Energy Facility Siting in North Dakota." 52 *North Dakota Law Review* 703 (1976).

Guttmann, J.M., "Pennsylvania's Technologically Impossible Air Pollution Standards Upheld." 12 *Natural Resources Journal* 395 (1981).

Hamilton, M.S., *Power Plant Sitings.* Monticello, Ill.: Council of Planning Librarians, Exchange Bibliography No. 1359-1360, September, 1977.

Henderson, R.J., "Ecology and Environmental Analysis." 99 *Public Utilities Fortnightly* 16 (May 26, 1977).

Hopping, W.L., and Raepple, C.S., "Solution to the Regulatory Maze: The Transmission Line Siting Act." 8 *Florida State University Law Review* 441 (1980).

House, P.W., and Train, R., *Trading Off Environment, Economics and Energy.* Lexington, Mass.: Lexington Books, 1977.

Jopling, D.G., "Plant Siting at the Florida Power and Light Company." 91 *Public Utilities Fortnightly* 27 (June 21, 1973).

Joskow, J., "Cost-Benefit Analysis for Environmental Impact Statement." 91 *Public Utilities Fortnightly* 21 (January 18, 1973).

Journey, D.D., "Power Plant Siting — A Road Map of the Problem." 48 *Notre Dame Lawyer* 273 (1972).

Kennedy, W.F., "Nuclear Electric Power and the Environment — New Regulatory Structures and Procedures." 13 *Atomic Energy Law Journal* 293 (1972).

Kindt, J.W., "Offshore Siting of Nuclear Power Plants." 8 *Ocean Development and International Law* 57 (1980).

Kneese, A.V., *Measuring the Benefits of Clean Air and Water.* Washington, D.C.: Resources for the Future, 1984.

Lalor, W.G., Jr., "Sulfur Oxides, Sulfates, and Sanity." 95 *Public Utilities Fortnightly* 16 (April 10, 1975).

Mackay, K., "Environmentally Related Work at EPRI." 97 *Public Utilities Fortnightly* 21 (May 6, 1976).

McDaniel, B.D., "Thermal Electric Power and Water Pollution: A Siting Approach." 46 *Indiana Law Journal* 61 (1970).

McKean, R.N., "Enforcement Costs in Environmental and Safety Regulation." 6 *Policy Analysis* 269 (1980).

Melnick, R.S., *Regulation and the Courts: The Case of the Clean Air Act.* Washington, D.C.: The Brookings Institution, 1983.

Nassikas, J.N., "Coordination of Electric Power and Environmental Policy." 4 *Natural Resources Lawyer* 268 (1971).

Nolan, V., "The National Environmental Policy Act After United States v. SCRAP: The Timing Question and Substantive Review." 4 *Hofstra Law Review* 213 (1976).

Patterson, W.D., "Progress in Satisfying Environmental Requirements." 94 *Public Utilities Fortnightly* 13 (August 1, 1974).

Ramey, J.T., and Malsch, M.G., "Environmental Quality and the Need for Electric Power — Legislative Reforms to Improve the Balancing Process." 47 *Notre Dame Lawyer* 1139 (1972).

Reis, R.I., "Environmental Activism: Thermal Pollution — AEC and State Jurisdictional Considerations." 13 *Boston College Industrial and Commercial Law Review* 633 (1972).

Rhodes, R.M., "Streamlining State Environmental Permitting — The Florida Experience." 12 *Natural Resources Lawyer* 727 (1979).

Russell, C.S., et al., *Enforcing Pollution Control Laws.* Washington, D.C.: Resources for the Future, 1986.

Schelling, T.C. (ed.), *Incentives for Environmental Protection.* Cambridge: The MIT Press, 1983.

Schlottmann, A., "A Regional Analysis of Air Quality Standards, Coal Conversion, and the Steam-Electric Coal Market." 16 *Journal of Regional Science* 375 (1976).

Schurr, S.H., et al., *Energy in America's Future.* Baltimore: The Johns Hopkins Press, 1979.

Schwing, A.T., "The Federal Power Commission's Noncompliance with the National Environmental Policy Act: Statutory Impossibility and Delegation." 55 *Boston University Law Review* 575 (1975).

Sherman, J.C., "Environmental Law: A Burden Established in Eminent Domain Proceedings." 14 *Washburn Law Journal* 355 (1975).

Showalter, D.W., "Environmental Impact of the Texas Public Utility Regulatory Act." 28 *Baylor Law Review* 1101 (1976).

Smith, G.P., II, "Electricity and the Environment: A Season of Discontent." 33 *Federal Bar Journal* 271 (1974).

Steinham, M., *Energy and Environmental Issues.* Lexington, Mass.: Lexington Books, 1979.

Strauss, P.L., "The NRC Role and Plant Siting." 4 *Journal of Contemporary Law* 96 (1977).

Tybout, R.A., "Pricing Pollution and Other Negative Externalities." 3 *Bell Journal of Economics and Management Science* 252 (1972).

————, "Pricing of Pollution: Reply." 4 *Bell Journal of Economics and Management Science* 320 (1972).

Tyler, G.F., "Let's Define 'Environment' Correctly and Put National Environmental Policy Back on Course." 98 *Public Utilities Fortnightly* 15 (July 1, 1976).

Vig, N.J., and Kraft, M.E. (eds.), *Environmental Policy in the 1980s: Reagan's New Agenda.* Washington, D.C.: Congressional Quarterly Press, 1984.

Watson, W.D., "Costs of Air Pollution Control in the Coal-Fired Electric Power Industry." 12 *Quarterly Review of Economics and Business* 63 (Autumn 1972).

Webster, J.K., (ed.), *Toxic and Hazardous Materials: A Sourcebook and Guide to Information Sources*. Westport, Conn.: Greenwood Press, 1987.

Weinberg, P., "Power Plant Siting in New York: High Tension Issue." 25 *New York Law School Law Review* 569 (1980).

Westerby, D.A., "Power Plant and Transmission Line Siting: Improving Arizona's Legislative Approach." 1973 *Law and The Social Order* 519.

Willrich, M., "Energy-Environment Conflict: Siting Electric Power Facilities." 58 *Virginia Law Review* 257 (1972).

Wilson, R., and Jones, W.J., *Energy, Ecology and the Environment*. New York: Academic Press, 1974.

Wise, S.W., "Sierra Club v. Ruckelshaus — Symptom of a Dilemma." 94 *Public Utilities Fortnightly* 24 (November 7, 1974).

Yaffee, S.L., *Prohibitive Policy: Implementing the Federal Endangered Species Act*. Cambridge: The MIT Press, 1982.

Young, H.W., "Power Plant Siting and the Environment." 26 *Oklahoma Law Review* 193 (1973).

Notes

*National Conference of Commissioners on Uniform State Laws, Uniform Public Utilities Act, Section 11 (1928).

[1] See, *e.g.*, Andrew S. Carron and Paul W. MacAvoy, *The Decline of Service in the Regulated Industries* (Washington, D. C.: American Enterprise Institute, 1981).

[2] Cost increases may be partially offset by fuller utilization of plant and equipment or smaller maintenance expenditures.

[3] See, *e.g.*, Comment, "Rates Follow Service: The Power of the Public Utility Commission to Regulate Quality of Service," 28 *Baylor Law Review* 1137 (1976).

[4] C. Woody Thompson and Wendell R. Smith, *Public Utility Economics* (New York: McGraw-Hill Book Co., Inc., 1941), p. 430.

[5] Francis X. Welch, *Cases and Text on Public Utility Regulation* (rev. ed.; Arlington, Va.: Public Utilities Reports, Inc., 1968), p. 177. Service may be refused a customer when (*1*) used for unlawful purposes (bookmaking); (*2*) the customer refuses to pay for service used; (*3*) service regulations are violated or service facilities are destroyed; or (*4*) the utility is unable to supply the service "due to circumstances beyond its control." For a complete discussion of these points, see *ibid.*, chap. iv.

[6] *Time*, July 15, 1966, p. 72. See *e.g.*, *Northwest Airlines, Inc.*, E-24490 (CAB, 1966).

[7] Cited in *Re Rules Regulating Service of Electric Utilities*, 35 PUR4th 365, 374 (Colo., 1980).

[8] Cited in *Nancy J. Hogan et al. v. Hampden Teleph. Co.*, 36 PUR4th 480, 486 (Me., 1980).

[9] *Ibid.*, p. 487.

[10] Clair Wilcox, *Public Policies Toward Business* (3rd ed.; Homewood, Ill.: Richard D. Irwin, Inc., 1966), pp. 296-97.

[11] "The Public Service Commission and . . . You," issued by The Public Service Commission of New York, 1967, pp. 8-10.

[12] The reader should note that some of these service standards will be changed in the coming months as the domestic telephone industry is restructured.

[13]In addition to pressure from consumers, termination of service standards were contained in the Public Utility Regulatory Policies Act of 1978 : Sections 113(b)(4) and 115(g) for electric utilities and Sections 303(b)(1) and 304(a) for gas utilities. See, *e.g.*, *Re Termination of Electric and Gas Services*, Docket No. 792-88 (N.J., 1981); *Re Termination of Service Standards*, 83 PUR4th 444 (Mich., 1987). See also Jean H. Standish et al., *Disconnect Policies in the Fifty States: 1984 Survey* (Columbus, Ohio: National Regulatory Research Institute, 1985).

On the topic, see Note, "Light a Candle and Call an Attorney — The Utility Shutoff Cases," 58 *Iowa Law Review* 1161 (1973); Note, "Fourteenth Amendment Due Process in Terminations of Utility Services for Nonpayment," 86 *Harvard Law Review* 1477 (1973); James A. Maines, "Utility Terminations: Pay Now and Litigate Later," 27 *University of Florida Law Review* 855 (1975); Dale W. Bruckner, "Procedures for Termination of Utility Service: The Requirements of Due Process," 64 *Kentucky Law Journal* 180 (1975-76); Stephan Jurman, "Termination of Service by a State-Regulated Public Utility," 14 *Duquesne Law Review* 761 (1976); J. C. O'Brien, "Protecting the Consumer in Utility Service Terminations," 21 *St. Louis University Law Journal* 452 (1977).

[14]See also *Re Rules Concerning Discontinuance of Utilities Service*, 28 PUR4th 376 (N.M., 1979).

[15]*Re Rules Regulating Service of Electric Utilities*, *op. cit.*, p. 375. Service discontinuance notices must be mailed to each individual tenant of a single-metered, multiunit dwelling.

[16]*Ibid.*, pp. 376-77.

[17]*Ibid.*, p. 377.

[18]See Richard Norgaard and Isabel Jensen, "Winter Moratorium on Utility Bills," 116 *Public Utilities Fortnightly* 32 (December 12, 1985). See also "Utilities Fight Rules that Bar Disconnection During Winter," *The Wall Street Journal*, October 8, 1981, p. 35.

[19]*NARUC Bulletin* No. 49-1981 (December 7, 1981), p. 13. But see *Re Lansing Energy Action Project*, 36 PUR4th 235 (Mich., 1978), where a similar approach was rejected.

[20]These plans (known as "equal," "balanced," "budget," or "levelized" payment plans) generally provide level or budget payment opportunities to residential customers, based on estimated yearly bills, and involve a "settlement" month in which actual utility bills are reconciled each year with estimated utility bills. See "California PUC Reports on Levelized Payment Plans by Utility Customers," *NARUC Bulletin* No. 35-1982 (August 30, 1982), pp. 20-21.

[21]See, *e.g.*, *Re Residential Low Income Usage Reduction Regulations*, 84 PUR4th 140 (Pa., 1987). On one specific program, see William Michael Warren, Jr., "Operation Assist: Action to Help Needy Customers of an Alabama Gas Utility," 116 *Public Utilities Fortnightly* 23 (December 12, 1985).

[22]In a few states, where the local exchange carrier is the billing agent for an interexchange toll carrier, local exchange service may be disconnected for failure to pay for toll service. See, *e.g.*, *Re AT&T Communications of the Mountain States, Inc.*, 72 PUR4th 494 (Colo., 1986). But see, *e.g.*, *Re Chesapeake & Potomac Teleph. Co. of Maryland*, Order No. 67033 (Md., 1985).

[23]Compulsory extension of service is considered in the following section.

[24]See, *e.g.*, *Re Applications for Certificate to Operate a Telecommunications Public Utility*, 33 PUR4th 22 (Alaska, 1979).

[25]Entry with respect to the telephone industry is discussed in Chapter 15.

[26]Natural Gas Act, 52 Stat. 824 (June 21, 1938), as amended, 56 Stat. 83 (February 4, 1942), Section 717f(c). The latter amendment contained a grandfather clause which applied to natural gas companies that were "bona fide engaged in transportation or sale of natural gas . . . on February 7, 1942," if such companies applied for a certificate "within ninety days." *Ibid.* The commission's jurisdiction under the 1938 act was limited to the construction or operation of facilities for the "transportation of natural gas to a market in which natural gas is already being served by another natural-gas company."

[27]The power to attach reasonable terms and conditions, found in many commission statutes, has been broadly interpreted, particularly with respect to conditions aimed at minimizing adverse environmental impacts. See, *e.g., Re New York State Elec. & Gas Corp.,* Opinion No. 80-30 (N.Y., 1980); *Detroit Edison Co. v. Nuclear Regulatory Comm.,* 630 F. 2d 450 (6th Cir. 1980); *Re Alabama Power Co.,* Opinion No. 91 (FERC, 1980).

[28]In emergency conditions, the commission may issue a temporary certificate without notice or hearing "to assure maintenance of adequate service or to serve particular customers." Natural Gas Act, *op. cit.,* Section 717f(c).

[29]The landmark case is *Re Kansas Pipe Line & Gas Co.,* 2 FPC 29 (1939).

[30]Ralph K. Huitt, "Federal Regulation of the Users of Natural Gas," 46 *American Political Science Review* 455, 455-56 (1952) (footnote omitted).

[31]*Re Tennessee Gas Transmission Co.,* 9 FPC 264 (1953). See also *Charleston & Western Carolina Ry. Co. v. Federal Power Comm.,* 234 F. 2d 62 (D.C. Cir. 1956).

[32]*Re Columbia Gulf Transmission Co.,* 37 FPC 118 (1967), *aff'd sub nom. Atlantic Seaboard Corp. v. Federal Power Comm.,* 397 F. 2d 753 (4th Cir. 1968). See also *Panhandle Eastern Pipe Line Co. v. Federal Power Comm.,* 169 F. 2d 881 (D.C. Cir. 1948), *cert. denied,* 335 U.S. 854 (1949); *Re Algonquin Gas Transmission Co.,* 37 FPC 1128 (1967); *Re Alabama-Tennessee Nat. Gas Co.,* 38 FPC 1069 (1967), *aff'd,* 417 F. 2d 511 (5th Cir. 1969). For a review of the FPC's competitive certificate proceedings, see Nelson Lee Smith, "The Federal Power Commission and Pipeline Markets: How Much Competition?," 68 *Columbia Law Review* 664 (1968).

[33]*Re Mississippi River Fuel Corp.,* 12 FPC 102, 112 (1953).

[34]*Re Transcontinental Gas Pipe Line Corp.,* 21 FPC 139 (1959), *aff'd,* 365 U.S. 1 (1961). Yet, six years later, the FPC approved the sale of additional natural gas to Con Ed: "Since Transcontinental Gas Pipe Line Corporation is otherwise supported by the record in its proposal to increase its firm sales to Consolidated Edison Company by 55,000 Mcf per day, the effect of this sale on the New York air pollution problem is not controlling. Nevertheless, the serious air pollution problem in New York may be alleviated slightly by the proposal, and to that extent furnishes an additional benefit." *Re Transcontinental Gas Pipe Line Corp.,* 71 PUR3d 161, 166 (FPC, 1967).

[35]Natural Gas Act, *op. cit.,* Section 717f(a).

[36]The obligation to serve, as noted earlier in the chapter, is not absolute.

[37]*New York & Queens Gas Co. v. McCall,* 245 U.S. 345, 351 (1917). See also *Lukrawaka v. Spring Valley Water Co.,* 169 Cal. 318 (1915).

[38]*Bierbaum v. Union Elec. Co. of Illinois,* 52 PUR (NS) 129 (Ill., 1944); *Fairview Water Co. v. Pennsylvania Pub. Utility Comm.,* 422 A. 2d 1209 (1980). But a utility may not curtail service and/or postpone, defer, or cancel capital expenditures needed to maintain service in order to maintain its rate of return at a level acceptable to

company management. *Pollis v. New England Teleph. Co.*, 25 PUR4th 529 (Me., 1978); *Ex parte South Central Bell Teleph. Co.*, 41 PUR4th 298 (La., 1981).

[39]*Manufacturers Light & Heat Co. v. Federal Power Comm.*, 206 F. 2d 404 (3rd Cir. 1953). A commission, however, may not reallocate supplies among customers. *Granite City Steel Co. v. Federal Power Comm.*, 320 F. 2d 711 (D. C. Cir. 1963).

[40]*City of Sikeston v. Missouri Pub. Service Comm.*, 336 Mo. 985 (1935); *Metropolitan Edison Co. v. Pub. Service Comm.*, 19 PUR (NS) 55 (Pa., 1937); *Meyers v. Southwestern Bell Teleph. Co.*, 34 PUR3d 491 (Mo., 1960).

[41]Entry may be permitted even in the absence of a finding that a present certificate holder is not performing its utility obligations or refuses to furnish new service. See, *e.g.*, *Empire Elec. Ass'n, Inc. v. Utah Pub. Service Comm.*, 604 P. 2d 930 (1979).

[42]See, *e.g.*, *New York Pub. Service Comm. v. Bath Elec., Gas & Water Systems*, 42 PUR3d 353 (N.Y., 1962); *Re Braithwaite*, 44 PUR3d 205 (Wis., 1962).

[43]*Woodhaven Gas & Light Co. v. New York Pub. Service Comm.*, 269 U.S. 244, 248 (1925).

[44]*Interstate Commerce Comm. v. Oregon-Washington R.R. & Navigation Co.*, 288 U.S. 14, 40 (1933).

[45]*Ibid.*, p. 35. The ICC has refused to order extensions on several occasions. See, *e.g.*, *Cooke v. Chicago, B. & Q. R. Co.*, 60 ICC 452 (1922); *Pub. Service Comm. of Wyoming v. Chicago, B. & Q. R. Co.*, 185 ICC 741 (1932).

[46]Alternatively, if a company has excess earnings, the commission could require the extension of service rather than order rate reductions. The results are the same.

[47]Most state regulatory commissions have considered curtailment issues surrounding natural gas distributors. See, *e.g.*, *Re Michigan Consol. Gas Co.*, Case No. U-3802 (Mich., 1971); *Re Investigation of Supply of Natural Gas Within the State of Ohio*, No. 71-757-G (Ohio, 1972). See also *Missouri ex rel. Gas Service Co. v. Missouri Pub. Service Comm.*, 24 PUR4th 33, 562 S.W. 2d 757 (1978); *Indiana Forge & Machine Co., Inc. v. Northern Indiana Pub. Service Co.*, 396 N.E. 2d 910 (1979). A few state commissions have considered electric curtailment plans. See, *e.g.*, *Re Emergency Curtailment of Electric Service*, 21 PUR4th 86 (Or., 1977).

[48]Order No. 431, 45 FPC 570 (1971). "All customers" was subsequently held to include direct sales: *Federal Power Comm. v. Louisiana Power & Light Co.*, 406 U.S. 621 (1972).

[49]Order No 467, 49 FPC 85 (1973). A ninth curtailment priority was added in a subsequent modification: Order No. 467-B, 49 FPC 583 (1973).

[50]Petitions to review the order were dismissed in *Pacific Gas & Elec. Co. v. Federal Power Comm.*, 506 F. 2d 33 (D.C. Cir. 1974).

[51]El Paso Natural Gas Company, to illustrate, filed its proposed curtailment plan in July, 1971; a final plan was approved by the FERC in March, 1981. One complicating factor: Two circuit court decisions held that any final curtailment plan must incorporate an environmental impact statement, as required by the National Environment Policy Act of 1969.

[52]*Re Panhandle Eastern Pipe Line Co.*, Opinion No. 754 (FPC, 1976), *aff'd sub nom. Hercules Inc. v. Federal Power Comm.*, 559 F. 2d 1208 (3rd Cir. 1977). Other plans, however, were reserved in part. See, *e.g.*, *American Smelting Ref. Co. v. Federal Power Comm.*, 494 F. 2d 925 (D.C. Cir. 1974), *cert denied*, 419 U.S. 882 (1974); *City of Willcox and Arizona Elec. Power Co-op., Inc. v. Federal Power Comm.*, 567 F. 2d 394 (D.C. Cir. 1977).

[53]See, *e.g.*, *Louisiana v. Federal Power Comm.*, 503 F. 2d 844 (5th Cir. 1974).

[54]In a 1977 decision [*Re Cities Service Co.*, Opinion No. 805 (FPC, 1977)], the commission modified its past base period by requiring curtailments based on the actual requirements of customers attached to the distribution system on or before January 1, 1978, and prohibiting the sale of gas to serve new requirements (except for that gas supply created by conservation by existing customers). The decision was controversial, for its effect was to limit load growth and, in Opinion No. 805-A (FPC, 1977), the commission agreed to conduct further hearings.

[55]A typical compensation proposal: Customers being curtailed less than the system average would compensate those customers being curtailed more than the system average.

[56]See, *e.g.*, *Mississippi Pub. Service Comm. v. Federal Power Comm.*, 522 F. 2d 1345 (5th Cir. 1975); *Elizabethtown Gas Co. v. Federal Energy Regulatory Comm.*, 575 F. 2d 885 (D.C. Cir. 1978); *North Carolina v. Federal Energy Regulatory Comm.*, 584 F. 2d 1003 (D.C. Cir. 1978).

[57]But see *Fort Pierce Utilities Authority v. Federal Energy Regulatory Comm.*, 724 F. 2d 1167 (5th Cir. 1984); *Mississippi Power & Light Co. v. Federal Energy Regulatory Comm.*, 724 F. 2d 1197 (5th Cir. 1984).

[58]*CF Industries, Inc. v. Transcontinental Gas Pipe Line Corp.*, 452 F. Supp. 358 (W.D. N.C. 1979), *cert. to FERC*, 614 F. 2d 33 (4th Cir. 1980), decision on remand, Opinion No. 248, 35 FERC Par. 61,043 (1986), *appeal pending sub nom. Transcontinental Gas Pipe Line Corp. v. Federal Energy Regulatory Comm.*, No. 86-1358 (D.C. Cir. filed June 17, 1986). See also *Texasgulf, Inc. v. United Gas Pipeline Co.*, 610 F. Supp. 1329 (D. D.C. 1985).

[59]American Gas Association, *Regulation of the Gas Industry* (New York: Matthew Bender & Co., 1987 Supplement and Revision), Vol. 1, p. 11-27, n. 50.

[60]Pub. Law 95-91 (1977). The Secretary subsequently delegated that responsibility to the Economic Regulatory Administration. DOE Delegation Order No. 0204-4, 42 *Fed. Reg.* 60,726 (1977). See Notice of Proposed Rulemaking, Docket No. ERA-R-79-10-A (June 24, 1980).

[61]Pub. Law 95-621 (1978), Section 401(f)2. See, *e.g.*, *Atlanta Gas Light Co. v. Federal Energy Regulatory Comm.*, 756 F. 2d 191 (D.C. Cir. 1985).

[62]Pub. Law 95-621, Section 402(f)1. The curtailment priority for "essential agricultural use" is not applicable "[i]f the commission, in consultation with the Secretary of Agriculture, determines, by rule or order, that use of a fuel (other than natural gas) is economically practicable and that the fuel is reasonably available as an alternative for any agricultural use of natural gas. . . ." *Ibid.*, Section 401(b). See, *e.g.*, *Process Gas Consumers Group v. U.S. Dept. of Agriculture*, 657 F. 2d 459 (D.C. Cir. 1981), *rehearing en banc*, 694 F. 2d 778 (D.C. Cir. 1982).

[63]Pub. Law 95-621, Section 402(d)1. This curtailment priority also is only available when an alternate fuel is not "economically practicable" and not "reasonably available." *Ibid.*, Section 402(b).

[64]Pub. Law 95-617 (1978), Section 605.

[65]Emery Troxel, *Economics of Public Utilities* (New York: Holt, Rinehart & Winston, Inc., 1947), p. 480.

[66]Due to the natural gas shortage in the interstate market in the late 1960s and 1970s, the FPC and later the FERC began to scrutinize applications alleging "depletion" carefully. See, *e.g.*, *Re Texaco, Inc.*, Docket No. G-8820 (order issued Nov. 1, 1977). See also *Shell Oil Co. v. Federal Energy Regulatory Comm.*, 566 F. 2d 536 (5th Cir. 1978). Considerable controversy and litigation, moreover, surrounded the meaning of "abandonment." Thus, in 1966, the Supreme Court upheld an FPC ruling that the

refusal of a natural gas pipeline company to continue receiving gas from a producer, after its contract with the producer had expired and the producer had filed a price increase which was approved by the commission, constituted an abandonment of facilities and of a service. *Re United Gas Pipe Line Co.,* 53 PUR3d 257 (FPC, 1964), 54 PUR3d 275 (FPC, 1964), *aff'd,* 350 F. 2d 689 (5th Cir. 1965), 385 U.S. 83 (1966). Other issues included: (*1*) the commission's jurisdiction in situations where producers' contracts expired and they sought authorization to cease deliveries to the buyer and to initiate deliveries to another buyer [see, *e.g., Gulf Oil Corp. v. Federal Energy Regulatory Comm.,* 575 F. 2d 67 (3rd Cir. 1978); *Transcontinental Gas Pipe Line Corp. v. Federal Power Comm.,* 488 F. 2d 1325 (D.C. Cir. 1973), *cert. denied,* 471 U.S. 921 (1974)]; (2) the meaning of a "dedicated" or "committed" well or lease [see, *e.g., Texas Oil & Gas Corp. v. Michigan Wis. Pipeline Co.,* 601 F. 2d 1144 (10th Cir. 1979), *cert. denied,* 444 U.S. 991 (1979); *Amarex v. Federal Energy Regulatory Comm.,* 603 F. 2d 127 (10th Cir. 1979)]; and (3) whether the commission could order "paybacks" in case of unauthorized abandonments [see, *e.g., United Gas Pipe Line Co. v. McCombs,* 542 F. 2d 1144 (10th Cir. 1976), 570 F. 2d 1376 (10th Cir. 1978), *rev'd,* 442 U.S. 529 (1979), *on remand,* 705 F. 2d 1177 (10th Cir. 1980), *vacated and dismissed,* 710 F. 2d 611 (10th Cir. 1983)]. On state jurisdiction over intrastate abandonment, see *Re Abandonment of Natural Gas Sales under Natural Gas Pricing Act (1978),* 26 PUR4th 592 (N.M., 1978).

[67]*Texas Railroad Comm. v. Eastern Texas R.R. Co.,* 264 U.S. 79, 85 (1924). See also *Wolff Packing Co. v. Court of Industrial Relations,* 262 U.S. 522, 543 (1923).

[68]*Re Missouri Power & Light Co.,* 17 PUR (NS) 469, 472 (Mo., 1937).

[69]*Re Billings Gas Co.,* 26 PUR (NS) 328 (Mont., 1938); *Re Northern States Power Co.,* 35 PUR (NS) 241 (Wis., 1940).

[70]*Citizens of Washington v. Washington & Cherry Valley Teleph. Co.,* 36 PUR (NS) 190 (N.H., 1940).

[71]*New York Central R.R. Co. Abandonment,* 245 ICC 745, 761 (1944).

[72]*Fort Smith Light & Traction Co. v. Bourland,* 267 U.S. 330, 332-33 (1925). See also *Broad River Power Co. v. South Carolina,* 281 U.S. 537 (1930).

[73]*Colorado v. United States,* 271 U.S. 153, 163 (1926).

[74]See, *e.g., Re Greyhound Corp.,* 37 PUR3d 113 (N.C., 1961); *Greyhound Corp. v. Carter,* 40 PUR3d 306 (Fla. Sup. Ct., 1961); *Re Deep South Oil Co. of Texas,* 38 PUR3d 438 (FPC, 1961); *Re Southern P. Co.,* 37 PUR3d 196 (Cal., 1960); *Re Chicago, B. & Q. R. Co.,* 39 PUR3d 174 (Neb. Sup. Ct., 1961).

[75]See, *e.g., Pennsylvania Pub. Utility Comm. v. Metropolitan Edison Co.,* 37 PUR4th 77 (Pa., 1980).

[76]See, *e.g., Re Public Utilities Bd. of City of Brownsville,* 36 PUR4th 271 (Tex., 1980).

[77]*Re Redfield Teleph. Co., Inc.,* Docket No. U-2834 (Ark., 1978), *aff'd sub nom. Redfield Teleph. Co. v. Arkansas Pub. Service Comm.,* 621 S.W. 2d 470 (1981). Revocation has been used more frequently in transportation cases. The ICC, to illustrate, has revoked or suspended thousands of motor carrier certificates and permits for failure to comply with the Interstate Commerce Act or an order of the commission, fraud or misrepresentation, failure to file required annual reports, violations of state size and weight regulations, and when carriers voluntarily abandoned operations. See, *e.g., Smith Bros. Revocation of Certificate,* 33 MCC 465 (1942); *Pub. Utility Comm. of Ohio v. Riss and Co., Inc., et al.,* 72 MCC 659 (1957).

[78]*Re Pacific Gas & Elec. Co.,* 78 Cal. PUC 638, 737 (1975).

[79]See "Promoting Energy Conservation," 106 *Public Utilities Fortnightly* 58 (December 4, 1981).

[80]See "Energy Conservation: Spawning a billion-dollar business," *Business Week*, April 6, 1981, pp. 58-69.

[81]For a full description of these approaches, see *Re Pacific Gas & Elec. Co.*, 34 PUR4th 1 (Cal., 1980). For a case study of potential commercial and industrial applications, see *Utility Promotion of Investment in Energy Efficiency: Engineering, Legal, and Economic Analyses* (Washington, D.C.: Alliance to Save Energy, 1983).

[82]Pub. Law 95-619, 92 Stat. 3206 *et seq.* (1978). This act is one of five related pieces of legislation collectively known as the National Energy Legislation.

[83]Pub. Law 96-294, 94 Stat. 741 (1980). For evaluations of conservation efforts, see Clark W. Gellings and Dilip R. Limaye (eds.), *Electric Utility Conservation Programs* (New York: Praeger Publishers, 1986); John C. Sawhill and Richard Cotton (eds.), *Energy Conservation: Successes and Failures* (Washington, D.C.: The Brookings Institution, 1986). See also Eric Monnier et al. (eds.), *Consumer Behavior and Energy Policy: An International Perspective* (New York: Praeger Publishers, 1986).

[84]The requirements are applicable to electric and gas utilities with annual sales (other than resales) in excess of either 750 million kilowatt-hours of electric energy or 10 billion cubic feet of natural gas. Many states also have adopted conservation statutes. See, *e.g., Re Adoption of Residential Conservation Service Program*, 40 PUR4th 126 (N.Y., 1980).

[85]To secure such approval, the act requires that a utility-sponsored program must contain procedures to ensure (*1*) that the utility charges fair and reasonable prices and rates of interest; (*2*) that provisions are made for resolving complaints against persons selling or installing the conservation measures; (*3*) that adequate measures exist to prevent unfair, deceptive, or anticompetitive practices; (*4*) that the utility, in implementing energy inspections, does not unfairly discriminate against customers, contractors, or lenders; and (*5*) that persons who allege any injury resulting from a violation of a program provision receive redress under procedures established by the governor or the state regulatory agency.

[86]"Residential customers" are purchasers of electricity, gas, or home heating fuel who own or occupy residential buildings, defined as buildings with one to four dwelling units and buildings of more than four units with central heating and/or cooling systems.

[87]The act also provides for "Class B" energy audits which, in contrast to onsite inspections, require customers themselves to supply the necessary information to determine the conservation needs of their homes. See Peter Lazare and Eric Hirst, " 'Class B' Audits As a Residential Conservation Service Option," 107 *Public Utilities Fortnightly* 31 (May 21, 1981). See also Alan B. Brownstein and Paul O. Grace, "Are 'Class B' Audits Really a Residential Conservation Service Option?," 108 *Public Utilities Fortnightly* 28 (September 24, 1981).

[88]Contractors or lenders may appear on the approved list if they meet the minimum standards established by the Secretary of Energy.

[89]Many rules have been promulgated under the act. One establishes the maximum repayment period at ten years. Another requires each state to designate a lead agency for the full development of state plans for RCS programs. Many states have designated their energy office.

[90]Rate design is discussed in Chapters 10 and 11; alternate energy sources and load management are considered in Chapters 13 and 14.

[91]Charles J. Cicchetti and Rod Shaughnessy, "Is There a Free Lunch in the Northwest? (Utility-sponsored Energy Conservation Programs)," 106 *Public Utilities*

Fortnightly 11, 12 (December 18, 1980). See, *e.g.*, *Re Pacific Power & Light Co.*, 36 PUR4th 356 (Cal., 1980).

[92]*Re Pacific Gas & Elec. Co.*, 41 PUR4th 475 (Cal., 1981). See also *Re Pacific Gas & Elec. Co.*, Decision No. 83-12-068 (Cal., 1983).

[93]John E. Bryson and Jon F. Elliott, "California's Best Energy Supply Investment: Interest-free Loans for Conservation," 108 *Public Utilities Fortnightly* 19, 20 (November 5, 1981) (citations omitted). If a residence is sold during the repayment period, ZIP loans are payable in full. The ZIP program is financed through a newly incorporated PG&E subsidiary. PG&E will be permitted to recover all reasonable expenses associated with ZIP, including a return on its equity investment in the new subsidiary.

[94]*Ibid.*, pp. 20-21. The potential energy savings translate into 14.5 billion kilowatt-hours of electricity and 6.1 billion therms of natural gas through 2005. *Ibid.*, p. 21, n.5.

[95]For a more complete discussion, see *Utility Promotion of Investment in Energy Efficiency*, *op. cit.*, Appendix C, "Survey of State Regulatory Law." See also Douglas Norland and James L. Wolf, "Utility Conservation Programs: A Regulatory and Design Framework," 116 *Public Utilities Fortnightly* 15 (July 25, 1985) and "Utility Conservation Programs: Opportunities and Strategies," 116 *Public Utilities Fortnightly* 27 (August 8, 1985).

[96]See, *e.g.*, Eric Hirst, "Measuring the Effects of Utility Conservation Programs," 108 *Public Utilities Fortnightly* 35 (December 17, 1981); Michael A. Einhorn, "Measuring the Costs and Benefits of Conservation Programs," 116 *Public Utilities Fortnightly* 22 (July 25, 1985). On two specific programs, see Geoffrey C. Crandall, Devere L. Elgas, and Martin G. Kushler, "Making Residential Conservation Service Work: A Trilogy of Perspectives," 116 *Public Utilities Fortnightly* 28 (January 10, 1985); Eric Hirst, Dennis White, and Richard Goeltz, "The Electricity Saved in a Residential Weatherization Pilot Program," 116 *Public Utilities Fortnightly* 27 (July 25, 1985).

[97]Bryson and Elliott, *op. cit.*, p. 21.

[98]"PP&L has as a starting point a tariff structure which does not reflect information about its marginal cost. If a PP&L customer were currently paying the marginal cost of supplying electricity (6.5 cents per kilowatt-hour), that customer would have an incentive to make all conservation investments which provide a return of up to 6.5 cents per kilowatt-hour of reduced usage." Cicchetti and Shaughnessy, *op. cit.*, p. 13.

[99]"These include the relative effects of consumption and conservation on the environment, national security, the balance of payments, and employment patterns." Bryson and Elliott, *op. cit.*, p. 21.

[100]*Re Intermountain Gas Co.*, 43 PUR4th 267 (Idaho, 1981). See also *Re Residential Conservation Service Program*, Docket No. R-003 (Ark., 1981). But see *Re Michigan Power Co.*, Case No. U-6819 (Mich., 1981).

[101]Bryson and Elliott, *op. cit.*, p. 21. But see Cicchetti and Shaughnessy, *op. cit.*, pp. 13-14.

The PG&E plan even includes rental property. "Owners of individually metered rental properties will be allowed to keep the 40 percent state tax credit and still repay their ZIP loans over an extended 100-month period. When combined with other depreciation and investment credit provisions of federal and state tax laws, this further incentive renders energy conservation investments very inexpensive for owners of residential property. PG&E will also create a certification program for energy-efficient rentals, and will encourage newspapers to provide separate classified advertising listings for such units. This may result in higher rents for participating property owners." Bryson and Elliott, *op cit.*, p. 23.

[102]"There is little benefit to insulating an attic when heat is leaking through a hole in the wall." *Ibid.*, p. 22. The PG&E plan addresses both of these problems. Eligible low-income homeowners (as defined by the federal government for its Low-income Energy Assistance Program) are permitted to retain their 40 percent state tax credits, but to repay their loan balances over 100 months (at a rate of one percent per month). If structural repairs are found to be cost effective, additional zero-interest financing will be extended for as much as $200.

[103]See, *e.g.*, *Southern Cal. Gas Co. v. Cal. Pub. Utilities Comm.*, 596 P. 2d 1149 (Cal. 1979); *Iowa-Illinois Gas & Elec. Co., et al. v. State Commerce Comm.*, Case No. AA-9 (D. Iowa 1982), *aff'd*, 334 N.W. 2d 748 (Iowa 1983). See also "Residential Conservation Service Programs," 108 *Public Utilities Fortnightly* 56 (August 27, 1981); "Residential Conservation Service Programs: Is Utility Financing Mandatory?," 110 *Public Utilities Fortnightly* 62 (September 16, 1982); Peter Lazare, "A Case Study in Utility Financing for Residential Conservation Measures," 107 *Public Utilities Fortnightly* 28 (June 4, 1981); *Re Conservation Financing*, 47 PUR4th 443 (Wis. 1982).

[104]Occasionally, however, there are differences of opinion with respect to specific facilities or equipment. Thus, in a 1965 decision, the California commission found that the Bell System's handsets were "less safe and healthful" than the "Ericofon" (a non-Bell manufactured instrument) and ordered the Bell System either to allow a hospital to attach the latter equipment to its lines or to provide the hospital with such equipment. *Doctors General Hospital v. Pacific Teleph. & Teleg. Co.*, 59 PUR3d 297 (Cal., 1965) 62 PUR3d 409 (Cal. 1965). See "Safety of Utility Facilities," 81 *Public Utilities Fortnightly* 55 (January 4, 1968).

[105]See, *e.g.*, *Re Gas Utilities and Gas Pipeline Safety*, 46 PUR4th 647 (W. Va., 1982).

[106]There has been considerable concern over potential adverse biological effects from extra-high-voltage transmission lines. See, *e.g.*, "High-voltage Power Lines and Human Health," 103 *Public Utilities Fortnightly* 11 (January 4, 1979).

[107]82 Stat. 720 (1968), 90 Stat. 2073 (1976).

[108]Pub. Law 90-481, Section 3(a)(1).

[109]49 C.F.R. Section 191 *et seq.* (1978).

[110]Pub. Law 90-481, *op. cit.*, Section 6(a)(1).

[111]*Ibid.*, Section 6(a)(1). A violation of the act carries possible criminal penalties; *i.e.*, a maximum fine of $25,000 per offense and/or imprisonment for a maximum of fifteen years. *Ibid.*, Section 11(c)(1).

In addition to these safety standards, an LNG terminal is a "facility of particular hazard," subject to Coast Guard regulations regarding such matters as adequacy of guards, fire extinguishing equipment, and lighting. LNG tankers also are subject to Coast Guard regulations. The Ports and Waterways Safety Act of 1972, as amended by the Port and Tanker Safety Act of 1978, grants the Coast Guard further authority to regulate LNG vessel operations in connection with port safety. Safety and siting of LNG facilities are of concern to affected states, but such states may not place restraints on interstate commerce by means of unreasonable approval requirements for natural gas facilities. See, *e.g.*, *Transcontinental Gas Pipe Line Corp. v. Hackensack Meadowlands Dev. Comm.*, 464 F. 2d 1358 (3d Cir. 1972), *cert. denied*, 409 U.S. 1118 (1973); *Ray v. Atlantic Richfield*, 435 U.S. 529 (1978).

[112]Metropolitan Edison Company is the licensed operator for, and 50 percent owner of, the Three Mile Island Unit 2 nuclear power plant. The company, along

with Pennsylvania Electric Company and Jersey Central Power and Light Company, are the three wholly-owned operating subsidiaries of General Public Utilities Corporation.

[113]John F. Ahearne, "High Costs, Lower Demand Plague U.S. Nuclear Industry," *Resources,* Summer 1987, p. 8. "The United States led other countries in numbers of plants and total operating capacity in 1985. It was followed by the Soviet Union, France, Japan, West Germany, and the United Kingdom." *Ibid.* See, *e.g.,* Barbara Starr, "Europe Takes Lead in Nuclear Power: Regulatory and Economic Climate is More Favorable Than in U.S.," 248 *Europe* 20 (March/April 1985); Pierre Tanguy, "Safety and Nuclear Power Plant Standardization: The French Experience," 116 *Public Utilities Fortnightly* 20 (October 31, 1985).

[114]In a conventional power plant, heat is turned into steam, and steam into electricity. The required heat, in turn, is generated in a coal, gas, or oil burning furnace. Heat may be generated also in a nuclear reactor which uses fissionable materials as a fuel. Two types of reactors are being developed: converters (reactors that produce less fissionable material than they consume) and breeders (reactors that produce more fissionable material than they consume). Breeders are also of two types: fast breeders and thermal breeders. To date, most of the reactors in operation are of the converter type. A demonstration project for the fast breeder was approved in 1972 (the Clinch River breeder reactor project at Oak Ridge, Tennessee). See "The Next Step Is the Breeder Reactor," *Fortune,* March, 1967, pp. 121-23, 198-202. However, after spending $1.5 billion (with a projected total cost of $4.5 billion), the Senate voted to deny further federal funds to the project in October, 1983. See *The Wall Street Journal,* October 27, 1983, p. 3.

[115]"In the optimistic days of the early 1950s, nuclear power was regarded as the ultimate clean, low-cost resource of electricity. Some even claimed that electricity would be so cheap that it wouldn't pay to bill users." James Quirk and Katsuaki Terasawa, "Nuclear Regulation: An Historical Perspective," 21 *Natural Resources Journal* 833, 849 (1981).

[116]For a more complete discussion, see Philip Mullenbach, *Civilian Nuclear Power* (New York: The Twentieth Century Fund, 1963); Report of the Nuclear Energy Policy Study Group, *Nuclear Power Issues and Choices* (Cambridge: Ballinger Publishing Co., 1977).

[117]60 Stat. 755 (1946).

[118]The act also provided for (a) a Military Liaison Committee and a General Advisory Committee of scientists to assist the commission and (b) a Congressional Joint Committee on Atomic Energy (nine members from the Senate and nine members from the House) to supervise the commission. Relations between the AEC and Congress were not always harmonious. See Robert Dahl and Ralph Brown, Jr., *Domestic Control of Atomic Energy* (New York: Social Science Research Council, 1951); Morgan Thomas, *Atomic Energy and Congress* (Ann Arbor: The University of Michigan Press, 1956); Harold P. Green and Alan Rosenthal, *Government of the Atom: The Integration of Powers* (New York: Atherton Press, 1963).

[119]In 1953, Congress authorized funds for the construction of the country's first nuclear plant at Shippingport, Pennsylvania. The plant, subsequently built at a cost of $120 million, supplied electricity to the Duquesne Power and Light Company of Pittsburgh. Duquesne provided the site, invested $15 million in generating equipment, and contributed $5 million toward the reactor. The government supplied the remaining $100 million.

[120]68 Stat. 919 (1954).

[121]One of the major debates in Congress concerned public versus private power. Proponents of public power sought to authorize the AEC to generate and sell electricity, to give public agencies such as the TVA the same right as private industry to generate nuclear power, and to give municipal and cooperative systems preference in the distribution of public nuclear power. Opponents of public power sought to restrict the development of nuclear power by public agencies, contending that the development of a nuclear power industry would be accelerated under private enterprise. Today, the adversary relationship has largely ended. See Rebecca Johnson, "Co-ops: Their Stake in Nuclear Grows," *Nuclear Industry*, November, 1980.

[122]A second major Congressional debate concerned patents. Some feared that private ownership of patents would result in a few firms dominating the industry. The AEC had contracted much of its research and development work to a small number of private firms. The head start enjoyed by these firms might result in an unfair advantage over others who might wish to enter the field at a later date. On the commission's contract system, see Richard A. Tybout, *Government Contracting in Atomic Energy* (Ann Arbor: The University of Michigan Press, 1956). On patent issues, see Walter Adams, "Atomic Energy: The Congressional Abandonment of Competition," 55 *Columbia Law Review* 158 (1955); Bennett Boskey, "Some Patent Aspects of Atomic Power Development," 21 *Law and Contemporary Problems* 113 (1956). See also L. Cohen, "Innovation and Atomic Energy: Nuclear Power Regulation, 1966-Present," 43 *Law and Contemporary Problems* 67 (1979); S. Goldberg, "Controlling Basic Science: The Case of Nuclear Fusion," 68 *Georgetown Law Journal* 683 (1980).

[123]Atomic Energy Commission, *Civilian Nuclear Power: A Report to the President — 1962* (Washington, D.C., 1962), p. 29.

[124]*Ibid.*

[125]All AEC reactors were built and operated for publicly-owned utility systems, except at Shippingport.

[126]Mullenbach, *op. cit.*, pp. 166-75. Mandatory government ownership of special nuclear material was terminated in 1964 (Pub. Law 88-489).

Until the mid-1970s, the government provided the only commercial uranium enrichment services in the free world at three plants: Oak Ridge, Tennessee; Paducah, Kentucky; and Portsmouth, Ohio. In 1985, the Department of Energy mothballed the Oak Ridge plant and abandoned a $2.6 billion plant (with a $10 billion estimated total cost), also in Portsmouth, to produce fuel by the centrifuge method, citing a decline in demand for nuclear fuel and strong competition from foreign enrichers. See, *e.g.*, Tom Alexander, "America's Costliest Government Boondoggle," *Fortune*, November 1, 1982, pp. 106-12; "Doubts Pervade Nuclear Fuel Industry," *The Wall Street Journal*, October 7, 1985, p. 6; "High Court to Decide if Energy Agency Must Curb Foreign-Uranium Processing," *ibid.*, January 12, 1988, p. 7. On the international uranium market, see Anthony David Owen, *Economics of Uranium* (New York: Praeger Publishers, 1985).

[127]Under the Price-Anderson Act of 1957 (Pub. Law 85-256, 71 Stat. 576), damage settlements against a utility for a nuclear accident ("incident") could not exceed a total of $500 million plus the amount of liability insurance available on the private market — approximately $60 million in 1957. Thus, the government was liable for the bulk of the coverage. The $560 million limitation on liability was continued when Congress, in 1975, extended the act's coverage until 1987 (Pub. Law 94-197, 89 Stat. 1111). However, under an amendment, each utility with a commercial nuclear reac-

tor was to provide $5 million per reactor [an amount set by the NRC, 42 *Fed. Reg.* 46 (1977)], to be assessed retroactively in the event of a nuclear accident. As a result, when the 80th reactor operating license was issued on November 15, 1982, the government's liability was eliminated: $160 million was being provided by private underwriters, and $400 million by those utilities with commercial reactors. [The Congressional limitation on liability for nuclear accidents was upheld in *Duke Power Co. v. Carolina Environmental Study Group, Inc.,* 438 U.S. 59 (1978). See also Harold P. Green, "Nuclear Power: Risk, Liability and Indemnity," 71 *Michigan Law Review* 479 (1973).] Congress failed, however, to meet the August 1, 1987, expiration date of the Price-Anderson Act (although the force of the law remains in effect until extended by legislation).

[128]Pub. Law 93-438, 88 Stat. 1233.

[129]Pub. Law 91-190, 83 Stat. 853 (1970).

[130]The NRC may fine utilities for failing to meet standards (*e.g.,* General Public Utilities Corporation was fined $155,000 for the Three Mile Island accident in 1979 and $205,000 for safety violations at its Oyster Creek plant in 1987; Boston Edison Company was fined $550,000 for admitted safety violations at its Pilgrim plant in 1982; Toledo Edison Company was fined $900,000 for twelve malfunctions of safety equipment at the Davis-Besse nuclear plant in 1985; Detroit Edison was fined a total of $600,000 for a series of violations at its Fermi 2 plant in 1986-1987). The NRC also may suspend permits and licenses (*e.g.,* Pacific Gas & Electric Company's preliminary start-up license at its Diablo Canyon plant was suspended in November, 1981; Cincinnati Gas and Electric Company was ordered to halt all safety-related construction at its nearly-completed Zimmer plant in November, 1982; Long Island Lighting Company's license for low-power tests at the Shoreham plant was revoked in February, 1985).

[131]*Report of the President's Commission on the Accident at Three Mile Island* (Kemeny Commission) (Washington, D.C.: U.S. Government Printing Office, 1979), p. 11. In addition to several NRC and industry investigations, there were numerous Congressional studies and hearings [see, *e.g., Nuclear Accident and Recovery at Three Mile Island* (Staff Studies, Committee Print, Subcommittee on Nuclear Regulation for the Committee on Environment and Public Works, Senate) (Washington, D.C.: U.S. Government Printing Office, 1980)] and private studies [see, *e.g.,* Thomas H. Moss and David L. Sills (eds.), *The Three Mile Island Nuclear Accident: Lessons and Implications* (New York: New York Academy of Sciences, 1981).]

The accident raised many other important issues and resulted in countless suits. In 1983, the Supreme Court held that the National Environmental Policy Act does not require the NRC to consider the issue of psychological harm to area residents in reactivating a nuclear plant. [*People Against Nuclear Energy, et al. v. Nuclear Regulatory Comm.,* 678 F. 2d 222 (D.C. Cir. 1982), *rev'd sub nom. Metropolitan Edison Co. v. People Against Nuclear Energy, et al.,* 103 S. Ct. 1556, 52 PUR4th 189 (1983).] In 1987, a federal appeals court vacated the NRC's backfit rule, holding that the commission may not take costs into account in deciding whether to order safety-enhancing modifications to existing nuclear plants. [*Union of Concerned Scientists v. Nuclear Regulatory Comm.,* 56 U.S. L.W. 2108 (D.C. Cir. 1987). See "The NRC's Backfit Rule: An Update," 120 *Public Utilities Fortnightly* 32 (November 12, 1987).] GPU filed $4 billion suits against both the NRC [*dismissed, General Pub. Utilities Corp. v. United States,* 745 F. F. 2d 239 (3rd Cir. 1984), *cert. denied,* 105 S. Ct. 1227 (1985)] and the reactor manufacturer, Babcock & Wilcox [settled in early 1983 for $37 million]. Two class action suits were filed against GPU: one by local residents and businesses [*Fantasky v. General Pub. Utilities Corp.*, Consolidated Class Action No. 79-432 (M.D. Pa. 1979); settled in 1981 for $25 million] and the other by its shareholders [*Gildenblatt v. General Pub. Utilities Corp.*, Civil Action No. 79-1420 (D. N.J. 1979); settled in 1983 for about $11 million plus a distribution of additional shares]. Hundreds of claims for alleged injuries caused by the accident have been filed and settled, including a 1985 settlement of 280 such claims. "This settlement included $3.9 million for 19 claims brought by children of area residents." [William O. Doub and James R. Shoemaker, "Who Pays the Costs of Industrial Accidents Like Three Mile Island?," 115 *Public Utilities Fortnightly* 13, 16 (May 16, 1985.] In the meantime, the cleanup at Three Mile Island continues [with an estimated total cost of $1 billion; one-fourth of which is being paid by the ratepayers of GPU's three operating subsidiaries]. And it is reported that the industry has been able to secure coverage of up to $1 billion for property damage at nuclear plants and replacement power insurance of $250 million. [*Electrical Week*, August 31, 1981, p. 9.]

[132]"NRC Action Plan Developed as a Result of the TMI-2 Accident," NUREG-0660 (May, 1980). See also "TMI-Related Requirements for New Operating Licenses," NUREG-0694 (June, 1980); "Further Commission Guidance for power Reactor Operating Licenses," 45 *Fed. Reg.* 41,738 (1980); "Clarification of TMI Action Plan Requirements," NUREG-0737 (November, 1980); "Further Commission Guidance for Power Reactor Operating Licenses," 45 *Fed. Reg.* 85,236 (1980).

[133]"Emergency Planning," 45 *Fed. Reg.* 55,402 (1980). But in October, 1987, the commission approved a rule [52 *Fed. Reg.* 6,980 (1987)] to allow it to consider granting operating licenses to plants where local and state officials refuse to assist in drawing up the required emergency evacuation plans for surrounding towns. [*The Wall Street Journal*, October 30, 1987, p. 4.] Two fully constructed nuclear plants, Seabrook in New Hampshire and Shoreham in New York, are at immediate issue. In the case of Seabrook, however, it is the State of Massachusetts that has refused to cooperate; the plant is two miles from the Massachusetts border. A court challenge seems certain.

[134]1980 *U.S. Code Cong. & Ad. News* 1339, 1693. For an assessment of the NRC, see William C. Wood, *Nuclear Safety: Risks and Regulation* (Washington, D.C.: American Enterprise Institute, 1983).

[135]See, *e.g.*, Marie Mastin Newman, "TMI-2: Making Strides in Research and Recovery," *Electric Perspectives* 9 (Fall 1982).

[136]For a case study of Consumers Power Company's Midland nuclear power plant, see Romney Wheeler, "The Right Idea at the Wrong Time," *Electric Perspectives* 11 (Summer 1981). For an update, see "The Midland Cogeneration Project: New Horizons for Electrics, QFs, and Retail Customers," 119 *Public Utilities Fortnightly* 42 (April 16, 1987).

The NRC has made attempts to expedite licensing. See, *e.g.*, "Statement of Policy on Conduct of Licensing Proceedings," 46 *Fed. Reg.* 28,533 (1981); "Expediting the NRC Hearing Process," 46 *Fed. Reg.* 30,328 (1981); "Commission Review Procedures for Power Reactor Operating Licenses; Immediate Effectiveness Rule," 46 *Fed. Reg.* 47,764 (1981). But see "Ills of Nuclear Aren't Likely to End with Faster Licensing," *The Wall Street Journal*, October 30, 1982, pp. 1, 8. See also Michael A. Kutsch, "How to Stabilize and Rationalize the Nuclear Licensing Process," 103 *Public Utilities Fortnightly* 28 (May 24, 1979).

[137]*Richmond Times-Dispatch*, November 16, 1982, p. A-13.

[138]See "Nuclear Power Fears," *Newsweek*, April 19, 1981, pp. 101-102. See also Union of Concerned Scientists, "The Nuclear Power Controversy" (Washington, D.C., 1982).

[139]"Nuclear waste management is a process that consists of at least four phases. The first phase involves treatment of nuclear wastes, including potentially significant changes in the physical or chemical characteristics of the reactor fuel. The second phase involves transportation, that is, the shipment of spent fuel or radioactive waste to treatment, storage and disposal sites. The third phase involves storage, that is, the safeguarding of radioactive waste until the fourth phase, the permanent disposal of the waste." Alfred C. Aman, Jr., *Energy and Natural Resources Law: The Regulatory Dialogue* (New York: Matthew Bender & Co., 1983), p. 7-66. See, *e.g.*, David A. Deese, *Nuclear Power and Radioactive Waste* (Lexington, Mass.: Lexington Books, 1978); D. Hansell, "Regulation of Low-level Nuclear Waste," 15 *Tulsa Law Journal* 249 (1979); E. Jaksetic, "Legal Aspects of Radioactive High-level Waste Management," 9 *Environmental Law* 347 (1979); Richard Ausness, "High-level Radioactive Waste Management: The Nuclear Dilemma," 1979 *Wisconsin Law Review* 707; Henry Cheung and John W. McKlveen, "Nuclear Wastes: A History of Deferrals," 106 *Public Utilities Fortnightly* 15 (November 20, 1980); "Symposium: Nuclear Waste Management," 32 *South Carolina Law Review* 639 (1981).

After years of debate, Congress enacted the Nuclear Waste Policy Act in 1982 (Pub. Law 97-425). The act, among other things, requires (*a*) the federal government and the states to come up with a schedule for the orderly disposal of wastes; (*b*) the President to choose the nation's first permanent nuclear waste repository by March 31, 1988 and a second site by March 31, 1991; and (*c*) those utilities which create the wastes to pay for their treatment and perpetual storage. [See, *e.g.*, *Re Indiana & Michigan Elec. Co.*, 52 PUR4th 340 (Ind., 1983).] But after the President approved three sites in the West as candidates for the first repository (Yucca Mountain, Nevada; Smith county, Texas; Hanford, Washington) and after the Department of Energy had identified twelve sites in seven mid-western and eastern states as potential candidates for a second repository, the entire selection process became embroiled in political controversy and a moratorium was imposed by Congress. See "High-level Nuclear Waste: A Continuing Dilemma," 120 *Public Utilities Fortnightly* 33 (November 12, 1987).

[140]See *Implications of the Accident at Chernobyl for Safety Regulation of Commercial Nuclear Power Plants in the United States* (NRC draft report, September 1987). See also "Utilities From 30 Nations to Form Information Body," *The Wall Street Journal*, October 7, 1987, p. 31.

[141]*Bluefield Water Works & Imp. Co. v. Pub. Service Comm. of West Virginia*, 262 U.S. 679, 693 (1923).

[142]Argues Kahn: "Freezing rates for the period of the lag imposes penalties for inefficiency, excessive conservatism, and wrong guesses, and offers rewards for their opposites: companies can for a time keep the higher profits they reap from a superior performance and have to suffer the losses from a poor one." Alfred E. Kahn, *The Economics of Regulation* (New York: John Wiley & Sons, Inc., 1971), Vol. 2, p. 48. Others believe that in the economic environment of the 1970s and early 1980s, regulatory lag "is at best an undifferentiating device to promote utility efficiency." Elizabeth Warren, "The Regulatory Lag Fallacy," 106 *Public Utilities Fortnightly* 15 (August 14, 1980).

[143]Thomas K. Standish, "Integrating Efficiency Standards into the Regulatory

Process," in Harry M. Trebing (ed.), *Issues in Public Utility Regulation* (East Lansing: MSU Public Utilities Papers, 1979) p. 527. Kahn has warned, however, that "[r]egulation is ill-equipped to treat the more important aspects of performance — efficiency, service innovation, risk taking, and probing the elasticity of demand." Kahn, *op. cit.*, p. 326.

[144]Kenneth W. Costello and Rodney E. Stevenson, "The Application of Performance Measures in Public Utility Regulation" (paper delivered at the Transportation and Public Utility Session on "Public Utility Performance," Washington, D.C., December 29, 1981, mimeographed), p. 1. See also Thomas G. Cowing and Rodney E. Stevenson, *Productivity Measurement in Regulated Industries* (New York: Academic Press, 1981). Further, far too little is known about the general effects of regulation on technological progress. See, *e.g.*, Sunit K. Khanna, "Economic Regulation and Technological Change: A Review of the Literature," 109 *Public Utilities Fortnightly* 35 (January 21, 1982).

[145]David B. Hertz and Peter C.M.S. Braun, "The Management Audit Fad for Utilities," 99 *Public Utilities Fortnightly* 19 (March 17, 1977). See also Ronald Doades, "The Mentality of Management Audits," 101 *Public Utilities Fortnightly* 25 (February 16, 1978); Howard Sargent, "Fishbowl Planning in Management Audits," 101 *Public Utilities Fortnightly* 22 (March 16, 1978); Edward P. Larkin, "Management Audits: Costs and Benefits," 101 *Public Utilities Fortnightly* 11 (June 8, 1978); Robert E. Dellon "The Management Audit Process: Room for Improvement," 103 *Public Utilities Fortnightly* 15 (February 1, 1979).

[146]See, *e.g.*, Bruce H. Nesbit and Carol S. Penskar, "Making the Most of a Mandated Management Audit," 108 *Public Utilities Fortnightly* 24 (December 17, 1981); Raymond Krasniewski et al., *The Management Audit as a Regulatory Tool: Recent Developments and Prospects for the Future* (Columbus, Ohio: National Regulatory Research Institute, 1981); Ralph C. Mitchell, III and Richard J. Metzler, "The Second-generation Management Audit," 111 *Public Utilities Fortnightly* 21 (May 12, 1983). See also *Commission Ordered Management Audits of Gas and Electric Utilities* (Columbus, Ohio: National Regulatory Research Institute, 1979); Price Waterhouse & Co., "Survey of Management Audits in the Electric Utility Industry" (New York, 1979); *1985 Annual Report on Utility and Carrier Regulation* (Washington, D.C.: National Association of Regulatory Utility Commissioners, 1987), pp. 501-09.

[147]See, *e.g.*, *Rate Incentive Provisions: A Framework for Analysis and a Survey of Activities* (Columbus, Ohio: National Regulatory Research Institute, 1981); Federal Energy Regulatory Commission, *Incentive Regulation in the Electric Utility Industry*, Vols. 1 and 2 (Washington, D.C., 1983); "Incentive Regulation in the Electric Utility Industry" (Washington, D.C.: National Association of Regulatory Utility Commissioners, 1983); Leland L. Johnson, *Incentives to Improve Electric Utility Performance* (Santa Monica, Calif.: The Rand Corp., 1985); Paul L. Joskow and Richard Schmalensee, "Incentive Regulation for Electric Utilities," 4 *Yale Journal on Regulation* 1 (1986).

[148]See, *e.g.*, William J. Baumol, "Reasonable Rules for Rate Regulation: Plausible Policies for an Imperfect World," in Almarin Phillips and Oliver E. Williamson (eds.), *Prices: Issues in Theory, Practice and Public Policy* (Philadelphia: University of Pennsylvania Press, 1967), pp. 108-23.

[149]See *Incentive Regulation in the Electric Utility Industry*, *op. cit.*, Vol. 1, Appendix G.

[150]Order No. 31, Docket No. RM78-12 (FERC, 1979).

[151]*Re Virginia Elec & Power Co.*, Docket No. ER82-423 (1982). The subsequent settlement agreement is reproduced in *Incentive Regulation in the Electric Utility Indus-*

try, op. cit., Vol. 2, as Appendix B to comments by Vepco. The plan was implemented for a trial period of three years in 1983.

[152]Irston R. Barnes, *The Economics of Public Utility Regulation* (New York: F. S. Croft & Co., 1942), p. 237. See also Charles S. Morgan, *Regulation and the Management of Utilities* (Boston: Houghton Mifflin Co., 1923), pp. 154-87; Irving Bussing, *Public Utility Regulation and the So-Called Sliding Scale* (New York: Columbia University Press, 1936); Harry M. Trebing, "Toward an Incentive System of Regulation," 72 *Public Utilities Fortnightly* 22 (July 18, 1963).

[153]Kahn, *op. cit.,* p. 61. Barnes proposed a modification: all excess earnings would be credited to an "earnings-equalization" reserve or a "rate-equalization" reserve (accumulating up to 20 percent of the rate base). The reserve would be used to cover any future deficiencies in earnings and would be treated as a deduction from the rate base for ratemaking purposes. Barnes, *op. cit.,* pp. 570-71.

[154]Daniel J. Demlow, "Incentive Regulation," in Trebing, *Issues in Public Utility Regulation, op. cit.,* p. 537. The fuel cost portion operated automatically, but the purchased power cost portion required monthly public hearings.

[155]Michael Schmidt, *Automatic Adjustment Clauses: Theory and Application* (East Lansing: MSU Public Utilities Studies, 1980), pp. 53-54 (citation omitted). As the author notes, the program had drawbacks. *Ibid.,* pp. 54-56. See also *Re Consumers Power Co.,* 25 PUR4th 167 (Mich., 1978).

[156]Eric J. Schneidewind and Bruce A. Campbell, "Michigan Incentive Regulation: The Next Step," in Harry M. Trebing (ed.), *Challenges for Public Utility Regulation in the 1980s* (East Lansing: MSU Public Utilities Papers, 1981), p. 407. The authors admit that the results of the system "have been mixed." *Ibid.*

While the Michigan system was discontinued in 1983 (due to legislation forbidding automatic adjustments), it is typical of other incentive regulation programs that focus on individual components of utility costs. See Joskow and Schmalensee, *op. cit.,* pp. 48-49.

[157]This discussion is based on Bernard W. Tenenbaum and Haskell P. Wald, "Performance Indicators for Electric Utilities: Some Methodological Issues," in Walter L. Balk and Jay M. Shafritz (eds.), *Public Utility Productivity: Management and Measurement* (Albany: The New York State Department of Public Service, 1975), pp. 37-55 and Luc Anselin et al., *The Measurement of Electric Utility Performance: Preliminary Analysis* (Columbus, Ohio: National Regulatory Research Institute, 1981).

[158]*Performance Profiles: Private Electric Utilities in the United States 1963-1970* (1973). Based upon these indicators, the NARUC's J. Edward Smith, Jr., issued his "red flag" study in 1975. See *The Measurement of Electric Utility Efficiency* (Washington, D.C.: National Association of Regulatory Utility Commissioners, 1975). The study was highly controversial. See also *The Measurement of Electric Utility Cost Performance: A Proposed Methodology* (Washington, D.C.: National Association of Regulatory Utility Commissioners, 1976).

[159]Tenenbaum and Wald, *op. cit.,* p. 41.

[160]John W. Kendrick, *Productivity Trends in the United States* (Princeton: Princeton University Press, 1961).

[161]See several articles on the theory and application of the TFP approach in Cowing and Stevenson, *op. cit.* See also Luc Anselin and J. Stephen Henderson, *A Decision Support System for Utility Performance Evaluation* (Columbus, Ohio: National Regulatory Research Institute, 1985); M. Foley and R. Tucker, *Electric Utility Perfor-*

mance Study 1972-1984 (Washington, D.C.: National Association of Regulatory Utility Commissioners, 1986).

[162]In 1975, Illinois Bell Telephone Company's proposed "cost and efficiency" adjustment clause, which incorporated a total factor productivity index, was rejected by the Illinois commission. *Re Illinois Bell Teleph. Co.*, Case No. 58916 (Ill., 1975). See H. A. Latimer, "The Cost and Efficiency Revenue Adjustment Clause," 94 *Public Utilities Fortnightly* 19 (August 15, 1974); John W. Kendrick, "Efficiency Incentives and Cost Factors in Public Utility Automatic Revenue Adjustment Clauses," 6 *Bell Journal of Economics* 299 (1975); Schmidt, *op. cit.*, pp. 45-49. In 1979, the New York commission rejected the TFP approach for ratemaking purposes. See Frank S. Robinson, "Total Factor Productivity Studies as a Rate Case Tool," 105 *Public Utilities Fortnightly* 19 (March 13, 1980). In 1983, the Utah commission initiated a "Total Factor Productivity Cost Factoring Program" for Utah Power & Light Company; a program that was abandoned the following year because of "uncertainty over the legality of incentive regulation programs under Utah law." Joskow and Schmalensee, *op. cit.*, p. 42 (footnote omitted). See also E. Fred Sudit, "Automatic Rate Adjustments Based on Total Factor Productivity Performance in Public Utility Regulation," in Michael A. Crew (ed.), *Problems in Public Utility Economics and Regulation* (Lexington, Mass.: Lexington Books, 1979), pp. 55-71.

[163]"If, as an example, the level of kilowatt-hours of electricity generated increased by 20 percent over a given period of time and over the same period the weighted average rise in the level of inputs is 15 percent, the growth rate of TFP is 5 percent." Costello and Stevenson, *op. cit.*, p. 53, n. 5.

[164]William Iulo, *Electric Utilities — Costs and Performance* (Pullman: Washington State University Press, 1961).

[165]Joe Pace, "Relative Efficiency in the Electric Utility Industry" (unpublished Ph.D. dissertation, The University of Michigan, 1970).

[166]Tenenbaum and Wald, *op. cit.*, pp. 41-42 (citations omitted). For other approaches, see Yoram Barzel, "Productivity in the Electric Power Industry, 1929-1955," 45 *Review of Economics and Statistics* 401 (1963); Costello and Stevenson, *op. cit.*; Cowing and Stevenson, *op. cit.*; Anselin and Henderson, *op. cit.* See also James C. Cox and R. Mark Isaac, "Mechanisms for Incentive Regulation: Theory and Experiment," 18 *The Rand Journal of Economics* 348 (1987).

[167]Kahn, *op. cit.*, p. 64, n. 45. "Suppose an enterprising management succeeds, by vigorous promotional efforts, in increasing average residential consumption. The latter factor would be included among the (cost-reducing) variables that are assumed to be independent of managerial efficiency; so management would get no credit for its own efforts that produced this result. Indeed it would show up as inefficient, because the promotional expenses would cause actual costs to exceed those estimated by application of the independent variables." *Ibid.*

[168]Robinson, *op. cit.*, p. 24. See also Dennis Goins, "Can Incentive Regulation Improve Utility Performance? The Inherent Danger of a Simple Answer," 115 *Public Utilities Fortnightly* 20 (January 10, 1985). But see William J. Baumol, "Productivity Incentive Clauses and Rate Adjustments for Inflation," 110 *Public Utilities Fortnightly* 11 (July 22, 1982); Joskow and Schmalensee, *op. cit.*, esp. pp. 43-47.

[169]Carron and MacAvoy, *op. cit.*, p. 65.

[170]Cowing and Stevenson, *op. cit.*, p. 27 (citation omitted).

[171]Pub. Law 91-190, 83 Stat. 853 (1970), as amended, Pub. Law 94-83, 89 Stat. 424 (1975), Pub. Law 94-475, 90 Stat. 2071 (1976).

[172]Pub. Law 91-190, as amended, Section 102(C). The act also established, in the Executive Office of the President, the Council on Environmental Quality.

[173]Daniel C. Kasperski, "Licensing and Regulatory Affairs as an Engineering Discipline," 106 *Public Utilities Fortnightly* 28, 29 (July 3, 1980). See also Warren Freeman, *Federal Statutes on Environmental Protection: Regulation in the Public Interest* (Westport, Conn.: Quorum Books, 1987).

[174]At least three other factors contribute to the current situation. (*1*) The implementation of these statutes has resulted in constantly changing requirements, which is perhaps inevitable under new legislation. (*2*) Each governmental agency (federal and state) is generally required to give due notice and to permit comments from other interested parties before issuing a license or permit. (*3*) Under some federal legislation (*e.g.*, the Clean Air Act, as amended), the states must prepare plans (State Implementation Plans) which incorporate the federal standards and which must be approved by the Environmental Protection Agency. Until such approval is granted, an applicant must secure a permit from both the state agency and the EPA.

[175]This discussion is based upon American Gas Association, *Regulation of the Gas Industry, op. cit.*, Vol. 1, pp. 10-46 — 10-62. It should be noted that there are certain exemptions from some of these environmental quality control measures.

[176]Several efforts have been made to coordinate EPA and federal agency activities in preparing, reviewing, and commenting on Environmental Impact Statements. On such efforts between the EPA and the FERC, see *Ibid.*, pp. 10-23 — 10-24.

[177]Although not requiring a specific permit, a proposed project is subject to the Toxic Substances Control Act of 1980, which seeks to control and determine the toxicity of all chemical substances and mixtures that are manufactured, processed, and distributed in commerce. *Ibid.*, pp. 10-53 — 10-54.

[178]The EPA and the COE have joint responsibility. A Memorandum of Understanding between the two agencies was issued in July, 1980, under which "the transmission company is to send its application for dredging activities to the District Engineer, COE, who will make a jurisdictional determination. If the EPA is found to be the appropriate agency, the COE will pass on the application to the Regional Administrator, EPA." Generally, EPA jurisdiction is limited to cases "presenting scientific, technical, or policy complexities." *Ibid.*, p. 10-55.

[179]"A Memorandum of Understanding between the BLM and the USGS was signed in August, 1980, which placed pipelines which are not wholly contained within the boundaries of a single lease, unitized leases, or contiguous leases of the same owner/operator under the jurisdiction of the BLM, while the USGS has jurisdiction over pipelines which are wholly contained within such boundaries." *Ibid.*, p. 10-56.

[180]A Memorandum of Understanding between the Coast Guard and the EPA in August, 1979, clarifies which agency has jurisdiction over a particular oil spill incident. *Ibid.*, p. 10-58.

[181]"Many of the states have been charged with carrying out these policies locally so that in certain cases the application may be filed at the state rather than the federal level." *Ibid.*, p. 10-59.

[182]For a study of how six electric utilities — three private and three public — have confronted environmental issues, see Marc J. Roberts and Jeremy S. Bluhm, *The Choices of Power: Utilities Face the Environmental Challenge* (Cambridge: Harvard University Press, 1981).

[183]*Hill v. Tennessee Valley Authority*, 549 F. 2d 1064 (6th Cir. 1977), *aff'd*, 473 U.S.

153 (1978). The Tellico Dam was exempted from the Endangered Species Act by Congress in 1979. [See William Bruce Wheeler and Michael J. McDonald, *TVA and the Tellico Dam, 1936-1979: A Bureaucratic Crisis in Post-Industrial America* (Knoxville: The University of Tennessee Press, 1986).] The snail darter was removed from the endangered species list in 1984. [See *The Wall Street Journal,* July 6, 1984, p. 28.]

[184]See, *e.g.,* "Why the Growing Controversy over Acid Rain," *U.S. News & World Report,* November 29, 1982, pp. 84-86; "Who'll Stop the Acid Rain?," *Newsweek,* March 24, 1986, p. 60. See also "The Outlook for Acid Rain Control Legislation," 119 *Public Utilities Fortnightly* 27 (April 16, 1987).

[185]*Re Appalachian Power Co.,* 51 FPC 1906 (1974), *aff'd sub nom. North Carolina v. Federal Power Comm.,* 533 F. 2d 702 (D.C. Cir. 1976). In September, 1976, President Ford signed into law an amendment to the Wild and Scenic Rivers Act of 1968 which added a twenty-six-mile segment of the New River in North Carolina (within the reservoir area) to the National Wild and Scenic Rivers System. Pub. Law 94-407, 90 Stat. 2138 (1976).

[186]*Time,* November 23, 1987, p. 50. The Company also agreed to a $15 million fine. See also "Commonwealth Edison Settles EPA Suit, Agreeing to Clean Up PCBs at 300 Sites," *The Wall Street Journal,* September 30, 1986, p. 10.

[187]See, *e.g.,* Carl Pechman, "Equity, Efficiency, and Sulfur Emission Reductions," 115 *Public Utilities Fortnightly* 21 (May 16, 1985). See also Paul H. Weaver, "Behind the Great Scrubber Fracas," *Fortune,* February, 1975, pp. 106-114; Fraser Ross, "To Scrub or Not to Scrub?," 96 *Public Utilities Fortnightly* 33 (November 6, 1975); "EPA and Utility Seek to Agree on Scrubbers," 191 *Electrical World* 26 (April 15, 1979).

PART III

The Public
Utility
Industries

Chapter	THE ELECTRIC
13	POWER
	INDUSTRY

The factors requiring unified planning, construction, and operation of generating and transmission networks have been present from the very beginning of the industry, but the size of the area most efficiently covered by a single network has grown as advances in electric technology have increased the economic transmission distance and enlarged the savings from using larger scale equipment.

*—Federal Power Commission**

The combined functions of generating, transmitting, and distributing electric energy represent the nation's largest industry.[1] The industry also is one of the country's most important businesses, since virtually every home and commercial enterprise is served by it. With but 6 percent of the world's population, the United States accounts for about 36 percent of the world's production of electric energy.

The industry, however, has been affected materially by the changed economic environment. Until the late 1960s, the industry was financially strong and growing at an annual rate of 7 percent per year. The 1964 *National Power Survey* projected that technological advances and sales growth would result in an average unit price of 1.2 cents per kilowatt-hour by 1980 (as compared with 2.7 cents in 1926 and 1.7 cents in 1962).[2] But by 1980, the average nationwide rate stood at 4.43 cents per kilowatt-hour (and at 7.38 cents at the end of 1985), although rates varied considerably across the country.[3] As conservation, rather than promotion, became the basic objective, the issues changed: the long public-private dispute subsided, while the need to have adequate capacity to meet future requirements came to the fore.[4] Further capacity, however, would have to be consistent with environmental, health, and safety considerations and with least-cost planning, and would be met — at least in part — from alternative (nontraditional) sources and imports (particularly from Canada). The widespread reestablishment of holding companies indicates a desire to offset slower electric growth with diversification efforts and raises new policy issues. The electric power industry well illustrates the problems and challenges of regulating a dynamic industry, whose growth and financial health weakened during the 1970s and early 1980s, and within which both private and public enterprise operate.

Development and Structure

The electric power industry is relatively young.[5] As early as 1802, it was demonstrated that an electric current could be used to make a light, but it was not until 1879 that San Francisco could boast of possessing the first central station in the United States, furnishing electric power to its arc lamp system.[6] On October 21, 1879, Thomas A. Edison invented the first commercially practical incandescent lamp, and in December of that year he demonstrated a complete incandescent lighting system; a central plant generated the power which was then transmitted to several houses in which incandescent lamps had been installed. Three years later, on September 4, 1882, the first central station to furnish current for the Edison-type lamp was put into operation at Pearl Street in New York City. The station began by supplying some 400 lamps and had a generating capacity of 560 kilowatts.[7] Later in the year, at Appleton, Wisconsin, the nation's first hydroelectric station was put into operation. And, in 1903, the world's first all-turbine station, a 5,000-kilowatt unit, was installed in Chicago.

The current supplied by the earliest stations was direct, and direct current (at the then available voltages) was uneconomical when transmitted over long distances. In 1886, primarily due to the efforts of George Westinghouse, a practical alternating current system was developed. This development made it possible first to "step up" the voltage, through transformers, before the current was transmitted so it could be carried over long distances, then to "step down" the voltage prior to distribution. With respect to distance, in 1889 a demonstration of a thirteen-mile transmission of power took place. By 1900, while more and more power was being transmitted, twenty-five miles was still looked on as being an exceptional distance.

Direct current, inadequate transmission facilities, and limited demand resulted in the establishment of numerous small local companies. "Frequently, two, three, or more noninterconnected plants, operating under different patents and owned by different concerns, were established in the same city."[8] Competition was relied upon to serve the public interest. Thus, in 1887, six electric companies were organized in New York City. Five electric companies served Duluth, Minnesota, prior to 1895, while Scranton, Pennsylvania, was being served by four firms in 1906. And, in 1907, forty-five electric light firms had the legal right to operate in Chicago.[9]

Introduction of the transformer in 1886 led to the use of alternating current, higher distribution voltages, and an expansion of the distribution area that could be served by an individual plant. Improvements in generators made possible larger outputs at lower unit costs, while other technical improvements made it possible to supply incandescent and arc lights as well as direct and alternating current motor loads from the same power source. The increasing economies of scale in power production and the standardization of equipment led to many consolidations of the small electric companies serving given communities or areas. The diminution of competition resulting from these consolidations of power production plants and distribution systems was one of the factors leading to government regulation of public utilities. In a number of cases the local government acquired ownership of the electric system in an effort to provide electric power at lower rates for local consumers.[10]

The Holding Company: Consolidation

The number of electric systems steadily increased up to 1917, when a decline set in. The decline reflects the consolidation movement in this field during the late 1910s and throughout the 1920s. While this movement took place through merger and lease, consolidation by means of the holding company was paramount.[11]

A holding company is an enterprise that owns sufficient stock in another company or in a number of companies so that it may influence the management of the company whose stock it holds (see Figure 13-1). Sometimes the holding company is a stockholding firm entirely and operates no properties directly — a pure holding company. Other holding companies both hold securities and operate some properties in their own names — operating holding companies. By the early 1930s, many electric utility holding companies had assets of $1 billion or more. Further, by 1932, sixteen holding companies accounted for 76.4 percent of the energy generated, with three systems (United Corporation, Electric Bond and Share Company, and the Insull interests) accounting for 44.5 percent of the total electricity produced.[12]

Advantages of the Holding Company. The rapid growth of the holding company in the electric utility field was due to a variety of factors. In the

FIGURE 13-1

Electric Bond and Share Company, 1933

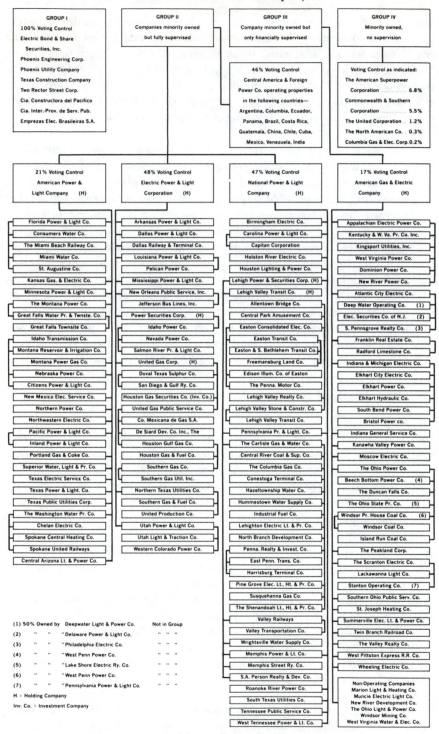

GROUP I	GROUP II	GROUP III	GROUP IV
100% Voting Control	Companies minority owned but fully supervised	Company minority owned but only financially supervised	Minority owned, no supervision

GROUP I

100% Voting Control

Electric Bond & Share

  Securities, Inc.

Phoenix Engineering Corp.

Phoenix Utility Company

Texas Construction Company

Two Rector Street Corp.

Cia. Constructora del Pacifico

Cia. Inter.-Prov. de Serv. Pub.

Emprezas Elec. Brasileiras S.A.

GROUP III

46% Voting Control
Central America & Foreign
Power Co. operating properties
in the following countries—
Argentina, Columbia, Ecuador,
Panama, Brazil, Costa Rica,
Guatemala, China, Chile, Cuba,
Mexico, Venezuela, India

GROUP IV

Voting Control as indicated:
The American Superpower
  Corporation 6.8%
Commonwealth & Southern
  Corporation 5.5%
The United Corporation .. 1.2%
The North American Co... 0.3%
Columbia Gas & Elec. Corp. 0.2%

21% Voting Control American Power & Light Company (H)	48% Voting Control Electric Power & Light Corporation (H)	47% Voting Control National Power & Light Company (H)	17% Voting Control American Gas & Electric Company (H)
Florida Power & Light Co.	Arkansas Power & Light Co.	Birmingham Electric Co.	Appalachian Electric Power Co.
Consumers Water Co.	Dallas Power & Light Co.	Carolina Power & Light Co.	Kentucky & W. Va. Pr. Co. Inc.
The Miami Beach Railway Co.	Dallas Railway & Terminal Co.	Capitan Corporation	Kingsport Utilities, Inc.
Miami Water Co.	Louisiana Power & Light Co.	Holston River Electric Co.	West Virginia Power Co.
St. Augustine Co.	Pelican Power Co.	Houston Lighting & Power Co.	Dominion Power Co.
Kansas Gas. & Electric Co.	Mississippi Power & Light Co.	Lehigh Power & Securities Corp. (H)	New River Power Co.
Minnesota Power & Light Co.	New Orleans Public Service, Inc.	Lehigh Valley Transit Co. (H)	Atlantic City Electric Co.
The Montana Power Co.	Jefferson Bus Lines, Inc.	Allentown Bridge Co.	Deep Water Operating Co. (1)
Great Falls Water Pr. & Twnste. Co.	Power Securities Corp. (H)	Central Park Amusement Co.	Elec. Securities Co. of N.J. (2)
Great Falls Townsite Co.	Idaho Power Co.	Easton Consolidated Elec. Co.	S. Pennsgrove Realty Co. (3)
Idaho Transmission Co.	Nevada Power Co.	Easton Transit Co.	Franklin Real Estate Co.
Montana Reservoir & Irrigation Co.	Salmon River Pr. & Light Co.	Easton & S. Bethlehem Transit Co.	Radford Limestone Co.
Montana Power Gas Co.	United Gas Corp. (H)	Freemansburg Land Co.	Indiana & Michigan Electric Co.
Nebraska Power Co.	Duval Texas Sulphur Co.	Edison Illum. Co. of Easton	Elkhart City Electric Co.
Citizens Power & Light Co.	San Diego & Gulf Ry. Co.	The Penna. Motor Co.	Elkhart Power Co.
New Mexico Elec. Service Co.	Houston Gas Securities Co. (Inv. Co.)	Lehigh Valley Realty Co.	Elkhart Hydraulic Co.
Northern Power Co.	United Gas Public Service Co.	Lehigh Valley Stone & Constr. Co.	South Bend Power Co.
Northwestern Electric Co.	Co. Mexicana de Gas S.A.	Lehigh Valley Transit Co.	Bristol Power co.
Pacific Power & Light Co.	De Siard Dev. Co. Inc., The	Pennsylvania Pr. & Light Co.	Indiana General Service Co.
Inland Power & Light Co.	Houston Gulf Gas Co.	The Carlisle Gas & Water Co.	Kanawha Valley Power Co.
Portland Gas & Coke Co.	Houston Gas & Fuel Co.	Central River Coal & Sup. Co.	Moscow Electric Co.
Superior Water, Light & Pr. Co.	Southern Gas Co.	The Columbia Gas Co.	The Ohio Power Co.
Texas Electric Service Co.	Southern Gas Util. Inc.	Conestoga Terminal Co.	Beech Bottom Power Co. (4)
Texas Power & Light. Co.	Northern Texas Utilities Co.	Hazeltownship Water Co.	The Duncan Falls Co.
Texas Public Utilities Corp.	Southern Gas & Fuel Co.	Hummestown Water Supply Co.	The Ohio State Pr. Co. (5)
The Washington Water Pr. Co.	United Production Co.	Industrial Fuel Co.	Windsor Pr. House Coal Co. (6)
Chelan Electric Co.	Utah Power & Light Co.	Lehighton Electric Lt. & Pr. Co.	Windsor Coal Co.
Spokane Central Heating Co.	Utah Light & Traction Co.	North Branch Development Co.	Island Run Coal Co.
Spokane United Railways	Western Colorado Power Co.	Penna. Realty & Invest. Co.	The Peakland Corp.
Central Arizona Lt. & Power Co.		East Penn. Trans. Co.	The Scranton Electric Co.
		Harrisburg Terminal Co.	Lackawanna Light Co.
		Pine Grove Elec. Lt. & Pr. Co.	Stanton Operating Co. (7)
		Susquehanna Gas Co.	Southern Ohio Public Serv. Co.
		The Shenandoah Lt., Ht. & Pr. Co.	St. Joseph Heating Co.
		Valley Railways	Summerville Elec. Lt. & Power Co.
		Valley Transportation Co.	Twin Branch Railroad Co.
		Wrightsville Water Supply Co.	The Valley Realty Co.
		Memphis Power & Lt. Co.	West Pittstton Express R.R. Co.
		Memphis Street Ry. Co.	Wheeling Electric Co.
		S.A. Person Realty & Dev. Co.	
		Roanoke River Power Co.	Non-Operating Companies Marion Light & Heating Co. Muncie Electric Light Co. New River Development Co. The Ohio Light & Power Co. Windsor Mining Co. West Virginia Water & Elec. Co.
		South Texas Utilities Co.	
		Tennessee Public Service Co.	
		West Tennessee Power & Lt. Co.	

(1) 50% Owned by Deepwater Light & Power Co.   Not in Group

(2) " " "Delaware Power & Light Co. " " "

(3) " " "Philadelphia Electric Co. " " "

(4) " " "West Penn Power Co. " " "

(5) " " "Lake Shore Electric Ry. Co. " " "

(6) " " "West Penn Power Co. " " "

(7) " " "Pennsylvania Power & Light Co. " " "

H = Holding Company

Inv. Co. = Investment Company

Source: Federal Trade Commission, *Utility Corporations* (Senate Doc. 92, 70th Cong., 1st sess.) (Washington D.C.: U.S. Government Printing Office, 1935), Part 72-A, Chart II facing p. 88.

main, two sets of forces were dominant. First, the holding company offered certain economies. Second, the holding company offered advantages to its owners which, while often producing harmful effects on the general welfare, encouraged its formation. Some systems (the Electric Bond and Share Company by the General Electric Company) were formed by electrical equipment manufacturers to find markets for their products. Others were organized by investment banking houses (United Corporation by J. P. Morgan and Company) engaged in the flotation of utility securities. Still others were promoted by engineering interests (such as Stone and Webster) which supplied technical services to operating utilities.[13] The basic motive, however, was profit.

1. *Economies.* The first advantage of the holding company arises from economies of large-scale generation. The introduction of alternating current made it feasible to generate electricity in large central stations and, thereby, to achieve lower costs. In turn, economical service could be rendered over wide areas. Interconnections further increased the service area.[14] In the second place, lower costs of financing were often possible through the holding company. Small companies usually are not well known; buyers for their securities are harder to find. A holding company can sell securities on itself at lower rates of interest and use such funds to buy securities of its operating companies at a lower interest rate than if the operating companies tried to find other buyers. As a result, by acting as fiscal agent, holding companies may offer a saving in cost of money to their operating affiliates.

In the third place, holding companies can perform an engineering and construction service for their operating companies. When the operating companies are small, they cannot afford an engineering staff. Construction jobs come at intervals so that a small operating company cannot be expert in carrying them out. However, a holding company with a large number of operating companies under its control can well afford to set up engineering and construction departments. Hence, if a local company wants to build a new plant, it can turn to its holding company's construction department and be sure that people with continual experience in that line of work will be in charge. Likewise, when an engineering problem arises which the staff of the operating company cannot solve, it can immediately be taken to the holding company's engineering department for solution.

Large-scale buying of supplies and equipment has proven to be a fourth source of savings in many fields. A holding company offers an ideal vehicle whereby a number of small companies can pool their purchases. Instead of each company going to a supply house to buy equipment, the orders of all companies are forwarded to the purchasing department of the holding company, which can then afford to go directly to the manufacturers and obtain substantial discounts. Such discounts can be passed on to the operating companies. Finally, many operating companies were originally begun by individuals with little knowledge of the electric utility business. As the field grew, many of these individuals grew with it and their plants were well managed. But a large number of plants were so small that they were unable to offer sufficient financial returns to attract capable managers. A holding company, by combining a number of these poorly managed plants, can group them so that able management may be given to each group.

2. *Profit Motive.* There can be little doubt that the formation of some holding companies was motivated by a desire to achieve economies. But the dominant motive arose from the profits that accrued to users of this system. By facilitating the pyramiding of control, the holding company affords an ideal means for those interested in controlling a large number of companies with a relatively small investment and, in addition, provides a large return on the money invested. Suppose that a holding company is constructed on the following assumptions (see Table 13-1):

A. There are twelve operating companies with a total capitalization of $48 million, divided in the following manner: 50 percent in 4 percent bonds, 25 percent in 5 percent preferred stock, and 25 percent in common stock.

B. The operating companies are divided into four groups of three each, with a father holding company over the groups. Each father company owns one-half of the common stock of its operating companies, requiring an investment of $1.5 million for each holding company or a total of $6 million for the four. The total capitalization is divided into 50 percent in 4 percent bonds, 25 percent in 5 percent preferred stock, and 25 percent in common stock.

C. The four father companies are now controlled by two grandfather holding companies. Their total capitalization, consisting of one-half of the common stock of the father companies, is $750,000, of which 50 percent is in 4 percent bonds, 25 percent in 5 percent preferred stock, and 25 percent in common stock.

D. A great-grandfather holding company controls the two grandfather companies. Its total capitalization is $93,750, representing one-half of the common stock of the grandfather companies, and is divided into 50 percent of 4 percent bonds, 25 percent of 5 percent preferred stock, and 25 percent in common stock.

If an individual group owns one-half of the common stock of the great-grandfather company — an investment of $11,718.75 — it controls the entire structure. Fanciful? In the case of the Associated Gas and Electric System, erected by H. C. Hopson and Associates, an investment of $300,000 at the top of the structure controlled a utility system having book assets in excess of $1 billion.[15]

The profit potential from the holding company structure also is illustrated in Table 13-1. If the hypothetical pyramid is permitted to earn 6 percent on its investment in the operating properties, then the correspond-

TABLE 13-1

Hypothetical Holding Company Pyramid

Company and Capital Structure	Investment	Rate of Return and Its Distribution			
		6 Percent	Percent	4 Percent	Percent
Operating companies					
50 percent bonds, 4%	$24,000,000	$ 960,000	4	$ 960,000	4
25 percent preferred stock, 5%	12,000,000	600,000	5	600,000	5
25 percent common stock	12,000,000	1,320,000	11	360,000	3
Total	$48,000,000	$2,880,000	6	$1,920,000	4
Father holding companies					
50 percent bonds, 4%	$ 3,000,000	$ 120,000	4	$ 120,000	4
25 percent preferred stock, 5%	1,500,000	75,000	5	60,000	4
25 percent common stock	1,500,000	465,000	31	...	...
Total	$ 6,000,000	$ 660,000	11	$ 180,000	3
Grandfather holding companies					
50 percent bonds, 4%	$ 375,000	$ 15,000	4	...	...
25 percent preferred stock, 5%	187,500	9,375	5	...	...
25 percent common stock	187,500	208,125	111	...	...
Total	$ 750,000	$ 232,500	28	...	...
Great-grandfather holding company					
50 percent bonds, 4%	$ 46,875	$ 1,875	4	...	...
25 percent preferred stock, 5%	23,437.50	1,171.88	5	...	...
25 percent common stock	23,437.50	101,015.62	431	...	...
Total	$ 93,750.00	$ 104,062.50	111	...	...

ing return on the common stock of the great-grandfather holding company is 431 percent. Obviously, this is a fantastic rate of return But large returns, in fact, were earned by several holding companies. According to the Federal Trade Commission, the earnings on the common stocks of five leading holding companies for 1924 and 1925 were as follows:[16]

	1924	*1925*
American Power & Light Co.	34.8%	40.5%
National Power & Light Co.	16.5	—
North American Co.	28.2	—
Middle West Utilities Co.	19.0	21.5
Standard Gas & Electric Co.	55.2	37.6
Average	30.7%	33.2%

Even larger profits accrued to the holding companies from their service contracts with operating companies. Again, according to the Federal Trade Commission, the following figures are illustrative: (*a*) from 1924 to 1929, the Associated Gas and Electric System had net income of $6.5 million for management and construction services alone, representing 193 percent net profit on its service cost; (*b*) in the same period, Electric Management and Engineering Corporation (owned by National Electric Power Company) received a "minimum" net profit from servicing of $2.9 million or 171 percent net on costs; and (*c*) from 1924 to 1927, W. S. Barstow and Company, Incorporated, and its subsidiary, W. S. Barstow Management Association, Incorporated, had a combined net income of $4 million or 321 percent on expenses.[17]

Abuses of the Holding Company. While there were advantages to the holding company in the electric utility field, there were also important abuses.[18] Three abuses stand out — pyramiding, write-ups, and excessive service fees.

1. *Pyramiding.* Pyramiding itself turned out to be an evil. In the words of the Federal Trade Commission:

The highly pyramided holding company group represents the holding company system at its worst. It is bad in that it allows one or two individuals, or a small coterie of capitalists, to control arbitrarily enormous amounts of investment supplied by many other people. In such a situation few men could be relied on to devote their attention to prudent management of the operating companies, because the speculative element is so overwhelming. It tends, apparently, to make them (1) neglect good management of operating companies, especially by failing to provide for adequate depreciation; (2) exaggerate profits by unsound, deceptive accounting; (3) seek exorbitant profits from service fees from subsidiaries; (4) disburse unearned dividends, because the apparent gains, so obtained, greatly magnify the rate of earnings for the top holding company; and (5) promote extravagant speculation in the prices of such equity stocks on the exchanges. Such concentration of control, even without that speculative pressure, appears objectionable as a matter of sound national welfare. . . . Finally, the exaggerated importance to the top holding company of comparatively small differences in the profit of the operating companies greatly enhances the incentive of the holding company to increase such profits, or to obtain a revenue through the exaction of service and other fees in addition to the ordinary revenue by way of dividends.[19]

The holding company structure is a fair-weather device. Consider again the data shown in Table 13-1. A 6 percent rate of return on the operating companies' investment would yield a 431 percent return on the common stock of the top holding company. But a 4 percent rate of return would not yield even enough revenue to meet the fixed obligations of the father holding companies. The entire structure, in other words, would collapse.

2. *Write-ups*. Closely connected was a second abuse — excessive write-ups, stock-watering, and inflated capital assets. The Federal Trade Commission estimated that write-ups exceeded $1.4 billion.[20] The Electric Bond and Share Company had total write-ups, for example, of $264 million. Sometimes write-ups occurred when property was purchased, but often they were the result of a revaluation of property already held. Thus, when the Cities Service Power and Light Company was established in 1924 to take over most of the securities held by the Cities Service Company, the former issued $99,999,000 of bonds, preferred stock, and common stock against a total investment of $40,057,852, and then recorded the securities on its books at $106,104,403, or at 165 percent more than the amount formerly recorded on the books of Cities Service Company.[21]

3. *Intracompany Transactions*. One of the major abuses of holding companies was charging excessive fees to their operating companies for services rendered. Usually, annual fees were collected in the form of a certain percentage of the operating company's gross revenue, and the resulting fees bore little relationship to the costs of the services furnished. Several examples of excessive fees were given above. Since they were hidden in the costs of the operating companies, excessive fees were covered in setting electric rates and thus paid by the consuming public.

Nor were excessive fees the only source of exploiting operating companies. The operating companies were weakened financially by inadequate depreciation charges, the payment of excessive dividends (sometimes out of capital), and the neglect of annual maintenance. Finally, it should be noted that since the holding company is a corporation separate from the corporation of the operating company whose stock it holds, it is not liable for the debts of the operating company. A holding company thus legally relieves its owners from financial responsibility toward its operating companies.

The Holding Company: Reorganization

State commissions were limited in their control of electric utilities in two specific ways: (*a*) by the interstate transmission of power and (*b*) by the development of holding companies. They could determine the retail rates at which interstate companies sold to local consumers, but not the wholesale rates at which interstate generators sold to local distributors.[22] They could investigate the cost of goods supplied and services rendered to operating companies only if the holding companies were intrastate.[23] Since the largest holding company systems were interstate, they were not within the state commissions' jurisdiction.[24] With the uncovering of holding company abuses, the federal government took steps to remedy these weaknesses in state regulation.

Congress enacted the Public Utility Act (the Wheeler-Rayburn Act) in 1935.[25] Title I of the act increased the jurisdiction of the Securities and Exchange Commission (SEC) over public utility securities, and gave the commission power to simplify the holding company structures of electric and gas utilities. Title II extended the jurisdiction of the Federal Power Commission over the interstate transmission and sale at wholesale of electric energy.

Legislative Provisions. Title I, known as the Public Utility Holding Company Act, is generally regarded as one of the most stringent corrective laws ever enacted by Congress. For purposes of the act, a holding company is defined as any company holding 10 percent or more of the voting stock of another holding company or of a public utility company, or one which has a "controlling influence over the management or policies" of such companies. Congress declared that its policy was to:

1. . . . eliminate the evils . . . connected with public utility holding companies which are engaged in interstate commerce.
2. . . . compel the simplification of public utility holding company systems. . . .
3. . . . provide as soon as practicable for the elimination of public utility holding companies except as otherwise expressly provided in this title.

The act contained many provisions aimed at eliminating holding company evils. The issuing of new securities by interstate holding companies was put under the control of the SEC. The commission was given a large degree of veto power over the purchase and sale of assets by holding companies. With certain exceptions, before a holding company may purchase other securities or property in another company it must file with the commission a detailed statement of its proposed purchase. If the proposal tends toward "economical and efficient development of an integrated public utility system" and its terms are such as to protect investors and consumers, it is to be approved by the commission. Otherwise, the SEC may state such changes in the proposed acquisition as it deems "necessary . . . in the public interest."[26] Interstate commerce loans must conform to "such rules and regulations . . . as the commission deems necessary . . . ." Payment of dividends by registered holding companies or any subsidiary company must conform to the commission's requirements. All service contracts were brought under the control of the SEC. And, finally, the commission was given power to prescribe the form and manner of accounting to be used by registered holding companies, affiliates of such companies, service companies, and "every person whose principal business is the performance of . . . contracts for public utility or holding companies."

The Death Sentence Clause. The major corrective provision of the 1935 act is contained in Section 11 (b), which reads, in part:

> It shall be the duty of the Commission, as soon as practicable after January 1, 1938:
>
> (1) To require by order, after notice and opportunity for hearing, that each registered holding company, and each subsidiary company thereof, shall take such action as the Commission shall find necessary to limit the operations of the holding-company system of which such company is a part to a single integrated public-utility system, and to such other businesses as are reasonably incidental, or economically necessary or appropriate to the operations of such integrated public-utility system. . . .
>
> (2) To require by order, after notice and opportunity for hearing, that each subsidiary company thereof, shall take steps as the Commission shall find necessary to ensure that the corporate structure or continued existence of any company in the holding-company system does not unduly or unnecessarily complicate the structure, or unfairly or inequitably distribute voting power among security holders, of such holding-company system. In carrying out the provisions of this paragraph the Commission shall require each registered holding company (and any company in the same holding-company system with such holding company) to take such action as the Commission shall find necessary in order that such holding company shall cease to be a holding company with respect to each of its subsidiary companies which itself has a subsidiary company which is a holding company. . . .

Thus, the act provides that all holding companies more than twice removed from their operating subsidiaries are to be abolished. This requirement is the famous "death sentence" clause of the Public Utility Act.[27]

Developments under the Act.[28] The commission's approach to its task of simplifying holding company structures was one of caution. It invited the companies affected to submit their own reorganization plans. It was not until 1940, therefore, that formal proceedings began. During the period June 15, 1938, to June 30, 1962, 2,419 electric and gas distribution utilities came under the jurisdiction of the commission either as registered holding companies or as subsidiaries thereof. Of these companies, 928 — with assets aggregating approximately $13 billion — were subject to divestiture.[29]

In compliance with the act, the SEC sought to establish integrated systems which were confined to a single area.[30] Further, the commission basically followed a "one-area rule," limiting a holding company to controlling only one utility system. Two systems could be controlled if three conditions are satisfied: (1) such control was needed to preserve substantial economies; (2) the systems were located in one state, in adjoining states, or in a contiguous foreign country; and (3) the resulting holding company was not so large as to impair the advantages of local management, efficient operation, or effective regulation.[31] The commission opposed the common control of electric and gas utilities unless it could be shown that there were substantial economies of joint operation.[32] It also opposed the ownership by a registered utility company of a nonutility enterprise unless that enterprise was (a) "reasonably incidental, or economically necessary or appropriate to the operations of" an integrated utility system and (b) in the public interest.[33] And, as previously noted, the SEC reorganized the capital structures of utility companies.[34]

The Public Utility Holding Company Act, by authorizing the reorganization of electric utility holding companies, removed a major obstacle to effective regulation of rates and service by state and federal commissions. It must not be inferred, however, that the effects of the holding company systems were entirely adverse or that the commission was completely successful in establishing economical integrated systems. It is undoubtedly true that the electric power industry today is far more advanced because of the contributions made by the early empire builders.[35] Moreover, as Troxel has pointed out, the commission made mistakes.

Emphasizing physical and geographic conditions, the SEC did not make careful cost studies as integrated operating systems were chosen. The most economical combinations of operating properties were not prescribed. Perhaps some systems represented the most economical units; others probably were smaller or larger than the economic optimums. The SEC could not be expected to make perfect choices. Careful cost studies took much time, were expensive, and were possible sources of extensive litigation. An optimum choice under current technical conditions could be upset by future technical changes. And a thorough integration necessitated a break-up of operating systems — a reshuffling of generating plants, transmission lines, and distribution systems in the electric industry. The SEC brought integration down to the level of the state commission. If operating properties, too, were carefully integrated, the state commissions were the proper authorities for the job. Neither the state legislatures nor state commissions showed any interest, however, in a reorganization of operating plants and marketing areas.[36]

Feeling that the purposes of the act had been achieved, the SEC recommended throughout the 1970s that its functions be transferred to the FPC/FERC and, in 1982, it recommended to Congress that the Public Utility Holding Company Act of 1935 be repealed.[37]

Current Structure

Electric power in the United States, notes Iulo,

> ... is supplied by a complex agglomeration of individual electric supply systems of widely differing economic and legal characteristics. These electric supply systems vary in nature from a small rural cooperative distributing power to a hundred or fewer customers to a large corporate utility serving the power needs of two or three million customers in an extensive metropolitan area. An industrial enterprise producing power primarily for its own use and a municipal light and power department provide additional examples of the diversity in electric supply systems' organization. An individual electric supply system may itself generate all the energy demanded by its customers, or it may obtain, by purchase or interchange, all or a portion of its needs from other utilities, government agencies, industrial enterprises, or it may utilize any combination of these sources. In many instances, the supplying of electric energy may be the sole activity of the electric supply system; in many other cases, electric service is only one aspect of an enterprise that may provide, in addition, gas, telephone, heating, water, or transportation services. The market served by an electric supply system may include only densely populated and industrialized sections within a relatively limited geographic area; or it may be comprised of sparsely populated rural territory spread over a wide geographic area; or the individual system may serve a region with both rural and metropolitan sections.[38]

There are approximately 3,500 separate electric systems, of which the largest 200 provide almost 90 percent of the industry's generating capacity and directly serve nearly 80 percent of the industry's ultimate customer load.[39] "In contrast, many of the remaining 3,300 systems have little or no generation or transmission facilities of their own, and function as distributors of electric energy purchased at wholesale from other utilities."[40] There are four distinct ownership segments (see Table 13-2); (*1*) privately owned systems[41] (approximately 250 systems possessing about 77 percent of the industry's generating capacity); (*2*) state, municipal, and local publicly owned

TABLE 13-2

Electric Energy Installed Generating Capacity and Production, by Class of Ownership, and Source of Energy, 1920-1985

	1920	1930	1940	1950	1960	1970	1980	1985
Installed Capacity (million kilowatt-hours)								
Privately Owned	12.7	32.4	39.9	68.9	168.0	341.1	613.7	688.7
Publicly Owned:	12.0	30.3	34.4	55.2	128.4	262.7	477.1	530.4
Cooperatives	a	a	a	.3	1.4	5.2	15.4	24.6
Municipal	.6	1.6	3.2	5.3	11.5	20.9	34.6	37.0
Federal	.01	.2	1.9	6.9	22.4	38.7	59.1	63.7
Power Districts, State Projects	.08	.3	.4	1.2	4.3	13.6	27.5	33.0
Production (billion kilowatt-hours)								
Privately Owned	39.4	91.1	141.8	329.1	753.3	1,531.6	2,286.4	2,469.8
Publicly Owned:	37.7	86.1	125.4	266.9	578.6	1,183.2	1,782.9	1,918.0
Cooperatives	a	a	a	.9	5.0	23.5	63.5	108.3
Municipal	1.4	3.6	6.7	16.1	36.9	71.4	86.6	73.9
Federal	.06	.5	8.6	40.4	112.3	185.7	235.1	233.0
Power Districts, State Projects	.3	.9	1.1	4.8	20.5	67.8	118.3	136.6
Source of Energy (percent):								
Coal[b]	53.1	55.8	54.6	47.1	53.5	46.1	51.0	57.2
Nuclear	b	b	b	b	.1	1.4	11.0	15.5
Oil	5.4	3.1	4.4	10.2	6.1	11.9	10.6	4.1
Gas	1.5	6.9	7.7	13.5	21.0	24.4	15.1	11.8
Hydro	40.0	34.2	33.3	29.2	19.3	16.2	12.1	11.4

[a]Included in Power Districts and State Projects.
[b]Includes small percentage from wood and waste, geothermal, petroleum coke, and (until 1960), nuclear fuels.
Source: U.S. Department of Commerce, *Historical Statistics of the United States* (Washington, D.C.: U.S. Government Printing Office, 1975), Vol. II; *Moody's Public Utility Manual* (1986 Edition); U.S. Department of Commerce, *Statistical Abstract of the United States: 1987* (Washington, D.C.: U.S. Government Printing Office, 1986), p. 554.

systems, including public utility districts and special authorities (approximately 2,200 systems accounting for 10.2 percent of the industry's generating capacity); (3) cooperatively owned systems (approximately 1,000 systems with 3.6 percent of the nation's generating capacity); and (4) federal agencies (accounting for 9.2 percent of the country's electric power supply). While the number of privately owned and municipal electric systems has declined over the past five decades, the number of rural electric cooperatives and federally owned systems has increased significantly.

Coordination

The electric power industry is highly coordinated, with nearly all of the 3,500 systems operating in electrical synchronism. Coordination is achieved in three ways: through regional reliability councils, interconnections, and power pools.

Regional Reliability Councils. The Northeast power failure of November 9-10, 1965, and the extensive power interruption in the Pennsylvania-New Jersey-Maryland Interconnection on June 5, 1967, dramatically raised the issue of reliability.[42] Interconnections among electric utility systems offer many economic advantages and interties have progressed rapidly, but the commission's power to require interconnections is limited. To prevent a failure in one part of a system from "cascading" or "snowballing" into other parts, coordinated planning, design, construction, and operation of generating and transmission facilities is required.

Following the Northeast power failure, the industry established nine regional reliability councils, accounting for virtually all of the electric power supply in the contiguous United States, the bordering provinces of Canada (in Ontario, British Columbia, Alberta, Manitoba, and New Brunswick), and northern Baja California, Mexico (see Figure 13-2). The councils

> ... provide mechanisms for coordination of operating practices and planning criteria and the exchange of bulk power plants by essentially all bulk power supply utilities within broad geographic areas. ... Each Council consists of a representative of each of the major utilities in the region and of groups of small utilities in some regions. The Council's develop voluntary standards for those aspects of bulk power supply that affect the regionwide reliability of service. For example, each Council has adopted design criteria for transmission facilities in an effort to prevent large-scale blackouts.[43]

In 1968, the North American Electric Reliability Council (NAERC) was formed to assist in the coordination of policy issues among the regional councils (and one affiliate, the Alaska Systems Coordinating Council). Rather than "a governing organization," the NAERC is "a consortium" of the re-

FIGURE 13-2

North American Electric Reliability Council

WSCC	—Western Systems Coordinating Council
MAPP	—Mid-Continent Area Power Pool
SPP	—Southwest Power Pool
ERCOT	—Electric Reliability Council of Texas
MAIN	—Mid-American Interpool Network
SERC	—Southeastern Electric Reliability Council
ECAR	—East Central Area Reliability Coordination Agreement
MAAC	—Mid-Atlantic Area Council
NPCC	—Northeast Power Coordinating Council

Source: John P. Williamson, "Does Electric Reliability Have a Future?," 119 *Public Utilities Fortnightly* 19, 20 (April 30, 1987).

gional councils, "focusing on interregional and national electric reliability issues."[44]

Interconnections. In a previous chapter, it was pointed out that the loads of electric utilities vary from hour to hour, day to day, and season to season. Each electric system must have access to enough power to supply the peak load, even though the peak occurs only for a short period of time once a year, as well as to maintain adequate reserves for emergencies and growth. The peak load for the entire country occurs in the summer, although growth in the use of electricity for heating results in a winter peak that is nearly as great. However, since the diversity factor for each utility system depends on the composition of its customers and its geographic location, different systems usually have different peak periods. Interconnections and pooling enable the industry to reduce the peak load of each system by taking advantage of differing diversity factors, thereby decreasing the amount of generating capacity needed. Put another way, when two or more systems are interconnected, their combined simultaneous peak load is less than the sum of the individual systems' peaks because of the diversity factor. Reserve capacity, which costs money but produces no revenue, can be reduced by interconnections.

Virtually all power generated by the electric power industry is produced by plants which are interconnected in three large networks. Each network consists of many systems tied together by interconnections. The largest of these networks embraces thirty-nine states and two Canadian provinces, covering the entire United States east of Texas and the Rocky Mountains and much of eastern Canada.[45]

Power Pools. In addition to interconnections, power pools have been, and are being, developed throughout the country. Such pools are of two basic types: *informal* and *formal*. The former "is a grouping of utilities that has agreed informally to establish common principles and practices for interconnected operation, to jointly review area power supply problems and establish criteria for power supply adequacy, to exchange generation and transmission construction plans, and to seek coordinated action for best economy and reliability, but which relies on voluntary adherence by members to pool principles and criteria."[46] The Northwest Power Pool is an example of an informal pool.[47] The latter refers to "two or more electric systems which coordinate the planning and/or operation of their bulk power facilities for the purpose of achieving greater economy and reliability in accordance with a contractual agreement that establishes each member's responsibilities."[48] Formal pools, in turn, may be categorized as either *tight* or *loose*. "In a tight pool, reserve requirements are enforced by penalties and single system operating economy is assured by central dispatch. A loose pool provides both operating and planning coordination, but generally does not include penalties or central dispatch provisions to enforce conformance with economic practices."[49] In 1981, the FERC identified nine tight power pools (four representing twelve corporately unaffiliated groups, with 44 percent of the nation's generating capacity, and five holding company pools, representing an additional 15 percent of the country's generating capacity). (See Table 13-3.) Three of these pools are located in the Northeast Region: the New England Power Pool (NEPOOL), the New York Power Pool (NYPP), and the Pennsylvania-New Jersey-Maryland Interconnection (PJM).[50] (See Figure 13-3.) These three tight pools have installed generating capacity of 95,942 megawatts (see Table 13-4) and jointly own seventeen base-load generating plants.

Coordination Issues. "Although coordination and pooling can result in improved efficiency, reliability, and conservation of energy, such efforts are not without problems, some general and some quite specific to the particular coordination opportunity."[51] Among the general issues are the loss of corporate sovereignty by the participants, particularly in a tight pool; the need to accept certain obligations, which may result in the exposure to some additional risks; and the need for decision making by a group whose members have diverse interests.[52] There also are regulatory delays (due to the need to secure multi-agency approvals and/or environmental considerations) which either delay or prevent effective coordination efforts.[53] Two additional problems deserve brief discussion: cost/benefit issues and competitive considerations.

1. *Cost/Benefit Issues.* Differences in the size and ownership of electric power systems raise complex cost/benefit issues. Smaller systems are likely to gain more proportionately from pooling than are larger systems which already realize significant economies of scale. "A small utility may gain immediate and major savings from pooling, through reduced operating reserve costs, increased opportunities to purchase economy energy, and reduced construction expenditures. Further, when new capacity is required, it can be purchased at lower cost through shared ownership of larger, more economical units."[54] Larger systems, however, "may not gain any further economies of scale from such pooling, the timing of their construction programs may not be significantly changed, and they may perceive substantial administrative problems in coordinating with smaller systems."[55] For these reasons larger systems, although "unlikely to experience any measurable economic disadvantages from pooling with smaller systems," often maintain "for reasons both of equity and maintenance of competitive relationships that they should receive a share of the savings that derive from such pooling above that provided by the usual arrangements."[56]

2. *Competitive Considerations.* Competition, both actual and potential, sometimes complicates attempts at coordination. At the bulk power supply level, the various forms of competition include: (*a*) competition among rival suppliers for firm wholesale loads; (*b*) competition among suppliers and purchasers for economy energy, emergency energy, short-term power, surplus power, and so forth; and (*c*) competition for ownership interests in generating facilities. None of these forms of competition appears to have inhibited

TABLE 13-3

Major Formal Power Pools in the
United States, 1980

Region	Generating Capability Summer 1979* (Megawatts)
NORTHEAST REGION	
New England Power Pool (NEPOOL)	21,294
New York Power Pool (NYPP)	29,742
Pennsylvania-New Jersey-Maryland Interconnection (PJM)	44,891
SOUTHEAST REGION	
Southern Company System (SOCO) (Holding Company)	23,909[1]
ECAR REGION	
Allegheny Power System, Inc. (APS) (Holding Company)	6,822
American Electric Power System (AEP) (Holding Company)	20,123
Central Area Power Coordination Group (CAPCO)	15,147
Michigan Electric Coordinated System (MECS)	15,791
MAIN-MARCA REGION	
Illinois-Missouri Pool (IL-MO)	13,480
Mid-Continent Area Power Pool (MAPP)	24,527
Wisconsin Power Pool (WPP)	3,681
SPP REGION	
Middle South Utilities, Inc. (MSU) (Holding Company)	12,177
Missouri-Kansas Pool (MOKAN)	8,879
ERCOT REGION	
Texas Municipal Power Pool (TMPP)	1,457
Texas Utilities Company (TUCO) (Holding Company)	17,336

TABLE 13-3 *(Continued)*

Region	Generating Capability Summer 1979* (Megawatts)
WESTERN REGION	
California Power Pool (CPP)	28,870
Pacific Northwest Coordination Agreement (PNCA)	32,292
TOTAL—Corporately Unaffiliated Pools	240,502
TOTAL—Holding Company Pools	80,367
Installed Capability—Contiguous United States	546,662

*As reported by NERC.

[1]Includes generation owned by the Municipal Electric Authority of Georgia and the Oglethorpe Power Corporation but operated by Georgia Power Company.

Source: Federal Energy Regulatory Commission, *Power Pooling in the United States* (Washington, D.C.: U.S. Government Printing Office, 1981), p. 9.

TABLE 13-4

Installed Generating Capacity in the Northeast Region
(Megawatts), Summer 1980

Type	PJM	NYPP	NEPOOL	Total Region	Percent of Total
Coal	14,912	3,519	455	18,886	19.7
Oil	20,227	18,153	13,129	51,509	53.7
Gas	254	30	0	284	.3
Nuclear	7,076	3,703	4,228	15,007	15.6
Hydroelectric	2,236	5,030	2,908	10,174	10.6
Other	50	32	0	82	0.1
TOTAL	44,755	30,467	20,720	95,942	100.0
Percent	46.6	31.8	21.6	100.0	

Source: Federal Energy Regulatory Commission, *Power Pooling in the United States* (Washington, D.C.: U.S. Government Printing Office, 1981), p. 71.

FIGURE 13-3

Northeast Region

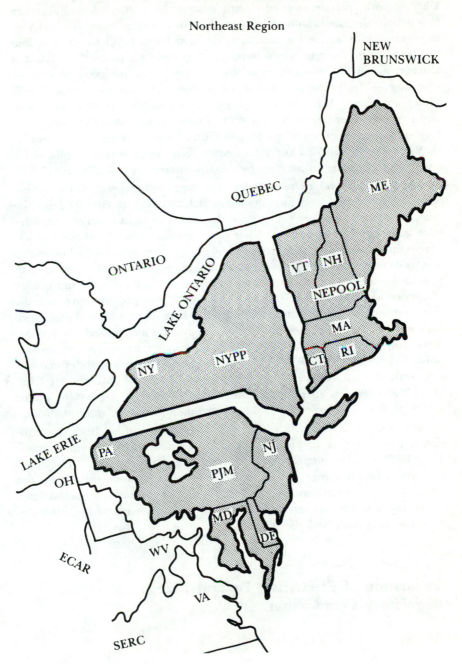

Source: Federal Energy Regulatory Commission, *Power Pooling in the United States* (Washington, D.C.: U.S. Government Printing Office, 1981), p. 70.

the development of coordination, although several raise policy problems.[57] Until recently, privately-owned electric systems have shown little interest in new wholesale loads, with the result that such competition has been of importance only where a municipality decided (*a*) to purchase the distribution system in order to take advantage of preference power[58] or (*b*), if it already owned the distribution system, to request transmission services — wheeling — from the investor-owned system so as to use another bulk power supplier.[59] Economy energy, emergency energy, short-term power, and surplus power generally were subject to filed rates. And, as in the New England Power Pool, there has long been an "active market . . . for ownership interests in baseload and intermediate load units. It is not unusual for ten or more utilities to have an ownership interest in a single plant."[60]

At the retail level, there are four basic types of competition: (*a*) competition for individual loads, usually industrial and commercial; (*b*) franchise competition, which involves rivalry for the exclusive right to serve a territory or a large block of customers; (*c*) fringe area competition, where a newly developing border area may be served by both a bulk power supplier and its wholesale customer; and (*d*) yardstick competition, "which refers to the competitive pressure felt by utilities from comparison of their rates and quality of service with those of neighboring utilities."[61] For present purposes, the most important types of competition are the first three, which almost inevitably involve rivalry between investor-owned systems and publicly-owned systems and, consequently, between large and small systems. In areas where public-private competition is weak and/or where there are well-defined service territories, coordination may be successfully carried out. The New England Power Pool is an example. But where there is strong rivalry and/or where preference power is available, coordination may be more difficult.

Any electric system which believes it has been excluded from transmission, interconnection, or pooling opportunities, has other avenues of relief. The FERC can order interconnections, coordination, or wheeling.[62] The FERC also has jurisdiction over power pools.[63] The electric power industry is not immune from the antitrust laws.[64] And, finally, all commercial nuclear reactor license applications are subject to prelicensing review by both the Department of Justice and the NRC.[65]

Regulation of Electricity: Federal Energy Regulatory Commission

The FERC has a twofold task with respect to its control of electricity — control of nonfederal hydroelectric projects on federal waterways and control of the interstate transmission and sale at wholesale of electricity.

Hydroelectric Projects

In 1920, the Federal Power Commission was created under the Federal Water Power Act to regulate construction and operation of nonfederal hydroelectric projects on navigable domestic waterways.[66] Jurisdiction over such waters results from the government's ownership of vast areas of land and from subsequent Supreme Court interpretations of the commerce clause.[67] The commission consisted of the Secretaries of Agriculture, Interior, and War. Since the Cabinet members were preoccupied with their own departmental duties and the commission was without its own staff, this structure proved to be unsatisfactory.[68] In 1930, the law was amended, providing for appointment of five full-time commissioners and a full-time staff.

The Licensing Process. A license must be obtained from the commission before a power plant can be constructed on a federal navigable waterway.[69] There are four types of licenses: the preliminary permit (usually not to exceed three years, during which time the applicant has priority with respect to a proposed project while doing the preliminary work prior to filing an application for a license),[70] the major license (not to exceed fifty years), the minor license (projects having an installed capacity of more than 100 horsepower, but not exceeding 2,000 horsepower), and the minor-part license (a minor part of a complete project or a complete project of less than 100 horsepower of installed capacity). Proposed projects also may qualify for an exemption from licensing, either on a case-specific basis (*i.e.,* hydroelectric generating facilities installed at existing dams or "certain natural water features" which are five megawatts or less; hydroelectric generating facilities of fifteen megawatts or less installed in conduits which were constructed for other purposes, such as the distribution of water for domestic, agricultural, or industrial purposes) or on a generic basis (*i.e.,* two classes of projects, subject to a certification procedure, one of five megawatts or less and the other of 100 kilowatts or less).[71]

The major licensee agrees to (*a*) keep the plant in good condition; (*b*) follow a prescribed accounting system; (*c*) make annual payments toward the costs of administration and "for the use, occupancy, and enjoyment" of United States land or other property; and (*d*) accept the rate, service, and security regulations of the commission where no state has jurisdiction or where states surrounding the federal waterway being developed find themselves unable to reach agreement on such regulation. At the end of the license period, the license may be renewed with the original company or granted to a new applicant, or the government can take over the project — except for state and municipal projects — by paying the net investment cost plus reasonable severance damages. During the first twenty years of a license, and if the states have not undertaken regulation, the licensee must make payments to the United States "for the expropriation to the Government of excessive profits." After the first twenty years, the licensee must establish an amortization reserve for the accumulation of excess earnings; that is, earnings which exceed the rate of return on net investment as specified in the license.[72] In granting a major license, the commission is to give priority to applications made by local and state governments,[73] and is to consider how the project will affect the conservation and utilization of the region's water resources for all purposes, such as power, flood control, navigation, and irrigation.[74]

As of September 30, 1986, 989 licenses were in effect: 666 for major projects, 307 for minor projects, seven for minor-part projects, and nine for projects involving transmission lines that cross federal lands. The major projects represent 51 million kilowatts of ultimate generating capacity. In addition, there were 546 preliminary permits in effect, involving the proposed installation of 6.5 million kilowatts of generating capacity. As a reflection of the renewed interest in hydroelectric power, there were 276 major licenses, 164 minor licenses, and 169 preliminary permits pending, totaling 14 million kilowatt-hours of ultimate generating capacity. Moreover, the FERC has issued 522 exemptions for projects of five megawatts or less, totaling 655 thousand kilowatts.[75]

Regulation and Reports. As most states have regulatory commissions, the FERC's authority to regulate the rates, services, and securities of its licensees is limited. The commission has prescribed and enforced a uniform system of accounts. It has enforced the requirement regarding amortization and has made countless inspections of all projects to insure compliance with licensing terms.[76] It has ordered over 200 net investment cost studies and has collected $166 million for headwater benefits provided by federally owned improvements.[77]

The commission has made several investigations and reports on the use of water resources in various regions, the waterpower industry, and waterpower sites; maintains a current inventory of information on developed and undeveloped hydroelectric power resources in the United States[78]; has located more than 3,000 retired plants that might be suitable for redevelopment[79]; and has an ongoing water resources appraisal program.[80] The chairman of the commission is a member of the Water Resources Council, a council established under the Water Resources Planning Act of 1965 to coordinate the activities of federal agencies engaged in water and land resources planning and development.[81]

Recreational Purposes. Section 10 (a) of the Federal Power Act requires the commission to take into consideration "recreational purposes" in granting a hydroelectric power project license.[82] For many years this mandate was carried out by including "general terms and conditions in licenses requiring free public access and use of project property for recreational purposes, and facilities for conservation of fish and wildlife resources."[83] Since 1963, however, this aspect of licensing has assumed greater importance. Beginning in that year, the FPC issued a series of orders designed to require license applicants "to develop — in consultation with appropriate Federal, State,

and local agencies — a comprehensive program for utilizing project properties for outdoor recreation and for enhancement of fish and wildlife
resources."[84] Subsequent court decisions broadened the phrase "recreational
purposes" to encompass the conservation of natural resources, the maintenance of natural beauty, and the preservation of historic sites.[85] Thus, if
overhead transmission structures would cause scenic damage, the commission must weigh the aesthetic advantages of underground lines against the
cost disadvantages.[86] As the Supreme Court stated in remanding a licensing
case to the Commission in 1967: in licensing proceedings, the commission
should keep in mind that, "in our affluent society, the cost of a project is
only one of several factors to be considered."[87] At the present time, FERC-
approved recreational plans cover more than 2.3 million acres and over
25,350 miles of shoreline. "Annual public use at licensed projects exceeds
102 million visitations."[88]

Relicensing or Recapture. Upon the expiration of a major license, the
Federal Power Act provides for either relicensing or recapture. After receiving an application from the original owner, the commission has three options:
grant the owner a new license, award the license to a competing applicant
who is deemed better able to operate the project, or recommend to Congress that the project be taken over by the federal government ("recapture").[89]
Until the late 1970s, the commission's general policy was to relicense the
original owner, as long as it could meet the statutory standards. But in the
late 1970s, two major events occurred:

1. Several municipalities petitioned the commission for licenses held by
   privately-owned utilities (*e.g.,* the city of Bountiful, Utah, for the
   Weber River Hydro Project, licensed to Utah Power and Light Company; the city of Santa Clara, California, for the Mokelumne River
   Project, licensed to Pacific Gas and Electric Company; the Clark-
   Cowlitz Joint Operating Agency for the Merwin Dam on the Lewis
   River in Washington state, licensed to Pacific Power & Light Company). The petitions cited the municipal preference provisions of the
   Federal Power Act (applicable to original licenses). The commission,
   in a 1980 decision, held that municipal preference does apply to
   relicensing actions, but that it would be used only as a "tie-breaker;"
   that is, it would be invoked only when the public interest factors are
   equally balanced between the original licensee and the competing
   state or municipal applicant. The commission's position was upheld
   on review.[90] But then, in a September, 1983, decision, after an administrative law judge had recommended a license be awarded to
   the Clark-Cowlitz Joint Operating Agency, the FERC reversed its
   1980 decision by holding that municipal preference does not apply
   in relicensing actions and relicensed the Pacific Power & Light Company for the Merwin Dam. The commission's position was reversed
   on review (in 1985), then upheld (in 1987).[91]

While the latter decision was on appeal, Congress enacted the Electric Consumers Protection Act of 1986[92] which, among other things, states that there is no municipal preference in future relicensing proceedings.[93]

2. Two projects were recommended for recapture by federal agencies: one by the Departments of Agriculture and Interior (the Chippewa Project, owned by Northern States Power Company), and the other by the Department of Interior (the Escondido Project, owned by Escondido Mutual Water Company). Both projects involve Indian lands. In the case of the latter project, the commission's decision to relicense Escondido Mutual Water Company was upheld by the Supreme Court in 1984.[94]

Interstate Transmission and Sale at Wholesale

Title II of the Public Utility Act of 1935, known as the Federal Power Act, gave the commission broad authority over the interstate transmission and sale at wholesale of electricity. In all those matters in which existing state regulation has proven ineffective or unconstitutional, the commission was authorized to regulate rates and earnings, prescribe an accounting system, control the issuance of securities, mergers,[95] and transfers of facilities, prevent interlocking officers and directors, and "to divide the country into regional districts for the voluntary interconnection and coordination of facilities for the generation, transmission, and sale of electric energy."[96] On application of a state commission or of any person engaged in either transmission or sale of electric energy, if such action is in the public interest and does not involve an enlargement of generating facilities, the commission may "direct a public utility to establish physical connection of its transmission facilities with the facilities of one or more other persons . . . to sell energy to or exchange energy with such persons." In 1978, Congress added three new sections to the act which expanded the commission's authority to order the interconnection and coordination of electric utility systems, either upon complaint or on its own motion, and gave the commission authority to order wheeling.[97] The commission also has responsibility for approving the rate schedules of public power sold by five federal power marketing agencies: Alaska Power Administration, Bonneville Power Administration,[98] Southeastern Power Administration, Southwestern Power Administration, and Western Area Power Administration.

The FERC's jurisdiction over wholesale electric rates amounts to approximately 28 percent of the industry's total domestic sales volume.[99] Prior to the early 1960s, however, few complaints had been filed with the commission, and few investigations had been undertaken on its own initiative. The commission did establish a uniform system of accounts and cooperated with numerous state commissions in resolving common regulatory problems. But by its own admission in 1962, the commission's "function of regulating interstate wholesale electric rates has not received the attention it deserves."[100] In that year, the commission reorganized its Bureau of Power and, the following year, initiated a program of reviewing all electric rate schedules on file and revised its regulations governing electric rate filings, thereby requiring more detailed cost data.[101] Since the mid-1960s, therefore, the commission's activity with respect to interstate transmission and wholesale electric rates has been of importance.

The Price Squeeze Problem.[102] The FERC's jurisdiction is limited to wholesale electric power rates, while retail electric power rates are subject to the jurisdiction of the state commissions. This divided authority raises the price squeeze problem under both the Federal Power Act and the antitrust laws: if wholesalers pay too high a price for purchased power, they may be unable to distribute and resell that power to their retail customers at rates competitive with those which vertically integrated power suppliers are charging their retail customers.[103] The issue only arises, of course, where there is competition among different suppliers for retail customers; a situation that exists in many areas of the country.

In FERC price squeeze cases,[104] the existence of price discrimination has been based upon a comparative rate of return analysis: the rate of return expected to be earned on the just and reasonable (but for price squeeze considerations) wholesale rate compared to the retail rate of return earned on that class of retail customers for which it is alleged competition exists.[105]

> .... If the analyses indicate that the rate of return from wholesale rates exceed that from the relevant retail rates, price discrimination is shown. At this point, the parties claiming injury are entitled to relief unless the utility shows that the discrimination is not undue. However, if the differential in prices to wholesale and retail customers is based on cost factors, no price discrimination has been demonstrated. The rule is based on the public policy that neither the utility's investors nor its other customers are required to subsidize the wholesale customers' ability to compete for retail business. . . .[106]

The commission has adopted a "presumption of competition" concept (*i.e.*, a "rebuttable presumption" that price discrimination has anticompetitive effects) and has eliminated the need to show "intent."[107] But is such discrimination "undue"? Discrimination has been considered undue unless noncost justified; "unless countervailing public policy or factual circumstances are of a nature that would cause the commission to conclude that the discrimination is not *undue.*"[108] Such mitigating circumstances have included "the paradox of dual utility rate regulation" (*e.g.*, different policies or procedures at the state and federal levels, timing differences between state and federal decisions).[109] Yet, while acknowledging the paradox, reviewing courts have not been persuaded that it provides a justification for discrimination.[110]

The price squeeze issue remains an "ongoing saga . . . in federal utility ratemaking."[111]

Public Power and Cooperatives

Public power and cooperatives are not new in the United States; their large-scale development dates from the 1930s. In 1935, they produced but 7.9 percent of the nation's electric energy, compared to 23 percent in 1985. Some groups see nonprivate entities as socialism, perhaps as the first step toward eventual nationalization of the entire industry, and as a source of unfair competition vis-a-vis private power. Others view nonprivate operations as a device to regulate and control privately operated electric utility companies (the so-called "yardstick" idea) and as a means of promoting regional development.[112]

Municipal Operations[113]

Municipal operations started in the early days of the electric industry, one such system being in operation as early as 1881. By 1921, when the number of municipal systems reached its peak, there were 2,581 such systems. Most of these systems were small: while accounting for nearly 41 percent of all electric systems, they generated but 4.7 percent of the total output of power. Many municipal power systems were built in small towns, and hundreds of them were sold to private companies during the consolidation movement of the 1920s.

During the 1930s, there was a considerable revival of interest in municipal operations. Some municipalities decided that operating their own electric systems might provide them with income which, in turn, might make possible some reduction in local taxation or, at least, check any tax increase. Other municipalities were interested in lower electric rates; the rate practices of the holding companies, in particular, led to demands for reform. Whatever the cause, the liberal loan policy of the federal government made it possible for many communities to realize their desires for their own electric systems. From 1933 to 1938, the federal government paid approximately 45 percent of the total cost of approved municipal projects and provided low-cost loans for the remaining 55 percent as part of its public works program (through the Public Works Administration).[114]

Numerically, municipal systems continue to be of significance, but their percentage of total power production has decreased slightly in the last forty-five years. A great majority of all municipal systems are found in federal power regions, where they buy preference power. The remaining municipal systems either produce their own electric energy or purchase it from bulk suppliers. No generalizations are possible concerning municipal rate policies: some operate at a profit or at cost, while others operate at a loss.[115]

Cooperatives[116]

In 1935, President Roosevelt, by executive order, established the Rural Electrification Administration (REA).[117] Statutory provision for the REA was made in the Rural Electrification Act of 1936 (the Norris-Rayburn bill). The basic purpose of the REA was to extend electric service to those rural areas of the country without central station service by providing government loans at low interest rates.[118] Cooperatives were formed by farmers to build power lines; private companies sold power to these co-ops at low wholesale rates. As of January 1, 1986, the REA had approved a cumulative total of $18.6 billion in loans (and had guaranteed an additional $33.1 billion) to over 1,000 cooperatives in forty-six states (all states but Connecticut, Hawaii, Massachusetts, and Rhode Island).[119]

The REA's success, ironically, is partly responsible for the debate over its future. First, it has been argued that in many cases the REA has been financing small, inefficient facilities[120]; a situation due to the fact that the typical rural electric system serves less than 6,000 customers. Second, many question the need of continuing two benefits long received by co-ops — their tax-exempt status and the low-cost money they can borrow. The tax benefit is similar to the one received by all users of public power; the loan benefit (of the insured variety) means that taxpayers are subsidizing the cooperatives.[121] Third, many of the larger cooperatives have received loans in order to expand into urban areas or to supply power to industrial users. Over the last two decades, nearly five out of every six new co-op customers were nonfarm. As a result, co-ops came into direct competition with private utilities.[122] Finally, beginning in the early 1960s, the REA began to make large loans to cooperatives for generating plants and transmission facilities (known as G&T loans).[123] Prior to 1961, the REA's policy was to limit such loans to those situations where power was not available from private companies or where private companies charged exorbitant wholesale rates. The new policy made such loans available when "necessary to protect the security and effectiveness of REA-financed systems,"[124] even though private companies had adequate facilities to supply power at reasonable rates.[125] Today, there are over fifty large G&T cooperatives that are fully integrated into regional power pools.[126]

Federal Operations

The federal government has become an important supplier of electric power. Significantly, its entry into the power field was by the back door. The major federal projects (see Table 13-5) were undertaken for other reasons: to prevent flood, to provide navigable waters, to supply water for irrigation, and to store water for urban and industrial consumers.[127] Yet, the dams constructed for these purposes also provided a source of electric power. The controversy which has focused on federal power projects was thus born.

TABLE 13-5

Major Federal Power Projects—Installed Capacity and
Investment Allocated to Electric Plant, 1978

Project or System	Capacity (1,000 Kw.)	Investment[a] ($1,000,000)
Central Valley:		
Bureau of Reclamation	1,141	$ 239
Columbia Basin:		
Bonneville Power Administration	b	1,969
Bureau of Reclamation	5,167	859
Corps of Engineers	10,774	3,383
Hoover and Parker-Davis:		
Bureau of Reclamation	1,705	236
Missouri Basin:		
Bureau of Reclamation	708	609
Corps of Engineers	2,055	733
Southeastern Power Administration:		
Corps of Engineers	2,651	956
Southwestern Power Administration:		
Southwest Power Administration	b	63
Corps of Engineers	1,926	615
Tennessee Valley Authority	27,032	10,926
Other projects	1,344	868
Total	54,503	$21,456

[a]Investment allocated to electric plant; partly estimated; reserves for depreciation not deducted.

[b]Transmission only.

Source: U.S. Bureau of the Census, *Statistical Abstract of the United States, 1981* (Washington, D.C.: U.S. Government Printing Office, 1981), Table 1015, p. 589.

In large measure, the controversy over public power is concerned with ideology and efficiency. Some believe that private enterprise is superior to public enterprise and that the private should prevail whenever possible. Others feel that government-operated enterprise tends to be inefficient; bureaucracy and apathetic management are familiar charges of those who oppose public enterprise. These two problems aside, public power development raises several issues worth contemplating.

The first issue concerns the yardstick concept — the idea that public power projects can serve as yardsticks against which the performance of private companies can be measured. In its earliest form, the concept assumed rate equality; that is, if the government could cover all costs, including a reasonable return, by adopting a particular schedule, then private companies' rates should be cut to these levels. Used in this sense, public power projects are not fair yardsticks. The cost of supplying public power tends to be lower than the cost of comparable private power and, unless costs are disregarded in establishing rates, the public rates must be lower than the private.[128] Others, such as Lilienthal, have used the yardstick concept in a different manner.[129] According to this notion, public power rates are properly used in an experimental way, namely, to examine the elasticity of demand for electric power. Used in this way, the yardstick concept makes more sense. Public power projects led the movement toward lower rates in the 1930s. The results are well known: consumption and production increased dramatically as it was shown that the demand for electric energy tends to be elastic. Private companies might have learned this lesson on their own, but it seems possible that the experience of public power projects accelerated the discovery.

A second issue, also of more historic than current interest, revolves around the disposition of water power. The federal government's entry into the generation, transmission, and distribution of power was not made mandatory by construction of dams. The falling water could have been sold to private companies who, in turn, would have built the necessary facilities. Instead, in all the major projects except one,[130] the government has built its own generating facilities and transmission lines. In the distribution of its power, the preference clause generally prevails and thus has been instrumental in promoting municipal and cooperative ownership of distribution systems.

A third issue concerns the important problem of allocating joint costs. When federal projects are multipurpose, how should the total cost be allocated to each purpose? Several methods have been used; each has its limitations. As Wilcox has concluded:

(1) It is suggested that an equal charge be made for each of the purposes for which a dam is used. This would be workable but purely arbitrary. (2) It is suggested that contributions to joint costs be made proportionate to the separate costs of the various uses of common

facilities. This, too, would be workable but arbitrary. (3) It is proposed that the contributions be made proportionate to the benefits received by the users of different services. This is justifiable but unworkable. The benefits of some services are difficult to measure. The benefits of others can be measured by the prices which they bring. But since these prices are in question, this method would involve circular reasoning. (4) It is proposed that the alternative cost of building a single-purpose dam for each of the purposes served by a project (where this would be economically justified) be computed, and contributions to joint costs be made proportionate to their respective shares in the total of single-purpose costs. The use of alternative possibilities as a basis for allocation has a certain logic. But this procedure necessitates an estimation of the cost of imaginary projects, an exercise in which personal judgment has free play and differences of opinion are certain to result. (5) It is proposed that the share of cost charged to each purpose be made proportionate to its use of reservoir capacity. This, too, makes sense. But the cost of different layers in a reservoir is difficult to estimate. The use of reservoir capacity for different purposes is even more so, since it differs from season to season and from day to day. The usefulness of a reservoir in producing power depends, moreover, not only on the volume of water that passes through the turbines but also on the head of water behind the dam. If this procedure were to be used, costs would have to be allocated, in the end, in accordance with an arbitrary rule. . . .[131]

In short, all methods of allocation rest ultimately on judgment, and the final decision is open to dispute. The Tennessee Valley Authority (TVA), for example, allocates 42 percent of the cost of dams and 40 percent of the cost of general administration to power.

The allocation of joint costs would be little more than an academic exercise were it not for a fourth issue — public power rates. Congress has specified two basic pricing objectives: repayment of the investment allocated to electric power and promotion of the widest possible usage of electricity. The two objectives might conflict. Rates based upon cost calculations might be too high, for instance, to promote widespread consumption in rural areas. In practice, rates have not been based strictly upon cost computations. Until the 1970s, emphasis was placed on low rates to encourage consumption; a policy that was highly successful.[132] Thus, residential rates in the TVA area averaged .89 cents per kilowatt-hour in 1967, compared with a national average of 2.18 cents; the number of farms electrified in the region rose from 3 percent in 1933 to more than 99 percent; the total consumption of power increased from 1.5 billion kilowatt-hours to 82.1 billion. During the same period, the established rates also resulted in "excess revenues" so that some of the public money invested in power projects was returned to the Treasury.[133]

A final, and related, issue concerns the expansion of public power projects. The entry of the federal government into the production of hydro-electric power was the result of undertaking multipurpose projects. But the government did not stop at that point. The TVA, for example, starting with a series of multipurpose dams, obtained both a regional monopoly by buying out private companies and an assured market by promoting public owner-ship of distribution facilities.[134] In addition to the twenty-nine hydroelectric plants it owns, it has continued to expand its power output by building twelve coal-fired generating plants,[135] four combustion turbine installations, a pumped-storage hydroelectric plant,[136] and, in 1967, announced plans to build nuclear facilities with seventeen reactors.[137] As a result, multipurpose projects — particularly the TVA — have tended to become giant utility enterprises, with similar problems confronted by investor-owned utilities.[138]

The Department of Energy and the National Energy Legislation

The Department of Energy (DOE) was created in 1977.[139] Prior to its establishment, some nineteen federal agencies had responsibilities relating to electric power. Many, but not all (*e.g.*, Nuclear Regulatory Commission, Rural Electrification Administration), of these functions were consolidated within the DOE. The Energy Research and Development Administration and the Federal Energy Administration were abolished and their duties transferred to the new department. Energy-related functions from the Inter-state Commerce Commission and the Departments of Housing and Urban Development, Interior, Commerce and Navy also were transferred to the DOE. An independent regulatory commission, the Federal Energy Regula-tory Commission, was created within the DOE and assumed most of the statutory duties of the abolished Federal Power Commission under the Fed-eral Power Act and the Natural Gas Act.[140]

A year later, Congress passed the national energy legislation. The major provisions of the legislation which apply to the electric power industry are as follows:

(1) *National Energy Conservation Policy Act.* The purpose of this act was to promote energy conservation by providing a variety of assistance programs, incentives, and mandatory standards and requirements. For residential customers, electric (and gas) utilities are required to establish programs to provide both information and assistance on conservation measures, including the financing of conservation mea-sures through utility bills. The DOE was required to establish man-datory energy efficiency standards for thirteen types of electrical appliances (*e.g.*, refrigerators and refrigerator-freezers, dishwashers, television sets, central air conditioners) and was given discretionary authority to establish such standards for other appliances.

(2) *Public Utility Regulatory Policies Act (PURPA)*. Title I of this act sought to foster conservation, more efficient energy utilization, and more "equitable" electric utility rates by requiring state commissions to consider and to adopt, if appropriate, eleven federal standards. Section 133 requires extensive gathering of information by electric utilities on cost of service. Title II increased the authority of the FERC to order interconnections and wheeling of electricity, and authorized the commission to undertake studies relating to pooling, wholesale ratemaking, and automatic adjustment clauses. Title II also encourages increased use of cogeneration and small power producers.

DOE was granted the right to intervene in any state commission electric ratemaking proceeding to advocate policies or methods of achieving the act's purposes.

(3) *Powerplant and Industrial Fuel Use Act*. This act was designed to foster greater utilization of coal in place of oil and natural gas, especially by high-volume users such as electric utilities and industrial installations. Basically, no new oil and gas burning plants are permitted, although there are a number of both temporary and permanent exemptions (*e.g.*, lack of alternate fuel supply, site limitations, or environmental requirements; use of synthetic fuels). A phase-out period is permitted for existing oil or gas users, but — again with several temporary and permanent exemptions — natural gas may not be used in such plants after 1990.

(4) *Natural Gas Policy Act (NGPA)*. This act, applicable mainly to the natural gas industry, represented a comprehensive revision of national policy concerning natural gas pricing and regulation. At least two provisions, however, are of importance to the electric power industry: (*a*) the "incremental pricing" provision, under which the higher cost of new gas supplies was to be allocated to certain industrial users, and (*b*) the curtailment policies developed under the act's guidelines.

(5) *Energy Tax Act*. This act was designed to reduce, through various tax incentives, the country's dependence on foreign oil and to encourage a switch to other energy sources (including solar, wind, or geothermal). The act contained a number of incentives to homeowners to insulate their homes and of tax credits to businesses to install energy-saving equipment. The act contained a provision for the rapid depreciation (early retirement) of oil and gas fired boilers if they are replaced with boilers using an alternative fuel. The act imposed a tax on fuel-inefficient automobiles. Finally, the act contained a number of tax measures with respect to intangible drilling costs for independent oil and gas producers and for producers of geothermal energy.

Developments under the Legislation. Much has been accomplished under the national energy legislation, but controversy surrounds certain provisions. Residential conservation programs have been developed[141]; most state commissions have considered, and adopted, the PURPA standards with respect to the termination of service[142] and advertising,[143] while others have adopted the standards with respect to rate design[144] and lifeline rates.[145] The industry has been analyzing and implementing

> . . . two general options or strategies for load management: (1) *direct load control* of specific customer appliances and (2) *energy storage*. Both forms of load management may be applied to customers in the residential, commercial, industrial, and agricultural sectors. Direct load control entails the interruption of customer equipment and appliances in response to peak-load levels on the utility system. Such interruptions can be singular or cyclical (for example, every fifteen minutes) and entail some inconvenience on the part of the customer. This option is generally applied to the customer's standard equipment or appliances. Use of thermal storage shifts load from peak periods to off-peak periods, generally on a repetitive basis (for example, daily), and if the storage unit is sized adequately, the customer experiences no inconvenience. The storage option is best accomplished through end-use-oriented load management equipment with storage capability (such as storage water heaters or storage space heaters), that take advantage of lower-cost off-peak energy. . . .[146]

The cost of service reporting requirements, particularly under Section 133 of PURPA, have been implemented.[147] The FERC has issued several of the required reports, including those on automatic adjustment clauses[148] and on power pooling.[149] Both cogeneration and small power producers have been encouraged, although a definitive definition of "full avoided costs" remains illusive.[150] Competitive bidding may be the ultimate solution.[151] The DOE has intervened in several state proceedings, basically with respect to rate design. However, after the DOE refused to issue efficiency standards for major electric and gas home appliances, Congress required that they be set by 1990.[152] Finally, the provisions giving the DOE power to order conversion of existing power plants to coal were modified in 1981, due to the improved natural gas supply situation,[153] and were substantially repealed in 1987.[154]

Diversification, Deregulation, Regionalism — and Adequate Future Capacity

Prior to the 1970s, the electric power industry was characterized by rapid technological change and bitter controversy. The demand for electricity doubled every decade; technological developments, as well as economies of scale, resulted in both a smaller number of larger systems and lower rates to consumers. Technical advances in the areas of generation and transmission made interconnections and pooling feasible, and resulted in the development of a network of regional pools. Yet, these achievements were often overshadowed by the struggle between proponents of private and public ownership; a struggle that Wildavsky referred to as "one of the most persistent and dramatic controversies in twentieth-century American politics."[155]

The decade of the 1970s, however, witnessed some dramatic changes. The emphasis gradually switched from growth to conservation; the industry's financial condition deteriorated. At least three new, but interrelated, policy debates replaced the long public-private conflict: diversification, deregulation, and regionalism. Diversification and deregulation of generation,[156] some contend, are means of regaining financial integrity, of assuring adequate future capacity, and of providing better incentives to management.[157] Others fear that diversification "will divert managements and regulators from the main issue: how to make regulation work"[158] and question the feasibility of deregulation.[159]

The third issue, regionalism, is closely related to the workability of regulation in the electric power industry. As a former commissioner has summarized:

> Our electric power regulatory system has evolved somewhat haphazardly into a crazy quilt of regulatory authorities and jurisdictions. State regulatory commissions regulate the retail rates and practices of investor-owned electric utilities pursuant to laws, regulations, and practices in most instances unlike those of contiguous states. Many of these utilities, however, are multistate enterprises. Wholesale transactions by these same utilities, even those solely within the borders of one state, are regulated by the Federal Energy Regulatory Commission under laws, regulations, and practices established with little regard to those of the states. Jurisdiction for safety, siting, certification of need, and securities issuance falls sometimes within, sometimes without, and sometimes astraddle the state and federal rate-making agencies. The utilities and power pools subject to this fragmented regulatory framework frequently serve territories not confined to or delineated by state boundary lines, and the related environmental and safety considerations often transcend state boundary lines. The result is a multitude of state and federal agencies governing the financing, construction, and return related to one new plant, transmission line, or even one class of service.[160]

While the need for regional planning has gained growing acceptance,[161] little attention has been given to regional regulation.[162] The issue suggests, however, that there must be innovations in institutional arrangements if the industry is to develop with maximum efficiency in the coming years.

Similarly, there must be changes in regulatory concepts. Schlesinger has argued that utilities have been encouraged in recent years to follow "a *strategy of capital minimization;* i.e., meticulously avoiding commitments that may unnecessarily force them into capital markets, avoiding commitments that may expose them to criticism and second-guessing by the regulatory bodies."[163] Consequently, there is a real danger that the industry will seek to meet the capacity shortages that seem certain before the end of the century (and perhaps sooner)[164] with short-term solutions, by (a) acquiring more combustion turbines (either oil- or gas-fired units) that have short construction periods and can gain rapid regulatory and environmental approvals, (b) acquiring more imports (particularly from Hydro-Quebec), (c) extending the lives of existing units, and/or (d) encouraging — even utilizing — decentralized technologies and cogeneration. Some of these solutions may be desirable, but they are not the only options and, therefore, may not represent the most economical solutions available by effective, long-term planning.[165]

Notes

*Federal Power Commission, *National Power Survey* (Washington, D.C.: U.S. Government Printing Office, 1964), Vol. 1, p. 13.

[1]"A conventional electric system consists of a prime mover driving an electrical generator, a transmission line, and an electric load. The prime mover can be a steam turbine, internal combustion engine, hydraulic turbine, or other means of producing shaft power. Electric energy in this conventional system cannot be stored, it can only be converted to other forms of energy, so that in any electric power system the electric energy produced is instantaneously consumed by the load. Consequently, as demand for electricity changes, the prime mover's power output and the electric generation must simultaneously be raised or lowered to match the load. . . . Utility systems typically install a number of generating units with a total generation capacity sufficient to both meet the load demands and allow for planned maintenance and possible forced outage of some units. . . ." Federal Energy Regulatory Commission, *Power Pooling in the United States* (Washington, D.C.: U.S. Government Printing Office, 1981), p. 25.

[2]*National Power Survey, op. cit.,* p. 277.

[3]In the summer of 1983, for example, the average cost per kilowatt-hour for residential service ranged from 2.00 cents (in Noxon, Montana, served by Washington Water Power) to 15.54 cents (in New York City, served by Consolidated Edison of New York). Regionally, the average cost per kilowatt-hour ranged from 3.77 cents (North West) to 11.35 cents (North East). *NARUC Bulletin* No. 5-1984 (January 30, 1984), pp. 13-14. See also "Residential Electric Bills, 1985-86" (Washington, D.C.: National Association of Regulatory Utility Commissioners, 1986).

[4]The basic concern, it should be emphasized, is adequate capacity in the long run. By the early 1980s, the industry (in total) had surplus capacity, due to the economic recession and conservation. See, *e.g.,* "Utilities are Tempting Big Customers to Turn Up the Juice," *Business Week,* September 31, 1983, pp. 121-24.

[5]For a more complete history, see John A. Miller, *At the Touch of a Button*

(Schenectady, N.Y.: Mohawk Development Service, Inc., 1962); Edwin Vennard, *The Electric Power Business* (New York: McGraw-Hill Book Co., 1962). But see Richard Munson, *The Power Makers: The Inside Story of America's Biggest Business . . . and Its Struggle to Control Tomorrow's Electricity* (Emmaus, Pa.: Rodale Press, 1985); Richard Rudolph and Scott Ridley, *Power Struggle: The Hundred-Year War Over Electricity* (New York: Harper & Row, Publishers, 1986).

A number of electric utilities have published company histories. See, *e.g.*, Nicholas B. Wainwright, *History of the Philadelphia Electric Company, 1881-1961* (Philadelphia, 1961); Nell C. Pogue, *South Carolina Electric & Gas Company, 1846-1964* (Columbia, 1964); John Dierdorff, *How Edison's Lamp Helped Light the West: The Story of Pacific Power & Light and Its Pioneer Forebears* (Portland, Or., 1971); John Hogan, *A Spirit Capable: The Story of Commonwealth Edison* (Chicago: Mobium Press, 1987).

[6]In 1875, a dynamo built by Professors William A. Anthony and George S. Moler of Cornell University was used to furnish the electricity lighting the arc lamps of the university's campus.

[7]"By the end of that year, the Edison Electric Illuminating Co. of New York was serving 500 customers using more than 10,000 lamps." *National Power Survey, op. cit.*, p. 10.

[8]Federal Power Commission, *The 1970 National Power Survey* (Washington, D.C.: U.S. Government Printing Office, 1971), Pt. I, p. I-2-1.

[9]Burton N. Behling, *Competition and Monopoly in Public Utility Industries* (Urbana: University of Illinois Press, 1938), p. 19.

[10]*The 1970 National Power Survey, op. cit.*, p. I-2-1.

[11]For a complete discussion of holding companies, see James C. Bonbright and Gardiner C. Means, *The Holding Company* (New York: McGraw-Hill Book Co., Inc., 1932); Irston R. Barnes, *The Economics of Public Utility Regulation* (New York: F. S. Crofts & Co., 1942), chap. iv.

[12]Barnes, *op. cit.*, p. 85.

[13]*Ibid.*, pp. 66-70.

[14]It should be noted, however, that many holding companies controlled operating companies which were scattered in various parts of the country, making integrated service impossible.

[15]Federal Trade Commission, *Utility Corporations* (Senate Doc. 92, 70th Cong., 1st sess.) (Washington, D.C.: U.S. Government Printing Office, 1935), Part 72-A, p. 356.

[16]Federal Trade Commission, *Control of Power Companies* (Senate Doc. 213, 69th Cong., 2d sess.) (Washington, D.C.: U.S. Government Printing Office, 1927), p. 45.

[17]*Utility Corporations, op. cit.*, pp. 662-63.

[18]The leading source on holding company abuses is *ibid.*

[19]*Ibid.*, p. 860.

[20]*Ibid.*, p. 302.

[21]*Ibid.*, pp. 240-41. These practices resulted in financial disaster for investors due to the stock market crash in 1929. See Chapter 6, p.p. 228-29.

[22]*Rhode Island Pub. Utils. Comm. v. Attleboro Steam & Elec. Co.*, 273 U.S. 83 (1927).

[23]*Smith v. Illinois Bell Teleph. Co.*, 282 U.S. 133 (1930).

[24]See, *e.g.*, D. E. Lilienthal, "The Regulation of Utility Holding Companies," 29 *Columbia Law Review* 404 (1929); Edwin T. Hellebrandt, "Public Utility Holding Companies and Their Regulation in Ohio," 15 *Harvard Business Review* 464 (1937).

[25]49 Stat. 803 (1935).

[26]See, *e.g.*, *Re Eastern Elec. Energy Sys.*, 45 SEC 684 (1975) (denying application to

merge two holding companies and an operating electric utility into a new holding company); *Re American Elec. Power Co., Inc.,* Holding Company Act Release No. 20633 (1978) (approving affiliation of Columbus & Southern Ohio Electric Company with American Electric Power System).

[27]The constitutionality of the act was immediately challenged. The SEC brought suit to compel the Electric Bond and Share Company to register, and the Supreme Court upheld the registration requirements. [*Electric Bond & Share Co. v. Securities and Exchange Comm.,* 303 U.S. 419 (1938).] The North American Company resisted reorganization, contending that the death sentence clause exceeded the powers of Congress under the commerce clause and that it deprived the company of property without due process of law. The Supreme Court rejected these arguments. [*North American Co. v. Securities and Exchange Comm.,* 327 U.S. 686 (1946).] Finally, the American Power and Light Company contested the simplification of its corporate structure, using the same arguments advanced by the North American Company, as well as the contention that the law involved an unconstitutional delegation of legislative power. Again, the Supreme Court upheld the act. [*American Power & Light Co. v. Securities and Exchange Comm.,* 329 U.S. 90 (1946).]

[28]See Douglas W. Hawes, *Utility Holding Companies* (New York: Clark Boardman Co., Inc., 1986).

[29]Securities and Exchange Commission, *Twenty-Eighth Annual Report* (1962), pp. 82-84. Of the remaining companies, 793 were released from the commission's jurisdiction as a result of dissolutions, mergers, and consolidations, and 514 by exemption. [See Securities and Exchange Commission, Division of Corporate Regulation, "Holding Companies Exempt from the Public Utility Holding Company Act of 1935 Pursuant to Rule 2 and Section 3(a)(1) and 3(a)(2) as of December 31, 1982" (undated).] Today, there are thirteen active holding companies registered under the act, the four largest being: Central and South West Corporation, The Southern Company, American Electric Power Company, and Middle South Utilities.

[30]Robert Blum, "SEC Integration of Holding Company Systems," 17 *Journal of Land & Public Utility Economics* 423 (1941).

[31]L. T. Fournier, "Simplification of Holding Company Systems," 13 *Journal of Land & Public Utility Economics* 138 (1937); *Re The Northern Nat. Gas Co.,* Holding Company Act Release No. 5657 (1945); *Re American Gas & Elec. Co.,* Holding Company Act Release No. 6333 (1945).

[32]*Re Columbia Gas & Elec. Corp.,* 8 SEC 443 (1941); *Re The United Gas Imp. Co.,* 9 SEC 52 (1941); *Re Philadelphia Elec. Co.,* 28 SEC 35 (1948), *aff'd,* 177 F. 2d 720 (D.C. Cir. 1949); *Re New England Elec. Sys.,* Holding Company Act Release No. 15035 (1964), *vacated,* 346 F. 2d 399 (1st Cir. 1965), *rev'd and rem'd,* 384 U.S. 176 (1966), *vacated,* 376 F. 2d 107 (1st Cir. 1967).

[33]*Re The North American Co.,* 11 SEC 194 (1942); *Re Peoples Light & Power Co.,* 13 SEC 81 (1943); *Re Cities Service Co.,* Holding Company Act Release No. 5028 (1944). The commission has long permitted service companies (with an applicable uniform systems of accounts). Reasonably incidental or functionally related activities have included the merchandising of appliances [*Re Engineers Pub. Service Co.,* 12 SEC 41 (1942)], railroads [*Re American Gas & Elec. Co., op. cit.*], coal properties [*Re North American Co.,* 29 SEC 521 (1949)], gas and oil exploration [*Re New England Elec. Sys.,* Holding Company Act Release No. 18635 (1974)], insulation [*Re Columbia Gas,* Holding Company Act Release No. 20561 (1978)], and rail-car facilities [*Re Ohio Power Co.,* Holding Company Act Release No. 21173 (1979)], but not pulpwood [*Re Northern*

New England Co., 20 SEC 832 (1945)] or housing construction [*Re Michigan Consol. Gas Co.*, Holding Company Act Release No. 16763 (1970), *aff'd*, 444 F. 2d 913 (D.C. Cir. 1971)]. Some of the permitted activities have involved the creation of joint ventures with unaffiliated energy resource companies.

[34]See Chapter 6, pp. 228-30.

[35]See, *e.g.*, Forrest McDonald, *Insull* (Chicago: University of Chicago Press, 1962).

[36]Emery Troxel, *Economics of Public Utilities* (New York: Holt, Rinehart & Winston, Inc., 1947), p. 189.

[37]Douglas W. Hawes, "Public Utility Holding Company Act of 1935 — Fossil or Foil?," 30 *Vanderbilt Law Review* 605, 605-07 (1977); American Bar Association Annual Report, Section of *Public Utility Law, 1982*, p. 227. The issue is controversial, in view of the trend toward the establishment of holding companies to diversify. [See, *e.g.*, *Re Boston Edison Co.*, 51 PUR4th 145 (Mass., 1983).] Yet, "one must also bear in mind that less than 1% of the SEC's total budget is devoted to the whole '35 Act activity and the Commission itself rarely has much interest in matters arising under the '35 Act." [Douglas W. Hawes, "Utility Diversification Under the '35 Act — SEC Light Changes from Red to Amber," in *Utility Diversification: Strategies and Issues* (Arlington, Va.: Public Utilities Reports, Inc., 1981), p. 95.] The SEC has encouraged electric and gas utilities that want to establish holding companies to do so under the exemption procedure provided by Rule 2. Under Rule 2, a utility simply files a form upon becoming a holding company claiming exemption; a claim that could be revoked by the commission at a later date under Rule 6.

[38]William Iulo, *Electric Utilities-Costs and Performance* (Pullman: Washington State University Press, 1961), pp. 1-2.

[39]*Power Pooling in the United States, op. cit.*, p. 5.

[40]*Ibid.*

[41]Called investor-owned utilities, but sometimes referred to as the "I.O.U.s" by their critics. See Lee Metcalf and Vic Reinemer, *Overcharge* (New York: David McKay Co., Inc., 1967).

[42]". . . [T]he term 'reliability' means the ability of a utility system or group of systems to maintain the supply of power. Reliability is gauged by the infrequency of interruption, the size of the area affected, and the quickness with which the bulk power supply is restored if interrupted." Federal Power Commission, *Prevention of Power Failures* (Washington, D.C.: U.S. Government Printing Office 1967), Vol. I, p. xiii. On the two major failures, see Federal Power Commission, *Northeast Power Failure* (Washington, D.C.: U.S. Government Printing Office, 1965), and *Power Interruption, Pennsylvania-New Jersey-Maryland Interconnection* (Washington, D.C., 1968). See also U.S. Department of Energy, *The National Electric Reliability Study* (Washington, D.C., 1981). For a different view, see William Rodgers, *Brown-Out* (New York: Stein and Day/Publishers, 1972).

[43]*Power Pooling in the United States, op. cit.*, p. 7.

[44]*Ibid.* The NAERC also "assumed responsibility for the development and maintenance of national standards for interconnected operation, a function previously performed by the North American Power Systems Interconnection Committee (NAPSIC). *Ibid.* On the reliability councils and the NAPSIC, see *The 1970 National Power Survey, op. cit.*, pp. I-17-14 — I-17-22. See also John P. Williamson, "Does Electric Reliability Have a Future?," 119 *Public Utilities Fortnightly* 19 (April 30, 1987).

[45]Early in 1967, an experimental East-West tie was successfully accomplished. The experiment involved making interconnections between 209 major publicly owned

and privately owned electric utilities; interconnections which linked together some 265,000 miles of transmission lines in both the United States and Canada and which represented nearly 95 percent of the nation's electrical supply. See Kenneth Holum, "The East-West Electrical Tie Closure," 79 *Public Utilities Fortnightly* 73 (April 27, 1967).

[46]*Power Pooling in the United States, op. cit.*, p. 6, n. 1.

[47]"It does not have a pooling contract, although it has a paid professional and clerical staff. It has functioned continuously since its inception during World War II and has recommended standard operating practices which have been adopted by members." *Ibid.* The Mid-Continent Area Power Pool started as an informal pool. See W. Stewart Nelson, *Mid-Continent Area Power Planners: A New Approach to Planning in the Electric Power Industry* (East Lansing: MSU Public Utilities Studies, 1968).

[48]*Power Pooling in the United States, op. cit.*, p. 9, n. 2.

[49]*Ibid.*

[50]NEPOOL consists of four holding companies; a Vermont group representing six investor-owned, two cooperative, and thirteen municipal systems; and individual memberships of eight investor-owned and thirty-three municipal systems. NYPP consists of seven major investor-owned utilities, plus the Power Authority of the State of New York. PJM consists of ten signatory utilities, plus three others that participate through separate agreements with one or more of the signatory members. *Ibid.*, p. 69, n. 2.

[51]*Ibid.*, p. 39. For a discussion of the benefits, see *ibid.*, esp. chap. 3.

[52]To illustrate: "Constructing new facilities on a joint-ownership basis entails risks similar to those of any partnership. In recent years, as a result of high inflation rates, some utilities have been unable to obtain the funds needed to continue their construction programs. If such a utility is a partner in a jointly owned construction project, other members will experience delay or stoppage of construction of facilities they may urgently need unless they provide funds to cover the obligation of the defaulting utility." *Ibid.*, p. 43. For a more complete discussion of these problems, see *ibid.*, esp. chap. 6.

[53]"Examples of regulatory delays in transmission construction and availability which effect coordination include the short section of 500-kV line in eastern Pennsylvania (Hosensack-Elroy), originally scheduled for service in 1974, which did not receive regulatory approval until December 1979, and was not in service until 1981. Whether justified or not on other grounds, its unavailability to the PJM pool has prevented the most economical use of the pool's generation and has required increased utilization of oil. In Montana, a 500-kV line from the Colstrip coal-fired generating plant to the transmission system of the Bonneville Power Administration has had its scheduled completion date set back from 1978 to 1983 because of environmental reviews. The line is said to be needed for most effective integration of coal-fired generation in Montana and Wyoming with the Pacific Northwest Region. A transmission line planned for construction from Colorado to New Mexico for improved electric coordination in those areas has been subjected to substantial delay because of the uncertainty of obtaining approval to cross Federal lands and lands in some local jurisdiction." *Ibid.*, p. 49.

[54]*Ibid.*, pp. 39-40.

[55]*Ibid.*, p. 40.

[56]*Ibid.*

[57]See *ibid.*, esp. chap. 8. Some of the specific policy issues, such as the "price squeeze" problem, are considered below.

[58]The preference clause, first included in the Reclamation Act of 1906, stated that preference for power generated at federal projects should be given to municipalities for such purposes as streetlighting. The current clause specifies that preference should be given to public entities and cooperatives, so that only "surplus" power is sold to investor-owned utilities. Further, contracts with investor-owned utilities can be canceled on five years' notice.

The allocation of "surplus" power, however, has generated substantial controversy. See, *e.g., Central Lincoln Peoples' Utility District v. Johnson,* 686 F. 2d 708 (9th Cir. 1982) (invalidating 1981 contracts between Bonneville Power Administration and industrial users), *rev'd and rem'd sub nom. Aluminum Co. of America v. Central Lincoln Peoples' Utility District,* 104 S. Ct. 2472, 60 PUR4th 1 (1984).

[59]On wheeling rates, see Chapter 10, pp. 441-42.

[60]*Power Pooling in the United States, op. cit.,* p. 66. Several recent events (*e.g.,* the development of surplus capacity, the expanded sales of economy energy, and the growth of nonutility-owned cogeneration and small power production) suggest more active competition in bulk power markets in the future, with the result that transmission access has become a highly controversial issues. [See, *e.g.,* Jerry L. Pfeffer, "Policies Governing Transmission Access and Pricing: The Wheeling Debate Revisited," 116 *Public Utilities Fortnightly* 26 (October 31, 1985).] The FERC, moreover, has encouraged competition through its bulk power experiments. [On the Western Systems Power Pool Experiment, see William J. Kemp, "The Western Systems Power Pool: A Bulk Power Free Market Experiment," 119 *Public Utilities Fortnightly* 23 (April 30, 1987). For a comparison with the earlier Southwest Bulk Power Market Experiment, see *ibid.,* Table 2, p. 24.]

[61]*Power Pooling in the United States, op. cit.,* p. 63. See also David W. Penn, James B. Delaney and T. Crawford Honeycutt, *Coordination, Competition, and Regulation in the Electric Utility Industry* (Springfield, Va.: National Technical Information Service, 1975); James F. Fairman and John C. Scott, "Transmission, Power Pools, and Competition in the Electric Utility Industry," 28 *Hastings Law Journal* 1159 (1977).

[62]See, *e.g., Shrewsbury Municipal Light Dept. v. New England Power Co.,* 32 FPC 846 (1964), *aff'd,* 349 F. 2d 258 (1st Cir. 1965); *Gainesville Utilities Dept. v. Florida Power Corp.,* 40 FPC 1227 (1968), *aff'd,* 402 U.D. Fla. 575 (1971).

[63]See, *e.g., Re New England Power Pool Agreement,* FPC Opinion No. 775 (1976), *aff'd sub nom. Municipalities of Groton, et al. v. Federal Energy Regulatory Comm.,* 587 F. 2d 1269 (D.C. Cir. 1978); *Re Mid-Continental Area Power Pool Agreement,* FPC Opinion No. 806 (1977), *aff'd sub nom. Central Iowa Power Cooperative v. Federal Energy Regulatory Comm.,* 606 F. 2d 1156 (D.C. Cir. 1979).

[64]See, *e.g., Otter Tail Power Co. v. United States,* 410 U.S. 366, 97 PUR3d 209 (1973); *City of Chanute, et al. v. Kansas Gas & Elec. Co.,* 564 F. Supp. 1416, 54 PUR4th 162 (D. Kan. 1983); *United States v. Florida Power Corp. and Tampa Elec. Co., 1971 Trade Cases,* Par. 73,637 (M.D. Fla. 1971).

[65]See, *e.g.,* DOE/ERA, *The National Power Grid Study* (Washington, D.C.: U.S. Government Printing Office, 1979), Vol. II, esp. chap. 14; *Alabama Power Co. v. Nuclear Regulatory Comm., et al., 1983-1 Trade Cases,* Par. 65,376 (11th Cir. 1982).

[66]Prior to 1920, licenses for such projects were granted by special acts of Congress.

[67]See *Gibbons v. Ogden,* 22 U.S. 1 (1824); *United States v. River Rouge Co.,* 269 U.S. 411 (1926). The Supreme Court has defined navigable waters broadly to include

streams that are not used by commercial traffic [*United States v. Utah*, 283 U.S. 64, 83 (1931)], waterways that would be navigable if improvements were undertaken [*United States v. Appalachian Elec. Power Co.*, 311 U.S. 377, 407 (1940)], and nonnavigable tributaries of navigable streams (*ibid.*). Then, in a 1965 decision, the Supreme Court held that a license may be required for a project on a nonnavigable stream if the electric output of the project enters into and affects interstate commerce. [*Federal Power Comm. v. Union Elec. Co.*, 381 U.S. 90 (1965), *reversing Union Elec. Co. v. Federal Power Comm.*, 326 F. 2d 535 (8th Cir. 1964).] See, *e.g.*, Harry A. Poth, Jr., and Abdul R. Sattar, "Some Implications of the 'Take Over' Provisions of the Federal Power Act," American Bar Association Annual Report, Section of *Public Utility Law, 1964*, p. 22. The latter decision required the commission to process and issue a number of licenses for constructed projects. See, *e.g.*, *Re Nantahala Power & Light Co.*, 36 FPC 119 (1966), *aff'd*, 384 F. 2d 200 (4th Cir. 1967), *cert. denied*, 390 U.S. 945 (1968); *Re Niagara Mohawk Power Corp.*, 41 FPC 77 (1969). But see *Farmington River Power Co. v. Federal Power Comm.*, 455 F. 2d 86 (2d Cir. 1972).

[68]"With all due respect to them, Congress might just as well have put the King of England, Mussolini, and Albert Einstein on the commission so far as any spontaneous, decisive action originating with the commissioners is concerned." Congressman Celler as quoted in Bernard Schwartz, *The Professor and the Commissions* (New York: Alfred A. Knopf, 1959), p. 33.

[69]When a stream over which Congress has jurisdiction is involved, a declaration of intention must be filed first. The commission undertakes an investigation of the proposed project, and if it finds that interstate or foreign commerce will be affected, a license must be obtained before construction can commence.

The commission also must approve all transfers of licenses. See, *e.g.*, *Re Niagara Mohawk Power Corp.*, *Re Henry Ford & Son, Inc.*, 37 FPC 1172 (1967).

[70]When two or more applications are filed for a preliminary permit, the commission has applied a general policy (*a*) favoring municipalities over nonmunicipalities and (*b*) applying the "first-filed" rule (or the "first-in-time" rule) when the competing applications are from like entities. [See, *e.g.*, *Re Arkansas Hydroelectric Develop. Corp.*, 14 FERC Par. 62,285 (1981), aff'd, 15 FERC Par. 61,152 (1981), rehearing denied, 16 FERC Par. 61,025 (1981), *aff'd sub nom. Delaware River Basin Comm. v. Federal Energy Regulatory Comm.*, 680 F. 2d 16 (3d Cir. 1982). However, private developers are joining together to file "hybrid" applications and more competing applications are being filed by unlike entities.

[71]See, *e.g.*, 45 *Fed. Reg.* 76115 (1980); 47 *Fed. Reg.* 4232 (1982).

[72]The reserve, in the discretion of the commission, is to be held until the termination of the license or to be applied from time to time in reduction of the net investment. The amortization reserve existing when the license expires serves to reduce the sum payable by the federal government if it decides to take over the project. See, *e.g.*, *Re Alabama Power Co.*, 89 PUR3d 473 (FPC, 1971), modified, 89 PUR3d 473 (FPC, 1971), *rem'd*, 482 F. 2d 1208 (5th Cir. 1973).

[73]The commission has held that the municipal and state preference does not apply to "hybrid" applications [see, *e.g.*, *Re City of Fayetteville Pub. Works Comm.*, 46 PUR4th 118 (FERC, 1981)].

[74]"Before issuing a license, the commission must review the application to determine if the project is best adapted to a comprehensive plan for improving or developing a waterway(s) for beneficial public use. The licensing procedure also provides for comments and recommendations by federal and state agencies and the public.

The objective here is to ensure the protection of fish, wildlife, and cultural resources, as well as provide for recreational uses of project lands and waters." Federal Energy Regulatory Commission, *Annual Report 1981*, p. 31. See, *e.g., National Wildlife Federation v. Gorsuch*, 530 F. Supp. 1291 (D. D.C. 1982), *rev'd*, 693 F. 2d. 156 (D.C. Cir. 1982) (reversing a district court ruling that the Environmental Protection Agency must regulate dams as "point sources" of pollution subject to the National Pollutant Discharge Elimination System program of the Clean Water Act, notwithstanding the fact that FERC-licensed projects must receive certification, under the Clean Water Act, that their operation will not result in violation of water quality standards).

[75]All data are from Federal Energy Regulatory Commission, *Annual Report 1986*, p. 32.

[76]Under the dam safety program — carried out under Section 10(c) of the Federal Power Act — the agency seeks to ensure that licensed projects are properly constructed, operated, and maintained for the protection of life, health, and property. During fiscal 1986, 1,929 dam safety inspections were conducted: 1,814 by the FERC's staff and 115 by independent consultants. *Ibid.*, p. 36. "As a result of the Commission's dam safety program, all FERC-licensed high hazard potential dams are considered safe or, where a safety problem exists, repairs are under way." *Ibid.*

[77]In addition to fees collected to cover the cost of administering the commission's licensing program, for federal lands and dams, and Indian lands [see, *e.g., Re The Montana Power Co.*, 38 FPC 766 (1967), *aff'd*, 459 F. 2d 863 (D.C. Cir. 1972)], the act authorizes the FERC to determine and assess payments for headwater benefits; *i.e.*, "how much an owner of a downstream non-Federal hydropower development must pay the United States, or a licensee, for benefits provided by an upstream project." Currently there are 329 headwater developments that provide benefits to 475 downstream powerplants. Federal Energy Regulatory Commission, *Annual Report 1986*, p. 39. See, *e.g., South Carolina Elec. & Gas Co. v. Federal Power Comm.*, 338 F. 2d 898 (4th Cir. 1964); *Re Alabama Power Co.*, 82 PUR3d 52 (FPC, 1970), *aff'd*, 450 F. 2d 716 (D.C. Cir. 1971).

[78]Federal Energy Regulatory Commission, *Hydropower Sites of the United States, Developed and Undeveloped, January 1986* (Washington, D.C.: U.S. Government Printing Office, 1986).

[79]Federal Energy Regulatory Commission, *Staff Report on Retired Hydroelectric Plants in the United States, December 1980* (Washington, D.C.: U.S. Government Printing Office, 1981).

[80]The commission makes two types of reports: (*a*) Planning Status Reports, which "identify and discuss existing and potential water resources projects for specific major river basins" and (*b*) Water Resources Appraisal Reports, which "examine the existing and proposed water resources developments that would affect or be affected by projects being considered for licensing action." Nearly 200 such reports have been issued. Federal Energy Regulatory Commission, *Annual Report 1981*, p. 32.

[81]Pub. Law 89-80 (1965). The council, which replaced the informal Inter-Agency Committee on Water Resources, is composed of six full members (the Secretaries of the Interior; Agriculture; Army; Health, Education, and Welfare; and Transportation; and the Chairman of the FERC), two associate members (the Secretaries of Commerce and of Housing and Urban Development), and interested observers (the Bureau of the Budget and the Attorney General). Six regional river basin commissions, two compact commissions, and three interagency committees have been established, with membership containing both state and federal agencies.

[82]Section 10 (a) provides: "That the project adopted, including the maps, plans, and specifications, shall be such as in the judgment of the commission will be best adapted to a comprehensive plan for improving or developing a waterway or waterways for the use or benefit of interstate and foreign commerce, for the improvement and utilization of water power development, and for other beneficial public uses, including recreational purposes."

[83]Federal Power Commission, *Annual Report, 1967,* p. 27.

[84]*Ibid.* See, *e.g., Re License Applications,* 29 FPC 777 (1963); *Re Hydroelectric Licenses — Applications — Recreational Plan Exhibits,* 33 FPC 32 (1965); *Re Recreational Development at Licensed Projects,* Order No. 313 (FPC, 1965), Order No. 375 (FPC, 1968) (requiring adequate measures and facilities for public safety). Guidelines for the preservation of scenic and historic resources in a project area were set forth in Order No. 414 (FPC, 1970). The commission requires licensees to submit a periodic inventory of recreational facilities at licensed projects. Order No. 330 (FPC, 1966).

[85]See, *e.g., Scenic Hudson Preservation Conference v. Federal Power Comm.,* 354 F. 2d 608 (2d Cir. 1965), *cert. denied,* 384 U.S. 941 (1966); *Washington Public Power Supply System v. Federal Power Comm.,* 358 F. 2d 840 (D.C. Cir. 1966), *rev'd and rem'd,* 387 U.S. 428 (1967).

[86]See Samuel G. Miller, "Electric Transmission Lines — To Bury, Not to Praise," 12 *Villanova Law Review* 497 (1967). See also *The Electric Utility Industry and the Environment* (A Report to the Citizens Advisory Committee on Recreation and Natural Beauty by the Electric Utility Industry Task Force on Environment) (New York, 1968); Working Committee on Utilities, *Report to the Vice President and to the President's Council on Recreation and Natural Beauty* (Washington, D.C., 1968).

[87]*Washington Public Power Supply System v. Federal Power Comm., op. cit.,* p. 435.

[88]Federal Energy Regulatory Commission, *Annual Report 1986,* p. 36. "Facilities are operated either by the licensee or through an agreement between the licensee and state and local governments, or by private concessionaries." Federal Energy Regulatory Commission, *Annual Report 1981,* p. 31.

[89]Projects owned by state and local governments are not subject to recapture. The FPC developed the following steps with respect to hydroelectric project licenses: (*1*) the annual publication of a table of expiring licenses subject to recapture within five years; (*2*) a request to other agencies for their comments five years prior to expiration; (*3*) the gathering of information from present licensees of their future development plans, including financing, rates, and taxes five years before expiration; and (*4*) a recommendation to Congress advising it on recapture two years before expiration. *Re Hydroelectric Project Licenses,* 55 PUR3d 113 (FPC, 1964).

Congress, in 1968, amended the Federal Power Act (Pub. Law 90-451, 82 Stat. 616). The legislation: (*1*) requires the commission to make a determination of whether to recommend takeover to Congress, or to proceed by itself with relicensing; (*2*) prohibits the commission from relicensing any project it decides should be recaptured; (*3*) requires the commission to solicit the views of federal agencies and other interested parties; (*4*) permits a federal agency, if unsuccessful in convincing the commission that it should recommend takeover, to obtain a two-year stay of a relicensing order to permit the agency to present its case to Congress; and (*5*) authorizes the relicensing of obsolete projects for nonpower purposes, subject to regulatory supervision by a state, municipal, or federal agency.

By the end of 1992, the licenses of forty-nine projects subject to relicensing or recapture will expire; during 1993, 162 more project licenses will expire. Federal Energy Regulatory Commission, *Annual Report 1986*, p. 34.

[90]*Re City of Bountiful*, 37 PUR4th 344 (FERC, 1980), *aff'd sub nom. Alabama Power Co. v. Federal Energy Regulatory Comm.*, 685 F. 2d 1311 (11th Cir. 1982), *cert. denied*, 463 U.S. 1230 (1983).

[91]*Re Pacific Power & Light Co.*, 56 PUR4th 1 (FERC, 1983), *rev'd and rem'd sub nom. Clark-Cowlitz Joint Operating Agency v. Federal Energy Regulatory Comm.*, 775 F. 2d 366, 69 PUR4th 543 (D.C. Cir. 1985), *en banc, aff'd in part and rem'd in part, CCH Utilities Law Reporter*, Par. 13,271 (D.C. Cir. 1987) (remanded only with respect to cost data). A petition for review has been filed with the Supreme Court.

[92]Pub. Law 99-495 (1986).

[93]The act establishes new priorities and procedures for the relicensing of existing hydroelectric projects, initiates new environmental provisions which apply to all licenses, and imposes a moratorium on the granting of PURPA benefits to hydroelectric facilities at new dams. See Amy S. Koch, "FERC Begins Implementation of the Electric Consumers Protection Act of 1986," 119 *Public Utilities Fortnightly* 41 (April 2, 1987).

[94]FERC Opinion No. 36 (1979), on rehearing, FERC Opinion No. 36-A (1979), *rev'd sub nom. Escondido Mutual Water Co. v. Federal Energy Regulatory Comm.*, 692 F. 2d 1223 (9th Cir. 1982), *amended*, 701 F. 2d 826 (9th Cir. 1983), *aff'd in part and rev'd in part*, 466 U.S. 765 (1984).

[95]Section 203 (a) covers mergers, consolidations, and partial acquisitions of jurisdictional facilities (such as segments of transmission lines). With respect to the commission's merger policy, see *Re Commonwealth Edison Co.*, 36 FPC 927 (1966), *aff'd sub nom. Utility Users League v. Federal Power Comm.*, 394 F. 2d 16 (7th Cir. 1968), *cert. denied*, 393 U.S. 953 (1968); *Re Delmarva Power & Light Co.*, Docket No. EL78-10 (FERC, 1978); *Re Florida Power & Light Co.*, Opinion No. 57 (FERC, 1979).

[96]Under Section 202 (a) of the act, the FPC divided the country into eight regions and promoted coordination arrangements within each region. See, *e.g., National Power Survey, op. cit.* Authority under Section 202 (a) was transferred to the Secretary of Energy under the Department of Energy Organization Act of 1977. See, *e.g.*, DOE/ERA, *The National Power Grid Study*, Vol. I, *Final Report* (Washington, D.C.: U.S. Government Printing Office, 1980). There is no enforcement authority in the section.

[97]The new sections are 210, 211, and 212. "Evidentiary prerequisites for such Commission action may include demonstrations of anticipated resource conservation, improved efficiency, or enhanced electrical reliability. Additionally, wheeling may be requested by a wholesale purchaser of bulk power in instances when its supplier proposes to terminate sales, forcing the buyer to seek remote alternative suppliers." *Power Pooling in the United States, op. cit.*, pp. 56-57. See, *e.g., Re Central Power & Light Co., et al.*, Docket No. EL79-8 (FERC).

[98]Congress enacted the Pacific Northwest Electric Power Planning and Conservation Act in 1980 (Pub. Law 96-501, 94 Stat. 2697), giving to the commission responsibility for approving the rates for both sales and purchases of the Bonneville Power Administration. The act is summarized in American Bar Association Annual Report, Section of *Public Utility Law*, 1982, pp. 62-64. See also *Re Bonneville Power Administration*, 54 PUR4th 513 (FERC, 1983) and 77 PUR4th 327 (FERC, 1986).

[99]While nearly three-quarters of the industry's sales volume is subject to state regulation, the FERC's "policies at times influence state regulatory bodies in oversee-

ing the retail rates of America's investor and publicly-owned electrics." Federal Energy Regulatory Commission, *Annual Report 1981,* p. 15.

A related issue: Under the "filed rate" doctrine, interstate electric rates filed with, or fixed by, the FERC must be given binding effect by state commissions in establishing intrastate electric rates. *Narragansett Elec. Co. v. Burke,* 381 A. 2d 1359, 23 PUR4th 509 (R.I. S.Ct. 1977), *cert. denied,* 435 U.S. 972 (1979). See also *Nantahala Power & Light Co. v. Thornburg,* 106 S. Ct. 2349, 74 PUR4th 464 (1986), *reversing North Carolina ex rel. Utilities Comm. v. Nantahala Power & Light Co.,* 332 S.E. 2d 397 (N.C. S.Ct. 1985). On the *Narragansett* doctrine, see Jerry L. Pfeffer and William W. Lindsay, *The Narragansett Doctrine: An Emerging Issue in Federal-State Electric Regulation* (Columbus, Ohio: National Regulatory Research Institute, 1984) and *The Narragansett Doctrine: A 1986 Update* (Columbus, Ohio: National Regulatory Research Institute, 1986).

[100]Federal Power Commission, *Annual Report 1962,* p. 69.

[101]See, *e.g.,* J. Rhoads Foster et al., "FPC Regulation of Electric Energy at Wholesale," 51 *Virginia Law Review* 76 (1965); Harry A. Poth, Jr., "Recent Trends in FPC Electric Rate Regulation," 78 *Public Utilities Fortnightly* 25 (August 4, 1966); Harry W. Keidan, "FPC Cost-of-Service Studies — Electric," 79 *Public Utilities Fortnightly* 39 (January 5, 1967).

[102]See, *e.g.,* three papers presented at the Iowa State Regulatory Conference (Iowa State University, May 23-25, 1979): George A. Avery, "'Price Squeeze' and Utility Rates;" David A. Leckie, "Price Squeeze: A Commission Staff Attorney's View;" and Sandra J. Streble, "Who Is Squeezed and What Can They Do About It?;" Richard D. Cudahy, "Price Squeeze Problems in Setting Wholesale Electric Rates," in Charles F. Phillips, Jr. (ed.), *Regulation and the Future Economic Environment — Air to Ground* (Lexington, Va.: Washington and Lee University, 1980), pp. 59-85.

[103]See, *e.g., United States v. Aluminum Company of America,* 148 F. 2d 416 (2d Cir. 1945). The price squeeze issue with respect to electric utilities was first raised in *Conway Corp. v. Federal Power Comm.,* 510 F. 2d 1264 (D.C. Cir. 1975), *aff'd,* 426 U.S. 271 (1976).

[104]The FPC issued a statement of policy [Order No. 563 (FPC, 1977), 42 *Fed. Reg.* 16,131 (1977)], subsequently codified in its regulations [18 CFR Section 2.17 (1979)], which outlined the parameters of a prima facie price squeeze case. See *Re Missouri Power & Light Co.,* 26 PUR4th 365 (FERC, 1978) and 30 PUR4th 401 (FERC, 1979).

[105]*Re So. California Edison Co.,* Opinion No. 62 (FERC, 1979); *Re Commonwealth Edison Co.,* Opinion No. 63 (FERC, 1979). The approach has been upheld. See, *e.g., Illinois Cities of Bethany, et al. v. Federal Energy Regulatory Comm.,* 661 F. 2d 1375 (D.C. Cir. 1981) (opinion withdrawn at court's request; rehearing granted), *supplemental opinion on rehearing,* 670 F. 2d 187 (D.C. Cir. 1981); *Cities of Batavia, et al. v. Federal Energy Regulatory Comm.,* 672 F. 2d 64 (D.C. Cir. 1982).

[106]*Re Pennsylvania Power Co.,* 50 PUR4th 635, 637 (FERC, 1982), *vacated in part sub nom. Boroughs of Ellwood City, etc. v. Federal Energy Regulatory Comm.,* 731 F. 2d 959 (D.C. Cir. 1984).

[107]On the rebuttable presumption, see *Re Boston Edison Co.,* 30 PUR4th 477 (FERC, 1979); *Re Connecticut Light & Power Co.,* 31 PUR4th 315 (FERC, 1979). On the issue of intent, see *Re Missouri Power & Light Co., op. cit.* (26 PUR4th 365). For an argument that intent is a critical consideration, see David C. Hjelmfelt, "A Price Squeeze Theory for Implementation of *Federal Power Commission v. Conway*," 50 *University of Colorado Law Review* 459 (1979).

[108]*Re Missouri Power & Light Co., op. cit.* (26 PUR4th 365), p. 371, n. 18 (emphasis in original).

[109]*Re Pennsylvania Power Co., op. cit.*, pp. 638-40. See also *Re Delmarva Power & Light Co.*, 55 PUR4th 31 (FERC, 1983) (a temporary difference in rates in two customer classes was not discriminatory).

[110]See, *e.g.*, *Boroughs of Ellwood City, etc. v. Federal Energy Regulatory Comm., op. cit.*

[111]*Ibid.*, p. 961. In September, 1987, the commission suggested that it would adopt a new policy, including the replacement of the "rebuttable presumption" with a requirement "that parties making price-squeeze claims come forward ... with evidence which demonstrates that the alleged price squeeze will have either an actual or a potential anticompetitive effect." *Inside F.E.R.C.*, September 28, 1987, p. 7.

The FERC does not have exclusive jurisdiction over a price squeeze claim. See, *e.g.*, *City of Mishawaka v. Indiana & Michigan Elec. Co.*, 560 F. 2d 1314 (7th Cir. 1977), *cert. denied*, 436 U.S. 922 (1978); *City of Groton v. Connecticut Light & Power Co.*, 497 F. Supp. 1040 (D. Conn. 1980), *aff'd in part*, 662 F. 2d 921 (2d Cir. 1981); *Borough of Ellwood City, et al. v. Pennsylvania Power Co., 1983-2 Trade Cases*, Par. 65,673 (W.D. Pa. 1983); Note, "The Applicability of Antitrust Laws to Price Squeezes in the Electric Utility Industry," 54 *St. John's Law Review* 103 (1979).

[112]For an analysis of these views, see Edwin Vennard, *Government in the Power Business* (New York: McGraw-Hill Book Co., 1968). The case for government-private competition is made by Richard Hellman, *Government Competition in the Electric Utility Industry: A Theoretical and Empirical Study* (New York: Praeger Publishers, 1972).

[113]Municipal systems vary in size from those serving a few hundred customers to the Los Angeles Department of Water and Power which serves over a million customers. In a few cases (*e.g.*, Cleveland, Ohio), a municipal system and an investor-owned system serve the same area. In some states, such as Nebraska and Washington, public utility districts — political subdivisions of the state — have been organized. Thus, the entire state of Nebraska is served by a public electric power system. [See Robert E. Firth, *Public Power in Nebraska* (Lincoln: University of Nebraska Press, 1962).] Other states, such as Arizona and New York, have established special authorities. The Power Authority of the State of New York, for instance, "supplies firm power to 45 municipal systems, 5 cooperative systems, and 3 upstate NYPP members, in addition to the City of New York, other public bodies in that city, 3 industrial plants, an Air Force base, and the State of Vermont." *Power Pooling in the United States, op. cit.*, p. 69, n. 3. See David Schap, *Municipal Ownership in the Electric Utility Industry: A Centennial View* (New York: Praeger Publishers, 1986).

[114]Rising electric rates resulted in another period of renewed interest in municipal operations throughout the 1970s. See, *e.g.*, "Vt. PSB Rejects Proposed Muni Takeover — Would Hurt Other Customers," *Electrical Week*, June 14, 1982, p. 6.

[115]See, *e.g.*, Thomas Gale Moore, "The Effectiveness of Regulation of Electric Utility Prices," 36 *Southern Economic Journal* 365 (1970); Sam Peltzman, "Pricing in Public and Private Enterprises: Electric Utilities in the United States," 14 *Journal of Law and Economics* 109 (1971); Louis DeAlessi, "An Economic Analysis of Government Ownership and Regulation: Theory and the Evidence from the Electric Power Industry," 19 *Public Choice* 1 (Fall, 1974); Leland G. Neuberg, "Two Issues in the Municipal Operation of Electric Power Distribution Systems," 8 *The Bell Journal of Economics* 303 (1977).

[116]On the rural electrification program, see Clyde T. Ellis, *A Giant Step* (New York: Vintage Books, 1966).

[117]Executive Order No. 7037 (issued May 11, 1935). The REA is an agency of the Department of Agriculture. The Administrator is named by the President with the consent of the Senate.

[118]Under the act, the interest rate was to be the average rate paid by the government on its long-term bonds in the preceding fiscal year, and loans could be made for a maximum of twenty-five years. In 1944, the Pace Act set the interest rate at 2 percent and extended the amortization period to thirty-five years.

In 1973, Congress established a new loan system (Pub. Law 93-32). (*1*) REA-insured loans come from the Rural Electrification and Telephone Revolving Fund and are made at a 5 percent rate, except for those borrowers who qualify for a special 2 percent rate (*e.g.*, co-ops with fewer than two customers per mile). Borrowers eligible for 5 percent insured loans may be required to finance up to 30 percent of the loan from outside sources (generally from a lending institution owned by the cooperatives, the National Rural Utilities Cooperative Finance Corporation). Congress establishes annually both a floor and a ceiling for REA-insured loans. (*2*) REA-guaranteed loans, from the Federal Financing Bank (created in 1973 to coordinate federal and federally assisted borrowings), at the cost of money to the U.S. Treasury plus .126 percent.

[119]REA loans may be made to other public entities, such as public utility districts. Cooperatives are exempt from regulation in a majority of the states and at the federal level. See, *e.g.*, *Re Dairyland Power Cooperative*, 37 FPC 12 (1967). But see *Arkansas Elec. Cooperative Corp. v. Arkansas Pub. Service Comm.*, 618 S.W. 2d 151 (1981), *aff'd*, 103 S. Ct. 1905, 52 PUR4th 514 (1983). Where they are regulated at the state level, there may be conflicts when a cooperative confronts financial difficulties. See, *e.g.*, "USDA Asserts Federal Rights Over States in Rate Regulation," *Rural Electric News Letter*, July 24, 1987, pp. 1-2; *Re Big Rivers Elec. Corp.*, Case Nos. 9613 and 9885 (Ky., 1987).

[120]See Charles E. Olson, "Inefficiency and Subsidy — A Conflict in Public Policy?," 81 *Public Utilities Fortnightly* 35 (June 6, 1968).

[121]See, *e.g.*, U.S. General Accounting Office, *Legislation Needed to Improve Administration of Tax Exempt Provisions for Electric Cooperatives* (Gaithersburg, Md., 1983). But see "Rural Utility Co-ops Fighting to Save Federal Loan Program," 42 *Cong. Quarterly* 53 (January 14, 1984); "Treasury Suspected of Closing Door on REA Guaranteed Loans," *Rural Electric News Letter*, September 18, 1987, pp. 1-2. See also "Senate Okays Debt Refinancing," *Ibid.*, June 5, 1987, p. 1.

[122]Court challenges of REA loans to finance competing facilities generally failed. See, *e.g.*, *Rural Electrification Administration v. Central Louisiana Elec. Co.*, 354 F. 2d 859 (5th Cir. 1966), *cert. denied*, 385 U.S. 815 (1966); *Northern States Power Co. v. Rural Electrification Administration*, 248 F. Supp. 616 (D. Minn. 1967), *cert. denied*, 387 U.S. 945 (1967). But see *Western Colorado Power Co. v. Colorado Pub. Utils. Comm.*, 411 P. 2d 785 (1966), *cert. denied*, 385 U.S. 22 (1966). Likewise, efforts by privately-owned utilities to restrict, by contract, the resale of power by municipalities and cooperatives to large industrial users failed. See, *e.g.*, *Re Georgia Power Co.*, 35 FPC 436 (1966), 35 FPC 818 (1966), *aff'd*, 373 F. 2d 484 (5th Cir. 1967); *Re Mississippi Power Co.*, Opinion No. 593 (FPC, 1971).

[123]REA loans also have been made to enable cooperatives to buy shares in nuclear power plants.

[124]*REA Bulletin* 20-6 (May 31, 1961).

[125]G&T loans are defended by Norman M. Clapp, "REA's Power Supply Pro-

gram," 81 *Public Utilities Fortnightly* 24 (June 6, 1968). The threat of G&T loans has tended to result in lower wholesale rates to cooperatives. See Nathaniel E. Shechter, "Low Purchased Energy Costs to the Rural Electric Cooperatives," 42 *Land Economics* 304 (1966). See also Robert T. Connery, "Generation and Transmission Loan Policy under the Rural Electrification Act," 43 *Denver Law Journal* 269 (1966). In more recent years, G&T loans have tended to be granted under the guaranteed, not insured, REA program. In 1981, for example, Deseret G&T Cooperative received an REA-guaranteed loan of $900 million to help construct a 360-megawatt, coal-fired generating unit, to develop a coal mine, and to string 276 miles of transmission line. However, the REA required that the additional $330 million estimated cost of the projects (for pollution control equipment) be obtained from private sources. *Rural Electric Newsletter,* September 4, 1981, p. 1.

[126]One additional note: Section 5 of the Rural Electrification Act authorizes loans "for the purpose of financing the wiring of the premises of persons in rural areas and the acquisition and installation of electric and plumbing appliances and equipment." Few loans have been made for these purposes, but REA loans were made (in the 1960s) to equip a ski resort in Illinois ($22,000) and to purchase gravel-crushing and gravel-washing machinery for a North Dakota firm ($25,000).

[127]River valley development has long been controversial, since it is closely tied to politics and many projects cannot be justified by economic criteria. See, *e.g.,* Otto Eckstein, *Water Resource Development* (Cambridge: Harvard University Press, 1958); John V. Krutilla and Otto Eckstein, *Multiple Purpose River Development* (Baltimore: Johns Hopkins Press, 1958); Stephen C. Smith and Emery N. Castle (eds.), *Economics and Public Policy in Water Resource Development* (Ames, Iowa: Iowa State University Press, 1964).

[128]Public power projects have lower capital costs and are not required to pay taxes (although some make voluntary payments to local and state governments "in lieu of taxes," while the federal government has made some payments to local and state governments in the Tennessee Valley area because of property removed from local taxing authority by navigation and flood-control projects). Some distribution companies have access to low-cost power from state or federal power marketing authorities. See Joe D. Pace, "The Subsidy Received by Publicly Owned Electric Utilities," 87 *Public Utilities Fortnightly* 19 (April 29, 1971). Further, since federal power projects are usually parts of multipurpose projects, there is the question (considered below) of how to allocate the total cost among the various purposes.

[129]David E. Lilienthal, *TVA: Democracy on the March* (New York: Harper & Bros., 1944), pp. 3-4.

[130]On the Colorado, Hoover Dam facilities have been leased to a private company and to a municipality. The lessees generate, transmit, and distribute the power.

[131]Clair Wilcox, *Public Policies Toward Business* (3d ed.; Homewood, Ill.: Richard D. Irwin, Inc., 1966), pp. 520-21. See also Eckstein, *op. cit.,* chap. ix; Joseph S. Ransmeier, *The Tennessee Valley Authority* (Nashville: Vanderbilt University Press, 1942), chaps. vi-xiv.

[132]See, *e.g.,* Gordon R. Clapp, *The TVA: An Approach to the Development of a Region* (Chicago: University of Chicago Press, 1955); Roscoe C. Martin (ed.), *TVA: The First Twenty Years* (University, Ala.: University of Alabama Press, 1956); John R. Moore (ed.), *The Economic Impact of TVA* (Knoxville: The University of Tennessee Press, 1967).

[133]Through 1958, the TVA paid $185 million of power proceeds and $41.5 million of nonpower proceeds into the Treasury. In 1959, Congress established a new

repayment schedule: beginning with fiscal 1961, payment of not less than $10 million for each of the first five fiscal years, $15 million for each of the next five years, and $20 million for each year thereafter until the remaining $1 billion of the Authority's debt has been repaid. The same legislation requires an annual payment from power proceeds of a return on the net appropriation investment in power facilities; a return based upon the computed average interest rate payable by the Treasury on its total marketable public obligations as of the beginning of each fiscal year.

From 1933 to 1959, the TVA received all of its construction funds from Congressional appropriations, except for $65 million borrowed from the Reconstruction Finance Corporation and the Treasury Department in fiscal years 1939-1941. The 1959 legislation permitted the TVA to sell its own debt obligations in the open market.

[134]The TVA is the only federal agency that has full responsibility for supplying all power requirements in the area of its operations (an 80,000 square mile area). In fiscal 1981, the Authority sold 13 percent of its output to federal agencies, 19.5 percent directly to private industries, and 76.7 percent to distributors. The distributors (including 160 municipal and cooperative electric systems, and one privately owned electric system) served over 2.8 million customers in parts of seven states. Data from Tennessee Valley Authority, *1981 Power Program Summary*.

[135]In addition to increasing demand, fossil-fuel steam generating plants were needed to "firm up" the supply because of the conflicting functions of multipurpose projects. The flow of water is regulated to meet the needs of flood control, irrigation, or navigation. Consequently, the flow at any given time may not coincide with the corresponding requirements of electric production. Steam plants, therefore, are built to supplement the irregular output of hydroelectric plants.

[136]Several methods of meeting peak loads have been developed by the industry. One of the most popular is a method known as "pumped storage." During periods of slack demand, power is used to pump water uphill to an upper reservoir. At peak hours, the water is permitted to pass through the turbines to a lower reservoir, thereby providing generation. Reversible units that can both pump and generate are now available, while the development of extra-high-voltage transmission lines has made it economical to transport power to and from the reservoirs.

[137]As of early 1986, the TVA had canceled eight of the seventeen reactors. Five reactors were closed for safety studies and four were under construction. See "TVA Cancels Work at 4 Partly Built Units, Will Write Off $1.85 Billion on Investment," *The Wall Street Journal*, August 26, 1982, p. 8; "Troubled Times for the TVA," *Newsweek*, January 27, 1986, pp. 23-24. See also Erwin C. Hargrove and Paul K. Conkin (eds.), *TVA: Fifty Years of Grass-Roots Bureaucracy* (Champaign: University of Illinois Press, 1983).

[138]Another federal agency, the Bonneville Power Administration, also was involved in controversy in the early 1980s. A municipal corporation, the Washington Public Power Supply System (WPPSS, commonly known as "Whoops"), was created in 1957 to acquire, build, and operate power plants and systems. WPPSS was authorized to issue revenue bonds to finance projects, payable from sales revenues. In the early 1970s, WPPSS started construction of five nuclear power plants. Two of the plants are partly owned by others [unit 3 is 30 percent owned by Pacific Power and Light Company (PacifiCorp.), Portland General Electric Company, Puget Sound Power and Light Company, and Washington Water Power Company; unit 5 is 10 percent owned by Pacific Power and Light Company (PacifiCorp.)]. WPPSS signed participants' agree-

ments with a number of entities to purchase the power and to make payments on bonds issued to finance the plants whether or not the projects were completed. Thus, the Bonneville Power Administration contracted to purchase all of the power from units 1 and 2, and 70 percent from unit 3; 88 of the region's utilities (including cooperatives, municipals, and public utility districts in six states) agreed to purchase all of the power from units 4 and 5. But construction costs for the five plants increased from $7.1 billion in 1976 to $25 billion in early 1983 and, combined with declining demand, forced WPPSS to cancel units 4 and 5, on which $2.25 billion in revenue bonds had been issued, and to halt construction of unit 3, which was almost 75 percent constructed. [The four investor-owned utilities involved in unit 3 have agreed to settle a $2 billion suit by swapping their collective 30 percent stake in the mothballed unit for 190,000 kilowatts of power from the Bonneville Power Administration over a thirty-year period. *The Wall Street Journal,* October 29, 1985, p. 6.]

The cancellation of units 4 and 5 subsequently resulted in default on the revenue bonds. [See, *e.g.,* "The Fallout from 'Whoops'," *Business Week,* July 11, 1983, pp. 80-87; "Whoops! A $2 Billion Blunder," *Time,* August 8, 1983, pp. 50-52. See also Peter Brimelow, "Shock Waves from Whoops Roll East," *Fortune,* July 25, 1983, pp. 46-48.] There are at least four issues. (*1*) Are the eighty-eight purchasers obligated to pay interest and debt service on the bonds? [The Idaho and Washington supreme courts have held that the municipalities and public utility districts did not have authority to enter into agreements with WPPSS and therefore were not obligated to pay off the bonds. *Asson v. City of Burley,* 670 P. 2d 839 (1983), *cert. denied,* 870 U.S. 1619 (1984); *Chemical Bank v. Washington Pub. Power Supply System,* 666 P. 2d 329 (1983), *aff'd,* 691 P. 2d 524 (1984), *cert. denied,* 471 U.S. 1258 (1985). The Oregon supreme court held otherwise. *DeFazio v. Washington Pub. Power Supply System,* 479 P. 2d 1316 (1984). See also *City of Springfield v. Washington Pub. Power Supply System,* 564 F. Supp. 90 (D. Or. 1983), *aff'd as modified,* 752 F. 2d 1423 (9th Cir. 1985), *cert. denied,* 474 U.S. 445 (1986). On the initial Washington court decision, see Comment, "Chemical Bank v. WPPSS: A Case of Judicial Meltdown," 5 *Journal of Energy Law & Policy* 273 (1984); Note, "Chemical Bank v. Washington Public Power Supply System: The Questionable Use of the Ultra Vires Doctrine to Invalidate Government Take-or-Pay Obligations," 69 *Cornell Law Review* 1094 (1984).] (*2*) Were the purchasers illegally pressured by the Bonneville Power Administration to participate in the two units? [See, *e.g.,* Norman Thorpe, "Bonneville Power is Criticized for Its Role in Planning Nuclear Power Plants for Northwest," *The Wall Street Journal,* February 16, 1983, p. 33; David L. Shapiro, "Whoops and the Hodel Connection," *ibid.,* May 20, 1983, p. 30.] (*3*) Were the buyers of the bonds given adequate information by the underwriters, the credit-rating agencies, the law firms that issued favorable legal opinions, and the engineering firms that prepared the cost estimates? [Three suits were pending against four securities firms, two law firms, and two engineering concerns, but two rating agencies were dismissed. *Ibid.,* August 9, 1983, p. 46. The underwriting firms have tentatively agreed to settle for $92 million. *Business Week,* November 2, 1987, p. 168.] (*4*) Was there securities fraud? [The SEC has completed a three-year investigation. See "SEC Concludes WPPSS Probe; Action Is Urged," *The Wall Street Journal,* February 26, 1987, p. 7. A massive consolidated class action securities-fraud suit (called by one lawyer "the largest securities case in the history of the world") is scheduled for trial in 1988, as is another consolidated class action suit (brought by several large institutional investors). *Business Week, op. cit.*]

See D. V. Anderson, *Illusions of Power: A History of the Washington Public Power*

Supply System (New York: Praeger Publishers, 1985); Daniel Jack Chasan, *The Fall of the House of WPPSS* (Seattle: Sasquatch Publishing, 1985); James Leigland and Robert Lamb, *WPP$$: Who Is to Blame for the WPPSS Disaster?* (New York: Ballinger Publishing Co., 1986).

[139]91 Stat. 569 (1977); Executive Order 12009 (1977). See, *e.g.*, Alfred C. Aman, Jr., "Institutionalizing the Energy Crisis: Some Structural and Procedural Lessons," 65 *Cornell Law Review* 491 (1980).

[140]Some former FPC matters were transferred directly to the Secretary of Energy who, in turn, delegated the responsibilities to the Economic Regulatory Administration (ERA). These duties included authority over exports and imports of both electric energy and natural gas, the setting of gas curtailment priorities (but not their implementation), the review of federal power marketing functions, and the ordering of emergency electric interconnections. The FERC also received some responsibilities not previously assigned to the FPC, including regulation of oil pipelines (formerly vested in the Interstate Commerce Commission) and certain duties related to the petroleum industry (*e.g.*, oil price and allocation regulations under the Emergency Petroleum Allocation Act).

[141]See Chapter 12, p. 525.

[142]See *ibid.*, pp. 513-15.

[143]See Chapter 7, pp. 251-53.

[144]See Chapter 10, pp. 437-41.

[145]See *ibid.*, pp. 425-28.

[146]Gary B. Ackerman and Ronald O. Mueller, "Determining the Benefits and Costs of Load Management Systematically," 107 *Public Utilities Fortnightly* 26, 27 (April 23, 1981). But see *Re Potomac Elec. Power Co.*, 72 PUR4th 168 (D.C., 1986).

By the mid-1980s, attention was being focused on least-cost planning, regarded by the industry "as integrated evaluation of supply and demand alternatives subject to risk and reliability constraints" and by regulators "as balanced evaluation of conservation and load management." Mary Sharpe Hayes and Richard M. Scheer, "Least-cost Planning: A National Perspective," 119 *Public Utilities Fortnightly* 13, 16 (March 19, 1987). See, *e.g.*, *Re Montana-Dakota Utilities Co.*, 81 PUR4th 90 (N.D., 1987). "The Department of Energy recently awarded a grant to the National Association of Regulatory Utility Commissioners to write a 'primer' that will provide uniform guidelines to regulators and utilities on the implementation of LCP." "Least-cost Planning: A State Survey," 119 *Public Utilities Fortnightly* 38 (May 14, 1987).

[147]However, a 1981 GAO report recommended their repeal as an "excessive undertaking" of limited use. See U.S. General Accounting Office, *Burdensome And Unnecessary Reporting Requirements of the Public Utility Regulatory Policies Act Need to be Changed* (Gaithersburg, Md., 1981).

[148]Federal Energy Regulatory Commission, *Automatic Adjustment Clauses in Public Utility Rate Schedules* (Washington, D.C., 1982).

[149]*Power Pooling in the United States, op. cit.*

[150]See Chapter 10, p. 442.

[151]See, *e.g.*, Renee Haman-Guild and Jerry L. Pfeffer, "Competitive Bidding for New Electric Power Supplies: Deregulation or Reregulation?," 120 *Public Utilities Fortnightly* 9 (September 17, 1987); William R. Meade, "Competitive Bidding and the Regulatory Balancing Act," 120 *ibid.* 22; Federal Energy Regulatory Commission, Office of Economic Policy, "Regulating Independent Power Producers: A Policy Analysis" (Staff paper, Washington, D.C., 1987). See also *Re Purchase of Electricity by Public*

Utilities from Qualifying Facilities, 89 PUR4th 185 (Va., 1988); "FERC Issues Competitive Initiatives; Strips Out Federal Preemption Rules," *Electric Utility Week Extra,* March 17, 1988.

[152]The National Appliance Energy Conservation Act of 1987 (Pub. Law 100-12). But see Doug Bandow, "Federal Appliance Standards: Inefficient at Best," *The Wall Street Journal,* February 19, 1987, p. 28.

[153]Under the Omnibus Budget Reconciliation Act of 1981 (Pub. Law 97-35), the DOE's authority to order conversion against the owner's will and the prohibition on gas use after 1990 were removed. See, *e.g.,* "Symposium on the Powerplant and Industrial Fuel Use Act of 1978," 29 *University of Kansas Law Review* 297 (1981); "More Utilities Shun Coal Conversion as Economic Benefits Start to Fade," *The Wall Street Journal,* May 16, 1983, p. 33. To encourage utilities to convert oil-fired generating units to coal, some state commissions and the FERC adopted incentive plans. To illustrate: The utility's customers financed the conversion through a surcharge on their monthly bills, which was partially offset by an "oil conservation adjustment" to the fuel clause (under which one-third of the cost savings were passed on immediately to ratepayers). *Business Week,* April 27, 1981, pp. 113-14.

[154]Repeal of Powerplant and Industrial Fuel Use Act Restrictions (Pub. Law 100-42). The legislation also repealed the incremental pricing provisions contained in the Natural Gas Policy Act. See "Restrictive FUA Provisions Repealed," 119 *Public Utilities Fortnightly* 37 (June 25, 1987).

[155]Aaron Wildavsky, *Dixon-Yates: A Study in Power Politics* (New Haven: Yale University Press, 1962), p. 5.

[156]The issues are carefully explored in James Plummer, Terry Ferrar, and William Hughes (eds.), *Electric Power Strategic Issues* (Arlington, Va.: Public Utilities Reports, Inc. and QED Research, Inc., 1983).

[157]See, *e.g.,* Tom Alexander, "The Surge to Deregulate Electricity," *Fortune,* July 13, 1981, pp. 98ff; Richard S. Bower, "Electricity's Unstable Regulatory Regime," 119 *Public Utilities Fortnightly* 13 (June 25, 1987). It should be noted that some urge deregulation of all generating capacity; others of only new generating capacity.

[158]Irwin M. Stelzer, "The Utilities as Venture Capitalists: Is This Diversification or Is It Diversion?," in *Utility Diversification: Strategies and Issues, op. cit.,* p. 21. See also Jordan D. Lewis and William Warfield Ross, "A Road Map for Utility Diversification," 110 *Public Utilities Fortnightly* 17 (December 23, 1982); Francis J. Andrews, Jr., "Diversification and the Public Utility Holding Company Act," 110 *Public Utilities Fortnightly* 24 (December 23, 1982); Stanley York and J. Robert Malko, "Utility Diversification: A Regulatory Perspective," 111 *Public Utilities Fortnightly* 15 (January 6, 1983); Elizabeth A. C. Murray and Malcolm J. Closterman, "How Utilities Are Becoming New Conglomerates," 118 *Public Utilities Fortnightly* 11 (August 7, 1986); Bruce Lipnick, "Investment Strategies in an Interval of Cash Surplus," 118 *Public Utilities Fortnightly* 34 (November 13, 1986).

[159]The issues are fully examined by Joe D. Pace, "Deregulating Electric Generation: An Economist's Perspective" and by William R. Hughes, "Issues in Deregulation of Electric Generation," in Albert L. Danielsen and David R. Kamerschen (eds.), *Current Issues in Public-Utility Economics* (Lexington, Mass.: D. C. Heath & Co., 1983), chaps. 20 and 21. See also Edison Electric Institute, *Deregulation of Electric Utilities: A Survey of Major Concepts and Issues* (Washington, D.C., 1982) and *Alternative Models of Electric Power Deregulation* (Washington, D.C., 1982); Paul L. Joskow and Richard Schmalensee, *Markets for Power: An Analysis of Electric Utility Deregulation* (Cambridge: The MIT

Press, 1983); John C. Moorhouse (ed.), *Electric Power: Deregulation and the Public Interest* (San Francisco: Pacific Research Institute for Public Policy, 1986).

[160]Larry J. Wallace, "Reregulation of the Electric Utility Industry — A Neglected Alternative," 110 *Public Utilities Fortnightly* 13 (November 25, 1982).

[161]See, *e.g.,* Sidney Saltzman and Richard E. Schuler (eds.), *The Future of Electrical Energy: A Regional Perspective of an Industry in Transition* (New York: Praeger Publishers, 1986); Michael C. Dotten and Jeffrey A. Boecker, "Regional Power Planning: The Pacific Northwest Experience," 118 *Public Utilities Fortnightly* 18 (September 18, 1986).

[162]See, *e.g.,* Douglas N. Jones et al., *Regional Regulation of Public Utilities: Issues and Prospects* (Columbus, Ohio: National Regulatory Research Institute, 1980); Report of the National Governors' Association Task Force on Electric Utility Regulation, *An Analysis of Options for Structural Reform in Electric Utility Regulation* (Washington, D.C., 1983). Argued Shipman, supporting regional regulation many years ago: "Of course, it will take much more than nuclear power and EHV transmission to bring about any such reordering of affairs; jurisdictional empires will be defended no matter how small or infirm. But, to paraphrase a famous remark by Bonbright, engineers who insist on pursuing technology across state lines must expect politics, sooner or later, to follow their example." William D. Shipman, "Some Economic Implications of Nuclear Power Generation in Large Central Stations," 40 *Land Economics* 1, 11 (1964) (citation omitted). For a more recent argument by Chairman Burke of the Rhode Island commission that regional regulation of the telephone industry is a model whose "time will come," see *NARUC Bulletin,* No. 8-1985, February 25, 1985, p. 23.

[163]James R. Schlesinger, "The Long-Run Security of the Energy Supply," in Saltzman and Schuler, *op. cit.,* pp. 37-38 (emphasis in original).

[164]See, *e.g., The Adequacy of U.S. Electricity Supply Through the Year 2000* (Washington, D.C.: Utility Data Institute, Inc., 1987); "Boston Bank Says New England Could Face Power Shortages by Early 1990s," *Electric Utility Week,* November 30, 1987, p. 7.

[165]The issues are discussed in Saltzman and Schuler, *op. cit.*

THE NATURAL GAS

INDUSTRY

In no other field of public service regulation is the controlling body confronted with factors so baffling as in the natural gas industry. . . .

—*Justice Brandeis**

Prior to the late 1920s, natural gas[1] was an unimportant source of domestic energy. It was used basically as a source of pressure to drive petroleum to the surface; then the gas was blown off (vented), burned off (flared), or used in nearby industrial plants. In the late twenties and early thirties, large new oil and gas fields were discovered in the Southwest. At the same time, improvements in pipeline construction, particularly the invention of seamless pipe, increased the distance over which natural gas could be economically transported. These two events radically altered the industry's role in the economy. Today, gas is transported to every part of the country and supplies just under one-fourth (22 percent in 1986) of the nation's total primary energy.

The necessity of regulating certain aspects of the natural gas industry, the most suitable method of regulation, and the feasibility of federal versus state control have been the subjects of constant debate. The issues, moreover, are complex. As the Supreme Court stated in a 1963 decision: "We recognize the unusual difficulties inherent in regulating the price of a commodity such as natural gas."[2] Both economics and politics have played roles in shaping public policy toward the industry. But in more recent years, some

627

of these long-standing issues have been overshadowed by the growing significance of competition.

Historical Development and Structure[3]

Jan Baptista van Helmont of Brussels is generally credited with discovering manufactured gas in 1609 (the word gas being derived from the German word for spirit, "Geist")[4] and Thomas Shirley with discovering natural gas in England in 1659.[5] The first use of gas for illumination is credited to William Murdock, a Scottish inventor and engineer employed by James Watt (the inventor of the steam engine). In 1792, Murdock "successfully transported gas through some seventy feet of iron and copper tubes to light his house" and in 1798, he "equipped the Boulton Watt Company at Soho in London with gas lighting."[6] In America, early in the nineteenth century, demonstrations of gas lighting were common. David Melville of Newport, Rhode Island, for example, illuminated his house in 1812 "with gas light produced by his own process which he patented the next year."[7] Baltimore was the first domestic city to permit a gas company — the Gas Light Company of Baltimore, granted a franchise in 1816 and formally incorporated in 1817 — to light its streets.[8] Boston followed in 1822, New York City in 1823, Brooklyn in 1825, New Orleans in 1835, Philadelphia and Pittsburgh in 1836, Louisville in 1838, Cincinnati in 1841, and Albany in 1845.[9] The Capitol grounds in Washington, D.C., were lighted with gas in 1847[10]; the Peoples Gas Light and Coke Company was organized in Chicago in 1850.[11]

The gas industry, particularly during the second half of the nineteenth century, expanded rapidly. According to Dorner:

> In 1860, the *American Gas-Light Journal* reported that as of December 31, 1859, 297 gas companies, with a total capitalization of $42,861,174, were supplying a population of 4,857,000 through 227,665 private meters. The second half of the nineteenth century saw equally remarkable expansion. *Brown's Directory of American Companies, 1899* showed 999 companies with a total capitalization of $400 million supplying a population of 24,500,000 in 885 towns with 60 billion cubic feet of gas. Thus, in the last forty years of the nineteenth century the number of companies tripled, the population served quintupled, and the capital invested increased tenfold.[12]

In the early years, manufactured (from soft or bituminous coal) gas competed with kerosene (which, in turn, had captured the lighting market from whale oil lamps and tallow candles). The invention by Bunsen, in 1855, of the blue flame burner made the industry's subsequent growth possible, since it provided "not only a more efficient but also a cheaper illuminant."[13] The Lowe Water-Gas Process was put into use in Pennsylvania in 1873, which "allowed water gas to hold a significant market well into the twentieth century."[14] Sales of manufactured gas increased each year until 1928, when nearly 500 billion cubic feet (bcf) were sold.[15]

The first domestic well for natural gas (twenty-seven feet deep) was drilled near Fredonia, New York, in 1821; the product was in use as an illuminant by 1824.[16] Centerville, Pennsylvania, discovered and utilized natural gas in 1840; Erie, Pennsylvania, in 1860; and Findley, Ohio, in 1872.[17] "Though obviously very inexpensive compared to manufactured gas, the transportation problems associated with natural gas inhibited market growth until the development of large diameter steel pipe in the late 1920s."[18] Indeed, even in the mid-1930s, less than half of the annual production of natural gas went into public utility uses.[19]

Electricity began to challenge the gas lighting market shortly after Edison patented the first incandescent electric lamp in 1878. The competition forced the gas industry to develop

> . . . other markets. In 1883, the Estate Gas Stove Company of Hamilton, Ohio, built the first commercial gas stove, which by the next year served several major hotels in New York. In 1884, T.S.C. Lowe patented a hot-air house heating furnace. In 1885, George D. Roper of Rockford, Illinois, patented the first residential gas range (known as the Eclipse). In 1889, the first automatic gas water heater was manufactured. In 1896, the first boiler for generating steam with gas as its fuel was demonstrated, and in 1897, the first gas steam radiator was invented and patented. . . .[20]

The Spectacular Growth of Natural Gas: 1945-1970

The dramatic growth of the natural gas industry dates from 1945, due in large part to technological improvements related to the design and construction of long-distance pipelines. Thus, in 1945, 87 percent of the natural gas produced and 68 percent of the natural gas consumed in the United States was concentrated in the six principal gas producing states — Texas, Louisiana, California, Oklahoma, West Virginia, and Kansas. In subsequent years, the construction of new pipelines from the Southwest to the Northeast and to the West Coast opened up large new markets. By the end of 1970, net sales of natural gas stood at 19 trillion cubic feet (versus 4.9 trillion cubic feet in 1950) and the percentage of domestic households heated by natural gas stood at 81.9 percent (versus 40.7 percent in 1950). Between 1945 and 1970 (see Table 14-1), the industry built 170,000 miles of transmission pipeline and 393,300 miles of distribution main. Estimated proved natural gas reserves rose each year from 147 trillion cubic feet in 1945 to a peak of 292.9 trillion cubic feet in 1967, but then began a steady decline (see Table 14-2).[21]

TABLE 14-1

Miles of Pipeline and Main[a]
1945-1985
(Thousands)

Year	Field and Gathering	Transmission Pipeline[b]	Distribution Main
1945	27.0	82.2	201.5
1950	32.8	113.1	241.6
1955	45.7	145.9	305.1
1960	55.8	183.7	391.4
1965	61.7	211.3	494.5
1970	66.3	252.2	594.8
1975	68.5	262.6	648.2
1980	83.5	266.5	701.8
1985	94.1	271.2	753.4

[a]Includes data for Hawaii subsequent to 1959 and for Alaska subsequent to 1960; excludes service pipe. Mileage shown as of end of year.

[b]Includes underground storage pipe in 1975, 1980, and 1985 (5.0 thousand miles, 6.2 thousand miles, and 6.0 thousand miles, respectively).

Source: *Moody's Public Utility Manual*, 1982, p. a50; *Gas Facts, 1986 Data* (Arlington, Va.: American Gas Association, 1987), p. 61.

Shortages and Curtailments: The 1970s

The decline in estimated proved reserves during the late 1960s and early 1970s brought the growth of the natural gas industry to a halt, and led to the curtailment of service in the early 1970s — particularly for industrial users — and to an acute shortage during the 1976-77 winter. As a result, the decade of the 1970s was one of significant change for the industry, as it sought to adjust to shortages. The development of curtailment policies[22] and of the wellhead price of natural gas[23] have previously been considered. Efforts to increase natural gas supplies by imports and developing supplemental sources will be discussed in a later section.

Surpluses and Competition: The 1980s

The natural gas supply situation began to improve in the early 1980s. In fact, a perceived temporary surplus (a "bubble") turned into a much more permanent surplus. This situation was due to three basic factors. First, the Natural Gas Policy Act (NGPA) of 1978 brought intrastate sales under

TABLE 14-2

Net Production and Proved Reserves
1945-1986
(Billions of Cubic Feet)

Year[a]	Net Production	Estimated Proved Reserves[b]	Change over Previous Year
1945	—	146,986.7	—
1950	6,855.2	184,584.7	5,183.1
1955	10,063.2	222,482.5	11,921.6
1960	13,019.4	262,326.3	1,155.9
1965	16,252.3	286,468.9	5,217.5
1970	21,960.8	290,746.4	15,637.6
1975	19,718.6	228,200.2	(8,932.3)
1976	19,542.0	216.026.1	(12,174.1)
1977	19,447.1	208,877.9	(7,148.2)
1978	19,311.0	200,301.7	(8,576.2)
1979	19,910.4	194,916.6	(5,385.1)
****			
1976	—	213,278	—
1977	18,843	207,413	(5,865)
1978	18,805	208,033	620
1979	19,257	200,997	(7,036)
1980	18,699	199,021	(1,976)
1981	18,737	201,730	2,709
1982	17,506	201,512	(218)
1983	15,788	200,247	(1,265)
1984	17,193	197,463	(2,784)
1985	15,985	193,369	(4,094)
1986	15,610	191,586	(1,783)

[a]1945-1979, old series; 1976-1986, new series.
[b]As of end of each year.
Source: *Moody's Public Utility Manual*, 1982, p. a49; *Gas Facts, 1986 Data* (Arlington, Va.: American Gas Association, 1987), .pp. 6, 8.

the same pricing rules as interstate sales, thereby ending a decade-long dominance of gas acquisitions by intrastate pipelines.[24] Second, producers responded to increased prices under the NGPA "with record drilling starts in 1980 and 1981."[25] Third, higher natural gas market prices encouraged consumers either to further conservation efforts or to alternate fuels (especially fuel oil). Explain Kalt and Schuller:

> ... the NGPA's escalation of "new" gas prices was aimed at bringing parity with the oil prices that Congress, acting in 1978, expected to prevail by 1985. But parity with oil came much faster than anticipated. By 1980 world oil prices had begun to tumble. From 1980 to 1982 oil prices declined from about $40 to $25 a barrel. Meanwhile, beginning in 1978 the prices of controlled natural gas escalated monthly in accordance with the provisions of the NGPA, and some decontrolled categories of gas swiftly topped $10 per thousand cubic feet (Mcf). This translated into an oil-equivalent price of roughly $60 a barrel. Such "above-market" levels were reached as pipelines faced with declining reserve commitments competed heatedly for decontrolled gas. They could sustain above-market prices for uncontrolled gas as long as the "rolled-in" average price of gas delivered to their customers did not exceed parity with oil, that is, as long as extra-high prices of decontrolled gas could be offset with a cushion of low-priced, permanently controlled gas. By 1982-1983, however, the steady decline of oil prices left many pipelines with even rolled-in average costs of delivered gas that were beginning to exceed oil-equivalent prices.[26]

These events, in turn, led to a series of new policy issues — off-system sales,[27] special marketing programs (SMPs),[28] changes in the allocation of fixed costs,[29] to mention but three — and to the rise of competition and restructuring proposals. The latter also will be considered in a later section.

Structure

As earlier explained,[30] supplying natural gas to consumers involves three functions and three corresponding marketing transactions: (*1*) the production and gathering of natural gas in the field — the "field price" or "wellhead price"; (*2*) the intra- and interstate transmission of the gas by pipeline from the producing field to consumer markets — the "city gate rate"; and (*3*) local distribution of the gas to consumers — the "resale rate." Since the natural gas industry, with some significant exceptions, is not integrated, the three marketing functions and transactions are carried out by separate companies, although there is overlap.

> ... For example, several integrated systems have production, transmission, and distribution functions. However, in most cases, their production function provided a relatively small percentage of their total gas supply. Some transporters and distributors also are engaged in production. Again, such production usually represents a relatively small per-

centage of their total gas supply. Distributors and in some cases large users are increasingly acquiring gas directly from producers and having it transported by transporters to their market areas.

Some transporters make direct sales to industry and electric generating plants. These sales are regulated only indirectly at the federal level and in varying degrees at the state level. Many such sales originated as a means of making offpeak seasonal sales, thereby achieving a higher load factor usage for the pipeline.[31]

Currently, there are over 5,000 natural gas producers, over 100 major intra- and interstate transmission companies, and approximately 1,303 distribution companies. Excluding independent producers, 1986 net income of $3.4 billion was allocated as follows: transporters, $1.3 billion; distributors, $747 million; integrated companies, $546 million; and combination (gas operations only) companies, $760 million.[32] In 1985, 94.5 percent of the nation's gas supply came from domestic sources (see Table 14-3).

TABLE 14-3

1985 Sources of Gas Supply

Source	Bcf	Percent Of Total
Domestic Onshore Production	11,524	66.5
Domestic Offshore Production	4,858	28.0
Imported Gas	950	5.5
Pipeline Gas from Canada	925	5.3
Pipeline Gas from Mexico	0	0
LNG	25	.2
Total	17,332	100.0

Source: American Gas Association (ed.), *Regulation of the Gas Industry* (New York: Matthew Bender & Co., Inc., 1987 Supplement and Revision), Vol. 1, pp. Int 7-8.

Regulation: The Regulatory Gap and Federal Control

Until 1938, regulation of the gas industry was largely a local and state matter. Local regulation predominated throughout the nineteenth century, at first through the issuance of exclusive franchises, and later through nonexclusive franchises. Competition, particularly in the larger cities, was relied upon to protect the public interest. In reality, however, "interminable rate wars" proved to be the frequent outcome.[33] A consolidation movement began in the last quarter of the nineteenth century, resulting in large holding companies (and combination companies) by the 1920s. Especially where local regulation proved ineffective, municipal operations were undertaken (*e.g.,* Philadelphia; Wheeling, West Virginia; Richmond, Danville, and Charlottesville, Virginia; and Hamilton, Ohio — in the period 1841 through 1890). State regulation increased in importance from 1907 on.

The states have long controlled the production of natural gas to conserve natural resources.[34] State regulation also has long prevailed over natural gas retail sales under the "affected with a public interest" doctrine. However, the Supreme Court consistently held that state regulatory authorities lacked power to control either the shipment of natural gas in interstate commerce[35] or the rates charged by interstate pipeline companies at the city gates.[36] A significant segment of the natural gas industry, therefore, was unregulated.[37] The Natural Gas Act of 1938 sought to remedy this situation by filling the regulatory gap.

The Natural Gas Act of 1938[38]

The Natural Gas Act of 1938 broadened the jurisdiction of the Federal Power Commission (now the Federal Energy Regulatory Commission) to include the interstate transmission of natural gas and its sale for resale. The act exempted production and gathering of natural gas and its local distribution. It required pipeline companies to file, publish, and adhere to their rate schedules, and to give thirty days' notice of proposed changes. The commission was empowered to suspend changes, except on sales for resale to industrial users, for a period not to exceed five months, and it was directed to establish "just and reasonable" rates as well as to prevent any "undue preference or advantage" to any person or any "unreasonable difference" in rates, service, or facilities among localities and among classes of service. The act also authorized the commission to prescribe and enforce accounting methods and to ascertain the "actual legitimate cost" of pipeline properties.

The commission was granted power to order a pipeline company to extend or improve its transportation facilities and to establish physical connections with, and to sell gas to, local distributors unless it finds that the ability of a company to render adequate service would be impaired by such an order. All voluntary extension of facilities and abandonment of service or facilities must be approved by the commission. Under a 1942 amendment, subject to a grandfather clause, certificates must be obtained from the commission for the extension of interstate facilities into a new territory unserved by a natural gas pipeline.[39] The commission may determine the service area to which each authorization is limited. Within such an area, a company is permitted to enlarge or extend its facilities without further approval. The commission, however, may issue a certificate to another pipeline company within a service area if it finds that additional service is necessary. The act authorized the commission to control imports and exports of natural gas. It also instructed the agency to cooperate with state regulatory agencies and provided for establishment of joint boards.

Finally, it should be noted that the commission was not given control over the security issues of interstate pipelines, nor was it empowered to order interconnections of facilities.

Developments under the Act. The FPC proceeded to develop its ratemaking principles for regulating the rates of jurisdictional pipelines. Particularly troublesome, however, were countless commission decisions, and judicial reviews, involving questions of jurisdiction. To illustrate: In 1950, the Supreme Court upheld the commission's jurisdiction (for reporting purposes) over an entirely in-state Ohio gas utility, which purchased natural gas from a jurisdictional interstate pipeline company at the Ohio state line, and which transported and distributed the gas solely in the state.[40] Four years later came the *Phillips* decision,[41] where the Supreme Court reversed an FPC decision by holding that the commission's jurisdiction extended to independent gatherers and producers whose sales of gas reached interstate pipeline purchasers. Thus began the commission's struggle to regulate the wellhead price of natural gas.[42] These and other cases suggest that

> . . . the limitations inherent in the Natural Gas Act have been subordinated to a policy of maximizing FPC control of the natural gas industry through legal interpretations which are policy-oriented rather than law-oriented. The effect of these decisions has been to expand FPC jurisdiction out of the limited exclusive federal segment upon which it was predicated and thus drive the states from what, as a minimum, were areas of concurrent jurisdiction on either side of the exclusive federal segment. State jurisdiction now is confined to local distribution in the narrowest sense (plus the limited cession back to the states represented by the Hinshaw amendment added to the act in 1954) on the one hand, and to physical regulation of producing properties, including producers' rates of production, on the other. In addition there is, of course, the limitation on the FPC inherent in the sale for resale structure of the Natural Gas Act. . . .[43]

Then, during the early 1970s, the commission had to deal with the growing natural gas shortage. In 1970, for example, the FPC initiated a series of rule-making proceedings to help cope with the situation. Exempt intrastate pipelines and intrastate distributors were authorized to make short-term emergency sales of natural gas to distributors or interstate pipelines without becoming subject to commission jurisdiction.[44] Independent producers were allowed to make emergency sales to pipelines for sixty-day periods without certificate authorization.[45] In 1971, limited-term certificates for above ceiling price sales by producers and pipelines were authorized for sales to jurisdictional pipelines experiencing severe gas shortages.[46] The commission adopted a policy favoring direct gas acquisitions by distributors.[47] In 1975, the commission issued a policy statement encouraging the transportation of gas sold directly by producers to nonresale industrial and commercial customers for Priority No. 2 and certain Priority No. 3 users.[48]

The National Energy Legislation of 1978

The major provisions of the national energy legislation of 1978 which apply to the natural gas industry are as follows:

(1) *National Energy Conservation Policy Act.* The purpose of this act was to promote energy conservation, by producing a variety of assistance programs, incentives, and mandatory standards and requirements. For residential customers, gas (and electric) utilities are required to establish programs to provide both information and assistance on conservation measures, including the financing of conservation measures through utility bills.

(2) *Public Utility Regulatory Policies Act (PURPA).* Title III of this act sought to foster conservation, more efficient energy utilization, and more "equitable" gas utility rates by requiring state commissions to consider, within two years, and to adopt, if appropriate, standards with respect to the termination of service and advertising. The former standard requires reasonable prior notice and forbids termination of customers who are unable to pay when such termination would endanger the customer's health. The latter standard requires that shareholders or owners of a company shall pay for all promotional or political advertising.

DOE was granted the right to intervene in any state commission gas ratemaking proceeding to advocate policies or methods of achieving the act's purposes. DOE was required to undertake a gas utility rate design study and to submit the study to Congress by May, 1980.

(3) *Powerplant and Industrial Fuel Use Act.* This act was designed to foster greater utilization of coal in place of oil and natural gas, especially by high-volume users such as electric utilities and industrial installations. Basically, no new oil and gas burning plants are permitted, although there are a number of both temporary and permanent exemptions (*e.g.*, lack of alternate fuel supply, site limitations, or environmental requirements; use of synthetic fuels). A phase-out period is permitted for existing oil or gas users, but — again with several temporary and permanent exemptions — natural gas may not be used in such plants after 1990.

(4) *Natural Gas Policy Act (NGPA).* This act represented a comprehensive revision of national policy concerning natural gas pricing and regulation. It was designed to gradually decontrol the wellhead price of

certain categories of natural gas by January 1, 1985, or July 1, 1987, through a phased-in program of monthly price escalations. (See Tables 14-4 and 14-5.) During the decontrol period (*a*) federal price control was applied to intrastate gas and (*b*) the higher cost of new gas supplies was to be allocated to certain industrial users ("incremental pricing"). After the decontrol period, but not before July 1, 1985, nor later than June 30, 1987, either the President or Congress may reimpose price controls on first sales of natural gas from all deregulated gas for a period of eighteen months.

The act contained emergency authority and requirements. The President may declare a natural gas supply emergency (for a period up to 120 days) if a severe natural gas shortage exists or if natural gas supplies for high priority users are in short supply. If an emergency is declared, the President (*a*) may authorize any interstate pipeline or local distribution company to contract for the purchase of emergency supplies of natural gas (with the contracts not to exceed four months unless the President authorizes renewal) and (*b*) may allocate supplies of natural gas, by order, to: any interstate pipeline, certain local distribution companies, and/or to any person for meeting requirements of high-priority use. All prices under such emergency conditions will be set by the President.

Finally, the act requires the FERC to prohibit interstate pipelines from curtailing deliveries of natural gas for any essential agricultural use and for essential industrial process or feedstock use. The Secretary of the Department of Energy was authorized to establish and review priorities for curtailment, with the FERC implementing the priorities.

(5) *Energy Tax Act.* This act was designed to reduce, through various tax incentives, the country's dependence on foreign oil and to encourage a switch to other energy sources (including solar, wind, or geothermal). The act contained a number of incentives to homeowners to insulate their homes and of tax credits to businesses to install energy saving equipment. The act imposed a tax on fuel-inefficient automobiles. Finally, the act contained a number of tax measures with respect to intangible drilling costs for independent oil and gas producers and for producers of geothermal energy.

Developments under the Legislation. The national energy legislation ushered in a new era for the natural gas industry. The wellhead price of natural gas rose rapidly (see Table 14-6), although gas continues to maintain its relative price advantage, at least in the residential market (see Table 14-7).

TABLE 14-4

Natural Gas Price Ceilings
Under the Natural Gas Policy Act of 1978[a]

Category	Act Section	MMBtu Ceiling Price and Escalation	Price Deregulation Date
New Natural Gas New onshore wells New onshore reservoirs New OCS leases	102	$1.75 starting 4/20/77; annual inflation adjustment factor plus real growth adjustment factor	1/1/85
New Onshore Production Wells	103		
Producing below 5000′		$1.75 starting 4/20/77; annual inflation adjustment factor	1/1/85
Producing above 5000′		$1.75 starting 4/20/77 to 12/31/84; annual inflation adjustment factor	7/1/87
		Starting 1/1/85 the ceiling price will be midway between the price that would be computed for new natural gas and the price that would be computed for new, onshore production wells	
Old OCS Gas	102	$1.75 starting 4/20/77; annual inflation adjustment factor plus real growth adjustment factor	Not deregulated
High-Cost Natural Gas	107	$1.75 starting 4/20/77; annual inflation adjustment factor plus real growth adjustment factor	Effective date of FERC incremental pricing rules
Stripper Well Natural Gas	108	$2.09 starting 5/1/78; annual inflation adjustment factor plus real growth adjustment factor	Not deregulated
Natural Gas Dedicated to Interstate Commerce	104		
Gas produced from wells spudded on or after 1/1/75		$1.45 starting 4/20/77; annual inflation adjustment factor	Not deregulated
Wells spudded on or after 1/1/73 but before 1/1/75		$0.94 starting 4/20/77; annual inflation adjustment factor	Not deregulated
Wells spudded before 1/1/73		$0.295 starting 4/20/77; annual inflation adjustment factor	Not deregulated

TABLE 14-4 *(Continued)*

Category	Act Section	MMBtu Ceiling Price and Escalation	Price Deregulation Date
Other gas		Applicable rate; annual inflation adjustment factor	Not deregulated
Gas Sold under Existing Intrastate Contracts	105		
Contract price less than new natural gas price on enactment date		Contract price; escalate by contract up to the price of new natural gas	1/1/85 if contract price exceeds $1.00 on 12/31/84 and no indefinite price clause; if less than $1.00, not deregulated
Contract price greater than new natural gas price on enactment date		Contract price plus annual inflation adjustment factor until exceeded by escalated new natural gas price	1/1/85 if contract price exceeds $1.00 on 12/31/84 and no indefinite price clause; if less than $1.00, not deregulated
Gas Sold under Rollover Contracts	106		
Interstate		$0.54 or just and reasonable FERC price; annual inflation adjustment factor	Not deregulated
Intrastate		Higher of expired contract price or $1.00 at 4/20/77; annual inflation adjustment factor	1/1/85 if more than $1.00
Other Categories of Natural Gas	109		
Any natural gas not covered under any other section of the Act		$1.45 or other just and reasonable rate established by FERC at 4/20/77; annual inflation adjustment factor	Not deregulated
Natural gas produced from the Prudhoe Bay Area of Alaska		$1.45 or other just and reasonable rate established by FERC at 4/20/77; annual inflation adjustment factor	Not deregulated

[a]The *annual inflation adjustment factor* is based on the Gross National Product Implicit Price Deflator, and equals the Deflator adjusted by addition of a Consumer Price Index "correction factor" of 0.2 percentage points.

The *real growth adjustment factor* is 3.5 percent for any month beginning before April 20, 1981 (*i.e.*, from April 20, 1977, through April 30, 1981); and 4 percent for any month beginning after April 20, 1981.

Source: Price Waterhouse & Co., "The Natural Gas Policy Act of 1978" (New York, 1978).

TABLE 14-5

Definition of New Natural Gas

New Natural Gas (Act Section 102), is gas from:
  New onshore wells;
  New onshore reservoirs, and
  New Outer Continental Shelf leases

New Onshore Wells:
  A *new onshore well* is:
  —a new well at least 2.5 miles from the nearest marker well; or
  —a new well 1,000 feet deeper than the nearest deepest marker well within a 2.5 mile radius.
  A *new well* is any well:
  —the surface drilling of which began on or after February 19, 1977; or
  —the depth of which was increased by means of drilling on or after February 19, 1977 to a completion location which is located at least 1,000 feet below the depth of the deepest completion location of such well attained before February 19, 1977.
  A *marker well* is any well from which natural gas was produced in commercial quantities at any time after January 1, 1970 and before April 20, 1977.

New Onshore Reservoirs:
  Natural gas is considered produced from a *new onshore reservoir* if:
  —the gas could not have been produced in commercial quantities prior to April 20, 1977 from an old producing well (behind-the-pipe gas); or
  —the gas could not have been produced from a well where suitable delivery facilities were in existence on April 20, 1977 (withheld gas).

New Outer Continental Shelf Leases:
  A *new Outer Continental Shelf lease* is any lease of submerged acreage entered into on or after April 20, 1977.

Source: Price Waterhouse & Co., "The Natural Gas Policy Act of 1978" (New York, 1978), pp. 9-12.

TABLE 14-6

Average Gas Prices of Wellhead, City Gate, and End-User Levels, 1945-1986

Year	Wellhead ($/Mcf)*	City Gate ($/MMBtu)*	Cost to the Ultimate Customer ($/MMBtu)*
1945	0.046	NA	NA
1950	0.065	NA	NA
1955	0.104	0.271	0.518
1960	0.140	0.342	0.605
1965	0.156	0.339	0.618
1970	0.171	0.354	0.641
1975	0.445	0.798	1.285
1980	1.588	2.414	3.134
1985	2.511	3.821	5.017
1986	1.860	3.579	4.601

*Mcf and MMBtu prices are roughly comparable. On a MMBtu basis, the wellhead price would be slightly less.

NA = Not Available.

Source: *1968 Gas Facts* (New York: American Gas Association, 1968), p. 30; *Gas Facts, 1986 Data* (Arlington, Va.: American Gas Association, 1987), p. 112.

TABLE 14-7

Average Residential Costs, 1955-1986

Year	Gas ($/MMBtu)	Electric ($/MMBtu)	No. 2 Fuel Oil ($/MMBtu)
1955	0.90	7.77	1.04
1960	1.00	7.24	1.08
1965	1.01	6.59	1.15
1970	1.06	6.15	1.33
1975	1.69	9.40	2.81
1980	3.61	14.45	7.21
1985	5.95	21.69	7.78
1986	5.65	21.80	6.02

Source: *Gas Facts, 1981 Data* (Arlington, Va.: American Gas Association, 1982), p. 125; *Gas Facts, 1986 Data* (Arlington, Va.: American Gas Association, 1987), p. 116.

Drilling activity showed a corresponding increase[49] and more costly areas (*e.g.*, the Overthrust Belt of the Rocky Mountains; more distant, deeper fields offshore Louisiana and Texas) were opened. Intrastate gas prices became subject to the FERC's jurisdiction.[50] These three events (along with a recession) contributed to an improved natural gas supply situation, ending the shortage which existed throughout much of the preceding decade.

The improved supply situation also was aided by the incremental pricing provision of the NGPA. Instead of switching from natural gas and oil to coal, however, large industrial users began to switch from natural gas to oil and the domestic user was left "to pay for the more expensive gas plus the cost of transmission and distribution facilities which the industrial user formerly bore."[51] Further, as a result of the improved supply situation, the Economic Regulatory Administration (ERA)[52] was liberal in granting exemptions under the Powerplant and Industrial Fuel Use Act. And, in 1987, the act's restrictive provisions, along with the incremental pricing provision, were repealed.[53]

There have been several other developments under the national energy legislation that deserve review. Several user conservation programs were developed[54]; most state commissions have considered, and adopted, the PURPA standards with respect to the termination of service[55] and advertising[56]; and curtailment priorities, under the NGPA, were established.[57] The gas utility rate design study was submitted to Congress on schedule.[58] But after the DOE refused to issue efficiency standards for major electric and gas home appliances, Congress required that they be set by 1990.[59] Finally, as can be expected, there have been countless disputes surrounding the terms, phrases, scope, and applicability of each section of the NGPA, which have resulted in continuous judicial scrutiny of the FERC's rules, regulations, and orders.[60] The following seven cases are illustrative.

(1) Gas sold under Title I of the NGPA must be priced on the basis of the water-saturated standard used under the NGA, rather than on the basis of the number of Btu's actually delivered. (Gas assumed to be saturated with water, but not so saturated, results in an understatement of approximately 1.74 percent of the Btu's actually delivered.)[61]

(2) A pipeline's transfer of its own gas from its production department to its pipeline department is a "first sale" as defined by the NGPA and qualifies for the applicable NGPA price.[62]

(3) Indefinite price escalation clauses (including area rate clauses, favored nation clauses, and spiral escalation clauses) in existing intra- and interstate producer/pipeline contracts provide sufficient contractual authority to collect the maximum lawful prices prescribed in the NGPA.[63]

(4) The phrase "produced in commercial quantities" in Section 102 requires that gathering and transportation facilities be installed so that gas from a well will be available to consumers and does not include gas flared for testing purposes prior to the installation of treating, gathering, and pipeline facilities.[64]

(5) The Section 109 price, rather than the Section 104 price, applies to gas produced from the OCS, which was committed or dedicated to interstate commerce on November 8, 1978, under the NGPA, but which was not actually being sold in interstate commerce on that date.[65]

(6) In determining stripper well status under Section 108, the total volume of natural gas produced from a well with multiple completion locations is to be used in determining the well's daily production, since Congress used the term "well" rather than the term "reservoir."[66]

(7) Where gas produced from a well qualifies for two NGPA categories (*i.e.,* both a regulated and a deregulated category), the deregulated category applies after January 1, 1985.[67]

Competition: The Wellhead Price and Open Access

Over the past decade, there have been fundamental changes in the nation's natural gas policy. "Indeed, the nation is moving in the direction of a much more rational, responsive, and productive natural gas industry. The key to this development is an expansion of the realm of marketplace competition and a concomitant circumscription of the role of government regulation."[68]

The Wellhead Price

Passage of the NGPA in 1978 ended a debate over the necessity of regulating the wellhead price of natural gas that had been going on since the end of World War II. In the early days of the debate, the focus was on the degree of monopoly or market power that would exist absent regulation. Gradually, however, the focus shifted to the issue of economic rents.

Market Power.[69] "Restraint of market power," note Breyer and MacAvoy, "is a traditional economic rationale for regulation," and concern over "producer market power played an important role in the debate in the 1950s over the need for regulation of producers. . . ."[70] The basic argument advanced to support field price regulation was that gas production and new reserves in major fields were under the control of a few large producers, often petroleum companies with strong ties to interstate pipeline companies, with the result that they were able to earn extremely high profits.[71] Evidence gathered during the 1960s, however, cast doubt on the market power theory and, in a 1970 decision, the Fifth Circuit Court of Appeals stated: "There seems to be general agreement that the market is at least structurally competitive."[72] To summarize that evidence:

(1) In 1961, there were approximately 4,365 producers selling to interstate pipelines. The largest firm accounted for 8 percent of new sales to interstate pipelines, the largest five firms for 25 percent, the largest twenty firms for 53 percent. The 266 producers making sales of 2 Mcf or more either alone or as first named in combination with others supplied 91 percent of the total interstate pipeline purchases and received 92 percent of the total producer revenues.[73]

(2) In some gas producing fields, concentration was higher. Thus, in the Panhandle-Hugoton fields of North Texas, the largest four suppliers accounted for 72 percent of total new sales in 1950-53, while the largest five firms accounted for more than 50 percent of total new sales in the Permian Basin in 1960.[74] With respect to the claim of petroleum company dominance: "The four largest petroleum companies provided at most from 37 to 44 percent of new reserve sales in West Texas and New Mexico and a maximum of 26 to 28 per-

cent in the Texas Gulf region — all in the 1950-54 period just before the *Phillips* decision."[75] Such concentration data suggest that while production of natural gas does not represent a perfect market, "workable competition can prevail in such a market structure in the absence of collusion."[76]

(3) Entry into the gas-producing segment of the industry, as McKie argued, is relatively easy as indicated by the large number of producers. "A monopolist or a monopolizing group which did not control this open end of the supply could not hope to monopolize for long."[77] Further, while natural gas pipelines once laid down cannot be readily moved, extensions and branches can be built to other pipelines (interconnections) if a supplier or group of suppliers attempted to control the supply in any field. "If any gas producer should attempt to hold out for a higher price than the other producers, he will simply lose his market. If the producer attempts on his own to restrict supply and force up the price, other producers will quickly fill the gap. Pipelines can turn to other sources, and would not as a rule be crippled by the loss of any one source."[78]

(4) The rise in the wellhead price of natural gas during the 1950s (from 6.5 cents per Mcf in 1950 to fourteen cents per Mcf in 1960), some contended, was evidence of noncompetitive performance. MacAvoy found, however, after studying the markets for new contracts, that instead of anticompetitive producer behavior, the price increases were the result of pipeline competition. During the early 1950s, due to the presence of only one pipeline in many gas fields, monopsony pricing did prevail in the three major southwestern producing areas, which had the effect of depressing the wellhead price below the competitive level. But the rapid growth of the pipeline network in the 1950s radically altered the competitive situation; new entry raised the wellhead prices to a competitive level.[79] Moreover, as noted above, the cost of building an extension or branch is not prohibitive. "When a new field is discovered, several pipelines in the vicinity may bid for the gas and thus fix its price competitively even though only one of them finally gets it under contract and builds a single line to gather it."[80]

(5) Finally, with respect to profits, experts in the Permian Basin area proceedings "reported average returns on capital between 12 and 18 percent for oil and gas companies at a time when the average return in manufacturing was less than 8 percent. This profit comparison, however, is not enough to establish the presence of monopoly pricing, for three special features of returns in the gas producing industry must be recognized. First, lucky discoveries in a world of uncertainty might earn unusually efficient or fortunate producers a high economic rent in natural gas because of the importance of the discovery process. Second, the Permian Basin fig-

ures reflect profits only of firms still in business, not of those that failed. . . . Third, the profit figures . . . overstate the true return to capital because of the accounting procedures used. The rate-of-return estimates were calculated simply by dividing total profits that producers reported they had received by the total capital that they reported they had invested. This does not account for the extensive time lag in this industry before an investment begins to earn a return. The accounting return on a dollar invested here must be far lower in real terms than elsewhere if payment begins five years, rather than one year, after the investment is made; the simple bookkeeping profit rate must be adjusted to take the long lag between exploration and production into account. Producer witnesses in the Permian Basin case estimated that an 'apparent yield' of 16 to 18 percent was equivalent, because of the lag in production, to a 'true yield' of about 10 percent."[81]

For all of these reasons, there was a growing consensus in the 1960s that workable competition in the production of natural gas would exist in the absence of federal regulation. To cite MacAvoy:

As has been suggested by this long analysis of price formation in the 1950s, gas markets were diverse in structure and behavior, and were generally competitive or were changing from monopsony toward competition. It would seem possible that this could result in price level changes and in a revolution of pricing patterns in contrast with those associated with monopoly. Markets with such characteristics need not be regulated by the Federal Power Commission to prevent monopoly pricing.[82]

Economic Rents. The argument for producer regulation shifted toward another objective: controlling economic rents (often referred to as "windfall profits"). Explain Breyer and MacAvoy:

Even in a competitive market, the distribution of gains from production might be so unacceptable as to justify the regulation of prices. Price in a competitive market is equal to the cost of producing the marginal units that can be sold. Some producers can sell — at that market price — intramarginal units that are far less costly to produce, perhaps because they have special skill or expertise or because they control a resource that cannot easily be duplicated. Such producers realize economic rents, or returns in excess of those required to bring forth production. It has been claimed that these rents are exceptionally high in the oil and gas industries and therefore that price control systems should be devised that would deprive producers of such incomes and give them to consumers in the form of lower prices.[83]

To eliminate economic rents, without interfering with the market-clearing mechanism, would require regulation to set a separate price for each well; a task that would be "absurd. . . . It would also be unworkable and unnecessary."[84] Further, to redistribute income by taking away economic rents from producers and providing higher real income for consumers, requires great care to make sure that output is not affected. This objective

> . . . requires knowledge of the location and shape of the supply curve for both established and additional supply. Moreover, when reduced intramarginal prices bring about the increase in quantity demanded, the excess demand has to be limited by recourse to such rationing devices as classifying users and designating one or more classes as "low priority" so that they experience shortage. Finding the low-priority consumer — on some grounds other than willingness to pay — turns out to be a never-ending search.[85]

There are instances where the commission wrestled with the issue of economic rents, most notably in the area rate cases. There, the FPC adopted a vintaging system, in part to prevent producers from receiving economic rents on "old" gas, while permitting higher rates on "new" supplies in recognition of rising exploration and development costs.[86] Similarly, under the NGPA, an attempt was made to control economic rents by maintaining price controls on "old" gas, while providing for a phased decontrol of "new" gas supplies.

Partial Decontrol. Under the NGPA, approximately 50 percent of domestic gas production has been decontrolled. The predicted price "fly-up" or "spike" failed to materialize (on January 1, 1985, when most categories were decontrolled), due to falling oil prices and the gas surplus. Absent further legislation, controls on "old" gas will continue, although such controlled gas will account for only 25 percent of total production by 1994.[87] However, many support immediate, complete decontrol, contending that such action would provide incentives to prolong the life of old gas fields, thereby adding to domestic reserves,[88] and would simplify the task of downstream regulation.[89]

Supply Contract Provisions

Under traditional regulatory policy, pipeline companies were required to have "assurance" of an adequate supply of natural gas before a certificate to construct a line would be issued (and before a line could be financed).[90] But because market conditions could not be predicted accurately over long periods of time,[91] escalation clauses were inserted into producer-pipeline contracts. In addition, producers have generally required the inclusion of take-or-pay clauses in contracts with pipelines, while pipelines have generally required the inclusion of minimum bill clauses in contracts with local distribution companies and large end-users. Each type of clause will be discussed in turn.

Escalation Clauses. Escalation clauses, which contain provisions for adjusting the base prices at which deliveries are made, are of two basic types — "definite" and "indefinite" escalations. A definite or fixed-rate escalation clause provides for price increases either at a fixed dollar amount or at a set percentage at definite dates during the contract period.[92] Indefinite clauses provide for price increases under a variety of situations. (*1*) The "most favored nation" clause permits the base price to rise (*a*) under the two-party clause, if the buyer pays a higher price to another producer for comparable supplies in the same field or (*b*) under the third-party clause, if a third, unrelated party pays a higher price in the same area.[93] (*2*) The "deregulation" clause provides for a redetermination or renegotiation of base prices whenever there is a change in government authority or jurisdiction over the rates charged under the contract. Redetermination provisions provide for the price to be adjusted based on certain preselected factors, such as an average of the highest contracts in the same producing area or the price of fuel oil (either No. 2 or No. 6).[94] Renegotiation provisions provide for open-ended negotiations, stating that price should take into account prevailing market prices or the highest contract prices for "similar" gas in the same producing area. (*3*) The FPC/FERC highest regulated rate clause provides that prices will escalate to the highest regulated prices allowable by the FPC, FERC, or any successor agency. During the era of area rates, for example, some intrastate clauses (known as the "FPC clause") provided that the buyer would pay the effective FPC-regulated price at the time of contract, plus an additional charge.

By 1961, about 80 percent of the gas sales contracts on file with the FPC contained either the two-party favored nation or redetermination clauses or both.[95] A more recent sample of pre-NGPA interstate contracts found that 92 percent of the 1977 volume was covered by indefinite escalation clauses (66 percent by deregulation clauses; 26 percent by highest regulated rate clauses) and only 8 percent by definite escalation clauses (and all of the definite clauses were found in pre-1973 contracts). Equally important, of the 66 percent with deregulation clauses, the vast majority contained third-party favored nation clauses.[96]

Escalation clauses have been severely criticized. Some have objected to all such clauses, arguing that regulatory authorities should maintain prices at the levels specified in the original contracts. Such a policy, however, makes little economic sense. "If demand continues to increase," argued McKie in 1957, "the prices for new supply will continue to be bid up. If the prices on 'old' supply are arbitrarily kept down to lower levels, then demand will increase all the more and prices for new supply will go up all the faster, which will pull up the average price."[97] The most intense criticism has been reserved for indefinite escalation clauses, on two grounds. First, under third-party favored nation clauses, new base prices are determined by outside parties. Such criticism resulted in a 1961 FPC order outlawing all indefinite price escalation clauses, other than those providing for redetermination once every five years, in contracts executed after April 3, 1961. In the commission's words:

> Increases in producer prices, triggered by indefinite escalation clauses, have resulted in a flood of almost simultaneous filings. These filings bear no apparent relationship to the economic requirements of the producers who file them. The Natural Gas Act contemplates that prices, to be just and reasonable, be related to economic needs. The elimination of indefinite escalation provisions does not, of course, cut off other avenues by which a producer may make provision for filing for increased rates.[98]

Nevertheless, under the commission's area rate and national rate proceedings, escalations up to the prescribed ceilings were generally permitted,[99] and indefinite escalation clauses are not illegal under the NGPA.[100]

Second, many believe that indefinite escalation clauses complicate any attempt to deregulate completely the wellhead price of natural gas. In the event of complete deregulation, they believe, deregulation clauses — particularly those with redetermination provisions tied to favored nation clauses or to fuel oil prices — will trigger significant price increases. Others take the position that prices might well decline under complete deregulation, since sellers would not be able to market the offered supply at higher prices. Yet, only a small percentage of pre-1980 contracts contain buyer protection or "escape" clauses (*i.e.*, clauses which offer relief if the redetermination price exceeds fuel oil on a Btu equivalent).[101] Many post-1980 contracts, however, do contain "market out" clauses (*i.e.*, clauses which permit the purchaser of deregulated gas to either terminate a contract or reduce the price under a contract which, because of marketing circumstances, is "uneconomic or otherwise unreasonable").[102]

Take-or-Pay Contract Provisions. Take-or-pay, or minimum take, clauses obligate a pipeline (*a*) to take a specified quantity of gas over a specific period of time,[103] (*b*) to make prepayments to the producer for quantities of gas not so taken, and (*c*) to "make up" the volumes not taken but already covered by such prepayments, also over a specific period of time.[104] Producers contend that take-or-pay provisions are essential, first, to provide a reasonably steady return under a contract, so as to be able to produce gas in paying quantities and to prevent loss of revenues through "drainage" by other producers and, second, to ensure "that a pipeline does not effectively shut-in production from a well while taking gas from another producer."[105] During periods of surplus dedicated supplies (*i.e.*, 1960s, early 1980s), prepayments totaled millions of dollars due to existing contracts with both high take provisions and high base prices.[106]

In 1967, the FPC amended its regulations regarding these contract provisions. While permitting take-or-pay clauses, the make-up periods were set at a minimum of five years and the prepayment price would be the "total price" for the gas, in contracts executed after February 1, 1967.[107] Further amendments were proposed in a 1970 rule-making proceeding; a proceeding terminated the following year because the commission was convinced by the record "that the limitations proposed in the rule might reduce the flexibility of negotiations between producers and pipelines and could, thereby, reduce gas supplies for the interstate market."[108]

But in the late 1970s, producers began to demand gas contracts with extremely high deliverability (take) obligations and, frequently, with advance payments.[109] As a result, during periods of surpluses, pipelines tend to shut-in those reserves under contracts with low take provisions and base prices, while continuing to purchase gas with high take provisions and base prices.[110] In a 1982 policy statement, the FERC adopted "a rebuttable presumption in general rate cases" that prepayments made under take-or-pay provisions above 75 percent of annual deliverability "are inappropriate and should not be given rate-base treatment" and noted that by so doing the commission "has attempted to balance the need for pipeline flexibility in responding to changing market conditions against the need to assure a cash flow to producers to cover their costs."[111] And, in a 1985 policy statement, the commission said that pipelines may file to include "buy-out" payments (*i.e.*, payments made by pipelines to settle take-or-pay liabilities) in their rate bases.[112]

Demand Charges and Minimum Commodity Bills. Interstate pipelines generally provide "Contract Demand" ("CD") service to firm customers (*e.g.*, local distribution companies), under which a pipeline agrees to sell to the customer a specified maximum daily volume of gas. Typically, pipeline rate structures are two-tiered: a demand charge (for the right to be able to purchase up to the maximum volume on any day) and a commodity charge (for each unit of gas purchased). The demand charge is payable regardless of the customer's actual use. Consequently, if the demand charge as a proportion of total price is high, the customer faces a severe restraint on switching to another supplier or purchasing gas at the wellhead (and buying transportation service).[113]

In addition, some pipeline tariffs contain a minimum monthly bill clause, equal to the demand charge plus a minimum commodity purchase requirement.[114] The latter was often more constraining than take-or-pay producer contracts "because they were monthly, not annual, obligations and had no makeup provisions."[115] In a 1984 decision, the FERC ruled that pipelines may not recover variable costs unless actually incurred through minimum commodity bills.[116] In more recent cases, it has tried to reduce or eliminate minimum bills entirely, arguing that since the modified fixed-variable approach[117] virtually guaranteed recovery of all fixed costs, minimum commodity bills "have been rendered unnecessary."[118]

Open-Access Transportation

"If the 1970s was the decade for debate over federal regulation of natural gas wellhead markets, the 1980s is the decade for debate over federal regulation of the pipeline segment of the industry."[119] The need for change in gas transportation policy basically came about because some gas producers and customers (*i.e.*, local distribution companies and end users), in trying to arrange lower-cost gas sales and purchases directly with one another, were denied access to transportation facilities.[120]

Order No. 436.[121] In late 1985, the FERC adopted an optional, open-access natural gas transportation program containing five key elements:

(1) To take advantage of "blanket certification" of transportation authority, interstate pipelines must agree to provide transportation service on a nondiscriminatory basis.

(2) Transportation capacity must be allocated on a "first-come, first-served" basis whenever demand exceeds capacity.

(3) Rates for open-access transportation will be unregulated except to establish floors and ceilings. Minimum rates are to be based on the average variable costs of providing transportation service. Maximum rates, which are to vary between peak and off-peak periods and between firm and interruptible service, are to be based on the cost of providing service (fully allocated costs). A two-tiered rate structure was retained, with firm customers paying a "reservation" fee for the guaranteed right to use a certain amount of a pipeline's capacity and a "volumetric" fee to cover the variable costs of providing the service actually used. No demand charges or minimum bills will be permitted.

(4) An open-access pipeline must allow local distribution companies to either reduce their firm sales entitlements (CDs) or convert them to firm transportation service over a five-year period. (Customers may reduce or convert up to 15 percent during the first year, up to 30 percent the second year, up to 50 percent the third year, up to 75 percent the fourth year, and up to 100 percent the fifth year and thereafter.)

(5) The commission may issue optional, expedited certificates for new facilities, services, and operations under Section 7 of the NGA, with open-access pipelines assuming the entire economic risk.[122]

On review,[123] the D.C. Circuit Court upheld both "the substance" of the order and "the procedures the Commission employed in adopting it," but vacated and remanded the matter to the FERC to remedy certain "defects."[124] First, the contract demand adjustment conditions "suffer from a want of both legal authority and reasoned decisionmaking."[125] Second, the commission "failed to adequately explain some of its grandfathering decisions."[126] Third, the commission's refusal "to take any affirmative action to solve the problems posed by the uneconomic producer-pipeline contracts also fails to meet the standards of reasoned decisionmaking."[127] The various parts of the order, noted the court,

> . . . are interdependent. The nondiscriminatory access and CD adjustment provisions aggravate the pipelines' jeopardy from take-or-pay liability. When coupled with take-or-pay liability, those provisions may bring about a wasteful imbalance between pipeline sales and unbundled transportation service. Thus the Commission's apparent insouciance on take-or-pay taints the package. . . .[128]

Order No. 500.[129] In August 1987, the FERC issued an interim rule, designed to supplant Order No. 436. The order addressed the three issues remanded by the circuit court as follows:

(1) Local distribution companies' contract demand reduction rights were eliminated, but their conversion rights were maintained.
(2) The grandfathered existing transportation arrangements were retained. (All grandfathered transportation will end by 1990, the commission noted.)
(3) Three options were expressed for addressing pipelines' take-or-pay exposure: (*a*) producer credits to avoid the build-up of current take-or-pay costs, (*b*) a passthrough mechanism for past costs, and (*c*) a gas-supply charge for future costs. Additionally, the commission held out the possibility of future action under Section 5 of the NGA to directly modify contract problems, after analyzing information received from pipelines and producers as a result of a data request.

Some Implications for Local Distribution Companies

In an earlier chapter, it was noted that local distribution companies also have confronted numerous problems due to the changing natural gas industry. To compete for dual-fuel customers, for example, many have adopted "flexible" rates.[130] But any such solutions raise a number of policy and regulatory questions. To mention but three. What service obligation does a local distribution company have when customers elect to purchase their own supplies?[131] Should local distribution companies be permitted to purchase spot-market or lower-cost gas and dedicate that supply to interruptible customers or to a particular interruptible customer?[132] Should pipelines be permitted to "bypass" the local distribution company's system by directly serving end-users who are, or have previously been, customers of the certificated utility or, conversely, should local distribution companies (and intra-state pipelines) be required to transport gas for large end-users?[133] And underlying all of these issues is the central one: How are customers without alternate fuel capability to be protected?[134]

Natural Gas Supplies and Outlook

Estimated proved natural gas reserves increased through 1967, but then declined in the 1968 through 1980 period (with the notable exception of 1970, due to the inclusion of Alaskan reserves). Higher consumer prices and conservation, since 1973, have resulted in lower yearly net production (see Table 14-2). At the end of 1986, estimated proved natural gas reserves were 191.6 trillion cubic feet, including 33 trillion cubic feet of gas in Alaska.[135] Based on 1986 production of 15.6 trillion cubic feet, estimated proved reserves represent a 12.3 year supply (see Table 14-8).

TABLE 14-8

Gas Production and Proved Reserves, 1986

State/Federal	Production		Proved Gas Reserves[a]	
	Billions of Cubic Feet	*Percent of Total*	*Billions of Cubic Feet*	*Percent of Total*
Texas	4,620	29.60	40,574	21.18
Louisiana	1,741	11.15	12,930	6.75
Oklahoma	1,658	10.62	16,685	8.71
New Mexico	628	4.02	11,808	6.16
Kansas	461	2.95	10,509	5.49
Wyoming	402	2.58	9,756	5.09
California	372	2.38	3,928	2.05
Alaska	324	2.08	32,664	17.05
Colorado	188	1.20	3,027	1.58
Mississippi	165	1.06	1,300	.68
Other states[b]	1,033	6.62	14,182	7.40
Federal offshore	4,018	25.74	34,223	17.86
Totals	15,610	100.00%	191,586	100.00%

[a]As of December 31, 1986.

[b]Includes 21 states.

Source: *Gas Facts, 1986 Data* (Arlington, Va.: American Gas Association, 1987), pp. 10-11.

Supplemental Gas Supplies: The 1970s

During the gas shortage of the 1970s, three basic supplemental sources of gas supply were utilized and/or investigated. First, the 1970s saw the increasing importation of natural gas from Canada[136] and of LNG[137] from Algeria (see Table 14-9). Both the desirability of, and price for, imports have been controversial. With respect to Canadian imports, six major pipelines[138] had authority to import natural gas from Canada in 1970. During the decade, the border price increased from an average of 24.52 cents per MMBtu to $4.47 per MMBtu. "Prices thus became a diplomatic as well as a commercial concern. The Canadian National Energy Board first announced that it would review prices annually in 1974, and in 1979 it changed its method of pricing so as to closely follow world petroleum prices."[139] Early in 1980, the ERA questioned the need for Canadian imports and began to explore ways to decrease reliance on foreign sources.[140] The border price, raised to $4.94 per MMBtu in 1981, was reduced to $4.40 per MMBtu in 1983, with a $3.40 per MMBtu incentive price. Since that time, the Canadian government has liberalized its export and pricing policies,[141] with the result that the *average* border price (estimated) declined to $2.47 per MMBtu

TABLE 14-9

Natural Gas Imports
1955-1986
(Millions of Cubic Feet)

Year	Algeria[a]	Canada	Mexico	Total
1955	0	10,885	7	10,892
1960	0	108,657	46,989	155,646
1965	0	404,686	51,708	456,394
1970	757	778,687	41,336	820,780
1975	4,893	948,115	0	953,008
1980	85,850	796,507	102,410	984,767
1981	36,824	762,113	105,013	903,949
1982	55,136	783,407	94,794	933,336
1983	131,124	711,923	75,361	918,407
1984	36,191	755,368	51,502	843,060
1985	23,659	926,056	0	949,715
1986	1,669	747,709	0	749,378

[a]Quantities represent total LNG imports from overseas into the United States.
   Source: *Gas Facts, 1981 Data* (Arlington, Va.: American Gas Association, 1982), p. 33; *Gas Facts, 1986 Data* (Arlington, Va.: American Gas Association, 1987), p. 34.

in 1986[142] and short-term sales (less than twenty-four months) have increased dramatically.[143]

With respect to LNG, four companies were authorized to import LNG on a long-term (twenty years or more) basis in the 1970s: Distrigas Corporation in 1972[144]; El Paso LNG (the importer for Southern Energy Company, Consolidated Gas Supply Corporation, and Columbia LNG Corporation) in 1972[145]; Eascogas LNG, Inc., in 1973[146]; and Trunkline Gas Company in 1977.[147] LNG imports, which peaked at 253 Bcf in 1979, have met two stumbling blocks. Such imports require the building of expensive tankers and receiving terminals.[148] Import price also has been controversial and, in April, 1980, caused a virtual halt (all except for Distrigas Corporation) to imports from Algeria.

Algeria demanded that its gas be priced according to a new principle; that is, a price equivalent to the energy content of Algerian crude oil at the point of export. If Algeria were to obtain parity for gas, the LNG in early 1980 would have cost the United States about $8 per million Btu's (about $6.11 for the gas and $1.75 to $2.00 for transportation and regasification). At the time, average wellhead prices of domestic gas were about $1.30 per million Btu's, with legal maximums for new gas between $2.25 to $2.40 per million Btu's.[149] Then, after Panhandle Eastern Corporation reached an agreement with Sonatrach in 1982, a group of its utility and industrial customers objected to the price of $7.13 per MMBtu, and asked the FERC and ERA to suspend or revoke Trunkline's import license. Both agencies refused to do so[150] and in subsequent negotiations, Panhandle Eastern reached a $665 million settlement with Algeria.[151] Imports may resume at the Lake Charles facility during 1988.

Second, several research programs and projects were undertaken or planned to manufacture synthetic gas (*i.e.,* processed gas or SNG and gas from coal gasification). These programs and projects included:

1. An SNG pilot facility, built by Algonquin SNG, Inc., designed to produce 120,000 Mcf per day, utilizing naphtha.[152]
2. A $296 million coal gasification research program, funded by the Interior Department and the American Gas Association. "The first four years of the program were to be directed to developing the coal gasification process through the pilot plant stage, at a cost of approximately $30 million a year. The second four-year period, or demonstration phase, would cost about $176 million. Commercial coal gasification plants built after the eight-year research period were to be completely financed by private industry, with a single plant capable of producing 250 million cubic feet per day of synthetic gas expected to cost $250 million."[153]
3. The Transwestern Coal Gasification Company project, involving construction of a coal gasification plant in New Mexico and the conver-

sion of approximately 25,000 tons of coal per day into approximately 250 million cubic feet of gas per day.[154]

4. "Project SNG-Biomass," a $12.7 million project of United Gas Pipe Line Company to explore a process for converting a combination of municipal solid wastes, agricultural residues, and biomass into one million cubic feet of SNG per day.[155]

5. The Great Plains Gasification Associates project, designed to produce an average of 125,000 Mcf of gas per day from 14,000 tons of lignite per day (using the Lurgi process), with the plant to be located in North Dakota.[156]

Most of these projects, in the late 1970s and early 1980s, confronted a number of difficulties, including a natural gas surplus, lower oil prices, declining energy demand, rising construction costs, high interest rates, and regulatory problems. Thus, the Algonquin plant failed to produce at its designated maximum capacity and, in line with the commission's original opinion, the company was forced "to absorb substantial excess demand costs."[157] "Project SNG-Biomass," upon reevaluation by the sponsor in May, 1979, was phased out and integrated with a similar program being conducted by the Gas Research Institute (GRI).[158] The Great Plains Gasification Associates project received a setback when the FERC's decision to permit the costs of the project to be charged to the ratepayers of the five sponsoring pipelines was reversed on appeal.[159] But after further negotiations,[160] and after the $2.1 billion project received a Department of Energy loan guarantee, construction began in the fall of 1981 and initial operation began in 1985.[161] And, finally, the Synthetic Fuels Corporation proved to be less than enthusiastic about granting subsidies for synfuel projects.[162]

Third, planning and construction of the first segments of the Alaskan Natural Gas Transportation System (ANGTS) began, in order to bring natural gas from Prudhoe Bay to the lower forty-eight states and to assist Canada in developing its northern gas reserves. After years of negotiation, the Alcan route was finally selected by the Canadian National Energy Board and by the President in 1977, and approved by Congress later in the same year.[163] As the project evolved, two segments of the ANGTS would be "prebuilt" in the lower forty-eight states before the Alaskan segment. Construction of the Western leg (sponsored by Pacific Gas Transmission Company) was completed in 1981; construction of the Eastern leg (sponsored by Northern Border Pipeline Company) was completed in 1982. Canada has approved the sale and export of gas produced in Alberta for a number of years prior to the time the Alaskan segment of the ANGTS is completed.

The Alaskan segment (Northern leg), however, has confronted serious financial difficulties. The estimated cost of the segment skyrocketed from $3.3 billion to $27 billion. (The total cost of the entire 4,800-mile ANGTS escalated from $10 billion in 1975 to $43 billion in 1982, which would have resulted in a price for Alaska gas of approximately $15 per Mcf, if deliveries had begun in the mid-1980s.) As originally approved, the Alaskan oil producers were excluded from ownership in the ANGTS, except that they could provide guarantees for the project. Congress granted a waiver in 1981, thereby allowing producers to purchase an interest in the pipeline under the supervision of the Department of Justice. The eleven pipeline sponsors subsequently decided to allow three producers — Exxon, Atlantic Richfield, and Standard Oil (Ohio) — to assume a 30 percent ownership of the project.[164] To date, that waiver, plus another to permit higher Alaskan gas prices to domestic consumers,[165] have failed to get construction of the Alaskan segment under way. That event may require huge loan guarantees from the federal government and/or from the state of Alaska.[166]

Incremental and Nonconventional Sources of Gas

There exists a significant potential resource of gas from incremental and nonconventional sources. The former refers to gas from tight formations (*i.e.*, from tight sands and Devonian shales); the latter to gas from renewable sources (*i.e.*, biomass and urban waste) or nonrenewable sources (*i.e.*, geopressured zones). The FERC took steps in 1980 to encourage supplies from incremental sources by setting the maximum price for tight formation gas at 200 percent of the Section 103 new, onshore production ceiling price under the NGPA and by changing the Devonian Shale definition to permit gas produced in sandstone or silt stringers to qualify as Section 107 gas under the NGPA.[167] Further, as noted earlier, manufactured synthetic gas was held by the commission to be nonjurisdictional until mixed with natural gas.

Production from tight formations "is estimated to be as much as 1.4 Tcf, accounting for about 9% of total lower-48 natural gas production."[168] Gas from nonconventional sources "will be produced as new technologies are developed, existing technologies are refined, and the economics for natural gas supply change."[169]

The Outlook

Estimates of future domestic energy demand vary widely, depending upon such factors as conservation efforts, energy mix, and growth in the economy. A 1987 study by the American Gas Association reached two conclusions with respect to the gas industry's future. First, there would be sufficient gas energy to supply between 20 and 25 percent of the nation's total energy requirements in 2010. Second, total gas production in the year 2010 is estimated to be in the range of 18.9 to 28.2 Tcf (see Table 14-10).[170]

An Industry in Transition: The Need for Flexibility

A review of public policy toward natural gas production, over several

TABLE 14-10

Estimated Gas Supply, Year 2010

(TCF)	Actual 1986	Year 2010		
		Low Price Scenario[a]	High Price Scenario[b]	OPEC Dominance Scenario[c]
Lower-48				
Conventional	15.7	11.5	14.0	16.0
Incremental[d]	—	3.325	4.6	7.5
Imports				
Canada	0.7	1.7	2.5	2.5
Mexico	—	1.2	0.6	—
LNG	f	0.4	0.7	0.7
Alaskan Gas (pipeline) ..	—	0.7	1.2	1.2
Other[e]	f	0.035	0.195	0.315
Total Supply	16.5	18.860	23.795	28.215

[a]Oil at $29/bbl; gas at $4.75/MMBtu (in 1987 dollars).
[b]Oil at $40/bbl; gas at $6.20/MMBtu (in 1987 dollars).
[c]Oil at $60/bbl; gas at $9.30/MMBtu (in 1987 dollars).
[d]Includes gas from tight formations, coal seams, and co-production.
[e]Includes synthetics and nonconventional.
[f]Less than 100 Bcf.

Source: *The Gas Energy Supply Outlook: 1987-2010* (Arlington, Va.: American Gas Association, 1987).

decades, suggests "that regulation by commission is at best a clumsy tool for achieving economic goals."[171] Between the 1954 *Phillips* decision and the enactment in 1978 of the Natural Gas Policy Act, the FPC/FERC sought to develop a method for regulating the wellhead price of natural gas (a task which the commission, it must be emphasized, did not seek[172]). Each method — the attempt to regulate producers' rates on an individual company "cost of service" basis between 1954 and 1960; the "area-rate" approach between 1960 and 1971; the "national rate" method between 1971 and 1977; and the "rule making," "optional procedure," "emergency," and "limited-term" certificates, and other methods of providing higher rates on a selected basis between 1970 and 1978 — proved to be "cumbersome and time-consuming" and, of even greater importance, "the resulting price ceilings were far from the competitive level."[173]

As a result, producer/pipeline and pipeline/local distribution company contract terms were negotiated "in an unrealistic regulatory environment" and often did not reflect "market reality."[174] The resulting contracts, moreover, were too inflexible to permit the industry to adjust to rapidly changing market conditions. The ultimate scenarios are all too familiar: (*1*) a natural gas reserve shortage that developed in the 1960s, which led to a production shortage in the early 1970s and to curtailments and (*2*) a natural gas surplus that developed in the late 1970s, which resulted in supplies that either could not be sold at existing prices or could not be transported at lower prices.

The latter development, in particular, prompted the FERC to take the initiative in restructuring natural gas regulation. But the ultimate success of "a new regulatory era predicated on extensive competition"[175] depends upon a number of other changes in traditional regulatory practices. Pipeline rates must be structured so that the transportation and sales rates "will stimulate the maximum efficient use of the pipelines."[176] Renegotiated and future contracts, at both the wellhead and city-gate ends of the natural gas transportation network, must recognize that long-term obligations to serve "are incompatible with present market realities."[177] Retail rate structures of local distribution companies must reflect the fact that "[t]he end-use natural gas market is now a short-term market characterized by price and volume variability."[178] Moreover, many of the necessary changes involve the state commissions, to whom much of the responsibility for future gas supply and prices has been shifted. Argues Hall:

> . . . In the past, PUCs [public utility commissions] generally deferred to the FERC regulation with respect to prices of gas purchased by LDCs. Deregulation of wellhead prices, changes in pipeline regulations, and the increased mix of LDC supply options have changed this. PUCs must confront such issues as whether LDCs are assuming an inappropriate amount of risk or are being sufficiently aggressive in seeking bargains. This new regulatory challenge has serious risks. If PUC oversight becomes "heads-you-lose/tails-you-also-lose," or "Monday-morning quarterbacking," the ability of LDCs to use competition to benefit consumers will be deterred. At worst, there could be counterproductive conflict between federal and state officials over regulation of gas prices.[179]

And in undertaking these changes, the regulatory commissions must be ever mindful of their responsibilities to captive ("core") customers.[180]

There is a related issue. The 1978 national energy legislation turned out to be only a step — although an important one — in the development of a truly national energy policy. The continued search for, and development of, a national policy is a worthwhile effort.[181]

Notes

*Justice Brandeis, dissenting opinion in *Pennsylvania v. West Virginia*, 262 U.S. 553, 621 (1923).

[1]"'Natural gas' is a simple hydrocarbon that is gaseous when surfaced from an underground reservoir. This hydrocarbon is composed of 85 to 95 percent methane, and can be processed to provide 1,000 Btu per cubic foot of energy content, usually at a pressure of 14.65 pounds pressure per square inch. It is removed from reservoirs or 'traps' that are porous, permeable rock formations in a surrounding seal of impermeable rock and water. The permeable rock may be sand, sandstone, limestone, dolomite, or chalk and may be found from 1,000 to 16,000 feet below surface. The reservoirs may contain not only gas of the requisite quality, but also crude oil . . . and 'liquid petroleum gas'. . . . Typically a number of traps occur close together — side by side or one above the other — so that they form a 'field'." Paul W. MacAvoy, *Price Formation in Natural Gas Fields: A Study of Competition, Monopsony, and Regulation* (New Haven: Yale University Press, 1962), pp. 10-11.

[2]*Wisconsin v. Federal Power Comm.*, 373 U.S. 294, 310 (1963).

[3]There are four basic sources of information on the gas industry. (*1*) Federal Trade Commission, *Final Report*, S. Doc. No. 92, 70th Cong., 1st sess. (1936). This study was ordered by Congress in 1928 and involved an investigation of the entire structure of the gas industry. (*2*) FPC Docket No. G-580 (Natural Gas Investigation). Two reports were issued in 1948: one by Commissioners Smith and Wimberly, and the other by Commissioners Olds and Draper. (*3*) Federal Power Commission, *Natural Gas Survey* (Washington, D.C.: U.S. Government Printing Office, 1975), comprising five volumes: Volume I contains the FPC's recommendations; Volume II the Supply Task Force Reports; Volume III the Transmission Task Force Reports; Volume IV the Distribution Task Force Reports; and Volume V the Special Reports. (*4*) American Gas Association (ed.), *Regulation of the Gas Industry* (New York: Matthew Bender & Co., Inc., 1987 Supplement and Revision), consisting of four volumes.

[4]C. Woody Thompson and Wendell R. Smith, *Public Utility Economics* (New York: McGraw-Hill Book Co., Inc., 1941), p. 16.

[5]Martin G. Glaeser, *Public Utilities in American Capitalism* (New York: The Macmillan Co., 1957), p. 29, n. 4.

[6]Steven J. Dorner, "Beginnings of the Gas Industry," in *Regulation of the Gas Industry, op. cit.*, Vol. 1, p. 1-7.

[7]*Ibid.*

[8]Oscar E. Norman, *The Romance of the Gas Industry* (Chicago: A. C. McClurg & Co., 1922), p. 44.

[9]Glaeser, *op. cit.*, p. 29.

[10]The project was proposed by James Crutchett and financed by Congress with an appropriation of $17,500. "Mr. Crutchett then supervised the construction of a gas plant and gas holder on the lower (northwest) terrace of the Capitol grounds. He introduced gas into the building and placed on its wooden dome an eighty-foot mast of white pine. On the mast was a lantern, six feet in diameter, made of iron and copper, beautifully gilded and enclosed with glass. Gas tubes ran through the heavy mast and were connected with the main gas tubes from the gas holder at the bottom of the terrace. This huge gas lantern lighted the Capitol grounds and part of the surrounding area, and the light was seen many miles down the Potomac." Dorner, *op. cit.*, p. 1-9.

[11]Thompson and Smith, *op. cit.,* p. 16. "During this period, gas had only one use, lighting. In the larger cities, streets and the homes of the more well-to-do were lighted with gas. Because of high rates, its use was not extensive, and at best gas was poor in quality and inadequate as an illuminant." *Ibid.* Glaeser places the price of gas at between $6.00 and $15.00 per thousand cubic feet (Mcf). Glaeser, *op. cit.,* p. 30.

[12]Dorner, *op. cit.,* p. 1-10 (citations omitted).

[13]Thompson and Smith, *op. cit.,* p. 17.

[14]Dorner, *op. cit.,* p. 1-11.

[15]Thompson and Smith, *op. cit.*

[16]*Ibid.,* p. 18. The Fredonia Gas Light and Waterworks Company was organized in 1865 "to distribute gas to domestic users." *Ibid.,* p. 19.

[17]H. C. Zwetsch, *A Brief History of the Natural Gas Industry* (New York: Zwetsch, Heinzelmann & Co., 1927), pp. 5-7.

[18]Dorner, *op. cit.,* p. 1-12. "The early pipes were made of selected pine logs, turned and bored to the proper inside and outside dimensions. . . . The first successful long-distance cast-iron line, a 2-inch line completed in 1872, was built from a well to near-by Titusville, Pennsylvania, a distance of 5 miles." Thompson and Smith, *op. cit.,* p. 19.

[19]The other half went into field use, carbon-black production, petroleum refining, and electricity production. *Ibid.,* p. 20.

[20]Dorner, *op. cit.,* p. 1-13. See Dean Hale (ed.), *Diary of an Industry* (Dallas: Petroleum Engineering Publishing Co., 1959).

[21]Estimated proved reserves increased in 1970, due to the inclusion of Prudhoe Bay reserves in Alaska, although no pipeline facilities existed to transport those reserves out of the state.

[22]See Chapter 12, pp. 520-22.

[23]See Chapter 11, pp. 456-67.

[24]"In 1978 wellhead gas sold to interstate pipelines was about $0.80 per thousand cubic feet (Mcf), well below the $1.39 per Mcf paid in intrastate markets. The resulting shortages increased pressure on Congress to change the fundamental nature of natural gas market regulation. In response, in 1978 Congress passed the NGPA." John C. Sawhill, "The Outlook for Domestic Supply and Demand," in Joseph P. Kalt and Frank C. Schuller (eds.), *Drawing the Line on Natural Gas Regulation: The Harvard Study on the Future of Natural Gas* (New York: Quorum Books, 1987), p. 16 (footnote omitted).

[25]Richard M. Merriman and Peyton G. Bowman, III, "The Early 1980's — The Promises and Developments of NGPA," in *Regulation of the Gas Industry, op. cit.,* Vol. 1, p. 5A-3.

[26]From the editors' "Introduction: Natural Gas Policy in Turmoil," in Kalt and Schuller, *op. cit.,* p. 5.

[27]"In contrast to SMPs, whose stated purpose is to retain the pipeline's current market, off-system sales involve sales on the systems of other pipelines. Such sales are almost always opposed as market raiding. The commission, however, does not prohibit such sales unless the objecting pipeline can show that the off-system sale actually displaces a sale it is currently making." Richard M. Merriman and Peyton G. Bowman, III, "The Mid 1980s Grappling with the Natural Gas Surplus," in *Regulation of the Gas Industry, op. cit.,* Vol. 1, p. 5B-7.

[28]See Chapter 11, p. 472.

[29]See *ibid.*, pp. 467-69.

[30]*Ibid.*, pp. 455-56.

[31]Richard A. Rosan and David J. Muchow, "Introduction," in *Regulation of the Gas Industry, op. cit.*, Vol. 1, p. Int.-4.

[32]*Gas Facts, 1986 Data* (Arlington, Va.: American Gas Association, 1987), p. 141.

[33]"The situation in New York City alone, prior to the major gas company consolidations, threatened municipal chaos." Francis X. Welch, "The Odyssey of Gas — A Record of Industrial Courage," 23 *Public Utilities Fortnightly* 501, 502 (October 12, 1939).

[34]*Ohio Oil Co. v. Indiana,* 177 U.S. 190 (1900); *Champlin Refining Co. v. Corporation Comm.,* 286 U.S. 210 (1932); *Thompson v. Consolidated Gas Utilities Corp.,* 300 U.S. 55 (1937); *Henderson Co. v. Thompson,* 300 U.S. 258 (1937).

State conservation laws to prevent some of the most serious forms of waste were enacted before the turn of the century. An 1891 Indiana law, for example, prevented the venting or flaring of natural gas. Following the large oil and gas discoveries in the 1925 to 1931 period, during which the production of both resources outran market demand and transportation facilities, the governors of the major oil- and gas-producing states adopted an Interstate Compact to Conserve Oil and Gas, submitted it for ratification to the legislatures of their states, and then submitted it to Congress for approval. The Compact received Congressional approval in 1935; it has been renewed without amendment ever since. The thirty-three member states agree to enact and continue laws "to conserve oil and gas by the prevention of physical waste thereof, from any cause." The Compact Commission, whose members are the governors of the signatory states, has no power to compel uniform state policies; it can only advise and recommend.

Diversity rather than uniformity is the rule. Present state laws cover such matters as the prevention of physical waste, overproduction, discrimination, and the use of gas for certain purposes (such as the manufacture of carbon black). See *A Study of Conservation of Oil and Gas in the United States, 1964* (Oklahoma City: Interstate Oil Compact Commission, 1964); *General Rules and Regulations for the Conservation of Oil and Gas* (Oklahoma City: Interstate Oil Compact Commission, 1969).

[35]*West v. Kansas Nat. Gas Co.,* 221 U.S. 229 (1911).

[36]*Pub. Utilities Comm. v. Landon,* 249 U.S. 236 (1918); *Missouri v. Kansas Nat. Gas Co.,* 265 U.S. 298 (1924).

[37]Interstate gas pipelines, for example, were specifically excluded, by amendment, from the jurisdiction of the Interstate Commerce Commission in 1906 [34 Stat. 584 (1906)] and were not subject to the Public Utility Holding Company Act of 1935.

[38]52 Stat. 821 (1938). On the legislative history of the act, see Dozier A. DeVane, "Highlights of Legislative History of the Federal Power Act of 1935 and the Natural Gas Act of 1938," 14 *George Washington Law Review* 30 (1945); William J. Flittie and James L. Armour, "The Natural Gas Act Experience — A Study in Regulatory Aggression and Congressional Failure to Control the Legislative Process," 19 *Southwestern Law Journal* 448, 448-54 (1965).

[39]56 Stat. 83 (1942). While the commission lacked authority to control extensions, such lines became jurisdictional upon completion.

[40]*Federal Power Comm. v. East Ohio Gas Co.,* 338 U.S. 464 (1950). Stated Justice Jackson in his dissenting opinion: "I can well understand the zeal of the Federal Power Commission to expand its control over the natural gas industry. It sprawls over

many states. . . . Its regulation cannot be uniform if the Federal Power Commission controls only a middle segment, with production on one end and distribution on the other committed to the control of different states. . . . This obviously subdivides regulation of what has to operate as a unitary enterprise. . . ." *Ibid.*, p. 488.

In response, Congress passed the Hinshaw amendment in 1954 (68 Stat. 36) which exempted from federal jurisdiction any person engaged in the transportation or sale for resale in interstate commerce of natural gas received within or at the boundary of a state "if all the natural gas so received is ultimately consumed within such state" and if the rates, service, and facilities of the person concerned are "subject to regulation by a state commission." The commission must grant an exemption under the amendment, although certification by a state commission that it was exercising jurisdiction was held to be conclusive evidence of the state's regulatory power.

[41]*Phillips Petroleum Co. v. Wisconsin*, 347 U.S. 672 (1954).

[42]See Chapter 11, pp. 456-67.

[43]Flittie and Armour, *op. cit.*, p. 471 (citation omitted). The Supreme Court, for example, held that minimum price orders of Oklahoma and Kansas were superseded by the National Gas Act. [*Nat. Gas Pipeline Co. v. Corp. Comm. of Okla.*, 272 P. 2d 425 (Okla. 1954), *rev'd*, 349 U.S. 44 (1954); *Cities Service Gas Co. v. State Corp. Comm. of Kan.*, 304 P. 2d 528 (Kan. 1956), *rev'd*, 355 U.S. 391 (1958)], while the commission's jurisdiction over all producers and types of sales was generally upheld [see, *e.g.*, *Saturn Oil & Gas Co. v. Federal Power Comm.*, 250 F. 2d 61 (10th Cir. 1957), *cert. denied*, 355 U.S. 956 (1958); *Re Lo-Vaca Gathering Co.*, 26 FPC 606 (1961), *rev'd*, 323 F. 2d 190 (5th Cir. 1963), *rev'd sub nom. California v. Lo-Vaca Gathering Co.*, 379 U.S. 366 (1965); *Re Texas Eastern Trans. Corp.*, 29 FPC 249 (1963), *rev'd sub nom. Marr v. Federal Power Comm.*, 336 F. 2d 320 (5th Cir. 1964), *rev'd sub nom. United Gas Imp. Co. v. Continental Oil Co.*, 381 U.S. 392 (1965); *Southland Royalty Co. v. Federal Power Comm.*, 543 F. 2d 1134 (5th Cir. 1976), *rev'd sub nom. California v. Southland Royalty Co.*, 436 U.S. 519 (1978)]. See Willard W. Gatchell, "Independent Producers under the Natural Gas Act," 26 *George Washington Law Review* 373 (1958); A. J. G. Priest, "Supreme Court Decisions on Gas Rate Cases," 82 *Public Utilities Fortnightly* 29 (October 10, 1968).

[44]Order No. 402, 43 FPC 707 (1970). The exemption was expanded to include LNG in 1975, Order No. 402-B, 6 FPS 5-933 (FPC, 1975).

[45]Order No. 418, 44 FPC 1574 (1970).

[46]Order No. 431, 45 FPC 570 (1971); Order No. 431-A, 48 FPC 193 (1972). The commission's 1973 order, extending the sixty-day period to 180 days (Order No. 491, 50 FPC 742), was set aside in 1975 [*Consumer Fed'n of Am. v. Federal Power Comm.*, 515 F. 2d 347 (D.C. Cir. 1975), *cert. denied*, 423 U.S. 906 (1975)].

[47]See *Re Northern Michigan Exploration Co.*, 50 FPC 1143 (1973); *Re Michigan Gas Storage Co.*, 11 FPS 5-270 (FPC, 1977).

[48]Order No. 533, 54 FPC 861 (1975); Order No. 533-A, 54 FPC 2058 (1975). The policy was upheld in *Am. Pub. Gas Ass'n v. Federal Energy Regulatory Comm.*, 587 F. 2d 1089 (D.C. Cir. 1978).

[49]In 1980, for example, 17,132 new gas wells were completed, a 109.7 percent increase over the 8,169 gas wells completed in 1975. *Gas Facts, 1986 Data, op. cit.*, p. 40.

[50]Intrastate regulation was upheld in *Oklahoma v. Federal Energy Regulatory Comm.*, 494 F. Supp. 636 (W.D. Okla. 1980), *aff'd*, 661 F. 2d 832 (10th Cir. 1981), *cert. denied sub nom. Texas v. Federal Energy Regulatory Comm.*, 102 S. Ct. 2902 (1982). While states

may regulate intrastate gas prices [see, *e.g.*, *Energy Reserves Group v. Kansas Power & Light Co.*, 630 F. 2d 1142 (Kan. S. Ct. 1981), *aff'd*, 459 U.S. 400 (1983)], state regulation may not interfere with the deregulation of the wellhead price of gas under the NGPA [see *Transcontinental Gas Pipe Line Corp. v. Mississippi State Oil & Gas Board*, 106 S. Ct. 709 (1986)].

The basic purpose of the provision in the NGPA was to eliminate the competitive advantage enjoyed (during the 1970s) by the intrastate market and, thereby, to alleviate the imbalances in supply between the intra- and interstate markets. (One exception: All reserves located in Offshore Federal Domain are committed by law to the interstate market.) There is evidence, however, that interstate purchasers had a slight advantage due to the fact that they had larger quantities of lower-priced controlled gas and could outbid intrastate purchasers for new gas supplies on a rolled-in pricing basis. See Energy Information Administration, *Intrastate and Interstate Supply Markets Under the Natural Gas Policy Act* (Washington, D.C.: U.S. Government Printing Office, 1981) and *An Analysis of Post-NGPA Interstate Pipeline Wellhead Purchases* (Washington, D.C.: U.S. Government Printing Office, 1982).

[51]Richard M. Merriman and Peyton G. Bowman, III, "The 1970's — A Period of Momentous Change," in *Regulation of the Gas Industry, op. cit.*, Vol. 1, pp. 5-69 — 5-70.

[52]Under the Department of Energy Organization Act of 1977, some of the FPC's responsibilities were transferred to the Secretary of Energy who, in turn, delegated those responsibilities to the ERA, an agency within the DOE. Among those responsibilities are authority over exports and imports of natural gas (and electric energy), and the setting of curtailment priorities (but not their implementation).

[53]Repeal of Powerplant and Industrial Fuel Use Act Restrictions (Pub. Law 100-42). See "Restrictive FUA Provisions Repealed," 119 *Public Utilities Fortnightly* 37 (June 25, 1987). Earlier changes were made in the act under the Omnibus Budget Reconciliation Act of 1981 (Pub. Law 97-35), including the removal (*a*) of the DOE's authority to order conversion against the owner's will and (*b*) of the prohibition on gas use after 1990.

[54]See Chapter 12, pp. 524-29.

[55]See *ibid.*, pp. 513-15.

[56]See Chapter 7, pp. 251-53.

[57]See Chapter 12, pp. 520-22.

[58]See Chapter 11, p. 474. "The study's proposals were not intended to take effect until well into the 1980's." Merriman and Bowman, *op. cit.*, p. 5-69. Other required reports also have been submitted. See, *e.g.*, U.S. Department of Energy, *Increasing Competition in the Natural Gas Market: Second Report Required by Section 123 of the Natural Gas Policy Act of 1978* (Washington, D.C.: U.S. Government Printing Office, 1985) (hereinafter referred to as *Second Report*).

[59]The National Appliance Energy Conservation Act of 1987 (Pub. Law 100-12). But see Doug Bandow, "Federal Appliance Standards: Inefficient at Best," *The Wall Street Journal*, February 19, 1987, p. 28.

[60]By the end of 1980, "not less than twenty-five appellate court proceedings were pending in cases involving Title I of the NGPA alone." Carroll L. Gilliam, "Wellhead Regulation Under the Natural Gas Act and the Natural Gas Policy Act," in *Regulation of the Gas Industry, op. cit.*, Vol. 1, p. 20-106. Most of the commission's rules implementing Titles I and V of the NGPA were affirmed in *Ecee, Inc. v. Federal Energy Regulatory Comm.*, 645 F. 2d 339 (5th Cir. 1981) and *Pennzoil Co. v. Federal Energy*

Regulatory Comm., 645 F. 2d 360 (5th Cir. 1981), *cert. denied*, 454 U.S. 1142 (1982). The significant exceptions were the rules implementing Sections 105 and 110. The latter section has been particularly troublesome, for it provides that the maximum lawful prices proscribed by Sections 102 through 109 *may be* exceeded to permit recovery of state severance taxes and "production-related" costs (*i.e.*, dehydration, compression, gathering, processing, and treating), thereby shifting such costs from producers to buyers. The commission's rule with respect to state severance taxes was issued in 1980 [Order No. 108] and modified in 1983 [Order No. 108-A]. The commission's interim rates and rules with respect to production-related costs were issued in 1980 [Opinion No. 90; Order No. 94], but were remanded for expeditious action on various applications for rehearing [*Texas Eastern Trans. Corp. v. Federal Energy Regulatory Comm.*, No. 80-1928 (5th Cir. 1981)]. In response to the remand, Order Nos. 94-A and 94-B were issued in 1983. [At the time the new rules were announced, nearly 3,000 cases were being held on the FERC's docket pending a decision on the issue. *NARUC Bulletin* No. 5-1983, January 31, 1983, p. 6.] The procedures used in Order No. 94-A were affirmed [*Texas Eastern Trans. Corp. v. Federal Energy Regulatory Comm.*, 769 F. 2d 1053 (5th Cir. 1985)], but both orders were vacated and remanded in 1987 [*Columbia Gas Trans. Corp. v. Federal Energy Regulatory Comm.*, No. 85-1846 (D.C. Cir. 1987) (holding that direct billing by pipelines for production-related costs incurred in past periods constitutes retroactive ratemaking)].

[61]Order Nos. 93 (FERC, 1980) and 93-A (FERC, 1981), *vacated sub nom. Interstate Nat. Gas Ass'n of America v. Federal Energy Regulatory Comm.*, 716 F. 2d 1 (D.C. Cir. 1983), *cert. denied*, 465 U.S. 1108 (1984). Subsequently, the commission implemented the water-saturated standard and ordered refunds for past overcharges. Order Nos. 399 (FERC, 1984) and 399-A (FERC, 1984).

[62]Order Nos. 58 (FERC, 1979) and 98 (FERC, 1980), *rev'd sub nom. Mid Louisiana Gas Co. v. Federal Energy Regulatory Comm.*, 664 F. 2d 530 (5th Cir. 1981), *vacated and remanded sub nom. N.Y. Pub. Service Comm. v. Mid Louisiana Gas Co.*, 103 S. Ct. 3024, 53 PUR4th 175 (1983). On the commission's subsequent regulations, see 49 *Fed. Reg.* 33,849 (1984).

[63]*Pennzoil Co. v. Federal Energy Regulatory Comm., op. cit.*

[64]*True Oil Co. v. Federal Energy Regulatory Comm.*, 663 F. 2d 75 (10th Cir. 1981).

[65]*Tenneco Exploration, Ltd. v. Federal Energy Regulatory Comm.*, 649 F. 2d. 376 (5th Cir. 1981).

[66]*Ecee, Inc. v. Federal Energy Regulatory Comm., op. cit.*, p. 355.

[67]*Re Deregulation and Other Pricing Changes Under the NGPA*, 64 PUR4th 197, 204-09 (FERC, 1984), *rev'd sub nom. Martin Exploration Management Co. v. Federal Energy Regulatory Comm.*, 813 F. 2d 1059 (10th Cir. 1987), *cert. granted*, 56 U.S.L.W. 3378 (1987).

[68]Kalt and Schuller, *op. cit.*, p. 1.

[69]For a summary of the market power theory, see *Natural Gas Policy Issues and Options: A Staff Analysis* (Senate, Committee on Interior and Insular Affairs, 93rd Cong., 1st sess.) (Washington, D.C.: U.S. Government Printing Office, 1973), pp. 10-14.

[70]Stephen G. Breyer and Paul W. MacAvoy, *Energy Regulation by the Federal Power Commission* (Washington, D.C.: The Brookings Institution, 1974), pp. 59, 60.

[71]See, *e.g.*, Paul H. Douglas, "Federal Regulation of Independent Natural Gas

Producers is Essential," 65 *Public Utilities Fortnightly* 622 (1955) and "The Case for the Consumer of Natural Gas," 44 *Georgetown Law Journal* 566 (1956); Joseph C. Swidler, "The Public Interest in Effective Natural Gas Regulation," 74 *Public Utilities Fortnightly* 34 (October 8, 1964); Statements of David A. Schwartz and John W. Wilson in *Hearings on the Natural Gas Industry* (Senate, Antitrust and Monopoly Subcommittee, 93rd Cong., 2d sess.) (Washington, D.C.: U.S. Government Printing Office, 1974). Dirlam, in supporting wellhead regulation, argued that "it is extremely doubtful whether any practically conceivable change in the field price of gas could result in any faintly predictable corresponding change in its long-run supply." Joel B. Dirlam, "Natural Gas: Cost, Conservation, and Pricing," 48 *American Economic Review* 491, 494 (1958).

[72]*Southern Louisiana Area Rate Cases*, 428 F. 2d 407, 416 (5th Cir., 1970).

[73]Federal Power Commission, *Sales by Producers of Natural Gas to Interstate Pipeline Companies, 1961* (Washington, D.C.: U.S. Government Printing Office, 1962).

[74]MacAvoy, *op. cit.*, p. 215; *In re Permian Basin Area Rate Cases*, 390 U.S. 747, 793, n. 62 (1968).

[75]Breyer and MacAvoy, *op. cit.*, p. 61.

[76]Martin L. Lindahl, "Federal Regulation of Natural Gas Producers and Gatherers," 46 *American Economic Review* 532, 541 (1956).

[77]James W. McKie, *The Regulation of Natural Gas* (Washington, D.C.: American Enterprise Association, Inc., 1957), pp. 32-33.

[78]*Ibid.*, p. 31.

[79]MacAvoy, *op. cit.*, pp. 243-45.

[80]McKie, *op. cit.*, p. 32.

[81]Breyer and MacAvoy, *op. cit.*, p. 63.

[82]MacAvoy, *op. cit.*, p. 265. Similar conclusions are reached by M. A. Adelman, *The Supply and Price of Natural Gas* (Oxford: B.H. Blackwell Ltd., 1962); L. Cookenboo, Jr., *Competition in the Field Market for Natural Gas* (Houston: Rice Institution, 1958); Lindahl, *op. cit.*; McKie, *op. cit.* Neuner concludes that "if field price regulation is to be avoided, it is essential that contractually imposed barriers to market adjustment be removed." Edward J. Neuner, *The Natural Gas Industry: Monopoly and Competition in Field Markets* (Norman: University of Oklahoma Press, 1960), p. 290. Connole suggested that the FPC's regulatory authority over gas producers be suspended for a period of years "while the Congress and the public judged the performance of the industry operating without any price regulation." William R. Connole, "Can Producer Regulation be Temporarily Suspended?," 83 *Public Utilities Fortnightly* 13 (January 30, 1969).

[83]Breyer and MacAvoy, *op. cit.*, p. 64.

[84]William G. Shepherd, *Public Policies Toward Business* (7th ed.; Homewood, Ill.: Richard D. Irwin, Inc., 1985), p. 415.

[85]Breyer and MacAvoy, *op. cit.*, p. 65. The commission has tackled the issue of "inferior" and "superior" uses, especially in the curtailment proceedings of the 1970s. Those lengthy cases clearly indicated that the task was immense: an inferior use to one person was a superior use to another, while the classification of such uses changed over time. Using natural gas as a boiler fuel, for instance, may seem like an inferior use when alternative resources are compared, but not when environmental considerations are dominant.

[86]See Chapter 11, pp. 462-65.

[87]Sawhill, *op. cit.*, p. 27. While the NGPA made no provision for decontrolling

"old" interstate gas, it allowed for escalation to reflect general price inflation and authorized the FERC to raise the former ceiling prices to higher "just and reasonable" levels. The FERC exercised this authority in 1986. Order No. 451 (FERC, 1986), *review pending sub nom. Mobil Oil Corp. v. Federal Energy Regulatory Comm.*, No. 86-4940 (5th Cir., filed December 15, 1986).

[88]The Department of Energy estimated that decontrol would add 27 to 48 Tcf to reserves. See *Second Report, op. cit.* For a slightly lower estimate (23 to 30 Tcf), see Office of Technology Assessment, *U.S. Natural Gas Availability* (Washington, D.C.: U.S. Government Printing Office, 1985).

[89]See Sawhill, *op. cit.*

[90]Prior to the 1970s, the FPC generally required that a twenty-year supply be committed to a new pipeline project and that the field be able to deliver enough gas to support systemwide sales for twelve years. [See, *e.g., Re Midwestern Gas Trans. Co.*, 21 FPC 653, 656 (1959).] The commission began to change its requirements in the 1970s, by allowing contingent agreements (*i.e.*, an agreement giving a pipeline an exclusive option to purchase undiscovered reserves in return for advance payments) or potential agreements (*i.e.*, an agreement still in the negotiation stage involving reserves which are in preliminary exploration). [See, *e.g., Re High Island Offshore System*, Docket No. CP75-104 (FPC, 1976); *Re Cities Service Gas Co.*, Docket No. CP 76-500 (FPC, 1978).]

[91]"Since 1970, when substantially all interstate contracts were for 20-year terms, the trend has been declining. By 1975, nearly half of the new contracts for offshore supplies were for terms of 10 years or less, whereas 25 percent contained terms of five years or less. For the total United States, interstate contracts with less than a 20-year term increased from 8 percent in 1971 to 45 percent in 1974 and 50 percent in 1975, with more than 30 percent of the 1975 contracts having a term of five years or less. . . ." *Re Getty Oil Co.*, Opinion No. 767 (FPC, 1976).

[92]Some contracts also contain a tax reimbursement clause which provides that the seller will be reimbursed for increases in production or severance taxes after a specified date.

[93]"If at any time during the term of this Agreement, Buyer is paying a price for gas produced from a new onshore production well as determined and described in the NGPA in the county wherein the dedicated gas is situated, which price is higher than the current price under this Agreement, exclusive of any tax and facilities reimbursement, then the price to be paid for all gas delivered under this Agreement shall be increased to the level of such higher price effective of the date the next regular price escalation is to occur." "Pipeline Gas Supplies," in *Regulation of the Gas Industry, op. cit.*, Vol. 1, pp. 12-19 — 12-20.

[94]"If, during the term of this Contract the price at which Seller shall see any portion of the natural gas produced from the lands dedicated hereto is no longer subject to FERC jurisdiction, then the price payable hereunder for such deregulated gas shall be equal to the Alternate Fuel Cost (a defined term) effective on the first day of the month following the date of such deregulation." *Ibid.*, p. 12-24.

[95]*Report of the National Fuels and Energy Supply Group on an Assessment of Available Information on Energy in the United States* (Senate, 87th Cong., 2d sess.) (Washington, D.C.: U.S. Government Printing Office, 1962), p. 226.

[96]Energy Information Administration, *Natural Gas Pipeline/Producer Contracts; A Preliminary Analysis* (Washington, D.C.: U.S. Government Printing Office, 1982), p. 8. On post-NGPA contracts, see Energy Information Administration, *The Current State of*

the Natural Gas Market (Washington, D.C.: U.S. Government Printing Office, 1982), esp. pt. 5.

[97]McKie, *op. cit.*, p. 36.

[98]*Re Automatic Escalation and Favored Nation Clauses*, 25 FPC 379, 609 (1961), 27 FPC 339, 340 (1962). The commission was upheld in *Texaco, Inc., v. Federal Power Comm.*, 317 F. 2d 796 (10th Cir. 1963), *rev'd*, 377 U.S. 33 (1964). See also *Superior Oil Co. v. Federal Power Comm.*, 322 F. 2d 601 (9th Cir. 1963), *cert. denied*, 377 U.S. 922 (1964), *rehearing denied*, 377 U.S. 960 (1964). Congress has considered indefinite escalation clauses for many years. See, *e.g., Amendments to the Natural Gas Act* (Hearings before the Senate Committee on Interstate and Foreign Commerce, 84th Cong., 1st sess.) (Washington, D.C.: U.S. Government Printing Office, 1955).

[99]See, *e.g.,* Opinion Nos. 699, 51 FPC 2212 (1974) and 699-H, 52 FPC 1604 (1974).

[100]See, *e.g., Pennzoil Co. v. Federal Energy Regulatory Comm., op. cit.*

Since the FERC has taken the position that it will not decide contract issues in intrastate contracts [see Order No. 23, Docket No. RM79-22 (FERC, 1979); *Re Deregulation and Other Pricing Changes Under the NGPA, op. cit.,* p. 212], several cases involving intrastate contracts have been filed. In one, the Tenth Circuit Court of Appeals reversed a Wisconsin court ruling that indefinite clauses in intrastate contracts are unconscionable and void as against public policy. See *Kerr-McGee Corp. v. Northern Utils., Inc.,* 500 F. Supp. 624, 634 (D. Wyo, 1980), *rev'd,* 673 F. 2d 323 (10th Cir. 1982). See also *Energy Reserves Group, Inc. v. Kansas Power & Light Co., op. cit.*

[101]See *Natural Gas Pipeline/Producer Contracts, op. cit.,* pt. 4; Richard J. Pierce, Jr., "Natural Gas Regulation, Deregulation, and Contracts," 68 *Virginia Law Review* 63 (1982).

[102]"Pipeline Gas Supplies," in *Regulation of the Gas Industry, op. cit.,* p. 12-24.

[103]"The two forms of minimum take provision in current common use are the 'deliverability' and the 'reserve-based' take formula. The first is expressed as a percentage of the well's tested ability to produce within legal and physical limits. The latter is expressed as a rate of average daily quantity to provide recoverable reserves (*e.g.,* 1 MMcf per day per 7.3 Bcf of proved recoverable reserves). . . . Several other common contract obligations may also determine takes. The buyer is usually obligated to take gas ratably, in accordance with reserves and deliverability of available gas. Another obligation of the pipeline buyer is to take gas in sufficient volume to permit the seller to maintain his leases. A matter becoming increasingly important in highly competitive areas is an obligation of the buyer to protect his seller against drainage." *Ibid.,* pp. 12-30 — 12-30.8 (citation omitted).

[104]"'Makeup' gas may be 'quantities taken in excess of the daily contract quantity for any month or months within the agreed upon period after payment for the gas not taken is made, or a certain percentage of the volumes taken in each succeeding month during the agreed upon period, until the volume represented by the percentage equals the deficiency volume.'" *Ibid.* (citation omitted).

[105]*Natural Gas Pipeline/Producer Contracts, op. cit.,* p. 19.

[106]Prepayments under take or pay contracts are not permitted to be passed through purchased gas adjustment (PGA) clauses. Instead, they are treated, for ratemaking purposes, as a cost of service.

[107]Alternatively, "if there had been a change of price between the date the gas was paid for but not taken and the date of make-up, to provide that the price otherwise effective at the time of make-up could be applied to the make-up vol-

umes." Gilliam, *op. cit.*, p. 20-46. See *Re New Regulations on Gas Prepayments*, Docket No. R-199, Order No. 334 (FPC, 1967).

[108]*Re Limitations on Provisions in Natural Gas Rate Schedules Relating to Minimum Take Provisions*, 45 FPC 543, 544 (1971), terminating Notice of Proposed Rulemaking, Docket No. R-400 (FPC, 1970).

[109]Beginning in the late 1960s, the FPC permitted interstate pipelines to make advance payments to producers to finance exploration and development. "The usual form of advance payment agreement and gas contract contained provisions covering the option to purchase gas, price, rate of take, time of advance payments, supplemental advance, repayment, and releases." "Pipeline Gas Supplies," in *Regulation of the Gas Industry, op. cit.*, p. 12-30.11 (citation omitted). Initially, pipelines were granted rate base treatment of advance payments, but such advance payments were restricted under the NGPA. See, *e.g.*, *Tennessee Gas Pipeline Co. v. Federal Energy Regulatory Comm.*, 606 F. 2d 1094 (D.C. Cir. 1979), *cert. denied*, 445 U.S. 920 (1980); *Ashland Exploration Inc. v. Federal Energy Regulatory Comm.*, 631 F. 2d 817 (D.C. Cir. 1980).

[110]"Indeed, the anomaly of a natural gas market producing gas at $10.00 per Mcf while shutting in $1.50 gas has been more responsible than any other factor for the current upheaval in public policy." Kalt and Schuller, *op. cit.*, p. 5. On pipeline cutback practices, see U.S. Department of Energy, *Recent Market Activities of Major Interstate Pipeline Companies* (Washington, D.C.: U.S. Government Printing Office, 1984); *Re Columbia Gas Trans. Corp.*, 58 PUR4th 43 (FERC, 1984), on rehearing, 59 PUR4th 196 (FERC, 1984), *aff'd in part and rev'd in part sub nom. Office of Consumers' Counsel v. Federal Energy Regulatory Comm.*, 783 F. 2d 206 (D.C. Cir. 1986).

[111]*Inside F.E.R.C.*, December 20, 1982, pp. 1, 2. The commission may preclude an interstate pipeline from passing through costs paid to producers where it determines that payments arose out of "fraud or abuse" [Section 601(c)(2) of the NGPA] or where costs were not "prudently" incurred. In a 1984 decision, the commission found that Columbia Gas Transmission Corporation's gas acquisition practices were not abusive conduct warranting denial of passthrough, but that its high (85-90 percent) take-or-pay contracts resulted in prices that violated Section 5 of the Natural Gas Act. The commission urged the company "to take decisive action" with respect to existing contracts. The circuit court, on review, remanded the decision to the commission for a better remedy. *Re Columbia Gas Trans. Corp., op. cit.*

[112]*Re Regulatory Treatment of Payments Made in Lieu of Take-or-Pay Obligations*, 50 Fed. Reg. 16,076 (1985). [See also *Re Recovery of Take-or-Pay Buy-Out and Buy-Down Costs by Interstate Natural Gas Pipelines*, 38 FERC Par. 61,230 (1987).] It was to help reduce potential payments under restrictive take-or-pay contracts that the FERC permitted some pipelines to enter into off-system sales and to develop special marketing programs.

Unable to buy-out or renegotiate enough contracts, several pipelines abrogated some of their agreements, invoking *force majeure* (acts-of-God) provisions and claiming that the contracts they were breaking had become "commercially impracticable." "The value of broken contracts could amount to more than $7 billion by 1986." ["A Stunning Challenge to the Sanctity of Contracts," *Business Week*, August 22, 1983, p. 76.] Oneok Inc., for example, reports that it is facing nine producer damage suits, with a total liability of $324 million (excluding any punitive damages). The company's net worth is $323.6 million. ["Oneok Inc. Suggests It May Ask Protection of Bankruptcy Court," *The Wall Street Journal*, December 9, 1987, p. 16.] The courts have generally upheld the validity of take-or-pay clauses. See, *e.g.,* *Universal Resources Corp. v. Panhandle Eastern Pipe Line Co.,* CA 3-85-0723-R (N.D. Tex. 1986).

Congress has considered several proposed amendments to the NGPA, including various provisions with respect to contract renegotiation and take-or-pay clauses. One amendment, for example, would have dropped takes to 50 percent. *Oil & Gas Journal,* August 8, 1983, pp. 41-43.

[113]"Thus, if the demand charge is $1 and the commodity charge $3, the customer will switch to an alternative supply only when the alternative's total cost (transportation and gas) is under $3, even though (in a sense) gas at $3.50 would be a better bargain. (It is better only 'in a sense' because the customer gets a security of supply from its pipeline supplier that it does not get in the spot market." *Associated Gas Distributors v. Federal Energy Regulatory Comm.,* 824 F. 2d 981, 83 PUR4th 459, 493 (D.C. Cir. 1987), *cert. denied,* 56 U.S.L.W. 3715 (1988).

[114]"*CD Contracted Demand Service* is firm service of a specified maximum daily volume. Billing demand is contract demand. Minimum monthly bill equals the demand charge plus (commodity rate multiplied by 66 2/3% of the contract demand multiplied by number of days in the month). The 66 2/3% may be reduced dependant upon Seller's storage operations." Stephen H. Watts, II, "Distributor Gas Supply," in *Regulation of the Gas Industry, op. cit.,* Vol. 1, p. 17-54.

[115]Merriman and Bowman, *op. cit.,* p. 5A-28. Thus, in the summer of 1982, "Columbia Gas Transmission Corporation sent shock waves through the industry by declaring that because of the severely depressed nature of its markets, the *force majeure* clauses in its contracts excused it from its obligations to purchase gas at minimum bill levels from its six interstate pipeline suppliers. These suppliers provided approximately one-third of Columbia's entire system supply." *Ibid.,* p. 5A-25. See also *Colorado Interstate Gas Co. v. Federal Energy Regulatory Comm.,* 791 F. 2d 803 (10th Cir. 1986), *cert. denied,* 55 U.S.L.W. 3474 (1987) (upholding an FERC order granting retroactive relief from Colorado Interstate Gas Company's 90 percent minimum commodity bill).

[116]Order No. 380, 27 FERC Par. 310 (1984), *aff'd in part and rem'd in part sub nom. Wisconsin Gas Co. v. Federal Energy Regulatory Comm.,* 770 F. 2d 1144 (D.C. Cir. 1985), *cert. denied,* 106 S. Ct. 1969 (1986) (remanded with respect to commission's refusal to permit downstream pipelines to flow through the minimum bills of upstream suppliers). On remand, see Order No. 380-E, 35 FERC Par. 61,384 (1986).

[117]See Chapter 11, pp. 467-69.

[118]Richard M. Merriman and Peyton G. Bowman, III, "Significant Developments in Natural Gas Regulation During 1985 and 1986," in *Regulation of the Gas Industry, op. cit.,* Vol. 1, p. 5C-16.

[119]Harry G. Broadman, "Deregulating Entry and Access to Pipelines," in Kalt and Schuller, *op. cit.,* p. 125. See also Harry G. Broadman, W. David Montgomery, and Milton Russell, "Field Price Deregulation and the Common Carrier Status of Natural Gas Pipelines," 6 *The Energy Journal* 127 (1985); *Second Report, op. cit.,* chap. 7; Harry G. Broadman, "Elements of Market Power in the Natural Gas Pipeline Industry," 7 *The Energy Journal* 119 (1986).

[120]See "Antitrust Officials Are Probing Charges Pipelines Won't Ship Lower-Priced Gas," *The Wall Street Journal,* January 31, 1986, p. 6. Several antitrust suits have been filed against pipelines by those seeking transportation services. See, *e.g.,* Jeremiah D. Lambert and Nathalie P. Gilfoyle, "Reforming Natural Gas Markets: The Antitrust Alternative," 111 *Public Utilities Fortnightly* 15 (May 12, 1983); Jeremiah D.

Lambert and Jay D. Pedelty, "Mandatory Contract Carriage: The Changing Role of Pipelines in Competitive Natural Gas Markets," 115 *Public Utilities Fortnightly* 26 (February 7, 1985). Mandatory carriage legislation also has been introduced in Congress and in several state legislatures. See Robert J. Haggerty, William R. Duff, and Robert B. Raven, "Natural Gas Transportation," in *Regulation of the Gas Industry, op. cit.*, Vol. 1, Appendices A and B to chap. 8.

[121]50 *Fed. Reg.* 52,217 (1985). There were five subsequent commission orders: 436-A (1985), granting in part and denying in part applications for rehearing; 436-B (1986), postponing the trigger date for the CD reduction/conversion option; 436-C, 436-D, and 436-E (1986), denying various applications for rehearing and reconsiderations.

The commission also indicated a change in policy with respect to abandonment. See *Re Abandonment of Sales and Purchases of Natural Gas under Expired, Terminated, or Modified Contracts*, 39 FERC Par. 61,144 (1987).

[122]Certain existing transportation arrangements were grandfathered for varying periods of time.

[123]"Virtually every sector of the natural gas industry has challenged the Order, asserting a dazzling array of errors and omissions. They have filed some 85 briefs totaling about 2,000 pages. Oral argument spanned two days in a well-filled courtroom." *Associated Gas Distributors v. Federal Energy Regulatory Comm., op. cit.* (83 PUR4th 459), p. 470 (citation omitted).

[124]*Ibid.*, p. 529.

[125]*Ibid.*

[126]*Ibid.*

[127]*Ibid.*

[128]*Ibid.*

[129]*Re Regulation of Natural Gas Pipelines After Partial Wellhead Decontrol*, 89 PUR4th 312 (FERC, 1987). But see "Gas Prices Rise Sharply Due to U.S. Rule: Less-Expensive Supplies Are Being Withheld," *The Wall Street Journal*, December 8, 1987, p. 6.

[130]See Chapter 11, p. 476.

[131]"Clearly, if a customer elects transportation and should not also elect a standby service, the utility company does not have a continuing public service obligation to sell gas to that customer." *Re Natural Gas Industrial Rates and Transportation Policies*, 78 PUR4th 57, 70 (Va., 1986).

[132]"Economic purchases should not be made solely for elastic customers to the exclusion of purchases for system supply. The authority to make such a dedication to the most elastic customers would also eliminate one incentive for a company to minimize its general system costs." *Ibid.*, p. 66.

[133]Some state commissions have asserted jurisdiction "over the retail sales of gas from interstate pipelines to local consumers" to regulate bypass. [See, *e.g.*, *Re Transportation of Natural Gas*, 82 PUR4th 121, 129 (Mo., 1987).] Others have decided to handle the bypass issue through certification requirements. [See, *e.g.*, *Re Natural Gas Transportation Policies*, 81 PUR4th 453, 457 (W.Va., 1987).] And at least one commission "believes that appropriately designed embedded cost of service rates should eliminate the economic incentives for bypass." [See *Re Natural Gas Industrial Rates and Transportation Policies, op. cit.*, p. 70.]

[134]In California, for example, customers have been separated into two basic groups: a core market (consisting of customers that do not have alternate fuel capability) and a noncore market (consisting of customers with alternate fuel capability and of whole-

sale customers). Noncore customers may choose transportation-only service, or procurement service from either spot market supplies or firm supplies. See *Re New Regulatory Framework for Gas Utilities,* 79 PUR4th 1 (Cal., 1986) and *Re Rate Design for Unbundled Gas Utility Services,* 79 PUR4th 93 (Cal., 1986), rehearing denied and modified, 82 PUR4th 1 (Cal., 1987). See also *Re Transportation of Customer-Owned Gas,* 86 PUR4th 241 (Cal., 1987).

[135]The Alaska *potential* recoverable reserves are estimated to be 152 Tcf. *The Gas Energy Supply Outlook: 1987-2010* (Arlington, Va.: American Gas Association, 1987), p. 35.

[136]Imports from Mexico, which ranged between 40 and 51 Bcf per year in the 1960s, fell to zero in 1975. In December, 1980, the ERA authorized Border Gas Inc. to import 300,000 Mcf per day at an initial price of $3.625 per MMBtu (subsequently increased to $4.94 per MMBtu to maintain parity with the Canadian border price). [See Opinion and Order No. 31 (ERA, 1981).] Border Gas is owned by six domestic transmission companies. Those companies, with their respective percentage entitlements: Tennessee Gas Pipeline Company (37 1/2 percent), Texas Eastern Transmission Company (27 1/2 percent), El Paso Natural Gas Company (15 percent), Transcontinental Gas Pipeline Corporation (10 percent), Southern Natural Gas Company (6 2/3 percent), and Florida Gas Transmission Company (3 1/3 percent). The contract was between Border Gas and Petroleos Mexicanos (Pemex, the national oil and gas company of Mexico). Despite a later price decrease, both parties agreed to suspend deliveries for an indefinite period in October, 1984.

[137]Liquefied Natural Gas "is conventional natural gas which has been liquefied by reducing its temperature to minus 260°F and its volume to 1/600 of that gas in its vaporous state. This permits the transportation of large volumes of natural gas over great distances, across oceans or other terrain unsuitable for pipelines, as well as efficient storage near markets." David J. Muchow, "The Gas Industry — 1985-2010 — Major Problems and Suggested Solutions," in *Regulation of the Gas Industry, op. cit.,* Vol. 1, p. 6-36.

[138]El Paso Natural Gas Company, Great Lakes Transmission Company, Michigan-Wisconsin Pipeline, Midwestern Gas Transmission Company, Pacific Gas Transmission Company, and Tennessee Gas Pipeline. The importing parties changed slightly during the decade: El Paso divested itself of its northwest division, by order of the Supreme Court [*United States v. El Paso Nat. Gas Co.,* 358 F. Supp. 820 (D. Colo. 1972), *aff'd,* 410 U.S. 962 (1973)], substituting the Northwest Pipeline Corporation; Northern Natural Gas Company and InterCity Minnesota Pipelines Ltd. were granted new authorizations.

[139]Merriman and Bowman, *op. cit.,* p. 5-58.

[140]Opinion No. 14 (ERA, 1980). In 1984, the ERA announced new policy guidelines under which it would "assess the competitiveness of imports in terms of contract flexibility to permit pricing and volume adjustments as required by market conditions and available competing fuels. . . . The guidelines also mandated that in addition to competitiveness the ERA would consider need for the gas, national energy requirements, and security of gas supply." Merriman and Bowman, *op. cit.,* p. 5B-17. Despite curtailment problems in the 1970s, however, the FPC/FERC never approved advance payments to Canadian producers. See, *e.g., Re Northern Nat. Gas Co.,* 47 FPC 1202 (1972); 50 FPC 1419 (1973).

[141]On Canadian policy, see Henry Lee, "U.S. Links to North American Supply Markets," in Kalt and Schuller, *op. cit.,* chap. 3.

[142]The uniform border price was replaced with an adjacent-zone pricing concept in 1985. See *ibid.*, pp. 50-51.

[143]Several additional pipelines and distribution companies received import authorizations in the 1980s. [See, *e.g.*, 26 FERC Par. 61,114 (1984) (certificate granted to a consortium of fourteen gas distributors).] However, many long-term contracts have been delayed due to regulatory and environmental issues concerning the construction of necessary transmission facilities. [See "Greater Imports of Canadian Gas to the U.S. Are Stalled: Producers' Pipeline-Expansion Proposals Caught in Regulatory Tangle," *The Wall Street Journal*, April 21, 1987, p. 6.] Also important is the issue of how Canadian gas purchases are treated in domestic pipeline rates. Specifically, the FERC has held that domestic pipelines must flow through the costs of Canadian gas to domestic customers in the same manner in which they flow through the costs of domestic gas to domestic customers. [*Re Nat. Gas Pipeline Co. of America*, 79 PUR4th 209 (FERC, 1986), clarified, 84 PUR4th 413 (FERC, 1987). But see "Canada Lobbies to Reverse FERC Ruling That Could Cut Price of Gas Sold to U.S.," *The Wall Street Journal*, May 18, 1987, p. 16.]

[144]*Re Distrigas Corp.*, 47 FPC 752; 47 FPC 1465 (1972). The commission asserted jurisdiction over terminal, storage, and regasification facilities related to LNG imports in 1973 [49 FPC 1145 (1973), *aff'd and rem'd sub nom. Distrigas Corp. v. Federal Power Comm.*, 495 F. 2d 1057 (D.C. Cir, 1974)].

[145]*Re Columbia LNG Corp.*, 47 FPC 1624; 48 FPC 723 (1972). The commission's requirement of incremental, rather than rolled-in, pricing was remanded in 1974 [*Columbia LNG Corp. v. Federal Power Comm.*, 491 F. 2d 651 (5th Cir. 1974)]. The Commission approved rolled-in pricing in 1977 [*Re Columbia LNG Corp.*, 18 PUR4th 359 (FPC, 1977)].

[146]*Re Eascogas LNG, Inc.*, 50 FPC 2075 (1973).

[147]*Re Trunkline LNG Co.*, Opinion No. 796 (FPC, 1977). The commission subsequently approved rolled-in pricing [*Re Trunkline LNG Co.*, 20 PUR4th 310 (FPC, 1977)].

[148]In 1981, El Paso Company took a $365 million write-off on ships and LNG receiving facilities when it was unable to resolve a price dispute with Sonatrach (the Algerian national oil and gas company). [*Business Week*, August 23, 1982, p. 27.] Panhandle Eastern Corporation, through its Trunkline LNG Company subsidiary, had $567 million invested in a receiving terminal at Lake Charles, Louisiana, and $205 million (along with General Dynamics and Moore McCormack) in the construction of two LNG tankers. [*Ibid.*, September 27, 1982, p. 28.]

In addition to the Lake Charles facility, terminals have been constructed at Cove Point, Maryland; Elba Island, Georgia; and Everett, Massachusetts. All four terminals, with a total annual capacity of 750 Bcf, have been operational, but the Cove Point and Elba Island terminals are now inactive.

[149]Merriman and Bowman, *op. cit.*, p. 5-56 (citation omitted).

[150]*Re Trunkline LNG Co.*, 22 FERC Par. 61,245 (1983); *Re Trunkline LNG Co.*, Opinion and Order No. 50 (ERA, 1983).

[151]*The Wall Street Journal*, September 12, 1986, p. 15.

[152]SNG involves the processing of liquid hydrocarbons, such as naphtha, natural gas liquids, or liquefied petroleum gas. In its 1972 decision [*Re Algonquin SNG, Inc.*, 48 FPC 1216], the commission held that SNG was not "natural gas" under Section 2(5) of the NGA.

[153]Merriman and Bowman, *op. cit.*, p. 5-50.

[154]Opinion No. 728, 5 FPS 5-247 (FPC, 1975).

[155]*Re United Gas Pipeline Co.*, 15 FPS 5-959 (FERC, 1978).

[156]*Re Great Plains Gasification Associates*, 19 FPS 5-549 (FERC, 1979). The project was sponsored by American Natural Resources, MidCon Corporation, Tenneco Inc., Transco Energy Company, and Pacific Lighting Corporation.

[157]Merriman and Bowman, *op. cit.*, p. 5-51. On the cost recovery issue, see *Algonquin Gas Trans. Co. v. Federal Power Comm.*, 534 F. 2d 952 (D.C. Cir. 1976). However, fourteen SNG plants "achieved operational status during the 1970s." *The Gas Energy Supply Outlook: 1987-2010, op. cit.*, p. 39.

[158]The GRI was formed in 1976 to undertake a comprehensive research and development program with the goals of "ameliorating the pervasive and increasingly severe shortage of natural gas, improving the economics and operation of the gas industry, and developing improved conservation technology." Each year, the FERC approves the GRI's annual budget and reviews its updated five-year projected research, demonstration, and development program. State commissions are permitted to intervene in the annual proceedings. See, *e.g.*, *Re Gas Research Institute*, 9 FERC Par. 61,008 (1979), *aff'd sub nom. Public Util. Comm. of Colorado v. Federal Energy Regulatory Comm.*, 660 F. 2d 821 (D.C. Cir. 1981), *cert. denied*, 456 U.S. 944 (1982).

[159]*Office of Consumers' Counsel v. Federal Energy Regulatory Comm.*, 655 F. 2d 1132, 40 PUR 4th 473 (D.C. Cir. 1980).

[160]Opinion and Order No. 119 (FERC, 1981). The settlement provided that the gas would be sold to pipelines at the plant tailgate at an initial price of $6.75 per MMBtu, with quarterly adjustments reflecting inflation and the price of No. 2 fuel oil.

[161]Production costs (exclusive of capital charges) of gas from the plant are approximately $3.00 per MMBtu. [*The Gas Energy Supply Outlook: 1987-2010, op. cit.*, p. 37.] Since 1985, the project has been plagued by litigation and, after a request for $820 million in price supports was rejected by the government, the Department of Energy was successful in obtaining a foreclosure order. The DOE is operating the plant under contract and is seeking a buyer.

[162]Congress established the Synthetic Fuels Corporation in 1980 as a vehicle to provide financial assistance to synthetic fuel projects [Pub. Law 96-294, 94 Stat. 633 *et seq.* (1980). The act is Part B of Title I of the Energy Security Act, Pub. Law 96-294, 94 Stat. 611 (1980)]. See, *e.g.*, Robert C. Pozen, "Synthetic Fuels Corporation — Investment Bank or Government Agency?," 36 *Business Lawyer* 953 (1981); Richard B. Herzog and Robert M. Jenkins, III, "Price Guarantees and Purchase Agreements under the United States Synthetic Fuels Corporation Act of 1980," 36 *ibid.* 969; F. John Hagele and Joseph L. Lincoln, "Loan Guarantees and Loans under the United States Synthetic Fuels Corporation Act of 1980," 36 *ibid.* 995. The agency, "beset by internal problems from its earliest days and buffeted in recent years by marked changes in the energy environment," ceased operations in April, 1986. "SFC, RIP: Breaking a Link with the Energy Crisis," 117 *Public Utilities Fortnightly* 41 (February 20, 1986). Operations ceased under Pub. Law 99-190 (1985).

Proposed synthetic oil projects suffered similar difficulties. See, *e.g.*, "The Death of Synfuels," *Newsweek*, May 17, 1982, pp. 75-76; "Exxon's Abrupt Exit from Shale," *Fortune*, May 31, 1982, pp. 105-07; "Synfuels: Washington's $15 Billion Orphan," *U.S. News & World Report*, January 17, 1983, pp. 58-59.

[163]"Decision and Report to Congress on the Alaskan Natural Gas Transportation

System" (Executive Office of the President, September, 1977); Pub. Law 95-158, 91 Stat. 1268 (1977). The selection process occurred under the Alaska Natural Gas Transportation Act, Pub. Law 94-586, 90 Stat. 2903 (1976).

[164]*Business Week,* May 3, 1982, p. 39.

[165]An appeal regarding the constitutionality of the procedures used to pass the so-called "Waiver Package" and of the three subsequent FERC implementing orders was dismissed: *Metzenbaum v. Federal Energy Regulatory Comm.,* 675 F. 2d 1282 (D.C. Cir. 1982).

[166]An alternative under regulatory and environmental review: A multi-billion Trans Alaska Gas System (TAGS), with Yukon Pacific Corporation (owned by CSX Corporation, Supra Corporation, and Walter J. Hickel & Associates) as sponsor, to build a 796-mile pipeline to connect the reserves at Prudhoe Bay to the state's southern coast for liquefaction and export to markets in East Asia (particularly Japan and South Korea). There is also a rival proposal, sponsored by Alaskan Northwest Natural Gas Transportation Company (a unit of Williams Companies). See *The Wall Street Journal,* September 18, 1987, p. 21.

[167]See Order Nos. 78 and 99 (FERC, 1980).

[168]*The Gas Energy Supply Outlook: 1987-2010, op. cit.,* p. 19.

[169]*Ibid.,* p. 40. At the end of 1986, there were thirteen landfill methane recovery projects producing high-Btu gas. "These facilities are generally directly linked to nearby distribution systems and provide a secure local supply of gas for local utility companies." *Ibid.*

[170]For demand analyses, see *The Gas Energy Demand Outlook: 1981-2000* (Arlington, Va.: American Gas Association, 1982); *The Outlook for Gas Demand in New Markets: 1986-2010* (Arlington, Va.: American Gas Association, 1986).

[171]Breyer and MacAvoy, *op. cit.,* p. 123.

[172]And a task, according to a circuit court, that the *Phillips* decision did not require. "The Commission does not have to employ the area rate method, or for that matter regulate price directly at all, but it has chosen to fulfill its duty in that manner here." *Southern Louisiana Area Rate Cases, op. cit.,* p. 416, n. 9.

[173]Breyer and MacAvoy, *op. cit.* As the Fifth Circuit Court of Appeals noted in upholding the FPC's national approach in 1975: "The national rate structure under review is a unique combination of provisions which, along with the shift to a national rate itself, demonstrates that the Commission does not believe that any of the total rate structures which it developed in the area proceedings had the desired effect of providing developmental incentive while preventing exploitation. The Commission has been unsuccessful in generating additional natural gas reserved for the interstate market within the framework of its congressional mandate. In the face of growing demand for natural gas by the intrastate market, the effort to protect the consumer interest as to price is at odds with the long-range consumer interest in maintaining an adequate supply of natural gas for the interstate market. Finding and maintaining this point of delicate balance is a difficult task. . . ." *Shell Oil Co. v. Federal Power Comm.,* 520 F. 2d 1061, 1072 (5th Cir. 1975).

[174]"Natural-Gas Deregulation: Time to Act," *The Morgan Guaranty Survey,* January, 1983, p. 14.

[175]George R. Hall, "Getting Regulation from 'Here' to 'There'," in Kalt and Schuller, *op. cit.,* p. 251.

[176]*Ibid.,* p. 259. "Modified fixed/variable rates for sales have significant advantages in this regard. However, if pipelines are competing with their LDCs [local distribu-

tion companies], it is hard to see the justification for one competitor paying another a demand charge or fixed-cost minimum bill. Volumetric rates may be required to provide a fair basis for competition between pipeline and LDC." *Ibid.*

[177] *Ibid.*, p. 260.

[178] *Ibid.*, p. 259. "If LDCs reach the ceiling they can charge to industrial customers but cannot recoup their costs from other sources — whether from residential users or from transportation fees — their revenues may fail to meet fixed capital costs. Similarly, if LDCs are not free to lower prices to industrial users in response to interfuel competition and if prices to residential consumers remain unchanged, the resulting load losses could cause a prohibitive loss of revenue. Thus price rigidities in a dynamic market may result in unstable and inadequate revenues." Colin C. Blaydon, "State Policies under Pressure," in Kalt and Schuller, *op. cit.*, pp. 161-62.

[179] Hall, *op. cit.*, p. 260. See, *e.g.*, J. Stephen Henderson et al., *Natural Gas Producer-Distributor Contracts: State Regulatory Issues and Approaches* (Columbus, Ohio: National Regulatory Research Institute, 1988).

[180] See Carmen D. Legato, "The Role of Regulation in Risk Allocation," in Kalt and Schuller, *op. cit.*, chap. 9.

[181] See, *e.g.*, Sam H. Schurr et al., *Energy in America's Future: The Choices Before Us* (Baltimore: The Johns Hopkins Press, 1979); Craufurd D. Goodwin (ed.), *Energy Policy in Perspective: Today's Problems, Yesterday's Solutions* (Washington, D.C.: The Brookings Institution, 1981).

THE

TELECOMMUNICATIONS

INDUSTRY

The telecommunications industry plays a key role in modern, economic, social, and political life. Indeed many commentators have asserted that we are entering an age in which information will be the keystone of the economy. . . .

—*Judge Harold H. Greene**

It is reported that Andrew Jackson, for lack of speedy communications, fought the British at New Orleans after peace had been reached in the War of 1812.[1] The incident illustrates a vital point: modern civilization would be unthinkable without rapid communications. Today, as the result of a continuous flow of technological invention and innovation, the world is literally at one's fingertips and, in addition to telephone and telegraph messages, telecommunications includes the transmission of data, facsimile, and video.

Technological breakthroughs, however, converted the telegraph and telephone industries into the telecommunications industry and, more recently, into the information industry. In so doing, a series of regulatory and public policy issues were raised, leading to the restructuring of the telecommunications industry; the largest divestiture undertaken in our history. These options are considered at length in this chapter. A related issue — antitrust policy in a transitional era — is discussed in the Appendix.

Development of the Telegraph and Telephone Industries

Until the mid-1950s, the domestic public message system was divided into voice and record communications. The former — telephone — was supplied by the operating telephone company subsidiaries and the Long Lines Department of the American Telephone and Telegraph Company (AT&T) and by hundreds of independent telephone companies. The latter — telegraph — was supplied by the Western Union Telegraph Company.[2] This section briefly discusses the development of these two segments of the telecommunications industry.

The Telegraph Industry

The inventor of the telegraph, Samuel F. B. Morse (a professional portrait painter), began experimentation on an electrical communication system in 1832.[3] By 1838, he had shown that signals could be transmitted by wires and had made public demonstrations. However, it was not until 1843 that Congress passed the Telegraph Act, appropriating $30,000 to construct a commercial telegraph line between Washington and Baltimore. The first public message was sent by Morse on May 24, 1844: "What hath God wrought?" The line proved unprofitable, and after the government refused to buy the invention from Morse and his associates for $100,000 in 1845, the telegraph was developed by private ownership. Funds were raised by Morse and his associates, and the Magnetic Telegraph Company extended its lines to Philadelphia and New York in 1846. Several small telegraph companies, numbering about fifty by 1851, began operations in different sections of the country.[4] Also, in 1851, dispatching of trains by telegraph commenced; indeed, most of the early lines were constructed along the rights-of-way of railroads, and telegraph offices throughout the country were found in railroad stations.

The first telegraph installations consisted of a sending and receiving instrument in each city, connected by iron wire strung on glass bottlenecks fastened to poles as insulators. Only one message at a time could pass in either direction over this circuit.[5] A good operator could transmit forty to fifty words per minute. The duplex telegraph, which made possible transmission of two messages simultaneously (one in each direction) over a single wire, was introduced in 1872; the multiplex telegraph, to transmit eight messages simultaneously (four in each direction), was introduced in 1914; and the varioplex telegraph, passing seventy-two messages simultaneously (thirty-six in each direction), was introduced in 1936. Teletypewriter and teleprinter machines came into use around 1925.[6] High-speed switching systems date from 1937; automatic facsimile devices[7] from 1939. Generally, teletypewriters and teleprinters are used between cities where volume is heavy and between business offices and the city telegraph centers, while manual operations continue in areas where message volume is small.

In the late 1950s, Western Union started construction of a transcontinental microwave telegraph network.[8] The network opened in 1964 and is able to transmit 2,000 telegrams simultaneously in each direction. Further, the network is capable of handling all forms of communications, including voice, data, facsimile, and video, and is relatively immune from interruption due to storm damage and electrical interference.

The Western Union Telegraph Company. In 1851, the New York and Mississippi Valley Printing Telegraph Company was incorporated to develop a nationwide telegraph system. At first, the company used the House system of transmission, but the Morse system was in use by 1856. The company constructed a number of lines and acquired others by purchase. In 1856, its name was changed to The Western Union Telegraph Company. Five years later, the company built the first transcontinental telegraph line.

Western Union, in 1866, acquired two significant competitors — the American Telegraph Company and the United States Telegraph Company. In 1881, the Postal Telegraph System entered the field. This company was incorporated as a subsidiary of the Commercial Cable Company, which laid two transatlantic cables in the early 1880s. The development of a successful oceanic cable system required adequate landline connections to domestic points. Rather than contracting with Western Union for interchange, the company organized the Postal Telegraph Company to build a separate domestic telegraph system. The company was able to operate successfully for many years, but substantial annual deficits followed the stock market crash of 1929. At that time, Postal Telegraph handled about 15 percent of the total domestic telegraph traffic. In 1940, the FCC recommended to Congress that the existing telegraph carriers be consolidated into one or more unified systems. Two years later, Congress amended the Communications Act, and Western Union was permitted to acquire Postal Telegraph, a merger consummated late in 1943.[9]

The merger resulted in Western Union's dominance of the public telegraph industry; a dominance completed by its 1970 purchase of the Bell System's teletypewriter exchange (TWX) service.[10] Prior to the late 1970s, the company also provided telegraph service between the continental United States and Alaska, Canada, and Mexico and was the sole agency for landline handling of overseas and ship-shore messages originating or terminating in the continental United States (outside seven gateway cities, such as Boston and New York). Then, in 1979 and 1980, the FCC adopted a series of decisions which opened the domestic telegram market.[11] Congress, in turn, amended the Communications Act, first in 1980 to permit Western Union to provide service to Hawaii, and again in 1981 to authorize Western Union to provide international telecommunications services — in both instances in competition with the international record carriers.[12]

Faced with a declining demand for public telegram messages, Western Union (now a wholly owned subsidiary of Western Union Corporation) began to diversify into other communications services in the 1960s. In 1986, Western Union's telegram message, money transfer, and mailgram services accounted for only 34.45 percent of its gross operating revenues, with business network services[13] accounting for 39.03 percent and private wire, satellite and related services accounting for 19.77 percent (with the remaining 6.75 percent derived from other services).[14]

The Telephone Industry

On March 7, 1876, U.S. Patent No. 174,465, frequently referred to as the world's most valuable patent, was issued to Alexander Graham Bell. Three days later Bell spoke, and his assistant Thomas A. Watson heard, the first complete sentence ever transmitted by telephone: "Mr. Watson, come here, I want you."

In 1877, the first overhead telephone line was erected from Boston to Somerville, Massachusetts. By 1880, there were 47,900 telephones in the United States. In 1881, telephone service opened between Boston and Providence; in 1884, New York and Boston were connected. Service between New York and Chicago commenced in 1892. Originally, telephones were rented in pairs to individuals for local use, and subscribers had to put up their own lines to connect each other. The switchboard came into existence in Boston in 1877, and the following year New Haven, Connecticut, boasted of the first regular telephone exchange. The dial telephone was invented in 1889 by Almon B. Strowger, a Kansas City undertaker, and the first dial exchange was installed at LaPorte, Indiana, in 1895.

Overhead wires soon "blotted out the sky in many cities" and became obstacles to effective firefighting and efficient telephone communications (due to snow and sleet damage). The result was development of overhead and underground cables. The initial long-distance underground cables were placed in operation between New York and Newark, New Jersey, in 1902; between New York and Philadelphia in 1906; between Washington and New York in 1912; and between Washington and Boston in 1913. Transcontinental telephone service was inaugurated in 1915 and transcontinental cable service in 1942.

In addition to wire telephone service, radio telephone (wireless telephone) became of major significance in the 1960s. Radio telephony was first demonstrated in 1915 between Montauk Point on Long Island and Wilmington, Delaware. Transoceanic radio telephony between America and Europe was opened in 1927; between America and South America in 1930. In 1947, an experimental microwave relay system went into operation between New York and Boston; four years later, an improved system was being used to send telephone and telegraph messages and television programs across the country.

All these developments have resulted from continuous technical progress.[15] To illustrate: The first commercial coaxial cable (a copper tube about three-eighths of an inch in diameter with a single wire suspended inside it), installed between New York and Philadelphia in 1936, could carry 480 simultaneous conversations, compared with cables installed in more recent years that can carry 32,400 simultaneous conversations. One set of antennas can carry 17,000 simultaneous telephone conversations over the transcontinental microwave relay system. Direct distance dialing was introduced in 1951; today, it is widely available for both domestic and international calls. Electronic switching central offices, to handle alternative routing of message toll service[16] and to provide a wider range of services (*e.g.*, abbreviated dialing of frequently called numbers; automatic transfer of calls to another number), have replaced step-by-step and cross bar central offices. Fiber optics cable (*i.e.*, thin strands of glass over which voice, television signals, and computer data can be transmitted), came into use in 1977.[17]

The American Telephone and Telegraph Company.[18] Bell's experimentation with the telephone was financed by Thomas Sanders and Gardiner G. Hubbard who, with the inventor, in 1875 organized a partnership known as the Bell Patent Association. Yet, even after the first successful experiment in 1876, many doubted that the telephone had future significance. Western Union, for instance, in 1876 rejected an opportunity to buy the Bell patent for $100,000. In 1877, the partnership became a Massachusetts voluntary association known as the Bell Telephone Company. Its purpose was to own and control any patents resulting from Bell's experiments. The following year, the association was incorporated in Massachusetts under the name Bell Telephone Company, and in 1879 as the National Bell Telephone Company. In 1880, the Bell interests reorganized to form the American Bell Telephone Company. The company was to manufacture telephones and other equipment, and to construct and operate telephone lines throughout the United States, outside New England.[19]

In 1877, Western Union entered into competition, developing telephone exchanges throughout the country under the patents of Elisha Gray and Thomas A. Edison. American Bell filed suit for patent infringement against Western Union in 1878, a suit voluntarily terminated in 1879. Western Union acknowledged the priority of the Bell patents, granted American Bell an exclusive seventeen-year license to use all its patents, and agreed to pay 20 percent of the cost of any new telephone patents American Bell developed or acquired. American Bell agreed to pay Western Union 20 percent of the rentals or royalties it received for the use of its licenses of telephone instruments, to purchase Western Union's telephone system, and to withdraw from the public message telegraph business.[20]

Throughout this early period, American Bell licensed companies and individuals to operate, and leased telephone instruments to them. "By November, 1879, the parent organization had entered into 185 contracts for the provision of local telephone service; in fact, all of the more productive territory of the country was covered by these license agreements."[21] Five-year licenses were common because of the uncertainties of the new ventures. As the industry grew, American Bell granted permanent licenses, taking in return a stock interest in the licensees. The parent company's control was further strengthened by the purchase of additional stock and through consolidations and mergers. In 1881, the American Bell Telephone Company acquired a substantial interest in the Western Electric Manufacturing Company of Chicago and changed its name to the Western Electric Company. Thus, by this date, "a program that envisaged the coordination of all phases of the telephone industry was formulated: the supply of local exchange service, the development of long-distance service, and the organization of manufacturing affiliates to supply the necessary equipment were all developed under the control of the parent company."[22]

The American Telephone and Telegraph Company was incorporated in February, 1885, as a wholly owned subsidiary of American Bell.[23] Its primary purpose was to operate the long-distance network connecting the local exchanges of the operating companies. Early in 1900, American Bell transferred all investments in its subsidiaries to the American Company, and the following year the two companies were consolidated, with the American Company becoming the parent holding company. In 1924 Bell Telephone Laboratories, Inc., was established to take over the product development engineering, and a portion of the patent, departments of Western Electric. The parent company's Development and Research Department was transferred to the Labs in 1934.[24]

AT&T and its operating companies (prior to the 1984 divestiture) dominated the domestic telephone industry. The parent company was both a holding and an operating company. It held 100 percent of the stock of Western Electric Company, a manufacturer, purchaser, and installer of telephone equipment.[25] It owned Bell Telephone Laboratories jointly with Western Electric. And it owned 100 percent of the stock of twenty-two subsidiary telephone operating companies, and minority interest in two additional operating companies. AT&T, Western Electric, Bell Labs, and the operating companies were collectively known as the Bell System (see Table 15-1).[26] The parent company, AT&T Co., was divided into two operations — the General Departments and Long Lines Department. The General Departments provided services to the associated companies, such as basic research and development in telephony (performed by Bell Labs); advice and assistance in engineering, traffic, plant, commercial, accounting, and legal matters; and financial advice and assistance, including assistance in marketing securities and maintenance of a central pool of funds on which the operating companies could draw to meet day-to-day needs for new capital or for operations. The Long Lines Department provided landline and transoceanic facilities connecting the associated companies (and independents) into a worldwide system of long distance service.

TABLE 15-1

Bell System Companies, 1981

Affiliates	Capital Stock Owned By AT&T Co. (Percent)	Assets (Millions)	Telephones (Thousands)
Principal Telephone Subsidiaries:			
New England Tel. & Tel. Co.	100.0	$ 5,515.0	7,110
New York Tel. Co.	100.0	12,263.6	11,678
New Jersey Bell Tel. Co.	100.0	4,694.3	6,620
Bell Tel. Co. of Pennsylvania	100.0	5,263.1	7,951
Diamond State Tel. Co.	100.0	388.7	540
Chesapeake & Potomac Tel. Co.	100.0	850.6	1,092
Chesapeake & Potomac Tel. Co. of Maryland	100.0	2,420.0	3,606
Chesapeake & Potomac Tel. Co. of Virginia	100.0	2,712.2	3,111
Chesapeake & Potomac Tel. Co. of West Virginia	100.0	938.5	975
Southern Bell Tel. & Tel. Co.	100.0	12,074.5	13,035
South Central Bell Tel. Co.	100.0	9,725.9	10,678
Ohio Bell Tel. Co.	100.0	3,629.4	5,002
Michigan Bell Tel. Co.	100.0	4,613.5	6,280
Indiana Bell Tel. Co., Inc.	100.0	1,866.4	2,619
Wisconsin Tel. Co.	100.0	1,791.1	2,360
Illinois Bell Tel. Co.	100.0	5,632.0	8,481
Northwestern Bell Tel. Co.	100.0	4,810.0	5,656
Southwestern Bell Tel. Co.	100.0	15,949.3	16,993
Mountain States Tel. & Tel. Co.	100.0	7,487.4	8,096
Pacific Northwest Bell Tel. Co.	100.0	3,811.7	3,864
Pacific Tel. & Tel. Co.	91.5[a]	16,573.4	16,639
Bell Tel. Co. of Nevada[b]			
Totals		$123,010.6	142,386
Other Subsidiaries:			
Bell Telephone Laboratories, Inc.	50.0[c]		
Western Electric Co., Inc.	100.0	8,338.3	
195 Broadway Corp.	100.0		
AT&T International, Inc.	...		
Other Companies:			
The Southern New England Tel. Co.	21.1	1,891.4	2,618
Cincinnati Bell, Inc.	29.7	751.8	1,206
Cuban American Tel. & Tel. Co.	50.0	...	...

[a]Increased to 100 percent in May, 1982.
[b]Wholly owned subsidiary of Pacific Telephone & Telegraph Company.
[c]Remainder owned by Western Electric Company.
Source: American Telephone and Telegraph Company.

The growth of the Bell System was spectacular (see Table 15-2). In 1980, AT&T (the country's largest corporation with net telephone plant of $110 billion) accounted for 88 percent of total message toll revenues, 95.3 percent of WATS revenues, and 87.6 percent of toll private-line revenues.[27] The operating companies served about 80 percent of the nation's 180.4 million telephones. Western Electric (one of the country's largest industrial corporations with sales exceeding $12 billion) accounted for between 80 and 90 percent of the nation's installed terminal equipment, depending on the product line, and manufactured over 80 percent of all central office equipment produced or used in the country.[28] Bell Labs, perhaps best known for the discovery of the transistor and development work on lasers, fiber optics, and bubble memories, accounted for most of the Bell System's research and development expenditures of $1.4 billion.

The Independent Telephone Companies. On issuance of the basic Bell patent in 1876, many competing telephone companies were organized. Between 1877 and 1893, when the original Bell patent expired, American Bell instituted over 600 patent infringement suits. Since many of the defendants went out of business on being sued, only a few of the cases reached the Supreme Court. These cases were combined for purposes of hearings and, on March 19, 1888, the Court, in a 4-to-3 decision, upheld the Bell patents in their entirety.[29]

Consequently, the real growth of the independent telephone companies dates from 1894. Hundreds of companies were formed, primarily in rural areas, although a few entered into direct competition with the Bell System in urban areas. In 1899, the independent industry attempted to form a competing long-distance network, but the effort failed for lack of financial support.[30] By 1902, out of the 1,051 incorporated cities in the United States with a population of more than 4,000, 1,002 were provided with telephone facilities. Independent companies had exclusive service in 137 of these cities, the Bell interests served 414 cities, and the remaining 451 cities were served by both independents and Bell interests.[31]

AT&T carried out an aggressive acquisition policy in the early 1900s, buying out "independent telephone companies in virtually every major population center"[32] and, in 1909, a substantial stock interest in Western Union, an acquisition that was promptly criticized by Postal Telegraph as resulting in discrimination against Postal and in favor of Western Union. The independent companies also charged that the Bell System was refusing satisfactory long-distance interconnections. In 1913, in response to an antitrust suit, the so-called Kingsbury Commitment was made whereby AT&T agreed to sell its Western Union stock, agreed to interconnections with those independent telephone companies (which numbered over 8,000 firms) which met its equipment standards, and promised not to acquire control of competing telephone companies.[33] The Kingsbury Commitment was followed by the Hall Memorandum of 1922, which explained the Bell System's acquisition policy as one opposed to purchases or consolidations with connecting or

TABLE 15-2

The Bell System, 1920-1980

	1920	1940	1960	1980
Telephones	8,134,000	17,484,000	60,735,073	141,674,000
Average daily conversations:[a]				
Local	32,489,000	77,706,000	209,373,000	527,543,000
Long distance	636,000	1,597,000	9,720,000	52,687,000
Overseas conversations (total for year)	...	73,429	3,713,183	450,000,000
Net telephone plant[b]	$ 1,082,811	$ 3,386,777	$ 18,825,273	$110,027,700
Operating revenues[b]	$ 442,790	$ 1,174,322	$ 7,920,454	$ 50,709,385
Construction expenditures[b]	$ 169,000	$ 290,000	$ 2,658,381	$ 17,300,936
Operating taxes[b]	$ 27,452	$ 184,770	$ 1,847,702	$ 7,613,801
Employees:				
Telephone companies	228,943	275,317	580,405	847,768
Western Electric	39,650	43,746	143,352	174,372
Bell Tel. Laboratories	...	4,638	12,009	21,901
Total wages[b]	$ 314,959	$ 610,815	$ 4,174,500	$ 23,292,405
AT&T shareowners	139,448	630,902	1,911,484	3,026,080

[a]Conversations through central offices only.
[b]Thousands of dollars.
Source: American Telephone and Telegraph Company.

duplicating companies "except in special cases." The memorandum continued, in part:

> We should consider that such an exception was proved only in cases
> where it seemed to be demanded either:
> (1) For the convenience of the public as evidenced by the wishes of
> State authorities or by local public sentiment in or adjoining the terri-
> tory served; or
> (2) By special reason which made the transaction seem desirable and
> essential from the point of view of the protection of our own property
> or the general public service.

* * *

> Types of cases which might be expected to come up for consideration
> under the second general classification would be:
> 1. Companies in which we now have a disproportionately large invest-
> ment without actual control.
> 2. Cases where connecting company or other telephone property is
> pressed for sale, and where it seems that the general public service will
> be improved by its operation as an integral part of our service.[34]

Over the decades, the number of independent telephone companies
has declined continuously, to 1,380 at the end of 1986.[35] Mergers among
independents to achieve economies of scale, rather than Bell System acquisitions, provide the major explanation for the decline. The independent segment of the telephone industry (in 1986) had operating revenues of $18.5
billion, total plant investment of $50.7 billion, and employed 165,357 to
serve 25.2 million access lines (approximately 21 percent of the nation's
access lines).[36]

The largest independent telephone company is GTE Corporation, a holding company that served (in 1986) 11.1 million access lines in thirty-one
states, with operating revenues of $15.1 billion.[37] GTE Corporation began as
the General Telephone Corporation in 1935 — a company that emerged
from a bankruptcy proceeding against the Associated Telephone Utilities
Company. It has made numerous acquisitions of operating telephone companies and, throughout the 1950s, of equipment manufacturers — Leich
Electric Company, Automatic Electric Company (by purchasing Theodore
Gary and Company, its parent and the second largest independent telephone company), and Lenkurt Electric Company. In 1959, General Telephone merged with Sylvania Electronics Products (and became General Telephone and Electronics Corporation). The company owns a research facility
(GTE Laboratories) and has entered nearly every segment of the domestic
(and some international) telecommunications industry (*i.e.,* GTE Telenet Corporation, GTE Satellite Corporation, GTE International). In 1983, GTE Cor-

poration purchased Southern Pacific Company's communications units (Sprint, its long distance telephone service, and Spacenet, a planned satellite system). In 1986, GTE Sprint and US Telecom entered into a joint venture to form US Sprint Communications Company, the nation's third largest long distance communications carrier.[38]

Joint Network Planning. The telephone industry, after an initial period of competition, developed under monopoly and regulation. Local exchange service was provided under franchise by one of the Bell System operating companies or by one of the independent telephone companies. Long-distance toll service was provided by AT&T's Long Lines Department under joint network planning procedures with Bell and independent operating telephone companies.[39] End-to-end service was provided, with the telephone companies assuming joint responsibility for the service (including the purchase, installation, and maintenance of the hardware attached to the nationwide network[40]) and being reimbursed on a cost plus return on investment basis. Private-line services also were provided jointly, over the same facilities used for long-distance toll service.

Western Electric and the 1956 Consent Decree. Since its purchase, Western Electric has been the manufacturing and supply arm of the Bell System. As described by the FCC:

> Generally, its function is twofold: First, it is the manufacturing branch of the Bell System; and second, it is the purchasing and supply department of the Bell System. In connection with its latter function, Western is also a developer, storekeeper, installer, repairer, salvager, and junker of the Bell System.[41]

Western Electric and the Bell operating companies had a Standard Supply Contract which covered all the various functions performed by Western Electric for the associated companies. The contract read, in part:

> The Electric Company will manufacture or purchase materials which the Telephone Company may reasonably require for its business and which it may order from the Electric Company; provided, however, that nothing contained herein obligates the Telephone Company to purchase any materials from the Electric Company.[42]

Thus, under the contract, Western agreed to manufacture or purchase[43] materials reasonably required by an associated company, but permitted the company (as well as Long Lines Department) to purchase materials from any manufacturer it desired. However, since Western Electric's prices were usually lower than any other, few outside purchases were made by the associated companies.[44] The company also installed communication equipment systems (such as central office equipment) for the associated companies, and its distribution centers had facilities for inspecting, repairing, salvaging, and junking telephone equipment. While the FCC and state commissions lacked direct regulatory control over Western Electric, continuing studies were made of the company's costs, prices, and profits[45] and, in rate cases, the company's prices and profits were reviewed.[46]

On January 14, 1949, the government filed a civil antitrust suit against AT&T and Western Electric, charging that the companies had engaged in a continuing conspiracy to monopolize the manufacture, distribution, and sale of telephones, telephone apparatus, and equipment, in violation of Sections 1 and 2 of the Sherman Antitrust Act.[47] The government asked that: (*a*) Western Electric be separated from AT&T and dissolved into three competing manufacturing companies; (*b*) Western Electric be required to sell its 50 percent stock interest in Bell Labs; (*c*) AT&T, Western Electric, and Bell Labs license their patents to all applicants on a nondiscriminatory and reasonable royalty basis; and (*d*) the Bell operating companies be required to buy all equipment and supplies under competitive bidding.

The heart of the case, therefore, involved the vertical integration of AT&T and Western Electric. The government alleged that the situation created a "closed market" in which the operating companies bought, and Western Electric sold, telephone equipment at noncompetitive prices. As former Attorney General Clark pointed out, "the chief purpose of this action is to restore competition in the manufacture and sale of telephone equipment now produced and sold almost exclusively by Western Electric at noncompetitive prices."[48]

AT&T and Western Electric denied the charges and requested that the complaint be dismissed.[49] They contended that existing regulatory processes adequately protected the public in furnishing of communications services and in manufacturing of equipment by Western Electric for use in such services. Further, they emphasized that the unification of research and development, manufacturing, and operation in the Bell System was a leading factor in "promoting the efficiency, economy, and dependability of the telephone service." In the defendants' words:

> It makes available to the operating telephone companies equipment of advanced design and high quality at prices substantially lower than would be obtainable in the absence of such unification. It facilitates the standardization of equipment which is essential to efficient operation of an interconnected telephone system. It enables the manufacturing and supply unit to adapt its production and planning to the anticipated needs of the System, stocks of equipment and installation forces for the restoration of service in time of emergency. And it assures that all steps in the development and production of the equipment are planned and carried out with intimate knowledge of the needs of the operating units of the System and with a common incentive to fulfill those needs most effectively. The ultimate beneficiaries of this unification are the users of telephone service, who thereby obtain better service at lower cost.[50]

Seven years later, on January 24, 1956, the suit was settled by a consent decree.[51] AT&T and Western Electric were required to grant licenses to anyone under all existing and future patents. Virtually all patents issued prior to the date of the decree were to be licensed royalty-free; patents issued subsequent to the date of the decree were to be licensed at reasonable royalties. The defendants were not required, however, to grant any patent license unless the licensee grants to the Bell System licenses it wants for use in its regulated communications business, subject to reasonable royalties.[52] Western Electric was precluded from manufacturing and selling equipment not of a type sold to the telephone operating companies of the Bell System, except for manufacturing equipment or providing services for the government. Western Electric also was required to maintain cost accounting methods consistent with generally accepted accounting principles and to disclose its manufacturing costs. Finally, AT&T and its operating companies were enjoined from engaging in any business other than furnishing common carrier communications services and incidental operations (such as the directory advertising business).[53]

The government was criticized for signing the consent decree rather than continuing its case for divestiture. Sheahan has argued:

> The price of moving Western closer to a regulated public utility status is the sacrificed alternative of choosing instead to secure competition within the telephone equipment industry, and to turn Western toward open competition outside the industry. This alternative was a feasible choice.
>
> Two major steps were required to open up competition. First, Western would have had to be separated from the Bell System, so that equipment choices would no longer be systematically biased in its favor. The second major step is the very gain secured in the settlement: removal of patent restrictions keeping electrical equipment producers out of the telephone field. The change would have had real significance if AT&T no longer had any interest in directing equipment choices to Western. This vast market would have become a real possibility to any aggressive electrical equipment firm. Initially, Western would remain in a very strong position to hold all Bell business. But Federal and the smaller producers already provide important sources of supply to an informed buyer actively seeking the best alternative, and effective purchasing tactics by the Bell companies should have made it possible to open the field quite quickly.[54]

The Communications Act of 1934

Regulation of the telephone and telegraph companies expanded as their impact on the economy developed and grew. The operations of the telegraph companies, which from the beginning have been interstate in nature, were first regulated at the federal level. In 1866, Congress enacted the Post Roads Act, giving telegraph companies construction rights over the public domain, post roads, and navigable streams and waters, and authorizing the Postmaster General to fix rates annually for government telegrams.[55] In 1887, the Interstate Commerce Commission received congressional authority to require interconnections among telegraph companies.

The telephone companies, on the other hand, developed and remained for a number of years almost exclusively as local operations. The first regulation, therefore, was by means of municipal franchises covering rates and conditions of service. As their operations expanded beyond municipal boundaries, the various states began exercising jurisdiction over the telephone companies through their existing railroad and public utility commissions. Shortly after the turn of the century, the interstate operations began to assume greater significance, and federal regulation was deemed necessary. Under the Mann-Elkins Act of 1910,[56] broad regulatory powers over interstate and foreign telephone, telegraph, and cable services were delegated to the ICC. The commission was authorized to determine maximum and minimum rates, to establish uniform systems of accounts, and to make valuation studies. Carriers were required to file monthly and annual financial reports.

The ICC, preoccupied with railroad regulatory problems, was handicapped also by inadequate Congressional appropriations to perform effectively its additional responsibilities for the communications common carriers. It did make, however, two significant contributions to the regulatory process: a uniform system of accounts for telephone companies was developed, and valuation studies of communication companies' plants were undertaken. During the period of ICC jurisdiction, formal rate proceedings were at a minimum. Between 1910 and 1934, the commission dealt with telegraph rates in only eight cases, telephone rates in four cases, and cable rates in two cases.[57] In none of these cases were the issues of major importance. In addition, some complaints were filed with the commission and acted on.

From August 1, 1918, to July 31, 1919, the telephone and telegraph companies were taken over by the federal government and operated by the Post Office Department as a war-time measure. (Radio stations were operated by the U.S. Navy.) Under the Transportation Act of 1920,[58] the ICC was directed to prescribe depreciation rates and charges of telephone and telegraph companies. The Willis-Graham Act of 1921[59] extended the commission's authority to include telephone consolidations and acquisitions of control. In the same year, Congress enacted the Submarine Cable Act,[60] authorizing the Department of State to receive license applications for the landing or operating of ocean cables, while the President was authorized to grant or refuse such licenses. Six years later, regulation of radio communications and allocation of the radio spectrum were vested by Congress in the Federal Radio Commission.

Early in 1933, an interdepartmental committee was set up by the Secretary of Commerce to study communications regulation. The committee recommended the creation of a single agency to regulate all communications services.[61] In accordance with the committee's recommendations, President Roosevelt sent a special message to Congress on February 26, 1934, urging creation of the Federal Communications Commission. Bills were introduced the following day by Senator Dill and Representative Rayburn. The Senate bill passed the House on June 1, 1934; the conference report was adopted by both houses on June 9th; and the Communications Act of 1934 was signed by the President on June 19, 1934. The purpose of the act, as amended in 1937, was to provide for the regulation of interstate and foreign communications by wire and radio,

> ... so as to make available, so far as possible, to all the people of the United States a rapid, efficient, Nation-wide, and world-wide wire and radio communication service with adequate facilities at reasonable charges, for the purpose of the national defense, for the purpose of promoting safety of life and property through the use of wire and radio communication, and for the purpose of securing a more effective execution of this policy by centralizing authority with respect to interstate and foreign commerce in wire and radio communication. ... [62]

With respect to common carriers — telephone, telegraph, and cable — all companies were required to furnish adequate service "upon reasonable request."[63] The commission may order physical connections between carriers, and may establish through routes and charges and determine the division of such charges, when found to be "necessary or desirable in the public interest." All rates, practices, classifications, and regulations must be "just and reasonable"; "unjust or unreasonable" discrimination and "undue or unreasonable preference or advantage" are prohibited. Rates must be filed with the commission and adhered to, and proposed rates may be suspended for a period not to exceed three months (later increased to five months[64]) to permit an investigation.[65] Common carriers must obtain certificates of public convenience and necessity for the construction, acquisition, or operation of a new line or for the extension of an existing line.[66] The commission may prescribe uniform accounting systems and depreciation charges, and may require records and reports. The newly created Federal Communications Commission was authorized to make valuation studies, and Congress specified that, in making such studies, the commission "shall be free to adopt any method of valuation which shall be lawful." The FCC was given jurisdiction over consolidations.[67]

The act prohibits interlocking directorates without express commission approval. The FCC, however, was given no control over the security issues of common carriers. The commission was instructed to investigate all transactions between operating companies and affiliated companies, and to report such findings and recommendations, if any, to Congress. The commission also was instructed to inquire into the management of common carriers and to keep itself informed of technical developments and improvements "to the end that the benefits of new inventions and developments may be made available to the people of the United States." While Congress reserved to the states the regulation of intrastate communications and exchange services, the FCC's authority encompassed all "instrumentalities, facilities, apparatus and services ... incidental to such transmission." To encourage state and federal cooperation, Congress made provision for establishment of joint boards.[68]

The Telephone Investigations

There have been two major investigations of the telephone industry by the FCC since enactment of the Communications Act, one initiated in the mid-1930s and the other in the mid-1960s. Both are of historical significance, but deserve brief review.

Investigation of the 1930s. One of the first major actions of the newly created FCC was to initiate an investigation of the telephone industry; an investigation undertaken at the direction of Congress.[69] The investigation was carried out in three phases: collection of data from the records and files of AT&T and the associated companies, formal hearings in which evidence was taken and interpreted, and development of the fundamental data and background material relative to basic interstate telephone rate and regulatory problems on which continuing regulation could be built. On June 14, 1939, the commission unanimously adopted its final report, in which it concluded:

> The concentration of the Nation's telephone business, and in particular of its interstate telephone business, in the hands of the Bell Telephone System is such that, whereas the problem of regulation is one of large magnitude, it is relatively simplified by reason of this very integration, as contrasted with the railroad, gas, electric-power, maritime, and motor-carrier fields of Federal regulatory effort. The fundamental problem underlying the provision of effective regulation in the interstate telephone field appears to consist largely of developing ways and means, as well as positive and effective machinery, for the continuous acquisition of the basic factual data, and of providing methods for the prompt and adequate digestion and analysis of such facts in such form and manner as to render Commission action thereon readily possible.[70]

Following 1939, many of the practices questioned in the report were changed or modified. By 1949, telephone companies had restated their plant accounts on the basis of original cost, reducing by $43 million the net book values on which their rates of return are computed.[71] By 1954, the FCC had completed a program of prescribing depreciation rates for the Bell

System, lowering depreciation charges by $29 million annually.[72] Detailed separations procedures were developed by the FCC and the National Association of Regulatory Utility Commissioners for separating intra- and interstate plant, expenses, and revenues.[73] AT&T's license contracts and fees were investigated and approved.[74]

Equally important, the FCC's investigation formed the basis of — in fact, it made possible — the commission's regulatory procedure known as constant or continuing surveillance.[75] Without the data, detailed information, and knowledge about the telephone industry gathered in making the study, the FCC would have been unable to rely so heavily on informal procedures; procedures which resulted in over fifty negotiated changes in interstate rates between 1935 and 1967, resulting in an overall net savings to the public (based on 1967 volumes of business) of more than $1.5 billion annually.

Investigation of the 1960s and 1970s. On October 27, 1965, the FCC instituted a formal investigation of the rates charged by AT&T for interstate and foreign communications[76]; an investigation that was not to be completed until February 23, 1977.[77] The investigation was divided ultimately into three parts: Phase 1A — the fair rate of return, the effect of the Bell System's nonuse of accelerated depreciation for tax purposes on the fair rate of return, the justification for the claimed inclusion of three items (plant under construction, cash working capital, and materials and supplies) in the rate base,[78] and separations procedures; Phase 1B — the appropriate ratemaking principles and factors applicable to the Bell System's services; and Phase 2 — the amounts properly includable as the Bell System's net investment, expenses, and taxes, including the reasonableness of Western Electric's prices and profits.[79] The major findings:

Phase 1A. A unanimous interim decision was issued on July 5, 1967. The FCC: (*a*) found a fair rate of return in the range of 7 to 7 1/2 percent; (*b*) ruled that the nonuse of accelerated depreciation reduced the Bell System's risk, but deferred an evaluation of that policy until Phase 2; (*c*) included the amount claimed for plant under construction, but excluded the amounts claimed for cash working capital, and materials and supplies (ending with a negative working capital allowance and deferring its treatment to Phase 2); and (*d*) established a new proceeding (Docket No. 17975) to further consider separations procedures. The Bell System was ordered to reduce its interstate and foreign rates by $120 million — $100 million, effective November 1, 1967, and $20 million, effective August 1, 1968.[80]

Phase 1B. The FCC incorporated the *record* of Phase 1B into its hearings on AT&T's revision of rates for private-line services (Docket No. 18128) on July 29, 1969, and terminated Phase 1B "without decision" on February 18, 1970.[81] The record was described by the commission as "massive" and one in which "the economics of pricing has been explored in detail." The resulting "Statement of Rate-Making Principles and Factors," concluded the commission, "properly recognizes the relevance of both fully distributed and incremental costs in considering appropriate rate levels of specific classes of service. . . . It is the thrust of the statement that effective testing of the complex economic theories of costing and pricing which had been advanced in this record, and the reconciliation of opposing, or at least partially conflicting, views of expert witnesses, can best be accomplished by relating the principles advocated to specific rate proposals."[82]

Phase 2.   Phase 2 was incorporated into Docket No. 19129 after AT&T (November 20, 1970) filed tariff revisions for increased interstate rates. In Phase II of that docket, decided February 23, 1977, the commission "found nothing in the record which would call for a fundamental change in the Bell System structure as it relates to the Western Electric Company and Bell Telephone Laboratories. It found the overall performance of the Bell System excellent in terms of providing high-quality nationwide telecommunications service at reasonable cost to the public. However, it found that the procurement process of the Bell System operating companies needed greater autonomy from Western Electric. . . ."[83]

The Domestic Telegraph Investigation

Message telegraph volume declined sharply after 1945. To illustrate: During the period 1945 to 1966, the message telegraph volume fell 70 percent and the number of telegraph offices declined 41 percent, while eleven rate increases resulted in a cumulative increase of 160 percent in the price of message telegraph between 1945 and 1964.

In May, 1962, the FCC instituted an investigation of domestic telegraph operations and services. The report of the Telephone and Telegraph Committees (which conducted the inquiry) was issued in December, 1966.[84] The basic question raised was whether the decline in message telegraph service represented the expected response of the price system to a change in consumer demand or whether there were forces distorting the rate relationships between message telegraph and substitute services. If the relative prices confronting consumers adequately reflected the inherent value and cost-of-service characteristics of message telegraph and substitute services, then the decline in the former could be assumed to be the result of consumer choice. If there were forces which distorted these rate relationships, then consumer diversion would have to be explained as a reaction to a series of imperfections in the system of prices.

The report of the Telephone and Telegraph Committees concluded that

> ... the consumers' choice between public message service and alter-
> native communications media was conditioned by a successive series of
> rate increases needed to support a diversification program into new
> areas and to offset Bell's pricing practices in TWX and other competi-
> tive services. In such a setting, it is difficult to argue that the resultant
> price-volume relationships reflect a correct valuation of consumer re-
> quirements for the public message service. A different outcome might
> have been expected had prices been maintained at levels corresponding
> more closely to value and cost-of-service considerations for public mes-
> sage telegraph and other communications services. This does not neces-
> sarily mean that, had prices been permitted to reflect these factors
> more accurately, the message telegraph service would have retained the
> position of dominance which it held a half century ago. Nor is it
> suggested that, even if price had stabilized, message traffic would have
> enjoyed the same proportional growth as message toll telephone or
> TWX. But it does indicate that the accelerated decline in volume attrib-
> utable to the substantial increase in price in the postwar period need
> not have come to pass. Indeed, in a growing economy, it would not
> have been improbable to assume that message volume would have stabi-
> lized, or possibly demonstrated a slight absolute increase as new usage
> developed.[85]

Several recommendations were made, the most important being the
following. First, an integrated record message service should be created,
through the unification of message telegraph, Telex, and the Bell System's
TWX in one carrier — namely, Western Union; a recommendation implemented in 1970. Second, Western Union should be required to introduce a
program of promotional pricing "without delay" and to meet adequate speed
and quality-of-service standards so as to maximize usage of each type of
message service. Third, certain Bell System-Western Union relationships with
respect to facility leasing arrangements, interconnection of services, and minimum prices should be established and/or regulated.[86]

Efforts to Amend the Communications Act

Congress, beginning in the mid-1970s, has considered countless proposals and bills aimed at amending or rewriting the Communications Act; a
task that is essential in view of technological developments and both FCC
and court actions restructuring the industry. No consensus has emerged.[87] It
is important to note, however, that there has been a distinct shift in objectives. For example, under the "Consumer Communications Reform Act of
1976," the FCC's procompetitive policies in the terminal equipment and

private-line areas would have been reversed and the structure of the industry returned to its monopoly status. Within a short time, a majority of the bills under discussion (such as the "Communications Act of 1979" and the "Telecommunications Competition and Deregulation Act of 1981") were procompetitive, and would deregulate a substantial portion of the industry (and reduce regulatory powers). The events of the early 1980s, particularly the divestiture of the Bell System, may make a consensus possible.

Technology and the Competitive Challenge

In the post-World War II period,

> ... the market for communications services changed greatly. The demand for telephone services rose steeply while the demand for public message telegraph services declined sharply. In addition, demands increased for new types of communication services which had been developed to meet the needs of far-flung business firms: teletypewriter exchange, alternate voice/record, and voice/data services.[88]

The demand for new types of bulk communications services, combined with continuous technological change, confronted policymakers with a series of issues affecting the structure of the telecommunications industry. As will be discussed in this section, new markets and new potential suppliers raised the possibility of rendering obsolete the traditional monopoly concept under which the industry developed.

The Above 890 Decision

Domestic common carriers first began to utilize microwave systems in 1945. Until 1939, the FCC licensed private microwave communications systems to government and business users only when they had "special communications needs," including the lack of common carrier facilities.[89] Several companies announced plans to install microwave systems between selected Eastern cities as early as 1946,[90] but it was not until 1956 that the FCC was asked by prospective private users for access to radio frequencies above 890 megacycles to develop noncommon carrier microwave service. The suppliers of microwave equipment joined in the request.

The potential entrants contended that there were sufficient frequencies available for both private and common carriers, and that private entry would enhance consumer choice and promote competition in the communications equipment market. The common carriers questioned the adequacy of the frequency spectrum to support both private and common carriers and suggested that private entry might result in interference. They argued also that private entrants would engage in "cream skimming," by entering only on a selective basis. As a result, not only would they lose significant revenues, but smaller users would be burdened with higher rates since the overhead of the common carriers would be distributed over a smaller number of customers. They maintained that a closely controlled system of communications is necessary in time of emergency and for national defense, and suggested that they could provide and plan a more efficient national microwave system. Finally, they contended that since microwave is a part of the electronics industry — an industry that is competitive — there would be no problem of monopoly if they were permitted to develop a national system.

On July 30, 1959, the FCC removed all significant barriers to the installation and operation of private microwave systems.[91] The commission concluded that there were adequate frequencies above 890 Mc available "to take care of present and reasonably foreseeable future needs of both the common carriers and private users for point-to-point communications systems"; that there was "a demonstrated need for private point-to-point communications systems"; and that the entry of private systems would not "adversely affect, to any substantial degree, the ability of common carriers to provide service to the general public or adversely affect the users of such common carrier service."[92]

The MCI *and* Specialized Common Carriers *Decisions*

Microwave Communications, Inc. (MCI),[93] filed applications with the FCC in 1963 for construction permits to provide point-to-point private-line microwave service[94] from St. Louis to Chicago and nine intermediate points. MCI did not propose a complete microwave service; rather, it sought interconnections from its terminals to local telephone (distribution) facilities. However, MCI contended that its rates would be substantially lower than those charged by the common carriers, and that the service would provide greater flexibility in terms of the use of facilities.

The common carriers (*e.g.*, the Bell System, General Telephone, Western Union) objected to the applications on four basic grounds: that MCI was not financially or technically qualified to construct and operate the proposed facilities; that such services could be provided more economically by the existing common carriers; that the proposal, requiring additional microwave systems, would be duplicative and would represent an inefficient utilization of the frequency spectrum; and that MCI's entry would result in "cream skimming," since the company would have no general service responsibilities and would provide service only over the most profitable routes.[95]

But in 1969, on a 4-to-3 vote, the commission granted MCI's applications "to provide only point-to-point private line service not requiring connection to the nationwide switched network. . . ."[96] The commission found that: MCI was financially qualified; a need existed for "microwave service of acceptable quality at lower rates than offered by the existing carriers"; the

MCI proposal "may reasonably be expected to achieve a degree of reliability which, while not matching the high degree of reliability claimed by the major carriers, will provide an acceptable and marketable common carriers service"; and the benefits of MCI's proposal "outweigh the fact that MCI will not make the fullest possible use of its frequencies." The commission admitted that the case was

> ... very close ... and one which presents exceptionally difficult questions. ... However, it would be inconsistent with the public interest to deny MCI's applications and thus deprive the applicant of any opportunity to demonstrate that its proposed microwave facilities will bring to its subscribers the substantial benefits which it predicts and which we have found to be supported by the evidence in this proceeding.[97]

The commission's rather cautious approach proved to be short-lived. Within twelve months

> ... it was confronted with no fewer than thirty-seven applications by companies (ten of them associated with MCI), proposing to establish themselves as specialized common carriers. The proposals involved construction of 1713 microwave stations, more than one-third the number in the entire Bell System. The most dramatic of these, submitted by Data Transmission Co. (Datran), was for a $350,000,000 nationwide switched network solely for the transmission of data, providing end-to-end service in direct competition with the Bell System.[98]

In June, 1971, the commission announced a policy of free entry by new specialized common carriers which meet financial and technical standards. Concluded the FCC:

> We find that there is a public need and demand for the proposed facilities and for new and diverse sources of supply, competition in the specialized communications field is reasonably feasible, there are grounds for a reasonable expectation that new entry will have some beneficial effects, and there is no reason to anticipate that new entry would have any adverse impact on service to the public by existing carriers such as to outweigh the considerations supporting new entry. We further find that a general policy in favor of the entry of new carriers in the specialized communications field would serve the public interest, convenience and necessity.[99]

This decision was to lead to substantial controversy and litigation over both its scope and implementation and its jurisdictional implications. Before summarizing that controversy, it is important to note that the decision itself

... was hardly a model of clarity. The decision did not define the specialized services to which it referred, nor did it define the corresponding obligations that the FCC expected the general carriers (primarily AT&T) to assume in order to assist the new carriers. . . .[100]

Scope. It was the contention of AT&T that the specialized common carriers decision authorized point-to-point private-line services not requiring switched network connections and that the Bell System was required to provide local distribution facilities only for these services. AT&T entered into interim contracts with MCI in September, 1971, specifying the kinds of interconnections it would provide for MCI to provide these services on the Chicago to St. Louis route. MCI, in contrast, argued that the decision authorized the company to provide not only point-to-point private-line services, but also foreign exchange (FX) and common control switching (CCSA) type services (which require interconnection with local switching machines).[101] The interim contracts did not permit access to the local distribution network for FX and CCSA services. The issue was not to be resolved until a 1974 commission order and 1977 court decision established MCI's right to interconnections for both services.[102] In the meantime, a further test of the scope was to come about in the mid-1970s, as the specialized common carriers began to offer long-distance telephone service, in direct competition with MTS and WATS. (See Execunet *Decisions,* below.)

Jurisdiction. Implementation of the specialized common carrier decision also created a series of complex jurisdictional issues. The FCC has long had jurisdiction over the nationwide network of long-distance transmission facilities, primarily owned by AT&T's Long Lines Department. However, local exchange facilities and switching machines belong to the local telephone companies and have long been under state jurisdiction, even though they are used at each end of a regular long-distance call. (In the separations process, the costs associated with the private-line portion of interstate FX services have been assigned to the intrastate jurisdiction.) In a series of decisions, contested by the state commissions, the FCC gradually preempted jurisdiction over the states on matters relating to the terms and conditions of interconnection to the nationwide switched network.[103]

The Carterfone Decision: Foreign Attachments

For many years (and with certain exceptions), both intra- and interstate telephone tariffs prohibited the attachment of devices, other than those supplied by telephone companies themselves, and the interconnection of customer-owned communications systems directly to the telephone network. The purpose of this policy was to protect the network from harm (*e.g.,* hazardous voltages, excess signal power[104]), although it had the obvious effect of limiting competition in providing telephone equipment. In 1968, the

FCC held that AT&T's existing tariff was "unreasonable, discriminatory, and unlawful" since it prohibited "the use of interconnecting devices which do not adversely affect the telephone system." At the same time, the commission said that telephone companies "may submit new tariffs which will protect the telephone system against harmful devices, and may specify technical standards if they wish."[105]

AT&T filed new tariffs in October, 1968, under which the telephone network was opened to a wide variety of customer-provided equipment, including the interconnection of most private systems. The new tariffs, however, contained two restrictions: a "customer premises" provision in the interconnection tariff[106] and a provision that customer-provided terminal equipment had to be attached to the network through a protective connecting arrangement or data access arrangement. After the Department of Justice complained that the new tariffs did not comply fully with the *Carterfone* decision, the commission initiated a series of informal conferences and, subsequently, two advisory committees were appointed[107] and a Federal-State Joint Board was created, to evaluate the company's foreign attachment and interconnection policies.

In November, 1975, the commission announced a registration program for terminal equipment, under which users would be allowed to connect any terminal equipment to the nationwide network (*a*) if such equipment is connected through a protective circuity registered with the commission or (*b*) if such equipment is itself registered with the commission.[108] A year later, the registration program was extended to include main stations, private branch exchange (PBX) switchboards, and key telephone systems.[109] The effective date of the registration program was subsequently set at May 1, 1976.[110] And, finally, the commission began informal industry meetings on the development of uniform national standards for plugs and jacks to be used in conjunction with registered terminal equipment.[111]

First Computer Inquiry

The electronic computer can provide a wide variety of data processing, computational, and information storage and retrieval services to a large number of users at remote locations. It also can be utilized by communications common carriers as part of their networks as a message switching device. Thus, the convergence of communications and computer technologies made feasible the entry of equipment manufacturers and other firms into supplying communications systems and services, and the entry of common carriers into supplying data processing and specialized information services.[112]

In 1966, the FCC issued a Notice of Inquiry seeking to delineate the main issues in the growing interrelationship between communications and computer technologies.[113] Interested parties were invited to respond to a lengthy list of questions, after which the commission engaged the Stanford Research Institute to prepare an analysis of the issues.[114] The FCC's final decision was issued in March, 1971. In that decision, rules were adopted which prohibited common carriers (domestic and international) from buying data processing services from their own affiliates and which prohibited such data processing affiliates from using their parents' names or obtaining promotional or other assistance from them (the so-called "maximum separation" rule). Explained the FCC's majority:

> The specialized and variant nature of the data processing services, particularly with reference to costs and charges therof, is conducive to improprieties which are difficult to detect. Such improprieties could translate into inflated charges to customers of a carrier's regulated services which, in turn, could lead to lengthy administrative proceedings and other litigation.
>
> At the same time, such improprieties could cause irreparable harm to a carrier affiliate's data processing competitors and thus, to the essentially competitive market within which data processing service offerings currently exist. In other words, excessive payments by carriers to data processing affiliates would enable the affiliates to unfairly underprice their own competitors in the data processing market.
>
> Since the basic objective of our policy herein is the deterrence of foreseeable abuse from indirect carrier entry into data processing, we shall amend our rules to include a provision prohibiting a common carrier from obtaining any data processing service from its data affiliate.[115]

The Domsat *Decision: Domestic Communications Satellites*

The spectacular launching of Telstar I on July 10, 1962, opened a new era in intercontinental communications. Telstar I, owned by AT&T, was designed for experimental purposes, but its subsequent success in telephone, television, teletype, facsimile, and data transmission clearly indicated the feasibility of space communications.

Congress, in the same year, established the Communications Satellite Corporation (Comsat) to set up an international satellite system.[116] At that time, the economic feasibility of a domestic satellite system was in doubt. Within three years, however, the commission had received two major proposals: one from Comsat to put a domestic satellite system into operation on a trial basis and one from the American Broadcasting Company to launch a domestic satellite for television broadcast distribution. The commission thereupon invited suggestions from other interested parties.[117] Many proposals were received, including one from the Ford Foundation that recommended the establishment of a new nonprofit corporation to distribute television programs via satellite so as to help finance an improved and expanded educational television system. Then, early in 1970, the FCC received a policy statement from the White House, proposing a three- to five-year test of free entry and competition in the domestic satellite field.[118]

By mid-1971, eleven parties had filed applications with the FCC for authorizations to provide domestic satellite service.[119] In 1972, the commission established the policy of "multiple entry" (*i.e.*, unrestricted entry) into domestic communications satellites.[120] It required

> ... that each domestic system applicant, as a condition to its use of satellites, make available to all other authorized users of satellites, on reasonable and nondiscriminatory terms, available terrestrial and space segment interconnection facilities and services required by such users to deliver satellite services to their customers. The commission further required that each terrestrial carrier submit with its application for domestic satellite facilities a description and explanation of the kinds of interconnection arrangements it will make available to other authorized users to meet their interconnection requirements.[121]

By the end of 1973, the commission had approved the applications of more than six companies to construct and operate, either individually or jointly, communications satellite facilities for domestic use.[122] In 1983, the commission authorized thirty-eight additional satellites, to be in orbit by the late 1980s. Competition was further enhanced when the FCC authorized the sale of individual transponders on a non-common carrier basis and reduced satellite spacing to allow the placement of more satellites in orbit.[123]

Execunet *Decisions*

With facilities in place, it was perhaps inevitable that the specialized common carriers would become interested in offering public message switching services, in direct competition with the established common carriers. In 1976, after at least two of the specialized common carriers began to provide switched long-distance services (MCI with "Execunet," Southern Pacific with "Sprint"), the FCC rejected MCI's tariff offering Execunet service, holding that the service exceeded the scope of the private-line services authorized in its 1971 specialized carrier's decision. But the commission was reversed by a court of appeals the following year, when it held that neither the FCC's 1971 decision nor subsequent facility authorization proceedings contained adequate findings that MCI's services would be contrary to the public interest and that such findings are essential to support a restriction on MCI's use of its facilities.[124] In response, the FCC initiated a new investigation to determine whether the public interest requires that MTS and WATS, or their functional equivalents, should be provided on a monopoly (sole source) basis.[125]

Then, in a 1978 declaratory ruling, the commission held that AT&T did not have a present obligation under either the Communications Act or prior commission orders to provide connections to specialized common carriers for the provision of any service which is substantially equivalent to MTS and WATS. That decision also was reversed by a court of appeals, which ordered the commission to comply with its 1977 decision and to compel AT&T to provide local interconnection for MCI's Execunet services without further public interest hearings pursuant to the Communications Act.[126] In May, 1978, AT&T filed a new Exchange Network Facilities Interstate Access (ENFIA) agreement and tariff, on behalf of the Bell System operating companies, offering certain local distribution and interexchange facilities at negotiated rates. After negotiations under FCC auspices, a Memorandum of Understanding was signed in November, 1978, and approved by the FCC in April, 1979.[127]

In 1980, the FCC issued its MTS/WATS market structure decision, holding that these two public switched network services should be provided under competition rather than on a sole source basis.[128]

A Concluding Note

In the above decisions adopting a liberalized entry policy, the FCC (with the notable exception of the first two *Execunet* decisions) — and, subsequently, the courts (including the *Execunet* decisions) — concluded that selected entry into particular segments of the telecommunications industry would result in a greater range of choice to the consumer, in services which were not currently available, and in new options in terms of leasing or buying.[129] Kestenbaum, after reviewing the early decisions, concluded:

> No doubt, an entirely open and balanced weighing of the opposing contentions and expectations would have permitted a judgment either way on these issues. The Commission in effect resolved them by putting the burden on the common carrier system to justify the need for monopoly. Implicitly, it accepted the proposition that certain objectives of communications policy could not as equally be assured by a monopoly carrier subject to regulatory supervision. Or, at least, it implemented the legal-economic judgment that reliance upon regulation is a last resort, justified only when competition is not feasible or practical.[130]

The common carriers had difficulty in sustaining the justification burden. In general, they opposed a policy of liberalized entry on the grounds that the frequency spectrum is limited, so that entry would lead to its wasteful use; that the inherent duplication of facilities and cream skimming by entrants would be detrimental to maximum efficiency (*i.e.*, would make it difficult to achieve economies of scale) and would result in higher rates to many subscribers; and that customer-provided equipment might be detrimental to maintaining the integrity of the network. In each case, however, the common carriers failed to persuade or convince either the commission or the courts that these potential adverse consequences of liberalized entry outweighed the potential advantages of introducing competitive forces, particularly in the area of technological advance.[131] Ultimately, it was technology that led to the restructuring of the telecommunications industry.[132]

Deregulation and Divestiture: An Industry Is Restructured

By 1980, despite a liberalized entry policy and the subsequent growth of numerous competitors, the structure of the telecommunications industry had not substantially changed (see Tables 15-3 and 15-4). But a restructuring of the industry was to occur very shortly, due to the FCC's *Computer II* decision (as modified in its initial *Computer III* decision) and a district court's approval of the Modification of Final Judgment.

TABLE 15-3

Total Metered and Private Line Toll Revenues, 1980

	Revenues (Billions)	Percent of Total
Bell System	$26.14	79.6%
Independent Companies	5.90	18.0
Specialized Carriers	.41	1.2
Western Union	.16	.5
Domsats	.14	.4
Value Added Carriers	.08	.2
Miscellaneous Carriers	.03	.1
Total	$32.86	100.0%

Source: *Telecommunications in Transition: The Status of Competition in the Telecommunications Industry* (House Committee Print 97-V, 97th Cong., 1st sess.) (Washington, D.C.: U.S. Government Printing Office, 1981), p. 105.

Second Computer Inquiry

On May 2, 1980, the FCC issued its *Computer II* decision,[133] which significantly modified its regulation of the telecommunications industry.

First, the commission made a distinction between "basic" transmission services and "enhanced" services.

TABLE 15-4

Domestic Record Carriers, Total Operating Revenues, 1980

	Revenues (Millions)	Percent of Total
Western Union	$532.1	86.0%
Tymnet	34.9	5.6
GTE Telenet	32.6	5.3
Graphnet	18.9	3.1
Total	$618.5	100.0%

Source: *Telecommunications in Transition: The Status of Competition in the Telecommunications Industry* (House Committee Print 97-V, 97th Cong., 1st sess.) (Washington, D.C.: U.S. Government Printing Office, 1981), p. 126.

1. A basic transmission service is one that is limited to the common carrier offering of transmission capacity for the movement of information. In offering this capacity, a communications path is provided for the analog or digital transmission of voice data, video, etc., information.
2. An enhanced service is any offering over the telecommunications network which is more than a basic transmission service. In an enhanced service, for example, computer processing applications are used on the content, code, protocol, and other aspects of the subscriber's information. . . . Moreover, in an enhanced service the content of the information need not be changed and may simply involve subscriber interaction with stored information. . . .[134]

Thus, under this dichotomy, POTS ("plain old telephone service") is a basic service, while various ancillary services — such as voice storage or automatic call answering — are enhanced services.[135]

Second, the commission decided that enhanced services and customer-premises equipment (CPE) should not be regulated as common carrier offerings under the Communications Act. "This structure enables us to direct our attention to the regulation of basic services and to assuring nondiscriminatory access to common carrier telecommunications facilities by all providers of enhanced services."[136] With specific reference to terminal equipment, the commission found that such devices "are increasingly incorporating data processing characteristics," so that "technological evolution would quickly render obsolete any attempt to draw distinctions among customer-premises equipment based on processing functions."[137] All CPE was to be unbundled from the basic services and detariffed on March 1, 1982.[138]

Third, the commission concluded that common carriers should be allowed under the Communications Act to offer both enhanced services and CPE. Except for AT&T,[139] the commission eliminated the maximum separation rules developed in the *Computer I* decision (*i.e.*, the requirement that common carriers could offer data processing services only through a separate subsidiary), but held that those carriers owning common carrier transmission facilities and offering enhanced services "must acquire transmission capacity pursuant to the same prices, terms, and conditions reflected in their tariffs when their own facilities are utilized."[140] Concerning carriers affiliated with AT&T, the decision required maximum separation; the offering of enhanced services and CPE through a separate, but unregulated, corporate entity on a resale basis, with its "own operating, marketing, installation, and maintenance personnel for the services and equipment it offers."[141]

Some Implementation Issues. In its two orders on reconsideration, the commission extended the detariffing date to January 1, 1983,[142] and adopted a two-step approach (the "bifurcated" approach, as opposed to the "flash-cut" approach[143]):

1. New CPE and enhanced services, as well as all federally tariffed CPE, were to be unbundled from the basic services and detariffed on January 1, 1983.[144]
2. All installed or "embedded" CPE, including inventories, tariffed at the state level and subject to the separations process, would remain with the telephone companies on a tariffed basis. It was contemplated that embedded CPE would either be sold to customers[145] or eventually detariffed (or, in the case of AT&T, transferred to the deregulated subsidiary).

The detariffing of CPE required consideration "not only of transition procedures, but also of separations implications, depreciation rates, investment recovery, asset valuation, and transfer pricing."[146] All of these issues were considered in subsequent proceedings.[147] With respect to AT&T, a wholly owned subsidiary — American Bell, Inc. (later renamed AT&T Information Systems) — was formed on June 15, 1982, as the entity to provide detariffed new customer premises equipment,[148] and enhanced information and data services. The Bell System operating companies were permitted to provide installation and maintenance services, under contract to AT&T, for an eighteen-month period (January 1, 1983 to July 1, 1984).

Modification of Final Judgment

On August 24, 1982, Judge Harold H. Greene of the federal district court in Washington, D.C., approved a modified agreement (the "Modification of Final Judgment" or "MFJ") which terminated the civil antitrust suit filed by the government in 1974 against AT&T, Western Electric, and Bell Labs, and which required the divestiture of the Bell System operating companies.[149] The government had charged that the defendants had monopolized a broad variety of telecommunications services and equipment in violation of Section 2 of the Sherman Antitrust Act. Initially, the government sought the divestiture from AT&T of the Bell operating companies and of Western Electric.[150]

AT&T agreed to the divestiture of its twenty-two wholly-owned operating companies, within eighteen months after formal approval of the agreement. "Absent such control," argued Judge Greene, "AT&T will not have the ability to disadvantage competitors in the interexchange and equipment markets."[151] The company was permitted to maintain control of both Bell Labs and Western Electric. The judge noted that the former "has been a positive force both in basic and in applied research, and this research has had a beneficial effect on the nation's economic position in all of its varied aspects," while "the links between Bell Laboratories and the manufacturing and service arms of the Bell System have been of assistance in the achievement of these technological successes."[152] Further, the line of business restrictions and the patent licensing requirements imposed by the 1956 consent decree were removed, so that AT&T "would be free to compete in all facets of the marketplace,"[153] with two exceptions: AT&T may not reacquire the operating companies and may not engage in the field of electronic publishing for seven years.[154] All embedded customer premises equipment would be transferred to AT&T, and the license contracts between AT&T and the twenty-two wholly-owned operating companies (as well as with Cincinnati Bell and Southern New England Telephone) terminated. The decree, concluded Judge Greene,

> . . . will thus allow AT&T to become a vigorous competitor in the growing computer, computer-related, and information markets. Other large and experienced firms are presently operating in these markets, and there is therefore no reason to believe that AT&T will be able to achieve monopoly dominance in these industries as it did in telecommunications. At the same time, by use of its formidable scientific, engineering, and management resources, including particularly the capabilities of Bell Laboratories, AT&T should be able to make significant contributions to these fields, which are at the forefront of innovation and technology, to the benefit of American consumers, national defense, and the position of American industry vis-a-vis foreign competition.[155]

The operating companies, after divestiture, would be limited to providing "exchange telecommunications and exchange access services." They are prohibited from providing "any other product or service . . . that is not a natural monopoly service actually regulated by tariff"[156] and from engaging in three specific ("core") activities: the provision of interexchange services, the provision of information services (including electronic publishing),[157] and the manufacture of telecommunications products and customer premises equipment.[158] They are permitted to engage in the marketing and installing of new customer premises equipment, and they retained control over the "Yellow Pages" directories. They are prohibited from discriminating in the "establishment and dissemination of technical information and procurement and interconnection standards" and, by September 1, 1986, must provide access services to interexchange carriers and information service providers which are "equal in type, quality, and price" to the access services provided AT&T and its affiliates.[159]

The MFJ contained countless specific provisions and general guidelines for carrying out the divestiture. To illustrate: AT&T was required to provide to the divested operating companies "sufficient facilities, personnel, systems, and rights to technical information" to permit them to perform their exchange telecommunications and exchange access functions. Assets were to be divided between AT&T and the divested operating companies on the basis of net book value; at the time of transfer of ownership, the separated operating companies "shall have debt ratios of approximately 45 percent (except for Pacific Telephone and Telegraph Company which shall have a debt ratio of approximately 50 percent), and the quality of the debt shall be representative of the average terms and conditions of the consolidated debt."[160] Finally, the Court retained jurisdiction to approve the plan of reorganization and "to issue orders or directions for the construction or carrying out of this decree, for the enforcement of compliance therewith, and for the punishment of any violation thereof."[161]

Implementation Plans. The plan of reorganization was reviewed by the Court in two stages.

On October 4, 1982, AT&T and the operating companies filed new local exchange areas — known as LATAs (Local Access and Transport Areas); a proposal which called for the establishment of 161 LATAs (a few of which were subsequently modified).[162] These LATAs followed the criteria contained in the MFJ (*e.g.*, areas that serve "common social, economic, and other purposes"; every point served by the divested operating companies shall be included within a LATA; except with court approval, no LATA shall cross state lines) and, in addition, the proposal sought to preserve existing local calling and nonoptional extended area service arrangements. As a consequence of the final LATA designations, "about one-fourth of pre-divestiture AT&T's long-distance traffic was transferred to the BOCs as a result of divestiture."[163]

On December 16, 1982, AT&T filed its Plan of Reorganization.[164] The plan contained three key provisions:

1. The twenty-two operating companies would be reorganized into seven regional holding companies (see Table 15-5). Under the plan, the regional companies would get about 75 percent of total Bell System assets. A method was established for allocating assets, as specified in the MFJ: (*a*) those facilities that are used to provide local exchange service and access will remain with the regional companies; (*b*) equipment used to provide interexchange switching and transmission will go to AT&T; and (*c*) "multifunction" facilities (*e.g.*, central office equipment, outside plant, land and buildings, motor vehicles) will be assigned on the basis of "predominant usage" — all at net book value. AT&T stockholders will receive one share in each regional company for each ten shares of AT&T stock owned.

2. A Central Staff Organization (CSO, later named Bell Communications Research or Bellcore) will be created to provide technical assistance and other services to the regional companies after divestiture. Each regional company will own one-seventh of the CSO. Until 1987, AT&T will provide (*a*) research and development services to the regional companies on a priority basis and (*b*) royalty-free licenses under all existing patents and patents issued during the period. The CSO will provide "a single point of contact" for coordination of the regional companies "to meet the requirements of national security and emergency preparedness" (as the MFJ requires) and will handle future use of the Bell logo.

3. Seven regional organizations will be created to provide and maintain cellular mobile telephone service (a service defined in the MFJ as a local exchange service).

Before accepting the Plan of Reorganization, Judge Greene required several modifications, the three most important being the following:

1. If by January 1, 1994, the Operating Companies in the aggregate have not recovered the costs of providing equal access and network reconfiguration . . ., plus financing expenses, through their collection of access charges from the interexchange carriers, AT&T will reimburse the Operating Companies in the amount of any remaining deficit. . . . [165]

2. Beginning on the date of divestiture, AT&T will cease to use the word "Bell" in its corporate name and in the names of its subsidiaries or affiliates, other than Bell Laboratories and AT&T's foreign subsidiaries or affiliates; and beginning on the same date, AT&T will cease to use the "Bell" name and the Bell trademarks, or either, on any equipment sold by it in the United States after that date, except for equipment manufactured or purchased by AT&T prior to that date. . . . [166]

3. AT&T will grant to each Operating Company nonexclusive and per-

TABLE 15-5

Regional Holding Companies and Proposed LATAs

Holding Company Bell Operating Companies	Assets[a] (Billions)	LATAs[b]	
NYNEX CORP.	$ 17.39	11	
New England Tel. & Tel. Co.			6
New York Tel. Co.			5
BELL ATLANTIC CORP.	16.26	19	
Chesapeake & Potomac Tel. Co.			1
Chesapeake & Potomac Tel. Co. of Maryland			3
Chesapeake & Potomac Tel. Co. of Virginia			5
Chesapeake & Potomac Tel. Co. of West Virginia ...			2
Diamond State Tel. Co.			0
New Jersey Bell Tel. Co.			3
Bell Tel. Co. of Pennsylvania			5
AMERITECH CORP.	16.26	30	
Illinois Bell Tel. Co.			11
Indiana Bell Tel. Co., Inc.			5
Michigan Bell Tel. Co.			5
Ohio Bell Tel. Co.			5
Wisconsin Tel. Co.			4
BELLSOUTH CORP.	20.81	37	
Southern Bell Tel. & Tel. Co.			21
South Central Bell Tel. Co.			16
SOUTHWESTERN BELL CORP.	15.51	25	
Southwestern Bell Tel. Co.			25
U S WEST INC.	15.51	29	
Mountain States Tel. & Tel. Co.			11
Northwestern Bell Tel. Co.			14
Pacific Northwest Bell Tel. Co.			4
PACIFIC TELESIS GROUP	16.19	10	
Pacific Tel. & Tel. Co.			9
Bell Tel. Co. of Nevada			1
Totals	$117.47	161	

[a]AT&T's financial data, filed with the Securities and Exchange Commission, as reported in *The Wall Street Journal*, November 17, 1983, pp. 24-25 (pro forma basis as of June 30, 1983).

[b]Proposed LATAs as filed by AT&T with the District Court, October 4, 1982.

sonal royalty-free licenses to use telecommunications equipment and operational methods covered by all existing patents owned or controlled by AT&T and all other patents issued to AT&T on or before five years after the data of divestiture.

AT&T will grant to each Operating Company the right to sublicense all AT&T patents to manufacturers for use only in providing the Operating Companies with goods and services embodying the inventions of the patents.[167]

Divestiture, Line of Business Restrictions, and Controversy. The divestiture of the world's largest corporation was complex and costly,[168] but it was completed before the February 24, 1984, deadline. (The divestiture was effective January 1, 1984.) Moreover, it will be several years before a meaningful assessment of the divestiture can be undertaken.[169] Procedures had to be established[170]; several applications have been filed with the court for clarification and/or enforcement.[171] But it is the "line of business" restrictions on the regional holding companies that have become so highly controversial, as has Judge Greene's continued oversight.

Line of business restrictions were imposed because of a belief that local exchange service was a "natural monopoly"; a "local bottleneck," too expensive to duplicate. "In the absence of the restrictions, it is reasoned, the Operating Companies will be able (1) to subsidize their prices in competitive markets with supracompetitive profits earned in the monopoly market, and (2) to hinder competitors by restricting their access to the intraexchange network."[172] These arguments, contend MacAvoy and Robinson, "make little sense. . . . Local telephone operations, standing alone, are by no reasonable measure a prime potential source of funds for cross-subsidies. . . . Constraining BOC activities can only lessen the likelihood that the AT&T divestiture will yield tangible public dividends."[173]

To date, Judge Greene has granted over 160 waivers regarding entry into unrelated businesses (nontelecommunications markets) and, in fact, has removed that restriction entirely.[174] But in a September, 1987, decision, he denied motions filed by the Department of Justice[175] and the seven regional holding companies to remove the three specific (core) restrictions in the decree, holding that because bypass is so slight at the present time, "the bottlenecks are as pervasive as ever."[176] And he added: "Only when a practical and economically-sound method is found for large-scale bypass or for connecting local consumers by a different method — as microwaves and satellites were ultimately found to be feasible for handling long distance traffic — can the Regional Companies' local monopoly be regarded as eroded."[177]

Continuing judicial supervision of the decree also has become a source of controversy. Argue Crandall and Owen:

We see danger in indefinite close judicial supervision of this industry.

The divestiture, new technologies, a surge of new entrants, and the visible nature of local subscriber rate regulation will combine to create substantial pressures for a variety of rates and new service options. The continuing jurisdiction of the federal court will give those damaged by competitive thrusts an easy avenue for appeal of marketplace dictates. Moreover, the court's continuing jurisdiction will provide future opportunities for judicial intervention that would not normally occur.

Judge Greene is an uncommonly astute and hard-working jurist, with life tenure. But the MFJ will outlive him. The purported benefits of the MFJ are those of enhanced service and rate competition. Continued judicial supervision of the decree may impede the operation of these market forces, as it has, for example, in the *Paramount* decrees.[178]

Third Computer Inquiry

The commission initiated its third computer inquiry[179] in 1985, noting that efforts to protect competition through the maximum separation requirements in *Computer II* had suppressed (in some instances), rather than promoted, public access to enhanced services.[180] A year later, in its initial *Computer III* decision, the commission removed the maximum separation requirements imposed on AT&T and the regional holding companies, subject to two conditions: (*a*) implementation of "Open Network Architecture" plans (to be filed by February 1, 1988) that satisfy "Comparably Efficient Interconnection" requirements[181] and (*b*) the development of accounting procedures to allocate common and joint costs to prevent cross-subsidy.[182] Moreover, the commission issued a Supplemental Notice of Proposed Rulemaking raising five topics for further consideration (*e.g.*, the specific types of nonstructural safeguards that should be applied to the provision of enhanced services; whether the nonstructural safeguards should be applied to independent local exchange carriers; whether *Computer III* should be applied to international communications).[183] It seems clear that implementation of the initial *Computer III* decision is several years away.

The Future of the Domestic Telecommunications Industry

The domestic telecommunications industry is one in which the rapid pace of technology — which was to blur the traditional distinction between the communications and computer markets — has resulted in the restructuring of the industry; a restructuring that "signals the start of a remarkable era for an otherwise mature industry."[184]

There remain, however, significant challenges for the coming years. Access charges, bypass, cost-based rates, line of business restrictions on the regional holding companies, continuing judicial supervision of the consent decree, and state and federal regulation of imperfectly competitive markets,[185] are simply a few of the immediate issues.[186] Equally important, Congress needs to rewrite the Communications Act of 1934, so that its goals and provisions are both consistent and geared to the current and foreseeable needs of the telecommunications industry and its users.[187] Utilization of the frequency spectrum will demand far more attention in the future, since many of the new entrants and/or technologies require new frequency allocations (*e.g.*, cellular radio,[188] microwave distribution systems for video, low-power TV).

All of these tasks, moreover, will take place in an environment of rapidly changing technology, which will provide users with a variety of new products and services, but which will also disturb the restructuring of the industry which has so recently occurred. As Phillips has suggested:

> We have witnessed history's most pervasive structural disintegration of a large enterprise. Despite this massive atomization — and despite objectives that seem to have ordained its occurrence — there are reasons for believing that the new structural arrangements will be short lived. The present industry and regulatory structures contain elements of inherent instability. Rather than anticipating the attainment of near-term market and regulatory equilibria, a more likely scenario is one of continued performance upheavals, and unsettled and unsettling regulatory and, perhaps, legislative change. With these will come the eventual reemergence of a more integrated structure. . . .[189]

Appendix: Antitrust Policy in a Transitional Era

The large firm has long been particularly vulnerable to antitrust action and certainly AT&T qualifies as a large firm.[190] The telecommunications industry developed, however, under conditions of monopoly and regulation, so that antitrust activity was relatively rare.[191] But beginning with the *Carterfone* decision, as outlined in a previous section, the FCC adopted a liberalized entry policy into segments of the industry. During the next few years, countless firms entered (or tried to enter) and the industry, in turn, found itself facing a growing competitive challenge. Over fifty private antitrust suits were filed against the former Bell System alone,[192] alleging various antitrust violations during the transitional era (generally the period 1968-1982).[193] While many of these suits were settled out of court,[194] the cases raise some complex legal and economic policy issues that are summarized in this Appendix.

The Private Cases

A majority of the private suits were filed by large (*e.g.*, General Dynamics, ITT, Litton Systems) or small (*e.g.*, Gregg Communications Systems[195]) terminal equipment manufacturers, intra- and interstate private line and switched message service providers (*e.g.*, MCI, Southern Pacific), and by a number of firms seeking interconnections for specific purposes (*e.g.*, Interconnect Planning,[196] Phonetele,[197] Sound,[198] Western States Telephone,[199] and two class action suits by alarm system companies[200]). Many of the firms were relatively new to the telecommunications industry, as the following three examples illustrate:

1. *MCI Communications Corporation* (MCI) commenced operations in 1973, offering private line service between Chicago and St. Louis. The company was unprofitable until 1977 (losing $68.8 million in the period 1974 through 1976), when net profits totaled $2.5 million. MCI's sales have grown from $6.9 million in 1974 to $2.5 billion in 1985. In July 1985, IBM announced the purchase of 18 percent of MCI's stock.[201]

2. *Northeastern Telephone Company,* established in Connecticut in 1972, "started with only its two founders doing primarily maintenance work on telephone systems sold and installed by International Telephone & Telegraph; it now has over fifty employees. Initially, Northeastern operated out of part of a building that was formerly a church; since then, it has expanded at the rate of approximately one new office each year.... Northeastern's revenues its first year were approximately $70,000; in its seventh year, it posted sales of over $3,000,000."[202]

3. *Southern Pacific Communications Company* (SPCC) was formed in January 1970, as a wholly-owned subsidiary of the Southern Pacific Company, to provide private line service via microwave facilities (many already in place and owned by Southern Pacific Transportation Company). "SPCC has grown from a company with assets of $9,552,303 in 1973 to one with $278,484,000 in 1980.... To date, SPCC has yet to make a profit in private line with its losses going from $1,025,969 in 1973 to over $15,000,000 in 1980.... However, there is no dispute that SPCC is a presently profitable company, due principally to the provision of switched services, known as 'SPRINT'."[203] In 1983, GTE Corporation purchased SPCC.[204]

Where specific damages were stated in the complaints, they were large: Southern Pacific, in its private line case, originally sought $567 million (trebled to $1.7 billion), later reduced to $230.2 million (trebled to $690.6 million); Litton Systems sought $600 million (trebled to $1.8 billion); Dasa reportedly sought $156 million (trebled to $468 million)[205]; Phonetele originally sought $30 million (trebled to $90 million), later raised to $100 million (trebled to $300 million); and General Dynamics sought damages amounting to "many millions of dollars."[206] Some jury awards also have been large:[207] MCI was awarded $600 million (trebled to $1.8 billion), reduced on remand to $37.8 million (trebled to $113.4 million)[208]; Litton Systems was awarded $92.2 million (trebled to $276.6 million)[209]; Northeastern Telephone was awarded $5.5 million (trebled to $16.5 million)[210]; and Woodlands Telecommunications was awarded $18.4 million (trebled to $55.1 million).[211]

Three Key Legal Issues

In the private suits filed against the former Bell System, three key legal issues have been advanced: the question of immunity, the issue of regulatory impact, and the applicability of the doctrine of offensive collateral estoppel.

The Question of Immunity.[212] There are three potential questions regarding immunity that are commonly raised in antitrust suits involving public utilities (and other regulated industries). First, is the conduct immune from the antitrust laws, under the implied immunity doctrine, because of pervasive regulation under a public interest standard? Second, is the conduct exempt from antitrust prosecution due to "state action" under the *Parker* exclusion? Third, is the conduct exempt from competitive criteria because it is "political action" under the *Noerr-Pennington* immunity?

Implied Immunity. The first question arises in cases where there is no explicit exemption in a federal regulatory statute (as is true with the Communications Act of 1934) of activities from the antitrust laws. "Repeal of the antitrust laws by implication," the Supreme Court has held, "is not favored and not casually to be allowed. Only where there is a 'plain repugnance between the antitrust and regulatory provisions' will repeal be implied."[213] Further, "[r]epeal is to be regarded as implied only if necessary to make the [regulatory scheme] work, and even then only to the minimum extent necessary."[214] Thus, the implied immunity may be found in only two instances: first, "where the regulatory scheme established by Congress is so pervasive as to impliedly repeal the antitrust laws"[215] and, second, "where application of the antitrust laws to the particular conduct challenged . . . would conflict with the requirements of the regulatory scheme in such a way that the scheme would be rendered unworkable."[216]

Parker. The second question refers to immunity due to the "state action" doctrine enunciated in the *Parker* decision of 1943.[217] To protect farmers from calamitous price changes, the California legislature enacted the California Agricultural Prorate Act of 1933, which authorized a state commission to stabilize the price of agricultural commodities. Local committees were permitted to formulate the prorate (marketing) plans, subject to commission approval. The Supreme Court (in a challenge from a raisin producer and packer) held that although such practices might have anticompetitive effects, they were immune from antitrust attack since the Sherman and Clayton Acts were not designed to interfere with valid governmental action. Generally, then, the *Parker* exclusion

... applies to the rates and practices of public utilities enjoying monopoly status under state policy where their rates and practices are subjected to meaningful regulation and supervision by the state to the end that they are the result of considered judgment of the state regulatory authority.[218]

Several decisions since 1943[219] have considerably narrowed the *Parker* exclusion, with the result that its applicability requires

... three principal inquiries: first, whether under state law defendants are compelled to engage in the anticompetitive conduct; second, whether such conduct is pursuant to a "clearly articulated and affirmatively expressed goal" to "displace unfettered business freedom;" and third, whether the anticompetitive or predatory conduct is necessary to effectuate state policy. . . .[220]

Noerr-Pennington. The third question concerns conduct protected under the *Noerr-Pennington* doctrine, subject to the so-called "sham" exception. In *Noerr,* a trucking association challenged a deceptive political campaign advocating legislation favorable to the railroads. The Supreme Court held that "the Sherman Act . . . does not apply to . . . activities compris[ing] mere solicitation of government action with respect to the passage and enforcement of laws," irrespective of whether the activities might be considered fraudulent or deceptive.[221] In dictum, however, the Court added: "There may be situations in which a publicity campaign, ostensibly directed toward influencing governmental action, is a mere sham to cover what is actually nothing more than an attempt to interfere directly with the business relationships of a competitor and the application of the Sherman Act would be justified."[222]

In *Pennington,* an industry union and large firms urged the Secretary of Labor to establish minimum wage levels that would have forced out smaller firms. The Supreme Court held that "*Noerr* shields from the Sherman Act a concerted effort to influence public officials regardless of intent or purposes. . . . Joint efforts to influence public officials do not violate the antitrust laws even though intended to eliminate competition."[223]

Both cases involved state political activity, but the doctrine was held applicable to administrative and adjudicative proceedings in 1972.[224] In the context of the former Bell System private antitrust cases, therefore, the issue becomes the applicability of the doctrine when a utility files a tariff (or tariffs) with a regulatory commission, which is (are) subsequently adjudicated; *i.e.,* does such a filing constitute a request for governmental action under the *Noerr-Pennington* doctrine?

Applications. AT&T has had very limited success in the private cases in arguing for exemption under an implied immunity,[225] the *Parker* doctrine,[226] or the *Noerr-Pennington* exclusion.[227] Consider, to illustrate, the much-publicized decisions involving Southern Pacific Communications' $230.2 million suit, relative to private line services,[228] under Section 2 of the Sherman Act.[229] In the district court, Judge Richey, after examining each specific complaint in detail, concluded (in a 602-page decision) that:

1. ... all of the rates and practices of defendants challenged by SPCC in this case are subject to pervasive federal and state regulatory control under a public interest standard that is quite different from and inconsistent with the application of the antitrust laws.
2. ... every action complained of in this case could have been or should have been handled by the appropriate regulatory bodies, which responsibility the regulators miserably mishandled or failed to handle.[230]

SPCC's numerous problems, Judge Richey found,

... are typical of any new company, especially a fast growing company in a new and emerging field of unusual technicalities. The foregoing analysis and findings of the Court should make it obvious that these problems are not the result of any anticompetitive conduct of AT&T, but rather just normal growing pains of a new company. It is easy for a new company who enters the market with expectations of grandeur to attack a giant when their expectations do not pan out. However, the evidence is clear, that SPCC's non-profitability is not the result of any illegal anticompetitive conduct on the part of AT&T on the basis of this record.[231]

On appeal, the decision was affirmed, but the circuit court held that while the regulatory scheme was inadequate, "as implemented by the FCC, to prevent anticompetitive behavior,"[232] the district court erred in holding that AT&T enjoyed implied immunity.

... under the applicable regulatory scheme, the initial decision to file a tariff establishing rates or to provide interconnections to a competing specialized common carrier rests with AT&T, and AT&T's tariffs and interconnection decisions often become effective without FCC scrutiny or approval. At minimum, long regulatory delays often have preceded final FCC approval or disapproval of AT&T's allegedly predatory rates, refusals to interconnect, or unreasonable and discriminatory terms and conditions of access to local distribution facilities. As Judge Greene concluded in *United States v. AT&T*, "it would be a gross misconception of the realities to equate the instant statutory scheme, the relatively weak regulatory controls which have implemented that scheme, and defendants' alleged activities which offend both the antitrust laws and the regulatory purposes, with the kind of explicit regulation endorsing industry conduct which the Supreme Court has held in relatively few instances to be inconsistent with antitrust enforcement." . . .[233]

The Issue of Regulatory Impact. While the existence of regulation appears insufficient to immunize challenged conduct from the antitrust laws, there is evidence to support the view that the existence of regulation must be considered in an assessment of whether a utility's conduct violates those laws. In 1975, the Supreme Court held that application of the antitrust doctrine to bank mergers "must take into account the unique federal and state restraints on [defendants' conduct]. Failure to do so would produce misconceptions that go to the heart of the doctrine itself."[234] In a 1980 decision, the 5th Circuit held that the antitrust laws "are not so inflexible as to deny consideration of governmental regulation."[235] And, in a 1983 decision, the 7th Circuit stated:

> Our conclusion that AT&T is not entitled to antitrust immunity in the instant case does not mean that AT&T's status as a regulated common carrier is irrelevant to our evaluation of AT&T's conduct. On the contrary, an industry's regulated status is an important "fact of market life," the impact of which on pricing and other competitive decisions "is too obvious to be ignored." . . . For this reason, the Supreme Court has repeatedly recognized that consideration of federal and state regulation may be proper even after the issue of antitrust immunity has been resolved. . . .[236]

The impact of regulation has been recognized in several ways. Consider, for example, monopolization cases. In the case of a nonregulated firm, the Supreme Court has stated: "The offense of monopoly under Section 2 of the Sherman Act has two elements: (1) the possession of monopoly power in the relevant market and (2) the willful acquisition or maintenance of that power as distinguished from growth or development as a consequence of a superior product, business acumen, or historic accident."[237] But in the case of a regulated firm, "the presence of a substantial degree of regulation, although not sufficient to confer antitrust immunity, may affect both the shape of 'monopoly power' and the precise dimensions of the 'willful acquisition or maintenance' of that power."[238] Heavy reliance cannot be placed on market share data as an indicator of "monopoly power:" Public utilities generally are monopolies within a service area. "Indeed, while a regulated firm's dominant share of the market typically explains *why* it is subject to regulation, the firm's statistical dominance may also be the *result* of regulation."[239] Likewise, "willfulness" cannot be presumed from the mere possession of monopoly power: Public utilities often have an explicit statutory obligation to anticipate and to meet all reasonable demands for service within their service territories. "To apply the *Alcoa* presumption to such conduct would be tantamount to holding that adherence to a firm's regulatory obligations could, by itself, constitute improper willfulness in a section 2 monopolization case."[240]

Further, regulation may affect also a utility's requisite purpose or intent to violate the antitrust laws. In a 5th Circuit decision, it was held that a utility's refusal to interconnect, based upon a claimed reliance on the statutory public interest standard (specifically, the avoidance of unnecessary duplication of facilities), could be considered in assessing the company's alleged monopolistic purpose or intent.[241] In a 7th Circuit decision, the court held as proper the lower court's instructions to the jury that if AT&T's good faith refusal to interconnect was based upon such reasons as a belief that the utility had not been ordered to interconnect by the FCC, that the plaintiff was not authorized by the FCC to provide the service, and that "established regulatory policies" would have been violated by the interconnections, "then the refusal to provide the interconnections was not anticompetitive conduct and cannot be considered conduct engaged in for the purpose of maintaining a monopoly."[242]

Thus, it seems clear that an assessment of the existence of monopoly power "requires close scrutiny of the regulatory scheme in question," while allegations about the misuse of monopoly power permit a defendant "to assert a defense based on good faith adherence to its regulatory obligations."[243]

The Doctrine of Offensive Collateral Estoppel. A third issue raised in several of the private antitrust suits is offensive collateral estoppel or issue preclusion, under which "a defendant is precluded from relitigating identical issues that the defendant litigated and lost against another plaintiff."[244] As explained by the Supreme Court:

> Under the judicially-developed doctrine of collateral estoppel, once a court has decided an issue of fact or law necessary to its judgment, that decision is conclusive in a subsequent suit based on a different cause of action involving a party to the prior litigation. . . . Collateral estoppel . . . serves to "relieve parties of the cost and vexation of multiple lawsuits, conserve judicial resources, and, by preventing inconsistent decisions, encourage reliance on adjudication."[245]

Several prerequisites must be considered before a trial judge can grant a motion for collateral estoppel:

1. The party to be estopped must have been a party or in privity with a party to the prior action;
2. The issues to be estopped must be identical to issues actually litigated and finally determined;
3. The issues to be estopped must have been necessary to the prior judgment;
4. The party to be estopped must have had a full and fair opportunity to litigate the issues in the prior action; and

5. Application of the doctrine must not otherwise be unfair.[246]

The decisions in those private suits where motions for application of collateral estoppel have been made indicate that the doctrine "is too fraught with drumhead potential to allow its application without the specific limitations that the Supreme Court, other courts, and legal scholars have enunciated."[247] Many of the cases involving potential application of collateral estoppel followed the *Litton* decisions.[248] Each issue must be analyzed in detail. However, to give but one illustration: In a 1984 decision, the D.C. Circuit reversed a lower court's application of the doctrine as constituting "an abuse of discretion." Specifically, the court held that: (*a*) despite a finding by the circuit court in *Litton* that the exclusion of state regulatory decisions was a "harmless" error, its exclusion "is a serious obstacle to the plaintiffs' use of offensive estoppel on the issue of AT&T's liability"; (*b*) there was an inconsistent determination with respect to the *Noerr-Pennington* doctrine as applied in *Litton* and in the government's antitrust suit against AT&T; (*c*) the doctrine could not be applied to the relevant product market definition in *Litton* since the definition was stipulated in that case; and (*d*) collateral estoppel could not be applied to the *Litton* jury finding that AT&T intentionally delayed in providing and installing interface devices because there was no showing of similarity between Litton and the plaintiffs in the instant proceeding.[249]

The Major Antitrust Issues

The specific alleged illegal conduct involved in the private antitrust suits falls into three broad categories: the protective connecting arrangement, interconnections, and pricing. Each will be summarized, with examples.

Protective Connecting Arrangement (PCA). The FCC's *Carterfone* decision opened the terminal equipment market to competition. But in several cases, potential competitors and terminal equipment users charged that AT&T prevented or thwarted entry (and, thereby, monopolized that market) by requiring (in tariffs filed in 1968) customers to use an "interface device" or PCA between the AT&T network and non-AT&T equipment. All PCAs had to be leased from, and installed by, AT&T.

Such hardware, it was alleged, was either "unnecessary" and "discriminatory,"[250] or "overdesigned" (thereby making it more expensive than necessary "and designed in a way to require modification of non-Bell equipment or to require additional equipment and an external power source on the customer's premises"[251]). As part of the charge, it has been maintained that AT&T consistently opposed the adoption of certification standards for terminal equipment, which "amounted to an abuse of the administrative process within the sham exception to the *Noerr-Pennington* doctrine."[252]

The basic issue is clear: Was the PCA an honest ("good faith") effort by

AT&T to protect the integrity of the network in the post-*Carterfone* period or was the PCA an attempt (even a sham) to maintain control of the terminal equipment market?

Interconnections. The FCC's 1971 *Specialized Common Carriers* decision opened some segments of the telecommunications market to competition and, hence, raised the issue of appropriate interconnections. The specialized common carriers were authorized to provide their own microwave facilities for point-to-point private line services (for which local distribution facilities were required). Other interconnections were required in two instances: Where the specialized common carriers desired to offer end-to-end transmission and where they desired to offer service to locations they did not cover (*i.e.,* "multipoint" interconnections). Thus, there were two basic issues: (*a*) the provision of local distribution facilities and (*b*) the provision of interconnections for other specialized common carrier services intended by the FCC.

The jury, in the original *MCI* decision, found that "AT&T's refusal to interconnect a competitor to local distribution facilities that were essential for the competitor to offer its customers certain kinds of telecommunications service constituted an act of monopolization under the essential facilities doctrine" and that "AT&T did not act in good faith when it purportedly determined that the public interest justified its denial of [FX and CCSA] interconnections."[253] But the 7th Circuit, on review, reversed the jury's finding that AT&T denied interconnections for multipoint service "with the intent to retain its monopoly."[254] Judge Richey, in the *SPCC* decision, concluded that AT&T had negotiated with SPCC in good faith for the provision of local distribution facilities[255]; "that at the very least there was a legitimate dispute over plaintiff's authority to provide FX and CCSA, and once resolved, the necessary interconnections were provided"[256]; and that the 1971 FCC decision "clearly did not impose any obligation upon AT&T to lease intercity facilities to, or piece-out services with, the specialized common carriers."[257]

Pricing. In response to the FCC's liberalized entry policy, it has been alleged in several of the private suits that AT&T engaged in "predatory" pricing; *i.e.,* "the deliberate sacrifice of present revenues for the purpose of driving rivals out of the market and then recouping the losses through higher profits earned in the absence of competition."[258] Following the FCC's 1971 *Specialized Common Carriers* decision, AT&T filed two new tariffs for private line services: High/Low and MPL.[259] Further, as the competitive challenge in the terminal equipment market heightened, the Bell operating companies (and some independents) began to make the so-called two-tier payment option available to some of their business customers.[260]

The meaning of predatory pricing in antitrust cases is far from clear. The standard may be subjective (based upon predatory intent and ruinous competition) or objective (a cost-based standard). While the former has been used for many years,[261] the latter has received more emphasis in recent cases.[262] In the AT&T cases, three courts have adopted a marginal cost standard, rather than a fully distributed cost standard (as advocated during the 1970s by the FCC in rejecting the tariffs filed by AT&T). Said the 2d Circuit in the *Northeastern* decision:

> Adopting marginal cost as the proper test of predatory pricing is consistent with the pro-competitive thrust of the Sherman Act. When the price of a dominant firm's product equals the product's marginal costs, "only less efficient firms will suffer larger losses per unit of output; more efficient firms will be losing less or even operating profitably." . . . Marginal cost pricing thus fosters competition on the basis of relative efficiency. Establishing a pricing floor above marginal cost would encourage underutilization of productive resources and would provide a price "umbrella" under which less efficient firms could hide from the stresses and storms of competition. Moreover, marginal cost pricing maximizes short-run consumer welfare, since when price equals marginal cost, consumers are willing to pay the expense incurred in producing the last unit of output. At prices above marginal costs, *per contra*, output is restricted, and consumers are deprived of products the value of which exceed their costs of production.[263]

Consequently, under a marginal cost standard — the Areeda-Turner Rule[264] in *Northeastern,* long-run incremental cost in *MCI* and *SPCC* — the predatory pricing charges against AT&T were dismissed.

With respect to the two-tier payment option, the 2d Circuit on review in *Northeastern* held that the option was offered to meet a competitive challenge and concluded that:

> . . . the incentives operating on a SNET [Southern New England Telephone Company] customer who elects the two-tier plan are similar to those applicable to a new owner of a Northeastern PBX. Just as a SNET customer is unlikely to purchase Northeastern's product, the latter is unlikely to switch to SNET's terminal equipment. Thus, SNET's use of the two-tier plan is no more anticompetitive than Northeastern's practice of selling PBXs. Neither one is an action that is "possible or effective only if taken by a firm that dominates its smaller rivals." . . . On the contrary, both are "ordinary marketing methods available to all in the market."[265]

Some Concluding Observations

Antitrust and regulation may well support common goals, but they utilize different techniques. Antitrust seeks to promote the public interest by insisting upon unrestrained competition (free market forces) to control behavior in an industry. Regulation does not simply equate the public interest with competition; its public interest standard is broader and, at the same time, requires consistency with the relevant regulatory statutes. Nationwide averaging and internal subsidies, promoted in telecommunications under the regulatory public interest standard, are but two examples of the different techniques, since neither could be maintained in a competitive market. The courts have long recognized the uneasy relationship between antitrust and regulation, as illustrated by their implied immunity, state action, and political action deliberations and by their view that the existence of regulation must be considered in an assessment of whether a utility's conduct violates the antitrust laws.

The AT&T private antitrust actions, however, are further complicated by the fact that the FCC (during the transitional era) was attempting to promote a form of "regulated competition" in some segments of the telecommunications industry; a form of competition that also differs substantially from the unfettered type of competition promoted by the antitrust laws. As the FCC put it in a 1977 decision:

> Even in those instances where we warrant that the public interest will be served by competition, the "competition" so permitted is required to be consistent with the regulatory requirements of the Communications Act. An applicant is still required to demonstrate legal, technical and financial qualifications ("fitness"), to be subject to conditions and control over entry and exit from common carriage, be subject to control over price and terms of service, and provide service on a nondiscriminatory basis and upon reasonable demand. Thus, even in concluding that the policy of limited open entry was preferable in the domestic satellite field, we noted that our policy did not constitute true open entry as in an unregulated field. We had no intention of abandoning our regulatory responsibilities in favor of permitting free market forces unfettered rein to regulate entry or behavior in this area.[266]

Thus, the FCC insisted upon a fully distributed cost standard throughout the 1970's, consistently rejecting AT&T's pleadings to adopt an incremental cost standard. The former *may* have been rational in a regulatory context, but it is of no relevance in an antitrust setting. Indeed, what is so unique about the private antitrust cases discussed above is the fact that almost every response that the former Bell System made to the FCC's new policy of "regulated competition" has been challenged under the antitrust laws as "anticompetitive." Whatever the merits of those suits, it can truly be said that AT&T was being forced to serve two masters during the transitional era.[267]

The private antitrust cases also suggest two important, but perhaps obvious, implications for regulatory commissions. They reinforce, in the first place, the need for the decisions and orders of the agencies to be written with greater clarity. The FCC's 1971 *Specialized Common Carriers* decision, for example, has been criticized by at least three courts. They require, in the second place, that greater emphasis be placed upon antitrust considerations in agency decisionmaking (*e.g.*, pricing, marketing programs, entry). This emphasis is particularly necessary in view of the trend towards competition that has been so evident in recent years.

Notes

*Judge Greene, *United States v. American Teleph. & Teleg. Co., 1982-2 Trade Cases*, Par. 64,979, p. 73,098 (D. D.C., 1982).

[1]Federal Communications Commission, *Annual Report, 1959*, p. 167.

[2]The telephone companies also leased private lines to their customers for various purposes, including record services, and offered teletypewriter exchange service.

[3]For a more complete history of the telegraph industry, upon which this discussion is largely based, see "The Telegraph Industry" in John G. Glover and Rudolph L. Lagai (eds.), *The Development of American Industries* (4th ed.; New York: Simmons-Boardman Publishing Corp., 1959), chap. xxxii. See also H. H. Goldin, "Government Policy and the Domestic Telegraph Industry," 7 *Journal of Economic History* 53 (1947).

[4]The Morse patent covered the transmission of messages by dots and dashes. Most of the early telegraph companies received licenses under this patent. A few, however, used the House printing telegraph, which transmitted messages by printing in Roman letters. While this system did not prove economical, it was the forerunner of automatic printing telegraphy.

[5]G. Lloyd Wilson, *Transportation and Communications* (New York: Appleton-Century-Crofts, Inc., 1945), p. 689.

[6]Teletypewriter messages are written by an operator using a keyboard very similar to a typewriter. As the keys are struck, holes are perforated into a narrow, moving paper tape. The tape passes into a transmitter, and the impulses caused by electrical contacts controlled by the holes in the tape flash out over the wire. At the receiving end, the impulses are automatically translated back into characters, printed on tape, and gummed by the operator to message blanks. In contrast, the teleprinter is a printing telegraph sending and receiving machine.

[7]A facsimile machine in a corporate office connects that office with the nearest telegraph center. Subscribers can send and receive telegrams instantly in picture form.

[8]"In essence, microwave systems send signals in the high-frequency range, amplify them at intermediate stations, and retransmit them until they reach their destination. Microwaves (which are electromagnetic) are between one and three inches long. Like light waves, they travel in straight lines and do not follow the curvature of the earth. They are focused sharply and aimed from point to point. Less than one watt of power — about the amount needed to light a pocket flashlight bulb — is sufficient to send them on their way between stations on a radio relay route." Herbert H. Goetschius, "Microwave Today and Tomorrow," 43 *Bell Telephone Magazine* 15, 15-16 (Summer, 1964). Microwave relay towers are approximately thirty miles apart.

[9]Pub. Law 4 (1943). Western Union was required to divest itself of its international telegraph operations. Divestiture was completed on September 30, 1963, when the cable facilities were sold to Western Union International Inc. (now owned by MCI Communications Corporation).

[10]*Re Western Union Teleg. Co. (TWX)*, 24 FCC 638 (1970).

[11]See, *e.g., Re Provision of Domestic Public Message Services*, 71 FCC 2d 471 (1979), 75 FCC 2d 345 (1980); *Re International Record Carriers' Scope of Operations (Gateways)*, FCC 2d 79-841 (1980) (which expanded the operation of the international record carriers from seven gateway cities to twenty-one areas, encompassing major metropolitan centers and satellite earth stations, with the condition that the carriers unbundle terminal equipment and local access loops); *Re Interconnection of International Telex*, 76 FCC 2d 61 (1979) (which allowed the international record carriers to interconnect with domestic telex services, with the condition that the carriers unbundle charges for telex machines and access lines). The latter two decisions were affirmed in 1981: *Western Union Teleg. Co. and TRT Telecommunications Corp. v. Federal Communications Comm.*, 665 F. 2d 1126 (D.C. Cir. 1981).

[12]Pub. Law 95-590 (1980); Pub. Law 97-130 (1981). The latter amendment followed a circuit court's reversal of a 1979 FCC order which had authorized Western Union to provide overseas service by connecting with facilities maintained by Canadian and Mexican communications entities. *Re Western Union Teleg. Co.*, 75 FCC 2d 461 (1979), *rev'd sub nom. ITT World Communications, Inc. v. Federal Communications Comm.*, 635 F. 2d 45 (2d Cir. 1980).

In 1981, Congress enacted the Record Carrier Competition Act, which directed the FCC to promote competition among record carriers and preempted state jurisdiction over such carriers' rates and services. In December, 1982, the FCC removed all restrictions on direct competition between voice and record transmitters in the international communications industry. Thus, AT&T was freed to offer international record and data services, while International Telephone and Telegraph Corporation, Western Union International, RCA Global Communications, and FTC Communications were freed to offer international voice service. *The Wall Street Journal*, December 9, 1982, p. 3.

[13]Such services include Telex, Economy Telex, and EasyLink, which permit subscribers to dial direct connections with other subscribers for the worldwide transmission of messages (*i.e.*, electronic mail) and data.

[14]*Moody's Public Utility Manual, 1987*, Vol. 2, p. 3662. Under severe financial pressure, due primarily to higher access charges and increasing competition, the company has announced plans to merge with its parent and form a new company — Western Union Telegraph Company. See "The Sad Saga of Western Union's Decline," *Business Week*, December 14, 1987, pp. 108-14.

[15]See Francis Bello, "The World's Greatest Industrial Laboratory," *Fortune*, November, 1958, pp. 148ff.

[16]The alternative routing system "works by assigning every telephone line a ten-digit number — an area code, an exchange, and a line number. Each line is at the end of a switching hierarchy. The local loop, ordinarily a pair of wires, connects the subscriber with a wire center, or class 5 local office. Trunks, or four wire connections, link the local office with a toll office, a primary center, a sectional center, and a regional center. These offices are numbered class 4, 3, 2, and 1, respectively.

"It is possible for a long distance call to travel all the way up the switching hierarchy and all the way down the chain of offices in which the called party is located. In practice, however, the call seldom follows this path (called the 'final route'). Special trunks ('high usage groups') are constructed between those intermediate stations that experience relatively heavy traffic. In fact, today most intercity traffic is transmitted between class 4 offices. 'Multiplexing' allows large numbers of conversations to travel over these trunks." *Telecommunications in Transition: The Status of Compe-*

tition in the Telecommunications Industry (House Committee Print 97-V, 97th Cong., 1st sess.) (Washington, D.C.: U.S. Government Printing Office, 1981), p. 74, n. 16.

[17]Digital transmission via fiber optics is rapidly replacing analog transmission via copper wire, since it is capable of carrying enormous quantities of information (*e.g.*, over 8,000 phone calls simultaneously on a pair of fibers) without serious distortion and, due to technological advances, is becoming increasingly competitive with satellite and microwave transmission. See "Fiber Optics Promises High-Tech Revolution," *The Wall Street Journal*, September 9, 1986, p. 6.

[18]See Horace Coon, *American Tel and Tel: The Story of a Great Monopoly* (New York: Longmans, Green, 1939); Arthur W. Page, *The Bell Telephone System* (New York: Harper & Row, 1941); Joseph C. Goulden, *Monopoly* (New York: G. P. Putnam's Sons, 1968); John Brooks, *Telephone: The First Hundred Years* (New York: Harper & Row, 1976); Sonny Kleinfield, *The Biggest Company on Earth: A Profile of AT&T* (New York: Holt, Rinehart & Winston, 1981).

[19]Early in 1878, the New England Telephone Company was formed to provide service in that area. The American Bell Telephone Company acquired a portion of the company's stock. The New England Company agreed to lease and not to sell its telephone instruments. The Bell Company, in turn, agreed to cooperate in patent litigation and in establishing connecting lines.

[20]Federal Communications Commission, *Investigation of the Telephone Industry in the United States* (House Doc. 340, 76th Cong., 1st sess.) (Washington, D.C.: U.S. Government Printing Office, 1939), pp. 123-25. "The Vanderbilt interests controlled Western Union at the time and were anxious to forestall the efforts of Jay Gould to acquire the company or achieve a foothold in communications. So when the prospect of a Gould-Bell alliance appeared, Western Union sought a compromise through a patent settlement, even though it possessed patents for the Blake Transmitter which was allegedly superior to anything then available for telephone service. Interestingly, the compromise was not successful in blocking Gould's acquisition of Western Union or in preventing Bell's entry into the telegraph field via private-line telegraph service." Harry M. Trebing, "The Plight of the Telegraph Service," 15 *MSU Business Topics* 43, 54, n. 8 (Summer 1967).

[21]Irston R. Barnes, *The Economics of Public Utility Regulation* (New York: F. S. Crofts & Co., 1942), p. 8.

[22]*Ibid.*, p. 39. See Robert W. Garnet, *The Telephone Enterprise: The Evolution of the Bell System's Horizontal Structure, 1876-1909* (Baltimore: The Johns Hopkins University Press, 1985); George David Smith, *The Anatomy of a Business Strategy: Bell, Western Electric, and the Origins of the American Telephone Industry* (Baltimore: The Johns Hopkins University Press, 1985).

[23]AT&T is a New York corporation. Massachusetts law prevented American Bell from holding more than 30 percent of the capital stock of any corporation doing business in the state, paying dividends in its own stock, or selling its stock at less than the market price as fixed by the Massachusetts Commissioner of Corporations. The company also experienced difficulty in securing permission to increase its capitalization with the growth of its business.

[24]AT&T owned the telephone instruments until December, 1927, when they were sold to the associated companies.

[25]Western Electric had five major subsidiaries: Teletype Corp. (manufacturer of teleprinters and data transmission equipment); Nassau Recycle Corp. (engaged in recycling, reclamation, and sale of nonferrous scrap metals); Manufacturers' Junction

Railway Co. (operating an industrial railroad in and about Western's Hawthorne plant at Cicero, with rail connections with all railroad systems entering Chicago); Sandia Corp. (operates, on a nonprofit basis, the government's Sandia National Laboratories at Livermore, California, and Albuquerque, New Mexico); and Western Electric Co., Ltd. (performs patent services in foreign countries).

[26]AT&T Co. owned a number of other subsidiaries, including 195 Broadway Corp.; Advanced Mobile Phone Service Corp; AT&T International, Inc.; Transoceanic Cable Ship Co., Inc.; Transpacific Communications, Inc.; and Transoceanic Communications, Inc.

[27]*Telecommunications in Transition, op. cit.*, p. 7.

[28]*Ibid.*, p. 13. (In a few markets, such as microwave equipment, Western Electric's share was below that of other manufacturers.) Approximately 94 percent of Western Electric's sales were to the Bell System. In addition to sales to the government, the company sold a small amount of equipment to the Graybar Electric Company, a nonaffiliated firm which, in turn, sold the equipment to other non-Bell System purchasers.

[29]*The Telephone Cases*, 126 U.S. 1 (1888).

[30]*Telecommunications in Transition, op. cit.*, p. 70.

[31]Bureau of the Census, "Telephones and Telegrams, 1902," Bulletin No. 17, as cited in *Investigation of the Telephone Industry in the United States, op. cit.*, p. 132. By 1907, the Bell System owned 3.1 million stations, while the independents owned 3 million. Bureau of the Census, "Special Reports: Telephones, 1907," p. 22.

[32]*Telecommunications in Transition, op. cit.*, p. 70. See Richard Gabel, "The Early Competitive Era in Telephone Communications," 34 *Law and Contemporary Problems* 340 (1969); Gerald W. Brock, *The Telecommunications Industry: The Dynamics of Market Structure* (Cambridge: Harvard University Press, 1981), pp. 89-125.

[33]Letter from N. C. Kingsbury, vice-president of AT&T, to the Attorney General of the United States, December 19, 1913. See *Annual Report of AT&T, 1913*, pp. 24-26. A consent decree was signed in 1914. [*United States v. American Teleph. & Teleg. Co.*, 1 *Decrees & Judgments in Civil Federal Antitrust Cases* 554 (D. Ore. 1914).] In 1917, the Kingsbury Commitment was modified whereby AT&T agreed to acquire competing companies only if it gave up an equal number of telephones to an independent company. When, in 1921, the Willis-Graham Act permitted telephone companies to merge or consolidate with competing companies if approved by the state commissions and the ICC, the Kingsbury Commitment was terminated. See letter from the Attorney General of the United States to E. K. Hall, vice-president of AT&T, September 19, 1921.

[34]Letter from E. K. Hall, vice-president of AT&T, to F. B. MacKinnon, president of the United States Independent Telephone Association (USITA), June 14, 1922. AT&T also agreed to give thirty days notice to the USITA before filing with a regulatory commission for approval of such an acquisition. In subsequent years, and with some exceptions, the Bell System purchased only distressed companies and, in several instances, it made offsetting sales to independent companies.

[35]In the early 1930s, there were over 6,400 independent telephone companies, compared with 5,469 in 1951, 3,034 in 1961, 1,807 in 1971, and 1,459 at the end of 1981.

[36]*Moody's Public Utility Manual, 1987*, p. a61. In 1949, Congress amended the Rural Electrification Act to authorize the agency to make loans to provide, expand, or upgrade rural telephone service at relatively low interest rates. As of January 1,

1987, 1,033 telephone companies and cooperatives had received REA and/or Rural Telephone Bank loans and guarantees totaling more than $8 billion. "Today, 95 percent of American farms have telephone service, compared to 38 percent in 1950, and 84 percent of it is single-party." 49 *Telecommunications Reports* 10 (October 17, 1983).

[37]The next five independent companies, with 1986 revenues in parentheses: Contel Corporation ($3.1 billion), United Telecommunications, Inc. ($2.8 billion), Southern New England Telecommunications Corporation ($1.4 billion), Centel Corporation ($1.4 billion), Alltel Corporation ($697.1 million).

[38]The company's acquisition program has resulted in several antitrust suits. See, *e.g., United States v. General Teleph. & Electronics Corp.,* Civil Action No. 64-1912 (S.D. N.Y., filed June 19, 1964; dismissed by government, November 14, 1966) (challenging acquisition of four telephone companies, alleging acquisitions would foreclose market to equipment manufacturers); *International Teleph. & Teleg. Corp. v. General Teleph. & Electronics Corp.,* 296 F. Supp. 920 (D. Haw. 1969), 352 F. Supp. 1153 (D. Haw. 1972), *aff'd in part and rev'd in part,* 518 F. 2d 913 (9th Cir. 1975) (challenging acquisitions of Hawaiian Telephone Company and Northern Ohio Telephone Company); *United States v. GTE Corp.,* 603 F. Supp. 730 (D. D.C. 1984) (approving consent decree regarding acquisitions of telecommunications units of Southern Pacific Company).

[39]Joint network planning involves voluntary (*i.e.,* non-FCC intervention) procedures under which the participants "agree on what types of equipment should be provided where and by which carriers for a range of toll switching and transmission facilities. The costs and operating characteristics of alternative types of equipment and arrangements of facilities are evaluated jointly by the representatives of multiple companies and decisions on ownership of new facilities are made jointly." Warren G. Lavey, "Joint Network Planning in the Telephone Industry," 34 *Federal Communications Law Journal* 345 (1982).

Yet, in a 1980 report, the FCC concluded: "We do not see an overwhelming need for interdependence everywhere in the telecommunications system. . . . Inefficiencies, associated with large, long-term, inflexible commitments, standardized rules, and the difficulties of achieving coordination throughout the various levels of a complex intertwined system of corporate hierarchies, may more than outweigh the advantages of centralized planning and integration." *Re Economic Implications and Interrelationships Arising From Policies and Practices Relating to Customer Interconnection, Jurisdictional Separations, and Rate Structures,* 75 FCC 2d 506, 547-48 (1980).

[40]Said the California Railroad Commission in a 1933 decision: "The Commission has frequently expressed the opinion that a divided ownership of telephone equipment and responsibility for its maintenance is not compatible with efficient telephone service. It has frequently been declared that a telephone utility must own and maintain all facilities required for the transmission of messages from one subscriber to another. Almost without exception a similar view has been expressed by the regulatory commissions of other states." *City of Los Angeles v. So. Calif. Teleph. Co.,* 2 PUR (NS) 247, 249 (Cal. 1933).

[41]*Investigation of the Telephone Industry in the United States, op. cit.,* p. 35.

[42]Western Electric Company, *Standard Supply Contract,* June 2, 1930, and supplements, Art. I, Section 1.

[43]In 1966, for example, Western Electric's purchases included 900,000 ball-point pens, 5 million pencils and 9,000 sharpeners, 82 million paper clips, 120,000 type-

writer ribbons, 6.5 million erasers, and 36 tons of rubber bands. *The Wall Street Journal*, October 5, 1967, p. 1. In 1967, Western Electric purchased over 150,000 different items from some 45,000 suppliers.

[44]Typical is the following quotation from a 1966 decision: "In April, 1964, the actual price paid by Bell companies to Western was $10.53 [for the standard telephone handset], and the lowest price for which a similar set could have been purchased elsewhere was $21.63. Other illustrations are found in the record which testify to the fact that significant price differentials, likewise, exist with respect to every comparable item available from other manufacturers supplying the general trade." *Re So. Bell Teleph. & Teleg. Co.*, 66 PUR3d 1, 38 (Fla., 1966).

[45]NARUC-FCC Staff Committee on Telephone Regulatory Problems, *Report on Preliminary Survey and Investigation of Western Electric Company, Inc.* (New York, 1948). The study was updated annually, and two ten-year summaries have been published: NARUC-FCC Staff Committee on Telephone Regulatory Problems, *Report on Operating Results of Western Electric Company, Incorporated, Years 1947 to 1957, Inclusive* (New York, 1958) and NARUC-FCC Staff Subcommittee on Manufacturing and Service Affiliates, *Report on Operating Results of Western Electric Company, Incorporated, Years 1958 to 1967, Inclusive* (New York, 1968).

[46]See Chapter 7, pp. 254-56. For a comprehensive evaluation of Western Electric, see *A Study of Western Electric's Performance* (A Report Prepared by McKinsey & Co., Inc.) (New York: American Telephone & Telegraph Co., 1969).

[47]*United States v. Western Elec. Co., Inc. and American Teleph. & Teleg. Co., Inc.*, Civil Action No. 17-49 (D. N.J., filed January 14, 1949). The *Complaint* is reprinted in *Consent Decree Program of the Department of Justice* (Hearings before the Antitrust Subcommittee of the Committee on the Judiciary, House, 85th Cong., 2d sess.) (Washington, D.C.: U.S. Government Printing Office, 1958), Part II, Vol. 1, pp. 1723-95.

[48]*Ibid.*, p. 1796.

[49]The *Answer* is reprinted in *ibid.*, pp. 1799-1844.

[50]*Ibid.*, p. 1807.

[51]The *Final Judgment* is reprinted in *ibid.*, pp. 1845-63.

[52]An exception to the licensing agreements was made with General Electric Company, Radio Corporation of America, and Westinghouse Electric Corporation. These companies, together with AT&T and Western Electric, had been parties to patent license agreements dated July 1, 1932. The decree did not require licenses to these companies under existing patents to be royalty-free unless they, in turn, granted similar royalty-free licenses to the Bell System.

On several occasions, AT&T licensing agreements have been cited as resulting in the company's control of related industries. See, *e.g.*, N. R. Danielian, *A.T.&T.: The Story of Industrial Conquest* (New York: Vanguard Press, 1939), chaps. v-vii.

[53]As a result of the decree, Western Electric was required to divest itself of Westrex Corporation (which leased and sold equipment in the motion picture field), the Teletypesetter Corporation (a subsidiary of Teletype Corporation, manufacturing automatic typesetting equipment), and its inventory of train dispatching apparatus and the facilities used in their manufacture, while the Bell System was required to discontinue rendering certain communications services then being provided on a private contract basis.

[54]John Sheahan, "Integration and Exclusion in the Telephone Equipment Industry," 70 *Quarterly Journal of Economics* 249, 267 (1956). See also *Report of the Antitrust*

Subcommittee on the Consent Decree Program of the Department of Justice (House, 86th Cong., 1st sess.) (Washington, D.C.: U.S. Government Printing Office, 1959, pp. 96-120; Manley R. Irwin and Robert E. McKee, "Vertical Integration and the Communication Equipment Industry: Alternatives for Public Policy," 53 *Cornell Law Review* 446 (1968), reprinted in 22 *Federal Communications Bar Journal* 131 (1968); Manley R. Irwin, *Telecommunications Policy: Integration vs. Competition* (New York: Praeger Publishers, 1971).

[55]The Post Roads Act was repealed in 1947, thereby ending special domestic telegraph rates for the federal government.

Federal power to regulate interstate and foreign communications rests on both the commerce and postal clauses of the Constitution. See *Pensacola Teleg. Co. v. Western Union Teleg. Co.*, 96 U.S. 1 (1877).

[56]Pub. Law 218, 36 Stat. 539 (1910).

[57]James M. Herring and Gerald C. Gross, *Telecommunications* (New York: McGraw-Hill Book Co., Inc., 1936), p. 220.

[58]41 Stat. 456 (1920).

[59]Pub. Law 25, 42 Stat. 27 (1921).

[60]42 Stat. 8 (1921).

[61]*Preliminary Report on Communication Companies* (H. Rep. No. 1273, 73d Cong., 2d sess.) (Washington, D.C.: U.S. Government Printing Office, 1934) (known as the Splawn Report).

[62]The Communications Act of 1934, as amended, 50 Stat. 189, Section 1 (1937). See "The Communications Act of 1934 as Amended and Other Selected Provisions of Law" (Washington, D.C.: U.S. Government Printing Office, 1983).

[63]With the concurrence of the Secretary of State and the Department of Defense, the commission may authorize a company to land submarine cables in this country to connect with other countries.

[64]Pub. Law 94-376, 90 Stat. 1080 (1976).

[65]Several of the FCC's tariff filing practices generated substantial controversy in the 1970s. See, *e.g.*, *American Teleph. & Teleg. Co. v. Federal Communications Comm.*, 487 F. 2d 865 (2d Cir. 1973) (rejecting commission's 1972 requirement — in Docket No. 18128 — that AT&T secure "special permission" before it could file a tariff adjusting its private-line rates); *Aeronautical Radio, Inc. v. Federal Communications Comm.*, 642 F. 2d 1221 (D.C. Cir. 1980) (ruling that the commission's decision not to reject — as well as not to suspend or investigate — a tariff filing is not subject to judicial review), *cert. denied*, 451 U.S. 920 (1981); *MCI Telecommunications Corp. v. Federal Communications Comm.*, 627 F. 2d 322 (D.C. Cir. 1980) (adopting a "rule of reason" approach in reviewing the commission's practice of permitting a tariff, which had gone into effect and later was found to be unlawful, to remain in effect pending further action).

[66]There are three exemptions to this requirement: (*1*) a line within a single state unless the line constitutes part of an interstate line; (*2*) local, branch, or terminal lines not exceeding ten miles in length; or (*3*) any lines acquired by the consolidation of telephone or telegraph companies.

[67]The act prohibits consolidation of a domestic telegraph carrier with an international telegraph carrier; the combination of wire and radio companies is forbidden if the purpose or effect may be "substantially to lessen competition."

[68]A new subsection 410(c), added by Congress in 1971 (Pub. Law 92-131), reads: "The Commission shall refer any proceeding regarding the jurisdictional separation of common carrier property and expenses between interstate and intrastate opera-

tions, which it institutes pursuant to a notice of proposed rulemaking and, except as provided in Section 409 of this Act [the general provisions relating to commission adjudicatory proceedings], may refer any other matter, relating to common carrier communications of joint Federal-State concern, to a Federal-State Joint Board."

[69]Pub. Res. 8, 74th Cong., 49 Stat. 43 (1935). The initial resolution appropriated $750,000 to carry out the mandate of Congress. Two additional appropriations were made in 1936 and 1937, providing a total of $1.5 million for the entire investigation. More than 300 people, primarily lawyers, accountants, and engineers, were engaged in the investigation which lasted over four years.

[70]Federal Communications Commission, *Investigation of the Telephone Industry in the United States, op. cit.,* p. 596. For a different interpretation of the history of the company during the same period covered by the report, see Danielian, *op. cit.*

[71]Federal Communications Commission, *Annual Report, 1949,* p. 104. The commission's decision to use original cost valuations was upheld in *American Teleph. & Teleg. Co. v. United States,* 299 U.S. 232 (1936).

[72]Federal Communications Commission, *Annual Report, 1954,* p. 40.

[73]See Chapter 6, pp. 215-18.

[74]National Association of Regulatory Utility Commissioners, *Report on Service Charges by the American Telephone and Telegraph Company to the Associated Bell Telephone Companies and Long Lines Department* (New York, 1945). See also *Consent Decree Program of the Department of Justice,* Part II, Vol. II, *op. cit.,* pp. 2508-20.

[75]See Chapter 5, pp. 190-91.

[76]Memorandum Opinion and Order, Docket No. 16258, 2 FCC 2d 871 (1965). See, *e.g.,* Charles F. Phillips, Jr., "Some Observations on the FCC's Telephone Investigation," 77 *Public Utilities Fortnightly* 23 (February 17, 1966); Ben W. Lewis, "The Great AT&T Investigation," 14 *Challenge* 5 (May-June, 1966).

[77]The investigation was completed as Phase II of Docket No. 19129, FCC 77-150 (1977).

[78]The commission had excluded these items in *Re American Teleph. & Teleg. Co. and Western Union Private Line Cases,* 34 FCC 217 (1963), 34 FCC 1094 (1963), *aff'd sub nom. Wilson & Co. v. United States,* 335 F. 2d 788 (7th Cir. 1964), *cert. denied,* 380 U.S. 951 (1965).

[79]The three phases involved 274 hearing days and over 43,000 pages of transcript. In Phases 1A and 1B, there were 103 intervenors. See Charles F. Phillips, Jr., "Interveners in the Telephone Investigation," 78 *Public Utilities Fortnightly* 26 (December 22, 1966).

[80]*Re American Teleph. & Teleg. Co.,* 70 PUR3d 129 (FCC, 1967), on recon., 71 PUR3d 273 (FCC, 1967). See Charles F. Phillips, Jr., "Phase 1A of the Telephone Investigation," 80 *Public Utilities Fortnightly* 15 (August 31, 1967) and "The FCC's Phase 1A Interim Order on Reconsideration," 80 *Public Utilities Fortnightly* 51 (October 12, 1967); Eugene M. Lerner, "The FCC's 7.5 Per Cent Ruling," 80 *Public Utilities Fortnightly* 40 (October 12, 1967); A. J. G. Priest, "Bell System Interstate and Foreign Rates and Services," 80 *Public Utilities Fortnightly* 20 (December 21, 1967); George A. Prendergast, "The FCC Proceedings — Issues and Implications," 82 *Public Utilities Fortnightly* 17 (September 26, 1968). The separations issues were resolved early in 1969. See Report and Order, Docket No. 17975, FCC 69-65 (January 29, 1969).

[81]Memorandum Opinion and Order, Docket No. 16258, 18 FCC 2d 761 (1969), FCC 70-191 (1970). See Charles F. Phillips, Jr., "Phase 1B of the Telephone Investigation," 87 *Public Utilities Fortnightly* 20 (April 15, 1971).

[82]FCC 69-842 (July 29, 1969), pp. 3-4. The record was subsequently incorporated into two additional hearings: on revision of AT&T's tariffs for program transmission services (Docket No. 18684) and for TWX services (Docket No. 18718). The commission was too optimistic; see Chapter 11, pp. 484-87.

[83]American Bar Association Annual Report, Section of *Public Utility Law, 1977,* p. 216.

[84]*Report of the Telephone and Telegraph Committees in the Domestic Telegraph Investigation,* Docket No. 14650 (FCC, December 21, 1966). See also *Report of the Common Carrier Bureau of the Federal Communications Commission in the Domestic Telegraph Investigation* (Washington, D.C., 1965).

[85]Federal Communications Commission, *Public Notice* (No. 93561, December 22, 1966), p. 7.

[86]The committees found that: "AT&T also imposed interconnection and inter-change of facilities restrictions on Western Union which served to limit the latter's capacity to compete in the private line voice and alternate voice-record fields." *Ibid.,* p. 5. This conclusion, along with others, is open to dispute. Trebing, on the basis of the record developed in the investigation, concluded that "it is difficult to argue that the Bell System has employed these restrictions in such a way as to effect the devel-opment and promotion of the message telegraph service. Leasing charges are a small element in message telegraph cost, and the Bell System has made circuits readily available." Trebing, "The Plight of the Telegraph Service," *op. cit.,* p. 49.

[87]The Senate passed the "Telecommunications Competition and Deregulation Act of 1981" (S. 898), S. Rep. No. 170, 97th Cong., 1st sess. (1981). The House Subcom-mittee on Telecommunications, Consumer Protection and Finance passed the "Tele-communications Act of 1982" (H.R. 5158), 97th Cong., 2d sess. (1982), but the bill never was reported out of the Committee on Energy and Commerce. Thus, "the 97th Congress, like its predecessors, was unable to update the Communications Act to reflect the tremendous technological advances which have occurred since 1934." Com-ment, "Resale, Shared Use and Deregulation: Can the 'Invisible Hand' Hold on to Ma Bell?," 35 *Federal Communications Law Journal* 209, 228-29 (1983). See Bro Uttal, "How to Deregulate AT&T," *Fortune,* November 30, 1981, pp. 70-75.

[88]Kurt Borchardt, *Structure and Performance of the U.S. Communications Industry* (Boston: Division of Research, Harvard Business School, 1970), pp. 25-26 (citation omitted).

[89]"This limited approach restricted licenses, other than communications common carriers, to governmental safety organizations such as fire and police and to busi-nesses such as electric utilities, pipeline companies, and the railroad companies." Bernard P. Herber. "The Impact of Microwave on the Telephone Business," 70 *Public Utilities Fortnightly* 214, 215 (1962). See also Manley R. Irwin, "The Communication Industry and the Policy of Competition," 14 *Buffalo Law Review* 256 (1964).

[90]Donald C. Beelar, "Cables in the Sky and the Struggle for Their Control," 21 *Federal Communications Bar Journal* 26, 27-33 (1967).

[91]*Re Allocation of Microwave Frequencies Above 890 Mc.,* Docket No. 11866, 27 FCC 359 (1959), aff'd on rehearing, 29 FCC 825 (1960).

[92]27 FCC 359 (1959). See Bernard P. Herber, "Telephone Industry Reaction to Microwave Competition," 70 *Public Utilities Fortnightly* 627 (1962).

[93]Microwave Communications, Inc. (now MCI Communications Corporation) is referred to as MCI. Among its subsidiaries is MCI Telecommunications, the nation's second largest long distance carrier. On the company, see Brian O'Reilly, "More Than

Cheap Talk Propels MCI," *Fortune*, January 24, 1983, pp. 68-72; Larry Kahaner, *On The Line: The Men of MCI — Who Took on AT&T, Risked Everything, and Won!* (New York: Warner Books, Inc., 1986).

[94]"Point-to-point private line service is a term which denotes a *dedicated* or private local channel at each end, connecting the customer's premises to the carrier's local central office, and an interexchange channel (IXC) which connects the central offices. At the customer's premises, the local channel is connected with a telephone, private branch exchange (PBX), teletypewriter, or other terminal equipment. The local channel at each end is dedicated solely to the private line service." *Re MCI Telecommunications Corp.*, 60 FCC 2d 25, 43 (1976).

[95]The cream-skimming controversy includes the "piece-out" problem, which "refers to any attempt of a specialized competitor or private firm to provide only an intermediate portion of the facilities needed for end-to-end communications service. If 'piece-out' is permitted, the cheap facilities may be provided by the specialized firm seeking to interconnect while the general service carrier will be required to provide service over costly facilities at averaged rates which may not recover the high cost of serving its portion of the 'pieced-out' route. . . ." *So. Pacific Communications Co. v. American Teleph. & Teleg. Co., 1982-83 Trade Cases*, Par. 65,219, p. 71,921, n. 21 (D. D.C. 1982). The problem can be prevented either by a restrictive interconnection policy or by adopting a cost-based structure.

[96]*MCI Communications Corp. v. American Teleph. & Teleg. Co., 1982-83 Trade Cases*, Par. 65,137, p. 71,358 (7th Cir. 1983), citing 18 FCC 2d 953, 953-54 (1969).

[97]*Re Applications of Microwave Communications, Inc.*, Docket No. 16509, 18 FCC 2d 953, 957, 963, 965, 966 (1969). See also 21 FCC 2d 190 (1970). Commissioner Johnson, in a separate statement, said that he was still looking "for ways to add a little salt and pepper of competition to the rather tasteless stew of regulatory protection that this commission and Bell have cooked up." 18 FCC 2d 953, 978 (1969).

[98]Alfred E. Kahn, *The Economics of Regulation* (New York: John Wiley & Sons, Inc., 1971), Vol. II, p. 135.

[99]*Re Specialized Common Carrier Services*, Docket No. 18920, Notice of Inquiry, 24 FCC 2d 318 (1970), First Report and Order, 29 FCC 2d 870, 920 (1971), recon. denied, 31 FCC 2d 1106 (1971), *aff'd sub nom. Washington Utils. & Transp. Comm. v. Federal Communications Comm.*, 513 F. 2d 1142 (9th Cir. 1974), *cert. denied*, 423 U.S. 836 (1975).

There are other specialized carriers. (*1*) In 1974, the FCC authorized the entry of "value added carriers." [See *Re Graphnet Systems, Inc.*, Memorandum Opinion, Order and Certificate, 44 FCC 2d 800 (1974); *Re Telenet Communications Corp.*, Memorandum Opinion, Order and Certificate, 46 FCC 2d 680 (1974).] These carriers lease facilities and enhance common carriers' basic channel capacity to provide additional service features under voluntarily filed tariffs. (*2*) Following the FCC's decisions authorizing the resale and unlimited sharing of private-line services [*Re Regulatory Policies Concerning Resale and Shared Use of Common Carrier Services*, 60 FCC 2d 261 (1976), on recon., 62 FCC 2d 588 (1977), *aff'd sub nom. American Teleph. & Teleg. Co. v. Federal Communications Comm.*, 572 F. 2d 17 (2d Cir. 1978), *cert. denied*, 439 U.S. 875 (1978)], and of interstate MTS and WATS [*Re Regulatory Policies Concerning Resale and Shared Use of Common Carrier Domestic Public Switched Network Services*, 83 FCC 2d 167 (1981)], several "resale carriers" (*e.g.*, U.S. Telephone) began to offer private-line and switched services on a nationwide basis. These carriers purchase services from common carriers and then resell them to customers on a shared basis. (*3*) There are several "miscellaneous common carriers" (*e.g.*, Western Telecommunications, United Video) which offer transmission services for radio and television programming through microwave facilities.

[100]*MCI Communications Corp. v. American Teleph. & Teleg. Co., op. cit.*, p. 71,359. Other courts, reviewing the decision, have reached similar conclusions. For example, the district court judge in the same case "characterized the decision as an 'abomination' and 'one of the worst examples of legal draftsmanship I have ever seen'." *Ibid.* A circuit court found the decision to be "unclear" on what services were authorized and that a "legitimate dispute" over its scope existed. *MCI Communications Corp. v. American Teleph. & Teleg. Co.*, 496 F. 2d 214, 221, 224 (3d Cir. 1974).

[101]"FX (foreign exchange) service permits a customer to make or receive local calls through a distant switching center by effectively providing a long extension cord in the form of a dedicated line between the customer's location and a telephone company switching system in the distant location (the foreign exchange). . . . CCSA (common control switching arrangement) is essentially a miniature AT&T long distance network, except for the fact that it is used by only one customer, albeit a customer, such as the federal government, with large telecommunications needs." *United States v. American Teleph. & Teleg. Co., op. cit.*, p. 73,095, n. 124.

[102]A preliminary injunction was sought by MCI in 1973 to obtain interconnections, but was later vacated on appeal. *MCI Communications Corp. v. American Teleph. & Teleg. Co.*, 369 F. Supp. 1004 (E.D. Pa. 1973), *vacated on primary jurisdiction grounds*, 496 F. 2d 214 (3d Cir. 1974). In 1974, the FCC issued a show cause order, holding that its 1971 decision required the interconnections MCI sought. *Re Bell System Tariff Offering of Local Distribution Facilities for Use by Other Carriers*, Docket No. 19896, Notice of Inquiry, 44 FCC 2d 245 (1973), Final Decision, 46 FCC 2d 413 (1974), *aff'd sub nom. Bell Teleph. Co. of Pennsylvania v. Federal Communications Comm.*, 503 F. 2d 1250 (3d Cir. 1974), *cert. denied*, 422 U.S. 1026 (1975). In 1977, a circuit court interpreted the 1971 decision as placing no limits on the services MCI could provide. *MCI Telecommunications Corp. v. Federal Communications Comm.*, 561 F. 2d 365 (D.C. Cir. 1977), *cert. denied*, 434 U.S. 1040 (1978).

[103]See, *e.g.*, *MCI Communications Corp. v. American Teleph. & Teleg. Co.*, 369 F. Supp. 1004 (E.D. Pa. 1973) (holding that transmission facilities located entirely in one state are not immune from FCC regulation if used in interstate transmission); *Re Telerent Leasing Corp.*, 45 FCC 2d 204 (1974), *aff'd sub nom. North Carolina Utils. Comm. v. Federal Communications Comm.*, 537F. 2d 787 (4th Cir. 1975), *cert. denied*, 429 U.S. 1027 (1976) (upholding FCC's jurisdiction over the interconnection of customer-provided equipment to the subscriber's telephone terminal); *Re American Teleph. & Teleg. Co., Interconnection with Specialized Carriers in Furnishing Interstate Foreign Exchange (FX) Service and Common Control Switching Arrangements (CCSA)*, 56 FCC 2d 14 (1975), *aff'd sub nom. California v. Federal Communications Comm.*, 567 F. 2d 84 (D.C. Cir. 1977), *cert. denied*, 434 U.S. 1010 (1978) (upholding FCC jurisdiction over FX and CCSA services and an order to provide interconnection to a specialized common carrier for such services in California and Oklahoma); 76 FCC 2d 349 (1980), recon. denied, 80-488 (1980), *aff'd sub nom. New York Teleph. Co. v. Federal Communications Comm.*, 631 F. 2d 1059 (2d Cir. 1980) (upholding FCC's exclusive jurisdiction over establishing access-type charges for interstate FX and CCSA services). In response, several state commissions have ruled that local exchange costs associated with interstate FX service should be reclassified and treated as wholly interstate. See, *e.g.*, *Re Mountain States Teleph. & Teleg. Co.*, Order No. 4786b (Mont. 1981); *Re Cincinnati*

Bell Teleph. Co., Case No. 80-476-TP-ATR (Ohio 1981). But see *Re New England Teleph. & Teleg. Co.*, Order No. 10513 (R.I. 1981).

[104]See, *e.g.*, Panel on Common Carrier/User Interconnections, *Technical Analysis of the Common Carrier/User Interconnections Area* (National Academy of Sciences, 1970).

[105]*Re Use of the Carterfone Device in Message Toll Telephone Service*, 13 FCC 2d 420, 423, 426 (1968), recon. denied, 14 FCC 2d 571 (1968). See also *Hush-A-Phone Corp. v. United States*, 238 F. 2d 266 (D.C. Cir. 1956), decision on remand, 22 FCC 2d 112 (1957).

The Carterfone was "a cradle that would connect an ordinary telephone to a mobile radio transmitter," while the Hush-A-Phone was a "cup-like" device "that attached to telephones in order to provide privacy to the speaker." *Telecommunications in Transition, op. cit.*, p. 169.

[106]"Under this provision, a competitor could interconnect with the AT&T network only if the interconnection occurred in switching equipment located on the customer's premises where the telecommunication originated or terminated." *United States v. American Teleph. & Teleg. Co., op. cit.*, p. 73,095, n. 123. This restriction prevented cream skimming of the "piece-out" variety.

[107]Advisory committees are established under the Federal Advisory Committee Act of 1972 (Pub. Law 92-463).

[108]*Re Interstate and Foreign MTS and WATS*, Docket No. 19528, 56 FCC 2d 593 (1975), *aff'd sub nom. North Carolina Utils. Comm. v. Federal Communications Commission*, 552 F. 2d 1036 (4th Cir. 1977), *cert. denied*, 434 U.S. 874 (1977), modified, 58 FCC 2d 716 (1976), 59 FCC 2d 83 (1976), 64 FCC 2d 1039 (1977), 67 FCC 2d 1255 (1978).

[109]59 FCC 2d 83 (1976).

[110]58 FCC 2d 716 (1976). See 47 C.F.R. Part 68 (1980) on regulations for the registration program.

[111]Docket No. 20774, FCC 76-319 (1976).

[112]"Inasmuch as computers have become standard communications gear, the common carrier networks are no longer confining their service offerings to purely communications service. Taking advantage of the versatility and capacity of their computers, certain carriers are now programming them to provide data processing and information storage and retrieval services in combination with their traditional communications services. At the same time, we find that the nonregulated computer service bureaus, and other entities providing specialized information services over communications channels leased from the carriers, are seeking to furnish their customers with message switching services, an activity which heretofore has been limited to the communications common carriers." Bernard Strassburg, "Communications and Computers: How Shall the Twain Meet?," 82 *Public Utilities Fortnightly* 69, 70 (September 12, 1968). See also C. C. Barnett, Jr., and Associates, *The Future of the Computer Utility* (New York: American Management Association, 1967); Manley R. Irwin, "The Computer Utility: Competition or Regulation?," 76 *Yale Law Journal* 1299 (1967) and "The Computer Utility: A Public Policy Overview," in *Selected Structure and Allocation Problems in the Regulated Industries* (East Lansing: MSU Public Utilities Studies, 1969), pp. 1-18; Stuart L. Mathison and Philip M. Walker, *Computers and Telecommunications: Issues in Public Policy* (Englewood Cliffs: Prentice-Hall, Inc., 1970).

[113]*Re Regulatory and Policy Problems Presented by the Interdependence of Computer and Communications Services and Facilities*, Docket No. 16979 (*Computer I*), Notice of Inquiry, 7 FCC 2d 11 (1966), Supplemental Notice of Inquiry, 7 FCC 2d 19 (1966),

Report and Further Notice of Inquiry, 17 FCC 2d 587 (1969), Notice of Proposed Rulemaking and Tentative Decision, 28 FCC 2d 291 (1970), Final Decision and Order, 28 FCC 2d 267 (1971), *aff'd in part and rev'd in part sub nom. GTE Service Corp. v. Federal Communications Comm.,* 474 F. 2d 724 (2d Cir. 1973), decision on remand, 40 FCC 293 (1973).

[114]Donald A. Dunn et al., *Stanford Research Institute Research Report Prepared for the FCC* (Docket No. 16979, 1969). See also Donald A. Dunn, "Policy Issues Presented by the Interdependence of Computer and Communications Services," 34 *Law and Contemporary Problems* 369 (1969).

[115]37 *Telecommunications Reports* 1, 7-8 (March 22, 1971). Argued Chairman Burch in his dissenting statement: "It seems to me that we all are losers in this proceeding— the industry, because in the name of competition, competition has been lessened; the Commission, because its efforts to get on top of a problem before it became a problem have come a cropper; the public generally, because they will lose the benefits of competition; and common carrier users specifically, because they alone will lose the benefits of any lower prices otherwise available from carrier affiliates." *Ibid.,* p. 6. At the time of the inquiry, Western Union — but not the Bell System — was in the process of establishing computer centers. Under the terms of the 1956 consent decree, which prohibited the Bell System's entrance into other than regulated common carrier offerings, the System would have been forced to tariff computer offerings and, as a result, might not have been competitive.

For another example of the commission's maximum separation policy, see *Re GTE-Telent Merger Authorization,* 72 FCC 2d 111 (1979), modified, 72 FCC 2d 516 (1979), recon. denied, 74 FCC 2d 561 (1979).

[116]The Communications Satellite Act, Pub. Law 87-624, 76 Stat. 419 (1962). Concern was expressed that a privately-owned space communications project would be dominated by AT&T [see *Antitrust Problems of the Space Satellite Communications System* (Hearings before the Subcommittee on Antitrust and Monopoly, Senate, 87th Cong., 2d sess.) (Washington, D.C.: U.S. Government Printing Office, 1962), Parts 1 and 2] or be in a position to charge discriminatory rates [see Leland L. Johnson, *Communications, Satellites and Telephone Rates: Problems of Government Regulation* (Santa Monica: The Rand Corp., 1961)]. Congress established Comsat as a privately-owned, publicly-regulated (by the FCC) corporation. [See S. Rep. No. 1584 (1962); *The Communications Satellite Act of 1962* (Hearings before the Committee on Foreign Relations, Senate, 87th Cong., 2d sess.) (Washington, D.C.: U.S. Government Printing Office, 1962); Note, "The Communications Satellite Act of 1962," 76 *Harvard Law Review* 388 (1962); Harvey J. Levin, "Organization and Control of Communications Satellites," 113 *University of Pennsylvania Law Review* 315 (1965).] Comsat owns 25 percent of the International Telecommunications Satellite Organization ("Intelsat"), a 113-nation consortium that owns the international satellite communications system. In 1966, the FCC adopted a balanced-loading policy, requiring AT&T to use Comsat facilities for approximately 60 percent of its overseas calls. In 1987, the commission proposed to eliminate or phase-out that policy. [*The Wall Street Journal,* March 20, 1987, p. 12. See also "Comsat, AT&T Reach Accord on Traffic Level," *The Wall Street Journal,* October 12, 1987, p. 5.]

[117]*Re Establishment of Domestic Communications-Satellite Facilities by Non-Governmental Entities (Domsat),* Notice of Inquiry, 2 FCC 2d 668 (1966), First Report and Order, 22 FCC 2d 86 (1970), Second Report and Order, 35 FCC 2d 844 (1972), *aff'd sub nom. Network Project v. Federal Communications Comm.,* 511 F. 2d 786 (D.C. Cir. 1975).

[118]The White House, "Memorandum for the Honorable Dean Burch, Chairman of the Federal Communications Commission" (mimeographed, January 23, 1970). See also President's Task Force on Communications Policy, *Final Report* (Washington, D.C.: U.S. Government Printing Office, 1969), esp. chap. 5.

[119]37 *Telecommunications Reports* 1-6, 43-62 (May 17, 1971).

[120]35 FCC 2d 844 (1972).

[121]American Bar Association Annual Report, Section of *Public Utility Law, 1974,* p. 183. The commission imposed some restrictions on AT&T; *i.e.,* the company was prohibited from using its satellite facilities for competitive private line services for (*a*) a three-year period following the start of domestic satellite operations by AT&T or (*b*) until such time as other common carriers achieved substantial utilization of their satellite capacity, whichever occurred first. In 1979, the restrictions were removed. *Re American Teleph. & Teleg. Co. (Domestic Satellite for Specialized Services),* 70 FCC 2d 635 (1979).

[122]See, *e.g., Re Western Union Teleg. Co.,* 38 FCC 2d 1197 (1973), *Re American Satellite Corp.,* 43 FCC 2d 348 (1973), *Re National Satellite Service, Inc., and GTE Satellite Corp.,* 43 FCC 2d 1141 (1973).

[123]*Re Domestic Fixed Satellite Transponder Sales,* 90 FCC 2d 1238 (1982); *Re Satellite Orbital Spacing,* FCC 83-184 (August 16, 1983). Further, transmitter power has been increased, permitting smaller and less expensive earth stations; more powerful satellites have been aided by the arrival of Ku-band transmission. See, *e.g.,* "Increasing Competition in Transmission Market is Fueled by New Technology, Declining Costs," *Communications Week,* July 29, 1985, p. C1.

The first fourteen satellites in commercial operation, built by either RCA or Hughes Aircraft, carried a total of 270 transponders. ["One transponder can relay a television signal, 1200 voice channels, 50,000 telegram channels or 60 megabits per second of data." *Telecommunications in Transition, op. cit.,* pp. 98-99.] These satellites were launched by the National Aeronautics and Space Administration on a cost-reimbursable basis. [The first thirteen were launched by rockets, at a cost of $30 million each; the fourteenth was taken into space (in 1982) on the shuttle Columbia. See John Cooney, "Lowering Skies for the Satellite Business," *Fortune,* December 13, 1982, pp. 148ff.] More recent rocket failures have slowed further development. [See "Is the U.S. Headed for a Satellite Crisis?," *Business Week,* May 19, 1986, p. 49.]

[124]*Re MCI Telecommunications Corp.,* 60 FCC 2d 25 (1976), *rev'd,* 561 F. 2d 365 (D.C. Cir. 1977) *(Execunet I), cert. denied sub nom. U.S. Independent Teleph. Ass'n v. Federal Communications Comm.,* 434 U.S. 1040 (1978). The court did not address the FCC's determination that Execunet service is not a private-line service. Similarly, it did not consider "whether competition like that posed by Execunet is in the public interest. That will be the question for the Commission to decide should it elect to continue the proceeding." 561 F. 2d 365, 380.

In 1976, the commission also rejected (and without hearings) two tariffs filed by MCI and Southern Pacific on the grounds that they were subject to the same objections as Execunet and similarly unauthorized: *Re MCI Telecommunications Corp.,* 61 FCC 2d 131 (1976), *Re Southern Pacific Communications Co.,* 61 FCC 2d 144 (1976), both *vacated sub nom. MCI Telecommunications Corp. v. Federal Communications Comm.,* 561 F. 2d 365 (D.C. Cir. 1977), *cert. denied,* 434 U.S. 1040 (1978).

[125]*Re MTS and WATS Market Structure,* CC Docket No. 78-72, Notice of Inquiry and Proposed Rulemaking, 67 FCC 2d 757 (1978), Supplemental Notice, 73 FCC 2d 222 (1979), Second Supplemental Notice, 77 FCC 2d 224 (1980).

[126]*Re American Teleph. & Teleg. Co. Petition for Declaratory Relief,* 67 FCC 2d 1455 (1978), *rev'd sub nom. MCI Telecommunications Corp. v. Federal Communications Comm.,* 580 F. 2d 590 (D.C. Cir. 1978) *(Execunet II),* cert. denied, 439 U.S. 980 (1978). A year later, the commission ordered an independent company to provide MCI with the interconnections necessary to provide Execunet service. *Re Lincoln Teleph. & Teleg. Co.,* 72 FCC 2d 724 (1979), aff'd, 659 F. 2d 1092 (D.C. Cir. 1981) *(Execunet III).*

[127]*Re Exchange Network Facilities for Interstate Access (ENFIA),* 71 FCC 2d 440 (1979). [The new agreement replaced an interim agreement (with specialized common carriers, international record carriers, Western Union, and domestic satellite carriers) approved in 1975. See 52 FCC 2d 727 (1975), aff'd sub nom. *Carpenter v. Federal Communications Comm.,* 539 F. 2d 242 (D.C. Cir. 1976).] The agreement was extended for an additional two years [90 FCC 2d 6 (1982), *aff'd in part and rem'd in part sub nom. MCI Telecommunications Corp. v. Federal Communications Comm.,* 712 F. 2d 517 (D.C. Cir. 1983) (remanded with respect to the issue of retroactive relief)], when it was to be replaced with switched access charges [*Re Investigation of Access and Divestiture Related Tariffs* (Contract Extension), FCC 84-106 (March 28, 1984)].

The rates paid by specialized common carriers (by FCC action) were substantially below the settlements paid by AT&T. "Until 1984, the leading competitive carrier, MCI, paid only about $235 per local line per month; AT&T paid settlements on average of $600 per line per month." [Paul W. MacAvoy and Kenneth Robinson, "Losing By Judicial Policymaking: The First Year of the AT&T Divestiture," 2 *Yale Journal on Regulation* 225, 232 (1985).] MCI argued that the "discount" was proper, since it was discriminated against in access to toll-switching functions. Under ENFIA arrangements, for example, a user of MCI's Execunet service had to dial up to fourteen digits more than if MTS were used. The additional digits were "required for access to an MCI switch and for MCI's billing." [Lavey, *op. cit.,* p. 371, n. 101.] Moreover, the commission had continuous opposition to reducing the discount. [See, e.g., FCC 80-382 (July 15, 1980), *rev'd sub nom. MCI Telecommunications Corp. v. Federal Communications Comm.,* 665 F. 2d 1300 (D.C. Cir. 1981).]

[128]*Re MTS and WATS Market Structure,* Report and Third Supplemental Notice, 81 FCC 2d 177 (1980). (The commission stated that its decision did not apply to Alaska, which would be the subject of further investigation.) The docket was kept open to replace separations procedures with access charges. See Fourth Supplemental Notice, 90 FCC 2d 135 (1982).

[129]Harry M. Trebing, "Common Carrier Regulation — The Silent Crisis," 34 *Law and Contemporary Problems* 299, 313 (1969).

[130]Lionel Kestenbaum, "Competition in Communications," 16 *Antitrust Bulletin* 769, 776 (1971).

[131]In its 1976 first report on the question of the economic implications of its policies promoting competition, to illustrate, the commission "found that there was no apparent basis for the telephone industry's claims that private-line and terminal equipment competition either have or are soon likely to have any significant impact on telephone company revenues or on the rates for basic telephone services. Specifically, the FCC found no evidence to support the industry's claims that these services currently provide any contribution of excess or revenues over costs, which helps maintain low rates for basic telephone service." American Bar Association Annual Report, Section of *Public Utility Law, 1977,* p. 224. The responses to the commission's inquiry in Docket No. 20003 were analyzed, under contract, by T + E, Inc. See Chester G. Fenton and Robert F. Stone, "Competition in the Terminal Equipment Market,"

99 *Public Utilities Fortnightly* 25 (March 31, 1977). See also William G. Shepherd, "The Competitive Margin in Communications," in W. Capron (ed.), *Technological Change in Regulated Industries* (Washington, D.C.: The Brookings Institution, 1971), pp. 86-122.

[132]See, *e.g.*, John R. Meyer et al., *The Economics of Competition in the Telecommunications Industry* (Cambridge: Oelgeschlager, Gunn & Hain, Publishers, Inc., 1980); Brock, *op. cit.; Telecommunications in Transition, op. cit.*

[133]*Re Amendment of Section 64.702 of the Commission's Rules and Regulations,* Docket No. 20828 (*Computer II*), Notice of Inquiry and Proposed Rulemaking, 61 FCC 2d 103 (1976), Supplemental Notice and Enlargement of Proposed Rulemaking, 64 FCC 2d 771 (1977), Tentative Decision and Further Notice of Inquiry and Rulemaking, 72 FCC 2d 358 (1979), Final Decision, 77 FCC 2d 384, 35 PUR4th 143 (1980), modified on recon., 84 FCC 2d 50, 39 PUR4th 319 (1980), modified on further recon., 88 FCC 2d 512 (1981), *aff'd sub nom. Computer & Communications Industry Ass'n v. Federal Communications Comm.,* 693 F. 2d 198 (D.C. Cir. 1982), *cert. denied,* 103 S. Ct. 2109 (1983). See Comment, "The Computer Inquiries: Mapping the Communications/ Information Processing Terrain," 33 *Federal Communications Law Journal* 55 (1981); Note, "Effect of the Second Computer Inquiry on Telecommunications and Data Processing," 27 *Wayne Law Review* 1537 (1981).

[134]35 PUR4th 143, 179, 180 (1980) (footnote omitted). Significantly, the commission decided "that the public interest would not be served by any classification scheme that attempts to distinguish enhanced services based on the communications or data processing nature of the computer processing activity performed." *Ibid.,* p. 187.

[135]Examples are Dial-It, which involves messages stored and delivered to callers from regional network switching centers, and Custom Calling II, which involves the storage of messages in the network for subsequent sending or retrieval. (Goodyear Tire & Rubber, for instance, sponsors the Dial-It 900 National Sports line.)

[136]35 PUR4th 143, 188 (1980).

[137]*Ibid.,* p. 195. See, *e.g., Re American Teleph. & Teleg. Co. (Dataspeed 40/4),* 62 FCC 2d 21 (1977), *aff'd sub nom. International Business Machs. Corp. v. Federal Communications Comm.,* 570 F. 2d 452 (2d Cir. 1978).

[138]To ease the impact on residential subscribers, the commission stated that each telephone company which chooses to remain in the CPE business "must offer to existing residential subscribers in its franchise area ... the opportunity to continue leasing the instrument(s) (including maintenance) in place at the terminal equipment tariff rate prevailing immediately prior to deregulation for the life of the instrument(s)." 35 PUR4th 143, 206 (1980).

[139]The exception originally applied to GTE as well, but was removed upon reconsideration: 39 PUR4th 319, 342-43 (1980). Just prior to divestiture, the FCC extended most of these requirements to the Bell operating companies. *Re Policy and Rules Concerning the Furnishing of Customer Premises Equipment, Enhanced Services and Cellular Communications Services by the Bell Operating Companies,* 95 FCC 2d 1117 (1983), *aff'd sub nom. Illinois Bell Teleph. Co. v. Federal Communications Comm.,* 740 F. 2d 465 (7th Cir. 1984), on recon., 49 Fed. Reg. 26,056 (1984), *aff'd sub nom. North American Telecommunications Ass'n v. Federal Communications Comm.,* 772 F. 2d 1282 (7th Cir. 1985).

[140]35 PUR4th 143, 229 (1980).

[141]*Ibid.,* p. 231. The decision also required AT&T and GTE to disclose to nonaffiliated suppliers of enhanced services or CPE (*a*) "information relating to network design and technical standards, including interface specifications, information affect-

ing changes which are being contemplated to the telecommunications network that would affect either intercarrier interconnection or the manner in which CPE is connected to the interstate network, and information concerning construction plans" and (*b*) "information which finds a principal use in marketing, such as customer proprietary information. . . ." *Ibid.*, pp. 234, 235.

There was some uncertainty as to whether the decision was in conflict with the 1956 consent decree. On March 4, 1981, AT&T and Western Electric filed a "Motion for Construction" of that decree with the District Court in New Jersey, requesting a ruling that the decree would not bar AT&T and its affiliates from furnishing the unregulated services authorized by *Computer II*. The request was opposed by the government, but on September 11, 1981, the court granted the request. [*United States v. Western Electric Co., Inc., et al., 1981-2 Trade Cases,* Par. 64,275 (D. N.J. 1981)]. The government appealed but, after a proposed settlement in the 1974 antitrust case was filed, the court of appeals ordered the district court to vacate the order [*United States v. Western Electric, Inc., et al.,* No. 81-1960 (3d Cir., February 2, 1982)]. The district court vacated the order on March 12, 1982 [*United States v. Western Electric Co., Inc., et al.,* No. 49-17 (D. N.J., 1982)].

[142]88 FCC 2d 512 (1981).

[143]39 PUR4th 319, 334-40 (1980).

[144]In a 1983 decision, however, the commission granted a modified version of a NARUC petition, permitting state commissions to order independent telephone companies to furnish CPE on an untariffed basis until June 30, 1985. The decision was "aimed primarily at rural, remote, or sparsely populated areas where it is feared no unregulated supplier of new CPE would be available to meet subscriber needs unless directed to do so by the state regulatory commissions." 49 *Telecommunications Reports* 1 (May 16, 1983).

[145]The Bell System operating companies, for example, filed "purchase option plans" with the state commissions, under which single-line residence and business customers could purchase their embedded base telephones.

[146]39 PUR4th 319, 340 (1980).

[147]For example, the commission approved a Federal-State Joint Board recommendation (CC Docket No. 80-286) that CPE be phased out of the separations process over a five-year period [FCC 82-492 (November 4, 1982)]. New accounting rules governing station connections (*i.e.*, inside wiring) and sale of terminal equipment were prescribed in CC Docket No. 79-105. [But see *Louisiana Pub. Service Comm. v. Federal Communications Comm.,* 106 S. Ct. 1890, 74 PUR4th 1 (1986) (precluding federal preemption of depreciation or accounting procedures).]

[148]The commission subsequently approved a capitalization plan of approximately $5 billion. FCC 82-496 (November 2, 1982). An additional capitalization of $8.7 million was approved for providing Picturephone meeting service. 48 *Telecommunications Reports* 8 (October 11, 1982). American Bell began operations with 28,000 employees.

[149]*United States v. Western Elec. Co., 1982-2 Trade Cases,* Par. 64,900, 552 F. Supp. 131 (D. D.C. 1982), *aff'd sub nom. Maryland v. United States,* 460 U.S. 1001 (1983). The original agreement between AT&T and the Department of Justice was published in 47 *Fed. Reg.* 4166 (1982). Judge Greene indicated approval of the agreement, but only with modifications. *United States v. American Teleph. & Teleg. Co., 1982-2 Trade Cases,* Par. 64,979 (D. D.C. 1982). However, he rejected some modifications proposed by the government relating to customer premises equipment: *1982-2 Trade Cases,* Par. 64,980 (D. D.C. 1982).

The original agreement was filed with the district court in New Jersey as a "modification" of the 1956 consent decree. On January 11, 1982, Judge Biunno approved the agreement. The next day, he transferred the entire *Western Electric* action to the District Court for the District of Columbia, where the 1974 suit was being heard. [The government had completed its case; the court had denied the defendants' motion to dismiss: 524 F. Supp. 1336 (D. D.C. 1981); and the defendants were presenting their evidence when the agreement was filed.] The D.C. court vacated the order of January 11, 1982, consolidated the *Western Electric* action with the *AT&T* case, and ordered that procedures equivalent to those required by the Tunney Act (including a sixty-day comment period, publication of a competitive impact statement by the Department of Justice, a sixty-day period of receipt of public comments, and a determination by the court that "the entry of such judgment is in the public interest") be applied to the consolidated actions. See *1982-2 Trade Cases*, Par. 64,979, pp. 73,085-73,089. The Modification of Final Judgment technically modified the 1956 consent decree; the 1974 *AT&T* case was dismissed [*1982-2 Trade Cases*, Par. 64,981 (D. D.C. 1982)]. The competitive impact statement was published in 47 *Fed. Reg.* 7170 (1982).

On the events leading to the agreement, see Alvin von Auw, *Heritage & Destiny: Reflections on the Bell System in Transition* (New York: Praeger Publishers, 1983); Steve Coll, *The Deal of the Century: The Break Up of AT&T* (New York: Atheneum, 1986). On the government's position, see David S. Evans (ed.), *Breaking Up Bell: Essays on Industrial Organization and Regulation* (New York: Elsevier Science Publishing Co., 1983).

[150]"While the action was pending, the government changed its relief requests several times asking, at various times or in various alternatives, for the divestiture from AT&T of Western Electric and portions of the Bell Laboratories." *1982-2 Trade Cases*, Par. 64,979, p. 73,077.

[151]*Ibid.*, p. 73,099.

[152]*Ibid.*, p. 73,100. But see "Bell Labs: The Threatened Star of U.S. Research," *Business Week*, July 5, 1982, pp. 46ff; Jeremy Bernstein, *Three Degrees Above Zero: The Bell Labs in the Information Age* (New York: Scribners, 1984).

[153]*1982-2 Trade Cases*, Par. 64,979, p. 73,103. But see Peter Petre, "AT&T's Epic Push in Computers," *Fortune*, May 25, 1987, pp. 42-50.

[154]Electronic publishing means "the provision of any information which a provider or publisher has, or has caused to be originated, authored, compiled, collected, or edited, or in which he has a direct or indirect financial or proprietary interest, and which is disseminated to an unaffiliated person through some electronic means." *Ibid.*, p. 73,112. See, *e.g.*, Arthur W. Lewis, "The Great Electronic Mail Shootout," *Fortune*, August 20, 1984, pp. 167-72.

[155]*1982-2 Trade Cases*, Par. 64,979, p. 73,146.

[156]The Court would "waive" the unrelated businesses ("nontelecommunications") restriction upon a showing that "there was no realistic possibility of abuse of monopoly power. . . ." *Ibid.*, p. 73,123, n. 267.

[157]Information services in the MFJ are roughly equivalent to enhanced services in *Computer II*. In the former, information services are defined as "the offering of a capability for generating, acquiring, storing, transforming, processing, retrieving, utilizing or making available information which may be conveyed via telecommunications. . . ." *Ibid.*, p. 73,110. In 1983, the regional holding companies were granted a waiver to provide time and weather services. *United States v. Western Elec. Co., 1983-2 Trade Cases*, Par. 65,748 (D. D.C. 1983). In 1987, Judge Greene exempted from the

information services restriction the transmission "of information services originated by others." *United States v. Western Elec. Co., 1987-2 Trade Cases,* Par. 67,815, p. 59,471 (D. D.C. 1987). See also *1988-1 Trade Cases,* Par. 67,918 (D. D.C. 1988).

[158]The Court would remove the line of business or core restrictions "upon a showing by the petitioning BOC [Bell Operating Company] that there is no substantial possibility that it could use its monopoly power to impede competition in the market it seeks to enter." *1982-2 Trade Cases,* Par. 64,979, p. 73,123. The Department of Justice "has undertaken to report to the Court every three years concerning the continuing need for the restrictions imposed by the decree." *Ibid.*

[159]There is one exception: The divested operating companies may provide billing services for only one interexchange carrier. They may provide billing services for more than one, but they are not required to do so. *Ibid.,* p. 73,126. On subsequent billing problems, see "Customers Battle Phone Industry Over Billings for Unconnected Calls," *The Wall Street Journal,* May 21, 1987, p. 33. On customers' choice of an interexchange carrier, see Stuart Gannes, "The Phone Fight's Frenzied Finale," *Fortune,* April 14, 1986, pp. 52-60.

[160]*1982-2 Trade Cases,* Par. 64,979, p. 73,148.

[161]*Ibid.,* p. 73,149.

[162]"Most simply, a LATA marks the boundaries beyond which a Bell Operating Company may not carry telephone calls. What the Operating Companies will do in the services field after divestiture is (1) to engage in exchange telecommunications, that is, to transport traffic between telephones located within a LATA, and (2) to provide exchange access within a LATA, that is, to link a subscriber's telephone to the nearest transmission facility of AT&T or one of AT&T's long-haul competitors." *United States v. Western Elec. Co., 1983-1 Trade Cases,* Par. 65,333, p. 69,970, 569 F. Supp. 990 (D. D.C. 1983) (footnotes omitted).

[163]McAvoy and Robinson, *op. cit.,* p. 225, n. 53.

[164]*United States v. Western Elec. Co., 1983-2 Trade Cases,* Par. 65,756, 569 F. Supp. 1057 (D. D.C. 1983), *aff'd sub nom. California v. United States,* 464 U.S. 1013 (1983).

[165]*Ibid.,* p. 69,876. It was estimated that equal access would cost $2.47 billion and network reconfiguration $73 million. *Ibid.,* p. 69,851. Judge Greene held, however, that "AT&T need not provide a guarantee with respect to costs which remain unrecovered as a consequence of actions by Operating Companies or regulators designed improperly to divert such costs to AT&T." 569 F. Supp. 1057, 1126.

[166]*1983-2 Trade Cases,* Par. 65,756, p. 69,876.

[167]*Ibid.*

[168]Two illustrations: (*1*) Embedded equipment ($8.5 billion in annual revenues), involved 120 million telephones, the maintenance of nearly 50 million business station records, the processing of nearly 70 million service orders annually, and 45,000 employees (business CPE installation and maintenance force). The FCC ruled that all embedded CPE could be transferred to AT&T on an unregulated basis, although AT&T guaranteed prices for the leased equipment for a two-year period. *The Wall Street Journal,* November 25, 1983, p. 3. (*2*) With respect to the seven regional holding companies, the 267-page prospectus required "about 98 truckloads to move the 3.9 million pounds of paper" for its printing and, after printing, the document was mailed "to 2.9 million names on AT&T's mailing list." *The Wall Street Journal,* November 18, 1983, p. 60. The printing of the new stock certificates "cost $2 million. Distributing them and dealing with other transfer details of the new issue required an AT&T staff of 1,400, housed in a three-story building in Jacksonville." *Time,*

November 21, 1983, p. 61. The dissolution added 1.6 billion shares to The New York
Stock Exchange, "not one of which anyone has chosen to purchase." Robert Rubin,
as quoted by Jeremy Main, "AT&T's Holiday Gift to Wall Street," *Fortune*, November
28, 1983, p. 67. It is reported that total divestiture-related costs will exceed $1 billion.
The Wall Street Journal, December 2, 1983, p. 3. See W. Brooke Tunstall, *Disconnecting
Parties — Managing the Bell System Break-Up: An Inside View* (New York: McGraw-Hill
Book Co., 1985).

[169]See, *e.g.*, Paul W. MacAvoy and Kenneth Robinson, "Winning By Losing: The
AT&T Settlement and Its Impact on Telecommunications," 1 *Yale Journal on Regulation*
1 (1983); Edward P. Larkin, "Telephone: It Will Never Be the Same," 111 *Public
Utilities Fortnightly* 15 (April 14, 1983); Michael L. Katz and Robert D. Willig, "The
Case for Freeing AT&T," 7 *Regulation* 43 (July/August, 1983); "Special Report: Did It
Make Sense to Break Up AT&T?," *Business Week*, December 3, 1984, pp. 86-124;
Harry M. Shooshan (ed.), *Disconnecting Bell: The Impact of the AT&T Divestiture* (New
York: Pergamon Press, 1984); Geoffrey M. Peters, "Is the Third Time the Charm? A
Comparison of the Government's Major Antitrust Settlements with AT&T This Cen-
tury," 15 *Seton Hall Law Review* 252 (1985).

[170]See, *e.g.*, *United States v. Western Elec. Co.*, 578 F. Supp. 677 (D. D.C. 1983)
(establishing procedures for the participation of third parties); *United States v. Western
Elec. Co.*, 592 F. Supp. 846 (D. D.C. 1984), *aff'd sub nom. U.S. West v. United States*,
1985-2 Trade Cases, Par. 66,862 (D.C. Cir. 1985) (establishing procedures for reviewing waiver requests from divested regional holding companies).

[171]See, *e.g.*, *United States v. Western Elec. Co.*, *1984-1 Trade Cases*, Par. 65,938, 583 F.
Supp. 1257 (D. D.C. 1984) (ordering Pacific Bell to grant access to its lines for
services originating from AT&T's coinless public telephones); *United States v. American
Teleph. & Teleg. Co.*, *1986-1 Trade Cases*, Par. 66,913, 627 F. Supp. 1090 (D. D.C.
1986), *aff'd in part and rev'd in part sub nom. United States v. Western Elec. Co.*, *1986-2
Trade Cases*, Par. 67,234, 797 F. 2d 1082 (D.C. Cir. 1986) (reversing holding that the
decree prevents regional holding companies from providing exchange services outside their geographic regions without obtaining a waiver); *United States v. Western Elec.
Co.*, *1987-2 Trade Cases*, Par. 59,217 (D. D.C. 1987) (clarifying the term "manufacturing" in the decree — manufacturing means "design, development, and fabrication"
— and discussing Department of Justice's failure to investigate or take other enforcement action against alleged violations of the decree by some regional holding
companies).

[172]*1982-2 Trade Cases*, Par. 64,979, p. 73,116.

[173]MacAvoy and Robinson, "Losing by Judicial Policymaking. . . ." *op. cit.*, p. 255.
See also Almarin Phillips, "Humpty Dumpty Had A Great Fall," 118 *Public Utilities
Fortnightly* 19 (October 2, 1986). But see Timothy J. Brennan, "Why Regulated Firms
Should Be Kept Out of Unregulated Markets: Understanding the Divestiture in
United States v. AT&T," 32 *The Antitrust Bulletin* 741 (1987).

[174]See, *e.g.*, *United States v. Western Elec. Co.*, *1984-1 Trade Cases*, Par. 66,312 (D.
D.C. 1984) (waivers granted for "the leasing of word processing, data processing, and
photocopying equipment; foreign business ventures; real estate services; offshore
cellular radio systems; office equipment leasing, sales, installations, maintenance, and
training; and computer sales and services"); *United States v. Western Elec. Co.*, *1986-1
Trade Cases*, Par. 66,987 (D. D.C. 1986) (waiver granted to acquire cellular radio
services). The restriction was removed in 1987. See *1987-2 Trade Cases*, Par. 67,815,
pp. 59,466-59,468. In removing the restriction, the Court also removed the condi-

tions generally imposed as part of the waiver grants (*e.g.,* "that the new competitive business be operated through a separate subsidiary"; "that the subsidiary obtain its own debt financing on its own credit"). *Ibid.,* p. 59,467. On diversification, see, *e.g.,* "The Baby Bells Take Giant Steps," *Business Week,* December 2, 1985, pp. 94-104; "Baby Bells Diversify into Non-Phone Areas, Spark Much Concern," *The Wall Street Journal,* December 10, 1986, pp. 1, 24. On rivalry for directories, see, *e.g.,* "Here a Phone Book, There a Phone Book," *Business Week,* March 3, 1986, pp. 40-41; "Invasion of the Yellow Pages," *Time,* October 5, 1987, p. 52.

[175]The Department supported removal of the information services and manufacturing restrictions, but was more cautious with respect to the interexchange service restriction. See "Justice Agency Urges Judge to Remove Curbs on Businesses of Ex-Bell Firms," *The Wall Street Journal,* February 3, 1987, p. 3; "Justice Department Urges the Removal of Curbs on Regional Bell Companies," *The Wall Street Journal,* June 30, 1987, p. 8. The Department's first report to the Court was accompanied by a consulting report prepared by Peter W. Huber. See U.S. Department of Justice, *The Geodesic Network: 1987 Report on Competition in the Telephone Industry* (Washington, D.C.: U.S. Government Printing Office, 1987).

[176]*1987-2 Trade Cases,* Par. 67,815, p. 59,423. "The complete lack of merit of arguments that economic, technological, or legal changes have substantially eroded or impaired the Regional Company bottleneck power is demonstrated by the fact that *only one-tenth of one percent of inter-LATA traffic volume, generated by one customer out of one million, is carried through non-Regional Company facilities* to reach an interexchange carrier." *Ibid.,* p. 59,417 (emphasis in original; citation omitted).

[177]*Ibid.,* p. 59,421. Nor is the relevant issue equal access (which has not been fully attained). "[E]qual access is not an objective that, once achieved, remains fixed and cannot be undone. On the contrary, to the extent that the Regional Companies have an incentive, the ability, and the freedom under the decree to do so, they may be expected to chip away at equal access as new configurations, changed technologies, and novel services provide the requisite opportunities." *Ibid.,* p. 59,424.

[178]Robert W. Crandall and Bruce M. Owen, "The Marketplace: Economic Implications of Divestiture," in Shooshan, *op. cit.,* p. 65. See, *e.g.,* "U.S. Agency Plans Move to Challenge Court's Jurisdiction Over Phone Industry," *The Wall Street Journal,* November 24, 1987, p. 3; "White House Holding Talks with Bell Firms," *The Wall Street Journal,* December 14, 1987, p. 6. But see "The Reluctant Wizard of Telecom," *Communications Week,* December 14, 1987, p. 4 (special section).

[179]"Trying to tell the difference [between computing and communicating] is a little like trying to determine the sex of a snake. From the outside it's impossible to tell and, for all practical purposes, it doesn't matter anyway." John Gantz, "Commentary," 30 *Telecommunication Products + Technology* 49 (September 1985).

[180]*Re Amendment of Section 64.702 of the Commission's Rules and Regulations,* CC Docket No. 85-229 (*Computer III*), Notice of Proposed Rulemaking, 50 *Fed. Reg.* 33,581 (1985), Report and Order, FCC 86-252 (May 15, 1986), Supplemental Notice of Proposed Rulemaking, FCC 86-253 (May 15, 1986). See "FCC Seeks to End Rule That Requires Phone Firms to Separate Data Services," *The Wall Street Journal,* July 26, 1985, p. 4. AT&T has estimated that relief from maximum separation requirements would save over $1 billion per year in duplicate costs. 51 *Telecommunications Reports* 1 (September 23, 1985).

Maximum separation requirements with respect to AT&T's provision of CPE were eliminated in: *Re Furnishing of Customer Premises Equipment and Enhanced Services by American Telephone and Telegraph Co.*, 102 FCC 2d 655 (1985), modified on recon., FCC 86-341 (1986). Such requirements will be eliminated for the regional holding companies upon development of nonstructural safeguards: *Re Furnishing of Customer Premises Equipment by the Bell Operating Companies and the Independent Telephone Companies*, FCC 86-529 (1987).

[181]Open Network Architecture "would theoretically unbundle the components of exchange services and permit the purchase of each component or 'basic service element' under tariff on an 'equal access' basis." *1987-2 Trade Cases*, Par. 67,815, p. 59,447, n. 226. Comparably Efficient Interconnection "requires the Regional Companies to offer to enhanced service providers, with some exceptions, the same interconnection features on an unbundled basis and at the same price, as are enjoyed by these companies for their own equivalent services." *Ibid.*, n. 225. The commission maintained, with some modifications, the public information requirements of *Computer II. Supra*, n. 141.

[182]*Re Separation of Costs of Regulated Telephone Service From Costs of Nonregulated Activities*, CC Docket No. 86-111, FCC 86-146 (April 17, 1986).

[183]See *NARUC Bulletin* No. 21-1986 (May 26, 1986), pp. 10-13. See also David A. Reams, "Computer III and Independent Value-added Telephone Networks," 117 *Public Utilities Fortnightly* 45 (March 20, 1986).

[184]John F. Dealy, "Telecommunications: Policy Issues and Options for the 1980s," 1 *The Brookings Review* 30 (Winter 1982). See Manley R. Irwin, *Telecommunications America: Markets Without Boundaries* (Westport, Conn.: Quorum Books, 1984); Gerald R. Faulhaber, *Telecommunications in Turmoil: Technology and Public Policy* (Cambridge: Ballinger Publishing Co., 1987).

[185]See, *e.g.*, John Haring, "Implications of Asymmetric Regulation for Competition Policy Analysis" (Washington, D.C., mimeographed, 1985); Jane R. Racster (ed.), *Issues in Regulating Imperfectly Competitive Telecommunications Markets* (Columbus, Ohio: National Regulatory Research Institute, 1986); Mark S. Fowler, Albert Halprin, and James D. Schlichting, "'Back to the Future:' A Model for Telecommunications," 38 *Federal Communications Law Journal* 145 (1986); "Market Structure Criteria to Evaluate Lessening Telecommunications Regulation" (Washington, D.C.: National Association of Regulatory Utility Commissioners, 1987).

[186]See, *e.g.*, Albert L. Danielsen and David R. Kamerschen (eds.), *Telecommunications in the Post-Divestiture Era* (Lexington, Mass.: D.C. Heath & Co., 1986). The issues also include foreign limits on domestic telecommunications imports. See "Telecommunications: Looking to Hill for Help," *Cong. Quarterly* 194 (February 1, 1986).

[187]"The [Communications Act] provided the impetus for achieving the overriding telecommunications objective of that time — universal service. But this objective has, for all practical purposes, been fulfilled. With no new objective to focus on, policy has drifted, with each regulatory body defending the interests of its own constituency." David L. Wenner, "Phone Companies Ought to 'Bundle'," *The Wall Street Journal*, October 15, 1987, p. 32.

[188]See *Re Cellular Communications Systems*, 68 FCC 2d 469 (1981), on recon., 89 FCC 2d 58 (1982), on further recon., 90 FCC 2d 571 (1982), *appeal dismissed sub nom. United States v. Federal Communications Comm.*, No. 82-1526 (D.C. Cir. 1983). See also John W. Dizard, "Gold Rush at the FCC," *Fortune*, July 12, 1982, pp. 102-12; Harold Ware, "The Competitive Potentials of Cellular Mobile Telecommunications," 111 *Public Utilities Fortnightly* 28 (February 3, 1983); Stuart Gannes, "Behold, The Bell

Tel Cell War," *Fortune,* December 22, 1986, pp. 97ff; "Hello Anywhere: The Cellular Phone Boom Will Change the Way You Live," *Business Week,* September 21, 1987, pp. 84-92.

[189]Almarin Phillips, "The Reintegration of Telecommunications: An Interim View," in Michael A. Crew (ed.), *Analyzing the Impact of Regulatory Change in Public Utilities* (Lexington, Mass.: D.C. Heath & Co., 1985), pp. 5-6. See also Warren G. Lavey, "The Public Policies That Changed the Telephone Industry Into Regulated Monopolies: Lessons from Around 1915," 39 *Federal Communications Law Journal* 171 (1987). See, *e.g.,* "Independent Phone Firms Join to Bring Long-Distance Options to Rural Areas," *The Wall Street Journal,* October 7, 1986, p. 18; "The Long-Distance Wars Get Hotter: Despite Hugh Losses, AT&T's Rivals Aren't About to Give Up," *Business Week,* March 23, 1987, pp. 150-56.

[190]AT&T was referred to as "a mammoth and legendary enterprise" by Judge Kaufman in *Northeastern Teleph. Co. v. American Teleph. & Teleg. Co., 1981-1 Trade Cases,* Par. 64,027, p. 76,308 (2d Cir. 1981).

[191]Antitrust activity typically was confined to acquisitions or to the authorization of specific services. See, *e.g., Re Satellite Business Systems,* 62 FCC 2d 997 (1977), recon. denied, 64 FCC 2d 872 (1977), *aff'd sub nom. United States v. Federal Communications Comm.,* 652 F. 2d 72 (D.C. Cir. 1980).

[192]"AT&T Loses Big Antitrust Cases, Opening Door to Costly Damages," *The Wall Street Journal,* February 11, 1983, pp. 23, 33. See also *KWF Industries, Inc. v. American Teleph. & Teleg. Co., 1984-2 Trade Cases,* Par. 66,095 (D. D.C. 1984) (motion to dismiss on statute of limitation grounds denied).

[193]"This is an industry that talks to each other through lawsuits." William McGowan, Chairman of MCI Communications, as quoted in *Newsweek,* June 10, 1985, p. 64.

"Feisty MCI Communications Corp. is in litigation so often that some Wall Street veterans call it 'a law firm with an antenna on the roof'." *Business Week,* April 22, 1985, p. 37.

[194]See, *e.g., International Teleph. & Teleg. Corp. v. American Teleph. & Teleg. Co.,* No. 77 Civ. 2854 (S.D. N.Y.) (settled in 1980; AT&T agreed to buy as much as $2 billion in goods and services from ITT over a ten-year period); *Essential Communications Sys., Inc. v. American Teleph. & Teleg. Co., 1978-1 Trade Cases,* Par. 61,962 (D. N.J. 1978), *rev'd, 1979-2 Trade Cases,* Par. 62,978 (3d Cir. 1979) (dismissed in 1980 at parties' request; no terms disclosed); *TeleSciences, Inc. v. American Teleph. & Teleg. Co.,* (settled in 1981; AT&T agreed to pay TeleSciences forty cents for every dollar below $300 million in purchases over an eight-year period, with a $40 million advance payment to support inventory buildup by the firm) [but see *Conrac Corp. v. American Teleph. & Teleg. Co., 1982-2 Trade Cases,* Par. 64,920 (S.D. N.Y. 1982) (stayed charges that the agreement between AT&T and TeleSciences violated the antitrust laws by foreclosing competition for sale of equipment to AT&T) (settled in 1984; AT&T agreed to pay $24 million over a six-year period)]; *Gregg Communications Sys., Inc. v. American Teleph. & Teleg. Co., 1983-2 Trade Cases,* Par. 65,610 (N.D. Ill. 1983) (settled in 1984; AT&T agreed to pay $15 million). MCI Communications also settled its second antitrust suit against the Bell System. See *infra,* n. 228.

[195]The ten plaintiffs are manufacturers and/or dealers of such telephone accessory devices as the Code-a-phone automatic answering device and the Soft-Touch device, as well as call diverters, call sequencers, and automatic dialers. *Gregg Communications Sys. Inc. v. American Teleph. & Teleg. Co., 1983-2 Trade Cases,* Par. 65,610 (N.D. Ill. 1983).

[196]The company "manufactures sophisticated 'multiple position order equipment' for use in large financial institutions, such as banks and brokerage houses, to facilitate trading in securities, commodities, and currency." *Interconnect Planning Corp. v. American Teleph. & Teleg. Co., 1979-1 Trade Cases,* Par. 62,655, p. 77,701 (S.D. N.Y. 1978).

[197]The company manufacturers a device called a "Phonemaster." Once attached to the telephone network, it prevents "the completion of unauthorized or misdialed long-distance calls. . . ." *Phonetele, Inc. v. American Teleph. & Teleg. Co., 1977-2 Trade Cases,* Par. 61,570, p. 72,311 (C.D. Cal. 1977), *rev'd and remanded, 1981-2 Trade Cases,* Par. 64,413 (9th Cir. 1981), *cert. denied,* 103 S. Ct. 785 (1983), *1984-1 Trade Cases,* Par. 65,921 (C.D. Cal. 1984) (denying motion for offensive collateral estoppel).

[198]The company began to sell and lease key telephone terminal equipment in Cedar Rapids, Des Moines and Waterloo, Iowa, in 1970. It ceased operations in 1975. *Sound, Inc. v. American Teleph. & Teleg. Co., 1979-2 Trade Cases,* Par. 62,974 (S.D. Iowa 1979), *aff'd, 1980-2 Trade Cases,* Par. 63,514 (8th Cir. 1980).

[199]The company sold "antique French" cradle telephones that could be plugged into jacks. *Western States Teleph. Co. v. American Teleph. & Teleg. Co., 1977-1 Trade Cases,* Par. 61,502 (C.D. Cal. 1977) (dismissing antitrust claim more than nine years after company went out of business as an active competitor), *summary judgment vacated and remanded sub nom. Segal v. American Teleph. & Teleg. Co., 1979-2 Trade Cases,* Par. 62,825 (9th Cir. 1979).

[200]In the first case, twenty-nine alarm companies "charged that the Bell companies have controlled the rates for remote alarm services and 'have excluded competition, actual and potential, in the furnishing of equipment associated with remote alarm system services'." 48 *Telecommunications Reports* 2 (October 18, 1982) (Civil Action No. 82-2907, D. D.C.). In the second case, forty-two remote alarm system companies affiliated with the Sonitrol system "charged the American Telephone & Telegraph Co. and all of its affiliates with 'manipulating' private line rates and taking other actions to monopolize the alarm service field." 49 *Telecommunications Reports* 5 (August 15, 1983). See *Sonitrol of Fresno, Inc. v. American Teleph. & Teleg. Co., 1986-1 Trade Cases,* Par. 67,080 (D. D.C. 1986) (holding less than wholly-owned subsidiaries were capable of conspiring), *1986-1 Trade Cases,* Par. 67,107 (D. D.C. 1986) (granting AT&T's motion for summary judgment).

There is also a class action suit, filed by fifteen unaffiliated individuals or business entities, engaged in the distribution of a mobile telephone device called "Melabs Attache Phone." *Chastain v. American Teleph. & Teleg. Co., 1973-1 Trade Cases,* Par. 74,281 (D. D.C. 1972) (referred to FCC under doctrine of primary jurisdiction), *Re Referral of Chastain v. American Tel. & Tel. Co.,* 43 FCC 2d 1079 (1973), *1975-2 Trade Cases,* Par. 60,519 (D. D.C. 1975) (summary judgment denied).

At least three applications for certification of class action have been denied: *San Antonio Teleph. Co., Inc. v. American Teleph. & Teleg. Co., 1974-2 Trade Cases,* Par. 75,219 (5th Cir. 1974), *1975-2 Trade Cases,* Par. 60,421 (W.D. Tex. 1975); *AM/COMM Sys., Inc. v. American Teleph. & Teleg. Co., 1984-1 Trade Cases,* Par. 65,920 (E.D. Pa. 1984); *Glictronix Corp. v. American Teleph. & Teleg. Co., 1985-1 Trade Cases,* Par. 66,340 (D. N.J. 1984).

One litigant has been permanently enjoined "from instituting any further actions in any court," after filing five suits against the former Bell System in one year. *Morgan Consultants v. American Teleph. & Teleg. Co., 1982-2 Trade Cases,* Par. 64,939 (S.D. N.Y. 1982).

[201]*Business Week,* July 8, 1985, p. 25.

[202]*Northeastern Teleph. Co. v. American Teleph. & Teleg. Co., 1980-81 Trade Cases,* Par. 63,593, p. 77,151 (D. Conn. 1980).

[203]*So. Pacific Communications Co. v. American Teleph. & Teleg. Co., 1982-83 Trade Cases,* Par. 65,219, p. 71,915 (citations omitted) (D. D.C. 1982).

[204]*The Wall Street Journal,* April 25, 1983, p. 14. Early in 1986, Sprint was combined with United Telecommunications' long-distance unit into a separate company called US Sprint Communications Co. *The Wall Street Journal,* January 17, 1986, p. 3.

[205]The suit was unique in that the company organized a limited partnership (thirty units at $50,000 each) to finance the suit. The partners were promised 5 percent or $3 million, whichever was larger, of any resulting award. The case was filed in the Philadelphia district court on June 1, 1983. *Boston Globe,* June 28, 1983, pp. 45, 50. The case was settled in 1984, with AT&T agreeing to pay $25.5 million over a six-year period. *The Wall Street Journal,* July 11, 1984, p. 3.

[206]*The Wall Street Journal,* December 30, 1982, p. 2.

[207]Upon the January 1, 1984 dissolution of the Bell System, the allocation of contingent antitrust liabilities are to be "shared by the entities of the System on the same basis as their receipt of the System's assets and equity." *United States v. Western Elec. Co., 1983-2 Trade Cases,* Par. 65,756, p. 69,853 (footnote omitted) (D. D.C. 1983).

After the dissolution, MCI Communications settled its second antitrust suit directly with the Bell operating companies. *The Wall Street Journal,* April 3, 1985, p. 6.

[208]The original award was reversed on appeal and remanded to reconsider damages with respect to seven of the ten allegations: *MCI Communications Corp. v. American Teleph. & Teleg. Co.,* No. 74-C-633 (N.D. Ill. 1980), *aff'd in part & rev'd in part, 1982-83 Trade Cases,* Par. 65,137 (7th Cir. 1983), *modified & rehearing denied, 1983-2 Trade Cases,* Par. 65,520 (7th Cir. 1983), *cert. denied,* 52 USLW 3291 (1983). At the new trial, MCI sought $5.8 billion in damages. But see "MCI's Tactics in AT&T Antitrust Case Led to Lower Award, Lawyers Contend," *The Wall Street Journal,* May 30, 1985, p. 6.

[209]The award was affirmed on appeal. However, Litton was denied all costs and attorneys' fees — over $10 million — because of misconduct in responding to discovery orders. (See "Costly Cover-Up," *The Wall Street Journal,* June 21, 1983, pp. 1, 18.) *Litton Sys., Inc. v. American Teleph. & Teleg. Co., 1981-2 Trade Cases,* Par. 64,306 (S.D. N.Y. 1981), *aff'd, 1982-83 Trade Cases,* Par. 65,194 (2d Cir. 1983), *cert. denied,* 104 S. Ct. 984 (1984). [Litton was awarded costs and attorneys fees — $1.5 million — for its successful defense of the original award judgment on appeal. *Litton Sys., Inc. v. American Teleph. & Teleg. Co., 1985-2 Trade Cases,* Par. 66,697 (S.D. N.Y. 1985).]

In 1982, Congress enacted legislation that increased the rate of post-judgment interest (Federal Courts Improvement Act of 1982, Pub. Law No. 97-164). Litton sought to have the 1981 jury award, which provided for a post-judgment interest rate of 9 percent, amended to provide for a 14.82 percent interest rate (equivalent to an additional $55 million). The court declined Litton's motion. *Litton Sys., Inc. v. American Teleph. & Teleg. Co., 1983-2 Trade Cases,* Par. 65,570 (S.D. N.Y. 1983), *aff'd, 1984-2 Trade Cases,* Par. 66,239 (2d Cir. 1984).

[210]The award was reversed on appeal and the case remanded for retrial on one of the five allegations: *Northeastern Teleph. Co. v. American Teleph. & Teleg. Co., 1980-81 Trade Cases,* Par. 63,593 (D. Conn. 1980), *rev'd & remanded, 1981-1 Trade Cases,* Par. 64,027 (2d Cir. 1981), *cert. denied,* 455 U.S. 943 (1982).

[211]The award was reversed on appeal and the case remanded for a new trial:

Mid-Texas Communications Sys., Inc. v. American Teleph. & Teleg. Co., 1978-1 Trade Cases, Par. 62,051 (S.D. Tex. 1978), *rev'd & remanded, 1980-2 Trade Cases,* Par. 63,314 (5th Cir. 1980), *cert. denied,* 449 U.S. 912 (1980).

[212]See, *e.g.,* Phillip E. Areeda, "Antitrust Laws and Public Utility Regulation," 3 *Bell Journal of Economics & Management Science* 42 (1972); Marlene B. Jones, "Immunities from the Antitrust Laws for Regulated Entities," 115 *Public Utilities Fortnightly* 37 (May 30, 1985).

[213]*Gordon v. New York Stock Exchange,* 422 U.S. 659, 682 (1975), citing *United States v. Philadelphia Nat. Bank,* 374 U.S. 321, 350-51 (1963).

[214]*Silver v. New York Stock Exchange,* 373 U.S. 341, 357 (1963).

[215]*Northeastern Teleph. Co. v. American Teleph. & Teleg. Co., 1980-81 Trade Cases,* Par. 63,593, p. 77,154 (D. Conn. 1980). See, e.g., *Otter Tail Power Co. v. United States,* 410 U.S. 366, 372-75 (1973); *United States v. Nat. Ass'n of Securities Dealers, Inc.,* 422 U.S. 694, 730-35 (1975).

[216]*Northeastern Teleph. Co. v. American Teleph. & Teleg. Co., 1980-81 Trade Cases,* Par. 63,593, p. 77,154 (D. Conn. 1980). See *Gordon v. New York Stock Exchange, op. cit.,* pp. 685-86, 691.

[217]*Parker v. Brown,* 317 U.S. 341 (1943).

[218]*Jeffrey v. Southwestern Bell, 1974-2 Trade Cases,* Par. 75,167 (N.D. Tex. 1974), *aff'd, 1975-2 Trade Cases,* Par. 60,482, p. 67,143 (5th Cir. 1975).

[219]See *Goldfarb v. Virginia State Bar,* 421 U.S. 773, 791 (1975) ("anticompetitive activities must be compelled by direction of the state acting as a sovereign"); *Cantor v. Detroit Edison Co.,* 428 U.S. 579 (1976) (the option to have a free light bulb program was "primarily" Detroit Edison's); *Bates v. State Bar of Arizona,* 433 U.S. 350 (1977) (prohibition of attorney advertising was a "clear articulation of the state's policy" and "at the core of the state's power to protect the public"); *Lafayette v. Louisiana Power & Light Co.,* 435 U.S. 389 (1978) (municipal utility operator not exempt, since there was no "active supervision by the policymaker").

"The ... issue raised by this ... quartet of decisions is whether anyone can make sense of what the Supreme Court is letting us know about the state action doctrine." Milton Handler, "Antitrust — 1978," 78 *Columbia Law Review* 1363, 1376 (1978). See also "Antitrust Jurisdiction over Regulated Utilities," 103 *Public Utilities Fortnightly* 45 (March 15, 1979); "The Antitrust State Action Exemption," 107 *Public Utilities Fortnightly* 50 (January 15, 1981).

[220]*Northeastern Teleph. Co. v. American Teleph. & Teleg. Co., 1980-81 Trade Cases,* Par. 63,593, p. 77,155 (D. Conn. 1980). But see *Mobilfone of Pa., Inc. v. Commonwealth Teleph. Co.,* 571 F. 2d 141 (3d Cir. 1978). In 1980, the Supreme Court articulated two standards: first, "the challenged restraint must be 'one clearly articulated and affirmatively expressed as state policy';" and, second, "the policy must be 'actively supervised by the state itself'." *Cal. Retail Liquor Dealers Ass'n v. Midcal Aluminum, Inc.,* 445 U.S. 97, 105 (1980), citing *Lafayette v. Louisiana Power & Light Co., op. cit.* See J. L. Harrison, "State Antitrust Immunity and State 'Neutrality' in Regulated and Compelled Activities," 55 *North Carolina Law Review* 270 (1977); Richard W. Pierce, "Antitrust and State Action: Lights Out for a Regulated Utility," 28 *Mercer Law Review* 733 (1977).

[221]*Eastern Railroad Presidents Conference v. Noerr Motor Freight, Inc.,* 365 U.S. 127, 138 (1961).

[222]*Ibid.,* p. 144.

[223]*United Mine Workers v. Pennington,* 381 U.S. 657, 670 (1965). See Daniel R.

Fischel, "Antitrust Liability for Attempts to Influence Governmental Action: The Basis and Limits of the *Noerr-Pennington Doctrine*," 45 *University of Chicago Law Review* 80 (1977); Thomas A. Balmer, "Sham Litigation and the Antitrust Laws," 29 *Buffalo Law Review* 39 (1980).

[224]*Cal. Motor Transport Co. v. Trucking Unlimited*, 404 U.S. 508 (1972).

[225]See, *e.g.*, *Jarvis, Inc. v. American Teleph. & Teleg. Co.,1978-2 Trade Cases*, Par. 62,197, p. 75,339 (D. D.C. 1978) (FCC regulation of the post-*Carterfone* tariffs "is not so pervasive or extensive that the range of optional behavior left to the carriers is *de minimis*"); *MCI Communications Corp. v. American Teleph. & Teleg. Co.*, *1979-1 Trade Cases*, Par. 62,491 (N.D. Ill. 1978) (refused to dismiss since there was no clear repugnancy between the regulatory scheme and the antitrust laws); *Northeastern Teleph. Co. v. American Teleph. & Teleg. Co.*, *1979-1 Trade Cases*, Par. 62,548, p. 77,179 (D. Conn. 1978) (FCC's supervisory role appears "to be too general and potentially passive to support an implied immunity. . . ."); *Litton Sys., Inc. v. American Teleph. & Teleg. Co.*, *1980-81 Trade Cases*, Par. 63,246, p. 78,213 (S.D. N.Y. 1980) (court found nothing in the 1934 Act or in its legislative history "which suggests that Congress intended that the regulation of communications carriers by the FCC would exempt from the antitrust laws all of the activities of such carriers. . . ."); *U.S. Transmission Sys., Inc. v. American Teleph. & Teleg. Co.*, *1983-1 Trade Cases*, Par. 65,287, p. 69,697 (S.D. N.Y. 1983) (court suggested that "labels such as 'primary jurisdiction,' 'exclusive jurisdiction,' or, indeed, 'implied immunity' serve more to confuse than enlighten"). See also Note, "AT&T and the Antitrust Laws: A Strict Test for Implied Immunity," 85 *Yale Law Journal* 254 (1975); Comment, "The Application of Antitrust Law to Telecommunications," 69 *California Law Review* 497 (1981); dissenting opinion of Judge Claiborne in *Phonetele, Inc. v. American Teleph. & Teleg. Co.*, *1981-2 Trade Cases*, Par. 64,413, pp. 75,019-75,028 (9th Cir. 1981).

[226]See, *e.g.*, *Essential Communications Sys., Inc. v. American Teleph. & Teleg. Co.*, *1978-1 Trade Cases*, Par, 61,962 (D. N.J. 1978), *rev'd*, *1979-2 Trade Cases*, Par. 62,978, p. 79,569 (3d Cir. 1979) (utility initiated tariffs "do not furnish a predicate for a *Parker v. Brown* exemption from antitrust claims by competitors injured as a result of compliance with the tariffs"). But see *Jeffrey v. Southwestern Bell*, *1974-2 Trade Cases*, Par. 75,167 (N.D. Tex. 1974), *aff'd*, *1975-2 Trade Cases*, Par. 60,482, p. 67,143 (5th Cir. 1975) (regulation by Dallas City Council "of the rates to be charged by a public utility are a classic example of the *Parker v. Brown* exemption"); *Sonitrol of Fresno, Inc. v. American Teleph. & Teleg. Co.*, *1986-1 Trade Cases*, Par. 67,107, p. 62,693 (D. D.C. 1986) (summary judgment granted; "the telephone companies' private line rates, which had been approved by appropriate state regulatory authorities, could not be used as bases of antitrust liability, nor could injuries resulting from the rates be considered as damages"); *North v. New York Teleph. Co.*, No. 80-Civ. 1028 (S.D. N.Y. 1981).

[227]See, *e.g.*, *MCI Communications Corp. v. American Teleph. & Teleg. Co.*, *1982-83 Trade Cases*, Par. 65,137, pp. 71,408-71,413 (7th Cir. 1983) (upholding jury finding that AT&T filed "sham" interconnection tariffs for local distribution facilities with forty-nine state commissions); *Litton Sys., Inc. v. American Teleph. & Teleg. Co.*, *1982-83 Trade Cases*, Par. 65,194, p. 71,777 (2d Cir. 1983) ("The fact that the FCC might ultimately set aside a tariff filing does not transform AT&T's independent decisions as to how it will conduct its business into a 'request' for governmental action or an 'expression' of political opinion."). See also *Sound, Inc. v. American Teleph. & Teleg. Co.*, *1980-2 Trade Cases*, Par. 63,514, p. 76,736 (8th Cir. 1980) ("Bell, not the FCC, proposes its rates,

regulations and restrictions, subject, of course, to FCC approval. In filing each tariff, Bell implements its own business judgment. . . ."); *Phonetele, Inc. v. American Teleph. & Teleg. Co., 1981-2 Trade Cases,* Par, 64,413, p. 75,012 (9th Cir. 1981), *cert. denied,* 103 S. Ct. 785 (1983) (tariff filings are "the product of the regulated entity's independent initiative and judgment").

[228]Both MCI and SPCC filed second suits against the former Bell System (and some independent companies) relative to their switched message services (Execunet and Sprint). [These two suits, along with one filed by U.S. Transmission Systems, were consolidated. 49 *Telecommunications Reports* 14 (October 3, 1983).] Just prior to the trial, MCI settled with the defendants. See "MCI Says It Settled Two Antitrust Suits Against AT&T, Former Bell Companies," *The Wall Street Journal,* November 19, 1985, p. 2.

[229]*So. Pacific Communications Co. v. American Teleph. & Teleg. Co., 1982-83 Trade Cases,* Par. 65,219 (D. D.C. 1982), *modified & amended, 1983-1 Trade Cases,* Par. 65,373 (D. D.C. 1983), *motion to vacate denied, 1983-2 Trade Cases,* Par. 66,675 (D. D.C. 1983), *aff'd, 1984-2 Trade Cases,* Par. 66,077 (D.C. Cir. 1984), *motion to vacate denied, 1984-2 Trade Cases,* Par. 66,132 (D.C. Cir. 1984), *cert. denied,* 470 U.S. 1055 (1985).

[230]*Ibid.* (Par. 65,219), pp. 72,120-72,121 (footnotes omitted). Noting the many pending private antitrust suits against AT&T, Judge Richey said: "Had the FCC not engaged in its usual regulatory lag and dealt forthrightly and properly with the problems as they arose, then few, if any, of the cases would now be before the antitrust Courts, such as this one." *Ibid.,* p. 72,121.

[231]*Ibid.,* p. 72,122.

[232]*Ibid.* (Par. 66,077), p. 65,999, n. 21.

[233]*Ibid.,* citing *United States v. American Teleph. & Teleg. Co.,* 461 F. Supp. 1314, 1328 (footnotes omitted) (D. D.C. 1978).

The case was "lamentably tainted with charges of judicial bias. The central issue at trial was whether AT&T had wrongfully used monopoly power to exclude competition. Yet, in his Memorandum Opinion, the District Judge strongly expressed his personal view that an AT&T monopoly, and not competition, is in the public interest in the telecommunications industry. Moreover, in drafting his extremely lengthy Memorandum Opinion, the trial judge simply copied — word-for-word (including even typographical errors) — most of AT&T's proposed findings of fact and conclusions of law. Virtually every assessment of the credibility of witnesses, finding of fact and conclusion of law is in favor of AT&T. Finally, almost as if to ensure a preferred result, the trial court's judgment is supported by layer upon layer of alternative holdings on the issues of implied antitrust immunity, monopoly power, unlawful maintenance of monopoly power, injury-in-fact and proof of damages. . . . Despite our dismay over this matter, we have concluded . . . that SPCC has failed to prove that the District Judge allowed his personal, legal and policy views impermissibly to affect his decisionmaking." *Ibid.,* pp. 65,986, 65,987.

[234]*United States v. Marine Bancorp.,* 418 U.S. 602, 627 (1975).

[235]*Mid-Texas Communications Sys., Inc. v. American Teleph. & Teleg. Co., 1980-2 Trade Cases,* Par. 63,314, p. 75,636 (5th Cir. 1980), *cert. denied,* 449 U.S. 912 (1980). On the need to instruct a jury properly on the issue of regulatory impact, see *ibid.,* pp. 75,636-75,641.

[236]*MCI Communications Corp. v. American Teleph. & Teleg. Co., 1982-83 Trade Cases,* Par. 65,137, p. 71,368 (7th Cir. 1983), citing *International Teleph. & Teleg. Corp. v.*

General Teleph. & Electronics Corp., 1971-1 Trade Cases, Par. 60,291, p. 66,153 (footnote omitted) (9th Cir. 1975) and *United States v. Marine Bancorp., op. cit.*

[237]*United States v. Grinnell*, 384 U.S. 563, 570-71 (1966).

[238]*MCI Communications Corp. v. American Teleph. & Teleg. Co., 1982-83 Trade Cases*, Par. 65,137, p. 71,369 (7th Cir. 1983), citing Keith S. Watson and Thomas W. Brunner, "Monopolization by Regulated 'Monopolies:' The Search for Substantive Standards," 22 *The Antitrust Bulletin* 559, 563 (1977).

[239]*Ibid.*

[240]*Ibid.*, p. 71,370.

[241]*Mid-Texas Communications Sys., Inc. v. American Teleph. & Teleg. Co., 1980-2 Trade Cases*, Par. 63,314, pp. 75,639-75,640 (5th Cir. 1980).

[242]*MCI Communications Corp. v. American Teleph. & Teleg. Co., 1982-83 Trade Cases*, Par. 65,137, p. 71,371 (7th Cir. 1983).

[243]*Ibid.*, pp. 71,369 (footnote omitted), 71,371. In *Otter Tail*, the Supreme Court noted that in fashioning a remedy, a court "should [not] be impervious to a [utility's] assertion that a compulsory interconnection or wheeling will erode its integrated system and threaten its capacity to serve adequately the public." *Otter Tail Power Co. v. United States, op. cit.*, p. 381.

[244]*Jack Faucett Assocs., Inc. v. American Teleph. & Teleg. Co., 1984-2 Trade Cases*, Par. 66,186, p. 66,677 (D.C. Cir. 1984), *reversing 1983-1 Trade Cases*, Par. 65,470 (D. D.C. 1983), *cert. denied*, 469 U.S. 1196 (1985).

The Faucett case was a class of seven business users of customer-provided PBX and key telephone systems, who made payments for the installation or use of PCAs (protective connecting arrangement), that was certified in 1983: *1983-1 Trade Cases*, Par. 65,285 (D. D.C. 1983). The action consolidated five class action antitrust suits. Late in 1985, the court accepted a settlement, under which the participating class members will recover approximately 50 percent of potential single damages over a seven-year period (a mimimum of $15,000,000): *1986-1 Trade Cases*, Par. 66,904 (D. D.C. 1985).

[245]*United States v. Mendoza*, 104 S. Ct. 568, 571 (1984), quoting *Allen v. McCurry*, 449 U.S. 90, 94 (1980).

[246]*Selectron, Inc. v. American Teleph. & Teleg. Co., 1984-2 Trade Cases*, Par. 66,111, pp. 66,212-66,213 (D. Ore. 1984). [The original *Selectron* case, filed in 1976 (No. 76-965-BE), was dismissed following the *Phonetele* decision: *1977-2 Trade Cases*, Par. 61,570 (C.D. Cal. 1977). The dismissal was reversed by the ninth circuit for the reasons stated in *Phonetele: 1981-2 Trade Cases*, Par. 64,413 (9th Cir. 1981).]

"Collateral estoppel is an equitable doctrine. Offensive collateral estoppel is even a cut above that in the scale of equitable values. It is a doctrine of equitable discretion to be applied only when the alignment of the parties and the legal and factual issues raised warrant it.... Its application is controlled by the principles of equity.... [F]airness to both parties must be considered when it is applied." *Nations v. Sun Oil Co. (Delaware)* 705 F. 2d 742, 744-45 (5th Cir. 1983), *cert. denied*, 104 S. Ct. 239 (1983). See also *Parklane Hosiery Co. v. Shore*, 439 U.S. 322 (1979).

[247]*Jack Faucett Assocs., Inc., v. American Teleph. & Teleg. Co., 1984-2 Trade Cases*, Par. 66,186, p. 66,684 (D.C. Cir. 1984). The court cautioned: "The doctrine is detailed, difficult, and potentially dangerous." *Ibid.*, p. 66,677.

[248]*Supra*, n. 209. See *Jack Faucett Assocs., Inc., v. American Teleph. & Teleg. Co., 1984-2 Trade Cases*, Par. 66,186 (D.C. Cir. 1984); *Glictronix Corp. v. American Teleph. & Teleg. Co., 1985-1 Trade Cases*, Par. 66,340 (D. N.J. 1984) (collateral estoppel denied;

motion for class certification denied); *Phonetele, Inc. v. American Teleph. & Teleg Co.,* *1984-1 Trade Cases,* Par. 65,921 (C.D. Cal. 1984) (denying motion for collateral estoppel); *Selectron, Inc. v. American Teleph. & Teleg. Co., 1984-2 Trade Cases,* Par. 66,111 (D. Ore. 1984) (motion for a partial summary judgment granted in part and denied in part); *Wrede v. American Teleph. & Teleg. Co.,* Civil Action No. 83-283-1-MAC (M.D. Ga. 1984) (denying motion for collateral estoppel).

[249]*Jack Faucett Assocs., Inc. v. American Teleph. & Teleg. Co., 1984-2 Trade Cases,* Par. 66,186, pp. 66,673, 66,680, 66,683 (D.C. Cir. 1984).

[250]See, *e.g., Macom Prods. Corp. v. American Teleph. & Teleg.Co., 1973-2 Trade Cases,* Par. 74,598 (C.D. Cal. 1973); *Essential Communications Sys., Inc. v. American Teleph. & Teleg. Co., 1978-1 Trade Cases,* Par. 61,962 (D. N.J. 1978); *Monitor Business Machs., Inc. v. American Teleph. & Teleg. Co., 1978-1 Trade Cases,* Par. 62,030 (C.D. Cal. 1978); *Sound, Inc. v. American Teleph. & Teleg. Co., 1979-2 Trade Cases,* Par. 62,974 (S.D. Iowa 1979); *Litton Sys., Inc. v. American Teleph. & Teleg. Co., 1982-83 Trade Cases,* Par. 65,194 (2d Cir. 1983); *Jack Faucett Assocs., Inc. v. American Teleph. & Teleg. Co., 1983-1 Trade Cases,* Par. 65,285 (D. D.C. 1983); *Selectron, Inc. v. American Teleph. & Teleg. Co., 1984-2 Trade Cases,* Par. 66,111 (D. Ore. 1984); *Wyly Corp. v. American Teleph. & Teleg. Co.,* Civil Action No. 76-1544 (D. D.C.).

[251]*Northeastern Teleph. Co. v. American Teleph. & Teleg. Co., 1980-81 Trade Cases,* Par. 63,593, p. 77,161 (D. Conn. 1980).

[252]*Litton Sys., Inc. v. American Teleph. & Teleg. Co., 1982-83 Trade Cases,* Par. 65,194, p. 71,761 (2d Cir. 1983). In this case, the jury also found that AT&T orchestrated shortages of PCAs, engaged in abusive practices in the sale of customer "inside wiring," and delayed "final customer conversions to non-AT&T equipment." *Ibid.*

[253]*MCI Communications Corp. v. American Teleph. & Teleg. Co., 1982-83 Trade Cases,* Par. 65,137, pp. 71,398 (7th Cir. 1983).

"MCI also contended . . . that AT&T was obligated to provide it with local distribution facilities at the same rate at which AT&T provided such facilities to Western Union, under a long-standing contract between those two carriers. AT&T disagreed, claiming that the contract then in effect with Western Union did not reflect AT&T's current costs, and that the price charged to MCI for local distribution facilities should be set so as to recover AT&T's costs on a current basis." *Ibid.,* p. 71,359. The jury accepted AT&T's position on the issue.

[254]"Contrary to MCI's assertion, multipoint interconnection was substantially different in character from the other types of interconnections sought by MCI. Multipoint interconnection was the device through which MCI sought access to the full scope of AT&T's nationwide long distance network. Granting MCI multipoint interconnections would have enabled MCI to compete with AT&T for long distance traffic into areas where MCI may have made no significant capital investment. At the time in question, the FCC may or may not have intended (or indeed may or may not now or in the future intend) to effect such a significant change in the structure of the national telecommunications industry, and to impose upon AT&T the extraordinary obligation to fill in the gaps in its competitor's network." *Ibid.,* pp. 71,404-71,405.

[255]*So. Pacific Communications Co. v. American Teleph. & Teleg. Co., 1982-83 Trade Cases,* Par. 65,219, p. 72,040 (D. D.C. 1982). The Bell System's provision of local distribution facilities (after May, 1975) were "governed by tariffs that reflected the Settlement Agreement in Docket No. 20099 negotiated under the aegis of the FCC, signed by various carriers — including SPCC and AT&T — and accepted by the Commission as being in the public interest and as an 'acceptable compromise' on

matters then in dispute between the parties. . . ." *Ibid.* Nor could the court find any discrimination in the terms and conditions under which local distribution facilities were offered.

[256]*Ibid.*, p. 72,016.

[257]*Ibid.*, p. 72,021. The court held that intercity facilities were "nonessential" and could have been provided by SPCC itself. "There is an important distinction between a refusal to 'deal' and a refusal to assist a competitor by sharing nonessential facilities. Thus, although some cases have suggested that a monopolist may be liable under the Sherman Act for refusing to sell to a competitor when its refusal was motivated by an intent to drive the competitor out of the market by unfair means, the Court is unaware of any case holding that a monopolist must assist its competitors by sharing its nonessential facilities as if it were engaged in a joint venture with the competitors." *Ibid.*, p. 72,017 (citation omitted).

See also *Mid-Texas Communications Sys., Inc. v. American Teleph. & Teleg. Co., 1980-2 Trade Cases*, Par. 63,314 (5th Cir. 1980) (remanding an $18.4 million award, trebled to $55.1 million, in an interconnection case).

[258]Phillip Areeda and Donald F. Turner, *Antitrust Law* (Boston: Little, Brown & Co., 1978), Vol. III, p. 151. There is an alternative concept of predatory pricing that has been advanced in some antitrust cases; namely, setting price below the "profit maximization" level, particularly where barriers to entry are great. Compare, *e.g.*, *ILC Peripherals Leasing Corp. v. International Business Machs. Corp.*, 458 F. Supp. 423, 432 (N.D. Cal. 1978), *aff'd per curiam sub nom. Memorex Corp. v. International Business Machs. Corp.*, 636 F. 2d 1188 (9th Cir. 1980), *cert. denied*, 452 U.S. 972 (1981) with *MCI Communications Corp. v. American Teleph. & Teleg. Co., 1982-83 Trade Cases*, Par. 65,137, p. 71,375 (7th Cir. 1982), *cert. denied*, 52 USLW 3291 (1983).

[259]See Chapter 11, pp. 486-87. Also at issue in the pricing cases was a third AT&T private line tariff, Telpak, originally filed in January, 1961. See *So. Pacific Communications Co. v. American Teleph. & Teleg. Co., 1982-83 Trade Cases*, Par. 65,219, pp. 71,967-71,968 (D. D.C. 1982).

[260]In place of the traditional flat monthly charge, which covered both the capital costs of the equipment and the related operating expenses, the two-tier plan had two monthly payments: Tier A covered the capital equipment costs (equal monthly installments over an agreed upon fixed period of time, commonly one to ten years) and Tier B covered operating costs (monthly payments for as long as the equipment was used). If the operating company received a rate increase (or decrease), only the Tier B payment would be affected. The Tier A payment, however, was subject to a termination charge and/or credit: if a customer ended the arrangement before the end of the contractual period, the termination charge was the discounted present value of the remaining Tier A payments, while the termination credit was the value of the equipment if used to provide service for another customer.

The Bell System's flexible pricing tariffs were subject to much scrutiny by the state commissions. See, *e.g.*, "Flexible Pricing for Terminal Equipment," 107 *Public Utilities Fortnightly* 53 (May 21, 1981); American Bar Association Annual Report, Section of *Public Utility Law, 1982*, pp. 154-57.

[261]See, *e.g.*, *Porto Rican Am. Tobacco Co. v. American Tobacco Co.*, 30 F. 2d 234 (2d Cir. 1929), *cert. denied*, 279 U.S. 858 (1929); *Forster Mfg. Co. v. Federal Trade Comm.*, 335 F. 2d 47 (1st Cir. 1964), *cert. denied*, 380 U.S. 906 (1965).

[262]See, *e.g.*, *California Computer Products, Inc. v. International Business Machs. Corp.*, 613 F. 2d 727, 742-43 (9th Cir. 1979) (directed verdict proper where plaintiff "failed

to produce evidence of pricing below marginal or average variable cost"); *SuperTurf, Inc. v. Monsanto Co.,* 660 F. 2d 1275, 1281 (8th Cir. 1981) ("Even if Monsanto is a monopolist, it was within its rights to respond to the lower prices of its competitors while still pricing above its marginal costs.").

[263]*Northeastern Teleph. Co. v. American Teleph. & Teleg. Co., 1981-1 Trade Cases,* Par. 64,027, pp. 76,315-76,316 (footnotes omitted) (2d Cir. 1981), citing Phillip Areeda and Donald F. Turner, "Predatory Pricing and Related Practices Under Section 2 of the Sherman Act," 88 *Harvard Law Review* 697, 711 (1975).

"Although the FCC adopted fully distributed cost in Docket No. 18128 as the standard for pricing of telecommunications services, the record here shows that this was not a foregone conclusion and may have been primarily motivated by a desire to protect inefficient new carriers such as SPCC from the full economic consequences of competition, rather than on a reasoned economic basis.... In any event, the Court is convinced that a predatory pricing standard based upon fully distributed costs would be inconsistent with sound legal and economic principles...." *So. Pacific Communications Co. v. American Teleph. & Teleg. Co., 1982-83 Trade Cases,* Par. 65,219, pp. 71,975, 71,976 (D. D.C. 1982).

"In particular, FDC [fully distributed cost] fails as a relevant measure of cost in a competitive market. FDC is, at best, a rough indicator of an appropriate rate *ceiling* for regulatory purposes and should not be used as a measure of the minimum price permissible in a competitive market." *MCI Communications Corp. v. American Teleph. & Teleg. Co., 1982-83 Trade Cases,* Par. 65,137, p. 71,378 (7th Cir. 1983). But see dissenting opinion of Judge Wood, *ibid.,* pp. 71,426-71,443; "Ruling in AT&T-MCI Case Indicates Courts' Confusion on Predatory Pricing," *The Wall Street Journal,* January 21, 1983, p. 7.

[264]There has been substantial controversy over the Areeda-Turner rule: pricing below short-run marginal cost (using average variable cost as a proxy, due to the difficulties of deriving short-run marginal costs from conventional accounting methods) should be deemed as predatory and unlawful. See Areeda and Turner, "Predatory Pricing and Related Practices . . . ," *op. cit.* and *Antitrust Law, op. cit.,* Vol. III, pp. 148-94; Phillip Areeda, "Predatory Pricing (1980)," 49 *Antitrust Law Journal* 897 (1980). On the controversy, see F. M. Scherer, "Predatory Pricing and the Sherman Act: A Comment," 89 *Harvard Law Review* 869 (1976); Phillip Areeda and Donald F. Turner, "Scherer on Predatory Pricing: A Reply," 89 *Harvard Law Review* 891 (1976); F. M. Scherer, "Some Last Words on Predatory Pricing," 89 *Harvard Law Review* 901 (1976); Oliver Williamson, "Predatory Pricing: A Strategic and Welfare Analysis," 87 *Yale Law Journal* 284 (1977); Phillip Areeda and Donald F. Turner, "Williamson on Predatory Pricing," 87 *Yale Law Journal* 1337 (1978); Oliver Williamson, "A Preliminary Response," 87 *Yale Law Journal* 1353 (1978) and "Williamson on Predatory Pricing II," 88 *Yale Law Journal* 1183 (1979); William J. Baumol, "Quasi-Permanence of Price Reductions: A Policy for Prevention of Predatory Pricing," 89 *Yale Law Journal* 1 (1979); Paul L. Joskow and Alvin K. Klevorick, "A Framework for Analyzing Predatory Pricing Policy," 89 *Yale Law Journal* 213 (1979); D. F. Greer, "A Critique of Areeda and Turner's Standard for Predatory Practices," 24 *The Antitrust Bulletin* 233 (1979); John S. McGee, "Predatory Pricing Revisited," 23 *Journal of Law & Economics* 289 (1980); Joseph F. Brodley and George A. Hay, "Predatory Pricing: Competing Economic Theories and the Evaluation of Legal Standards," 66 *Cornell Law Review* 738 (1981).

[265]*Northeastern Teleph. Co. v. American Teleph. & Teleg. Co., 1981-1 Trade Cases,* Par.

64,027, p. 76,320 (2d Cir. 1981), citing *Berkey Photo, Inc. v. Eastman Kodak Co.,* 603 F. 2d 263, 275 (2d Cir. 1979), *cert. denied,* 444 U.S. 1093 (1980) and *Telex Corp. v. International Business Machs. Corp.,* 510 F. 2d 894, 926 (10th Cir. 1975), *cert. dismissed,* 423 U.S. 802 (1975).

[266]*Re Satellite Business Systems,* 62 FCC 2d 997, 1070 (1977).

[267]Harold S. Levy, "Deregulation-Antitrust: Must Utilities Serve Two Masters?" (speech delivered at the "Utility Regulatory Conference," sponsored by Public Utilities Reports, Washington, D.C., October 4, 1978) (mimeographed). See also G. E. Hale and Rosemary D. Hale, "The Otter Tail Power Case: Regulation by Commission or Antitrust Laws," *1973 Supreme Court Review* 99, 121-22.

Chapter	THE WATER
16	INDUSTRY

> *The water utility industry is unlike other utility groups which are regulated. The supply side of the business is not subject to substitution nor technological breakthrough. The quality of the end product must meet increasingly stringent legislative mandates. The need to be individually self-sufficient in a local as opposed to a regional, statewide, or even broader area prevents economy of scale. . . .*
>
> —*Loren D. Mellendorf**

The water industry, long held to be a public utility, is one that supplies an indispensable service (and a commodity for which there are no substitutes), but one that is dominated by small, rural systems and public enterprise. Consequently, it is an industry that presents unique regulatory challenges. Yet, compared with other utility industries, the water industry has been neglected. Such neglect

... can be attributed to such factors as water service constituting a relatively minor portion of consumer expenditures (and firm production costs), the dominance of public health issues in water supply, and the relative abundance in the past of cheap and easily accessible water supplies. In addition, the traditional engineering emphasis in water supply has tended to relegate pricing to a minor role in water policy decision making. Since 1970, energy issues have further reduced the general public's perception of the importance of water issues, except for the occasional drought-induced concern for adequate water supply. In brief, the public has had difficulty recognizing that water service, even though a necessity, does not have sacred qualities that preclude it from being subjected to economic analysis.[1]

The situation has changed dramatically in the past few years. While per capita consumption of water has continued to rise, potential reservoir sites have become increasingly scarce, ground sources have become more limited in availability, and increased environmental regulation has imposed higher-quality standards on public water systems. These factors, combined with the economic environment that prevailed throughout the 1970s, resulted in a new emphasis on water industry problems, as numerous rate cases were filed before the forty-five state commissions that have jurisdiction (often limited) over such utilities. Particularly has attention been focused on the problems confronted by small water companies, water conservation, and innovative rate design.

This chapter seeks to outline briefly the development of the water in-dustry and its current structure, to discuss the issues confronting both the industry and its regulators, and to consider present rate structures and proposed changes. As such, the focus is on the economic regulation of the industry, thereby omitting consideration of an equally important public pol-icy issue: the growing scarcity of water supplies in some sections of the country.

Historical Development and Structure

"The development of water works has been largely devoid of dramatic incidents. Most of the industry's growth has occurred since the opening of the nineteenth century."[2] Indeed, prior to 1800, there were only sixteen water supply systems in the United States (see Table 16-1). All but one were privately owned. The earliest water system was constructed in Boston, Massa-chusetts, in 1652; a gravity system consisting of wooden pipes and conduits conveying water from nearby wells and springs to a single disposal point (a wooden tank). The first water system to use machinery was completed in Bethlehem, Pennsylvania, in 1754; "its equipment consisting of a wooden pump, a wooden reservoir, and a log line."[3] The third water system was constructed in Schaefferstown, Pennsylvania, in 1764; a system which in-volved a farmer who piped water from his farm to the community.[4] The first municipally owned water system was constructed in Winchester, Virginia, shortly before 1800.[5]

By 1850, the number of public water supply systems had increased to eighty-three; by 1896, to 3,196. Between these years, there was a steady increase in the proportion of publicly owned water systems; from 39.7 to 53.2 percent.[6] By 1927, the number of water systems had grown to approxi-mately 9,800, of which 70 percent were municipally owned.[7] Today, the

TABLE 16-1

Water Systems in the United States,
1800-1896

Year	Publicly Owned	Privately Owned	Total	Percent of Total Public	Percent of Total Private
1800	1	15	16	6.3	93.7
1810	5	21	26	19.2	80.8
1820	5	25	30	16.6	83.4
1830	9	35	44	20.5	79.5
1840	23	41	64	35.9	64.1
1850	33	50	83	39.7	60.3
1860	57	79	136	41.9	58.1
1870	116	127	243	47.7	52.3
1880	293	305	598	49.0	51.0
1890	806	1,072	1,878	42.9	57.1
1896	1,690	1,489	3,179[a]	53.2	46.8

[a]There were seventeen additional water systems, of which twelve were of joint ownership and five of unknown ownership.

Source: M. N. Baker, "Water Works," in Edward W. Bemis (ed.), *Municipal Monopolies* (New York: Thomas Crowell & Co., 1899), p. 15.

public water sector is comprised of 34,631 systems (see Table 16-2), with a capital investment of over $125 billion and nearly 12 million miles of transmission and distribution lines,[8] serving some 192.2 million people.

Central Water Systems

A central water system[9] must acquire, collect, process, and deliver to its customers' premises a safe and potable supply of water. There are three primary water sources: ground, surface, and purchased (see Table 16-3). The majority (75 percent) of central water systems rely upon ground sources (*i.e.,* sources tapped by wells), but they account for less than 40 percent of service volume. Other (13 percent) central water systems rely upon surface sources (*i.e.,* impounding reservoirs, lakes, and rivers), but they account for nearly 40 percent of public water output. The remaining systems (12 percent) rely upon purchases from other water systems. As already noted, rising per capita consumption, coupled with a growing scarcity of potential reservoir sites and the imposition of strict quality standards on public water service,[10] have forced the industry to consider and implement a number of conservation programs (including waste water recycling and changes in rate design).[11]

TABLE 16-2

Central Water Systems and Population Served
in the 48 Contiguous States, 1976

Total Population Served		Number Of Systems	Percent Of Systems	Population Served (Millions)
25-	99	6,308	18	0.4
100-	499	11,714	34	2.8
500-	999	4,932	14	3.4
1,000-	2,499	4,850	14	7.6
2,500-	4,999	2,496	7	8.7
5,000-	9,999	1,646	5	10.4
10,000-	99,999	2,442	7	73.8
100,000-999,999		232	1	58.9
> 1.0 million		11		26.2
Total		34,631	100	192.2

Source: U.S. Environmental Protection Agency, *Survey of Operating and Financial Characteristics of Community Water Systems* (Washington, D.C.: Report prepared by Temple, Barker, and Sloane, April, 1977), p. II-4.

TABLE 16-3

Operating Characteristics of Central Water Systems
in the 48 Contiguous States, 1976

Total Population Served		Number Of Systems	Average Daily Production[a]	Number of Systems Primary Water Source		
				Ground	Surface	Purchased
25-	99	6,308	.006	5,930	63	315
100-	499	11,714	.025	9,488	586	1,640
500-	999	4,932	.075	3,452	888	592
1,000-	2,499	4,850	.200	3,347	824	679
2,500-	4,999	2,496	.480	1,448	674	374
5,000-	9,999	1,646	.921	1,053	428	165
10,000-	99,999	2,442	5.059	1,270	757	415
100,000-999,999 ...		232	48.003	65	137	30
> 1.0 million ...		11	496.660	1	10	0
Total		34,631		26,054	4,367	4,210

[a]Millions of gallons daily (MGD).

Source: U.S. Environmental Protection Agency, *Survey of Operating and Financial Characteristics of Community Water Systems* (Washington, D.C.: Report prepared by Temple, Barker, and Sloane, April, 1977), p. II-7.

After its collection, the water must be treated before it enters the distribution system. Treatment costs depend upon the source of water (*e.g.*, surface water generally requires more treatment than ground water; some water requires only chlorination, while other water requires complex processing that may include softening) and upon state and federal requirements (*e.g.*, some states have minimum education standards for personnel operating treatment plants). Passage of the Safe Water Drinking Act has tended to raise water treatment and purification costs across the country. Finally, distribution

> . . . takes place through a network of mains and service connections, with the water driven by pressure created as the result of sufficient elevation in the system. Water systems make use of storage facilities, which are often located in the areas where it is consumed. Storage facilities assist in meeting peak demands — which would otherwise fall on the facilities serving to supply, treat, pump, and distribute water.[12]

A central water system, like other utilities, is designed to meet peak demands. Such peaks may be time-of-day (hourly or weekly) and seasonal. It is important to recognize that

> . . . water system components are generally designed to meet different types of demands. For example, raw water storage facilities (e.g., reservoirs) are generally designed to meet average annual demand; transmission and treatment facilities as well as major feeder mains are generally designed to absorb maximum day demand; and distribution mains, pumping stations, and local storage facilities are designed to meet maximum hour demand, or maximum day demand plus fire protection flow requirements, whichever is greatest. . . . The obvious implication is that water systems with identical average demands must be designed differently if their peak demands differ.[13]

For most central water systems, the peak demand period occurs during the summer months, June through September. Residential lawn and garden sprinkling, along with golf course sprinkling and swimming pool use, are the primary contributors to the summer peak period. While such usage is related to income,[14] it is particularly sensitive to climatic factors, such as temperature, precipitation, and the evapotranspiration rate.[15] For water systems, the summer peak period raises at least two problems. First, the summer peak period — which generally occurs when the sources of water supply are at their lowest — may be 1.5 to three times the average daily demand. It is not uncommon, therefore, for water systems to control residential lawn and garden sprinkling in two basic ways: a water utility's tariff (*a*) may prohibit residential lawn and garden sprinkling between specific hours or (*b*) may impose higher residential rates during the summer months.

Second, the existence of a summer peak results in significant amounts of underutilized capacity during the eight off-peak months. In contrast to electric utilities, for instance, water systems tend to confront deteriorating load factors: no new types of winter water uses have emerged to offset the growing summer peak loads.

Some Important Characteristics

The water industry differs in several important respects from other public utilities. As succinctly summarized by Mellendorf:

> Water utilities have developed where there has been a concentration of people. Their service areas have remained local and thus their size has remained small. Even the largest are very small in comparison to other utilities. Characteristically, they require huge sums of capital investment, are not normally interconnected because of the extreme investment necessary to traverse sparsely populated areas, have had to be self-sufficient under whatever weather conditions prevail, and have had to treat an ever-poorer raw material to an ever-more stringent quality standard. Technology changes have been slow and limited; therefore, obsolescence has not been a problem and facilities have had a very long life. However, that same lack of technological change has prevented any noticeable improvement in productivity and has meant that each new increment of capacity is more costly. . . . The furnishing of water utility service has been, and will continue to be, both capital and labor intensive, and it is a service which has required, and will continue to require, an ever-increasing price.[16]

The water industry, as a result of these characteristics, is exceedingly diverse. Of the nearly 35,000 central water systems, approximately 20,000 or 57 percent are located in rural areas. They are small, often serve only a few customers, commonly confront severe financial difficulties, and are unable to achieve economies of scale with their deteriorating physical facilities.[17] Concludes a National Regulatory Research Institute (NRRI) report:

> . . . Like other types of public utilities, small water utilities are capital intensive, yet because of their small size and weak financial structure, they often lack the ability to attract capital through the same mechanisms available to large electric, gas, telephone, and water utilities. Indeed, many small water utilities lack a significant rate base because the original cost of all or most of the water systems was included in and recovered in the purchase price of each property owner in a housing sub-division. Without a substantial rate base, equity, or physical assets to serve as collateral, small water utilities find it difficult and expensive to

raise capital. Stories of the very small water utility owner faced with using his house or car as collateral are widely circulated and are, at least, illustrative of the capital acquisition problem.

Inadequate capital for construction and maintenance activities is often accompanied by inadequate management, both financial and otherwise. The problem here is circular. Lack of funds, it is argued, leads to an inability to support a management structure adequate to maintain stringent financial records and to attract capital. Further, it appears that these small water systems are too small to command much high quality management effort. Managing a small water utility is usually a second job, and often more than the utility owner bargained for: he went into the business to sell land or housing, not water. The owner can tend to view his utility as an adjunct to his normal business and not as a regulated public service. Rather than feeling an obligation to serve, he may be concerned with recovering his money and moving on to other business opportunities.[18]

Moreover, there is evidence that "smaller systems tend to have increasing problems with leakage, incorrect meter readings, meter failure, and illegal withdrawals."[19]

Ownership and Regulation

Of the 34,631 central water systems,[20] 56 percent are public and 44 percent are private. However, the public systems (either municipal systems or public water districts) serve 84 percent of the population served by central systems. There is a wide diversity in the size of both public and private systems: the largest systems (8 percent) serve nearly 83 percent of the population, while the smallest systems (80 percent) serve about 7 percent of the population.[21] Diversity also characterizes system investment: while the average water system investment is approximately $260 per capita served, the range to serve a residential family (of three persons) is from $200 for the largest systems to $1,600 for the smallest systems.

Some private water systems are regulated by state commissions.[22] Where such regulation prevails, it generally encompasses wholesale and retail rates, financing, depreciation rates, and extensions, as well as uniform systems of accounts. Since most of these private systems are small, they present a number of complex regulatory problems. To illustrate: countless water utilities were originated by land developers. Many subsequently seek to become compensatory, under traditional regulatory standards, despite the fact that the price the customers paid to the real estate firm "for the developed lots or houses must have reflected the price that they were to be charged for the water. . . ."[23]

Of the 527 utility rate cases filed in 1985 before the state commissions,

292 or just over 55 percent involved water, sewer, or combination water and sewer filings.[24] A survey report by NRRI suggests that those commissions regulating water utilities have modified their traditional procedures to deal with small water companies. These modifications include: (*1*) use of stipulated proceedings[25]; (*2*) use of simplified or shortened forms required to be filed for a rate case[26]; and (*3*) use of simplified procedures (such as the authority to waive a formal hearing; the use of "staff-assisted rate cases"[27]). The NRRI report suggests a number of other approaches that have been, or could be, implemented by the state commissions, including: (*1*) policy changes to reduce the demand for the creation of small water utilities[28]; (*2*) steps to enhance the economic viability of small water companies[29]; (*3*) steps to improve the operation of small water utilities (such as regionalization[30]; training for owners and operators); and (*4*) deregulation (especially for the smallest water utilities)[31] and/or wider use of automatic adjustment clauses.[32]

In contrast to private water companies, most public systems are regulated at the local level; *i.e.*, by city councils, water commissions, and so forth. These systems

> . . . vary from an integral part of local government to an operation independent of local government. As an agency of local government, budget, rate structure, and other policies are generally subject to city council approval; system expansion is financed by general obligation bonds. As an independent agency, rate structure and budget are under the jurisdiction of an elected or appointed commission with water system expansion financed by general revenue bonds. Many variations between these two extremes exist with few if any municipally owned water utilities operating completely free of local control. Although there are differences in the type of regulation, the actual operation of publicly owned firms in many respects can be similar to that of investor-owned firms.[33]

Public Fire Protection

A central water system performs three basic functions. First, it delivers water of proper quality to its customers. Second, it makes possible the operation of a network of sewers, since "a water-carrying system is the most economical method of collecting and disposing of community sewage."[34] Third, it provides water for public fire protection. This latter function is extremely important in the proper design of a central water system. Explain Garfield and Lovejoy:

> Another economic characteristic of water utilities is the joint nature of their supply function, arising from the fact that they provide both water service to utility customers and fire-protection service to the gen-

eral public. This is sometimes referred to as service to "users" and "nonusers," respectively. The users of water service, of course, are the conventional and special classes of utility customers. The nonusers are the beneficiaries of the capacity installed by water utilities for the purpose of supplying water to the fire departments in their communities. Stated more specifically, the beneficiaries of public fire-protection water service are the owners of property in the community. The importance of such service relates far more to the value of the property protected than to the amount of water consumed. Private fire-protection service, in the form of service to interior sprinkler systems and additional hydrants, is provided to commercial and industrial customers. This is a service different from public fire protection and amounts to a special class of service. Water supply and distribution systems are designed with due regard for the needs of both users and nonusers. Therefore, in order to provide public fire-protection service, water utilities must invest in more plant capacity than would be required to supply service solely to water users. This takes the form of larger supply capacity and mains, hydrants, extra valves, larger pumps, and additional storage capacity. Accordingly, the costs of providing public fire-protection service are almost entirely composed of readiness-to-serve costs, or fixed costs, largely associated with the plant capacity required. The amount of water used for this purpose is comparatively unimportant.[35]

Investor-owned central water systems are generally compensated for public fire-protection service, either by an annual lump sum charge or by an annual hydrant charge.[36] "Since the property tax is the principal source of revenues to local governments, the fire-protection payment to the investor-owned water utility is essentially supported by the property which received the benefit of the fire protection."[37] Publicly-owned central water systems are usually not compensated for public fire-protection service, with such costs being charged to water users or absorbed in the general fund. If fire-protection costs are charged to water users, there may be "a haphazard mixing of the respective burdens that should be borne by water users and property owners, and it is only a matter of chance that these burdens will be fairly distributed and borne."[38]

Water Utility Rate Structures

The diversity which characterizes the size of central water supply systems results in a corresponding diversity in water rates and in pricing objectives. Take just two examples. (*1*) Approximately 50 percent of the water systems in the smallest size category (25-99 population served) are in mobile home parks, and the vast majority do not charge for the water service directly; the trailer park generally incorporates the water charge in the rental rate. (2) For years, many of the smaller municipal systems, particularly those regulated by city councils, set water rates to cover both the associated costs[39] and to permit some revenues to flow into the general fund. But local governments also may have a variety of other objectives in mind when establishing water rates, such as community acceptance, rates of nearby communities, and annexation policies.[40]

Existing Rate Structures[41]

In the case of those water systems regulated by water or state commissions, the traditional steps in rate determination apply; *i.e.*, establishment of the revenue requirement, a cost-of-service study, the allocation of costs to specific customer groups, and the design of a rate schedule (or rate schedules).[42] The revenue requirement may be determined on a utility basis (operating expenses, depreciation, taxes, and return on rate base) or on a cash basis (operating and maintenance expense, debt service, payment in lieu of taxes, and plant extensions, replacements, and improvements).[43] Costs may be classified by the base-extra capacity method or by the commodity-demand method.[44] Under the former, costs are classified as base costs (costs associated with service to customers under average load conditions), extra capacity costs (costs associated with use requirements in excess of the average), customer costs (meter reading, billing, accounting and collection expenses), and direct fire-protection costs (public fire hydrants, related branch mains and valves). Under the latter, costs are classified as commodity costs (treatment and other operating expenses), demand costs (investment to meet system peak demand), customer costs, and direct fire-protection costs. Base costs and commodity costs are commonly allocated on the basis of usage volume; extra capacity costs and demand costs on the basis of the noncoincident peak method; and customer costs on the basis of the number of customers.

The final rate structure may be either flat or declining (in the case of most water systems). Early rate structures, as well as current unmetered service (and most small water utilities provide unmetered service), were and continue to be flat, as illustrated by the following two residential rate structures. First, the 1932 rate schedule for the Seymour Water Company:[45]

	Per Year
Dwelling houses—each family:	
For sink	$ 8.00
Sink and set tub	9.00
Sink and toilet	11.00
Sink, toilet, and bowl	12.00
Sink, toilet, and bath	15.00
Sink, toilet, bath, and bowl	17.00
Sink, toilet, bath, bowl and set tub	19.00

Each additional sink, bowl, or set tub 1.00
Each additional toilet or bath 2.00
Each additional faucet in stable or garage 3.00

Hose—For hand use only 6.00
For revolving sprinklers, sprays, or hose other
than by hand 12.00

Second, the 1984-85 rate structure for the Tisbury Water Works:[46]

	Per Annum
Dwelling houses. House occupied by one family, supplied by one faucet	$ 54.21
Each additional faucet	9.05
One water closet of approved kind	16.40
Each additional water closet	9.90
One bath tub	12.60
Each additional bath tub	8.20
One self-closing urinal, none other allowed	10.80
Dishwasher	14.45
One set tub or automatic washer	14.45
Each additional set tub	4.30
Outside shower	12.60
Turn On	10.00
Turn Off	10.00

Hose. For sprinklers of not over 1/4 inch orifice used for watering lawns, gardens, and other similar uses, the use being limited as follows: Y branches and soaker hose over 50 feet are prohibited.

One hose from 4 p.m. to 8 p.m.	$ 36.15
Each additional hose used at same time	36.15
One hose from 8 a.m. to 8 p.m.	108.50
Each additional hose used at same time	108.50

The use of hose for above purposes must cease at 8 p.m. For each violation of the above rules concerning the use of hose, a fine of $10.00 will be imposed, and added to the annual billing.

Such flat rates tend to encourage waste. "Leaky fixtures and pipes are neglected; more water is used than is actually needed; excessive quantities may be used for sprinkling the lawn; et cetera. Waste cannot be controlled through raising the price of service, since a higher price on a flat rate only leads to a curtailment of the number of outlets and approximately the same quantity of water may be wasted as before."[47]

Metered rates commonly are declining, but with a single rate schedule applicable to all retail customers. In the case of a three-block rate schedule, the initial block may be for residential users, the second block for commercial users, and the final block for large industrial users.[48] In the case of a four-block rate schedule, the initial block may be designed to recover customer costs and the costs of serving small residential users, the second block designed for large residential and small commercial users, the third block designed for large commercial and small industrial users, and the tail block designed for large industrial and special users.[49] Such rate schedules generally contain a graduated minimum charge that increases as the size of the meter increases and may contain a purchased water surcharge or purchased water adjustment clause.[50] The following four rate schedules are illustrative. First, a three-block water rate structure, with a related sewer rate structure:[51]

		Per 1,000 gallons per Month
Water Service		
First	15,000 gallons	$ 3.30
Next	15,000 gallons	2.50
All over	30,000 gallons	2.10
Minimum Bill		$13.20
(includes first 4,000 gallons)		
Sewer Service		
First	4,000 gallons	$ 4.15
Next	12,000 gallons	1.56
Minimum Bill		$16.60
(includes first 4,000 gallons)		
Maximum Bill		$32.32
(usage over 16,000 gallons)		

Second, a three-block water rate structure, with a graduated minimum charge:[52]

	Gallons per		Rate per
RATE:	*Month*	*Quarter*	*1,000 Gallons*
For the first	2,000	6,000	at minimum charge
For the next	13,000	39,000	$1.081
For all over	15,000	45,000	.944

MINIMUM CHARGE:

No bill will be rendered for less than the minimum charges set forth below:

Size of Meter	Per Month	Per Quarter
⅝ inch	$ 4.71	$ 14.13
¾ inch	7.07	21.21
1 inch	11.78	35.34
1½ inch	23.56	70.68
2 inch	37.69	113.07
3 inch	70.66	211.98
4 inch	117.75	353.25
6 inch	235.50	706.50
8 inch	376.80	1,130.40

SERVICE CONNECTION CHARGE:

¾ inch Service Connection	$ 610.00
Service Connection over ¾ inch	Actual cost to company including overhead and Federal Income Tax

PURCHASED WATER SURCHARGE:

$0.29 per 1,000 gallons

Third, a five-block water rate structure for all retail service, also with a graduated minimum charge:[53]

RATE:

		Rate per 1,000 Gallons per Month
First	2,000 gallons	at minimum charge
Next	28,000 gallons	$3.210
Next	970,000 gallons	1.830
Next	9,000,000 gallons	1.336
All over	10,000,000 gallons	1.044

MINIMUM CHARGE:

No bill will be rendered for less than the following amount according to the size of each meter installed, to wit: for customers having multiple meter settings, the minimum charge will be the sum of the minimum charges for each of the individual meters:

Size of Meter	Per Month
⅝ inch meter or less	$ 8.65
¾ inch meter	12.95

1 inch meter	21.55
1½ inch meter	43.15
2 inch meter	69.00
3 inch meter	129.45
4 inch meter	215.65
6 inch meter	431.40
8 inch meter	690.25

Fourth, two five-block water rate structures for a company with both a gravity service area and a pumped service area:[54]

GRAVITY SERVICE AREA

RATES:

Quarterly Consumption		*Monthly Consumption*		
In Excess of	*600 cu ft*	*In Excess of*	*200 cu ft*	*Gravity Service*
First	8,400 cu ft	First	2,800 cu ft	$0.546/100 cu ft
Next	81,000 cu ft	Next	27,000 cu ft	0.433/100 cu ft
Next	810,000 cu ft	Next	270,000 cu ft	0.383/100 cu ft
Next	1,200,000 cu ft	Next	400,000 cu ft	0.299/100 cu ft
Excess		Excess		0.192/100 cu ft

MINIMUM CHARGES AND ALLOWANCES:

	Quarterly Accounts		*Monthly Accounts*	
Meter Size (inches)	*Allowance (100 cu ft)*	*Minimum Charge Gravity*	*Allowance (100 cu ft)*	*Minimum Charge Gravity*
⅝ & ¾	6	$ 11.84	2	$ 3.95
1	6	20.33	2	6.78
1½	6	34.48	2	11.49
2	6	51.46	2	17.15
3	6	96.74	2	32.25
4	6	147.68	2	49.23
6	6	289.18	2	96.39
8	6	657.08	2	219.03

PUMPED SERVICE AREA

RATES:

Quarterly Consumption		*Monthly Consumption*		
In Excess of	*600 cu ft*	*In Excess of*	*200 cu ft*	*Pumped Service*
First	8,400 cu ft	First	2,800 cu ft	$0.777/100 cu ft
Next	81,000 cu ft	Next	27,000 cu ft	0.664/100 cu ft
Next	810,000 cu ft	Next	270,000 cu ft	0.614/100 cu ft
Next	1,200,000 cu ft	Next	400,000 cu ft	0.530/100 cu ft
Excess		Excess		0.423/100 cu ft

MINIMUM CHARGES AND ALLOWANCES:

Meter Size	Quarterly Accounts		Monthly Accounts	
	Allowance (100 cu ft)	Minimum Charge Pumped	Allowance (100 cu ft)	Minimum Charge Pumped
⅝ & ¾	6	$ 13.22	2	$ 4.41
1	6	21.71	2	7.24
1½	6	35.86	2	11.95
2	6	52.84	2	17.61
3	6	98.12	2	32.71
4	6	149.06	2	46.69
6	6	290.56	2	96.85
8	6	658.46	2	219.49

Declining block rates, despite their tendency to minimize revenue instability (usage fluctuations occur primarily in the tail blocks), often fail to track costs, just as the allocation of demand costs by the noncoincident peak demand method fails to distinguish between peak and off-peak usage. Declining block rates cannot be justified unless the system tends to experience decreasing unit costs with increased usage (from improvements in capacity utilization in the short run and from economies of scale in the long run), but it appears that many water systems have exhausted such economies of scale. Expansion costs have increased for a variety of reasons, including "the exhaustion of economies of scale in treatment, the depletion of the more accessible sources of supply, and diseconomies in distribution. Therefore, increasing use in the short-run may justify declining charges given load factor improvements; but if this increased usage triggers an increase in required system capacity with the elevation of unit costs, then the promotion of use in the short-run conflicts with increasing use in the long run."[55] The ultimate effects of both a single rate structure for all users and a declining block rate structure not cost justified are price discrimination among customers and a failure to encourage water conservation.

Future Rate Structures: Issues and Problems

Increased operating and construction costs, along with increased costs of new water facilities (increased storage requirements, for example) and stricter quality standards, have forced the water industry to reevaluate existing rate schedules.[56] There has been a trend toward the elimination of blocks.[57] Some have urged the development of separate rate schedules for different customer classes to reduce price discrimination and other adverse effects of rate "averaging."[58] Others have urged the adoption of zonal pricing, whereby rates would vary with zones within a service area. Such a proposal assumes that water service costs are a direct function of the distance between the production center (treatment plant) and the consumer's water intake point; an assumption that may not hold for a number of water systems.[59] Still others urge the adoption of either time-of-day peak-load pricing or of seasonal peak-load pricing.[60] The former would require the installation of demand meters, thereby raising a cost/benefit issue, particularly for residential users; the latter would not, if peak and off-peak rates (as is true with summer/winter differentials in the electric utility industry) are confined to specific billing periods. And, finally, there are those who urge adoption of an inverted rate structure, largely on grounds of conservation.[61]

Rate reform, however, is exceedingly difficult in the water industry. Concludes Mann:

> The application of the cost of service criterion to water rates is not a simple task. One significant problem with the cost approach is the subjectivity in cost measurement for specific services and specific user groups. The subjectivity is a function of the lack of knowledge regarding cost of specific water services, costs of supplying specific consumer groups, and cost of peak versus off-peak consumption. The cost of service principle can also generate a conflict between efficiency and simplicity. A rate structure or level based on costs of service may not be publicly acceptable and may not be easy to administer. Given the many participants (*e.g.,* city administrators, utility managements, customer groups, special users, bondholders, stockholders, and regulators) who can influence the rate setting mechanism, it is not difficult to perceive why water rates incorporate non-cost elements. One can generally observe a wide variation in rates across water systems in the United States even within categories of the same size, ownership, and source of supply.[62]

A Host of Unresolved Issues

Over the years, far too little attention has been given to the economics of providing water service.[63] Instead, the major emphasis has been on cost/benefit evaluation of various water projects (reservoirs and dams) and on regional development.[64] The public has taken the provision of water service for granted, except during periods of drought-induced shortages (*e.g.,* California, 1976-1977; New Jersey, 1980-1981) or when controversial issues (*e.g.,* interbasin transfers[65]; coal slurry pipelines[66]) arise. Much has been written about the water "crisis," particularly in the West, and the long-standing conflict between Arizona and California for Colorado River rights.[67] But is there truly a crisis? Answers Castle:

> . . . water availability varies greatly with geography, and general statements about the subject are suspect. Since the seasonal distribution as

well as total amounts of rainfall differ greatly from place to place, the cost of making water available at a given place and time also varies widely. But this is very different than saying water is not physically available, or that water of a quality necessary for certain kinds of human activity is unavailable. Therefore, crisis is not an appropriate term to apply to most areas of the United States when describing water issues. And that includes most of the West.[68]

What is all too obvious is that the country faces significant cost increases in the future to obtain additional quantities of high-quality water. Given the diversity of water supply systems, the challenge is immense. Present economic regulation of the water industry is limited, with both supply and environmental responsibilities shared by numerous state and federal agencies. Such fragmentation makes solutions to the nation's future water supplies more difficult to fashion and to implement. But one thing seems certain: the challenge for water policy in the coming years "will be to provide incentives that will result in water being viewed as an increasingly scarce resource."[69]

Notes

*Loren D. Mellendorf, "The Water Utility Industry and Its Problems," 111 *Public Utilities Fortnightly* 17 (March 17, 1983).

[1]Patrick C. Mann, *Water Service: Regulation and Rate Reform* (Columbus, Ohio: National Regulatory Research Institute, Occasional Paper No. 4, 1981), p. ix. See also J. Hirshleifer et al., *Water Supply Economics, Technology and Policy* (Chicago: University of Chicago Press, 1960); Diana C. Gibbons, *The Economic Value of Water* (Washington, D.C.: Resources for the Future, 1986).

[2]Irston R. Barnes, *The Economics of Public Utility Regulation* (New York: F. S. Crofts & Co., 1942), p. 24.

[3]*Ibid.*

[4]Other early water systems included Providence, Rhode Island (1772); Geneva, New York (1787); Plymouth and Salem, Massachusetts (both in 1796); Hartford, Connecticut (1797); Portsmouth, New Hampshire (1798); Worcester, Massachusetts (1798); Albany, New York (1798); Lynchburg, Virginia (1799); Peabody, Massachusetts (1799); Morristown, New Jersey (1799); and Newark, New Jersey (1800).

[5]See J. Michael La Nier, "Historical Development of Municipal Water Systems in the United States," 68 *Journal of the American Water Works Association* 173 (1976).

[6]By 1896, fourteen of the original fifteen private water systems had been converted to municipal ownership. "The trend from private to public ownership with respect to the supply of water is less a reflection of the inability of private enterprise to supply the service profitably than it is of public dissatisfaction with the profits which private companies were assumed to be earning and of a realization that the maintenance of sanitary standards of living require that water service be rendered at the lowest possible cost. The technical aspects of water supply are sufficiently simple and the market sufficiently stable so that these features have constituted no obstacle

to the successful construction or operation of waterworks by governmental units." Barnes, *op. cit.*, p. 25.

[7]Roland E. Eustler, "Public and Private Ownership of Water Supply Utilities," 201 *Annals of the American Academy of Political and Social Sciences* 89 (1939).

[8]La Nier, *op. cit.*

[9]Some water service is "noncentral" or self-supplied service (as opposed to "centralized" service). The Soil Conservation Service, for example, defines a self-supply system as one that serves five or less households from an individual source (*e.g.*, a well). Under this definition, it has been estimated that in 1975 approximately 36 million people were served by self-supply systems. Self-supply systems include farm irrigation and industrial firm water systems.

[10]Quality standards are particularly important under the Safe Drinking Water Act of 1974 (Pub. Law 92-253), which provides for the protection of underground sources, as well as drinking water quality standards, and is applicable to virtually all public water supply systems. See, *e.g.*, Robert M. Clark and Richard G. Stevie, "Meeting the Drinking Water Standards: The Price of Regulation," in Clifford S. Russell (ed.), *Safe Drinking Water: Current and Future Problems* (Washington, D.C.: Resources for the Future, 1978), pp. 271-317; Robert M. Clark et al., "Cost of Water Supply: Selected Case Studies," 105 *Journal of the Environmental Engineering Division-ASCE* 89 (1979). Even more stringent requirements were imposed when the act was extended, in 1986, for another five-year period (Pub. Law 99-339); *e.g.*, the EPA is required to set standards for eighty-three contaminants within three years; the EPA must specify criteria for filtration of surface water supplies by 1988 and for disinfection of surface and groundwater supplies by 1990. See, *e.g.*, "Water Treatment Enters a New Era," *Chemical Week*, October 26, 1986, pp. 21-22; Gordon I. Culp, "Big Changes Ahead for Drinking Water Industry," *Water Engineering and Management*, March 1987, pp. 24ff; G. Richard Dreese and Vivian Witkind Davis, *Briefing Paper on the Economic Impact of the Safe Drinking Water Act Amendments of 1986* (Columbus, Ohio: National Regulatory Research Institute, 1987); Vivian Witkind Davis et al., *A Preliminary Review of Certain Costs of the Safe Drinking Water Act Amendments of 1986 for Commission-Regulated Ground Water Utilities* (Columbus, Ohio: National Regulatory Research Institute, 1987).

Other significant federal water quality standards are contained in the Clean Water Act of 1972 (as amended in 1977, 1981, and 1986), which regulates the discharge of pollutants into surface waters, and the Resource Conservation and Recovery Act of 1976 (as amended in 1984), which regulates the disposal of solid and hazardous waste and further protects surface and groundwater quality.

[11]See Duane D. Baumann and Daniel Dworkin, "The Challenge to Management," in David Holtz and Scott Sebastian (eds.), *Municipal Water Supply: The Challenge for Urban Resource Management* (Bloomington: Indiana University Press, 1978), pp. 293-99.

[12]Paul J. Garfield and Wallace F. Lovejoy, *Public Utility Economics* (Englewood Cliffs: Prentice-Hall, Inc., 1964), p. 221.

[13]Mann, *op. cit.*, p. 30 (citations omitted).

[14]See, *e.g.*, Charles Headley, "The Relation of Family Incomes and Use of Water for Residential and Commercial Purposes in the San Francisco-Oakland Metropolitan Area," 39 *Land Economics* 441 (1963); Kenneth Gibbs, "Price Variance in Residential Water Demand Models," 14 *Water Resources Research* 15 (1978).

[15]See, *e.g.*, W. Douglas Morgan, "Climatic Indicators in the Estimation of Municipal Water Demand," 12 *Water Resources Bulletin* 511 (1976). During arid periods, to

illustrate, lawn sprinkling may account for as much as 80 percent of the residential hourly peak. Mann, *op. cit.*, p. 31.

[16]Mellendorf, *op. cit.*

[17]See, *e.g.*, Benjamin V. Dall and Hsiu-Hsiung Chen, *Economics and Finance of Nevada Public Water Systems* (Reno: Center for Water Resources Research, University of Nevada, 1975).

[18]Raymond W. Lawton and Vivian Witkind Davis, *Commission Regulation of Small Water Utilities: Some Issues and Solutions* (Columbus, Ohio: National Regulatory Research Institute, 1983), pp. 5-6 (citation omitted).

[19]Mann, *op. cit.*, p. 16. See, *e.g.*, Charles W. Keller, "Analysis of Unaccounted-for Water," 68 *Journal of the American Water Works Association* 159 (1976).

[20]The data in this section are from two Environmental Protection Agency reports: *Inventory of Water Supply Systems* (Washington, D.C., 1976) and *Survey of Operating and Financial Characteristics of Community Water Systems* (Washington, D.C., 1977). The EPA data reflect only those central water systems serving a minimum of twenty-five persons and/or having fifteen customer connections, and exclude federally-owned systems, systems in Alaska and Hawaii, and systems serving only wholesale customers (*e.g.*, the Metropolitan Water District of Southern California).

[21]Private systems dominate the smaller population categories: 86 percent of the systems serving less than 100 persons are investor-owned [see National Demonstration Water Project, *Drinking Water Supplies in Rural America* (1979)], with most of these located in mobile home parks and/or small rural communities.

[22]*1985 Annual Report on Utility and Carrier Regulation* (Washington, D.C.: National Association of Regulatory Utility Commissioners, 1987), p. 738. Even where state commissions have jurisdiction over private systems, there are many limitations, *e.g.*, in Florida, jurisdiction is limited to systems serving more than 100 persons and having at least forty connections; in Louisiana, to systems serving at least ten customers; in Michigan, to systems serving over seventy-five customers; in Nevada, to systems serving over twenty-five customers and having at least $5,000 in annual revenues; and in Virginia, to systems with at least fifty customers. *Ibid.*

[23]Alfred E. Kahn, "Recent Developments in Cost Analysis and Rate Design," in *Proceedings of the 1977 Symposium on Problems of Regulated Industries* (Columbia: University of Missouri-Columbia, 1978), p. 19. See, *e.g.*, *Re Crestview Services, Inc.*, Order No. 65118 (Md., 1981).

[24]*1985 Annual Report on Utility and Carrier Regulation, op. cit.*, pp. 332-86. Despite the abundance of rate increase cases, "the real price of residential and commercial water service has declined during the past decade, whereas the real price of industrial water service has increased in the same period." Patrick C. Mann and Paul R. LeFrancois, "Trends in the Real Price of Water," 75 *Journal of the American Water Works Association* 441, 443 (1983).

[25]"In a stipulated proceeding, the staff of the petitioning utility and the commission meet in advance of the formal commission hearing, agree on certain data and/or facts, and present the stipulated portion to the commissioners as an area where the utility and the commission staff are in agreement. The commissioners are not bound by the stipulations, but where they accept them, time in formal hearings is saved for both regulators and the utility." Lawton and Davis, *op. cit.*, pp. 31-32.

[26]"The authorization of a simplified form by a commission is in explicit recognition of the significant differences that exist in managerial structure, accounting systems, operating revenues, number of customers, and the homogeneity of customer

classes between small utilities and medium or large utilities. . . . One common, highly specialized, division in most utilities is the division or office of regulatory affairs, which has the primary responsibility for rate case applications and general compliance with commission orders. Small water utilities lack the size necessary to specialize and may have an owner-operator simultaneously serving as the chief executive officer, head engineer, accountant, and financial officer. Lacking a sufficient management and accounting system, the attention of the owner-operator tends to be on daily, operational concerns and not on compliance with regulatory forms and procedures." *Ibid.,* pp. 34-35. The NARUC also has offered assistance to small water companies and their regulators. See, *e.g.,* "Model Record-Keeping Manual for Small Water Companies" (Washington, D.C., 1978), "Depreciation Practices for Small Water Utilities" (Washington, D.C., 1979), "Model Simplified Annual Report for Small Water Utilities" (Washington, D.C., 1979), and "Depreciation Practices for Very Small Water Utilities" (Washington, D.C., 1981).

[27]"In a few states the burden of preparing a rate case application and assessing the need for changing rates devolves almost entirely to commission staff. . . . In these commissions, the staff has essentially taken on the job of preparing rate applications for the small water utilities." Lawton and Davis, *op. cit.,* pp. 38, 57.

[28]"The California commission in 1979 began a policy of denying new certificates for privately owned water companies considered unlikely to be economically viable." *Ibid.,* p. 69 (citation omitted).

[29]"The state of Pennsylvania . . . has established a substantial fund to aid water supply systems. Voters in Pennsylvania in 1981 approved $300 million in general obligation bonds for loans for water improvements, including $220 million for 'community water systems.' The other $80 million is for flood control and port facilities. The bonds are exempt from state and local taxes. The legislation created a 'Water Facilities Loan Board' within the Department of Environmental Resources to manage the loan program. The 11-member Board is composed of seven state agency heads, including the chairman of the public utility commission, two state senators, and two state representatives." *Ibid.,* pp. 74-75.

[30]"In West Virginia, for example, public service districts occasionally contract with a company for management functions. Utilities pay a service fee, but save the costs of hiring someone themselves. . . . Not only regional management, but regional ownership has been encouraged in West Virginia. The West Virginia Water Company recently took over a financially troubled rural water company with the provision that they would be allowed to charge the same rates as in the main district of the water company. . . ." *Ibid.,* p. 80. See Committee Report, "Regionalization of Water Utilities: A Survey," 71 *Journal of the American Water Works Association* 702 (1979); Edward W. Limbach, "Single Tariff Pricing," 76 *Journal of the American Water Works Association* 52 (1984).

On central management services provided by larger water utilities, see Michael M. Stump, "Private Operation of U.S. Water Utilities," 78 *Journal of the American Water Works Association* 49 (1986). On private sector financing of what otherwise would be publicly-owned facilities, see Ronald D. Doctor, "Private Sector Financing of Water," 78 *Journal of the American Water Works Association* 52 (1986). On the incentives (disincentives) that encourage (discourage) the acquisition of small, financially troubled water utilities, see Patrick C. Mann et al., *Commission Regulation of Small Water Utilities: Mergers and Acquisitions* (Columbus, Ohio: National Regulatory Research Institute, 1986).

[31]Many commissions, as already noted, exempt very small companies. Further, most water companies are subject to other state agencies that monitor and enforce quality standards. In Georgia, for example, where water utilities are unregulated, they are supervised by the state Department of Natural Resources. See Vivian Witkind Davis et al., *Commission Regulation of Small Water Utilities: Outside Resources and Their Effective Uses* (Columbus, Ohio: National Regulatory Research Institute, 1984). The pros and cons of deregulation are discussed in Lawton and Davis, *op. cit.*, pp. 88-101.

[32]Eight state commissions permit automatic rate increases for purchased water, five for fuel (for pumping), and two for taxes. *Ibid.*, p. 105. See, *e.g.*, *Re Kentucky-American Water Co.*, Case No. 8571 (Ky., 1983); *Re New Rochelle Water Co.*, Opinion No. 84-21 (N.Y., 1984); *Re Sebastian Lake Pub. Utility*, Order No. 3 (Ark., 1984).

[33]Mann, *op. cit.*, pp. 11-12. With respect to water system financing: "Capital investment in transmission, treatment, and reservoirs are generally financed by debt (for both investor-owned and publicly-owned firms) and equity (by investor-owned firms only) borrowing. Distribution system expansion is generally financed by developer and user hook-up charges with some reliance on borrowing. Operation costs and minor system improvements are generally financed by commodity rates; however, in the case of municipally owned systems, rate financing is occasionally supplemented by municipal subsidies." *Ibid.*, p. 7. It is important to note that under the Tax Reform Act of 1986, all contributions in aid of construction (received after December 31, 1986) must be treated as taxable income.

[34]Garfield and Lovejoy, *op. cit.*, p. 220.

[35]*Ibid.*, pp. 224-25. "The proportion of the capacity costs which are attributable to fire-protection service depends upon the size of the community and the size of the company: the proportion of cost is higher for the small company and falls sharply as the size of the community increases. Of course, a part of the capital investment is not influenced by the requirements of fire protection, for water for fire-protection purposes need not be filtered and purified; however, these treatments must be provided for domestic consumption." Barnes, *op. cit.*, p. 360 (citation omitted). On private fire protection, see, *e.g.*, *Re Gallup Water Service Inc.*, 33 PUR4th 413 (Conn., 1980). On public fire protection, see, *e.g.*, *Re Village of McFarland*, 41 PUR4th 114 (Wis., 1980).

[36]"The charge per hydrant is not a wholly satisfactory basis of collecting for fire protection. The cost is not proportional to the number of hydrants, and if the rate per hydrant is high the quality of fire protection may suffer because of the hesitancy of the city to install additional hydrants. Actually, the cost of fire protection may be smaller if many hydrants are installed, since the nearness of one or more hydrants to the fire may aid in bringing a fire under early control. Theoretically, the charge for fire protection should reflect simply the cost of installing the hydrants, if the hydrants are purchased and installed by the water utility instead of the municipality, plus a demand charge which reflects the probable capacity which the fire-protection service will require. Thus, an increase in the area of the community or an increase in the number of dwellings will presumably have little effect upon the capacity which the water company needs to supply, except in mains; but an increase in the congestion of the municipality or in height of buildings increases the fire risk, and compels the utility to provide more powerful pumping equipment and larger reserve capacity." Barnes, *op. cit.*, p. 363.

[37]Garfield and Lovejoy, *op. cit.*, p. 25.

[38]*Ibid.*, p. 226. Compare *Re Boise Water Co.*, Order No. 15617 (Idaho, 1980) with *Re HVL Utilities, Inc.*, 53 PUR4th 508 (Ind.,1983).

[39]In addition to the normal allocation problems, many municipal systems operate both water and sewer departments with one set of records and accounts. Indeed, in some municipalities, the sewage rate is based upon the prevailing water rate.

[40]See, *e.g.*, Hamdy H. Afifi and V. Lewis Bassie, *Water Pricing Theory and Practice in Illinois* (Urbana: Bureau of Business and Economic Research, University of Illinois, 1969); William L. Patterson, "Application of Water Rates," 65 *Journal of the American Water Works Association* 677 (1973).

[41]For a more complete discussion, see American Water Works Association, *Water Rates* (3d ed.; New York, 1983). See also Louis R. Howson, "Review of Rate Making Theories," 58 *Journal of the American Water Works Association* 849 (1966); John C. Adams and Vito F. Pennachio, "Handling Revenue and Cost Elements in Rate Setting," 62 *Journal of the American Water Works Association* 754 (1970); Stewart H. Fonda, "Financing a Capital Improvement Program: Revenue Requirements, Cost of Service Analysis, and Rate Design," 71 *Journal of the American Water Works Association* 187 (1979).

[42]See, *e.g.*, *Re Wakefield Water Co.*, 32 PUR4th 476 (R.I., 1980); *Re Trans-Sierra Water Service, Inc.*, 37 PUR4th 536 (Nev., 1980); *Re Jacksonville Suburban Utilities Co.*, 39 PUR4th 1 (Fla., 1980); *Re Davenport Water Co.*, 49 PUR4th 616 (Iowa, 1982); *Re General Waterworks Corp. of Pine Bluff, Arkansas, Inc.*, 56 PUR4th 352 (Ark., 1983); *Re Indianapolis Water Co.*, 65 PUR4th 368 (Ind., 1985); *Re Tennessee-American Water Co.*, 67 PUR4th 630 (Tenn., 1985); *Re Lake Erie Utilities Co.*, 81 PUR4th 201 (Ohio, 1986).

[43]The cash basis is the commonly used method of determining revenue requirements for publicly-owned utilities. See, *e.g.*, *Re Town of Kingsford Heights*, 83 PUR4th 303 (Ind., 1987). See also *Re Lake Monticello Service Co.*, 57 PUR4th 155 (Va., 1983).

[44]A third method of classifying costs, not widely used, is by function; *i.e.*, production and transmission, distribution, customer services, and fire protection. See *Water Rates, op. cit.*, pp. 20-22; Peter K. MacEwen, "Municipal and Industrial Water Rates," 69 *Journal of the American Water Works Association* 519 (1977).

[45]*Selectmen v. Seymour Water Co.*, PUR1932B, 175, 185 (Conn., 1932).

[46]Tisbury Water Works (Vineyard Haven, Massachusetts), "Residential Fixtured Accounts," 1984-85 fiscal year.

[47]Barnes, *op. cit.*, p. 361.

[48]Charles W. Keller, "Pricing of Water," 69 *Journal of the American Water Works Association* 19 (1977).

[49]*Water Rates, op. cit.*, Sec. 4. Afifi and Bassie, *op. cit.*, found a range of two to thirteen blocks in Illinois water rate schedules.

[50]See., *e.g.*, *Re Masury Water Co.*, 48 PUR4th 628 (Ohio, 1982).

[51]*Re Camelot Utilities, Inc.*, 53 PUR4th 681, 683 (Ill., 1983). The rate structures shown are as of the time the company filed for a rate increase. In its final order, the Illinois commission adopted a common three-block structure for both water and sewer service: First 4,000 gallons per month, next 12,000 gallons per month, and over 16,000 gallons per month. *Ibid.*

[52]*Re Virginia-American Water Co.* (Alexandria District), Case No. PUE 820077 (Va., 1983).

[53]*Re West Virginia Water Co.*, Case No. 82-561-W-42T (W.Va., 1983).

[54]*Re The Ansonia Derby Water Co.*, Docket No. 790711 (Conn., 1979).

[55]Patrick C. Mann, "The Water Industry: Economic and Policy Issues," in Charles F. Phillips, Jr. (ed.), *Regulation, Competition and Deregulation — An Economic Grab Bag* (Lexington, Va.: Washington and Lee University, 1979), p. 104. See also Steve H.

Hanke and Robert K. Davis, "Potential for Marginal Cost Pricing in Water Resource Management," 9 *Water Resources Research* 808 (1973); Patrick C. Mann and Donald L. Schlenger, "Marginal Cost and Seasonal Pricing of Water Service," 74 *Journal of the American Water Works Association* 6 (1982).

[56]For summaries of price elasticity of demand estimates, see Steven H. Hanke, "A Method for Integrating Engineering and Economic Planning," 70 *Journal of the American Water Works Association* 487 (1978); Leon E. Danielson, "An Analysis of Residential Demand for Water Using Micro Time-Series Data," 15 *Water Resources Research* 763 (1979).

[57]See "Trends in Setting Water Utility Rates," 115 *Public Utilities Fortnightly* 52 (January 24, 1985).

[58]See, *e.g.,* John D. Russell, "Rate Design for Equity Among Customers," 71 *Journal of the American Water Works Association* 184 (1979).

[59]There is one commonly used form of zonal pricing: municipally owned water systems often charge higher rates to consumers residing outside of the municipality. Such rates, however, are frequently based on noncost considerations. See, *e.g.,* Afifi and Bassie, *op. cit.* "The city of Seattle, Washington, has initiated rate differentials based on 'old water,' for city customers who originally financed the system, and 'new water,' for the growing suburban customer population." "Trends in Setting Water Utility Rates," *op. cit.,* p. 54.

[60]The issues associated with both proposals are explored in detail by Mann, *Water Service: Regulation and Rate Reform, op. cit.* On time-of-day peak-load pricing, based upon marginal costs, see Stephen L. Feldman, "On the Peak Load Pricing of Urban Water Supply," 11 *Water Resources Research* 355 (1975) and "Peak Load Pricing through Demand Metering," 67 *Journal of the American Water Works Association* 490 (1975); J. Ernest Flack and George J. Roussos, "Water Consumption under Peak Responsibility Pricing," 70 *Journal of the American Water Works Association* 121 (1978). On seasonal peak-load pricing, also based upon marginal costs, see Steve H. Hanke, "Pricing Urban Water," in Selma Mushkin (ed.), *Public Prices for Public Products* (Washington, D.C.: The Urban Institute, 1972), pp. 283-304; Hanke and Davis, *op. cit.;* Steve H. Hanke, "Water Rates: An Assessment of Current Issues," 67 *Journal of the American Water Works Association* 215 (1975).

[61]See, *e.g.,* A. P. Lino Grima, "The Impact of Policy Variables on Residential Water Demand and Related Investment Requirements," 9 *Water Resources Bulletin* 703 (1973); Marshall Gysi, "A 'Radical' Policy for the Energy and Environmental Crisis," 11 *Water Resources Bulletin* 551 (1975). One proposal suggests an inverted block rate structure along with an initial lifeline rate. Jeremy J. Warford and De Anne S. Julius, "Water Rate Policy: Lessons from Less Developed Countries," 71 *Journal of the American Water Works Association* 199 (1979). A few systems have adopted inverted rates, including an inverted block rate structure for summer consumption in Dallas, Texas [I.M. Rice and L.G. Shaw, "Water Conservation — A Practical Approach," 70 *Journal of the American Water Works Association* 480 (1978)], a year-round inverted block rate structure implemented by the Washington Suburban Sanitation Commission [Robert S. McGarry and John M. Brusnighan, "Increasing Water and Sewer Rate Schedules," 71 *Journal of the American Water Works Association* 474 (1979)], and a uniform commodity charge coupled with a summer "excess use" charge by the Fairfax County (Virginia) Water Authority [Fred P. Griffith, "An Innovative Approach to Rate Making," 69 *Journal of the American Water Works Association* 89 (1977)].

The industry has taken a number of approaches to conservation, including public education stressing voluntary reductions, the use of water conservation devices (*e.g.*, shower flow controls, toilet inserts), and mandatory reductions (limitations of usage, particularly for lawn sprinkling, car washing, and so forth). See, *e.g.*, Brian G. Stone, "Suppression of Water Use by Physical Methods," 70 *Journal of the American Water Works Association* 483 (1978); William E. Sharpe, "Municipal Water Conservation Alternatives," 14 Water *Resources Bulletin* 1080 (1978). See also William E. Martin et al., *Saving Water in a Desert City* (Baltimore: The Johns Hopkins University Press, 1984).

[62]Mann, "The Water Industry: Economic and Policy Issues," *op. cit.*, pp. 105-06.

[63]But see Gibbons, *op. cit.*; Kenneth D. Frederick (ed.), *Scarce Water and Institutional Change* (Baltimore: The Johns Hopkins University Press, 1986).

[64]See, *e.g.*, Constance M. Boris and John V. Krutilla, *Water Rights and Energy Development in the Yellowstone River Basin* (Baltimore: The Johns Hopkins University Press, 1980); Allen V. Kneese and F. Lee Brown, *The Southwest Under Stress* (Baltimore: The Johns Hopkins University Press, 1981).

[65]See, *e.g.*, Bruce R. Beattie, et al., *Economic Consequences of Interbasin Water Transfers* (Corvallis: Oregon State University Agricultural Experimental Station, Technical Bulletin 116, 1971).

[66]See, *e.g.*, Note, "Do State Restrictions on Water Use by Slurry Pipelines Violate the Commerce Clause?," 53 *University of Colorado Law Review* 655 (1982).

[67]Walter O. Spofford, Jr., Alfred Parker, and Allen V. Kneese (eds.), *Energy Development in the Southwest: Problems of Water, Fish, and Wildlife in the Upper Colorado River Basin* (Baltimore: The Johns Hopkins University Press, 1980).

[68]Emery N. Castle, "Water Availability — The Crisis of the Eighties?," *Resources*, June, 1983, p. 8. But see, *e.g.*, Terry L. Anderson, *Water Crisis: Ending the Policy Drought* (Baltimore: The Johns Hopkins University Press and Washington, D.C.: Cato Institute, 1983).

[69]Castle, *op. cit.*, p. 9.

PART IV

An Appraisal —
And a Challenge

Chapter	AN APPRAISAL OF
17	REGULATION

Regulation is a peculiarly American institution. All nations use political and legal processes to constrain the economic activities of their citizens, but most other countries implement such policies by giving government officials great direct authority. Important industries are nationalized, or regulatory decisions are entrusted to a controlling bureaucracy that has far more power than the typical U.S. regulatory agency.

—*Roger G. Noll and Bruce M. Owen**

Independent regulatory commissions are a unique American institution. Although there are signs of change, the public utility sector has been owned and operated by governmental agencies in most other countries. From the very beginning, however, the American economy has been fundamentally a competitive, free-enterprise system. When it became apparent that direct competition between suppliers of utility services was ineffective in securing the public interest, public control was established, but private ownership (with exceptions) was maintained.[1] The early forms of control — franchises, charters, courts, and legislatures — proved little more satisfactory than reliance on competition. Consequently, the independent regulatory commission evolved late in the nineteenth century and has been the major form of public regulation since that time.

Government regulation of private enterprise raises many difficult questions. Even today, after over a century of experience, the answers to these questions do not command general agreement. Perhaps the most funda-

783

mental issue is the balance between government control and private property rights. Some economists and political scientists hold that the provision of utility services is essentially a government operation and emphasize the control function of regulation. Others argue that since the utility industries have no outstanding differences from other private enterprises, primary reliance should be placed on incentives to attain the social objectives expected from competition. The basic issue has been stated by Brynes to be whether a licensed monopoly "should be regulated as an enterprise selling a service, or as a concessionaire providing all there is to be had of it for a cost plus a fixed fee.... In this view a public utility is created primarily for public purposes and has the status of a trustee; it carries out a function of the state."[2]

Many questions concerning regulatory procedure stem from this basic issue. Some see the necessity for regulation to control every aspect of utility operations, while others feel that regulation should be concerned only with results. Some view regulation as a conflict between the public good and private property rights, requiring a judicial atmosphere and formal proceedings. Others advocate informal administrative methods as ordinarily being the most expeditious means of obtaining the benefits of regulation.

Another major area of disagreement concerns the necessity for, and effectiveness of, regulation. For many years, criticism came mainly from those who held that public regulation was both unnecessary and undesirable.[3] As this type of criticism diminished, new questions were raised concerning the results of regulation and the possibility of obtaining better performance by substituting other forms of regulation for the independent commissions. More recently, attention has shifted back to the issue of necessity, as the deregulation of at least some utility activities has been widely debated.

It is the purpose of this concluding chapter to review these questions, assuming both that some government regulation of the utility industries is essential and that government regulation is superior to public ownership. Emphasis is on regulation as a method of control,[4] rather than on the various regulatory problems such as determination of the rate base or the rate of return. The concluding sections offer some comments on the role of competition (including deregulation) and on the future.

The Regulatory Process

The independent regulatory commission combines in the same body legislative, judicial, and executive functions in the regulation of an industry. A number of advantages were assumed to accrue to regulatory commissions, including continuity of policy, expertise, impartiality, experimentation, and flexibility in procedures. And independence was designed to gain for commissions the isolation from politics enjoyed by the judiciary. Today, however, all these supposed virtues have been challenged.

Independence from Political Control

Independence was thought to isolate the regulatory commissions from undue political pressures, thereby assuring their devotion to the public interest and their impartiality in carrying out their statutory tasks. But commissions, as is true with most other branches of government, operate within a political environment.[5] They are dependent on the executive for their members (except in a few states), their budgets must be approved by the executive, their court cases (with a few exceptions) initiated by the attorney general's office, and, in some cases, the executive has statutory control over a commission's internal structure. They get their legal authority and their financial support from the legislative branch, and they are subject to legislative investigation as to personnel and performance. Finally, their authority is subject to judicial interpretation and their decisions to judicial review. The net effect has been to put the regulatory commissions, in Corwin's words, "in the uncomfortable halfway situation of Mahomet's coffin, suspended 'twix Heaven and earth.'"[6]

Independence, therefore, is difficult to achieve and, even if obtainable, many question its desirability. It is difficult to achieve because commissions must operate within the existing framework of government and, therefore, must coordinate their activities and policies with other branches of government. It is undesirable, according to some, because independence isolates the commissions from the political support and leadership that is essential for the success of regulation and tends to curtail commission participation in the achievement of national economic objectives.

Outside Pressures. Some observers believe that the regulatory commissions have been subject to improper outside pressures. Schwartz, for example, has argued that the federal commissions have been subjected to pressures from both the executive and legislative branches, thereby resulting in partisan political decisions rather than unprejudiced determinations.[7] Other types of improper pressures were pointed out by Landis:

> Much attention has recently been centered on efforts, unfortunately too frequently successful, to sway the judgment of the members of regulatory agencies by so-called *ex parte* approaches or arguments, usually personalized, made off the record in proceedings that should be decided on the record. The extent of these *ex parte* approaches has only partially been revealed. They come from various sources — the office of the President, members of Congress, and the regulated industries. Some are made in good faith; others to further a personal desire regardless of the public interest. Many of them emanate from lawyers striving to press their clients' cause, indeed, one of the worst phases of this situation is the existence of groups of lawyers, concentrated in Washington itself, who implicitly hold out to clients that they have means of access

to various regulatory agencies off the record that are more important than those that can be made on the record. . . .

Instances have also recently been uncovered of actual malfeasance in the sense of bribery among high administrative officials. More serious than these are the subtle but pervasive methods pursued by regulated industries to influence regulatory agencies by social favors, promises of later employment in the industry itself, and other similar means.[8]

The problem of outside pressures is not unique to the regulatory commissions, nor is it an easy one to solve. Laws exist which make malfeasance a crime. But commissioners and their staffs must keep in constant contact with the industries under their jurisdiction, and the line between proper and improper *ex parte* contacts is often a fine one to draw. Some have suggested a code of ethics for federal and state employees, but, as McFarland has observed: "An alert and devoted public service is the best insurance against improper 'influence' from outsiders. . . . Indeed, it is probably the only way to care for the problem — for such influence takes every variety and quality of forms so that no 'code' could begin to comprehend them."[9] Others have focused on the issue of eliminating conflicts of interest.

. . . Popular wisdom identifies a partial cause of regulation's failure with the fact that many regulators have a financial stake in the well-being of the industry or firms that they regulate. This stake may consist of the ownership of stock in companies affected by regulatory action. It may arise out of hoped-for future employment, for many commissioners and agency staff leave the agency for work in regulated industry or law firms or other professional groups that serve industry. Or it may arise out of past associations and loyalties, because staff and commissioners often come from regulated companies or their law firms.[10]

Many proposals have been made to eliminate conflicts of interest, ranging from annual public financial disclosure statements (now required only from top officials, but not from top executive branch staff) to government contracts prohibiting employees from working, representing, or accepting any compensation from any company or organization that was affected by proceedings in which they participated for two years after leaving the government (the so-called "revolving door" proposals).[11] Yet, as Breyer has observed, such proposals may deny to government the very expertise that is often required.[12] Effective solutions to the "revolving door" issue, moreover,

. . . imply a major change in the nature of governmental employment. They move the country in the direction of a more professional, more permanent career service less open to penetration by temporary appointees from business or the professions. They suggest a civil service more like that of France or Great Britain. Whether such a system is desirable, whether it would be technically ignorant, whether it would prove more skilled and efficient — all are questions that have not been answered but that must be addressed before one can seriously undertake this type of regulatory reform.[13]

Finally, as Gormley has argued: "If regulated industries dominate the regulatory process, it is through the control of information, not personnel."[14]

Better Qualified Personnel. It has been contended by many that the ultimate solution to the problems of both outside pressures and commission performance is personnel. According to Landis: "The prime key to the improvement of the administrative process is the selection of qualified personnel. Good men make poor laws workable; poor men will wreck havoc with good laws."[15] The Ash Council noted that the regulatory agencies had difficulties in "attracting highly qualified commissioners and retaining executive staff."[16] And the Senate Governmental Affairs Committee found: "The pre-eminent problem with the regulatory appointments process, as it has operated in the past, is that it has not consistently resulted in the selection of people best equipped to handle regulatory responsibilities. For much of the past fifteen years, neither the White House nor the Senate has demonstrated a sustained commitment to high quality regulatory appointments."[17]

Higher salaries, particularly at the state level, and longer tenures (perhaps ten to fifteen years)[18] might be steps in the right direction. So, too, might be steps to encourage better qualified people to apply for commission jobs, such as the creation of a public interest talent bank (as advocated by Common Cause), the establishment of an "independent" board to evaluate nominees, or the development of more meaningful standards for selection.[19] The quality of staff personnel might be improved, as Gormley suggests, by "declassification," so that commissioners are able "to hire and promote job applicants whose skills match the challenges of the future rather than the challenges of the past."[20] But equally important, steps must be taken to insure that the challenge of the job is appealing.

Independence and Political Control. Other observers contend that independence from political control may be undesirable. Bernstein argues:

> "Independence" is a device to escape popular politics. It facilitates maximum responsiveness by a commission to the demands and interests of regulated groups. It provides maximum freedom from exposure to popular political forces. It tends to alienate commissions from sources of political strength, especially the president, upon whom regulatory progress may largely depend. Independence acquires a sacred inviolability because it reduces the effectiveness of regulation and seems to satisfy the Congressional desire to lessen the power and authority of the president.[21]

Separation of Functions. Some who support this position advocate drastic structural changes in regulatory commissions. One often-voiced concern is with the combination of functions assigned to commissions — administrative, policymaking, and adjudication; a belief that these functions are incompatible and should be separated. The American Bar Association has long supported the transfer of judicial functions to an administrative court, similar to the tax court; a position also taken by the President's Committee on Administrative Management in 1937, by the Hoover Commission in 1955, and by the Ash Council in 1971.[22] Two former chairmen of federal agencies, Hector of the CAB and Minow of the FCC, have advocated the transfer of all policymaking, planning, and administrative work of the regulatory commissions to an executive agency, with all judicial duties being transferred to an administrative court and all responsibility for investigation and prosecution given to an executive department or agency, such as the Department of Justice.[23] And a former member of the ICC has suggested that managerial or administrative duties can best be performed by a single administrator and has urged that those duties be separated from the commission.[24]

Such drastic surgery has not been forthcoming. Jaffe has noted that there is little in our history to suggest "that an executive agency will be much different from an independent agency in periods when public opinion or statutory policy is slack, indeterminate, or lacking in conviction. The odds are that it will respond in much the same way to the climate of opinion."[25] Boyd asks: "How would regulated industries fare if policies of regulation became campaign issues, as they well could under the proposed separation?"[26] Further, policymaking and adjudication are so closely related that their separation seems neither desirable nor feasible. In Judge Friendly's words:

> Let me illustrate this from the field of railway rates. If the question is whether a shipment comes within one classification of a tariff or another, that is adjudication clearly enough, with no element of policy making. But a case concerning the fairness or the prejudicial character of rates involves elements of policy, and this even though it arises as a demand for reparations. The policy considerations inherent in such proceedings range from the trivial to the gravest, as in cases relating to the overall rate level or to differentials, or the lack of them, between different ports or between traffic that has or has not moved all the way by rail. To call such cases adjudication and place their decision in an administrative court would deprive the public of the benefits of the very expertise that is a principal *raison d'etre* of the regulatory agency. Moreover, reparations cases and cases involving future rates cannot possibly be divided — often a single case will involve both; yet the fixing of future rates is surely not a "judicial" function.
>
> ... But even when separation is feasible from a formal standpoint, how can one characterize as adjudication and not policy making a

decision whether the service should be operated by an existing airline or by a newly organized enterprise, or the weight to be given to better immediate service to the public as against the benefits thought to be ultimately realizable from fortifying weak carriers against the strong? To analogize decisions on such matters to the ordinary work of the courts is to let words and methods obscure substance.[27]

Less drastic separation of functions *within* the regulatory agencies have been made. After detailed studies of the agencies, a majority of the Attorney General's Committee on Administrative Procedure in 1941 endorsed an internal separation of the prosecution and adjudication functions.[28] Such a separation was subsequently required by the Administrative Procedure Act of 1946.[29] The act established an independent class of hearing examiners (now administrative law judges), whose appointment, promotion, salary, and tenure are determined by the Civil Service Commission. Further, administrative law judges may not be assigned to other duties, and cases are to be assigned to them in rotation.[30] And, finally, based upon the Landis Report, federal commission chairmen received increased powers and their terms were redefined so as to serve "at the pleasure of the President."

Control, Coordination, and Oversight. Landis, in his 1960 report, rejected a division of functions, urging instead the preservation of the regulatory agencies' integrity and independence.[31] However, he proposed that executive leadership be provided by (*1*) the creation of a new White House office ("Office for the Oversight of Regulatory Agencies") to oversee the regulatory commissions and (*2*) executive authority to select the chairman of each commission.

Congress subsequently adopted the second proposal, as noted above, but the first proved more controversial. The "Overseer," Landis argued, should not be "a mere Inspector-General," but should be a source of "imaginative and creative activity."[32] The office should watch such matters as regulatory delay and failure to implement statutory policies, and should coordinate policies, particularly in the fields of communications, energy, and transportation.[33] Clearly, the chief executive has the duty to see that the agencies are carrying out the laws they were established to administer. Congress has a similar duty, as indicated by the action of the House Committee on Interstate and Foreign Commerce in establishing a permanent Legislative Oversight Subcommittee.[34] If, therefore, the role of the "Overseer" were not to compromise the independence of current agencies and if this could be assured by carefully defining the purposes and limits of the office before it were established, there would be little opposition. But if the "Overseer" were to use the post "as a funnel for regulatory policies originating at the White House,"[35] the effect would be to lessen the independence of the commissions.[36] Many believe that independence is still an essential ingredient of the regulatory process.[37]

Control and oversight, however, must be distinguished from coordination. A persistent criticism of regulation has been the failure to develop meaningful interagency policy standards where, at the federal level, a number of agencies and executive departments share complementary and often overlapping responsibilities.[38] The establishment of the Department of Transportation in 1966[39] and of the Department of Energy in 1977,[40] which brought many nonregulatory transport and energy activities of the federal government, respectively, under one jurisdiction, represented a step toward achieving better policy formulation. So, too, did the creation of the Water Resources Council by the Water Resources Planning Act of 1965.[41] Various administrations have established interagency committees to coordinate policy.[42] And a majority of the states have established energy offices to coordinate nonregulatory energy activities of state governments.

Many believe that further efforts are vitally needed to deal with the problem. Landis recommended the creation of three coordinating offices (for communications, energy, and transportation) within the Executive Office of the President.[43] Some, including former ICC Commissioner Tucker, have urged the uniting of federal transport regulatory activities by the creation of a National Transportation Commission; a merger that would result in a stronger regulatory body "more capable of dealing with transport problems in an equitable and coordinated fashion responsive to the public demands for transport service rather than modal policy."[44] Others, such as Redford[45] and Cutler and Johnson,[46] have proposed a statute

> . . . that would allow the president to direct an agency to take up and to decide any regulatory issue within a specified period of time or to modify or reverse an agency rule or policy. In other words, the president himself, acting under certain procedural constraints, could reverse most agency policy making. Presidential action would be subject to congressional review either through a legislative veto process or by requiring Congress to renew the president's authority at regular intervals.[47]

Such a statute would involve the executive more directly in regulatory matters, thereby offering the opportunity for increased interagency coordination. But the proposal also has its drawbacks.

> . . . For one thing, will it mean that groups adversely affected by agency action simply come to the White House for a second opportunity to defeat it? For another, even if a president is less willing to protect a special interest than is, say, a subcommittee chairman, his agenda is still highly political. Arguably, political considerations should not be brought to bear piecemeal upon individual agency regulations. Moreover, why is the president's policy likely to be so much more sensible than the agency's? The president may have higher-quality advice available in the Council of Economic Advisers or the Bureau of the Budget, but the agency has many more facts at its disposal and is more familiar with them.

Would the proposal require a much larger White House staff? Further, if the president follows the advice of his economists will he inject economic considerations where Congress specifically did not want them? In the final analysis, the direction that any reform takes under the proposal depends upon the substantive policy directions preferred by the president. The proposal itself produces little pressure to move in any one direction.[48]

The need for greater policy coordination is clear; the best means of achieving this goal have yet to be agreed upon.

The Issue of Legitimacy

The capture and interest group theories of regulation,[49] in particular, raise the issue of legitimacy. Asks Judge Breyer: ". . . if agency decisions are not controlled by Congress, if they are not scientifically determined, if agency decision makers are not elected, what right does the agency have to make its policies? What makes the agency's decision legitimate?"[50] He answers:

> In the past decade, the courts and the agencies, as well as Congress, have sought to find a partial answer to the question of legitimacy — and to improve agency decisions — by broadening the degree of participation in agency decision making. Consumer groups, public interest law firms, environmental groups, and others claiming to represent those who cannot readily organize themselves have not only been allowed to appear before agencies but their appearance has been encouraged, sometimes by governmental payment of their costs and by an expansion of their rights to appeal agency decisions to the courts. At the same time, Congress had enacted laws allowing greater access to agency information and forcing the agencies to meet and to make decisions in public. These laws, together with court decisions increasing the formality of informal rulemaking have transformed the decision-making process into an open forum, in which lawyers represent a wide variety of interest groups, including public interest groups, and decisions emerge out of their evidence, argument, and negotiation. The emergence of this "interest representation" model of the administrative process characterizes the procedural change since 1970.[51]

Broader representation before agencies, however desirable on grounds of fairness or due process,[52] is unlikely to provide a satisfactory solution to the issue of legitimacy. Consider two examples. First, in the hearings before the FPC on natural gas prices, "both sides had a legitimate claim to representing the consumer — one stressing lower prices and the other stressing the need to avert a shortage. It becomes more difficult to decide which

position a public or consumer representative should take when industry and
consumer are not necessarily at odds and when the agency is not necessarily
captured by industry — instances that are fairly common."[53] Second, if a
license is granted in a nuclear power plant licensing proceeding, the public
interest representative "may not accept the result as legitimate. Indeed, he
may not describe his loss as 'reasonable' but may view it as an agency
mistake, resulting from his opponent's superior financial or informational
resources. If so, increased participation in an *adversary* process will not [make]
legitimate or win acceptance for an adverse agency decision."[54]

A solution to the problem of legitimacy, in the case of rule-making
proceedings, has been proposed by Harter.[55] The relevant agency would
select an independent third party, empowered to do two things: first, to
decide which interests should be represented in the proceeding and, second,
to mediate and manage negotiations. The negotiating group could jointly
conduct any factual research that might be needed to help reach a consensus on a proposed rule. If such a consensus were reached, and in the
absence of a good reason not to do so, the relevant agency would publish
the plan as a notice of proposed rule making. As a consequence of this
procedure, all interested parties would be familiar with the details of the
rule and its development.

Lack of Meaningful (Consistent) Policy Standards

Judge Friendly has argued that a justifiable dissatisfaction with the
regulatory process "is the failure to develop standards sufficiently definite to
permit decisions to be fairly predictable and the reasons for them to be
understood; this failure can and must be remedied."[56] He continues:

> There have been failures, perhaps excusable, by Congress at the time
> of initial enactment, failures by the agencies to sharpen the vague con-
> tours of the original statute, failures by the legislature to supply more
> definite standards as growing experience has permitted or even de-
> manded, and failures by the executive to spur the legislature into activ-
> ity. All these failures have been interdependent: failure by the agency to
> make clear what it is doing impedes both executive challenge and legis-
> lative response. I do not assert that failure has been universal; [there
> have been] victories as well as defeats. The victories help to show the
> defeats need not have been suffered.[57]

The regulatory commissions operate under broad standards established
by the legislatures. There are many examples: "just and reasonable" rates,
"undue preference or prejudice," "compensatory," "destructive competition,"
"public convenience and necessity," and "public interest," to cite but six.
These standards, largely resulting from the inability of the legislature to

resolve important issues and from the need for flexibility to meet changing conditions in dynamic industries, endow the commissions "with a discretion so wide that they can offer a more or less plausible explanation for any conclusion they choose to reach with respect to many, perhaps the great majority, of the matters coming before them."[58] As Davis has put it: "Because of history or context, vague phrases of this sort may sometimes have considerable meaning. But sometimes they do not have. Sometimes telling the agency to do what is in the public interest is the practical equivalent of instructing it: 'Here is the problem. Deal with it.' . . ."[59]

It would be clearly desirable if the legislature could be more specific at the outset. It is difficult to see how an agency can be expected to make policy when the legislature is unable to do so because of conflicting forces. Nevertheless, "fairly broad standards in initial legislative grants to administrative agencies are likely to remain with us, as to some extent, when the statute deals with a novel field, they should."[60] But there is little justification, as Fair has pointed out, for initial statutes that fail to provide a commission with the power to carry out stated policy or that contain inconsistencies in the law.

> For example, there is no just basis to criticize the Interstate Commerce Commission for not carrying out a general plan of consolidation of the railroads, a policy which in the Transportation Act of 1920 was held to be in the public interest, since the Act provided for acquisition of control by stock purchases independent of any consolidation plan and since the Commission was given no power to carry out its plan. Again the Interstate Commerce Act preamble calls for a coordinated and integrated transportation system, yet does not provide for the establishment of through routes between motor carriers and other surface carriers under the Act and actually discourages or restricts acquisition of a carrier by one or another mode of transportation.[61]

Even if it is conceded that the initial standards must be broad, both the legislature and the commission should define and clarify these standards as experience dictates. However, the statutes which our regulatory agencies seek to enforce are, in the opinion of Rostow,

> . . . usually out of date, often confused, ill-drawn, and needlessly complex. Many of their rules echo forgotten battles, and guard against dangers which no longer exist. They comprise vast codes, understood only by a jealous priesthood which protects these swamps and thickets from all prying eyes. In the main, the agencies follow routines established for the control of local gas companies and street railways. The relevance of the model is not immediately apparent, in dealing with progressive and expanding industries like air transport or trucking.[62]

Consider the ICC's minimum rate power. The power was conferred by Congress in the Transportation Act of 1920, at a time when the railroads enjoyed a virtual monopoly of the nation's transportation system. It was revised by Congress on two occasions: in 1940, "with language so encompassing as to create as many contradictions as were dissipated," and again in 1958, with "legislation that took with one hand much of what was given to the other."[63] Throughout this period, the commission failed to define the relevant cost standards or to explain the rationale for its use of a particular one. Fulda thus concluded: "Regrettably one searches in vain for an unambiguous pronouncement of general policy with respect to the various measures of compensativeness. Indeed, the reading of the decisions creates the impression that the Commission selects whichever theory appears best to fit the case at hand."[64] And Williams, after analyzing some 900 railroad cases, concluded:

> The treatment of the declaration of policy both by the Commission and by the courts, therefore, leaves in doubt the nature of the general objective toward which the Commission should work. In effect the average case is decided without reference to any such objective. In those few instances in which construction of the policy seems almost unavoidable care is taken to skirt the edges; to reach an acceptable decision in the instant case, but one which may not be relied upon as a guide to the decision of future cases.[65]

Or, consider the former CAB's domestic air route certification power. Under Section 2 of the Civil Aeronautics Act, the board was directed to consider a number of factors in issuing competitive certificates. In carrying out this directive, however, the board vacillated and changed its policy on several occasions, and never spelled out the standards it would apply in situations arising under the section. Judge Friendly contended:

> ... It is no answer to take refuge in such cliches as that "no mechanical formula exists whereby statistics can be fed into a machine and an ultimate route decision obtained" — as if anyone had ever contended that it did — and that "the outcome depends upon a balancing and weighing" of many factors such as "diversion, subsidy, cost, need for service, strengthening of weak carrier, competitive balance, [and] adequacy of existing service." The Board ought to have been able to say *something* as to *how* these factors would be weighed — which were more important and which less — and to develop some useful tests of these and other factors through careful economic study. ...
> The Board's history is a prime example of how an agency's failure to grasp the nettle can make a relatively easy problem hard.[66]

The statutes also are ambiguous concerning the relationship between regulation and antitrust policy.[67] A few statutes give antitrust immunity to some or all commission decisions.[68] Generally, however, an exemption from the antitrust laws is not expressly stated. Thus, in consolidation cases, most regulatory statutes provide that the transaction be "consistent with the public interest."[69] When antitrust exemptions are not specified, conflicts between regulatory standards and antitrust standards may arise.[70]

It is not being suggested that regulatory standards can be completely free of ambiguities. Regulation must be flexible enough to adapt to changing economic conditions and technological developments. At the same time, "during three-quarters of a century of regulatory experience in the railroad field and several decades in others, many patterns have recurred frequently enough so that by now it should be possible to articulate bases of administrative determination more specific than we have generally had, even though these cannot be expected to be as immutable as the law of the Medes and Persians."[71] What is needed, argues Bernstein, is an appropriate balance between broad and vague policies (which "generally prove to be unsatisfactory guides to decision in adjudicated cases") and policies that are too tight and specific (which "may be applicable only to a relatively few cases").[72]

Policy formulation also might be improved if the decisions and orders of the agencies were written with greater clarity and by the commissioners themselves. Commented Justice Black on a decision of the ICC: "I am compelled to say that the Commission could have informed me just as well if it had written its so-called findings in an ancient Sanskrit."[73] Landis argued: "Opinions of the Interstate Commerce Commission are presently in the poorest category of all administrative agency opinions. Their source is unknown and the practice has grown up of parsimony in discussing the applicable laws in making a determination. Lengthy recitals of the contentions of the various parties are made as a prelude to a succinct conclusion devoid of real rationalization."[74] And the Office of Management and Budget concluded that it had "identified the single, most important problem in the regulatory process as the lack of consistent and effective policy oversight of regulatory decisions by the heads of regulatory agencies. . . . The officials who signed regulations often had no idea of what was in them. Those who wrote regulations were not held accountable for their actions."[75]

The work loads of the commissions often prevent the commissioners from writing opinions. Consequently, opinion writing is delegated to staff personnel, commonly (at the federal level) within an independent Opinion Writing Office. Yet, effective regulation requires that the commissioners take responsibility for all phases of opinions. The Special Subcommittee on Legislative Oversight concluded:

> The subcommittee has been impressed with the need for change in the practices followed by some commissions of letting the commission staff rather than individual commissioners assume responsibility for the preparation of commission decisions and opinions. It is the view of the

subcommittee that inconsistencies in commission decisions over the years are traceable to a considerable extent to the failure of following the practice of having the commission, or the majority of the commission, designate individual commissioners to assume responsibility for the preparation of the decisions or opinions of the commission, or the majority of the commission. It is the view of the subcommittee that this practice, which is traditional with the courts and which has been followed by some commissions, should be adopted by all commissions. It is the hope of the subcommittee that this change will produce a sense of personal responsibility of individual commissioners for the decisions and opinions of the commission and will avoid the practice of having commission staffs assume the burden of reconciling inconsistent decisions reached by the commissions.[76]

Regulatory Delay

The Achilles' heel of the regulatory process is delay.[77] The Senate Committee on Governmental Affairs found:

> ... From start to finish, the proceedings averaged more than 19 months for licensing, 21 months for ratemaking, and over 3 years for enforcement actions. Each stage of the three types of proceedings was very time-consuming. In licensing and ratemaking proceedings, it took about 160 days for matters to even reach the hearing state; for enforcement actions, it averaged well over a year before a hearing was convened. Protracted hearings also characterized the proceedings, and once again enforcement was the lengthiest of the three — just under 18 months devoted to hearings, which was nearly double the time spent for ratemaking and licensing hearings. Finally, the time necessary for agency review and decision-making accounted for about 25 percent to 30 percent of the total agency time on the case. For licensing the agency review took more time than either of the two preceding stages individually.[78]

Regulatory delay adversely affects the public welfare in several ways. Delay in the regulatory process may hamper the progress and efficiency of the utility industries. Delay may prevent consumers from receiving their share of the benefits flowing from progress and efficiency. The first may occur when a rate increase is in order; the second when technological advances indicate a rate decrease. And both occur when the introduction of a new or improved service is postponed.[79] Delay is costly — "costly in terms of the human energies expended by the managements of regulated industries in obtaining approval to do those things which must be done; costly in terms of legal fees and the expenses of management personnel engaged in the long-drawn-out proceedings before regulatory agencies."[80] Delay may postpone or even deny justice and/or change; it favors "those who gain from the status quo."[81] Delay causes further delay: When the FERC has a gas pipeline case pending, the affected state commissions are unable to determine proper rates for local distributors. Finally, delay aggravates the problem of *ex parte* influences.

The causes of regulatory delay are numerous. A major factor is the increasing work loads of the commissions. As previously noted, the volume of work (and its complexity) has been expanded by court decisions (the Supreme Court's 1954 *Phillips* decision), by new legislation (the national energy legislation of 1978), and by the economic environment (inflation during the 1970s).[82] Another cause is inadequate budgets. To handle increasing work loads, the commissions must have adequate appropriations and staffs.[83] The lack of clearly defined standards and policies is a third cause of delay. Commissions must interpret broad statutory provisions in regulating a particular industry. Sometimes these statutes are conflicting (regulatory versus promotional duties); other times they are outdated, resulting in overregulation (transportation industry).[84] Poor personnel contributes to the problem. "While regulatory agencies are blessed with a number of highly competent hearing examiners, they are cursed with an equal number of weak ones. The latter compound the problem of regulatory lag through failing their responsibility of determining admissibility of the evidence. This is why some hearings continue ad infinitum."[85] All of these are important causes, but they are subordinate to the problem of administrative procedures.

Administrative Procedures. The "judicialization" of proceedings — that is, the tendency to introduce trial-type processes into administrative proceedings — has long been a source of controversy. The Landis Report commented on this as follows:

> Beginning about 1938 concerted efforts were made to deal with these [procedural] problems. At the outset, spurred on by an antagonism to the very powers exercised by the regulatory agencies, the bar as a whole sought to impose the straightjackets of traditional judicial procedure on the agencies. They were countered by other forces which sought to retain the value of the administrative process but still advocated reforms that would assure fairness in the exercise of powers delegated to the agencies. Some eight years thereafter a compromise between these two opposing views was effected by the enactment of the Administrative Procedure Act of 1946. That Act, however one may evaluate it, is far from a definitive solution of the problems with which it dealt. It has achieved some uniformity of procedure, some assurance of the application of fairer standards, but with its emphasis on "judicialization" has made for delay in the handling of many matters before these agencies.[86]

The basic problem then is to reconcile the legal and constitutional requirements of due process of law in agency decisions with the demands of promptness and efficiency in achieving statutory duties.[87] Equally important, it is difficult to evaluate the many recommendations for improving administrative procedures, since "the practical and theoretical motivations of reformers differ. Each group seeking change views the administrative process in terms of one aspect of its operation; thus, the official viewpoint of the American Bar Association is based above all on the need to protect the rights of private parties in administrative proceedings, while administrative-minded reformers seek to increase efficiency."[88]

The regulatory commissions have adopted many of the proposals advanced to streamline administrative procedures. Prehearing conferences are used to determine the areas of agreement and of dispute. Previously prepared and filed (so-called "canned") testimony generally is required to limit the necessary hearing time. Informal proceedings have been used increasingly in place of formal proceedings to establish major commission policy, but their use has not been without controversy.[89] Yet, further remedies would seem desirable. The number of intervenors, in many cases, could be limited without any loss to interested parties. "There can be no quarrel with any party presenting his point of view to a regulatory commission, but when the same points of view have been already adequately presented by the public service company or by the staff of the commission, it is a needless waste of time for other groups to plow the same ground a second or third time."[90]

Many believe that the key to cutting down procedural delay lies with the administrative law judge. Welch argues:

> Too often he has been governed by the understandable tendency to let questionable material go into the record so as to give the offering parties the "benefit of the doubt" and make his own position less vulnerable on appeal. This may result in a mass of extraneous material which commissioners and eventually appellate courts are supposed to read. It takes real courage and a good deal of ability to kick irrelevant material out of the record, to cut off counsel mid-flight in the pursuit of testimony obviously not germane, and cutting through the downright "gobbledy-gook" of obscure expert testimony.[91]

Case-by-case adjudication is a slow, costly, and inadequate process for resolving the complex economic issues that characterize the regulation of industry. To be sure, fairness and impartiality must be maintained and informal procedures cannot be used in all instances. But the commissions should be permitted to use informal procedures when applicable. The FCC's policy of primary reliance on continuous surveillance and informal procedures in its regulation of the former Bell System is an outstanding example of the benefits that can be derived. Rate reductions made possible by increased efficiency and new equipment were passed on quickly to subscribers. Innovations in ratemaking were made possible and new services were introduced.

In an effort to provide for the constant improvement of administrative procedures, the Administrative Conference of the United States was established by Congress in 1964.[92] A permanent, independent government agency, the Administrative Conference has the responsibility of studying and making recommendations for improvement in all federal agency functions which involve "the determination of the rights, privileges, and obligations of private persons through rule making, adjudication, licensing, or investigation." The Administrative Conference issues an annual report, and works with federal agencies in implementing its recommendations.[93]

Regulation as a Substitute for Competition

Criticisms of the regulatory process are numerous and varied. Yet, the shortcomings of regulation cannot be attributed solely to the lack of political control, *ex parte* influences, industry-mindedness, the failure to develop meaningful policy standards, and undue delay. If all these defects could be remedied, regulation would be more effective, but it would still fall short, in the opinion of some, of the competitive standard.

The Inherent Difficulties

Wilcox has argued that "the difficulties of regulation are largely inherent in the nature of the undertaking itself." In his view:

Taking the place of competition as the method of control, regulation should be expected to yield comparable results. It should not only prevent the regulated industry from charging a monopoly price, impairing the quality of its service, and enjoying a monopoly profit. It should provide an incentive to adopt new methods, to improve quality, to increase efficiency and cut costs, to develop mass markets and expand output by selling at a lower price. It does none of these things.

Regulation, at best, is a pallid substitute for competition. It cannot prescribe quality, force efficiency, or require innovation, because such action would invade the sphere of management. But when it leaves these matters to the discretion of industry, it denies consumers the protection that competition would afford. Regulation cannot set prices below an industry's costs however excessive they may be. Competition does so, and the high-cost company is compelled to discover means whereby its costs can be reduced. Regulation does not enlarge consumption by setting prices at the lowest level consistent with a fair return. Competition has this effect. Regulation fails to encourage performance in the public interest by offering rewards and penalties. Competition offers both.

Regulation is static, backward-looking, preoccupied with the problems of the past. It does nothing to stimulate change, seeking to maintain order on the basis of the old technology. It is slow to adapt to change: new problems appear, but regulatory thinking lags. Competition, by contrast, is dynamic. . . .

Regulation is slower than competition. It must satisfy the requirements of due process: investigate, give notice, hold hearings, study the record, make findings, issue orders, permit appeals. All this takes time and delays action. In some cases, delay may be harmful, as when it permits earnings to rise well above or to fall far below the return required to attract new capital. In other cases, it may be helpful, as when it brakes an inflationary spiral of wages and prices. But here, the merit of regulation lies, not in its efficiency, but in its inefficiency.[94]

It can be argued that Wilcox appears to be comparing some of the alleged shortcomings of regulation as it actually exists with the idealistic benefits of the theoretical competitive model. If true, he has arrived at a view of regulation which seems too pessimistic, particularly with respect to the nontransport utilities.[95] Put another way, if regulation were as unsuccessful as Wilcox suggests, the communications, electric, and gas utilities could not have contributed so largely to the nation's economy, particularly in the pre-1968 period. At least two hypotheses are possible: that the utilities achieved these results under the incentives provided by regulation or, alternatively, that these results were achieved despite regulation, in large measure due to a supportive economic environment.[96] But regardless of which view one accepts, the inherent defects of regulation became more apparent during the 1970s.[97]

The Role of Competition

Those who believe that regulation is superior to public ownership almost unanimously recommend that a greater reliance be placed on competitive forces.[98] Typical are the following comments by Turner (in 1969) and Breyer (in 1982):

> . . . the difficulties and inadequacies of direct regulation, theoretical as well as practical, suggest that it should be confined to cases in which strong elements of natural monopoly are plainly present. They also suggest that, even where some direct regulation is thought necessary, the regulatory agency should take advantage of whatever competitive possibilities exist.[99]

* * *

In other words, increased efforts to fine-tune regulation often will not yield results. Regulators of great intelligence, with genuine good will, working extremely hard, are nonetheless unlikely to deal effectively with borderline cases. The defects and difficulties inherent in the system make regulation a crude weapon of government intervention — a blunderbuss, not a rifle. These defects are embedded in the process to such an extent that they cannot readily be changed.[100]

The transportation industry is an obvious case in point. Competitive forces were restrained by restrictions on the entry of new firms. The allocation of both traffic and resources was distorted by commission policy and public aids. The growth of private and unregulated carriers was encouraged by regulatory statutes and failure to develop rate structures which met modern conditions.[101] And, in far too many instances, innovation was delayed or stifled. Here was a situation, as Barber pointed out, in which technology over a forty-year period

> ... has not only radically changed the character of American transportation but in the process has rendered transport regulation largely anachronistic. Greatly assisted by various forms of government aid, the newer forms of transportation have displaced the once dominant position of the railroads, and have undermined the older regulatory apparatus which rested on the assumption that the ICC was in effective control of the transportation system. It no longer is; competition, albeit limited, has replaced the rail monopoly; and increasing amounts of freight traffic are unregulated. . . .[102]

Deregulation: Some Issues.[103] The task of permitting freer play to competitive forces has not proven to be an easy one.[104] Cramton has noted that "a regulatory scheme is likely to generate interests that make deregulation extremely difficult."[105] Regulators, moreover, tend to develop a presumption in favor of regulation. Summarized Jaffe, with respect to transportation: "In this thinking, competition becomes the equivalent of 'chaos,' of 'waste,' and of 'destruction;' regulation will assure neat, explicable, rationalized ordering of transportation resources, each with its duly appointed role."[106] Stated another way, competitive forces tend to complicate the regulatory process. In the case of partial deregulation, for instance, how should a regulatory commission handle such a situation to insure that a regulated company will not use the power at its disposal in the monopoly (regulated) area of its business to gain an unfair advantage over its rivals in the competitive (nonregulated) area?[107] Nor, it should be noted, is deregulation the only viable alternative to economic regulation. Judge Breyer, for example, considers six additional options: disclosure, taxes, marketable rights, disability rules, bargaining, and nationalization.[108]

Equally important, as Foster has argued,

> . . . regulatory concepts evolve and strategies change in response to the effects of advancing technology and the economic and social forces which determine the economic characteristics and market structures of individual industries. . . . The drawing of boundaries between competition and economic regulation of specific industries is not an easy task in a complex, unstable environment. . . .[109]

Deregulation, however, has its costs and critics. There may be transitional costs, such as when deregulation generates windfall gains for either investors at the expense of consumers or for consumers at the expense of investors. Deregulation also may impose substantial, and unequal costs, upon various consumer and/or industry interests. The controversy surrounding deregulation of the wellhead price of natural gas is a clear example.[110] So, too, is the deregulation of portions of the telecommunications industry. To cite Foster again:

> A change in public policy is in the public interest if the present worth of the prospective net benefits is in excess of all transitional cost. New entrants benefit relative to existing firms because their investment decisions are made according to the new "rules of the game;" unless alternative uses are available, the existing capital of established firms is "sunk." Competition will grow most rapidly in the denser, more attractive markets, so that existing firms in those markets may be disadvantaged in greater degree. New entrants with lower non-union labor costs may force cost and staff reductions by established firms. New entrants focus on price-sensitive segments of the total market to the disadvantage of consumers in other segments. Alternatively, specialized services may be offered in markets which are not highly price-sensitive.[111]

Critics of deregulation express concerns over service, safety, and oligopolistic behavior. Summarizes Reagan, with respect to transportation deregulation:

> Service cuts: with the CAB defunct and the ICC permitting abandonment of routes by rail and motor carriers more easily than in the past, some consumers, particularly those in rural areas, find themselves with fewer transportation options than in the past. In one ironic reaction, the city of Fresno, California, became an investor in a commuter airline, in order to maintain service to the community. Thus, deregulation led to local socialism.
> Deregulated airline prices have risen substantially on the less compet-

itive routes, somewhat diminishing the enthusiasm of those consumers whose travel is other than between major coast-to-coast stops. Also, as of mid-1986, concerns were rising about airline mergers that were proceeding at such a pace as to threaten oligopolistic pricing . . . in a number of markets.

Lifting of restrictions on entry may bring back some of what was called "destructive competition" in the 1930s. The first result of trucking deregulation, for example, was to increase the number of truckers substantially. Since the amount of goods to be carried did not increase proportionately, the second effect in the first few years has arguably been to produce a lot of bankruptcies among small truckers, and increase the concentration ratio among the remaining firms. The ultimate fear is that the long-term result could be the gobbling up of the small by the big until the point is reached at which so few firms are left that pricing becomes notably oligopolistic — and then the cry for regulation will appear again.[112]

Contends Thayer: "Social regulation of health and safety standards cannot be effective (or can become effective only at very high costs) unless it is accompanied by economic regulation."[113] Competition in the airline industry, he argues, will lead to cutting corners (*i.e.,* on maintenance, use of inexperienced pilots). This factor, in turn, will require more FAA inspectors and greater enforcement expenditures. The entry of new firms, moreover, raises issues concerning the air traffic control system and airport access.[114]

In short: "Whether the benefits outweigh the costs, whether the freedoms are worth the risks, whether the reduction in governmental oversight outweighs the ignorance of consumers — these are the questions that remain unanswered in the deregulated society."[115]

Institutional Competition. Adams and Gray would go even further.[116] In those cases where market competition is not feasible, they have recommended development of "institutional" competition. By institutional competition they mean rivalry among different types of utility organizations — private, public, and cooperatives. Institutional competition has two important limitations. First, a meaningful yardstick with which to compare the performance of the different forms of organization would have to be developed. Such a yardstick would be extremely difficult to obtain.[117] Second, as Trebing has pointed out, institutional competition would be unable "to accomplish in a positive fashion the ends which it seeks. Under market competition, profits are the stimulus and losses the penalty that eventually drive the inefficient out of business. Institutional competition, on the other hand, possesses at best hazy stimuli and almost completely ineffectual penalties."[118] He concludes:

Given these limitations, any general attempt to enforce institutional competition is certain to lead to adverse social effects or losses. If the yardstick is based primarily on rates, then service may be allowed to deteriorate in the interests of low prices. Service may also be adversely affected if a particular utility firm falls behind the yardstick standard and, rather than endeavor to improve performance, chooses to recapture its capital through deferred maintenance and replacement. But perhaps the most telling effects of institutional competition will be on the cost of capital, especially for private utilities. The threat of public ownership, whether real or illusory, will give rise to greater feelings of uncertainty among investors, thereby leading to a demand for a greater return on capital devoted to these enterprises. Repercussions, however, would be cumulative and would carry beyond this point, for once the cost of capital increases, the relative yardstick performance of private utilities worsens, thereby triggering a fresh round of anxiety among investors. Ultimately, private utility investment could become less and less profitable as capital costs rise with consequent depressing effects on investment spending and national income.[119]

In summary, while institutional competition seems impracticable, the forces of market competition should be strengthened and used wherever possible. By so doing, the inherent difficulties of regulation can be minimized so that regulation can become a more effective substitute for competition.

Management: Divided Responsibility

Regulation creates another basic problem by dividing the responsibility for management.[120] A company's management, not a regulatory commission, is responsible for the financial success of a firm. Yet, the regulator can and often does interfere with management and, in so doing, may discourage entrepreneurial initiative and diminish the sense of responsibility.

If the regulator is given a clear mandate to remove a perceived evil, he has an adequate and limited basis for validating his interference with management, and management has a basis for calculating the effects of the interference. But in the absence of a clear mandate, it is not only inevitable, but appropriate that regulation take the form of an accommodation in which industry is the senior partner. This is the essence of "industry-orientation."[121]

Of course, if it could be assumed that most of the regulator's business judgments were superior to those of management, this duplicative effort might result in a net gain. Such an assumption, however, is dubious. As two former commissioners have put it:

> Members of a regulatory agency must not live in an ivory tower, thinking they know how to operate an airline better than those actually in the business who know the job firsthand and from the ground up.[122]

* * *

> Commissioners have neither the training, nor the skills, nor the incentives to manage.[123]

Further, even if commissioners could be assumed to be the better businessmen, "there would be offsetting costs." Explains Wilcox:

> Duplication costs money; two managements impose a heavier administrative burden than does one. Negotiation between the managements takes time; decisions are inevitably delayed. Division of authority saps the vitality of an enterprise; diverts energy from the solution of external problems to the prosecution of internal disputes. Managements come to direct their attention more to outsmarting the regulators than to introducing innovations, improving service, and reducing costs.
>
> Regulation dissipates responsibility. The ICC is required, in setting rates, to consider their probable effect upon the volume of traffic. In doing so, it may substitute its own judgment for that of railway managements. And here, if earnings fall, there is no one whom the owners of the roads can hold responsible. The managements are deprived of power; the Commission has power but lacks responsibility. And even if managements are not reversed, decisions are often so delayed that substantial losses are sustained. In cases such as this, management escapes accountability by blaming the regulators. And the regulators are not made accountable by law.[124]

A Continuing Challenge

Private industries in the United States frequently are classified as belonging to either the unregulated sector or the regulated sector. In the unregulated, competition is assumed to prevail; in the regulated, competition is assumed to be limited, at best, and public regulation is undertaken as a substitute. Despite this dichotomy, both competition and regulation have the same basic objectives: the efficient allocation of resources and the protection of consumers against exploitation. It is the means to these ends that are notably different. Competition operates through profit incentives and penalties determined by prices set in the marketplace. Regulation, however, must set rates itself, thereby determining the profit incentives and penalties.

The lengthy experience of this country with regulation clearly indicates that, like competition, regulation falls short of perfection. Opinions as to the degree of imperfection, however, vary considerably. In the words of Lewis:

> The record of public utility regulation generally since 1907 is neither impressive, nor yet too disheartening. The excessive costs and delays of regulation, its rigidities, and its apparent lack of purpose beyond the settlement of individual controversies, cannot fairly be overlooked. On the other hand, the utilities industries have experienced an enormous physical growth, the increasingly complex problems of regulation have been met by the improvisation of elaborate regulatory machinery, and the period of adjustment has, after all, been short.[125]

According to Bauer:

> Under the conditions that have existed, the wonder is that regulation has worked as well as it has. Although far from satisfactory, it has not been a complete and unmitigated failure. While the commissions have not measured up to high standards, perhaps they have done, in the main, the best they could under all the circumstances. They have carried on their work in an easy going, nonalert way, but they have seldom deliberately flouted the public interest.[126]

In the opinion of Cramton:

> There are inherent limitations on the effectiveness of economic regulation even where public policy is fairly clear and the regulatory task, relatively speaking, is confined and manageable. The simpler case of economic regulation — the determination of maximum rates of a conventional public utility — has not been performed with obvious success. I do not assert that public utility regulation has been a failure. I do maintain, however, that unqualified assertions of its effectiveness would be unwarranted. The lesson of a half-century of experience is that the environment generates enduring problems which limit the potential effectiveness of rate regulation.[127]

And, finally, Noll concludes in his review of the Ash Council Report:

> The preceding discussion of regulatory failures only summarizes a vast literature in which regulators are accused of being excessively concerned about the welfare of the regulated. The Ash Council raises the issue only once, then quickly dismisses it as one of several effects,

rather than a cause, of the deficiencies of regulation. According to the Council, "it would be easy to attribute dissatisfaction with the performance of regulatory commissions . . . to overidentification with the industries regulated. . . . In our view, however, these and other points of dissatisfaction are symptoms. The cause is more fundamental." With a bit of nostalgia for old regulatory problems and apparently a belief that regulation was more effective in the past, the Council identifies the real problem as the inability of the organizational structure of regulation to cope with the growing demands placed upon it. Thus, "the commissions, perhaps suitable to a simpler day, have not been freed from structural restraints that are antithetic to the accomplishment of their new missions."

The complaints outlined above indicate that the problem of regulation runs far deeper than ineptitude by the agencies. According to the alternative view, the regulatory agencies, by attempting to maintain the status quo in regulated industries, are making policies that are not in the public interest. Consequently, the performance of regulated industries falls short of a reasonable, attainable social objective because the regulators have a different definition of the public interest than does society generally.[128]

Lacking perfection, there is room for improvement. Regulation is, after all, an evolutionary process. In its earlier days, regulation was conceived to be an essentially negative or restrictive force to limit the monopoly power of certain industries and, thereby, to protect utility users from inequitable price discrimination and exorbitant profits. To carry out this task, commissions developed such tools and concepts as establishment of uniform systems of accounts, separations procedures, measures for determining valuation and depreciation, and theoretical principles to use in arriving at a fair rate of return. All these and other regulatory tools were and are essential to effective regulation.

Yet, the great challenge to regulation is to improve its adaptability to a rapidly changing economic environment. Today, regulation must be more than a protector. It cannot attain its objectives merely by protecting consumers from monopoly profits, utility investors from confiscation of their investment, nor utilities from competition. It would be highly desirable if the goals and policies of regulation were more explicit and if the regulatory process could be stripped of its needlessly complex, costly, and often confusing procedures, thus permitting greater flexibility. But above all, regulation needs to adopt dynamic standards to meet the needs of a changing economy, and to evaluate both performance and policy.

The Need for Dynamic Standards

The establishment of dynamic standards will not be easy. A commission must formulate long-range policies or plans and must develop the means to effectuate its policies. Consider the role of profits. Dynamic progress requires technological advance; profits provide the basic incentive for progressiveness. "Cost-plus" regulation, with major emphasis upon limiting profit rates, offers no explicit incentives to a regulated firm. Indeed, as others have observed, regulatory lag may be the most important incentive to efficiency under such a scheme.[129] To encourage efficiency and innovation, therefore, incentive regulatory techniques must be developed.[130] It is not being implied that the rate of return currently being earned by any particular firm is too low. The point is that in determining the proper level of earnings for a utility, a commission must not be obsessed with limiting profits; rather, regulation must be a positive system, with consideration given to the role of profits as incentives, in addition to the level of earnings needed to attract capital.[131] The point of reference, moreover, must be long term, for technological progress commonly requires a long-time horizon.

Dynamic standards require basic changes in regulatory thinking and in regulatory techniques. With respect to regulatory thinking, more effective economic analysis is needed. Commissioner Johnson, for example, in the telephone investigation of the 1960s, listed a series of questions which he thought the FCC should direct its attention toward, "other than (or in addition to) the rate-of-return focus dictated by nineteenth century public utility philosophy:"

> What are the forces encouraging, or retarding, technological innovation in telephone equipment and service?
>
> What are the most appropriate rates of change in making new equipment available to the subscriber?
>
> What are the implications for national communications behavior of the ways in which we price telephone service?
>
> What should be the standards by which some rate discrimination (or subsidies) are encouraged and others discouraged?
>
> How should the pricing of telephone service respond as new techniques (satellites, wave guide, lasers) transform an industry of limited capacity into one of excess capacity?
>
> In what ways would more, or less, competition in providing telephone service be useful?
>
> By what procedures and institutional means can the needs and interests of both shareholders and subscribers best be formulated and translated into corporate or national policy?[132]

These questions shift traditional regulatory thinking, and place greater emphasis upon the economic effects of regulation. In turn, the goal or objective of regulation would become incentive regulation, rather than the traditional, profit limitation goal.[133]

The Need for Performance Evaluation

If regulation is to serve as an effective substitute for competition, methods or criteria for evaluating the performance of the regulatory process must be developed. Lewis succinctly summarized the problem several years ago:

Data are available to show the steady increase in the use of electric power, and the general lowering of electric rates — broken down for types of uses, sizes of markets, etc. But these indicate merely what has happened under the exact circumstances that have in fact obtained. There is no universal, objective standard against which the achievements of this industry under regulation may be measured; no way of knowing what the industry might have accomplished if regulatory conditions had been different. Similarly, data are available showing the earnings of the industry, its "profitability," and the ease with which it has been able to market its securities; likewise, cost ratio data, throwing light on changes in the efficiency of its operations; but with reference to all of these it must still be said that they throw little light either on how much of what has been accomplished has been due to regulation, or what might have been accomplished under regulation of another kind.[134]

In the past, evaluation of regulatory performance has concentrated on procedure. But issues of procedure and organization, while they can either help or hinder the resolution of policy issues, "avoid the important consequences of other types of governmental activities."[135] Further, the effectiveness of the regulatory process cannot be judged by an enumeration of regulatory policies. As Stigler and Friedland have noted, such an enumeration only indicates a desire to regulate, not the effectiveness of regulation. The relevant question, they contend, is whether regulation makes a difference in the behavior of an industry.[136]

Consider, for instance, the argument advanced several years ago by Averch and Johnson that regulation has a tendency to result in overinvestment, or excessive rate base expansion. In their words:

. . . if the rate of return allowed by the regulatory agency is greater than the cost of capital but less than the rate of return that would be enjoyed by the firm were it free to maximize profit without regulatory constraint, then the firm will substitute capital for the other factor of production and operate at an output where cost is not minimized.[137]

Given these assumptions, and on the basis of a careful analysis, they conclude that regulated firms have an incentive to use more capital and that the general level of utility rates will be higher than would be the case if returns were held to cost-of-capital levels.[138]

The Averch-Johnson thesis, which suggests that rate base regulation is deficient, has been the subject of considerable discussion.[139] First, are their assumptions valid? Do utilities (or did utilities in the pre-1968 period) earn rates of return that are (were) in excess of cost-of-capital levels? Expert opinion differs on this question. Second, to what extent does the model describe the functioning of the utility industry? Further, could it be that regulatory lag offsets the potential adverse effects of the Averch-Johnson thesis? Third, as Weintraub has noted, the Averch-Johnson analysis, on grounds of efficient resource allocation, "must be correct.... But do we want merely to improve resource allocation, or do we intend to advance production techniques? ... The very incentives to use 'excess' equipment, which Averch and Johnson deplore, may well be forces of some importance in enhancing productivity in the public utility sector and the economy generally.... Some allocational inefficiency may be a cost of technological externalities."[140] And, finally, Kahn has argued that the Averch-Johnson effect may have a beneficial aspect in that the incentive to overinvestment may offset the monopolist's tendency to restrict output.[141]

The Averch-Johnson thesis thus raises significant questions concerning the behavior and performance of firms under regulation. Whether one agrees with their findings or not, it is clear that too little is known about how the market performance of an industry is affected by regulation.[142]

The Need for Policy Review

Along with performance measures and evaluation, there is a need for periodic policy review, for at least two purposes. First, where regulation is deemed necessary, there should be a periodic review of a commission's statutory duties, organization, personnel, and performance. Out-of-date statutes, inadequate staffs and budgets, and poor performance can all be corrected, and the legislative branch has an obligation to undertake such a review. Second, there should be a periodic review of the need for continued regulation and of the alternatives to traditional economic regulation. Here, disagreement continues over who is responsible for such a review — the legislative or the executive branch — although many believe that both must play a role.[143]

Several mechanisms have been proposed. One such mechanism is the *impact statement.* Agencies are required by the National Environmental Policy Act of 1969 to

> ... include in every recommendation or report on proposals for legislation and other major Federal actions significantly affecting the quality of the human environment, a detailed statement by the responsible official on—

(i) the environmental impact of the proposed action,
(ii) any adverse environmental effects which cannot be avoided should the proposal be implemented,
(iii) alternatives to the proposed action,
(iv) the relationship between local short-term uses of man's environment and the maintenance and enhancement of long-term productivity, and
(v) any irreversible and irretrievable commitments of resources which would be involved in the proposed action should it be implemented.[144]

Before taking any major action, agencies were required by an order issued by President Carter to undertake a "regulatory impact statement," detailing the agency's objectives and alternative ways of achieving them, and justifying its action as better than any alternative.[145] Before taking any major action, agencies are required by an order issued by President Reagan to undertake a "regulatory impact analysis," which requires — in addition to objectives and alternatives — that a cost-benefit test be applied and met.[146]

At the federal level, impact statements

> . . . provide a justification for the Office of Management and Budget, the Council of Economic Advisers, the Council on Wage and Price Stability, and the Department of Justice (Antitrust Division) to intervene in agency proceedings and to present their views. These agencies are institutionally disposed to stress the need for competition, the importance of incentives, and the difficulties of classical regulation. Their presence in the proceeding can force the agency to take more serious account of these considerations. Thus, the Council on Wage and Price Stability has intervened in several agency proceedings and shown that the agency's proposed action would have involved costs out of proportion to probable benefits. Intervention based upon the impact statement can also force the White House staff to pay attention to issues and decisions that might otherwise pass unnoticed. Involvement by the Council of Economic Advisers in some major regulatory proceedings, for example, has led the White House to develop a firm position, which, in turn, has strongly influenced the agency's decision toward less restrictive regulation. Finally, if the impact statement is reviewable in court, action that is unreasonable in terms of the statement can be set aside. Thus, the Justice Department might urge the courts to set aside ICC action that impeded entry into the trucking business on the grounds that the ICC had not written (indeed, could not write) a competitive impact statement showing that a restrictive entry policy was needed to carry out the purposes of trucking regulation.[147]

Another mechanism is *sunset legislation*. Under such legislation, an agency ceases to exist on a specific date, unless its life is extended by new legislation. Several states have adopted sunset laws (including Colorado and Florida), and Congress has adopted sunset provisions in a few instances (such as with the Federal Energy Administration). Given a threat of extinction, the legislative body should be impelled to reconsider the need for the agency before its life is terminated. However, there is the danger that the legislative body will simply reenact the old program automatically, as Congress did with the Federal Energy Administration, or "may simply attack administrative waste without examining the fundamental objectives of the program."[148] Further, sunset legislation "may condemn to extinction those agencies that are the subject of serious political controversy."[149] Despite these potential weaknesses, the 1980 review by the Florida legislature of its public service commission "led to major revisions of the commission's decision-making process."[150]

A third mechanism is the *regulatory budget*. First proposed by Crandall,[151] the regulatory budget

> . . . would operate by close analogy to the conventional fiscal process. Each year (or at some longer interval), the federal government would establish an upper limit on the cost of its regulatory activities to the economy and would apportion this sum among the individual regulatory agencies. This would presumably involve a budget proposal developed by OMB in negotiation with the regulatory agencies, approved by the President, and submitted to Congress for review, revision, and passage. Once the President had signed the final budget appropriations into law, each agency would be obligated to live within its regulatory budget for the time period in question. The budget would cover the total costs of all regulations past and present, not just new ones. Thus, for a given budget period, an agency could issue and enforce new regulations only to the extent that the costs imposed, when added to the current costs imposed by regulations issued in previous years, were within the agency's total budget. The policies of individual regulatory statutes would have to be implemented within this budget constraint, just as they now must be implemented within the constraint of the expenditure budget.[152]

Supporters of the regulatory budget admit that there are a number of practical difficulties, including (*a*) "the problem of collecting and analyzing the vast quantities of cost information that would be needed to establish and enforce the budget"; (*b*) "the measure of costs to be employed in the budgeting process"; and (*c*) "the source of the budget constraint under a regulatory budget."[153] In view of these difficulties, Bardach and Kagan have proposed a *retrospective* regulatory budget:

> . . . Instead of trying to control the costs of future regulations, perhaps the focus should be on trimming back the costs of regulations

already on the books. Suppose that agencies were obligated periodically to decrease the compliance costs of existing regulations by some percentage, say 5-10 percent every three or four years. Compared with the estimates of future costs, already incurred costs are relatively (though not completely) certain and measurable. Suppose further that agencies were obliged to accept nominations from outside sources, for example, regulated firms and institutions, academics, other government agencies, and legislators, as to which regulations most urgently deserved revision. Any successes at actually cutting down compliance costs could be entered into the political display of performance statistics that agencies now engage in with respect to fines levied or sites inspected.[154]

Others have proposed less formal mechanisms. Gormley, for instance, stresses the need to promote important values, including democratization, professionalism, and administrative efficiency. In his words:

> . . . Intervenor funding promotes democratization by facilitating the participation of grassroots advocacy groups in public utility commission proceedings. In addition, it encourages professionalism by improving the technical expertise of grassroots advocacy groups. Declassification promotes professionalism by enabling commissioners to hire and promote job applicants whose skills match the challenges of the future rather than the challenges of the past. It also encourages administrative efficiency by expediting hiring and firing decisions. Rule-making promotes administrative efficiency by channeling important controversies into generic proceedings rather than a repetitive series of ad hoc decisions. In addition, it encourages leadership by providing state legislators with more meaningful opportunities for oversight. The initiative promotes leadership by encouraging reluctant governors and legislators to act. It also promotes democratization by affording the electorate an opportunity to make policy through the ballot box.[155]

The Future

The decade of the 1970s placed a tremendous strain on the regulatory process. A radically different economic environment (*e.g.,* rapid annual rates of inflation, high interest rates, soaring construction costs and fuel prices) confronted a regulatory process geared to periodic rate cases, and which generally involved rate reductions. Concurrently, legislatures enacted new social regulations at a steady pace, particularly early in the decade, often forcing the traditional regulatory agencies to consider broader and more complex issues in carrying out their duties. The regulatory process (as well as the regulated utilities) tried desperately to adapt and adjust to these changes, but not too successfully, many contend.

There were two other trends which confronted the regulatory process. First, there developed an underlying struggle — legislative versus executive oversight and initiative, for one example; regulation by commission or antitrust policy, for another. Several examples have already been provided,[156] but to quote the Hales with respect to the latter:

> ... many conflicts occur between the commands of public utility commissions and their organic laws, on the one hand, and the antitrust statutes, on the other. The uncertainty over which set of controls might be applicable to any given situation would be costly and time-consuming. Almost any move by a public utility firm could be questioned under both means of control. This is scarcely a time — if ever there was one — to add needless costs to public utility service. Long periods of uncertainty, possibly extending for five or more decades, might be required to ascertain what activities of the utilities remained under interventionist regulation and which would be attacked under the antitrust laws. In short, the utility companies can scarcely be expected to serve two masters. Hence this issue should be put to the legislative branch of government for resolution. . . .[157]

This struggle caused AT&T's chairman to remark: "And there is a very real question as to whether AT&T is master of its own destiny — or whether the FCC is or the Justice Department is or Congress is."[158]

Second, regulation became mired in procedural requirements, as hundreds of interest groups were formed (with both public and private funding) to intervene in regulatory proceedings. Nor were such groups averse to appealing "unfavorable" decisions; appeals which resulted in delay but, more importantly, in the courts becoming active participants. This participation resulted in a warning from Justice Rehnquist in a 1978 decision:

> ... The fundamental policy questions appropriately resolved in Congress and in the state legislatures are *not* subject to reexamination in the federal courts under the guise of judicial review of agency action. Time may prove wrong the decision to develop nuclear energy, but it is Congress or the States within their appropriate agencies which must eventually make that judgment. In the meantime courts should perform their appointed function. NEPA does set forth significant substantive goals for the Nation, but its mandate to the agencies is essentially procedural. . . . It is to insure a fully informed and well-considered decision, not necessarily a decision the judges of the Court of Appeals or of this Court would have reached had they been members of the decisionmaking unit of the agency. Administrative decisions should be set aside in this context, as in every other, only for substantial procedural or substantive reasons as mandated by statute . . . not simply because the court is unhappy with the result reached. . . .[159]

Given these four basic trends, it is little wonder that, for the first time in our history, substantial deregulation occurred, if for no other reason (and there were many other good reasons) than the inability of understaffed and overworked regulatory agencies to handle the growing work loads and the conflicting pressures.

Countless proposals have been made to reform regulation and, after careful analysis and review, some of them deserve implementation. But the fact remains that regulation can, and will, only be as effective and as imaginative as its personnel. With all due respect for those who toiled against incredible odds, the regulatory agencies lacked the leadership of a Joseph B. Eastman or a James M. Landis,[160] although the contributions of Alfred E. Kahn must not be minimized.[161] To be effective, there must be a regulatory incentive system, to attract and to retain high caliber personnel (commissioners, staffs, and administrative law judges).[162] Such a goal will require updated statutes and adequate funding from the legislative branch, and both proper restraint and support from the executive and judicial branches.[163] Given the trends of the past decade and a half, such a regulatory incentive system may seem academic. Yet, the price of failing to develop such a system (and a better balance among conflicting objectives) will be significant, including higher utility rates, poorer utility service, and slower economic growth.

What is required, in the future, is far more cooperation between the regulator and the regulated — and far more understanding of the basic issues by interested parties — if the public utility sector, under regulation or partial regulation, is to reach its maximum potential. So, too, must there be far more cooperation between the federal government and the states. New tools and concepts must be developed, old ones discarded as their usefulness diminishes.[164] The emphasis, moreover, must be not only on restricting the regulated firms (minimum rates of return, minimum valuation of assets, minimum depreciation rates), but also on promotion (via incentives), with long-run goals and objectives. Stated another way, regulation must never become an end in itself. Both the utilities and the commissions must cooperate in developing the required new tools and concepts, and in finding new ways to serve the American public, with the assistance of the executive, legislative, and judicial branches. And, finally, research must continue on the development of dynamic standards and on the effectiveness of regulation, with periodic public policy review to make sure that regulation, where still justified, is up-to-date.

For all of these reasons, effective regulation — in an era of greater complexity and conflict[165] — continues to offer "a challenging opportunity for creative and constructive action."[166]

Notes

*Roger G. Noll and Bruce M. Owen, "What Makes Reform Happen?," 7 *Regulation* 19 (March/April, 1983).

¹"The American regulatory process is a reflection of the democratic and egalitarian principles held by the Founding Fathers, especially their fear of centralized government power. Its organizing principle is that decisions should be based on objective analysis and made only after the views of all who are likely to be affected are heard and considered. Elaborate rules regarding rights of participation, the evidence pertaining to a decision, and the statutory basis for a policy action have developed to serve this principle. Thus, like many American legal processes, regulation is designed to serve principles of equity and the public interest in a rational way in an environment populated primarily by advocates of particular economic interests. . . ." *Ibid.*

²Asher Brynes, "A $500 Million Mistake," *The New Republic*, September 26, 1964, p. 12.

³See, *e.g.*, three articles by Philip Cabot, "Public Utility Rate Regulation," 7 *Harvard Business Review* 257 (1929), 7 *ibid.* 413, and "Four Fallacious Dogmas of Utility Regulation," 7 *Public Utilities Fortnightly* 719 (1931).

⁴For some comparisons, see W. T. Stanbury and Fred Thompson, *Regulatory Reform in Canada* (Montreal: Institute for Research on Public Policy, 1982).

⁵See Chapter 4, pp. 138-43.

⁶Edwin Corwin, as quoted in Samuel Krislov and Lloyd D. Musolf (eds.), *The Politics of Regulation* (Boston: Houghton Mifflin Co., 1964), p. 93.

⁷Bernard Schwartz, "Crisis in the Commissions," *The Progressive*, August, 1959, p. 13.

⁸James M. Landis, *Report on Regulatory Agencies to the President-Elect* (Reprinted as a Committee Print by the Committee on the Judiciary, Senate, 86th Cong., 2d sess.) (Washington, D.C.: U.S. Government Printing Office, 1960), pp. 13-14 (hereinafter referred to as Landis Report). See also *Independent Regulatory Commissions* (Report of the Special Subcommittee on Legislative Oversight of the Committee on Interstate and Foreign Commerce, House Report No. 2238) (Washington, D.C.: U.S. Government Printing Office, 1961); *Re Contacts Between Public Utilities and Former Commissioners*, 82 PUR4th 559 (Minn., 1987).

⁹Carl McFarland, "Landis Report: The Voice of One Crying in the Wilderness," 47 *Virginia Law Review* 373, 415 (1961).

¹⁰Stephen Breyer, *Regulation and Its Reform* (Cambridge: Harvard University Press, 1982), p. 344 (citation omitted). One study by Common Cause, to illustrate, found that: (*a*) "52 percent (or twenty-two) of the forty-two regulatory commissioners who were appointed during the fiscal years 1971-1975 came from companies regulated by their agency, or from such companies' law firms" and (*b*) "48 percent (or seventeen) of the thirty-six commissioners who left during this five-year period went to work for regulated industries or their law firms." Stephen G. Breyer and Richard B. Stewart, *Administrative Law and Regulatory Policy* (Boston: Little, Brown & Co., 1979), p. 141. See *Serving Two Masters: A Common Cause Study of Conflicts of Interest in the Executive Branch* (Washington, D.C.: Common Cause, 1976). See also Robert C. Fellmeth et al., *The Interstate Commerce Omission* (New York: Grossman Publishers, 1970), esp. chap. 1. There is, according to *Fortune*, a new revolving door, "in which deregulators leave the agencies they've gutted and take up high-paying jobs in the newly deregulated industries they've helped shape." "The New Revolving Door," *Fortune*, October 17, 1983, p. 58.

¹¹In 1978, Congress enacted the Ethics in Government Act (Pub. Law 95-521) which, among other things, places time restrictions on departing commissioners and

designated staff personnel before they may work for a public utility. [On the FCC's implementation of the act, see *NARUC Bulletin* No. 40-1983 (October 3, 1983), pp. 15-16.] Twenty-three states have adopted some restrictions. See *1985 Annual Report on Utility and Carrier Regulation* (Washington, D.C.: National Association of Regulatory Utility Commissioners, 1987), pp. 817-20.

[12]"Those familiar enough with the industry to possess the necessary qualifications for appointment to many agencies are likely to have had some prior industry connection. Moreover, if younger employees cannot look for future employment in the regulated industry or the law firms that will serve it, will they seek jobs in regulatory agencies? Must they choose between permanent careers in government and careers totally outside it?" Breyer, *op. cit.*, p. 345.

[13]*Ibid.* See, *e.g.*, William T. Gormley, Jr., "A Test of the Revolving Door Hypothesis at the FCC," 23 *American Journal of Political Science* 665 (1979); Jeffrey E. Cohen, "The Dynamics of the 'Revolving Door' on the FCC," 30 *American Journal of Political Science* 689 (1986). See also Paul Quirk, *Industry Influence in Federal Regulatory Agencies* (Princeton: Princeton University Press, 1981), esp. pp. 62-69.

[14]William T. Gormley, Jr., *The Politics of Public Utility Regulation* (Pittsburgh: University of Pittsburgh Press, 1983), p. 31.

[15]Landis Report, *op. cit.*, p. 66. See also Cornelius J. Peck, "Regulation and Control of Ex Parte Communications with Administrative Agencies," 76 *Harvard Law Review* 233 (1962).

[16]President's Advisory Council on Executive Organization, *A New Regulatory Framework: Report on Selected Independent Regulatory Agencies* (Washington, D.C.: U.S. Government Printing Office, 1971), p. 4 (hereinafter referred to as Ash Council Report).

[17]*Study on Federal Regulation, Vol. I: The Regulatory Appointments Process* (Committee on Government Operations, Senate, 95th Cong., 1st sess.) (Washington, D.C.: U.S. Government Printing Office, 1977), p. xxxi. At the state level, Gormley has concluded: "The independence of public utility commissions is not a principle to which politicians have solemnly committed themselves, but neither is it a myth. Public utility commissions remain independent not because politicians respect their integrity but because they recognize a political liability when they see one. Public utility commissions today have little to fear from the governor or the state legislature." Gormley, *The Politics of Public Utility Regulation, op. cit.*, p. 88.

[18]Geller suggests fifteen-year, nonrenewable terms. See Henry Geller, "A Modest Proposal for Modest Reform of the Federal Communications Commission," 63 *Georgetown Law Journal* 705, 722 (1975). But Robinson is skeptical of the proposal: "I cannot think of anything worse for the regulatory process than creating a class of regulators who want to die with their regulatory boots on." Glen Robinson, "The Federal Communications Commission: An Essay on Regulatory Watchdogs," 64 *Virginia Law Review* 169, 213, n. 99 (1978). Yet, as Howard Morgan wrote to President Kennedy (in 1963), stating his unwillingness to seek another term on the FPC: "The big problem in the regulatory field is not influence peddling and corruption as that word is commonly understood. In my experience as a regulatory official I have been approached only once with a veiled intimation that money or stock was available in return for a favorable decision, and that was at the state level, not here in Washington. But abandonment of the public interest can be caused by many things, of which timidity and a desire for personal security are the most insidious. This commission, for example, must make hundreds and even thousands of decisions each year, a

good many of which involve literally scores and hundreds of millions of dollars in a single case. A commissioner can find it very easy to consider whether his vote might arouse an industry campaign against his reconfirmation by the Senate." Quoted in Louis M. Kohlmeier, Jr., *The Regulators* (New York: Harper & Row, Publishers, 1969), p. 82.

[19]See, *e.g.*, *Quality of Regulators* (Hearings before the Subcommittee on Oversight and Investigation of the Committee on Interstate and Foreign Commerce, House, 94th Cong., 1st sess.) (Washington, D.C.: U.S. Government Printing Office, 1975).

Breyer questions the value of such proposals. To illustrate: ". . . as long as the President appoints and the Senate confirms, the appointment process will remain political. If the politics of the day favor the appointment of an experienced person of great integrity, that is likely to be done, in the presence or in the absence of advisory commissions, standards, and 'close looks.' If not, it is unlikely that standards and so forth will make much difference. Indeed, the extent to which politicians heed the advice of advisory committees or of various members itself depends upon political factors. And advisory committees, too, can develop politics of their own. It is difficult to find examples of advisory committees or standards improving a basically political selection process." Further, "developing a meaningful set of standards is close to impossible. Those suggested tend to be embarrassingly general, such as the suggestion by the Governmental Affairs Committee that 'by reason of background, training, or experience, the nominee' be 'affirmatively qualified for the office to which he or she is nominated.' . . ." Breyer, *op. cit.*, p. 343.

[20]Gormley, *The Politics of Public Utility Regulation, op. cit.*, p. 210. Declassification "also encourages administrative efficiency by expediting hiring and firing decisions." *Ibid.*

[21]Marver H. Bernstein, *Regulating Business by Independent Commission* (Princeton: Princeton University Press, 1955), p. 101.

[22]59 *A.B.A. Rep.* 539-64 (1934); 81 *A.B.A. Rep.* 491-535 (1956); President's Committee on Administrative Management (Brownlow Committee), *Report with Special Studies* (Washington, D.C.: U.S. Government Printing Office 1937); Commission on Organization of the Executive Branch of the Government (Hoover Commission), *Task Force Report on Legal Services and Procedure* (Washington, D.C.: U.S. Government Printing Office, 1955), pp. 84-88; Ash Council Report, *op. cit.* For a summary, see Robert S. Lorch, "The Federal Administrative Court Idea," 52 *A.B.A. Journal* 635 (1966).

The Mann-Elkins Act of 1910 provided for a Commerce Court to expedite judicial review and enforcement of ICC orders. The court was to be composed of five judges from the federal circuit courts, appointed by the President, for five-year terms. The court was impractical and was abandoned in 1913. See S. O. Dunn, "The Commerce Court Question," 3 *American Economic Review* 20 (1913); I. Leo Sharfman, *The Interstate Commerce Commission* (New York: Commonwealth Fund, 1935), Vol. I, pp. 52-70. Several proposals have been made for a specialized court or technical committee to review environmental controversies. See, *e.g.*, Comment, "Attorney General's Report Rejects Establishing an Environmental Court," 4 *Environmental Law Reporter* 10019 (1974); Joel Yellin, "High Technology and the Courts: Nuclear Power and the Need for Institutional Reform," 94 *Harvard Law Review* 489 (1981).

Several alternatives to the creation of an administrative court have been made, including (*a*) the creation of a board of experts in technical disciplines to act as advisors to agencies and judges [see, *e.g.*, Bruce A. Ackerman et al., *The Uncertain Search for Environmental Quality* (New York: The Free Press, 1974), pp. 147-61; A.

Kantrowitz, "Controlling Technology Democratically," 63 *American Scientist* 505 (1975); but see Earl Callen, "The Science Court" (Letter), 193 *Science* 950 (1976)]; (*b*) the creation of an ombudsman to examine commission procedures and practices, and to investigate citizen complaints [see, *e.g.,* Walter Gellhorn, *Ombudsmen and Others: Citizens' Protectors in Nine Countries* (Cambridge: Harvard University Press, 1966); Bernard Frank, "State Ombudsman Legislation in the United States," 29 *University of Miami Law Review* 397 (1975); Larry Hill, *The Model Ombudsman* (Princeton: Princeton University Press, 1976]; and (*c*) the creation of a Consumer Protection Agency to advocate the consumer's position before both regulatory commissions and legislative bodies [see *e.g., Report on the Consumer Protection Organization Act* (Senate Rep. No. 92-1100, 92d Cong., 2d sess.) (Washington, D.C.: U.S. Government Printing Office, 1972)].

[23]Louis J. Hector, "Problems of the CAB and the Independent Regulatory Commissions," 69 *Yale Law Journal* 931, 960-64 (1960); Letter from Newton N. Minow to the President, May 31, 1963 (mimeographed). See also Bernard Schwartz, "Administrative Justice and Its Place in the Legal Order," 30 *New York University Law Review* 1390 (1955).

[24]Anthony F. Apraia, "The Brass Tacks of the ICC Administrative Problem," 65 *Public Utilities Fortnightly* 443, 439-40 (1960). The Hoover Commissions (1949 and 1955), Landis (1960), and the Ash Council (1971) recommended that federal regulatory agencies be directed by a single administrative head responsible to the President. Concluded the first Hoover Commission, for example: chairmen are "too frequently merely presiding officers at commission meetings. No one has been responsible for planning and guiding the general program of commission activity." See Commission on Organization of the Executive Branch of the Government, *The Independent Regulatory Commissions: A Report with Recommendations* (Washington, D.C.: U.S. Government Printing Office, 1949) and *Task Force Report on Legal Services and Procedure, op. cit.; Landis Report, op. cit.;* Ash Council Report, *op. cit.* Breyer, however, asks: "Why should a single head improve the quality of a multi-member agency's performance? Critics of the Federal Trade Commission's performance during the 1960s felt that its current chairman had too much power, not too little. They argued that his policies and programs served to hinder rather than further competition throughout the economy. They urged that the other members of the FTC be given more power, not less. Two subsequent chairmen of the Federal Trade Commission reformed it despite their membership in a collegial body where the chairman did not possess full powers. Similarly, Alfred Kahn reformed the Civil Aeronautics Board without total power; he was chairman of a collegial body with five members." Breyer, *op. cit.,* p. 355 (footnotes omitted).

[25]Louis L. Jaffe, Book Review, "The Independent Agency — A New Scapegoat," 65 *Yale Law Journal* 1068, 1074 (1956). See also, by the same author, "The Illusion of the Ideal Administration," 86 *Harvard Law Review* 1183 (1973).

[26]Alan S. Boyd, "The Scope and Philosophy of Regulatory Commissions," 65 *Public Utilities Fortnightly* 909, 911 (1960).

[27]Henry J. Friendly, "A Look at the Federal Administrative Agencies," 60 *Columbia Law Review* 429, 441-42 (1960). A former chairman of the Securities and Exchange Commission concludes: "To divorce the adjudicatory from the rule making and administrative functions would fragment the regulatory responsibility and deprive both the adjudicators and the rule makers of the valuable feedback between the two regulatory processes." William L. Cary, *Politics and the Regulatory Agencies*

(New York: McGraw-Hill Book Co., 1967), pp. 133-34. See also the testimony of Robert W. Ginnane, *Administrative Process and Ethical Questions* (Hearings before the Special Subcommittee on Legislative Oversight of the Committee on Interstate and Foreign Commerce, House, 85th Cong., 2d sess.) (Washington, D.C.: U.S. Government Printing Office, 1958), pp. 3-7; Carl A. Auerbach, "Should Administrative Agencies Perform Adjudicatory Functions?," *1959 Wisconsin Law Review* 95 and "Some Thoughts on the Hector Memorandum," *1960 Wisconsin Law Review* 183; Earl W. Kintner, "The Current Ordeal of the Administrative Process: In Reply to Mr. Hector," 69 *Yale Law Journal* 965 (1960); William L. Cary, "Why I Oppose the Divorce of the Judicial Function from Federal Regulatory Agencies," 51 *A.B.A. Journal* 33 (1965); Philip Elman, "A Note on Administrative Adjudication," 74 *Yale Law Journal* 652 (1965).

[28]Attorney General's Committee on Administrative Procedure, *Final Report* (Senate Doc. No. 8, 77th Cong., 1st sess.) (Washington, D.C.: U.S. Government Printing Office, 1941). For a reproduction of the major portions of the Report, see *Administrative Procedure in Government Agencies* (Charlottesville, Va.: The University Press of Virginia, 1968).

[29]60 Stat. 237 (1946) (currently 5 U.S.C. Sections 551-706).

[30]Woll has noted that the independence of administrative law judges "is an important achievement. The separation of functions must be based upon an independent class of hearing officers; once such independence has been destroyed, the prosecuting arm of the agency can easily influence adjudicative decisions." Peter Woll, *Administrative Law: The Informal Process* (Berkeley and Los Angeles: University of California Press, 1963), p. 21.

[31]Landis Report, *op. cit.,* pp. 82-87.

[32]*Ibid.,* p. 82.

[33]There is "an almost complete barrenness" of policy formulation among these various groups. "The few interagency committees that have been set up have accomplished too little in conducting their separate approaches to a common problem." *Ibid.,* p. 24.

[34]67 *Public Utilities Fortnightly* 461 (1961). On Congressional oversight, see, *e.g.,* A. Ribicoff, "Congressional Oversight and Regulatory Reform," 28 *Administrative Law Review* 415 (1976); *Study on Federal Regulation,* Vol. II: *Congressional Oversight of Regulatory Agencies* (Committee on Government Operations, Senate, 95th Cong., 1st sess.) (Washington, D.C.: U.S. Government Printing Office, 1977); Breyer and Stewart, *op. cit.,* pp. 144-49; Barry R. Weingast and Mark J. Moran, "The Myth of Runaway Bureaucracy: The Case of the FTC," 6 *Regulation* 33 (May/June, 1982); Michael D. Reagan, *Regulation: The Politics of Policy* (Boston: Little, Brown & Co., 1987), esp. chap. 7.

[35]Francis X. Welch, "The Effectiveness of Commission Regulation of Public Utility Enterprise," 49 *Georgetown Law Journal* 639, 669 (1961).

[36]Or worse: "The principal disadvantage of the proposal is its inherent potential for disaster. An administration elected on issues that are unrelated to regulation not only could promulgate regulatory policies that were uniformly disastrous, but could also coordinate its disastrous policies effectively." Roger G. Noll, *Reforming Regulation* (Washington, D.C.: The Brookings Institution, 1971), p. 90.

[37]See, *e.g.,* R. W. Lishman, "'Independence' in the Independent Regulatory Agencies," 13 *Administrative Law Review* 133 (1960); Cary, *Politics and the Regulatory Agencies, op. cit.,* pp. 20-23.

[38]"The authority of the President to control and supervise executive policymaking is derived from the Constitution; the desirability of such control is demonstrable from the practical realities of administrative rulemaking. Regulations such as those involved here demand a careful weighing of cost, environmental, and energy considerations. They also have broad implications for national economic policy. Our form of government simply could not function effectively or rationally if key executive policymakers were isolated from each other and from the Chief Executive. Single mission agencies do not always have the answers to complex regulatory problems. An overworked administrator exposed on a 24-hour basis to a dedicated but zealous staff needs to know the arguments and ideas of policymakers in other agencies as well as in the White House." *Sierra Club v. Costle,* 657 F. 2d 298, 406 (D.C. Cir. 1981).

[39]Prior to the establishment of the Department of Transportation, numerous proposals had been made to deal with the lack of coordination. See, *e.g.,* Report to the President from the Secretary of Commerce, *Unified and Coordinated Federal Program for Transportation* (Sawyer Report) (Washington, D.C.: U.S. Government Printing Office, 1949); Commission on the Organization of the Executive Branch of the Government, *Task Force Report on Regulatory Commissions* (Washington, D.C.: U.S. Government Printing Office, 1949), Appendix N, chap. iv; *National Transportation Policy, op. cit.,* pp. 107-15; D. I. Mackie, "The Necessity for a Federal Department of Transportation," 8 *Journal of Public Law* 1 (1959).

[40]See Chapter 13, p. 603. See also *Study on Federal Regulation,* Vol. V: *Regulatory Organization and Coordination* (Committee on Government Operations, Senate, 95th Cong., 1st sess.) (Washington, D.C.: U.S. Government Printing Office, 1977); Alfred C. Aman, Jr., "Institutionalizing the Energy Crisis: Some Structural and Procedural Lessons," 65 *Cornell Law Review* 491 (1980).

[41]Pub. Law 89-80 (1965). See Federal Power Commission, *Annual Report* (1967), pp. 33-34.

[42]The Carter Administration (Executive Order 12044, March, 1978) utilized the Regulatory Analysis Review Group — an interagency group chaired by the chairman of the Council of Economic Advisers, staffed by technicians from the Council on Wage and Price Stability, and administered by the Office of Management and Budget. See, *e.g.,* Susan J. Tolchin, "Presidential Power and the Politics of RARG," 3 *Regulation* 44 (July/August, 1979); Christopher C. DeMuth, "Constraining Regulatory Costs — Part I: The White House Review Programs," 4 *Regulation* 13 (January/ February, 1980). ["In late 1978, the heads of 35 regulatory agencies countered by forming the Regulatory Council, which proceeded to commission studies to produce better methods of demonstrating regulatory benefits." Eugene Bardach and Robert A. Kagan, *Going by the Book: The Problem of Regulatory Unreasonableness* (Philadelphia: Temple University Press, 1982, p. 308.] The Reagan Administration (Executive Order 12291, February, 1981) transferred regulatory oversight responsibilities to the Office of Information and Regulatory Affairs within the Office of Management and Budget. See, *e.g.,* George C. Eads, "Harnessing Regulation: The Evolving Role of White House Oversight," 5 *Regulation* 19 (May/June, 1981) and "White House Oversight of Executive Regulation," in Eugene Bardach and Robert A. Kagan (eds.), *Social Regulation: Strategies for Reform* (San Francisco: Institute for Contemporary Studies, 1982), chap. 8; George C. Eads and Michael Fix (eds.), *The Reagan Regulatory Strategy* (Washington, D.C.: Urban Institute Press, 1984); Reagan, *op. cit.* See also Paul R. Verkuil, "Jawboning Administrative Agencies: Ex Parte Contacts by the White House," 80 *Columbia Law Review* 943 (1980); Howard Ball, *Controlling Regulatory Sprawl: Presi-*

dential Strategies from Nixon to Reagan (Westport, Conn.: Greenwood Press, 1984); Marshall B. Goodman and Margaret T. Wrightson, *Managing Regulatory Reform: The Reagan Strategy and Its Impact* (New York: Praeger Publishers, 1987).

"In 1979 the administration began to issue a semiannual regulatory calendar (published in November and May each year), listing federal regulatory activities that have economic impacts estimated to exceed $100 million a year. Independent agencies, such as executive branch agencies and other regulatory commissions, are not required to submit data concerning their projects, however." Kenneth W. Clarkson and Roger LeRoy Miller, *Industrial Organization: Theory, Evidence, and Public Policy* (New York: McGraw-Hill Book Co., 1982), p. 488 (footnote omitted).

[43]Landis Report, *op. cit.*, pp. 74-81. Cary has argued that the proposal "has much to be said for it in theory," but seems "unduly optimistic" since it "would accentuate existing political antagonisms." Cary, *Politics and the Regulatory Agencies, op. cit.*, p. 34. Noll believes that "the incremental danger of the czar proposal over the Ash proposal does not seem great: once the regulatory agencies crawl inside the executive branch, the danger of destructive presidential leadership will have been accepted. The issue here is only a slightly altered version of the traditional debate over independence versus political control." Noll, *op. cit.*, pp. 90-91.

[44]William H. Tucker, "Government Organization and Federal Transportation Regulation" (speech before the Board of Directors of the American Trucking Associations, Chicago, October 19, 1967) (mimeographed). Former FCC Commissioner Bartley suggested the abolition of that agency, and the establishment of two new independent agencies (one to regulate broadcasting and the other for common carrier regulation) and a new authority for frequency allocations. Robert T. Bartley, "Let's Abolish the F.C.C." (address before the Illinois Broadcasters Association, Quincy, May 23, 1968) (mimeographed). See *The Wall Street Journal*, May 24, 1968, p. 12.

[45]Emmette S. Redford, "The President and the Regulatory Commissions" (prepared for the President's Advisory Committee on Government Organization, mimeographed, 1960). For a revised version, see Emmette S. Redford, "The President and the Regulatory Commissions," 44 *Texas Law Review* 288 (1965).

[46]Lloyd Cutler and David Johnson, "Regulation and the Political Process," 84 *Yale Law Journal* 1395 (1975). In the authors' view: "Regulatory 'failure' . . . occurs when an agency has not done what elected officials would have done had they exercised the power conferred on them by virtue of their ultimate political responsibility. Agencies would be said to fail when they reach substantive policy decisions (including decisions not to act) that do not coincide with what the politically accountable branches of government would have done if they had possessed the time, the information, and the will to make such decisions." *Ibid.*, p. 1399.

[47]Breyer, *op. cit.*, p. 359 (citation omitted). The proposal was endorsed by the American Bar Association's Commission on Law and the Economy, *Federal Regulation: Roads to Reform* (Chicago, 1979).

[48]Breyer, *op. cit.*, pp. 359-60. See, *e.g.*, Clark Byse, "Comments on a Structural Reform Proposal: Presidential Directives to Independent Agencies," 29 *Administrative Law Review* 157 (1977).

The Supreme Court, in a 1983 decision, held that a one-house veto was unconstitutional: *Immigration and Naturalization Service v. Chadha*, 103 S. Ct. 2764 (1983). See, *e.g.*, Harold H. Bruff and Ernest Gellhorn, "Congressional Control of Administrative Regulation: A Study of Legislative Vetoes," 90 *Harvard Law Review* 1369 (1977).

As an alternative, some have recommended increased supervisory powers to the courts. But see, *e.g.*, Breyer, *op. cit.*, pp. 360-61; R. Shep Melnick, *Regulation and the Courts: The Case of the Clean Air Act* (Washington, D. C.: The Brookings Institution, 1983).

[49]See Chapter 5, pp. 175-78.

[50]Breyer, *op. cit.*, p. 351.

[51]*Ibid.* (footnotes omitted). "Under our system of government, the very legitimacy of general policymaking performed by unelected administrators depends in no small part upon the openness, accessibility, and amenability of these officials to the needs and ideas of the public from whom their ultimate authority derives, and upon whom their commands must fall." *Sierra Club v. Costle, op. cit.*, pp. 400-01.

See, *e.g.*, J. Freedman, "Crisis and Legitimacy in the Administrative Process," 27 *Stanford Law Review* 1041 (1975); R. B. Stewart, "The Reformation of American Administrative Law," 88 *Harvard Law Review* 1667 (1975); Breyer and Stewart, *op. cit.*, chap. 10. Greater access to federal agency information was provided by the Freedom of Information Act, 5 U.S.C. Section 552 (1966); public decisions were required by the Government in the Sunshine Act, 5 U.S.C. Section 552b (1976). On the former, see, *e.g.*, Note, "The Freedom of Information Act: A Seven-Year Assessment," 74 *Columbia Law Review* 895 (1974); on the latter, see, *e.g.*, Note, "Government in the Sunshine Act: Opening Federal Agency Meetings," 26 *American University Law Review* 154 (1976). Most states have similar statutes.

[52]See, *e.g.*, Roger C. Cramton, "The Why, Where, and How of Broadened Public Participation in the Administrative Process," 60 *Georgetown Law Journal* 525 (1972); Robert L. Rabin, "Lawyers for Social Change: Perspectives on Public Interest Law," 28 *Stanford Law Review* 207 (1976); *Study on Federal Regulation*, Vol. III: *Public Participation in Regulatory Agency Proceedings* (Committee on Governmental Affairs, Senate, 95th Cong., 1st sess.) (Washington, D.C.: U.S. Government Printing Office, 1977); Burton A. Weisbrod, *Public Interest Law: An Economic and Institutional Analysis* (Berkeley: University of California Press, 1978).

The expansion of rights to participation and review to public interest groups, "to a considerable degree, has transformed the traditional model of administrative law (the basic purpose of which was to limit the coercive power of government officials) into an interest representation model of administrative law (the basic purpose of which is to ensure the equitable exercise of discretionary policy-making power by administrators)." Breyer and Stewart, *op. cit.*, p. 1014 (with a citation to Stewart, *op. cit.*). See, *e.g.*, Paul A. Sabatier, "Social Movements and Regulatory Agencies: Toward a More Adequate — and Less Pessimistic — Theory of 'Clientele Capture'," 6 *Policy Sciences* 301 (1975).

[53]Breyer, *op. cit.*, p. 352.

[54]*Ibid.*, p. 354. Judge Breyer considers other issues, such as the lack of adequate funding and the difficulty confronted by public interest representatives to compromise because of their inability to secure their clients' consent. *Ibid.*, pp. 352-53. Various steps have been taken to overcome these problems. See, *e.g.*, "Reimbursing Intervenors for Attorney's Fees," 105 *Public Utilities Fortnightly* 42 (February 28, 1980); William T. Gormley, Jr., "Statewide Remedies for Public Underrepresentation in Regulatory Proceedings," 41 *Public Administration Review* 454 (1981). To illustrate. (*1*) With respect to funding, the Michigan legislature, late in 1982, created a Utility Consumer Representation Fund, administered by a five-member Utility Consumer Protection Board. "One-half of the money is allocated automatically to the attorney general; the

remainder is distributed on a competitive basis to nonprofit organizations and local governments that promote the interests of residential consumers." The fund is financed by the state's electric and gas utilities and, ultimately, by ratepayers. Gormley, *The Politics of Public Utility Regulation, op. cit.,* p. 188. (2) With respect to accountability, the Wisconsin legislature, in 1979, created a nonprofit Citizens Utilities Board (CUB), whose members are those citizens who contribute $3 or more to the organization. "CUB is headed by a board of directors, elected by members in each congressional district. . . . At the present time, CUB has a membership of 55,000 and an annual budget of $300,000." *Ibid.,* p. 186 (footnote omitted).

[55]Philip J. Harter, "Negotiating Regulations: A Cure for Malaise," 71 *Georgetown Law Journal* 1 (1982).

[56]Henry J. Friendly, *The Federal Administrative Agencies: The Need for Better Definition of Standards* (Cambridge: Harvard University Press, 1962), pp. 5-6. See also Theodore Lowi, *The End of Liberalism: Ideology, Policy, and the Crisis of Public Authority* (2d ed.; New York: W. W. Norton & Co., 1979).

[57]Friendly, *The Federal Administrative Agencies, op. cit.,* p. 6. See also Harry M. Trebing, "A Critique of the Planning Function in Regulation," 79 *Public Utilities Fortnightly* 21 (March 16, 1967) and "Toward Improved Regulatory Planning," 79 *Public Utilities Fortnightly* 15 (March 30, 1967).

The issue, it should be noted, is not the lack of standards; it is the existence of too many standards. "The effect of many standards, however, is virtually the same as having none at all. There is no clear indication of which standards are more important, how they are to be individually applied, or how varying degrees of conformity are to be balanced. The existence of so many standards effectively allows the agency near-total discretion in making a decision." Breyer, *op. cit.,* p. 79.

[58]*Independent Regulatory Commissions* (Staff Report to the Special Subcommittee on Legislative Oversight of the Committee on Interstate and Foreign Commerce, House) (Washington, D.C.: U.S. Government Printing Office, 1960), p. 6.

[59]Kenneth C. Davis, *Administrative Law Treatise* (St. Paul: West Publishing Co., 1958), Vol. 1, p. 82 (citation omitted).

[60]Friendly, *The Federal Administrative Agencies, op. cit.,* p. 14.

[61]Marvin L. Fair, "Some Observations on the Theory and Performance of the Independent Regulatory Agencies in Regulating the Public Utility Industries," 27 *I.C.C. Practitioners' Journal* 957, 967 (1960).

[62]Eugene V. Rostow, *Planning for Freedom* (New Haven: Yale University Press, 1959), pp. 311-12.

[63]Friendly, *The Federal Administrative Agencies, op. cit.,* p. 140.

[64]C. H. Fulda, *Competition in the Regulated Industries: Transportation* (Boston: Little, Brown & Co., 1961), p. 370. See also David Boies, Jr., "Experiment in Mercantilism: Minimum Rate Regulation by the Interstate Commerce Commission," 68 *Columbia Law Review* 599 (1968).

[65]Ernest W. Williams, Jr., *The Regulation of Rail-Motor Rate Competition* (New York: Harper & Bros., 1958), pp. 208-09. The Doyle Report argued that "the Commission in its written decisions and its statements to congressional committees provides the best documentation of the thesis that the meaning of minimum rate policy is less certain and its application more confusing than before the addition" of the 1958 amendment. *National Transportation Policy* (Preliminary Draft of a Report Prepared for the Committee on Interstate and Foreign Commerce by the Special Study Group on

Transportation Policies in the United States, Senate, 87th Cong., 1st sess.) (Washington, D.C.: U.S. Government Printing Office, 1961), p. 405.

[66]Friendly, *The Federal Administrative Agencies, op. cit.,* pp. 103-04, 105. See also Howard C. Westwood, "Choice of the Air Carrier for New Air Transport Routes," Part I: 16 *George Washington Law Review* 1 (1947), Part II: 16 *George Washington Law Review* 159 (1948); *Civil Aeronautics Board Practices and Procedures* (Report of the Subcommittee on Administrative Practice and Procedure, Senate, 94th Cong., 1st sess.) (Washington, D.C.: U.S. Government Printing Office, 1975).

There are many other examples, particularly in the FCC's awarding of broadcast licenses. See, *e.g.,* Robert Anthony, "Towards Simplicity and Rationality in Comparative Broadcast Licensing Proceedings," 24 *Stanford Law Review* 1 (1971); R. G. Noll, M. J. Peck, and J. J. McGowan, *Economics Aspects of Television Regulation* (Washington, D.C.: The Brookings Institution, 1973).

Former FCC Commissioner Hyde has defended indefinite standards, arguing that the adoption of more definite standards "would press applicants into a mold, . . . thus deterring perhaps better qualified applicants from applying; it would preclude significant consideration of material differences among applicants and result in automatic preferences of applicants slavishly conforming to the model and eventually for the Commission to decide cases on trivial differences among applicants." Dissenting statement in *1965 Policy Statement,* 1 FCC 2d 400.

[67]See *Report of the Attorney General's National Committee to Study the Antitrust Laws* (Washington, D.C.: U.S. Government Printing Office, 1955), pp. 261-93.

[68]The Interstate Commerce Act, for example, provides that "any carriers . . . participating in a transaction approved or authorized . . . are relieved from the operation of the antitrust laws. . . ." 49 U.S.C. Section 5 (11) (1952). Similar relief is granted for ratemaking agreements. 49 U.S.C. Section 5b (9) (1952). In such circumstances, the Department of Justice may intervene in a case before the commission.

[69]See, *e.g.,* Federal Communications Act, 47 U.S.C. Sections 221a, 222(c)(1) (1952).

[70]Argued Justice Harlan in a 1964 concurring opinion: This case "affords another example of the unsatisfactoriness of the existing bifurcated system of antitrust and other regulation in various fields. . . . It would be unrealistic not to recognize that this state of affairs has the effect of placing the Department of Justice in the driver's seat even though Congress has lodged primary regulatory authority elsewhere. It does seem to me that the time has come when this duplicative and, I venture to say, anachronistic system of dual regulation should be reexamined. . . ." *United States v. El Paso Nat. Gas Co.,* 376 U.S. 651, 663-64 (1964).

See, *e.g.,* Irwin Stelzer, "Antitrust and Regulatory Policies: An Introduction and Overview," 16 *The Antitrust Bulletin* 669 (1971); Phillip E. Areeda, "Antitrust Laws and Public Utility Regulation," 3 *Bell Journal of Economics and Management Science* 42 (1972); Note, "Applicability of the Federal Antitrust Laws to State-Regulated Activities," 18 *Boston College Industrial and Commercial Law Review* 370 (1977); E. E. Bailey, "Contestability and the Design of Regulatory and Antitrust Policy," 71 *American Economic Review* 178 (1981); Comment, "Vanishing Immunity: The Antitrust Assault on Regulated Industries," 27 *Loyola Law Review* 187 (1981); Franklin M. Fisher (ed.), *Antitrust and Regulation* (Cambridge: The MIT Press, 1985); David C. Hjelmfelt, *Antitrust and Regulated Industries* (New York: Wiley Law Publications, 1986). For cases dealing with the interaction of antitrust and regulatory standards, see Thomas D. Morgan et al., *The Economic Regulation of Business: Cases and Materials* (2d ed.; St. Paul:

West Publishing Co., 1985). See also "Special Issue on Antitrust Implications of Deregulation," 28 *The Antitrust Bulletin* 1 (1983).

[71]Friendly, *The Federal Administrative Agencies, op. cit.*, p. 18.

[72]Marvin H. Bernstein, "The Regulatory Process: A Framework for Analysis," 26 *Law and Contemporary Problems* 329, 332 (1961).

[73]Dissenting opinion, *Chicago & Eastern Illinois R. Co. v. United States*, 375 U.S. 150, 154 (1963).

[74]Landis Report, *op. cit.*, p. 39. As former FCC Chairman Henry said: ". . . many of our hearing records and many of our decisions contain some of the world's greatest collection of useless information." Quoted in *The Wall Street Journal*, January 21, 1966, p. 1.

[75]*Regulatory Reform* (Hearings before the Committee on the Judiciary, Senate, 96th Cong., 1st sess.) (Washington, D.C.: U.S. Government Printing Office, 1979), Pt. 1, p. 61.

[76]*Independent Regulatory Commissions* (Report of the Special Subcommittee on Legislative Oversight of the Committee on Interstate and Foreign Commerce, House Report No. 2711) (Washington, D.C.: U.S. Government Printing Office, 1959), p. 41. Bardach and Kagan agree: "If it were possible for outsiders to pin the blame for sloppy analytical work — or to give credit for good analytical work — on the responsible *individuals*, sloppiness might be somewhat discouraged, as might be the disposition to err in the direction favored by one's immediate boss or peer group. This adjustment in the way government agencies go about their work might not dramatically improve regulation, but it would probably not hurt and, in any case, might be endorsed on the more general grounds of reducing anomie in the bureaucracy." Bardach and Kagan, *Going by the Book, op. cit.*, p. 311.

[77]Boyd, *op. cit.*, p. 911.

[78]*Study on Federal Regulation*, Vol. IV: *Delay in the Regulatory Process* (Committee on Governmental Affairs, Senate, 95th Cong., 1st sess.) (Washington, D.C.: U.S. Government Printing Office, 1977), p. 7. For earlier studies of regulatory delay, see *Statistical Data Related to Administrative Proceedings Conducted by Federal Agencies — Fiscal 1963* (Committee Print, Committee on the Judiciary, Senate, 88th Cong., 2d sess.) (Washington, D.C.: U.S. Government Printing Office, 1964); *Questionnaire Survey on Delay in Administrative Proceedings* (Committee Print, Prepared for the Committee on the Judiciary by its Subcommittee on Administrative Practice and Procedure, Senate, 89th Cong., 2d sess.) (Washington, D.C.: U.S. Government Printing Office, 1966); *Evaluation Charts on Delay in Administrative Proceedings* (Committee Print, Prepared for the Committee on the Judiciary by its Subcommittee on Administrative Practice and Procedure, 89th Cong., 2d sess.) (Washington, D.C.: U.S. Government Printing Office, 1966); *Federal Regulation and Regulatory Reform* (Subcommittee on Oversight and Investigations of the Committee on Interstate and Foreign Commerce, House, 94th Cong., 2d sess.) (Washington, D.C.: U.S. Government Printing Office, 1976), esp. pp. 581-85.

[79]See, *e.g.*, Paul W. MacAvoy and James Sloss, *Regulation of Transport Innovation: The ICC and Unit Coal Trains to the East Coast* (New York: Random House, 1967).

[80]*Public Regulation of Utility Enterprises* (New York: New York Chamber of Commerce, 1960), p. 21. See, *e.g.*, Robert W. Gerwig, "Natural Gas Production: A Study of Costs of Regulation," 5 *Journal of Law and Economics* 69 (1962); Arthur Andersen & Co., *Cost of Government Regulation Study: Executive Summary* (New York: The Business Roundtable, 1979).

[81]Bruce M. Owen and Ronald Braeutigam, *The Regulation Game: Strategic Use of the Administrative Process* (Cambridge: Ballinger Publishing Co., 1978), p. 23.

[82]See Chapter 4, pp. 133, 136.

[83]Landis Report, *op. cit.*, pp. 6-7. As former Commissioner Bartley noted, after explaining the rapidly expanding responsibilities of the FCC: "But the FCC's manpower, as authorized by Congress, instead of keeping pace with the expansion — steadily decreased until 1955, and did not even reach the 1947 level again until 1963. And, in 1967, we had only 71 more employees than in 1947. And many of these were consumed by new management procedures and techniques imposed upon the Commission." Bartley, *op. cit.*, p. 4.

[84]"Comprehensive statutory revision should have been effected long ago and should certainly not be postponed any longer. *Every* state system of regulation is outdated. It is too indefinite as to objectives, standards, and procedures. It is not well-suited either for the conservation and promotion of the public interest in the great public services entrusted to private organization, or for clear and consistent protection of the private interests. For the purpose of statutory revision, every state should conduct a comprehensive inquiry as to conditions and needs." John Bauer, *Updating Public Utility Regulation* (Chicago: Public Administration Service, 1966), p. 181.

[85]Boyd, *op. cit.*, p. 912.

[86]Landis Report, *op. cit.*, p. 16. In more recent years, as Stewart has argued, consumer groups (in particular) have insisted on formal administrative procedures. "Unorganized interests may remain at a considerable disadvantage in the formal process of agency decision-making because their comparative lack of cohesion and financial resources prevents them from having as effective representation as organized concerns. It may therefore be to the advantage of unorganized interests to force administrative decision-making into the formal mode, even if their chances of ultimately prevailing are slim. The delay costs that can be imposed on opponents by resort to formal proceedings present tactical advantages that lawyers are unlikely to forego." Stewart, *op. cit.*, p. 1771.

[87]*Independent Regulatory Commissions*, Staff Report, *op. cit.*, p. 7. See, *e.g.*, Robert E. Burns, *Administrative Procedures for Proactive Regulation* (Columbus, Ohio: National Regulatory Research Institute, 1988).

[88]Woll, *op. cit.*, p. 177.

[89]Davis, for example, has referred to informal rule making as "one of the greatest inventions of modern government." [Kenneth C. Davis, letter in *Reform of Federal Regulation* (Joint Report of the Committee on Governmental Affairs and the Committee on the Judiciary, Senate Rep. 96-1018, 96th Cong., 2d sess.) (Washington, D.C.: U.S. Government Printing Office, 1980), Pt. 2, p. 51.] Critics tend to view informal procedures as an unfair denial of due process and as providing little or no check upon a commission's freedom to act. And the courts have tended, in recent years, to require administrative agencies to conduct informal rule making proceedings "with greater formality, giving all parties greater opportunity to examine the evidence upon which the agency bases its decision." [Breyer, *op. cit.*, p. 346 (footnote omitted).] See, *e.g.*, *Mobil Oil Corp. v. Federal Power Comm.*, 483 F. 2d 1238 (D.C. Cir. 1973); *Home Box Office, Inc. v. Federal Communications Comm.* 567 F. 2d 9 (D.C. Cir. 1977), *cert. denied*, 434 U.S. 829 (1977). But see *Vermont Yankee Nuclear Power Corp. v. Natural Resources Defense Council, Inc.*, 435 U.S. 519 (1978).

[90]*Public Regulation of Utility Enterprises*, *op. cit.*, pp. 23-24. As Welch has observed:

"The coal industry and affiliated mining labor interests have almost automatically intervened in every major pipeline certificate case before the FPC for the obvious reason that granting such certificates to build pipelines would mean delivery of gas to markets previously enjoyed by coal or other fuels." Welch, "The Effectiveness of Commission Regulation . . .," *op. cit.*, p. 663, n. 63. For a discussion of the procedures adopted to expedite the telephone investigation initiated in the mid-1960s, see Charles F. Phillips, Jr., "Interveners in the Telephone Investigation," 78 *Public Utilities Fortnightly* 26, 34-36 (December 22, 1966). See also William H. Tucker, "Renovating the Decisional Process in an Independent Regulatory Commission," 35 *I.C.C. Practitioners' Journal* 207 (1968).

[91]Welch, "The Effectiveness of Commission Regulation . . . ," *op. cit.*, pp. 665-66. See, *e.g.*, E. Barrett Prettyman, "The President's Conference on Administrative Procedure," 55 *Public Utilities Fortnightly* 61, 67 (1955); *Selected Reports of the Administrative Conference of the United States* (Senate Doc. No. 24) (Washington, D.C.: U.S. Government Printing Office, 1963), esp. pp. 69-114; "ICC Members Blame Some Regulatory Lag on Examiners, Parties, and Budget Limits," *Traffic World*, December 24, 1966, pp. 5-6; Arthur A. Gladstone, "The Role of the Hearing Examiner," 83 *Public Utilities Fortnightly* 22 (January 16, 1969). After years of study, one of the major recommendations of the Senate Governmental Affairs Committee was to revamp the selection process for administrative law judges. See *Study on Federal Regulation*, Vol. IV: *Delay in the Regulatory Process, op. cit.*, pp. 105-12.

[92]The chairman, appointed by the President with the advice and consent of the Senate for a five-year term, is the only paid full-time member of the conference. The members represent practitioners, academics, and representatives of federal agencies.

[93]See Jerre S. Williams, "Problems Confronting the Administrative Conference," 82 *Public Utilities Fortnightly* 86 (September 12, 1968).

[94]Clair Wilcox, *Public Policies Toward Business* (3d ed.: Homewood, Ill.: Richard D. Irwin, Inc., 1966), pp. 476-77. See also, *e.g.*, Ben W. Lewis, "Ambivalence in Public Policy toward Regulated Industries," 53 *American Economic Review* 38, 44-45 (1963); Roger C. Cramton, "The Effectiveness of Economic Regulation: A Legal View," 54 *American Economic Review* 182 (1964).

[95]"The myriad criticisms from different perspectives suggest the complexity of the issues, but do not support a presumption that the public interest is always best served by free competition. Study of relative advantages and disadvantages should not assume the existence of either perfect regulation or perfect competition. Unfettered competition, like ineffectual regulation, may yield results incompatible with economic efficiency or other public policy objectives. Rational analysis requires comparisons between regulation as it is actually practiced and the imperfect performance of competitive markets. An inappropriate regulatory structure, uninformed or incompetent personnel, inadequate staff resources, and procedural rigidities may contribute to ineffectual performance, but the primary causes of failure are substantive and related to limitations inherent in the political process." J. Rhoads Foster, "Commentary on Boundaries Between Competition and Economic Regulation," in J. Rhoads Foster et al. (eds.), *Airline Deregulation: Lessons for Public Policy Formation* (Washington, D.C.: Institute for Study of Regulation, 1983), p. 22.

[96]Argues Kahn: "[I]t is forces almost totally outside the control of utility companies and regulators, preponderantly, that determine how well these industries perform. The happy record of the 1950s and 1960s, it has become abundantly clear, was the product primarily of exogenous factors. The most important of these were very

modest rates of inflation in the economy at large, correspondingly low interest rates, rapid technological progress — in electricity generation and transmission, in the long-distance transmission of natural gas, in telephony, and in the production of the primary energy sources, oil and gas — and finally, very satisfactory rates of growth in the United States economy generally. These, along with declining real prices of public utility services, translated into rapid, exponential growth in demand. One did not have to be very smart in those circumstances, whether as a regulator or a manager of one of these companies, to look good." Alfred E. Kahn, "A Critique of Proposed Changes," in Sidney Saltzman and Richard E. Schuler (eds.), *The Future of Electrical Energy: A Regional Perspective of an Industry in Transition* (New York: Praeger Publishers, 1986), p. 341.

[97]"By the end of the decade," contends MacAvoy, "these regulated industries rather than leading in investment and production lagged behind the rest of the economy." Paul W. MacAvoy, *The Regulated Industries and the Economy* (New York: W. W. Norton & Co., 1979), p. 29. See also Andrew S. Carron and Paul W. MacAvoy, *The Decline of Service in the Regulated Industries* (Washington, D.C.: American Enterprise Institute, 1981). In comparison, see Paul W. McCracken, *Economic Progress and the Utility Industry* (Ann Arbor: Bureau of Business Research, The University of Michigan, 1964).

[98]See, *e.g.*, Noll, *op. cit.;* Breyer, *op. cit.;* David S. Evans (ed.), *Breaking Up Bell* (New York: Elsevier Science Publishing Co., 1983).

[99]Donald F. Turner, "The Scope of Antitrust and Other Economic Regulatory Policies," 82 *Harvard Law Review* 1207, 1232 (1969). See also Walter Adams, "The Role of Competition in the Regulated Industries," 48 *American Economic Review* 527 (1958); James R. Nelson, "The Role of Competition in the Regulated Industries," 11 *The Antitrust Bulletin* 1 (1966); Frederick M. Rowe, "Antitrust and Monopoly Policy in the Communications Industry," 13 *The Antitrust Bulletin* 871 (1968); Almarin Phillips (ed.), *Promoting Competition in Regulated Markets* (Washington, D.C.: The Brookings Institution, 1975).

[100]Breyer, *op. cit.*, p. 185. "[R]ecent history carries an important message about the American experience with regulation: in every regulatory determination there ought to be a presumption — open to rebuttal — in favor of using competitive market approaches for achieving effective social control of business. Arguments against deregulation based on a desire either to avoid competition or to preserve interests inadvertently created by regulation itself deserve short shrift." Noll and Owen, "What Makes Reform Happen?," *op. cit.*, p. 24.

[101]Regulation also may have contributed to the overdevelopment of highway trucking transport and the underdevelopment of railroad transport and, in turn, may have exaggerated such problems as those of congestion, noise, smog, transit, and rail passenger service.

[102]Richard J. Barber," Technological Change in American Transportation: The Role of Government Action," 50 *Virginia Law Review* 824, 884-85 (1964). See, *e.g.*, John R. Meyer et al., *The Economics of Competition in the Transportation Industries* (Cambridge: Harvard University Press, 1959). "Interrailroad competition is no more reliable as an economizing instrument than it ever was, but interindustry (rail, water, air, motor transport, and private motor transport) competition is a very lively affair. We cannot and should not ignore it; we should use it (shaping it in the process) and strengthen it." Lewis, "Ambivalence in Public Policy toward Regulated Industries," *op. cit.*, p. 51.

[103]See, *e.g.*, Werner Sichel (ed.), *Salvaging Public Utility Regulation* (Lexington,

Mass.: D. C. Heath & Co., 1976); Donald L. Martin and Warren F. Schwartz (eds.), *Deregulating American Industry: Legal and Economic Problems* (Lexington, Mass.: D. C. Heath & Co., 1977); Robert W. Poole, Jr., *Unnatural Monopolies: The Case for Deregulating Public Utilities* (Lexington, Mass.: D. C. Heath & Co., 1985). But see, *e.g.*, Martin T. Farris, "The Case Against Deregulation in Transportation, Power, and Communications," 45 *I.C.C. Practitioners' Journal* 306 (1978); Susan J. Tolchin and Martin Tolchin, *Dismantling America: The Rush to Deregulate* (New York: Oxford University Press, 1983); Frederick C. Thayer, *Rebuilding America: The Case for Economic Regulation* (New York: Praeger Publishers, 1984).

[104]It also may run in cycles. See, *e.g.*, "Deregulation's Lost Momentum," *The Morgan Guaranty Survey*, June, 1983, pp. 7-10; "A Farewell to Deregulation," *Fortune*, September 19, 1983, pp. 49-52. In mid-1982, for example, President Reagan disbanded the Task Force on Regulatory Relief (headed by Vice President Bush).

[105]Cramton, "The Effectiveness of Economic Regulation . . . ," *op. cit.*, p. 191. See also Robert A. Nelson, "Interest Conflicts in Transportation," 37 *Journal of Business of the University of Chicago* 167 (1964); Roger G. Noll and Bruce M. Owen (eds.), *The Political Economy of Deregulation: Interest Groups in the Regulatory Process* (Washington, D.C.: American Enterprise Institute, 1983); Martha Derthick and Paul J. Quirk, *The Politics of Deregulation* (Washington, D.C.: THe Brookings Institution, 1985). On airline deregulation, see Breyer, *op. cit.*, chap. 16; Stephen G. Breyer and Leonard R. Stein, "Airline Deregulation: The Anatomy of Reform," in Robert W. Poole, Jr. (ed.), *Instead of Regulation: Alternatives to Federal Regulatory Agencies* (Lexington, Mass.: D. C. Heath & Co., 1982), chap. 1.

[106]Louis L. Jaffe, "The Effective Limits of the Administrative Process: A Reevaluation," 67 *Harvard Law Review* 1105, 1115-16 (1954). Or, as Adams has argued: "Regulation breeds regulation. Competition, even at the margin, is a source of disturbance, annoyance, and embarrassment to the bureaucracy. By providing a yardstick for performance, an outlet for innovation, and a laboratory for experiment, competition subverts the orthodox conformity prescribed by the regulatory establishment. It undermines the static, conservative, and unimaginative scheme of bureaucratic controls, and erodes the artificial values created by protective restrictionism. From the regulator's point of view, therefore, competition must be suppressed wherever it may arise." Walter Adams, "Business Exemptions from the Antitrust Laws: Their Extent and Rationale," in Almarin Phillips (ed.), *Perspectives on Antitrust Policy* (Princeton: Princeton University Press, 1965), p. 283. "Regulation-mindedness," states Wilcox, is endemic to regulation as such. . . . The regulator's concern is less with the purpose of regulation than with the instrument of regulation itself." Wilcox, *op. cit.*, p. 477.

[107]". . . even where competitive forces are powerful, there remains one case in which regulatory oversight may continue to be considered appropriate. That is the case in which at least one of the firms participating in a market which is clearly competitive also sells other goods or services in which it holds a monopoly or a near monopoly. In that case, the standard concern is that this supplier not compete unfairly by selling the competitive products at prices that are unacceptably low; i.e., that the prices not be 'uncompensatory' with the resulting shortfall covered by overcharging consumers in its monopoly markets." William J. Baumol, "On Regulation of Utilities under Deregulation," in *Proceedings of the 1981 Rate Symposium on Problems of Regulated Industries* (Columbia: University of Missouri-Columbia, 1982), p. 13.

[108]Breyer, *op. cit.*, chap. 8. See also Barry M. Mitnick, *The Political Economy of*

Regulation (New York: Columbia University Press, 1980); Poole, *op. cit.;* Alan Stone, *Regulation and Its Alternatives* (Washington, D.C.: Congressional Quarterly Press, 1982).

[109]Foster, *op. cit.,* p. 20. See also J. Rhoads Foster et al. (eds.), *Boundaries Between Competition and Economic Regulation* (Washington, D.C.: Institute for Study of Regulation, 1983).

[110]See, *e.g.,* Foster Associates, Inc., "A Comparison and Appraisal of Ten Natural Gas Deregulation Studies" (Prepared for the Chemical Manufacturers Association) (Washington, D.C., 1982); Edward J. Mitchell (ed.), *The Deregulation of Natural Gas* (Washington, D.C.: American Enterprise Institute, 1983).

[111]Foster, "Commentary on Boundaries Between Competition and Economic Regulation," *op. cit.,* p. 26. See also James N. Heller, *Coal Transportation and Deregulation* (Washington, D.C.: Serif Press, 1983).

[112]Reagan, *op. cit.,* p. 80. See also U.S. General Accounting Office, *Telephone Communications: Issues Affecting Rural Telephone Service* (Washington, D.C.: U.S. Government Printing Office, 1987).

[113]Thayer, *op. cit.,* p. 73.

[114]See, *e.g.,* John J. Nance, *Blind Trust: How Deregulation Has Jeopardized Airline Safety and What You Can Do About It* (New York: William Morrow Co., 1986). But see John R. Meyer and Clinton V. Oster, Jr. (eds.), *Airline Deregulation: The Early Experience* (Boston: Auburn House Publishing Co., 1981); John R. Meyer et al., *Deregulation and the New Airline Entrepreneurs* (Cambridge: The MIT Press, 1984); Elizabeth E. Bailey et al., *Deregulating the Airlines* (Cambridge: The MIT Press, 1985); Steven Morrison and Clifford Winston, *The Economic Effects of Airline Deregulation* (Washington, D.C.: The Brookings Institution, 1986).

[115]Larry N. Gerston et al., *The Deregulated Society* (Pacific Grove, Calif.: Brooks/Cole Publishing Co., 1988), p. 235.

[116]Walter Adams and Horace M. Gray, *Monopoly in America* (New York: Macmillan Co., 1955), chap. iii. See also Richard Hellman, *Government Competition in the Electric Utility Industry: A Theoretical and Empirical Study* (New York: Praeger Publishers, 1972); Walter J. Primeaux, *Direct Electric Utility Competition: The Natural Monopoly Myth* (New York: Praeger Publishers, 1986).

[117]See Chapter 13, p. 601.

[118]Harry M. Trebing, "What's Wrong with Commission Regulation?," Part II, 65 *Public Utilities Fortnightly* 738, 747 (1960).

[119]*Ibid.*

[120]See, *e.g.,* Frederick F. Blachly and Miriam E. Oatman, *Federal Regulatory Action and Control* (Washington, D.C.: The Brookings Institution, 1940), pp. 18-25.

[121]Jaffe, "The Independent Agency: A New Scapegoat," *op. cit.,* p. 1074.

[122]Former CAB Commissioner Chan Gurney, quoted in 73 *Public Utilities Fortnightly* 11 (January 2, 1964).

[123]Former New Jersey Commissioner Richard B. McGlynn, "The Regulator as Manager" (paper presented at the Third Annual Utility Regulatory Conference, Washington, D.C., October 7, 1980) (mimeographed), p. 8.

[124]Wilcox, *op. cit.,* p. 478. See also Owen and Braeutigam, *op. cit.*

In recent years, to illustrate, there have been several state commission decisions ordering either the cancellation or the suspension of nuclear power plants. See, *e.g., Re Pub. Service Co. of N.H.,* 47 PUR4th 167 (N.H., 1982), *rev'd sub nom. Appeal of Pub. Service Co. of N.H.,* 454 A. 2d 435, 51 PUR4th 298 (N.H. S. Ct. 1982); *Re Limerick Nuclear Generating Station,* 48 PUR4th 190 (Pa., 1982), stay denied, 49 PUR4th 165

(Pa., 1982), *rev'd sub nom. Philadelphia Elec. Co. v. Pennsylvania Pub. Util. Comm.*, 455 A. 2d 1244 (Commonwealth Ct. of Pa., 1983), *rev'd*, 460 A. 2d 734 (Pa. S. Ct. 1983). Some state commissions have ordered utilities subject to their jurisdiction to sell their shares in nuclear plants or to persuade their co-owners to halt construction. See, *e.g.*, "Seabrook, N.H., Nuclear Plant's 2nd Unit Should Be Canceled, 2 More Utilities Say," *The Wall Street Journal*, August 29, 1983, p. 7; "Utilities in Maine Told to Find Buyers For Seabrook Stakes," *The Wall Street Journal*, December 14, 1984, p. 19. Several senior utility executives have "retired" in part because of pressure by state commissions. See, *e.g.*, "Departure of Consumers Power Head is Urged by State Official in Rate Case," *The Wall Street Journal*, August 6, 1984, p. 5; "Boston Edison Bid on Rate Rise Fails; Firm is Criticized," *The Wall Street Journal*, June 27, 1986, p. 12. Investment decisions also may be reviewed before the related expenditures take place. See Russell J. Profozich et al., *Commission Preapproval of Utility Investments* (Columbus, Ohio: National Regulatory Research Institute, 1981).

[125]Ben W. Lewis, "Public Utilities," in Leverett S. Lyon and Victor Abramson (eds.), *Government and Economic Life* (Washington, D.C.: The Brookings Institution, 1940), Vol. II, p. 744.

[126]John Bauer, *Transforming Public Utility Regulation* (New York: Harper & Bros., 1950), pp. 137-38.

[127]Cramton, "The Effectiveness of Economic Regulation . . . ," *op. cit.*, p. 186.

[128]Noll, *op. cit.*, p. 31. (The quotations from the Ash Council Report are pp. 31, 31-32.) Posner, however, has concluded that "public utility regulation is probably not a useful exertion of governmental powers; that its benefits cannot be shown to outweigh its costs; and that even in markets where efficiency dictates monopoly we might do better to allow natural economic forces to determine business conduct and performance subject only to the constraints of antitrust policy." Richard A. Posner, "Natural Monopoly and Its Regulation," 21 *Stanford Law Review* 548, 549 (1969). See also, Adams, "Business Exemptions from the Antitrust Laws. . .," *op. cit.*, pp. 278-79; Harold Demsetz, "Why Regulate Utilities?," 11 *Journal of Law and Economics* 55 (1968); Yale Brozen, "Is Government the Source of Monopoly?" 5 *The Intercollegiate Review* 67 (Winter 1968-69).

[129]"Essentially, this is an allegation that imperfections in the regulatory process induce efficiency in production! If true, it intimates that the regulatory process is even more futile than contended by even its most stalwart critics: The argument is that it works well through its imperfections!" Sidney Weintraub, "Rate Making and an Incentive Rate of Return," 81 *Public Utilities Fortnightly* 23, 30 (April 25, 1968).

[130]See, *e.g.*, Harold H. Wein, "Fair Rate of Return and Incentives — Some General Considerations," in Harry M. Trebing (ed.), *Performance under Regulation* (East Lansing: MSU Public Utilities Studies, 1968), pp. 39-67; Eric J. Schneidewind and Bruce A. Campbell, "Michigan Incentive Regulation: The Next Step," in Harry M. Trebing (ed.), *Challenges for Public Utility Regulation in the 1980s* (East Lansing: MSU Public Utilities Papers, 1981), pp. 397-415; Raymond W. Harr, "A Cost Effectiveness Measure Applied to Incentive Rates in Ohio," in *Award Papers in Public Utility Economics and Regulation* (East Lansing, MSU Public Utilities Papers, 1982), pp. 103-50. On incentive systems, see Chapter 12, pp. 535-38.

[131]In Butler's words: ". . . I would argue that the goal of regulation is not minimum profits in the regulated industries but rather maximum service to the public at the lowest feasible costs. In many cases, these two requirements may coin-

cide, but I suspect that there may be many other cases where incentives in the form of reasonable rewards through profits could make genuine and lasting contributions to improved service and to reduction in real costs over the longer run." William F. Butler, "The Business Outlook Plus Some Thoughts on Business Regulation," *Telephony,* September 19, 1964, p. 25. See, *e.g.,* William M. Capron (ed.), *Technological Change in Regulated Industries* (Washington, D.C.: The Brookings Institution, 1971).

[132]Johnson, *op. cit.,* pp. 233-34.

[133]See, *e.g.,* Lee Loevinger, "Regulation and Competition as Alternatives," 11 *The Antitrust Bulletin* 101 (1966); the books published by The Brookings Institution in its Studies in the Regulation of Economic Activity series and by The MIT Press in its Regulation of Economic Activities series. See also Patricia M. Wald, "Judicial Review of Economic Analyses," 1 *Yale Journal on Regulation* 43 (1983).

[134]Lewis, "Public Utilities," *op. cit.,* p. 744, n. 225. See also, *e.g.,* Mark S. Massel, "The Regulatory Process," 26 *Law and Contemporary Problems* 181 (1961); Richard E. Caves, "Direct Regulation and Market Performance in the American Economy," 54 *American Economic Review* 172 (1964); the articles in Trebing, *Performance under Regulation, op. cit.;* Elizabeth E. Bailey (ed.), *Public Regulation: New Perspectives on Institutions and Policies* (Cambridge: The MIT Press, 1987).

[135]Massel, *op. cit.,* p. 202.

[136]George J. Stigler and Claire Friedland, "What Can Regulators Regulate? The Case of Electricity," 5 *Journal of Law and Economics* 1 (1962).

[137]Harvey Averch and Leland Johnson, "Behavior of the Firm under Regulatory Constraint," 52 *American Economic Review* 1052, 1053 (1962).

[138]The authors also conclude that regulated firms have an incentive "to operate in some markets even at a loss." *Ibid.,* p. 1063. On the basis of the Averch-Johnson thesis: (*a*) Westfield has argued that utilities are willing to pay increased equipment prices (since this behavior expands the rate base) and (*b*) Klevorick has proposed that "after some point the maximum allowable rate of return on capital would decline with increases in the amount of capital used." See Fred M. Westfield, "Regulation and Conspiracy," 55 *American Economic Review* 424 (1965); Alvin K. Klevorick, "The Graduated Fair Return: A Regulatory Proposal," 56 *American Economic Review* 477 (1966). But see Alfred E. Kahn, "The Graduated Fair Return: Comment," 58 *American Economic Review* 170 (1968).

[139]See, *e.g.,* William G. Shepherd, "Regulatory Constraints and Public Utility Investment," 42 *Land Economics* 348 (1966); William R. Hughes, "Comment," in Trebing, *Performance under Regulation, op. cit.,* pp. 73-87; E. E. Zajac, "A Geometric Treatment of Averch-Johnson's Behavior of the Firm Model," 60 *American Economic Review* 117 (1970); Elizabeth E. Bailey, *Economic Theory of Regulatory Constraint* (Lexington, Mass.: D. C. Heath & Co., 1973); Robert M. Spann, "Rate of Return Regulation and Efficiency in Production: An Empirical Test of the Averch-Johnson Thesis," 5 *The Bell Journal of Economics and Management Science* 38 (1974); Leon Courville, "Regulation and Efficiency in the Electric Utility Industry," 5 *The Bell Journal of Economics and Management Science* 53 (1974); H. Craig Petersen, "An Empirical Test of Regulatory Effects," 6 *The Bell Journal of Economics* 111 (1975); Paul M. Hayashi and John M. Trapani, "Rate of Return Regulation and the Regulated Firm's Choice of Capital-Labor Ratio: Further Empirical Evidence on the Averch-Johnson Model," 43 *Southern Economic Journal* 384 (1976); William J. Boyes, "An Empirical Examination of the Averch-Johnson Effect," 14 *Economic Inquiry* 25 (1976).

[140]Weintraub, *op. cit.,* pp. 30-31.

[141]Kahn, *op. cit.*

[142]Two approaches to the problem have been suggested by Caves: (*1*) a comparison of a regulated industry's performance with "an ideal norm derived from the familiar optimum conditions of economic theory" and (*2*) a comparison of a regulated industry's performance with the performance of an industry not subject to regulation. Caves, *op. cit.*, p. 175. While both approaches involve numerous problems [see Ronald H. Coase, "Discussion," 54 *American Economic Review* 194, 194-96 (1964)], they appear worthy of further research. On the development of performance measures, see Chapter 12, pp. 537-38.

[143]Airline deregulation, it should be remembered, "would not have been realized without the concerted effort of two presidents, several legislators, and two reform-minded CAB chairmen." Breyer and Stein, *op. cit.*, p. 36. See also Derthick and Quirk, *op. cit.*

[144]Pub. Law 91-190, 42 U.S.C. Section 4332(C).

[145]Executive Order No. 12044, 43 *Fed. Reg.* 12663 (1978).

[146]Executive Order No. 12291, 46 *Fed. Reg.* 13193 (1981). See, *e.g.*, Eads, *op. cit.*; *Use of Cost-Benefit Analysis by Regulatory Agencies* (Hearings before the Committee on Interstate and Foreign Commerce, House, 96th Cong., 1st sess.) (Washington, D.C.: U.S. Government Printing Office, 1979); J. Miller and S. Yandle, *Benefit-Cost Analyses of Social Regulation: Case Studies from the Council on Wage and Price Stability* (Washington, D.C.: American Enterprise Institute, 1979); Edward M. Gramlich, *Benefit/Cost Analysis of Government Programs* (Englewood Cliffs: Prentice-Hall, Inc., 1981).

[147]Breyer, *op. cit.*, p. 364 (footnotes omitted). On such intervention, see, *e.g.*, Donald Baker, "The Antitrust Division, Department of Justice: The Role of Competition in Regulated Industries," 11 *Boston College Industrial and Commercial Review* 571 (1970); Miller and Yandle, *op. cit.*

[148]Breyer, *op. cit.*, p. 366.

[149]*Ibid.* See, *e.g.*, Gerald H. Kopel, "Sunset in the West," 49 *State Government* 135 (1976); Benjamin Shimberg, "The Sunset Approach: The Key to Regulatory Reform?," 49 *State Government* 140 (1976); Robert D. Behn, "The False Dawn of the Sunset Laws, 49 *The Public Interest* 103 (1977).

[150]Gormley, *The Politics of Public Utility Regulation, op. cit.*, p. 87.

A modified sunset approach was proposed by Senator Kennedy in 1979 (S. 1291, 96th Cong., 1st sess.), which would involve a presidential review of regulatory programs on a specific schedule (*i.e.*, two or three programs per year for a ten-year period), with the advice of a special committee (whose members might include the chairman of the Council of Economic Advisers, the attorney general, or the chairman of the FTC, the president's consumer representative, the head of the agency under review and, perhaps, members of Congress) and with all proposals for change developed by the president being transmitted to Congress. "The proposals will remain in committee for one year, after which they, or alternative proposals developed by the committee, will be automatically discharged for a vote upon the floor of the house. They would be privileged on the floor, thus receiving priority attention. Since any member could offer the president's original reform proposals as an amendment, the president is guaranteed [a] vote upon those proposals after one year." Breyer, *op. cit.*, p. 367.

[151]Robert W. Crandall, "Federal Government Incentives to Reduce the Price Level," in Arthur M. Okun and George L. Perry (eds.), *Curing Chronic Inflation* (Washington, D.C.: The Brookings Institution, 1978), p. 2.

[152]Christopher C. DeMuth, "Constraining Regulatory Costs — Part II: The Regulatory Budget," 4 *Regulation* 29, 30-31 (March/April, 1980).

[153]*Ibid.*, pp. 38, 42. With respect to the third factor: ". . . the regulatory budget would be a one-sided ledger: there would be no tax receipts with which to compare spending levels, and no familiar norms for rhetorical support such as the analogy of the family budget and the prudence of budget balancing." *Ibid.*, p. 42.

[154]Bardach and Kagan, *Going by the Book, op. cit.*, p. 314 (footnote omitted).

[155]Gormley, *The Politics of Public Utility Regulation, op. cit.*, p. 211. See also Bardach and Kagan, *Going by the Book, op. cit.*, pp. 316-23, for a discussion on "the ethic of professionalism."

[156]Moreover, they often overlapped. Congress, to illustrate, tried for several years to rewrite the Communications Act and, at least toward the end of the decade, to even go beyond the FCC's procompetitive policy. Yet, when a major restructuring of the industry occurred, under antitrust policy, Congress suddenly became concerned about the impact of higher local rates on universal service.

[157]G. E. Hale and Rosemary D. Hale, "The Otter Tail Power Case: Regulation by Commission or Antitrust Laws," 1973 *Supreme Court Review* 99, 121-22. See also Baker, *op. cit.*

[158]Charles L. Brown, opening remarks to Bell System Presidents' Conference, La Quinta, California, October 29, 1979, as quoted in Alvin von Auw, *Heritage & Destiny: Reflections on the Bell System in Transition* (New York: Praeger Publishers, 1983), p. 14.

[159]*Vermont Yankee Nuclear Power Corp. v. Natural Resources Defense Council, op. cit.*, p. 558. Stated one editorial: "Altogether, the courts — and most recently the federal district court of Judge Harold H. Greene — have involved themselves far too deeply in the telephone case. Starting with an admittedly complex matter of antitrust law, the courts have taken an ever more active role in shaping the future of the telecommunications industry." "A Judge Who Went Too Far," *Business Week*, December 12, 1983, p. 140.

[160]See, *e.g.*, Donald A. Ritchie, *James M. Landis: Dean of the Regulators* (Cambridge: Harvard University Press, 1980).

[161]See, *e.g.*, Thomas K. McCraw, *Prophets of Regulation* (Cambridge: The Belknap Press of Harvard University Press, 1984), "Kahn and the Economist's Hour," chap. 7.

[162]". . . I remind you that only slightly more than half of the regulators of electricity have managed (or wanted) to survive in office more than four years; that less than 40 percent have served more than three years; and that more than 25 percent have served less than two years." Larry J. Wallace, Presentation to the Westinghouse Power Systems Marketing Department at "A Seminar on Electric Utility Finance and Regulation" (Pittsburgh, Pa., October, 1982) (mimeographed), p. 5.

[163]The organization, composition, and structure of the regulatory agencies also may require major changes. Commissioner Stalon (of the FERC), for example, has argued that agencies "all too often lack the ability to synthesize information well enough even to oversee their own operation; they lack the tools, especially with respect to electricity, to offer real leadership at the national level; and these bodies simply by their nature lack the attitudinal commitments (guts, if you will) to make realistic forecasts. The major reasons for this failure are the peculiar relationships among commissioners and the relationships between commissioners and the commission staff. Both of these relationships are substantially determined by law." Charles G. Stalon, "Analysis and Synthesis in Quasi-Judicial Multimember Regulatory Agencies," in Saltzman and Schuler, *op. cit.*, p. 330.

[164]The electric power industry, with interconnections and power pools, provides an obvious example of an industry that transcends traditional federal-state jurisdictional boundaries, and calls for both regional power planning and regional regulation. "Interregional transactions could be regulated by joint boards comprising representatives of the involved regional commissions or, perhaps, could be regulated by the FERC. Appeals from decisions could go directly to a federal circuit court of appeals. Accountability to the states within the regions could *and should* be provided for by appointment of the membership of the regional commissions by the governors of the states within the regions." Larry J. Wallace, "Reregulation of the Electric Utility Industry — A Neglected Alternative," 110 *Public Utilities Fortnightly* 13, 14 (November 25, 1982). See also Report of the National Governors' Association Task Force on Electric Utility Regulation, *An Analysis of Options for Structural Reform in Electric Utility Regulation* (Washington, D.C., 1983); Saltzman and Schuler, *op. cit.*

[165]"Complexity and conflict do not require more painful choices, but they do require more painful thinking." Gormley, *The Politics of Public Utility Regulation, op. cit.*, p. 218.

[166]Walter A. Morton, "Creative Regulation," 39 *Land Economics* 367, 374 (1963).

Index of Cases

Index of Names

Index of Subjects